Microsoft Project Server 2013
Managing Projects and Portfolios

Gary L. Chefetz
Margaret Wallace

Microsoft Project Server 2013

Managing Projects and Portfolios

Publisher: Chefetz LLC
Authors: Gary L. Chefetz, Margaret Wallace
Copy Editor: Rodney L. Walker
Cover Design: Emily Baker

ISBN: 978-1-934240-28-1

LCCN: 2013948831

Published and distributed by Chefetz LLC dba MSProjectExperts, 90 John Street, Suite 404, New York, NY 10038. (646) 736-1688 http://www.msprojectexperts.com

MSProjectExperts publishes a complete series of role-based training/reference manuals for Microsoft's Enterprise Project Management software including Microsoft Project and Microsoft Project Server. Use our books for self-study or for classroom learning delivered by professional trainers and corporate training programs. To learn more about our books and courseware series for Administrators, Implementers, Project Managers, Portfolio Managers, Resource Managers, Executives, Team Members, and Developers, or to obtain instructor companion products and materials, contact MSProjectExperts by phone (646) 736-1688 or by email info@msprojectexperts.com

Contents

About the Authors

Gary Chefetz is the founder and President of MSProjectExperts, which exists to support businesses and organizations that choose the Microsoft project and portfolio management platform. Gary has worked with Microsoft Project since 1995 and has supported Microsoft Project users since the introduction of Project Central in early 2000. Gary continues to receive the prestigious Microsoft Project Most Valuable Professional (MVP) award for his contributions to the Project community and possesses the Microsoft Certified IT Professional (MCITP) and the Microsoft Certified Trainer (MCT) certifications. As a long-time MVP and Project Advisory Council member, he works closely with the Microsoft Project product team and support organizations. Gary is dedicated to supporting Microsoft Project Server implementations through his business efforts with clients and through his contributions in TechNet forums, LinkedIn and Twitter. Contact Gary Chefetz on LinkedIn, e-mail or Twitter.

gary.chefetz@msprojectexperts.com • Twitter: @gchefetz

Margaret Wallace has worked with many Fortune 500 Companies across multiple industries. She has over three years of experience as a Project Server administrator in state government and in the utility industry. She has over 12 years of Project Management experience, and over 7 years of Project Server experience, including global implementations. Margaret is married to Andy of Delaware County, Ohio. She has a Bachelor of Science in Computer Information Systems with a focus in Project Management and Technical Writing from DeVry University and Master of Project Management from Keller Graduate School of Management. Margaret is a Microsoft Certified Technology Specialist (MCTS) with certifications in Microsoft Project, Project Server, and SharePoint. She is a Principal Consultant with MSProjectExperts, and enjoys blogging with Project Server related tips & tricks.

margaret.wallace@msprojectexperts.com • Twitter: @MSExpertGrrl

Download Errata and Supplemental Files

As we become aware of errors in the book, changes to the software, we update material included in the book, or we publish supplemental material, we update the download package located at:

http://www.msprojectexperts.com/managing2013

Introduction

After ten years in the market, the "blue book," also known as *Managing Enterprise Projects...,"* changes its moniker to *Microsoft Project Server 2013: Managing Projects and Portfolios* to reflect the new direction for this book. Heavily influenced by the objective domain for the Microsoft Certified Professional Exam 74-344, it also reflects a new capabilities emphasis driven by Project Online, Microsoft's Project Server in the cloud.

After presenting you with a big picture overview of "the new Project Server," the way Microsoft would like us to start thinking about their software; we dive right into the topics of most interest to portfolio managers, executives, managers and senior project managers. In fact, you can think of the first five modules of the book as portfolio management essentials. You learn all of the fundamental functionality to implement and support ideation, demand and capacity management, portfolio analyses and project governance.

Modules 06 through 11 focus on core project management functions from creating enterprise projects, assignment planning, and resourcing, to tracking and analysis. For those of you who could use a basic skills brush-up, we provide a rigorous basic assignment skills review. The balance of the book shows you how to use the various collaborative tools provided by Project Server as well as a deep dive into creating views and using the business intelligence center.

Throughout each module, you get a generous amount of Notes, Warnings, and Best Practices. Notes call your attention to important additional information about a subject. Warnings help you avoid the most common problems experienced by others and Best Practices provide tips for using the tool based on our field experience.

With this book, we believe that you can become more effective at using Microsoft Project and Portfolio Management tools. If you have questions about the book or are interested in our professional services, please contact us at our office. If you have questions about Microsoft Project or Project Server, join the conversation in our LinkedIn group at http://linkd.in/YG7UdJ

Gary L. Chefetz

Margaret Wallace

Supporting Courseware

This book is designed to for use with MSProjectExperts courses:

- Project Server 2013 74-344 Certification Boot Camp
- Project Server 2013 Portfolio Management Essentials
- Project Server 2013 Managing Enterprise Projects

For more information about MSProjectExperts courses or courseware, contact info@msprojectexperts.com

Module 01

Introduction and Project Server Overview

Learning Objectives

After completing this module, you will be able to:

- Understand the components in the Microsoft PPM platform
- Understand Project Server 2013's project portfolio management terminology
- Understand the Enterprise Resource Pool and the Enterprise Global file
- Describe the new features in Project Server 2013
- Understand the PPM platform technology stack
- Understand the Project Server 2013 installation types
- Name the databases used by Project Server 2013 and Windows SharePoint Services
- Describe the project communications lifecycle used in Project Server 2013
- Understand and utilize Project Server 2013 team collaboration tools
- Understand the concept of publishing with Project Server 2013
- Acquire an overview understanding of OLAP cubes and Data Analysis views

Inside Module 01

Welcome to Project Server 2013

You can consider Project Server 2013 as a landmark release for a number of reasons, first, because it ascends into the Microsoft cloud and secondly because it re-introduces accessibility for smaller organizations not only through cloud accessibility but also by pushing more intelligent project management tools into SharePoint. In this module, I begin by quickly highlighting the changes for Project Server 2013 for you old hands and finish with important "getting started" concepts for Project Server neophytes. This book covers and applies to both Project Online, the name for Project Server in Microsoft's Office 365 environment, and on-premises Project Server. I note the differences wherever applicable throughout the book.

Year of the Cloud

Microsoft Project marketing calls Project 2013 and Project Server 2013 a "landmark release," due to its entry into Microsoft's online service called Office 365. It is big news because what was an enterprise-only solution is now highly accessible to smaller businesses and business units; and because of the architectural changes that the move to Office 365 forced into Project Pro and Project Server 2013. Microsoft's multi-tenant cloud infrastructure for SharePoint demands that Project Server 2013 meet performance and scalability measures that required some significant architectural changes and that have produced the performance results necessary to play in the cloud without sacrificing functionality.

> **Information**: It is time to consider that in the cloud, multi-year product cycles producing versions labeled by year released, become less relevant because the cloud supports a more fluid release model. The new way of thinking about this is always having the "latest version" and no need for installing updates. The cloud does it for you.

Along with the architectural changes necessary to support Office 365 performance demands, Microsoft introduces a bundle of new project and work management oriented functionality into SharePoint 2013. This new functionality provides lightweight project management capabilities you can employ for a variety of management maturities and styles. From improved task list capability, to task aggregation, to a vastly improved harmony between Project 2013 and SharePoint 2013, some of the biggest news for 2013 actually falls just outside the traditional Project Server boundaries. While the lines between the two applications continue to blur, it is rewarding to see how well these applications play together after several iterations of a clunky relationship. The non-restrictive way you can mix lightweight and more-structured processes side-by-side to accommodate multiple groups operating at varying levels of maturity or create tiered systems that provide and enforce varying levels of formality for different business requirements, are a giant leap forward.

Certainly one of the biggest headlines for Project Server 2013 is that it now supports SharePoint designer for building Project Server demand management and governance workflow. This change unleashes one of the great strengths of the SharePoint platform, its ability to eliminate or greatly reduce the need for developers to implement business rules. This change puts the true power of Project Server's portfolio management capabilities in your hands. More than ever, for you to appreciate Project 2013 and Project Server 2013 fully, you must also appreciate SharePoint Server 2013 Enterprise Edition. Project Server 2013 is completely dependent on SharePoint Server 2013.

My favorite way to describe the progression of Project Server into the SharePoint architecture is that Project Server and SharePoint started dating in 2003. By the time Microsoft released the 2007 versions of these products, they were living together. With the introduction of Microsoft's 2010 Office computing platform, Project Server and SharePoint were married. Now, with the 2013 release, it has gotten to the point that they are completing each other's sentences. All kidding aside, if you want to have your way with Project Server, and you want to get the most out of the work management and project management capabilities of the platform, you need to be able to take control of SharePoint because you achieve your best potential by leveraging SharePoint and Project Server together.

Project Management available on Office 365

Microsoft's move to offer the SharePoint 2013 and Project Server 2013 enterprise solution as part of Office 365 lowers almost all of the barriers to using Project Server for smaller businesses and business units that do not have IT budgets, and for some smaller organizations, that do not have IT departments. Office 365 even allows users to start a free trial without providing so much as a credit card as shown in Figure 1 - 1. Not only are the upfront costs of hardware and software deferred into reasonable monthly payments, the online model places no additional technical burden on the organization. Understanding how to administer both SharePoint and Project Server is a requisite for success with these enterprise-class applications, but you no longer need to have the technical skills to manage the server platform.

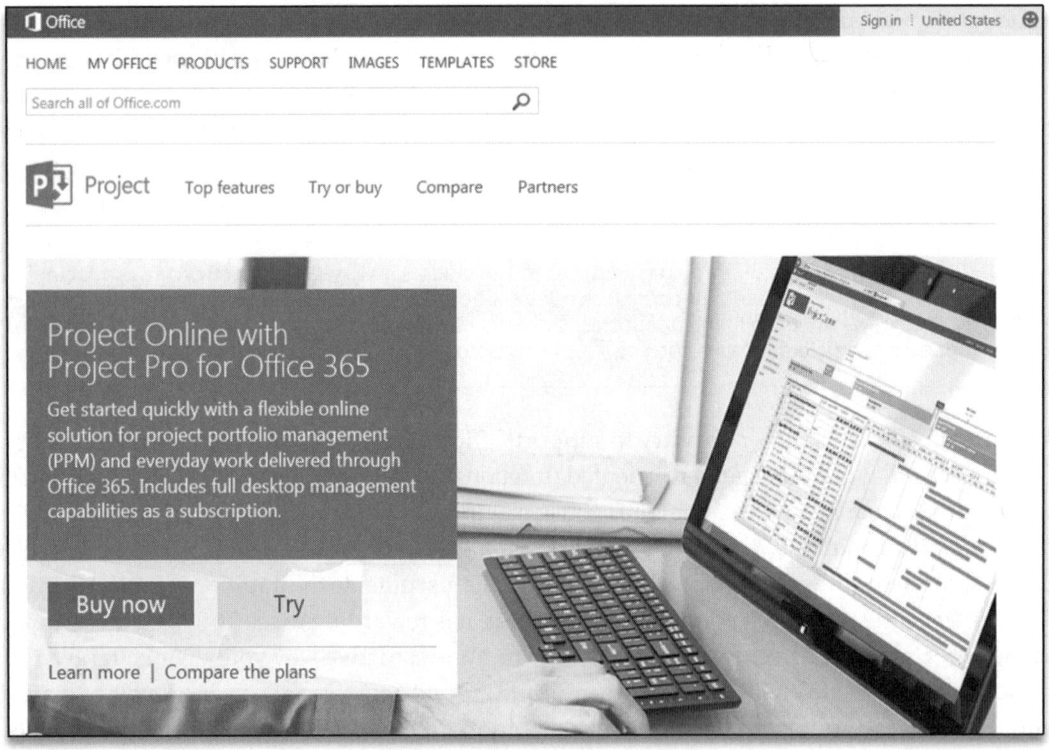

Figure 1 - 1: Office 365 home page

Throughout this book, I highlight the differences between managing Project Online and Project Server 2013 installed on premises. The good news for Project Server maintenance is that most of the management experience for Project Server is identical in either environment, kudos to Microsoft for that. The most significant differences between the online offering and implementing the solution on premises are the items you can no longer control. For instance, the online version provides no direct database access. Similarly, you do not have OLAP cubes available to you online. To overcome the database access limitation Microsoft added oData support to provide the foundation for business intelligence. I cover oData extensively in Module 18: *Working with Business Intelligence and Reporting*. oData is an open-standard for providing data access via HTTP and HTTPS protocols. That means that the Office Data Connection files use oData links and queries rather than connection strings and SQL queries. The experience for the report author changes, but the user experience remains the same.

Important general capabilities of Office 365 include single-sign-on through AD synchronization, it supports the use of SharePoint designer for workflow including Project Server 2013 demand management, and it introduces a new extensibility story for Microsoft, adopting the app store model in its new Office Marketplace. The Office 365 administration pages and controls are easy to use even for less-technically-inclined users. Even managing such things as alternate access mappings (host headers) is a simple task.

Microsoft does not currently provide an easy migration path between an existing on-premises Project Server installation to Project Online. Currently, the only way to migrate is to configure a fresh environment online and then move the resource pool and projects manually. At the time of this writing, at least one Microsoft partner has a migration tool available in the app store.

Project Pro 2013 Available as Click-To-Run

Project Professional 2013 -- or as I refer to it throughout this book, Project Pro 2013 -- arrives in the Office 365 stack as a click-to-run application like its Office system cousins. Microsoft calls it Project Pro 2013 when you purchase a subscription and Project Professional when you purchase the old-fashioned way. Click-to-run uses streaming technology to deliver applications to the end-user and requires a much smaller footprint on your local machines. One of the advantages is that you are always using the latest version of the software when you are connected. You can run a click-to-run version of Office alongside a local version allowing you to have multiple copies of the software as well as multiple versions. The market changer is, once again, accessibility. It has never been easier to try or to acquire Microsoft Project than through Office 365. A major advantage of acquiring Project Pro 2013 this way is that your backstage information roams with you on all five devices on which you may install it.

New Trade Dress

The entire Office product stack gets a fresh new Windows 8-inspired look with fresh clean lines and tiles all over the place. Most notably, Microsoft removed the chrome from the interface freeing up precious screen real estate following the flat UI design trend, which better adapts to multiple devices. One aspect of the user experience that Microsoft focused on for this release is the "getting started" story. In the Office clients, this manifests itself by not automatically starting a new document or project, in favor of the way most people work, typically wanting to begin with a previous item. In Project Web App, the new "getting started" story includes the top row of tiles shown in the carousel in Figure 1 - 2. Below the *Get Started with Project Web App* carousel, appears the *Track your work* carousel of live tiles. Live tiles not only provide navigation, they provide valuable information as you can see in the *Approvals* and *Tasks* tiles in the figure. The *Get Started with Project Web App* carousel provides new users with the information they need to get off to a good start. You can hide this feature or expose it at any time.

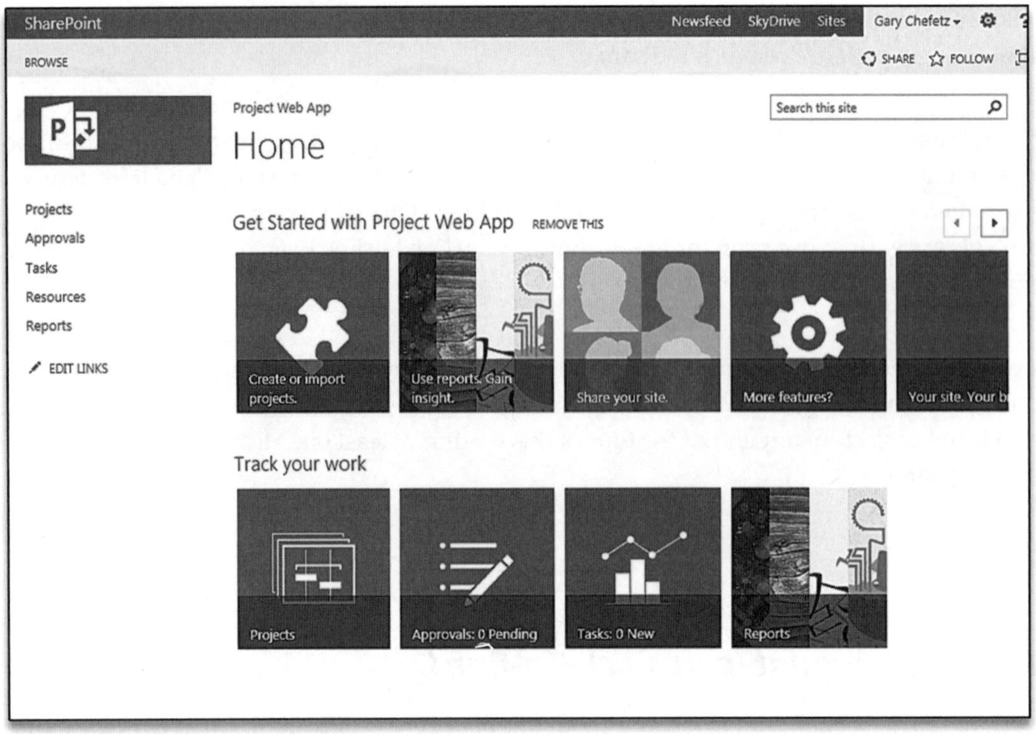

Figure 1 - 2: A new look for Project Web App

New for Demand Management and Governance

Portfolio management in Project Server 2013 allows you to measure strategic alignment and evaluate a portfolio of proposed projects against cost and resource constraints as well as other custom cost or cost benefit measures. It provides an objectified approach to analyzing what is typically a very subjective exercise in most organizations supporting intelligent decisions to determine how best to distribute limited resources. Because constraint analysis requires data collection that may or may not be possible at an early stage of ideation, Project Server's built-in, more formal construct, is a bit heavy-handed for early stage idea development.

Project Server 2013 liberates early-stage ideation from the formal data collection requirements to perform detailed portfolio analysis. Actually, SharePoint is the liberator; Project Server accommodates the transition from informal ideation to formal constraint analysis by providing an easy path between the two. Essentially, your ideation lists that you create using simple SharePoint lists, are on-ramps to either a project that becomes a project in Project Server without going through a portfolio management process or one that does go through a formal selection process. Understand that you can build multiple on-ramps to one or more selection processes and you can build your own selection process in SharePoint, avoiding Project Server portfolio selection altogether. Figure 1 - 3 illustrates a fully integrated process from ideation in SharePoint through execution phases in Project Server 2013.

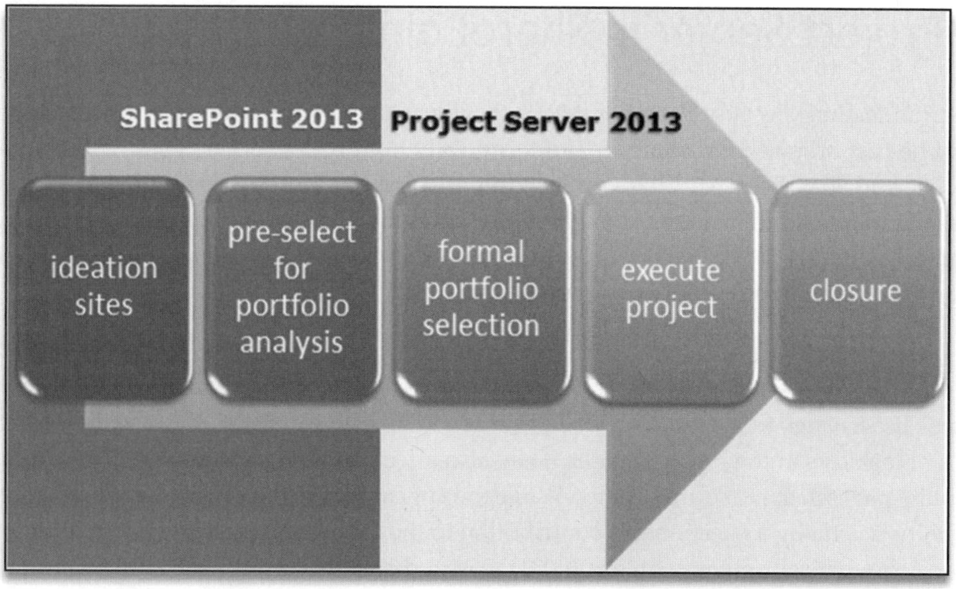

Figure 1 - 3: Integration into the entire lifecycle from idea through project closure

Collecting Ideas

Collecting ideas for new projects is as easy as creating a new SharePoint list. Essentially, you can use any list with any fields, although at some point, if you are going to grow the ideas into Project Server, you may want to think past the first week or two in the life of the list. For instance, both SharePoint and Project Server 2013 allow you to ignore factoids like estimated cost and work, and even strategic alignment throughout the ideation process; but you know that you will want to get to those facts at some point, so the question you must ask yourself and your stakeholders is when do we get to it? Do you collect this data before the idea hits Project Server 2013 or after?

I want you to appreciate both how easy Microsoft has made it to collect ideas, and how incredibly disorganized this completely free-form setup can end up. You should plan this feature carefully, lay out the rules of engagement for entering ideas, and have a plan for bringing these ideas into the formal Project Server portfolio.

With native SharePoint as your battleground for ideation, you have a cache of weapons at your disposal. Not unlike other Microsoft solutions, you can swat your flies with everything from flyswatters to ray guns. Although all you really need is a list on an existing site, I think it is worth creating a site for your ideation or request center so that you can add other SharePoint enhancements to the ideation process and experience. The two primary elements of SharePoint that you use for ideation include a list and optional workflow. You can make this as simple and easy as you want, or you can build an ideation empire. I provide you with more ideas about this in a future module.

Support for SharePoint Designer Workflow

Project Server 2010 introduced a new demand management platform based on workflow, but many organizations hesitated to implement this functionality because workflows are expensive to develop. Because third party tools available for non-developers to create Project Server workflows are rather costly, adoption of workflow-managed intake and execution was limited in 2010. I expect this to explode with the addition of SharePoint Designer support for Project Server 2013 workflow. You can now use either SharePoint Designer or Visio to design declarative workflows, which are XML based, rather than coded solutions you develop in Visual Studio. These now support loops with conditions and other parameters and can call other web services through REST or SOAP interfaces, and you can extend them with custom activities.

New for Project Server in SharePoint

No, this is not a trick heading, because SharePoint now provides functionality that Project Server can consume, which ultimately might be part of your PPM solution, but technically not Project Server. These elements include the new SharePoint task list, and SharePoint My Sites with task aggregation. It is not surprising that the Project team actually built the new task list feature, but it belongs to SharePoint Foundation. Not only are these part of a new lightweight project management story for Project Server 2013, they support an organization just starting out with project management and provide a path into project management maturity.

Visibility Projects

You can make task lists created in the same site collection as PWA, visible in PWA. You can then see the projects managed in SharePoint task lists in the Project Center. They also affect resource availability, so you can see them in the resource availability pages in the Resource Center. While the appearance in the Project Center is benign, the impact on resource availability is actually a questionable contribution to the resource-capacity-management purist unless you actually have projects where all assignments are 100% measured only in full days of 8 hours. These Visibility Projects are best suited for organizations that are not interested in tracking time on projects, as you cannot add these tasks to the timesheet, an important component in a project management system that estimates and measures work in order to measure resource capacity. This end-user feature does not require special implementation or management considerations from Project Server; however, I cover this in context with new Project Site behaviors in Module 02, *Tasks List, Project Sites and News Feed* and you can find more information in Dale Howard's *Ultimate Study Guide: Foundations Microsoft Project 2013.* You can also promote these and other projects contained in SharePoint lists to enterprise projects in Project Server 2013.

My Sites and Work Management Service Application

The My Sites feature in SharePoint is not new; but it works in a new way when you add the new Work Management Service Application to SharePoint, which can aggregate tasks across SharePoint sites and site collections, Outlook tasks through Exchange Integration, and tasks from Project Server 2013. This provides the user with an all-my-work-in-one-place view of their assignments across the organization. Using My Sites and the Work Management Service application are optional for Project Server 2013 deployments. Deploying My Sites in SharePoint deserves its own considerations and you should get a good book on SharePoint 2013 that explains this feature in depth.

One of the big investments for SharePoint in this release is a new work management service that performs user task aggregation across the SharePoint farm, across multiple SharePoint farms and from sources such as Project Server, Outlook, and Exchange as illustrated in Figure 1 - 4. This feature works with the new My *Tasks* web part on the user's *My Sites* page. To some degree, you can liken My Sites to Facebook for the corporate intranet. It provides a central location for members of the organization to post their skills, tell their stories, store their documents, manage lists, and collaborate with other team members. With the new task aggregation capability, My Sites has to be part of your architectural consideration. You can begin to see why much of the PWA interface arrives hidden. If you want to take advantage of task aggregation, implementing this option dictates that people naturally status their tasks in their My Sites or Outlook, rather than PWA. The Work Management Service uses a provider model and is, therefore, easily extensible to include tasks from sources such as help desk systems or other service management systems.

If your business requirements call for effort-based planning and tracking and intend to use timesheets, this feature may not be applicable to your goals. If your business requirements call for simplified task tracking, then task aggregation in My Sites is a compelling value for the end user and a new weapon in the arsenal. Making it easier to access and manipulate task data increases the likelihood that users will status their tasks. Placing the task status apparatus inside a productivity hub like My Sites provides a one-stop experience that adds a timesaving convenience for the user.

Figure 1 - 4: Task Aggregation in SharePoint

Single database per Project Web App instance

Each Project Server 2013 instance now has only one schematized database. Rather than keeping separate databases for draft, published, reporting, and archive, all tables combine into a single database each labeled with one of four prefixes:

- dbo. Tables with this prefix replace the reporting database in previous versions.
- draft. Tables with this prefix replace the draft database in previous versions.
- pub. Tables with this prefix replace the published database in previous versions.
- ver. Tables with this prefix replace the archive database in previous versions.

Warning: Microsoft does not support development against any of these tables except for the reporting tables as it reserves the right to change the schemas of the other tables at any time. In order to ensure that your customizations do not break one day when you install a cumulative update to your system, remember this rule.

The database is at your disposal for on-premises deployment or private cloud implementation; but when using Microsoft's online version, you only have access to reporting data using OData.

Improved Queue Mechanism

For Project Server 2013, Microsoft completely re-engineered the queue system from a continuous polling mechanism to a push technology, which significantly reduces its overhead. In addition, the queue system now has a self-healing system whereby it looks for, detects, and automatically retries failed push jobs. Another significant performance gain for the queue is that timesheet jobs no longer process through the queue, eliminating what could become quite a processing backup at certain high-activity times such as Friday afternoons when everyone is rushing to enter their time cards. Timesheet reporting jobs, however, continue to use the queue.

You now manage the queue settings through central administration. Each instance of a Project Server service application has a single queue service, so all sites using that service application share the same queue settings. Microsoft also added additional logging capabilities that you access through the new Log Level Manager capability that you invoke and manipulate through PowerShell.

Performance Improvements

Anyone who has used Project Server during previous generations knows all too well that there were a number of bottlenecks in the system that sometimes made performance less than desirable. Even with the many performance gains in the 2010 release, page load times and response times could sometimes be very slow. Consequently, Project Server 2010 was under the cloud rather than in it. For the 2013 release, the Project team had no choice but to concentrate on performance improvement making very substantial investments under the hood.

Among these improvements, at the web tier, the team focused on page load times, WAN optimization, and eliminated the queue wherever possible. At the application level the optimized queue and reduced database activity contributes to significant performance gains. Microsoft completely reengineered AD Synch. Besides consolidating databases, Microsoft made some very substantial improvements at the database tier by optimizing security validation. Any developer who has worked with the PSI is going to cheer for this one! Project Server administrators have reason to rejoice as well because the product team baked SQL best practices into the database, which now performs all of its own SQL maintenance eliminating the need for SQL Server maintenance plans other than for backup purposes. Thank you, Redmond!

New Server-Side Scheduling Engine

After years of user frustration with differences between Project Web App calculations, particularly with custom fields, Microsoft has finally brought the full Project scheduling engine to the web, which runs under a new Windows Service called *Project Calculation Services.* It is important to note that the PSI continues to use the old PWA scheduling engine for backward compatibility, which may also provide some awkward compatibility. I assume that after a while, this too shall pass.

New Permissions Mode

Project Server 2013 supports two permissions modes. The classic Project Server permissions mode based on groups and categories remains available, but you can now run your system using SharePoint security only. When you create a new Project Server instance with a new database, Project Server 2013 wakes up in SharePoint security mode. You can switch to classic mode by running a PowerShell cmdlet or by flipping a switch in your online tenant. When you run in SharePoint permissions mode, you use SharePoint groups that map to Project Server groups to authorize access to your users, which invisibly applies the default Project Server security model and disables RBS-relation-based security options in the interface and at the application level making it unavailable to developers as well.

Timesheet Improvements

When you launch timesheets in Project Server 2013, the UI changes are immediately apparent in the streamlined ribbon. Microsoft also added the ability to report multiple lines against administrative time buckets making this feature much more useful than it has been in the past. The timesheet now supports carry-forward administration lines, allows users to group and sort on the front end, and allows administrators to set these attributes on the backend with more control over view defaults. You now manage timesheet managers through a list for non-fixed approval routing, simplifying the process for end users.

Introducing the Microsoft 2013 PPM Platform

Microsoft uses the term Project Portfolio Management (PPM) to refer to its offering of tools for coordinating and standardizing portfolio and project management as an enterprise platform. Microsoft's PPM platform facilitates project selection, project collaboration between project managers, team members, executives, and other stakeholders. This toolset includes:

- Office 365 Project Online
- Project Pro 2013
- Project Server 2013
- Project Web App 2013 (part of Project Server)
- Windows SharePoint 2013 Enterprise
- SQL Server 2008 R2 SP1 or 2012 (2012 preferred)
- SQL Server Analysis Services
- SQL Reporting Services (Optional)
- Windows Access Server (WAC Server) (Optional)

When you implement PPM, you employ all of these technologies across a Windows server farm consisting of one or more servers. The number of servers you use depends on the scale of your deployment, determined in part by the number of system users, the number of projects to support, and the amount of associated content you plan to store in your PPM environment.

This book does not extensively cover SharePoint Server Enterprise, but the extent to which you intend to use it is an important consideration for almost everyone evaluating PPM. SharePoint Server is an approachable platform for building enterprise content management solutions, including portals, communities, document management sites, and too many more to describe in a sentence.

Applying PPM Terminology to Project Server

In the world of enterprise project management, you hear terms like project, program, and portfolio. How do these terms apply to your organization's project management environment? Unless I otherwise note, this book accepts the Project Management Institute (PMI) definition of a **project**: "a temporary endeavor undertaken to create a unique product or service." A project is temporary, meaning that it has a beginning and an end. A project is unique, meaning that it is something that your organization has not done before. In the real world, many projects are unique enough to be treated as a separate management object; however much of the work contained within the project is highly repetitive.

For the purposes of this book, a **program** is "a collection of related projects" and a **portfolio** is "a collection of programs and/or projects within a business unit or across an entire enterprise." Project and Program Management collectively refers to the practice and management principles that organizations apply during project execution. Portfolio Management, on the other hand, is the process an organization uses to select which projects to execute. Many companies have their own interpretation of these terms, reflecting their approach to project management. Sometimes the sheer size of the organization drives these definitions.

The concept of a portfolio is flexible, depending on the size of the company. A smaller organization may have a single portfolio of projects, whereas a larger business may conceive of an enterprise portfolio made up of numerous departmental or line-of-business portfolios, each containing its own set of programs and projects. Regardless of the way a business conceives these terms, you can model them in Project Server 2013 as shown in the hierarchy illustrated in Figure 1 - 5.

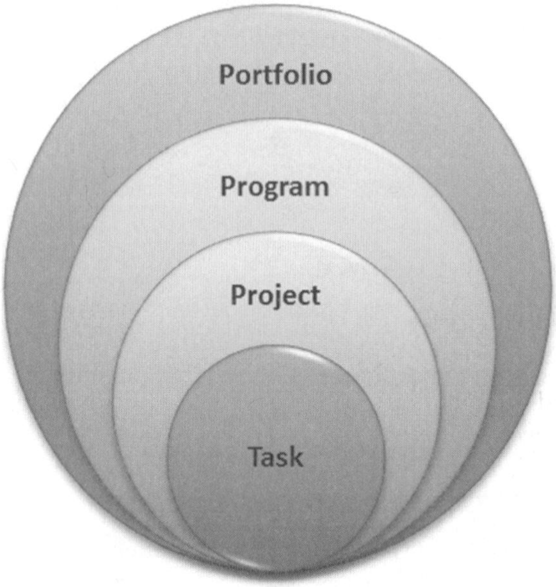

Figure 1 - 5: Portfolio Hierarchy

Understanding Project Server Terminology

Two terms that you must understand in the context of the Project Server 2013 environment are **enterprise project** and **enterprise resource**. Very specific criteria determine whether a project is an enterprise or non-enterprise project, and whether a resource is an enterprise or local resource. When an object is an "enterprise" object in Project Server 2013, you manage centrally using Project Server. Enterprise objects support uniformity for processes as well as for object management, particularly when you attach workflows to them.

Enterprise Project

A project is an **enterprise project** when one of the following two conditions is true:

- You create the project using the Project Pro 2013 client while connected to Project Server 2013 and save the project in the Project Server database.

- You create the project using Project Web App, which is Project Server's web-based front-end.

Any project not stored in the Project Server database, such as a project saved as a .mpp file, is termed a non-enterprise project or a local project. The only other way to create an enterprise project is to use third-party tools or workflows that move the project into Project Server 2013.

Enterprise Resource

A resource is an **enterprise resource** when one of the following two conditions is true:

- You create the resource in the Enterprise Resource Pool using the Project Pro 2013 client while connected to Project Server 2013, or you create the resource using Project Web App.
- You connect Project Server 2013 to your Active Directory or other directory service to import the users into the central Project Server database.

If a resource exists in an enterprise project but does not exist in the Enterprise Resource Pool, then this resource is termed a **local resource**, meaning that it is local to the particular project only.

Check In and Check Out

The terms **check in** and **check out** apply to enterprise projects, enterprise resources, the Enterprise Global file and other objects in the Project Server system. A user must check out any of these before editing, so that others have *Read-only* access until the user checks them in.

Portfolio Analyses

When you encounter this term in Project Server 2013 it refers to the collection of individual analysis studies performed by various users in the system to determine the viability of proposed project investments in the system.

Portfolio Analysis

The term **portfolio analysis** refers to an analysis of a batch or group of projects in the system for the purposes of selecting projects for execution by best matching the strategic objectives of the organization and fit within resource and cost constraints set by management consensus.

Enterprise Resource Pool Overview

A centralized Enterprise Resource Pool is the centerpiece of advanced resource management functionality in Project Server 2013. This resource pool contains resources and resource attribution that drives functionality to match people to tasks using skills comparisons or other attributes based on department, location or other criteria that you configure in the system. You must define these resource attributes in enterprise custom fields using the facilities provided in Project Web App administration. Typical resource attribution can contain all manners of details, such as practice groups, location, department, or any other company-specific information that project and resource managers use to assign resources to task assignments. You can use these same management tools to drive reporting and analysis. After defining custom fields for your organization, your Project Server administrator assigns values to these fields to each resource in the Enterprise Resource Pool.

After you complete the task planning process in Project Pro 2013, you begin the resource management process by building a team for your project using resources from the Enterprise Resource Pool. Initial resource management activities include assembling the project team and making specific task assignments. Using team-building tools such as the *Build Team from Enterprise* dialog and the *Assign Resources* dialog, Project Server 2013 allows you to locate resources by both skill and availability, even if you are using a large resource pool. This simplifies the project staffing process not only by leveraging the custom attributes in the pool, but also by providing instant access to availability data enhanced with graphical representations of current and future workload and availability.

Enterprise Global Overview

Every time a project manager launches Project Pro 2013 and connects to Project Server 2013, the system opens a copy of two global files in the background. One is the Global.mpt file and the other is the Enterprise Global file. Both Global files contain a library of project objects including views, tables, filters, groups, reports, etc.

The Global.mpt file contains the standard set of Project objects shipped with the Project Pro 2013 client, as well as any custom objects created by the individual user to whom the profile belongs. The Enterprise Global file is your organization's "library" of custom enterprise objects. This gives your project managers access to all custom objects stored for enterprise-wide use, including custom enterprise views. The Enterprise Global file is the vehicle through which an organization can standardize objects across a user population.

Understanding the PPM Platform Technology Stack

Prior to 2010, Project Server leveraged the free Windows SharePoint Services (WSS) to provide team collaboration on issues, risks, and documents. With the release of the 2010 version, Project Server became a service running under the SharePoint umbrella, and its web interface became a Windows SharePoint application. Project Server 2013 is the largest SharePoint application in existence. Because Project Server 2013 Web App is a Windows SharePoint application, you must implement Project Server with SharePoint Server 2013 Enterprise. If you do not have WSS Enterprise preinstalled on your server, it installs with your Project Server installation.

You must procure a copy of Project Pro 2013 for each user who manages projects in the PPM system and requires the advanced scheduling capabilities found only in the Project client, for each application administrator, and possibly for other managers depending upon the responsibilities you define for their role. The most common extended use requirement is for resource managers to take on resource management responsibilities that require the Project client. Understand that there are two available editions of Project 2013, just as there were for 2010. Along with some feature differentiators, the primary difference between the two editions is that the Standard edition cannot connect to Project Server whereas the Pro edition can. If you do not intend to implement Project Server, you may not need to purchase the more expensive professional edition unless you want features such as the Team Planner and the ability to publish projects to SharePoint without third-party tools.

Information: You must use Project Pro 2013 to connect to Project Server 2013. You cannot use Project Professional 2010 to connect to Project Server 2013. There is no *Backward Compatibility* mode, which was available for people upgrading to 2010, Project Pro 2013 is **not compatible** with any earlier version of Project Server.

PPM mix is Microsoft SharePoint Server 2013 (MSS) which provides a rich set of content management tools, including rich document versioning and a powerful workflow engine that allows you to bake best-practice process into the content store. These capabilities open the door to building solutions that control workflow at the deliverable level, reducing the need to capture these individual steps in the work breakdown structure, and providing the capability of gathering progress data without relying upon resources to report it. You should evaluate the inclusion of SharePoint features early in your deployment planning, as it is a feature-rich and powerful tool.

Microsoft's Office technologies suite combined with Project Server 2013 and Microsoft Office desktop tools, as well as other data integration technologies, provide the tools necessary to build complete Enterprise Content Management (ECM) solutions. As is typical for Microsoft, the price points for these technologies make them accessible to a much broader audience by removing the cost barriers set by other vendors whose products are unapproachable for all but large companies that can entertain seven-figure technology investments. For this reason, you should carefully consider how to leverage other benefits by deploying the 2013 Office desktop technologies, which feature tighter integration to the latest SharePoint technologies. This is particularly an important consideration if you plan to make heavy use of SharePoint collaboration tools.

When you deploy the Microsoft 2013 PPM platform, you commit yourself to a number of supporting Microsoft technologies at the most basic level, and you have options to deploy an extended set of closely related and generally related Microsoft technologies as well. For instance, a basic Project Server 2013 implementation includes Windows Server, SQL Server, SQL Analysis Server, Windows SharePoint Server, Internet Information Services, and the Dot Net Framework 4.0. In addition to this base configuration, you can elect to add SQL Reporting Services, additional service applications that are part of SharePoint Server, and other 2013 Office components. Note that I include Analysis Services and SQL Reporting Services in the SQL Server layer. These are not required, but you can implement them at no extra charge if you maintain them on a single SQL Server box.

Yes, it is a lot of software! However, the breadth and the strength of the SharePoint Server collaboration platform give the PPM platform its greatest competitive advantage. No other PPM product supports the range of solutions that the Microsoft 2013 PPM platform can support. In fact, it is difficult even to refer to any of the competing products as a "platform," while there is no question that Microsoft provides a customizable solution platform. This is an important distinction to remember when comparison-shopping.

> **Information**: For your consideration, a number of Microsoft partners provide connector solutions for integrating Microsoft PPM to various popular ERP systems including the Microsoft Dynamics solutions.

Understanding the Project Communications Lifecycle

Project Server's core functionality provides a cyclical assignment and update process between project managers and team members. This cycle is the heart of Project Server's work and resource management system. Work assignments flow from the plan to resources performing the work, and resources report progress data back to the plan. This project communication cycle flows through the following steps:

1. The project manager saves the project plan in the Project Server database, as illustrated in Figure 1 - 6. This action saves the project in the *Draft* tables only. Project information is not visible in the Project Center and assignments are not visible to team members.

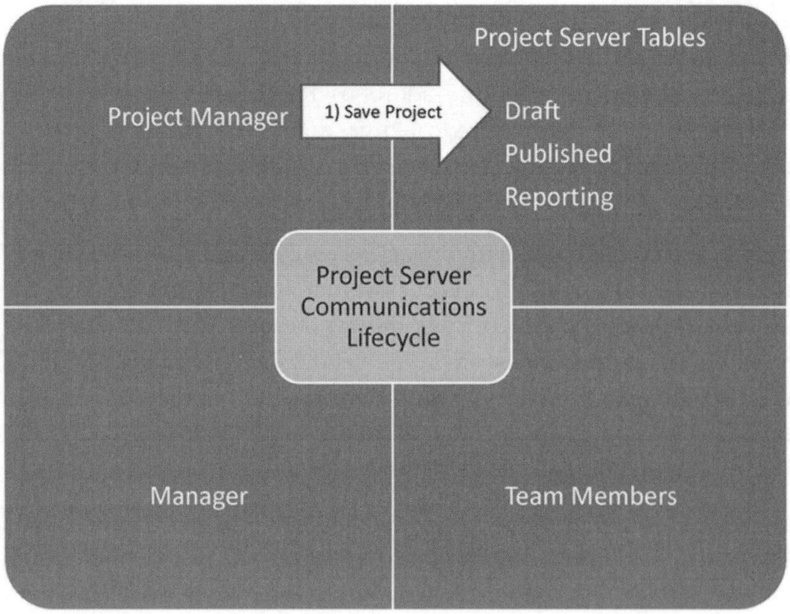

Figure 1 - 6: Save the project in Project Server Draft database

2. When the project manager publishes a project, as illustrated in Figure 1 - 7, the system writes the project data to the *Published* and *Reporting* tables. If you enable Project Server's notification feature, Project Server 2013 optionally activates a messaging service and sends an email to each resource notifying them of their new task assignments. Using an embedded link in the email message, team members can quickly click the link to view their task assignments in the project through Project Web App or through Outlook. Publishing makes project data visible in the *Project Center* and *Project Detail* views, and the project data is included in the next cube build.

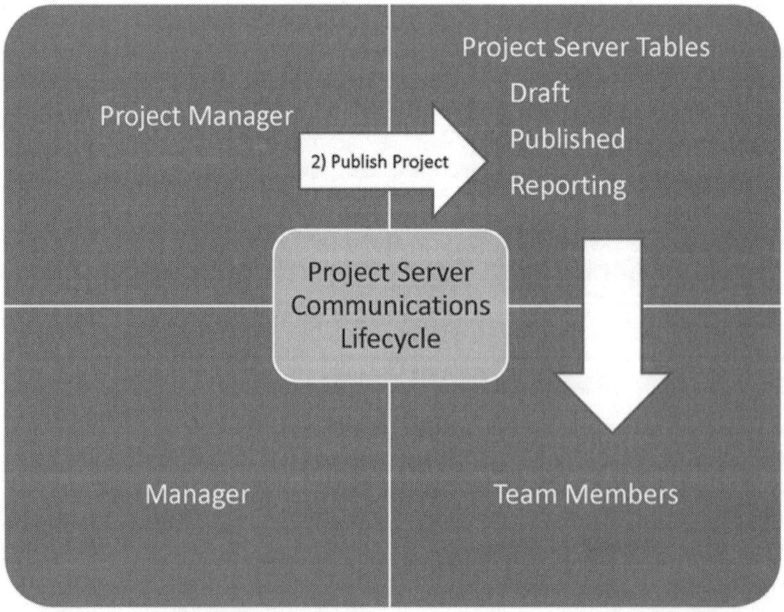

Figure 1 - 7: Publish the project with e-mail sent to team members

3. At the end of each reporting period, team members optionally update their timesheets, if you enable timesheets in your configuration. They then update their actual progress on the project and send the updates to the project manager via the Project Web App interface as illustrated in Figure 1 - 8. Actual progress includes completion percentages and/or hours worked on each task, based on your organization's reporting method. The updates are visible to the project manager, but they do not flow into the plan until the project manager accepts the updates in the next step or unless the project manager uses automation rules.

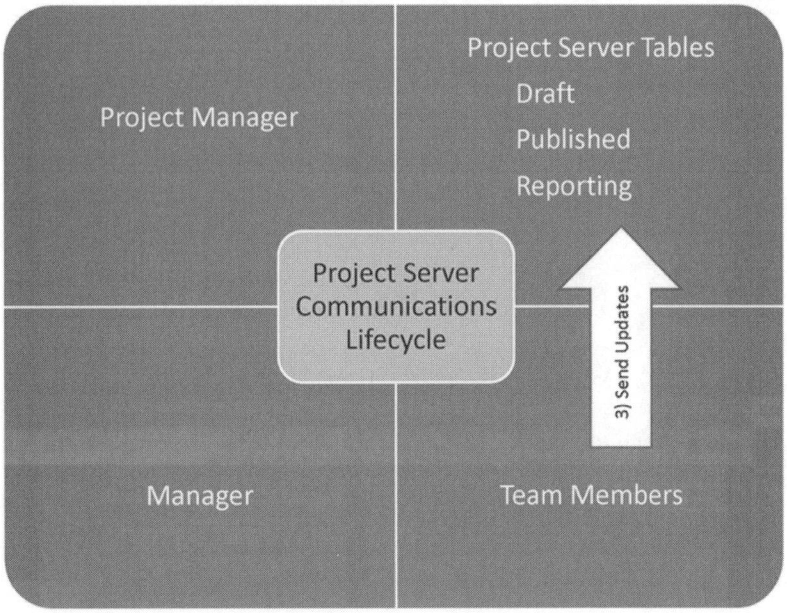

Figure 1 - 8: Team members submit actual progress

4. The project manager receives and reviews each set of task updates from project team members as illustrated in Figure 1 - 9. The project manager can individually accept or reject each task update or process them in total or in batches using automation tools.

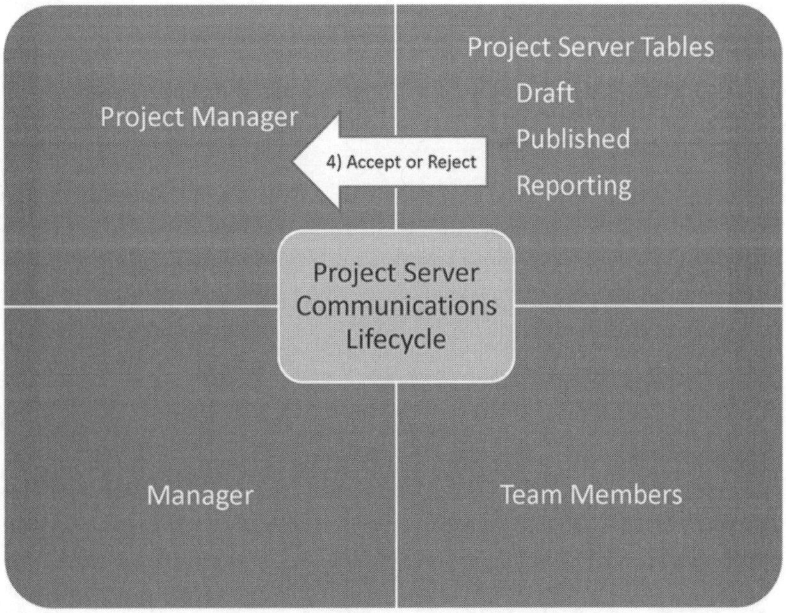

Figure 1 - 9: Project manager reviews and processes updates

5. After accepting or rejecting each task update, the project manager saves the latest schedule changes in the *Draft* tables. After saving the project, the project manager publishes the latest project schedule changes to the *Published* and *Reporting* tables, as illustrated in Figure 1 - 10. This makes the schedule changes visible in the *Project Center*, the *Reporting* tables, the next OLAP cube build, and the *Timesheet* and *Tasks* pages for team members.

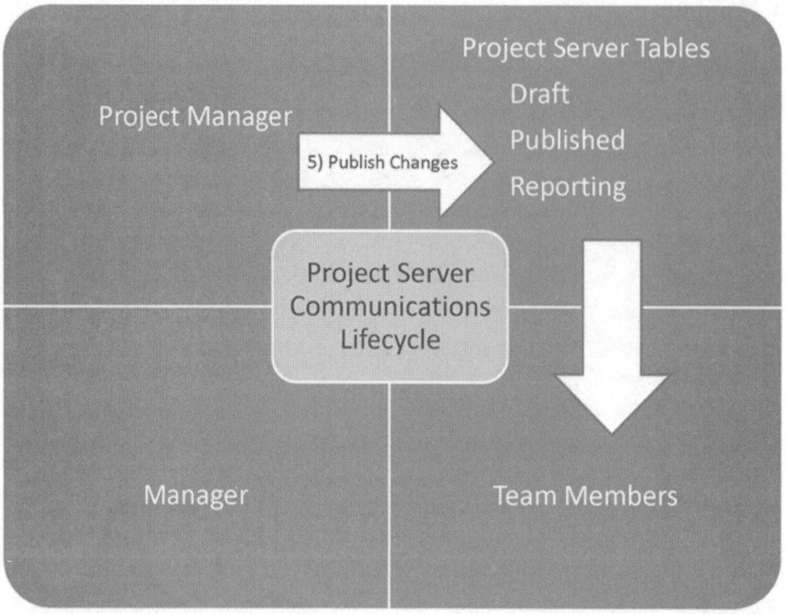

Figure 1 - 10: Project manager publishes the latest schedule changes

6. At any time throughout the life of the project, executives within the organization can view all projects or individual projects in the organization's portfolio, as illustrated in Figure 1 - 11. Project Server 2013 provides numerous view entry points, including the *Project Center*, which is also the gateway to detailed project views, and the *Resource Center*, which provides resource data and a gateway to resource details. In addition, Project Server 2013 provides a rich data analysis theater leveraging SQL Analysis Services.

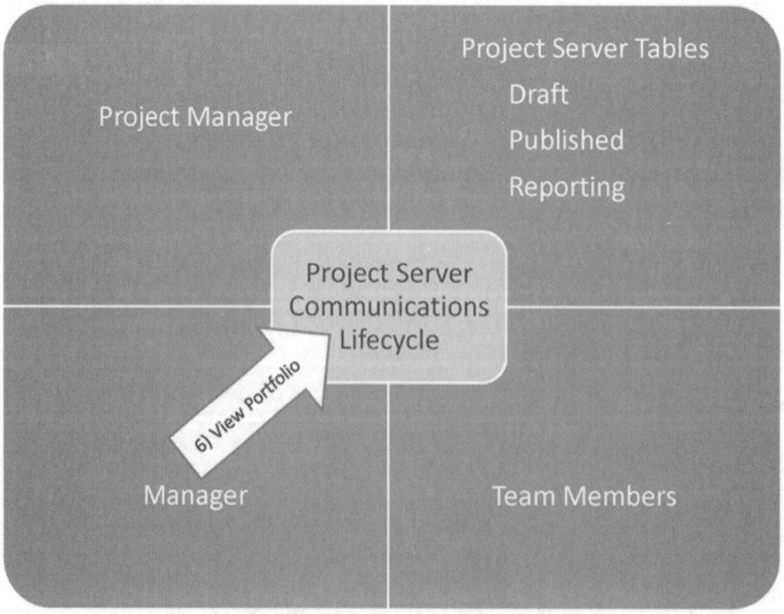

Figure 1 - 11: Executives view the organization's project portfolio

> **Information**: Project managers can create automation rules to process updates from resources automatically. Project managers can use a combination of rules and manual actions to maintain their projects by accepting updates from resources. Automation rules also allow the project manager to automatically publish as well as accept the updates.

Collaboration and Management Tools Overview

Beyond the core communication between project managers and project team members, Project Server 2013 provides additional features for project team collaboration. Some of these features are native to Project Server 2013, whereas others leverage integration with Windows SharePoint Server (WSS) and Windows SharePoint Foundation. The features that are native to Project Server 2013 include:

- **Status Reports** – Status reports allow project managers, resource managers, and executives to establish single or periodic status reports to which team members must respond. Team members may also create their own unrequested reports and submit them at any time. The *Status Report* feature can save a manager time, as it automatically compiles a team report from individual responses.
- **Automated Alerts and Reminders** – Project Server 2013 features an automated reminder system that generates email notices for a variety of situations, including reminding team members of upcoming and overdue task work, and of status reports that are due. In addition to reminders, alerts provide instant notification when certain events occur, such as a new task assignment. All users have the ability to set their own alerts and reminders, and managers have the added ability to set reminders for their resources.
- **Exchange Integration** – This feature allows users to display Project Web App tasks in SharePoint My Sites and synchronizes user's out of office information to create exceptions on Project Server resource calendars.
- **Task Reassignment** – The system supports a team lead structure where functional leaders participate in the work distribution and management process. If the project manager enables task reassignment for team members in a project, team members can transfer work to each other, subject to the project manager's approval.
- **Ad hoc Reporting** – You can quickly print information from data grids in Project Web App, selecting and ordering fields and formatting the results. You can also export grid data and analysis cube data to Excel for additional manipulation and reporting.
- **Issues** – Team members log and track project issues from creation to resolution using the Project Server Issues list created as part of each project's Project Workspace. You can link issues to risks, tasks, documents, and other issues. The links create indicators that appear in Project Center views, where the system flags a project with an icon indicating it contains issues. Similarly, the system flags tasks in Project views when they have issues linked to them.
- **Risks** – Team members can identify, prioritize, and track project risks using the Issues List created as part of each project's workspace. Risks use a different field array than issues, but each function the same when it comes to linking and the flagging that the system performs in response.
- **Documents** – Project Web App provides a general public document library available to all system users. The public document library is an excellent place to make common process documentation available as part of a standardized environment. Each project has its own document library within the Project Workspace into which users can load documents and link them to tasks, issues, risks, and other documents in the system.
- **Project Proposals** – System users can create and submit project proposals for consideration and approval. This feature enables the enterprise to build a demand-management system for new projects in the enterprise. You can tailor the approval process to meet your organization's workflow.

- **Resource Plans –** Used in conjunction with project proposals and projects, resource plans provide a means to estimate and measure future resource loads.
- **Timesheets –** Timesheets provide enterprise users with fully functional time reporting capabilities that can collect time at any reporting level. Most importantly, the timesheet feature includes the ability to create a full audit trail, allowing system implementers to create regulatory-compliant solutions. You can use timesheet data to drive task progress or maintain this data without using it to drive task updates. You can also use the *Tasks* page to collect task progress as in previous versions of Project Server.
- **Deliverables –** Project managers can define deliverables linked to tasks that other project managers can consume in their projects, thereby creating a new way of cross-linking projects. With the addition of SharePoint Server to the server farm, managers can apply SharePoint workflows to the deliverables.

The following modules walk you through configuring and using Project Server 2013 and Project Online in a logical systematic workflow. Each module builds upon the learning of the previous module to increase your understanding of the toolset and provides you with the learning necessary for each step of the PPM process.

Module 02

Task Lists and Project Sites

Learning Objectives

After completing this module, you will be able to:

- Use Project Server and SharePoint to manage projects
- Understand the SharePoint content management model
- Understand Managed Metadata Service and Enterprise Content Types
- Understand new Project Site behaviors and permissions modes
- Manage Project Sites and their contents

Inside Module 02

SharePoint Concepts

SharePoint Foundation and SharePoint Server 2013 are base technologies in the platform for Microsoft Project Server 2013. Together, the industry recognizes these tools as making up a Portfolio and Project Management (PPM) platform. Microsoft Project Server 2013 surfaces itself to most users by way of a web-based interface called Project Web App (PWA).

SharePoint Foundation provides the building blocks for the PWA user interface. When users create projects in PWA, each project is typically given a collaboration site which I refer to as a *Project site.* SharePoint Server 2013 provides a collection of enterprise features such as Excel Services for business intelligence, Business Connectivity Services for line of business integration, an extensive library of web parts, and expanded searching capabilities to name just a few.

All pages that users see in Project Web App are SharePoint pages. As demonstrated in Figure 2 - 1, SharePoint Foundation provides the web interface for PWA and the Project Sites that include features such as risks, issues, documents, and deliverables. The Project Server 2013 application builds upon SharePoint Foundation by adding a project and resource scheduling engine, the mechanisms for task updating, and a project and resource reporting engine.

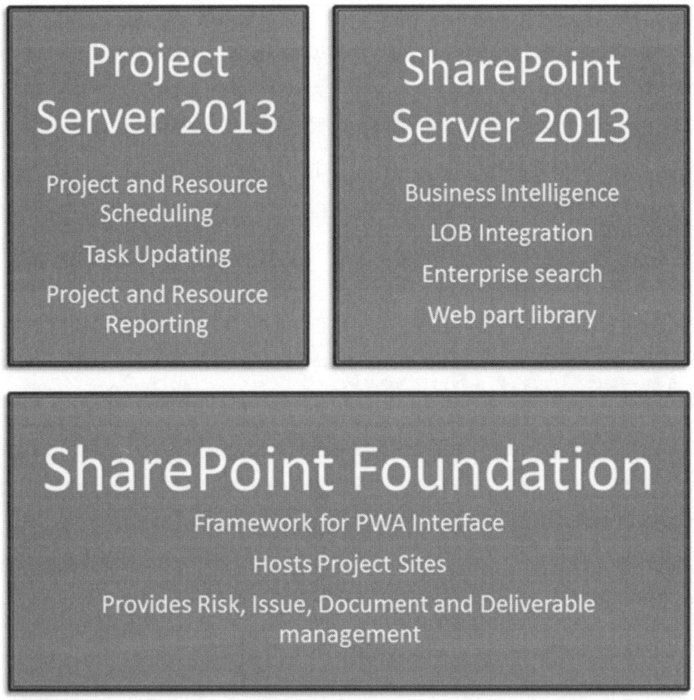

Figure 2 - 1: SharePoint Project Server features

If you configure Project Server 2013 to provision Project Sites automatically, then the system provisions a new Project Site when a project manager publishes a new project for the first time. If you configure Project Server 2013 to provision Project Sites manually, then the system provisions a new Project Site only when the project manager chooses to do so. The Project Site provides a central collaboration area for the project team. Figure 2 - 2 represents the publishing and provisioning sequence.

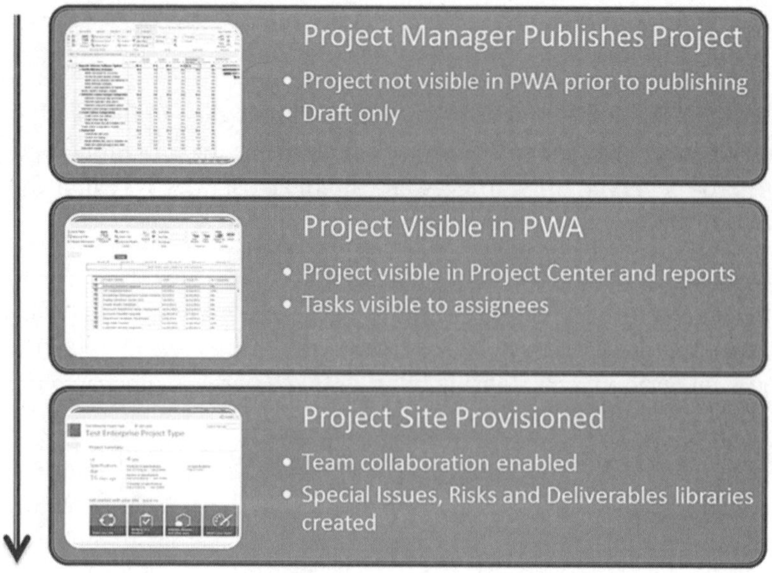
Project Manager Publishes Project
• Project not visible in PWA prior to publishing
• Draft only
Project Visible in PWA
• Project visible in Project Center and reports
• Tasks visible to assignees
Project Site Provisioned
• Team collaboration enabled
• Special Issues, Risks and Deliverables libraries created

Figure 2 - 2: Publishing and provisioning sequence

The first topics in this module familiarize you with the basic SharePoint model, including some of the core concepts of collaboration and content management. Next, you learn how to work with the tools within the PWA interface to control SharePoint provisioning for new Project Sites and for managing existing sites.

It is extremely helpful for you to understand general SharePoint administration. You should understand the SharePoint architecture and how to perform basic configuration and troubleshooting tasks in SharePoint. As this book focuses on Project Server 2013, the following provides "bare bones" knowledge to get you moving in the right direction. To dive deeper into working with SharePoint technologies, you should consider acquiring additional reference materials and training.

Understanding the SharePoint Hierarchy

At a high level, SharePoint is a family of tools for creating and managing websites for teams to collaborate and share many different types of structured and unstructured information or content. Table 2 - 1 lists examples of both structured and unstructured content in SharePoint.

Structured Content	Unstructured Content
• Task lists • Risk logs • Issue logs • Event calendars • Discussion forums • Surveys	• Documents • Forms • Web pages • Images • Wiki pages

Table 2 - 1: Structured and unstructured content examples

Structured content is a collection of data stored and organized in tables, whereas **unstructured content** is stored in files, such as Microsoft Word or Excel files. SharePoint stores structured content in SharePoint lists, and unstructured content in SharePoint libraries.

Although SharePoint exists in two distinct flavors, SharePoint Foundation and SharePoint Server 2013, many people use the word SharePoint as a generic term to describe the collection of storage and collaboration features offered by this family of products. Figure 2 - 3 illustrates the SharePoint architecture, with SharePoint Foundation serving as a base layer for both Project Server 2013 and SharePoint Server.

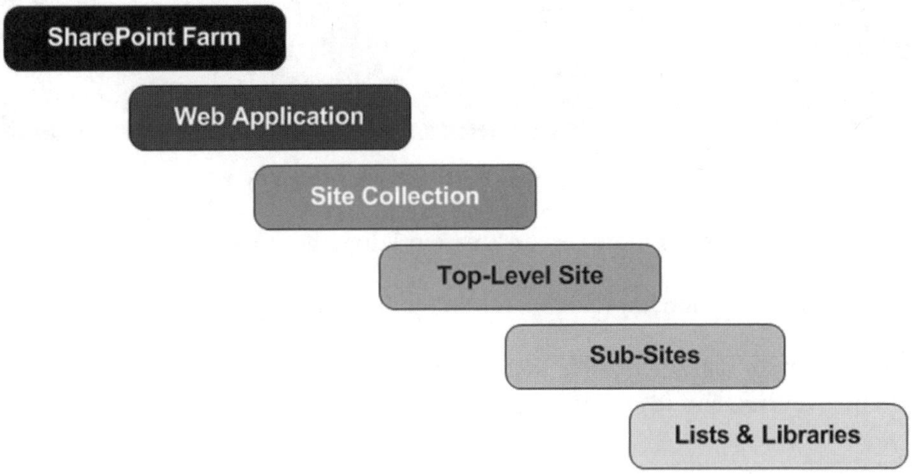

Figure 2 - 3: SharePoint architecture

SharePoint helps to organize data and enables collaboration. Regardless of the type of data, there are several main concepts that recur throughout the system, including the following:

- Storage
- Administration
- Security
- Templates
- Recycle bins
- Metadata
- Version Control
- Alerts
- Workflow

Understanding SharePoint Storage

SharePoint stores and organizes your content according to the nested hierarchical model shown in Figure 2 - 4.

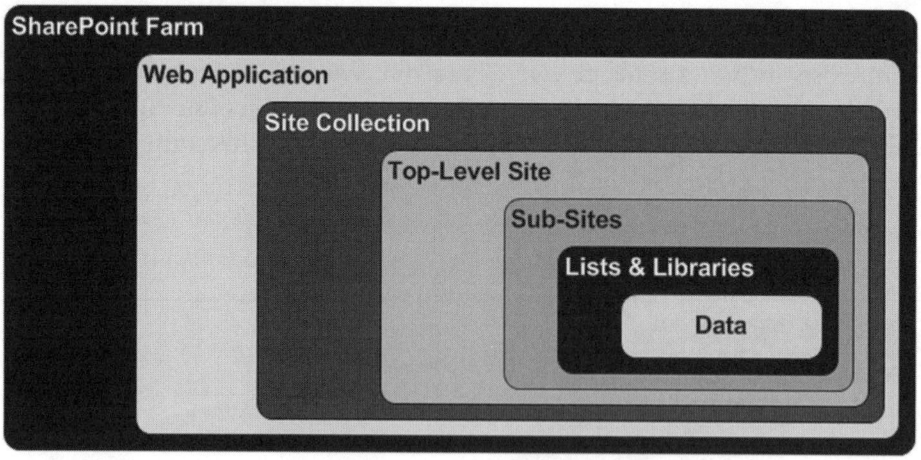

Figure 2 - 4: SharePoint storage hierarchy

SharePoint Farm: A collection of one or more servers that work together to serve SharePoint functionality.

Web Application: An IIS website extended with SharePoint to host Site Collections.

Site Collection: A collection of SharePoint sites that contains a top-level site and optional child sites, and is the base unit for ownership, security, and recovery.

Top-Level Site: The top-most user-accessible site in a SharePoint Site Collection, which can contain pages, lists, libraries, and child sites.

Sub-Sites: Child sites in a SharePoint Site Collection organized in a hierarchical fashion below a Top-Level site, and can contain pages, lists, libraries, and other child sites.

Apps (Lists and Libraries): Containers that hold structured and unstructured data within a SharePoint site.

Each subsequent level within this storage and management structure has an increasing level of granularity for administration, security, and control over the data stored within.

Understanding Project Site Security in Project Server Permissions Mode

As I mention in Module 01, there are two types of security modes in Project Server 2013. As with previous versions of Project Server, administrators can create their own security groups, permissions and categories. When using these granular permissions you are using Project Server permissions mode. Project Server permissions are very powerful but have the potential to add significant maintenance and complexity to your deployment. For administrators that want a seamless, out-of-the-box experience, Microsoft Project Server 2013 offers SharePoint permissions mode. I cover Project Server permissions mode and SharePoint permissions mode in this section.

You use Project Server security groups to manage users, groups, and permissions when your system runs in Project Server permissions mode. A user is an individual who can access the system and use its features. Permissions are specific functions available to users of the system. You grant access to permissions in SharePoint by first adding users to Project Server security groups, and then by adding people to project teams and task assignments. Table 2 - 2 shows examples of Project Server groups and their respective permissions.

Users	Groups	Permissions
Jan Michael	Portfolio Viewers	View Risks View Issues View Documents View Deliverables
Jim Dwight Angela	Project Managers	Edit Risks Edit Issues Edit Documents Edit Deliverables
Kevin Pam Andy Oscar	Team Members	Edit Risks Edit Issues Edit Documents View Deliverables

Table 2 - 2: Users, groups, and permissions

When your system is set to Project Server permissions mode, Project Server 2013 manages security for your Project Sites through a synchronization process. When a project stored in Project Server 2013 has a Project Site associated with it, the synchronization process runs automatically when the project manager republishes the project to PWA, as shown in Figure 2 - 5. I discuss the specific configuration options for this synchronization process later in this module.

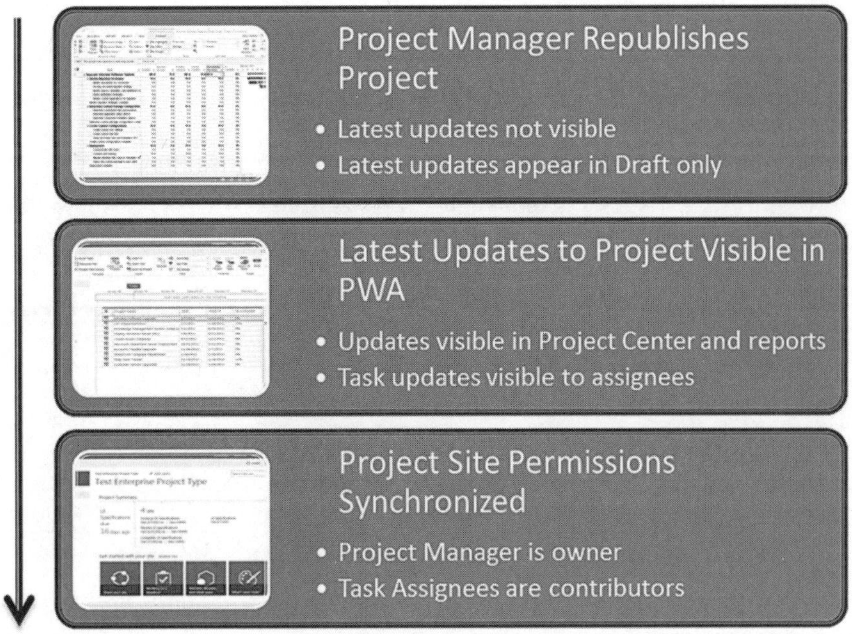

Figure 2 - 5: Republish a project to synchronize the Project Site permissions

A user's effective rights are determined by their group membership and association with a project. For instance, the system grants *Read-Only* access to a Project Site to a user who is a member of the project team, but does not have a task assignment. On the other hand, a team member who is assigned to a task on the project has the right to contribute items to the site. The project manager is the owner of the Project Site.

Project Server 2013 configures the user, group, and permission settings within a Project Site at the site level, and those settings cascade down to each library and list within the site as well as to each data item stored within each library and list. However, if your business processes require it, you can break this security inheritance, allowing you to independently control which users have access to which data within the site. Understand that once you break the inheritance, you must manage security for the site manually.

Understanding Project Site Security in SharePoint Permissions Mode

When you run your system in SharePoint permissions mode, the system assumes that the Project Site is the central focus and the project manager, owner of the site, controls access through normal SharePoint-style sharing. There is no connection between PWA access and access to Project Sites in this mode. Therefore, you must manage each separately just as if you would individual SharePoint sites.

Site and List Templates

SharePoint helps you streamline site and list creation by employing site templates and list templates. The quantity and selection of site and list templates installed in your system depends on the version of SharePoint you deploy. If none of the built-in templates meet your needs, you can create your own tailored templates, which you can use to create future sites or lists within your SharePoint environment.

Information: Note that when you update a site template, it does not update sites previously created from the template.

When Project Server 2013 provisions a new Project Site for a project, it uses a template. As a Project Server administrator, you can create new templates for associating with various Enterprise Project Types in your organization and update the default template, causing all future Project Sites to reflect the changes you implement in the new site template. Examples of list templates that are included in both versions of SharePoint are:

- Announcements
- Contacts
- Discussion Board
- Links
- Calendar
- Tasks
- Survey

List templates are not necessary for creating new lists within a SharePoint site. Rather, they streamline the process of creating a new list if the type of data that you want to store is similar to one of the existing templates.

Recycle Bins

Similar to a PC desktop, SharePoint offers site-level recycle bin functionality. Each site has a recycle bin that stores files and list items when you delete them from libraries and lists within that SharePoint site, allowing you to easily restore them to their original locations. SharePoint includes a 2-stage recycle bin process. When a person deletes an item from the site-level recycle bin, the item moves to a site collection administrative recycle bin for a period of time. This second-stage recycle bin is accessible only by a SharePoint administrator.

Version Control

SharePoint provides automatic version control, a mechanism for tracking updates contributed by members of a team. When you enable this functionality you can track major versions (1.0, 2.0, 3.0, etc.) for each item of structured content in a SharePoint list. Each time you make a change to an item stored in a list, the system automatically increments the version number and stores the previous version of the item for later review and retrieval. You can also track both major and minor versions (1.0, 1.1, 1.2, 2.0, etc.) for each unstructured content item that you store in a SharePoint library. When you enable minor versioning for files in a library, these minor versions are drafts. When you enable versioning for a list or library within a SharePoint site, the system includes all of the content items stored in that list or library.

Alerts

As a SharePoint user, you can use two different notification mechanisms to learn about content changes in a SharePoint list or library. SharePoint provides both email alerts and RSS feeds. Assuming that you configured the email notification functionality by connecting to an SMTP server for sending outbound messages, you can request that the system send an email notification whenever a user creates, changes, or deletes all or certain items in a list or library. If you enable RSS feeds in SharePoint, each list or library in a SharePoint site can provide its own feed, which lists any recent alterations including additions, changes, and deletions that users make to its content. Any user with access to the list or library can subscribe to this feed with an RSS reader such as Microsoft Outlook 2010, which automatically harvests the feed on a regular basis and displays the updates for the user on their desktop without requiring a site visit.

Workflow

A workflow in SharePoint is an electronic representation of a business process. More specifically, it is a way of attaching business logic to content stored and managed in a SharePoint site. Whether you want to represent a review and approval process, an issue escalation process, or a project proposal process, you can break down each process into a set of activities or tasks that the SharePoint workflow engine represents, stores, and tracks. Each workflow can automatically perform actions on content stored in a SharePoint list or library, such as update a status field from "Submitted" to "Approved" or move an expense report from one location to another. Workflows can also initiate a request to a person to perform an action on an item, such as review a project issue and assign it to the appropriate team member for resolution. You can use a number of options and tools for creating workflows in SharePoint, including each of the following:

- **Built-in Workflows:** Because Project Server 2013 installs with SharePoint Server, the system provides a number of built-in workflows for SharePoint Server lifecycle management. You do not need to have custom code development capabilities to use and configure built-in workflows.
- **Microsoft SharePoint Designer:** This Microsoft desktop application has a convenient wizard-style interface for building workflows for non-developers. It allows you to represent sophisticated processes that may have several process steps and can contain conditional logic as well as perform several types of ac-

tions on the content stored in a SharePoint list or library. These workflows are limited, in that they can interact within the scope of only a single site.

- **Microsoft Visual Studio:** You can use this developer tool to build much more sophisticated SharePoint workflows, including custom interactive forms, interaction with multiple lists and libraries, and interaction with other applications or Line of Business systems. Leveraging this power and flexibility comes at a price: you must be proficient with the tool and have knowledge of .NET application development and deployment.

- **Third-Party Tools:** There are various third-party tools available for building SharePoint workflows. These tools combine the ease of use provided by SharePoint Designer with the power and flexibility of Visual Studio workflows.

I cover only some of the built-in workflows in this module. If you are interested in learning more about building workflows with SharePoint Designer, Visual Studio, or third party tools, you should consider acquiring additional reference materials and training.

Managed Metadata and Enterprise Content Types

Rather than keeping this section summarized and part of the previous content, I thought that these two very powerful SharePoint features need more prominent consideration as they are often overlooked during Project Server deployments and are more relevant to Project Server 2013 than ever given the option to run Project Site-centric. In order to run under SharePoint permissions mode and maintain some consistency, you should at least deploy Enterprise Content Types. The most powerful way to deploy Enterprise Content Types is by leveraging the SharePoint Managed Metadata Service, so I would be remiss if I did not encourage you to deploy that as well.

What is the Managed Metadata Service?

You can think of the Managed Metadata Service as a master lexicon, both dictionary and thesaurus for the business, one that allows people to interact with the system using familiar terms, but tightly controls taxonomy management in the background. In other words, the Managed Metadata Service is a term store capable of standardizing and storing term hierarchies as well as countless synonyms that help users tag content correctly.

Consider the following example where I show a real-world scenario where a company has grown by acquisition leaving behind a scattered corporate lexicon. To standardize data capture in the content store, a savvy SharePoint administrator can leverage Managed Metadata Services to help users find the correct term. Here I examine the term set "Division," which itself has multiple synonyms as well as an information hierarchy, or related terms in the term set. Each of the terms in bold are preferred metadata usage while the italicized entries represent synonyms that the users might enter for each preferred term.

- **Division,** *Department, Dept., Core, Silo, Practice Group*
- **Finance**, *Fin, $, Accounting, Payables, Receivables*
- **HR**, *Human Resources, People Services, Recruiting*
- **IT**, *IS, I.S., Information Services, Information Technology*

One of the powerful constructs is to use these defined terms as selectable column values in SharePoint. The benefit to the end user is ease of use such as the system suggesting "IT" when the user types "IS." The benefit to the business is consistent metadata architecture across the enterprise. As a Project Server administrator you benefit from a level of control over your Project Site metadata using a best practice approach and your users will benefit from improved search results.

I hope that I thoroughly whetted your appetite. The Managed Metadata Service is well-thought-out with surprisingly rich options that would take an entire book to fully articulate. It really deserves more attention from both of us. I am limited by sheer page count. You do not have that excuse.

What are Enterprise Content Types?

Experienced Project Server administrators can think of these as the logical native SharePoint equivalent to Enterprise Project Types in Project Server 2013. Enterprise Content Types bring together templates, metadata, and workflow into an easy-to-reuse package. Combined with the Managed Metadata Service this could be a data steward's paradise. What makes it so powerful is that sites consume content types as a service. The system publishes content type updates so that consumer sites always have the most current published data.

Enterprise Content Types can contain both managed and non-managed metadata as columns and they can contain managed metadata from multiple sources. You can also cascade Enterprise Content Types by defining one that is based upon another. For example, you have a business requirement that every issue entered into the system must contain several mandated corporate PMO fields while other user groups, such as Finance, want to add its own. You can create a corporate change management content type and then create a Finance change management content type consuming the corporate change management content type.

Another powerful use of Enterprise Content Types is the ability to create document libraries that contain common Microsoft Word, PowerPoint, or Excel templates. For example, if your organization's PMO has a standard scope statement document template, you can implement that as a content type. Now, project teams can go to the document library and create a new scope statement from the scope statement template.

Before customizing your Project Site templates for your Enterprise Content Types, it is a good idea to determine whether your deployment can benefit from deploying the Managed Metadata Service and Enterprise Content Types. It makes more sense to configure your custom Project Site templates using ECT's rather than configuring each one individually.

Importance of Managed Metadata and Enterprise Content Types

The Managed Metadata Service and Enterprise Content Types are not new for SharePoint 2013, but they suddenly take on more importance when you consider their potential impact in two areas: Ideation, or Pre-Portfolio analytics, and for supporting the SharePoint-site centric approach and the "grow into a project" scenario that I describe in the next main topical section, *Understanding Special Project Site 2013 Behaviors.* When you consider that SharePoint becomes the primary source of data when you use the lightweight approach, or when you use SharePoint lists for ideation, enforcing a uniform metadata model that can easily and consistently map to Project Server 2013 fields becomes much more important. Plus, I would be surprised if Project Server starts consuming managed metadata in a near future version. I would certainly push the "like" button for that.

Content Type Hubs

Content type hubs are site collections designated as a content type dispensary for an instance of a Managed Metadata Service. Used together, a Managed Metadata Service and a content type hub provide a complete metadata syndication system allowing administrators to publish, retract, or refresh metadata stores on all sites that consume managed metadata through Enterprise Content Types as illustrated in Figure 2 - 6.

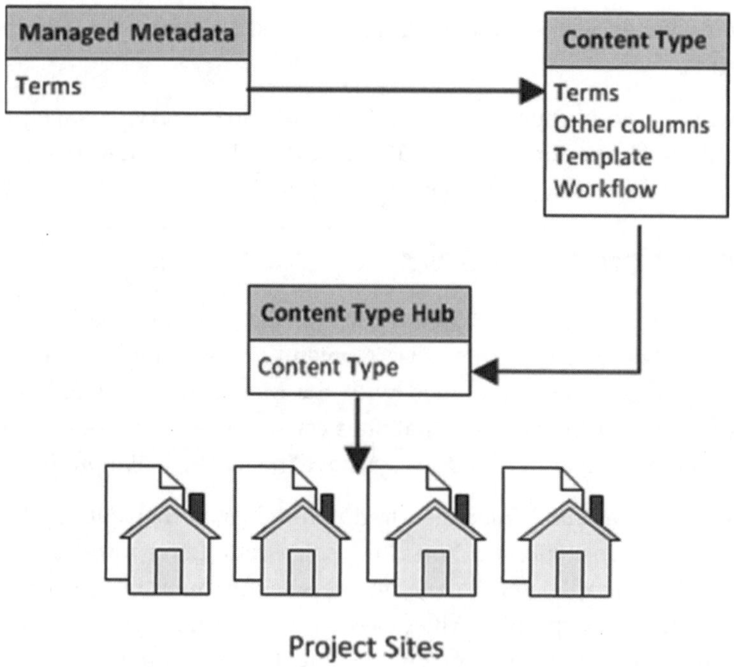

Figure 2 - 6: Managed metadata delivered through an Enterprise Content Type

The advantage to using this scenario is that you can selectively publish changes in the content store through content types to the consuming SharePoint sites allowing you to refresh metadata throughout the system from a single command. The disadvantage to this approach is that it takes more planning time; much more planning time.

Understanding Special Project Site 2013 Behaviors

As I mentioned in Module 01, *Introduction and Project Server Overview,* Project Sites take on new meaning in the SharePoint 2013 Foundation platform as they now support a "grow-up" or maturity growth path into Project Server. As a Project Server administrator, you may encounter business requirements that have you maintaining systems that support a combination of agile and less formal approaches and the more traditional formal project management scenarios with which Project Server is typically associated. Using the new and improved tools in both the SharePoint 2013 and Project Server 2013 platform, you can move entire organizations along a maturity path or you can move ideas along a maturity path. To make this all the more confusing, you can blend these capabilities in practice or you can use them as stepping-stones in a process maturity path as illustrated conceptually in Figure 2 - 7.

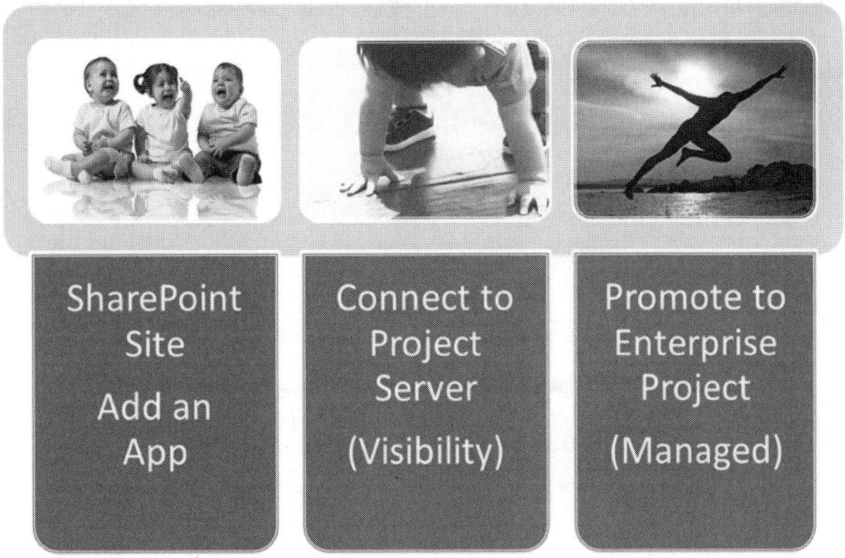

Figure 2 - 7: SharePoint and Project Server support a maturity path

Starting with a SharePoint Team Site

To understand how this works with maturing an idea or an everyday task such as identifying and solving a problem, consider a real world scenario where Marian is a technical manager in logistics who believes that her company has a problem with its product allocation process in the fulfillment center. She bases this on the fact that numerous allocators have told her that they are experiencing partial pick rejections on numerous orders when the stock system indicates that the stock is available, yet at the end of the week, the stock audits never indicate unusual variance. The stated facts are contradictory in that if the stock is available, the pickers should be able to pick the orders the system generates. Marian is a skilled business analyst who also runs logistic projects that involve technology. The first thing Marian needs to do is gather more data as she not only wants to verify the veracity of the allocators claims, she wants as much discovery as she can get her hands on to try to identify the cause of the problem. As a project manager she takes the following steps:

1. Navigates to PWA.

2. Clicks the *Gear* icon and selects the *Site Settings* item.

3. From the *Site Administration* section of the *Site Settings* page, Marian clicks the *Sites and Workspaces* link. The system displays the *Site Settings* ▸ *Sites and Workspaces* page shown in Figure 2 - 8.

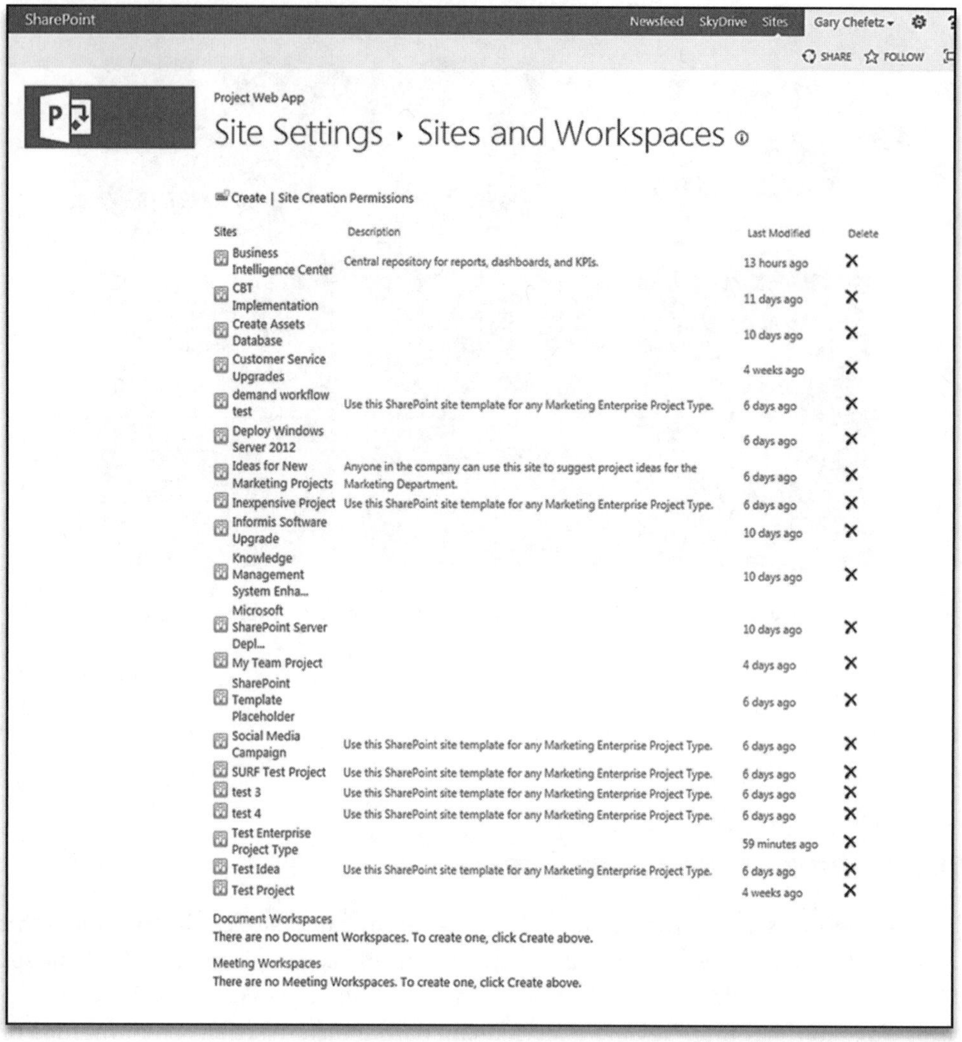

Figure 2 - 8: Site Settings ▸ Sites and Workspaces page

4. Next, from the selections below the page title, Marian clicks the *Create* link. The system displays the *Site Contents ▸ New SharePoint Site* page shown in Figure 2 - 9.

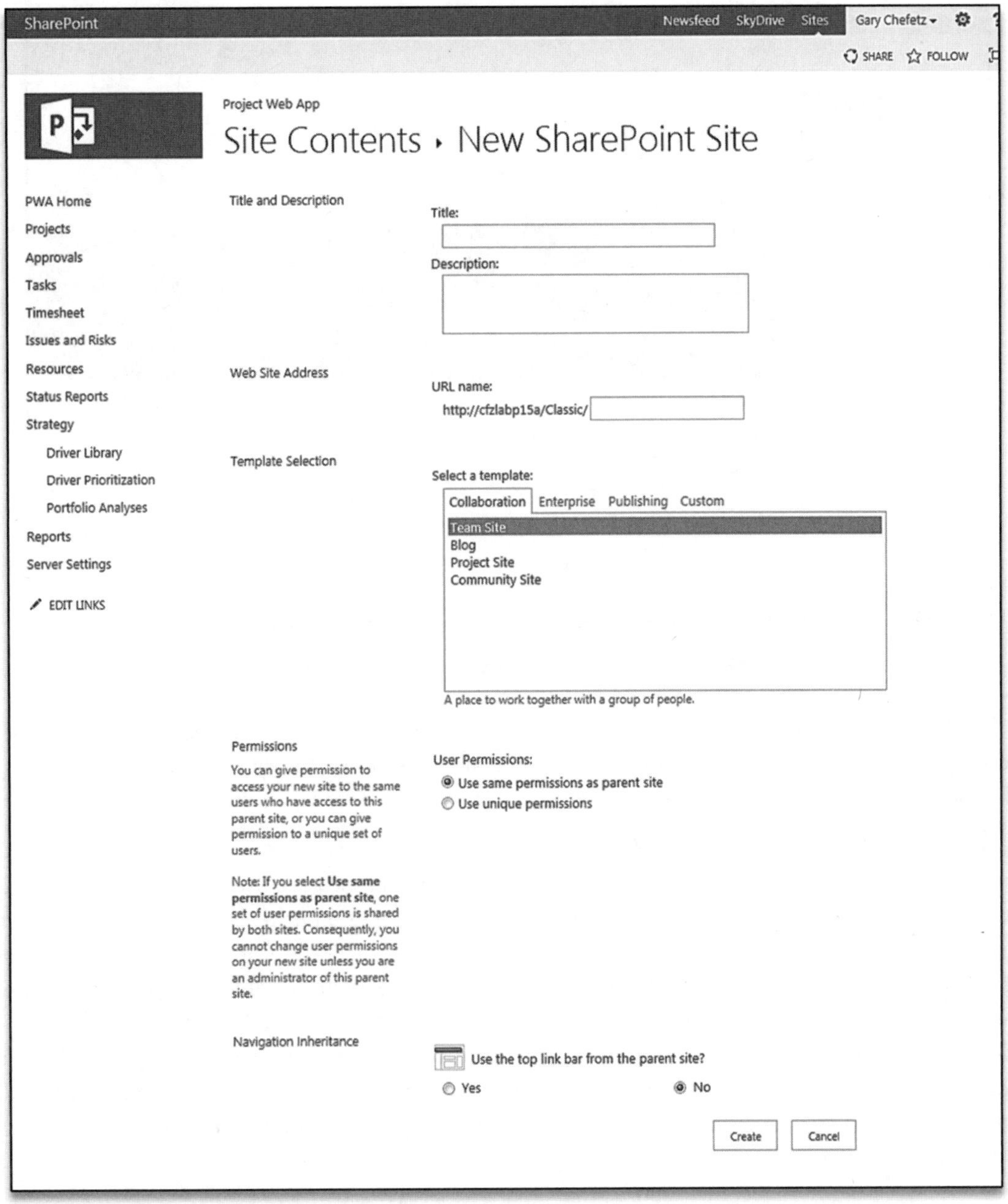

Figure 2 - 9: Site Contents ▸ New SharePoint Site page

5. After naming her site and entering a description, in the *Template* section Marian selects the *Team Site* item to create a simple collaboration site with a document library to house the documentation and evidence she needs to investigate the anomaly. After clicking the *Create* button, the system navigates to Marian's new site as shown in Figure 2 - 10.

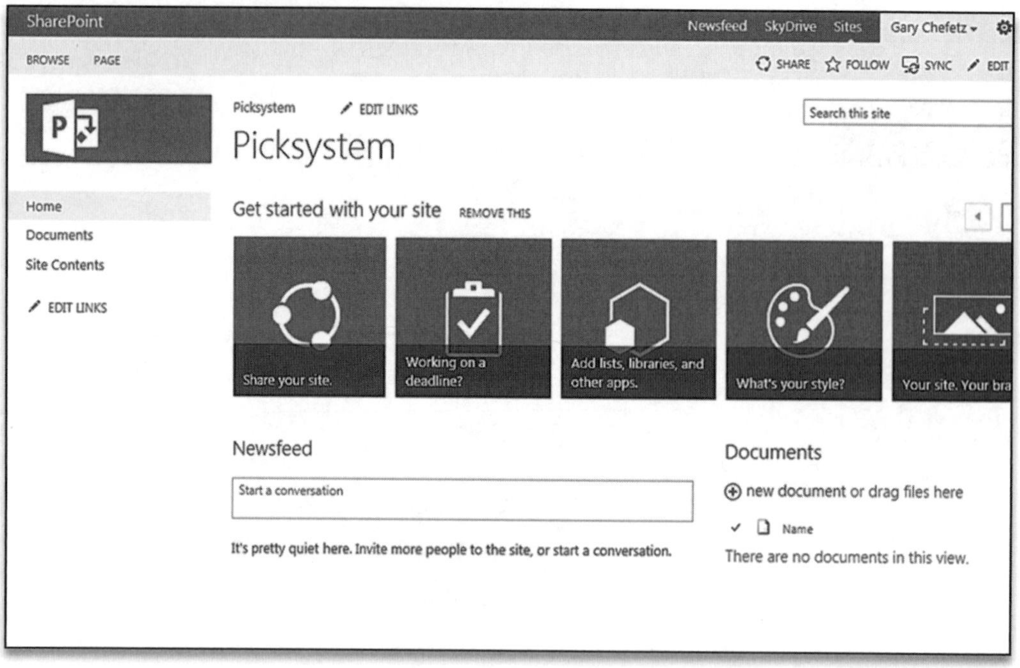

Figure 2 - 10: Picksystem SharePoint Team site

Notice that the *Getting started with your site* carousel for a new SharePoint site provides the most logical next steps for users the way the same carousel works for PWA. You can also see that the site includes a document library by default and that Marian can now add documents, share the site, or add additional SharePoint elements now called *Apps* in SharePoint 2013.

For the moment, Marian wants to build some Excel workbooks to analyze inventory and picking system data. The Project Server administrator created a trusted file location record for the entire PWA site, and Marian has data-reader role on the SQL databases she needs to query, so she is free to create workbooks and pivot tables to analyze the data, which she can later publish to stakeholders if her investigation yields results. Lo and behold, after days of looking at the data, slicing it various ways, she notices that the picking troubles seem to begin on Wednesdays and carry through the week, so she calls the fulfillment center manager, Margaret Wallace, with her findings to ask whether she knew of any reason why things would be going awry midweek. Naturally, the distribution manager wanted to see the data, so Marian clicks the *Share your site* tile in the carousel and the system displays the *Share* dialog shown in Figure 2 - 11.

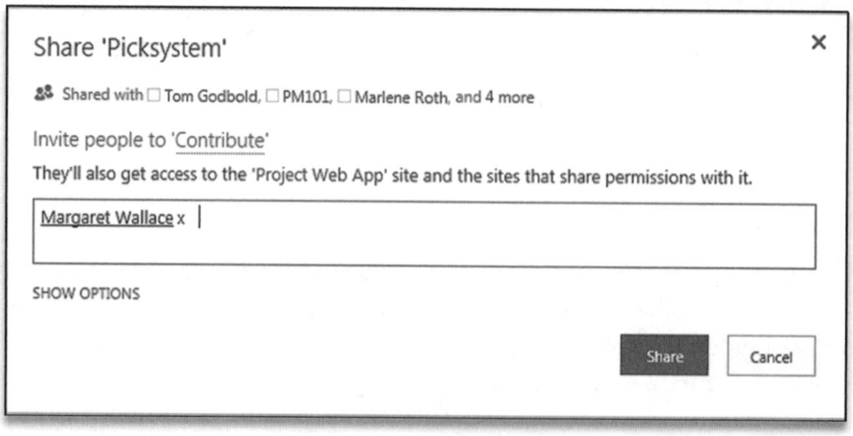

Figure 2 - 11: Share dialog

Although impressed with Marian's trend analysis report showing that picking problems spiked on Wednesday, Margaret had no ready answers. Marian and Margaret agree that the best course of action is to meet at the fulfillment center after their shift at 5:30 the next Wednesday to conduct a physical inspection. Marian arrives at the fulfillment center the following Wednesday evening armed with copies of the day's non-pickable tickets. Marian's inventory spot check affirms that the stock showing as available in the system is not hanging on the racks, so Marian and Margaret walk through the physical fulfillment process. This is an informative exercise but reveals nothing. Finally, Marian asks, "What is the process when the picker cannot complete the pick?" "The pickers are supposed to take the picked stock to this holding area," Margaret replies as she walks Marian to a tucked away area of the warehouse, "they're supposed to get back to these orders and complete them or return the items to stock the same day," Margaret said. As the two entered the holding area, the cause of the problem became clear; the missing inventory was stacked up in the holding area causing cascading picking problems.

Adding Apps to Your Site

The next day, Marian schedules a meeting with the VP of Logistics who, after Marian explains the issue, asks Marian to flesh out a project for reviewing the fulfillment process end-to-end rather than applying a spot fix. Marian returns to her *Picksystem* site and clicks the *Working on a Deadline* tile, the second in the carousel shown previously in Figure 2 - 10. The system displays the *Working on a deadline?* dialog shown in Figure 2 - 12.

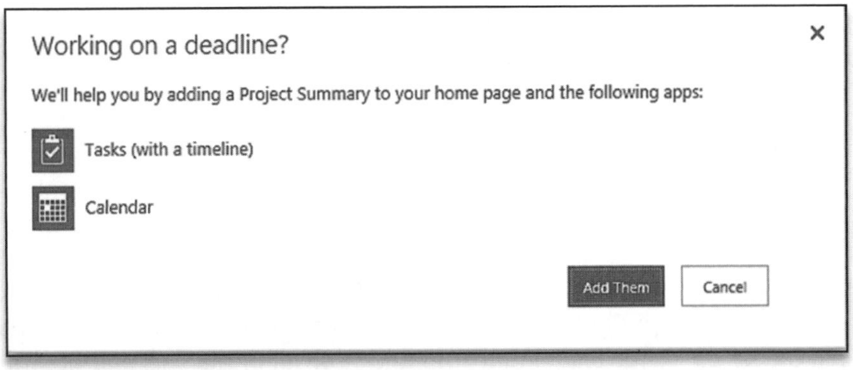
Working on a deadline?
We'll help you by adding a Project Summary to your home page and the following apps:
Tasks (with a timeline)
Calendar
Add Them
Cancel

Figure 2 - 12: Working on a deadline? dialog

In the dialog, Marian confirms the additions proposed by the system by clicking the *Add Them* button. The system redisplays Marian's site as shown in Figure 2 - 13.

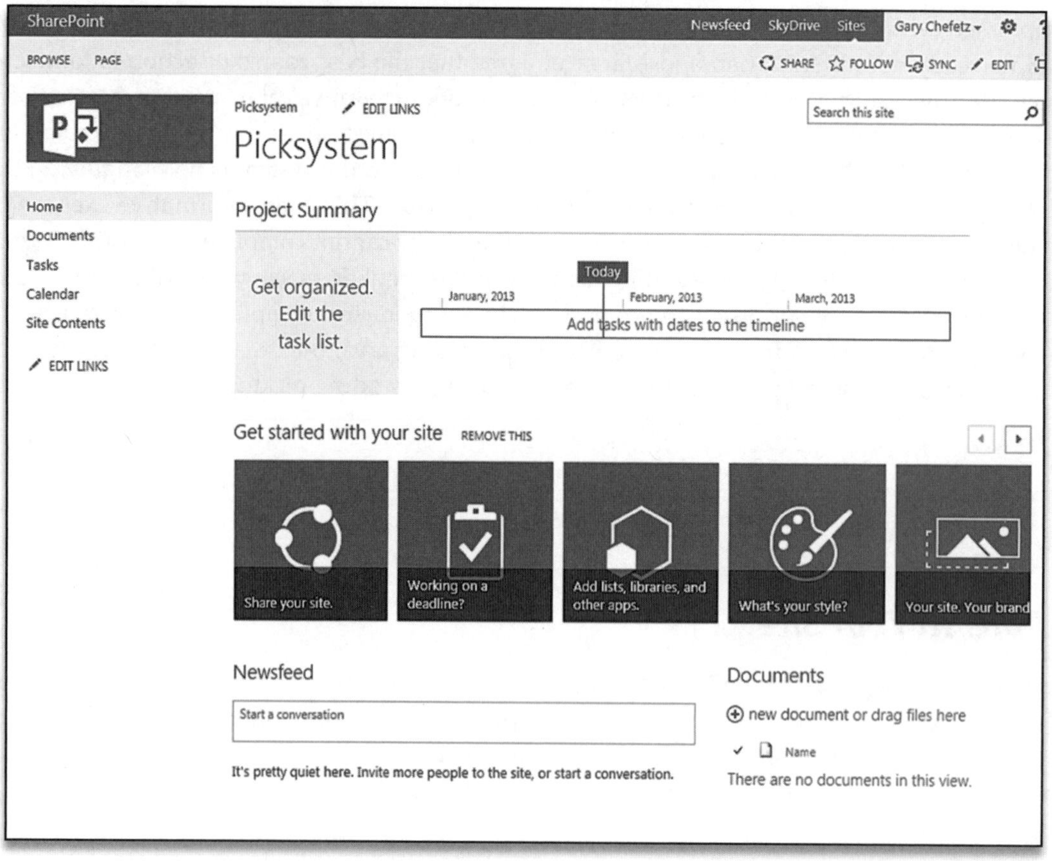

Figure 2 - 13: Picksystem site with Project Summary section and calendar additions

In this case, the system added two *Apps* to the site. Those of you familiar with previous versions know these as lists. Microsoft changed the language for SharePoint 2013 and now all of the lists and libraries you can add to a site in SharePoint are called "*Apps.*" The system dispenses built-in SharePoint apps, SharePoint apps from the Microsoft Office app store, or custom apps that you build and make available to your users. The traditional way for an administrator or user to add an app to a site is to click the *Gear* icon and select the *Add an app* item on the menu. The system displays the *Site Contents* ▸ *Your Apps* page shown in Figure 2 - 14.

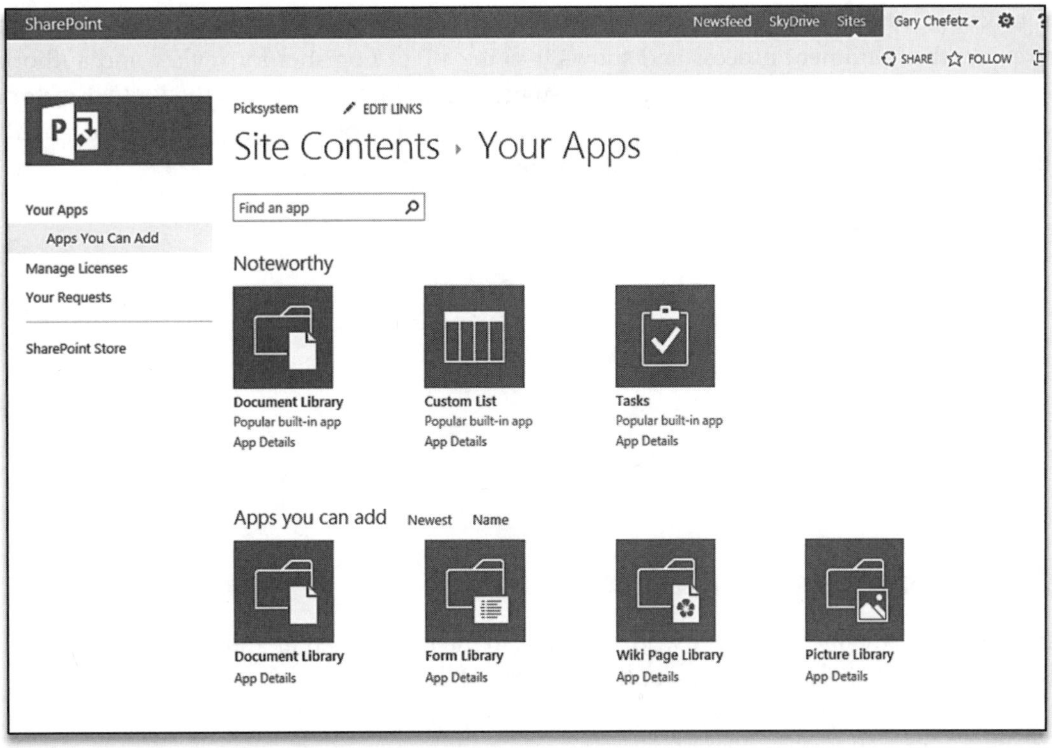

Figure 2 - 14: Site Contents ▸ Your Apps page

Meanwhile, Marian clicks the *Edit the Task List* link to the left of the timeline shown previously in Figure 2 - 13 and the system takes her to the *Tasks* page shown in Figure 2 - 15.

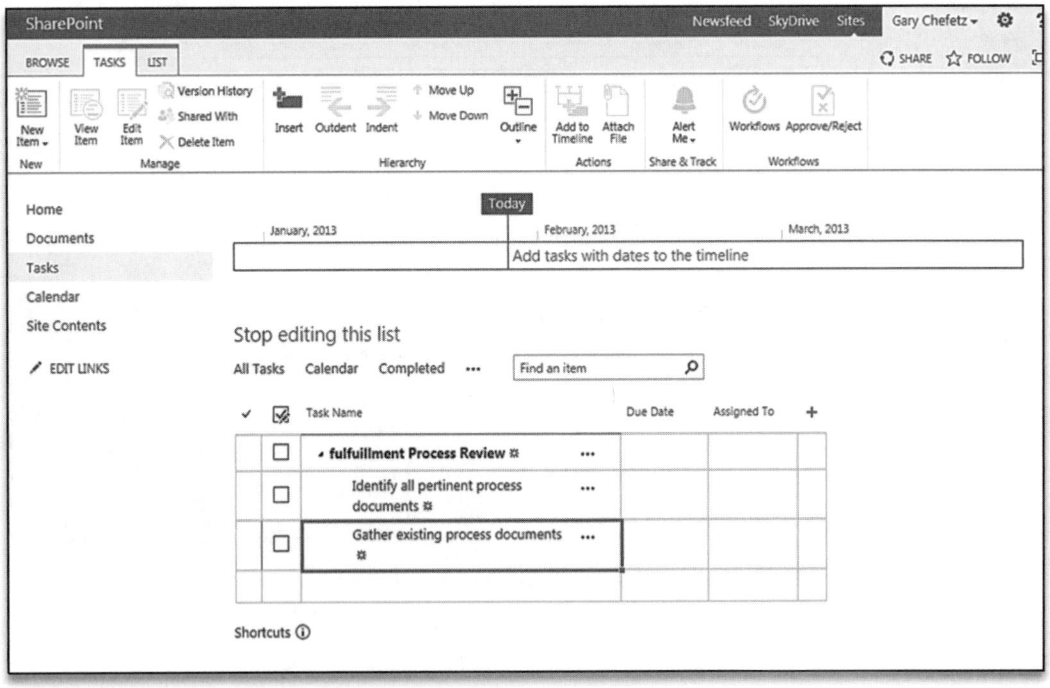

Figure 2 - 15: Tasks page

Marian adds tasks and summary lines to her new project until she creates a work breakdown structure (WBS) for the effort to review the fulfillment process and shows it to the VP of Logistics for review and authorization. The VP, surprised at first by the complexity of the project, suggests that Marian contacts the PMO director to have the project added to Project Server 2013 for visibility because the level of effort looks significant. He added, "I want to know why this started to happen in January. What changed?"

Adding SharePoint Sites to Project Web App

Marian sends an email to the PMO director who navigates to the Project Center and from the *Project* section of the *Projects* ribbon, clicks the *Add SharePoint Sites* button shown in Figure 2 - 16.

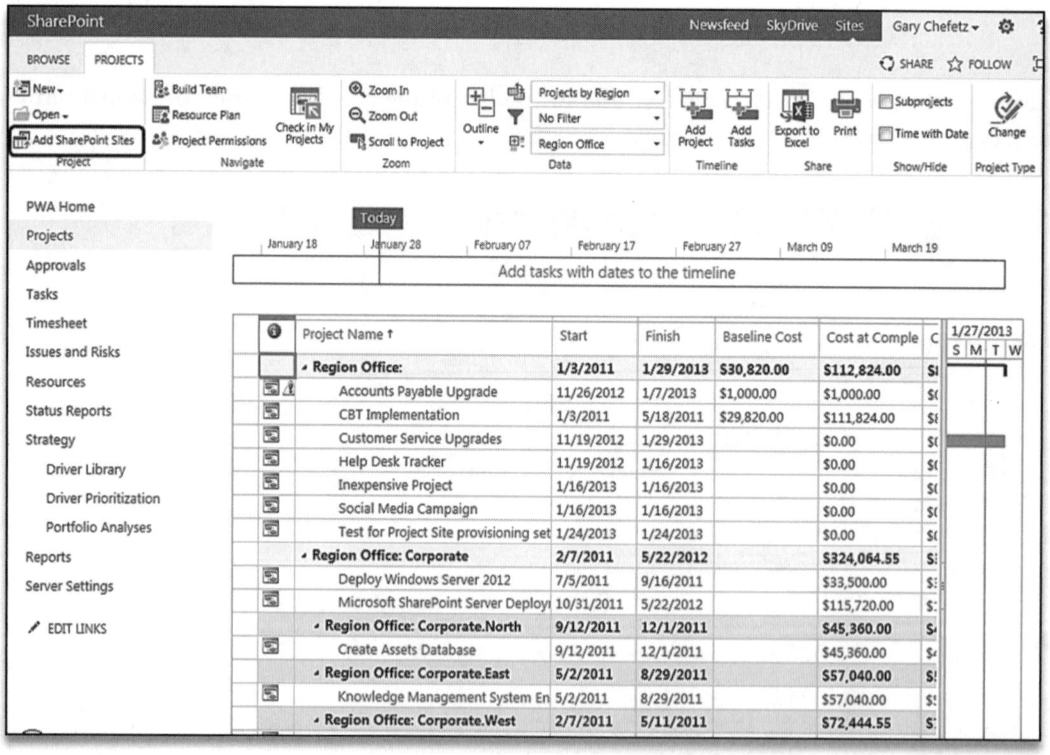

Figure 2 - 16: Click the Add SharePoint Sites button

After clicking the button, the system opens the *Add SharePoint Sites to Project Web App* dialog shown in Figure 2 - 17.

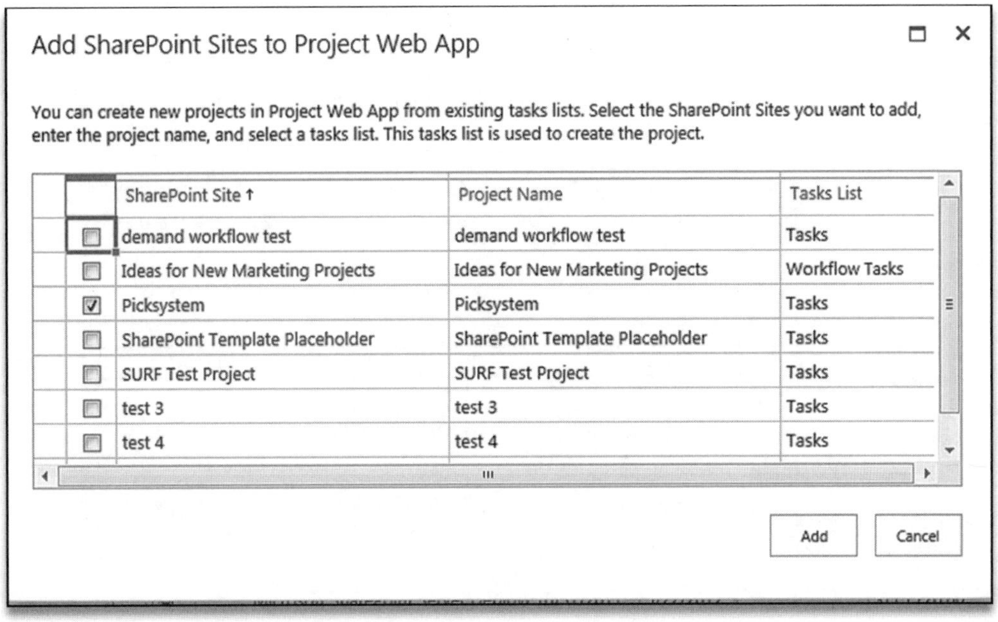

Figure 2 - 17: Add SharePoint Sites to Project Web App dialog

The PMO director selects the checkbox for the *Picksystem* site and the clicks the *Add* button. The system displays the confirmation shown in Figure 2 - 18.

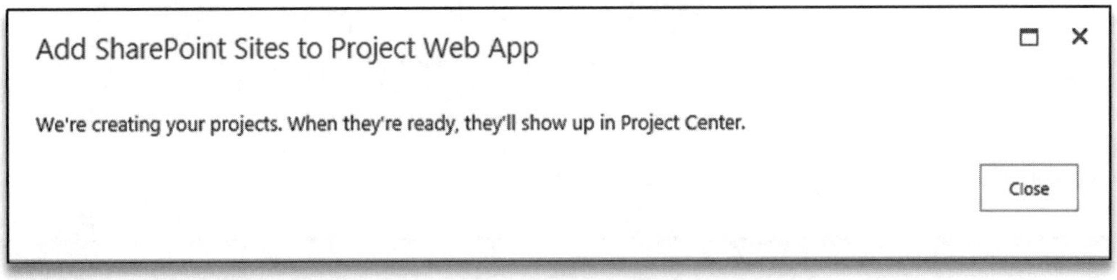

Figure 2 - 18: Add SharePoint Sites to Project Web App confirmation

Clicking the *Close* button returns the PMO director to the Project Center where the project is now visible as shown in Figure 2 - 19.

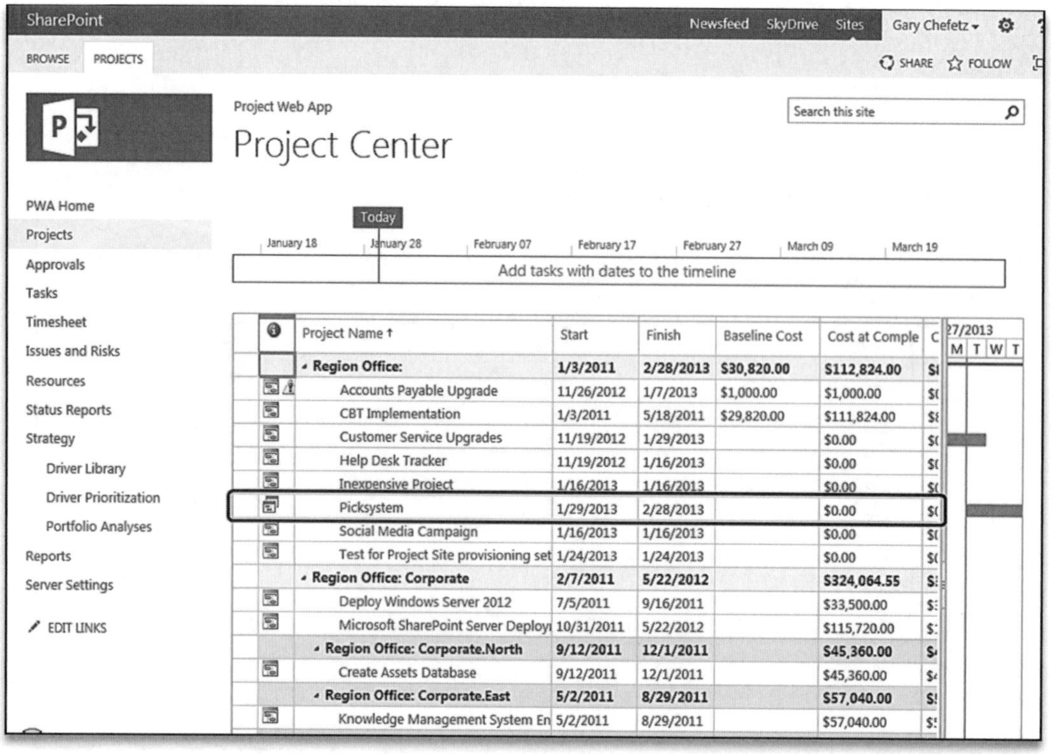

Figure 2 - 19: SharePoint site visible in Project Center

Not only is the project now visible in the Project Center, but the task assignments become visible in Project Web App in two other areas; the *Resource Assignments* and *Resource Availability* pages that you reach from the Resource Center. Figure 2 - 20 shows the *Picksystem* tasks for Margaret Wallace.

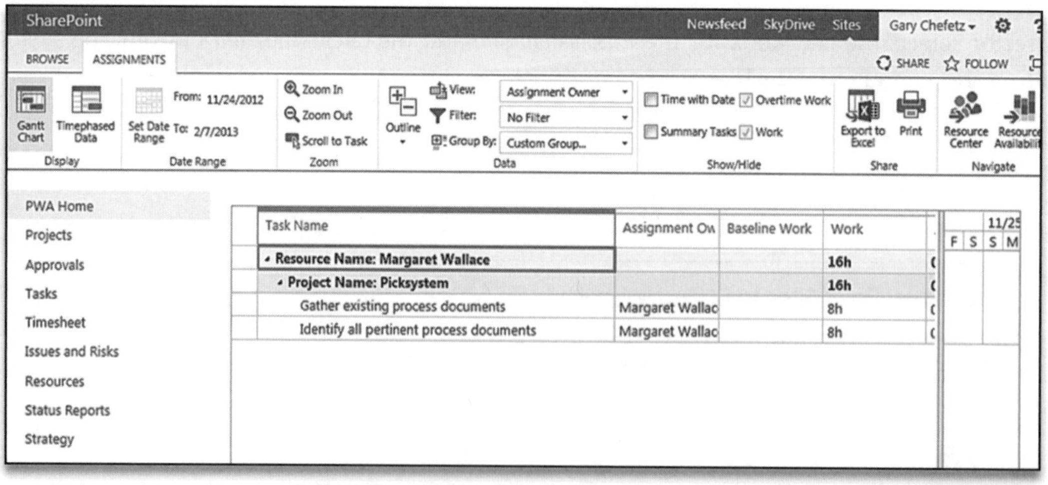

Figure 2 - 20: Resource Assignments page

These tasks also impact resource availability calculations and show up on the *Resource Availability* page as well, after the nightly timer job processes. Notice that each of these tasks shows as 8 hours of work. Based on the due date set in the task list the system calculates one full day of work for each task. The true effort behind the task is unknown. Either of these tasks might take only an hour, or one might take a week's effort for Margaret, but the system uses a very simple algorithm to calculate work for these tasks.

> **Best Practice**: MSProjectExperts recommends that you do not connect SharePoint task lists to Project Web App if you are serious about modeling work/effort in your system unless you are managing the SharePoint lists using Project Pro 2013, as these tasks do not support work values or accurate duration estimates. If you do choose to use these, then you should consider filtering them out of your resource availability calculation by using reporting methods other than the *Resource Availability* page you reach from the Project Center or sample reports.

Converting a Task List to a Project Managed in Project Pro 2013

Based on her discussion with the VP of Logistics, Marian decides to interview some of the pickers during the lunch hour to attempt to figure out what changed at the beginning of the year that caused the problem to begin with. After talking casually with a number of workers in the lunch room Marian is able to determine that the new incentive program implemented in January triggered the problem because it rewards workers for the number of orders processed, ignoring other key performance metrics. The well-intended incentive caused the workers to change their behavior as desired and caused them to focus on orders-out-the-door rather than the entire process. In their haste to make their bonuses, they were allowing other tasks to slip in favor of picking more orders. The backup in the return-to-stock area is an unintended consequence of the new incentive program.

After reporting her findings, the VP of Logistics asks Marian to expand the project to include a complete review of the incentive program. At this point Marian realizes that a simple task list is not going to work for her given the growing complexity of the project, deciding it's time to switch from the list to Project Pro 2013 to meet the complexity demands. Marian navigates to the Project Center in PWA, selects her project in the data grid, and then clicks the *Open* pick list and selects the *In Microsoft Project for Editing* item as shown in Figure 2 - 21.

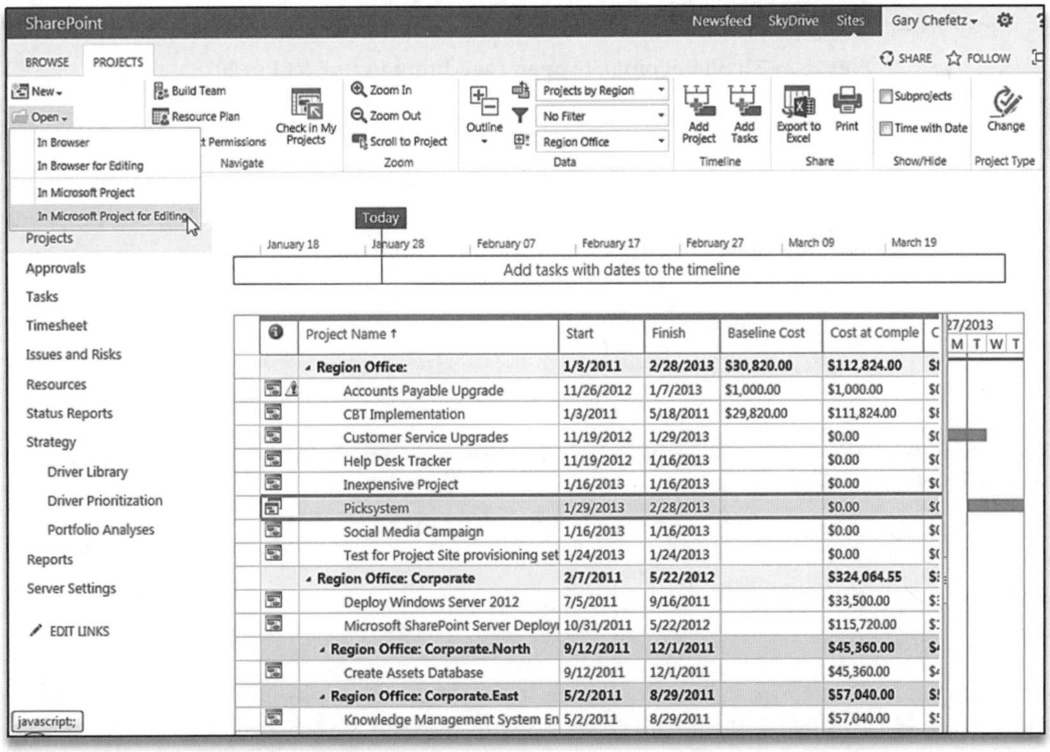

Figure 2 - 21: Open SharePoint list in Microsoft Project for Editing

The system opens the SharePoint list in Project Pro 2013 as shown in Figure 2 - 22.

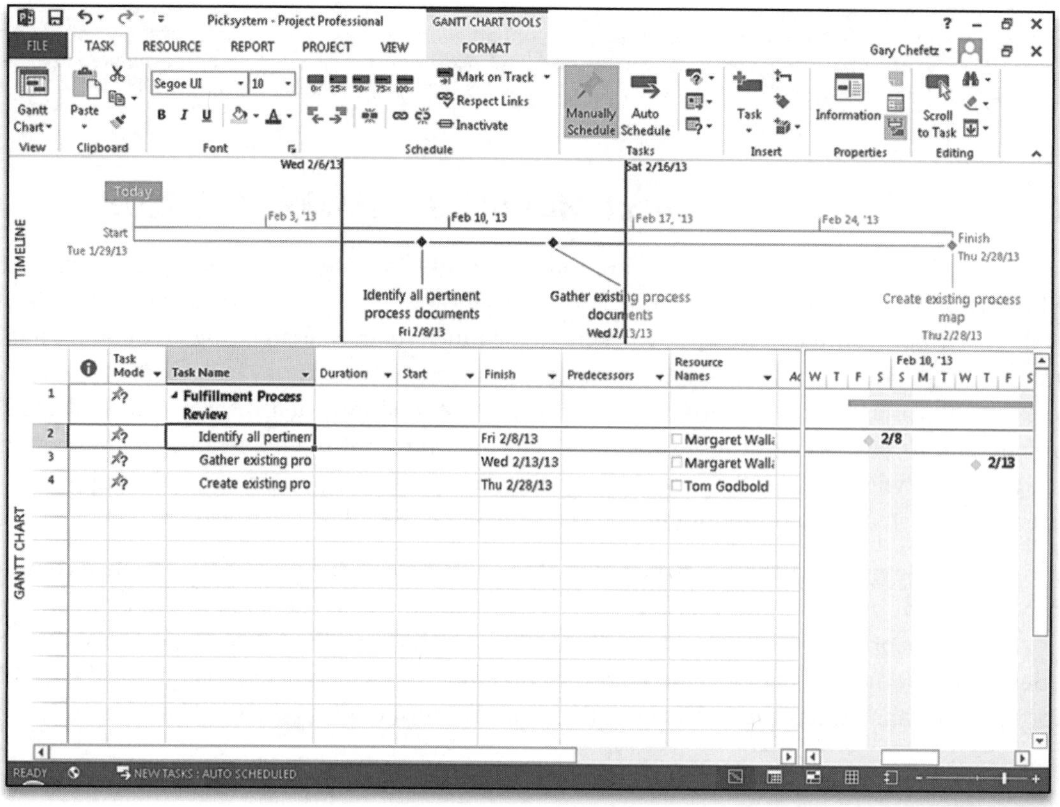

Figure 2 - 22: SharePoint site open for editing in Project Pro 2013

Now that the task list is open in Project Pro 2013, Marian begins to flesh out the WBS by adding dependencies, setting task durations, and assigning level of effort using resource units to create a more realistic view of the work and workflow.

Information: When you open a SharePoint list with Project Pro 2013, Project Pro saves the file to the *Site Assets* library.

After saving her project Marian's *Picksystem* site, shown in Figure 2 - 23, looks a bit different. Notice that the system automatically added *Deliverables, Risks,* and *Issues* apps to the site. Notice also, that the timeline now reflects durations for tasks, not simply due dates marked as milestones.

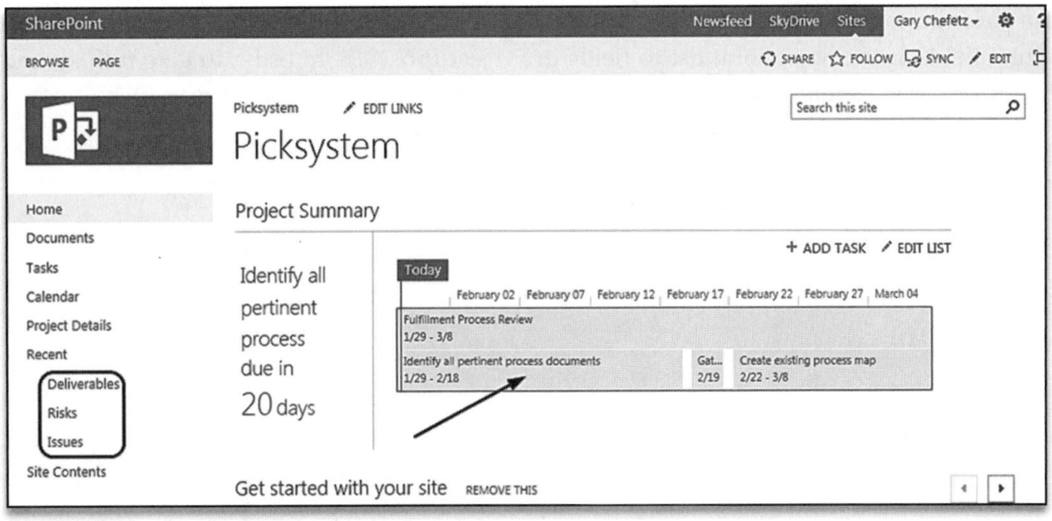

Figure 2 - 23: Picksystem site after saving with Project Pro 2013

A glance at the *Info* page of the *Backstage* in Project Pro 2013 reveals another addition, the *Save and Sync Your Project* section and the *Map Fields* button as shown in Figure 2 - 24.

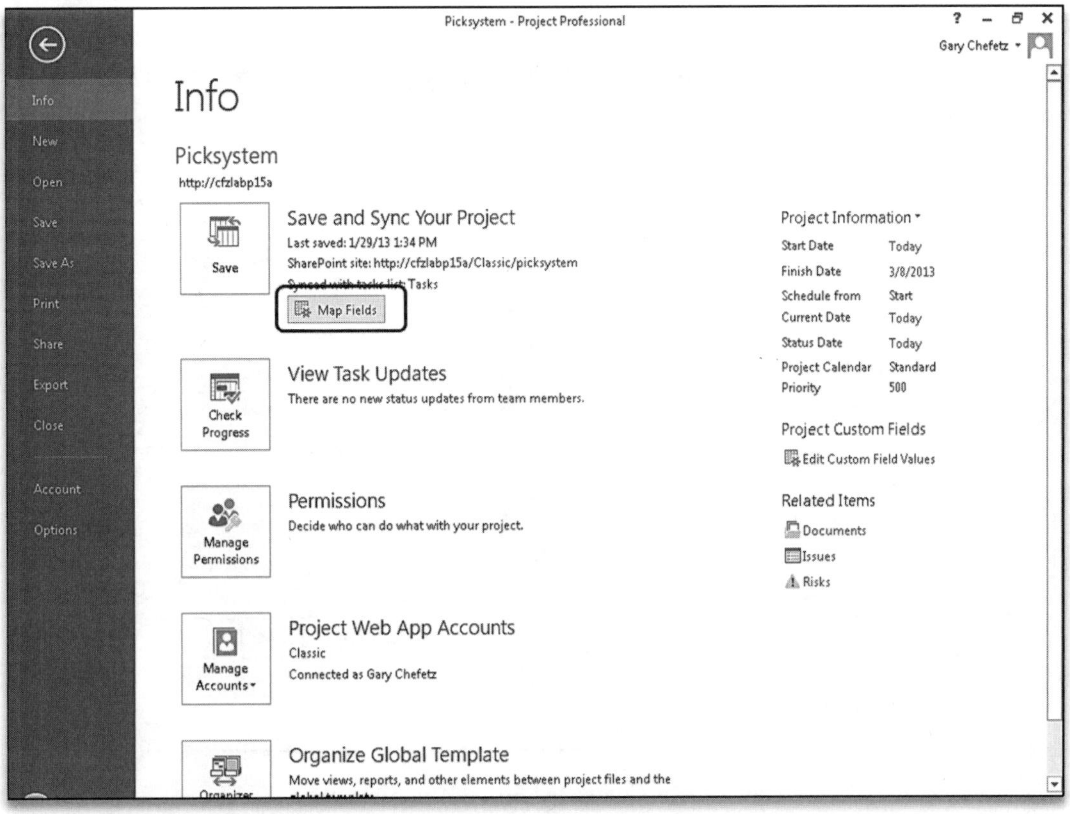

Figure 2 - 24: Project Backstage showing Save and Sync Your Project section

Click the *Map Fields* button to display the *Map Fields* dialog shown in Figure 2 - 25. This dialog allows the project manager to map fields in the SharePoint list to fields in Project Pro 2013. In order to take full advantage of field mapping, the project owner must add custom fields to the SharePoint list in order to map them.

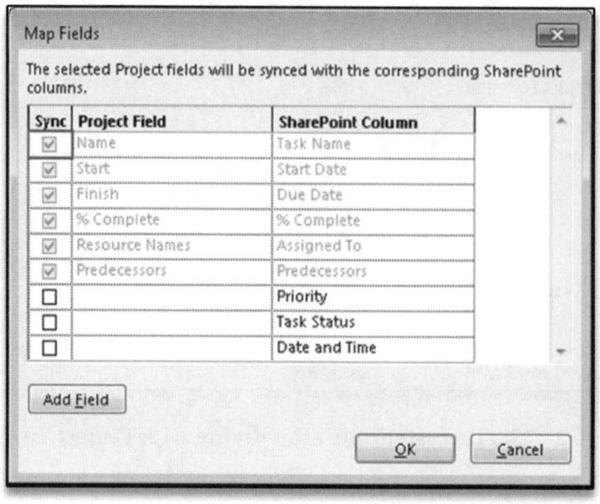

Figure 2 - 25: Map Fields dialog

Promoting a SharePoint list to an Enterprise Project

As the project expands in scope, it is now time for Marian to move her project up the ladder to a full-scale enterprise project. She asks her Project Server 2013 administrator to add enterprise features to her project. To do this, the administrator navigates to the *PWA Settings* page and from the *Operational Policies* section selects the *Connected SharePoint Sites* item. The system displays the *Connected SharePoint Sites* page shown in Figure 2 - 26.

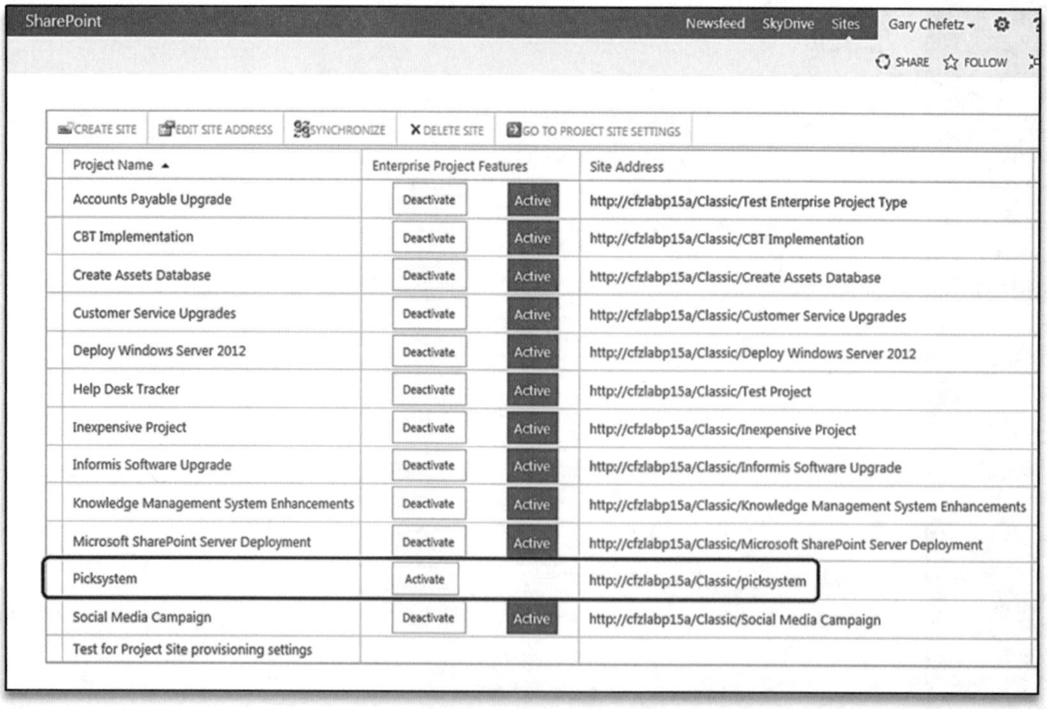

Figure 2 - 26: Connected SharePoint Sites page

The administrator clicks the *Activate* button to add enterprise features to Marian's growing project. The system displays the warning shown in Figure 2 - 27.

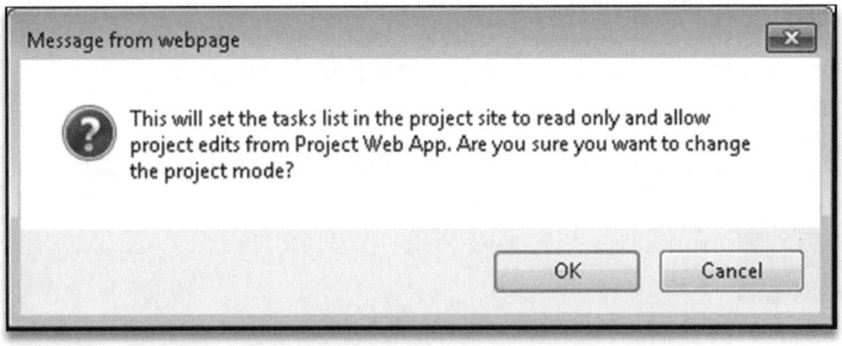

Figure 2 - 27: Changing Project Mode warning

After clicking the *OK* button, the system treats the project like any other enterprise project. When Marian navigates to the Project Center, selects her projects and opens them in the browser for editing, the system takes her to Project Web App rather than the Project Site. The system also locks the tasks list in the Project Site for editing as shown in Figure 2 - 28.

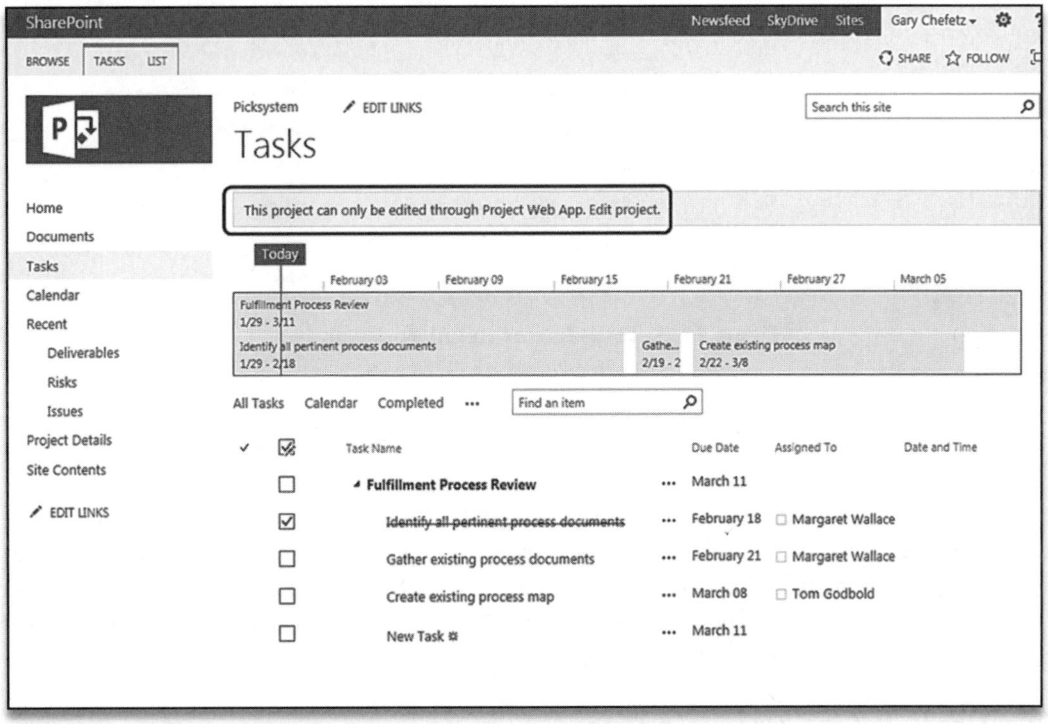

Figure 2 - 28: Project Site locked for editing

> **Warning**: The first time you open a SharePoint list in Project Pro 2013, and you are connected to Project Server, the RTM version of Project Server 2013 allows you to use the *Save* or *Save As* features and save the project to Project Server rather than saving the project to the *Site Assets* library. If you do this before connecting the SharePoint site to Project Server, there is no way to promote the project to an enterprise project.

Enterprise Project Tasks now Synchronize to the Project Site Tasks List

When you create a new enterprise project in Project Server 2013 and then publish and create a new Project Site, the system automatically synchronizes the tasks in the project to the tasks list in the Project Site. Figure 2 - 29 shows a task list for an enterprise project. Notice the warning below the page title stating "This project can only be edited through Project Web App."

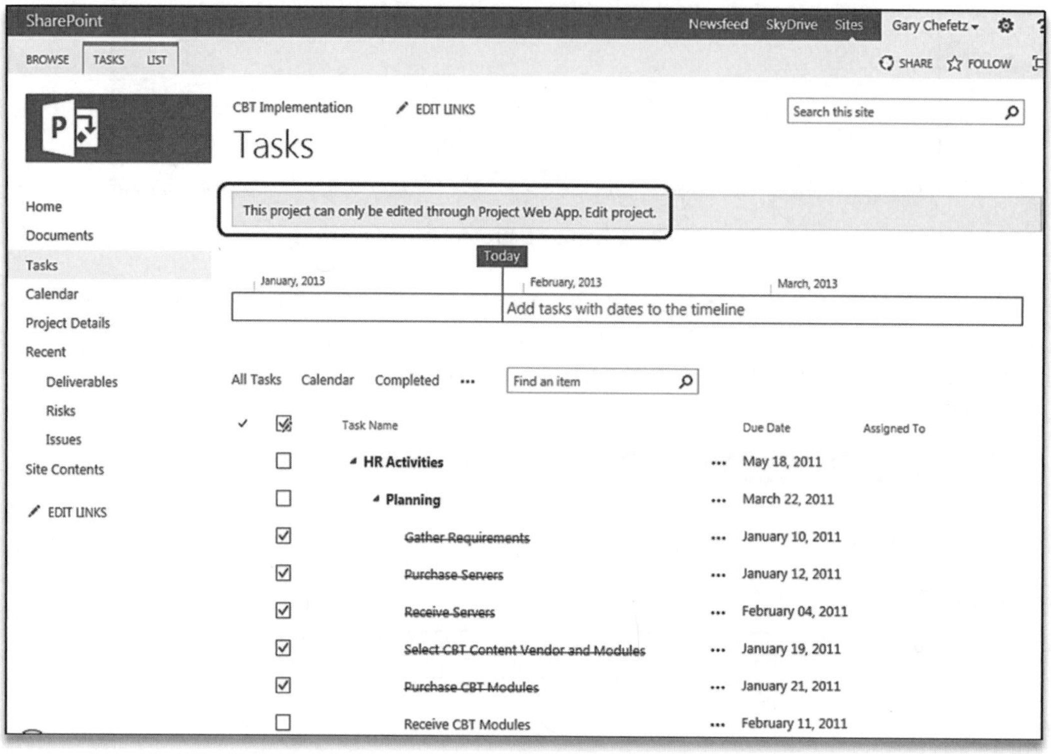

Figure 2 - 29: Tasks list for an Enterprise project

Managing the SharePoint/Project Server Connection

There are three administration pages within Project Web App that you use to set Project Site provisioning settings and to administer existing Project Sites. Because Project Web App is a SharePoint application, you can also leverage many SharePoint tools embedded in each PWA page to change the look and feel of your PWA instance and to change the content of pages to tailor them to your organizational requirements. These built-in features provide you with an unprecedented ability to mold your application.

Managing Project Site Provisioning

If you are using Project Online, you cannot change these settings, however you should know that your default settings for each Project Server instance online, is that sites are created in the PWA site collection to which they belong, and the *Automatic Provisioning* option is set to *Allow users to manually create project sites in Project Server.* By setting this as the default for Project Online, Microsoft makes it possible for online users to selectively create sites as sub-sites of other sites, a popular construct for a collection of related projects managed as a program.

For on-premises and cloud implementations that provide server-level access, you manage these settings from the *PWA Settings* page that you reach through SharePoint Central Admin. From the *Operational Policies* section of the

PWA Settings page, click the *Project Site Provisioning Settings* link. Project Server 2013 displays the *Project Site Provisioning Settings* page shown in Figure 2 - 30.

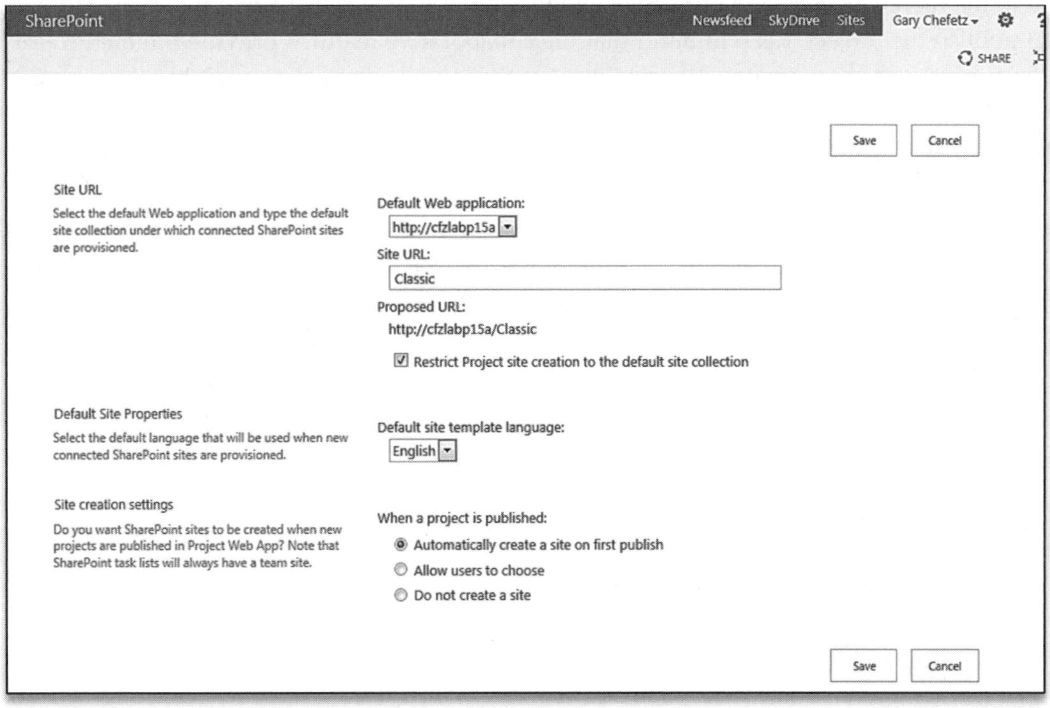
SharePoint
Newsfeed
SkyDrive
Sites
Gary Chefetz
SHARE
Save
Cancel
Site URL
Select the default Web application and type the default site collection under which connected SharePoint sites are provisioned.
Default Web application:
http://cfzlabp15a
Site URL:
Classic
Proposed URL:
http://cfzlabp15a/Classic
Restrict Project site creation to the default site collection
Default Site Properties
Select the default language that will be used when new connected SharePoint sites are provisioned.
Default site template language:
English
Site creation settings
Do you want SharePoint sites to be created when new projects are published in Project Web App? Note that SharePoint task lists will always have a team site.
When a project is published:
Automatically create a site on first publish
Allow users to choose
Do not create a site
Save
Cancel

Figure 2 - 30: Project Site Provisioning Settings page

When you first access the *Project Site Provisioning Settings* page, the system displays the default settings for provisioning Project Sites. In the *Site URL* section, you can change the default web application under which the system creates your sites, although in most circumstances, you should not change this setting. The system derives the values in the *Default Web application* field and the *Site URL* field from the information you supplied during Project Server 2013 installation, or while creating a new Project Server instance.

In the *Default Site Properties* section, you can change the language settings for new site provisioning and change the base template that the system uses to create the sites. The system specifies your language in the *Default site template language* field.

In the *Site creation settings* section, the system pre-selects the *Automatically create a project site for each project when first published to Project Server* option to automatically create a Project Site when a project manager publishes a project for the first time. Whether you use this automatic provisioning option or set your provisioning mode to "manual" depends on your requirements. In most cases, automatic provisioning makes sense. With automatic provisioning, the system forces the creation of a Project Site for every project published in the system.

When does it make sense to use the *Allow users to manually create project sites in Project Server* option? You might choose this setting if most of your projects are rolled up into programs, and you have a need to create the component projects before you create the program's master project. Because Project Server 2013 gives you the choice to create your Project Site as a sub-site of another Project Site, you can create a program site with individual Project Sites below it in the hierarchy. Setting your provisioning mode to *Manual* gives you the chance to create a Project Site after you publish the project. Keep in mind that the collaborative features provided in the Project Site are not available to your users until you create a Project Site. Another instance when you might select manual provisioning is when you simply do not intend to use Project Sites, including the *Risks, Issues, Documents,* and *Deliverables* features in your environment.

When you set your system to *Manual,* your project managers see the *Publish Project* dialog shown in Figure 2 - 31. Notice that the *Do not create a site at this time* option is the default. This dialog continues to appear during each publish operation until the project manager chooses to provision the Project Site or until an administrator provisions one.

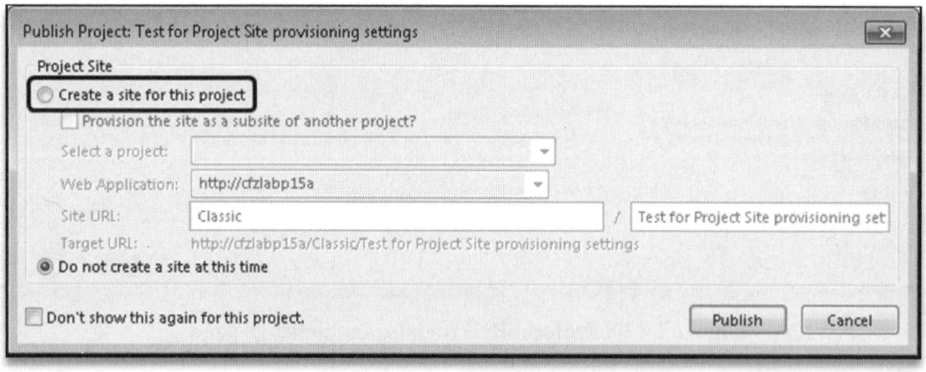

Figure 2 - 31: Publish Project dialog

In the *Project Site Permissions* section of the *Project Site Provisioning Settings* page, the system pre-selects the option to provision sites with automatic user synchronization. Leave this option selected if you want the system to automatically manage user permissions for you. Notice that the information on the page clearly defines the permissions synchronization that occurs when you select this option. In most cases, selecting this option is appropriate. If you deselect this option, you must manually manage these permissions in the system or provide your own synchronization routine. Click the *Save* button to save any changes you make on this page.

Information: With the exception of the *Project Site Permissions* option, changes you make on the *Project Site Provisioning Settings* page affect sites created after the change date. In the case of Project Site Permissions, any user permissions already synchronized to a site remain unchanged when you turn off automatic synchronization. Deselecting this option stops future synchronization on current sites.

Managing User Synchronization

Whether you are using Project Online or using Project Server 2013 on premises, you can control the synchronization behaviors in the system. From the *Security* section of the *PWA Settings* page, click the *Manage User Sync Settings* link to display the *Project Permission Sync Settings* page shown in Figure 2 - 32.

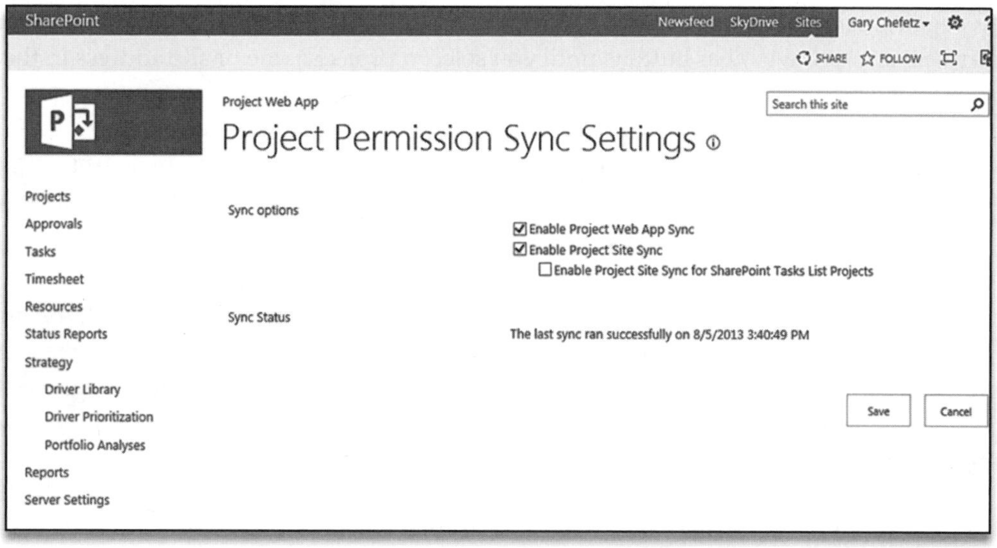

Figure 2 - 32: Project Permission Sync Settings page

The options on this page pertain to Project Server permissions mode only. The *Enable Project Web App Sync* option, instructs the system to not only create a resource record for the Active Directory record, it and adds the person to the *Team Members for PWA* security group. In other words, this option causes the user account to be created. This action occurs on the first synchronization only. Group synchronization with Active Directory is a separate operation not affected by these settings. Selecting the *Enable Project Site Sync* option causes the system to synchronize user permissions from Project Server to the Project Sites. These two options are selected by default when you convert to Project Server permissions mode, or upgrade a Project Server 2010 database. The final option, *Enable Project Site Sync for SharePoint Tasks List Projects,* causes the system to synchronize to this new type of project in Project Server.

Managing Project Sites

In the *Operational Policies* section of the *PWA Settings* page, click the *Connected SharePoint Sites* link to manually provision or delete Project Sites, or to manage existing sites. The system displays the *Connected SharePoint Sites* page shown in Figure 2 - 33.

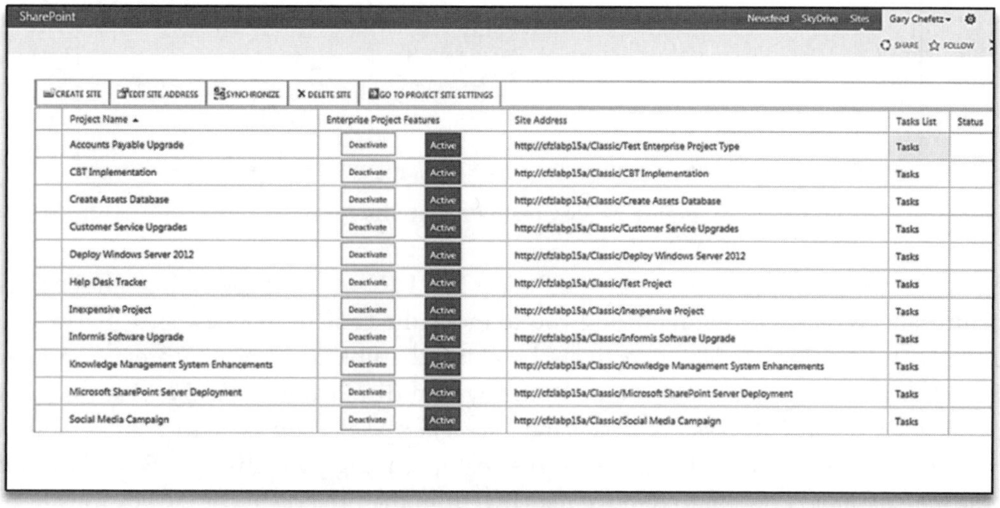

SharePoint
Newsfeed
SkyDrive
Sites
Gary Chefetz
SHARE
FOLLOW
CREATE SITE
EDIT SITE ADDRESS
SYNCHRONIZE
DELETE SITE
GO TO PROJECT SITE SETTINGS
Project Name
Enterprise Project Features
Site Address
Tasks List
Status
Accounts Payable Upgrade
CBT Implementation
Create Assets Database
Customer Service Upgrades
Deploy Windows Server 2012
Help Desk Tracker
Inexpensive Project
Informis Software Upgrade
Knowledge Management System Enhancements
Microsoft SharePoint Server Deployment
Social Media Campaign
Deactivate
Active
http://cfzlabp15a/Classic/Test Enterprise Project Type
http://cfzlabp15a/Classic/CBT Implementation
http://cfzlabp15a/Classic/Create Assets Database
http://cfzlabp15a/Classic/Customer Service Upgrades
http://cfzlabp15a/Classic/Deploy Windows Server 2012
http://cfzlabp15a/Classic/Test Project
http://cfzlabp15a/Classic/Inexpensive Project
http://cfzlabp15a/Classic/Informis Software Upgrade
http://cfzlabp15a/Classic/Knowledge Management System Enhancements
http://cfzlabp15a/Classic/Microsoft SharePoint Server Deployment
http://cfzlabp15a/Classic/Social Media Campaign
Tasks

Figure 2 - 33: Connected SharePoint Sites page

Notice that the page contains a data grid with a toolbar running across the top as shown in Figure 2 - 34. The system does not activate any of the toolbar buttons until you select a project name or site address in the grid.

Figure 2 - 34: Connected SharePoint Sites toolbar

The *Site Address* column contains a link to the Project Site for the specified project. If you click the link for any project in the *Site Address* column, the system navigates to the selected Project Site. The *Site Address* column should always contain a link for every project when you select the automatic provisioning option, unless the provisioning process fails, which leaves the *Site Address* column blank. This page gives you the ability to recover from a failed automatic provisioning by allowing you to manually provision a site.

The *Project Sites* toolbar offers you five options, which are as follows:

- **Create Site** causes the system to create a site for the selected project. If the project does not have a URL in the *Site Address* column, the Project Site does not exist for that project. Click the *Create Site* button to manually provision a Project Site. Select the project for which you want to create a site and click the *Create Site* button. The system displays the *Create Project Site* form shown in Figure 2 - 35. You can both select the web application under which to provision the site and also determine the URL. The URL defaults to the project name, and this is usually the best naming convention to use.

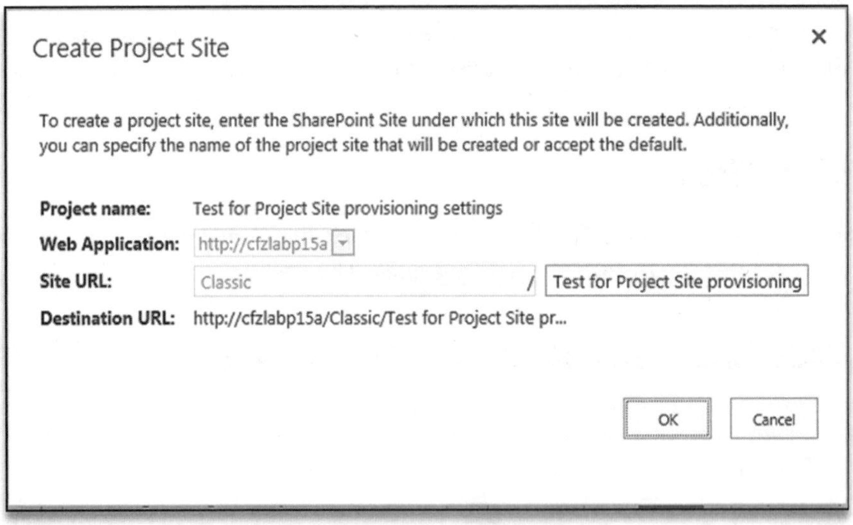

Figure 2 - 35: Create Project Site form

- **Edit Site Address** allows you to change the Project Site URL for the project as might be necessary should an existing site become corrupt, requiring you to move the content to a new site. It also allows you to remove the URL for a Project Site, effectively breaking the link between the project and the Project Site. When you click the *Edit Site Address* button, the system displays the *Edit Site Address* form shown in in Figure 2 - 36. By default, the system selects the *Type a new SharePoint site URL* option. Make sure that you click the *Test URL* button to test the site address before saving your changes. Select the *Unlink the SharePoint site from the project* option to remove the URL from the project's record. Click the *OK* button to complete your action or the *Cancel* button to abort the change.

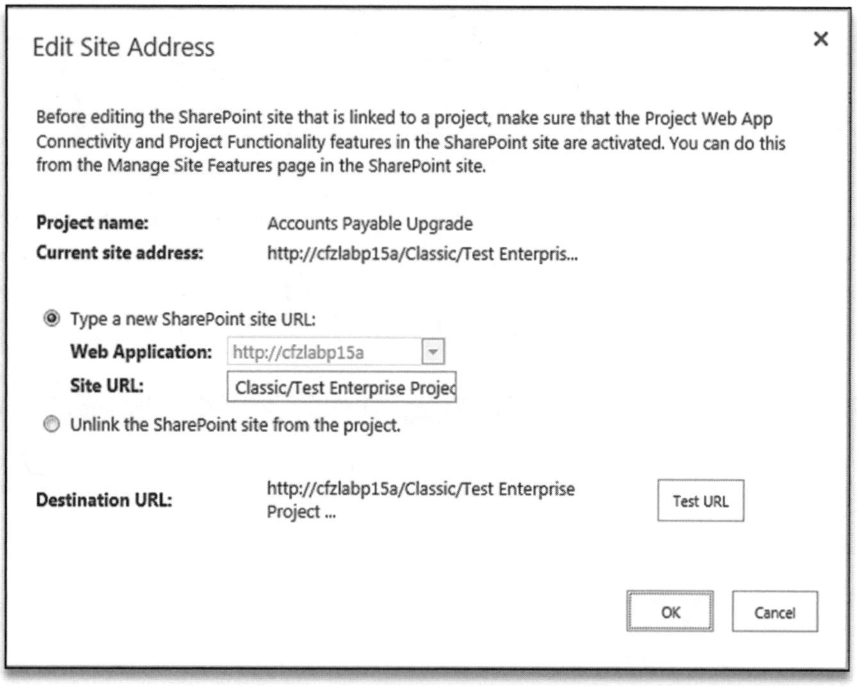
Edit Site Address
×
Before editing the SharePoint site that is linked to a project, make sure that the Project Web App Connectivity and Project Functionality features in the SharePoint site are activated. You can do this from the Manage Site Features page in the SharePoint site.
Project name:
Accounts Payable Upgrade
Current site address:
http://cfzlabp15a/Classic/Test Enterpris...
Type a new SharePoint site URL:
Web Application:
http://cfzlabp15a
Site URL:
Classic/Test Enterprise Projec
Unlink the SharePoint site from the project.
Destination URL:
http://cfzlabp15a/Classic/Test Enterprise Project ...
Test URL
OK
Cancel

Figure 2 - 36: Edit Site Address form

Best Practice: MSProjectExperts recommends that you use a short title without spaces or a nickname for your project as the URL. This makes it easier for users to remember the URL without having to go to the Project page to navigate to the project site.

- **Synchronize** allows you to force a permissions synchronization to occur for the project you select in the grid. The system places a synchronization job in the Project Server queue when you click this button and redisplays the *Project Sites* page. It does not give you any additional feedback; however, you can verify that the job succeeded through the *Manage Queue Jobs* page.
- **Delete Site** gives you the ability to completely remove a Project Site including all of its content. Use this feature when you archive a project and do not want to retain the Project Site, or if you have a need to recreate a site. When you click the *Delete Site* button, the system displays the dialog shown in Figure 2 - 37. Click the *OK* button to continue removing the site and all of its contents. Click the *Cancel* button to exit without deleting the site.

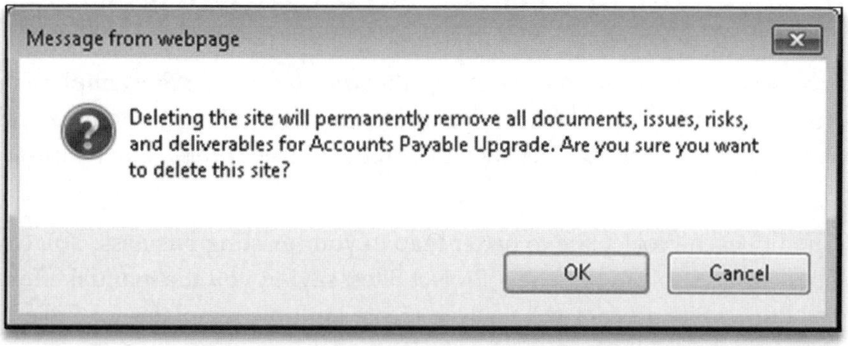
Message from webpage
Deleting the site will permanently remove all documents, issues, risks, and deliverables for Accounts Payable Upgrade. Are you sure you want to delete this site?
OK
Cancel

Figure 2 - 37: Delete Project Site warning dialog

> **Warning**: When you delete a site, the system does not place the site or its contents in a recycle bin. Therefore, there is no undo available to reverse this action. Use this feature very judiciously.

- **Go to Project Site Settings** takes you directly to the *Site Settings* page for the selected Project Site as shown in Figure 2 - 38. From the *Site Settings* page, you can manage the look and feel of your Project Site, perform site administration, and control several other site features. SharePoint gives you built-in tools to customize the site and add content through its user interface without requiring custom coding.

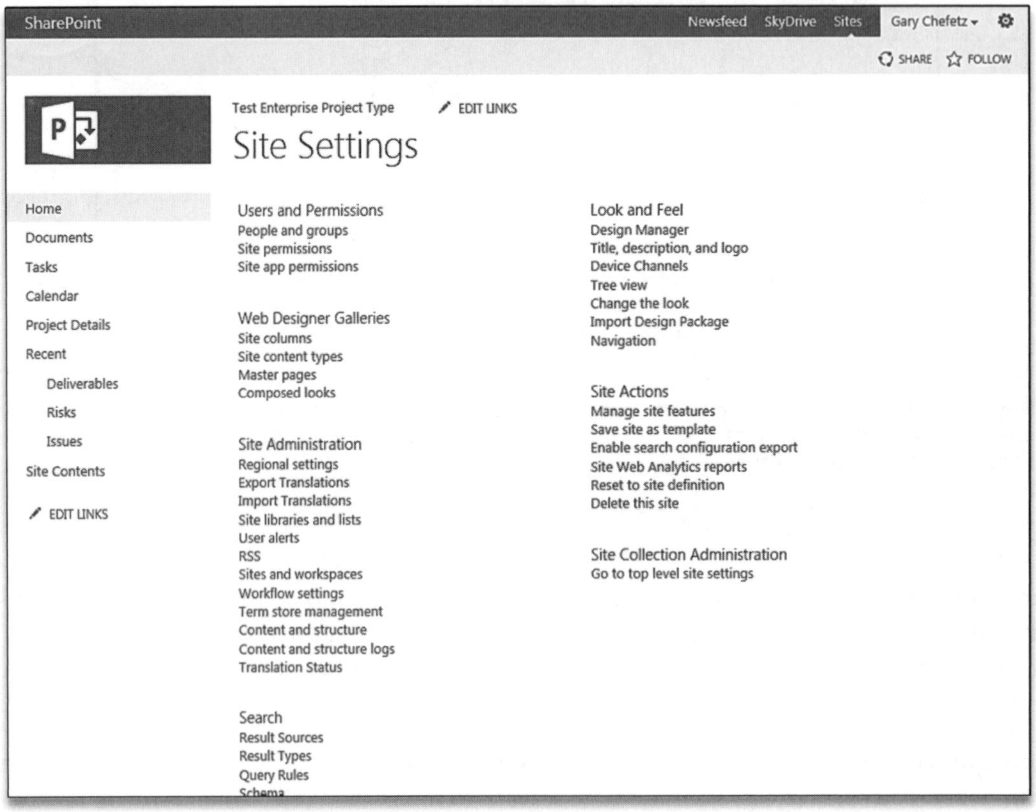

Figure 2 - 38: Site Settings page

Creating and Modifying Project Site Columns

Each Project Site that the system creates for a project uses the *Microsoft Project Site* template that installs with Project Server 2013. Because every company, department, and team may follow different processes; and, therefore, operate with different requirements, the features included in the built-in *Project Site* template may not meet all of your business process needs.

Fortunately, you can modify each Project Site to better map to your existing business. You can also customize the site template that the system uses to generate new Project Sites, saving you the manual effort required to modify each newly provisioned Project Site process and you can create multiple templates for Project Sites. Project Server 2013 supports multiple site templates through the *Enterprise Project Type* feature.

Managing List and Library Metadata

SharePoint stores both structured content and unstructured content, SharePoint lists act as containers for structured content, and SharePoint libraries act as containers for unstructured content. A SharePoint list stores a collection of structured data items similar to a bulleted list of values, and a SharePoint library stores a collection of unstructured items in the form of files. Because the functionality and configuration options are so similar for lists and libraries, I primarily present instructions and examples for lists in this section, but the information I present typically applies to libraries as well, with only minor differences.

Regardless of whether it is in a list or library, each item stored in SharePoint has descriptive metadata to help classify the items for sorting, grouping, filtering, or otherwise locating specific items of interest. This is especially helpful when lists or libraries contain hundreds or thousands of items. SharePoint columns are the pieces of descriptive metadata that you can use to classify items in lists and libraries.

SharePoint columns are a fundamental building block for lists and libraries. In the event that your business process requires you to capture additional metadata to describe or categorize the items in a list or library, the system allows you to modify existing columns or create new custom columns in the Project Site for a selected project. Although Microsoft uses the word *column* to describe this feature, it is very similar to a custom *field* in Project Server.

Best Practice: MSProjectExperts recommends that you use content types and the SharePoint term store to create and manage SharePoint custom fields as much as you can. This provides central visibility to what metadata people are using and how they are using it. Allowing users to add ad-hoc metadata is also important because it helps the end user and it promotes metadata maturity. Your goal should be to periodically review the list and site columns added by users and evaluate them as candidates for the formal publishing process.

Figure 2 - 39 displays a form for editing or logging a new project issue. You can see in this form that there are several metadata columns (*Title, Owner, Assigned To, Status,* etc.) that describe and classify the issue that you log in the *Issues* list.

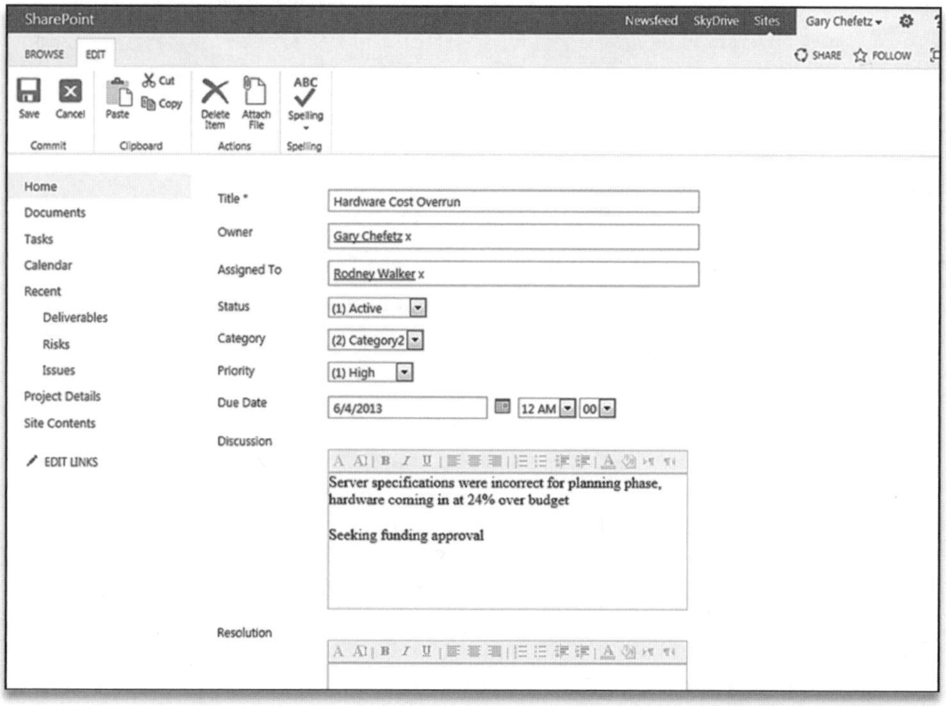

Figure 2 - 39: Issue Form with several metadata columns

Creating a New Column

Creating custom fields for a list, site, or for metadata publishing in SharePoint shares mostly the same interface with few variances. The skills I cover here are essential basics you need to know and are transferrable to any level. It is important that you understand that custom fields cascade downward in the SharePoint hierarchy so it matters where you create them as this determines where you can use them.

To create a new column within a SharePoint list, navigate to the list, click the *List* ribbon tab, and from the *Manage Views* section, click the *Create Column* button as shown in Figure 2 - 40.

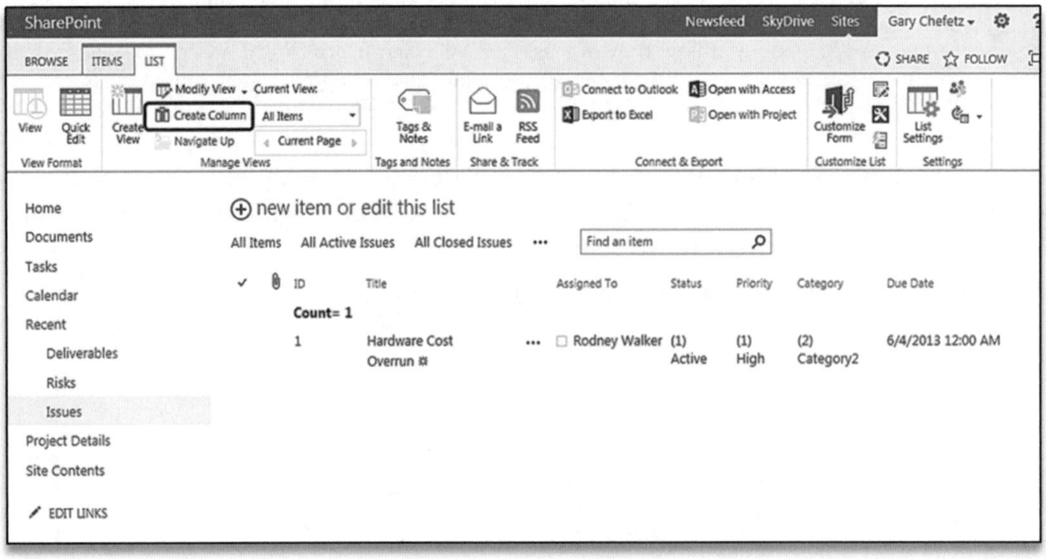

Figure 2 - 40: Clicking the Create Column button on the Issues page

The system displays the *Create Column* dialog shown in Figure 2 - 41.

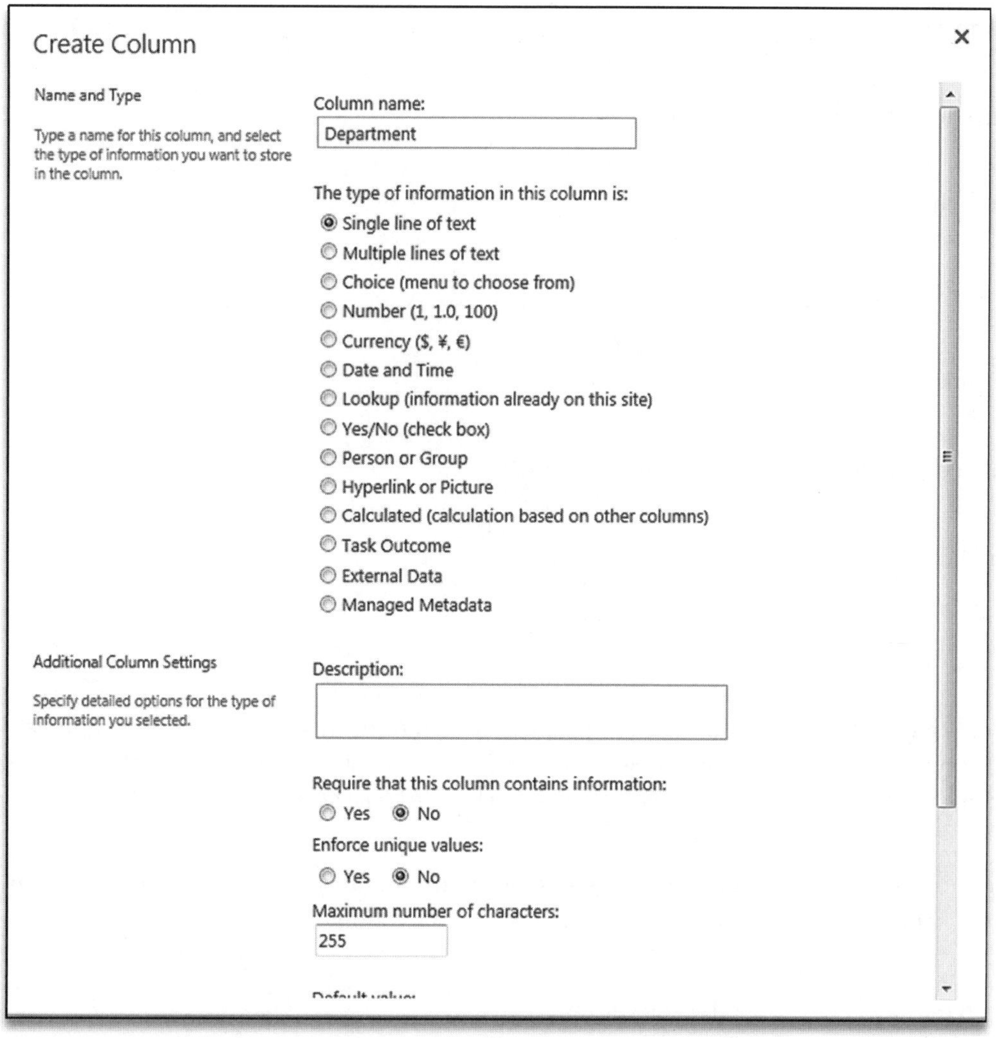

Figure 2 - 41: Create Column form for the Issues list

To create the new custom column, enter a descriptive name for the column in the *Column name* field, then select an option that describes the data type for the information in the column. The system offers a number of data types, including each of the following:

- Single line of text
- Multiple lines of text
- Choice (menu to choose from)
- Number (1, 1.0, 100)
- Currency ($, ¥, €)

- Date and Time
- Lookup (information already on this site)
- Yes/No (check box)
- Person or Group
- Hyperlink or Picture
- Calculated (calculation based on other columns)
- External Data
- Managed Metadata

When you select an option for the column data type, the system redraws the *Additional Column Settings* section of the form for the type of data you select. For example, Figure 2 - 42 shows the *Additional Column Settings* section after I selected the *Choice (menu to choose from)* option from the *The type of information in this column* section.

In the *Additional Column Settings* section of the form, select your options for the new custom column. For example, when using the *Choice* data type for the column, you must do the following:

- Enter an optional description for the column.
- Specify whether the field is required.
- Specify whether to enforce unique values.
- Enter the list of choices.
- Determine how the system displays the choices (as a pick list menu, as radio buttons, or as checkboxes).
- Determine whether to allow a user to append the list with additional choices.
- Specify a default value in the column.
- Determine whether to add the column to the default view.

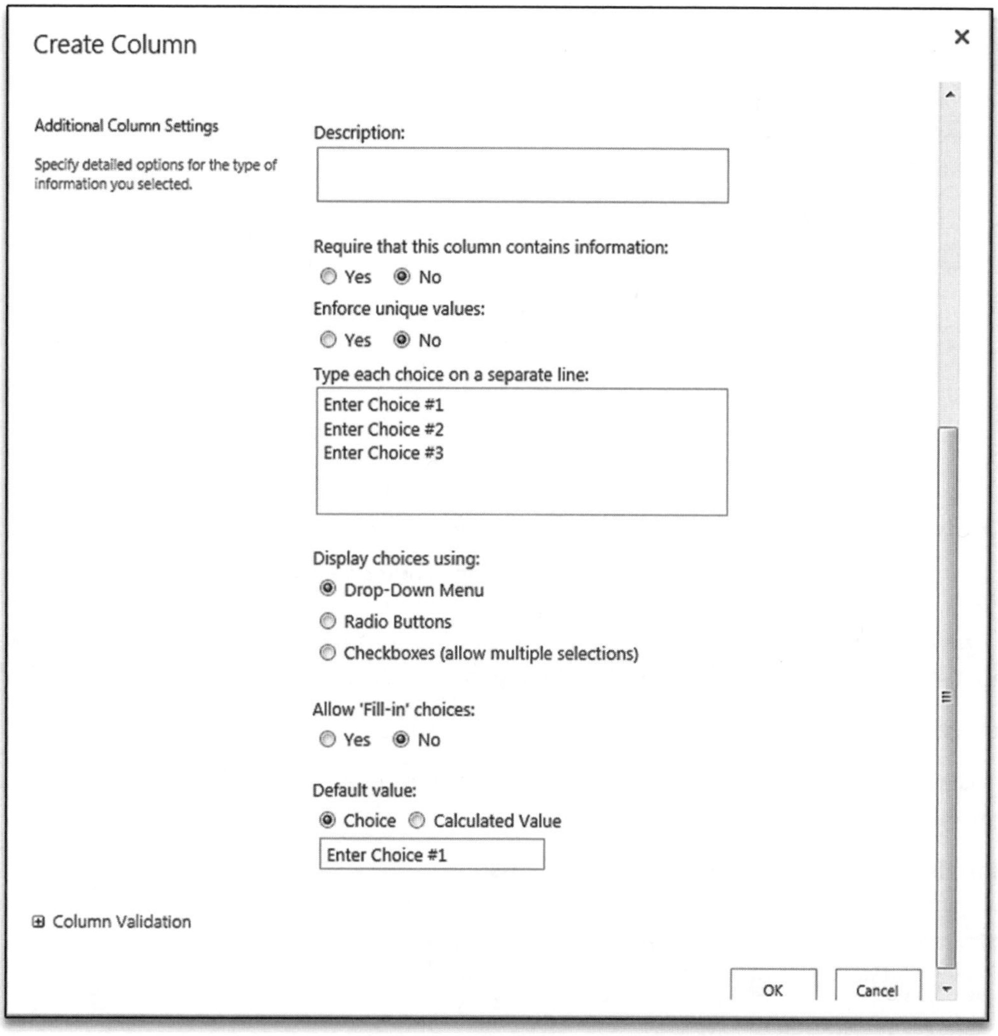

Figure 2 - 42: Additional Column Settings section for the Choice data type

Finally, there is an optional *Column Validation* section at the end of the *Create Column* form; you need to click the heading to expand this section. As shown in Figure 2 - 43, you may enter a validation formula that prevents people from entering incorrect data into the column. To enter a validation rule for data entered into this column, enter an expression into the *Formula* text box using similar syntax as you use for SharePoint calculated columns, based on Microsoft Excel formulas.

If a user enters data into the column that does not comply with the validation rule that you enter, SharePoint does not save the item and spawns an alert message to the user. You can determine this message when you enter a custom alert message into the *User message* text box.

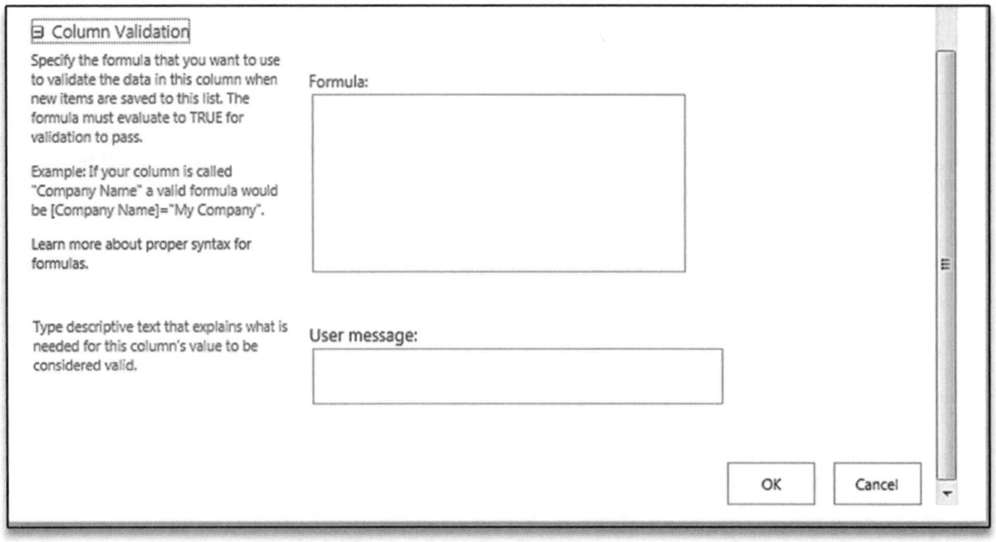
Column Validation
Specify the formula that you want to use to validate the data in this column when new items are saved to this list. The formula must evaluate to TRUE for validation to pass.
Example: If your column is called "Company Name" a valid formula would be [Company Name]="My Company".
Learn more about proper syntax for formulas.
Formula:
Type descriptive text that explains what is needed for this column's value to be considered valid.
User message:
OK
Cancel

Figure 2 - 43: Column Validation options in the Create Column form

For example, one of your business process requirements states that the customer number for any item entered into the list must start with the text "Cust-". The validation formula for this scenario is:

=LEFT([Customer],5)="Cust-"

This formula tests that the left 5 characters of the data entered into the *Customer* column equals "Cust-". The user alert message for this scenario is:

You must begin the customer number with the text "Cust-".

Information: It is unlikely that you would use this type of data validation with a *Choice (menu to choose from)* field, rather you would use this with a *Single line of text* field type.

Information: A column validation formula cannot refer to any columns other than itself. For example, you cannot enter a column validation formula for the *Due Date* column that compares it against the *Created* column. You can accomplish this through list validation settings, which I cover later in this module.

Warning: Multiple columns within the same list can have unique column validation rules; be careful not to enter rules that conflict with one another, resulting in preventing people from entering any new items into the list.

After you configure all of the settings for the new custom column, click the *OK* button at the bottom of the form. The system adds the column to the list and adds the column to the default view. When you add a new column to a list with existing records, and the column is not self-populating, you must then edit each of the items in the list to populate the new metadata. For example, Figure 2 - 44 shows the new field at the bottom of the *Issues* edit form, along with the values available on the choice list.

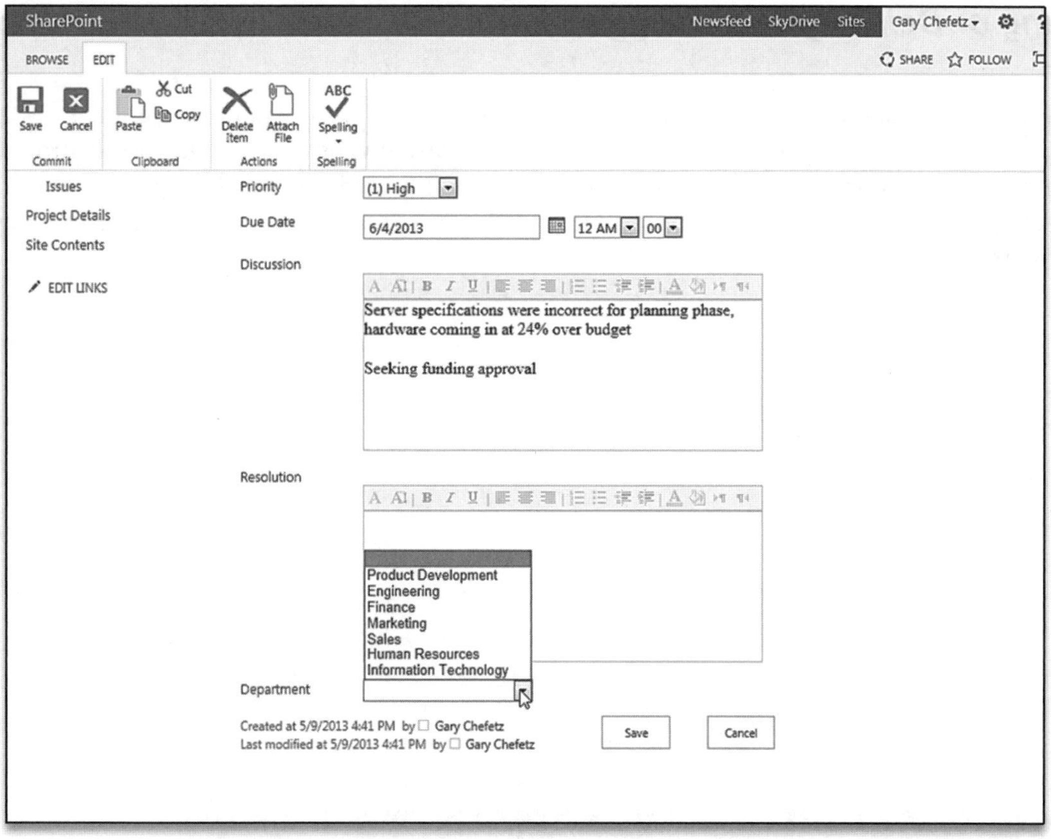

Figure 2 - 44: Department column at bottom of Issue form

Information: A column that you create within a SharePoint list or library is available only to the list or library in which you create it. Later in this module, you learn how to create a *Site* column, which allows you to create a column that you can use in any list or library within that site.

Best Practice: MSProjectExperts recommends that if you have a generalized need for Project Site customizations, such as new or modified columns, you should modify the base template for Project Sites. If you are using the *Enterprise Project Types* feature in Project Server 2013, each project type can utilize its own Project Site template that has unique customizations for that Project Type.

Modifying or Deleting an Existing Column

Please observe the warning that follows about editing Project Sites. If you plan on using the *Issues* feature, you probably want to make the *Category* field meaningful. This is a built-in custom field that uses a drop-down menu like the *Department* field I used in the previous example. To modify or delete an existing column within a SharePoint list, navigate to the list, click the *List* ribbon tab, then in the *Settings* section, click the *List Settings* button as shown in Figure 2 - 45.

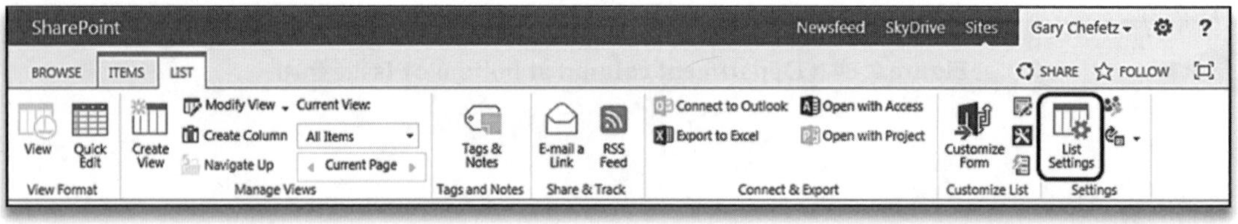

Figure 2 - 45: Selecting the List Settings Button on the Issues Page

The system displays the *List Settings* page shown in Figure 2 - 46, containing links to all of the administrative configuration options for the list.

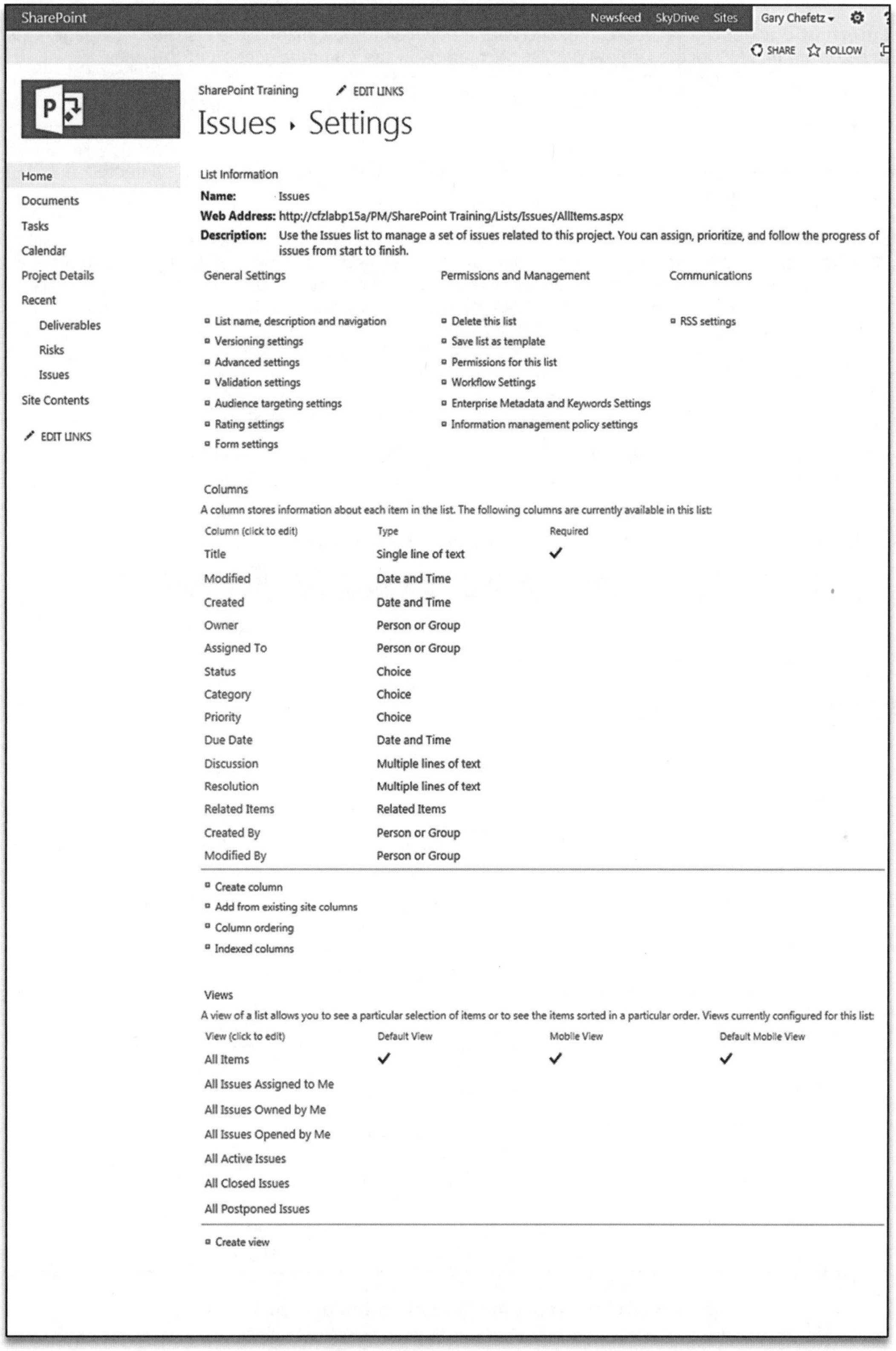

Figure 2 - 46: List Settings page for the Issues list

Information: Notice that you can also create a new column by visiting the *List Settings* page, then clicking the *Create column* link, located below the list of columns in the *Columns* section of the page.

The *Columns* section of the *List Settings* page displays the entire list of columns for the selected list. To modify one of the existing columns, click the name of the column in the list.

Best Practice: MSProjectExperts recommends that you modify the built-in *Category* column and enter choice values that are relevant to your organization's business processes. Further, you should modify the base template for your Project Site(s) with this modification. I show you how to create a new Project Site template in Module 05, *Working with Portfolio and Project Governance.*

The system displays the *Edit Column* page shown in Figure 2 - 47, which contains the same column configuration options that are available on the *Create Column* form shown in the previous section. When you finish modifying the behavior of the column, as shown in Figure 2 - 47 where I change the *Category* choice values, click the *OK* button at the bottom of the page. Notice that you can delete the column from the list by clicking the *Delete* button at the bottom of the page. Do not delete any field contained in the *Issues* list.

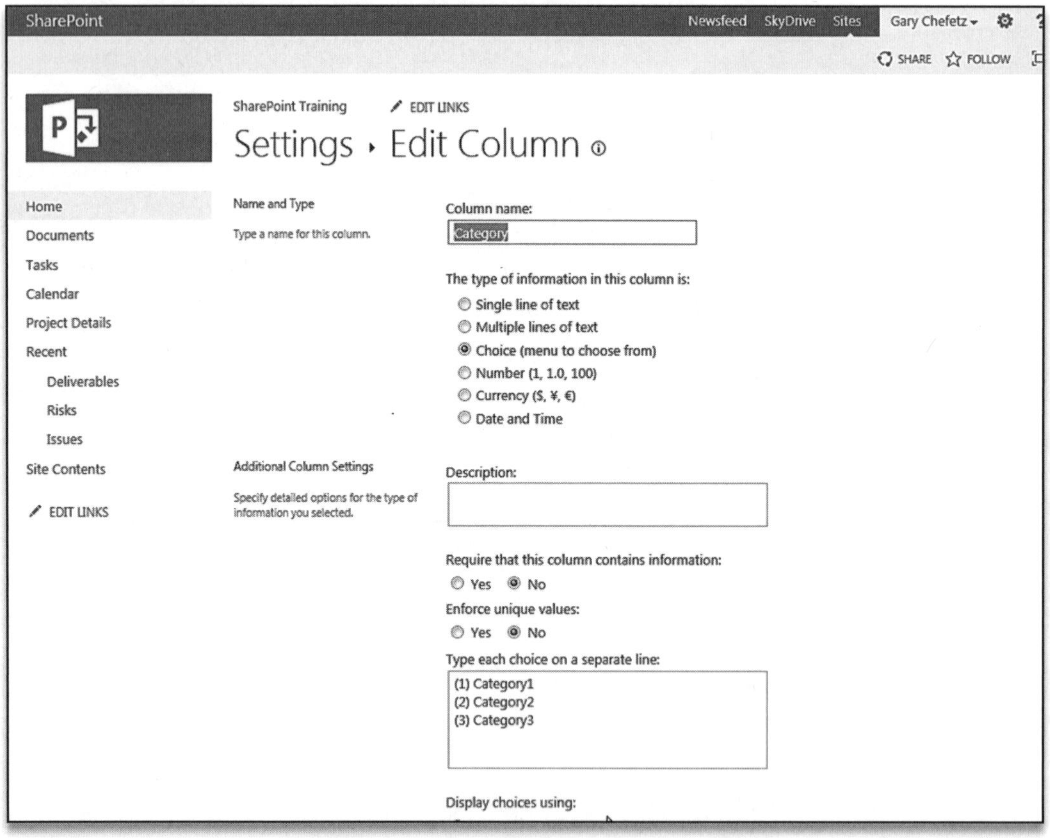

Figure 2 - 47: Modifying the Category column in the Issues list

Warning: Do not delete or hide any built-in columns from the Risks, Issues, Deliverables lists, or from the Project Documents library. Doing so will prevent Project Server 2013 from synchronizing properly with the Project Site.

Creating a New Site Column

You may need to add the same column to multiple lists and libraries within a Project Site; if you have this requirement you can create a *Site* column reusable throughout the entire site. You can then easily add this *Site* column to any list to capture metadata.

To create a new *Site* column, click the *Site Actions* menu from any page within the Project Site, then select the *Site settings* item, as shown in Figure 2 - 48.

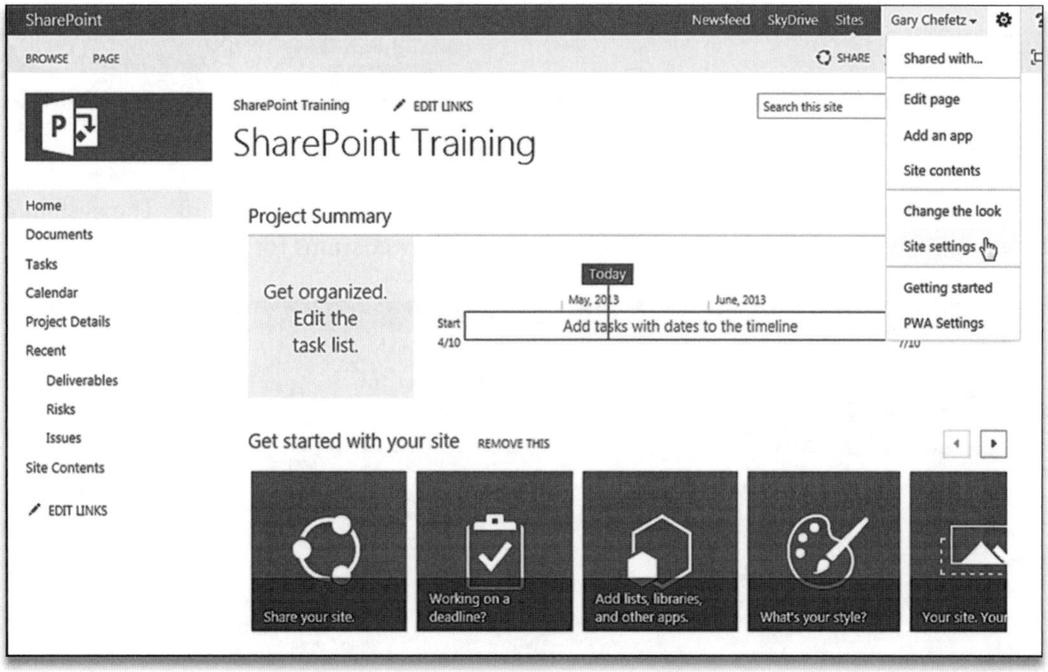

Figure 2 - 48: Opening the Site Actions menu

The system displays the *Site Settings* page shown in Figure 2 - 49, which contains the links to all of the administrative configuration options for the Project Site available to administrators. Depending on your role in the system, not all of the selections may be available to you.

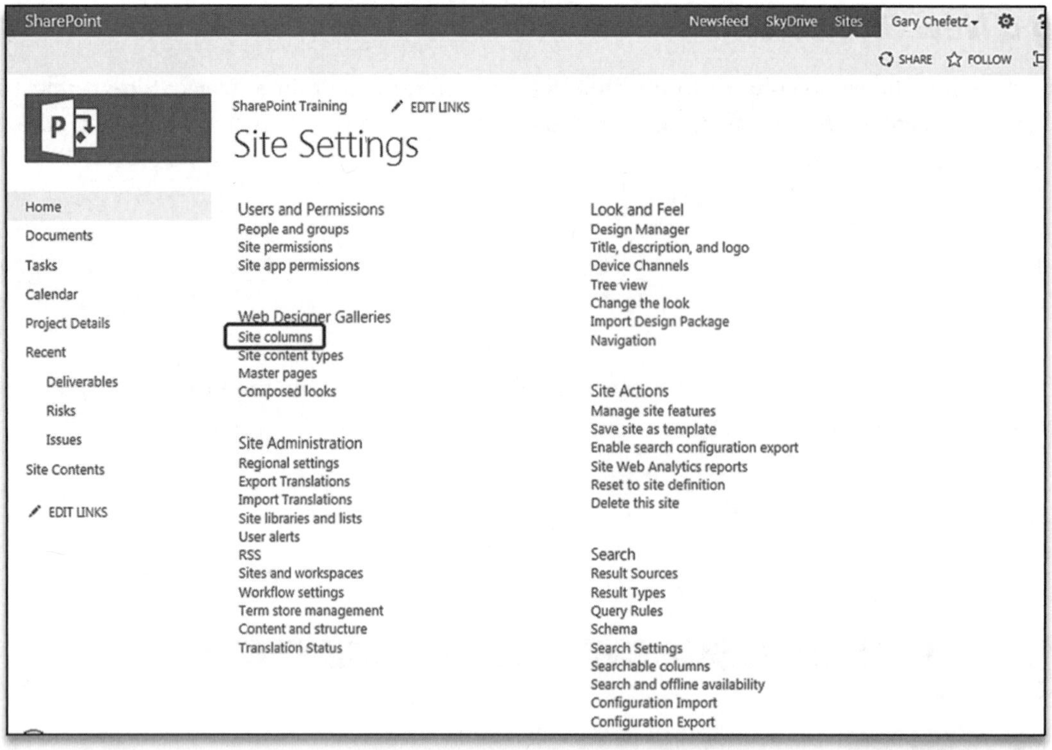

Figure 2 - 49: Site Settings page

In the *Web Designer Galleries* section of the *Site Settings* page, click the *Site columns* link. The system displays the *Site Columns* page shown partially in Figure 2 - 50, displaying all *Site* columns for the Project Site.

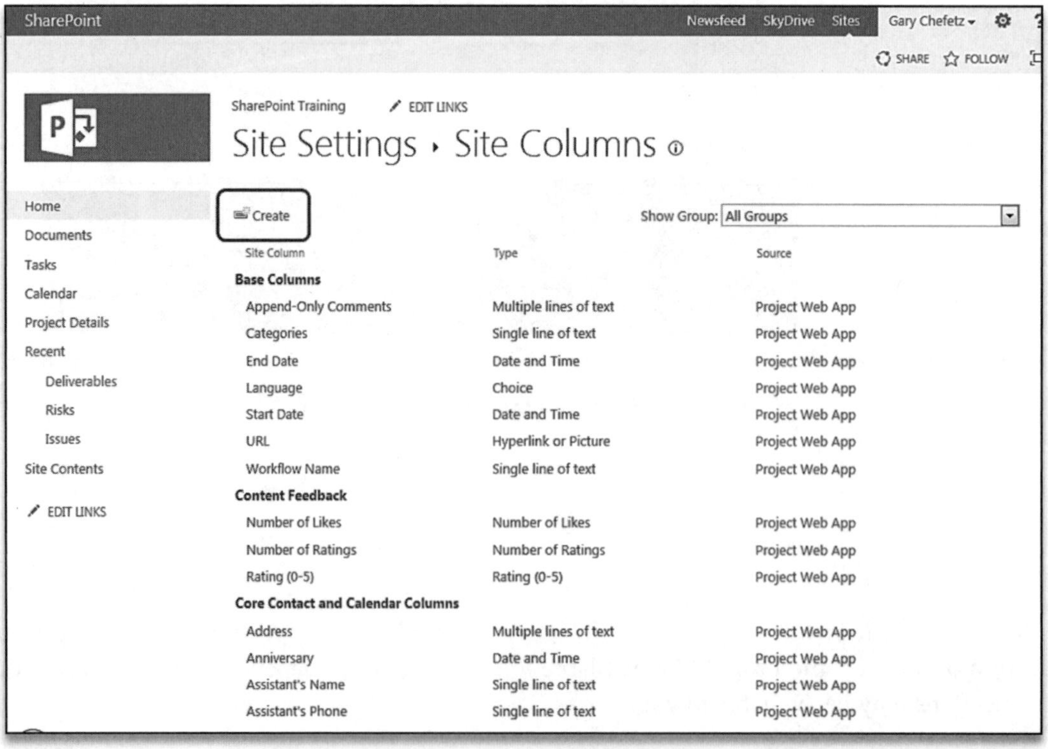

Figure 2 - 50: Site Columns page

Click the *Create* link, located near the top of the page, to create a new *Site* column. The system displays the *New Site Column* page shown in Figure 2 - 51. Here you see options very similar to those you saw when you created a new custom column for the *Issues* list. The primary difference is the addition of the *Group* section of the page, which allows you to place your new *Site* column into a group when it appears on the *Site Columns* page. You may select from an existing group or create your own group as shown previously in Figure 2 - 50. When you finish specifying all of the options for the new *Site* column, click the *OK* button at the bottom of the page.

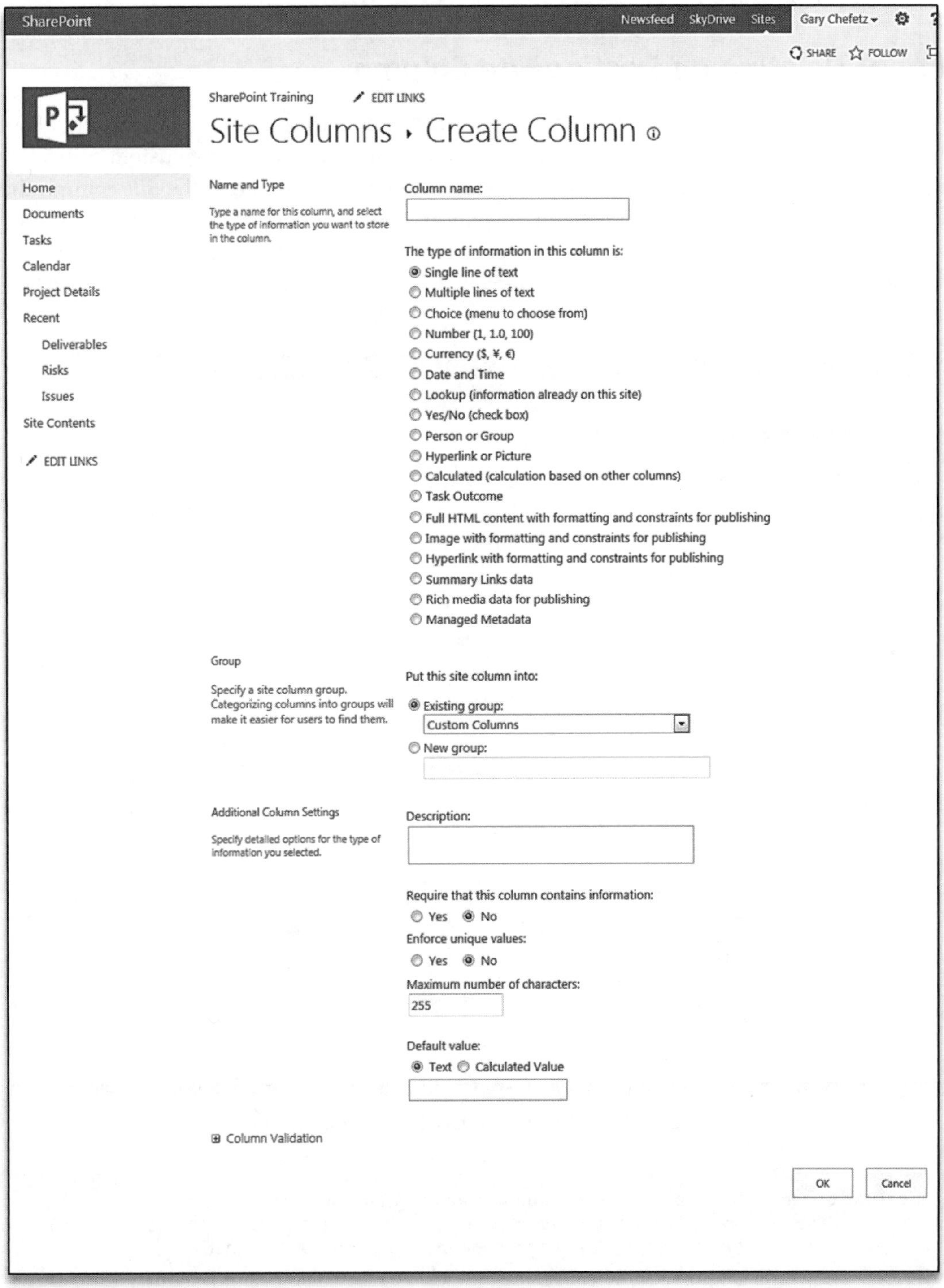

Figure 2 - 51: New Site Column page

Best Practice: MSProjectExperts recommends that you create a new group to categorize any new *Site* columns that you create in a Project Site. This will make it easier to separate and find your custom *Site* columns in the future.

The system displays the *Site Columns* page again, and you can scroll the page to find your new *Site* column listed in the group that you specified.

Modifying or Deleting an Existing Site Column

Although you cannot modify or delete any of the built-in *Site* columns from a Project Site, you may need to modify or delete a custom *Site* column that you previously created. To modify an existing custom column, visit the *Site Columns* page in the Project Site as shown in the previous section. In the list, locate the *Site* column that you want to modify or delete, then click its name. The system displays the *Site Columns ▸ Edit Column* page shown in Figure 2 - 52, allowing you to make any modifications necessary to the selected *Site* column. Click the *OK* button at the bottom of the page, or if you need to delete the column entirely from the Project Site, click the *Delete* button at the bottom of the page.

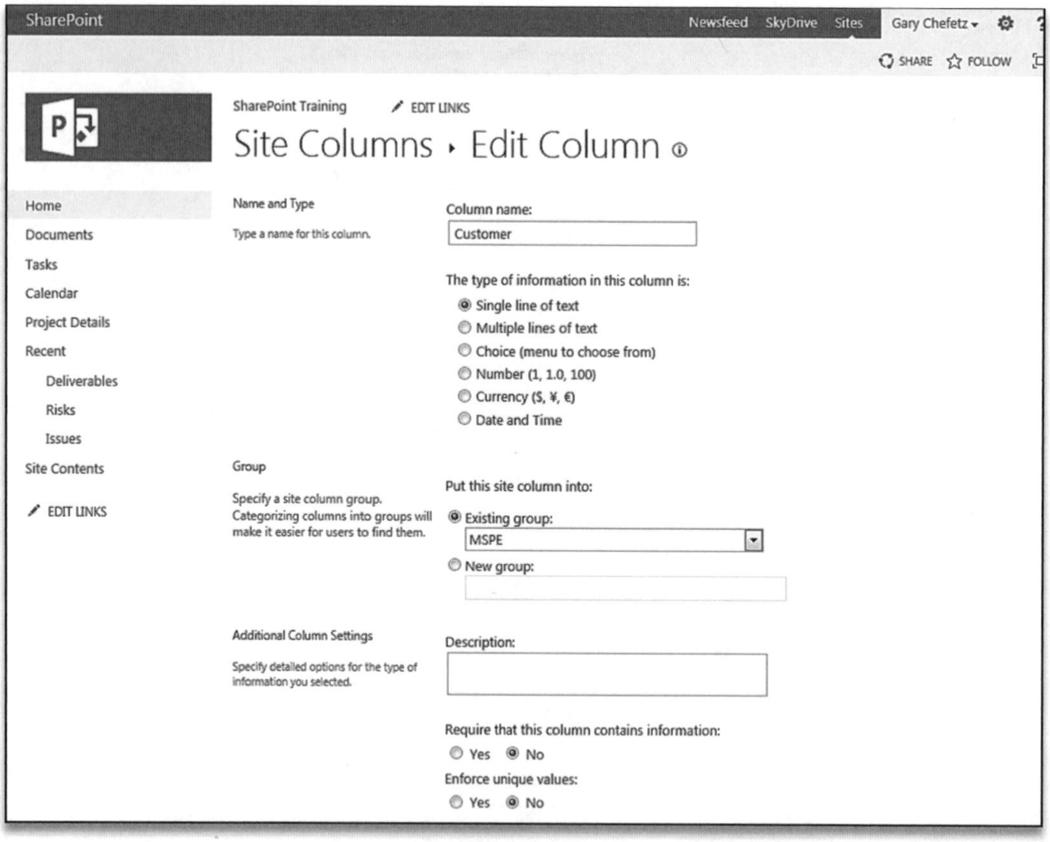

Figure 2 - 52: Site Columns ▸ Edit Column page

Information: Deleting a "parent" *Site* column from a Project Site will not remove any associated "child" columns from lists or libraries within the site. However, all "child" instances of the column become orphans and they will continue to function; but they will function independently of one another.

Adding a Site Column to a List

Once you create a new custom *Site* column for a Project Site, you can add that *Site* column to one or more lists or libraries within that site. To add a *Site* column to a list, navigate to the list, click the *List* tab, then in the *Settings* section of the ribbon, click the *List Settings* button. On the *List Settings* page, scroll to the *Columns* section and click the *Add from existing site columns* link, located below the column listing. The system displays the *Add Columns from Site Columns* page, as shown in Figure 2 - 53.

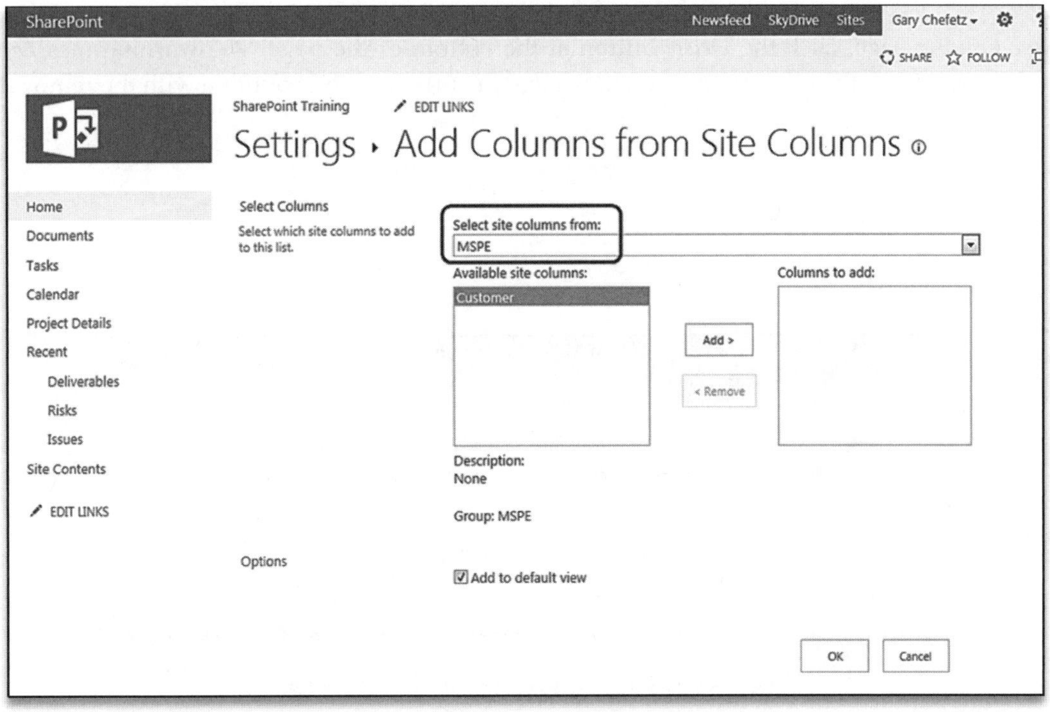

Figure 2 - 53: Add Columns from Site Columns page

The *Add Columns from Site Columns* page allows you to select your custom *Site* columns to add to the current list. The *Select site columns from* pick list displays all *Groups*; therefore, all *Site* columns from all groups appear in the *Available site columns* list. If you created a *Site* column and placed it into a new custom group, select the group from the *Select site columns from* pick list. Your custom *Site* column appears in the *Available site columns* list, as shown previously in Figure 2 - 53. Select the new *Site* column and click the *Add* button. To add the *Site* column to the default view for the list, select the *Add to default view* option, then click the *OK* button at the bottom of the page. The system returns to the *List Settings* page and displays the newly-added *Site* column in the *Columns* section of the page. If you selected the *Add to default view* option, return to the list and view the *Site* column in the default view.

Removing a Site Column from a List

Removing a *Site* column from a list is similar to deleting a standard column. Navigate to the list, click the *List* tab, then in the *Settings* section of the ribbon, click the *List Settings* button. On the *List Settings* page, scroll to the *Columns* section and click the name of the *Site* column that you need to remove.

Information: The *List Settings* page does not indicate which columns were created from *Site* columns.

On the *Change Column* page, click the *Delete* button at the bottom of the page. The warning message shown in Figure 2 - 54 displays. Click the *OK* button to acknowledge the message and continue with the removal of the column.

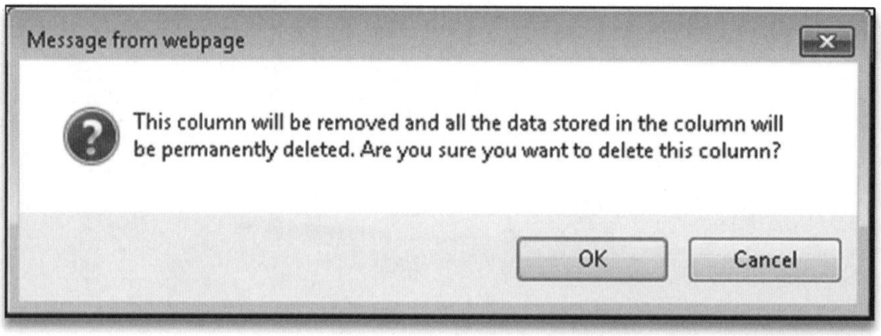
Message from webpage
This column will be removed and all the data stored in the column will be permanently deleted. Are you sure you want to delete this column?
OK
Cancel

Figure 2 - 54: Delete column warning message

Information: Deleting a *Site* column from a list or library will not delete the *Site* column entirely from the Project Site. It will remain in any other lists or libraries that are using it.

Controlling Column Ordering in Forms

When you create new columns in a list or add columns from existing *Site* columns, the system adds new columns to the bottom of the *New Item* and *Edit Item* forms. Depending upon your business process requirements, you may need to change the order of the columns in these forms. To control column ordering in list and library forms, navigate to the list, click the *List* tab, then in the *Settings* section of the ribbon, click the *List Settings* button. On the *List Settings* page, scroll to the *Columns* section and click the *Column ordering* link, located below the collection of columns. The system displays the *Change Column Ordering* page, shown in Figure 2 - 55.

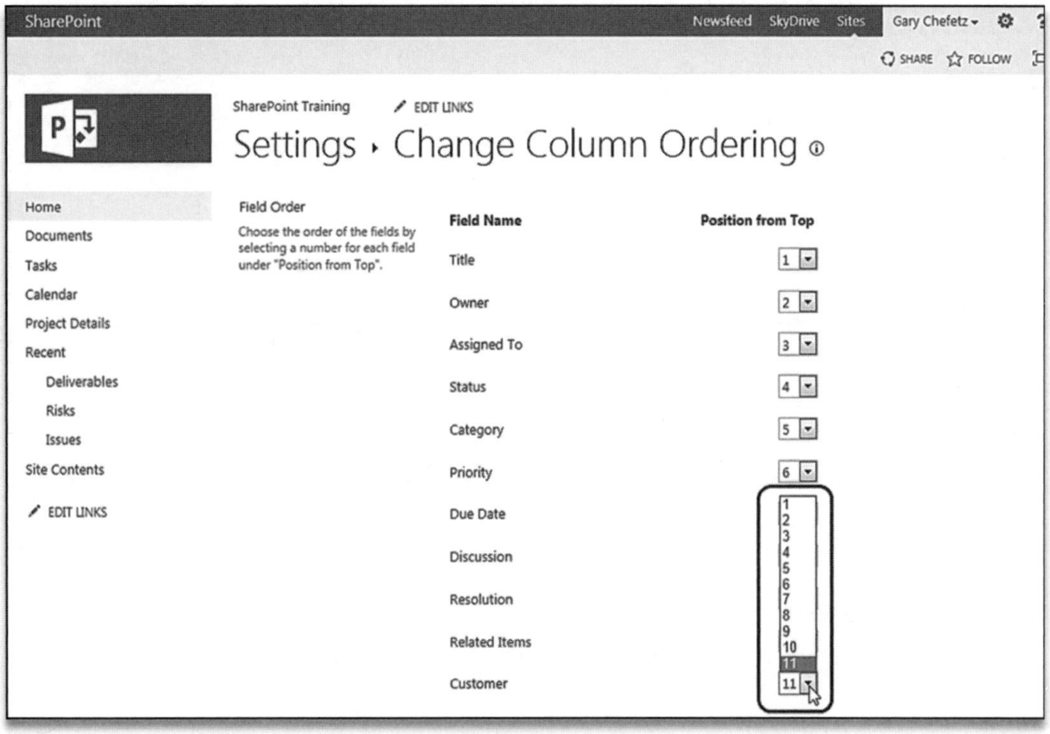

Figure 2 - 55: Change Column Ordering page

Information: Do not be confused here! Even though this page refers to "fields," you are working with SharePoint columns within the selected list or library. The term *Column* and the term *Field* are interchangeable.

The *Change Column Ordering* page displays all of the columns associated with the list in the order in which they displayed in the *New Item* and *Edit Item* forms. To change their order in the forms, select the appropriate numeric value next to each column; the system re-arranges the columns automatically to show the current order. Click the *OK* button at the bottom of the page to accept the column ordering.

Notice in Figure 2 - 56 that the columns displayed on the *New Item* form now reflect the new ordering I selected on the *Change Column Ordering* page to move my custom *Customer* field to position three.

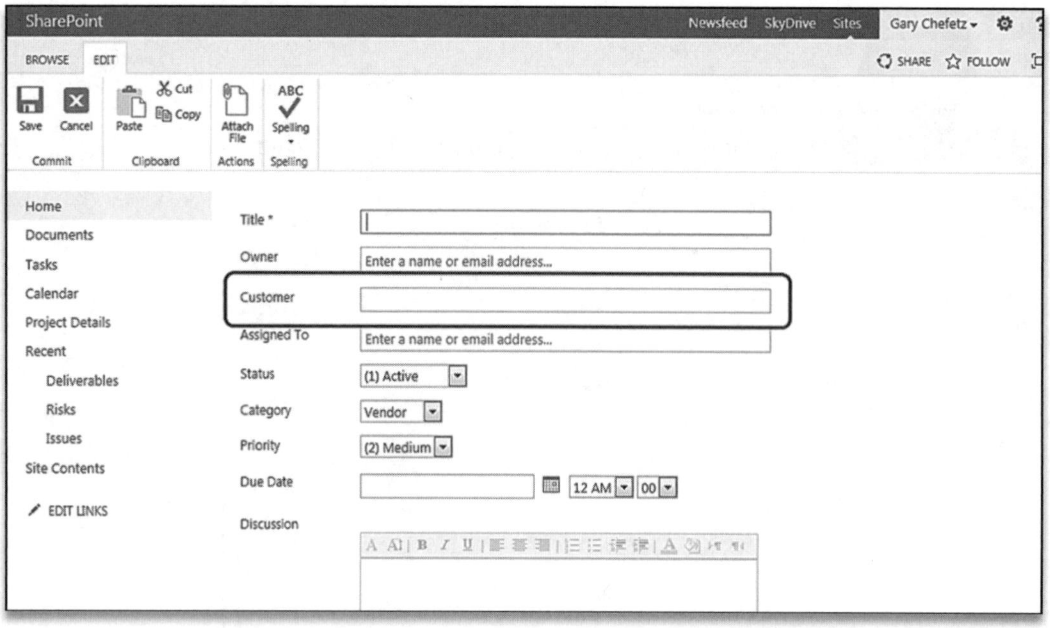

Figure 2 - 56: New Item form after changing column ordering

Managing List and Library Views

As I mentioned previously in this module, the system creates each new Project Site from a site template; this site template includes not only several lists and libraries in which to store project data, deliverables, and artifacts, but it also includes several built-in views for each list and library. In the event that your business process requires you to interact with the data differently, the system allows you to modify existing views or create new custom views in the Project Site for a selected project.

Figure 2 - 57 displays a view of the *Issues* list for a project; notice that the view displays a listing of issue items in table format, including a collection of columns that hold additional information describing each issue item.

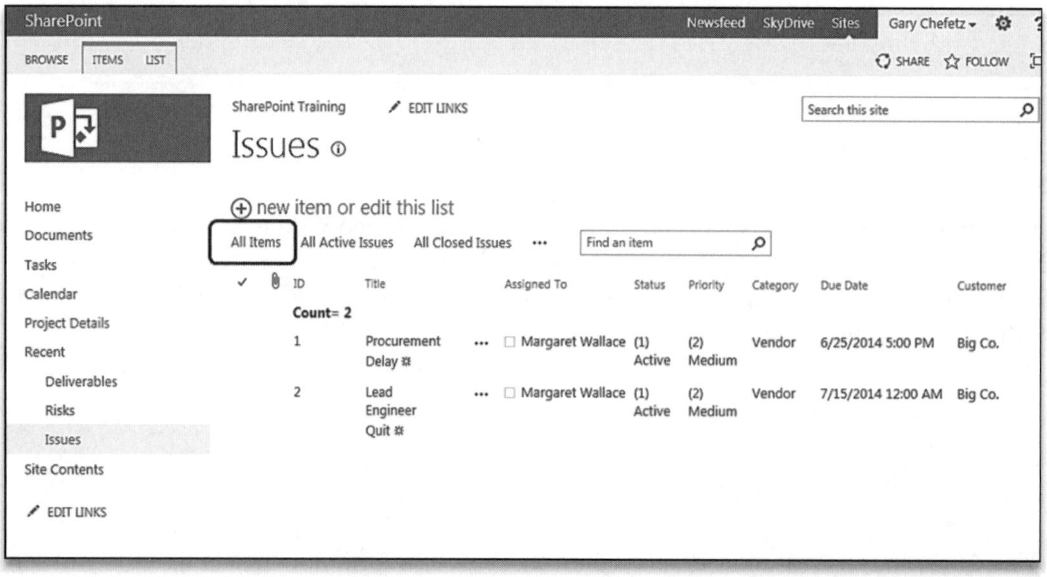

Figure 2 - 57: Issues list All Items view

When customizing an existing view or creating a new view for a SharePoint list or library, you need to ask yourself or your stakeholders the following questions:

- Which items do you need to see? Should you see all items in the list or library, or only specific items of interest?
- When displaying items in a view, which columns of metadata do you need to see for each item, and in which order should the view display them?
- When displaying items in a view, should the view sort the rows into a specific order?
- When displaying items in a view, should the view create groupings of similar items?

The answers to these questions are useful when you define list and library views in a Project Site.

Modifying or Deleting an Existing View

To modify an existing view in a list, navigate to the list, click the *List* tab, in the *Manage Views* section of the ribbon, select the desired view from the *Current View* pick list, and then click the *Modify View* button. The system displays the *Edit View* page shown in Figure 2 - 58. Select the appropriate options as described below and then click the *OK* button.

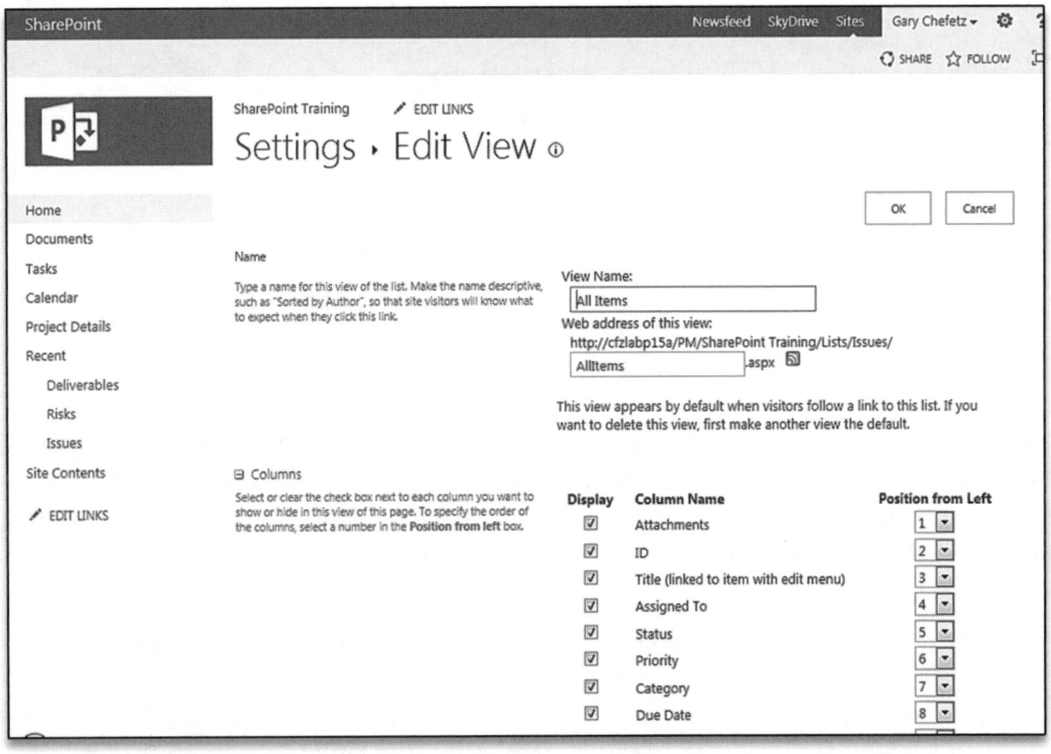

Figure 2 - 58: Edit View page

Information: You can also access the *Edit View* page by navigating to the list or library, clicking the *List* tab, and in the *Settings* section of the ribbon, clicking the *List Settings* button. On the *List Settings* page, scroll to the *Views* section of the page and click the name of the view.

In the *Name* section of the page rename the view or change the unique URL of the view, as necessary. Enter a new name into the *View Name* text box, or enter a new URL ending into the *Web address of this view* text box.

In the *Columns* section of the page, you can change which columns appear in the view and the ordering of those columns. Select your desired columns by selecting the *Display* option next to each and then adjust the ordering of the selected columns by adjusting the *Position from Left* values next to each column.

In the *Sort* section of the page shown in Figure 2 - 59, change the sort order of the item rows in the view. Select a column to use for sorting from the *First sort by the column* pick list, then select whether the rows sort in ascending or descending order, based on the values in that column. To sort the rows based on multiple columns, select a second column using the *Then sort by the column* pick list and pick a sort order.

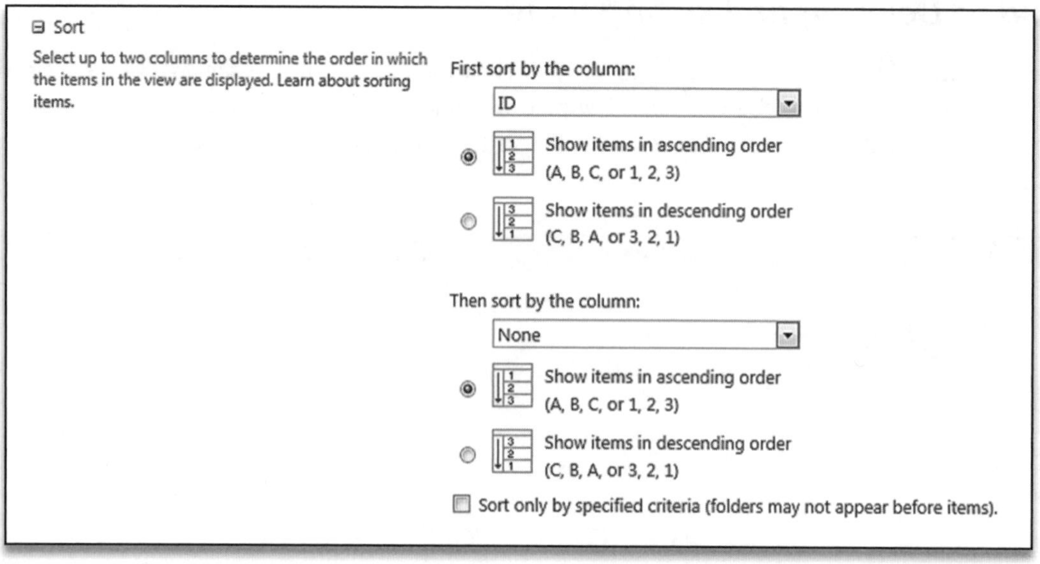

Figure 2 - 59: Sort section of the Edit View page

In the *Filter* section of the page shown in Figure 2 - 60, display only specific items of interest in the view, rather than all of the items in the list. Select the *Show items only when the following is true* option and then configure one or more conditions that each item must meet before appearing in the view. To configure a conditional test, select a column from the first pick list, select a test from the second pick list, and enter a value in the text box.

For example, to show items that belong to the Human Resources Department, you may create a condition such as:

Column	Test	Value
Department	is equal to	Human Resources

To configure multiple conditional tests, select the appropriate *And / Or* option after the first conditional test, then configure a second conditional test using the second set of options in the *Filter* section. To configure more than two conditional tests, click the *Show More Columns* link.

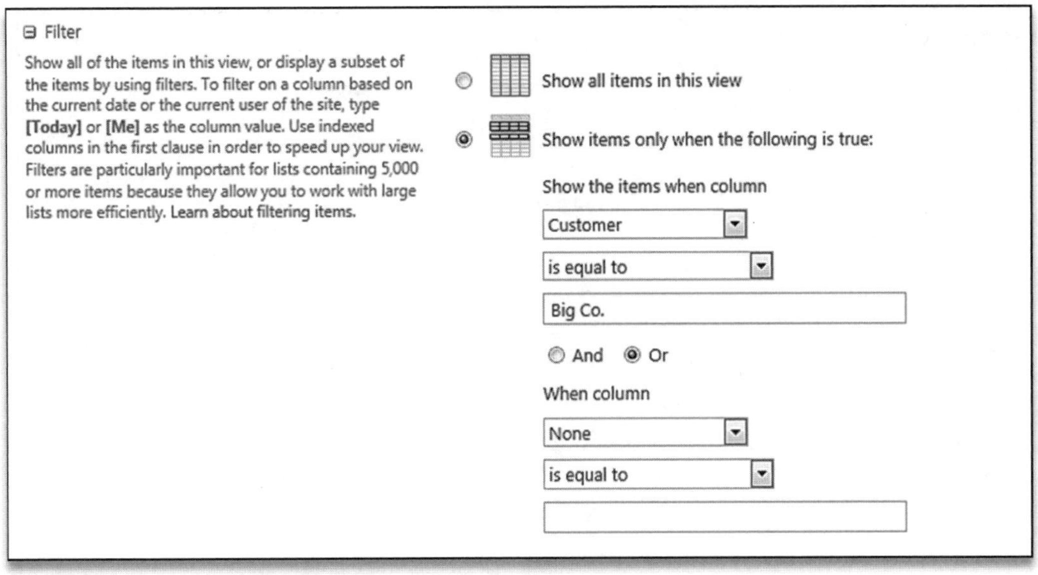
Filter
Show all of the items in this view, or display a subset of the items by using filters. To filter on a column based on the current date or the current user of the site, type [Today] or [Me] as the column value. Use indexed columns in the first clause in order to speed up your view. Filters are particularly important for lists containing 5,000 or more items because they allow you to work with large lists more efficiently. Learn about filtering items.
Show all items in this view
Show items only when the following is true:
Show the items when column
Customer
is equal to
Big Co.
And
Or
When column
None
is equal to

Figure 2 - 60: Filter section of the Edit View page

In the *Tabular View* section of the page shown in Figure 2 - 61, you can allow people to select multiple item rows in the view for certain operations such as multi-item deletion. Select the *Allow individual item checkboxes* option to allow multi-item selection in the view. In the *Group By* section of the page shown in Figure 2 - 61, you can rearrange the rows in the view to group similar items together under common headings. Select a column from the *First group by the column* pick list, then select whether the group headings sort in ascending or descending order. To create a second level of nested groupings within the first level of groupings, select another column using the *Then group by the column* pick list, then select whether the nested group headings sort in ascending or descending order. Select whether the groupings appear collapsed or expanded by selecting the appropriate *By default, show groupings* option. Finally, enter a value for *Number of groups to display per page* in the text box. If there is more than the specified number of groupings in the view, SharePoint displays links to navigate between multiple pages of items.

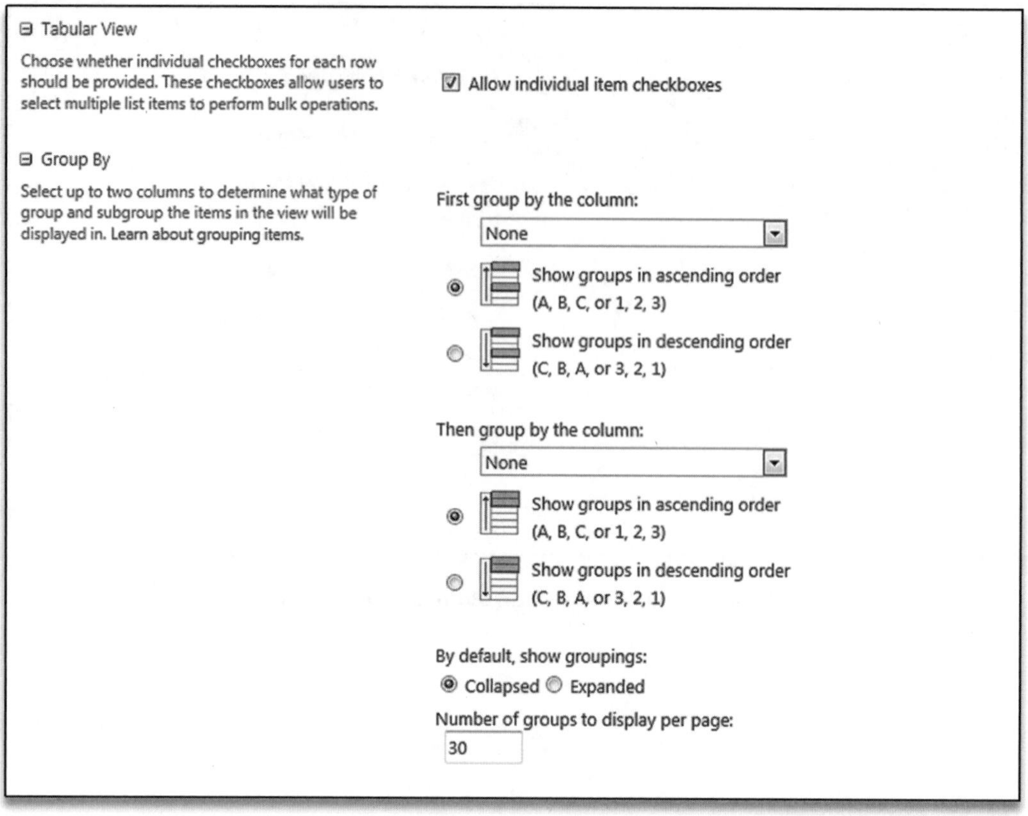

Figure 2 - 61: Tabular View and Group By section of the Edit View page

In the *Totals* section of the page shown in Figure 2 - 62, you can display totals at the bottom of any column in the view. The page displays a listing of all of the columns selected to appear in the view, as well as the option to display a total for each column. Select the appropriate option for each listed column.

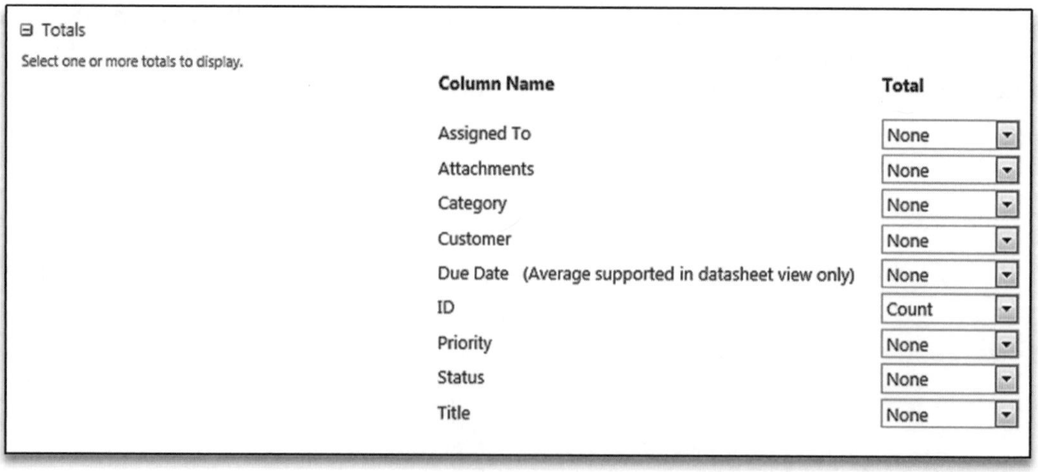

Figure 2 - 62: Totals section of the Edit View page

In the *Style* section of the page shown in Figure 2 - 63, you control the formatting of the items displayed in the view. Select the desired formatting option from the *View Style* pick list.

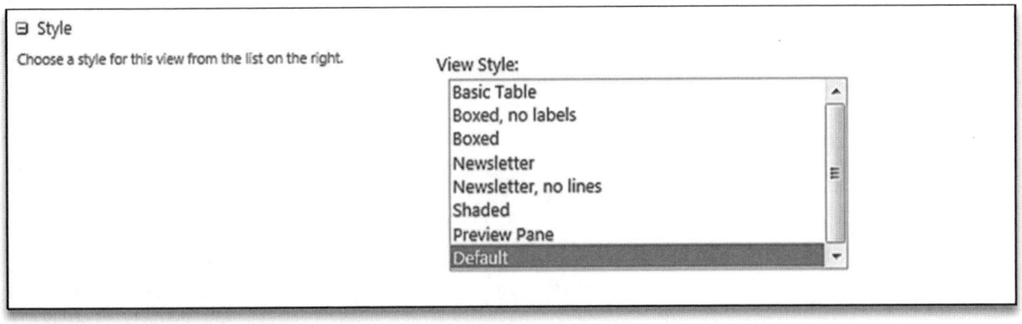
Style
Choose a style for this view from the list on the right.
View Style:
Basic Table
Boxed, no labels
Boxed
Newsletter
Newsletter, no lines
Shaded
Preview Pane
Default

Figure 2 - 63: Style section of the Edit View page

In the *Folders* section of the page shown in Figure 2 - 64, you control whether folders appear in the view. Select the *Show items inside folders* option or the *Show all items without folders* option, depending on your requirements. In the *Item Limit* section of the page shown in Figure 2 - 64, you control how many item rows appear on each page in the view. Enter a number in the *Number of items to display* text box, then select the *Display items in batches of the specified size* option or the *Limit the total number of items returned to the specified amount* option, depending on your requirements.

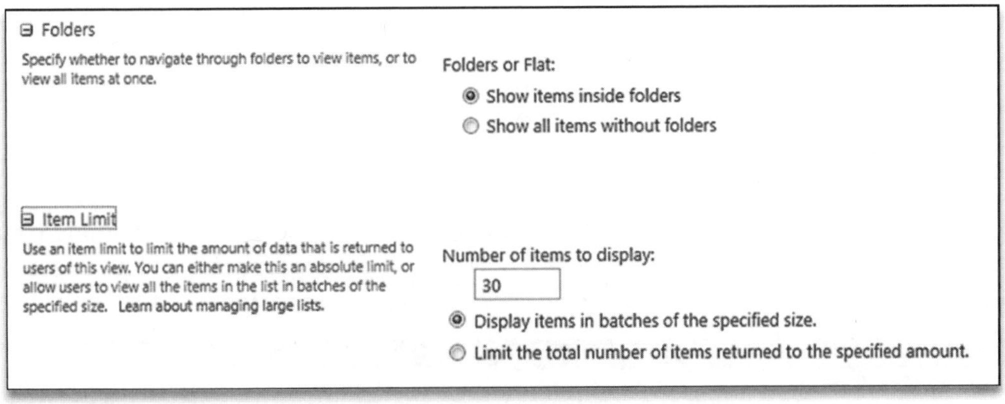
Folders
Specify whether to navigate through folders to view items, or to view all items at once.
Folders or Flat:
Show items inside folders
Show all items without folders
Item Limit
Use an item limit to limit the amount of data that is returned to users of this view. You can either make this an absolute limit, or allow users to view all the items in the list in batches of the specified size. Learn about managing large lists.
Number of items to display:
30
Display items in batches of the specified size.
Limit the total number of items returned to the specified amount.

Figure 2 - 64: Folders and Item Limit sections of the Edit View page

Information: A large number of items displayed in a view could have adverse effects on system performance.

In the *Mobile* section of the page shown in Figure 2 - 65, you can control mobile options for the view. Select the *Enable this view for mobile access* option to format the view optimally for mobile devices with small screens such as PDAs or mobile phones. Select the *Make this view the default view for mobile access* option to configure the view as the default mobile view. To limit the number of items displayed in the mobile view, enter a number in the *Number of items to display in list view web part for this view* text box.

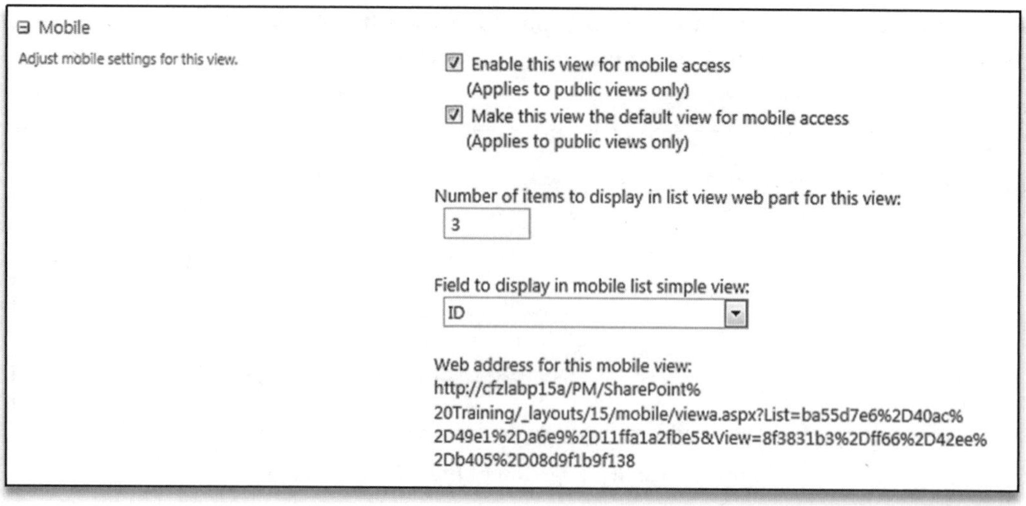

Figure 2 - 65: Mobile section of the Edit View page

Best Practice: MSProjectExperts recommends that if you have a generalized need for Project Site customizations, such as new or modified views, your Project Server administrator modify the base template for Project Sites. If you are using the *Enterprise Project Types* feature in Project Server 2013, each project type can utilize its own Project Site template that has unique customizations for that Project Type.

Creating a New Standard View

A standard view is a basic SharePoint list view that displays items in table format with rows and columns. Figure 2 - 66 shows an example of a standard view. To create a new standard view for a list, navigate to the list, click the *List* tab, then in the *Manage Views* section of the ribbon, click the *Create View* button.

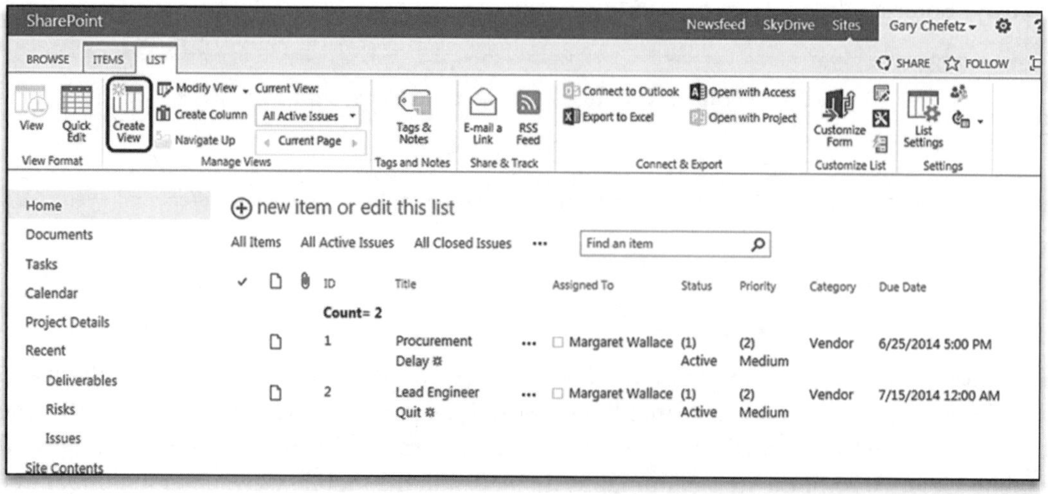

Figure 2 - 66: Example of a Standard view

In the *Choose a view format* section of the *View Type* page shown in Figure 2 - 67, click the *Standard View* link.

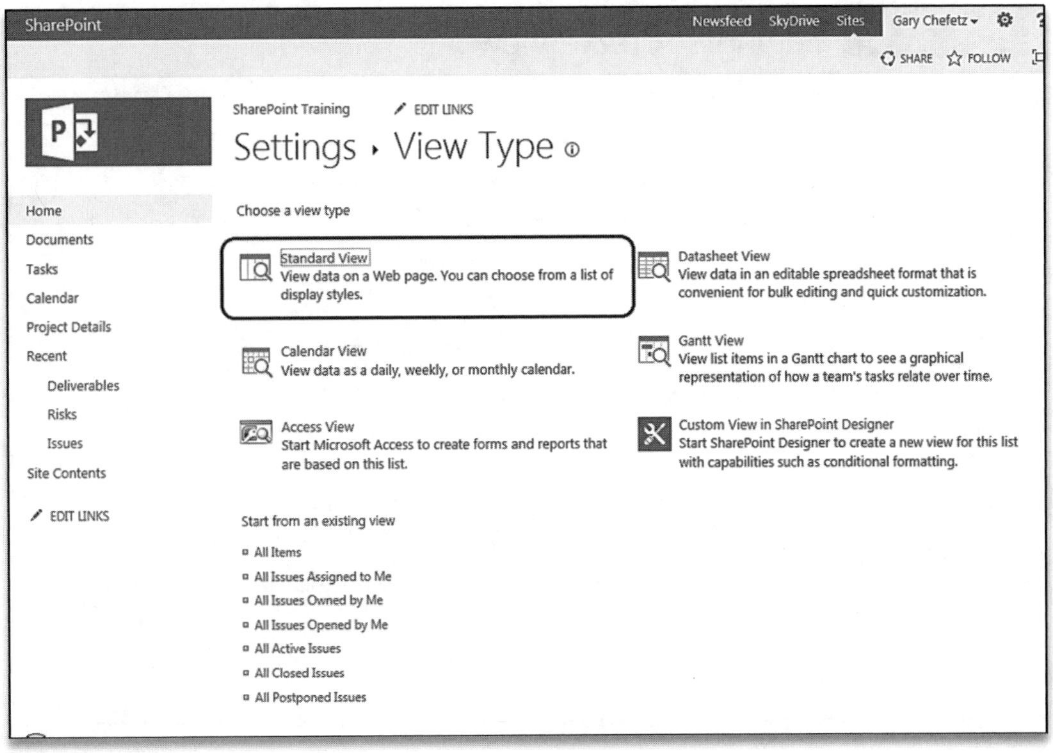
SharePoint
Newsfeed
SkyDrive
Sites
Gary Chefetz
SHARE
FOLLOW
SharePoint Training
EDIT LINKS
Settings › View Type
Home
Documents
Tasks
Calendar
Project Details
Recent
Deliverables
Risks
Issues
Site Contents
EDIT LINKS
Choose a view type
Standard View
View data on a Web page. You can choose from a list of display styles.
Datasheet View
View data in an editable spreadsheet format that is convenient for bulk editing and quick customization.
Calendar View
View data as a daily, weekly, or monthly calendar.
Gantt View
View list items in a Gantt chart to see a graphical representation of how a team's tasks relate over time.
Access View
Start Microsoft Access to create forms and reports that are based on this list.
Custom View in SharePoint Designer
Start SharePoint Designer to create a new view for this list with capabilities such as conditional formatting.
Start from an existing view
All Items
All Issues Assigned to Me
All Issues Owned by Me
All Issues Opened by Me
All Active Issues
All Closed Issues
All Postponed Issues

Figure 2 - 67: View Type page

The system displays the *Create View* page shown in Figure 2 - 68, which is very similar to the *Edit View* page shown previously. Enter a name for the new view in the *View Name* text box, and then select the *Make this the default view* option if you want this view to be the default view for everyone who visits the list. Next, to create a view that is visible only to you, in the *View Audience* pick list for the new view, select the *Create a Personal View* item, or to create a view that is visible to everyone, select the *Create a Public View* item. Select the other options on the page as described in the previous section, then click the *OK* button.

Information: You can only set a Public View as the default view for a list or library.

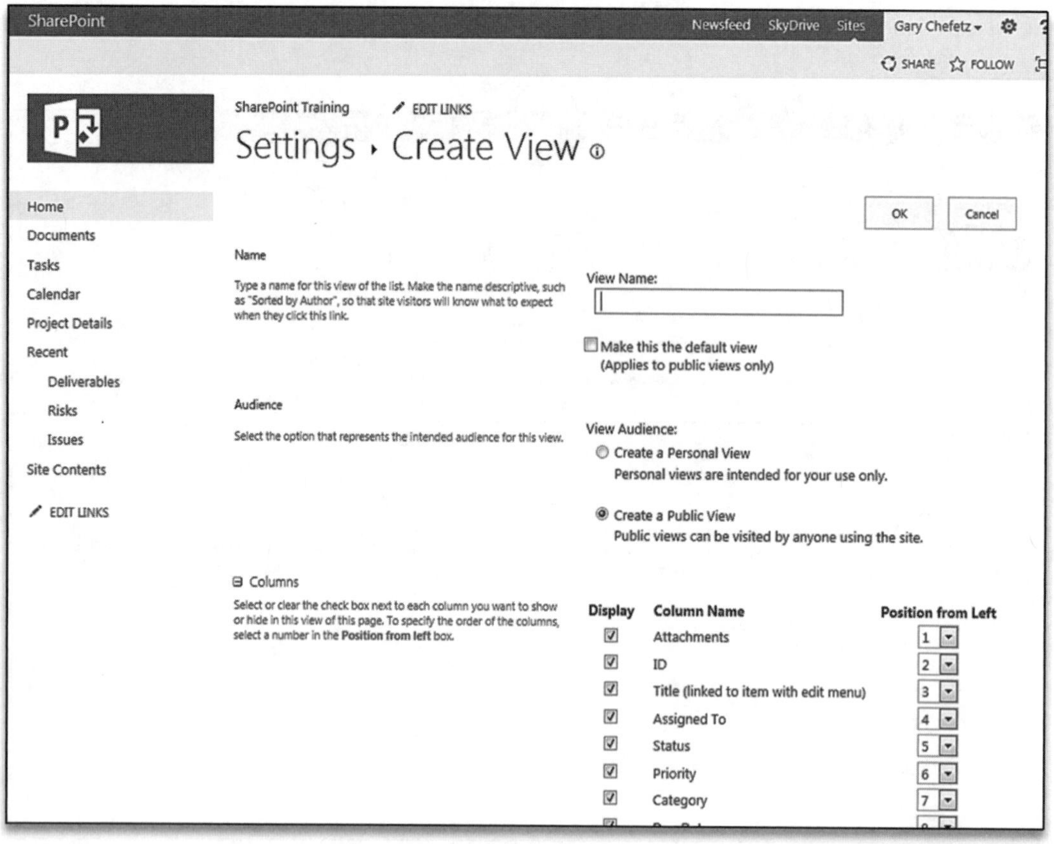
SharePoint
Newsfeed
SkyDrive
Sites
Gary Chefetz
SHARE
FOLLOW
SharePoint Training
EDIT LINKS
Settings › Create View
OK
Cancel
Home
Documents
Tasks
Calendar
Project Details
Recent
Deliverables
Risks
Issues
Site Contents
EDIT LINKS
Name
Type a name for this view of the list. Make the name descriptive, such as "Sorted by Author", so that site visitors will know what to expect when they click this link.
View Name:
Make this the default view
(Applies to public views only)
Audience
Select the option that represents the intended audience for this view.
View Audience:
Create a Personal View
Personal views are intended for your use only.
Create a Public View
Public views can be visited by anyone using the site.
Columns
Select or clear the check box next to each column you want to show or hide in this view of this page. To specify the order of the columns, select a number in the Position from left box.
Display
Column Name
Position from Left
Attachments
ID
Title (linked to item with edit menu)
Assigned To
Status
Priority
Category

Figure 2 - 68: Create View page

Information: You can also access the *Create View* page by navigating to the list or library, clicking the *List or Library* tab, and clicking the *List or Library Settings* button in the *Settings* section of the ribbon. Once on the *List or Library Settings* page, scroll to the *Views* section of the page and click the *Create view* link.

Creating a New Calendar View

A *Calendar* view is a SharePoint list view that displays items in monthly, weekly, or daily calendar format. Figure 2 - 69 shows the default *Calendar* view for the default calendar list in a Project Site.

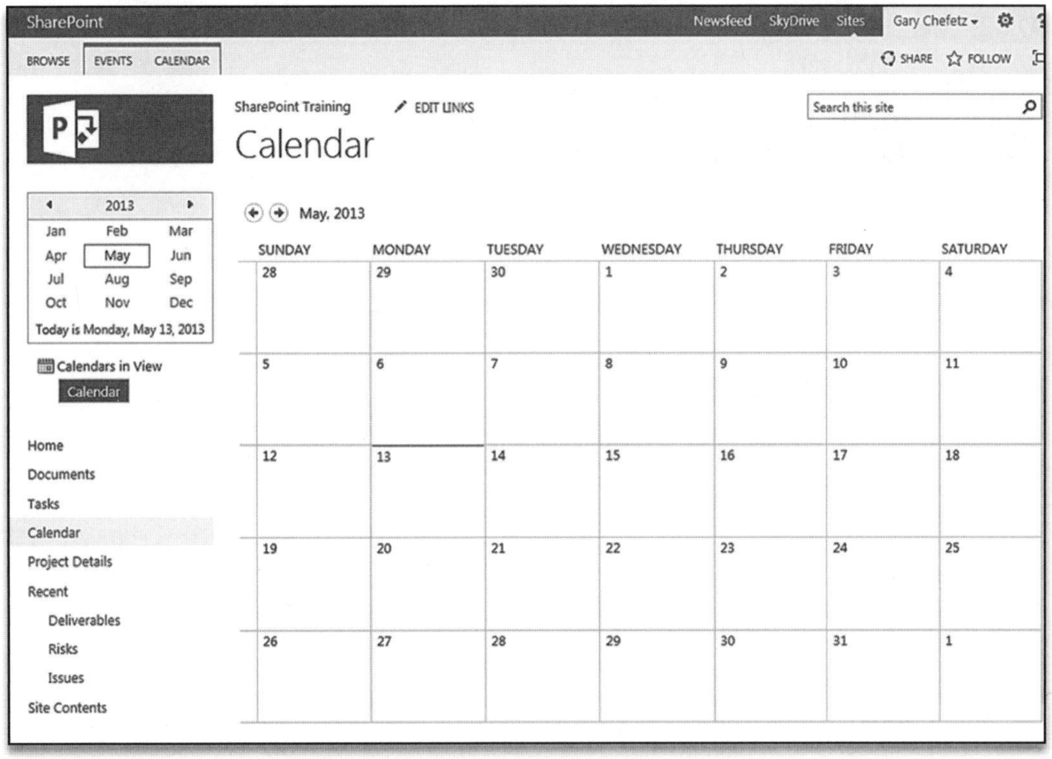

Figure 2 - 69: Example of a Calendar view

Information: Calendar views are most useful for viewing lists of tasks, events, or other date-driven items.

To create a new *Calendar* view for a list, navigate to the list, click the *List* tab, then in the *Manage Views* section of the ribbon, click the *Create View* button. In the *Choose a view type* section of the *View Type* page, click the *Calendar View* link. The system displays the *Create Calendar View* page, shown in Figure 2 - 70. Select the appropriate options as described below and then click the *OK* button.

The *Create Calendar View* page has several sections and options; some are similar to those for creating a standard view as described previously, and some are unique to *Calendar* views. To control when each item begins and ends on the timeline, scroll to the *Time Interval* section of the *Create Calendar View* page also shown in Figure 2 - 70. Select the column that contains the begin date for each item from the *Begin* pick list, and select the column that contains the end date for each item from the *End* pick list.

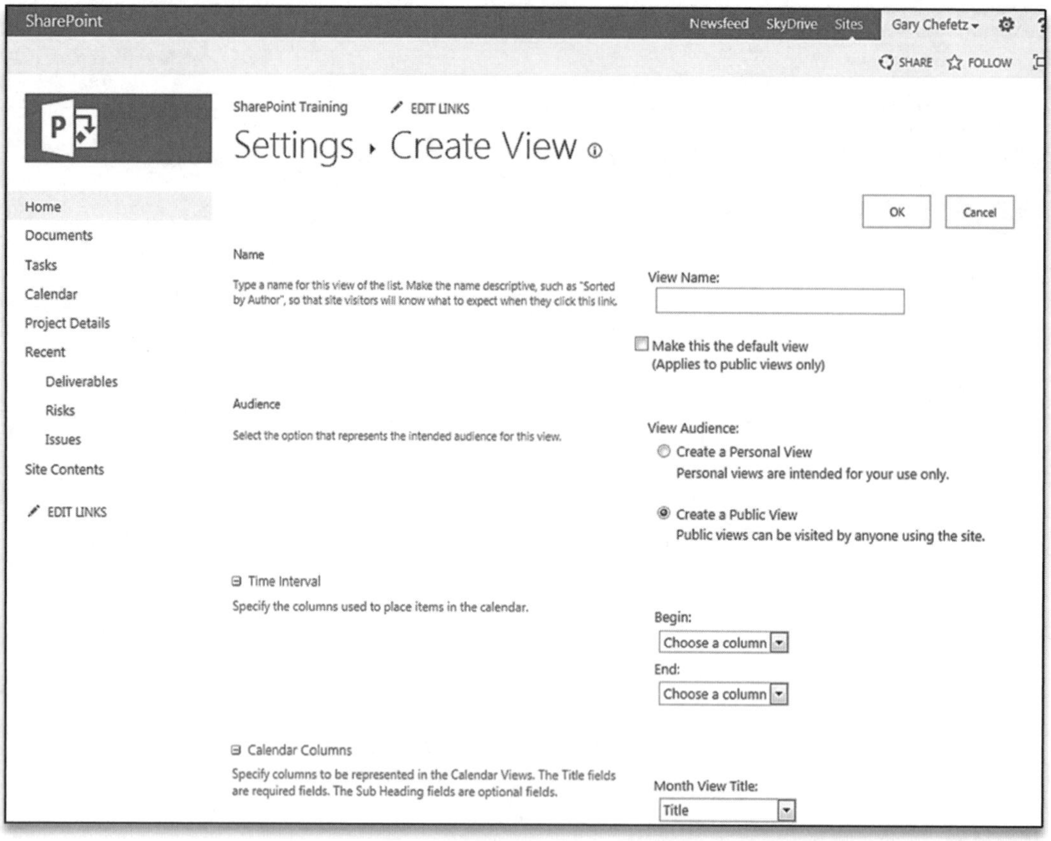
SharePoint
Newsfeed
SkyDrive
Sites
Gary Chefetz
SHARE
FOLLOW
SharePoint Training
EDIT LINKS
Settings › Create View
Home
Documents
Tasks
Calendar
Project Details
Recent
Deliverables
Risks
Issues
Site Contents
EDIT LINKS
OK
Cancel
Name
Type a name for this view of the list. Make the name descriptive, such as "Sorted by Author", so that site visitors will know what to expect when they click this link.
View Name:
Make this the default view
(Applies to public views only)
Audience
Select the option that represents the intended audience for this view.
View Audience:
Create a Personal View
Personal views are intended for your use only.
Create a Public View
Public views can be visited by anyone using the site.
Time Interval
Specify the columns used to place items in the calendar.
Begin:
Choose a column
End:
Choose a column
Calendar Columns
Specify columns to be represented in the Calendar Views. The Title fields are required fields. The Sub Heading fields are optional fields.
Month View Title:
Title

Figure 2 - 70: Create View page for Calendar view (top of page)

> **Information**: You must select a column in both the *Begin* and *End* pick lists. The system uses the dates in the selected columns to display items graphically on the calendar. Only columns that contain date information appear in the *Begin* and *End* pick lists.

To control which columns of data appear for each item in the *Calendar* view, scroll to the *Calendar Columns* section of the *Create Calendar View* page shown in Figure 2 - 71. Because you can display a *Calendar* view in daily, weekly, or monthly format, you can configure a different column to appear as the title for each item in each of these types of views. To specify the title that appears for each item in the monthly *Calendar* view, select the appropriate column from the *Month View Title* pick list. To specify the title that appears for each item in the weekly *Calendar* view, select the appropriate column from the *Week View Title* pick list. To specify the title that appears for each item in the daily *Calendar* view, select the appropriate column from the *Day View Title* pick list. Optionally, select a sub-heading to appear for each item in the weekly *Calendar* view or the daily *Calendar* view by selecting the appropriate column in the *Week View Sub Heading* pick list and the *Day View Sub Heading* pick list.

To control whether the system displays the default *Calendar* view in daily, weekly, or monthly calendar format, scroll to the *Default Scope* section of the *Create Calendar View* page shown in Figure 2 - 71 and select the appropriate *Default scope* option.

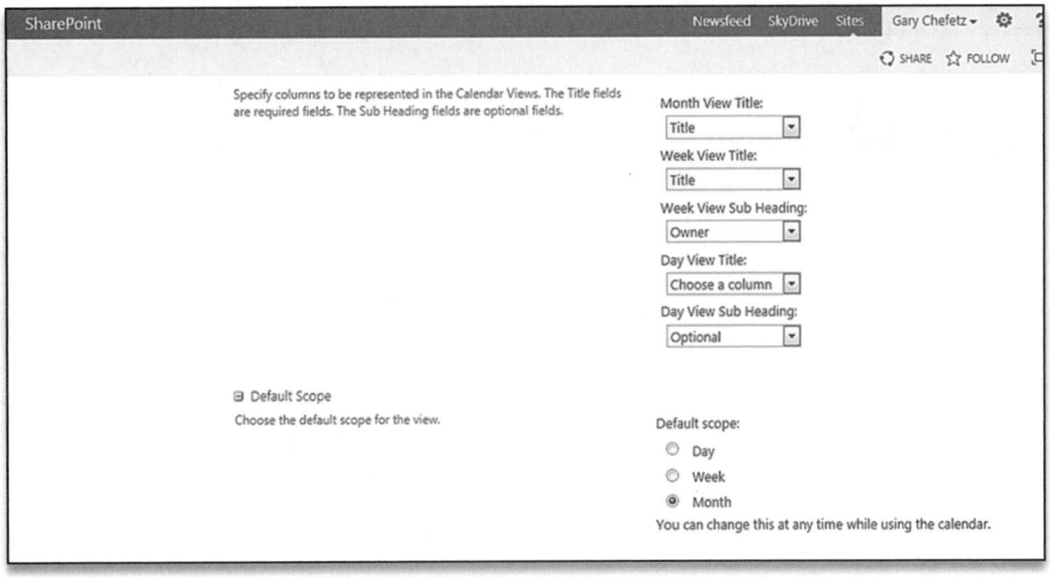

Figure 2 - 71: Create View page for Calendar view (middle of page)

The remaining sections of the *Create View* page are identical to standard list views, so I do not cover them again here.

Creating a New Datasheet View

A *Datasheet* view is an interactive SharePoint view that displays items in table format with rows and columns and allows in-page editing of the data, including the addition and deletion of items, as if you are working in an embedded spreadsheet. Figure 2 - 72 shows an example of a *Datasheet* view.

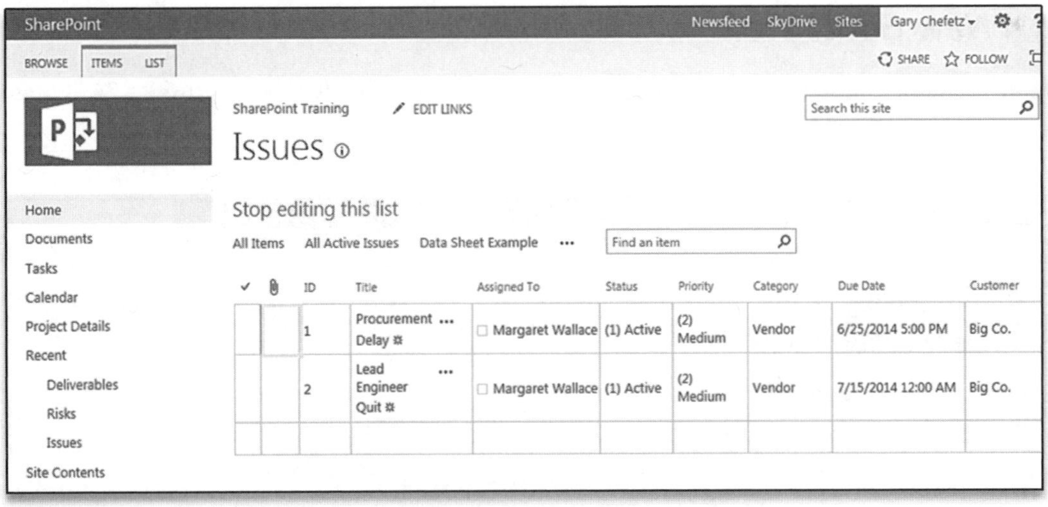

Figure 2 - 72: Example of a Datasheet view

To create a new *Datasheet* view for a list, navigate to the list, click the *List* tab, then in the *Manage Views* section of the ribbon, click the *Create View* button. In the *Choose a view format* section of the *Create View* page, click the *Datasheet View* option. The system displays the *Create Datasheet View* page shown in Figure 2 - 73. The sections and options available to configure the view are nearly identical to those available for creating a standard view described previously. Select the appropriate options for the view and then click the *OK* button.

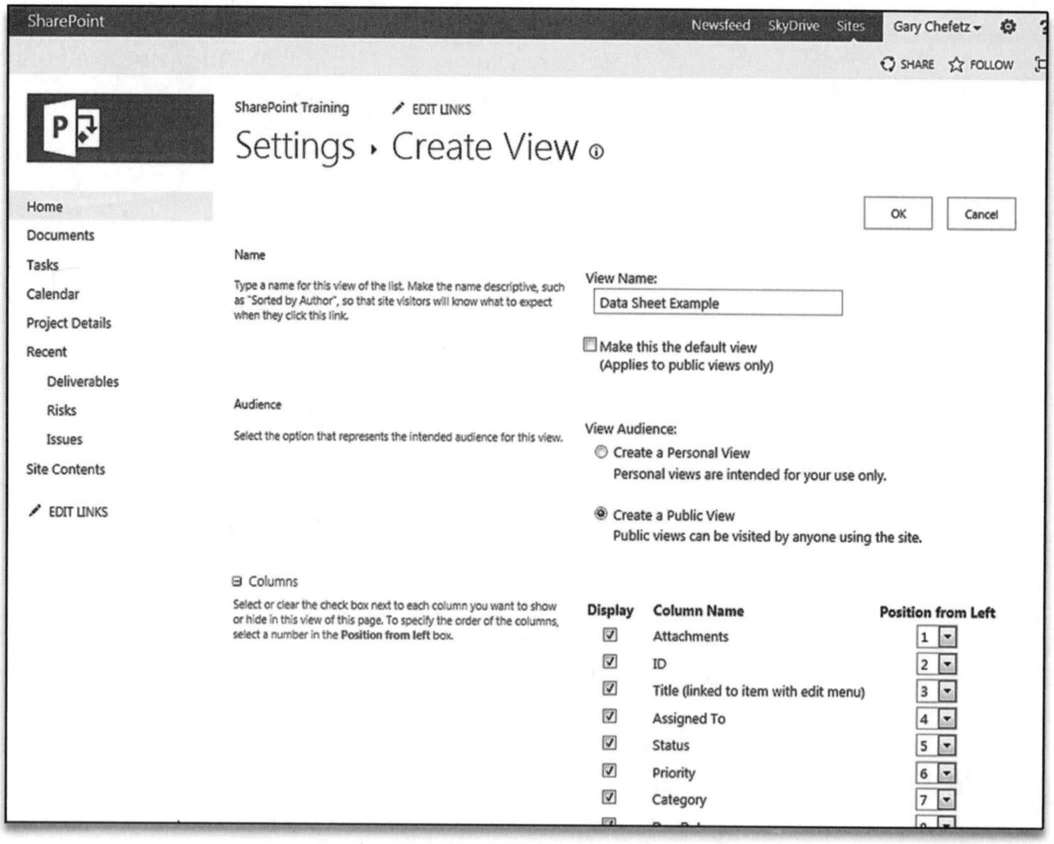

Figure 2 - 73: Create View page for a Datasheet view

Creating a New Gantt View

A *Gantt* view is a SharePoint list view that displays items in Gantt chart format. Figure 2 - 74 shows the default view for the *Deliverables* list for a Project Site, which is a *Gantt* view.

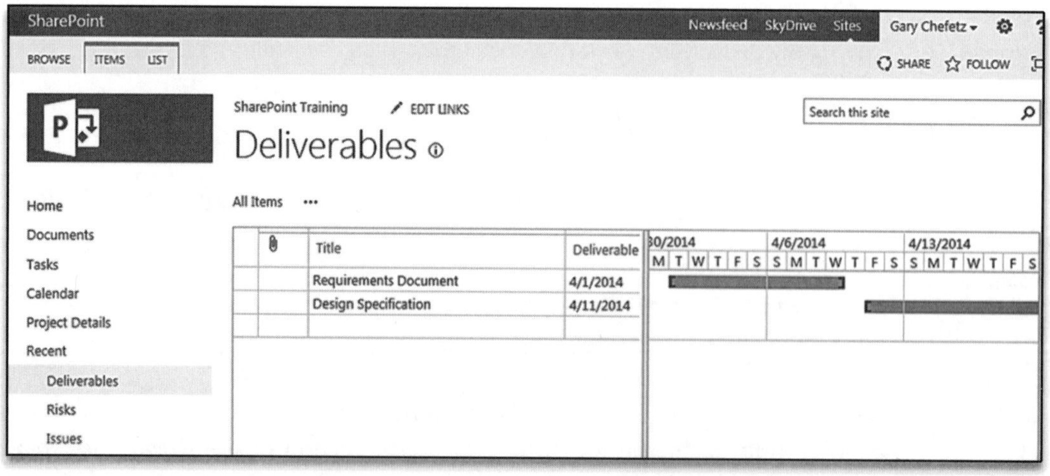

Figure 2 - 74: The Deliverables default view is an example of a Gantt view

Information: Gantt views are most useful for viewing lists of tasks, events, or other date-driven items. This is out-of-box functionality and does not require Microsoft Project Pro or Project Server to create a Gantt view.

To create a new *Gantt* view for a list, navigate to the list, click the *List* tab, then in the *Manage Views* section of the ribbon, click the *Create View* button. In the *Choose a view format* section of the *Create View* page, click the *Gantt View* link. The system displays the *Create Gantt View* page shown in Figure 2 - 75. Select the appropriate options as described below and then click the *OK* button.

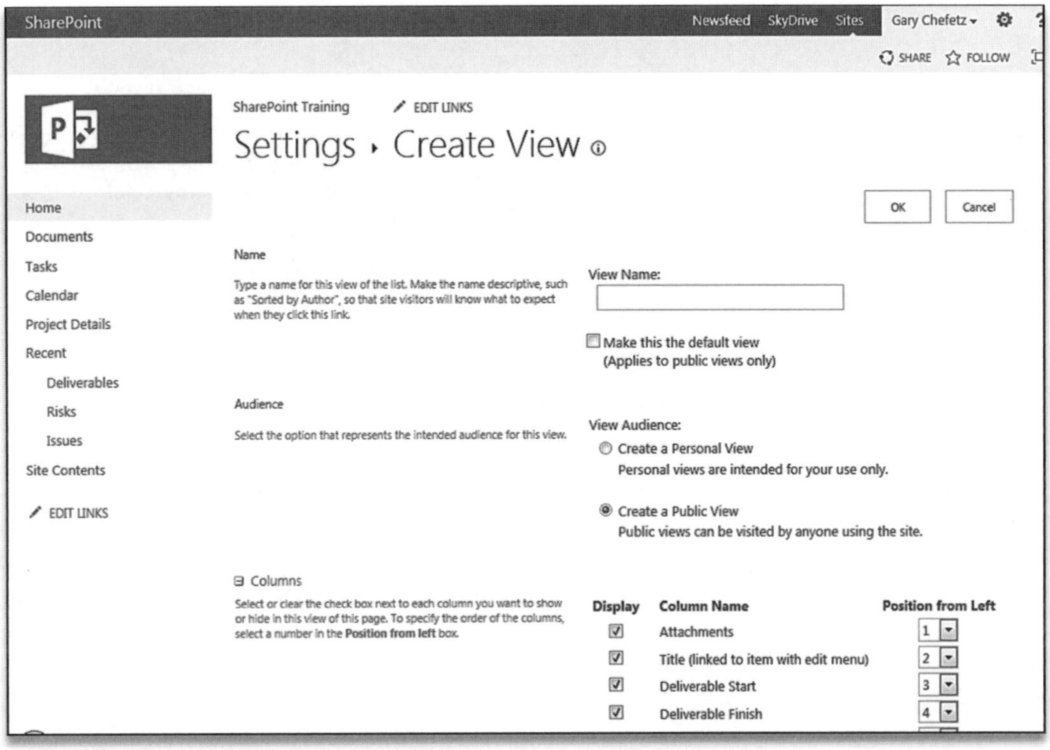
SharePoint
Newsfeed
SkyDrive
Sites
Gary Chefetz
SHARE
FOLLOW
SharePoint Training
EDIT LINKS
Settings › Create View
OK
Cancel
Home
Documents
Tasks
Calendar
Project Details
Recent
Deliverables
Risks
Issues
Site Contents
EDIT LINKS
Name
Type a name for this view of the list. Make the name descriptive, such as "Sorted by Author", so that site visitors will know what to expect when they click this link.
View Name:
Make this the default view
(Applies to public views only)
Audience
Select the option that represents the intended audience for this view.
View Audience:
Create a Personal View
Personal views are intended for your use only.
Create a Public View
Public views can be visited by anyone using the site.
Columns
Select or clear the check box next to each column you want to show or hide in this view of this page. To specify the order of the columns, select a number in the Position from left box.
Display
Column Name
Position from Left
Attachments
Title (linked to item with edit menu)
Deliverable Start
Deliverable Finish

Figure 2 - 75: Create View page for Gantt view (top of page)

The *Create Gantt View* page has several sections and options; some are similar to those for creating a standard view as described previously, and some are unique to *Gantt* views. To control which columns represent the title for each Gantt bar, the date when each item begins and ends on the timeline, as well as the progress and predecessors for each Gantt bar, scroll to the *Gantt Columns* section of the *Create Gantt View* page shown in Figure 2 - 76. Select the column that contains the title for each Gantt bar from the *Title* pick list, select the column that contains the begin date for each item from the *Start Date* pick list, and select the column that contains the end date for each item from the *Due Date* pick list. Optionally select the column that contains the progress value for each Gantt bar from the *Percent Complete* pick list, and optionally select the column that contains the predecessor information for each Gantt bar from the *Predecessors* pick list.

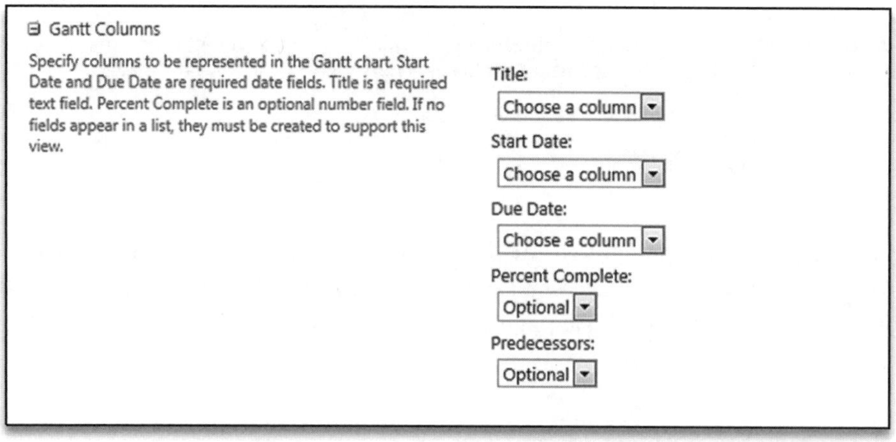
Gantt Columns
Specify columns to be represented in the Gantt chart. Start Date and Due Date are required date fields. Title is a required text field. Percent Complete is an optional number field. If no fields appear in a list, they must be created to support this view.
Title:
Choose a column
Start Date:
Choose a column
Due Date:
Choose a column
Percent Complete:
Optional
Predecessors:
Optional

Figure 2 - 76: Gantt Columns section of the Create View page for a Gantt view

> **Information**: You **must** select a column in both the *Start Date* and *Due Date* pick lists. The system uses the dates in the selected columns to display items graphically on the Gantt chart. Only columns that contain date information will appear in the *Start Date* and *Due Date* pick lists.

Creating a New View Based on an Existing View

Perhaps the easiest way to create a new view for a SharePoint list is by making a copy of an existing view, then making slight adjustments to achieve a view that meets your business requirements. To create a new view based on an existing one, navigate to the list, click the *List* tab, then in the *Manage Views* section of the ribbon, click the *Create View* button. In the *Start from an existing view* section of the *Create View* page, click the name of the existing view upon which you want to base the new view. The system displays the *Create View* page, shown previously. Notice that if you scroll through the various sections of the page, the options match the existing view that you copied. Enter a name for the new view and select or adjust the appropriate options depending upon the type of view, then click the *OK* button.

Modifying List and Library General Settings

SharePoint organizes structured and unstructured content into list and library containers within a Project Site. You learned how to work with columns and views for these repositories, but there are additional ways you can control the behavior of lists and libraries affecting all of the items stored in them. To view and adjust the configuration settings for a list, navigate to the list, click the *List* tab, then in the *Settings* section of the ribbon, click the *List Settings* button to open the *List Settings* page shown in Figure 2 - 77. I cover many of these topics, but not all of them, because you must have Administrator rights to fully leverage some of these. Some of these features require additional administrative setup and configuration.

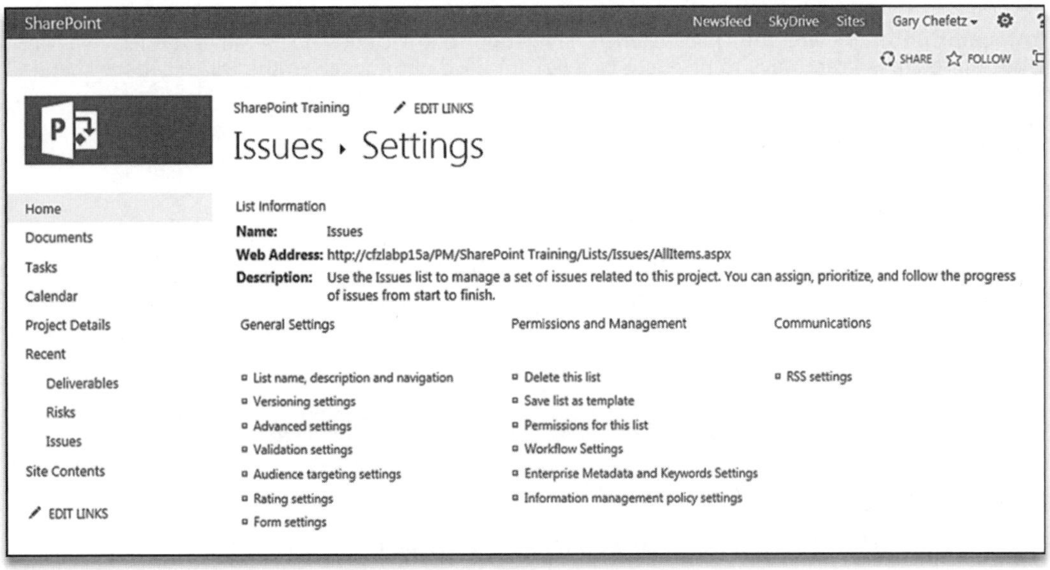

Figure 2 - 77: List Settings page
General Settings, Permissions and Management, and Communications sections

Specifying Title, Description, and Navigation Settings

To change the name or description for a list or to control whether the list is easily accessible from the *Quick Launch* menu, on the *List Settings* page, click the *List name, description and navigation* link located below the *General Settings* heading. The system displays the *General Settings* page shown in Figure 2 - 78.

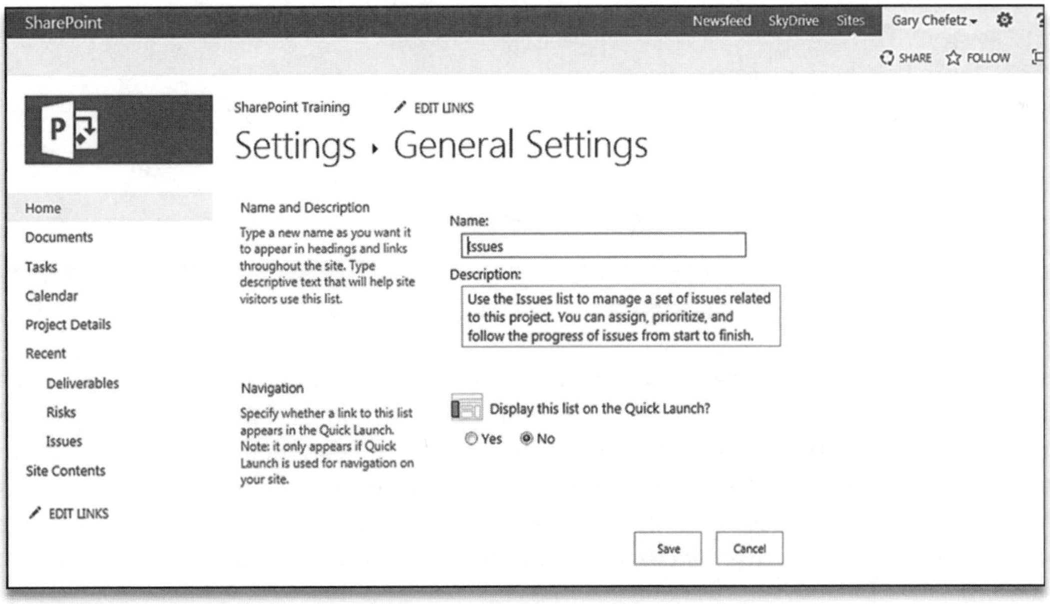

Figure 2 - 78: General Settings page

To change the name of the list, update the contents of the *Name* text box. To change the description of the list, update the contents of the *Description* text box. To control the *Quick Launch* navigation to the list, select the appropriate option for *Display this list on the Quick Launch*. Select the *Yes* option to display the list on the *Quick Launch* menu, or select the *No* option to prevent the list from appearing on the menu.

Information: Removing the *Quick Launch* navigation to a list does not remove the list itself from the Project Site; there are indirect ways to navigate to a list if it does not appear on the *Quick Launch* menu.

Specifying List Versioning Settings

For many organizations, the ability to automate version control for issues, risks, and documents is a great advantage. You can take advantage of this feature by clicking the *Versioning Settings* link on the *List Settings* page, located below the *General Settings* heading. The system displays the *Versioning Settings* page shown in Figure 2 - 79.

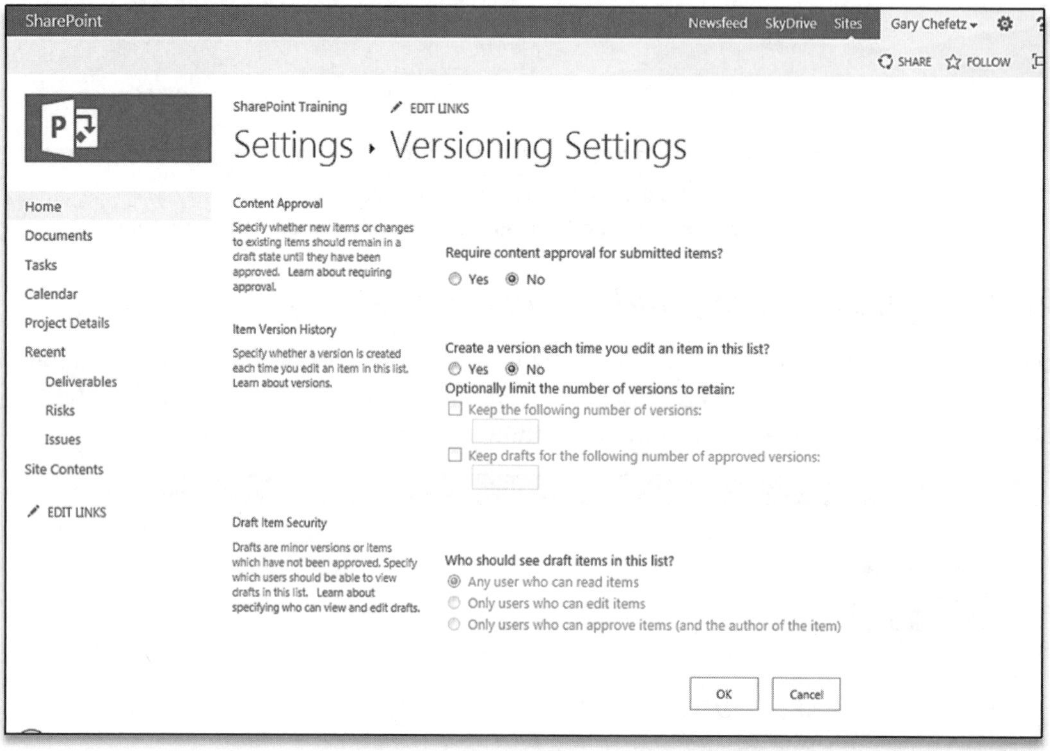
SharePoint
Newsfeed
SkyDrive
Sites
Gary Chefetz
SHARE
FOLLOW
SharePoint Training
EDIT LINKS
Settings › Versioning Settings
Home
Documents
Tasks
Calendar
Project Details
Recent
Deliverables
Risks
Issues
Site Contents
EDIT LINKS
Content Approval
Specify whether new items or changes to existing items should remain in a draft state until they have been approved. Learn about requiring approval.
Require content approval for submitted items?
Yes
No
Item Version History
Specify whether a version is created each time you edit an item in this list. Learn about versions.
Create a version each time you edit an item in this list?
Yes
No
Optionally limit the number of versions to retain:
Keep the following number of versions:
Keep drafts for the following number of approved versions:
Draft Item Security
Drafts are minor versions or items which have not been approved. Specify which users should be able to view drafts in this list. Learn about specifying who can view and edit drafts.
Who should see draft items in this list?
Any user who can read items
Only users who can edit items
Only users who can approve items (and the author of the item)
OK
Cancel

Figure 2 - 79: Versioning Settings page

In the *Content Approval* section of the page, you can set the list to require a designated person or group to approve items before they become publicly visible in the list. Enabling content approval places a hold on all item submissions until someone with the appropriate permissions approves them. Submitted content items are not visible to the rest of the project team until approved. Select the *Yes* option to enable content approval for the list, or select the *No* option to disable content approval. When you select the *Content Approval* option, the system enables the *Draft Item Security* section options at the bottom of the page where you can determine who can see the items in the list, pending approval.

In the *Item Version History* section of the page, you can enable item version control. When you enable item versioning, the system creates a new copy of an item each time someone edits the item. Select the *Yes* option for the *Create a version each time you edit an item in this list?* option to enable item versioning for the list, or select the *No* option to disable versioning. When you enable this option, you should set a version retention policy to limit the number of copies held by the system to avoid overusing your data storage capacity. This consideration is more important for libraries than for lists. Select the *Keep the following number of versions* option and then enter a number of versions into the text box. When you enable both content approval and version control, you can also specify the retention policy for draft versions in the *Keep drafts for the following number of approved versions* option.

Best Practice: MSProjectExperts recommends that you **do not** enable content approval in most cases for lists and libraries. Doing so can impose an unnecessary process bottleneck, because project team members will not be able to see items such as new risks, issues, and project documents until they are approved.

Best Practice: MSProjectExperts recommends that you enable item version control and set a reasonable retention policy in lists and libraries. Doing so can provide valuable historical information for artifacts stored in a Project Site.

Deleting a List

To delete a list from the Project Site, in the *Permissions and Management* section, click the *Delete this list* link. The system displays the confirmation dialog shown in Figure 2 - 80.

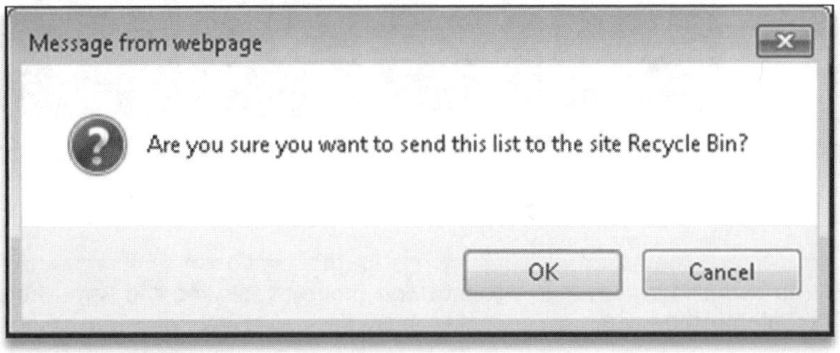
Message from webpage
Are you sure you want to send this list to the site Recycle Bin?
OK
Cancel

Figure 2 - 80: Warning dialog when deleting a list

Click the *OK* button to confirm the list deletion. The system then deletes the list, places it into the site recycle bin, and displays the *All Site Content* page.

Creating and Editing Pages

In addition to the list and library repositories that the system creates for storing and managing content within a Project Site, SharePoint also provides *pages* for presenting that content in an organized and meaningful manner to Project Site visitors. Each Project Site contains a single *Home* page that can act as a central landing page or dashboard, and you can create additional pages based on your business process needs. SharePoint provides a user-friendly, web browser-based interface for creating and editing pages, and new pages reside in libraries, much like other types of unstructured SharePoint content. The exception is the *Home* page, which does not reside in a library.

Editing the Project Site Home Page

The Project Site *Home* page is a web part page, which allows placement of one or more web parts onto the page, organized into one or more web part zones. A web part is a page component that allows you to add content or functionality to a page; a web part zone is an area on the page where you may place one or more web parts. To edit the Project Site *Home* page in order to manipulate the web parts on the page, select the *Edit page* item from the *Site Actions* menu, as shown in Figure 2 - 81.

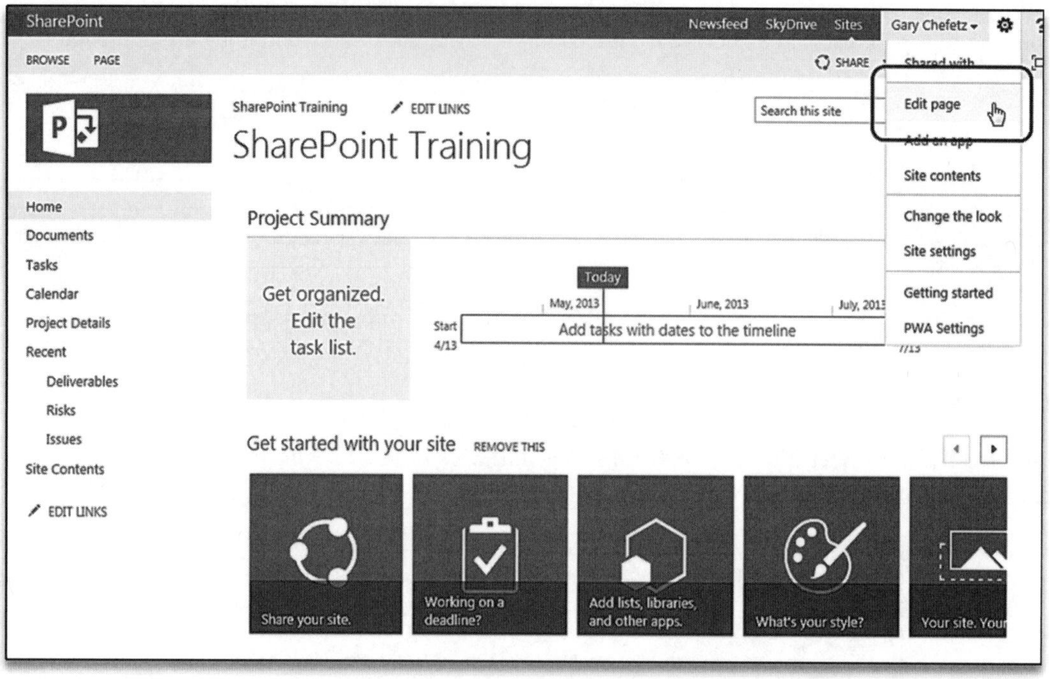

Figure 2 - 81: Selecting Edit Page from the Site Actions menu

Information: You can also switch the page into *Edit* mode by clicking the *Page* tab on the ribbon menu, then clicking the *Edit Page* button.

The system displays the *Home* page in editing mode as shown in Figure 2 - 82, allowing you to manipulate the contents of the page in any of the following ways:

- Add a web part to a web part zone
- Reposition a web part within a web part zone
- Move a web part to a different web part zone
- Remove a web part from the page

Notice that the *Home* page contains six web parts by default:

- The *Welcome to your site* web part, located in the *Left* web part zone, which displays a welcome message and general site use instructions
- The *Deliverables* web part, located in the *Left* web part zone, which displays items in the *Deliverables* list
- The *Issues* web part, located in the *Left* web part zone, which displays items in the *Issues* list
- The *Risks* web part, located in the *Left* web part zone, which displays items in the *Risks* list
- The *Site Image* web part, located in the *Right* web part zone, which displays a predefined image
- The *Links* web part, located in the *Right* web part zone, which displays items in the *Links* list

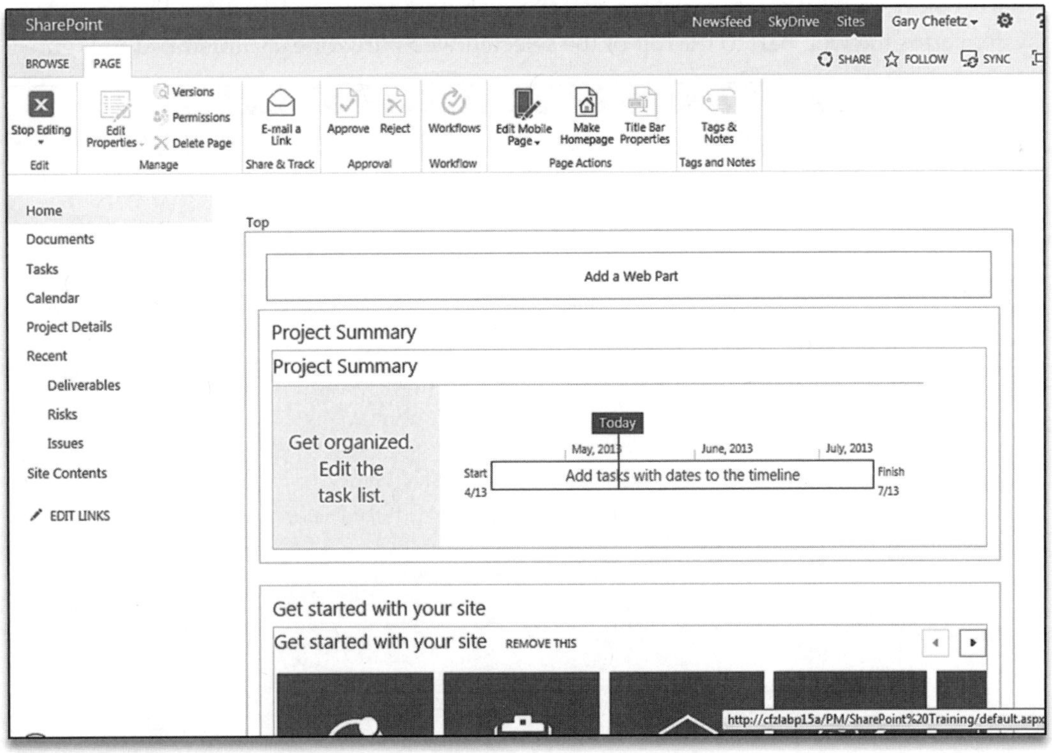

Figure 2 - 82: Home page in Edit mode

To add a web part to the *Home* page, click the *Add a Web Part* link near the top of both the *Left* web part zone and the *Right* web part zone. The system displays a panel below the ribbon that lists web parts available to add to the page, as shown in Figure 2 - 83.

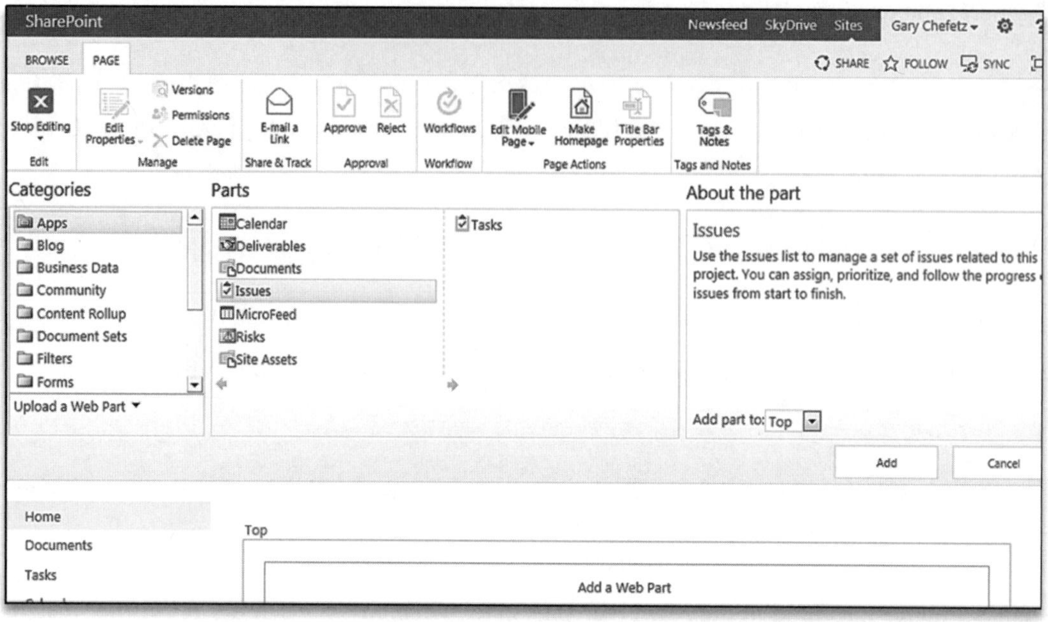

Figure 2 - 83: List of web parts available to add to the page

Select a web part type from the *Categories* listing, select a web part from the *Web Parts* listing, then click the *Add* button. The system adds the web part to the top of the selected web part zone, as illustrated in Figure 2 - 84.

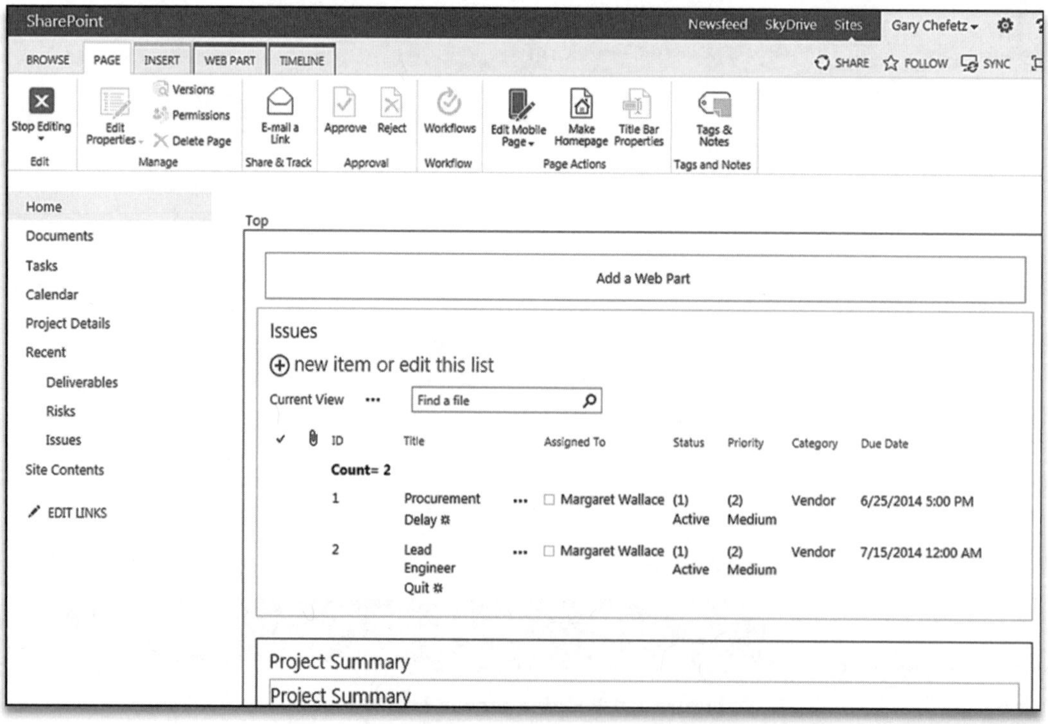

Figure 2 - 84: Page with Issues web part added to top of the web part zone

To reposition a web part within a web part zone or to move it to a different zone, click the title bar of the web part and drag it into the desired position on the page, as shown in Figure 2 - 85. Notice that a blue bar indicates positions where you may drop the web part on the page.

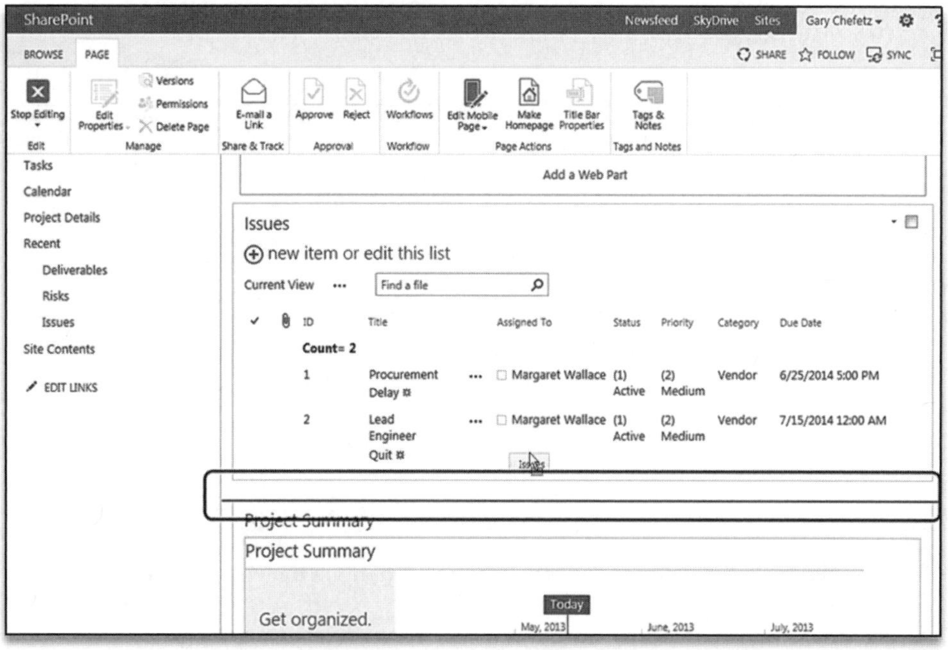

Figure 2 - 85: Repositioning the Issues web part on the page

The system displays the repositioned web part on the page, as shown in Figure 2 - 86. Notice that the Issues list now appears below the carousel.

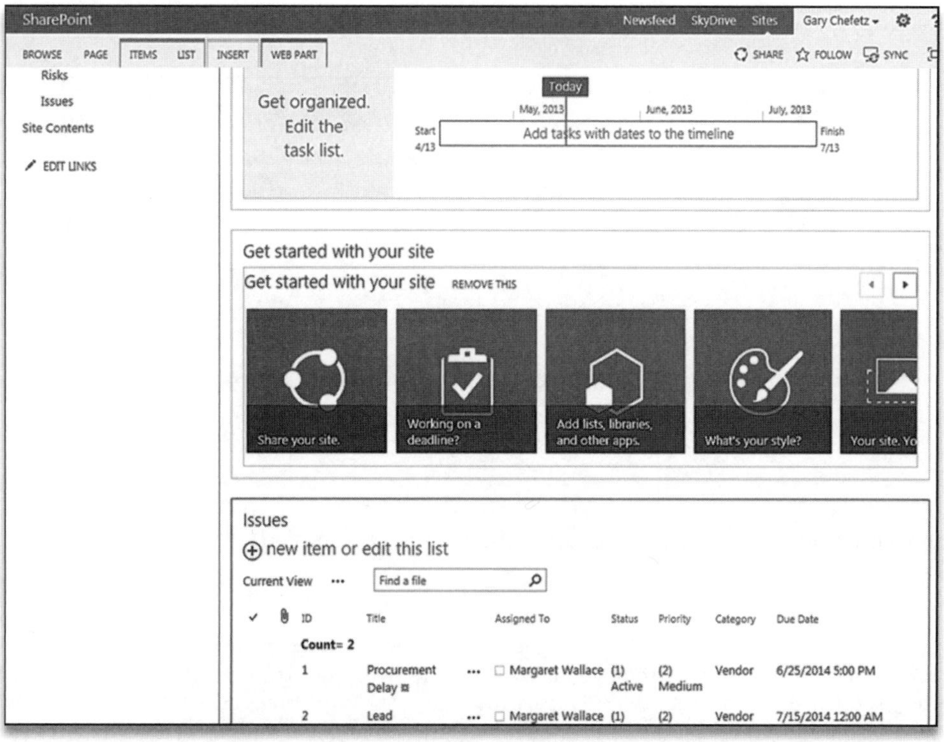

Figure 2 - 86: Updated page with repositioned Issues web part

To remove a web part from the page, float the mouse cursor over the web part title bar to activate the web part menu, indicated by a tiny downward-pointing arrow in the upper right corner of the web part. Click the arrow to open the web part menu and select the *Delete* option, as shown in Figure 2 - 87.

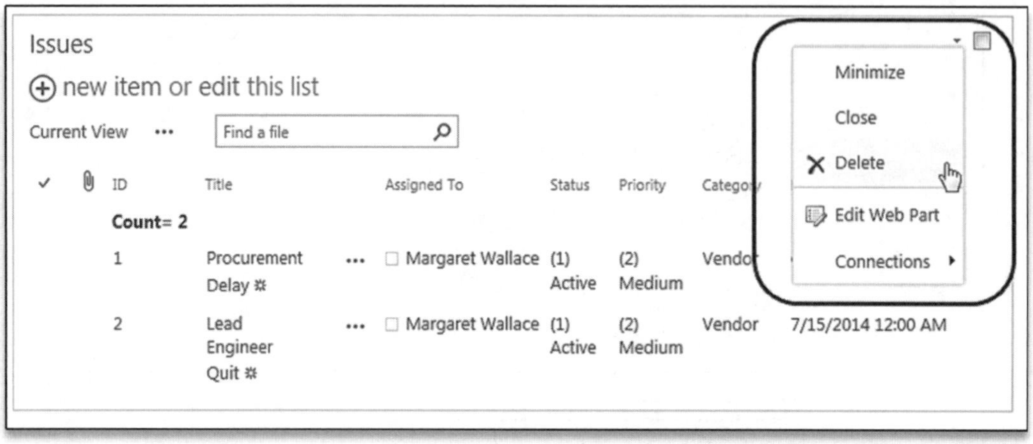

Figure 2 - 87: Deleting the Site Image web part via the web part menu

The system displays the warning dialog shown in Figure 2 - 88; click the *OK* button to acknowledge the message and proceed with the web part deletion.

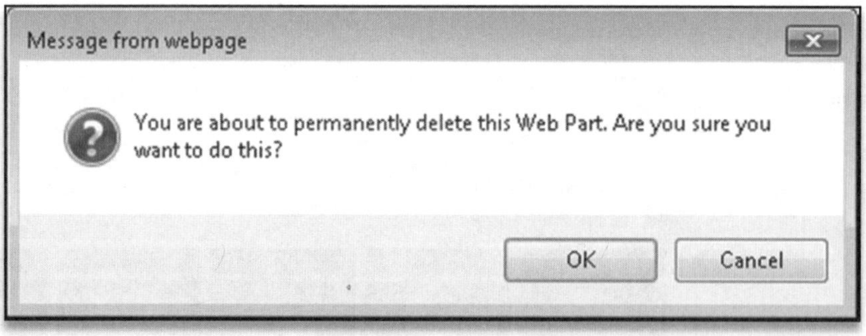

Figure 2 - 88: Web part deletion warning dialog

The system displays the updated web part page with the web part removed.

Warning: Deleting a web part removes it **completely** from the page but does not delete it from the system. Selecting the *Close* option from the web part menu or clicking the **X** in the upper right corner of the web part hides it on the page, but it remains embedded in the underlying code of the page.

To stop editing the page, on the *Page* tab, click the *Stop Editing* button on the ribbon. The system displays the final version of the page in *View* mode as shown in Figure 2 - 89.

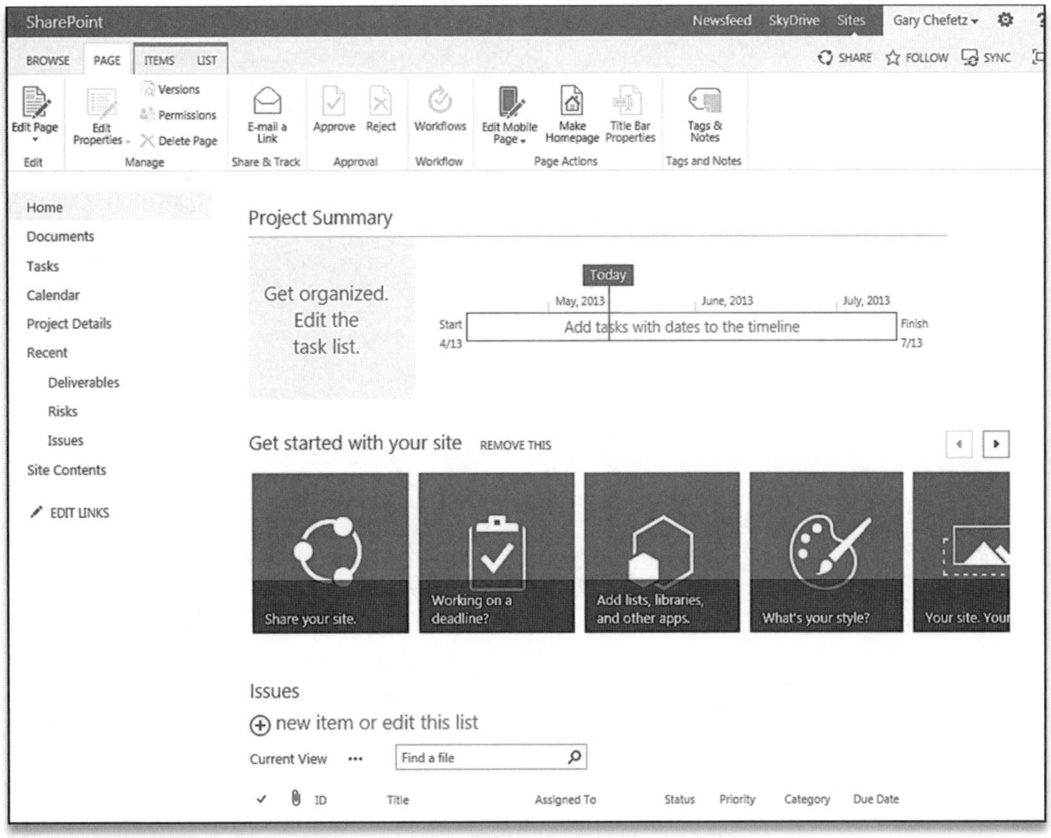

Figure 2 - 89: Updated page in View mode

Information: Depending upon your last page editing action, you may need to click the *Page* tab on the ribbon to display the *Stop Editing* button.

Module 03

Introducing Project Web App 2013

Learning Objectives

After completing this module, you will be able to:

- Locate administrative functions in the new distributed administration model
- Understand the 2013 Project Web App interface and how to modify it
- Understand the impact of using SharePoint permissions mode
- Change permissions mode online and on-premise
- Transform the default configuration of Project Web App to Project Server Classic
- Work with the Project Web App interface and interface components

Inside Module 03

Introducing Project Web App 2013

Project Web App, or PWA, is a browser-based interface to Project Server. PWA is a central point to access and manage nearly all project data. While PWA offers many features, the core functionality is as follows:

- **Project Center:** View projects, their current workflow progress, and edit their metadata. Project Center also offers lightweight project management functionality for editing a Gantt chart.

- **Resource Center:** Project Server 2013 utilizes a centralized pool of resources called the Enterprise Resource Pool. Project managers assign enterprise resources to their projects. The Resource Center provides a central location to view resource assignments and utilization.

- **Tasks and Timesheet:** PWA provides the means for resources to update their task status using various tracking methods including timesheet functionality where resources enter their time on a regular basis governed by an optional management approval workflow.

- **Business Intelligence (Reports):** PWA leverages the SharePoint Business Intelligence Center (BI Center) that brings all of the potential of the SharePoint business intelligence tools to the end user for the creation, management, and viewing of reports, key performance indicators (KPI), and dashboards.

- **Collaboration:** Any project can have its own SharePoint website for document management, issues and risks tracking, and more. PWA manages the links between the projects themselves and the SharePoint collaboration website.

- **Portfolio Management and Project Governance:** Project Server 2013 provides advanced capabilities to allow for the selection and oversight management of all projects in the system. This system includes business driver management, cost constraint analysis, resource constraint analysis, and governance workflow.

- **Application Administration:** Each PWA instance provides a rich set of administration tools necessary to manage a complex portfolio and project management information system.

Experienced project managers may not view PWA as a usable solution to perform detailed project management where Gantt charts and resource management are required. For project managers, Project Pro 2013 remains indispensable. Project Pro 2013 can connect to Project Server 2013 and publish to PWA allowing users to view and interact with the plan. Figure 3 - 1 shows how people are likely to use the toolset based on their role in the organization. Note that application administrators also need Project Pro 2013 to manage the system effectively.

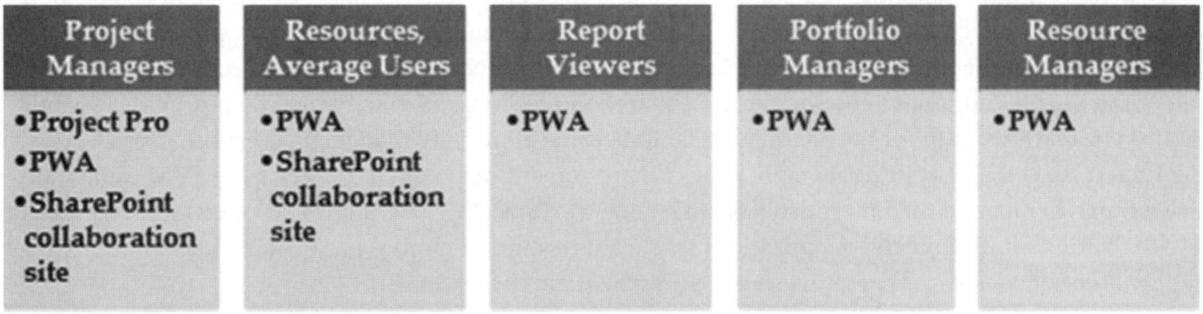

Project Managers
•Project Pro
•PWA
•SharePoint collaboration site
Resources, Average Users
•PWA
•SharePoint collaboration site
Report Viewers
•PWA
Portfolio Managers
•PWA
Resource Managers
•PWA

Figure 3 - 1: General user base for Project Pro, PWA and SharePoint collaboration sites.

A Major Decision Point

By the time you read half way through this module, you must decide whether you want to run your new PWA instance in SharePoint permissions mode or Project Server classic permissions mode. To a large degree, this is a decision about building a system to support a task-management environment versus a system to support an effort-based or work management environment. Because Microsoft uses the concept of task management and work management interchangeably, I want to be clear where I draw the line for this canvas. For the purposes of this book, effort-based planning and tracking models use work values as the primary determining factor for duration and other scheduling calculations, whereas task-based planning and tracking models use some degree of doneness to measure duration and completion, usually a percentage of completion and duration is the primary planning unit. The simplest task management approach tracks done or not done.

For many organizations, implementing a PPM tool is an enabling force in maturing business practices. The brass ring that these organizations reach for is a working model for measuring resource availability and demand. In order to get there using any tool, you must build a resource pool model and a loading model in the form of a time-phased schedule. Notice that I do not specify a detailed project schedule; rather I use the term *loading model* generically to indicate that the schedule must model resource demand at a minimum.

Another way of looking at this is a decision between implementing tools for a formal approach or lightweight approach to your project management and portfolio management process as shown in the diagram in Figure 3 - 2.

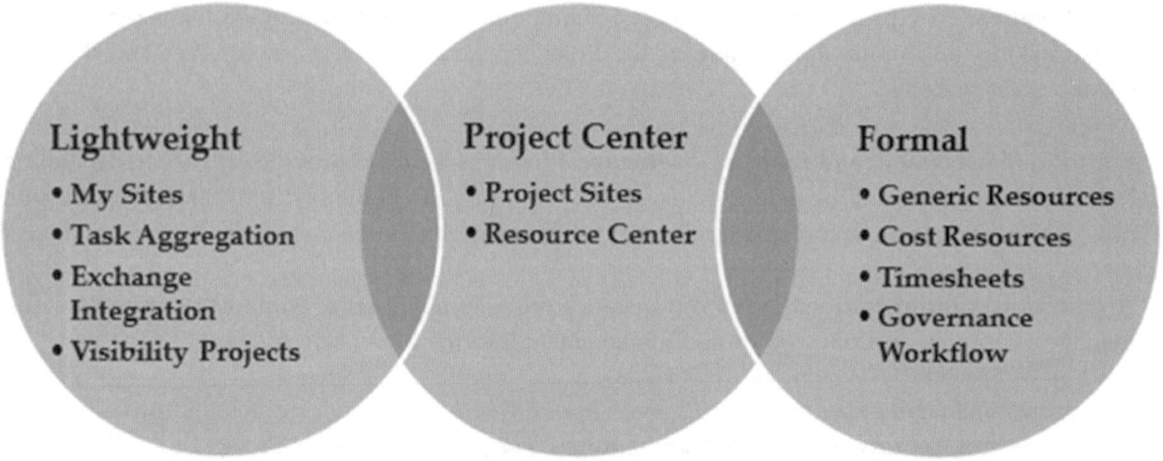

Figure 3 - 2: Formal versus Lightweight tools

On the lightweight side of the toolset, News Feed (My Sites), task aggregation via the *Work Management* service, and Exchange integration are available for SharePoint 2013 users without Project Server. You can apply Project Server 2013 to either a lightweight or a formally managed environment, and you can support both practices simultaneously. When you add Project Server 2013 to the lightweight environment, you introduce the ability to connect all of the distributed project environments in SharePoint to Project Server, which then provides visibility and a migration or maturity path for the SharePoint list to become a formally managed enterprise project. After introducing Project Server 2013 your lightweight project management can begin to benefit from PPM capabilities such as the Resource Center and the Enterprise Resource Pool, the Project Center, and the business intelligence connections with SharePoint. Ultimately, organizations that want to support mature project management practices make heavy use of various resource types, timesheets, and governance workflows.

In the simplest terms, if you intend to model and track work, you should strongly consider enabling Project Server 2013 in classic mode. The lightweight features, including task aggregation, are probably of little interest to you if your goal includes demand and capacity management. If you are looking to build a task-oriented system with task aggregation in News Feed or Outlook, the new lightweight task management tools in SharePoint make a lot of sense, especially when you pair them with Project Pro 2013 and use them in a planned way to improve your management process.

What's New in Project Web App 2013 Interface?

> **Information**: This module provides a walkthrough of Project Server 2013 functionality. You will find that some screens contain information that may not be on yours. This is because I am stepping ahead in my configuration in order to show you the impacts of the decisions you are making.

Project Web App veterans are initially shocked when they see the new *Home* page shown in Figure 3 - 3, as it displays in SharePoint permissions mode for a user with Project Server administrator permissions. The Project Web App *Home* page consists of two parts: a *Quick Launch* menu on the left and a main content area.

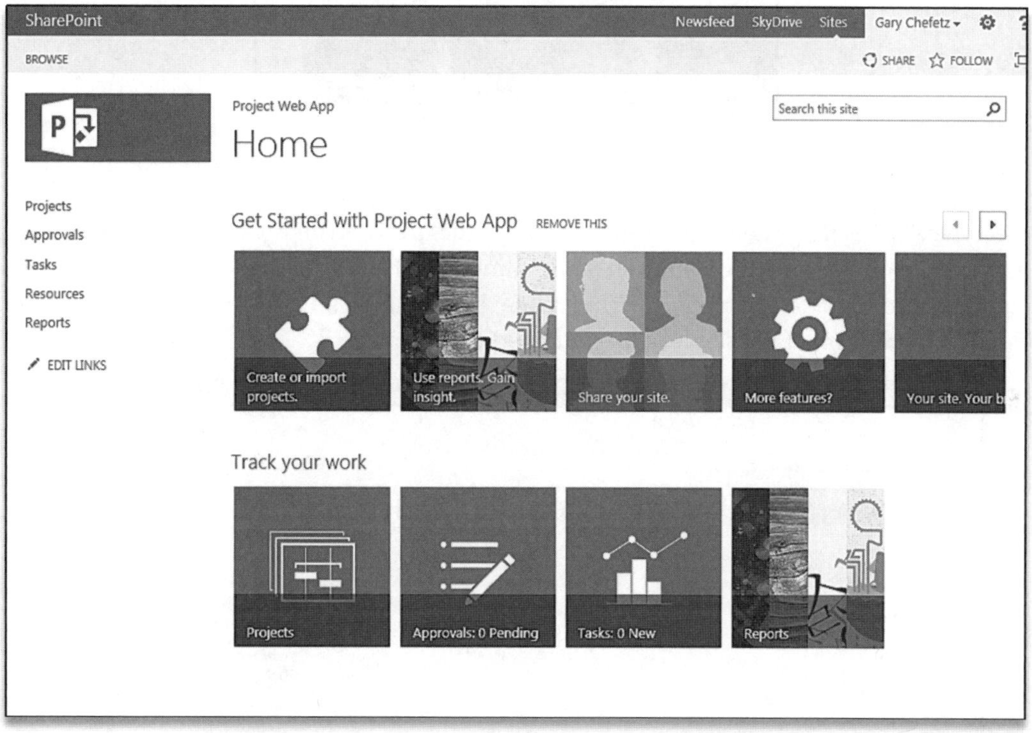

Figure 3 - 3: Project Web App Home page for an administrator

A default new instance of Project Server 2013 presents itself very differently than previous versions. The most important change is not immediately apparent; Project Web App defaults to SharePoint permissions mode, a new way you can manage security in PWA. Simply put, in this mode you manage PWA like SharePoint. The new Windows 8 interface design trend makes a strong appearance in Project Server 2013 with two new carousel web parts, the *Get Started with Project Web App* carousel containing user-scenario-based navigation choices at the top and the *Track your work* carousel containing live tiles that provide both navigation and current insight into your project world. The carousel is highly customizable and has the ability to display many more live tiles than it displays by default. Even though the clean elegant interface distracts you for a moment, it is what you do not see that starts to disturb you. You start to wonder what happened to all the *Quick Launch* menu choices. They remain available on the *Quick Launch* menu; however many now default to hidden. This provides you with the option to construct new types of user experiences that leverage other parts of SharePoint.

The SharePoint way of accessing PWA server settings is by clicking the *Gear* icon in the upper right part of the page to reveal the *Site Actions* menu shown in Figure 3 - 4.

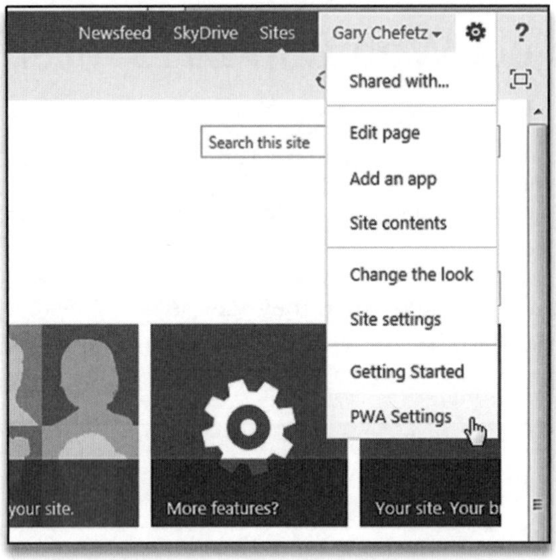

Figure 3 - 4: Site Actions menu open

When you select the *PWA Settings* item, the system displays the, *PWA Settings for* page shown in Figure 3 - 5. This is your first look at Project Server administration's migration into the SharePoint model. In SharePoint terms, this page is the equivalent to the SharePoint *Site Settings* page; but it handles Project Server functionality. All administration you expect to perform at the site level is contained on this page.

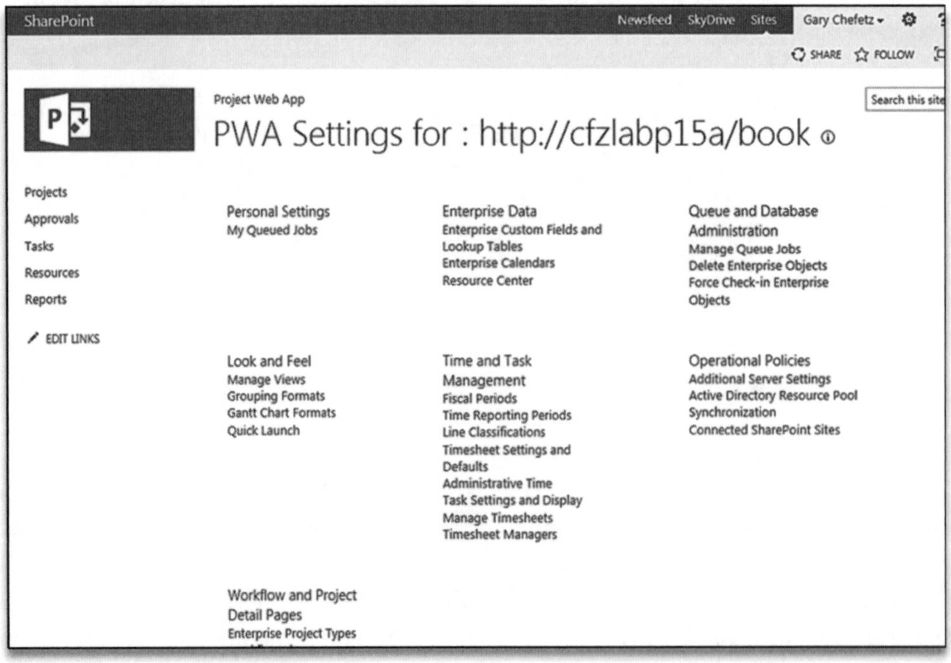

Figure 3 - 5: PWA Settings page in SharePoint permissions mode

To be more precise, the page is representative of a *PWA Settings* page for a site running in SharePoint permissions mode. In SharePoint permissions mode the system omits the entire *Security* category on this page. SharePoint permissions mode removes Project Server security controls because, when in this mode, you perform user management the same way you do for SharePoint, the only difference is that you use SharePoint security groups pre-configured for Project Server.

Did the *PWA Settings* page shown previously in Figure 3 - 5 look like it is missing something more to you? Good catch! In redistributing administration into the SharePoint model, the product team logically separated those tasks performed at the site level from the application or site collection level, which you now access through SharePoint Central Administration.

Using the following three tables, I show you which Project Server administration tasks you must now go to SharePoint Central Administration to perform and which ones you can find through site administration.

Queue and Database Administration

Notice that Microsoft is drawing an arbitrary line between what it expects a technical administrator should do in the system versus a PMO person assuming that the PMO person is acting at the site level in the following tables. I have been preaching for years about this dichotomy and here is substantiation from Microsoft of what I call the "Application Administrator role" as listed in Table 3 - 1. Do you agree with Microsoft's division of administrative responsibility shown in the following tables? If you are using Project Online, then you do not have access to any of the administration normally performed through SharePoint Central Administration.

Action	PWA Site	Central Admin
Manage Queue Jobs	Y	Y
Daily Schedule Backup	N	Y
Administrative Backup	N	Y
Administrative Restore	N	Y
OLAP Database Management	N	Y
Delete Enterprise Objects	Y	N
Force Check-in Enterprise Objects	Y	N

Table 3 - 1: Queue and Database Administration actions

Operational Policies

As you can see, there are quite a few overlapping actions in the Operational Policies group shown in Table 3 - 2.

Action	PWA Site	Central Admin
Alerts and Reminders	N	Y
Additional Server Settings	Y	Y
Project Professional Versions	N	Y
Enterprise Settings	Y	Y
Currency Settings	Y	Y
Resource Capacity Settings	Y	Y
Resource Plan Day	Y	Y
Exchange Server Details	N	Y
Task Mode Settings	Y	Y
Server Side Event Handlers	N	Y
Project Site Provisioning Settings	N	Y
Bulk Update Connected SharePoint Sites	N	Y
Active Directory Resource Pool Synchronization	Y	N
Connected SharePoint Sites	Y	N

Table 3 - 2: Operational Policies actions

Workflow and Project Detail Pages

The single option available in Central Administration is for setting the workflow proxy account as shown in Table 3 - 3.

Action	PWA Site	Central Admin
Project Workflow Settings (Proxy Account)	N	Y

Table 3 - 3: Workflow and Project Detail Pages settings

Introducing SharePoint Permissions Mode

Continuing the progression of aligning Project Server to the SharePoint management model, Project Server 2013 introduces SharePoint permissions mode. In SharePoint permissions mode, SharePoint groups replace Project Server groups one for one. However, in SharePoint permissions mode you cannot manage individual permissions, global permissions for groups, or category permissions. SharePoint permissions mode behaves as if you are using only the default permissions for groups in Project Server.

SharePoint permissions mode has some other serious consequences. It essentially shuts down resource-based security in Project Server 2013 including those security functions in the Project Server Interface (PSI). It makes the Resource Breakdown Structure (RBS) useless for anything but reporting, and it disables the use of delegation in the system, as SharePoint has no construct for impersonation. This represents a complete paradigm shift where SharePoint brokers all access, even Project Site access, which you manage independently. Using the Project Server classic permissions mode, Project Server controls access, including access to Project Sites. Project Server permissions modes are site-specific as illustrated in Figure 3 - 6. When you upgrade a Project Server 2010 database, the system automatically sets the site to Project Server classic permissions mode. When you create a new instance of Project Server using a new database, the system automatically sets the site to SharePoint permissions mode.

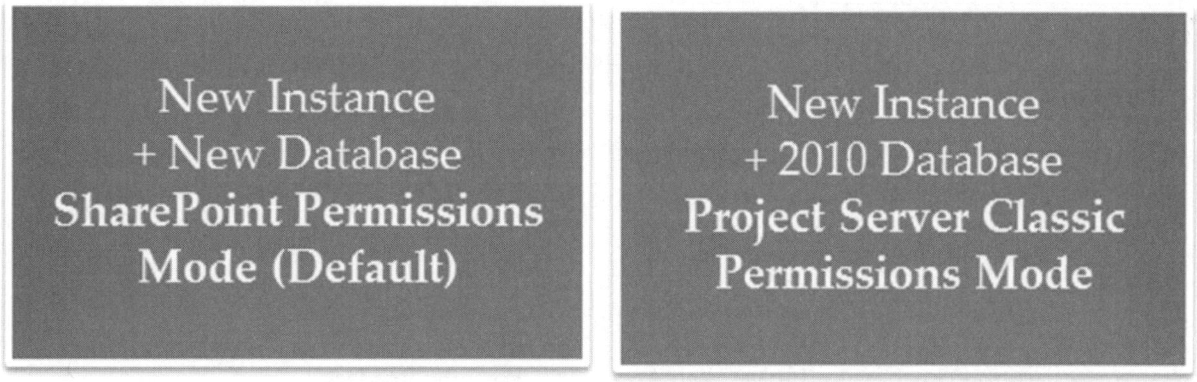

Figure 3 - 6: Permissions Modes are site specific

Using SharePoint permissions mode makes managing a PPM environment more familiar to SharePoint administrators. It also simplifies the task of user management. The primary advantages are:

- Shifts user management to SharePoint (Eliminates users management in Project Server)
- Simplifies permissions model
- Enables solutions based on the SharePoint user object model
- Easy to use AD groups
- Easy to use Custom Claims
- Best Supports SharePoint Task lists in Project Server (Visibility Projects)
- Will automatically create a logon in PWA upon first sign-on for all Resource Pool members

The most significant downside to using this model is the lack of granular security control and the loss of impersonation. For some implementations, either security requirements or the ability to impersonate may be so critical as to render the SharePoint security model a non-option. Considerations for using the SharePoint permissions model include:

- Cannot use Resource Delegation (Impersonation)
- Cannot use PSI to manipulate security
- Disables RBS-driven security
- No access to *Category* and *Group* permissions
- No way to connect SharePoint users with existing resources in Project Server
- No permissions customization in SharePoint permissions mode
- No reporting structure representation without RBS
- When in SharePoint permissions mode, the system uses a set of SharePoint security groups that correspond to standard Project Server security groups that apply when running Project Server permissions mode as shown in Table 3 - 4.

SharePoint Group	Project Server Group
Administrators for Project Web App	Administrators
Portfolio Managers for Project Web App	Portfolio Managers
Portfolio Readers for Project Web App (Previously Executives)	Portfolio Readers
Project Managers for Project Web App	Project Managers
Team Members for Project Web App	Team Members
Team Leads for Project Web App	Team Leads
Resource Managers for Project Web App	Resource Managers

Table 3 - 4: SharePoint and corresponding Project Server Security Groups

Microsoft characterizes SharePoint permissions mode by the following:

- Permissions published from SharePoint to Project Server
- You define users in SharePoint
- Resources managed in Project Server
- Team Site role determines Project Server role

Microsoft characterizes Project Server permissions mode by the following:

- Project Site permissions controlled from Project Server
- Permissions publish to SharePoint PWA site from Project Server
- Resources and users managed in Project Server
- Enables granular control/customization of groups/categories/RBS
- Project Server role and Project role determines Project Site role

Best Practice: When using the SharePoint permissions mode, set up AD Sync and synchronize the resource pool first, then add AD groups to Project Server groups for SharePoint.

Adding Users in SharePoint Permissions Mode

SharePoint makes it easier than ever to share your site with others by putting the ever-present *Share* button in the application navigation in the top right corner. Click the *Share* button and the system displays the *Share Project Web App* dialog shown in Figure 3 - 7. This dialog allows you to see with whom the administrator already shared the site.

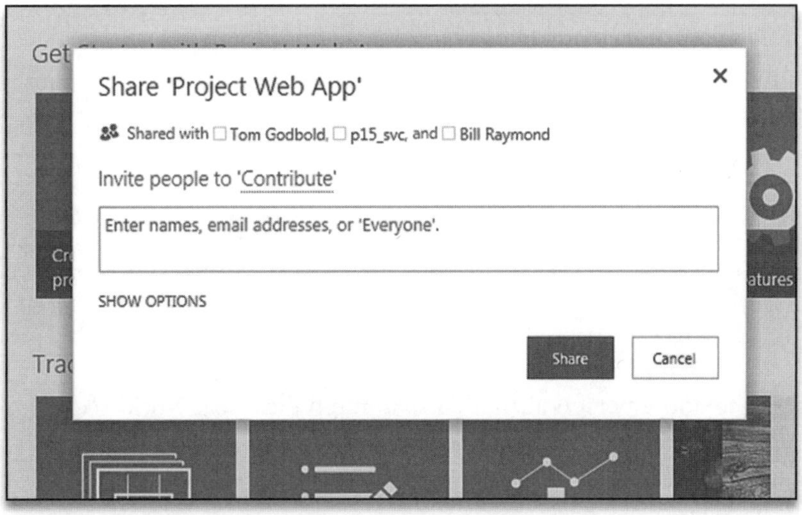

Figure 3 - 7: Share Project Web App dialog

Click the *Show Options* link and the system expands the *Share Project Web App* dialog to reveal the *Select a group or permission level* pick list shown in Figure 3 - 8. In order to grant access to Project Web App securable objects, you must use the groups that include "for Project Web App" in the name.

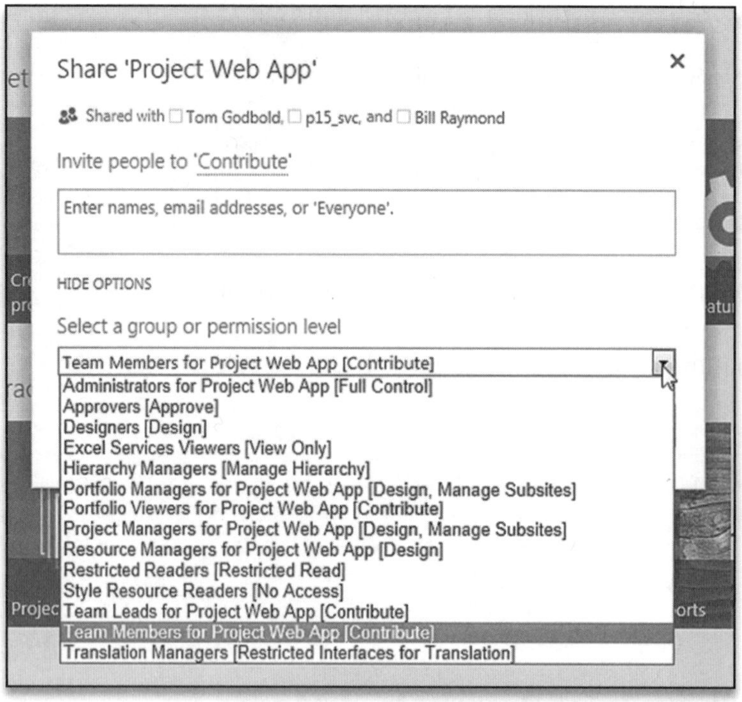

Figure 3 - 8: Share Project Web App dialog
Select a group or permission level pick list

To add a new user using SharePoint permissions mode:

1. Enter a user or users in the *Invite People* list
2. Click the *Show Options* link to expose the *Select a group or permission level* pick list
3. Select a Project Web App group
4. Click the *Share* button

Information: Adding a user to your site in SharePoint permissions mode does not create a resource pool record for the user. If your intention is to have this person available as a resource in the resource pool, you must add them to the resource pool through AD sync (recommended) or manually.

You are not actually going to add a person individually in the typical real world scenario; rather you use Active Directory groups and add them to the SharePoint Security groups for Project Server. Otherwise, managing individuals is added manual work. If you are using Project Online for a small group, adding individual users manually might be your typical scenario.

Best Practice: Use Active Directory security enabled groups to grant access to your PWA site. You can use mail-enabled distribution groups or security groups.

Warning: The RTM version of Project Server 2013 does not support nested AD groups. Look for an early-cycle update to restore this ability.

Understanding the Default Project Web App 2013 Interface

More than ever, the new default Project Web App user interface conforms to the SharePoint site layout standard. All of the Project Web App pages function just like any other SharePoint site. In fact, you can easily customize your Project Web App site by dragging and dropping web parts from the SharePoint web part gallery just as you would for any other SharePoint application. Across SharePoint, you find the new Windows-8-styled *Get Started* experience.

Working with the Track your work carousel web part

To make the PWA homepage a compelling site to visit, the new *Track Your Work* carousel includes a set of standard live tiles that you can make visible to users personalizing their PWA experience. Like any other SharePoint web part, you must put the page into *Edit* mode before you can edit the web part. Go to your PWA site, click the *Gear* icon in the upper right, and select the *Edit page* item as shown in Figure 3 - 9.

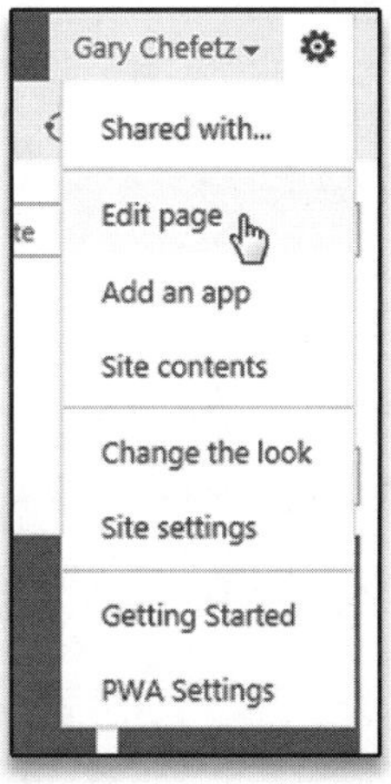

Figure 3 - 9: Site Actions menu, Select Edit Page

When the page redisplays in *Edit* mode (not shown) locate the pick list menu in the upper right hand corner of the *Track your work* web part and select the *Edit Web Part* item as shown in Figure 3 - 10.

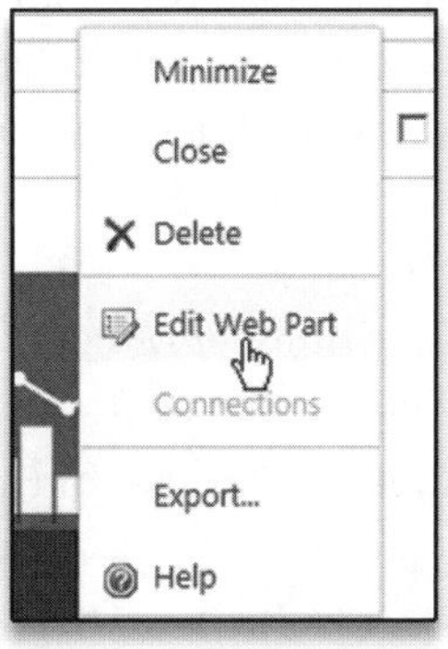

Figure 3 - 10: Edit Web Part pick list

Expand the *Track your work* web part control panel as shown in Figure 3 - 11. Notice that Project Server 2013 provides a dozen live tile options that you can enable. By default, only four display to the user: Projects, Pending tasks, Tasks, and Reports. You can enable as many of these as you want until you clutter your PWA homepage. Keep the old adage about "too much of a good thing" in mind before you start checking boxes. Make sure you provide just what your users want and need. More importantly, make sure that there is relevant data to display before turning them on.

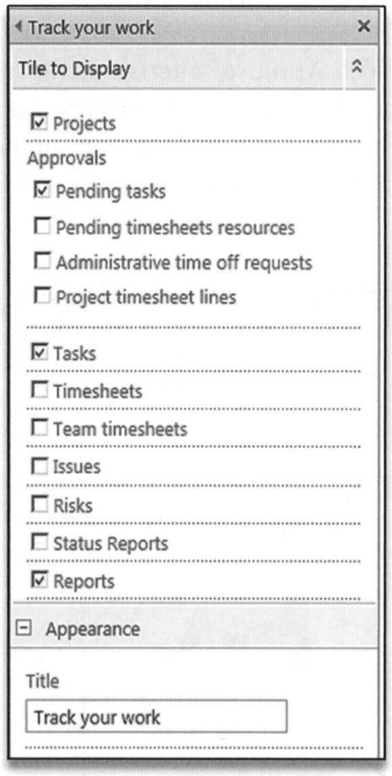

Figure 3 - 11: Track your work web part control panel

The *Track your work* web part provides live tiles for the following uses:

Tiles	Uses
Projects	Navigates to the Project Center
Approvals	Displays the total number of approvals in the system. Selecting the checkboxes for pending tasks, pending timesheets resources, administrative time off requests, and project timesheet lines includes these approvals in the total count.
Tasks	Displays number of new tasks assigned to me
Timesheets	Displays the number of timesheets I have due
Team timesheets	Timesheets due from your resources

Tiles	Uses
Issues	Number of active issues assigned to me
Risks	Number of active risks assigned to me
Status Reports	Number of status reports that I have due
Reports	Navigates to the BI Center

Best Practice: Enable only the live tiles relevant to your implementation. If your user base does not use timesheets, it is unnecessary to enable live tiles for timesheets and project timesheet lines.

Understanding the Site Action Menu

You have already used the *Site Actions* menu to navigate to the *PWA Settings* page and to put the page in *Edit* mode. The complete list of options available on the *Site Actions* menu shown previously in Figure 3 - 9 include:

1. The *Shared with...* link navigates to the dialog shown in Figure 3 - 12. Notice that the dialog provides a scrolling list of members and three selections below the name, *Invite People, Email Everyone,* and *Advanced.* Clicking the *Invite People* link takes you to the *Share* dialog shown previously in Figure 3 - 7. Clicking the *Email Everyone* link generates a new Outlook email to every member of the current group. Finally, clicking the *Advanced* link navigates to the SharePoint permissions page for the current site.

Figure 3 - 12: Shared With dialog

Warning: You should be aware of which permissions mode your system is using before making changes here, particularly if you are in a Project Site governed by Project Server classic permissions mode connected to an enterprise project, in which case the system is likely to override your changes.

2. The *Edit page* selection allows you to put the page in *Edit* mode to introduce additional web parts or change the page layout. When you edit the page from this menu selection, the changes you make affect all users.

3. The *Add an app* selection takes you to the page shown in Figure 3 - 13. "App" is the new term for familiar SharePoint objects such as sites, customized lists, and document libraries. Microsoft fully embraces the app store approach in 2013 providing a service application for administrators to manage their own app stores, as well as the ability to connect to external app stores such as the Office App store or independently owned stores.

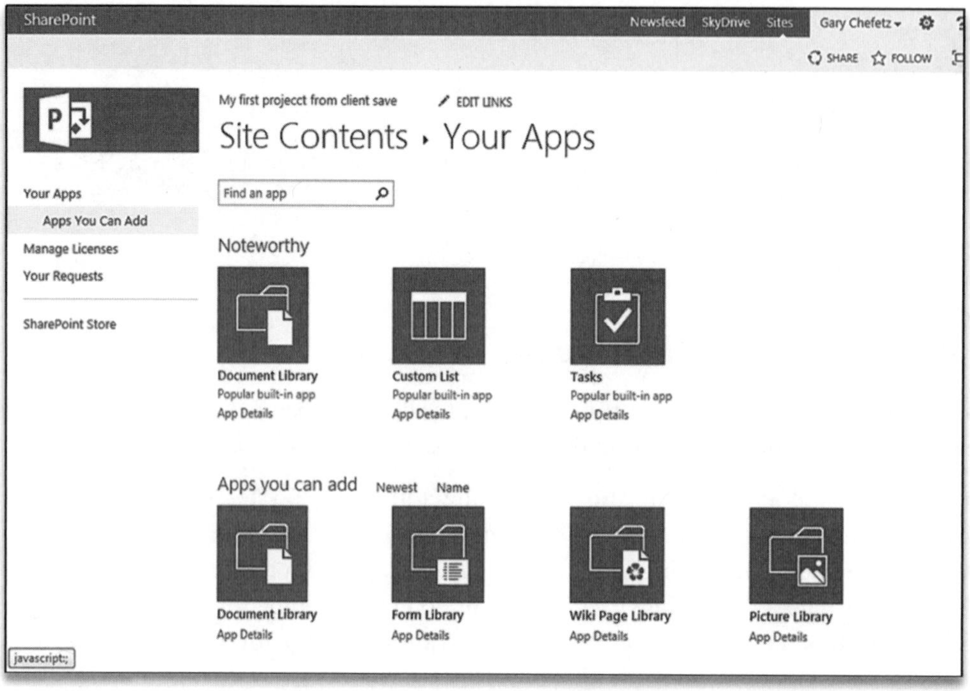

Figure 3 - 13: Add an App page (partial)

4. The *Site contents* selection is the new name for the *View All Site Content* selection in prior versions taking you to a view that summarizes all of the contents from the current site and summarizes the sub-sites associated with it.

5. The *Change the look* selection takes you to the *Change the Look* page, which allows you to apply various built-in themes to your site.

6. The *Site settings* selection takes you to the full administration page for the SharePoint site.

7. The *Getting Started* link navigates you to the *Get Started with Project Web App* page, which is the homepage for the *Getting Started* carousel. Users can reach this page even if the Project Server administrator closes the web part on the Project Web App home page.

8. The *PWA Settings* selection takes you to the *PWA Settings* page shown previously in Figure 3 - 5.

Project Web App inherits the *Browse* tab from SharePoint, and it is visible throughout the site. In PWA, this contains title information only, and serves no functional purpose in the PWA user interface other than sometimes providing you with a quick way to access the Project Web App homepage.

In Figure 3 - 14, notice that your name appears in the upper-right corner with a pull down menu shown in Figure 3 - 15. This menu contains selections that allow you to change your personal settings, personalize the page, or sign out.

Figure 3 - 14: Personal Site Action Menu

Information: SharePoint 2013 no longer supports logging in as a different user. Use Windows switch user feature instead when you need to test multiple logins.

You are already familiar with the *Gear* icon and the *Share* button. The *Question Mark* icon takes you to a *Help* menu. The *Follow* button adds the site or selected document to your followed site or followed document list in your My Site. This feature allows you to bookmark SharePoint objects instantly with one-click convenience. Lastly, the new *Focus on Content* icon that looks a bit like a page zoom control, allows you to remove SharePoint navigation from view affording you more display real estate devoted to content. Figure 3 - 15 shows the personal action choices available.

Figure 3 - 15: Personal Site Action Menu Expanded

When you click the *About Me* link, the system navigates to your *My Sites Profile* page. The *Personalize this Page* option gives you the ability to personalize the page or your personal view of the page.

Information: Note the navigation elements in the blue band at the top of the browser window include Newsfeeds, SkyDrive, and Sites. These elements provide one-click access to your followed sites, and newsfeeds in My Sites and quick access to your SkyDrive account, if you have one. Hint, hint!

Using the Quick Launch Menu

The Project Web App user interface offers a *Quick Launch* menu on the left side of every primary page. As previously discussed, Microsoft trimmed the initial presentation of this menu in 2013. This menu lists your viewable selections based on your role in the project management environment.

Click the *Gear* icon and select the *PWA Settings* item from the menu to display the *PWA Settings for* page. From the *Look and Feel* section, click the *Quick Launch* link at the bottom of the category. The system displays the *Modify Quick Launch Items* page shown in Figure 3 - 16. Notice that only a small subset displays by default.

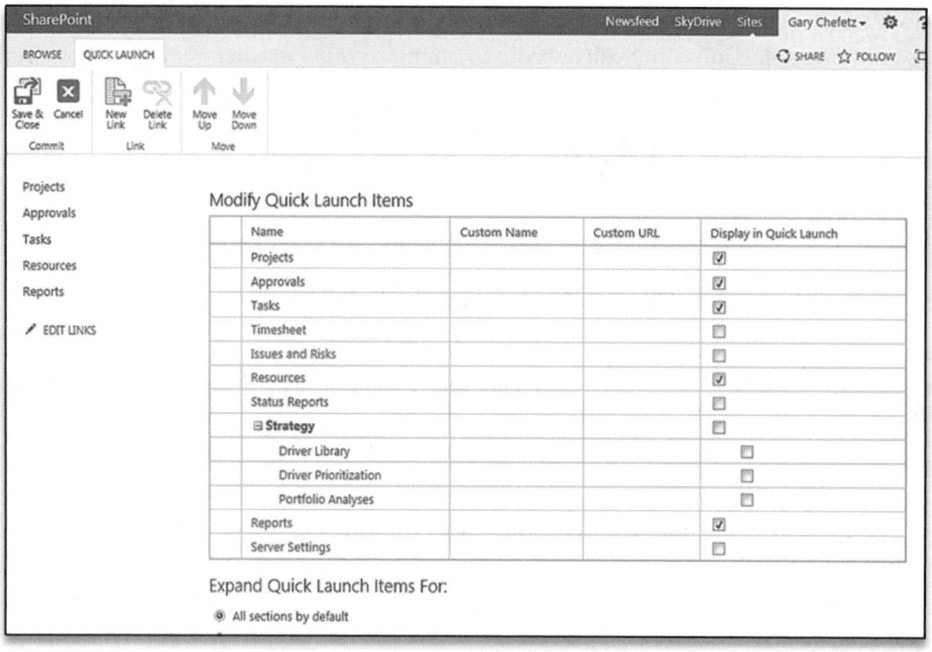

Figure 3 - 16: Modify Quick Launch Items page

Notice on the *Modify Quick Launch Items* page that many of the *Quick Launch* items from 2010 carry forward; however, many of them do not display by default. If you want your new default Project Web App site to take on the navigation feel of Project Web App 2010, you must enable the links that you want to expose. If you opt to display the *Server Settings* link, you may want to change the link name to *PWA Settings* to remain consistent with the new page name.

In Figure 3 - 17, I exposed all of the Project Server classic *Quick Launch* selections still available. This is what a Project Server administrator sees including all possible selections.

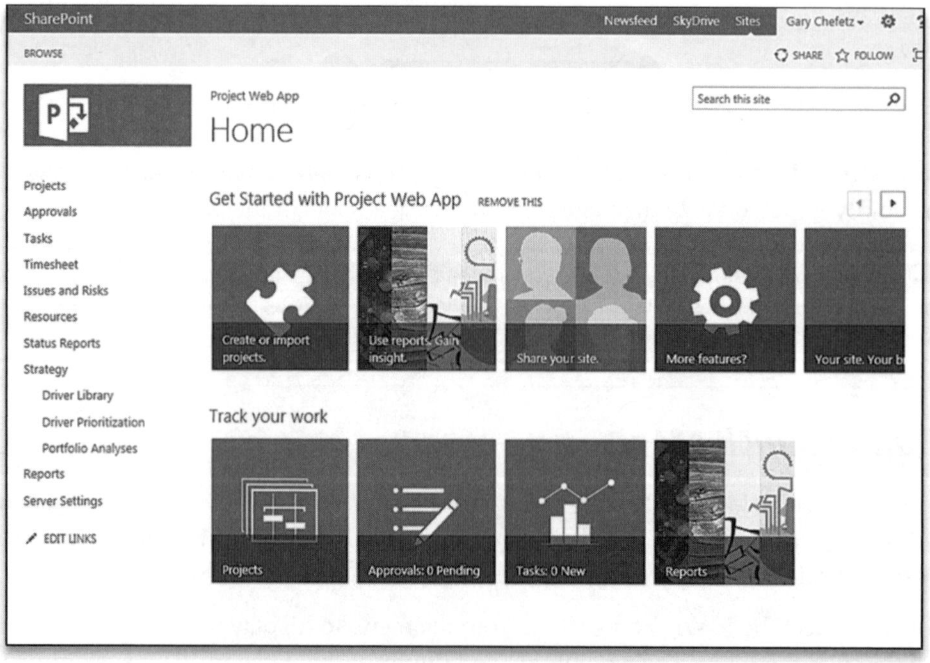

Figure 3 - 17: Full Quick Launch menu

The options available on the *Quick Launch* menu include:

- Click the *Projects* link to navigate to the *Project Center* page where you can view your project portfolio.

- Click the *Approvals* link to view and navigate to the *Task Updates* page, where you approve task updates (task progress) from your team members.

- Click the *Tasks* link to view tasks assigned to you.

- Click the *Timesheet* link to view your timesheet for the current reporting period.

- Click the *Issues and Risks* link to view issues and risks assigned to you in all of your projects.

- Click the *Resources* link to navigate to the *Resource Center* page where you can view and work with resource information.

- Click the *Status Reports* link to navigate to the *Status Reports* page where you can create or respond to a *Status Report* request.

- The *Strategy* section contains three links. Click the *Driver Library* link to navigate to the *Driver Library* page and view a list of your organization's business drivers for projects. Click the *Driver Prioritization* link to navigate to the *Driver Prioritization* page and see your organization's priorities for business drivers. Click the *Portfolio Analyses* link to navigate to the *Portfolio Analyses* page and access the executive decision making tool provided separately as Portfolio Server in a previous Project Server version.

- Click the *Reports* link to access the Business Intelligence center in Project Server, where you can view reports and perform project data analysis.

- Click the *Server Settings* link to access the *PWA Settings for* page.

Notice that the *Settings* section is gone from Project Server 2013. Users can access their personal settings using the *Site Actions* menu. Like all parts of SharePoint and Project Server, Microsoft bases the options available to the user on their rights in the system. Users now select the *PWA Settings* link to access personal settings where they can set up e-mail subscriptions for Alerts and Reminders, manage queued jobs, set up Alerts and Reminders for resources, manage delegates, or act as a delegate. The default shared library with Project Server for several versions is now gone as well.

Touring the Interface

Every Project Web App page that contains a data grid includes a ribbon with one or more ribbon tabs at the top of the page. When you click a ribbon tab, Project Server 2013 displays one or more buttons on the ribbon, depending on your Project Server permissions.

Projects Link

Figure 3 - 18 shows the *Project Center* page for a user with administrator permissions. Notice the *Projects* ribbon at the top of the page showing under the *Projects* tab.

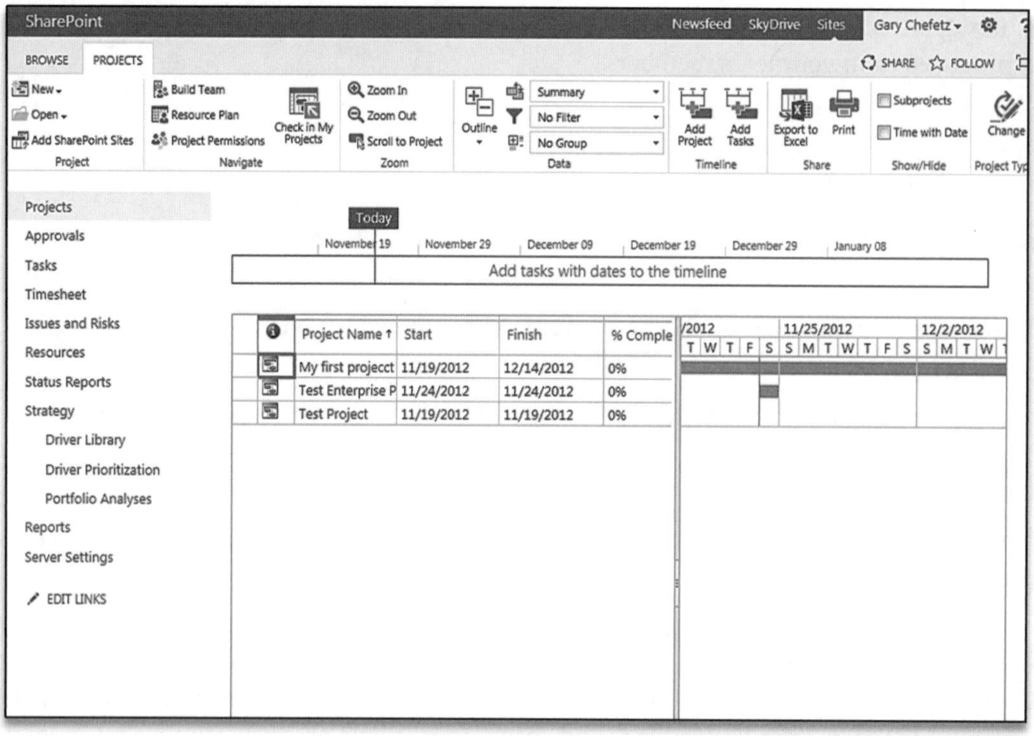

Figure 3 - 18: Project Center page

The first thing you might notice in the figure is that the timeline makes its debut in PWA 2013. The timeline is now available on the *Project Center* page and on the *Project Schedule* page for individual projects, for the SharePoint Tasks List, and for My Tasks. The Project Center has one context-sensitive tab, the *Projects* tab. Some pages contain only the *Browse* tab when the page contains all of the functionality. In one particular case, the *Browse* tab actually contains an additional navigation element, but I cover that later. The *Projects* ribbon contains menu selections in eight sections: *Project, Navigate, Zoom, Data, Timeline, Share, Show/Hide,* and *Project Type*. If you have experience with Project Server 2010, you can see right away that this ribbon is mostly unchanged. The *Project* section gives you the ability to create new proposals and projects, open projects for editing in the browser or Project client, as well as the ability to connect SharePoint sites with tasks lists to Project Server in visibility mode, another new feature for 2013. This replaces the 2010 Synchronize to SharePoint sites. The *Navigate* section provides familiar functions carried forward including *Build Team, Resource Plan, Check in My Projects, Close Tasks to Update,* and *Project Permissions;* however, Microsoft omitted the button to navigate to the Project Site for a selected project presumably to avoid confusion because stand-alone Project Sites can now display in the Project Center. You must now drill down to the individual project to find a link to the Project Site. If you deploy My Sites, you can use the *Follow* feature to organize your Project Sites.

Some pages contain more than one context-sensitive tab, such as the *Project Details* page, which contains three such tabs, *Project* as well as *Task* and *Options,* as shown in Figure 3 - 19. You navigate to the *Project Details* page by clicking the name of a project from the *Project Center* page. The *Project Details* page contains both a *Project* and a *Task* tab because you must access both project-level and task-level functions to leverage the features on this page. Notice the convenient status bar notification just below the ribbon.

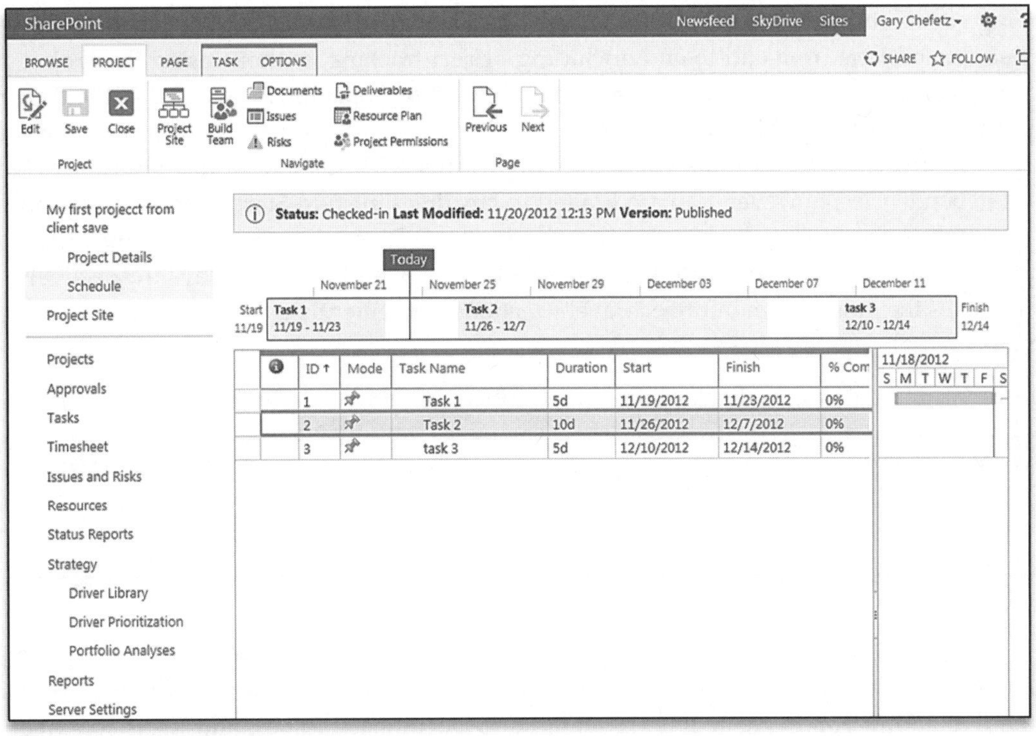

Figure 3 - 19: Project Details Schedule page showing Project ribbon

> **Information**: Note that the *Projects* tab in the Project Center differs significantly from the *Project* tab you see in the *Project Details* page. The operations available in the Project Center apply to all projects available in the Project Center while the *Project* tab available in a *Project Details* page contains operations that you use to act on a selected project.

The *Project* section on the *Project Details* page shown previously in Figure 3 - 19 provides redundant *Edit* and *Save* buttons and provides the only way to close and check in a project after editing on the web via the *Close* button. The *Navigate* section provides navigation to the Project Site homepage using the *Project Site* button or to any of the four primary Project Site features using the *Documents, Issues, Risks,* and *Deliverables* buttons to reach their respective destinations. You also find *Build Team* and *Resource Plan* buttons to activate these two features and a new *Project Permissions* button that allows you to set project-level permissions specific to your selected project. Finally, the *Previous* and *Next* buttons allow you to switch between schedule pages and the *Project Fields* page where you can edit the *Project Name, Project Start Date,* and *Project Owner* fields as well as any enterprise custom fields applicable to the specific project.

The *Task* ribbon shown in Figure 3 - 20 continues to provide the *Clipboard* section on the far left and the *Editing* and *Tasks* sections in the center. These three sections contain the web-based project editing tools available in Project Server 2013 using familiar iconography similar to what you find in the Project client. New for Project Server 2013, is the ability to set a baseline using PWA. In the *Editing* section, notice the new *Set Baseline* pick list.

Figure 3 - 20: Task ribbon

The web editing capability in PWA allows numerous users to participate in project schedule development, or even manage simple projects from end-to-end, including project tracking, without using the Project 2013 client. I say "simple" projects as these tools are a small subset of the editing capabilities you find in the Project client and are limited in their functionality. Most notably, while you can assign resources or even multiple resources to a task, you cannot control the percent-units value for assignments with 100% as your only choice. Similarly, you can create task dependencies; however, you are limited to creating Finish-to-Start dependencies and cannot enter lag values as you can in the Project client and you cannot manage constraints. Notice that the *Data* and *Zoom* sections provide you with tools to manipulate the data display and Gantt chart displays, respectively. Finally, the *Project* section makes the most common project-level functions conveniently available without the need to switch to the *Project* tab.

Click the *Options* tab and the system displays the *Options* ribbon shown in Figure 3 - 21.

Figure 3 - 21: Project Details Page, Options ribbon

From the *Share* section, you can choose to print the project or export to Excel. The *Link To* section contains a *Related Items* button that allows you to create links from tasks to Documents, Issues, and Risks contained in the project's *Project Site*. You can even create any one of these objects and link them all in one operation. The *Show/Hide* section allows you to display the Project Summary Task in the current view and allows you to change the date/time format.

Approvals Link

Working your way down the *Quick Launch* menu, the next stop is the *Approvals* link, which navigates to the Approval Center. The system displays the *Approval Center* homepage where you process task status updates, administrative time requests, timesheet lines, and timesheet updates from your resources as shown in Figure 3 - 22.

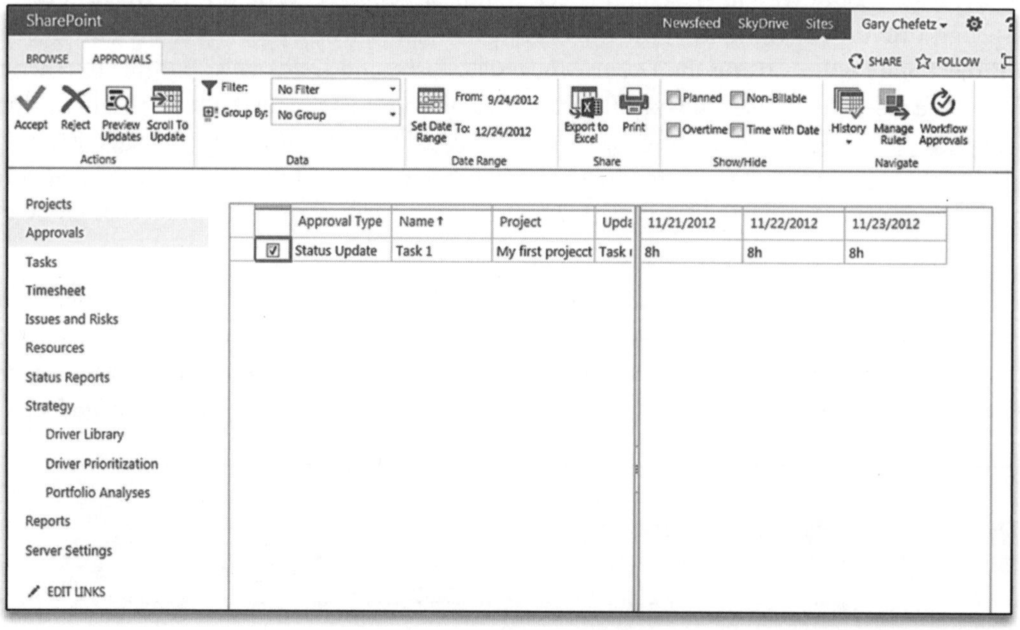

Figure 3 - 22: Approval Center

Notice that the *Approvals* ribbon contains buttons in the *Actions* section to accept, reject, and preview the impact that updates have on your schedule. In the *Data* section, you can filter or group the data on the page. Use the *Date Range* section to set a date range for the data display. Like many pages in PWA, the *Approvals* ribbon contains a *Share* section for exporting the data to Excel or for printing the data grid. The *Show/Hide* section contains check-boxes to selectively control data display options such as showing planned work values, non-billable work entries, overtime work entries, and to display the time with the date. Finally, you can use the *Navigate* section to display the *Rules* page by clicking the *Manage Rules* button. You can also navigate to either the *Status Updates* history or the *Timesheets* history pages by clicking the *History* pick list button. Project Server 2010 users should take note that you now access workflow approvals using the *Workflow Approvals* button, which appears on this page exclusively, rather than on the *Quick Launch* menu as it had in Project Server 2010. From the *Actions* section, click the *Preview Updates* button and the system opens the *Preview Updates* page containing the *Preview* ribbon shown in Figure 3 - 23.

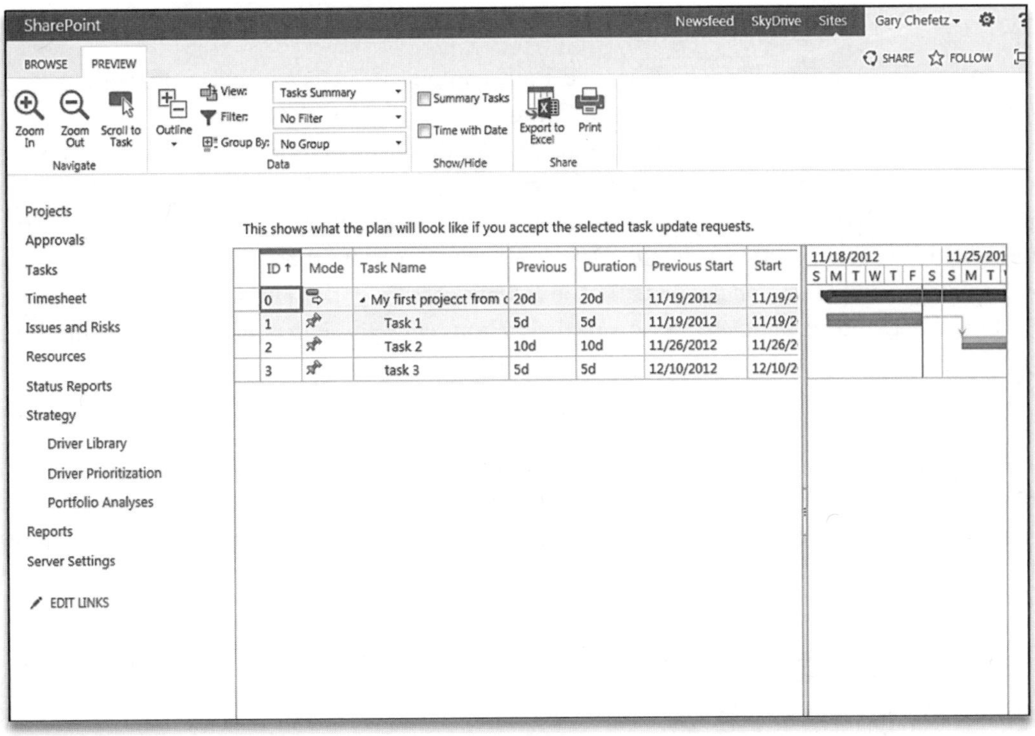

Figure 3 - 23: Preview Updates page and ribbon

The *Preview Updates* page contains a Gantt chart displaying a tracking view of the project that you select to pre-view; and, therefore, the ribbon contains buttons in the *Navigate* section to allow you to zoom in or out as well as scroll to the selected task on the Gantt chart. The *Data* section contains controls to switch views, set a filter, group by value, and an *Outline* pick list button to select the outline level displayed. In the *Show/Hide* section, you can opt to show or hide summary tasks and decide whether to show the time as well as the date in date fields. Finally, the ribbon contains the standard *Share* section for exporting to Excel or printing the data grid to a printer.

When you click the *History* pick list button from the *Approvals* page shown previously in Figure 3 - 22, you have a choice of either *Status Updates* ribbon or *Timesheets* ribbon. These display their respective update histories as shown in Figure 3 - 24 and Figure 3 - 25.

Figure 3 - 24: Status Updates History ribbon

Figure 3 - 25: Timesheets History ribbon

Both ribbons contain the standard *Share* section and both contain a *Navigate* section. In both cases, clicking the *Approval Center* button returns you to the Approval Center shown previously in Figure 3 - 22. When you click the *History* pick list, you have the option to navigate to the history details page not currently displayed. You use these to toggle back and forth between the *Status Updates* history ribbon and the *Timesheets* history ribbon. On the *Status Updates* ribbon, from the *Actions* section, you can click the *Delete Item* button to delete a history entry, or the *Publish* button to publish the selected items. In the *Date Range* section, click the *Set Date Range* button to set a date range for the display on the *Status Updates* page. In the *Actions* section of the *Timesheets* ribbon, click the *Recall* button to recall a timesheet, and in the *Data* section of the ribbon, click the *Filters* button to set filter criteria for the data displayed on the page.

Finally, the last selection on the *Approvals* ribbon, shown previously in Figure 3 - 22, is the *Manage Rules* button in the *Navigate* section of the ribbon. Click the *Manage Rules* button to navigate to the *Rules* page where you can create rules for automatically approving updates using the tools accessed through the *Rules* menu ribbon shown in Figure 3 - 26.

Figure 3 - 26: Rules ribbon

In the *Rule* section, the ribbon contains buttons for creating, editing, copying, and deleting rules including *New, Edit, Copy,* and *Delete* selections. The *Run* section contains the *Run Selected* button to run rules that you select in the page and a *Run All* button to run all of your rules immediately. Like most ribbon menus in the system, the *Rules* ribbon contains the standard *Share* section.

When you click the *Workflow Approvals* button from the *Approvals* ribbon, shown previously in Figure 3 - 22, the system displays the *Project Server Workflow Tasks* page shown in Figure 3 - 27 with the *Tasks* ribbon exposed. As you can see, this page uses the standard SharePoint tasks list.

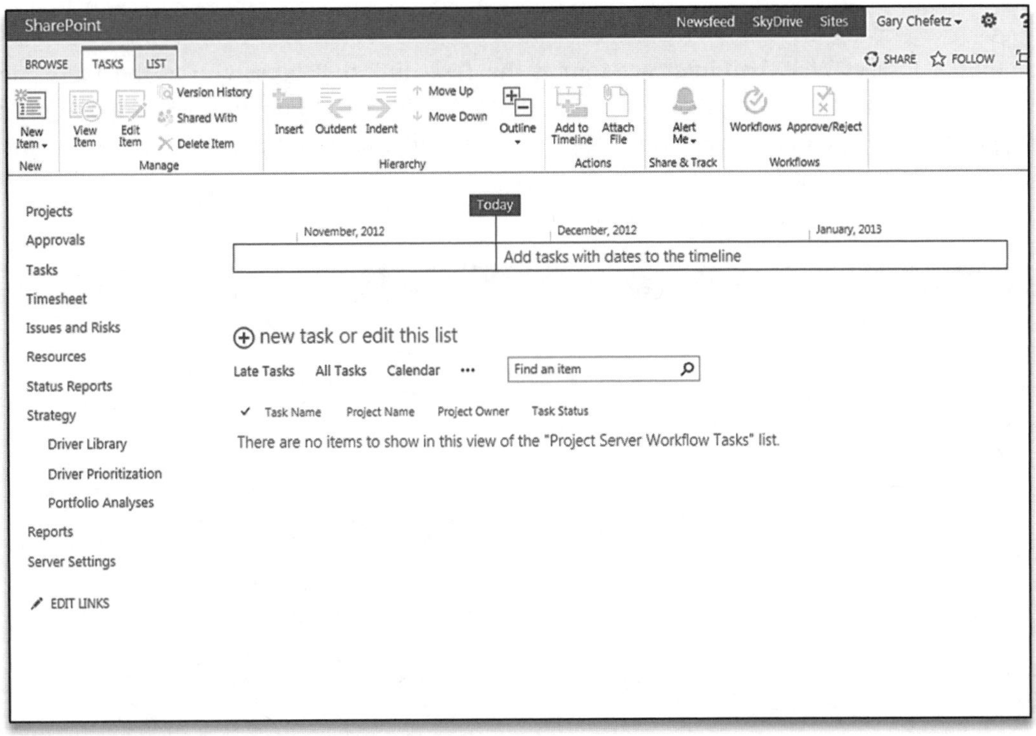

Figure 3 - 27: Project Server Workflow Tasks page

Because this page uses a standard SharePoint list to contain its data, it inherits the standard SharePoint *List Tools* ribbons for manipulating SharePoint lists. You will encounter these menu ribbons when you use any standard SharePoint list. The *Tasks* ribbon appears previously in Figure 3 - 27 and the *List* ribbon appears in Figure 3 - 28.

Figure 3 - 28: List ribbon

> **Information**: Note that not all standard SharePoint menu items are applicable to Project Server 2013 pages where they might appear. Further, your permissions in the system may prevent you from selecting various actions from the menu.

Tasks Link

The next stop on the Project Web App interface tour is the *Tasks* link that takes you to the *Tasks* page shown in Figure 3 - 29. This page contains a single ribbon menu that provides functionality for manipulating data and the display in the page. Team members use the *Tasks* page to submit progress updates to project managers whose projects to which they are assigned.

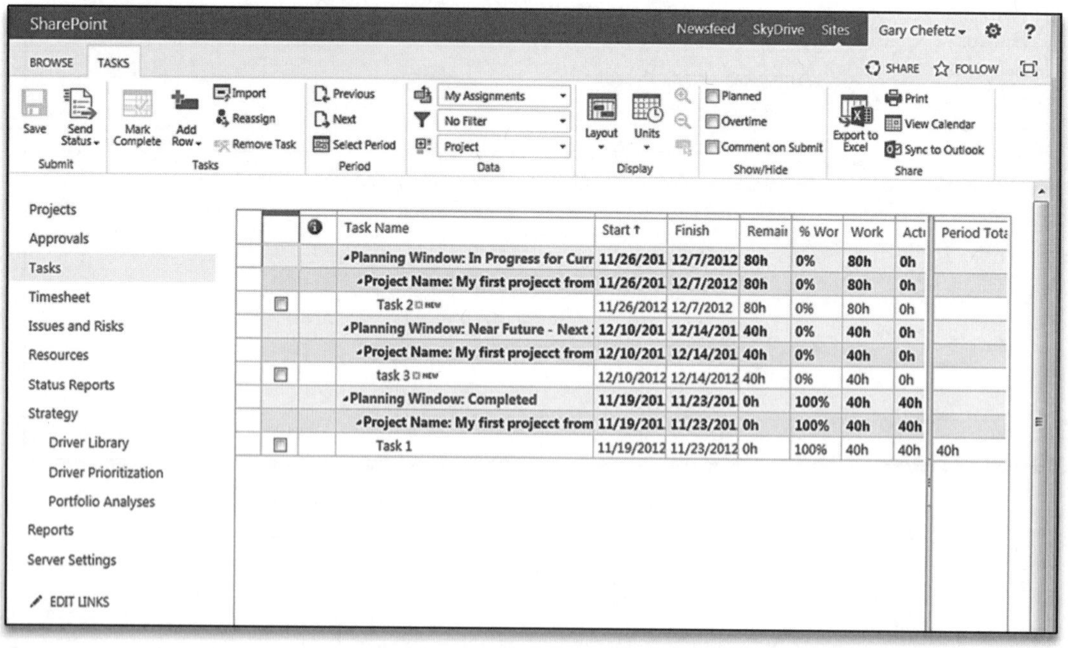

Figure 3 - 29: Tasks page and ribbon

In the *Submit* section of the ribbon you can save your updates for later submission using the *Save* button, or send a status update for all tasks or selected tasks using the *Send Status* pick list. The *Tasks* section contains an *Add Row* pick list that allows you to add a new task, assign yourself to an existing task, or add a team task to your *Tasks reporting* screen. Use the *Import* button to import data from your timesheet, the *Reassign* button to assign a selected task to another resource, and the *Remove Task* button to remove a task from your *Tasks* page. The buttons in the *Period* section allow you to navigate to other reporting periods using the *Previous* and *Next* buttons, or the *Select Period* button. The *Data* section provides selectors to choose a view, filter, and group-by values for the view. The *Display* section contains a *Layout* pick list that allows you to choose between three layouts: *Gantt chart, Time-phased,* and *Sheet* layout. The *Units* pick list allows you to choose a format for displaying duration work, and dates in the page, and the *Zoom* buttons and *Scroll to Task* button provide familiar navigation options when the *Gantt chart* layout is active. The *Show/Hide* section contains checkboxes that allow you to show *Planned* and *Overtime* rows selectively as well as to determine whether the system prompts you for comments when submitting updates. The *Share* section contains the typical *Export to Excel* and *Print* selections as well as a special *View Calendar* button that activates a calendar view of your *Tasks* page.

Timesheet Link

The *Timesheet* page ribbon, shown in Figure 3 - 30, contains the tools you need to manipulate the display and data on the *Timesheet* page.

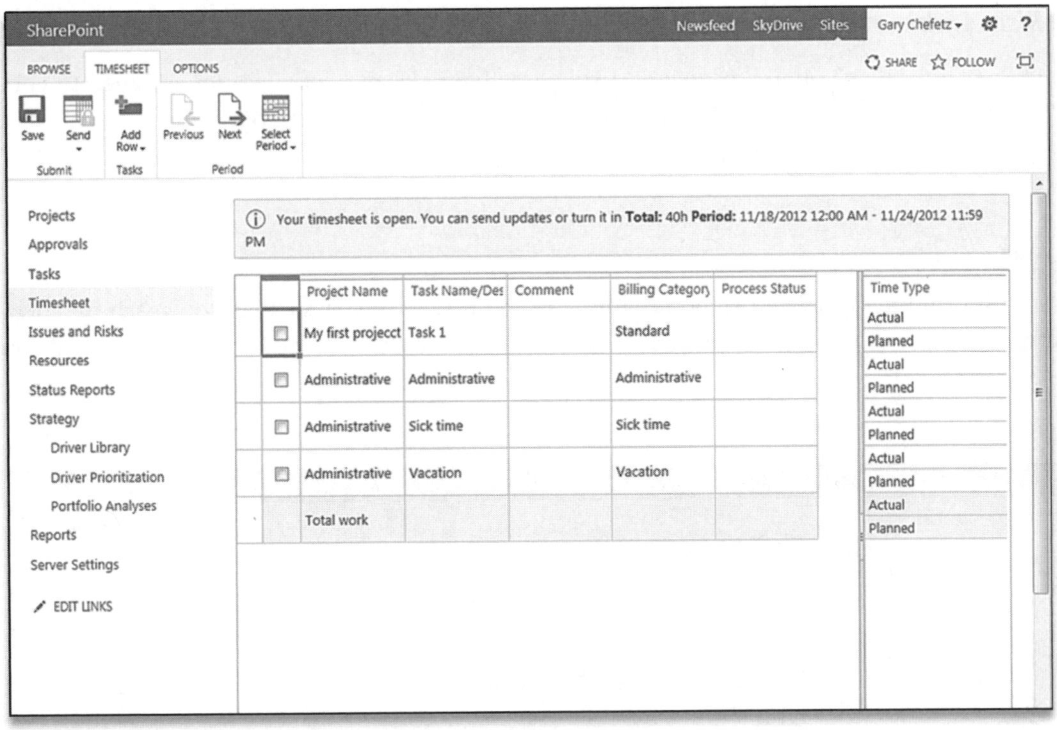

Figure 3 - 30: Timesheet ribbon

From the *Submit* section, click the *Save* button to save your entries for a later date. Click the *Send* pick list button to send status on specific tasks or to lock and submit your entire timesheet. The *Tasks* section contains only the *Add Row* pick list button. Microsoft moved the *Import* and *Remove Task* buttons to the *Options* tab. This indicates that they believe these to be the least used of these options. Essentially, these buttons provide the same capabilities that I discussed in the *Tasks* ribbon. In the *Period* section, the *Previous* and *Next* buttons allow you to navigate forward and backward through time periods and the *Select Period* pick list opens a dialog that allows you to quickly navigate to a specific time period. Some functionality that used to be front and center now appear on the *Options* ribbon shown in Figure 3 - 31.

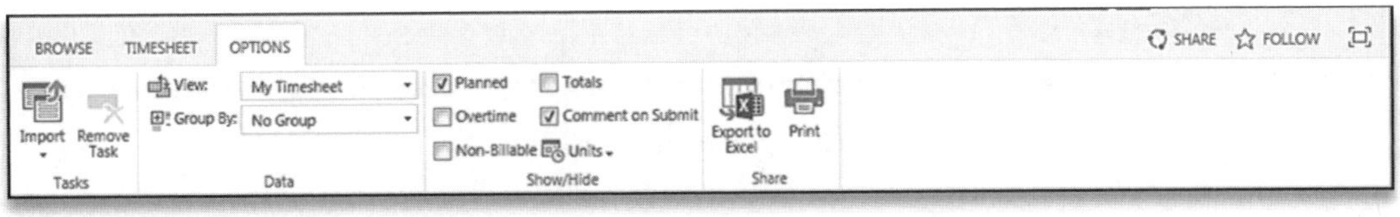

Figure 3 - 31: Timesheet Options ribbon

The *Tasks* section now contains the *Import* and *Remove Task* buttons. The *Data* section includes pick lists to change the view or group-by values while the *Show/Hide* section contains checkboxes to show or hide data rows for *Planned* work, *Overtime* work, and *Non-Billable* work. The *Totals* checkbox lets you determine whether or not to show totals by day in daily timesheet columns, the *Comment on Submit* checkbox enables the system to prompt you for comments when submitting updates, and the *Units* pick list allows you to define how the system displays duration, work, and dates on this page. Finally, the *Share* section provides the standard options for exporting to Excel or printing.

Issues and Risks Link

The *Issues and Risks* link takes you to a page that displays active risks and active issues assigned to you. This page is for display purposes only and does not allow you to interact with data; however, it does provide a nice personal summary.

Resources Link

The next place you find a specialized ribbon menu is in the Resource Center that you reach by clicking the *Resources* heading or *Resources* link from the *Quick Launch* menu. The *Resource Center* and *Resources* ribbon displays in Figure 3 - 32.

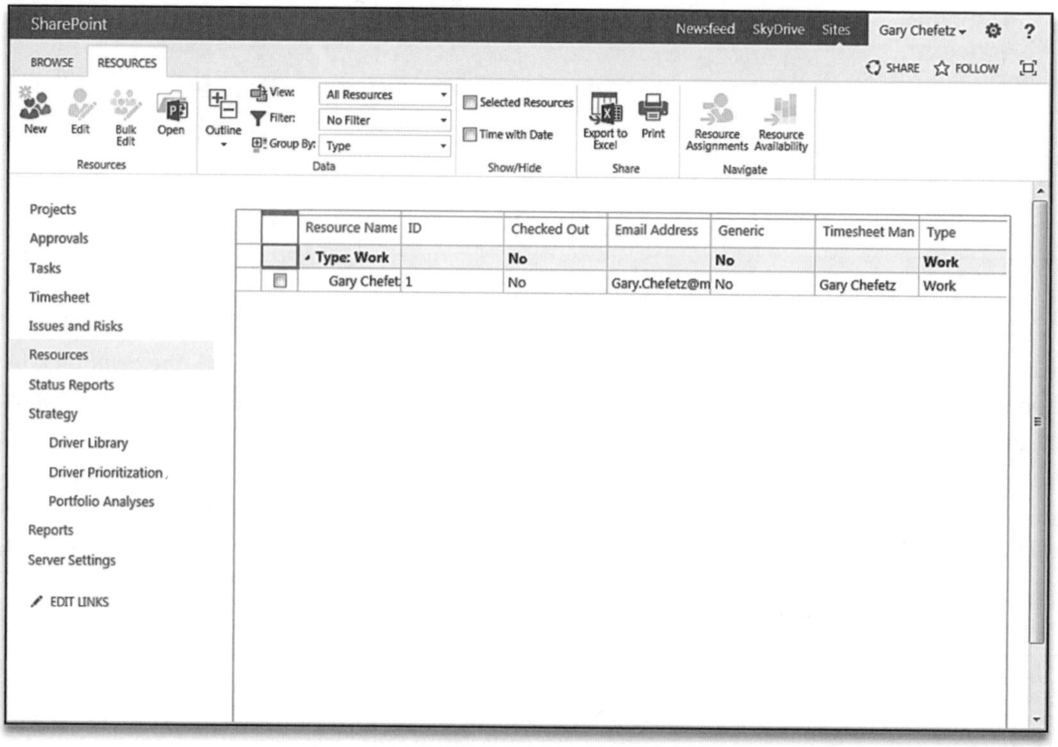

Figure 3 - 32: Resources ribbon

From the *Resources* section of the *Resources* ribbon, you click the *New* button to create a new resource, click the *Edit* button to edit both an individual resource and multiple resources by batch. The *Bulk Edit* button takes you to a screen that allows you to bulk-edit resources by providing values for resources that apply to multiple entries. The *Open* button opens the selected resources for editing in the Project client. Familiar selections adorn the *Data* section with options to choose an outline level for the display, and selectors to choose a view, filter, and group-by values. The *Show/Hide* section contains checkboxes to show the list of selected resources alongside the selection grid and add the time to the date format. The *Share* section provides the usual *Share* options while the *Navigate* section provides links to two resource views via the *Resource Assignments* and *Resource Availability* buttons. Click the *Resource Assignments* button to reach the *Resource Assignments* page containing the ribbon shown in Figure 3 - 33.

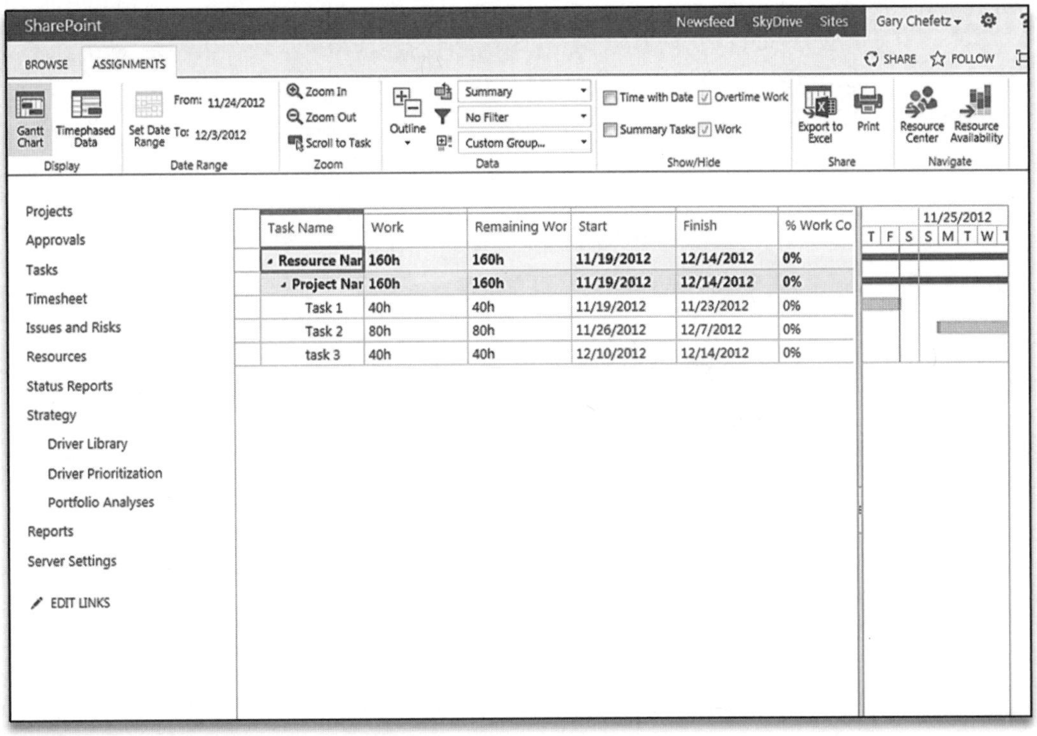

Figure 3 - 33: Resource Assignments page

The *Assignments* ribbon contains display and navigation options, as this page is not actionable. Note that the *Display* section provides buttons to change the view to *Gantt Chart* or *Timephased Data*. The *Set Date Range* button allows you to select a date range for the display while the buttons in the *Zoom* section control zooming on the Gantt chart as well as a *Scroll to Task* button to scroll the Gantt chart to the selected task. The *Data* section contains buttons to set the outline level display, select a view, set a filter, and group-by options. The *Show/Hide* section contains checkboxes to show time with date, summary tasks, overtime work, and work. Use the options in the *Share* section as you would with any other ribbon and the *Navigate* section to go back to the *Resource Center* page, or click the *Resource Availability* button to navigate to the *Resource Availability* page with the ribbon shown in Figure 3 - 34.

Figure 3 - 34: Resource Availability page

The *Availability* ribbon contains a *View* pick list to choose a view in the *Views* section. The usual *Share* options are available from the ribbon and the *Navigate* section allows you to return to the *Resource Center* page or the *Resource Assignments* page.

Status Reports Link

Clicking the *Status Reports* link takes you to the *Status Report* page where users can request and submit status reports. This functionality is a legacy feature that has not changed since Microsoft removed the ability to interact with actual project data. More importantly, this is an end-user feature and of little concern to Project Server 2013 administrators.

Strategy Links

The next stop on the interface tour is a quick look at the screens and ribbon menus for the *Strategy* section. The selections you find under the *Strategy* section are the pages that contain the portfolio analysis capability that Microsoft fully integrated into Project Server 2010. Click the *Driver Library* link from the *Strategy* section to see the *Driver* ribbon shown in Figure 3 - 35.

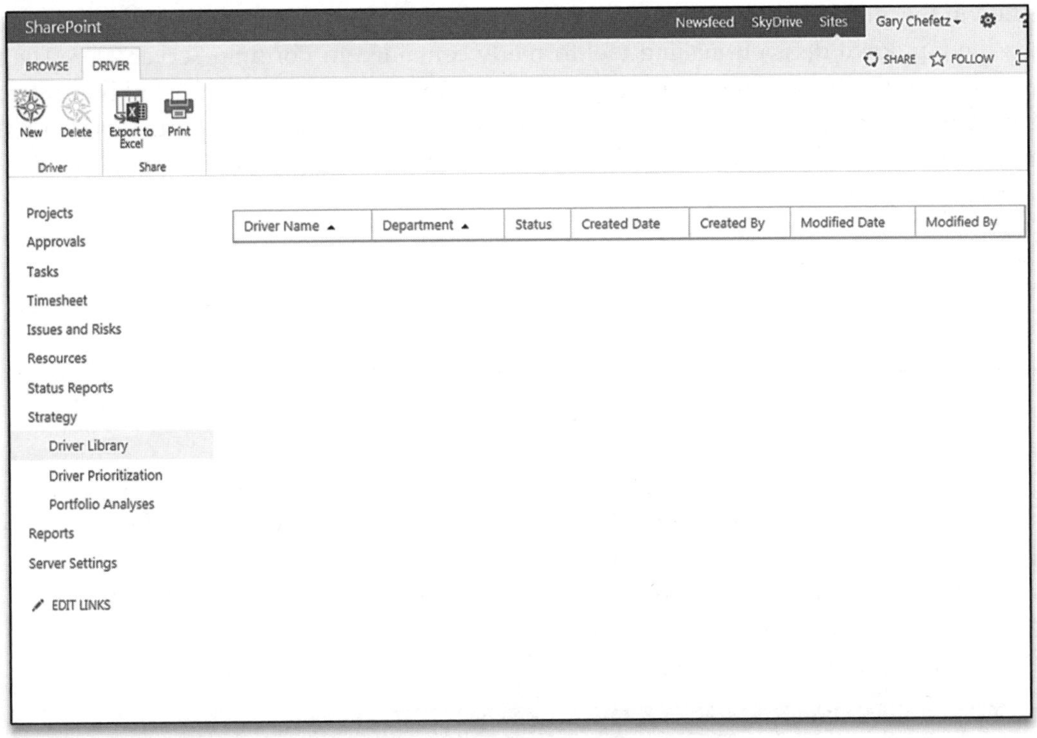

Figure 3 - 35: Driver Library ribbon

The ribbon functionality for business drivers is very simple; you can either create a new business driver, or delete an existing one. You have the exact capabilities with the first ribbon you encounter in the *Business Driver Prioritization* process as shown in Figure 3 - 36.

Figure 3 - 36: New Driver Prioritization ribbon

The second ribbon menu that you encounter during the *Business Driver Prioritization* process, shown in Figure 3 - 37, contains buttons in the *Navigate* section for the logical steps involved in the process: *Define Properties, Prioritize Drivers,* and *Review Priorities.* These align with the steps that the system walks you through while performing a prioritization exercise. Note that all three of these ribbons in the *Strategy* section of the *Quick Launch* menu contain the *Share* section with the usual options and that the *Prioritization* ribbon contains a *Close* button to complete the prioritization and a *Save* button to save your prioritization.

Figure 3 - 37: Driver Prioritization ribbon

The last selection in the *Strategy* section is the *Portfolio Analyses* link, which contains Project Server specific ribbon menus. This is the top-down decision-making tool formerly contained in Portfolio Server 2007. The first step in the analysis process is to create a new analysis or work with an existing one. The ribbon menu shown in Figure 3 - 38 contains *New* and *Delete* buttons for creating new or deleting existing portfolios in the *Analysis* section. The *Project Dependencies* button allows you to define dependencies and inclusive or exclusive relationships between projects in your analysis.

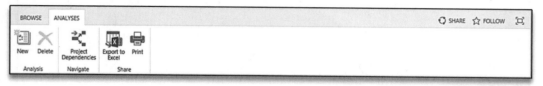

Figure 3 - 38: Portfolio Analysis ribbon

Once you have created the initial analysis and defined your project dependencies, the system walks you through the analysis process. The next step is to define the properties for the analysis such as what projects to consider, and to set other properties and constraints for the analysis. The ribbon menu that supports this process displays in Figure 3 - 39. Note that the next two steps that follow use almost identical ribbon menus, as shown in Figure 3 - 40 for prioritizing your selected projects and in Figure 3 - 41 for reviewing your priorities before you use the system tools to perform the actual analysis.

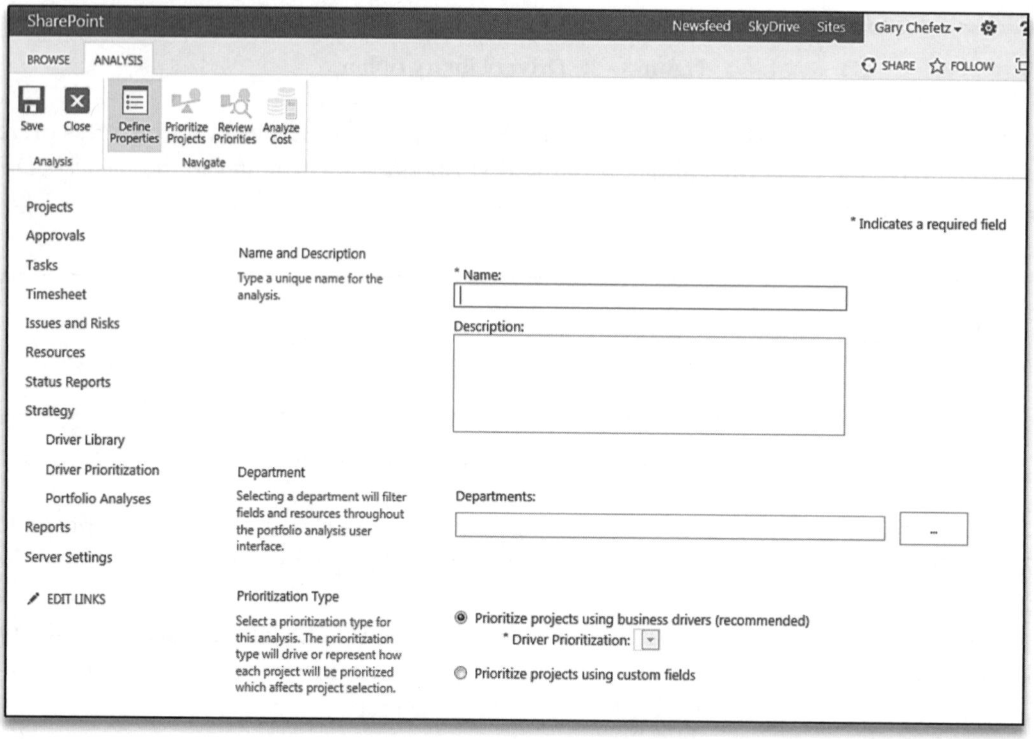

Figure 3 - 39: Define Properties

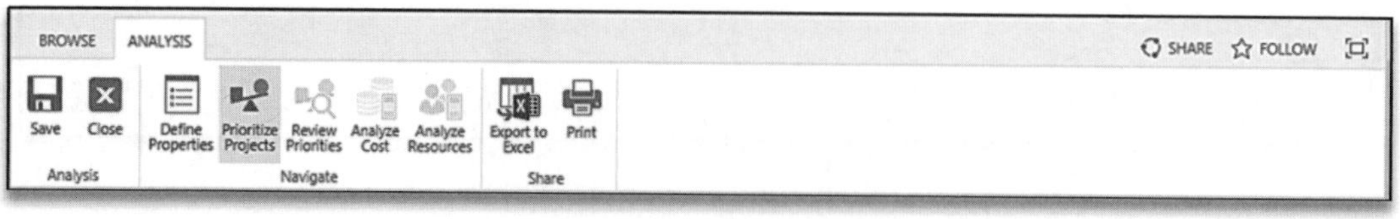

Figure 3 - 40: Prioritize Projects

Figure 3 - 41: Review Priorities

Information: Note that the *Share* section appears on pages with data grids. Pages, such as the *Define Properties* page, do not contain data grids; and, therefore, do not display ribbon menus that include the *Share* section.

After you have defined your analysis selections, the next step you take is to perform the analysis using the tools provided by the system. The first analysis is cost-driven. The ribbon menu for cost analysis, shown in Figure 3 - 42, introduces two new sections to the ribbon including *Portfolio Selection* and *Projects*. The *Portfolio Selection* section is common to both cost analysis and resource analysis as shown in the *Analyze Resources* ribbon in Figure 3 - 43 with the only difference being that the *Analyze Resources* ribbon also contains a *Reports* pick list. Both ribbons also include a *Projects* section that offers additional tools that pertain to the specific type of analysis.

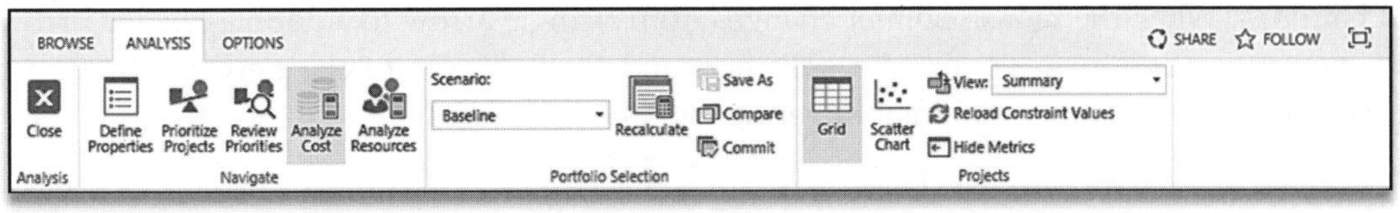

Figure 3 - 42: Analyze Cost

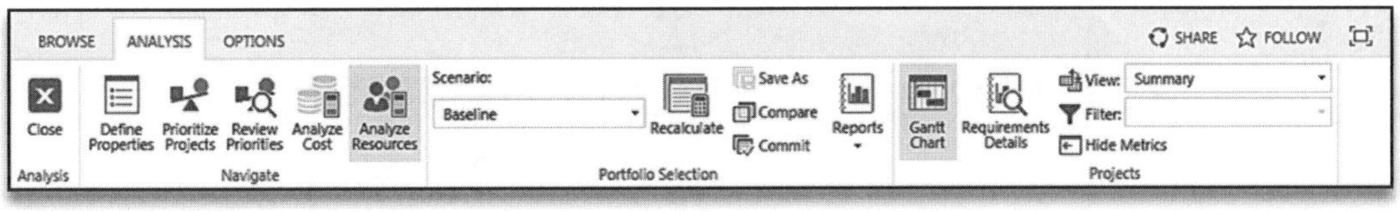

Figure 3 - 43: Analyze Resources

In the two figures shown previously, notice that both contain an additional tab selection, the *Options* tab, which displays the *Options* ribbon shown in Figure 3 - 44. This ribbon provides additional option settings for both cost and resource analysis scenarios.

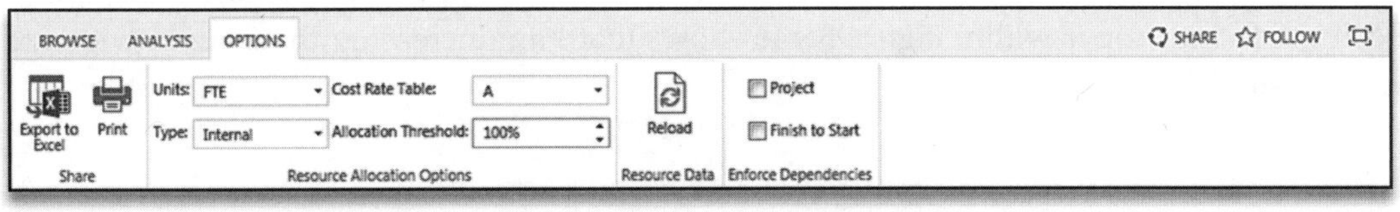

Figure 3 - 44: Options ribbon

Reports Link

Clicking this link navigates to the SharePoint BI Center wired up for Project Server 2013, which I cover in Module 18, *Working with Business Intelligence and Reporting*.

Server Settings Link

For more information about this link, see the last topical section of this module, *Using the Administration Interface for a PWA Instance.*

You have now explored the major components of the *Quick Launch* menu of the Project Server PWA user interface, focusing on the various ribbon menus that you encounter. If you have used one of the prior versions of Project Server, by this time the breadth of the new functionality available in Project Server 2013 no doubt, impresses you and, by the way, the new ribbons surface this functionality in a more intuitive arrangement than prior versions.

Manipulating the Data Grid

As I previously mentioned, a number of Project Web App pages contain a data grid that displays task, resource, and assignment data. Some data grids, such as the *Project Center* page, have a vertical split bar separating the grid into two sections, while other pages contain a single grid only. For example, notice that the *Project Center* page, shown previously in Figure 3 - 18, consists of two sections: the project list on the left side of the split bar, and the Gantt chart on the right side. To work with the data in the grid most effectively, it is important to know how to take the following actions:

- **Move the Split Bar**: You move the split bar in the grid by floating your mouse pointer anywhere over the split bar itself. When the mouse pointer changes from a single arrow to a double-headed arrow, click and hold the mouse button to "grab" the split bar, and then drag it to the new position on the screen. Figure 3 - 45 shows the mouse pointer hovering over the split bar.

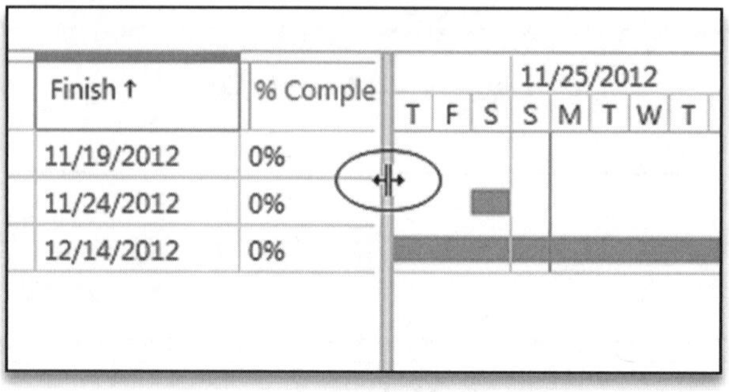

Figure 3 - 45: Mouse Pointer over Split Bar

- **Change Column Widths**: To change the width of any column in the grid, position the mouse pointer anywhere on the right edge of the column in the header row. The mouse pointer changes from a single arrow to a double-headed arrow. Click and hold to "grab" the right edge of the column, and drag the edge of the column to the proper width. Figure 3 - 46 shows that I am increasing the column width of the *Project Name* column.

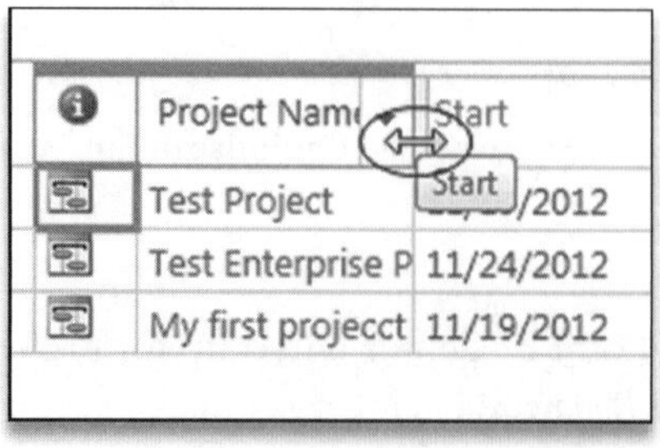

Figure 3 - 46: Widen the Project Name Column

Information: To widen any column to "best fit" the data in the column, you can use the Excel trick by double-clicking the gridline on the right edge of the column.

- **Move Columns**: To move any column in the grid, click and hold the column header of the column you want to move, then drag the column and drop it into its new position in the grid. The column snaps to the grid at the locations where you can place the column. Notice in Figure 3 - 47 that I am dragging the *Finish* column to a new position. Notice how the column floats over the other columns in a transparent format as I move it across the other columns.

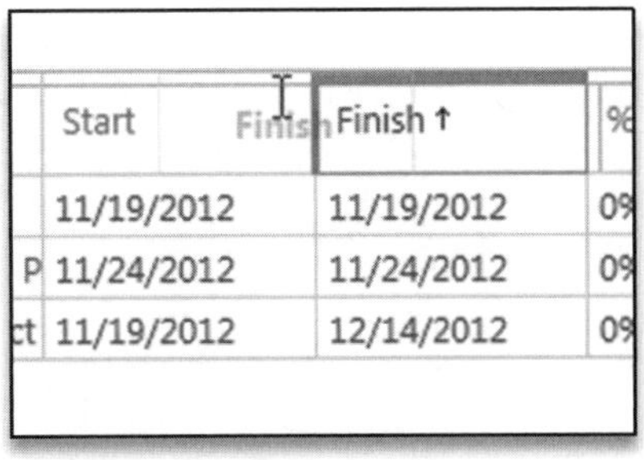

Figure 3 - 47: Dragging the Finish Column

- **Hide and Unhide Columns**: To hide any column, float your mouse pointer over the column header of the column you want to hide, and then click the pick list button that appears at the right edge of the column. Project Server 2013 displays the pick list menu shown in Figure 3 - 48. On the pick list menu, select the *Hide Column* item.

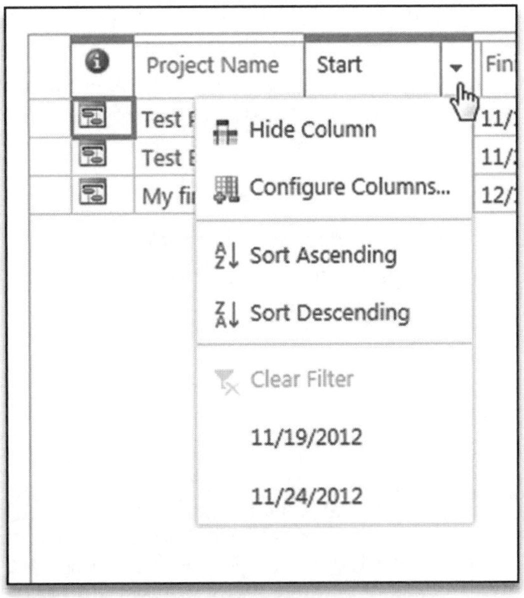

Figure 3 - 48: Hide Column

- To unhide a column, float your mouse pointer over any column header, click the pick list button, and select the *Configure Columns* item on the pick list menu shown previously in Figure 3 - 48. The system displays the *Configure Columns* dialog shown in Figure 3 - 49. In the *Configure Columns* dialog, select the checkbox for the column(s) you want to unhide and then click the *OK* button.

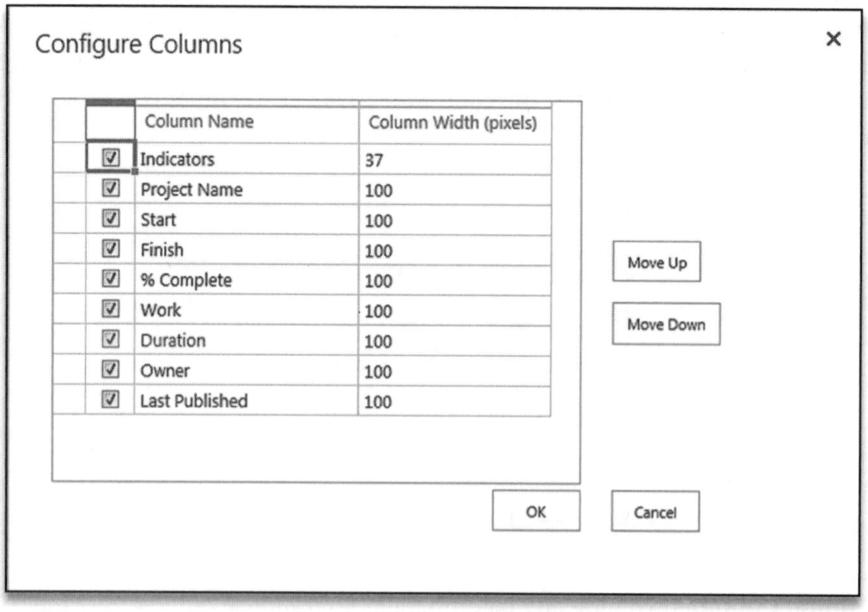

Figure 3 - 49: Unhide column in the Configure Columns dialog

- Notice in the dialog shown in Figure 3 - 49 that Project Server 2013 also allows you to set column widths and the column display order. To change the width of any column, enter the width in pixels in the *Column Width* field. To change the display order of columns, select any column and use the *Move Up* and *Move Down* buttons. Click the *OK* button when finished.

- **Sort Columns:** To sort the data in the grid, float your mouse pointer over the column header of the column that you want to sort, click the pick list button, and then select the *Sort Ascending* or *Sort Descending* item on the pick list menu.

Information: Project Server 2013 automatically saves any changes you make to the layout of a grid (such as column order, column width, etc.) in your user profile. The layout of the grid reappears the next time you return to the page. These changes affect the current user only. A Project Server administrator must use the *Manage Views* selection from the *Server Settings* menu to make these changes universal for all users.

Printing the Data Grid

Project Server 2013 allows you to print a report from a data grid or export the data grid information to Excel. To print a data grid, click the *Print* option in the *Share* section on the ribbon. The system opens the *Print Grid* dialog in its own Internet Explorer window. Figure 3 - 50 shows the *Print Grid* dialog for the *Project Center* page.

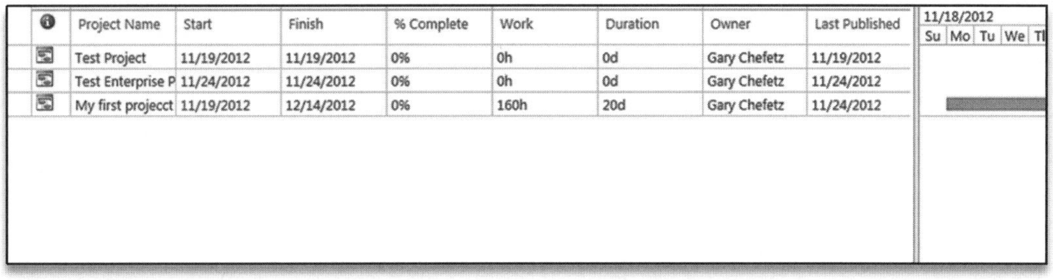

	Project Name	Start	Finish	% Complete	Work	Duration	Owner	Last Published
	Test Project	11/19/2012	11/19/2012	0%	0h	0d	Gary Chefetz	11/19/2012
	Test Enterprise P	11/24/2012	11/24/2012	0%	0h	0d	Gary Chefetz	11/24/2012
	My first projecct	11/19/2012	12/14/2012	0%	160h	20d	Gary Chefetz	11/24/2012

Figure 3 - 50: Print Grid dialog

Notice that the *Print Grid* dialog is a duplicate of the grid in the parent window. In this window, you can rearrange and resize the columns using the same techniques you used to move columns in the parent window; however, you cannot hide columns. Instead, you must hide the columns that you do not want to print before you open the *Print Grid* dialog. If you do hide columns for printing, do not forget to restore them in your view.

Information: Project Server 2013 prints both the data grid and the Gantt chart components. The ability to print the Gantt chart was new for 2010. In prior versions, you could apply additional formatting to the grid prior to printing; however, that feature is not available in Project Server 2013.

Warning: If you attempt to print a data grid, and the data grid exceeds 100 lines of information, Project Server 2013 does not allow you to print the data grid. Instead, the system forces you to export the data grid to Excel. From Excel, you can then print the data grid.

Exporting the Data Grid to Excel

In addition to printing the data grid, you can also export it to an Excel workbook by clicking the *Export to Excel* button from the *Share* section of the ribbon on a page containing a data grid. When you select this option, the system displays the *File Download* dialog shown in Figure 3 - 51.

Figure 3 - 51: File Download dialog

Click the *Open* button to open the file in Excel. The system opens Excel and exports the grid as shown in Figure 3 - 52.

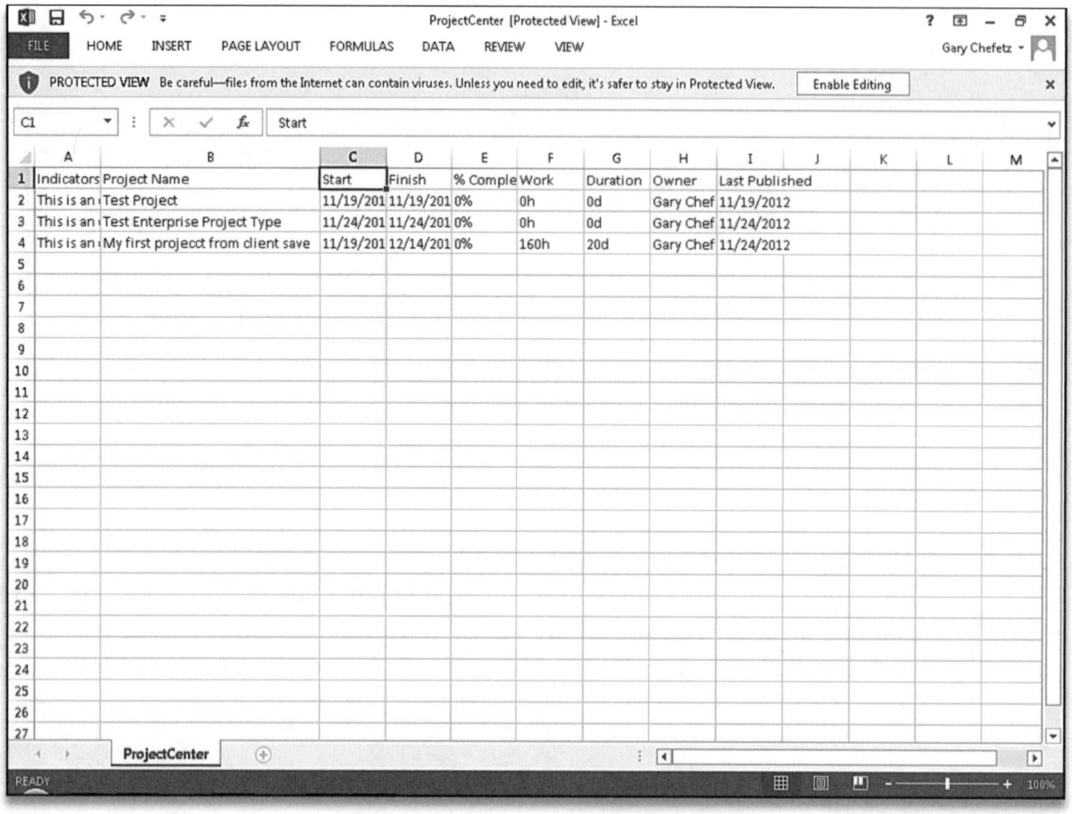

Figure 3 - 52: Tasks Exported to Excel

Using the Administration Interface for a PWA Instance

To access the administration features of the system at the site or PWA instance level, log in to Project Web App using an account with administrator permissions and then click the *Gear* icon in the upper right corner. If you are running in Project Server permissions mode, the system displays the *PWA Settings* page shown in Figure 3 - 53. If you are running in SharePoint permissions mode, the system displays the *PWA Settings* page shown in Figure 3 - 54.

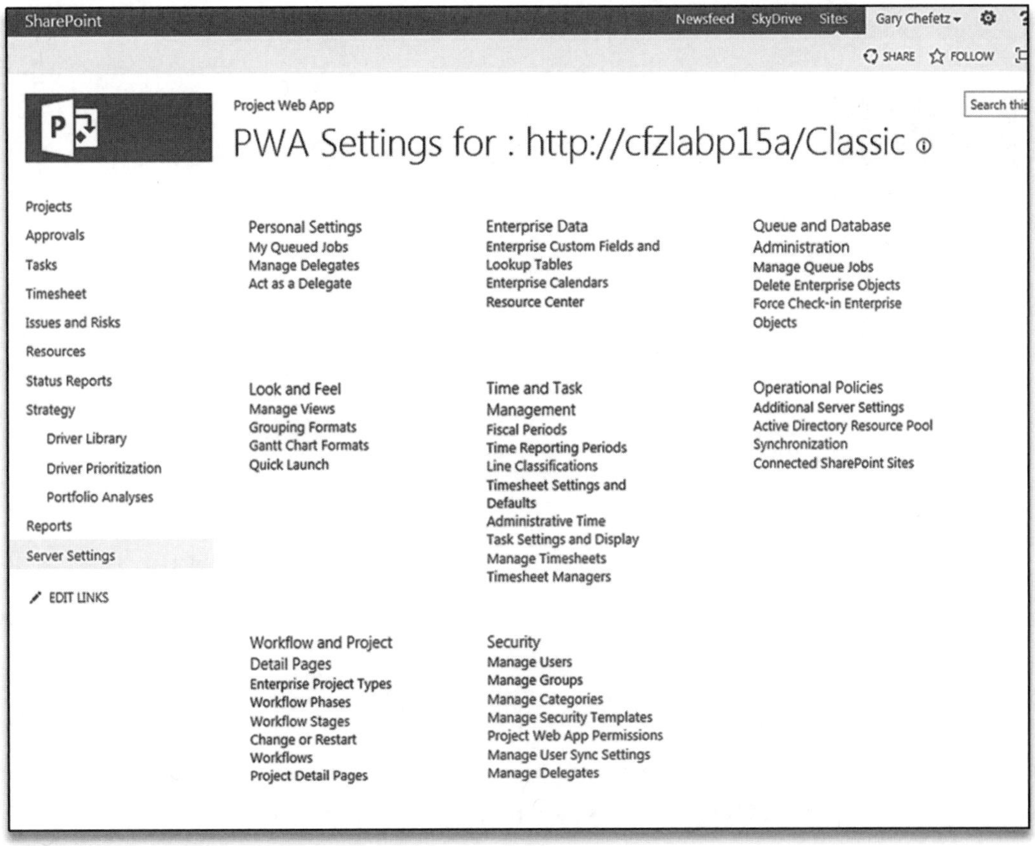

Figure 3 - 53: PWA Settings page for Project Server permissions mode

The *PWA Settings* page for Project Server permissions mode organizes administrator functions into logical sections, including *Personal Settings, Enterprise Data, Queue and Database Administration, Look and Feel, Time and Task Management, Operational Policies, Workflow and Project Detail Pages,* and *Security*. Each section contains links for the functions you perform as the Project Server administrator. For example, use the functions in the *Security* section to manage users, groups, categories, security templates, Project Web App permissions, and to manage delegates.

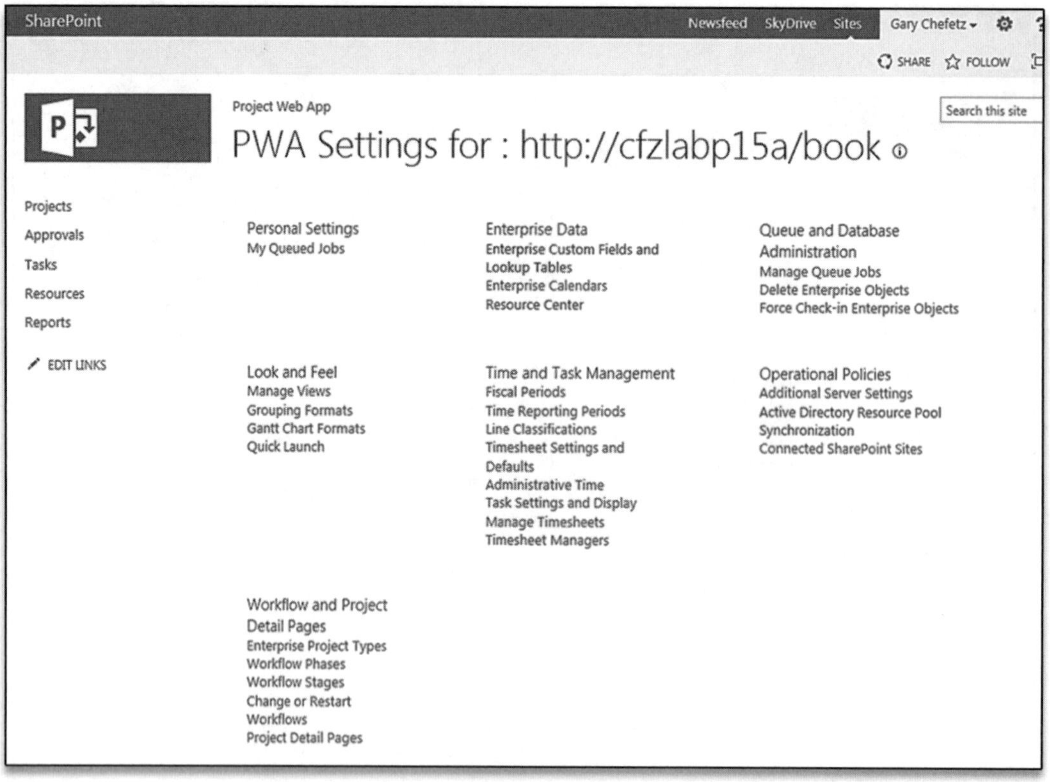

Figure 3 - 54: PWA Settings page for SharePoint permissions mode

Notice in Figure 3 - 54 that the *Security* section does not appear when you are running in SharePoint permissions mode. Notice also under the *Personal Settings* section that the two links *Manage Delegates* and *Act as a Delegate* disappear from the display because the *Delegate* feature relies upon Project Server permissions mode and is not usable in SharePoint permissions mode. Table 3 - 5 through Table 3 - 11 contain brief descriptions of the functions available in each section of the *PWA Settings* page for a PWA instance running in Project Server permissions mode. Those items marked with an asterisk (*) do not apply in SharePoint permissions mode.

Security Functions*	
Function	**Description**
Manage Users*	Add, modify, and deactivate users. Set groups, categories, permissions, and custom field values.
Manage Groups*	Add, modify, and delete user groups. Set Active Directory group mappings for user groups with synchronization frequencies. Manage user and category associations to groups and global permissions.
Manage Categories*	Add, modify, and delete categories. Associate users, groups, projects, resources, and views with each category.
Manage Security Templates*	Add, modify, and delete the security templates used to set category permissions and global permissions in groups.

Security Functions*	
Function	**Description**
Project Web App Permissions*	Enable or disable the high-level permissions that are available in Project Server 2013 for category and global permissions.
Manage User Sync Settings*	Configure Active Directory user synchronization.
Manage Delegates*	Add or delete delegates in the system.

Table 3 - 5: Security Functions

Enterprise Data Functions	
Function	**Description**
Enterprise Custom Fields and Lookup Tables	Create, modify, and delete custom enterprise fields and lookup tables. Modify built-in custom enterprise fields and lookup tables.
Enterprise Calendars	Create, modify, and delete custom enterprise calendars. Modify the built-in enterprise standard calendar.
Resource Center	Navigate to the Resource Center page to create new resources, to modify existing resource information individually or using a bulk modification, or to view resource availability and resource assignments.

Table 3 - 6: Enterprise Data Functions

Queue and Database Administration Functions	
Function	**Description**
Manage Queue Jobs	View the status of queue jobs and take administrative action on them.
Delete Enterprise Objects	Delete projects, resources and user accounts, Status Report responses, timesheets, and user delegations from the Project Server database.
Force Check-in Enterprise Objects	Check in projects, resources, custom fields, calendars, lookup tables, or resource plans left in a checked-out state.

Table 3 - 7: Database Administration functions

Look and Feel Functions	
Function	**Description**
Manage Views	Create, modify, copy, or delete any type of view displayed in Project Web App.
Grouping Formats	Customize the grouping formats used in Project Web App views.
Gantt Chart Formats	Customize the formats for Gantt charts used in Project Web App views.
Quick Launch	Add, edit, delete, or reorder the links in the Quick Launch menu in Project Web App.

Table 3 - 8: Look and Feel functions

Time and Task Management Functions	
Function	**Description**
Fiscal Periods	Define, modify, and delete financial periods and set Fiscal Year options.
Time Reporting Periods	Define time periods used for timesheets in Project Web App.
Line Classifications	Create duplicate timesheet lines for business or accounting purposes.
Timesheet Settings and Defaults	Specify all options related to timesheet display and usage in Project Web App. Tie the My Timesheet page to the My Tasks page for a single point of time entry in Project Web App.
Administrative Time	Add and delete categories used for tracking administrative time.
Task Settings and Display	Specify the default and/or locked-down reporting methods for reporting and tracking task progress in Project Web App.
Manage Timesheets	Alter submitted timesheets.
Timesheet Managers	Manage the list of timesheet managers

Table 3 - 9: Time and Task Management functions

Operational Policies Functions	
Function	**Description**
Additional Server Settings	Specify connectivity options for users with Project Pro 2013. Specify whether to allow master project publishing and allow project managers to use local base calendars, set the default currency, specify resource capacity and resource plan workday settings, and determine the behavior of the built-in custom State field. Synchronize Project Web App tasks with each user's Exchange Server account.
Active Directory Resource Pool Synchronization	Set options for synchronizing the Enterprise Resource Pool with Active Directory.
Connected SharePoint Sites	Create, edit, and delete SharePoint sites and synchronize user access to a site. Link to a Site Administration page for a specific SharePoint site.

Table 3 - 10: Operational Policies functions

Workflow and Project Detail Pages Functions	
Function	**Description**
Enterprise Project Types	Create, modify, and delete project types used with an associated workflow process to approve proposal projects.
Workflow Phases	Create, modify, and delete the phases used in the workflow process.
Workflow Stages	Create, modify, and delete the stages used in each phase of the workflow process.
Change or Restart Workflows	Change or restart the workflow process for individual proposal projects or enterprise projects.
Project Detail Pages	Change the properties or modify the layout of the Project Detail pages used in the workflow process in Project Web App.

Table 3 - 11: Workflow and Project Detail Pages functions

Your overview tour of the Project Web App user interface is complete. Although you have not seen every ribbon menu in the system, you have covered most of them, including those for the most significant pages. Some of the pages that you use to administer Project Server 2013 also contain ribbon menus; however, they are very simple and you learn about them as you encounter them in upcoming modules.

Module 04

Configuring Enterprise Objects and Options

Learning Objectives

After completing this module, you will be able to:

- Understand department filtering
- Understand the importance of custom enterprise fields
- Edit built-in lookup tables
- Create a custom lookup table
- Create custom enterprise fields using lookup tables, formulas, and graphical indicators
- Edit custom enterprise fields and lookup tables
- Delete custom enterprise fields and lookup tables
- Set the working schedule on the enterprise standard calendar
- Create custom enterprise base calendars
- Import a base calendar from a non-enterprise project
- Understand and implement tracking methods

Inside Module 04

Introduction

The topics I cover in this module are specifically for those of you who are preparing for the 74-344 certification; however, I go a step beyond Microsoft's objective domain requirements with my coverage of configuring tracking settings. The OD has a section titled *Select a Tracking Method* in the domain of *Track and Collaborate on an Enterprise Project.* That it appears under "Track and Collaborate" presumes that you have a choice when you create an enterprise project. In all likelihood, if you are a project manager, chances are you do not have a choice. If you are a program or portfolio manager, chances are you do not want the project managers to have a choice. Choice is good unless it conflicts with your business objectives. Consistency is almost an absolute requisite for any type of intelligent portfolio analysis.

If you are a project manager, it is incredibly helpful if you understand what the system is capable of and how each tracking selection affects the way you interact with the system. If you are a Project Server professional, you must know how to guide an organization through the decision making process of selecting a tracking method. If you are a program or portfolio manager you need to understand how to maintain consistency for reliable analytics and how to consume the resource usage data Microsoft Project 2013, and Project Server 2013 produces. Because tracking touches everyone in the organization, taking a deep dive into this topic is beneficial but not required for the 74-344 exam.

Understanding Project Server 2013 Metadata Architecture

Project Pro 2013 is a scheduling tool used primarily by Project Managers. Project Server 2013 is a Project and Portfolio Management information system, one that is transitioning from a singular focus on project management to an all-encompassing work management system capable of delivering project, work, and resource management capabilities. More than ever, Project Server 2013 requires a carefully planned metadata architecture, which is especially true for leveraging the tool's demand management, lifecycle management, and portfolio management capabilities.

As with a ERP financial system or a CRM customer management tool, you must mold the raw functionality provided in Project Server 2013 to shape and channel information to your organization's specific requirements. Although the built-in generic information streams provide useful tracking and statistical data, the information becomes meaningful only when you seed the database with custom attributes. These attributes exist in Project Server 2013 as custom fields. Do not worry, the term *custom* does not mean you are changing product functionality or need a software developer. As you will see in this module, it is quite simple to create custom fields and Microsoft encourages their use.

Custom fields come in two flavors: enterprise and local. For the most part, you manage enterprise field definitions centrally using the Project Web App interface rather than through Project Pro 2013. Only administrators or portfolio managers specifically granted administrator permissions can modify the field definitions. Project managers can create and modify their own local custom fields for their projects on a project-by-project basis, as well as in project templates and in their local Global.mpt file.

Introducing Departments

Project Server 2010 introduced a new powerful construct to the metadata arena, *Departments*. This construct overcomes a limitation that made it difficult to deploy Project Server with a single instance serving multiple departments with diverse metadata requirements. In previous versions of Project Server, every custom field was visible to every user. This could become particularly annoying when project managers have to enter this information in the *Project Information* dialog where they might have to find their ten departmental fields among a selection of fifty or more. In

Artist:

Mon Tue

Date:

If you are unable to keep your appointment, please [illegible] so you do not lose your dep[illegible]

You can see the [illegible] *Data* section of the P[illegible] plays the *Enterprise Custom Fields and Lookup Tables* page with the default set of custom fields [illegible] Server 2013 shown in Figure 4 - 1.

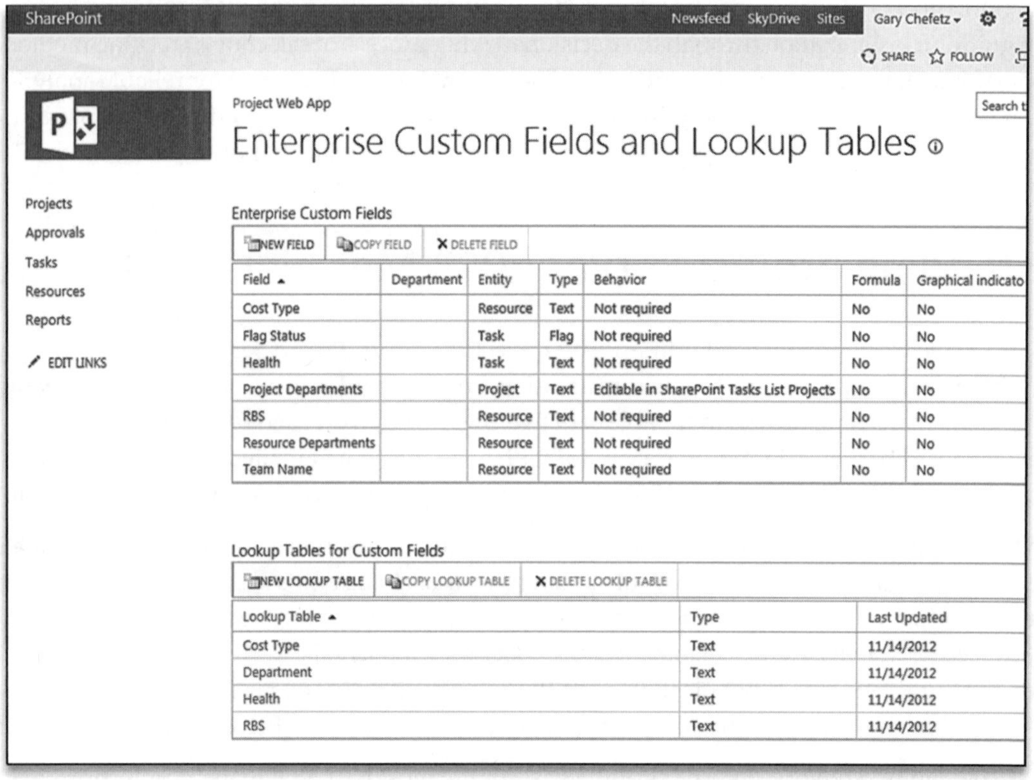

Figure 4 - 1: Enterprise Custom Fields and Lookup Tables page

Notice in the figure that under the *Enterprise Custom Fields* section you find two fields referencing "departments," *Project Departments* and *Resource Departments*. These two built-in custom enterprise fields both use the *Department* lookup table you see in the *Lookup Tables for Custom Fields* section at the bottom of the page. The *Department* lookup table is blank when you install Project Server 2013. Notice also the *Department* column in the *Enterprise Custom Fields* section. If you plan to use this feature, you should consider it first before you create other objects in Project Server 2013 because it applies to important system artifacts including:

- Projects
- Resources
- Enterprise Custom Fields

- Project Types

- Business Drivers

- OLAP Cubes

As you might have surmised by now, your design for the *Department* lookup table determines the granular
filtering capability using *Departments* in Project Server 2013. When you use department attribution, both
prise Resource/User and the Enterprise Object (Project, Custom Field…) must have matching attribution
is not visible in the system. I cover editing the *Department* lookup table later in this module.

Working with Enterprise Custom Fields and Lookup Tab

Enterprise Custom Fields provide the necessary building blocks for making Project Server 2013 data interesting to
your everyday users, as well as management stakeholders. Without metadata attribution, management would have
difficulty accessing relevant project information across a portfolio of projects. Project Web App gives you the opportunity to capture and display this information in views you create and through a plethora of reporting capabilities
leveraging OLAP cubes and Reporting Database data through Excel Services. Metadata brings project information to
life, such as budget and schedule variance. In the *Project Center* view shown in Figure 4 - 2, I include the project *Cost
Status* and project *Schedule Status* custom enterprise project fields to enrich the view. Each of these fields displays a
green, yellow, or red stoplight indicator to show the severity of budget or schedule variance. Using this view, project
stakeholders, and executives can easily determine the variance for each project across the portfolio of projects.

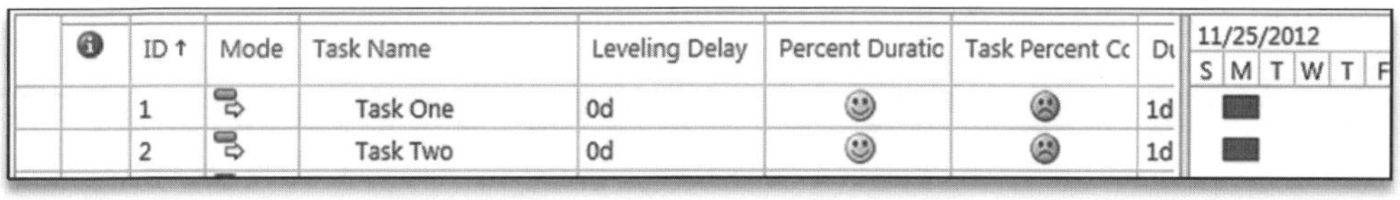

❶	ID ↑	Mode	Task Name	Leveling Delay	Percent Duratic	Task Percent Cc	Dι	11/25/2012					
									S	M	T	W	T	F
		1	⇨	Task One	0d	☺	☹	1d	■					
		2	⇨	Task Two	0d	☺	☹	1d	■					

Figure 4 - 2: Project Detail view

 Information: When initially building your custom field set in Project Server 2013, you work with the *Custom Fields* section of the Requirements and Configuration Specification document deliverable.

Understanding Enterprise Field Types

Project Server 2013 offers six types of custom enterprise fields at the task, resource, and project levels. Earlier versions
of Project Server offered you a limited number of custom fields; however, Project Server 2010 introduced an **unlimited
number** of each of the following field types:

- Enterprise **Cost**

- Enterprise **Date**

- Enterprise **Duration**

- Enterprise **Flag**

- Enterprise **Number**

- Enterprise **Text**

> **Information**: For those of you upgrading from Project Server 2003, Project Server 2013 treats text fields the same way Project Server 2007 and 2010 does, and does not offer outline codes; but offers the same functionality using enterprise fields containing a hierarchical lookup table structure.

Understanding Built-In Fields and Lookup Tables

Project Server 2013 ships with seven built-in fields and four built-in lookup tables. To view the built-in fields and lookup tables, complete the following steps:

1. Log in to Project Web App with administrator permissions.
2. Click the *Gear* icon and select the *PWA Settings* item from the menu.
3. In the *Enterprise Data* section of the *PWA Settings* page, click the *Enterprise Custom Fields and Lookup Tables* link.

The system displays the *Enterprise Custom Fields and Lookup Tables* page shown in Figure 4 - 3. The *Enterprise Custom Fields and Lookup Tables* page consists of two sections. Use the options in the *Enterprise Custom Fields* section to create new enterprise fields, or to copy, edit, or delete an existing field. Use the options in the *Lookup Tables for Custom Fields* section to create a new lookup table, or to copy, edit, or delete an existing lookup table. Project Server 2013 users will find this page largely unchanged since 2007; however, you should note the important addition of the *Behavior* column on this page that replaces the *Required* column in 2007 and indicates one of three possible values: "Not required," "Required," or "Workflow-controlled." When custom fields indicate that they are *Workflow-controlled,* users cannot edit these outside the context of a workflow in the system. Consequently, these appear in *Read-Only* mode in all views except for Project Detail Pages when the system presents custom fields as part of workflow stages. You learn more about workflows in Module 05, *Working with Portfolio and Project Governance.*

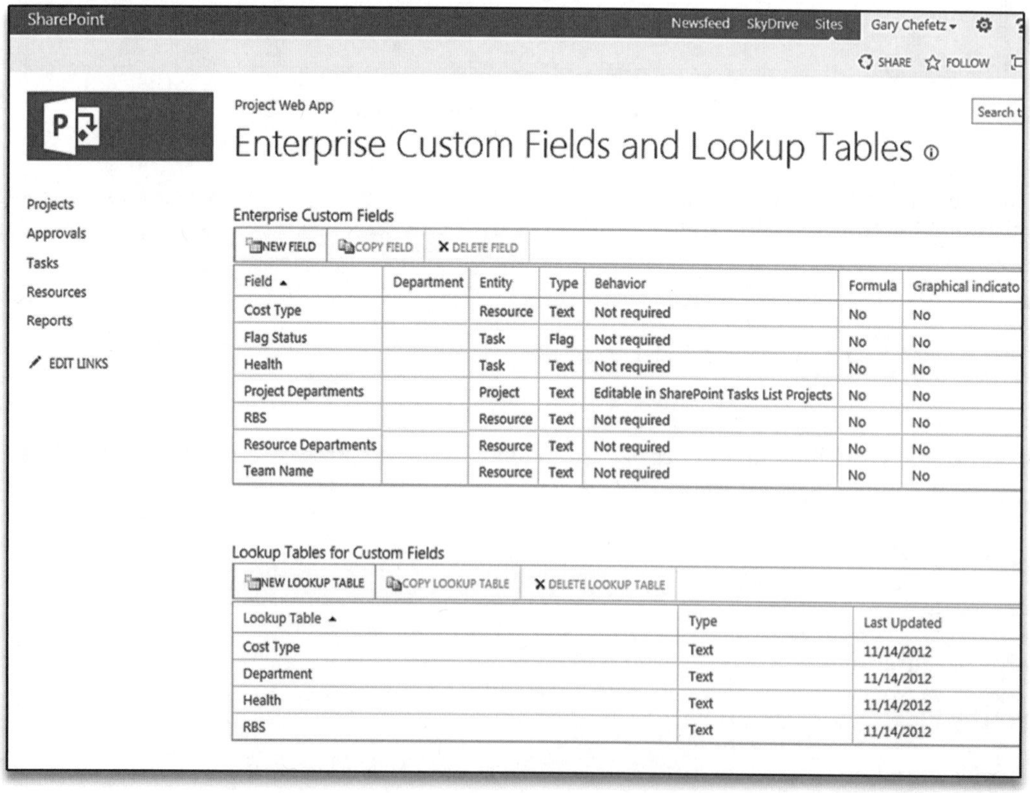

Figure 4 - 3: Custom Fields and Lookup Tables page

Project Server 2013 contains seven built-in custom fields and four built-in lookup tables. Unlike Project Server 2010, Project Server 2013 does not ship with a sample workflow and sample custom fields to support the sample workflow. The built-in enterprise custom fields include:

- The **Cost Type field** is a resource text field containing the **Cost Type lookup table**. The *Cost Type* lookup table contains a single-level code mask, but contains no values in the actual lookup table. You must customize the *Cost Type* lookup table to mold its functionality to your organization's requirements. You can use this field, or any other resource field, to match resources in the Enterprise Resource Pool to roles in Portfolio Analyses in Project Server 2013.

- The **Health field** is a task text field containing the **Health lookup table**. The *Health* lookup table contains a single-level code mask with six values in the actual lookup table. You can use these values "as is" or you may customize them according to your organization's task tracking requirements.

- The **Project Departments field** is a project text field containing the **Departments lookup table**. The *Departments* lookup table contains a single-level code mask, but contains no values in the actual lookup table. You must customize the *Departments* lookup table according to your organization's requirements for filtering the view of enterprise objects by department.

- The **RBS field** is a resource text field containing the **RBS lookup table**. The *RBS* lookup table contains a single-level code mask, but contains no values in the actual lookup table. If you want to use the RBS to define and manage relationship-based Project Server 2013 security, you must customize the *RBS* lookup table to reflect the reporting structure in your organization. Remember that the system deactivates relationship-based security using the RBS in SharePoint permissions mode.

> **Information**: Keep in mind that the RBS **rarely** reflects the exact structure of an organization. Rather, it is a "pseudo organizational chart" that can be anything from representative to nearly literal.

- The **Resource Departments field** is a resource text field containing the **Departments lookup table**. The *Departments* lookup table contains a single-level code mask, but contains no values in the actual lookup table. You must customize the *Departments* lookup table according to your organization's requirements for filtering enterprise objects by department.

- The **Team Name** field is a resource text field that does not contain a lookup table. I recommend that you create a lookup table for this field if you want to use the *Team Name* field to assign a group of resources (a team) to tasks. Obviously, you must customize the lookup table to match the teams available in your organization.

> **Warning**: Project Server 2013 **does not** include an empty lookup table associated with the *Team Name* field. Because the *Edit Custom Field* page defaults to the last lookup table in the list, it is very easy to assign the *RBS* lookup table to this field accidentally if you absentmindedly open and save the *Team Name* field. MSProjectExperts recommends that you immediately create a *Team Names* lookup table and then assign it in the *Team Name* field to avoid this problem. This is a serious vulnerability because the system does not allow you to change the lookup table assigned to a custom field once you apply it, requiring you to delete the custom field instead. Because you cannot delete the built-in custom fields, you must repair the misapplication of an incorrect lookup table directly in the database.

Creating Lookup Tables

Lookup tables are benign in that there is little to them that can cause problems in the system; however, they are the fundamental building blocks of your codified metadata in Project Server. Lookup tables are the stored values that matter most to your metadata architecture; the very language you speak. As a critical input to your ability to derive business intelligence from the system, it is very important that you invest enough time in capturing these requirements during the planning phase and maintain them, as business needs change.

Defining Programs using Metadata

One of the most important uses of metadata is for grouping and filtering in views and reports. You use metadata, such as a Project enterprise custom field with a value list to associate like projects in the database such as for identifying projects that are part of a program.

Creating a Program Lookup Table

The first step in creating the metadata to define my program is to create the lookup table using the following steps:

1. From the *Enterprise Data* section of the *PWA Settings* page, click the *Enterprise Custom Fields and Lookup Tables* link. Scroll to the bottom of the page to reveal the *Lookup Tables for Custom Fields* section shown in Figure 4 - 4.

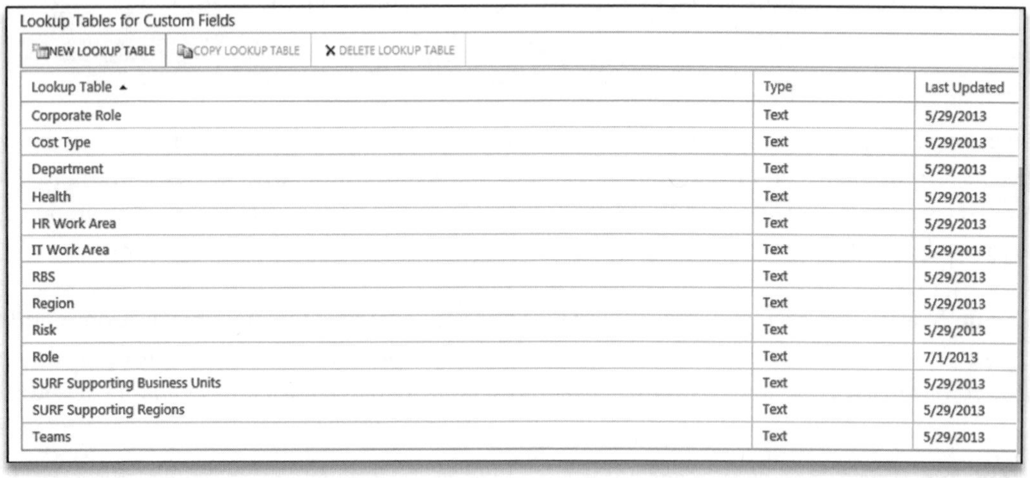

Lookup Table ▲	Type	Last Updated
Corporate Role	Text	5/29/2013
Cost Type	Text	5/29/2013
Department	Text	5/29/2013
Health	Text	5/29/2013
HR Work Area	Text	5/29/2013
IT Work Area	Text	5/29/2013
RBS	Text	5/29/2013
Region	Text	5/29/2013
Risk	Text	5/29/2013
Role	Text	7/1/2013
SURF Supporting Business Units	Text	5/29/2013
SURF Supporting Regions	Text	5/29/2013
Teams	Text	5/29/2013

Figure 4 - 4: Lookup Tables for Custom Fields section

2. Click the *NEW LOOKUP TABLE* button on the toolbar above the grid. The system displays the *New Lookup Table* page shown in Figure 4 - 5.

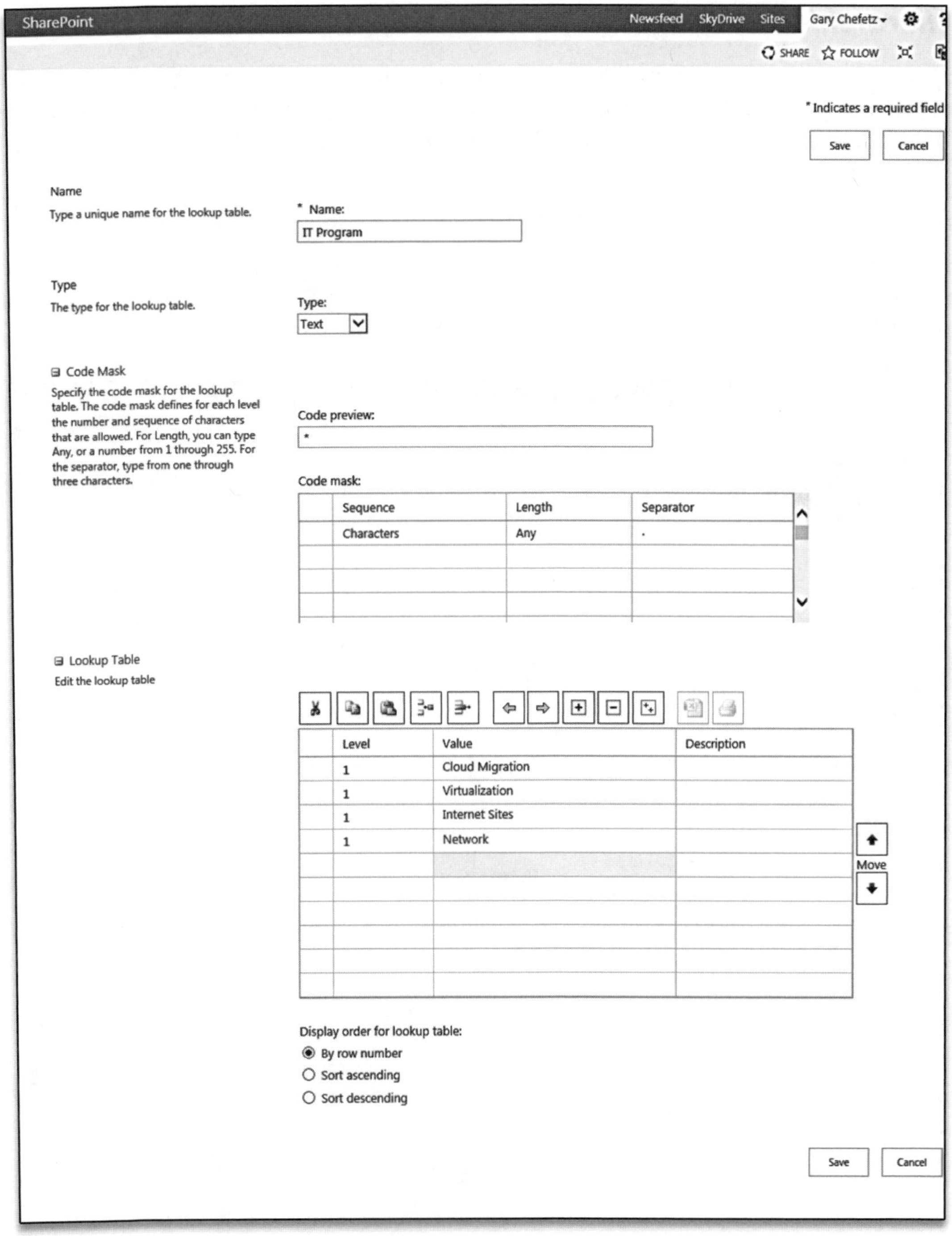

Figure 4 - 5: New Lookup Table page

3. Notice in the figure that I entered the *Programs,* (related projects) for my organization in the *Lookup Table* section. Click the *Save* button (not shown) to save your changes.

Create Hierarchical Lookup Tables

My organization requires several lookup tables and custom fields to meet my reporting needs for tracking tasks, resources, and projects. For example, I need a *Risks* lookup table containing a list of project risk levels (High, Medium, and Low). I need a *Locations* lookup table containing the locations of my company's regional offices in the US and Europe.

To create a new lookup table, complete the following steps from the *Custom Fields and Lookup Tables* page:

1. Click the *NEW LOOKUP TABLE* button. The system displays the *New Lookup table* page shown in Figure 4 - 6. The *New Lookup table* page contains sections in which to enter the *Name* of the lookup table, select the *Type* of lookup table, set up the *Code Mask*, and enter the actual lookup table values.

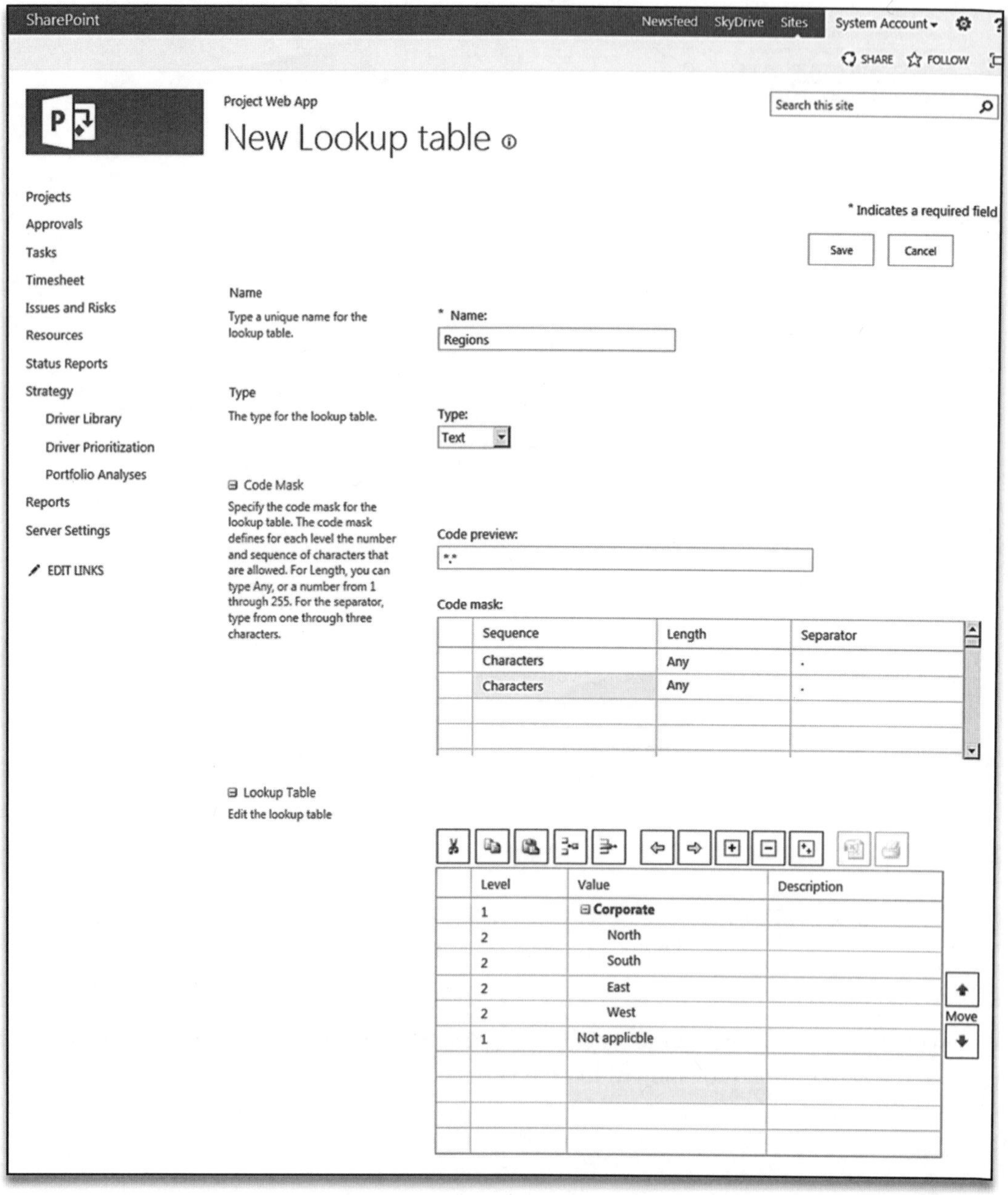

Figure 4 - 6: New Lookup Table page

2. Enter a name for the lookup table in the *Name* field.

3. Click the *Type* pick list and select the type of lookup table you want to create. Project Server 2013 allows you to create five types of lookup tables: *Cost, Date, Duration, Number*, and *Text*. If you select the *Text* option, the system presents the *New Lookup table* page shown previously in Figure 4 - 6 and requires you to supply a code mask for the lookup table. If you select any of the other four types, the system allows you to define a single-level lookup table and displays the *New Lookup table* page shown in Figure 4 - 7 for a blank lookup table.

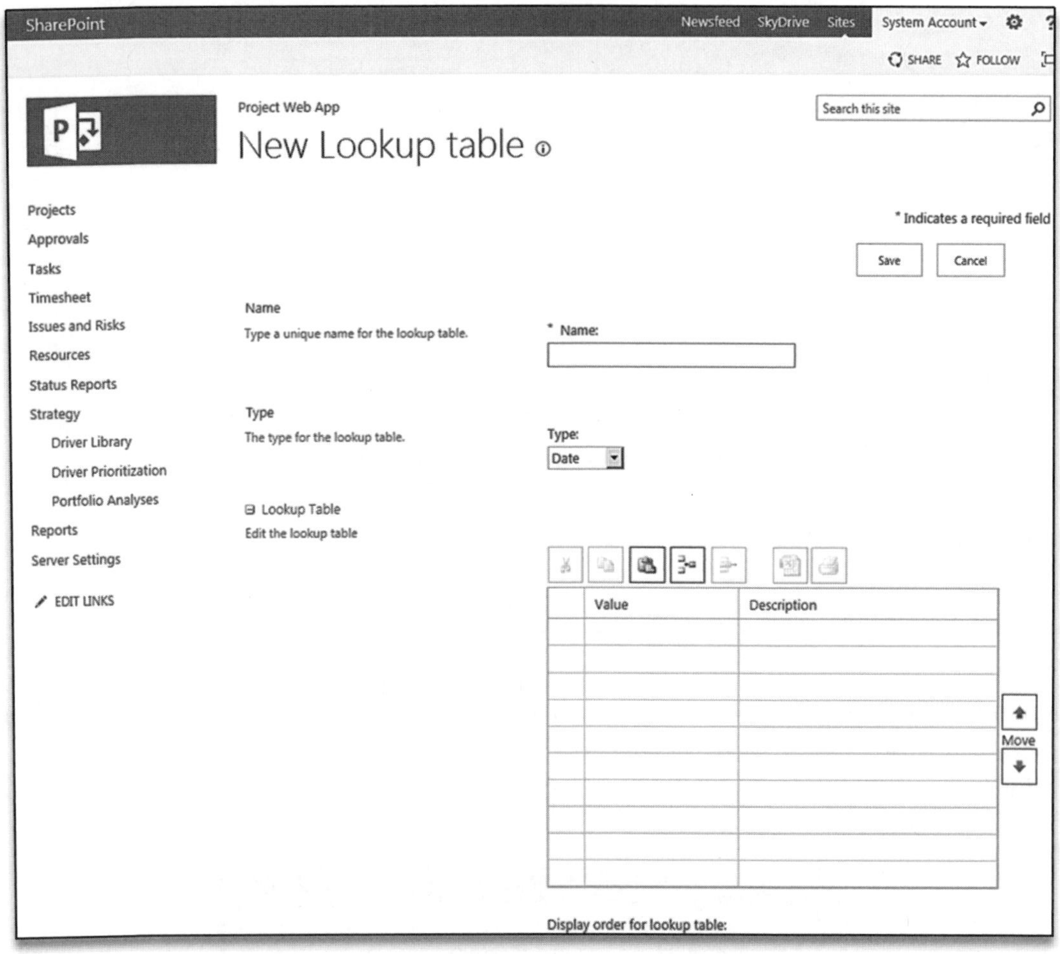

Figure 4 - 7: New Lookup Table page for the Date type

4. If you selected the *Text* type, create the code mask required for the type of lookup table you want to create.

5. Enter data in the *Lookup Table* section of the page and confirm that the lookup table data conforms to the code mask that you specified. Figure 4 - 8 shows the completed definition of the *Regions* lookup table. Notice that I specified a two-level code mask that accepts any type of characters on the first level and any type of characters on the second level. Notice also that my lookup table values conform to the code mask.

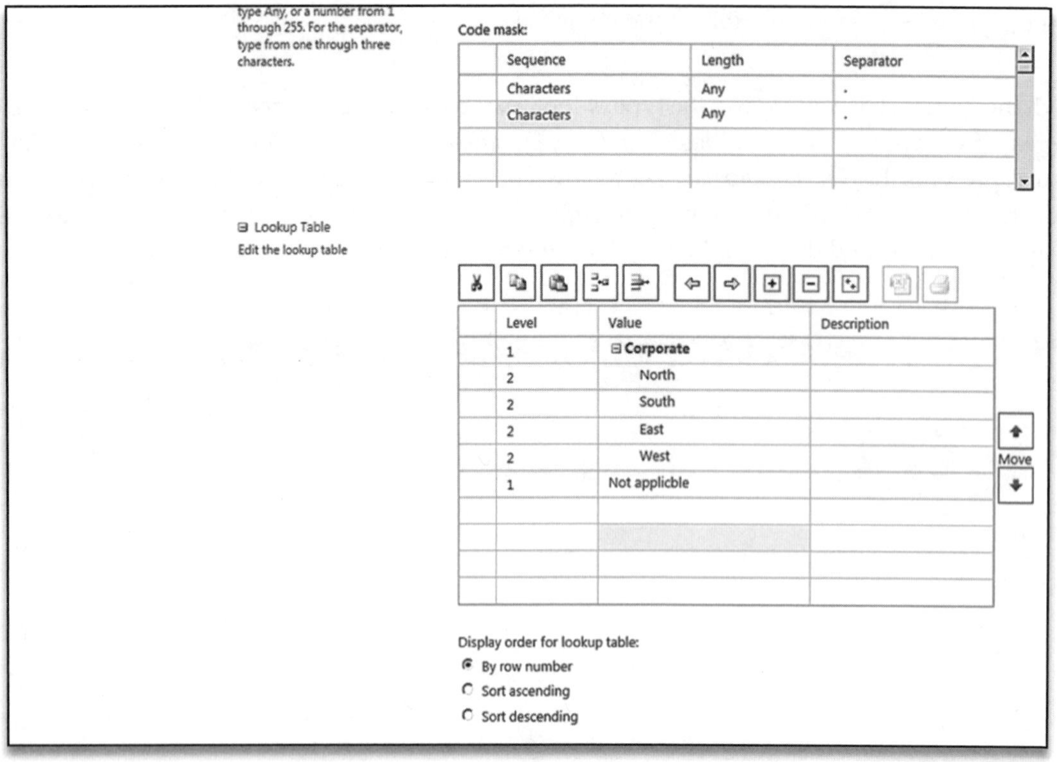

Figure 4 - 8: Locations Lookup Table Definition

6. Select a sort order at the bottom of the *Lookup Table* section, as needed.

7. Click the *Save* button to save your new lookup table.

If you attempt to save the lookup table with an illegal character as a separator in the code mask, the system displays the error message shown in Figure 4 - 9. In this case, the system displayed the warning dialog when I attempted to use a comma character as a separator character in the code mask.

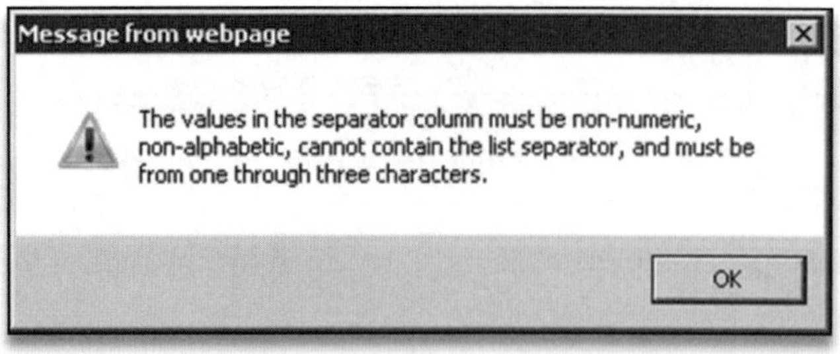

Figure 4 - 9: Warning dialog about illegal separator character

If you do not enter the lookup table values according to your specified code mask, the system presents an error message in red text at the top of the page as shown in Figure 4 - 10. The system does not allow you to save the lookup table until you correct the errors.

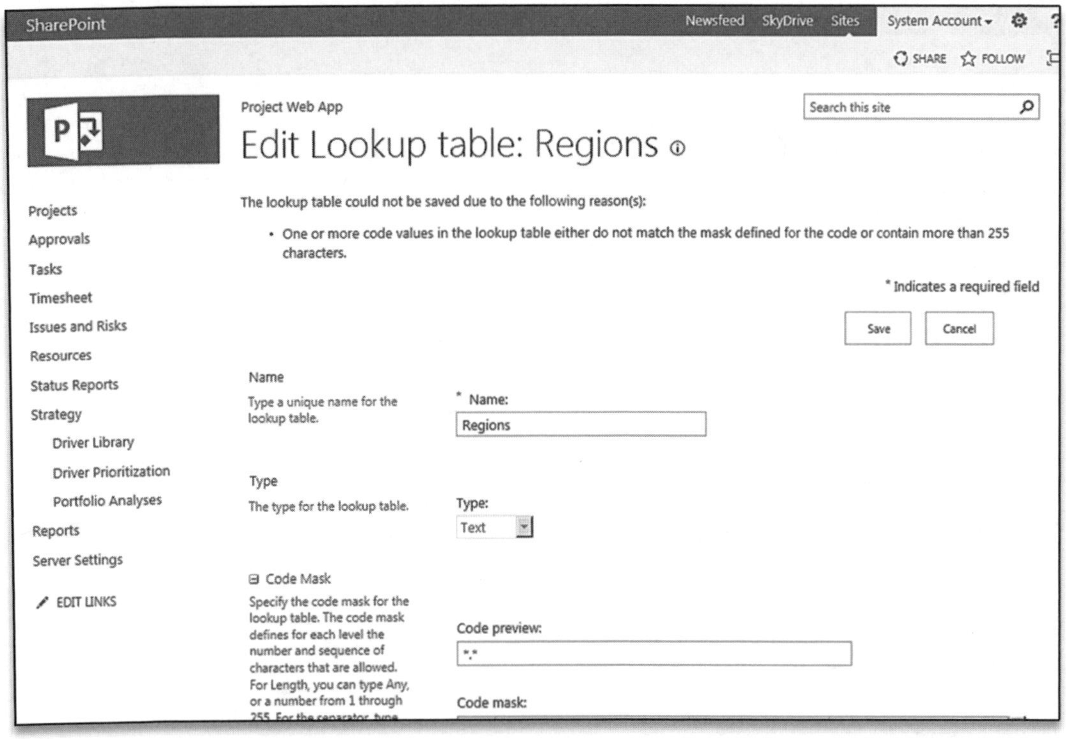
SharePoint
Newsfeed
SkyDrive
Sites
System Account
SHARE
FOLLOW
Project Web App
Edit Lookup table: Regions
Search this site
Projects
Approvals
Tasks
Timesheet
Issues and Risks
Resources
Status Reports
Strategy
Driver Library
Driver Prioritization
Portfolio Analyses
Reports
Server Settings
EDIT LINKS
The lookup table could not be saved due to the following reason(s):
One or more code values in the lookup table either do not match the mask defined for the code or contain more than 255 characters.
* Indicates a required field
Save
Cancel
Name
Type a unique name for the lookup table.
* Name:
Regions
Type
The type for the lookup table.
Type:
Text
Code Mask
Specify the code mask for the lookup table. The code mask defines for each level the number and sequence of characters that are allowed. For Length, you can type Any, or a number from 1 through
Code preview:
Code mask:

Figure 4 - 10: Lookup Table values do not conform to the code mask

Modifying Built-In Lookup Tables

As I noted earlier in this module, Project Server 2013 includes four built-in lookup tables: *Cost Type, Department, Health,* and *RBS.* If you need to use *Cost Type, Department,* or *RBS* built-in lookup tables, you must enter the lookup table values. If you intend to use department filtering, I recommend that you begin the process of working with custom fields and lookup tables by determining and modifying the values in the *Department* lookup table, as many of the enterprise custom fields you create require this attribution. Although you can always go back and edit your enterprise custom fields to add the *Department* value later, you save a lot of time by enabling yourself to complete your definitions during field creation. To modify any of the built-in lookup tables, complete the following steps:

1. Navigate to the *Enterprise Custom Fields and Lookup Tables* page in Project Web App.

2. In the *Lookup Tables for Custom Fields* section on the bottom half of the page, click the name of the lookup table you want to edit. The system displays the *Edit Lookup Table* page for the selected lookup table. For example, Figure 4 - 11 shows the *Edit Lookup Table* page for the *Department* lookup table.

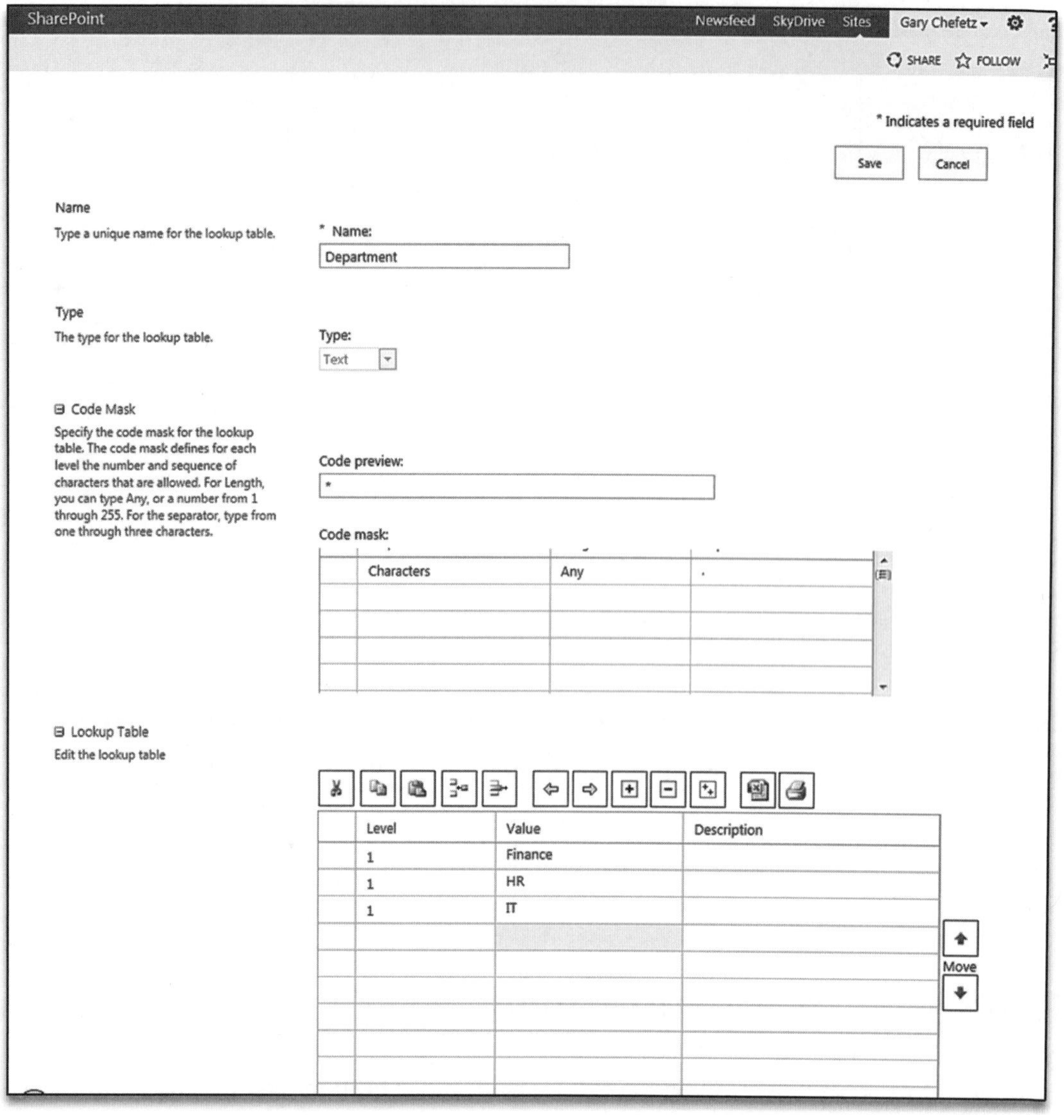

Figure 4 - 11: Edit Lookup Table page for Department lookup table

3. Edit the *Code Mask* as needed using the tools and information listed in the following bulleted list:

- To create a code mask you must supply values for each level in the *Sequence, Length,* and *Separator* columns. Project Server 2013 defaults to a single-level code mask that uses characters of any length with the period character as the separator in the code mask. You may edit this first level and add additional levels, as needed.

- To create a new level in the code mask, click the first blank line in the *Sequence* column, click the pick list button, and select the type of data for the outline code segment. You may select *Numbers, Uppercase Letters, Lowercase Letters,* or *Characters.* When you select any of these, the values for each code segment must adhere to the type of data specified. Selecting the *Characters* item gives you the most flexibility, as you may use any character in defining your values. Use one of the other selections to reflect non-flexible formalized values in your enterprise.

- Click in the *Length* column on the selected line and enter the length for the code segment. The default choice allows any length, but you can delete this choice and enter a number representing the maximum number of characters allowed, up to a maximum of 255 characters.

- Click in the *Separator* column on the selected line and enter the character used as the separator between code segments. You can use up to three characters as the separator, including characters like the period (the default option), a dash, a plus sign, or a forward slash. You can also use other non-numeric and non-alphabetic characters, such as those found above the number keys on a keyboard.

> **Information**: In the *Lookup Table* section of the page, you can use any of the buttons at the top of the section to modify the data you enter. For example, use the *Indent* and *Outdent* buttons to structure the lookup table entries to match your code mask.

> **Information**: You can use the *Paste* button to paste values into the lookup table from another application, such as Microsoft Word or Excel.

- You enter the values in the *Lookup Table* section according to the structure you build in the code mask. If you need only a "flat file" list of values, you can use the single-level code mask included by default in each built-in lookup table. If you want a hierarchical lookup table, however, you must add additional lines to the code mask.
- Project Server 2013 defaults the *Department* field to a single-level code mask that uses characters of any length with the period character as the separator in the code mask. You may edit this first level and add additional levels, as needed. To create a new level in the code mask, click the first blank line in the *Sequence* column, click the pick list button, and select the type of data for the outline code segment. You may select *Numbers, Uppercase Letters, Lowercase Letters*, or *Characters*. When you select any of these, the values for each code segment must adhere to the type of data specified. Selecting the *Characters* item gives you the most flexibility, as you may use any character in defining your values. Use one of the other selections to reflect non-flexible formalized values in your enterprise.
- Click in the *Length* column on the selected line and enter the length for the code segment. The default choice allows any length, but you can delete this choice and enter a number representing the maximum number of characters allowed, up to a maximum of 255 characters.
- Click in the *Separator* column on the selected line and enter the character used as the separator between code segments. You can use up to three characters as the separator, including characters like the period (the default option), a dash, a plus sign, or a forward slash. You can also use other non-numeric and non-alphabetic characters, such as those found above the number keys on your keyboard.

4. Edit the existing values in the *Lookup Table* section or add new values, as needed.

5. Add optional information in the *Description* field for each of the lookup table values.

When you select an existing value in the *Lookup Table* section, the system activates the toolbar at the top of the *Lookup Table* section, as shown in Figure 4 - 12. The first three buttons on the toolbar are the standard *Cut, Copy*, and *Paste* buttons found in Microsoft Office products. Use the *Insert Row* and *Delete Row* buttons to add a new row between two existing rows or to delete an existing row. Use the *Indent* and *Outdent* buttons to control the level of indenture for any row of information in the lookup table and to build a hierarchical structure. Use the *Expand, Collapse*, and *Expand All* buttons to expand or collapse a hierarchical lookup table. Use the *Export to Excel* and *Print* buttons to export the data to Excel or to print the data on paper.

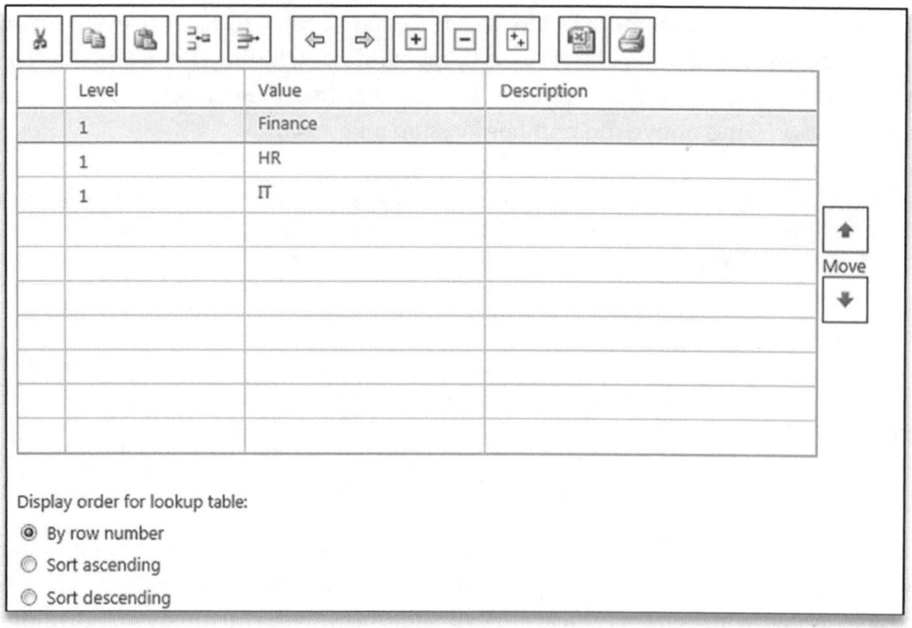

Figure 4 - 12: Lookup Table toolbar

6. To export the lookup table data to Excel, click the *Export to Excel* button. The system displays the *File Download* dialog shown in Figure 4 - 13.

Figure 4 - 13: File Download dialog for export to Excel

7. Click the *Open* button to continue the export process or click the *Save* button to save the lookup table data as an Excel workbook file to your default download location. If you click the *Open* button, the system displays the Excel warning dialog shown in Figure 4 - 14.

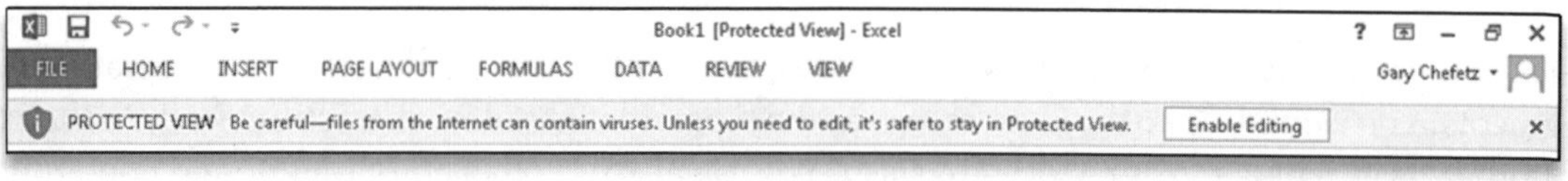

Figure 4 - 14: Microsoft Office Excel warning dialog

8. Click the *Yes* button in the dialog to continue the process of exporting the lookup table data to Excel. When finished, the system displays the exported lookup table data in an Excel workbook. For example, Figure 4 - 15 shows the exported data in Excel for my new *Departments* lookup table.

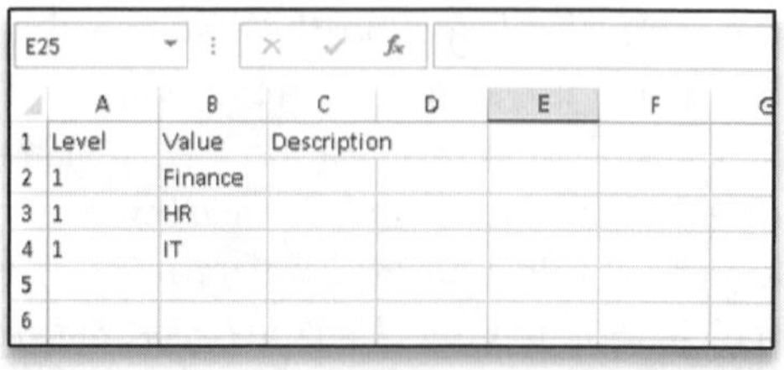

Figure 4 - 15: Lookup Table exported to an Excel workbook

Information: In order to use the *Export to Excel* feature, you must first save your lookup table changes. It is generally a good idea to do this in a reasonable amount of time; otherwise, you risk losing your security context for the page.

9. To print the lookup table, click the *Print* button in the *Lookup Table* section of the *Edit Lookup Table* page. The system displays the lookup table data as a web page in Internet Explorer as shown in Figure 4 - 16. To print the lookup table data, you must use Internet Explorer's print functionality.

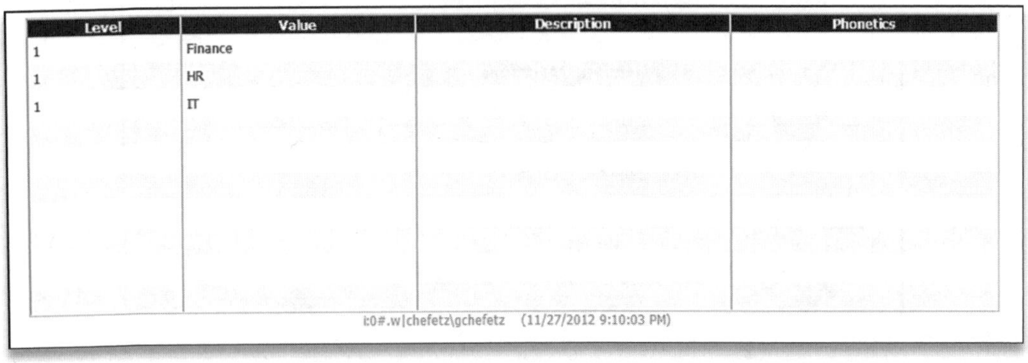

Level	Value	Description	Phonetics
1	Finance		
1	HR		
1	IT		

i:0#.w|chefetz\gchefetz (11/27/2012 9:10:03 PM)

Figure 4 - 16: Print Preview page displays Lookup Table data

To complete the process of editing the *Lookup Table*, continue with the following final steps:

10. Change the sorting order of the values in the lookup table as needed. Project Server 2013 allows you to sort the data in the lookup table in three ways: by row number, ascending order, and descending order. The system offers you these three sort options at the bottom of the lookup table list. If you select the *By row number* option, the system retains the order in which you entered the values in the lookup table. Use this option when you need to display the lookup table in a specific order that is neither ascending nor descending. When you select the *Sort ascending* option, the system sorts the lookup table list in ascending order (A-Z and 0-9). When you select the *Sort descending* option, the system sorts the lookup table list in descending order (Z-A and 9-0).

11. Click the *Save* button to save your changes to the selected built-in lookup table.

Modifying the RBS Lookup Table

You use the *RBS* field to control Project Server 2013 security by defining a pseudo-org chart for your organization. Refer *Implementing and Administering Microsoft Project Server 2013* for other RBS design decisions you must tackle while creating your Requirements and Configuration Specification deliverable. You should populate your *RBS* lookup table before importing your resource pool so that you are able to attribute resources correctly after loading them.

Like assigning each resource a place in an org chart, the *RBS* field shows Project Server 2013 "who reports to whom." You can control a manager's ability to see project and resource data through subordination in the *RBS* field. These resource-reporting constructs drive very powerful Project Server 2013 relationship-based security features.

When you open the *RBS* lookup table for editing, you find a single-level code mask with no values in the lookup table. Because the *RBS* lookup table is a blank slate by default, it is your responsibility to design and configure it specifically for your organization. Keep in mind that lookup table values can be hierarchical, which is exactly what you need for this purpose.

Based on your requirements, you should create an *RBS* lookup table that reflects your organization's management reporting structure. For example, an organization that uses Project Server 2013 only in the IS department may have a very simple reporting structure within IS. Based on that reporting structure, I created a 4-level code mask and populated the *RBS* lookup table shown in Figure 4 - 17.

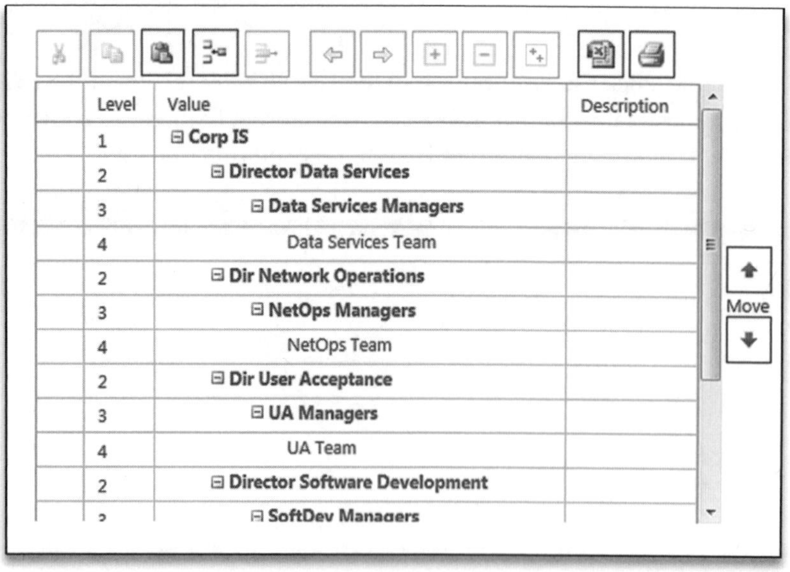

Figure 4 - 17: Sample RBS Lookup Table structure

You can configure the Project Server security environment as follows:

- Place company executives and Project Server administrators at the *Corporate IS* level where they can view resource information for all resources in the system because all of the resources fall below them in the RBS structure.
- Place directors and their peers, such as their admins, at their respective *Director* levels in the tree structure. Senior managers at this level can see only those resources below them in their branch of the RBS structure. For example, the Director of Data Services sees only those resources at the *Manager* and *Team Member* levels of the Data Services branch.
- Place project managers and resource managers at the *Manager* level of the appropriate branch of the RBS structure. For example, place the project managers for the Software Development team at the *Manager* level of the Software Development branch. The Software Development project managers see only those resources at the *Team Member* level of the Software Development branch.
- Place team members at the *Team Member* level of the branch to which they belong.

Information: Depending on how you set up security categories, you can configure Project Server 2013 so that people can see other people at the same level of the *RBS* lookup table. This means that senior managers at the *Database* level can see all resources below them in their branch, plus all other senior managers at the *Database* level.

Warning: Be very careful about the placement of project managers in your organization's RBS. You must place any project manager who manages cross-functional project teams at a high level in the RBS to access resources across the organization. Using the previous example, if a project manager must manage projects that include members of all four departmental teams, you must place the project manager at the *Corporate IS* level of the RBS to gain access to the resources for all four teams.

Your RBS complexity follows your deployment scope. If you are deploying a single implementation across many departments, and each department distributes resource maintenance to its managers, your RBS structure may have many top-level branches with many descending levels. On the other hand, if your installation is for a single department, and only one person is responsible for handling resource data, then you may not need to use the *RBS* field at all, or you may need to use it for reporting only. Assessing the value of the RBS to your organization is an important system design decision. You should fully understand the Project Server security model to make these decisions.

Creating Custom Fields

After you edit the built-in lookup tables and create custom lookup tables for the fields you want to create with value lists, you are ready to create custom enterprise fields. Organizations typically need custom fields to track unique information about projects, resources, and tasks in projects. You can create all types of custom enterprise project, resource, and task fields, including the following:

- Free entry fields that allow the user to manually enter any value
- Fields that require the user to select a value from a lookup table of allowable values
- Fields that contain a formula that automatically calculates a value using data in other fields
- Fields that display graphical indicators instead of data

I discuss how to create all of these types of fields in the succeeding sections of this module. Project Server 2013 allows you to create custom enterprise fields in two locations:

- You can create custom enterprise project, resource, and task fields using Project Web App.
- You can use Project Pro 2013 to create only task and resource fields, which you can then import into Project Server 2013.

Using the Project Web App interface, I show you how to create free entry fields and fields that contain a lookup table. Using the Project Pro 2013 interface, I show you how to create fields that contain a formula and/or display graphical indicators instead of data.

Creating Free Entry Custom Fields

Use a free entry custom field to allow users to enter any value in the field, as defined by the field type. This means that the system allows a user to enter any alphanumeric data in a text field, but restricts the user to entering numeric cost data in a cost field. My organization needs a custom enterprise task text field into which users can type an optional billing number for each task. To create this task text field, complete the following steps from the *Enterprise Custom Fields and Lookup Tables* page:

1. Click the *New Field* button. Project Server 2013 displays the *New Custom Field* page shown in Figure 4 - 18.

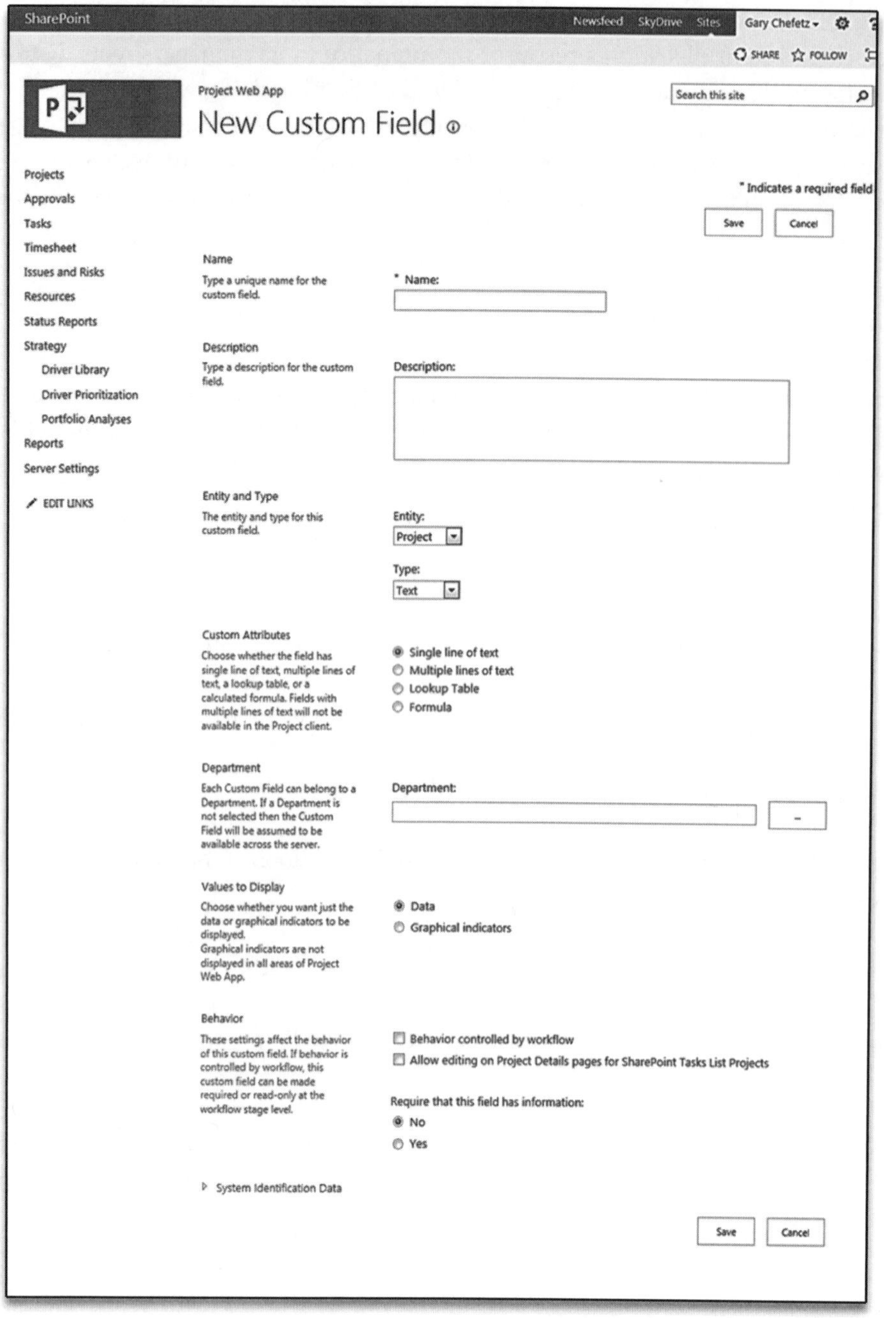
SharePoint
Newsfeed
SkyDrive
Sites
Gary Chefetz
SHARE
FOLLOW
Project Web App
New Custom Field
Search this site
Projects
Approvals
Tasks
Timesheet
Issues and Risks
Resources
Status Reports
Strategy
Driver Library
Driver Prioritization
Portfolio Analyses
Reports
Server Settings
EDIT LINKS
* Indicates a required field
Save
Cancel
Name
Type a unique name for the custom field.
* Name:
Description
Type a description for the custom field.
Description:
Entity and Type
The entity and type for this custom field.
Entity:
Project
Type:
Text
Custom Attributes
Choose whether the field has single line of text, multiple lines of text, a lookup table, or a calculated formula. Fields with multiple lines of text will not be available in the Project client.
Single line of text
Multiple lines of text
Lookup Table
Formula
Department
Each Custom Field can belong to a Department. If a Department is not selected then the Custom Field will be assumed to be available across the server.
Department:
Values to Display
Choose whether you want just the data or graphical indicators to be displayed.
Graphical indicators are not displayed in all areas of Project Web App.
Data
Graphical indicators
Behavior
These settings affect the behavior of this custom field. If behavior is controlled by workflow, this custom field can be made required or read-only at the workflow stage level.
Behavior controlled by workflow
Allow editing on Project Details pages for SharePoint Tasks List Projects
Require that this field has information:
No
Yes
System Identification Data
Save
Cancel

Figure 4 - 18: New Custom Field page

2. Enter a name for the new custom field, such as *Billing Entity*, in the *Name* field and enter an optional description in the *Description* field.

3. Click the *Entity* pick list and select the *Task* entity from the pick list. When you select the *Task* entity (or the *Resource* entity), Project Server 2013 displays the *Edit Custom Field* page, which includes two additional sections, as shown in Figure 4 - 19. The *Calculation for Summary Rows* section contains options used with a formula. If you do not include a formula in the field, the system allows only the *None* option in this section. The *Calculation for Assignment Rows* section offers options that determine whether the system displays editable information for task assignments on the *Tasks* page.

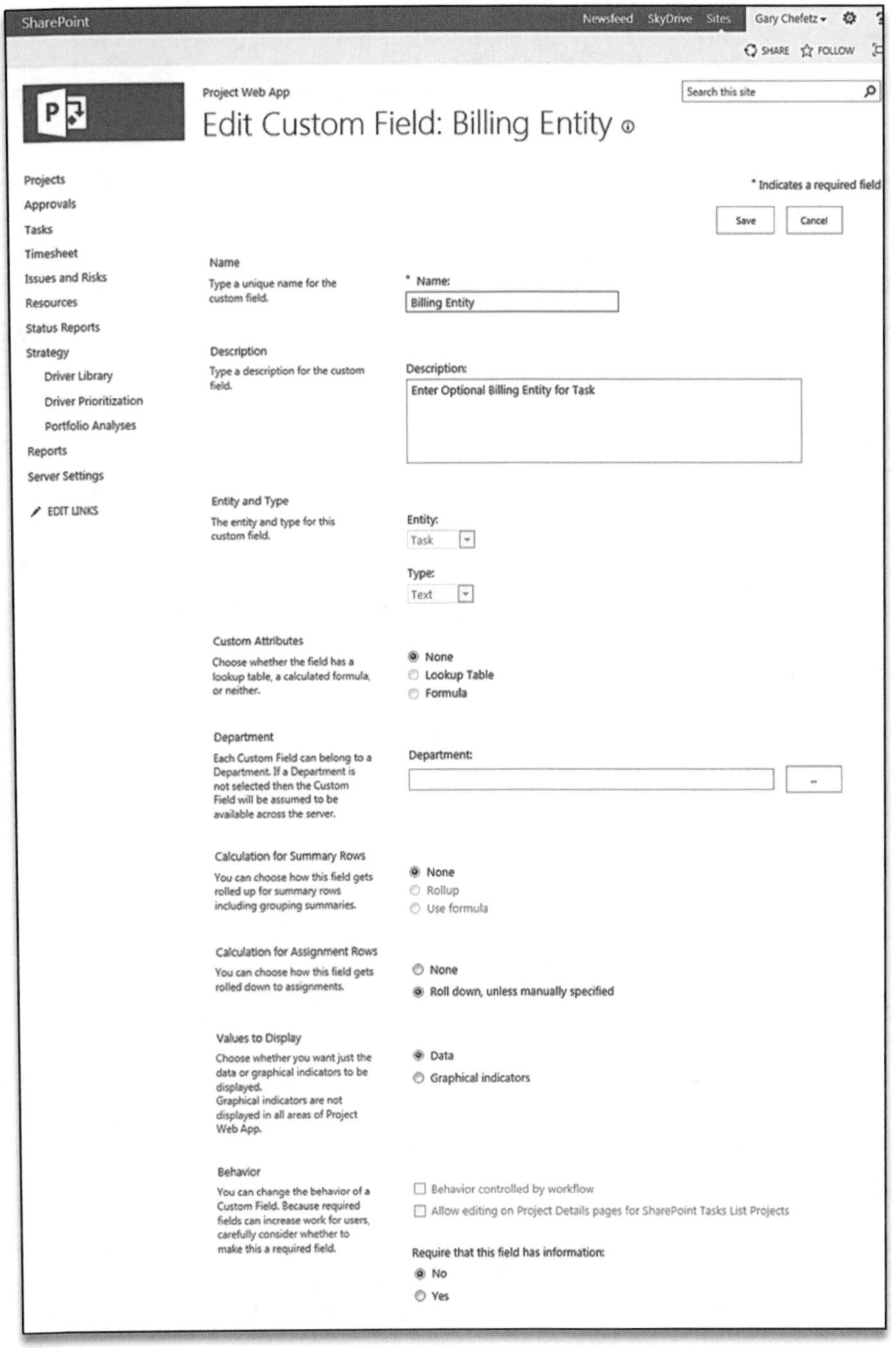
SharePoint
Newsfeed SkyDrive Sites
Gary Chefetz
SHARE FOLLOW
Search this site
Project Web App
Edit Custom Field: Billing Entity
Projects
Approvals
Tasks
Timesheet
Issues and Risks
Resources
Status Reports
Strategy
Driver Library
Driver Prioritization
Portfolio Analyses
Reports
Server Settings
EDIT LINKS
* Indicates a required field
Save
Cancel
Name
Type a unique name for the custom field.
* Name:
Billing Entity
Description
Type a description for the custom field.
Description:
Enter Optional Billing Entity for Task
Entity and Type
The entity and type for this custom field.
Entity:
Task
Type:
Text
Custom Attributes
Choose whether the field has a lookup table, a calculated formula, or neither.
None
Lookup Table
Formula
Department
Each Custom Field can belong to a Department. If a Department is not selected then the Custom Field will be assumed to be available across the server.
Department:
Calculation for Summary Rows
You can choose how this field gets rolled up for summary rows including grouping summaries.
None
Rollup
Use formula
Calculation for Assignment Rows
You can choose how this field gets rolled down to assignments.
None
Roll down, unless manually specified
Values to Display
Choose whether you want just the data or graphical indicators to be displayed.
Graphical indicators are not displayed in all areas of Project Web App.
Data
Graphical indicators
Behavior
You can change the behavior of a Custom Field. Because required fields can increase work for users, carefully consider whether to make this a required field.
Behavior controlled by workflow
Allow editing on Project Details pages for SharePoint Tasks List Projects
Require that this field has information:
No
Yes

Figure 4 - 19: Edit Custom Field page

4. Click the *Type* pick list and select the *Text* type from the pick list.

> **Information**: For custom enterprise project, resource, and task fields, Project Server 2013 allows you to create *Cost, Date, Duration, Flag, Number*, and *Text* fields.

5. In the *Custom Attributes* section, select the *None* option.

Information: When you create a new custom enterprise project text field, the system offers two special options in the *Custom Attributes* section. Select the *Single Line of Text* option to limit users to entering only a single line of text in the field. Select the *Multiple Lines of Text* option to allow users to enter two or more lines of text in the field.

6. If you want to control user visibility for this field using the Department filter, click the Department (...) button to the right of the Department field and select the Department(s) that you want to see this field.

Information: If you do not select a value in the Department field, all users in your Project Server 2013 system can see the field.

7. In the *Calculation for Assignment Rows* section, select one of the available options.

Warning: If you intend to include a custom enterprise *Task* field in the *Tasks* page and need to allow users to enter a value in the field, you must select the *Roll down, unless manually specified* option in the *Calculation for Assignment Rows* section. For a free entry field, this allows users to type a value in the field manually. For a field containing a lookup table, this allows users to select a value from the list of values in the lookup table. This also makes the data available in assignment views such as the *Resource Usage* and *Task Usage* views.

8. In the *Values to Display* section, select the *Data* option.
9. In the *Behavior* section, select the *Yes* option to require the user to enter a value in the field. Select the *No* option if you want to make data entry optional in the field.
10. When you finish, click the *Save* button to save the new custom field.

Working with Behavior Options

Project Server 2010 introduced yet another option in the *Behavior* section of the *New Custom Field* page. The top option is *Behavior controlled by workflow* followed by a new option *Allow editing on Project Detail pages for SharePoint Task List Projects.* The latter means quite literally, what it says. When you select this new option, you allow users to edit the field in a Project Detail Page assigned to the SharePoint List enterprise project type. When you select the *Behavior controlled by workflow* option, the field's appearance depends on the existence of a workflow.

Making Fields Required

There are actually two ways to make fields required: (1) make it a required field on a PDP displayed under a workflow by selecting the *Behavior controlled by workflow* option, or (2) set the *Require that this field has information* option to *Yes*.

When you select the *Yes* option in the *Behavior controlled by workflow* section for a custom enterprise field, this allows you to define when the field will be required. For example, if you are creating a brand new project, you may not yet know the data to fill in to your custom fields. You can design a workflow that decides the appropriate time to make a field required. If you select the *Require that this field has information* option, you should understand that required field's impact users in the following manner:

- For a required enterprise project field, project managers must enter or select a value in the field before they can save a new project to the Project Server database.
- When you define a required enterprise task field, project managers must enter or select a value for **every task** in the project before they can save the project.

- For a required enterprise resource field, your Resource Pool administrators must enter or select a value for **every resource** before they can save the resource in the Enterprise Resource Pool.

> **Warning**: If you plan to use Active Directory synchronization to help maintain your resource pool, using required resource fields can prevent the synchronization job from completing successfully, as you cannot map these values from AD using the built-in functionality provided in the system.

If users fail to enter a value in any required field, the system warns them in a dialog and then documents the error in the required field. For example, Figure 4 - 20 shows the warning dialog the system displays when I fail to enter a value in a required project field before saving a new enterprise project. Before the system allows me to save my project, I must select a value for this project.

Microsoft Project
Project cannot save the project to Project Server.
You must first specify values for all required project fields. These fields are indicated with an asterisk in the Project Information dialog box, available from the Project tab.
OK

Figure 4 - 20: Required field dialog

> **Using Required Fields**
>
> You must give careful thought to your organization's use of required fields. For example, it must be reasonable to expect that users have a value for a required field when they encounter them. You must also anticipate exceptions to validated values when opting to use them. In the case of required resource fields for instance, you must consider whether you have applicable values for *Generic, Material*, and *Cost* resources, if your configuration includes them. For example, a required *Regional Office* field does not make sense for a *Generic* resource unless you are creating a geographically specific generic resource. In this case, providing an "NA" value in the lookup table may suffice.

Creating a Custom Field with a Lookup Table

After creating and saving the *IT Program* lookup table earlier, I must create the *IT Program* field and apply the new *IT Program* lookup table. To create a new field, navigate to the *Enterprise Custom Fields and Lookup Tables* page and click the *New Field* button at the top of the data grid. The system opens the *New Custom Field* page shown in Figure 4 - 21.

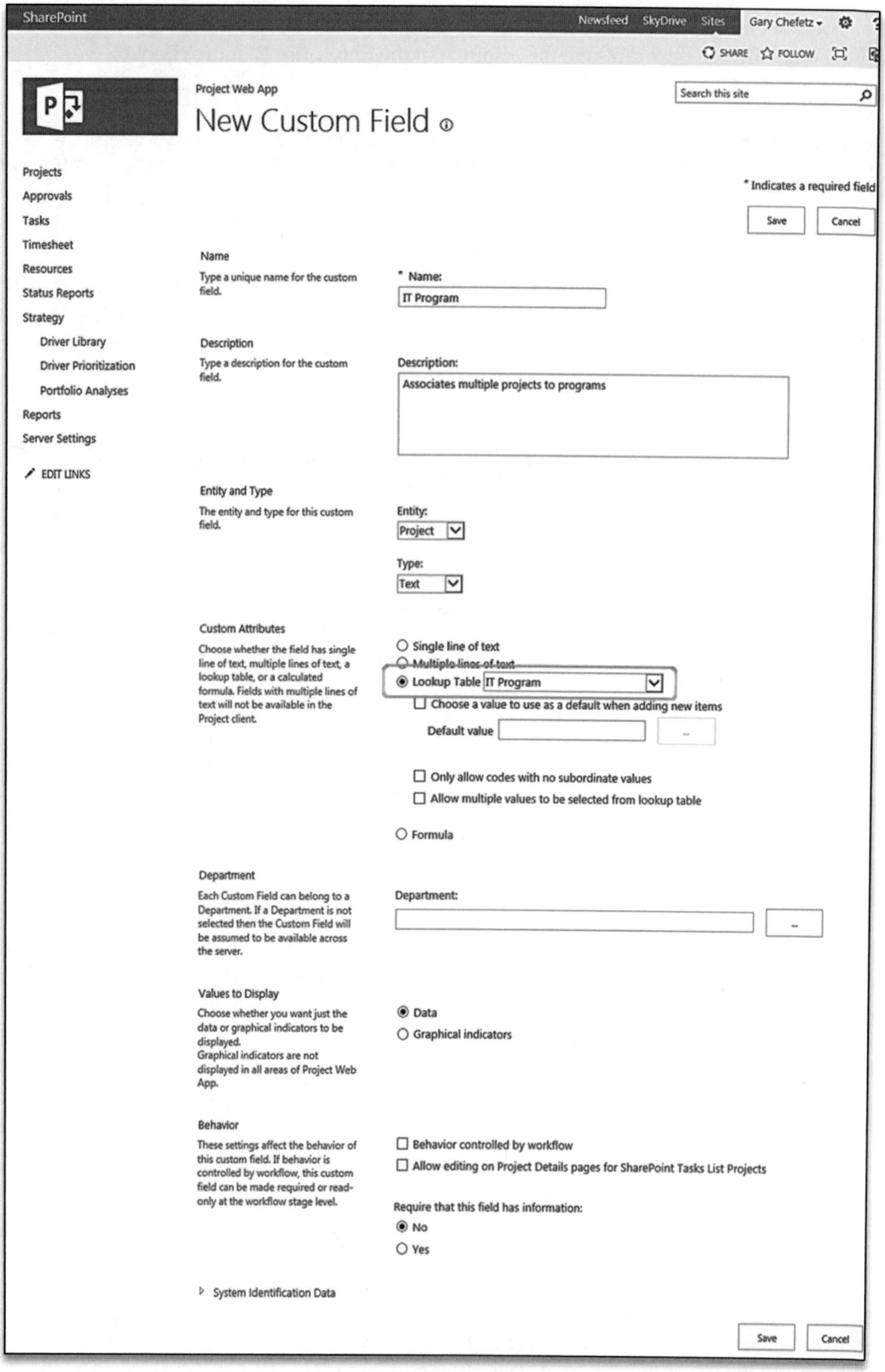

Figure 4 - 21: New Custom Field page for IT Program field

Notice in the figure that I selected the new *IT Program* lookup table I created in the last step, and assigned it to the *IT Program* enterprise custom field as highlighted in the image. Click the *Save* button to save your changes.

Creating Custom Fields sharing Lookup Tables

Custom fields can share lookup tables. For example, our organization needs to identify projects by their regional focus, and employees by the regional office where they work. Although you need to create one enterprise custom resource field to satisfy the latter need, you must create a separate enterprise custom project field for the former requirement. In this case, they can both use the same lookup table.

The first step is to create a custom enterprise project field containing the *Regions* lookup table. Using the lookup table in this field, users must select the Regional Office where they are performing the project. Next, create the enterprise custom resource field that also contains the *Regions* lookup table. To create a custom project field using the *Regions* lookup table, complete the following steps from the *Custom Fields and Lookup Tables* page:

1. Click the *New Field* button. Project Server 2013 displays the *New Custom Field* page shown previously in Figure 4 - 18.

2. Enter "Region Office" for your new custom field, in the *Name* field.

3. Click the *Entity* pick list and select the *Project* entity from the pick list.

4. Click the *Type* pick list and select the *Text* type.

5. In the *Custom Attributes* section, select the *Lookup Table* option and then select the *Regions* lookup table from the *Lookup Table* pick list. The system expands the *Custom Attributes* section to include lookup table information as shown in Figure 4 - 22.

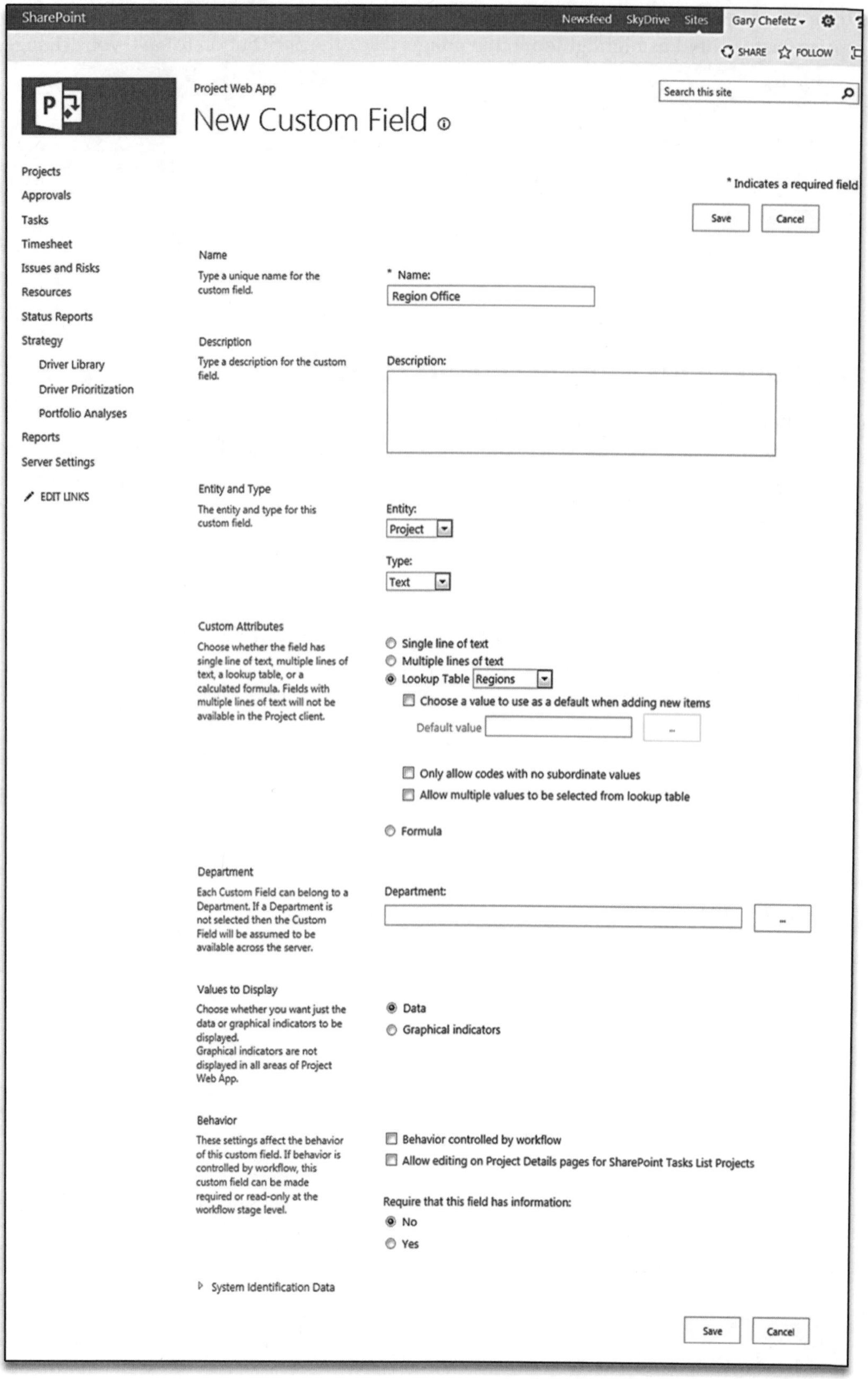

Figure 4 - 22: Custom Attributes section with Lookup Table options

Optionally, the *Custom Attributes* section allows you to set three additional attributes for the lookup table you select. Use these options as follows:

- Select the *Choose a value to use as a default when adding new items* option to specify the default value for the field. When you select this option, you must click the *Select Value* (...) button to the right of the *Default value* field and then pick a value from the lookup table, as shown in Figure 4 - 23.

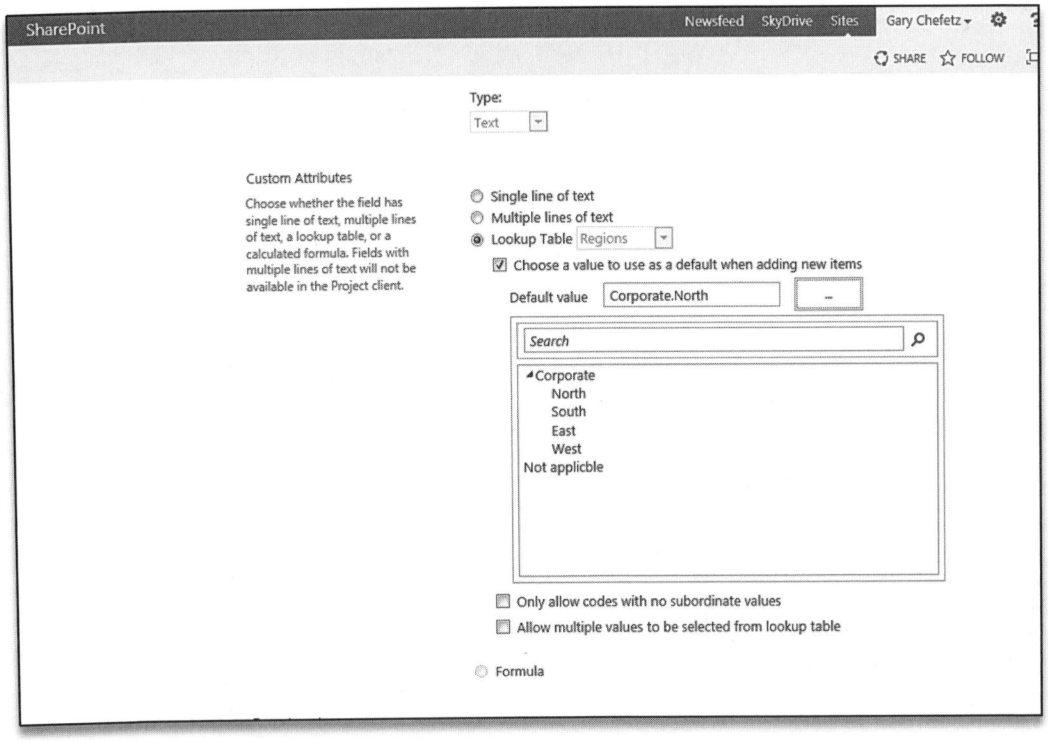

Figure 4 - 23: Select a Default value for the Office Location field

> **Information**: If you enter descriptions for your field values, the system displays the *Description* field information for each value in the lookup table.

- Select the *Only allow codes with no subordinate values* option to require users to select a value at the lowest level of the lookup table. If you select this option for the *Regions* field, the system allows users to select the values below the *Corporate* selection; however it does not allow them to select the *Corporate* value because it has subordinate values.

- Select the *Allow multiple values to be selected from lookup table* option to make the field a *Multi-Value (MV)* field. When you create an *MV* field, users can select one or more values in the field. If you do not select this option, the system allows users to select only a single value in the field.

> **Warning**: If you intend to use a custom field with a lookup table for data analysis, do not select the *Allow multiple values to be selected from lookup table* option. If you select this option, you are unable to use the field as a dimension in an OLAP cube.

Information: If you create a custom enterprise *Resource* field with a lookup table, the *Custom Attributes* section contains one additional option: the *Use This Field for Matching Generic Resources* option. Select this option if you want Project Server 2013 to use this field to match human resources with generic resources, such as with skill matching. Users can use the system's resource matching capabilities in either the *Build Team* dialog or the *Resource Substitution* wizard.

6. In the *Values to Display* section, select the *Data* option.

7. In the *Behavior* section, select the *Yes* option to require users to enter a value in the field or select the *No* option to make data entry optional for the field. You can also select the *Behavior controlled by workflow* option to control the new custom enterprise project field in a workflow process.

8. Click the *Save* button to save the new custom field.

Warning: At the time you select the *Lookup Table* option, make sure that you select the correct lookup table. If you select an incorrect lookup table and then save the new custom field, you cannot change the lookup table later. Instead, you must delete the custom field and create a new one using the correct lookup table.

Information: When you create a custom enterprise project field, you have the option to select the *Behavior controlled by workflow* checkbox in the *Behavior* section for fields that use a lookup table. When you select this option, Project Server 2013 adds the field to the list of fields controlled by workflow. After creating a custom enterprise field controlled by workflow, you must also add the field to one of the Project Detail Pages managed by a workflow or it will not be accessible from anywhere else in the system except for administration pages.

Modifying Built-In Project and Resource Department Fields

You may need to modify these fields if your organization intends to use the *Department* filtering feature to limit the display of projects, resources, enterprise custom fields, project types, business drivers, and OLAP cubes. The two fields involved are the *Project Departments* field and the *Resource Departments* field. Each of these fields contains the *Departments* lookup table.

By default, these two fields allow users to select a single value from the pick list and neither has a default value. You can change these to multi-value fields; however, you should understand this option removes your ability to use the field in reports or in resource capacity views. You should consider the impact before deciding to flip this switch, as you cannot undo this change. A more benign change that you can revisit is setting a default value for each field, or you may want to make it a required field. In the case of the *Resource Departments* field, you may also want to use the field for resource matching or for demand and capacity calculations.

To modify either one of these fields, click the name of the field in the *Enterprise Custom Fields* section of the *Enterprise Custom Fields and Lookup Tables* page. The system opens the field for editing in the *Edit Custom Field* page shown in Figure 4 - 24. Notice that the page does not contain a *Departments* section or selector, as all other enterprise custom fields do.

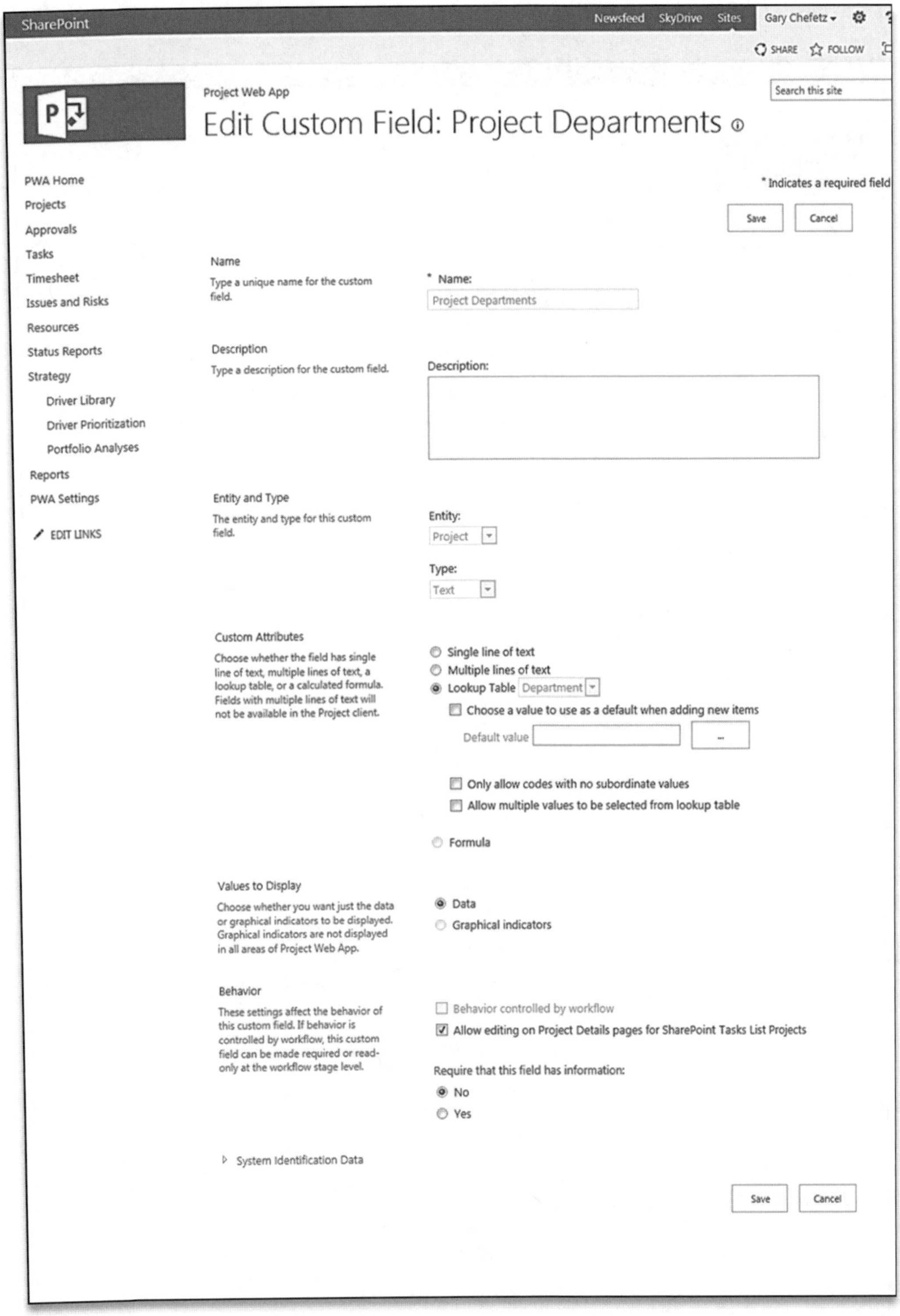

Figure 4 - 24: Edit Project Departments field page

The *Resource Departments* field uses a similarly limited *Edit Custom Field* page shown in Figure 4 - 25.

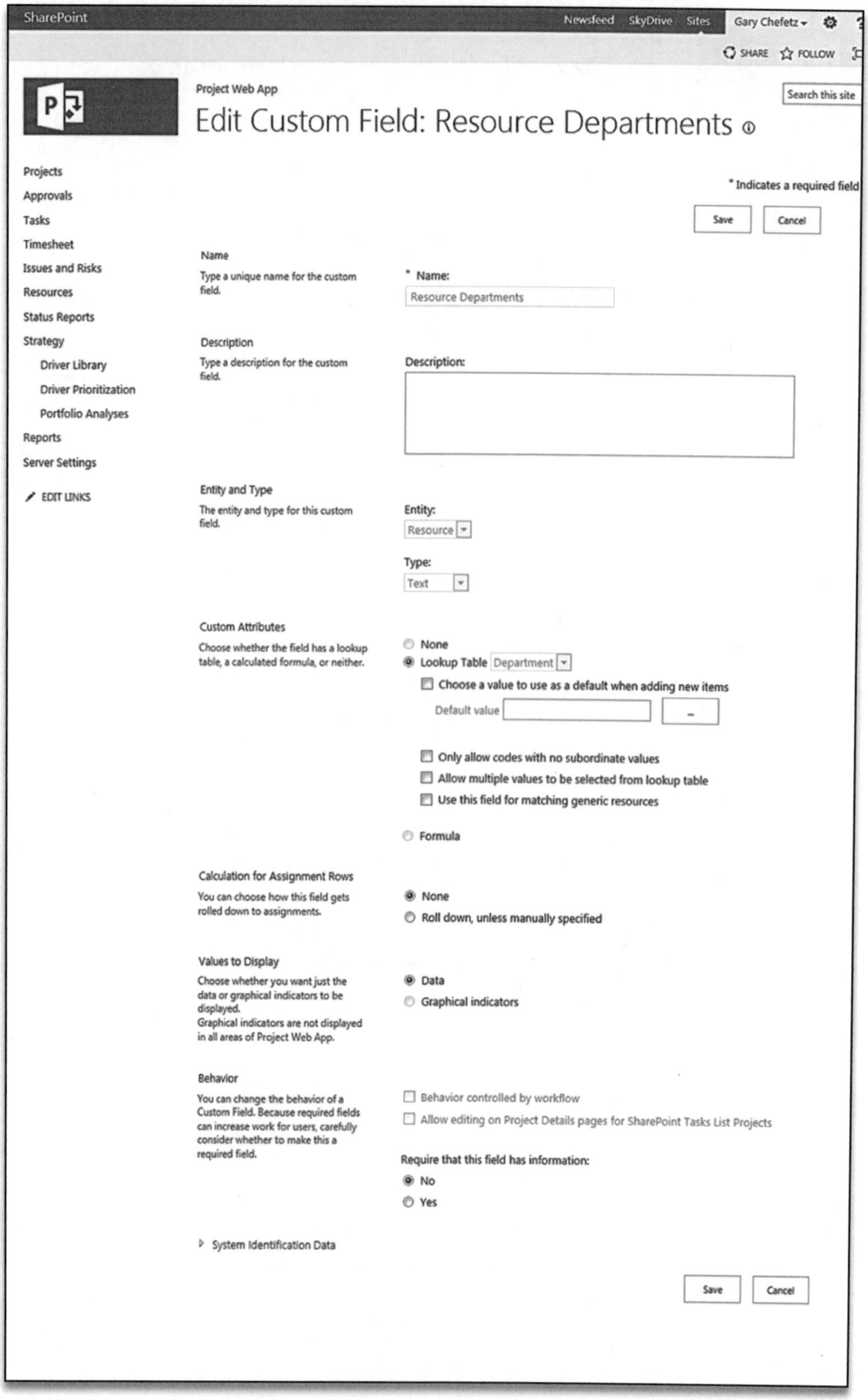

Figure 4 - 25: Edit Resource Departments field page

Notice that the *Custom Attributes* section shown previously in Figure 4 - 24 appears to allow you to select either the *Single line of text* or the *Multiple lines of text* options; however, the field will not save with either of these options if selected, and the system displays *An unknown error has occurred* message at the top of the page. While the resource-specific option to use the field for matching generic resources applies only to the *Resource Departments* field, you can set the same additional options for this field as you can for the *Project Departments* field. It is worth noting that the system also grays out the option to control both the *Project Departments* and *Resource Departments* fields via workflow for these fields and logically exposes the *Allow editing on Project Detail pages for SharePoint Tasks Lists Projects* option only to the *Project Departments* field.

Creating a Custom Field Controlled by Workflow

Designating a field controlled by workflow is as simple as selecting a checkbox on the *Edit Custom Field* page; but it is a very powerful construct because it allows you to present the field only in the context that you want to present it, and control when and where to make it a required value. Because you use workflow in association with project intake governance, or project execution governance, the types of fields you might want to control by workflow include any type of information you might want to gather and track at the project level.

A common application for workflow in Project Server 2013 is to govern the intake of project ideas for formal portfolio selection. As is typical for such a process, an intake workflow usually walks the project proposer through a series of information gathering and information analysis tasks that ultimately provide the input data that portfolio managers use to evaluate and measure projects against strategic business drivers and other constraints such as cost and resource availability. In order to use portfolio cost constraint analysis, you must define at least one custom enterprise cost field. You can define as many custom cost fields as you like against which you can perform portfolio cost constraint analysis.

For the following example, I have a business requirement that the organization wants to be able to perform cost constraint analysis against both a high estimate of cost for each project as well as low estimate of cost for each project. To meet the business requirement, I create two custom cost fields: *High Estimate* and *Low Estimate*. The process for creating each field is identical so I illustrate only one here. From the *Custom Fields and Lookup Tables* page, click the *New Field* button. The system displays the *New Custom Field* page shown in Figure 4 - 26 with the entries for a new *High Estimate* custom field.

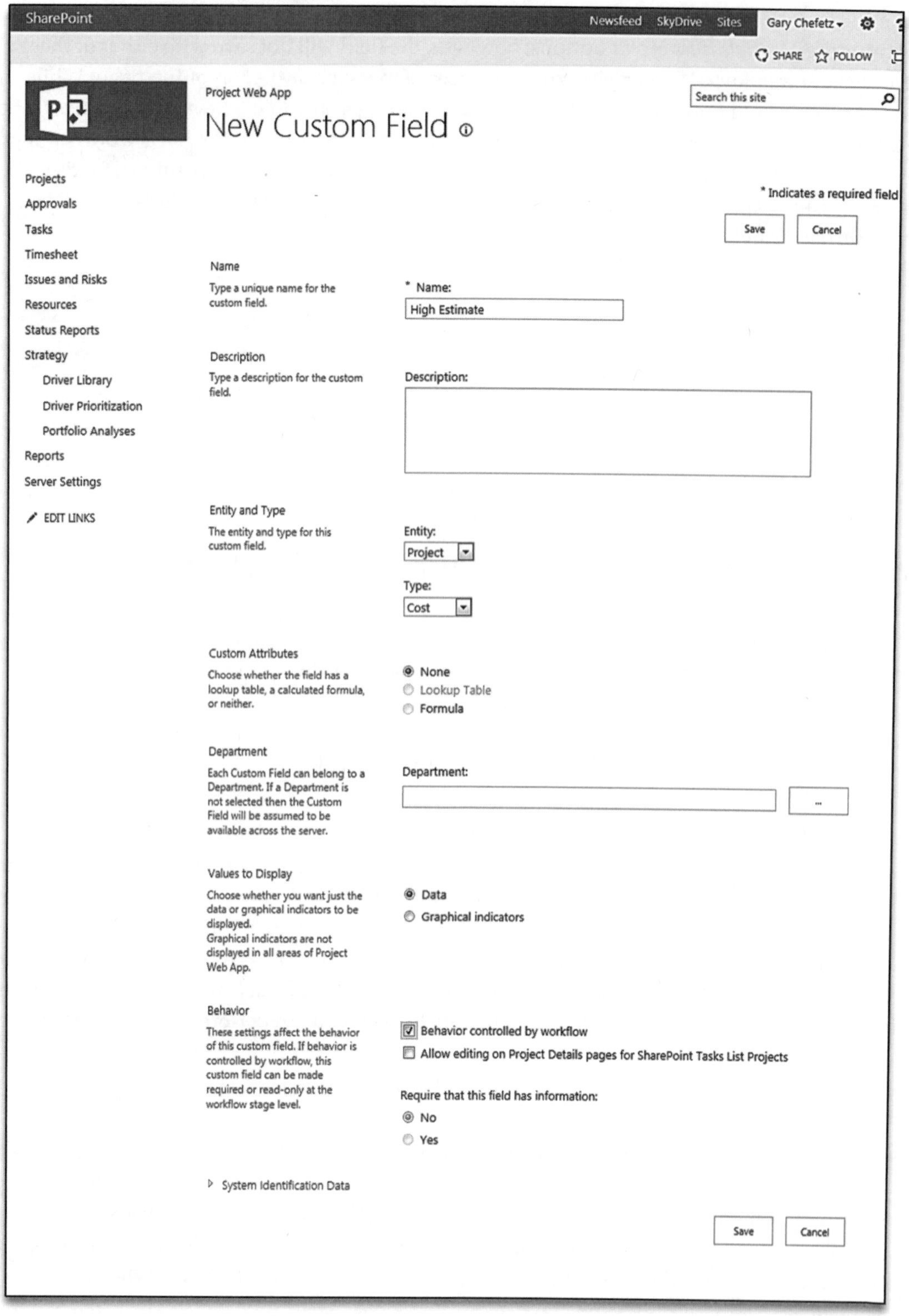

Figure 4 - 26: Cost Field controlled by workflow

Notice that once I select the *Behavior controlled by workflow* option, the system automatically disables the *Require that this field has information* option because this could create a contradiction in the system if the user tried to save a project record outside of the workflow, such as the case when someone creates a project using Project Pro 2013.

Creating a Custom Field with a Formula

Using a custom field with a formula provides a very flexible way to influence the output of views in both Project Pro 2013 and Project Web App. By using a formula in a custom field, you can perform compound financial calculations such as net present value or build business-specific key performance indicators (KPI's). You can also provide data conditioned to a specific business interpretation to accommodate non-project standard displays of duration and effort facts.

Information: As you create each custom enterprise field containing a formula, keep in mind that the formula can reference most standard or custom enterprise fields; but they cannot reference local custom fields. This is because local custom fields are not reliable data sources.

To define a custom field containing a formula, the system provides two methods:

- Project Web App
- Project Pro 2013.

The Project Web App interface can be useful but has its limitation. Creating formulas in PWA neither allows you to import a formula from another custom field or to test a formula in a project, nor does it allow you to access the *Help* articles to assist you with writing your formula. On the other hand, you can use Project Pro 2013 to define the field and create the formula, and then import the new custom field into Project Server 2013. The advantage of this approach is that you can import a formula from another custom field; you can test your formula on a real project before you import it, and you can access the *Help* library of documentation about all fields and functions available for use in your formulas. For the purpose of thoroughness, I document how to create a formula using both interfaces.

Best Practice: MSProjectExperts recommends that you always use Project Pro 2013 to define custom fields containing a formula. The user interface for creating a formula is much better than the one provided in Project Web App.

Best Practice: Before you create a field and formula using Project Pro 2013, MSProjectExperts recommends that you open any project saved as a .mpp file in *Read-Only* mode. This allows you to create and test your formulas in custom enterprise task fields. When finished, you can import the new field into Project Server 2013 and close the project without saving the changes.

Understanding Field Types with Formulas

Remember that Project Server 2013 offers you the following field types for formulas: *Cost, Date, Duration, Flag, Number*, and *Text*. Although you can create a formula in any of these field types, the mystery for most users is determining which field type to use for your formula. Consider the following examples on how to use formulas with each field type:

- Use a **Cost** field when you need to calculate any type of custom cost using your organization's default currency type. For example, my organization defines two custom enterprise task cost fields, *Internal Cost* and *Client Billable Cost*, to track project costs. I can define a third custom enterprise task cost field called *Profit* and create the following formula to calculate the profit:

```
[Client Billable Cost] - [Internal Cost]
```

- Use a **Date** field when you need to calculate any type of project date. For example, my organization defines a "drop dead" date for the completion of each task as the date 5 days later than the original *Baseline Finish* date. I can define a custom enterprise task date field called *Drop Dead Date* and use the following formula to calculate the drop dead date:

```
ProjDateAdd([Baseline Estimated Finish], "5d", "Standard")
```

> **Information**: In the preceding formula, I used the ProjDateAdd function to add 5 working days to the *Baseline Finish* date, as defined by the schedule shown in the enterprise *Standard* calendar.

- Use a **Duration** field when you need to calculate the duration between two dates. For example, my organization needs to calculate the time span (duration) between the *Baseline1 Finish* date and the *Baseline Finish* date for every task after a change control procedure. I can define a custom enterprise task duration field called *Baseline Slippage* and use the following formula to calculate the duration:

```
ProjDateDiff([Baseline1 Finish], [Baseline Estimated Finish], "Standard")
```

> **Information**: In the preceding formula, I used the ProjDateDiff function to determine the number of working days between the *Baseline1 Finish* date and the *Baseline Finish* date, as defined by the schedule shown in the enterprise *Standard* calendar.

- Use a **Flag** field to calculate a value where the answer must be in a *Yes/No* or *True/False* format. For example, my organization needs to flag new tasks that the project manager failed to baseline after a change control procedure. I can define a custom enterprise task *Flag* field called *Is Baselined* and use the following formula to determine whether each task has a *Baseline Finish* date value:

```
IIf([Baseline Estimated Finish]<>ProjDateValue("NA"), True, False)
```

- Use a **Number** field to calculate any type of unformatted numeric value. For example, my organization needs to calculate the percentage of duration variance for every task. I can define a custom enterprise task *Number* field called *Percent Duration Variance* and use the following formula to calculate that value:

```
IIf([Milestone], 0, IIf([Baseline Estimated Finish]<>ProjDateValue("NA"), [Duration
Variance]/[Baseline Duration], 0))
```

> **Information**: The preceding formula uses the IIf function to determine whether a task is a milestone. If so, the formula returns a 0 value. If the task is not a milestone, then the formula uses a second IIf function and the ProjDateValue function to determine whether the task has a *Baseline Finish* value, indicating that the task has been baselined. If so, the formula calculates the percentage of duration variance. If not, the formula returns a 0 value.

- Use a **Text** field to generate textual information resulting from a calculation, or to apply numeric formatting to a formula that generates a number. For example, my organization needs to calculate the percentage of duration variance for every task, but wants to display the number as an actual percentage value, such as 20%. I can define a custom enterprise task *Text* field called *Percent Duration Variance* and use the following formula to calculate that value and format the result as a percentage:

```
IIf([Milestone],"NA",IIf([Baseline Estimated Finish]<>ProjDateValue("NA"), ([Dura-
tion Variance]/[Baseline Duration]) * 100 & "%", "0%"))
```

Information: The preceding formula uses the IIf function to determine whether a task is a milestone. If so, the formula returns an "NA" text value. If the task is not a milestone, the formula uses another IIf function and the ProjDateValue function to determine whether the task has a *Baseline Finish* value, indicating that the task has a baseline. If so, the formula calculates the percentage of duration variance, multiplies the resulting value by 100, and appends the text string with the percent sign (%) to show a percentage value. If not, the formula returns a "0%" text value.

Using the type of formulas shown in last two examples you can also calculate the percentage of work variance or cost variance by substituting [Work Variance]/[Baseline Work] or [Cost Variance]/[Baseline Cost] in either of the preceding formulas.

Best Practice: Even though Project Pro 2013 does not allow you to create and import custom enterprise project fields, you can use this application to help you create *Project* fields that include a formula. Because a custom enterprise project field is essentially a special type of custom enterprise task field, do the following:

1. In Project Pro 2013, define a custom enterprise task field that mimics the custom enterprise project field you need.
2. Create the formula in the *Task* field.
3. Test the formula by examining the resulting value shown in the Project Summary Task (Row 0).
4. If the formula calculates correctly, copy and paste the formula into a Notepad file.
5. Close the temporary read-only project file in Project Pro 2013.
6. Begin the process of creating the custom enterprise project field in Project Web App.
7. Copy and paste the formula from the Notepad file.

MSProjectExperts recommends this process as a best practice because it allows you to test the functionality of the field (and its formula) before you actually define the field in Project Web App.

Creating a Formula Using Project Web App

As I stated earlier, you can create a custom enterprise field with a formula in either Project Web App or in Project Pro 2013. While creating the formula in Project Web App, you cannot test the formula before you save it to confirm that the formula functions as desired. This makes it much more difficult to create a formula for a custom enterprise **task** field, making Project Pro 2013 a much better option for creating the formula. On the other hand, Project Server 2013 does not allow you to use Project Pro 2013 to create a custom enterprise **project** field with a formula, which makes the Project Web App interface a better option.

As part of my organization's project tracking methodologies, I must calculate percentage of cost variance for each project. To accomplish this, I need to define a custom enterprise *Project* field containing a formula to perform the calculation. Because the field requires a formula, I can use either a custom enterprise task *Number* or *Text* field. For the purpose of this example, I plan to use a *Number* field, and I want the formula to "trap" tasks that do not have a baseline value set and for milestone tasks.

Before I show you how to create this custom field, I need a formula to calculate the percentage of cost variance. The formula is simply:

Cost Variance/Baseline Cost

How did I determine this formula? If the project cost is $125,000 when the baseline cost is only $100,000, then the cost variance is $25,000 (Cost – Baseline Cost). Applying the percentage of cost over budget formula, the task is 25% over budget (25,000/100,000 = .25 or 25%).

To create a custom enterprise field with a formula in Project Web App, complete the following steps:

1. On the *Enterprise Custom Fields and Lookup Tables* page, click the *New Field* button.

Project Server 2013 displays the *New Custom Field* page shown previously in Figure 4 - 18.

2. Enter a name for your new custom field, such as Percent Cost Variance, in the *Name* field.
3. Click the *Entity* pick list and select the *Project* item from the list.
4. Click the *Type* pick list and select the *Number* item.
5. In the *Custom Attributes* section, select the *Formula* option.

The system refreshes the *New Custom Field* page to show the formula workspace (blank canvas) and the formula tools in the *Custom Attributes* section, as shown in Figure 4 - 27. The formula tools include the *Pick field* button, the *Pick Function* button, and the *Pick Operator* button.

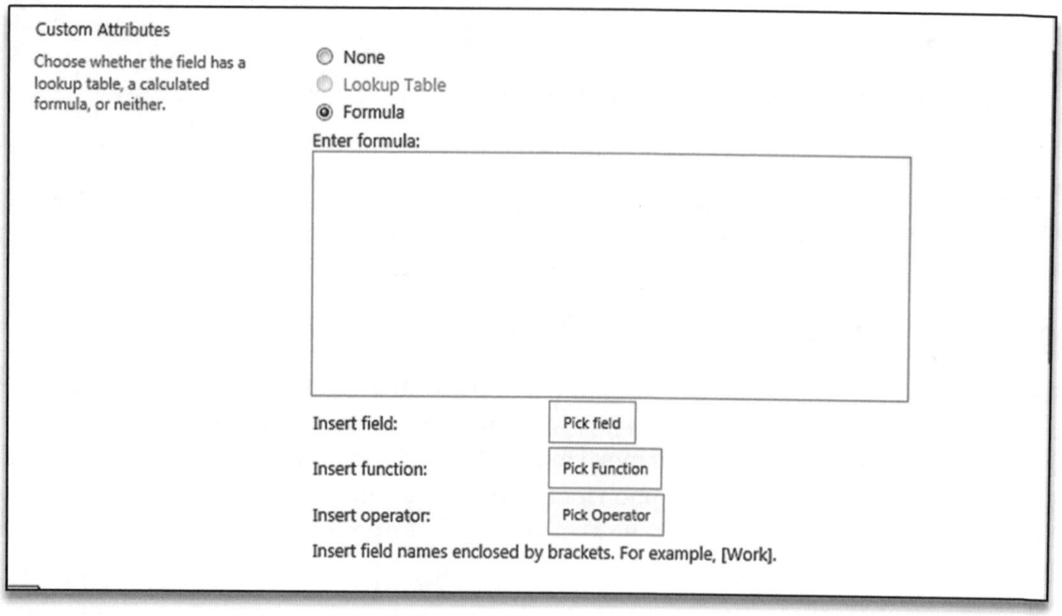

Figure 4 - 27: Formula buttons in the Custom Attributes section

6. Use the formula tools buttons to build your formula using custom enterprise fields, functions, and operators.

When you click the *Pick field* button, the system displays a list of all default and custom fields available. The system groups the default and custom fields into six categories, including *Cost, Date, Duration, Flag, Number,* and *Text.* Figure 4 - 28 shows the list of field types available by clicking the *Pick field* button.

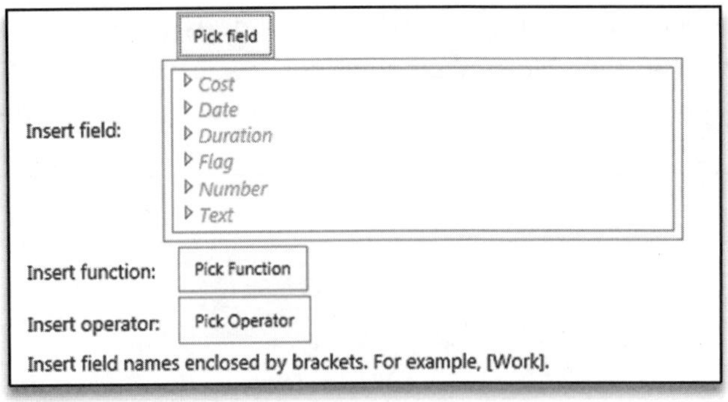

Figure 4 - 28: Field types available using the Pick field button

When you click the *Expand* (▸) button, the system displays the list of all fields available in that group. Figure 4 - 29 shows the list of *Cost* fields.

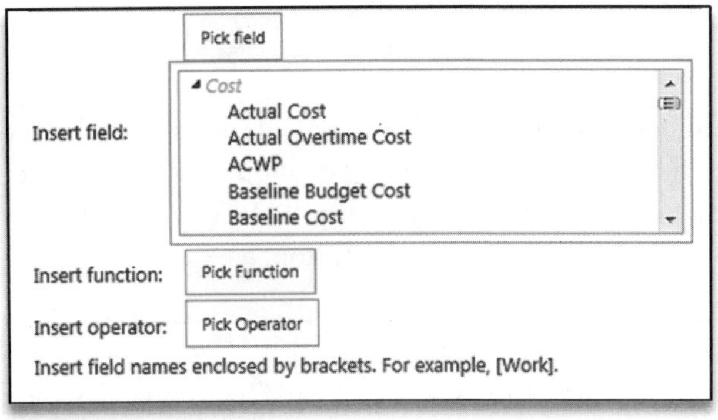

Figure 4 - 29: Cost fields

From the list of fields in the expanded section, click the first field you want to use in the formula. The system adds the field to the formula workspace and collapses the *Pick field* list, as shown in Figure 4 - 30.

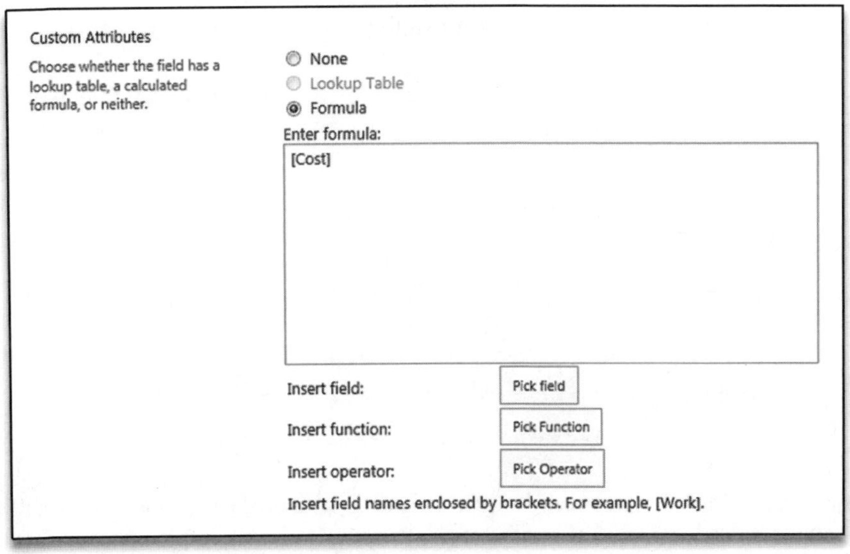

Figure 4 - 30: Formula workspace includes first selected field

If you need to use mathematical operators, such as multiplication or division operators, you can click the *Pick Operator* button. The system displays the list of available mathematical and Boolean operators, as shown in Figure 4 - 31. Select the operator you want to use in your formula and the system adds the operator to the formula workspace.

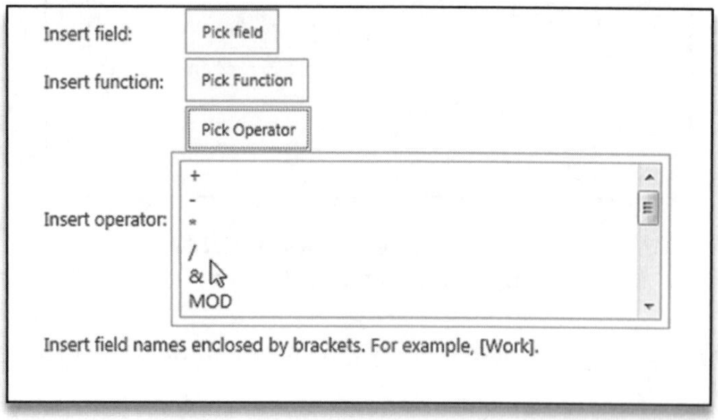

Figure 4 - 31: Mathematical operators on the Pick Operator list

Project Server 2013 includes a number of mathematical and logical functions to help you create your formula. When you click the *Pick Function* button, the system displays the list of all functions available. The system groups these functions into six categories, including *Conversion, Date/Time, General, Math, Microsoft Project,* and *Text.* Figure 4 - 32 shows the list of functions available by clicking the *Pick Function* button.

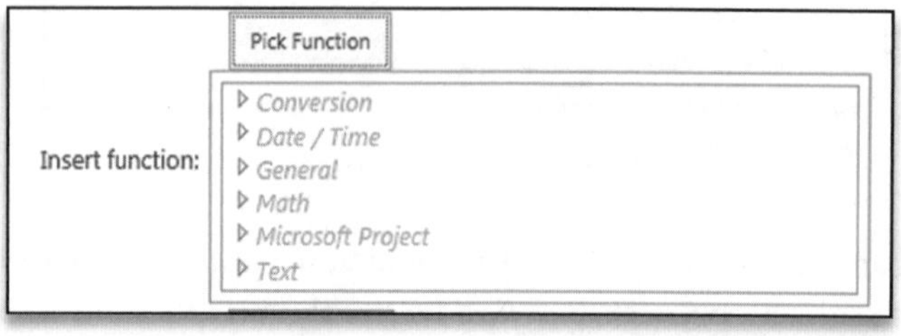

Figure 4 - 32: Functions available using the Pick Function button

When you click the *Expand* (+) button, the system displays the list of all functions available in that group. Figure 4 - 33 shows the list of functions in the *General* section.

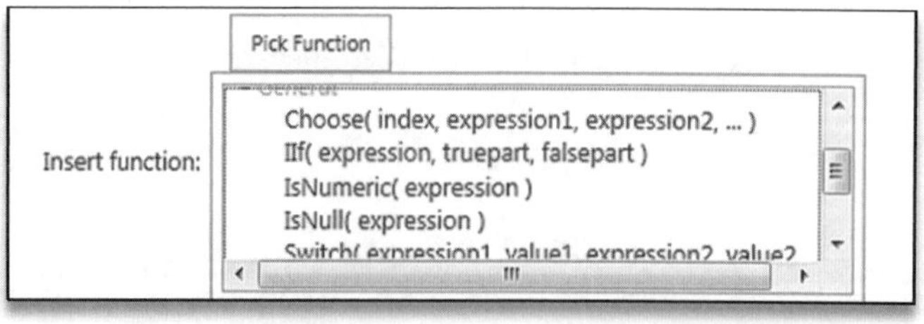

Figure 4 - 33: Functions in the General section

Several categories contain functions that are very helpful in building useful formulas in Project Pro 2013 and Project Web App. In the **Date/Time** category, consider using the following functions:

- Use the **Day** or **Month** function to isolate the day or month value in any date. For example, Day (10/21/2008) returns the 21 value.

- Use the **Now** function to return the current date, as specified on the system clock in your workstation.

In the **General** category, consider using the following functions:

- Use the **IIf** function to test for a condition, and then to return a certain value if the condition is true, or a different value if the condition is false. You can also nest *IIf* functions.

- Use the **Switch** function to test for a series of conditions, and to return a value for the first condition that generates a *True* value. In some cases, using the *Switch* function is much simpler than using a series of nested *IIf* functions.

In the **Microsoft Project** category, consider using the following functions:

- Use the **ProjDateAdd** function to add a specific number of days to a date using the working schedule on the calendar you specify.

- Use the **ProjDateDiff** function to determine the number of working days between two dates using the working schedule on the calendar you specify.

- Use the **ProjDateValue** function to test for the presence (or lack) of baseline information for a task. Project Pro 2013 indicates the lack of a baseline on a task by an *NA* value in either the *Baseline Start* or *Baseline Finish* fields. You normally use this function as part of a formula using an IIf statement. For example, the following formula tests for a baseline:

```
IIf([Baseline Finish] = ProjDateValue("NA"), truepart, falsepart)
```

From the list of functions in the expanded section, select a function that you want to use in the formula. The system adds the function to the formula workspace and collapses the *Pick Function* list. After I build a formula using functions, fields, and mathematical operators, Figure 4 - 34 shows the following completed formula in the formula workspace:

```
IIf([Baseline Finish] = ProjDateValue("NA"), -16000, [Cost Variance] / [Baseline
Cost])
```

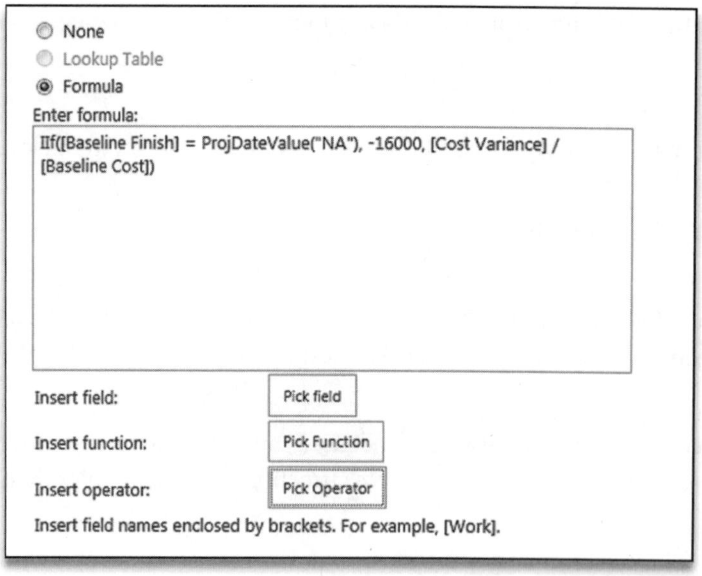

Figure 4 - 34: Percent Project Cost Variance formula

I used the following logic to create this formula:

- I used IIf([Baseline Finish] = ProjDateValue("NA") to test for the presence of a *Baseline Finish* date for each task.
- If there is no *Baseline Finish* date for the task, the formula returns a value of -16,000. I selected this value because the odds of it occurring as a result of the [Cost Variance] / [Baseline Cost] calculation are slim to none. In order for the [Cost Variance] / [Baseline Cost] calculation to return a value of -16,000, the task would need to be 1,600,000% under budget! Because I cannot use text in a *Number* field, I had to use a number that would indicate that a task has no *Baseline Finish* date.
- If the task has a *Baseline Finish* date, the formula applies the [Cost Variance] / [Baseline Cost] calculation to determine the percentage of cost variance.

Finish the process of creating the new field with a formula by completing the following steps:

7. In the *Values to Display* section, select the *Data* option.
8. Click the *Save* button.

Displaying Graphical Indicators in Custom Fields

Graphical indicators lend a powerful, popular, and eye-pleasing impact to views in both Project Pro 2013 and Project Web App. Many users find graphical indicators easier to understand than the raw numerical data. For example, almost anyone can figure out that a red stoplight indicator is not a good thing; while a green "smiley face" indicator is a sign of something very good indeed!

As with custom enterprise fields that contain a formula, there are two ways to create a custom enterprise field that uses graphical indicators:

- Project Web App
- Project Pro 2013

The advantages of using Project Pro 2013 are that you can import graphical indicators from another custom enterprise field, you can test your graphical indicators on a real project, and you can access the system's *Help* documentation. The Project Web App interface does not provide any of these three features. For the purpose of thoroughness, I document how to create graphical indicators using both interfaces.

Creating Graphical Indicators Using Project Web App

For ease of variance analysis, my company's project reporting methodology requires the use of stoplight indicators to show the percentage of project cost variance. Users need to see this information in a *Project Detail* view reached from the Project Center and in a custom view in Project Pro 2013. Therefore, I want to display a green, yellow, or red stoplight indicator for each value in the new *Percent Task Cost Variance* field that I created previously in this module. My company's criteria for displaying stoplights in this field are as follows:

- If the task has no *Baseline Finish* date (indicating that the project is not baselined), display a clock face icon.
- If the Task Percent Cost Variance is less than 2%, display a green smiley face icon.
- If the Task Percent Cost Variance is greater than or equal to 2%, but less than 5%, display a yellow serious face icon.
- If the Task Percent Cost Variance is greater than or equal to 5%, display a red unhappy face icon.

In addition, users need to be able to see the underlying value in the field for any task by floating the mouse pointer over the graphical indicator. To add graphical indicators to the *Task Percent Cost Variance* field, complete the following steps:

1. On the *Enterprise Custom Fields and Lookup Tables* page, click the name of the *Task Percent Cost Variance* field to open the field for editing.
2. In the *Values to Display* section of the page, select the *Graphical indicators* option. The system displays a graphical indicators data grid as shown in Figure 4 - 35.

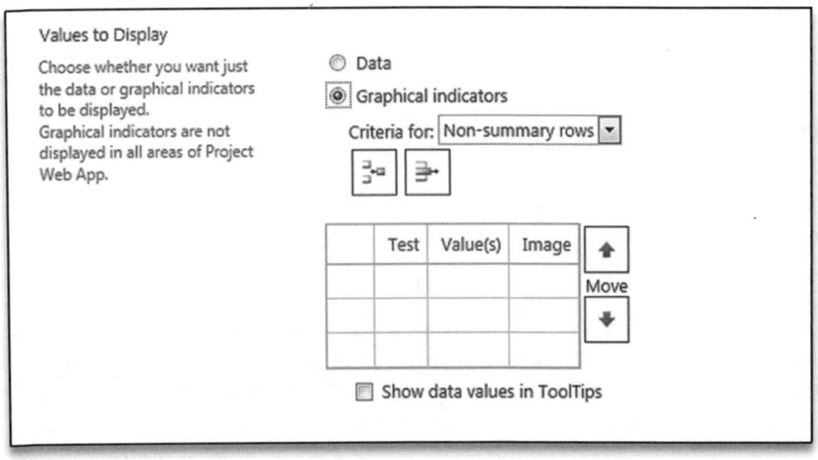

Figure 4 - 35: Graphical Indicators data grid on the Edit Custom Fields page

3. Enter your graphical indicator criteria in the Graphical indicators data grid.

Warning: If you use the Project Web App interface to create graphical indicators for a *Task* field, you must individually specify the criteria used for non-summary tasks (subtasks), summary tasks (such as phases and deliverables), and the Project Summary Task (Row 0). Selecting the items on the *Criteria for* pick list, the system allows you to set completely different criteria for each of the three types of tasks, or to specify that all summary rows (including the Project Summary Task) inherit their criteria from the non-summary rows.

To set up the criteria for the graphical indicators, you must specify multiple tests using the pick lists in the data grid. The order in which you enter your criteria is very important because the system processes the criteria list from the top to the bottom of the grid. When the system encounters the first "true" condition for a test, it stops processing the criteria and displays the graphical indicator for that test. This means that in some cases, you may need to enter the criteria in reverse order from your reporting requirements.

When you click the first blank cell in the *Test* column and then click the pick list, the system offers the following tests:

- Equals
- Does not equal
- Is greater than
- Is greater than or equal to
- Is less than
- Is less than or equal to
- Is within
- Is not within
- Contains
- Does not contain
- Contains exactly
- Is any value

Information: The *Is Any Value* test yields a positive result in all cases. This makes it useful as a "catchall" test to include at the bottom of the criteria list, as it will display an indicator to represent a value not otherwise defined.

The tests you select in the *Test* column apply to the values you select or enter in the *Value(s)* column. In the *Value(s)* column, you can select a standard or enterprise field, or you can enter a literal value. In the *Image* column, select a graphical indicator for each test. Table 4 - 1 shows the types of multi-colored graphical images available and the number of each type of image.

Image Type	Number
Blank indicator	1
Stoplights	13
Flags	8
Solid color squares	5
Plus signs	5
Minus signs	6
Solid color diamonds	3
Blue arrows	5
Semaphores	7
Light bulbs	2
Miscellaneous	5
"Smiley face" icons	6

Table 4 - 1: Graphical Indicators

Information: As you create your Graphical Indicator criteria, you need more than three default rows in the data grid. You can click the *Insert Row* button to add as many rows as you need.

To meet my organization's reporting requirements, the correct order of my graphical indicator criteria is as follows in Table 4 - 2:

Test	Value(s)	Image
Equals	-16000	Clock face
Is greater than or equal to	.50	Red unhappy face
Is greater than or equal to	.20	Yellow neutral face
Is less than	.20	Green smiley face

Table 4 - 2: Correct order for Graphical Indicator criteria

Because Project Server 2013 processes the graphical indicator criteria in the order listed, the system processes the criteria shown previously in Table 4 - 2 as follows:

- The system first determines if the value for the task equals -16,000. If true, it displays the Clock face graphical indicator and stops processing the list.
- If the previous test returns false, the system determines if the percent cost variance for the task is greater than or equal to 50%. If true, it displays the red unhappy face graphical indicator and stops processing the list.
- If the previous test returns false, the system determines if the percent cost variance for the task is greater than or equal to 20%. If true, it displays the yellow neutral graphical indicator and stops processing the list.
- If the previous test returns false, the system determines if the percent cost variance for the project is less than 20%. Again, if true, it displays the green smiley face graphical indicator and stops processing the list.
- If all test conditions return false, the system displays no symbol at all.

Because of how I created the formula and structured the graphical indicator criteria, the system will find a true condition for one of the four criteria for every project and will always display a resulting graphical indicator. Figure 4 - 36 shows the four criteria for the graphical indicators in the *Percent Project Cost Variance* field.

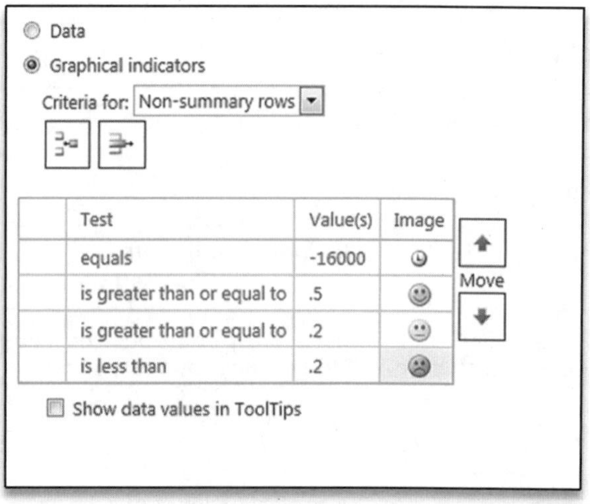

Figure 4 - 36: Completed graphical indicator criteria for the Task Percent Cost Variance field

4. If you want users to see the underlying data values by floating their mouse pointer over the graphical indicator, select the *Show data values in ToolTips* option.
5. Click the *Save* button to save the graphical indicator criteria as a part of the *Percent Task Cost Variance* field.

Understanding the Connection between Formulas and Graphical Indicators

If you know in advance that, you need to create graphical indicators in a custom field with a formula, give careful thought to the interaction between the formula and the graphical indicator criteria. Your reporting requirements ultimately determine what type of fields you use, how you write the formula, and how you list the graphical indicator criteria. Make sure you structure your formula to return consistent values that the system can test with graphical indicator criteria.

Keep in mind that Project Web App allows users to export data in a data grid to Excel. The *Project Center* page contains a data grid, for example, and is often the location for using custom enterprise project fields that contain a formula and display graphical indicators. When exporting to Excel from a data grid that displays graphical indicators, the system **does not** export the graphical indicators. Instead, it exports only the underlying value in each cell. Because of this, you may opt to use a *Text* field rather than a *Number* field when creating a formula with graphical indicators in the field.

For example, following are the three most common variance formulas you might want to use with graphical indicators in either *Task* fields or *Project* fields. To use any of these formulas, you must select a *Text* field type, rather than a *Number* field type. When exporting to Excel from a Project Web App data grid, keep in mind that the system exports the text values, giving useful information to the user in Excel.

Percent Cost Variance

```
Switch(([BaselineFinish]=ProjDateValue("NA")),"NoBaseline",[Milestone],
"Green",[CostVariance]<([BaselineCost]*0.05),"Green", [Cost Variance]<([Baseline
Cost]*0.1), "Yellow", [Cost Variance]>=([Baseline Cost]*0.1), "Red")
```

Information: The *Percent Cost Variance* formula shown above uses the *Switch* function to determine what text value to display in the field. It tests for the following conditions:

- Baseline Finish date = NA
- Milestone
- Percent cost variance < 5%
- Percent cost variance < 10%
- Percent cost variance >= 10%

The first condition that generates a "True" response forces the system to display the text specified for that test.

Percent Work Variance

```
Switch(([Baseline Finish]=ProjDateValue("NA")), "No Baseline", [Milestone], "Green",
[Work Variance]<([Baseline Work]*0.05), "Green", [Work Variance]<([Baseline
Work]*0.1), "Yellow", [Work Variance]>=([Baseline Work]*0.1), "Red")
```

Percent Duration Variance

```
Switch(([Baseline Finish]=ProjDateValue("NA")), "No Baseline", [Milestone], "Green",
[Duration Variance]<([Baseline Duration]*0.05), "Green", [Duration
Variance]<([Baseline Duration]*0.1), "Yellow",[Duration Variance]>=([Baseline
Duration]*0.1), "Red")
```

Information: If you use any of the above formulas in your own custom fields, you must specify your own organization's criteria for calculating how much variance results in a green, yellow, or red value in the formula. After creating these formulas in a field, you can create matching graphical indicator criteria.

Deleting a Custom Field or Lookup Table

To delete a custom enterprise field or lookup table, first navigate to the *Custom Fields and Lookup Tables* page in Project Web App. If you want to delete a custom field, select it in the data grid and then click the *Delete Field* button. When prompted, click the *Yes* button in the warning dialog to delete the field. If you want to delete a custom lookup table, select it in the data grid and then click the *Delete Lookup Table* button. When the system prompts, click the *Yes* button in the warning dialog to delete the lookup table.

Planning for Matching Generic Resources

Consider the following scenario in my organization to understand the need for matching human resources with generic resources:

- Project managers in my organization routinely plan projects that do not start until three months or more in the future.
- During the initial planning for a new project, project managers add generic resources to their project team and then assign the generic resources to the tasks.
- The generic resources are skill-based or placeholder resources that indicate the IT skills needed to perform each task.
- As the project start date approaches, project managers need to match generic resources with human resources who possess the same IT skills and have the availability to work on the project.

The preceding scenario is very common across the PPM community. Most organizations find generic resources a useful planning tool and need to do some form of matching between generic resources and human resources as they move project into execution. The most common need, as presented above, is to match skills between generic and human resources. Other common needs involve matching resources by availability, by position in the RBS structure, by region or location, and by language proficiency.

Scale is everything when you plan for matching generic resources with human resources. Project Server 2013 provides tools that instantly sift through hundreds or thousands of resources to locate one that has the preferred attributes for the job. If your organization does not have a large number of resources, then you may take a very light-handed approach to this capability or choose to ignore it completely.

Project Server 2013 provides project managers and planners two tools for skill matching generic-to-human or human-to-human resources: the *Build Team from Enterprise* tool and the *Resource Substitution* wizard. Using either tool, the system matches skills and other resource attributes by comparing enterprise resource fields that contain lookup tables and other criteria that the individual user can apply through the interface. Skill matching uses "contains" logic as it compares a generic resource with possible matching human resources, and does not require an exact match between the resources.

Your challenge as the Project Server business analyst or administrator is to provide thoughtful attribution values to enhance Project Server's team-building tools. If you are working with a large Enterprise Resource Pool, it is possible to build a significant matrix of attributes for team building. Distributed organizations may want location codes, while large organizations may want seniority codes and secondary skill identifiers. Remember that once you create a new attribute, you obligate yourself to provide a value for it for each resource in your Enterprise Resource Pool.

My organization's primary need is to match generic resources with human resources using IT skills. Using a skills assessment provided by our human resources staff, the IT skills that I need to track are as follows:

- **Admin Support**
- **Client**
- **Database Analyst**
- **Executive**
- **Network Administrator**
- **Project Manager**
- **Software Developer**
- **Software Tester**
- **Technical Writer**

Based on the above information, I can use a single enterprise field containing a lookup table to represent the available skills across the IT department. Because Project Server 2013 allows the use of multiple values in the lookup table, I can optionally set up the field to select multiple skills for each resource. To enable skill matching in my organization, I first created the IT Skills lookup table shown in Figure 4 - 37.

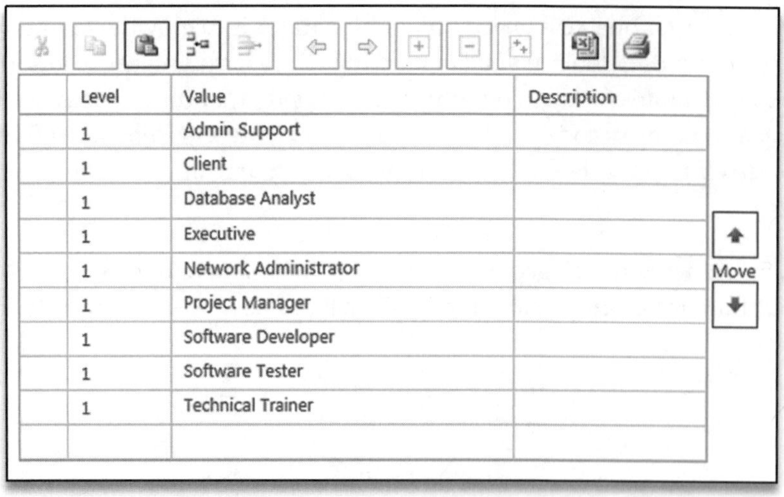

	Level	Value	Description
	1	Admin Support	
	1	Client	
	1	Database Analyst	
	1	Executive	
	1	Network Administrator	
	1	Project Manager	
	1	Software Developer	
	1	Software Tester	
	1	Technical Trainer	

Figure 4 - 37: Role lookup table

After creating the IT Skills lookup table, I created a custom enterprise resource field called *Role* using the *Role* lookup table shown previously in Figure 4 - 37. I set up the options in the *Role* field shown in Figure 4 - 38 to match the following requirements:

- The Enterprise Resource Pool administrator must select a specific IT skill for each resource.
- The field must not allow the user to select multiple values for each resource. I mandate this requirement because I intend to use this field as a dimension in the OLAP cubes, which do not display data for *Multi-Value (MV)* fields.
- You must use the field for matching generic resources with human resources.
- The field must not be a required field, so the system does not require the Enterprise Resource Pool administrator to select an IT Skill value for every resource in the pool. I mandate this requirement because the Enterprise Resource Pool will contain other types of resources, including material resources and cost resources that do not have a *Role* value.

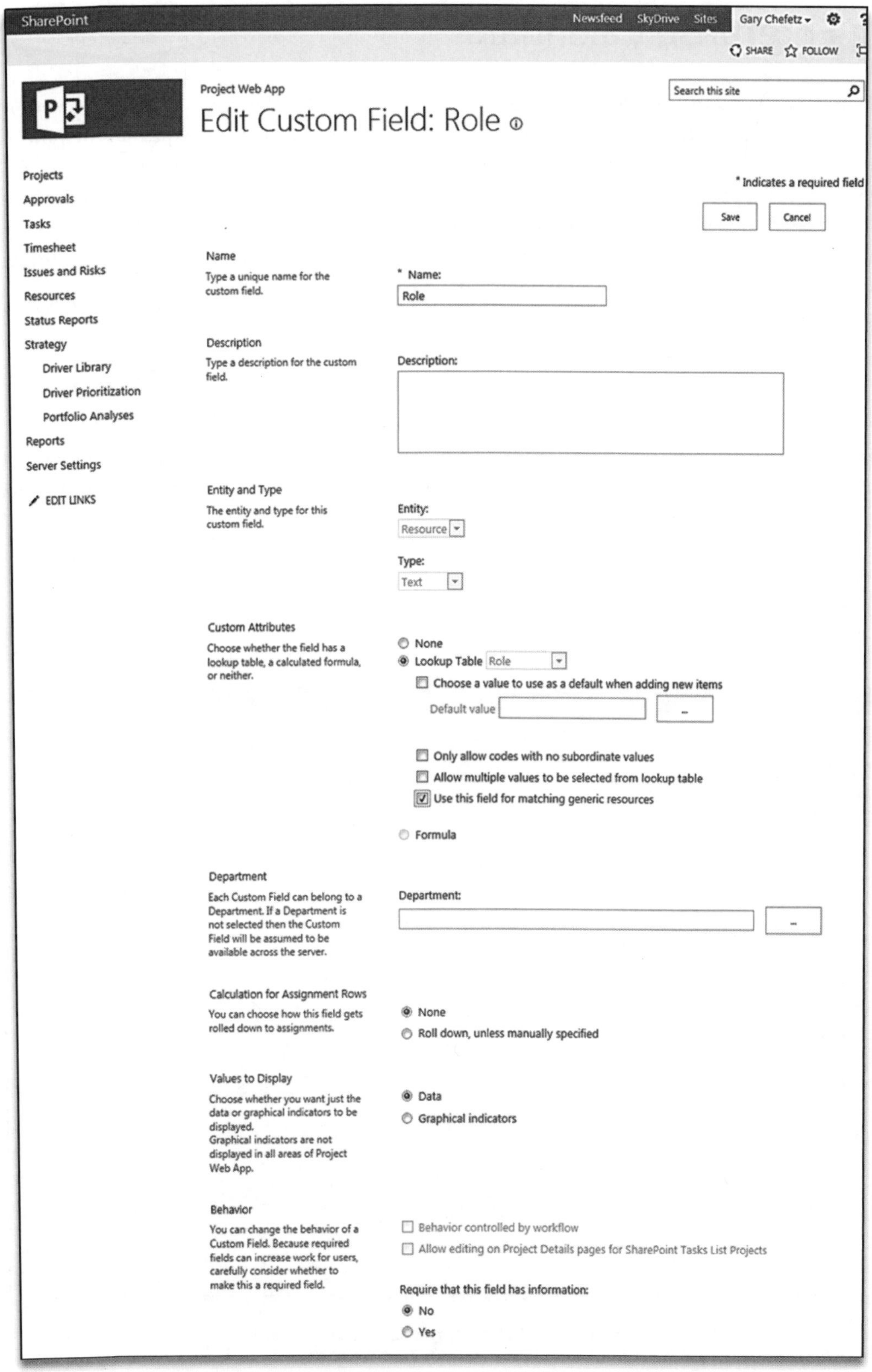
SharePoint
Newsfeed
SkyDrive
Sites
Gary Chefetz
SHARE
FOLLOW
Project Web App
Edit Custom Field: Role
Search this site
Projects
Approvals
Tasks
Timesheet
Issues and Risks
Resources
Status Reports
Strategy
Driver Library
Driver Prioritization
Portfolio Analyses
Reports
Server Settings
EDIT LINKS
* Indicates a required field
Save
Cancel
Name
Type a unique name for the custom field.
* Name:
Role
Description
Type a description for the custom field.
Description:
Entity and Type
The entity and type for this custom field.
Entity:
Resource
Type:
Text
Custom Attributes
Choose whether the field has a lookup table, a calculated formula, or neither.
None
Lookup Table
Role
Choose a value to use as a default when adding new items
Default value
Only allow codes with no subordinate values
Allow multiple values to be selected from lookup table
Use this field for matching generic resources
Formula
Department
Each Custom Field can belong to a Department. If a Department is not selected then the Custom Field will be assumed to be available across the server.
Department:
Calculation for Assignment Rows
You can choose how this field gets rolled down to assignments.
None
Roll down, unless manually specified
Values to Display
Choose whether you want just the data or graphical indicators to be displayed.
Graphical indicators are not displayed in all areas of Project Web App.
Data
Graphical indicators
Behavior
You can change the behavior of a Custom Field. Because required fields can increase work for users, carefully consider whether to make this a required field.
Behavior controlled by workflow
Allow editing on Project Details pages for SharePoint Tasks List Projects
Require that this field has information:
No
Yes

Figure 4 - 38: Role field linked to the Role lookup table

Creating Enterprise Calendars

Before you add resources and projects to your Project Server 2013 database, you must configure your organization's enterprise *Standard* calendar and create new base calendars as indicated in your Requirements and Configuration Specification document. The enterprise *Standard* calendar serves as the default project calendar for all new projects created in the system, and provides the base calendar for all resources. You create additional base calendars for the unique scheduling needs of your organization, such as for a resource who works four ten-hour work days each week, or for tasks that must occur on weekends only. At a minimum, you must add your company's holidays to the enterprise *Standard* calendar so that your project managers have realistic project schedules.

To work with enterprise calendars, navigate to the *PWA Settings* page in Project Web App and then in the *Enterprise Data* section of the page, click the *Enterprise Calendars* link. The system displays the *Enterprise Calendars* page shown in Figure 4 - 39.

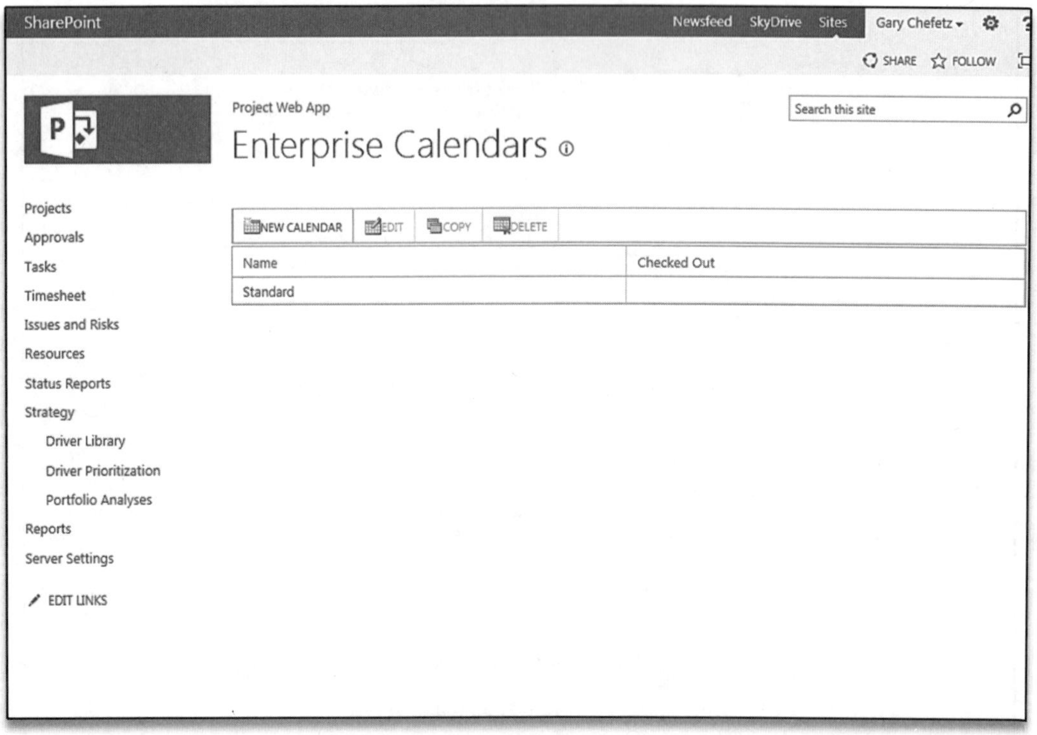

Figure 4 - 39: Enterprise Calendars page

Setting Company Holidays

To edit the *Standard* calendar, select the *Standard* calendar in the list of calendars and then click the *Edit Calendar* button. The system launches Project Pro 2013 if it is not already open and then opens the *Standard* calendar for editing in the *Change Working Time* dialog shown in Figure 4 - 40.

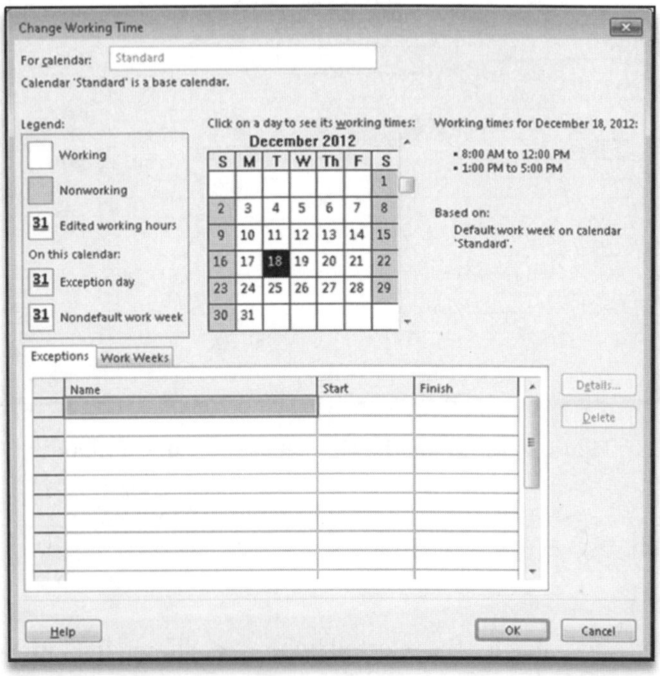

Figure 4 - 40: Change Working Time dialog for the Standard calendar

To add a non-working company holiday on the *Standard* calendar, complete the following steps:

1. In the calendar data grid, select the date of the next company holiday.

> **Information**: To set consecutive nonworking days, drag your mouse pointer to select a block of days. To select noncontiguous dates, select the first date, press and hold the **Ctrl** key on your computer keyboard, and then select additional dates.

2. On the *Exceptions* tab in the bottom half of the page, enter a name for the holiday, and then press the **Right-Arrow** key on your computer keyboard. Notice in Figure 4 - 41 that I set May 27, 2013 as the Memorial Day company holiday.

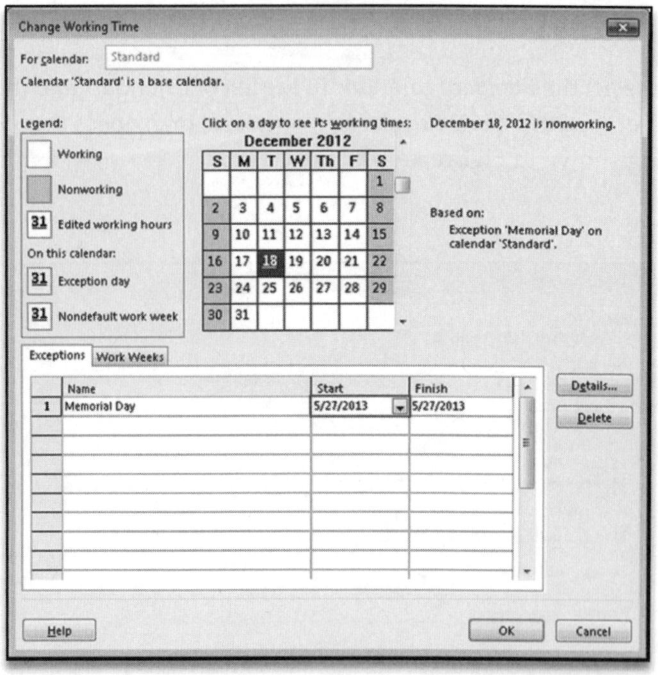

Figure 4 - 41: Memorial Day set as company holiday

3. Click the *Details* button.

The software displays the *Details for* dialog for the selected holiday, as shown in Figure 4 - 42 . You use the *Details for* dialog to create a recurring company holiday for a specified number of years into the future. For example, you might set each company holiday to recur for the next 5 years.

Information: The right side of the *Recurrence Pattern* section allows you to specify a hard date every year, such as January 1, or a floating date, such as the fourth Thursday of every November (Thanksgiving Day).

4. In the *Recurrence Pattern* section, select the *Yearly* option and then select your pattern of recurrence.

5. In the *Range of Recurrence* section, select the *End after* option and then select the number of years to repeat the holiday. Figure 4 - 42 shows the *Recurrence pattern* values set to *Yearly* on *The Fourth Monday of May* and the *Range of recurrence* values set to *End after 5 occurrences.*

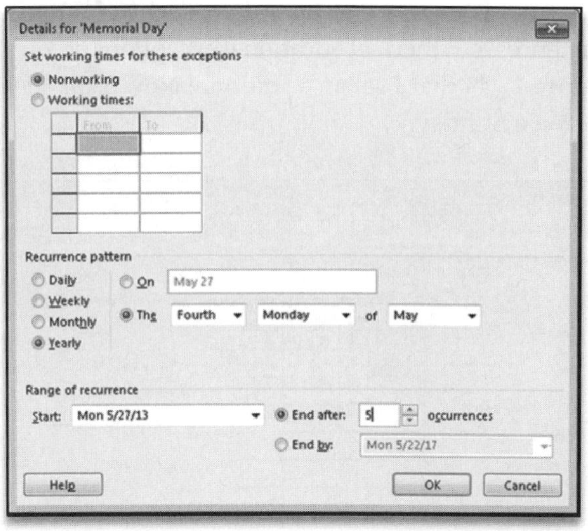

Figure 4 - 42: Details dialog for Memorial Day

6. Click the *OK* button. The system displays the *Change Working Time* dialog with the Memorial Day holiday set as shown in Figure 4 - 43.

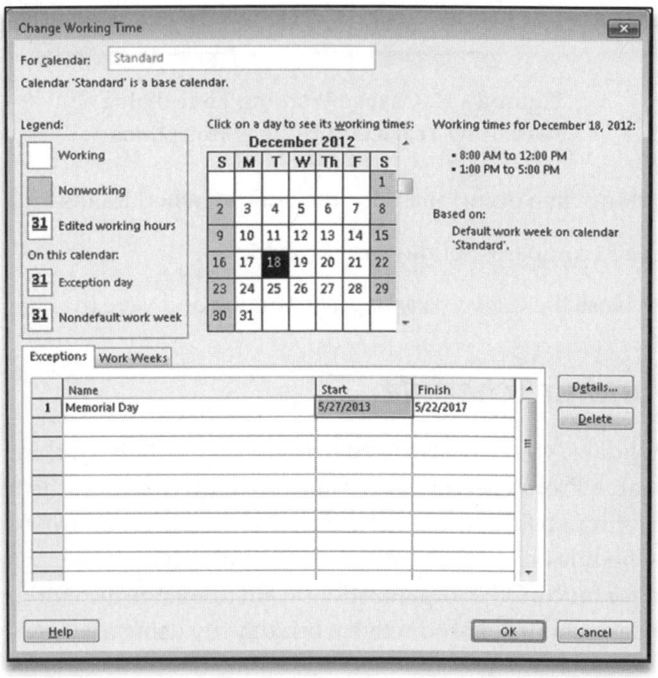

Figure 4 - 43: Change Working Time dialog with Memorial Day holiday

Warning: When you set a hard date as nonworking time, such as January 1, and then set the holiday to recur multiple times, some of the nonworking dates may fall on a weekend. Project Server 2013 does not automatically reset a Saturday holiday to the previous Friday, or reset a Sunday holiday to the following Monday. Instead, you must set these weekend occurrences as additional holidays on the *Exceptions* tab.

7. After you set a recurring company holiday on a hard date, such as January 1, scroll through the calendar grid looking for weekend occurrences and then set additional exceptions according to your organization's policies. For example, notice in Figure 4 - 44 that I set an additional New Year's Day holiday for January 2, 2017 because January 1, 2017 falls on a Sunday.

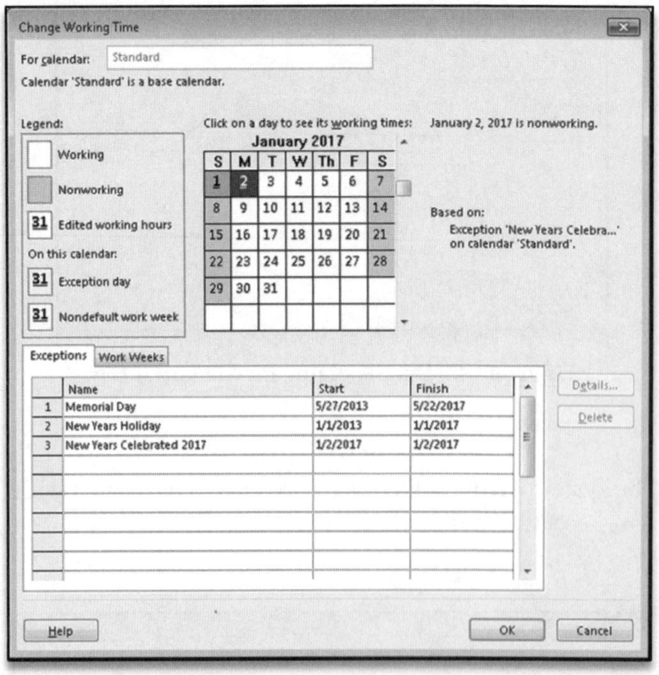

Figure 4 - 44: Change Working Time dialog with New Year's Day Holiday Exceptions

8. Set additional nonworking time occurrences for the holiday when it falls on a Saturday or Sunday.
9. Repeat steps #1-7 for each company holiday.
10. Click the *OK* button to close the *Change Working Time* dialog and save the changes to the *Standard* calendar.

Setting the Daily Working Schedule

After setting your company holidays, you may also need to establish the daily working schedule for your company. By default, the *Standard* calendar in Project Server 2013 assumes a daily working schedule of 8:00 AM – 5:00 PM with one hour off for lunch, Monday through Friday, with Saturday and Sunday as nonworking times. Some organizations want to change the working schedule on the *Standard* calendar to match their exact working schedule, such as 7:00 AM – 3:30 PM with a half-hour for lunch. Other organizations want to change the working schedule to match a typical worker's productive working day (6 hours of productive work/day) by using a 9:00 AM – 4:00 PM schedule with one hour for lunch.

Information: In the previous example, I am not recommending the use of a "productive working time" construct, such as setting the *Standard* calendar schedule to 6 hours per workday. Instead, I merely use it for illustration purposes. You must carefully make such decisions during your design phase.

To change the working schedule on the *Standard* calendar from the *Enterprise Calendars* page in Project Web App, complete the following steps:

1. Select the *Standard* calendar in the list of calendars and then click the *Edit Calendar* button.

The system launches Project Pro 2013 and opens the *Standard* calendar for editing in the *Change Working Time* dialog shown previously in Figure 4 - 44.

2. In the *Change Working Time* dialog, click the *Work Weeks* tab and then click the *Details* button. The software displays the *Details* dialog for the Default working schedule shown in Figure 4 - 45.

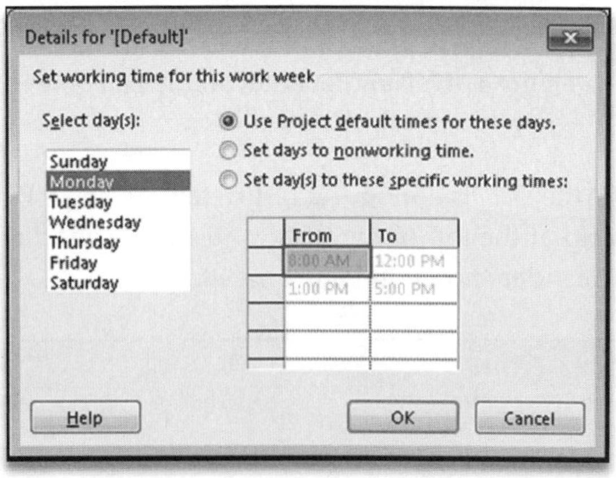

Figure 4 - 45: Details dialog for the Default working schedule

3. In the *Select day(s)* section, select and drag Monday through Friday in the list of days.

4. Select the *Set day(s) to these specific working times* option at the top of the dialog. The software displays the default 8:00 AM – 5:00 PM working time in the working times grid, shown in Figure 4 - 46.

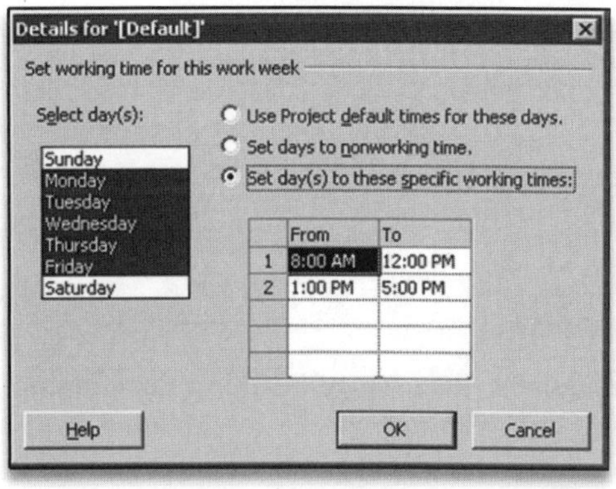

Figure 4 - 46: Default working schedule in the Details dialog

5. Change the *From* and *To* times to reflect your organization's working schedule. For example, Figure 4 - 47 shows a standard working schedule of 9:00 AM to 4:00 PM with an hour for lunch as if I wanted to reflect the productive working time of 6 hours per day for resources in my organization.

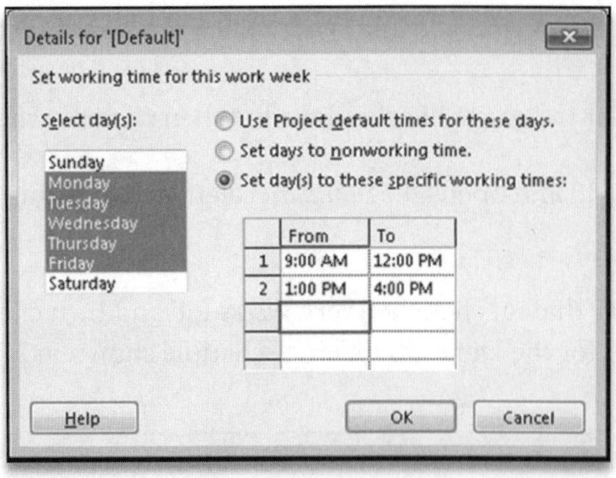

Figure 4 - 47: New default working schedule in the Details dialog

6. Click the *OK* button to close the *Details* dialog and return to the *Change Working Time* dialog. When you click any date in the calendar grid at the top of the *Change Working Time* dialog, you can see the new working schedule for the *Standard* calendar shown in Figure 4 - 48.

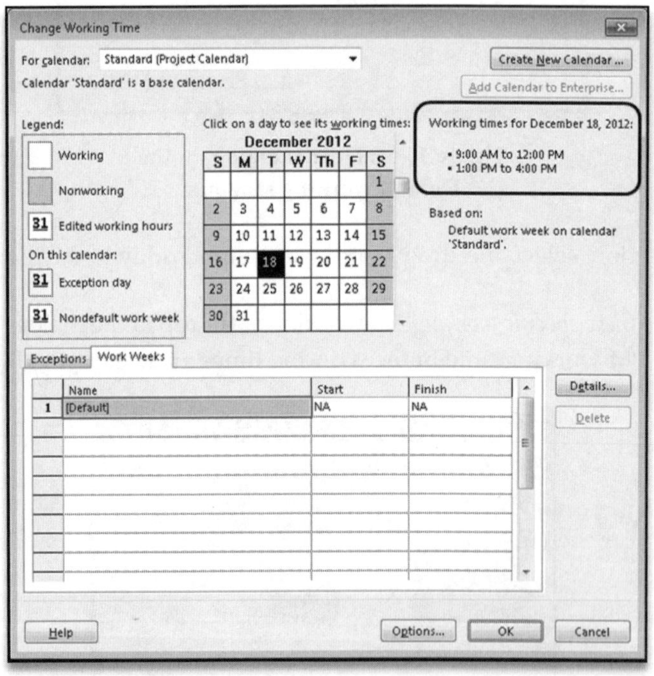

Figure 4 - 48: Change Working Time dialog with new working schedule

7. Click the *OK* button to close the *Change Working Time* dialog and save the new working schedule on the *Standard* calendar.

Warning: Synchronizing Working Time with Project Options

If you change the working schedule on the *Standard* calendar to any schedule different from the default 8:00 AM – 5:00 PM working schedule, and the *Standard* calendar is the default *Project* calendar for individual projects, your project managers must synchronize the calendar options in **every existing enterprise project** to match the schedule in the *Standard* calendar. To synchronize the calendar options, your project managers must complete the following steps:

1. Open an enterprise project.
2. Click *File* ➤ *Options* and then click the *Schedule* tab. Figure 4 - 49 shows the *Project Options* dialog with the *Schedule* page selected.

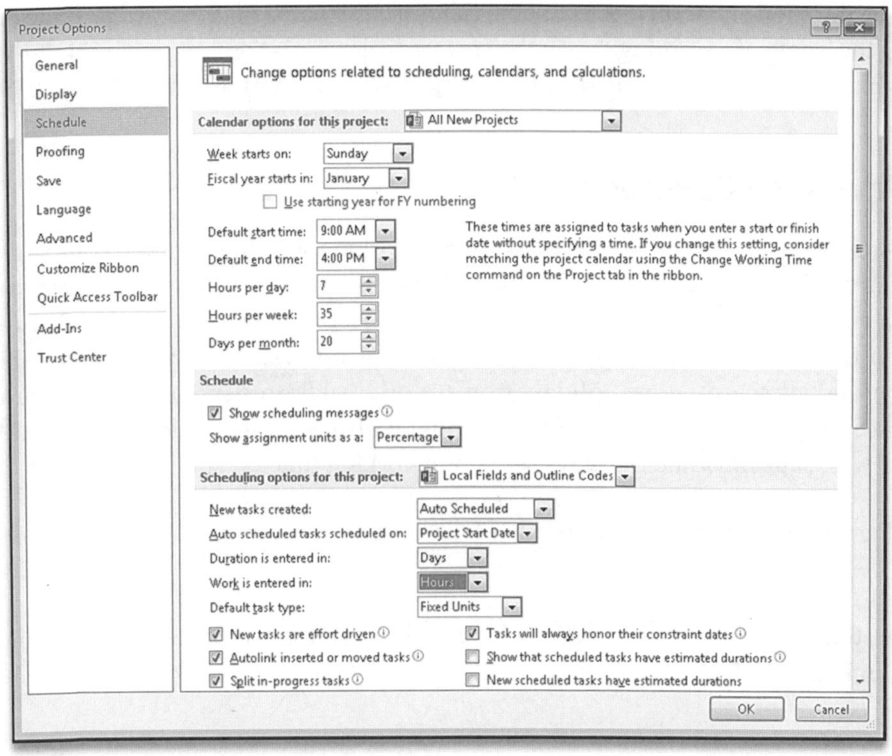

Figure 4 - 49: Project Options dialog, Schedule page

3. In the *Calendar options for this project* pick list, select the *All New Projects* option.
4. Set the *Default start time* and *Default end time* values to match the project calendar start time and end time.
5. Set the *Hours per day* and *Hours per week* values to match the working hours per day and per week on the *Project* calendar.
6. Click the *OK* button and then save the project.

For example, I set the working schedule on the *Standard* calendar from 9:00 AM to 4:00 PM, representing only a 7-hour working day and a 35-hour working week. In every enterprise project, each project manager must perform the following steps on the *Schedule* page of the *Project Options* dialog:

- Set the *Default start time* to 9:00 AM.
- Set the *Default end time* to 4:00 PM.
- Set the *Hours per day* value to 7 hours.
- Set the *Hours per week* value to 35 hours.

The *Hours per day* setting on the *Schedule* page determines how Project Pro 2013 calculates the duration of **every task** in the project. The duration equation is the formula used to calculate duration and you write it as follows:

Duration = **Work** ÷ (**Hours Per Day** x **Units**)

D = W ÷ (HPD x U)

The HPD value in the duration equation is actually the *Hours per day* value on the *Schedule* page of the *Project Options* dialog. Therefore, if the length of a working day in the *Standard* calendar is "out of sync" with the *Hours per day* setting on the *Schedule* page, you will see confusing duration values calculated in your Project Pro 2013 plans.

Creating a New Base Calendar

A *Base* calendar is a master calendar that represents a unique working schedule for your company. You should create custom base calendars to show a project schedule different from the one shown on the *Standard* calendar. Before you create a new *Base* calendar, you must determine whether to create it by copying an existing *Base* calendar or by creating the *Base* calendar from scratch. If you copy an existing *Base* calendar, such as the *Standard* calendar, the new *Base* calendar inherits the working schedule and holidays from the original *Base* calendar. If you create a new *Base* calendar from scratch, Project Server 2013 creates a new blank calendar with a work schedule from 8:00 AM – 5:00 PM with an hour for lunch, and with Saturdays and Sundays set as nonworking time.

To create a copy of an existing calendar, complete the following steps from the *Enterprise Calendars* page in Project Web App:

1. Select an existing calendar and then click the *Copy Calendar* button. The system displays the *Copy Calendar* dialog shown in Figure 4 - 50.

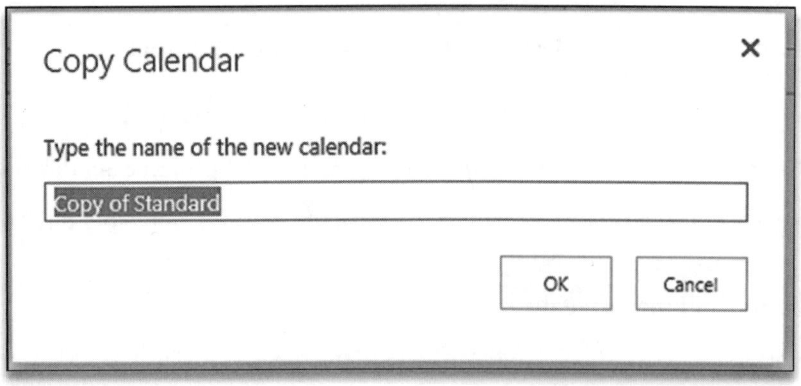

Figure 4 - 50: Copy Calendar dialog

2. Enter a name for the calendar in the *Name* field and then click the *OK* button. Project Server 2013 adds the new *Base* calendar to the list of calendars on the *Enterprise Calendars* page, as shown in Figure 4 - 51. Notice that I created a new *Base* calendar named *4 X 10* to reflect the working schedule of resources who work four 10-hour days.

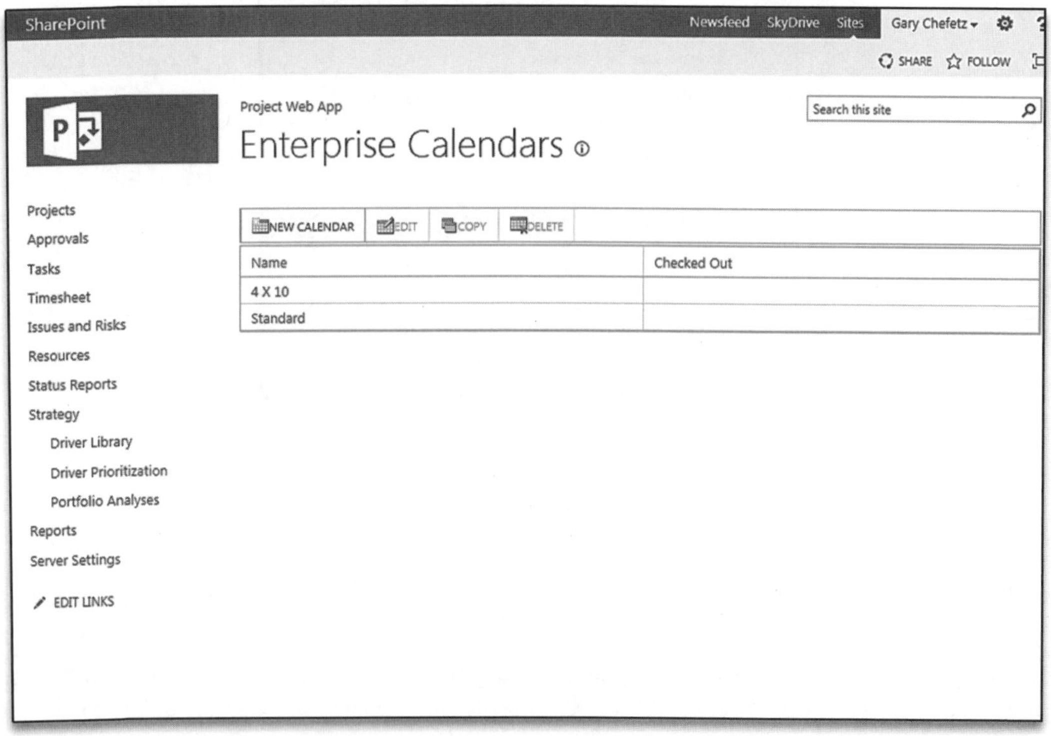

Figure 4 - 51: New Base Calendars created

3. Select the new *Base* calendar and click the *Edit Calendar* button. Project Server 2013 displays the *Change Working Time* dialog shown previously.
4. Click the *Work Weeks* tab and then click the *Details* button. Project Server 2013 displays the *Details* dialog shown previously.
5. In the *Details* dialog, select the daily working schedule for each day of the week. Figure 4 - 52 and Figure 4 - 53, together, show the *Details* dialog after I set the working schedule with 10 hours of work Monday through Thursday, with no work on Friday.

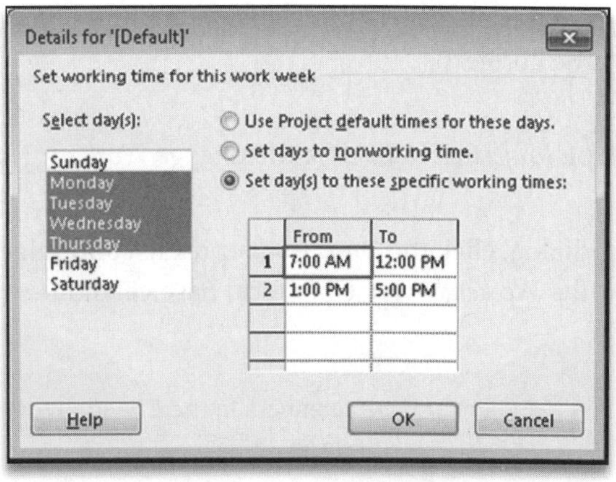

Figure 4 - 52: Details dialog shows Monday - Thursday schedule

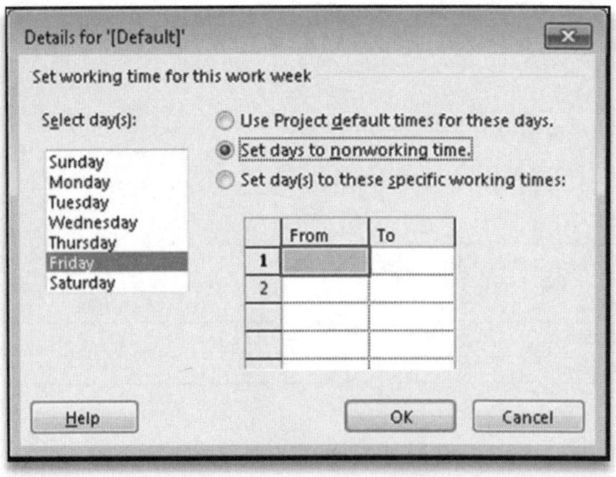

Figure 4 - 53: Details dialog shows Friday schedule

6. Click the *OK* button to close the *Details* dialog and return to the *Change Working Time* dialog.
7. Click the *OK* button to close the *Change Working Time* dialog and save the new *Base* calendar.

> **Information**: When you create a new blank *Base* calendar by clicking the *New Calendar* button on the *Enterprise Calendars* page, you must perform the same steps presented earlier in this section to set up your new blank *Base* calendar.

Importing a Base Calendar from a Project

Project Server 2013 allows you to import *Base* calendars created in local (non-enterprise) projects. For example, prior to my organization's implementation of Project Server 2013, a project manager created a special *Weekend Work* base calendar in a project to schedule tasks that must occur only on a Saturday or Sunday. To import this *Base* calendar as an enterprise *Base* calendar, I must complete the following steps:

1. Launch Project Pro 2013 and log in to Project Server 2013 with administrator permissions.

2. Open the local (non-enterprise) project.

3. In the *Properties* section of the *Project* ribbon, click the *Change Working Time* button.

4. In the *Change Working Time* dialog, click the *For calendar* pick list and select the local *Base* calendar. Notice in Figure 4 - 54 that I selected the *Weekend Work Only* local base calendar.

> **Information**: You can create additional *Base* calendars in the *Change Working Time* dialog using the *Create New Calendar* button and the *Add Calendar to Enterprise* button.

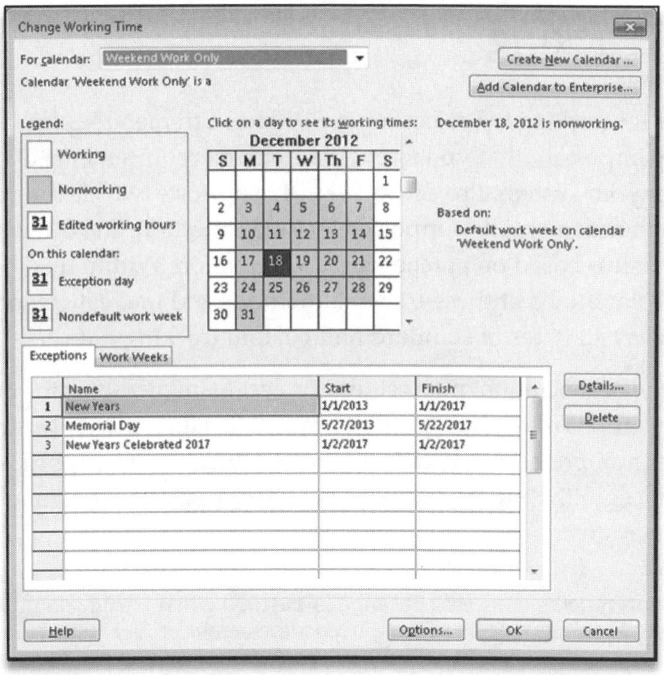

Figure 4 - 54: Change Working Time dialog shows local Base calendar

5. Click the *Add Calendar to Enterprise* button.

The system displays the *Add to Enterprise* dialog. In the *Add to Enterprise* dialog, enter a new name that conforms to your organizational standard for naming base calendars and then click the *OK* button.

6. Click the *OK* button to close the *Change Working Time* dialog.

Figure 4 - 55 shows the new *Weekend Work Only* calendar added to the calendars list on the *Enterprise Calendars* page in Project Web App.

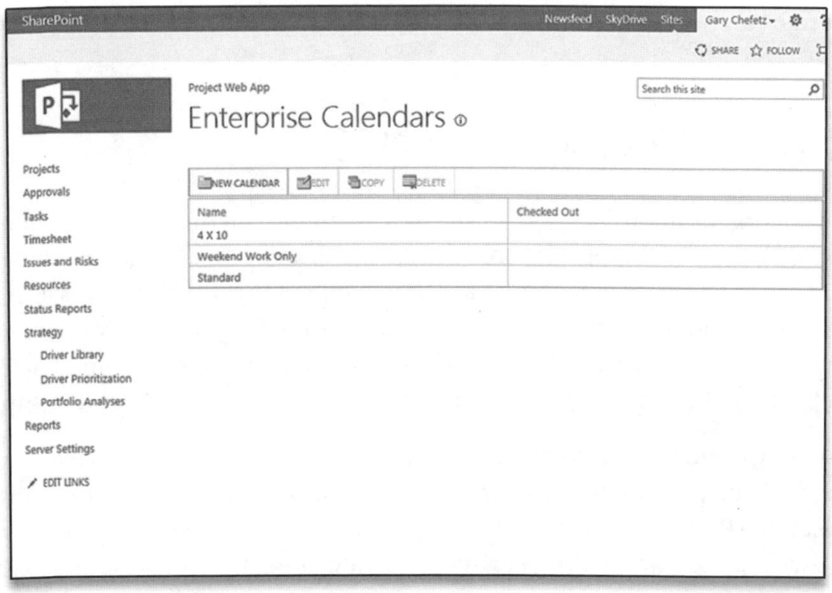

Figure 4 - 55: Enterprise Calendars page includes Weekend Work Only calendar

Understanding Tracking

The configuration you choose for tracking in Project Server 2013 has a tremendous impact on everyone in your organization. Therefore, it is vitally important that you know the tracking requirements of your organization before you configure tracking settings for your system. Project Server 2013 supports two classic approaches to task assignment tracking: effort-based tracking fundamentally supported by time collection, and duration-based tracking fundamentally supported by collecting status based on percentage of completion. Within this dichotomy, Project Server 2013 gives you the ability to create variations of these tracking methods and to create blended methods to support very specific requirements and collect all types of standard and custom tracking data.

In a normal repetitive cycle, the organization must require project team members to enter task-tracking information for enterprise projects. Organizations may need to collect time information in a daily timesheet to track the amount of time spent on activities such as non-project work, billable and non-billable time, or time spent on administrative work. Project Server 2013 also interfaces with third party ERP systems to support articulation of timesheet information to a billing, payroll, or accounting system.

Warning: Your organization's greatest challenge is **culture** when introducing the use of timesheets for the first time. If your organization has not previously used timesheets of any type, you will likely face a great deal of "pushback" from team members, and possibly even from project managers. Your leaders **must address this issue and plan accordingly**, or face the possibility of failure in implementing Project Server 2013 in your organization.

To configure Project Server 2013 for tracking, you must specify your organization's settings in each of the following areas, which I discuss individually:

- Fiscal periods
- Time periods for timesheets
- Timesheet options
- Default method of tracking task progress

For the purposes of this book, I assume that you or an administrator already defined fiscal periods and time periods in your system.

Configuring Time and Task Tracking

The tracking method your organization chooses has a significant impact on project team members and their interaction with the *Tasks* page in Project Web App. Not only do some of these options control what data a resource reports, but they also determine the appearance of the *Tasks* page. If you intend to configure your system to use timesheets to drive progress in single entry mode, the system sets and locks the tracking method for you. You must understand both the interface impact and your organization's tracking requirements to determine tracking method settings. Choose a tracking method that best fits the planning and tracking scenarios you intend to support.

- **Using Task Aggregation:** If you plan on having your users update all of their tasks in My Sites (News Feed) or Outlook because you plan to use task aggregation through the SharePoint Work Management Service, then you should select the *Percent of work complete* option for your tracking method. In this case, your users use neither the *Task* page nor the *Timesheet* page to update their task status. Using the task aggregation feature provides a simple mark-as-done interface using checkboxes next to each task. Using this scenario, your percent complete values will always be 0% or 100% and nothing in between.

- **Mixed Enterprise and Non-enterprise (Visibility) Projects**: You should also use *Percent of work complete* to support a mixed environment with some projects directly managed in Project Server 2013 and updated through the *Tasks* page, and other projects appearing as visibility projects managed at the Project-Site level. This is an ideal way to support both agile and formal project management methodologies.

- **Mixed Tracking Methods Enterprise**: If you need to support mixed tracking methods, your tracking method selection becomes the default, as you will not choose to lock it down. In this case, choose the most prevalent form of tracking for your enterprise projects. You can use the *Tasks* page to gather both. Understand that mixing tracking methods can confuse the users with the row format changes on the *Tasks* page.

- **Mixed Tracking Methods Enterprise with Task Page and Timesheet page:** When you decide to mix both of these user entry points; it is typically because you want to track time at a different level than tasks. For instance, users report time at the project level through the *Timesheet* page, but then report percent complete through the *Tasks* page. Although the system easily supports this, you must take extra care when training your users under this scenario.

- **Single Tracking Method Enterprise:** Select the method most appropriate for your business requirements. Always choose to lock down the tracking method.

- **Single Tracking Method Enterprise Timesheet-Driven**: If you intend to use timesheets collecting time by day, I strongly recommend that you run your system in Single Entry Mode (SEM). When you choose SEM, the system locks down certain selections on the *Task Settings and Display* page.

Best Practice: Because users cannot add tasks from visibility projects to their timesheets, and because they impact resource availability data with crude estimates, MSProjectExperts recommends that you not mix visibility projects into your environment unless you understand that this may render useless, the *Resource Availability* page in the Resource Center. You can adjust for this in reporting using BI tools.

Warning: If you selected the *Single Entry Mode* option on the *Timesheet Settings and Defaults* page, keep in mind that Project Server 2013 locks the *Tracking Settings* options at the top of the *Task Settings and Display* page.

Selecting the Tracking method

If you want to configure your system to support a timesheet-driven tracking environment, you should skip to the next major topical section, *Configuring Project Server 2013 for Time Reporting,* and then come back to the settings on this page. Otherwise, as part of your Project Server 2013 implementation, your organization must make two important decisions about tracking method settings:

- Determine which method of progress tracking to set as the default.
- Determine whether to "lock down" the default method of tracking, or to allow individual project managers to select their own tracking method for each project.

Project Server 2013 offers four methods for tracking task progress. The difference between each tracking method is the progress information entered by resources:

- **Percent of Work Complete** allows resources to enter an estimated *% Work Complete* value for each task assignment.

- **Actual Work Done and Work Remaining** allows resources to enter the cumulative amount of *Actual Work* and *Remaining Work* for each task assignment.

- **Hours of Work Done per Period** allows resources to enter the hours of *Actual Work* completed on a daily or weekly basis for each task assignment.

- **Free Form** allows resources to enter task progress using any of the three previous methods for each task assignment.

In addition, each of the four methods for tracking task progress allows resources to adjust the *Remaining Work* estimate for each task assignment.

Information: **Percent of Work Complete** is the system default method of tracking progress unless your organization selects another method.

Warning: The *Percent of Work Complete* and the *Actual Work Done and Work Remaining* methods of tracking progress impose tracking limitations on your project managers. Neither of these methods is date sensitive, which means that Project Server 2013 does not automatically reschedule uncompleted work for tasks that started late. Because of this limitation, I recommend that you customize the setup of the *Tasks* page to include the *Actual Start* and *Actual Finish* fields to make each method of tracking date sensitive. I document the recommended setup of the *Tasks* page in the next section of this module.

To configure the default method of tracking progress for your organization, in the *Time and Task Management* section of the *PWA Settings* page, click the *Task Settings and Display* link. Project Server 2013 displays the *Task Settings and Display* page shown in Figure 4 - 56. The *Task Settings and Display* page contains four sections of tracking options. I discuss the options in each section separately.

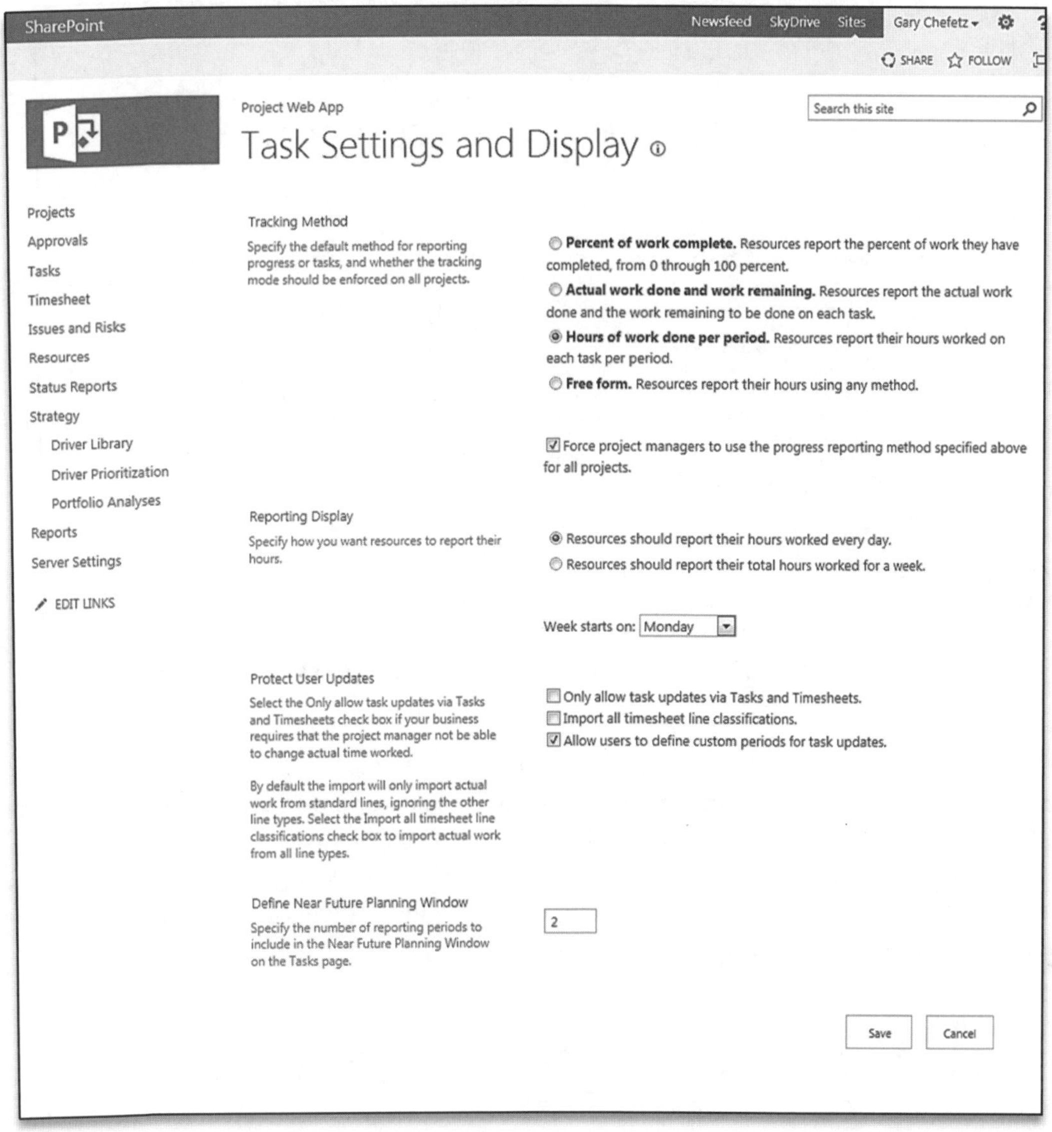
SharePoint
Newsfeed
SkyDrive
Sites
Gary Chefetz
SHARE
FOLLOW
Search this site
Project Web App
Task Settings and Display
Projects
Approvals
Tasks
Timesheet
Issues and Risks
Resources
Status Reports
Strategy
Driver Library
Driver Prioritization
Portfolio Analyses
Reports
Server Settings
EDIT LINKS
Tracking Method
Specify the default method for reporting progress or tasks, and whether the tracking mode should be enforced on all projects.
Percent of work complete. Resources report the percent of work they have completed, from 0 through 100 percent.
Actual work done and work remaining. Resources report the actual work done and the work remaining to be done on each task.
Hours of work done per period. Resources report their hours worked on each task per period.
Free form. Resources report their hours using any method.
Force project managers to use the progress reporting method specified above for all projects.
Reporting Display
Specify how you want resources to report their hours.
Resources should report their hours worked every day.
Resources should report their total hours worked for a week.
Week starts on: Monday
Protect User Updates
Select the Only allow task updates via Tasks and Timesheets check box if your business requires that the project manager not be able to change actual time worked.
By default the import will only import actual work from standard lines, ignoring the other line types. Select the Import all timesheet line classifications check box to import actual work from all line types.
Only allow task updates via Tasks and Timesheets.
Import all timesheet line classifications.
Allow users to define custom periods for task updates.
Define Near Future Planning Window
Specify the number of reporting periods to include in the Near Future Planning Window on the Tasks page.
2
Save
Cancel

Figure 4 - 56: Task Settings and Display page

Specifying the Tracking Method

In the *Tracking Method* section, specify one of the four tracking methods for your organization. If you select the **Percent of Work Complete** method of tracking, the system displays the *Tasks* page shown in Figure 4 - 57.

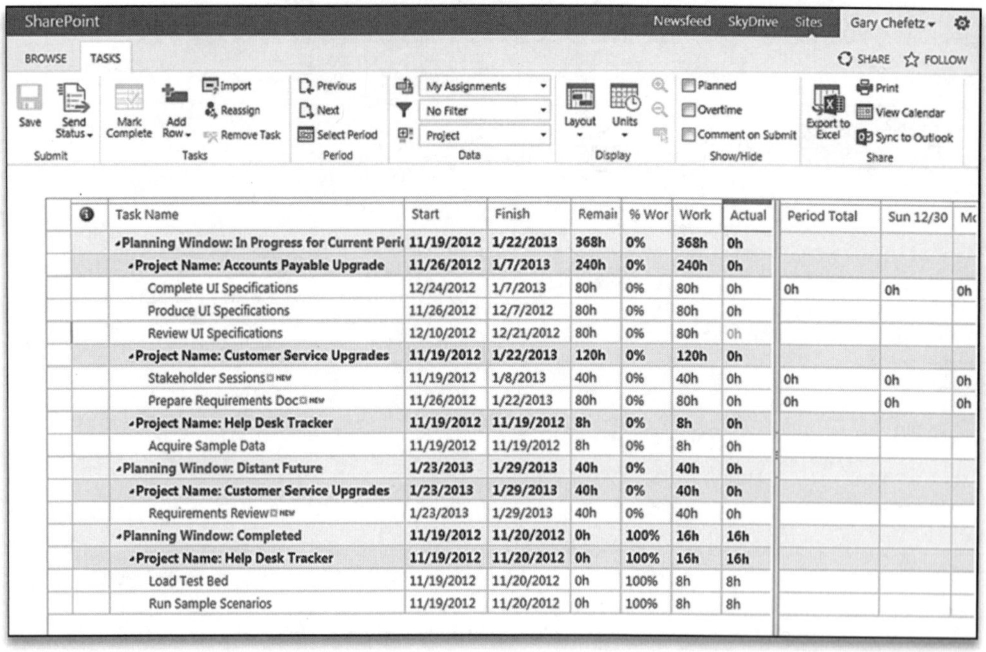

Figure 4 - 57: Tasks page using Percent of Work Complete tracking method

On the *Tasks* page, resources enter their cumulative *Percent Work Complete* value in the *% Work Complete* column. When you use the *Percent of Work Complete* tracking method, the system locks the *Actual Work* column and locks the cells in the timephased grid if the user opts to display the timephased grid by selecting this option from the *Layout* button pick list. Users can click a task in the *Task Name* column to display the *Assignment Details* page for the selected task, shown in Figure 4 - 58 and Figure 4 - 59.

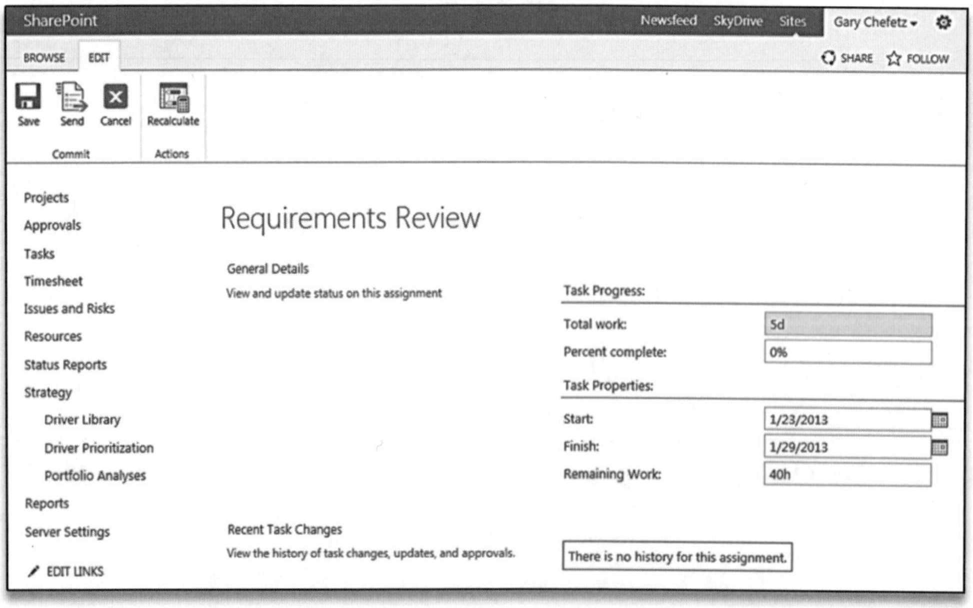

Figure 4 - 58: Task Details page for a selected task (part 1)

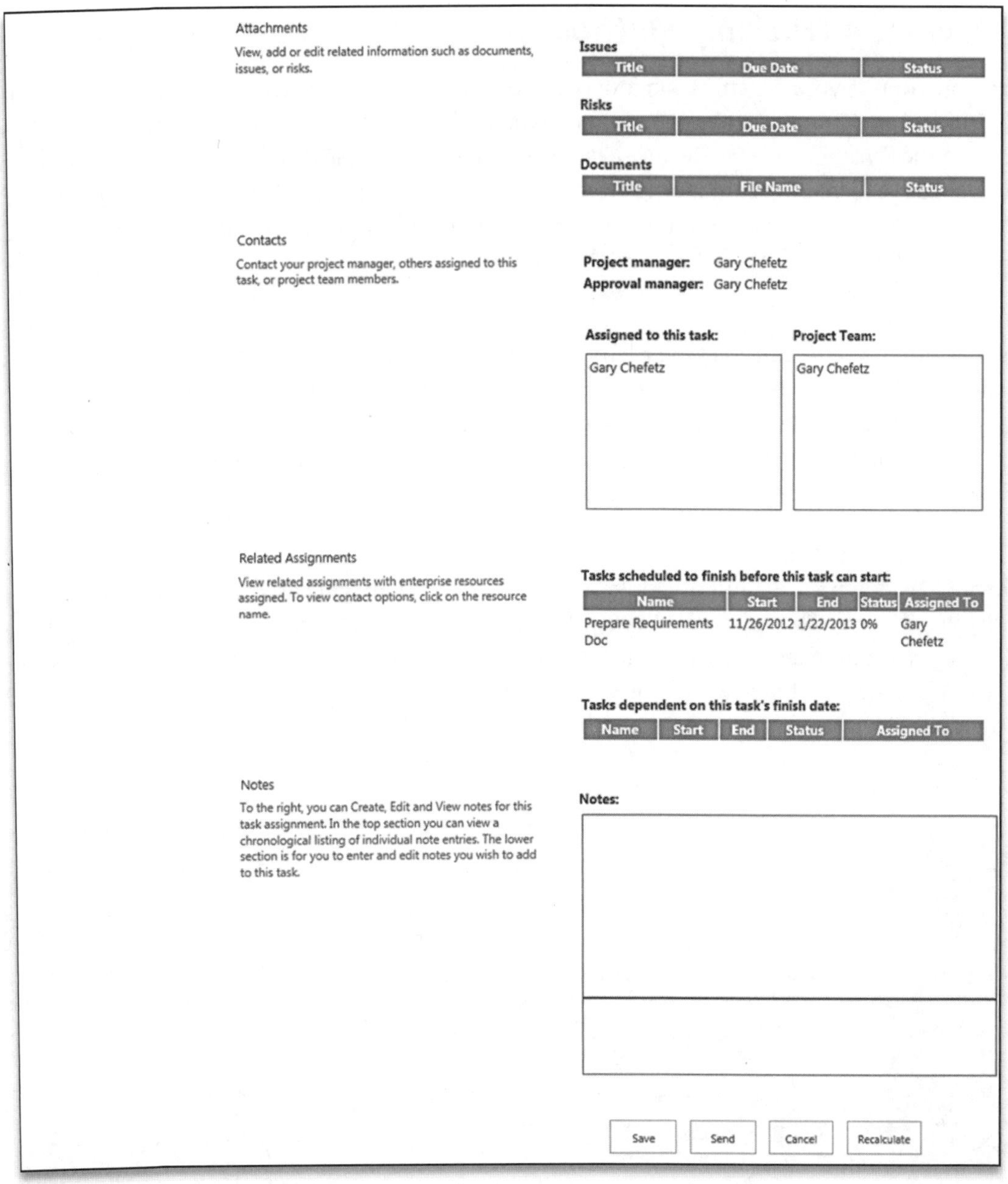
Attachments
View, add or edit related information such as documents, issues, or risks.
Issues
Title
Due Date
Status
Risks
Title
Due Date
Status
Documents
Title
File Name
Status
Contacts
Contact your project manager, others assigned to this task, or project team members.
Project manager: Gary Chefetz
Approval manager: Gary Chefetz
Assigned to this task:
Project Team:
Gary Chefetz
Gary Chefetz
Related Assignments
View related assignments with enterprise resources assigned. To view contact options, click on the resource name.
Tasks scheduled to finish before this task can start:
Name
Start
End
Status
Assigned To
Prepare Requirements Doc
11/26/2012
1/22/2013
0%
Gary Chefetz
Tasks dependent on this task's finish date:
Name
Start
End
Status
Assigned To
Notes
To the right, you can Create, Edit and View notes for this task assignment. In the top section you can view a chronological listing of individual note entries. The lower section is for you to enter and edit notes you wish to add to this task.
Notes:
Save
Send
Cancel
Recalculate

Figure 4 - 59: Task Details page for a selected task (Part 2)

If you select the **Actual Work Done and Work Remaining** method of tracking, on the *Tasks* page, resources enter their cumulative actual work value in the *Actual Work* column and remaining work value in the *Remaining Work* column. When you use this tracking setting, the system locks the *%Work Complete* column and the timephased grid for editing.

If you select the **Hours of Work Done per Period** tracking method, the system locks the *%Work Complete* column and the *Actual Work* column from editing on the left-hand data grid, while unlocking the timephased grid.

If you select the **Free Form** method of tracking, the system unlocks all progress columns for editing. Users must choose which columns to edit. This can be extremely confusing to users who do not understand the system scheduling paradigms.

Locking Down the Tracking Method

As I mentioned previously, your organization must decide whether to "lock down" the default method of tracking, or to allow individual project managers to select their own method of tracking for each project. To lock down the tracking method, select the *Force project managers to use the progress reporting method specified above for all projects* option. Most organizations choose to force project managers to use the default tracking method. The consequence of not locking this down is potential confusion in the minds of resources when their *Tasks* page displays tasks that use different tracking methods and have different fields available for editing.

If you do not lock down the default tracking method for the organization, a resource must know how to report progress using the different methods available. In certain implementations where project teams are static entities, or where specific groups represented within the system follow different uniform tracking methods, multiple reporting methods may be a viable option. As a general rule, I recommend you strive for simplicity rather than complexity in setting up Project Server 2013 for tracking task progress.

When you do not lock down the default tracking method, a project manager can change the method of tracking for a project by clicking the *File* tab and then clicking the *Info* tab in the *Backstage* in Project Pro 2013 as shown in Figure 4 - 60. The project manager can then select any one of the four methods of tracking progress in the *Tracking Method* pick list. After selecting the new method of tracking progress in the project, the project manager must save the project and then publish it to make the change apparent in Project Web App.

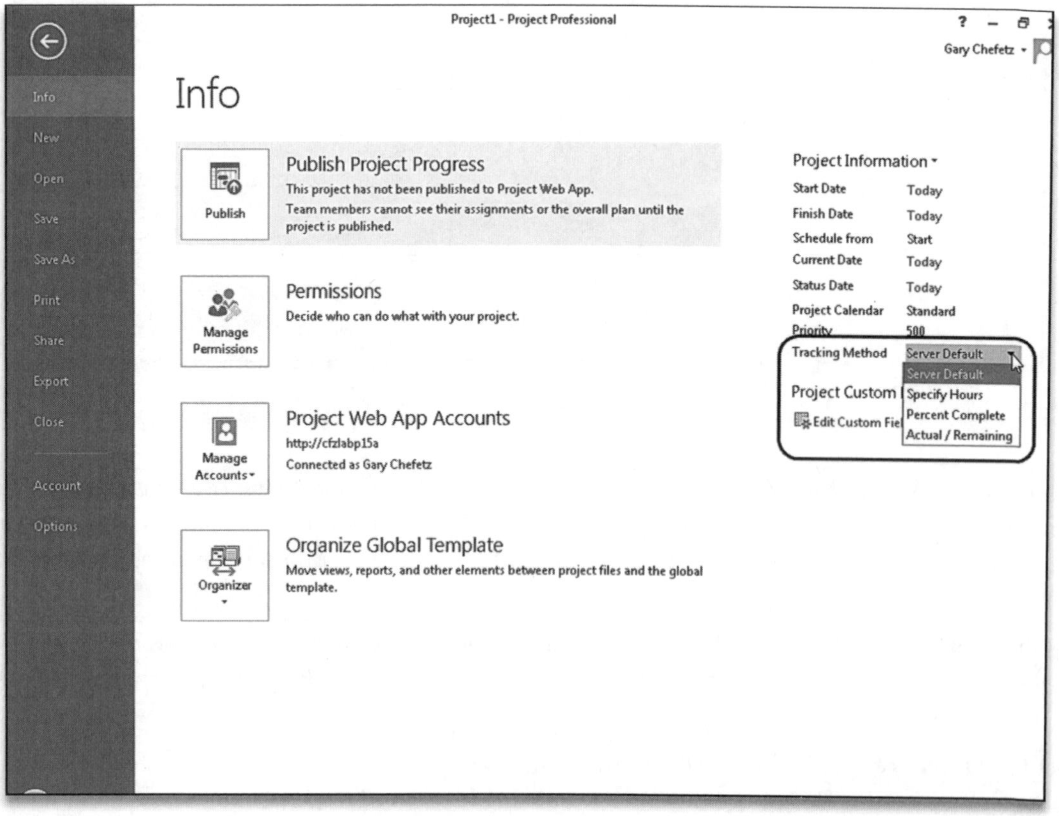

Figure 4 - 60: Change tracking method on the Info page in the Backstage

Information: Notice in Figure 4 - 60 that the default method of tracking progress is *Server Default*. Therefore, it only makes sense to select one of the three other options: *Specify Hours, Percent Complete*, or *Actual/Remaining.*

Tips for Using Tracking Methods

If your organization uses either the *Percent of Work Complete* method or the *Actual Work Done and Work Remaining* method of tracking, you should be aware of the default behavior of both Project Server 2013 and Project Pro 2013 when using these two methods. In the following sections, I present some tips for effectively using these two tracking methods after setting up the custom layout of the *Tasks* page detailed in the previous topical section.

Using Percent of Work Complete

The *Percent of Work Complete* method of tracking progress does not automatically capture an *Actual Start* date or an *Actual Finish* date when resources enter progress on tasks. Instead, when the resource enters a percentage value in the *Progress* field, the system assumes the task **started as scheduled**. When the resource enters 100% in the *% Work Complete* field, the system assumes the task **finished as scheduled**.

For example, Rhonda Epperson was to perform 40 hours of work beginning on Monday, but completed only 50% of her work because she actually started work on Wednesday. When she enters 50% in the *% Work Complete* field for the task, the software **assumes she started on Monday** even though she actually started on Wednesday. The result is that, even though the task will probably finish at least two days late, the system does not show the potential late finish.

MSProjectExperts recommends as a best practice that your organization require each resource to use the following methodology for entering progress on the *Tasks* page using this tracking method:

1. In the *Actual Start* field, enter the actual date when the resource began work on the task.
2. In the *% Work Complete* field, enter the cumulative percentage of how much work the resource completed to date.
3. Adjust the estimate in the *Remaining Work* field, if necessary.
4. If the resource adjusts the *Remaining Work* estimate, the resource should add a note to document the reason for the change.
5. In the *Actual Finish* field, enter the actual date when the task is complete, which causes the system to set the *% Work Complete* field to 100% for the task.

Using this methodology, resources should never enter 100% in the *% Work Complete* field because when the user enters an *Actual Finish* date, the system marks the task 100% complete automatically. The only time a user can safely enter 100% in the *% Work Complete* field is when the task starts and finishes as scheduled.

Using Actual Work Done and Work Remaining

The *Actual Work Done and Work Remaining* tracking method does not automatically capture an *Actual Start* date or an *Actual Finish* date when resources enter progress on tasks. Instead, when the resource enters actual hours, the system assumes the task **started as scheduled**. When the resource enters as many actual hours as originally planned in the *Actual Work* field or in the timephased grid, causing the *Remaining Hours* value to hit zero, the system assumes the task **finished as scheduled**.

For example, Rhonda Epperson was to perform 40 hours of work beginning on Monday. Rhonda completed only 20 hours of work because she actually started work on Wednesday. When she enters 20 hours in the *Actual Work* field for the task, the software **assumes she started on Monday** even though she actually started on Wednesday. The result is that the system does not show the potential late finish even though the task will probably finish at least two days late.

MSProjectExperts recommends as a best practice that your organization require each resource to use the following methodology for entering progress on the *Tasks* page using this tracking method:

1. In the *Actual Start* field, enter the actual date when the resource began work on the task.
2. In the *Actual Work* field, or in the timephased grid, enter the cumulative number of hours of actual work completed to date.
3. Adjust the estimate in the *Remaining Work* field, if necessary.
4. If the resource adjusts the *Remaining Work* estimate, the resource should add a note to document the reason for the change.
5. In the *Actual Finish* field, enter the actual date when the resource finishes work on the task.

As you can see, there are numerous options available to you when selecting tracking methods and configuring the system for task updates and time entry. I have tried to give you some pointers toward best practices, but each implementation and each organization has its own unique requirements. If you completely identify these before you begin your configuration, your configuration will take less time.

Setting the Reporting Display

The *Reporting Display* section of the *Task Settings and Display* page allows you to determine how Project Server 2013 displays the data grid when you select the *Hours of Work Done per Period* method of tracking. In this section, you must specify whether to show a daily grid or a weekly grid, and then specify the first day of each reporting period.

If you select the default *Resources should report their hours worked every day* option, the system displays a daily timesheet grid spanning seven days on the *Tasks* page. If you select the *Resources should report their total hours worked for a week* option, the system displays a weekly timesheet data grid spanning four weeks on the *Tasks* page.

In the *Reporting Display* section of the *Task Settings and Display* page, you must also select an option from the *Week starts on* pick list. If you select the default *Monday* value, the system sets up workweeks from Monday through the following Sunday. If you select the *Sunday* option, the system sets up workweeks from Sunday through the following Saturday.

Protecting User Updates

In the *Protect User Updates* section of the *Task Settings and Display* page, you specify how Project Server 2013 handles task updates from the *Tasks* page. If you select the *Only allow task updates via Tasks and Timesheets* option, you prevent your project managers from manually entering actual progress in their enterprise projects in Project Pro 2013. If your project managers need to enter actual progress manually in their enterprise projects, you must not select this option. Selecting this option enables the "Managed Time Periods" feature used previously in Project Server 2003 and 2007.

By default when users import their time entered in the *Timesheet* page to the *Tasks* page, the system only imports actual work from standard lines, ignoring the other line types. Select the *Import all timesheet line classifications* option to import actual work from all line types when your organization tracks both time and task progress using both the *Timesheet* page and the *Tasks* page in Project Web App.

The *Allow users to define custom periods for task updates* option allows users to define custom time reporting periods. For example, Figure 4 - 61 shows the *Select Period* dialog that a user reaches by clicking the *Select Period* button from the *Period* section of the *Tasks* ribbon.

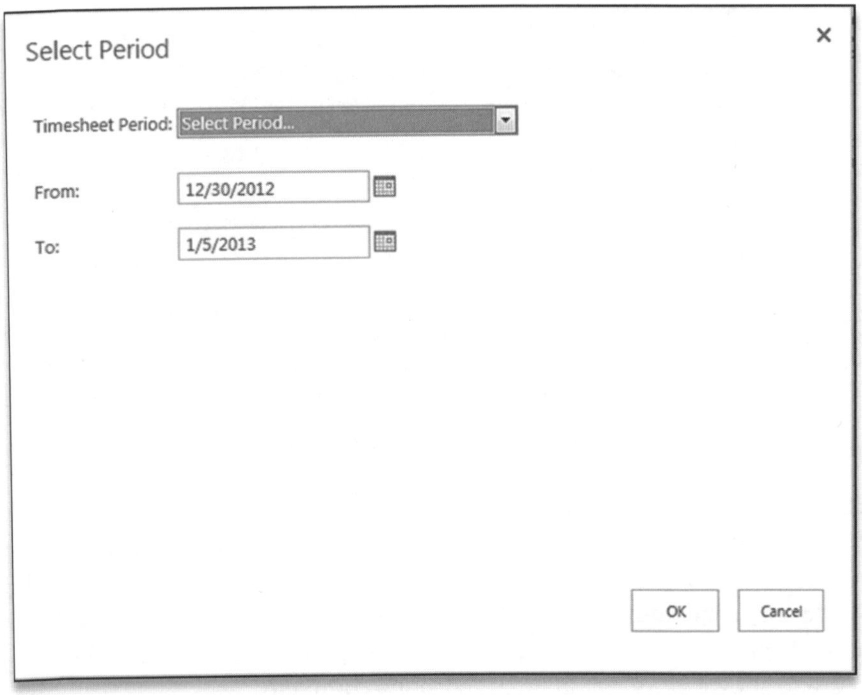

Figure 4 - 61: Select Period dialog

Notice in Figure 4 - 61 that the *From* and *To* fields display and are available for editing. When you select this option, each user can define their own reporting periods as they use the system. When you do not select this option, the *From* and *To* fields and their date pickers do not display in the *Select Period* dialog. Users are limited to using the *Timesheet Period* pick list. If you combine this option with the *Free Form* reporting option, your Project Server 2013 tracking system is off leash. Project Server 2010 was the first version to accommodate an unstructured time reporting paradigm. Note that this setting does not impact timesheets.

Defining the Near Future Planning Window

In the *Define Near Future Planning Window* section, enter the number of reporting periods that constitute the Near Future Planning Window. The default value in this section is 2 reporting periods, representing a two-week "look ahead" into the future. The system uses the value in this section to group the tasks on the *Tasks* page, as shown in Figure 4 - 62.

Task Name	Start	Finish	Remai	% Wor	Period Tota
Planning Window: In Progress for Current Peri	**11/19/2012**	**1/22/2013**	**504h**		
Project Name: Accounts Payable Upgrade	**11/26/2012**	**1/7/2013**	**240h**	**0%**	
Complete UI Specifications	12/24/2012	1/7/2013	80h	0%	0h
Produce UI Specifications	11/26/2012	12/7/2012	80h	0%	
Review UI Specifications	12/10/2012	12/21/2012	80h	0%	
Project Name: Customer Service Upgrades	**11/19/2012**	**1/22/2013**	**120h**	**0%**	
Stakeholder Sessions NEW	11/19/2012	1/8/2013	40h	0%	0h
Prepare Requirements Doc NEW	11/26/2012	1/22/2013	80h	0%	0h
Project Name: Help Desk Tracker	**11/19/2012**	**1/9/2013**	**144h**		
Acquire Sample Data	11/19/2012	11/19/2012	8h	0%	
Load Test Bed	11/19/2012	11/23/2012	28h	22%	
Analyze test result data NEW	1/3/2013	1/9/2013	40h	0%	0h
Run Sample Scenarios	11/19/2012	12/6/2012	68h	11%	
Planning Window: Near Future - Next 2 Period	**1/10/2013**	**1/16/2013**	**40h**	**0%**	
Project Name: Help Desk Tracker	**1/10/2013**	**1/16/2013**	**40h**	**0%**	
Compile analysis report NEW	1/10/2013	1/16/2013	40h	0%	
Planning Window: Distant Future	**1/23/2013**	**1/29/2013**	**40h**	**0%**	
Project Name: Customer Service Upgrades	**1/23/2013**	**1/29/2013**	**40h**	**0%**	
Requirements Review	1/23/2013	1/29/2013	40h	0%	

Figure 4 - 62: Planning Windows displayed on the Tasks page

Notice in Figure 4 - 62 that the system organizes all tasks on the *Tasks* page into four groups: *In Progress for Current Period, Near Future, Distant Future,* and *Completed* (not shown). The *In Progress* group includes any unstarted task with a start date in a previous reporting period or in the current reporting period, plus any task that is currently in-progress. The *Near Future* group includes tasks with a start date in the next "N" reporting periods where "N" is the value you set. The *Distant Future* group includes all tasks with a start date that falls after the *Near Future* grouping. Of course, the *Completed* group shows tasks that are marked 100% complete.

After you set your organization's task tracking settings, click the *Save* button. As you can clearly see, the tracking settings you select have a major impact on how team members interact with the system when entering actual progress. Before your project managers publish any projects, you should carefully consider how your organization measures project progress and then select the appropriate tracking settings values.

Warning: Carefully choose your method of tracking progress. If you choose the wrong method and then later need to change it in an environment where you force all project managers to use the Project Server default, all project managers must open each of their projects and publish them to force the new method to each team member's *Tasks* page in Project Web App. In an environment with a large number of projects, changing the default method of tracking progress may prove very frustrating to your project managers!

Configuring Project Server 2013 for Time Reporting

You have a series of two-choice selections you need to make as you decide how to configure your system for time reporting. The first two-choice selection is whether to use the timesheet feature in Project Server 2013 to collect time that you can keep completely separate from your project data, or to configure the system so that timesheet data drives progress on projects. If you choose to drive project progress with timesheet data, then your next two-choice selection is whether submitting timesheets submits tasks updates at the same time automatically, or whether this is a two-step process for the users where they must import the time sheet data into their tasks page and then submit task updates separately. Finally, if you opt to drive progress using timesheet data, you must decide whether to protect the actual work in project plans. Project Server timesheets and their data is completely separate from the information flow from the *Tasks* page, except that users can exchange data between the two, and you configure Project Server 2013 to act as if the two are connected.

Timesheet data does not drive project progress: Use this scenario when you want to collect timesheet data that you cannot use to drive progress on task assignments. For instance, your business requirements are to collect time data at the project level only, but to use Percent Work Complete to drive task status. In this and variations of this theme, the data you are collecting in the timesheets is at a different level than required for task progress or you simply choose not to drive task progress using timesheet data.

Timesheet data drives task progress manually: In this scenario users import some or all of their task progress from their timesheet entries. This is a legacy scenario that dates back to Project Server 2007, which introduced timesheets that supported only this scenario at release. There are few real-world situations where this configuration is not simply added work for the user and added complexity. If you are using timesheets and do not require your users to enter all data in the timesheets, you have one of those rare situations that separating the entry makes sense; but this is not a likely real-world scenario.

Timesheet data drives task progress automatically: This is the most common configuration for systems that use timesheet data to drive task progress and the least complex and confusing for your end users. By selecting *Single Entry Mode (SEM)*, timesheet data flows to both timesheet approvers and project managers for updating into the schedules automatically.

Protected User Updates: At first, this may sound like a good idea, but it adds a rigid construct to the system that requires your project managers to be relatively advanced users of Project or you risk heaps of frustration among them. This setting prevents project managers from making any change to the schedule that would change an actual work value, such as manually changing the percentage of completion of a task with resources assigned to it. With this setting active, actual work collected through PWA rules and system calculated actual work is strictly forbidden. Understand that changes that project managers make to their schedules that change actual work values do not affect timesheet data under any scenario; however, the *Tasks* page will inherit the new actual work values when the project manager publishes the changes. The best reason for using this setting is that your organization is contractually obligated to provide copies of the project schedules with actual work that matches the timesheet stream.

Configuring Timesheet Options

Two sets of options allow you to configure timesheets for your organization in Project Server 2013. You can create line classifications, if necessary, for business purposes or accounting needs. You may also change the default options for displaying timesheet periods in Project Web App. The values you set here show up on a user's timesheets as the *Billing Category* field, by default.

Creating Line Classifications

To create additional timesheet line classifications, in the *Time and Task Management* section of the *PWA Settings* page, click the *Line Classifications* link. The system displays the *Line Classifications* page shown in Figure 4 - 63.

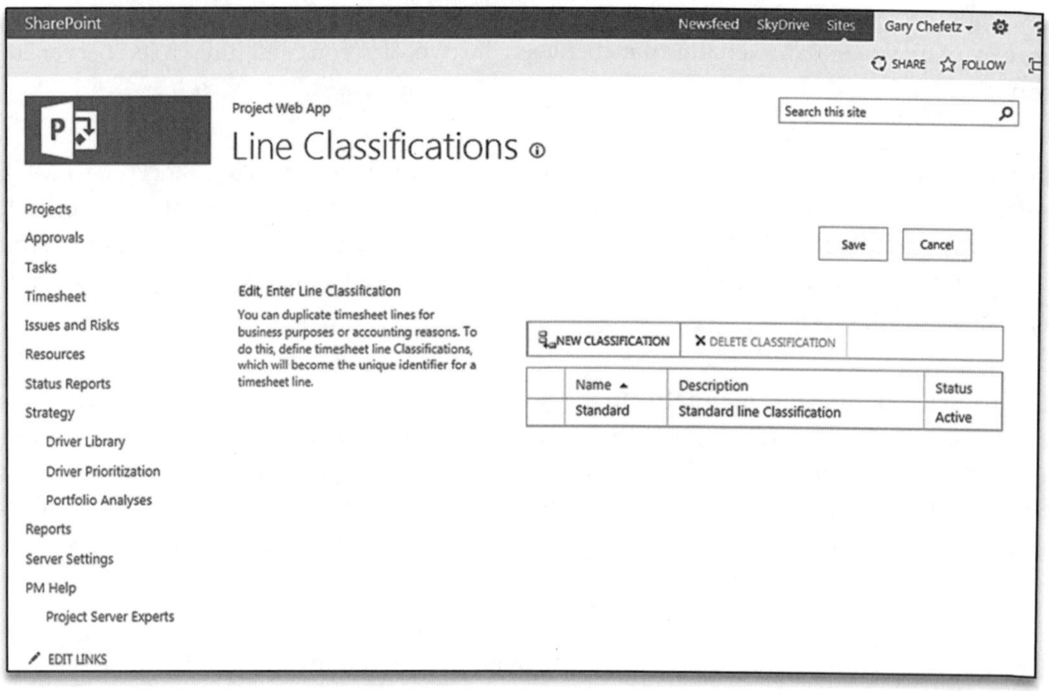

Figure 4 - 63: Line Classifications page

In the data grid, the system displays the *Standard* line classification for timesheet tasks. If your organization requires additional line classifications, click the *NEW CLASSIFICATION* button at the top of the data grid. Project Server 2013 adds the new, unnamed line classification as shown in Figure 4 - 64.

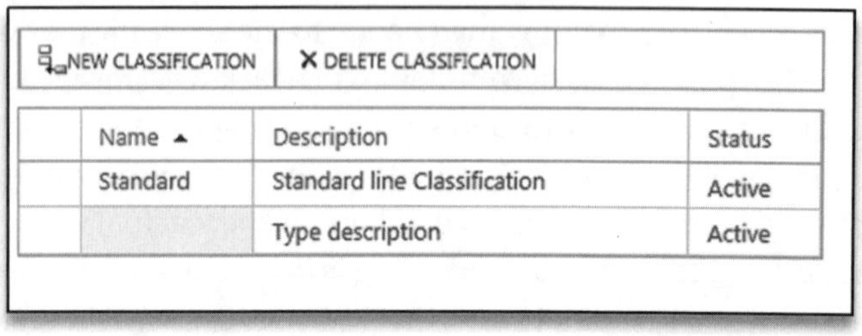

Figure 4 - 64: New unnamed line classification

Edit the information for the new line classification line by entering data in the *Name* and *Description* fields. If you do not want to use the new classification immediately, set its *Status* value to *Inactive*; otherwise, leave the *Status* value set to *Active*. Create as many additional line classifications as you need and then click the *Save* button when finished.

Warning: To preserve historical data, Project Server 2013 does not allow you to delete the new classification after you save it, If you create a new line that you no longer need, set the *Status* value to *Inactive*. The *DELETE CLASSIFICATION* button works only until you save your new entry.

Setting Timesheet Options

To set the options for displaying Project Server 2013 timesheets, in the *Time and Task Management* section of the *PWA Settings* page, click the *Timesheet Settings and Defaults* link. The system displays the *Timesheet Settings and Defaults* page shown in Figure 4 - 65. Notice that the first section of the page determines how the system displays the timesheet in Project Web App.

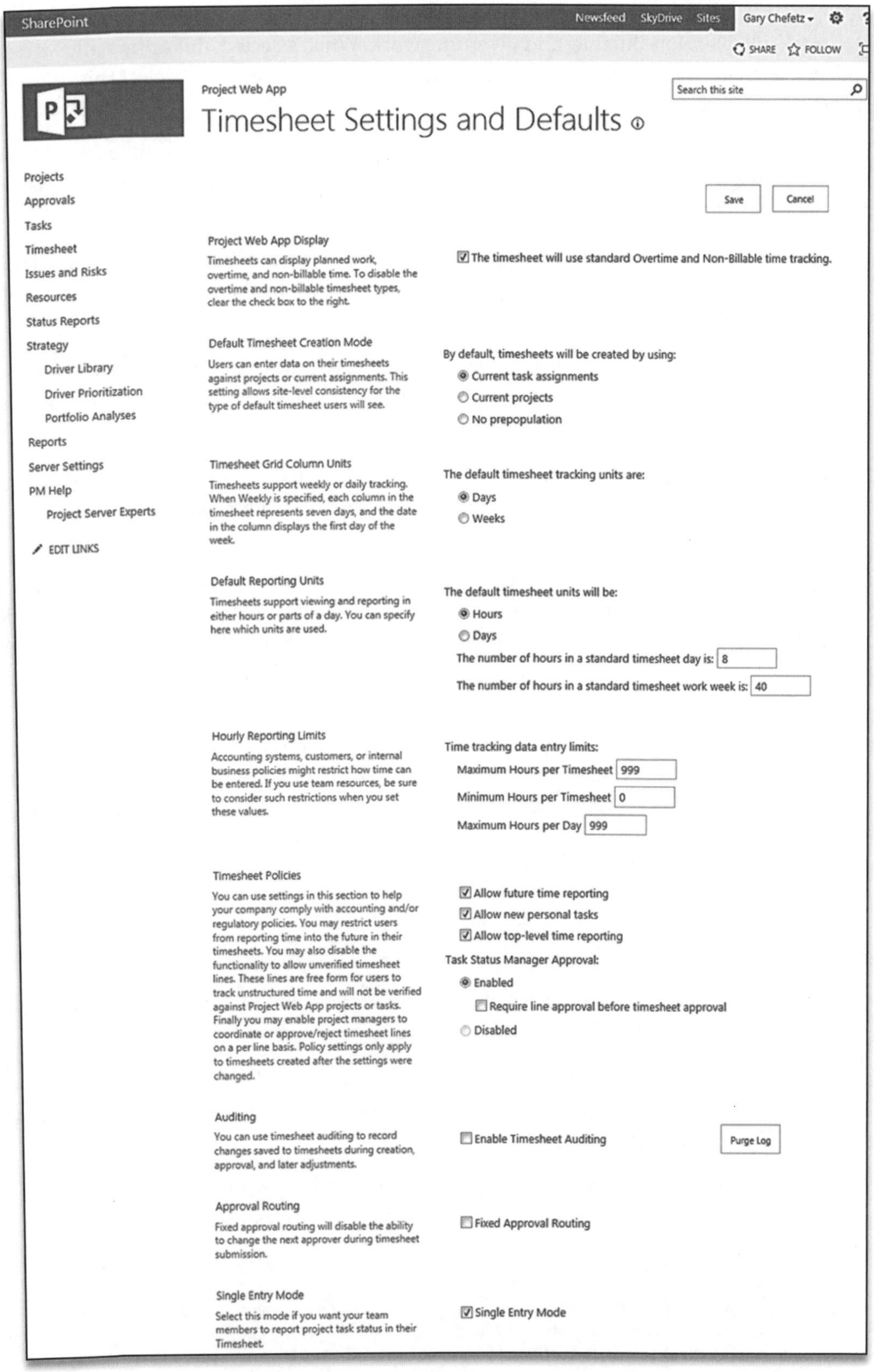
SharePoint
Newsfeed
SkyDrive
Sites
Gary Chefetz
SHARE
FOLLOW
Project Web App
Search this site
Timesheet Settings and Defaults
Projects
Approvals
Tasks
Timesheet
Issues and Risks
Resources
Status Reports
Strategy
Driver Library
Driver Prioritization
Portfolio Analyses
Reports
Server Settings
PM Help
Project Server Experts
EDIT LINKS
Save
Cancel
Project Web App Display
Timesheets can display planned work, overtime, and non-billable time. To disable the overtime and non-billable timesheet types, clear the check box to the right.
The timesheet will use standard Overtime and Non-Billable time tracking.
Default Timesheet Creation Mode
Users can enter data on their timesheets against projects or current assignments. This setting allows site-level consistency for the type of default timesheet users will see.
By default, timesheets will be created by using:
Current task assignments
Current projects
No prepopulation
Timesheet Grid Column Units
Timesheets support weekly or daily tracking. When Weekly is specified, each column in the timesheet represents seven days, and the date in the column displays the first day of the week.
The default timesheet tracking units are:
Days
Weeks
Default Reporting Units
Timesheets support viewing and reporting in either hours or parts of a day. You can specify here which units are used.
The default timesheet units will be:
Hours
Days
The number of hours in a standard timesheet day is: 8
The number of hours in a standard timesheet work week is: 40
Hourly Reporting Limits
Accounting systems, customers, or internal business policies might restrict how time can be entered. If you use team resources, be sure to consider such restrictions when you set these values.
Time tracking data entry limits:
Maximum Hours per Timesheet 999
Minimum Hours per Timesheet 0
Maximum Hours per Day 999
Timesheet Policies
You can use settings in this section to help your company comply with accounting and/or regulatory policies. You may restrict users from reporting time into the future in their timesheets. You may also disable the functionality to allow unverified timesheet lines. These lines are free form for users to track unstructured time and will not be verified against Project Web App projects or tasks. Finally you may enable project managers to coordinate or approve/reject timesheet lines on a per line basis. Policy settings only apply to timesheets created after the settings were changed.
Allow future time reporting
Allow new personal tasks
Allow top-level time reporting
Task Status Manager Approval:
Enabled
Require line approval before timesheet approval
Disabled
Auditing
You can use timesheet auditing to record changes saved to timesheets during creation, approval, and later adjustments.
Enable Timesheet Auditing
Purge Log
Approval Routing
Fixed approval routing will disable the ability to change the next approver during timesheet submission.
Fixed Approval Routing
Single Entry Mode
Select this mode if you want your team members to report project task status in their Timesheet.
Single Entry Mode

Figure 4 - 65: Timesheet Settings and Defaults page

In the *Project Web App Display* section, leave the default *The timesheet will use standard Overtime and Non-Billable tracking* option selected to track Billable, Non-Billable, and Overtime work. When selected, this option allows users to add the *Overtime, Non-Billable,* and *Overtime nonbillable* fields to their timesheets as needed. Deselect this option to track only actual work and scheduled work.

In the *Default Timesheet Creation Mode* section, Project Server 2013 offers three options for timesheet creation. The system uses the option you select when a user creates a new timesheet using the *Create with Default Setting* option. The three options in the *Default Timesheet Creation Mode* section are:

- Select the default *Current task assignments* option to force the system to create timesheets that include both administrative tasks and current task assignments. By default, a current task is any task with planned work during the time period for which the user creates a timesheet.
- Select the *Current projects* option to force the system to create timesheets that include both administrative tasks and only a single top-level line item for each project containing a current task. This option is for organizations that do not track time at the task level, and do not use time to drive task progress.
- Select the *No prepopulation* option to force the system to create blank timesheets that include only administrative tasks. Selecting this option forces the users to insert the tasks they want to see after they create a new timesheet.

In the *Timesheet Grid Column Units* section, select the default *Days* option to specify daily tracking with seven days/week on each user's timesheet. Selecting this option forces the system to set up timesheets with a 7-day data grid using the dates you selected for each timesheet period. Select the *Weeks* option to specify weekly tracking, where each column in the timesheet represents a seven day time period.

In the *Default Reporting Units* section, select the default *Hours* option to display planned work in hours, or select the *Days* option to display planned work in days. Regardless of which option you choose, Project Server 2013 allows team members to enter actual work in either hours or days. If a team member enters actual work in days, such as 1d, then the system converts the value to hours using the number you specify in *The number of hours in a standard timesheet day is* field. The default value in this field is *8*, so if a user enters .5d in a timesheet cell, the system converts the value to 4 hours. If you select the *Weeks* option in the *Timesheet Grid Column Units* section, and a user then enters an actual work value in weeks, such as 1w, the system converts the value to hours using the number you specify in *The number of hours in a standard timesheet week is* field. The default value in this field is 40, so if a user enters .75w in a timesheet cell, the system converts the value to 30 hours.

In the *Hourly Reporting Limits* section, set your upper and lower limits for time entry based on your organization's policies for time entry. These options are:

- In the *Maximum Hours per Timesheet* field, enter the largest number of hours each user can enter in a single timesheet. On a timesheet spanning one week, the theoretical upper limit is 168 hours (7 days x 24 hours/day). To set no upper limit, enter 999 in the field.
- In the *Minimum Hours per Timesheet* field, enter the smallest number of hours each user can enter in a single timesheet. The default value in this field is 0 hours, meaning that users are not required to enter more than 0 hours in any timesheet.

Information: If your organization mandates that each user enter a minimum number of hours during each timesheet period, such as 40 hours, enter that number in the *Minimum Hours per Timesheet* field. The system enforces this minimum value when the user attempts to submit the timesheet.

- In the *Maximum Hours per Day* field, enter the largest number of hours each user can enter in a single timesheet day. On a one day time period, the theoretical upper limit is 24 hours since there are only 24 hours in a day. If you wish to set no upper limit, enter 999 in the field.

> **Information**: Setting either the *Maximum Hours per Timesheet* value or *Maximum Hours per Day* value to 999 makes no sense unless your entries represent more than one actual resource. Therefore, determine your organization's policy for tracking time and enter those numbers accordingly.

In the *Timesheet Policies* section, Project Server 2013 offers options that you can set according to your organization's policies for using the timesheet functionality. These options are:

- Select the *Allow future time reporting* option to allow resources to enter time for tasks in the future, such as for vacation or planned sick leave. Deselect this option to allow resources to report time only in their current timesheet and in past open timesheets.

- Select the *Allow new personal tasks* option to permit users to create timesheet entries for personal tasks. A personal task is any task not included in any project in Project Server 2013. Deselect this option to prevent users from adding personal tasks to their timesheets.

- Select the *Allow top-level time reporting* option to allow users to enter time at the project level.

- Enable the *Task Status Manager Approval* option to include members of the Project Managers group in timesheet line item approvals.

- If you select the previous option, the system enables the *Require line approval before timesheet approval* option. Select this option to force project managers to approve timesheet lines from the projects they manage, or leave it deselected to make the timesheet line approval process optional.

In the *Auditing* section, select the *Enable Timesheet Auditing* option to allow timesheet auditing. The default state of this option is deselected. If you select the *Enable Timesheet Auditing* option, the system creates an auditing log of timesheet usage, which is not accessible through any standard view or report in Project Web App. You must write your own queries or application to retrieve and use this data. You can click the *Purge Log* button at any time to clear the auditing log file of all entries.

In the *Approval Routing* section, select the *Fixed Approval Routing* option to prevent users from manually selecting the next timesheet approver when they submit their timesheets for approval. Deselect this option to allow users to select the next timesheet approver when they submit their timesheets for approval, such as when your organization uses multiple timesheet approvers and users can select the approver.

The *Single Entry Mode* section contains one very important option that controls the behavior of the *Timesheet* page and the *Tasks* page. If you select the *Single Entry Mode* option, Project Server 2013 works as follows:

- A user enters time on *Task A* on the *Timesheet* page.

- The system automatically updates the task progress on *Task A* on the *Tasks* page.

- When the user submits the timesheet for approval to the timesheet manager, the system automatically sends the task update for approval to the status manager for the task.

Information: If you select the *Single Entry Mode* option, the system locks the options in the *Tracking Method* section of the *Task Settings* and *Display* page. These locked options force synchronization between the time entered on the *Timesheet* page and the task progress shown on the *Tasks* page. Keep in mind that when you select the *Single Entry Mode* option, the system automatically selects the *Hours of Work Done Per Period* option. You can still set the *Reporting Display* options to determine whether users enter their time in daily increments or in weekly buckets.

Configuring Administrative Time

You can configure Project Server 2013 to track administrative time. Administrative time consists of activities such as non-project time, unplanned work, support work, meetings, training, and non-working time such as vacation and sick leave. To configure the system to track administrative time on each user's timesheet, in the *Time and Task Management* section of the *PWA Settings* page, click the *Administrative Time* link. The system displays the *Administrative Time* page shown in Figure 4 - 66.

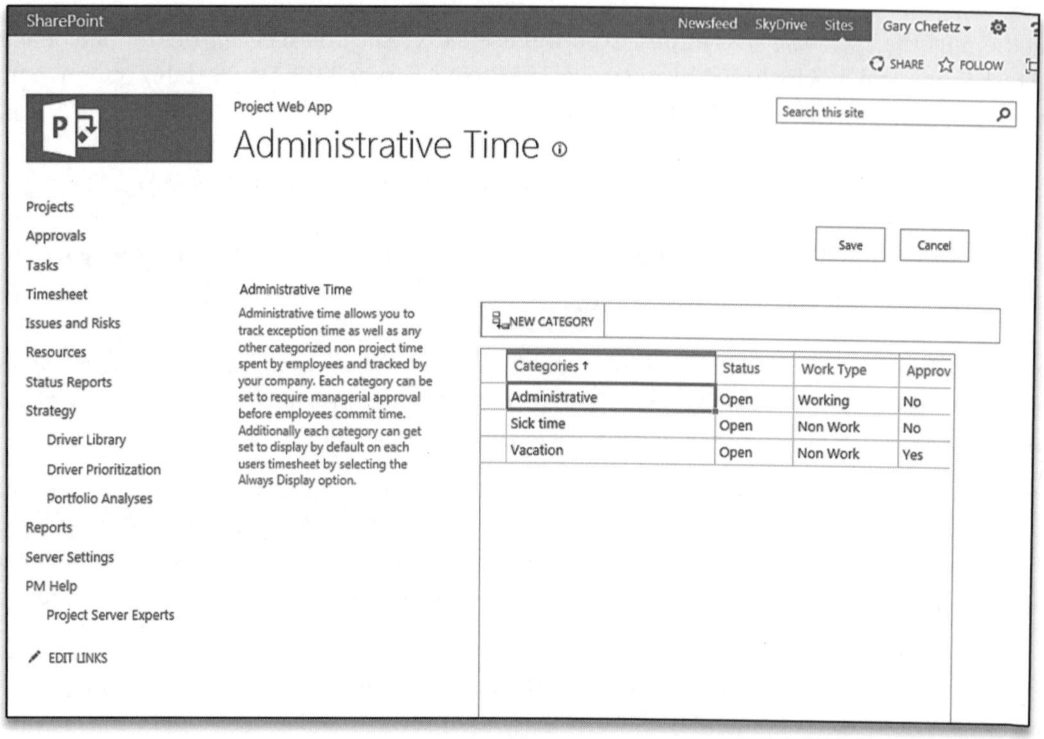

Figure 4 - 66: Administrative Time page

The *Administrative Time* page includes three default categories: *Administrative, Sick time,* and *Vacation*. You can edit each of these categories and add new categories. For each category of administrative time, you can set the following values:

- Enter a descriptive name for the category in the *Categories* field.
- In the *Status* field, set the status for the category as either *Open* or *Closed*. If you close a category, you prevent resources from entering time against it, even though it still appears on each user's timesheet.
- In the *Work Type* field, set the type to *Working* or *Non Work*.
- In the *Approve* field, select either the *Yes* or *No* value to indicate whether category submissions require managerial approval.

- Select the *Always Display* option (scroll to the right to reveal the column) to display the administrative time category on each user's timesheet. Deselect this option for a new category that you do not want users to see, and then select this option when you want users to see the category on their timesheets.

> **Best Practice**: MSProjectExperts strongly recommends that you determine your organization's default categories of administrative time, and then configure these categories before users actually begin using timesheets. If you deselect the *Always Display* option for a category after users create timesheets, the category continues to appear on existing timesheets, and does not appear on new timesheets.

> **Warning**: If your organization intends to use the planned *Sick time* and *Vacation* categories of administrative time, understand that Project Server 2013 reschedules project tasks around a resource's nonworking time automatically. When a resource submits planned *Sick time* or *Vacation*, and the timesheet manager approves the submission, the system automatically adds the planned *Sick time* or *Vacation* as a new nonworking time exception on the resource's calendar in the Enterprise Resource Pool. Unfortunately, Project Server 2013 **does not** indicate whether the non-working time is *Sick time* or *Vacation* on the resource's calendar, simply labeling the exception as "Timesheet." At least at this point, you can guess that it must be planned time for one of your non-working administrative time categories.

> **Best Practice**: MSProjectExperts recommends that you maintain a relatively **short list** of administrative time categories. The more categories you add, the longer the list of tasks on each user's timesheet, and the more cumbersome the time entry process becomes.

Figure 4 - 67 shows the administrative time categories that my organization uses. Notice that I added a new category called *Training*. After you create your organization's administrative time categories, click the *Save* button.

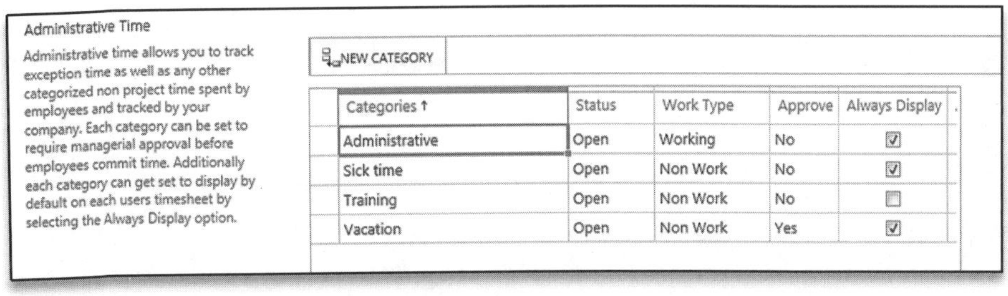
Administrative Time
Administrative time allows you to track exception time as well as any other categorized non project time spent by employees and tracked by your company. Each category can be set to require managerial approval before employees commit time. Additionally each category can get set to display by default on each users timesheet by selecting the Always Display option.
NEW CATEGORY
Categories
Status
Work Type
Approve
Always Display
Administrative
Open
Working
No
Sick time
Open
Non Work
No
Training
Open
Non Work
No
Vacation
Open
Non Work
Yes

Figure 4 - 67: New categories on the Administrative Time page

> **Warning**: To preserve historical data, Project Server 2013 does not allow you to delete the new administrative time category after you create it and then click the *Save* button. If you create a new category and do not need it, set the *Status* value to *Closed* and then deselect the *Always Display* option.

Module 05

Working with Project and Portfolio Governance

Learning Objectives

After completing this module, you will be able to:

- Understand portfolio and project governance
- Understand demand management
- Understand decision management
- Understand the configuration process for lifecycle management
- Create and manage new enterprise project types
- Create Project Detail Pages (PDP's)
- Create new phases and stages
- Understand the sample workflow
- Create and manage dynamic workflows

Inside Module 05

Portfolio Management and Project Governance Overview

By its name alone, Project Server 2013 suggests it is a project management tool to create project schedules, track resources, and collaborate with teams. While this is all true, Project Server is actually more than just a project management tool in that it also offers portfolio and project governance capabilities.

In short, portfolio and project governance is a combined set of capabilities in Project Server 2013 that allow you to configure standardized processes to select and monitor projects from ideation to closeout. Where portfolio and project governance is concerned with management oversight and commitment, project management is about the successful delivery of projects. While Project Server 2013 offers a wealth of features and capabilities, you can think of it as having three core components shown in Figure 5 - 1.

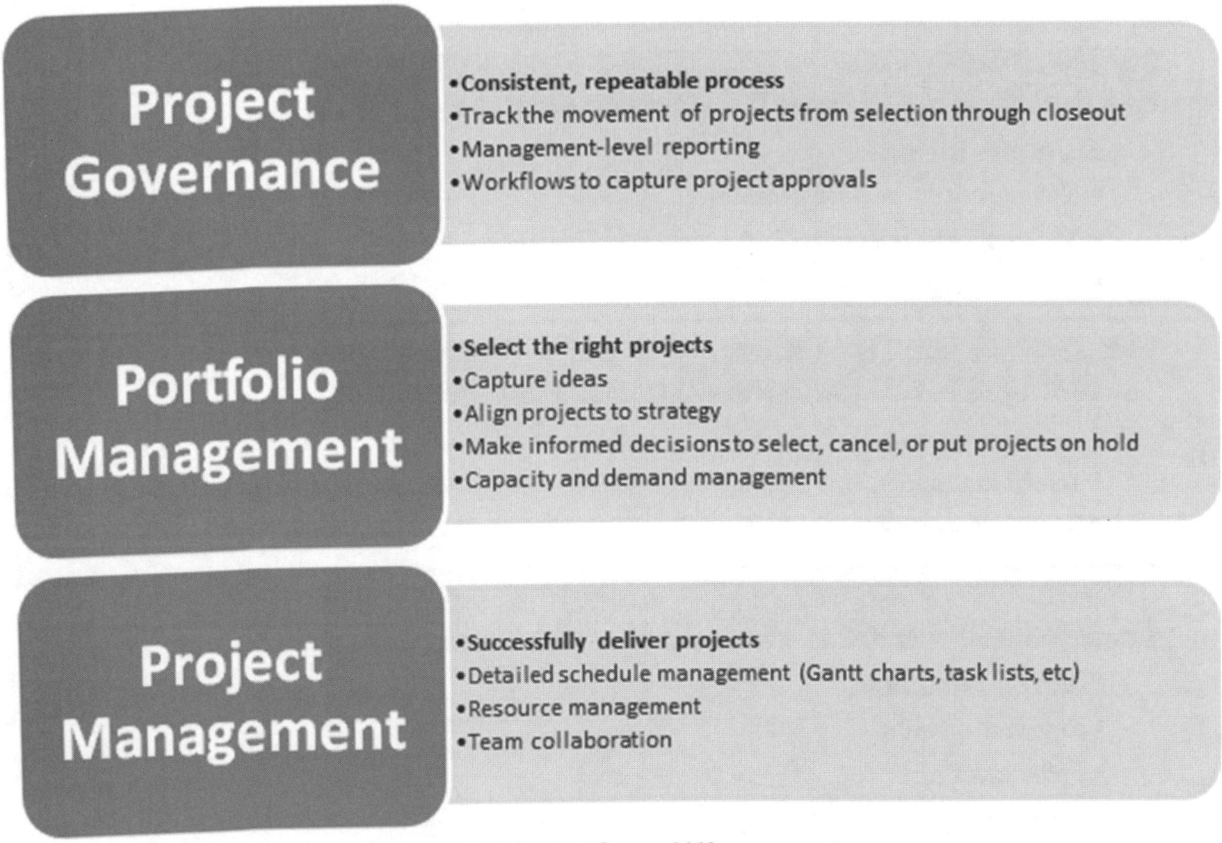

Project Governance
•Consistent, repeatable process
•Track the movement of projects from selection through closeout
•Management-level reporting
•Workflows to capture project approvals
Portfolio Management
•Select the right projects
•Capture ideas
•Align projects to strategy
•Make informed decisions to select, cancel, or put projects on hold
•Capacity and demand management
Project Management
•Successfully deliver projects
•Detailed schedule management (Gantt charts, task lists, etc)
•Resource management
•Team collaboration

Figure 5 - 1: Project Server 2013 components

Information: In the next section, I use real-world examples of these features working together. The rest of this module breaks down the components that you configure in Project Server 2013 to enable portfolio and project governance.

Understanding Project Governance: A Real-World Example

Imagine, for example, a marketing department at a large company that makes consumer goods. Everyone in the company has demands for marketing resources. The people creating products ask marketing to do research, announce new products, or market new uses for the products. The Human Resources department wants to attract new talent by sponsoring events at colleges. Marketing, itself, has a mandate to manage corporate trade events and sponsor the next big sporting event.

Understanding EPT's (Enterprise Project Types)

Just like departments in your company, the marketing department example must categorize its various projects. In this example case, the requirement is to define large, medium, and small projects. In Project Server 2013, the way to define these is as Enterprise Project Types (or EPT's) as shown in Figure 5 - 2.

Project Server EPT: Corporate Events (Large)

- **Examples include:**
  - New product release events
  - Major sporting events
  - Re-branding

Project Server EPT: Marketing Campaigns (Medium)

- **Examples include:**
  - Television spots
  - Brand awareness

Project Server EPT: Targeted Campaigns (Small)

- **Examples include:**
  - Regional events
  - Sales meetings
  - Sponsorships

Figure 5 - 2: Enterprise Project Types (EPT's) for a marketing department.

Information: The system associates all projects in Project Server 2013 with an EPT. If you do not create additional EPT's then Project Server uses the default EPT. You can create as many EPT's as you need in your Project Server environment.

You can optionally associate an EPT with a project template and a Project Site template. For example, the marketing department requires a work breakdown structure containing specific milestones for specific EPT's. To address this use case, you can create base project plans in Project Pro 2013 for each EPT and save these as templates in Project Server 2013 and then associate them with their respective EPT's.

If the marketing department required custom Project Site elements, you can build Project Site templates and associate them with the EPT's.

Information: You are not required to build your own custom project template or Project Site template.

Best Practice: Project Server 2013 is an enterprise system; so the more templates you create the more you have to manage them. A best practice is to create the smallest number of templates and EPT's as possible.

After you create EPT's and associate them with Project Pro and SharePoint templates, you are ready to create projects based on them. Later in this module, I walk you through the steps in the PWA interface; however, for now, I illustrate the process as shown in Figure 5 - 3.

Authorized users create new projects from the Project Center in PWA. First, the user selects the appropriate EPT for their project (the system prompts the user for a project name and other details). If a Project Pro template is associated with the EPT, Project Server 2013 automatically uses the template to create the new project plan. If a Project Site template is associated with the EPT, Project Server 2013 automatically generates the site using the template. The system does not require you to define or use templates or workflows when you create EPT's. These elements are optional.

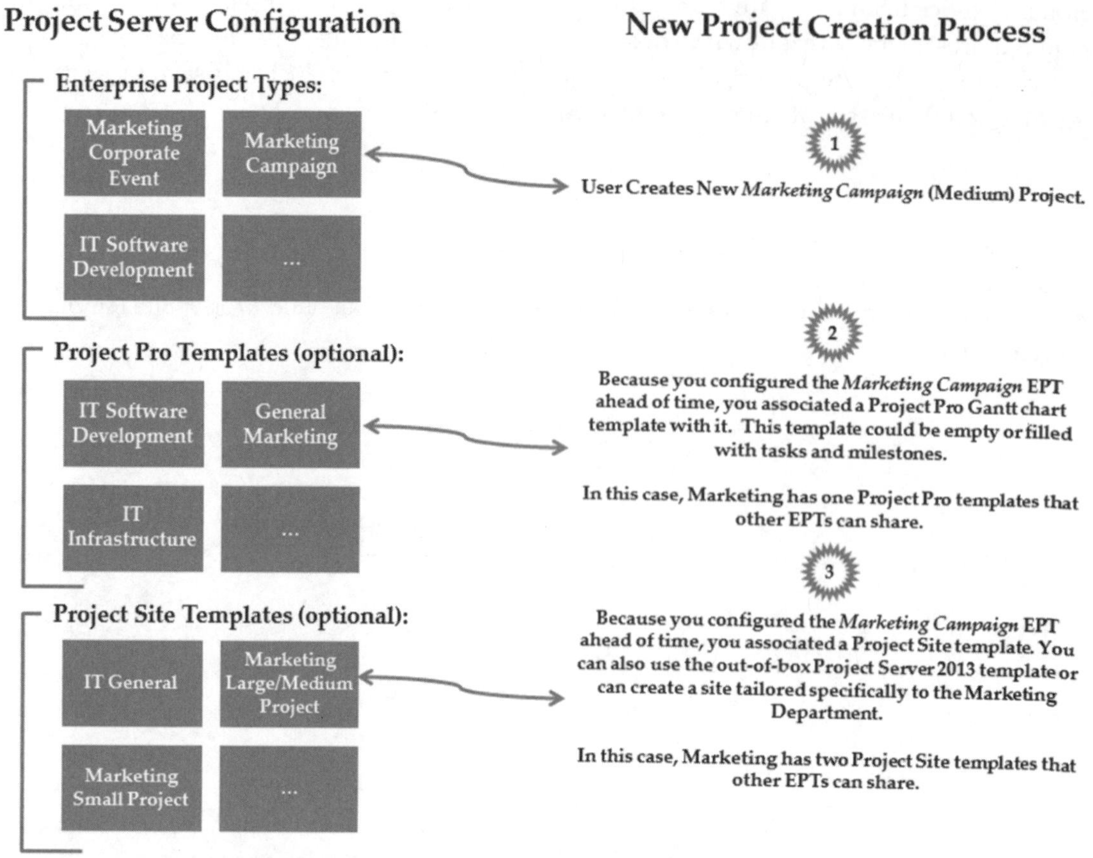
Project Server Configuration
New Project Creation Process
Enterprise Project Types:
Marketing Corporate Event
Marketing Campaign
IT Software Development
...
1
User Creates New Marketing Campaign (Medium) Project.
Project Pro Templates (optional):
IT Software Development
General Marketing
IT Infrastructure
...
2
Because you configured the Marketing Campaign EPT ahead of time, you associated a Project Pro Gantt chart template with it. This template could be empty or filled with tasks and milestones.
In this case, Marketing has one Project Pro templates that other EPTs can share.
Project Site Templates (optional):
IT General
Marketing Large/Medium Project
Marketing Small Project
...
3
Because you configured the Marketing Campaign EPT ahead of time, you associated a Project Site template. You can also use the out-of-box Project Server 2013 template or can create a site tailored specifically to the Marketing Department.
In this case, Marketing has two Project Site templates that other EPTs can share.

Figure 5 - 3: New project creation process in Project Server 2013

Given that templates are optional, if you are not familiar with the project governance features of Project Server 2013, you might be wondering how you can manage a project without a project plan or even a simple SharePoint site. Let me explain!

My fictional marketing department runs hundreds of projects a year. Some of these are small projects, such as creating a banner ad for a website or modifying an existing newspaper ad for another market. Other projects require many resource with multi-disciplined teams to accomplish major business objectives like launch a new product line. The marketing department can manage the smallest projects using a simple task list created in SharePoint while its larger projects require a detailed schedule model. A new feature in Project Server 2013 allows SharePoint task lists to **act** like project plans and allows for the reporting of this detail. EPT's are very powerful because they enable you to use templates to tailor the end user's experience.

Understanding Phases and Stages

As an executive overseeing this marketing department, I may not want to see the minute details for each project, but I do want to know generally how many projects require funding, how many are in progress, and so on. I certainly do not want to have to read detailed schedule models to determine whether a project has moved from a funding phase to a project management phase.

In order to get an executive level view of my projects and to bring more consistency to the funding and delivery process, I require every project to move through a stage gate process. Because this is a marketing department, I want it to be a little fun so I call the official process SURF (Select Underwrite Run Finalize). Project Server 2013 provides the ability to create these phases so I can see a visual depiction of where each project lies in the SURF process.

My management team must follow the SURF process and I want accountability so I ask them to sign off on key elements along the way. To obtain these approvals and visually see them in Project Server 2013, I define some unique stages under each phase. I assume that projects in the *Finalize* phase are to a point in the process where signoff is not required but all other phases have approval steps as shown in Figure 5 - 4.

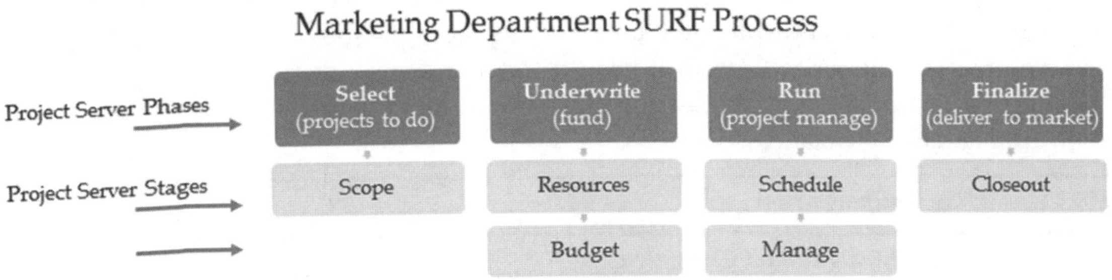

Figure 5 - 4: Phases and Stages for any given marketing project

Project Server 2013 does not require you to configure phases and does not require stages if you do not use a workflow. If you want to offer a project governance model, this is the best way to do it. You can create as many phases and stages as you like. Project Server 2013 offers a lot of flexibility, which I cover later in this module, but here are some important points to remember:

- Any department can have their own phases and stages. In my case, the marketing department uses the four-phase SURF process but product development uses its own eight-phase Product Lifecycle Methodology (PLM).
- If more than one department follows the same process, you can simply re-use the existing stages and phases. Keep in mind that reusing stages may not be a best practice because if one department has a few unique requirements, that change affects everyone sharing that stage.
- Each EPT can have a unique set of phases. For example, my marketing department requires four phases but smaller projects might only require one, two, or three.

Using Project Server's project governance functionality, you discover that consistency in reporting and a repeatable process has a real positive impact on your management success.

Understanding Project Detail Pages (PDP's)

To recap the scenario, I run a marketing department at a large consumer goods company. My first requirement is to have a unique set of project types representing my large, medium, and small projects. Project Server's Enterprise Project Types (EPT's) meet that need. I also need to track the flow of projects from selection through delivery using my internal SURF stage gate methodology. To use Project Server 2013's project governance capabilities to meet that need I create **phases** and **stages**.

PWA's Project Center has a built-in view that lists projects and their current phase and stage. While this is very helpful, I need to view project-related data like the proposed cost, geographic coverage area, and other pertinent data. This supporting information is the project metadata you learned about in the previous module. Project Server 2013 collects this metadata using enterprise fields.

Project Server 2013 allows you to create Project Detail Pages (PDP's), which are individual web pages you build using a web-based, drag-and-drop designer.

By creating PDP's you can lay out pages based on a natural categorization. In Figure 5 - 5, I show an example of a project called *New Product Campaign*. Notice this project derives from the *Marketing Campaign* EPT. When a user clicks on this project, they see five PDP's called *Project Details, Scope, Project Plan, Stage Criteria,* and *Strategy*. You build each of these PDP's and then assign them to the appropriate stage.

Note also in Figure 5 - 5 that the project is in the *Run* phase of the SURF stage gate methodology. You can see that I added a web part to this PDP that displays the progress graphic at the top of the page. Underneath the visual SURF process, you can see Enterprise Custom Fields (ECF's) that display metadata related to this project. The metadata I require, which includes *Proposed Cost* and *High Estimate,* are very basic. The *High Estimate* allows a project manager to estimate any potential cost overruns.

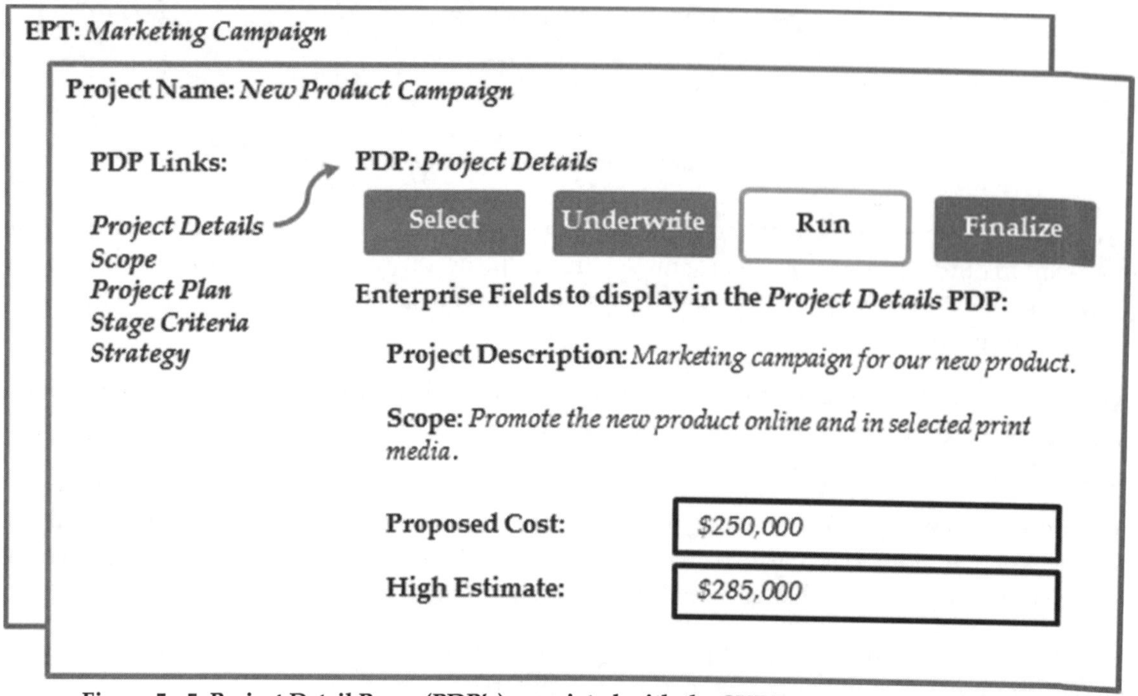

Figure 5 - 5: Project Detail Pages (PDP's) associated with the SURF stage gate methodology

Best Practice: Create at least one PDP for each of the following: ECF's, Project Plan (to display the Gantt chart when a detailed plan is required), and the current phase of the project.

Understanding Workflows

Assuming that I now have the SURF stage gate process configured using phases and stages, ECF's define the metadata for these projects, and PDP's nicely lay out the project details I need to see. The next requirement is to put a formal approval process in place. For example, I have a requirement that I must personally approve all large projects, which in my taxonomy is a *Corporate Event* EPT.

To move a project from one phase to the next (or even move it backwards), you need to implement a workflow. A workflow can send projects for approval or perform advanced functions such as updating a financial system with budget information. If you are familiar with Project Server 2013, you know that product was "Workflow Ready," which basically meant there were no built-in workflows and Project Server workflows require a developer to write significant amounts of code to provide even the simplest approval processes.

Project Server 2013 does not ship with ready-built workflows but the good news is that SharePoint Designer 2013, available as a free download, allows you to create workflows using a visual interface. Unlike Project Server 2013 that used only .NET workflows, Project Server 2013 also uses declarative SharePoint workflows.

You can easily build the simple management approval workflow shown in Figure 5 - 6, which uses e-mail and a SharePoint task list, with SharePoint Designer. More complex workflows that interface with financial systems or workflows that require advanced approval branching require software code or a third party product.

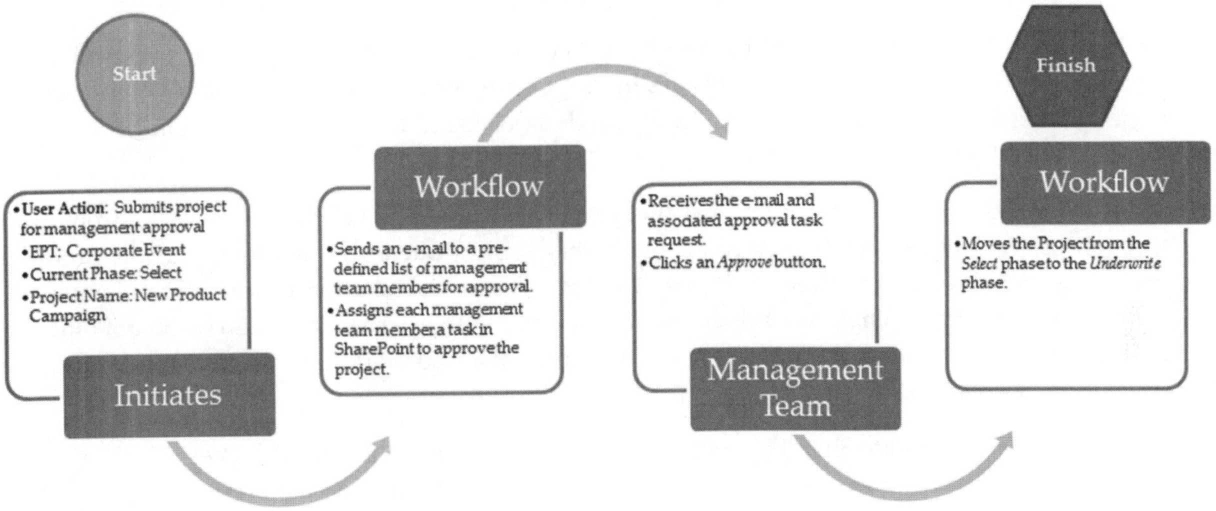
Start
Initiates
•User Action: Submits project for management approval
•EPT: Corporate Event
•Current Phase: Select
•Project Name: New Product Campaign
Workflow
•Sends an e-mail to a pre-defined list of management team members for approval.
•Assigns each management team member a task in SharePoint to approve the project.
Management Team
•Receives the e-mail and associated approval task request.
•Clicks an Approve button.
Workflow
•Moves the Project from the Select phase to the Underwrite phase.
Finish

Figure 5 - 6: Simple workflow approval process

Best Practice: SharePoint Designer is a very simple tool so your Project Server users may ask for functionality not supported by SharePoint workflows. Always make sure you test or mock up these requirements before committing to the final design.

Project Governance Conclusion

As you can see, Project Server 2013 provides a very powerful project governance solution that enables users to create and manage projects based on their process, rather than a pre-defined set of processes. Enterprise Project Types (EPT's) give you the flexibility to define a set of templates, processes, and workflows for each project. Figure 5 - 7 summarizes the complete EPT package.

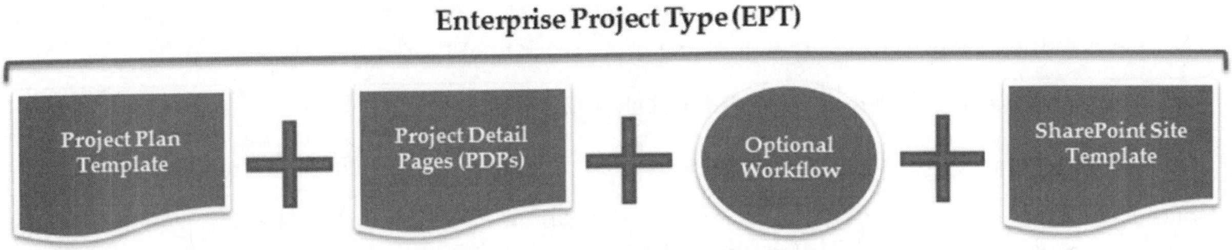
Enterprise Project Type (EPT)
Project Plan Template
Project Detail Pages (PDPs)
Optional Workflow
SharePoint Site Template

Figure 5 - 7: Project Type Representation

Information: When an Enterprise Project Type does not have an associated workflow, a Project Server administrator must specify the PDP's that display for the EPT. When an Enterprise Project Type does have a workflow, the workflow controls the display of PDP's.

- A **Project Plan Template** is a pre-built schedule model that ideally contains a well-structured schedule with generic resources assigned to tasks as well as duration and effort information that the author estimated in the template. To the degree that the template can eliminate manual schedule building, the more valuable it is to the managers who use them. When you do not specify a specific project template for a project type, the system uses a blank project template.
- **Project Detail Pages** are web-part based web pages that you create to display and collect project related information. You display Project Detail Pages in Project Server Web App. Project Detail Pages can contain Project Server Enterprise Custom Fields (ECF's), web parts, Excel data, and more. You must specify a new Project Detail Page for a project type.
- **Workflows** allow you to control the entire lifecycle flow of projects in Project Server 2013, from proposal through project closure. Workflows can contain very sophisticated business logic such as processing a project request through an automated criteria-based selection or rejection process. Complex workflows can contain multi-branching process logic and can interact with external data sources. SharePoint Designer 2013 can build simple workflows; however, for more advanced workflows you must use software code designed in Visual Studio.
- **Project Site Templates** are SharePoint sites that you tailor so the look-and-feel meets the user's expectations. You can place web parts on various pages, create list templates, or just make use of the out-of-box functionality.

Understanding Portfolio Management: A Real-World Example

In the previous section, I played the role of an executive at a marketing department for a large consumer goods company. I defined the marketing department's SURF stage gated methodology, where each letter represents a particular phase in the process. I am very happy with the solution as I now have a list of all projects in a central location but now I am thinking about making better decisions about which of these projects we should select for execution.

As a marketing executive, I have the following challenges to overcome:

- There are a lot of people in my company with great ideas and I want to hear them
- My budget is not increasing
- I have fewer resources to do more work
- My peers in the executive team are requesting more work than I can do
- Some projects are not strategically aligned and should not be selected
- Some projects were good ideas when they began, but it is time to kill them off to free up resources

Project Server 2013 provides computational models and a simple user interface, allowing senior management teams to make important decisions to address these challenges.

Understanding Demand Management

As a marketing executive, people in my company pull me aside in the cafeteria or in meetings and ask "why aren't we on social media?" or "why can't we market the product this way?" While I always listen to new ideas, I want to give all employees a voice to share their ideas and project proposals.

Naturally, I do not want everyone with a project idea going to Project Server and creating projects. I want my team to review these ideas first. Figure 5 - 8 depicts "Demand Management," a concept of collecting potential projects and ideas before they are formally accepted as a project. In the figure, note that the demand management process uses SharePoint as the front-end for capturing ideas and potential projects.

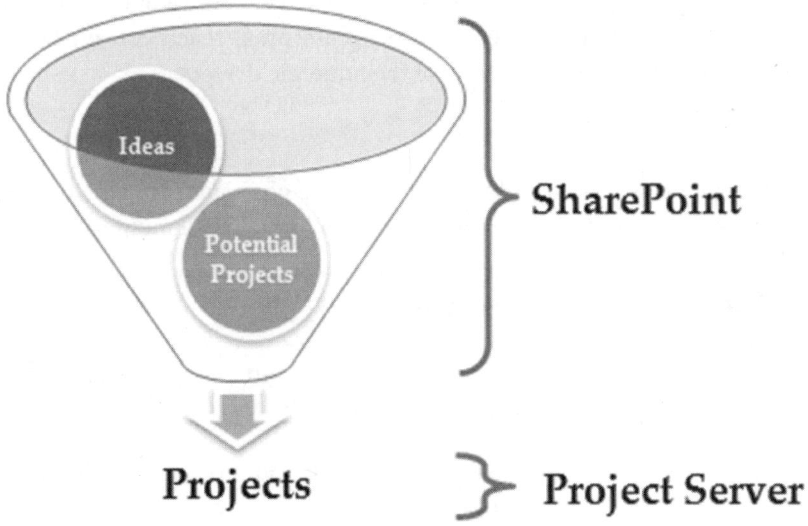

Figure 5 - 8: Demand Management

> **Information**: If you allow anyone to enter projects into Project Server 2013; that is perfectly acceptable. Just be aware of the administrative overhead for maintaining projects that may never see the light of day.

In my marketing organization, I want to enable demand management with the following three scenarios:

- **Enable employees to share ideas**: Anyone in the company can propose an idea upon which marketing can act. If the idea is accepted, an administrator moves it into Project Server 2013.
- **Enable project managers to formalize projects**: My marketing team has some projects that require initial due diligence and planning with little or no budget. My team calls these **potential projects** and can upload them to Project Server 2013 when they are ready.
- **Enable self-service for small projects**: The marketing department has many creative people that can do things like generate a banner ad for a website or create artwork for tradeshow posters. I want to give specific members of various departments the opportunity to input their project requests. If these requests fit within a defined budget and timeline, the team may automatically create the project in Project Server 2013.

Project Server 2013's new demand management features meet all of the above requirements. You can create workflows to automatically create new projects or allow for a manual intervention. At a minimum, I can meet the above requirements with three separate lists if not three separate SharePoint 2013 sites.

Understanding Portfolio Management

Even though I work for a large consumer goods company making a lot of money, my budget and resources are limited. There are certain projects I know there is a budget for, discretionary funds for special projects, and projects that will not move forward no matter how good an idea they are. Further, some projects just are not working out and I want to kill them before they become a drag on my hard working team. The last thing I want to do is walk up to one of my peers and say, "I am not doing this project" without having solid data as to why. I also want these same peers to have influence in our organizational project selection process. Because of this, I need a portfolio management process.

Portfolio management in Project Server 2013 allows the executive team to agree on a number of strategic drivers that impact projects selection. Ultimately, the executive team must reach consensus in rating each driver's importance. Every project must influence at least one of the strategic drivers.

Understanding Strategic Drivers

Relating projects to strategic drivers is important, but I also weight some strategic drivers as more important than others. Table 5 - 1 contains the final list of strategic drivers I want to implement in Project Server 2013.

Strategic Driver	Description
New home owner appeal	This project supports our efforts to gain market penetration with new homeowners.
Into the kitchen	This project supports our efforts to build our brand as a recognized leader in consumer kitchen products.
Earth-friendly products	This project supports our green initiatives to provide earth-friendly and recyclable products.
Premium products	This project supports our entry into premium products targeting affluent buyers.
Visual appeal	This project supports our renewed effort to make our products visually appealing in a household.

Table 5 - 1: Strategic Drivers

Each strategic business driver has its own impact statement. These impact statements should provide a measurable value rather than just using one work such as **strong.** In my example, I use the same weighting criteria for each strategic driver, which is as follows:

- **None** = No direct impact
- **Low** = Some impact to this strategic driver
- **Moderate** = 25% chance of supporting this strategic driver, resulting in significant consumer product awareness.
- **Strong** = Market penetration will grow at least 15% a year for two years
- **Extreme** = Fully supports this strategic driver and will guarantee market penetration of greater than a million new consumers within a six month period

> **Best Practice**: Each strategic driver should have its own impact statement. I repeat the same set to reduce complexity in the book.

Understanding Driver Prioritization

Now that the marketing department has a list of strategic drivers, when a project manager (or someone with similar security rights in Project Server 2013) edits a project, they can measure the project against the business drivers. My strategic drivers are very useful in that I know which projects have the most impact on the various business drivers.

In some ways, my marketing department is a service provider for other departments within my company. For example, I work with a department in charge of new product launches, another which deals with existing products, and so on. I want balance in my portfolio selection process, but I also want to give priority to those projects that our CEO and other executives have deemed as very important but at the same time prevent people from pushing projects by falsely rating them as strongly impacting business drivers. I meet with all the major executives to whom marketing provides a service and ask them to rate how important each business driver is when compared to the others. To do this, I ask them to use Project Server's pairwise comparison process to rate each strategic driver against the other.

This is part of a democratic approach to prioritizing strategic business drivers. Rather than someone standing up and saying, "my strategic driver belongs at the top," all the business owners must agree on how each one compares against the other as shown in the example in Table 5 - 2.

	Driver 1	Driver 2	Driver 3	Driver 4	Driver 5	Priority
Driver 1		3	4	2	4	31.03%
Driver 2			3	4	3	27.18%
Driver 3				4	5	15.6%
Driver 4					6	15.46
Driver 5						10.73%
TOTAL						**100%**

Table 5 - 2: Sample driver prioritization

Understanding Portfolio Analysis

As a marketing executive, I manage a balanced portfolio of projects that drives brand recognition, gains market share, and helps to drive new sales. Many projects can contribute to my goals, but I have a limited budget and only so many people to do the work.

Portfolio analysis is the action I take on a quarterly basis to review incoming and in-play projects in Project Server 2013. Because I assign every project ranking against strategic drivers, Project Server 2013 actually calculates an optimal portfolio for me based on the prioritization I choose. Obviously, I may not agree with Project Server 2013's project selections so I can analyze the portfolio by creating what-if scenarios. For example, here are some functions I can perform:

- Kill projects that are not producing.
- Sponsor new projects that have promise.
- Delay the start and finish dates for projects.
- Verify resource availability.
- If resources are not available, determine how many more I may need to hire.

These are just some of the things I can do with Project Server 2013's powerful portfolio management features.

Configuring Portfolio Management

In this section, I show you how to configure the typical components of Project Server 2013 to implement a portfolio management solution. To configure portfolio management, you typically configure Project Server in this order:

1. Enable the *Strategy* menu in the *Quick Launch* menu.
2. Define and weight the strategic drivers.
3. Prioritize the strategic drivers.
4. Add a PDP so individual projects can align to strategic drivers (I cover this topic in the next section of this module).
5. Perform a portfolio analysis.

Creating Strategic Drivers

To create strategic drivers, follow the steps below:

1. Log in to PWA as an administrator, such as the Farm Administrator service account. The system displays the PWA site.
2. From the *Quick Launch* menu at the left of the screen, click the *Driver Library* link. The system displays the *Driver Library* page as shown in Figure 5 - 9.
3. In the *Driver* section of the *Driver* tab at the top of the screen, click the *New* button.

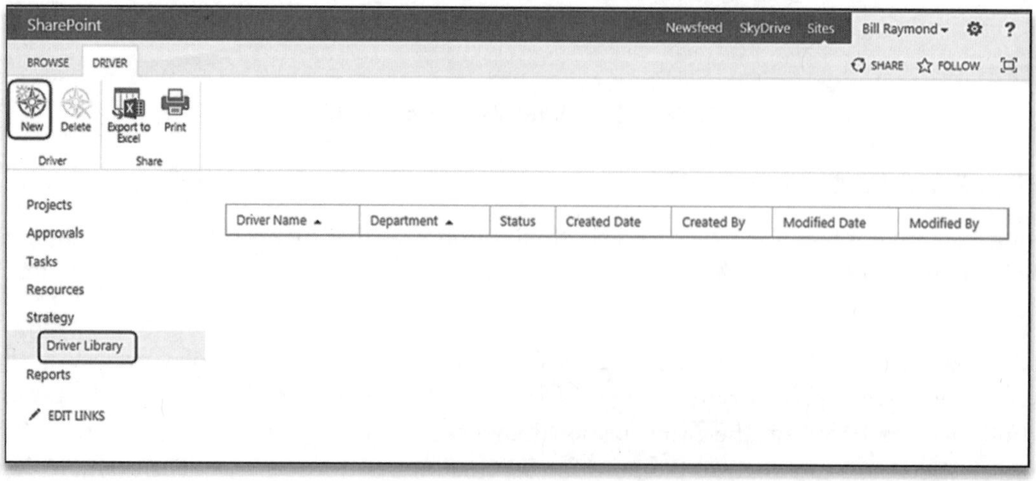

Figure 5 - 9: Driver Library

4. The system displays the *Create New Driver* dialog as shown in Figure 5 - 10 and Figure 5 - 11. Minimally, type a name for your first driver. In my case, I also enter *Description* and *Project Impact* statements. Click the *Save & Close* button.

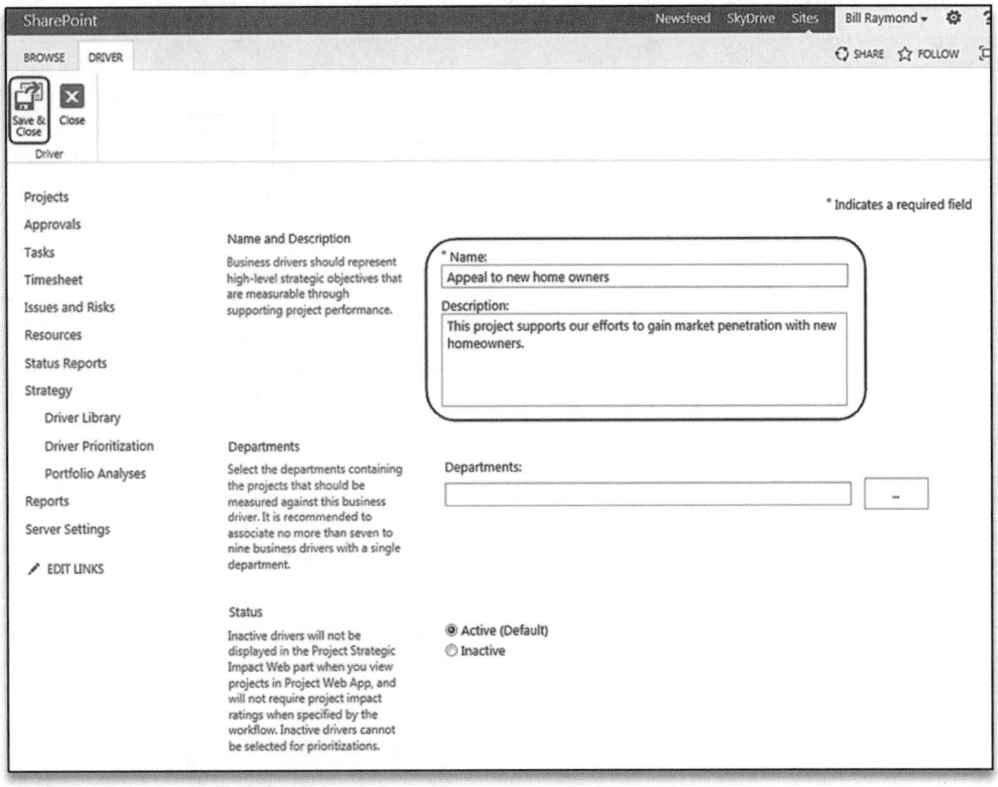
SharePoint
Newsfeed
SkyDrive
Sites
Bill Raymond
BROWSE
DRIVER
SHARE
FOLLOW
Save & Close
Close
Driver
Projects
Approvals
Tasks
Timesheet
Issues and Risks
Resources
Status Reports
Strategy
Driver Library
Driver Prioritization
Portfolio Analyses
Reports
Server Settings
EDIT LINKS
* Indicates a required field
Name and Description
Business drivers should represent high-level strategic objectives that are measurable through supporting project performance.
* Name:
Appeal to new home owners
Description:
This project supports our efforts to gain market penetration with new homeowners.
Departments
Select the departments containing the projects that should be measured against this business driver. It is recommended to associate no more than seven to nine business drivers with a single department.
Departments:
Status
Inactive drivers will not be displayed in the Project Strategic Impact Web part when you view projects in Project Web App, and will not require project impact ratings when specified by the workflow. Inactive drivers cannot be selected for prioritizations.
Active (Default)
Inactive

Figure 5 - 10: Create New Driver dialog, part 1

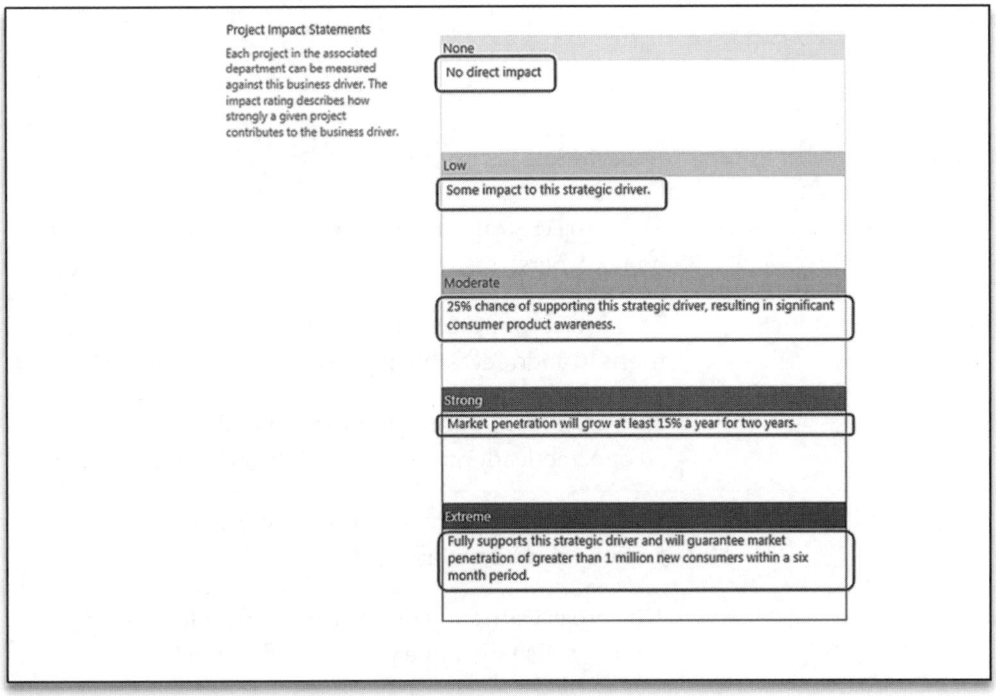
Project Impact Statements
Each project in the associated department can be measured against this business driver. The impact rating describes how strongly a given project contributes to the business driver.
None
No direct impact
Low
Some impact to this strategic driver.
Moderate
25% chance of supporting this strategic driver, resulting in significant consumer product awareness.
Strong
Market penetration will grow at least 15% a year for two years.
Extreme
Fully supports this strategic driver and will guarantee market penetration of greater than 1 million new consumers within a six month period.

Figure 5 - 11: Create New Driver dialog, part 2

5. The system displays the populated *Driver Library* as shown in Figure 5 - 12. Note that my colleague is also creating strategic drivers. Even though I can segment these different drivers into various departments, it is okay if they are not. If at any time I decide a certain driver is no longer important, I can add new ones. Note that all the settings I use are located at the end of this section.

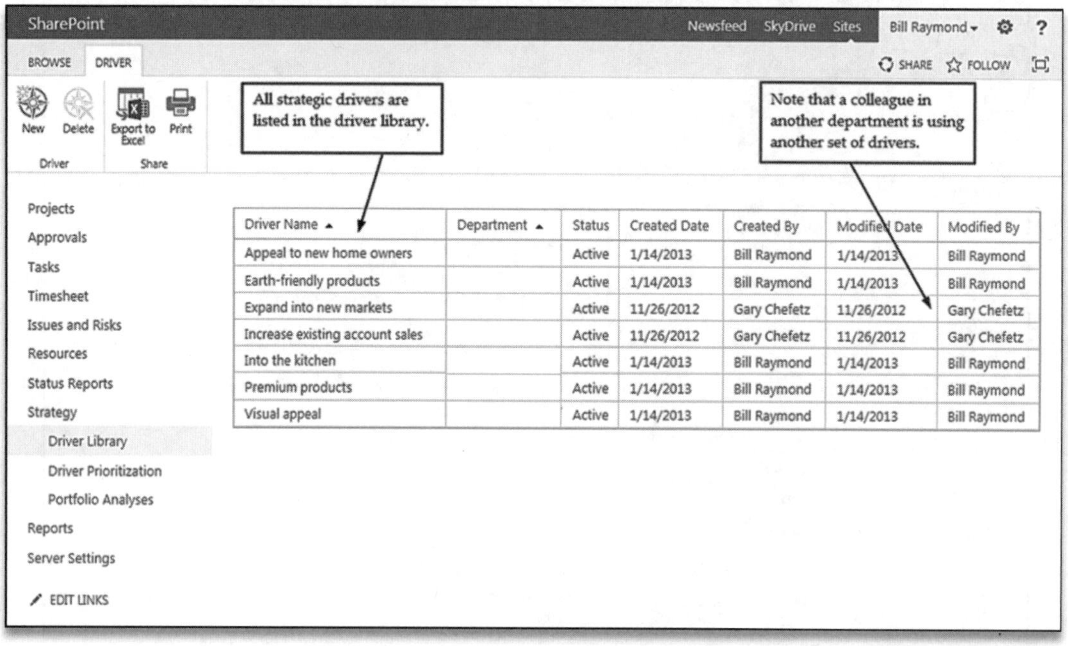

Figure 5 - 12: Populated Driver Library

Best Practice: You can create as many strategic drivers as you like, but it will not be possible to perform a good portfolio analysis with too many. It is best to use 5 to7 strategic drivers for any given portfolio.

Table 5 - 3 contains the drivers in my configuration:

Name	Description
Appeal to new home owners	This project supports our initiative to appeal to first-time homeowners.
Earth-friendly products	This project supports our green initiatives to provide earth-friendly and recyclable products.
Into the kitchen	This project supports our efforts to build our brand as a recognized leader in consumer kitchen products.
Premium products	This project supports our entry into premium products targetting affluent buyers.
Visual appeal	This project supports our renewed effort to make our products visually appealing in a household.

Table 5 - 3: Sample Business Drivers

For purposes of this book, I use the same strategic impact statements but ideally, you should use a unique, measurable statement for each driver. Below are the strategic impact statements I use for each driver:

- **None -** No direct impact
- **Low -** Some impact
- **Moderate -** 25% change of supporting this strategic driver, resulting in significant consumer awareness
- **Strong -** Market penetration will grow at least 15% for two years
- **Extreme -** Fully supports this strategic driver and will guarantee market penetration of greater than 1 million consumers within a 6-month period

Creating Driver Prioritizations

Pairwise Comparison is the process of prioritizing one driver against another. Because business drivers have varying degrees of impact on the business, this is a very important step. Using my example of a marketing department, if my objective is to value **Premium products** and **Earth-friendly products over other business drivers** then Project Server 2013 needs to know that in order to help me select the projects that align with my objectives.

> **Best Practice**: While anyone with the proper security rights can perform this analysis, it is best for the highest level of executives to do this analysis. Many organizations will hire a consultant versed in portfolio prioritization to guide the meetings.

To perform a driver prioritization, follow these steps:

1. Log in to PWA as a user with the security rights to perform a prioritization. Portfolio managers and administrators may perform these actions.
2. In the *Quick Launch* menu, click the *Driver Prioritization* link.
3. The system displays the *Driver Prioritization* page shown in Figure 5 - 13. Click the *New* button to create a new prioritization.

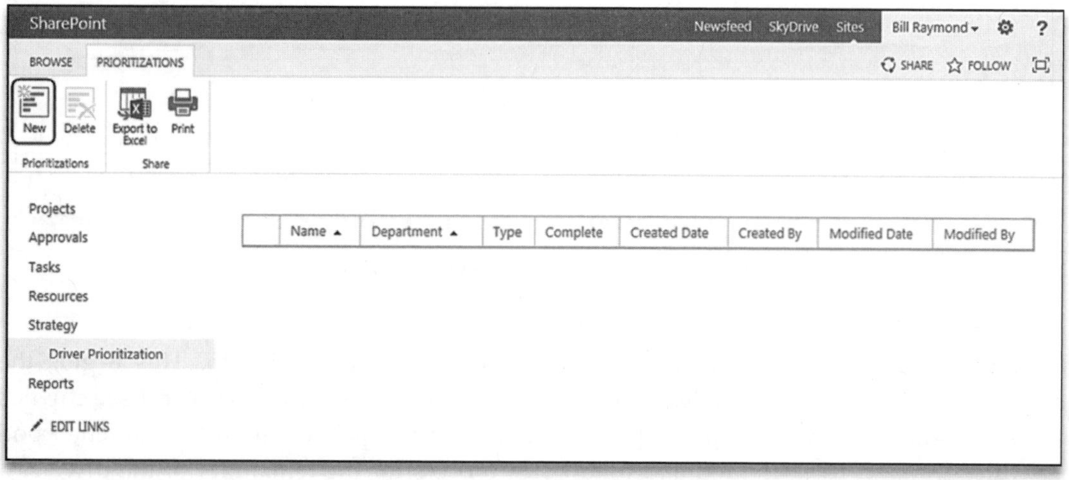

Figure 5 - 13: Driver Prioritization page.

4. The system displays the *Define Properties* dialog shown in Figure 5 - 14. Minimally, give the driver a name and select at least 2 drivers. In my case, I provide a *Name, Description,* and 5 of my strategic drivers. In the *Prioritization Type* section, I select the *Calculated* option, which drives the relative importance for each driver based on a pairwise comparison. If I want to manually enter the priority for each driver (and thus skipping the pairwise comparison), I select the *Manual* option. After completing your entries click the *Next: Prioritize Drivers* button.

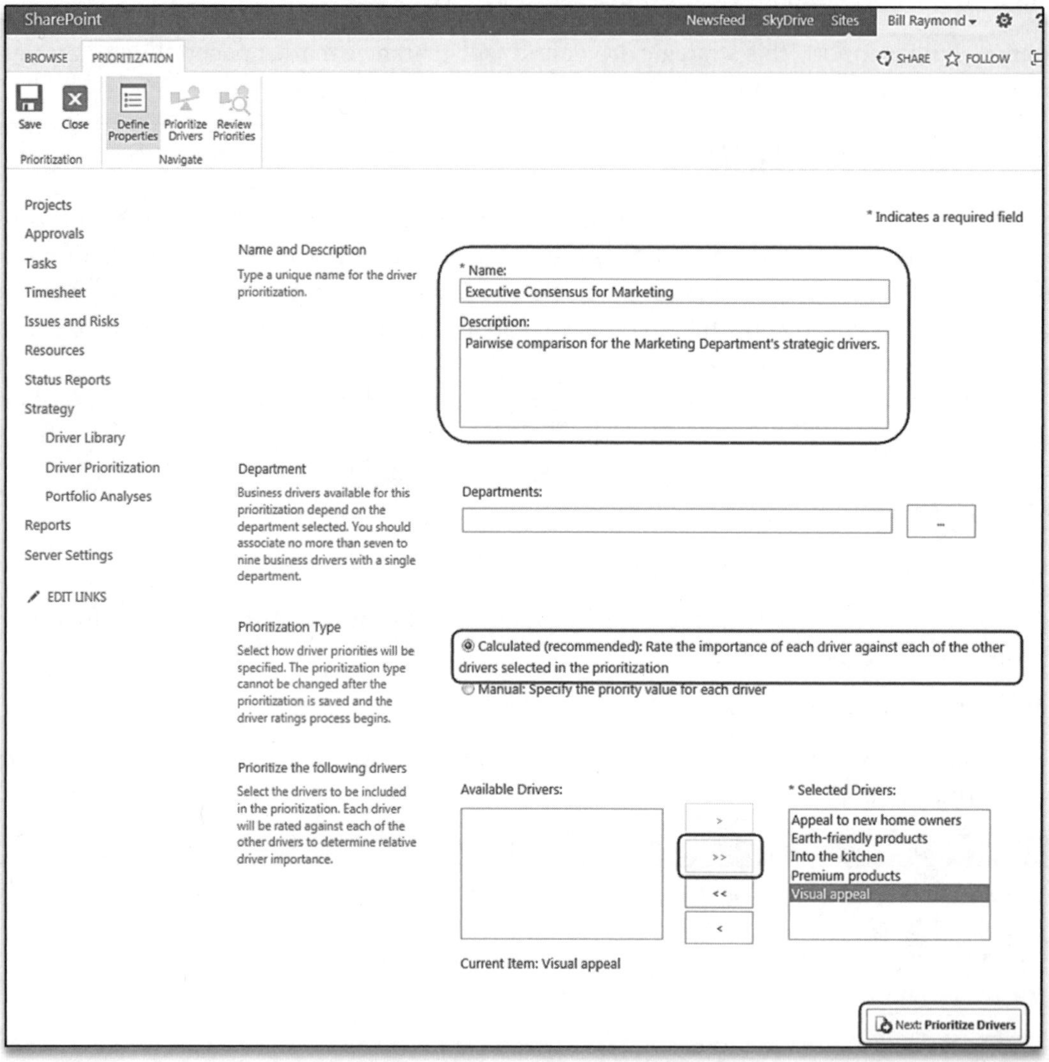
SharePoint
Newsfeed SkyDrive Sites
Bill Raymond
BROWSE PRIORITIZATION
SHARE FOLLOW
Save Close
Define Properties Prioritize Drivers Review Priorities
Prioritization Navigate
Projects
Approvals
Tasks
Timesheet
Issues and Risks
Resources
Status Reports
Strategy
Driver Library
Driver Prioritization
Portfolio Analyses
Reports
Server Settings
EDIT LINKS
* Indicates a required field
Name and Description
Type a unique name for the driver prioritization.
* Name:
Executive Consensus for Marketing
Description:
Pairwise comparison for the Marketing Department's strategic drivers.
Department
Business drivers available for this prioritization depend on the department selected. You should associate no more than seven to nine business drivers with a single department.
Departments:
Prioritization Type
Select how driver priorities will be specified. The prioritization type cannot be changed after the prioritization is saved and the driver ratings process begins.
Calculated (recommended): Rate the importance of each driver against each of the other drivers selected in the prioritization
Manual: Specify the priority value for each driver
Prioritize the following drivers
Select the drivers to be included in the prioritization. Each driver will be rated against each of the other drivers to determine relative driver importance.
Available Drivers:
* Selected Drivers:
Appeal to new home owners
Earth-friendly products
Into the kitchen
Premium products
Visual appeal
Current Item: Visual appeal
Next: Prioritize Drivers

Figure 5 - 14: Define Properties dialog

5. The system dispays the *Prioritize Drivers* dialog shown in Figure 5 - 15. This begins the pairwise comparison process. In my example, *Appeal to new home owners* is the first driver. I select whether all the other drivers are more or less important by choosing from the pick lists found in the center portion of the table. Click the *Next Driver* button and follow this process for the remainder of the drivers. Note that I provide the settings I use to create a successful prioritiation at the end of this section.

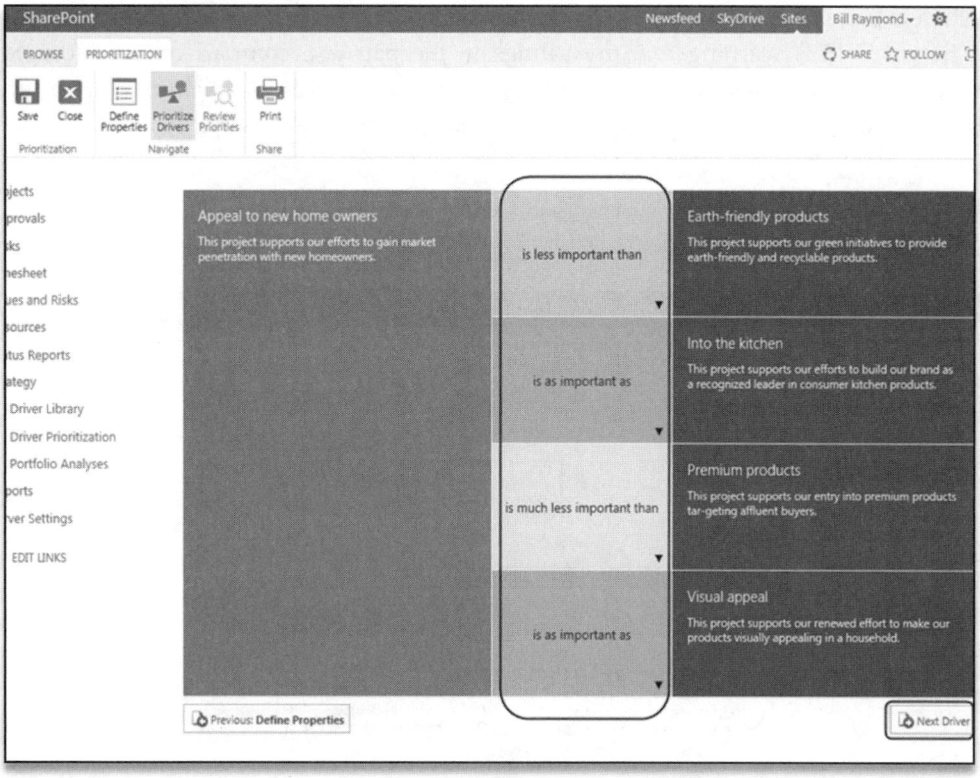

Figure 5 - 15: Prioritize Drivers dialog

6. When you complete your rating of the last driver, the system displays the *Review Priorities* dialog shown in Figure 5 - 16 and Figure 5 - 17. In my case, Project Server 2013 is warning me that I have a *low consistency ratio*. To learn more, click the *Consistency Ratio* link at the bottom of the page.

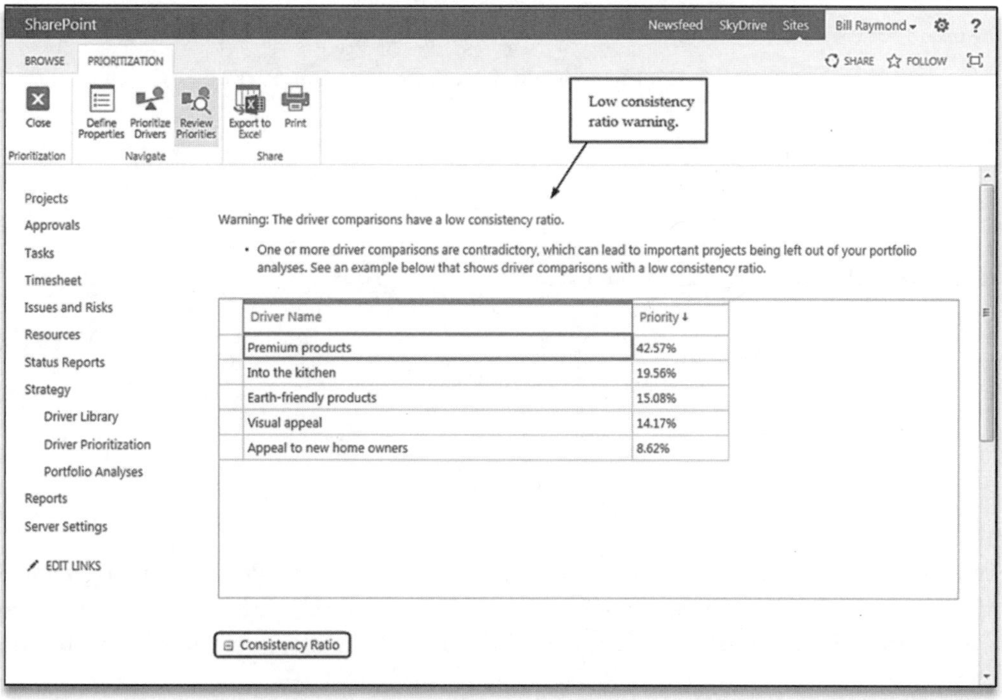

Figure 5 - 16: Inconsistent Driver Prioritization, Part 1

7. The system expands the *Consistency Ratio* portion of the *Review Priorities* dialog as shown in Figure 5 - 17. Project Server 2013 is warning that my ratings in the pairwise comparison are inconsistent. This also means a portfolio analysis based on this prioritization will not accurately align to my objectives. Click the *Previous: Prioritize Drivers* button to go back and adjust the pairwise comparison.

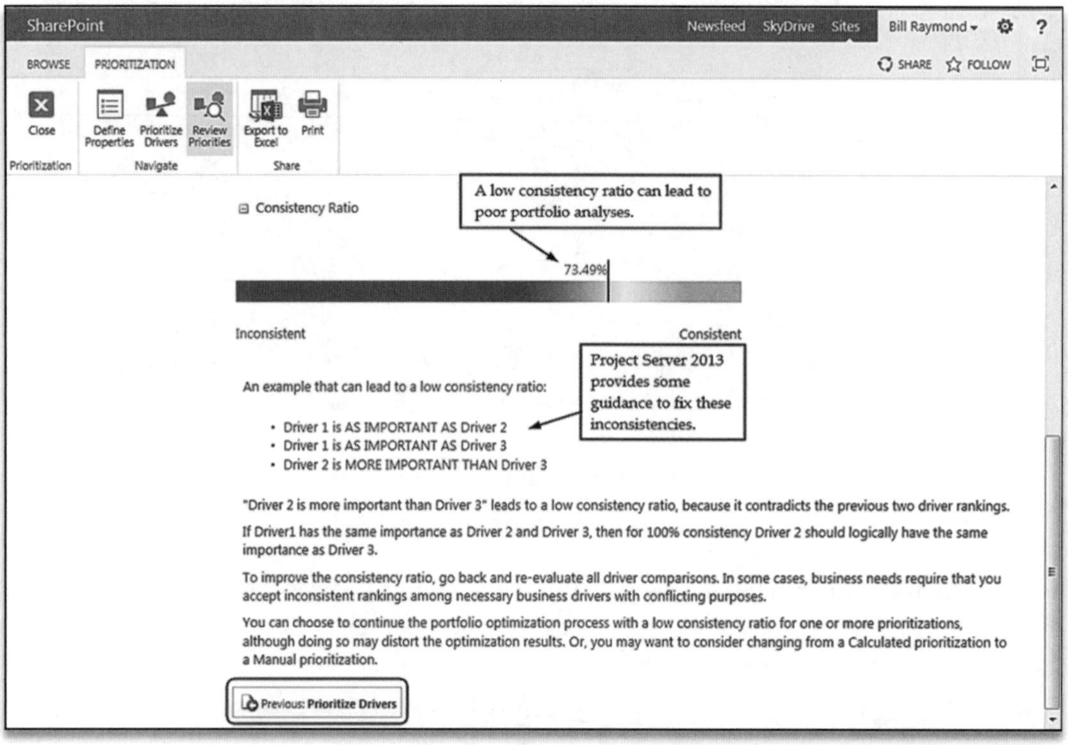
SharePoint
Newsfeed
SkyDrive
Sites
Bill Raymond
BROWSE
PRIORITIZATION
SHARE
FOLLOW
Close
Define Properties
Prioritize Drivers
Review Priorities
Export to Excel
Print
Prioritization
Navigate
Share
Consistency Ratio
A low consistency ratio can lead to poor portfolio analyses.
73.49%
Inconsistent
Consistent
Project Server 2013 provides some guidance to fix these inconsistencies.
An example that can lead to a low consistency ratio:
Driver 1 is AS IMPORTANT AS Driver 2
Driver 1 is AS IMPORTANT AS Driver 3
Driver 2 is MORE IMPORTANT THAN Driver 3
"Driver 2 is more important than Driver 3" leads to a low consistency ratio, because it contradicts the previous two driver rankings.
If Driver1 has the same importance as Driver 2 and Driver 3, then for 100% consistency Driver 2 should logically have the same importance as Driver 3.
To improve the consistency ratio, go back and re-evaluate all driver comparisons. In some cases, business needs require that you accept inconsistent rankings among necessary business drivers with conflicting purposes.
You can choose to continue the portfolio optimization process with a low consistency ratio for one or more prioritizations, although doing so may distort the optimization results. Or, you may want to consider changing from a Calculated prioritization to a Manual prioritization.
Previous: Prioritize Drivers

Figure 5 - 17: Inconsistent driver prioritization, Part 2

Best Practice: Try to keep the minimum consistency ratio to 80%.

8. Once you make the adjustments, the system displays the *Review Priorities* dialog showing that your prioritization is consistent. As you can see in Figure 5 - 18, there are still inconsistencies in my ratings but they are at least in a 'safe zone' ensuring an accurate portfolio analysis. Click the *Close* button.

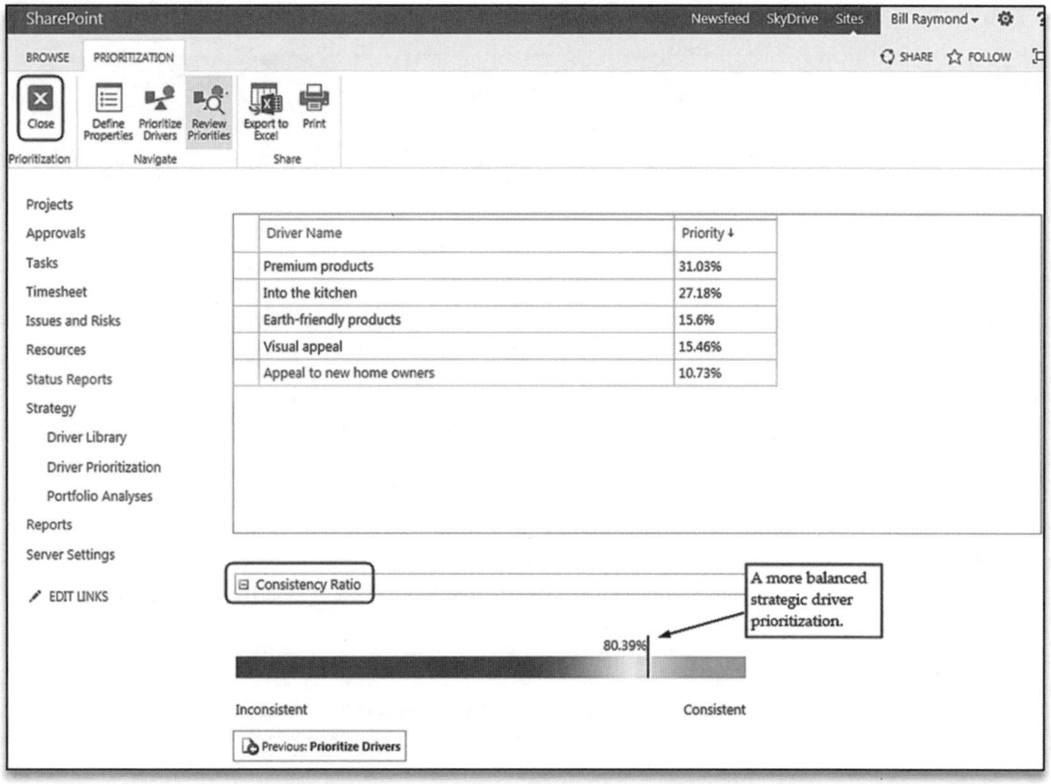

Figure 5 - 18: Consistent Driver Prioritization.

The system displays the populated *Driver Prioritization* window shown in Figure 5 - 19.

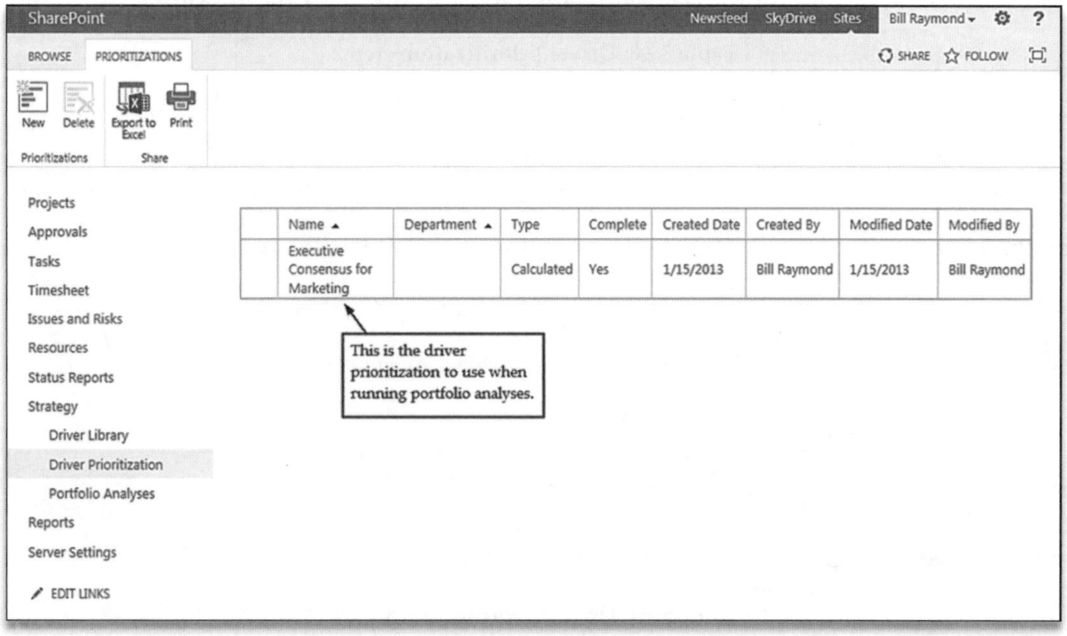

Figure 5 - 19: Populated Driver Prioritizations.

Table 5 - 4 contains the name and description of the driver prioritization I used:

Name	Description
Executive Consensus for Marketing	Pairwise comparison for the Marketing Department's strategic drivers.

Table 5 - 4: Driver Prioritization

Table 5 - 5 through Table 5 - 8 include the settings I used to create a successful driver prioritization:

Driver	Prioritization	Drivers
Appeal to new homeowners	is less important than	Earth-friendly products
	is as important as	Into the kitchen
	is much less important than	Premium products
	is as important as	Visual appeal

Table 5 - 5: Driver prioritization step 1

Driver	Prioritization	Drivers
Earth-friendly products	is less important than	Into the kitchen
	is as important as	Premium products
	is less important than	Visual appeal

Table 5 - 6: Driver prioritization step 2

Driver	Prioritization	Drivers
Into the kitchen	is as important as	Premium products
	is more important than	Visual appeal

Table 5 - 7: Driver prioritization step 3

Driver	Prioritization	Drivers
Premium products	is more important than	Visual appeal

Table 5 - 8: Driver prioritization step 4

Configuring Project Governance

In this section, I walk you through the steps to create a project governance process in Project Server 2013. The end objective is to have at least one enterprise project type that a user can start with when creating a new project. To achieve this, you must perform the steps shown in Figure 5 - 20.

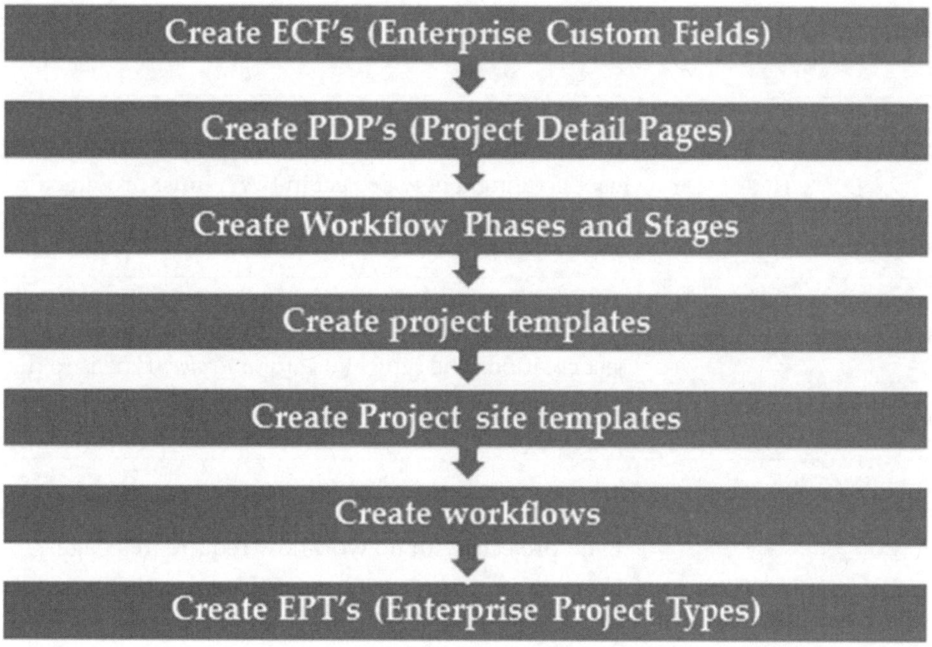

Figure 5 - 20: Project Governance steps

Best Practice: MSProjectExperts recommends that you fully map out your project types and workflow processes before you begin creating elements to support them; otherwise, you are likely to find yourself having to account for changes across many objects when you make even a simple change to one.

Configuring Enterprise Custom Fields

Because Module 04, *Configuring Enterprise Objects and Options* thoroughly covers Enterprise Custom Fields (ECF's), I do not cover that subject again in this module.

Configuring PDP's

Before you can organize your process into phases and stages, you must first create the Project Detail Pages (PDP's) that you want to use in each stage of the workflow. During each stage, users enter, modify, review, or process data on the PDP's used in that stage. While you create and edit PDP's using a common user interface, there are multiple types of PDP's you can create. You must create or re-use at least one PDP for every new EPT you create. Table 5 - 9 lists the various *Page Types* you can create:

PDP Page Type	Description
New Project	Use to allow the creation of a new project. At minimum, the user creating a new project in PWA must provide a project name and start date.
Project	Use to display information relating to the project after project creation. The typical use for a *Project* type is to display enterprise custom fields or *Gantt Chart* views.
Workflow Status	Use to display the current workflow status of a project. Even projects with no workflow require this page.

Table 5 - 9: PDP Page Types

Because a PDP is nothing more than a web part page, you can add nearly anything to these pages. For example, you can add a company logo, links to training sites, online video tutorials, custom web parts, and much more. I highly recommend you explore the various built-in components you can add to PDP's.

Information: Project Server 2013 ships with some basic pre-built PDP's. I walk you through creating a PDP in the steps that follow, and then I use built-in PDP's for the rest of my example.

To create a new PDP, complete the following steps:

1. Log in to PWA as an administrator.

2. At the top-right of the page, click the *Gear* icon and select the *PWA Settings* item.

3. The system displays the *PWA Settings* page shown in Figure 5 - 21. Locate the *Workflow and Project Detail Pages* section and click the *Project Detail Pages* link.

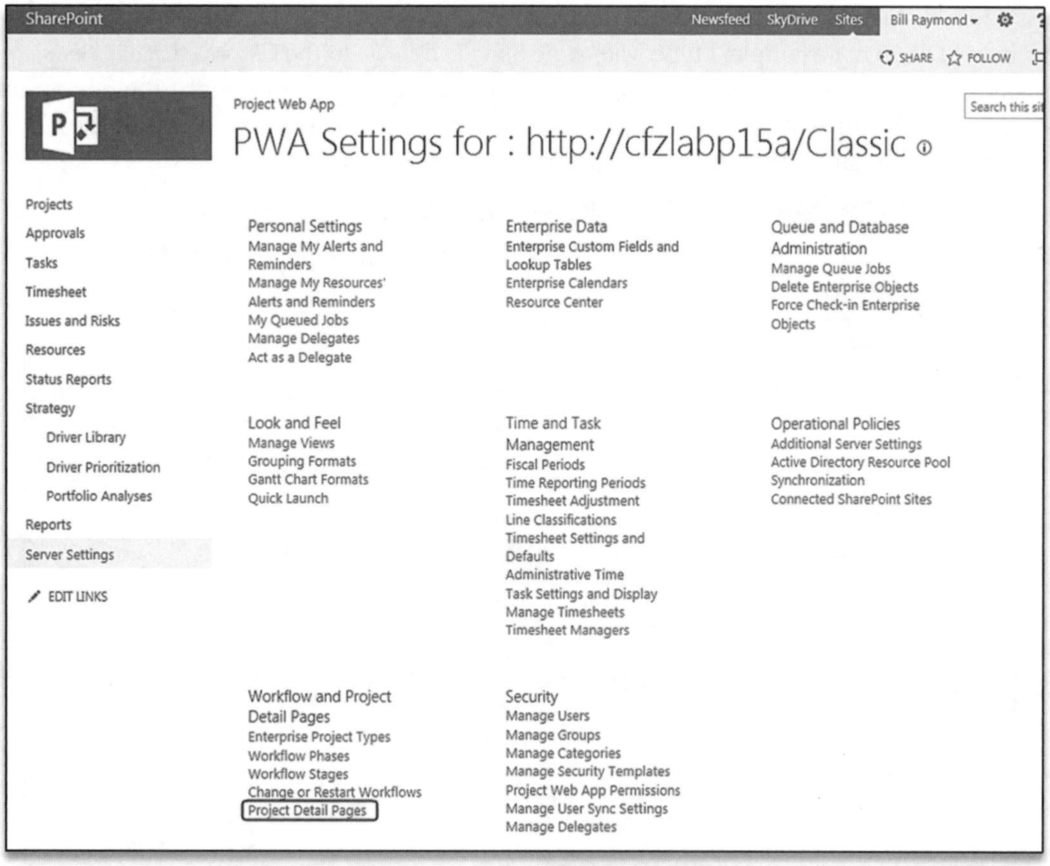

Figure 5 - 21: PWA Settings page

4. The system displays the *Project Detail Pages* library shown in Figure 5 - 22. Notice that the *Project Detail Pages* library already contains default PDP's that you can re-purpose. At the upper-left portion of the screen, click the *Files* tab and in the *New* section, click the *New Document* button.

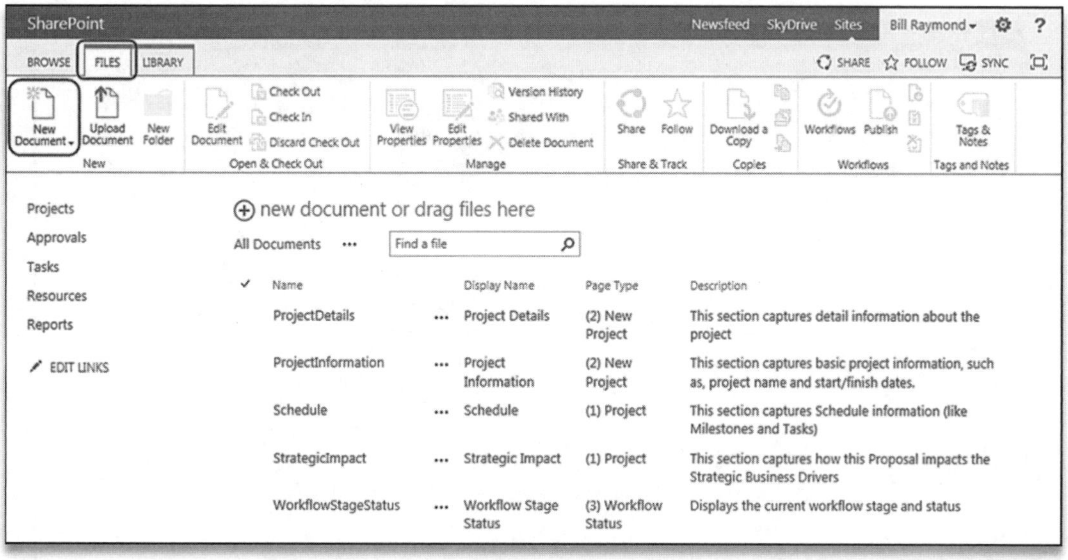

Figure 5 - 22: Project Detail Pages library

5. The system displays the *New Web Part* dialog shown in Figure 5 - 23. In the *Name* field, type a name for your new PDP. In my example, I type *Marketing Specific Details*. In the *Choose a Layout Template* field, select a layout template. Note that as you select the templates, the *Layout* graphic at the bottom-left animates, showing you what the template looks like. In most cases, the best layout for a PDP is the *Full Page, Vertical* option, which is what I select here. Click the *Create* button.

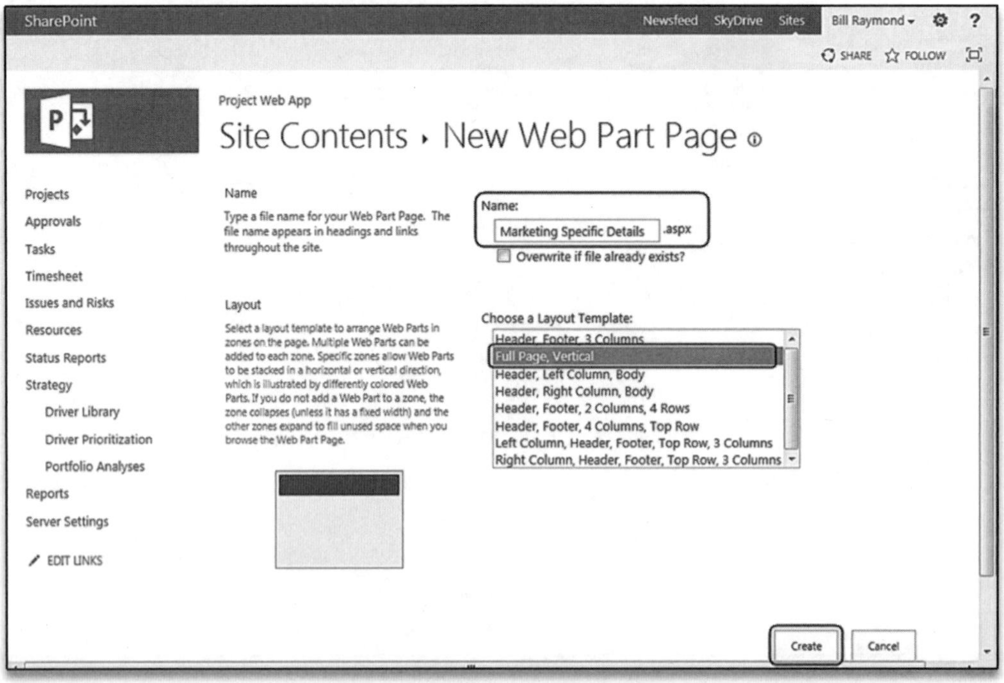

Figure 5 - 23: New Web Part page

6. The system displays the *Display Form* page shown in Figure 5 - 24 (note, if you want to see the title of the page, click the *Browse* tab at the top of the page). In the *Full Page* area of the web part page, click the *Add a Web Part* link.

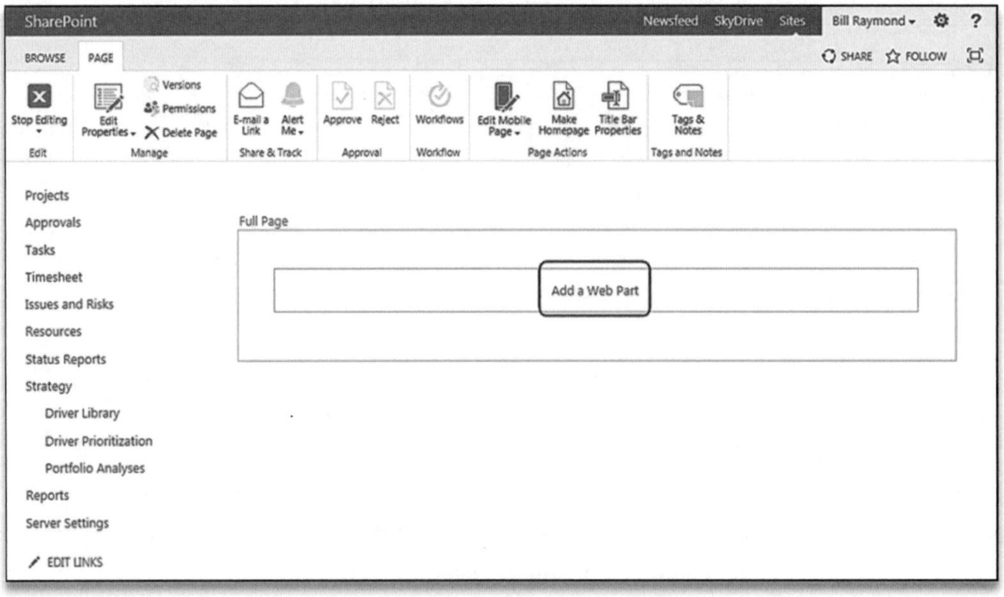

Figure 5 - 24: Display Form page

7. The system displays the *Select Web Part* dialog shown in Figure 5 - 25, which contains a list of all the web parts you can add to your PDP. In the *Categories* section, select the *Project Web App* item. The *Parts* section filters to show Project Server 2013-specific web parts. Note that clicking any web part displays a description in the *About the Part* section. Select the *Basic Info* item, and then click the *Add* button.

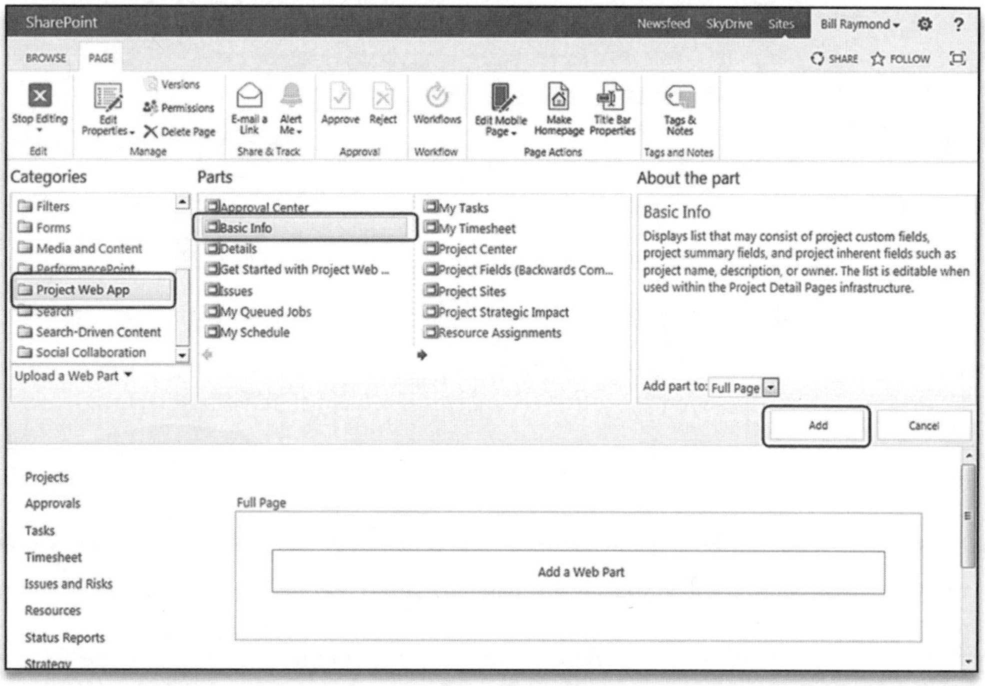

Figure 5 - 25: Select Web Part dialog

8. The system displays the *Display Form* page shown in Figure 5 - 26. Note the big change to this page is a *Basic Info* web part. Click the small arrow to the right of the *Basic Info* web part and select the *Edit Web Part* item.

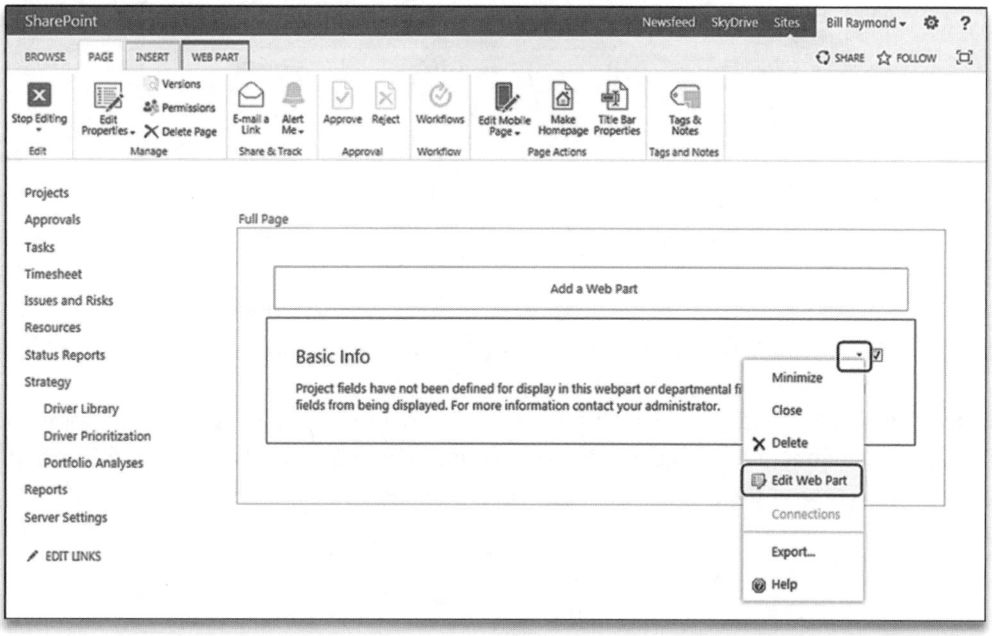

Figure 5 - 26: Display Form page, Basic Info web part added

9. The system displays the *Basic Info* web part panel at the right of the screen as shown in Figure 5 - 27. Locate the *Displayed Project Fields* section and click the *Modify* button.

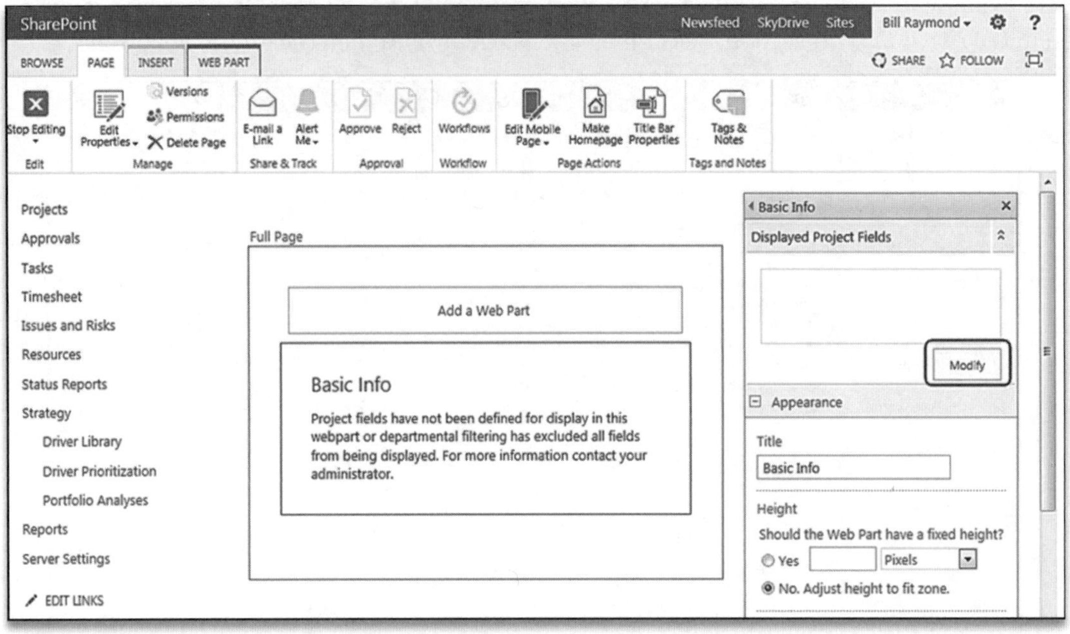

Figure 5 - 27: Basic Info web part panel, Displayed Project Fields section

10. The system displays the *Choose Project Fields* dialog shown in Figure 5 - 28. Here, you can add any ECF's to a PDP. Select any field you want under the *Project Fields* section, then click the > (single arrow) button to add the field. The web part displays the fields shown in the *Selected Project Fields* section of the dialog. In my case, I created two ECF's required for this page, the *Proposed Cost* and *High Estimate* fields. Click the *OK* button.

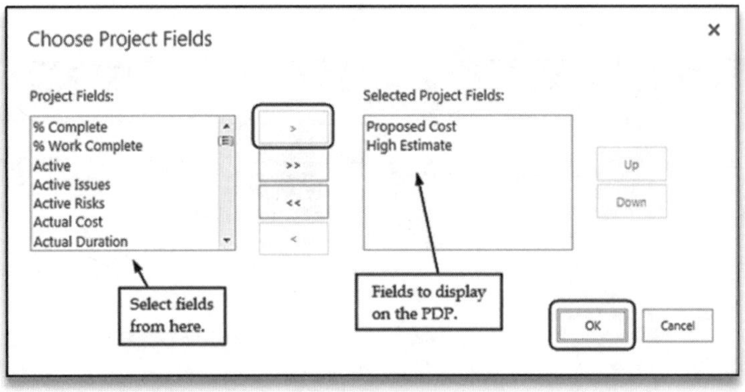

Figure 5 - 28: Choose Project Fields dialog

11. The system returns to the *Basic Info* web part panel shown in Figure 5 - 29. At this point, you can modify other areas or elements of the page to get the look and feel you want. In my case, I locate the *Title* field in the *Appearance* section of the panel and type *Required for the SURF process*. Scroll to the bottom of the page and click the *OK* button (not shown).

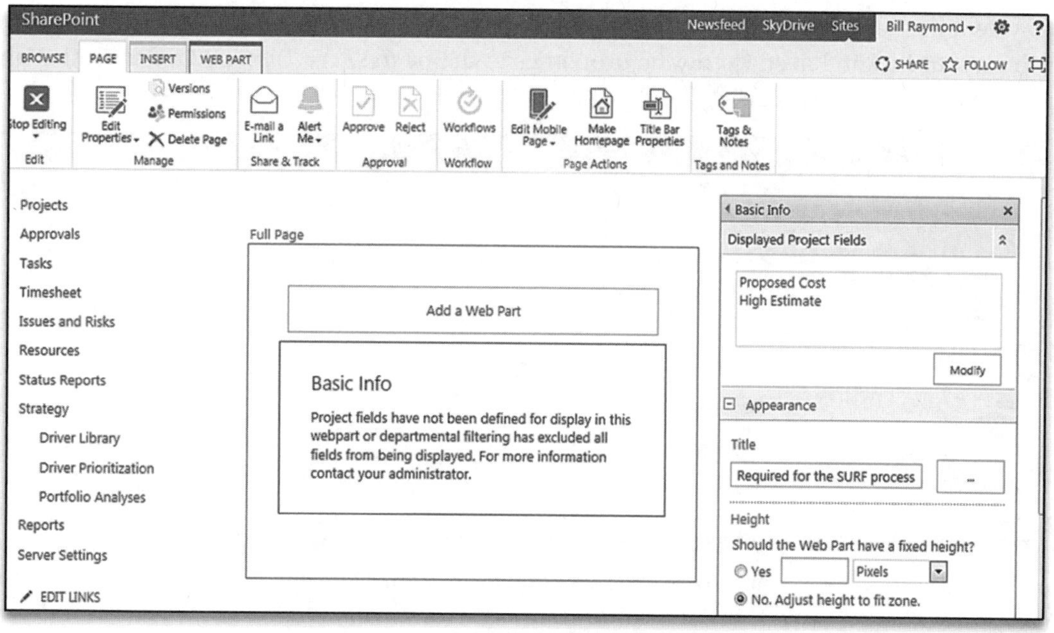

Figure 5 - 29: Basic Info web part editor dialog

12. The system refreshes the *Display Form* page shown in Figure 5 - 30. Note how the *Basic Info* web part's title is *Required for the SURF process* and that the *Proposed Cost* and *High Estimate* fields display. If you are following along with this book, make sure your page looks like this. At the top of the page, click the *Page* tab and then in the *Edit* section, click the *Stop Editing* button.

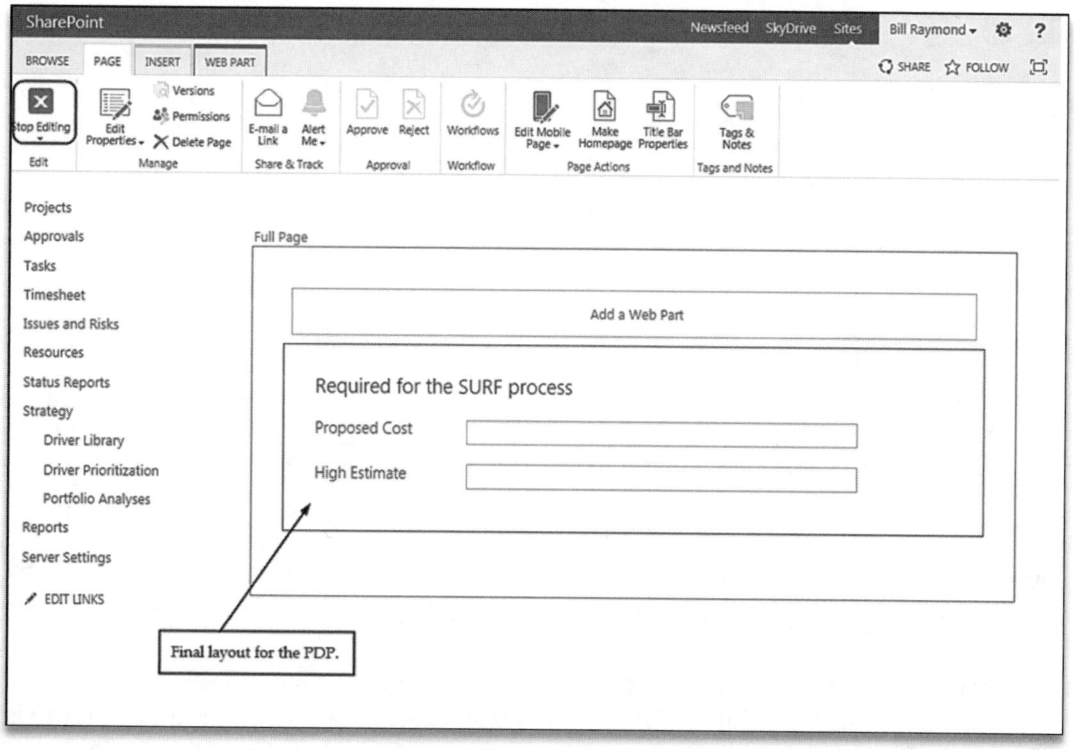

Figure 5 - 30: Display Form page with fields to display.

13. The system displays the *Display Form* page in *View-Only* mode, as shown in Figure 5 - 31. While this page has the layout I want, I need to edit the properties to define the *Page Type*, add a description and other details. At the top of this page, click the *Page* tab.

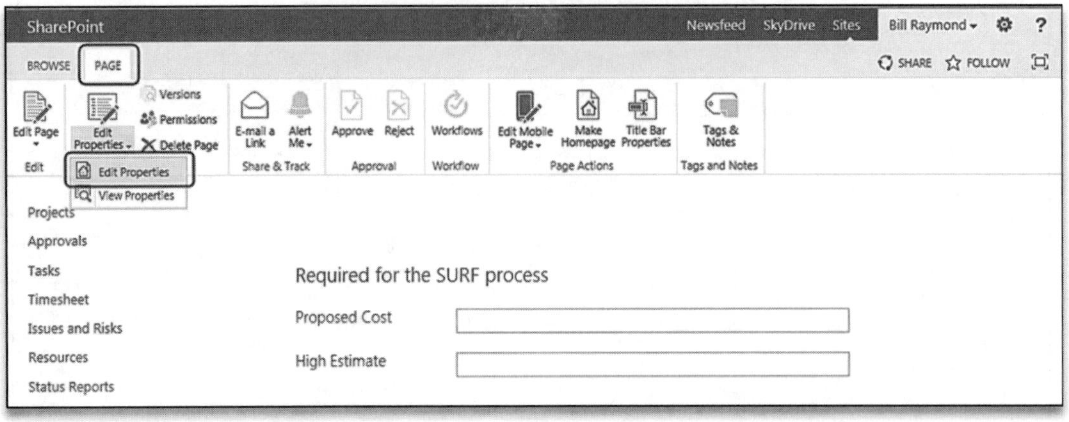

Figure 5 - 31: Display Form page, View-Only mode

14. The system displays the *Project Detail Pages* screen shown in Figure 5 - 32 where you edit the properties for the PDP. In my case, I type *SURF Fields* in the *Display Name* field and *These fields must be maintained for any project using the SURF process* in the *Description* field. Project Server 2013 frequently uses the *Display Name* as a friendly name seen by users. Click the *Save* button.

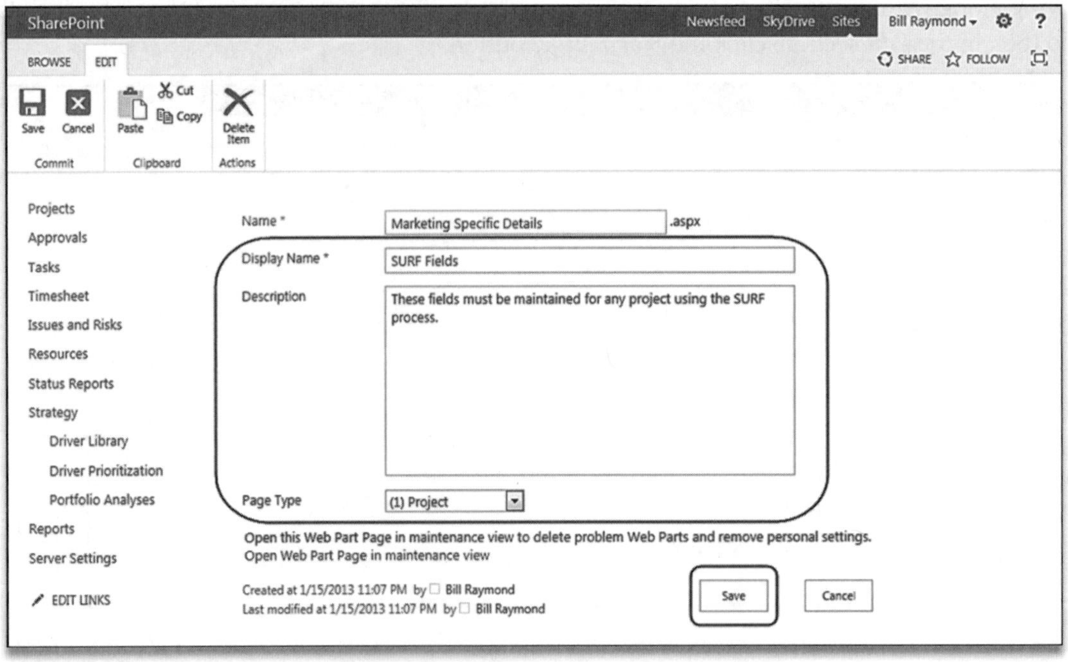

Figure 5 - 32: Project Detail Pages dialog

15. To review your changes, click the *Gear* icon at the top-right of the page and select the *PWA Settings* item. Click the *Project Detail Pages* link and the *Project Detail Pages* library displays as shown in Figure 5 - 33. Verify the new PDP reflects the property changes you made in the last step of this section.

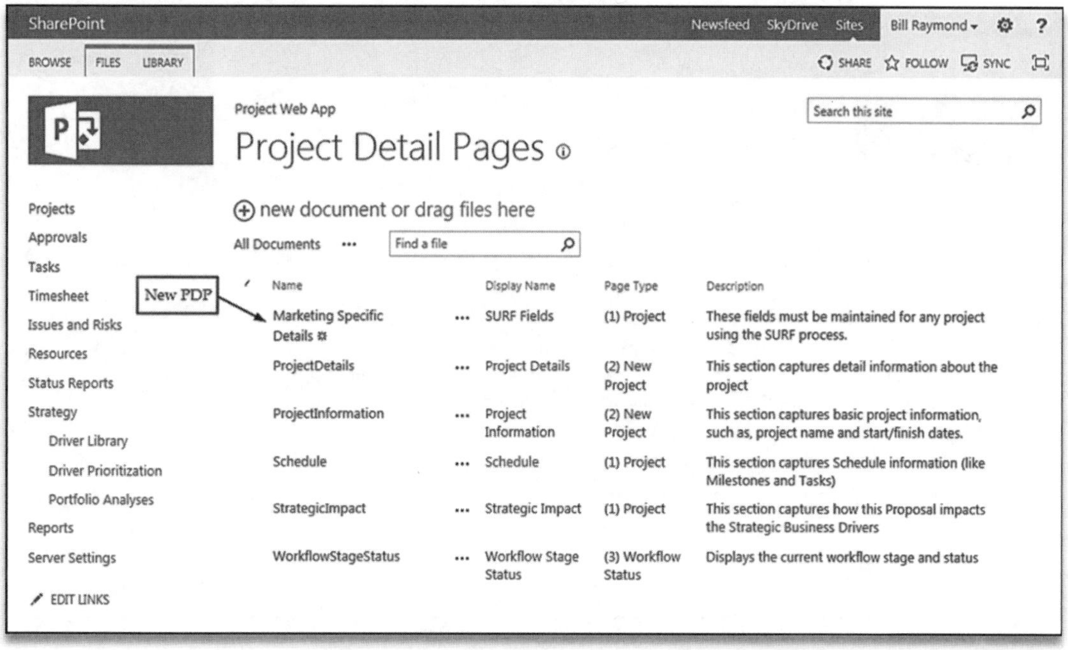

Figure 5 - 33: Project Detail Pages library

16. If necessary, edit your PDP by selecting the PDP you want to modify. The *Display Form* page displays in *View-Only* mode showing you the PDP you selected. At the top of the page, click the *Page* tab and then click the *Edit Page* button to make your changes.

Configuring Workflow Phases

Phases are an organizational unit for a collection of workflow stages. In Project Server 2013, you associate stages with phases, each of which represents a step or set of steps in the workflow process. By default, Project Server 2013 ships with a basic set of phases, which include:

- Create
- Select
- Plan
- Manage
- Finished

To view the system's default phases, or to create a new phase, complete the following steps:

1. Log in to PWA as an administrator, such as the Farm Administrator service account.
2. At the top-right of the screen, click the *Gear* icon and select the *PWA Settings* item.
3. In the *Workflow and Project Detail Pages* section of the *PWA Settings* page, click the *Workflow Phases* link.
4. The system displays the *Workflow Phases* page shown in Figure 5 - 34. Notice that the page displays five sample workflow phases, which are *Create, Finished, Manage, Plan,* and *Select.* Note that the system displays the default phases in alphabetical order rather than logical sequential order. If you want to edit a workflow phase, simply click the link for that phase. To create a new workflow phase, click the *New Workflow Phase* button.

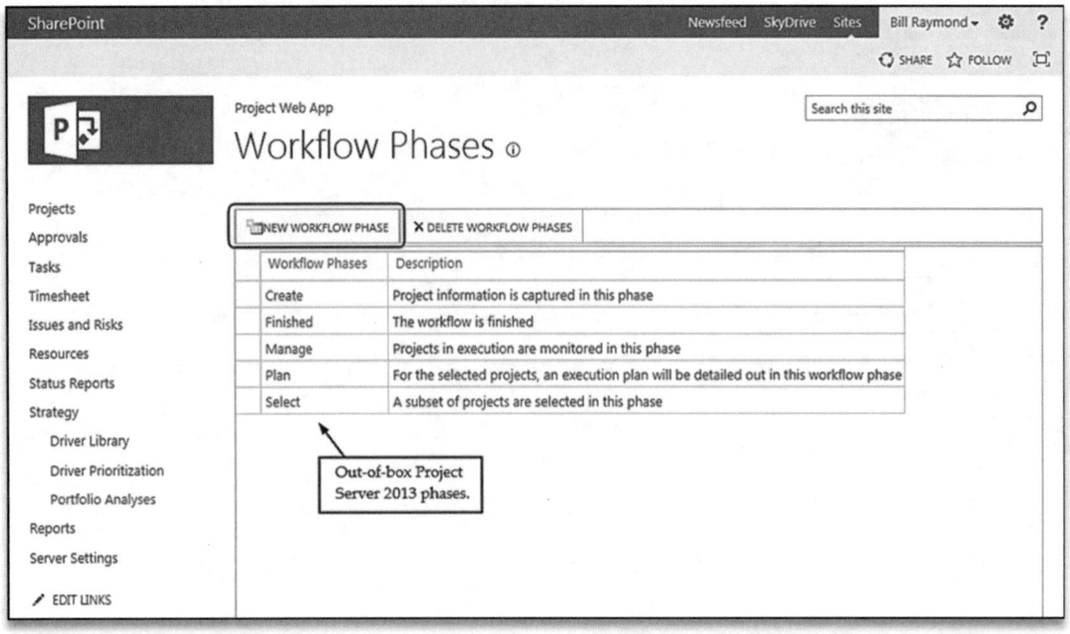

Figure 5 - 34: Workflow Phases page with built-in Project Server 2013 Workflow Phases

5. The system displays the *Add Workflow Phase* page shown in Figure 5 - 35. To add a workflow phase, type a name in the *Name* field. In my case, I type *SURF Select*. A description is not required but I type *This is the Select phase in the SURF process for the marketing department.* Click the *Save* button.

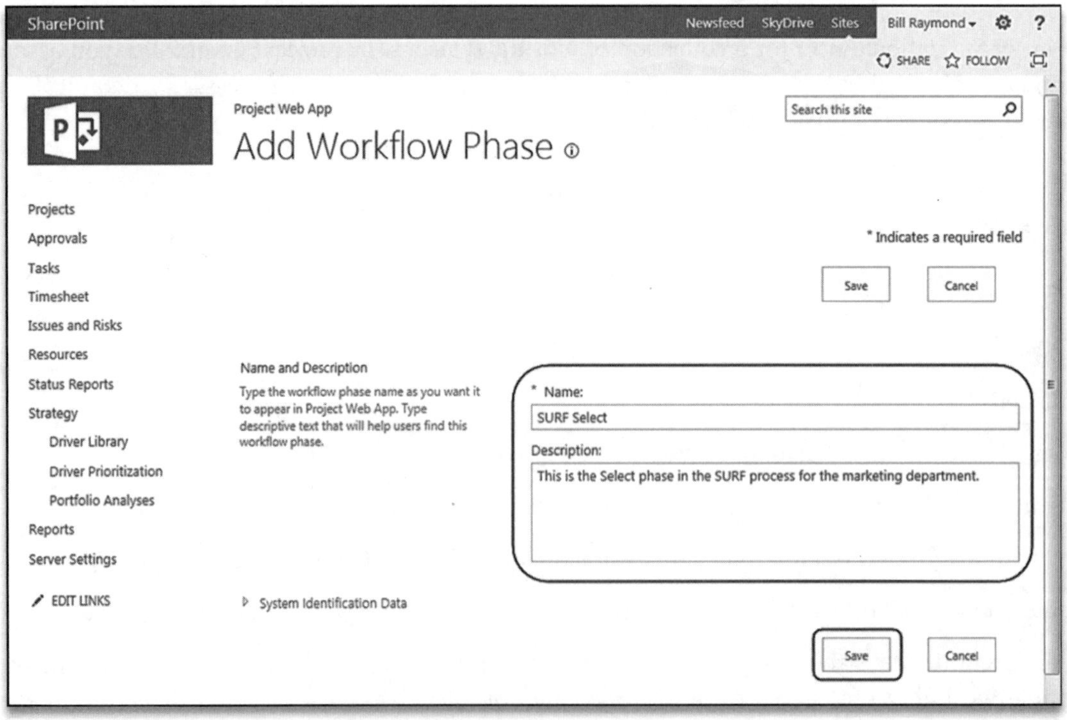

Figure 5 - 35: Add Workflow Phase page

When you save a workflow phase, the system displays the *Workflow Phases* library shown in Figure 5 - 36. Note that I followed the previous steps to create all the phases for my *SURF* marketing process described earlier in this module.

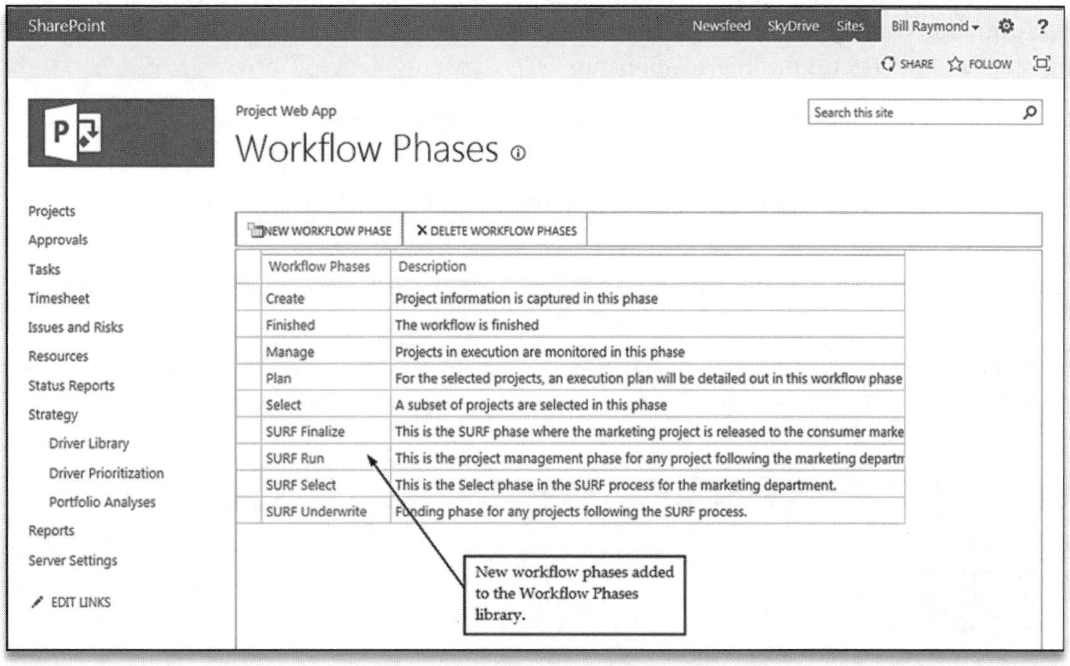
SharePoint
Newsfeed
SkyDrive
Sites
Bill Raymond
SHARE
FOLLOW
Project Web App
Workflow Phases
Search this site
Projects
Approvals
Tasks
Timesheet
Issues and Risks
Resources
Status Reports
Strategy
Driver Library
Driver Prioritization
Portfolio Analyses
Reports
Server Settings
EDIT LINKS
NEW WORKFLOW PHASE
DELETE WORKFLOW PHASES
Workflow Phases
Description
Create
Project information is captured in this phase
Finished
The workflow is finished
Manage
Projects in execution are monitored in this phase
Plan
For the selected projects, an execution plan will be detailed out in this workflow phase
Select
A subset of projects are selected in this phase
SURF Finalize
This is the SURF phase where the marketing project is released to the consumer marke
SURF Run
This is the project management phase for any project following the marketing departm
SURF Select
This is the Select phase in the SURF process for the marketing department.
SURF Underwrite
Funding phase for any projects following the SURF process.
New workflow phases added to the Workflow Phases library.

Figure 5 - 36: Workflow Phases library

If you want to configure your environment with my settings, use the workflow phases described in Table 5 - 10.

Workflow Phase Name	Phase Description
SURF Select	This is the Select phase in the SURF process for the marketing department.
SURF Underwrite	This is the Funding phase for projects following the SURF process.
SURF Run	This is the project management phase for any project following the marketing department's SURF process.
SURF Finalize	This is the SURF phase where the marketing project is released to the consumer market.

Table 5 - 10: Workflow Phases

As you can see, it is very simple to create phases for your project although they do not really **mean** anything to Project Server 2013 because you have not linked them to stages and EPT's.

Configuring Workflow Stages

Workflow stages allow you to determine how users interact with workflow phase transitions and Project Detail Pages. Each stage represents a step in the workflow process. Each stage can display one or more PDP's to display or capture information during that stage. Stages contain characteristics and properties that affect PDP behavior. Follow these steps to understand the interrelationship:

1. Log in to PWA as an administrator, such as the Farm Administrator service account.

2. At the top-right of the page, click the *Gear* icon and select the *PWA Settings* item.

3. From the *Workflow and Project Detail Pages* section of the *Server Settings* page, click the *Workflow Stages* link.

4. The system displays the *Workflow Stages* page shown in Figure 5 - 37. To create a new workflow stage, click the *New Workflow Stage* button.

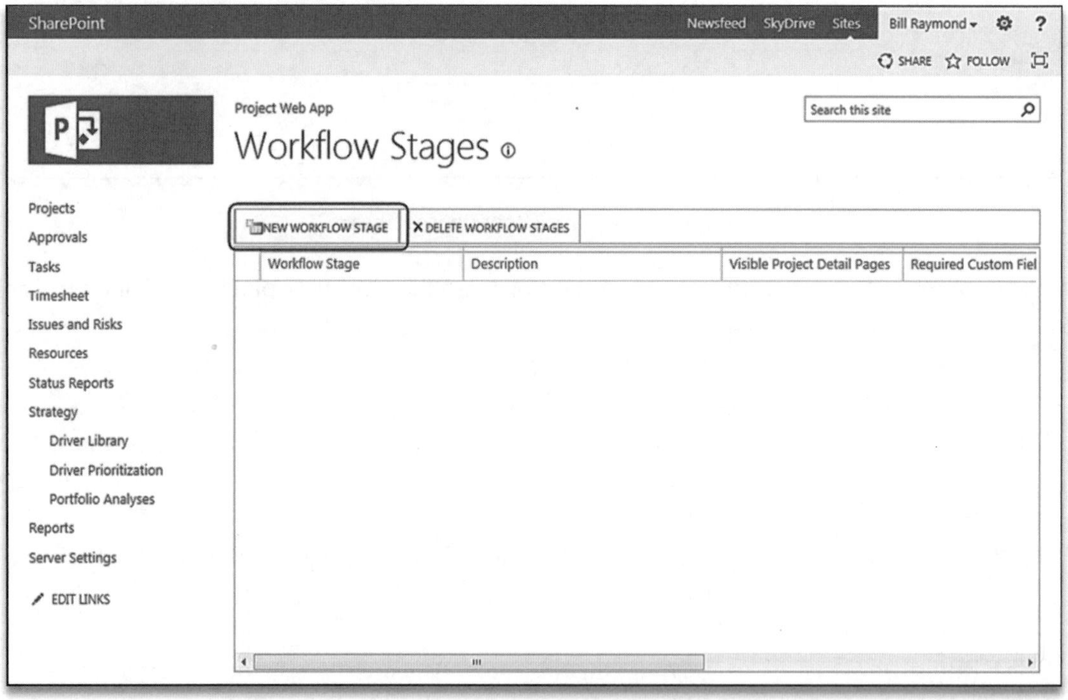

Figure 5 - 37: Workflow Stages page

5. The system displays the *Add Workflow Stage* page. Minimally, modify the *Name, Description, Workflow Phase, Workflow Status Project Detail Page,* and *Visible Project Detail Pages* sections. Table 5 - 11 through Table 5 - 16 outline the settings for my configuration. After completing your entries on the *Add Workflow Stage* page, click the *Save* button. Upon save, the system displays the *Workflow Stages* library as shown previously in Figure 5 - 37, which contains all stages in your Project Server 2013 configuration.

Name: SURF Scope	
Option	**Setting**
Description	This is the SURF Scoping stage required for the Select phase.
Description for submit	N/A
Workflow phase	SURF Select
Workflow status Project Detail Page	Workflow Stage status
Available Project Detail Pages	Project Details Strategic Impact
Additional Settings for the Visible Project Detail Pages	N/A
Required Custom Fields	N/A
Read-Only Custom Fields	N/A
Strategic Impact Behavior	Read/Write
Project Check-In Required	N/A

Table 5 - 11: SURF Scope

Name: SURF Resources	
Option	**Setting**
Description	This is the SURF Scoping stage required for the Underwriting phase.
Description for submit	N/A
Workflow phase	SURF Underwrite
Workflow status Project Detail Page	Workflow Stage status
Available Project Detail Pages	Project Details Schedule
Additional Settings for the Visible Project Detail Pages	N/A
Required Custom Fields	N/A

Name: SURF Resources	
Option	**Setting**
Read-Only Custom Fields	N/A
Strategic Impact Behavior	Read/Write
Project Check-In Required	N/A

Table 5 - 12: SURF Resources

Name: SURF Budget	
Option	**Setting**
Description	This is the SURF Budget stage required for the Underwriting phase.
Description for submit	N/A
Workflow phase	SURF Underwrite
Workflow status Project Detail Page	Workflow Stage status
Available Project Detail Pages	Project Details Schedule SURF fields
Additional Settings for the Visible Project Detail Pages	N/A
Required Custom Fields	High Estimate
Read-Only Custom Fields	N/A
Strategic Impact Behavior	Read/Write
Project Check-In Required	N/A

Table 5 - 13: SURF Budget

Name: SURF Schedule	
Option	**Setting**
Description	This is the SURF Scoping stage required for the Underwriting phase.
Description for submit	N/A
Workflow phase	SURF Run
Workflow status Project Detail Page	Workflow Stage status
Available Project Detail Pages	Project Details Schedule SURF fields
Additional Settings for the Visible Project Detail Pages	N/A
Required Custom Fields	N/A
Read-Only Custom Fields	High Estimate
Strategic Impact Behavior	Read/Write

Table 5 - 14: SURF Schedule

Name: SURF Manage	
Option	**Setting**
Description	This is the SURF Manage stage required for the Run phase.
Description for submit	N/A
Workflow phase	SURF Run
Workflow status Project Detail Page	Workflow Stage status
Available Project Detail Pages	Project Details Schedule SURF fields
Additional Settings for the Visible Project Detail Pages	N/A
Required Custom Fields	N/A

Name: SURF Manage	
Option	**Setting**
Read-Only Custom Fields	High Estimate
Strategic Impact Behavior	Read/Write
Project Check-In Required	N/A

Table 5 - 15: SURF Manage

Name: SURF Closeout	
Option	**Setting**
Description	This is the SURF Finalize stage required for the Run phase.
Description for submit	N/A
Workflow phase	SURF Finalize
Workflow status Project Detail Page	Workflow Stage status
Available Project Detail Pages	Project Details Project Information Schedule Strategic Impact SURF fields
Additional Settings for the Visible Project Detail Pages	N/A
Required Custom Fields	N/A
Read-Only Custom Fields	High Estimate
Strategic Impact Behavior	Read/Write
Project Check-In Required	N/A

Table 5 - 16: SURF Closeout

New projects require basic project information and alignment to strategic drivers. The *SURF Resource* stage requires a project plan containing a basic resource plan. The *SURF Budget* stage requires a cost estimate (*High Estimate*). An approved project in the *Run* phase allows the user to view the estimate in *Read-Only* mode. The *Schedule* and *Manage* stages have identical settings; the distinction is that someone approved the schedule via workflow and that reports show that the project is in the manage stage.

The *Workflow Stage* page is identical whether you are creating new stages or editing existing ones. When you create a new workflow stage, or edit an existing stage, you must assign each stage to a phase. Enter the name of the stage in the *Name* field, and enter an optional description in the *Description* field. The *Description for Submit* section contains a second *Description* field into which you enter the description that Project Server 2013 displays when a user clicks the *Submit* button to move beyond the current stage. The system limits you to no more than 255 characters in the *Description* field.

In the *Workflow Phase* section, click the *Phase* pick list and select the phase for the stage. In the *Workflow Stage Status Project Detail Page* section, click the *Choose Workflow Stage Status Project Detail Page* pick list and choose a *Project Detail Page* that is the *Workflow Status* type and contains the *Workflow Status* web part from the list. The system always makes this page visible during this stage of the workflow process. The example uses the *Proposal Stage Status* PDP that ships with the product.

In the *Visible Project Detail Pages* section, you select the PDP's you want visible to users during this stage of the workflow process. By default, the system selects no PDP other than the *Workflow Stage Status Detail Page* you selected, so you must select at least one PDP to support your data gathering and communication for this stage, because a stage cannot have only a *Workflow Status* page. You can select each PDP individually or use multi-selection techniques in the *Available Project Detail Pages* list and then click the *Add* button to add your selected pages to the list on the right. After adding the first page or all of your pages, you should enter a description for the page in the *Type the Workflow Stage Specific Description for the Visible Project Detail Page* text field. Note that the value changes for this field as you select each page on the right hand side of the *Choose Project Detail Pages* section. The system displays the *Stage Specific Description* with the name of the PDP in the *Workflow Status* page. The system limits you to no more than 1,024 characters in the description. If you need to mandate that the user take action in the PDP, select the option checkbox named *The Project Detail Page requires attention*. After completing this process for the first PDP in the *Visible Project Detail Pages* section, repeat the process for each additional PDP you add to this stage. The system allows you to enter information in the *Stage Specific Description* field and to select the option checkbox for each PDP individually.

The *Required Custom Fields* section allows you to determine the behavior of the fields in the PDP's and the stage. To make fields required for this stage, select one or more custom fields in the *Choose Custom Fields* list and then click the *Add* button to add them to the list on the right. If you want to include all of the available custom fields, click the *Add All* button.

Warning: The PDP's used in this stage must include the custom fields you select in the *Required Custom Fields* section. If you fail to include these custom fields in the PDP's, users cannot enter required values, and Project Server 2013 does not allow the workflow process to continue beyond this stage.

In the *Read Only Custom Fields* section, choose the fields that the system displays in *Read-Only* mode during this workflow stage. Select one or more custom fields in the *Choose Custom Fields* list and then click the *Add* button to add them to the list on the right. If you want to include all of the available custom fields, click the *Add All* button. When you mark a field as read-only for a stage, the field is not editable when displayed in the *Project Details* web part on any PDP included in this stage. *Required* and *Read-Only* attributes for fields during specific stages are an important control in managing the information flow within your workflow.

In the *Strategic Impact Behavior* section, the system allows you to specify the behavior of *Strategic Impact* values for the project proposal. Select the *Read Only* option or *Read Write* option, as you require. If you select the *Required* option, users must select a *Strategic Impact* value for **every** business driver in order to determine strategic alignment using portfolio analysis.

Information: If you select the *Required* option in the *Strategic Impact Behavior* section, make sure that you include the *Strategic Impact* web part on at least one of the PDP's used in this stage.

In the *Project Check In Required* section, you must choose whether the stage requires the user to check in the project. If you select this option, the user cannot submit the project proposal to the workflow without first checking in the project. You typically select this option if any updates occur to the project proposal in this stage. If you select the *Project check in is required* option and the user does not check in the project proposal, Project Server 2013 prevents the user from submitting the project to the next stage in the workflow. One reason for setting this flag is to allow the workflow to modify the project. If your workflow edits the project after the user clicks the *Submit* button, you must force the user to check it in. Otherwise, the workflow cannot check out the project, edit it, then check it back in. Setting this option is also a good way to ensure that the project is available for editing by the next person who needs to work the project through the next workflow stage. If you do not require the check in, you may find that you have many people complaining that they cannot edit the project to shepherd it though the next stage. Click the *Save* button when you complete your entries to save your new stage or modified stage.

Best Practice: When you are in the process of creating Phases and stages, I recommend you add a numbered prefix in front of each item. Because PWA displays items in alphabetical order, they will likely be out of order which can lead to confusion.

Creating Site Templates

Most project teams want a SharePoint site to collaborate on documents, issues, risks, and other pertinent information. Project Server 2013 ships with a Project Site template that is perfectly acceptable. Many organizations prefer to modify the template using the techniques you learned in Module 02, *Task lists, Project Sites and News Feed* and more.

Best Practice: The best approach to creating a new site template is to create a new project plan in PWA, modify that clean site, then save it as a template.

Saving a Project Site as a Template

In Module 02, *Task lists, Project Sites and News Feed,* I made numerous customizations to the SharePoint Training site. Now I can save that site as a template that I can assign to an enterprise project type.

1. At the top-right of the page, click the *Gear* icon and select the *Site Settings* item (note: **do not** select *PWA Settings*).
2. The system displays the *Site Settings* page. Locate the *Site Actions* section and click the *Save site as template* link as shown in Figure 5 - 38.

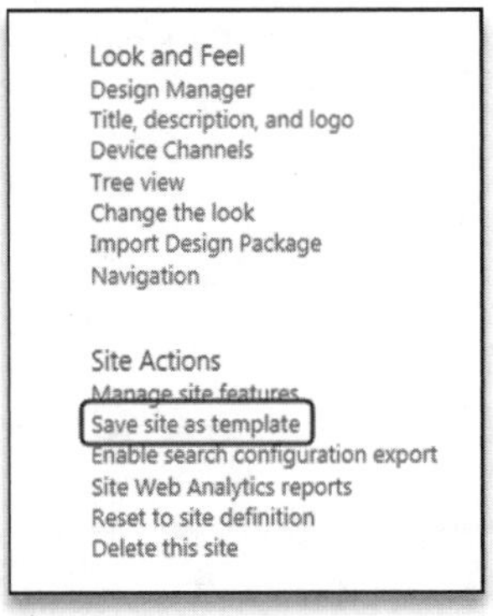
Look and Feel
Design Manager
Title, description, and logo
Device Channels
Tree view
Change the look
Import Design Package
Navigation
Site Actions
Manage site features
Save site as template
Enable search configuration export
Site Web Analytics reports
Reset to site definition
Delete this site

Figure 5 - 38: Site Settings page

3. The system displays the *Save as Template* page shown in Figure 5 - 39. In this example, I use the *File name* field to type *SURF SharePoint Site Template* and type the same entry into the *Template name* field. I also use the *Template description* field to type *Use this SharePoint site template for any Marketing Enterprise Project Type.* Select the *Include Content* option if you plan to include content such as documents or other items in the site. You make this choice during the template creation process. Click the *OK* button.

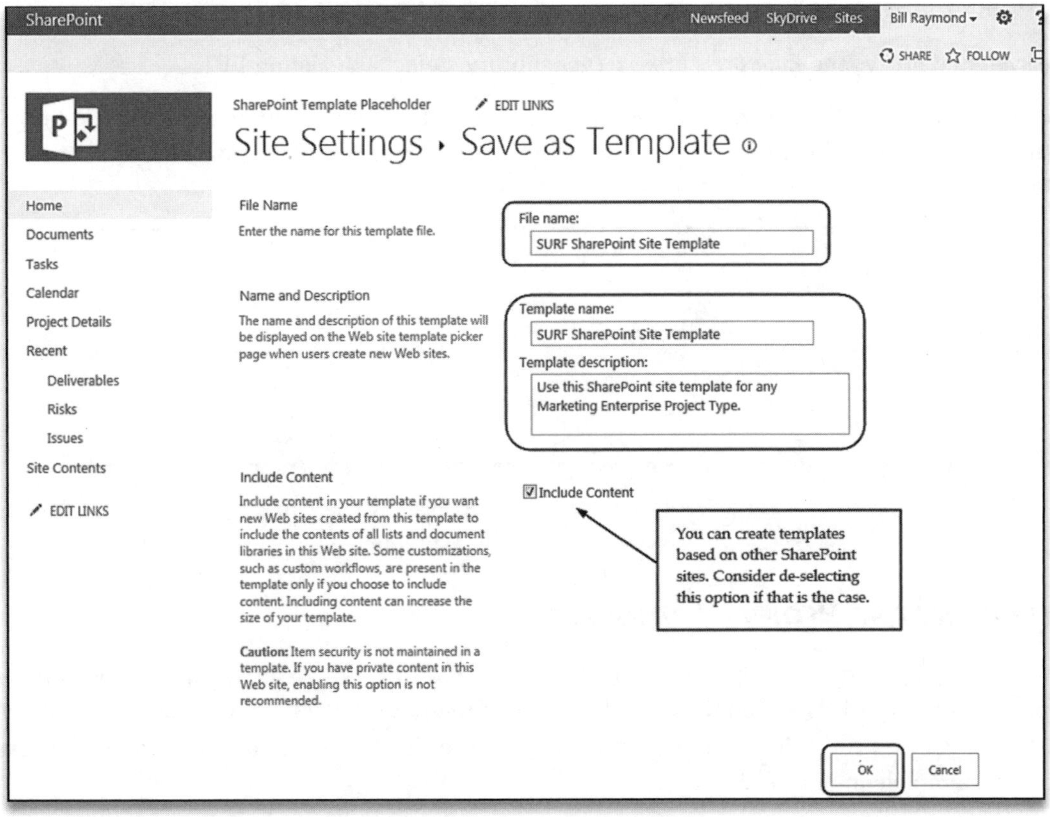
SharePoint
Newsfeed SkyDrive Sites
Bill Raymond
SHARE FOLLOW
SharePoint Template Placeholder
EDIT LINKS
Site Settings › Save as Template
Home
Documents
Tasks
Calendar
Project Details
Recent
Deliverables
Risks
Issues
Site Contents
EDIT LINKS
File Name
Enter the name for this template file.
File name:
SURF SharePoint Site Template
Name and Description
The name and description of this template will be displayed on the Web site template picker page when users create new Web sites.
Template name:
SURF SharePoint Site Template
Template description:
Use this SharePoint site template for any Marketing Enterprise Project Type.
Include Content
Include content in your template if you want new Web sites created from this template to include the contents of all lists and document libraries in this Web site. Some customizations, such as custom workflows, are present in the template only if you choose to include content. Including content can increase the size of your template.
Caution: Item security is not maintained in a template. If you have private content in this Web site, enabling this option is not recommended.
Include Content
You can create templates based on other SharePoint sites. Consider de-selecting this option if that is the case.
OK
Cancel

Figure 5 - 39: Save as Template page

4. After processing, the system displays the *Operation Completed Successfully* dialog shown in Figure 5 - 40. Click the *OK* button.

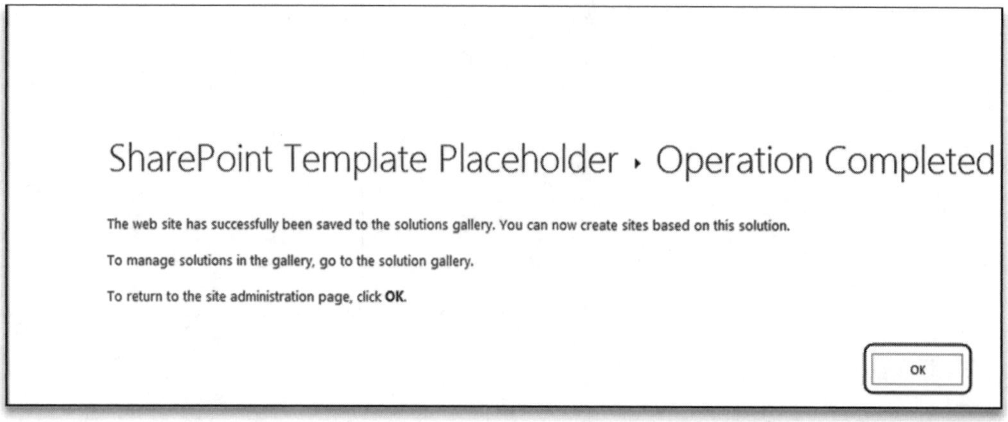
SharePoint Template Placeholder ▸ Operation Completed
The web site has successfully been saved to the solutions gallery. You can now create sites based on this solution.
To manage solutions in the gallery, go to the solution gallery.
To return to the site administration page, click OK.
OK

Figure 5 - 40: Operation completed successfully dialog

The system returns to the *SharePoint Site Template.* There are no more actions to take at this time. I use this template in another section of this module. To use this template on an existing EPT, follow these steps:

1. Log in to PWA as an administrator.
2. At the top-right of the screen, click the *Gear* icon and select the *PWA Settings* item.
3. Locate the *Workflow and Project Details* section and click the *Enterprise Project Types* link.
4. The system displays the *Enterprise Project Types* library. Select an existing EPT.
5. The system displays the *Enterprise Project* page as partially shown in Figure 5 - 41. Scroll down the page until you find the *Project Site Template* section and select your template from the pick list. Click the *Save* button.

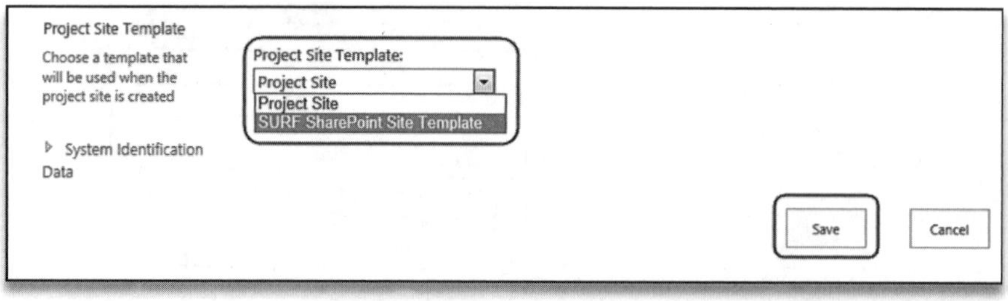
Project Site Template
Choose a template that will be used when the project site is created
Project Site Template:
Project Site
Project Site
SURF SharePoint Site Template
System Identification Data
Save
Cancel

Figure 5 - 41: Enterprise Project page where you select the Project Site Template.

Creating Enterprise Project Templates

Before you create your Enterprise Project Types (EPT's), you may want to create or import the enterprise project templates for use with your EPT's. To take full advantage of the power of EPT's, you have the option to create a corresponding enterprise project template for each EPT. As the Project Server administrator, you can create an enterprise project template in one of two ways:

- Create the enterprise project template manually.
- Import an existing project as an enterprise project template.

Best Practice: Before you attempt to create or import enterprise project templates, MSProjectExperts recommends that you enlist the aid of key project managers and executives to determine if workflow must govern certain types of projects. Once you determine your requirements, ask your project managers to help in the creation of appropriate enterprise project templates.

Creating an Enterprise Project Template

To create an enterprise project template, launch Project Pro 2013 and connect to your Project Server instance as an administrator. Create a project plan template according to your organization's project standards **or** open an existing project plan already on your server. There are no set rules to creating a project template but you typically include the following elements:

- Project tasks with duration estimates
- Summary tasks to organize the tasks into phase and deliverable sections
- Milestone tasks to represent significant points in the project
- Task dependencies linking tasks to one another
- Task notes, where applicable

Including generic resources with effort estimates, if applicable, reduces the workload on your project schedulers when creating a new project from the template. If you include resources, add generic resources to the resource sheet and assign them to tasks to indicate the skill types required for each task. Your enterprise project template should never include constraints or deadline dates on tasks, or named resources as your project managers need to add these according to the requirements for each individual production project.

As you can see in Figure 5 - 42, I have a very basic template following the SURF process. The assumption is a project manager knows the best tasks to add to their plan, connects the logic, and adds resources according to their best practices.

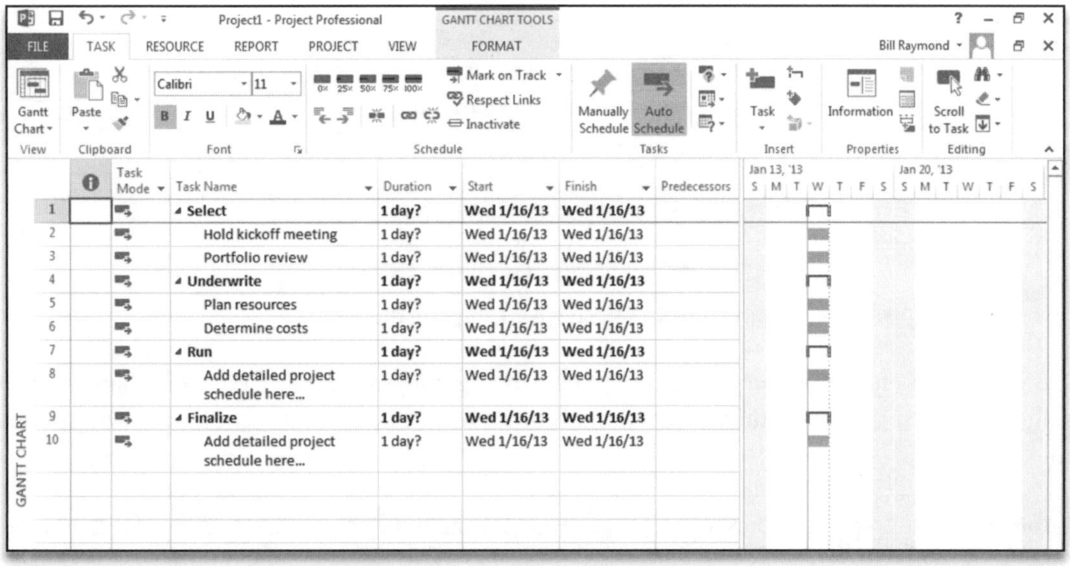

Figure 5 - 42: SURF Process template

When you finish creating the template, click *File* ➢ *Save*. The system displays the *Save to Project Web App* dialog shown in Figure 5 - 43. Type a name for the enterprise project template in the *Name* field. Click the *Type* pick list and select the *Template* item from the pick list. Optionally, select the appropriate calendar from the *Calendar* pick list and department from the *Department* pick list. Click the *Save* button.

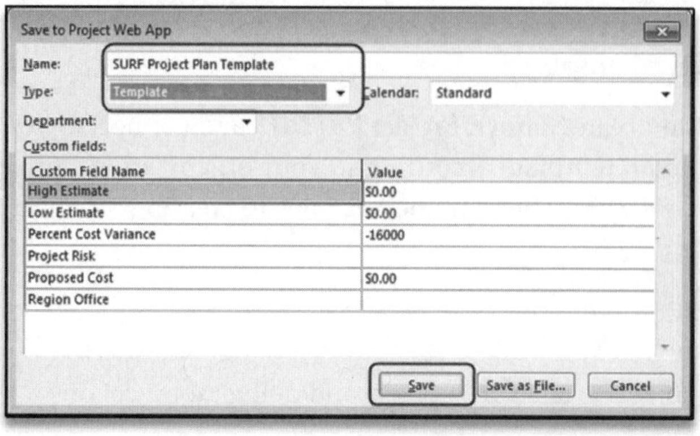

Figure 5 - 43: Save to Project Web App dialog

Information: When you save a project as an enterprise template, the system does not force you to enter values in required fields. If you choose to enter values in any custom enterprise fields, these become the default values for new projects created from the template. Project managers can then change these values when creating a new project. To guarantee that project managers supply a value for all required enterprise fields, do not enter any value in the required fields when you save the enterprise template. This forces your project managers to enter values in those fields before they can save an enterprise project in the Project Server database.

The system displays the *Save As Template* dialog shown in Figure 5 - 44. In the *Select the type of data that you want to remove from the template* section, select any checkbox with the type of data that would never exist in a new project. This step is for removing data from an existing project that you want to save as a template. Ultimately, you can decide which settings to keep and which to remove. Keep in mind that by checking these boxes, you are actually removing the data permanently from the template. Click the *Save* button, then close and exit Project Pro 2013.

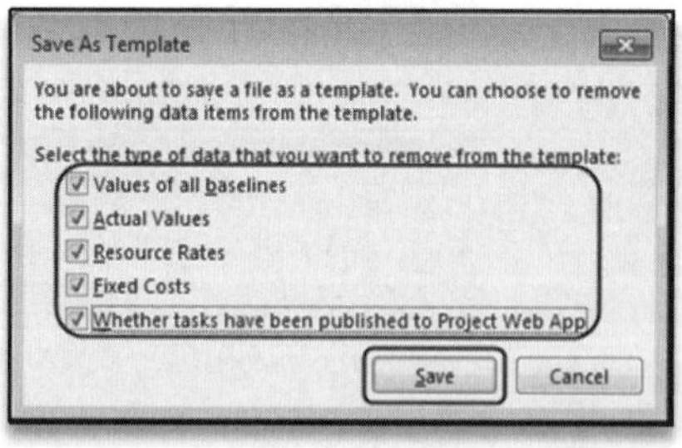

Figure 5 - 44: Save As Template dialog

You can also import an enterprise project template or existing project schedule as a template using the *Import Wizard.* Using the wizard gives you the ability to map local custom fields and resources to enterprise fields and resources.

Information: Creating project templates is optional. If no template is used, then Project Server 2013 will use a SharePoint list or a blank project plan based on how you define the EPT (Enterprise Project Type).

Configuring Workflows

Project Server 2013 is workflow enabled, which means there are no pre-defined workflows. Instead, you create workflows to match your specific business needs. With Project Server 2013, the only way to create workflows is to use Microsoft's solution starter, write software code in Visual Studio, or purchase a third-party software product. Microsoft now allows you to create basic SharePoint 2013 and Project Server 2013 workflows using the free SharePoint Designer 2013 product. If you have advanced workflow requirements, like complex branching workflows, or a need for the workflow to integrate with other systems, then Visual Studio or third-party products are still the way to go.

Best Practice: SharePoint Designer is very powerful in that anyone can quickly learn how to build workflows. However, it is a best practice for a technical person, such as a developer, to **own** the solution to ensure that it is streamlined and supportable in a production environment.

Before you begin, download a copy of SharePoint Designer from Microsoft's website, and install it on your workstation computer. While the product is free, you may find it best to download a copy of the software based on the licensing site Microsoft has provided you. You can also go to the following website and search for *SharePoint Designer 2013*:

http://www.microsoft.com/downloads

After you install SharePoint Designer on your workstation computer, follow these steps to create a Project Server workflow:

Warning: Many of the steps below require a significant amount of processing on the server. You will notice that SharePoint Designer may appear as if it is not responding or functioning properly. It is important that you wait until the processing completes and try to avoid clicking around the window to avoid frustration.

1. Press the **Windows** key on your computer keyboard and type *SharePoint Designer*. Click the *SharePoint Designer* link as shown in Figure 5 - 45.

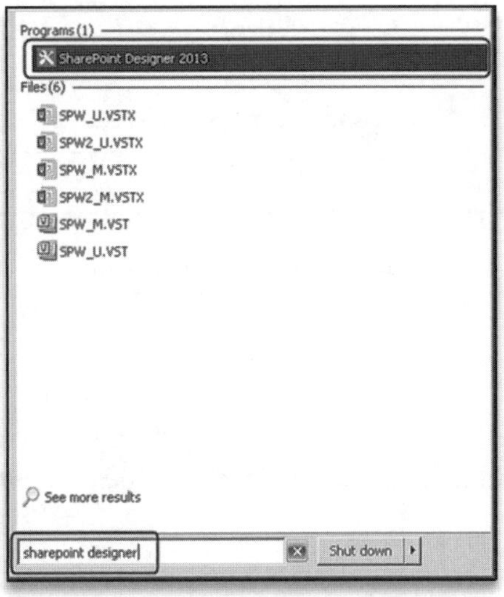

Figure 5 - 45: Windows Start menu

2. The system displays the SharePoint Designer *Backstage* shown in Figure 5 - 46. Click the *Open Site* button.

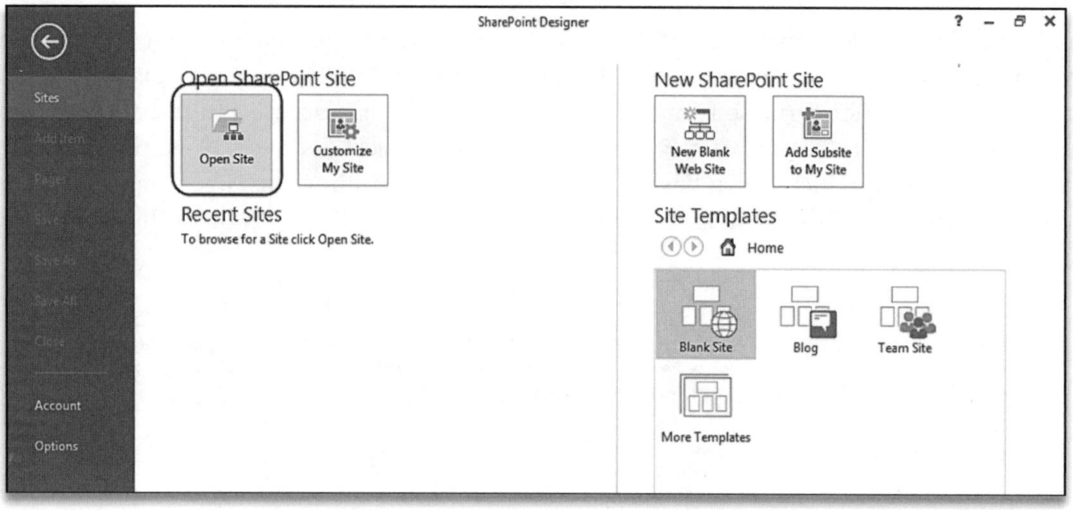

Figure 5 - 46: SharePoint Designer 2013 Backstage

3. The system displays the *Open Site* dialog shown in Figure 5 - 47. In the *Site name* field, type the URL path for your PWA instance and then click the *Open* button.

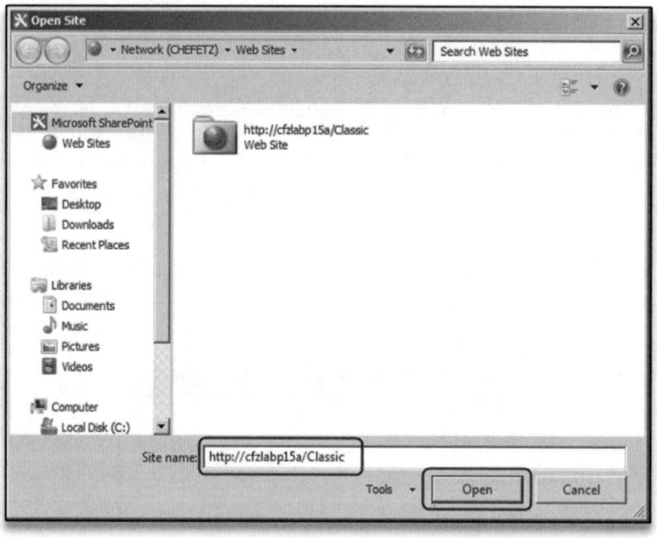

Figure 5 - 47: Open Site dialog

4. The system displays the SharePoint Designer user interface with your PWA site opened as shown in Figure 5 - 48. Click the *Site* tab, and then in the *New* section, click the *Site Workflow* button.

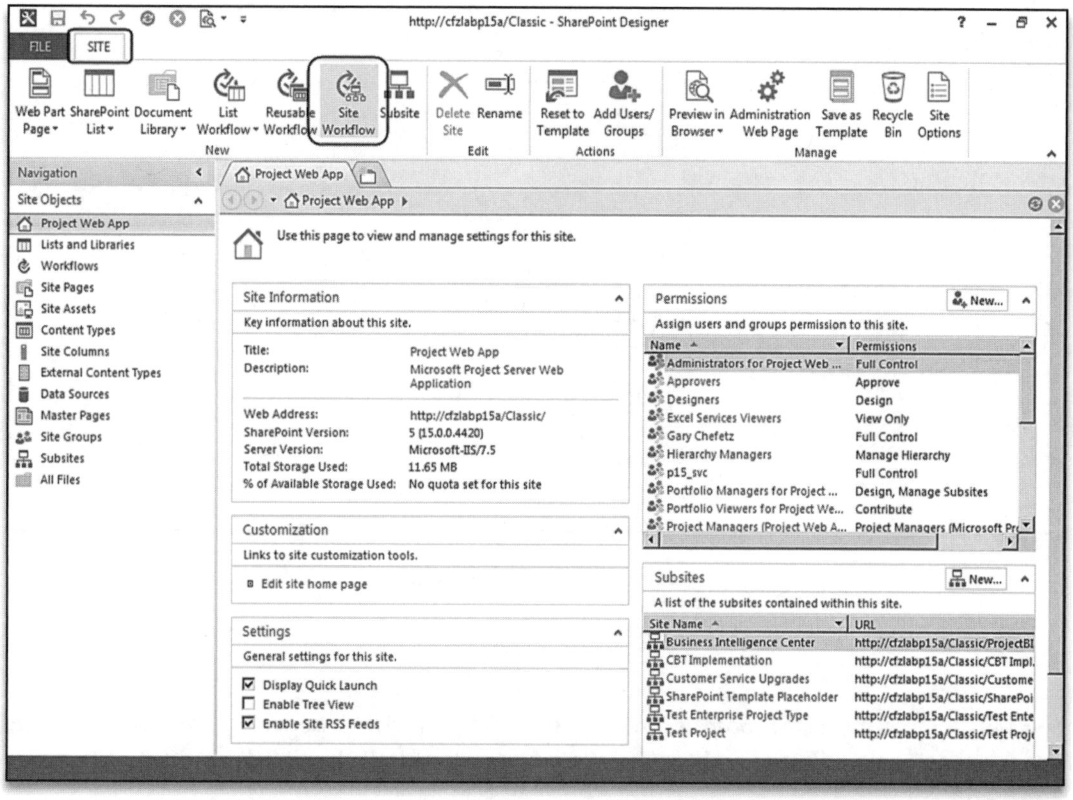

Figure 5 - 48: SharePoint Designer with an open PWA site

5. The system displays the *Create Site Workflow* dialog shown in Figure 5 - 49. In the *Name* field, type a name for the new workflow such as *SURF Workflow*. In the *Description* field, type a good description for the workflow such as *This workflow supports the Marketing department's SURF process.* In the *Platform Type* pick list, select the *SharePoint 2013 Workflow - Project Server* item and then click the *OK* button.

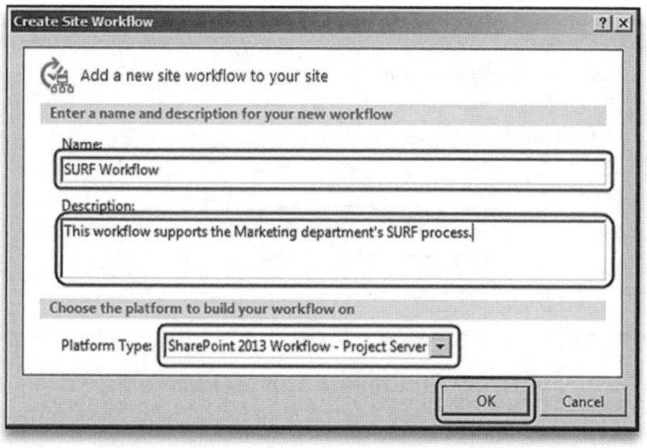

Figure 5 - 49: Create Site Workflow dialog

6. The system displays the *SURF Workflow* page shown in Figure 5 - 50. From the *Insert* section, click the *Stage* pick list button. Select the first stage in your governance process. In my example, I choose *SURF Scope.*

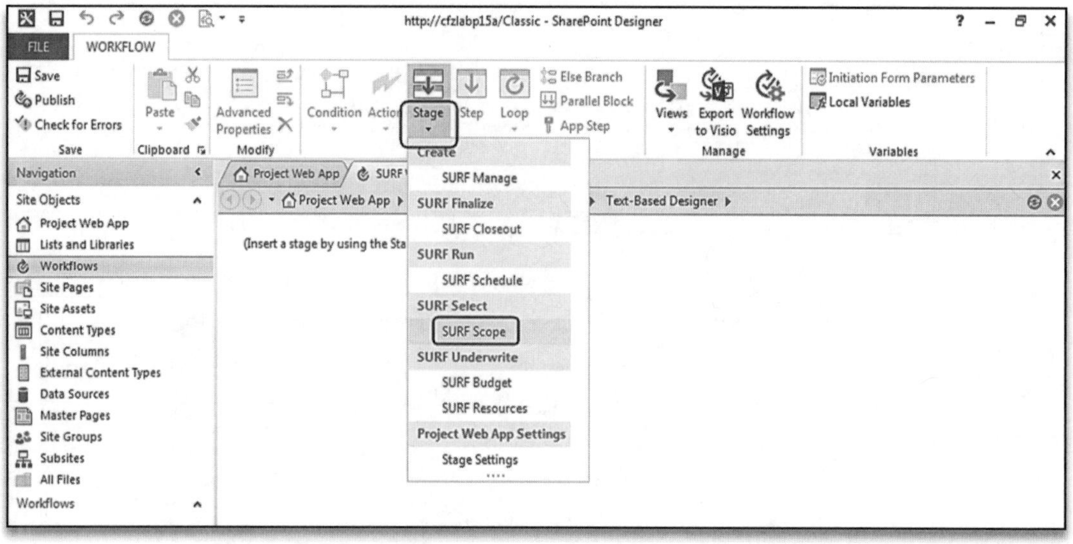

Figure 5 - 50: Add a Stage

7. The system places the *SURF Scope* item onto the *SURF Workflow* page. To add another stage, click the white space area directly under the *SURF Scope* item. I add all the SURF workflow stages as shown in Figure 5 - 51.

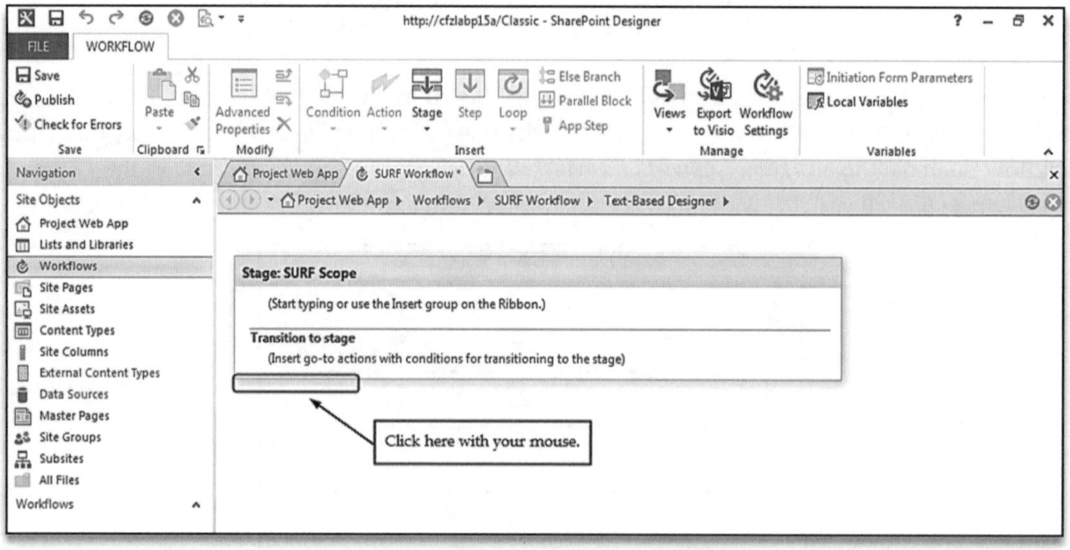

Figure 5 - 51: Prepare to add a new stage

8. The system places the stages you created underneath the previous stage. In my example, I add all the stages in the SURF process in the proper order, as shown in Figure 5 - 52. To finish the process, I add the last stage, that I call *SURF Closeout.*

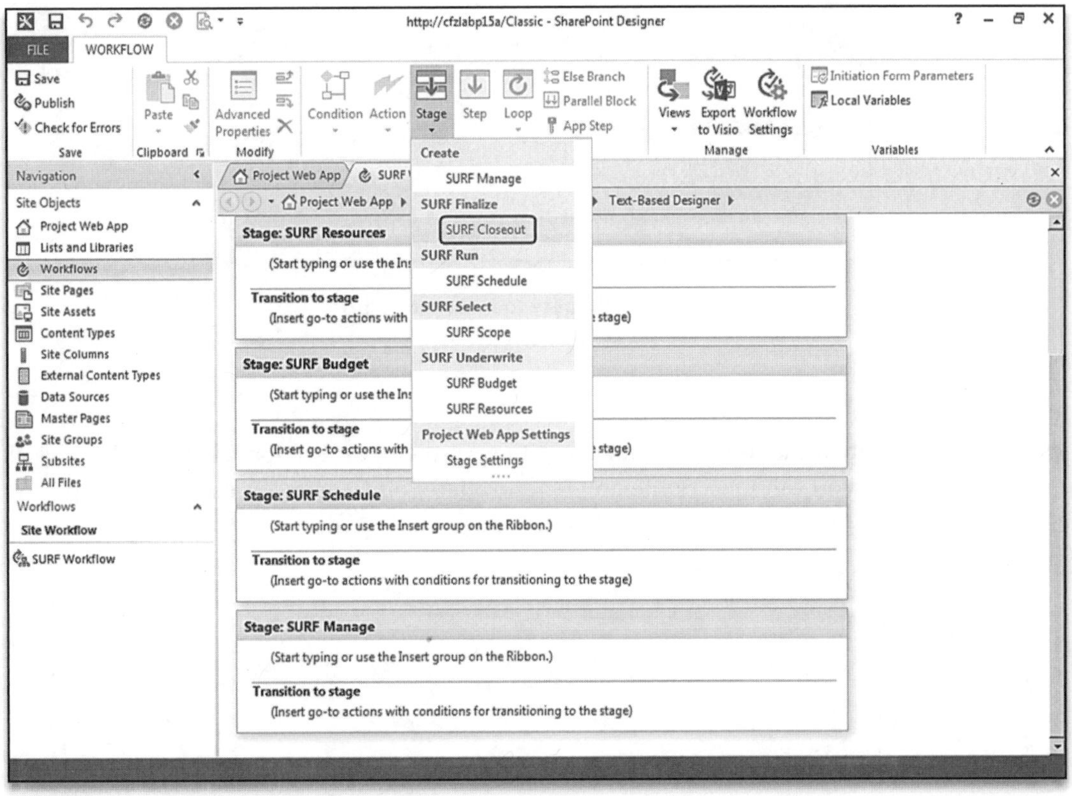

Figure 5 - 52: Select remaining stages in proper order

9. This workflow is incomplete but it is a good idea to save your work frequently. Saving is like creating a draft document in that the workflow is now stored in SharePoint but is inaccessible. Click the *Workflow* tab, then in the *Save* section, click the *Save* button as shown in Figure 5 - 53.

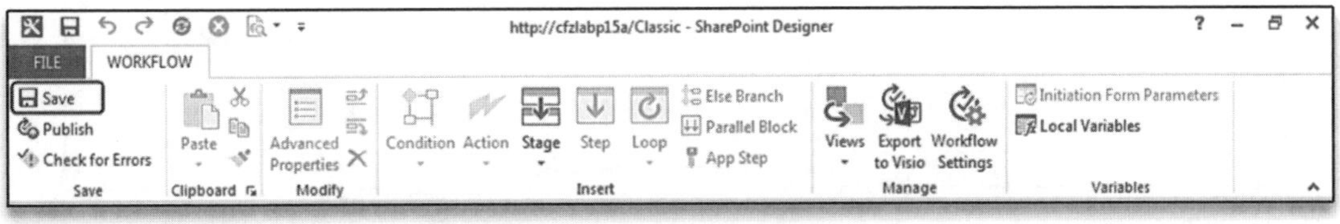

Figure 5 - 53: Save the workflow

10. In my example, I want to review new projects and then approve or reject them. When I approve the project, it will move to the next stage. When I reject the project, it typically means that I want more information but it can also mean I do not want the project to move forward. In an approval step, Project Server 2013 assigns a SharePoint approval task to me. When I open the task item, it provides a place to enter comments where I can express these directions. Because *Scope* is the first stage in the *SURF* process, I want to insert an action to assign a task. To insert an action, locate the *Stage: SURF Scope* item and click your mouse directly under the text titled *Start typing or use the Insert group on the Ribbon*. A glowing orange line appears as shown in Figure 5 - 54. As this is a very light color, it may not be very visible; therefore, make note of the call-out I drew in the figure.

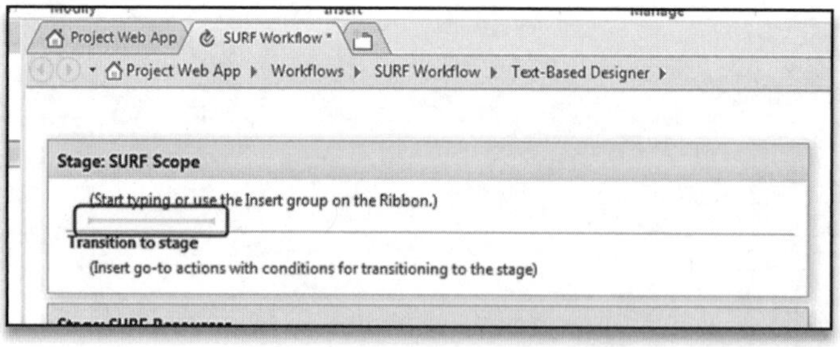

Figure 5 - 54: Prepare to insert an Action

11. Click the *Workflow* tab at the top of the page and then in the *Insert* section, click the *Action* pick list. Note the available actions you can take. Some are generic SharePoint actions and others are specific to Project Server 2013. You can use any of these actions interchangeably. Select the *Assign a task* item as shown in Figure 5 - 55.

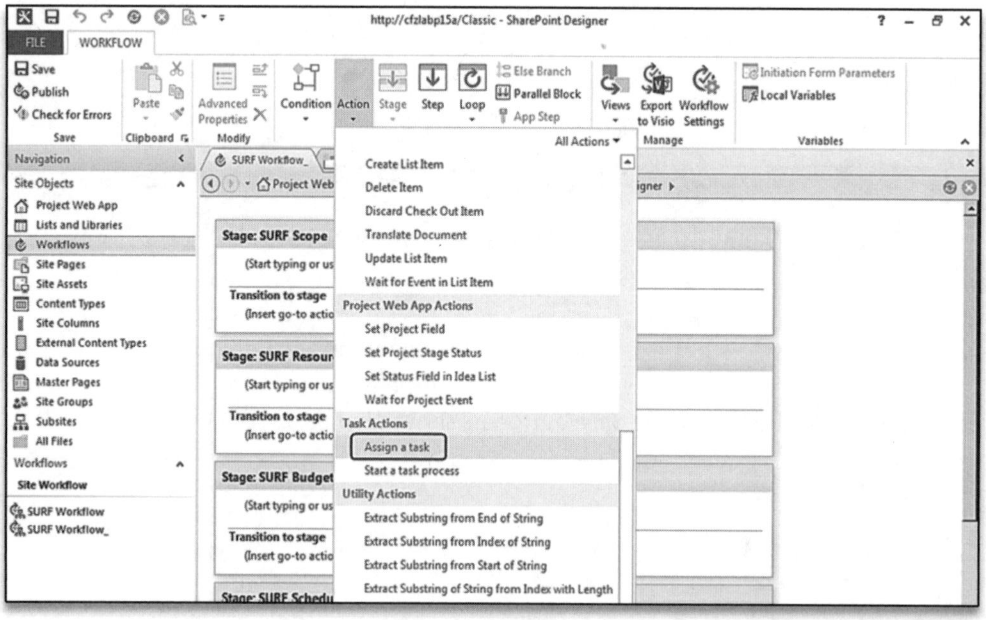

Figure 5 - 55: Insert an action

12. The system adds an *Assign a task to this user* action as shown in Figure 5 - 56. Click the *this user* hyperlink and the system displays the *Assign a Task* dialog. In the *Participant* field, select the person to receive the task assignment by clicking the … button. In the *Task Title* field, you build a string of information you want to display in the task. In my example, I first click the *fx* button and find the *Project Name* field. Next, I click the … button and add some text that provides context to the person assigned to the task. In the *Description* field, I enter some text that describes the workflow. There are many more settings but in my example, I do not make any more changes. Click the *OK* button.

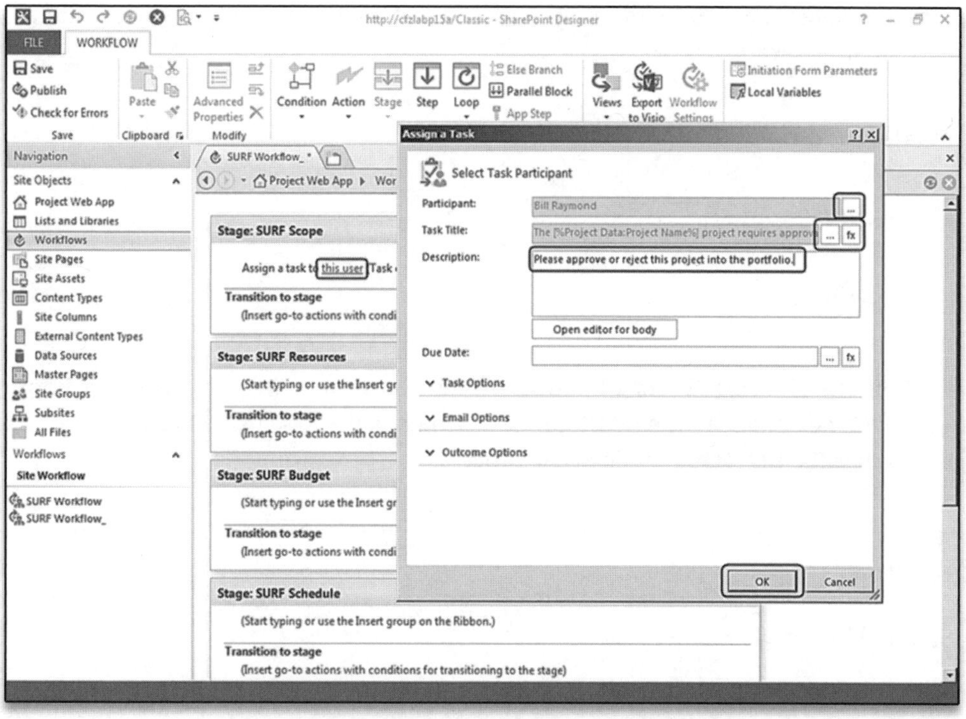

Figure 5 - 56: Assign a Task dialog

13. The workflow assigns a task to me but now it needs to know what to do if I approve or reject. The way you evaluate the condition is by clicking your mouse just under the help text where *Transition to stage* is located. With the area selected, click the *Workflow* tab and then in the *Insert* section, click the *Condition* button. Select the *If any value equals value* item as shown in Figure 5 - 57.

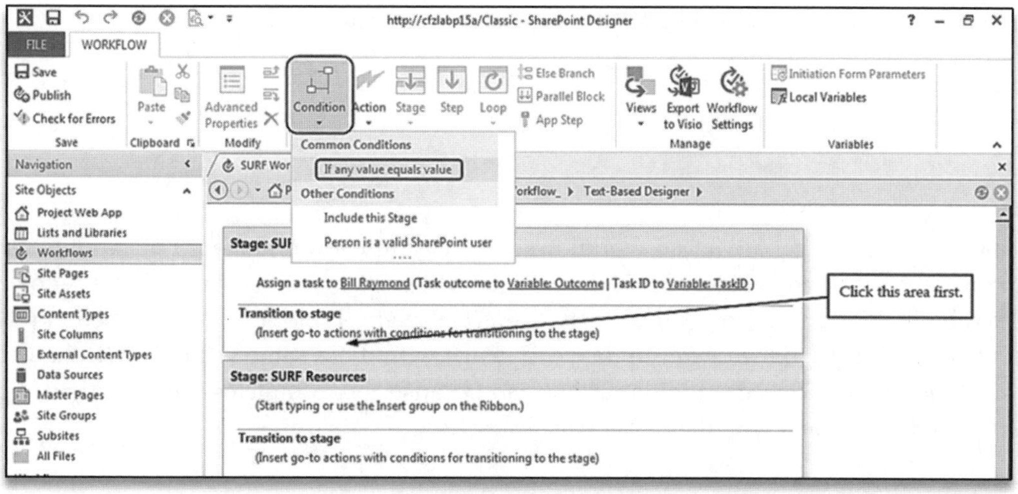

Figure 5 - 57: Insert a condition

14. The system populates the stage with an *if..then..else* statement that requires your attention as shown in Figure 5 - 58. In my example, I use:

    If: Workflow Variable: Outcome equals Approved

    Then: Go to SURF Resources

    Else: Go to SURF Scope

This statement is telling the *Transition to stage* element of the workflow to evaluate whether I approved or rejected. If I approve, go to the next stage in the SURF process, which is the *Resources* stage. If I reject, keep the project in the *Scope* stage, which is the first stage in the SURF process.

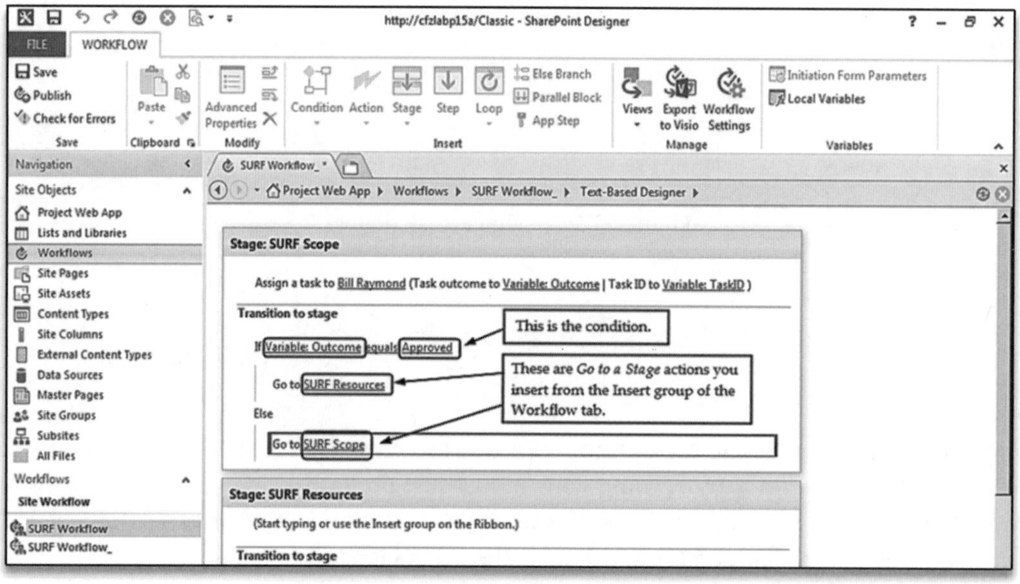

Stage: SURF Scope
Assign a task to Bill Raymond (Task outcome to Variable: Outcome | Task ID to Variable: TaskID)
Transition to stage
If Variable: Outcome equals Approved
Go to SURF Resources
Else
Go to SURF Scope
This is the condition.
These are Go to a Stage actions you insert from the Insert group of the Workflow tab.
Stage: SURF Resources
(Start typing or use the Insert group on the Ribbon.)
Transition to stage

Figure 5 - 58: Add condition and actions

15. I do not require any other advanced workflows for this simple example, but I do want to connect all the stages together as shown in Figure 5 - 59. In my example, I add a *Wait for Project Event* action that requires project submittal by a user. In the *Transition to Stage* element, I add a *Go to Stage* action that moves the project from one stage to the next. I update each stage with those same settings until the very last stage. The last stage does not need an initial action and because this completes the workflow, I populate the *Transition to stage* element with the *End of Workflow* setting.

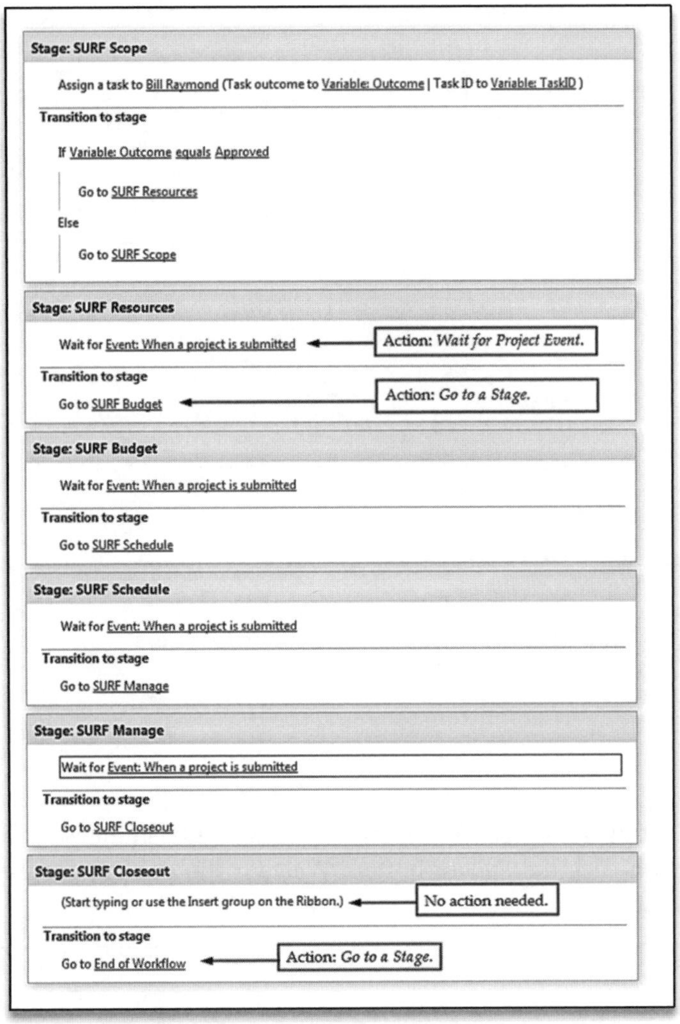
Stage: SURF Scope
Assign a task to Bill Raymond (Task outcome to Variable: Outcome | Task ID to Variable: TaskID)
Transition to stage
If Variable: Outcome equals Approved
Go to SURF Resources
Else
Go to SURF Scope
Stage: SURF Resources
Wait for Event: When a project is submitted
Action: Wait for Project Event.
Transition to stage
Go to SURF Budget
Action: Go to a Stage.
Stage: SURF Budget
Wait for Event: When a project is submitted
Transition to stage
Go to SURF Schedule
Stage: SURF Schedule
Wait for Event: When a project is submitted
Transition to stage
Go to SURF Manage
Stage: SURF Manage
Wait for Event: When a project is submitted
Transition to stage
Go to SURF Closeout
Stage: SURF Closeout
(Start typing or use the Insert group on the Ribbon.)
No action needed.
Transition to stage
Go to End of Workflow
Action: Go to a Stage.

Figure 5 - 59: Finalize workflow actions

16. As you can see, even simple workflows can have some complexities to them that make it difficult for the naked eye to find errors or other problems. SharePoint Designer can check your workflow for errors as shown in Figure 5 - 60. Click the *Workflow* tab, then in the *Save* section click the *Check for Errors* button. If there are no errors, click the *OK* button. If there are errors, go back and correct your workflow accordingly.

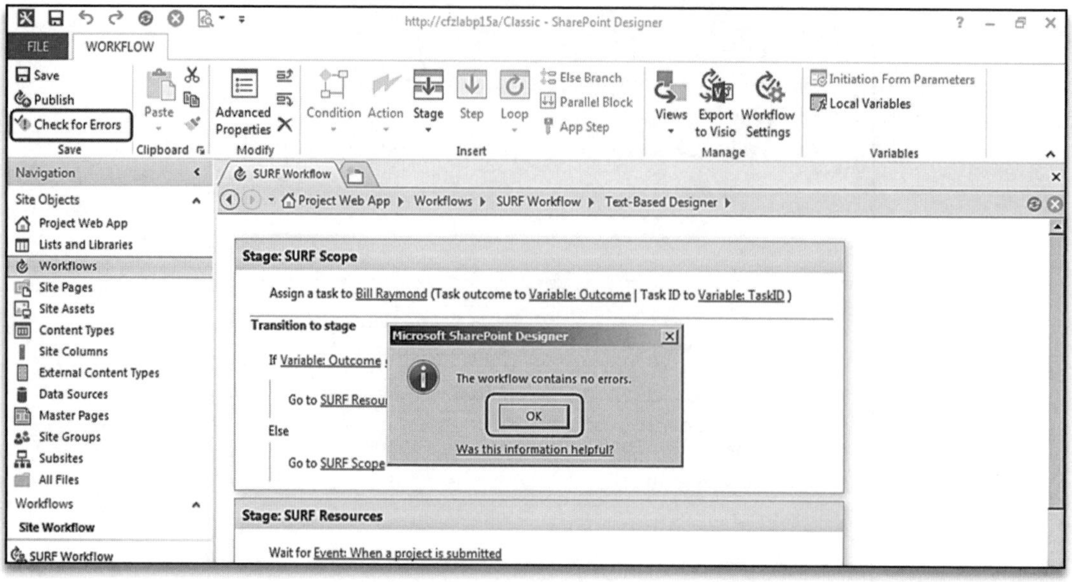

Figure 5 - 60: Check workflow for errors

17. Once you verify that your workflow has no errors, you can publish the workflow. Click the *Workflow* tab, then in the *Save* section click the *Publish* button. Wait for the publish process to complete as shown in Figure 5 - 61.

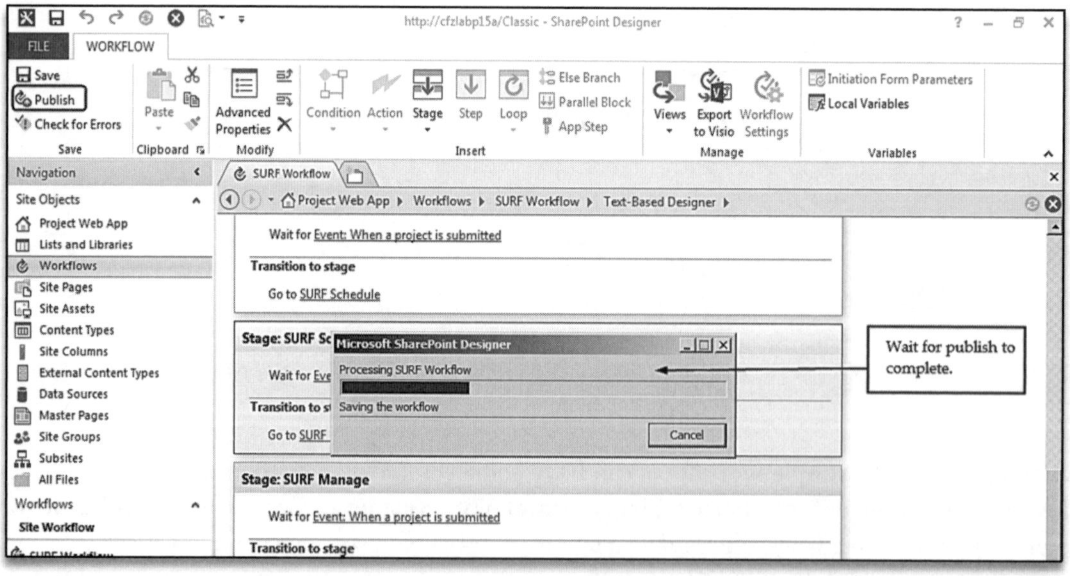

Figure 5 - 61: Publish a workflow

18. Exit SharePoint Designer.

Configuring EPT's (Enterprise Project Types)

Typically, organizations manage multiple types of projects, such as IT projects, engineering projects, HR projects, new product development projects, etc. In fact, each of these departments may have several types of projects that they manage as well. Out of the box, Project Server 2013 provides two basic EPT's:

- SharePoint Tasks List
- Enterprise Project

The **SharePoint Tasks List** EPT is for lightweight projects. Microsoft designed this type of project to use the SharePoint site and task lists to manage the project. The **Enterprise Project** EPT is for projects that make full use of PWA features and likely uses Gantt charts created in Project Pro 2013. As you may recall from a previous section, I used an example of a marketing department at a large consumer goods company. My department defined three project types:

- Corporate Events (Large)
- Marketing Campaigns (Medium)
- Targeted Campaigns (Small)

In this section, I create a *Marketing Campaigns* EPT. Because my project managers are required to use Project Pro 2013, I use an **Enterprise Project** EPT. To create an EPT, follow these steps:

1. Log in to PWA as an administrator, such as the Farm Administrator service account.
2. At the top-right of the PWA page, click the *Gear* icon and select the *PWA Settings* item.
3. In the *Workflow and Project Detail Pages* section of the *Server Settings* page, click the *Enterprise Project Types* link.
4. The system displays the *Enterprise Project Types* page shown in Figure 5 - 62. Notice that the page displays the two EPT's available in Project Server 2013 by default. Click the link to edit any of these EPT's. To create a new EPT, click the *New Enterprise Project Type* button.

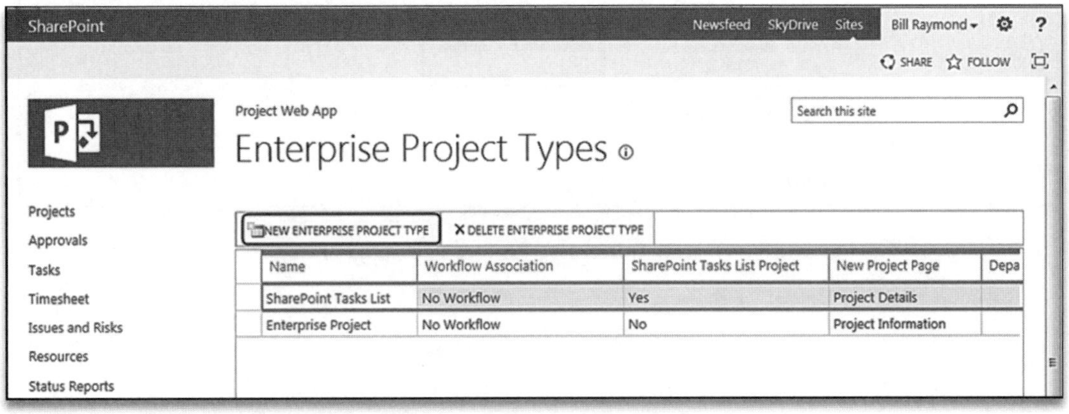

Figure 5 - 62: Enterprise Project Types page

5. The system displays the *Add Enterprise Project Type* page shown in Figure 5 - 63, Figure 5 - 64, and Figure 5 - 65. The *Add Enterprise Project Type* page contains a number of sections that contain online help under each heading. I describe each setting in more detail after these steps are complete. In my case, I type *SURF Marketing Campaign* in the *Name* field. In the *Description* field, I type *Any medium-size marketing project that follows the SURF process.* In the *Site Workflow Association* pick list, I select the *SURF Workflow* item I created with SharePoint Designer in the previous section. In the *New Project Page* pick list, I select the *Project Details* item. In the *Project Plan Template* pick list, I select the *SURF Project Plan Template* item. In the *Project Site Template* pick list, I select the *SURF SharePoint Site Template* item. Click the *Save* button to create the new EPT.

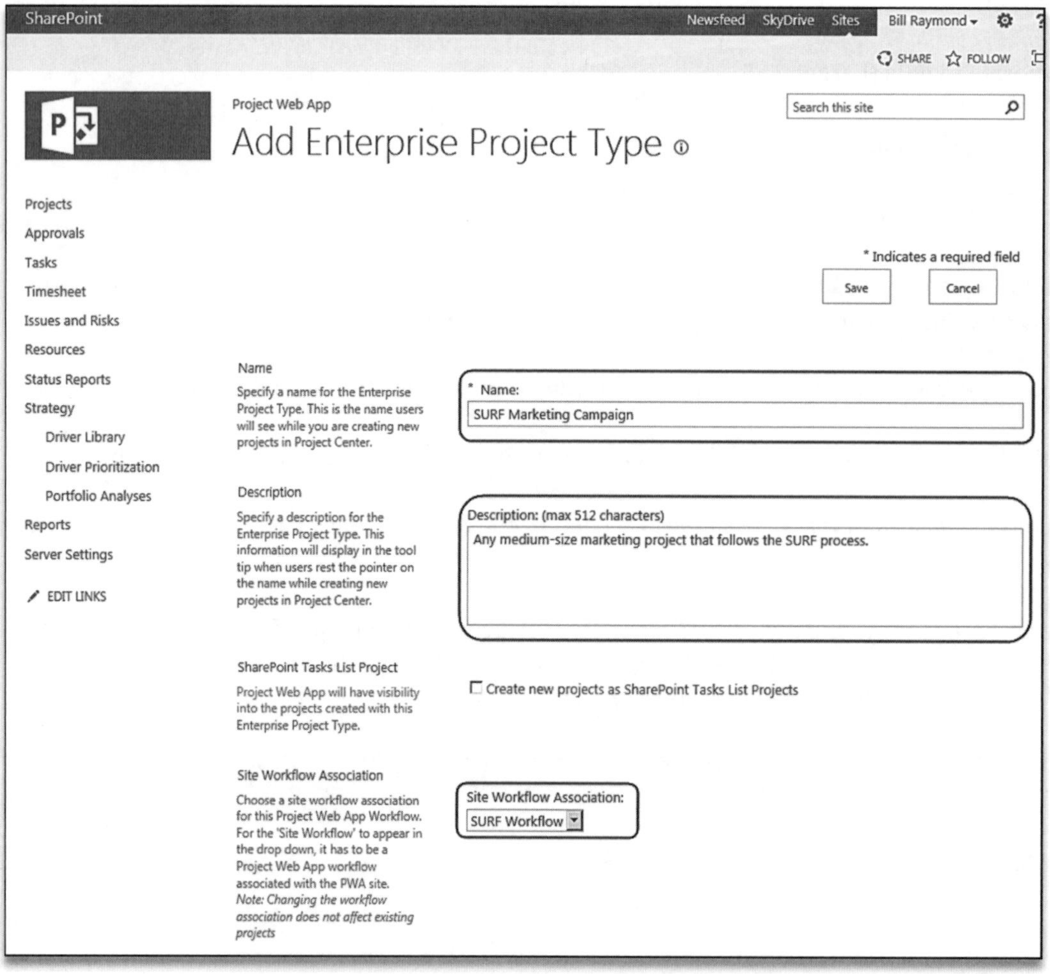
SharePoint
Newsfeed SkyDrive Sites
Bill Raymond
SHARE FOLLOW
Project Web App
Add Enterprise Project Type
Search this site
Projects
Approvals
Tasks
Timesheet
Issues and Risks
Resources
Status Reports
Strategy
Driver Library
Driver Prioritization
Portfolio Analyses
Reports
Server Settings
EDIT LINKS
* Indicates a required field
Save
Cancel
Name
Specify a name for the Enterprise Project Type. This is the name users will see while you are creating new projects in Project Center.
* Name:
SURF Marketing Campaign
Description
Specify a description for the Enterprise Project Type. This information will display in the tool tip when users rest the pointer on the name while creating new projects in Project Center.
Description: (max 512 characters)
Any medium-size marketing project that follows the SURF process.
SharePoint Tasks List Project
Project Web App will have visibility into the projects created with this Enterprise Project Type.
Create new projects as SharePoint Tasks List Projects
Site Workflow Association
Choose a site workflow association for this Project Web App Workflow. For the 'Site Workflow' to appear in the drop down, it has to be a Project Web App workflow associated with the PWA site.
Note: Changing the workflow association does not affect existing projects
Site Workflow Association:
SURF Workflow

Figure 5 - 63: New Enterprise Project Type page, Image 1

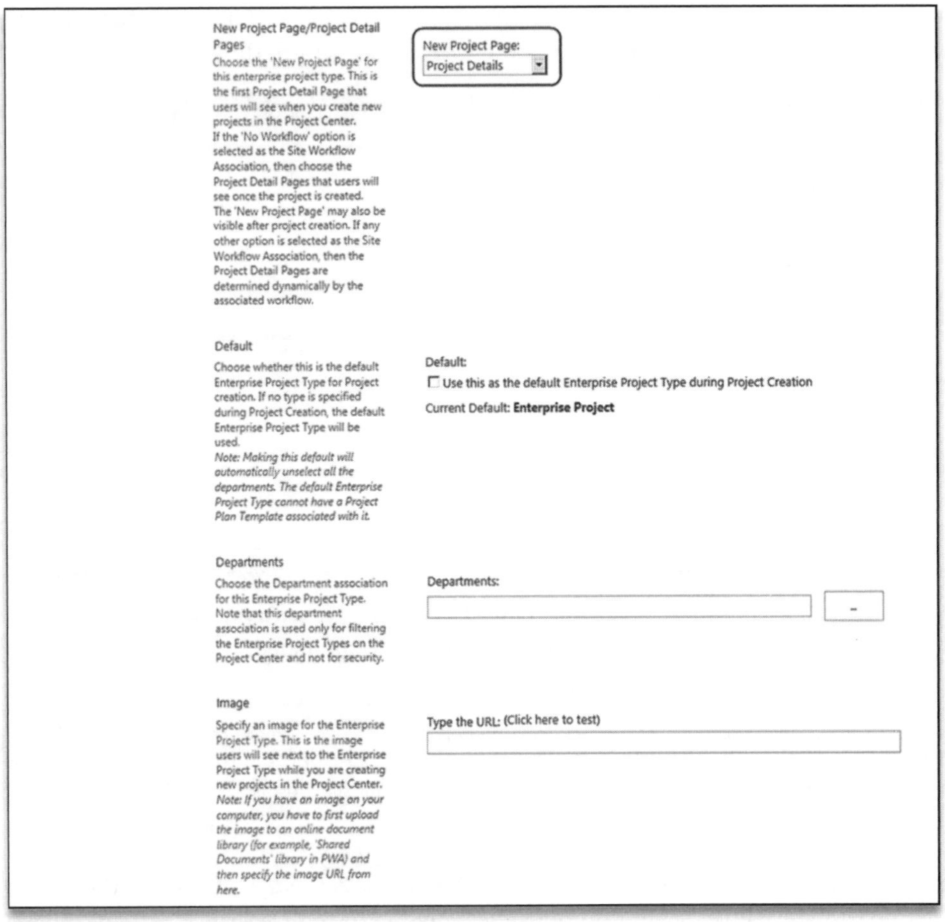
New Project Page/Project Detail Pages
Choose the 'New Project Page' for this enterprise project type. This is the first Project Detail Page that users will see when you create new projects in the Project Center.
If the 'No Workflow' option is selected as the Site Workflow Association, then choose the Project Detail Pages that users will see once the project is created.
The 'New Project Page' may also be visible after project creation. If any other option is selected as the Site Workflow Association, then the Project Detail Pages are determined dynamically by the associated workflow.
New Project Page:
Project Details
Default
Choose whether this is the default Enterprise Project Type for Project creation. If no type is specified during Project Creation, the default Enterprise Project Type will be used.
Note: Making this default will automatically unselect all the departments. The default Enterprise Project Type cannot have a Project Plan Template associated with it.
Default:
Use this as the default Enterprise Project Type during Project Creation
Current Default: Enterprise Project
Departments
Choose the Department association for this Enterprise Project Type. Note that this department association is used only for filtering the Enterprise Project Types on the Project Center and not for security.
Departments:
Image
Specify an image for the Enterprise Project Type. This is the image users will see next to the Enterprise Project Type while you are creating new projects in the Project Center.
Note: If you have an image on your computer, you have to first upload the image to an online document library (for example, 'Shared Documents' library in PWA) and then specify the image URL from here.
Type the URL: (Click here to test)

Figure 5 - 64: New Enterprise Project Type page, Image 2

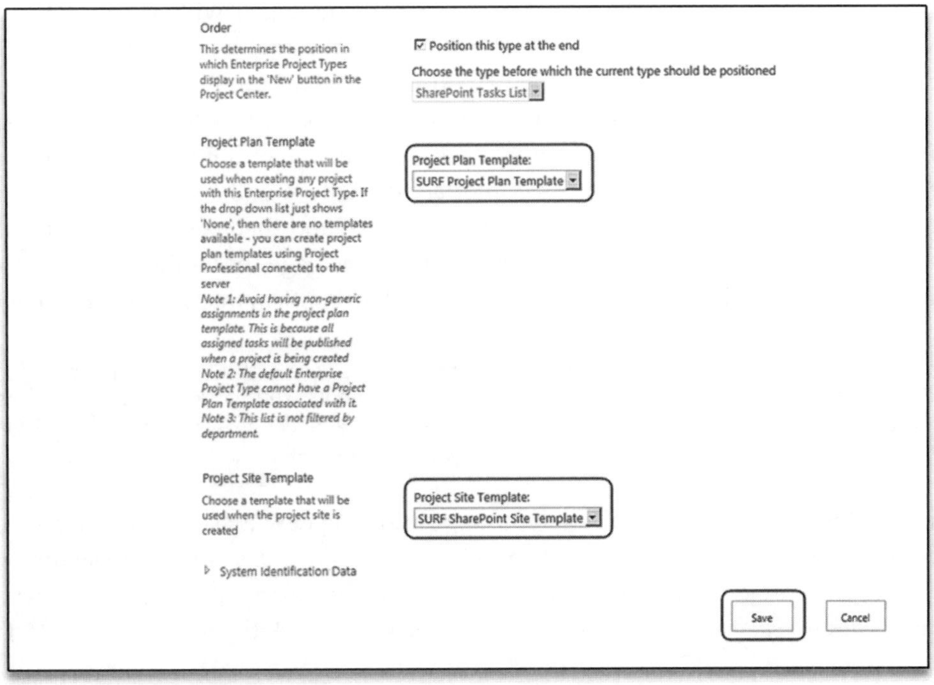
Order
This determines the position in which Enterprise Project Types display in the 'New' button in the Project Center.
Position this type at the end
Choose the type before which the current type should be positioned
SharePoint Tasks List
Project Plan Template
Choose a template that will be used when creating any project with this Enterprise Project Type. If the drop down list just shows 'None', then there are no templates available - you can create project plan templates using Project Professional connected to the server
Note 1: Avoid having non-generic assignments in the project plan template. This is because all assigned tasks will be published when a project is being created
Note 2: The default Enterprise Project Type cannot have a Project Plan Template associated with it.
Note 3: This list is not filtered by department.
Project Plan Template:
SURF Project Plan Template
Project Site Template
Choose a template that will be used when the project site is created
Project Site Template:
SURF SharePoint Site Template
System Identification Data
Save
Cancel

Figure 5 - 65: New Enterprise Project Type page, Image 3

The system returns to the *Enterprise Project Types* library shown in Figure 5 - 66. Verify that your new EPT appears in the list and the various settings are correct. To edit the EPT, click its hyperlink.

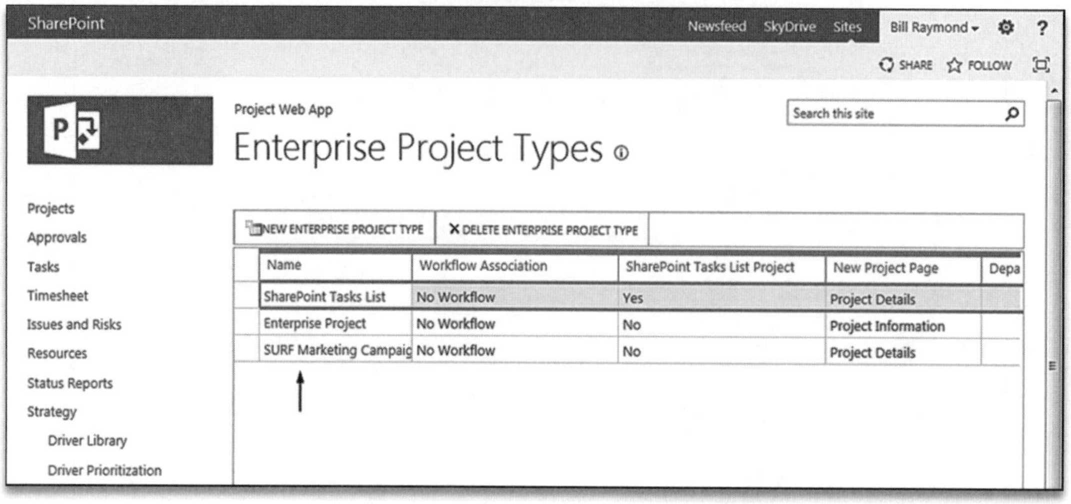

Figure 5 - 66: Enterprise Project Types library with the new SURF Marketing Campaign EPT populated.

Warning: If you are creating a non-workflow associated EPT, you must select at least one item on the *Available Project Detail Pages* list and add it to the list on the right. If you fail to do so, Project Server 2013 does not allow you to save the new EPT and reminds you to select at least one item on the *Available Project Detail Pages* list.

If you need to limit the users who can see the new EPT, click the *Select Value* button for the *Departments* field and select one or more department values. If you do not select a value in the *Departments* field, the new EPT becomes available for all users.

In the *Image* section of the page, you have the option to associate the new EPT with an image file. The system displays the image you select when a user creates a new project proposal using the new EPT. Before you associate an image with the EPT, you must upload the image file to a document library in Project Server 2013. The document library for public documents is one choice; however, you may want to save files like this in a separate library that you create specifically for this purpose. I like to create a separate document library for this purpose without displaying it on the *Quick Launch* menu so that users do not accidentally modify or delete these objects. After uploading the image file to the document library, select the image file, and then copy the URL for the image file to the clipboard. In the *Image* section of the *New Enterprise Project Type* page, paste the URL into the *Type the URL* field. After making your entry, click the *Click here to test* hyperlink to confirm the URL for the image file.

Information: You must scale the images you choose to associate with EPT's for the intended purpose, which is to display as an icon next to the selection on a pick list menu. Therefore, you should choose a graphic that works well as an icon in a very small format. Scale your images to 18 pixels wide by 18 pixels high for this purpose.

In the *Order* section of the page, the system allows you to position the new EPT on the *New* pick list when a user clicks the *New* button in the Project Center. The system selects the *Position this type at the end* option by default. To position the new enterprise project type anywhere else in the list, deselect this option. The system enables the *Choose the type before which the current type should be positioned* pick list. Click the pick list and select the location for the new EPT.

In the *Project Plan Template* section, you can optionally associate your new project template to a specific EPT. When you associate a *Project Plan* template to a project type, the system converts the project proposal into an enterprise project using the enterprise project template you select after it gains approval. Click the *Project Plan Template* pick list and select an enterprise project template from the list. If you leave the default *None* value selected in this field, the system creates a new blank project when users select the project type.

In the *Project Site Template* section, your final option is to select the project site template to use when creating the Project Site for projects created using your new EPT. By default, the system selects the *Microsoft Project Site* item in the *Project Site Template* field. If you want to use additional project site templates, you must create them.

The system returns to the *Enterprise Project Types* library. Verify that your new EPT exists in the list and the various settings are correct in the rest of the table. To edit the EPT, click on its hyperlink.

Verifying Project Governance Functionality

To verify all the project governance settings, you must create a project plan in Project Server 2013 and ensure the functionality works as expected.

> **Information**: Testing with an administrator account is a good first start. You should also test with other users that have appropriate security rights.

1. Log in to PWA as an administrator, such as the Farm Administrator service account.

2. In the *Quick Launch* menu in PWA, click the *Projects* tab. The system displays the *Project Center* page as shown in Figure 5 - 67. Click the *Projects* tab, and then click the *New* button. Select your new EPT. In my case, I select *SURF Marketing Campaign*.

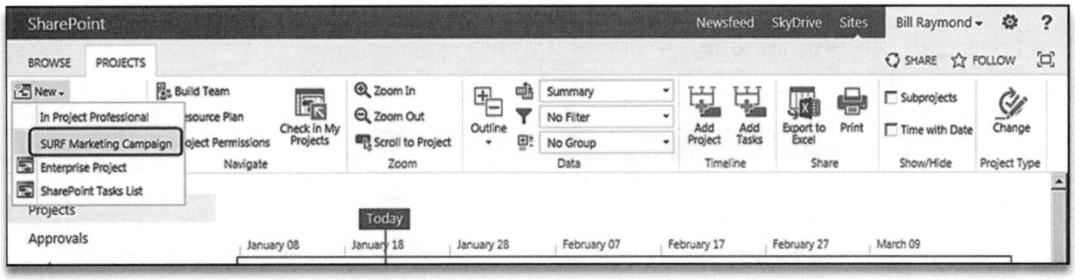

Figure 5 - 67: Create a new project in the Project Center

3. The system displays the *New Project* dialog shown in Figure 5 - 68. Enter required fields and optional fields as you choose. In my case, I select the *Name* field and type *SURF Test Project*. Note the *Start Date* field filled in for me automatically, so I did not make any changes. Click the *Save* button when you are ready to create your project.

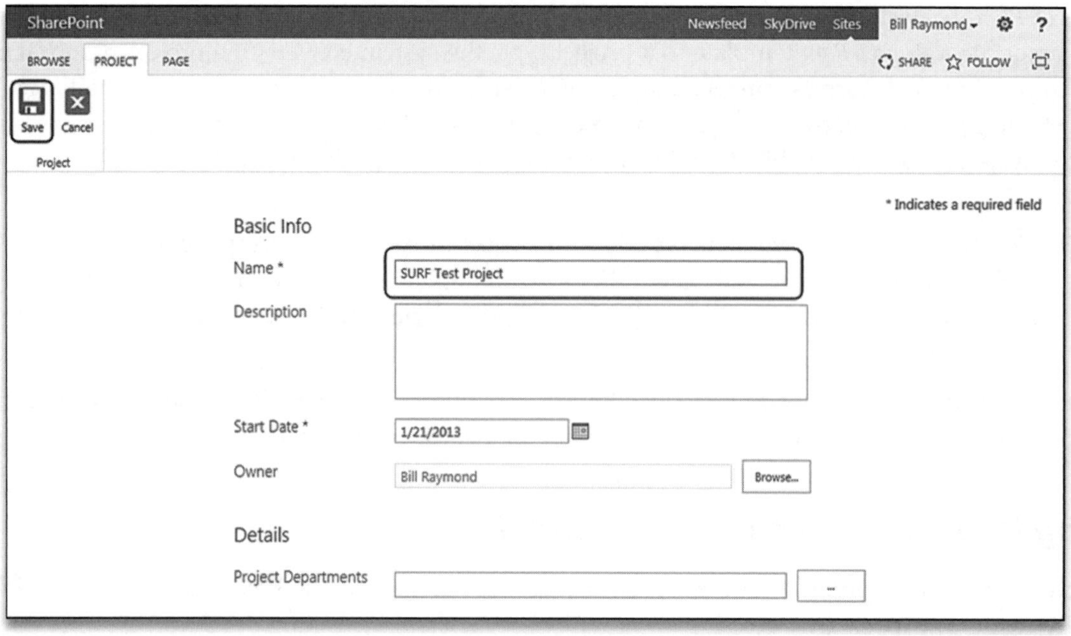

Figure 5 - 68: New Project dialog

4. After processing the save, the system displays the *Workflow Status* page shown in Figure 5 - 69. Verify the correct PDP's display above the *Quick Launch* menu. Also, verify the proper stage displays. In my case, the SURF process requires me to update the linkage between strategic drivers and my new project. Click the *Strategic Impact* link.

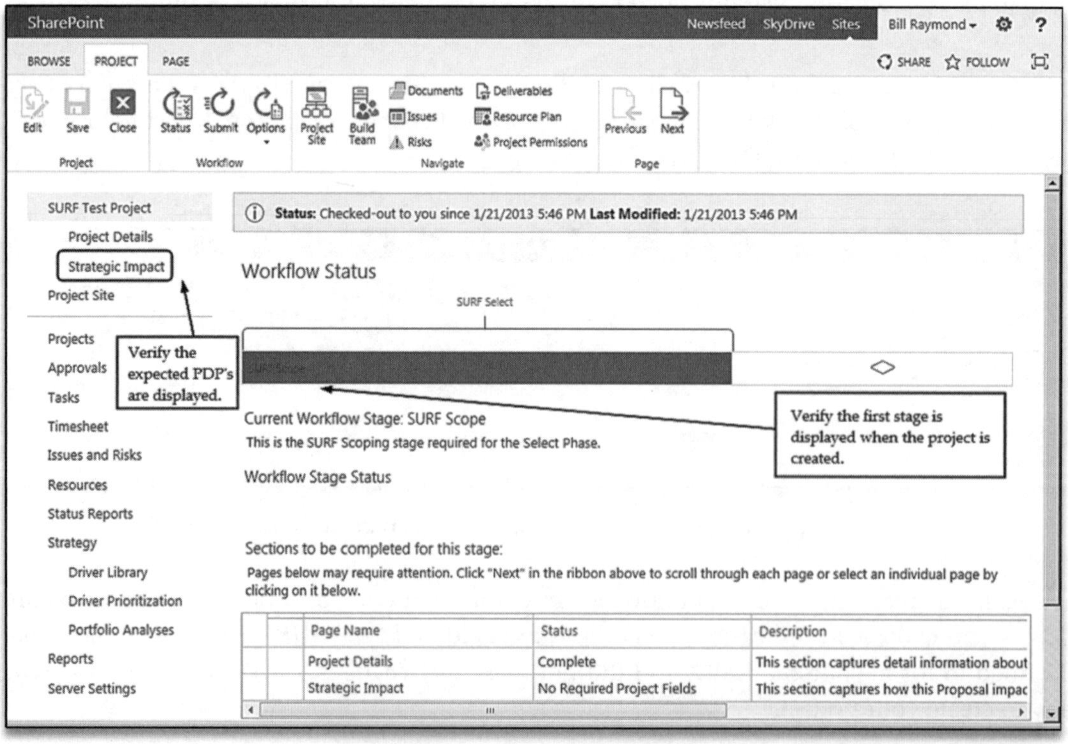

Figure 5 - 69: Workflow Status page

5. The system displays the *Project Strategic Impact* page shown in Figure 5 - 70. Select an impact statement for each strategic driver. Click the *Project* tab, and then in the *Project* section, click the *Save* button. Select the title for your project above the *Quick Launch* menu. In my case, I click the link labeled *SURF Test Project.*

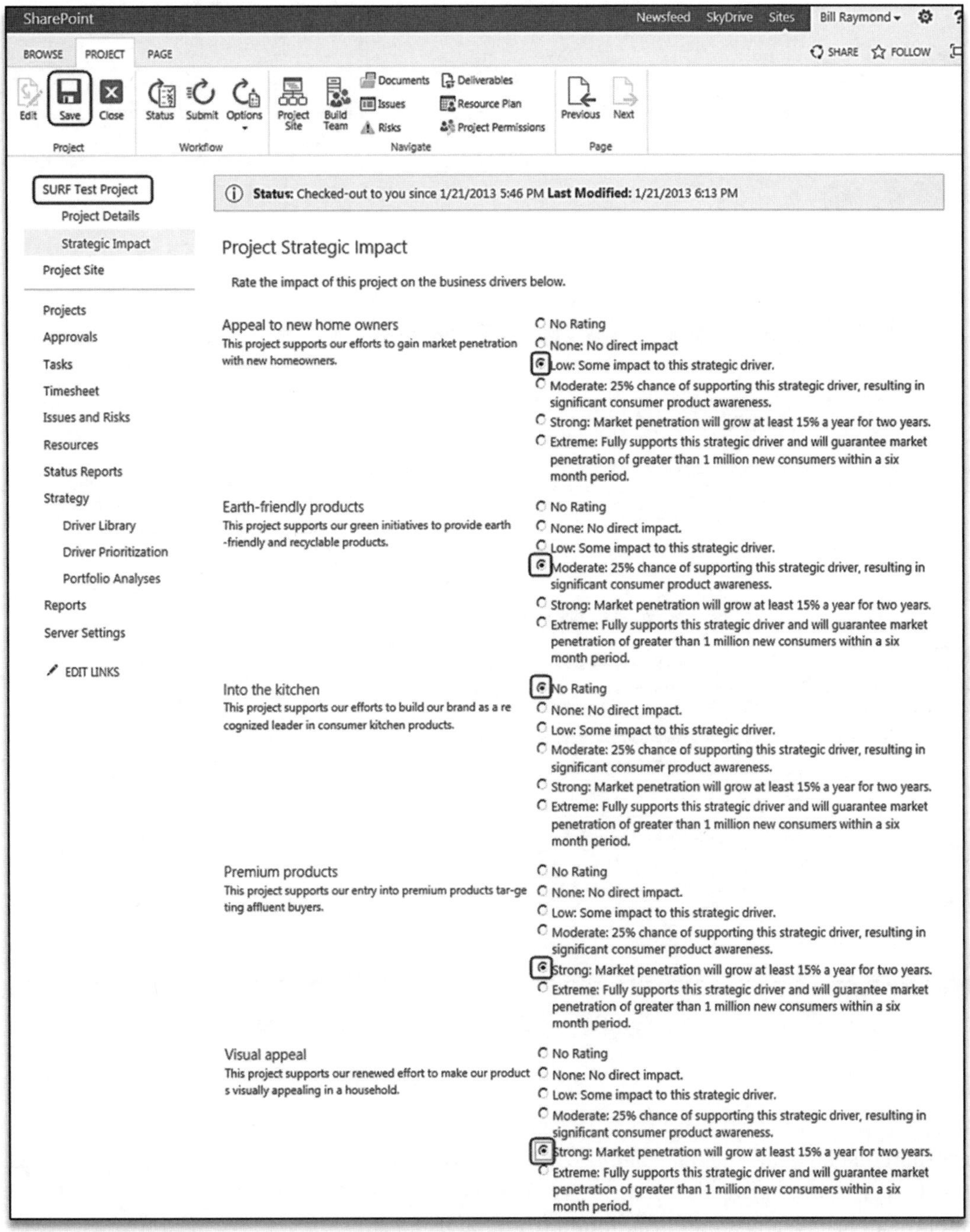

SharePoint
Newsfeed SkyDrive Sites
Bill Raymond
BROWSE PROJECT PAGE
SHARE FOLLOW
Edit Save Close
Status Submit Options
Project Site Build Team
Documents Deliverables
Issues Resource Plan
Risks Project Permissions
Previous Next
Project Workflow Navigate Page
SURF Test Project
Project Details
Strategic Impact
Project Site
Projects
Approvals
Tasks
Timesheet
Issues and Risks
Resources
Status Reports
Strategy
Driver Library
Driver Prioritization
Portfolio Analyses
Reports
Server Settings
EDIT LINKS
Status: Checked-out to you since 1/21/2013 5:46 PM Last Modified: 1/21/2013 6:13 PM
Project Strategic Impact
Rate the impact of this project on the business drivers below.
Appeal to new home owners
This project supports our efforts to gain market penetration with new homeowners.
Earth-friendly products
This project supports our green initiatives to provide earth -friendly and recyclable products.
Into the kitchen
This project supports our efforts to build our brand as a re cognized leader in consumer kitchen products.
Premium products
This project supports our entry into premium products tar-ge ting affluent buyers.
Visual appeal
This project supports our renewed effort to make our product s visually appealing in a household.
No Rating
None: No direct impact
Low: Some impact to this strategic driver.
Moderate: 25% chance of supporting this strategic driver, resulting in significant consumer product awareness.
Strong: Market penetration will grow at least 15% a year for two years.
Extreme: Fully supports this strategic driver and will guarantee market penetration of greater than 1 million new consumers within a six month period.

Figure 5 - 70: Project Strategic Impact page

6. The system displays the *Workflow Status* page for the project shown in Figure 5 - 71. Scroll to the bottom of the page and expand the *All Workflow Stages* item. The system displays a list of all workflow stages. Verify that the stages display in the proper order. In my example, I create a workflow step that requires an approval before the project can move to the next step. Click the *Additional Workflow Data* link located at the bottom of the page.

> **Information**: In a production environment, I would receive an e-mail requesting approval with a link to the task.

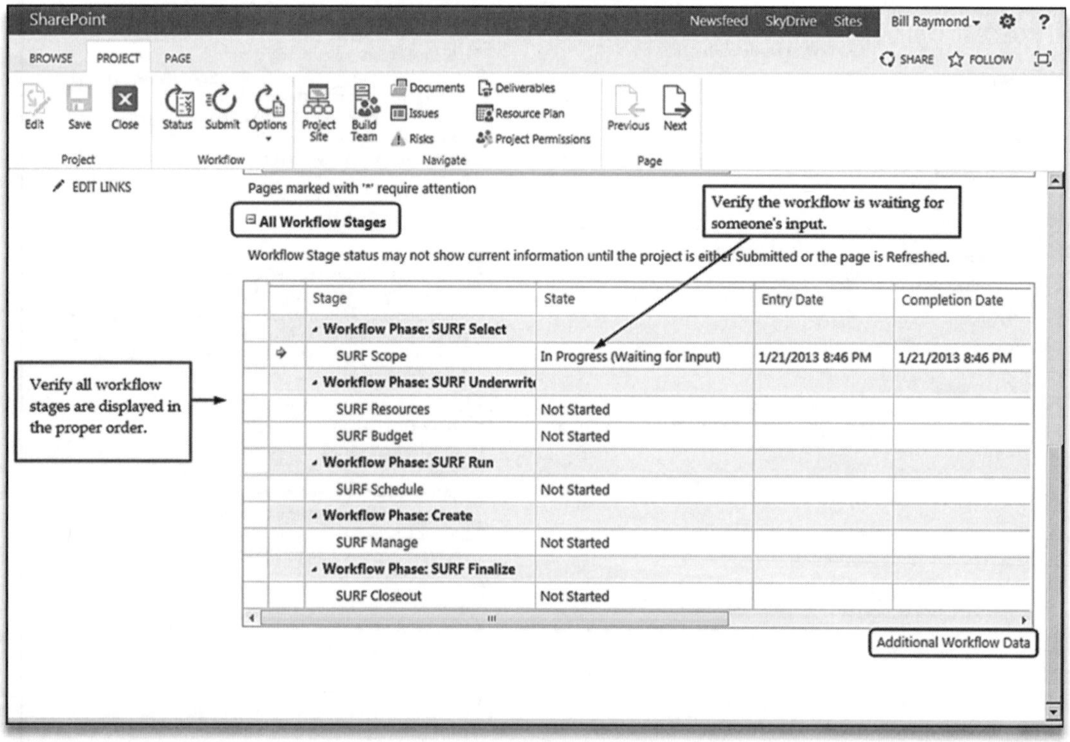

Figure 5 - 71: All workflow stages area on the Workflow Status page

7. The system displays the *Workflow Status (Additional Workflow Data)* page shown in Figure 5 - 72. In my example, I created an approval step. Move your mouse over the task assignment and click the arrow to the right of the item. Select the *Edit Item* option from the pick list.

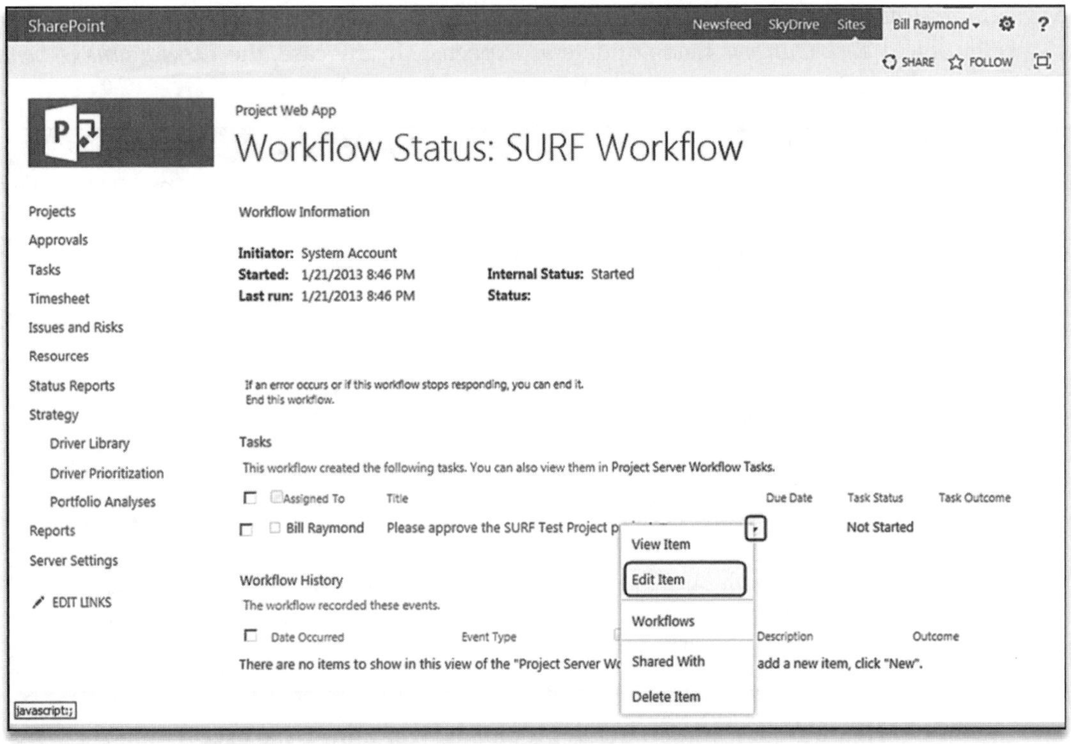

Figure 5 - 72: Workflow Status page - Additional Workflow Data

8. The system displays the *Edit Task* dialog shown in Figure 5 - 73. Click the *Approved* button.

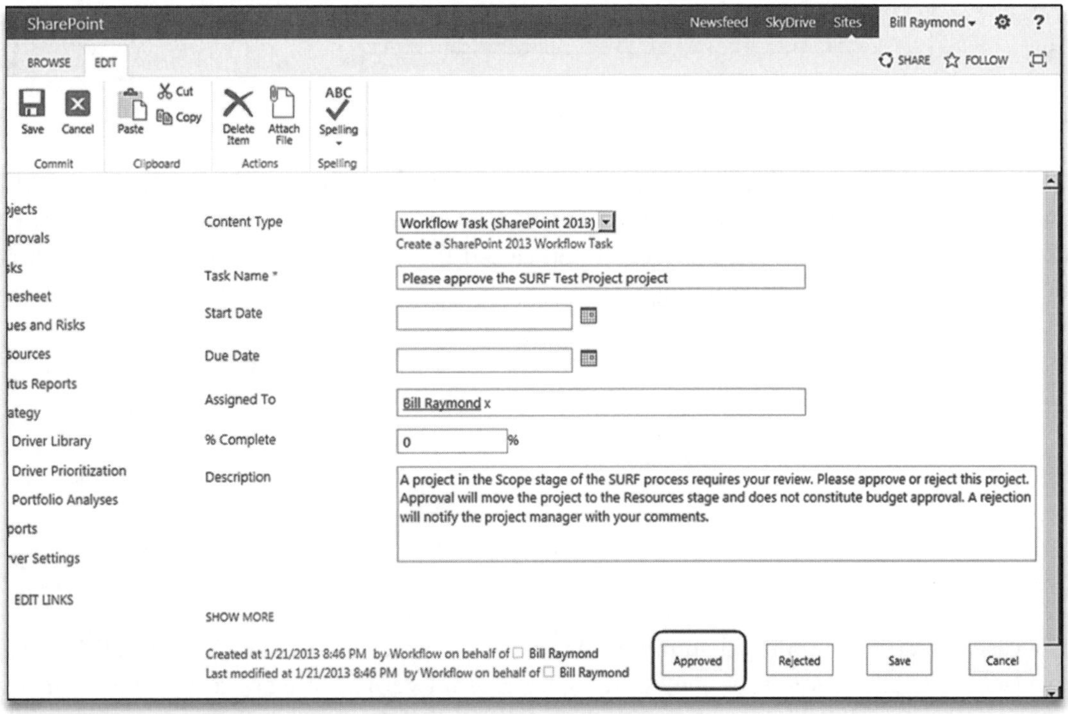

Figure 5 - 73: Edit Task dialog

9. The system returns to the *Workflow Status (Additional Workflow Data)* page shown in Figure 5 - 74. Verify the *Task Status* and *Task Outcome* fields update as expected. In my case, the *Tasks Status* is *Completed* and the *Task Outcome* is *Approved*.

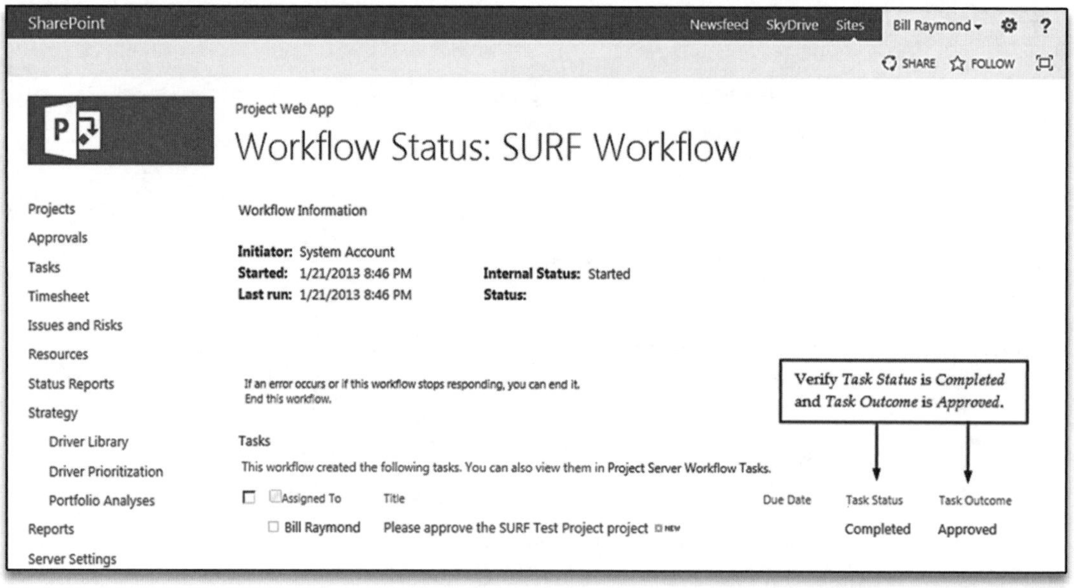

Figure 5 - 74: Workflow Status (Additional Workflow Data) page

10. At this point, you should see that the *Workflow Status (Additional Workflow Data)* page opened in another browser tab. If that is not the case, click the *Project Details Pages* tab again, select the original project, and click the *Refresh* button on your browser. If you closed the tab, then go back to the PWA Project Center and select the project you are verifying.

11. In my case, a workflow approval automatically moved the project to a stage called *SURF Resources* and a phase called *SURF Underwrite* as shown in Figure 5 - 75. I verify these are correct and I must verify that the project plan template is associated with this project. Click the *Schedule* PDP.

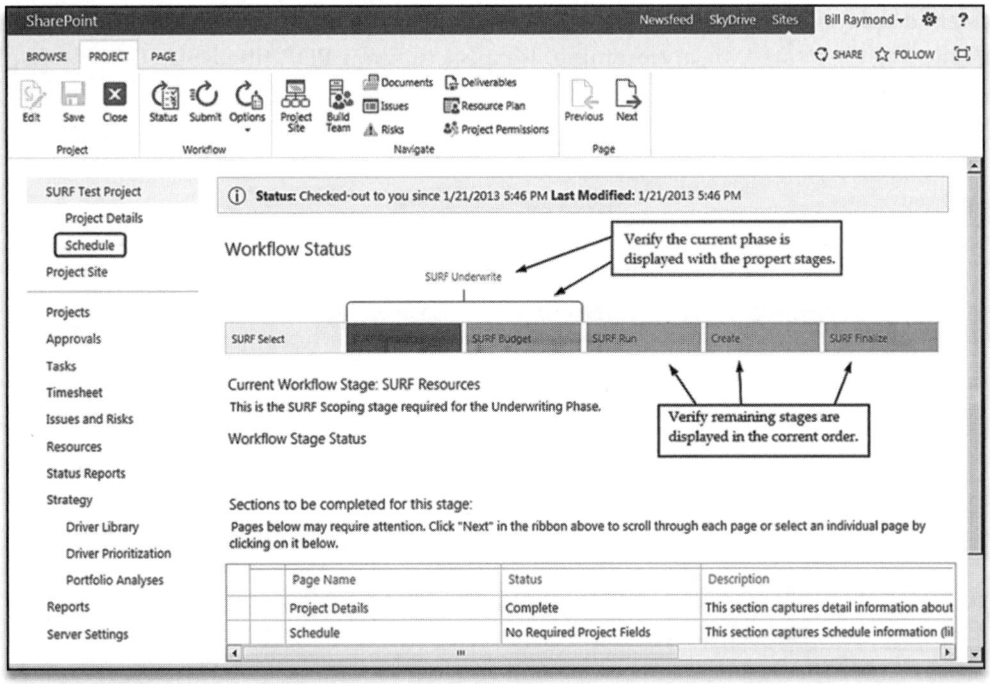

Figure 5 - 75: Workflow Status page for a project that is now in a new stage

12. The system displays the *Schedule* PDP as shown in Figure 5 - 76. Verify the project plan template displays the expected results. In my case, a very simple project plan template meets my expectations. If you did not select a project plan template for your project, the project plan displays with no data in the display grid.
13. I want to make sure that I can manually move my project to the next stage. Click the *Project* tab, and then in the *Workflow* section, click the *Submit* button. If prompted, click the *OK* button.

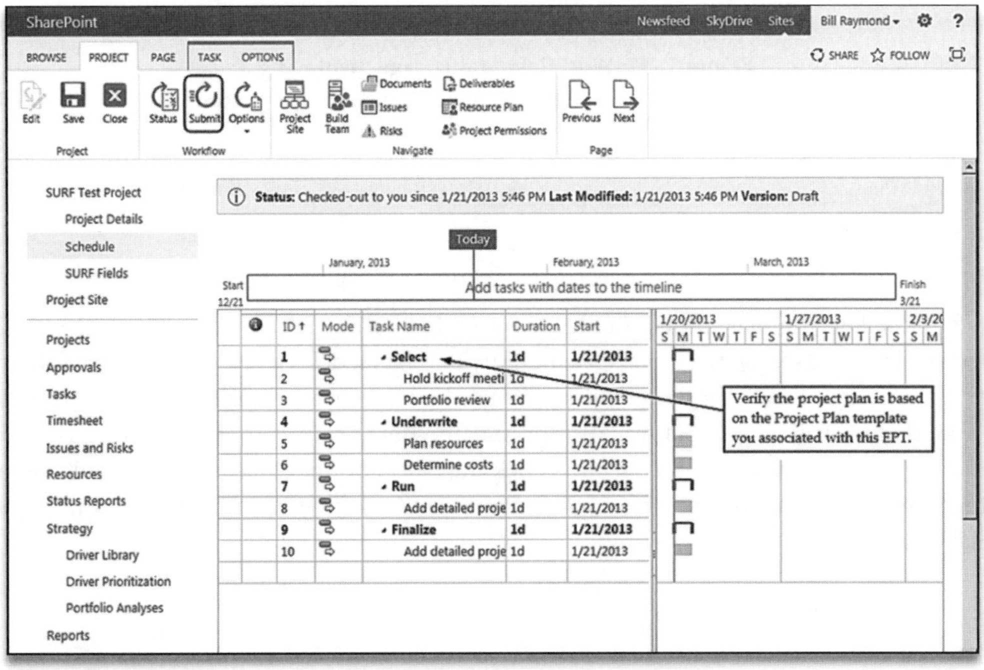

Figure 5 - 76: Schedule PDP

14. The system displays the *Workflow Status* page for the project shown in Figure 5 - 77. Verify the project has moved into the next stage. In my example, I expect to see a PDP titled *SURF Fields* display under the *Schedule* PDP so I click that link.

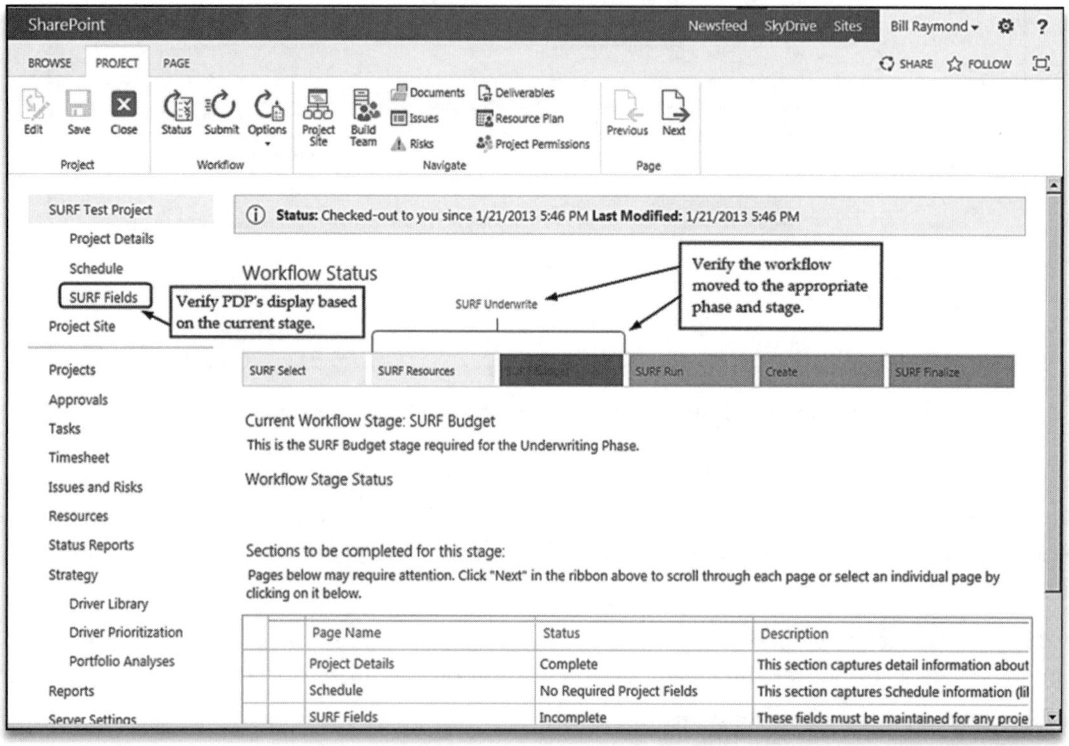

Figure 5 - 77: Workflow Status page displaying a project moved into the third stage of a governance process

15. The system displays the PDP shown in Figure 5 - 78. I call this PDP *SURF Fields*. Verify the fields display as expected. In my case, I expect to see two fields, one labeled *Proposed Cost*, and the other labeled *High Estimate*. I verify that I can edit both fields and that the *High Estimate* field is a required field. I enter data in these fields to verify Project Server 2013 formats the fields correctly after entering numbers into them. Click the *Project* tab, then in the *Save* section click the *Save* button. Once this project moves out of the current stage, the system should set the *High Estimate* to *Read-Only*. Click the *Project* tab, and then in the *Workflow* section, click the *Submit* button.

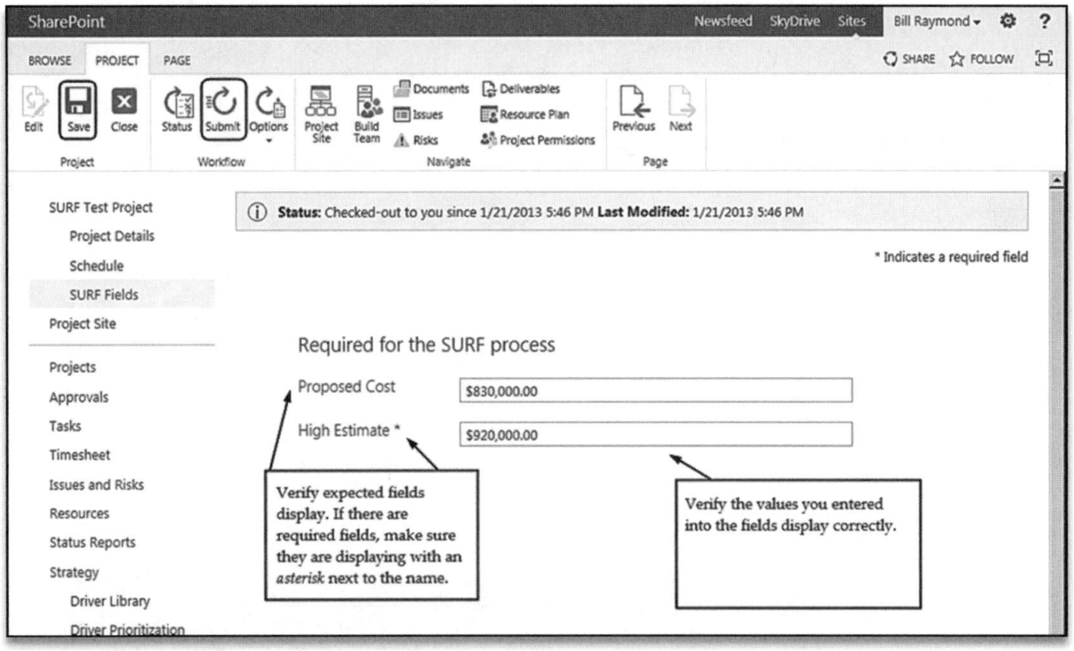

Figure 5 - 78: SURF Fields PDP

16. The system refreshes the page as shown in Figure 5 - 79. In my example, the *High Estimate* field should now be in *Read-Only* mode. Unless you specify otherwise, Project Server 2013 automatically creates a Project Site for new projects. In my example, I have a special SharePoint Site template that populates with this EPT. Click the *Project* tab, and then in the *Navigate* section, click the *Project Site* button.

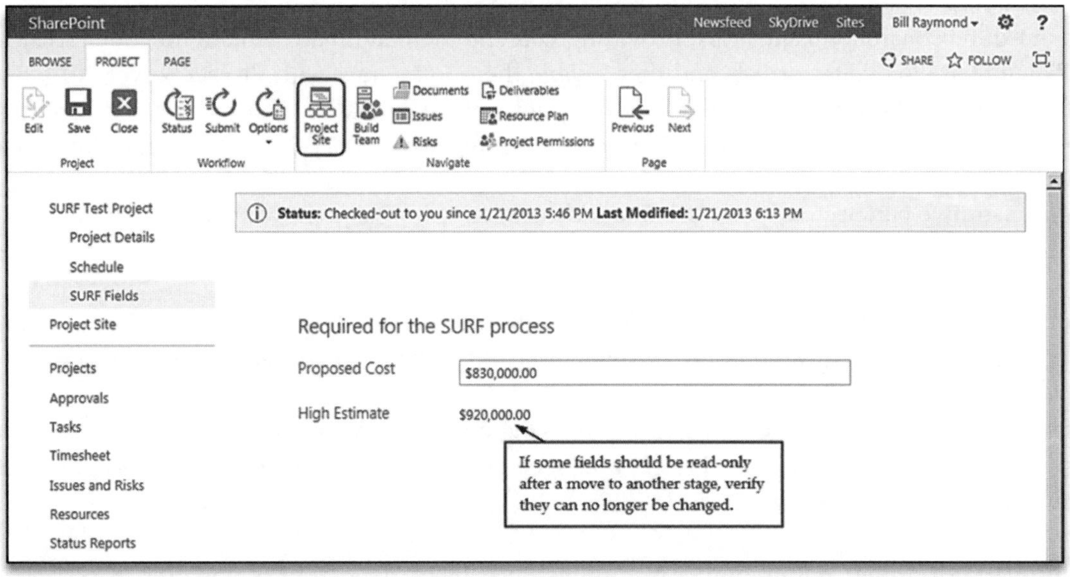

Figure 5 - 79: High Estimate field in Read-Only mode

17. The system displays the Project Site for the selected project shown in Figure 5 - 80. Verify the site contains the proper template modifications. In my case, I made one simple change that includes a sentence of text along the top of the page.

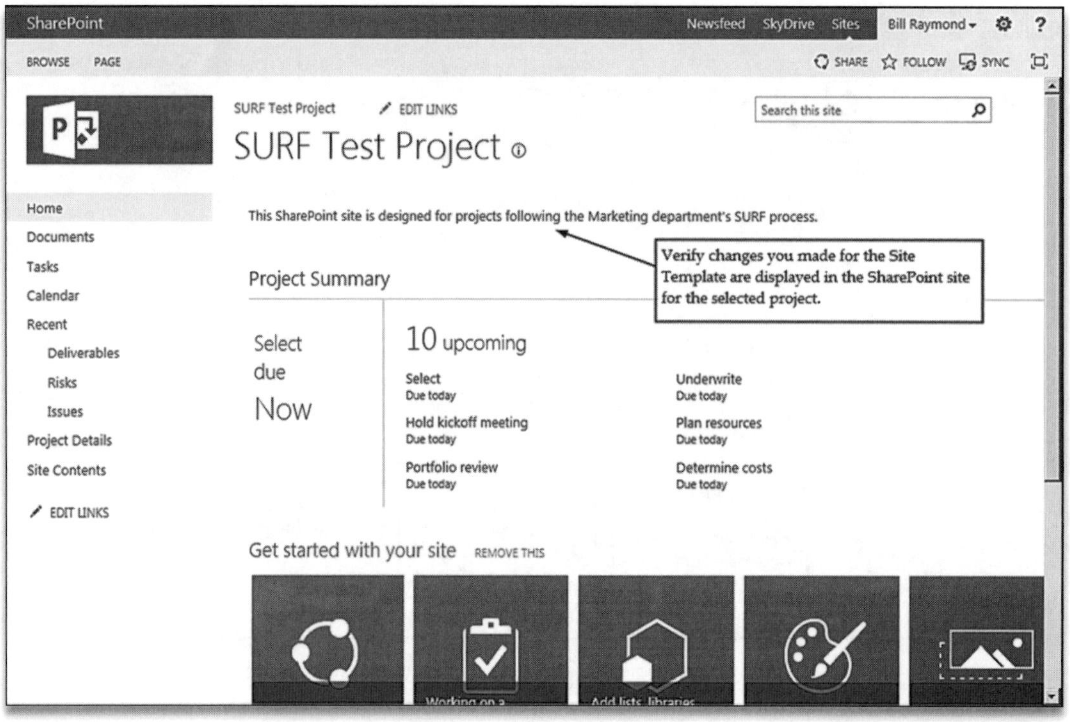

Figure 5 - 80: Project Site

Configuring Demand Management

There is no out-of-box SharePoint site or list providing you with demand management functionality. Instead, you create your own SharePoint sites or lists and then enable them to interact with Project Server 2013. Because any SharePoint list can feed Project Server's demand management functionality, you can create SharePoint lists for ideas, potential projects that are not ready to share more widely, or any other list that may turn into projects.

From an administrative perspective, you have many choices as to how you move this list data into Project Server 2013. Here are some examples:

- **Workflow-driven population**: A user enters data into a SharePoint list and a workflow populates Project Server 2013. This is an ideal solution for small projects like helpdesk tickets, or small projects.

- **User-driven manual population**: Someone working on the list manually publishes the list item to a project. This is an ideal solution for Project Management Offices that review ideas then handpick selected items to publish to Project Server 2013.

- **Administrator-driven population**: An administrator takes data from SharePoint list(s) and populates them in Project Server. This is an ideal solution for those companies that require tight controls over the criteria for creating projects in Project Server.

Project Server 20213 uses the term *Demand Management* because it makes no distinction between a list of ideas, new project requests, or any other inputs. You must define what types of projects feed into your Project Server environment.

Configuring a Demand Management Site

You can create as many sites or lists as you want to capture ideas, project requests, or other types of proposed projects. I create a new site for a marketing department to collect new ideas. To create the new site, follow these steps:

1. Log in to PWA as an administrator, such as the Farm Administrator service account.
2. The system displays the *PWA Home* page shown in Figure 5 - 81. At the top-right of the page, click the *Gear* icon and then select the *Site Settings* item.

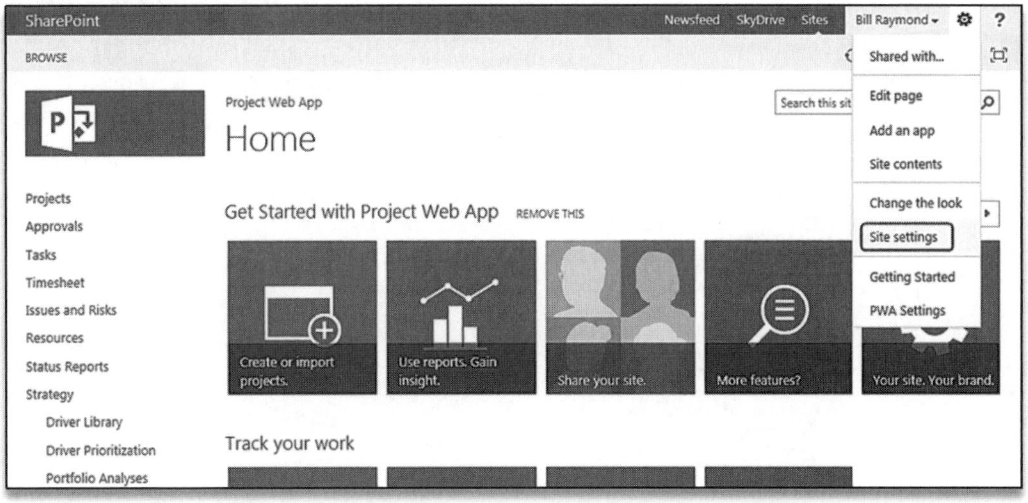

Figure 5 - 81: PWA Home page

3. The system displays the *Site Settings* page shown in Figure 5 - 82. Click the *Sites and workspaces* link.

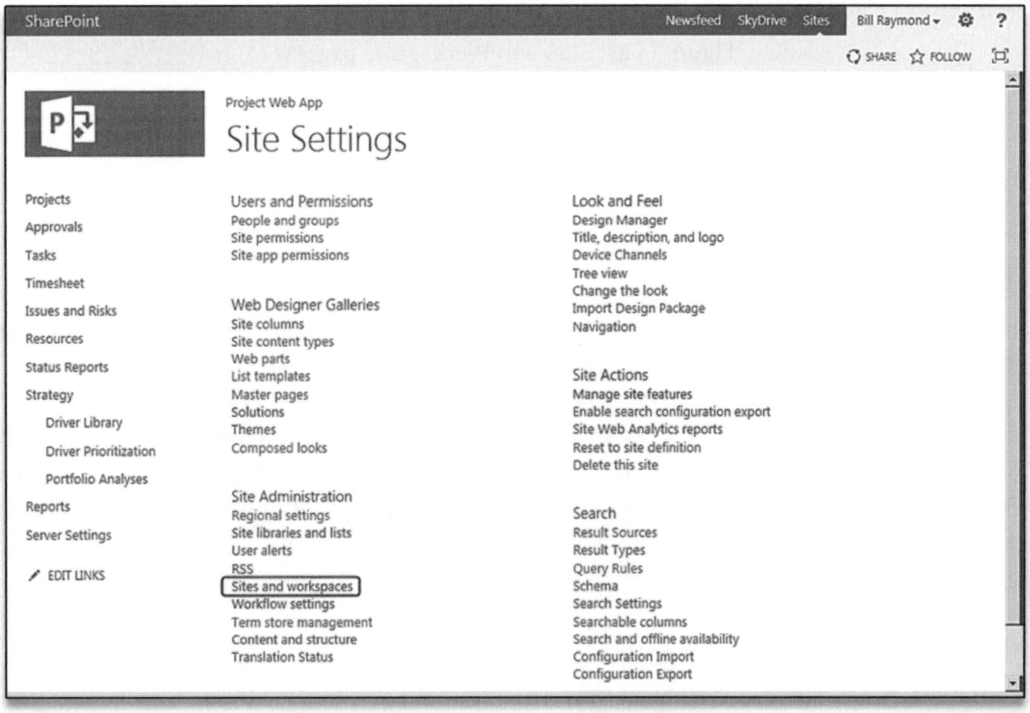

Figure 5 - 82: Site Settings page

4. The system displays the *Sites and Workspaces* page shown in Figure 5 - 83. Click the *Create* button.

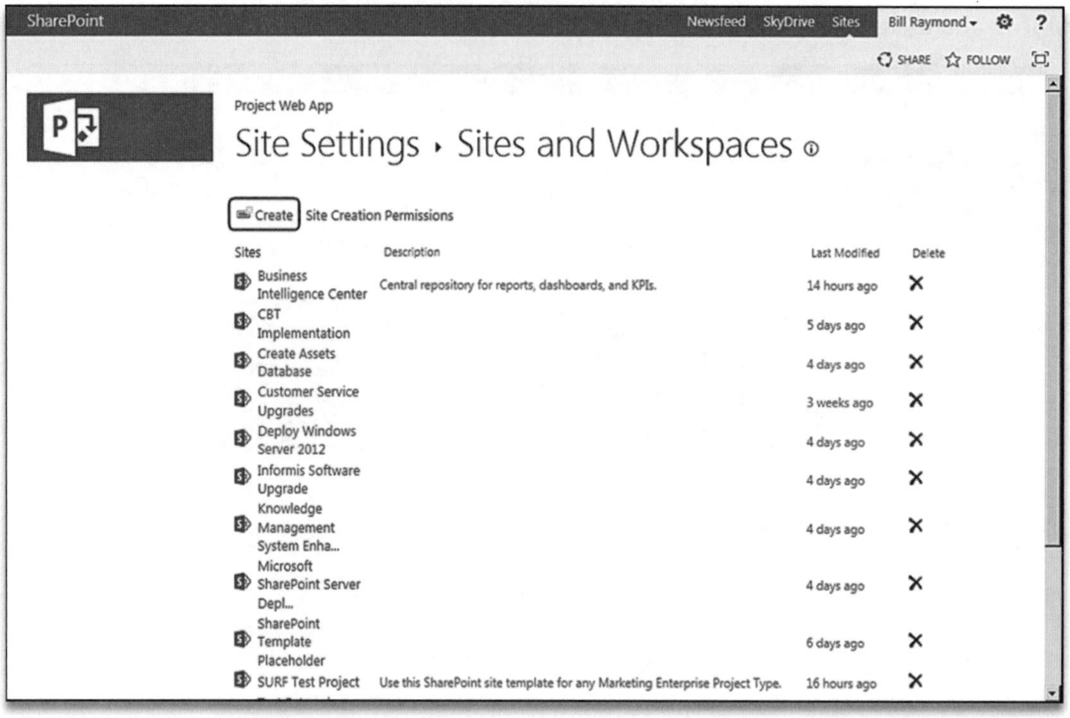

Figure 5 - 83: Sites and Workspaces page

5. The system displays the *New SharePoint Site* dialog shown in Figure 5 - 84. In my example, I type *Ideas for New Marketing Projects* in the *Title* field. In the *Description* field, I type *Anyone in the company can use this site to suggest project ideas for the Marketing Department*. In the *URL name* field, I type *MarketingIdeas* (note: I recommend you avoid using spaces or special characters). In the *Select a template* area, I click the *Collaboration* tab and select *Team Site* from the pick list. In the *Navigation Inheritance* section, I select the *Yes* option (this is optional as you can opt to manage the security manually without inheriting PWA settings). Click the *Create* button.

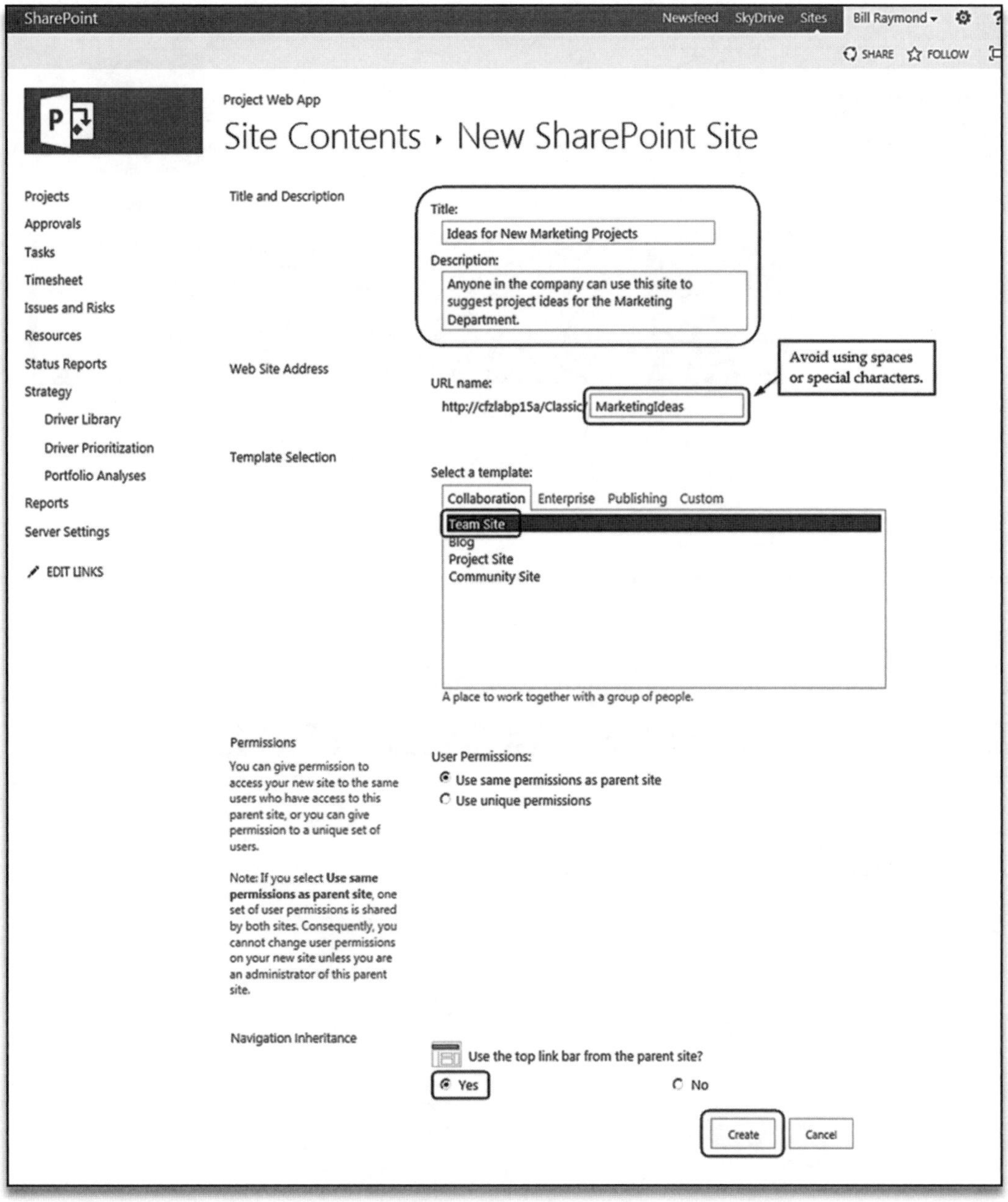

Figure 5 - 84: New SharePoint Site dialog

6. The system displays the *Ideas for New Marketing Projects* site as shown in Figure 5 - 85. At the top-right of the page, click the *Gear* icon and then select the *Site settings* item.

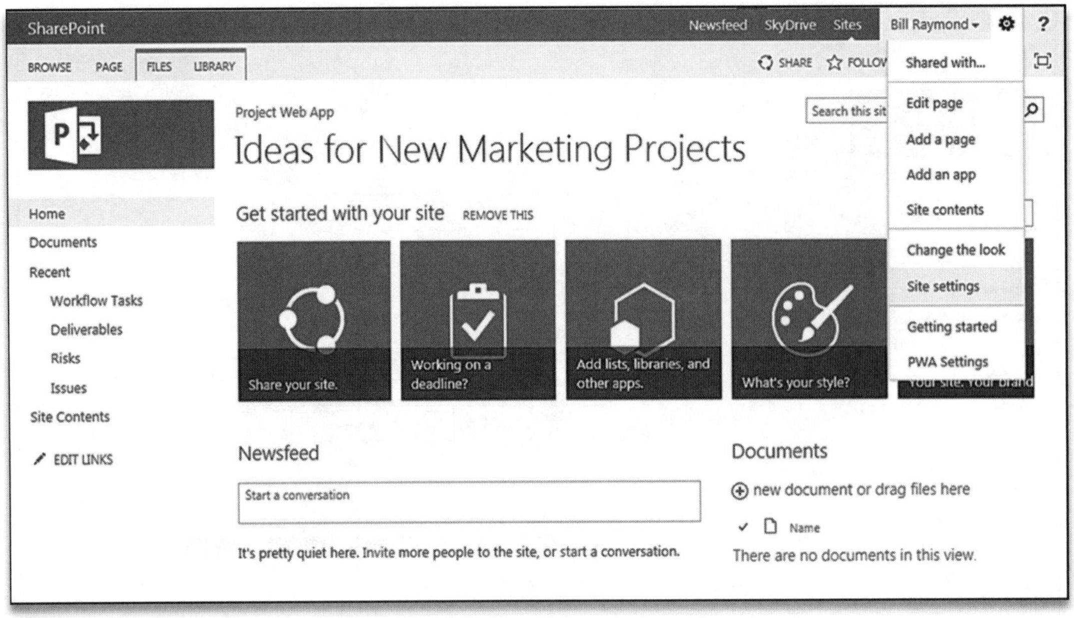

Figure 5 - 85: SharePoint site home page

7. The system displays the *Site Settings* page shown in Figure 5 - 86. Click the *Manage site features* link.

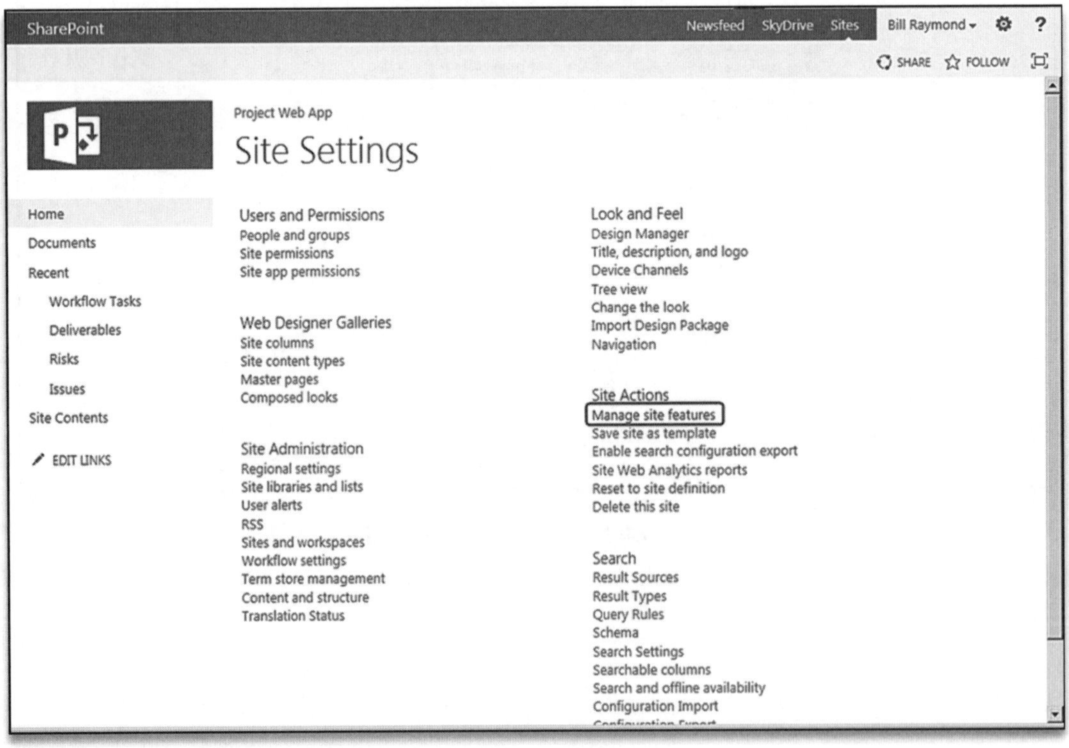

Figure 5 - 86: Site Settings page

8. The system displays the *Site Features* page as partially shown in Figure 5 - 87. Locate the feature called *Project Proposal Workflow* and click the *Activate* button (if already activated, you can skip this step).

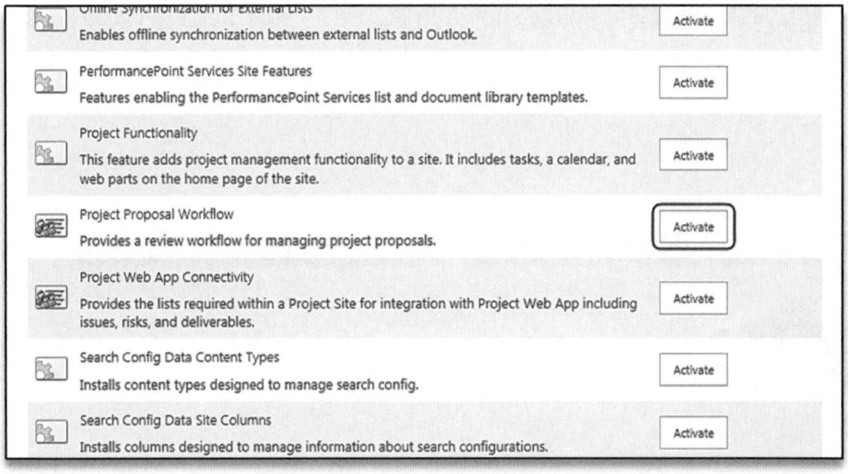

Figure 5 - 87: Site Features page

9. The system refreshes the *Site Features* page as previously shown in Figure 5 - 87. At this point, I recommend you confirm that the *Project Proposal Workflow* field is set to *Activated*. At the top of the page, click the *Sites* link.
10. The system displays the *Sites I'm following* page shown in Figure 5 - 88. Click the *Ideas for New Marketing Projects* link.

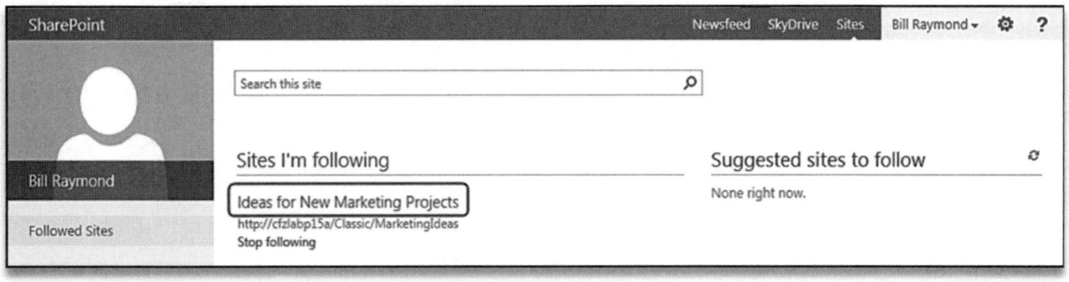

Figure 5 - 88: Sites library

11. The system displays the *Ideas for New Marketing Projects* site shown in Figure 5 - 89. At this point, I recommend you save this link as a bookmark in your browser. Click the *Add lists, libraries, and other apps* tile.

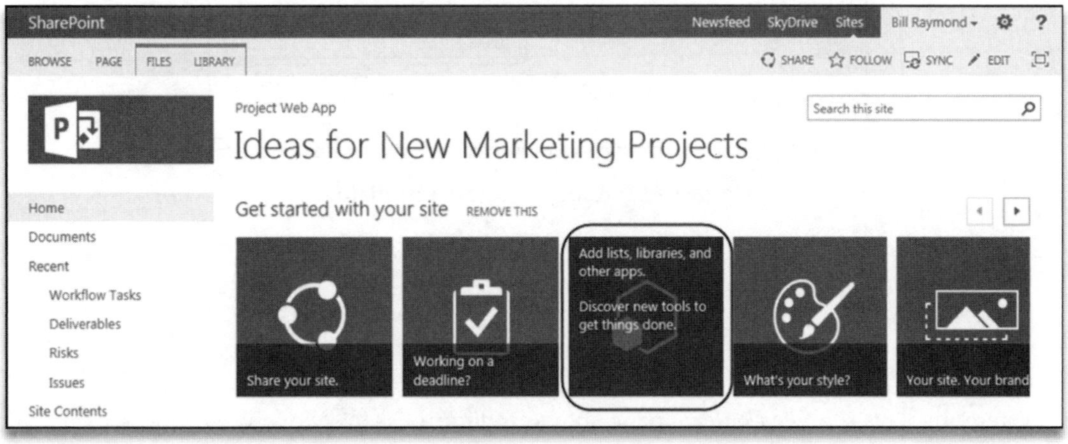

Figure 5 - 89: SharePoint site home page

12. The system displays the *Your Apps* page shown in Figure 5 - 90. Click the *Custom List* tile.

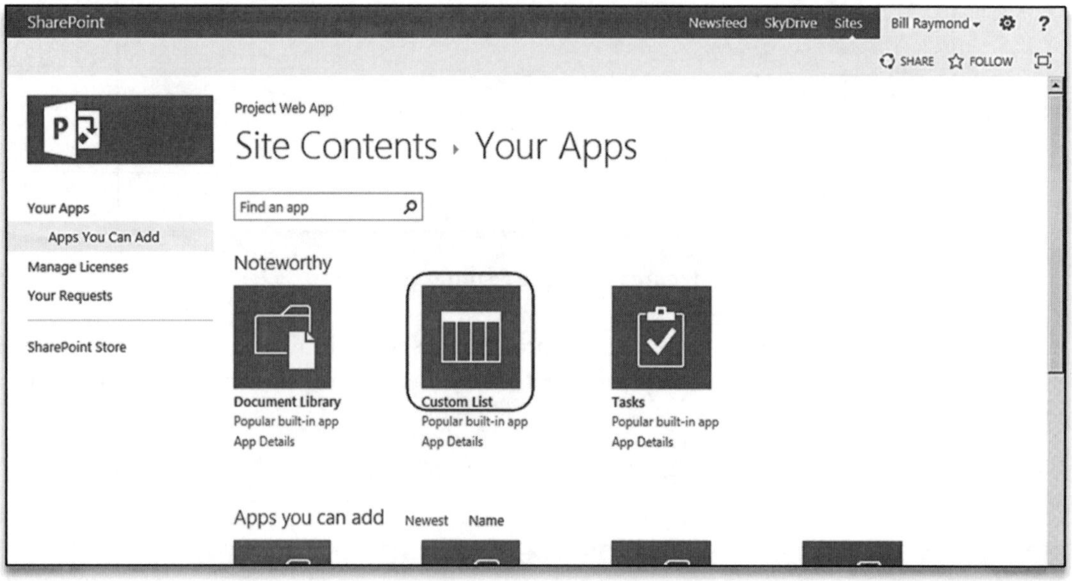

Figure 5 - 90: Your Apps page

13. The system displays the *Adding Custom List* dialog shown in Figure 5 - 91. Type a name for your list. In my example, I type *Marketing Ideas* in the *Name* field. Click the *Create* button.

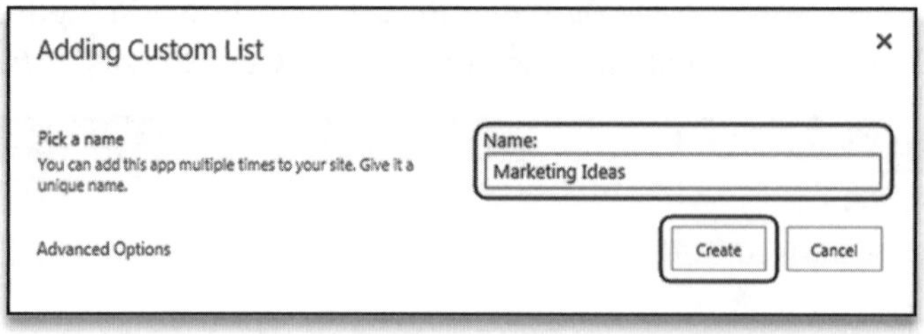

Figure 5 - 91: Adding Custom List dialog

14. The system displays the *Site Contents* page shown in Figure 5 - 92. Move your mouse over the newly created list and click the ... link. The system displays a small dialog, which I labeled *Marketing Ideas*. Click the *SETTINGS* link.

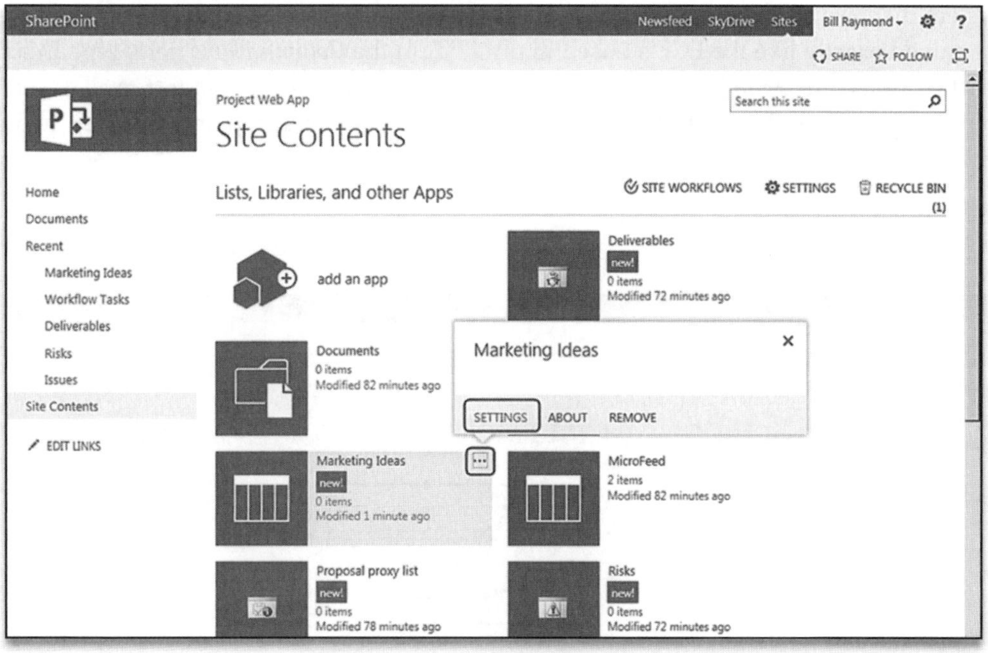

Figure 5 - 92: Site Contents page

15. The system displays the *Settings* page for the *Marketing Ideas* list as shown in Figure 5 - 93. Click the *Create column* link.

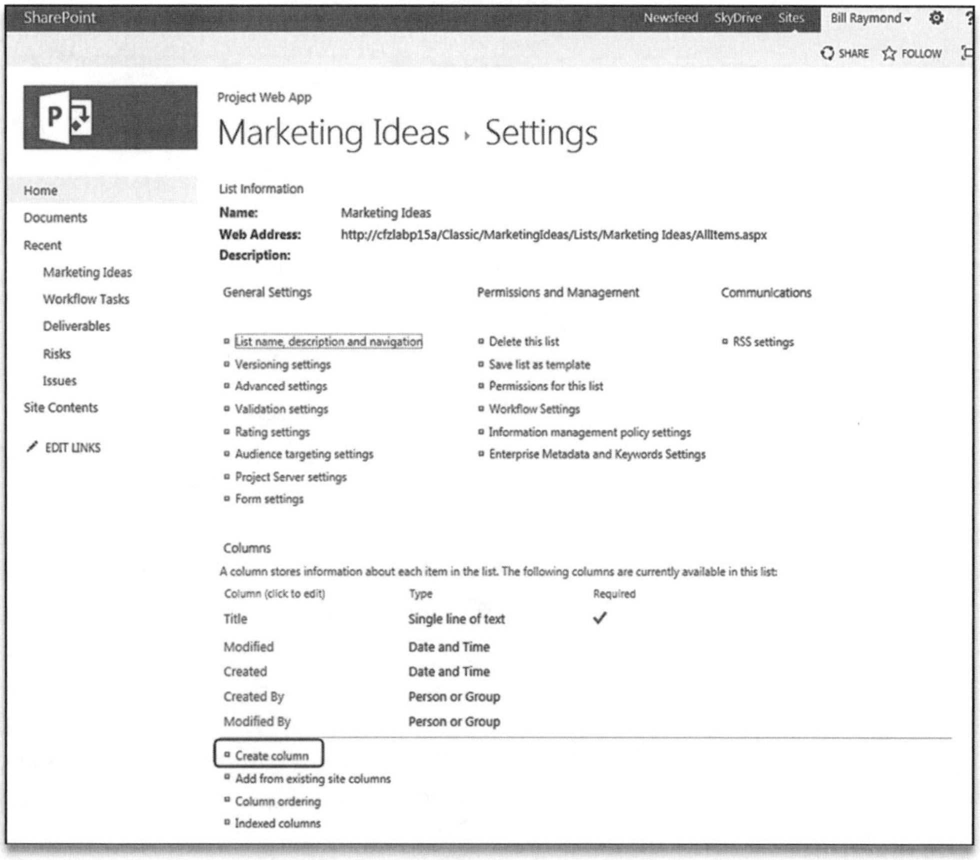

Figure 5 - 93: List Settings page

16. The system displays the *Create Column* dialog shown in Figure 5 - 94. In this case, I want to create fields in my list named exactly like the ECF's I used in my EPT. In the *Column Name* field, type *Description*. For the *Type* section, select the *Multiple lines of text* option. In the *Specify the type of text to allow* section, select the *Plain text* option. Click the *OK* button. **Note:** I repeat the previous step and this step two more times to create two currency fields called *Proposed Cost* and *High Estimate*.

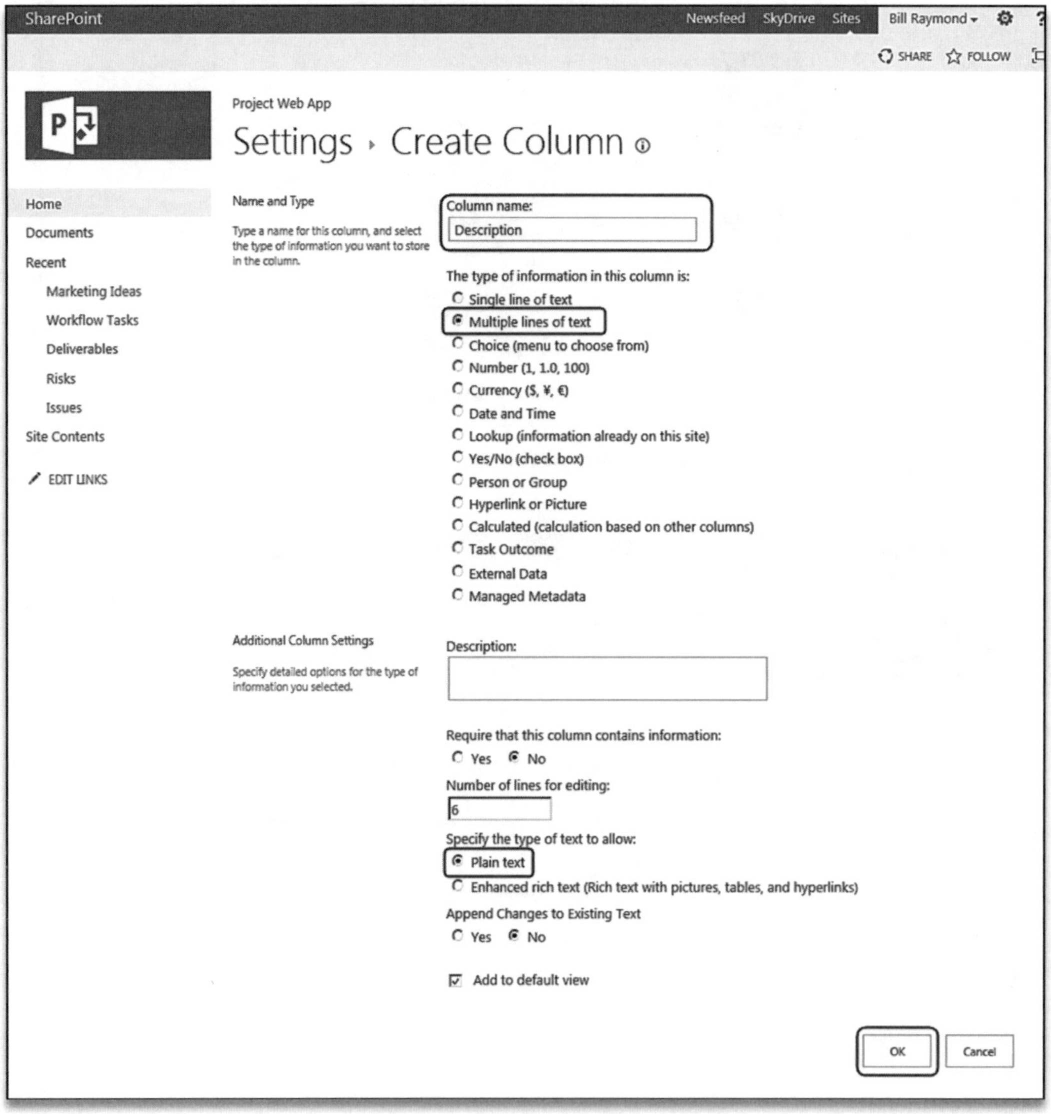

Figure 5 - 94: Create Column dialog

17. The system displays the *Marketing Ideas Settings* page shown in Figure 5 - 95. Verify the column(s) you created display in the *Columns* section. Click the *Marketing Ideas* breadcrumb link at the top of the page.

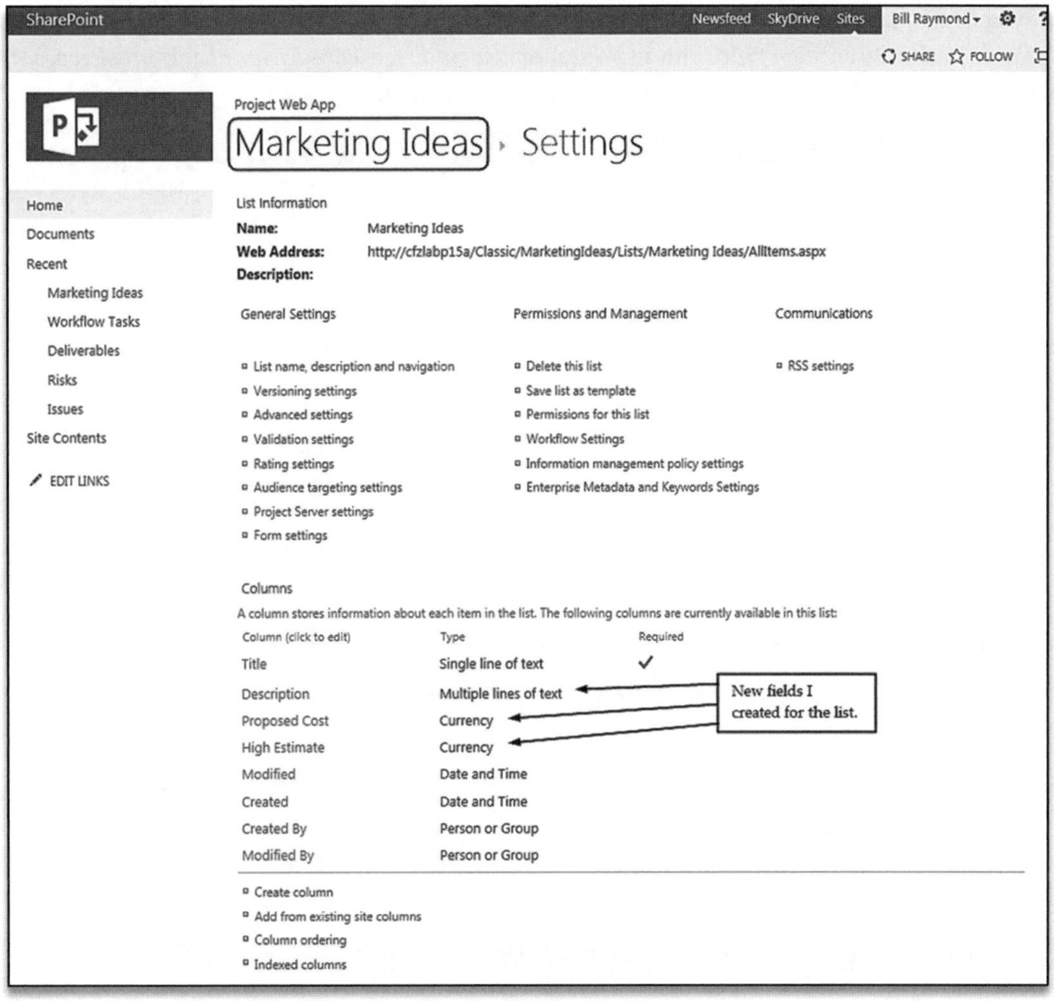

Figure 5 - 95: List Settings page

18. The system displays the *Marketing Ideas* page shown in Figure 5 - 96. Click the *new item* link under the list title.

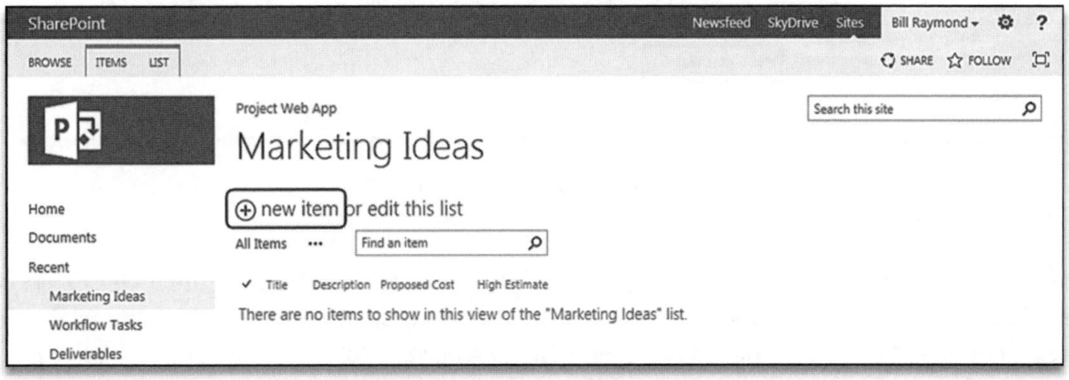

Figure 5 - 96: Marketing Ideas page

19. The system displays the *New List Item* dialog shown in Figure 5 - 97. I enter *Social Media Campaign* in the *Title* field. In the *Description* field, enter *Create a campaign directed at social media.* In the *Proposed Cost* field, I enter *10,000* and in the *High Estimate* field, I enter *15,000.* Click the *Save* button.

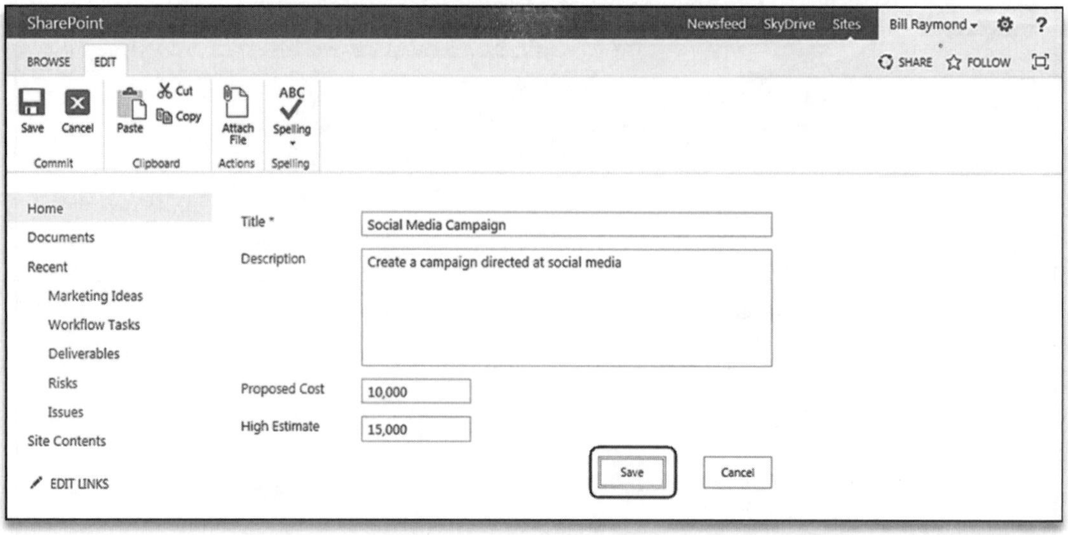

Figure 5 - 97: New List Item dialog

20. The system returns to the *Marketing Ideas* list shown in Figure 5 - 98. At this point, SharePoint knows there is a list called *Marketing Ideas* and one of the list item titles is *Social Media Campaign*. There is no correlation between this list and Project Server 2013. To create this correlation, at the top of the page, click the *Items* tab, then in the *Project Server* section, click the *Create Projects* button.

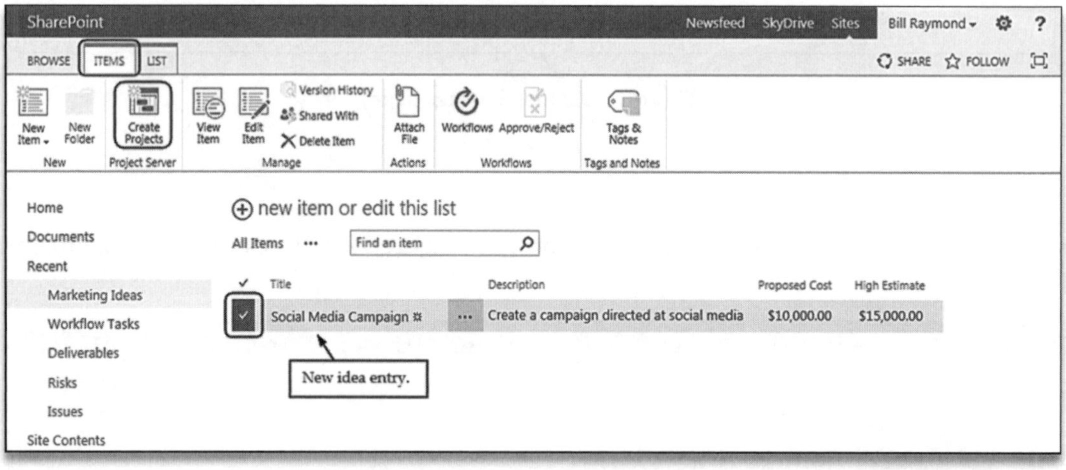

Figure 5 - 98: Marketing Ideas list

21. The system displays the *Create Projects in Project Web App* dialog shown in Figure 5 - 99. Select columns in the pick lists that you want to map between SharePoint (left side) and your PWA site (right side). In my case, I map the *Description, Proposed Cost,* and *High Estimate* fields. The *Enterprise Project Type* section already lists my *SURF Marketing Campaign* EPT as the default, but I could select another from the pick list. Click the *Create Project* button.

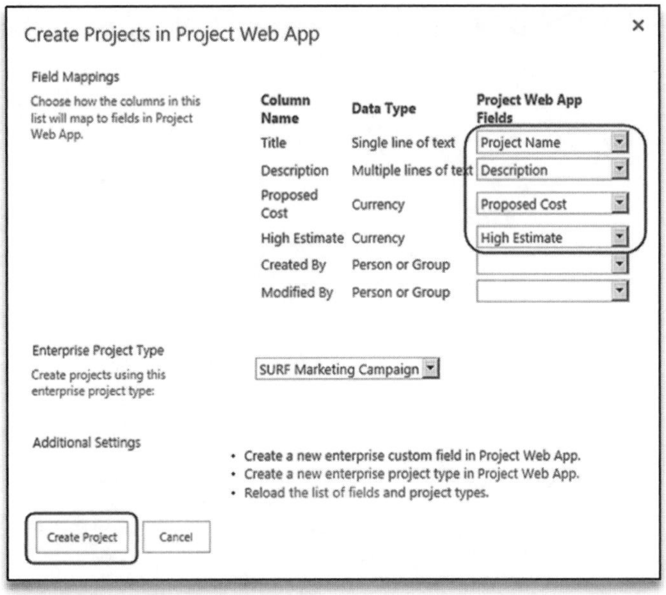

Figure 5 - 99: Create Projects in Project Web App dialog

22. The system refreshes the *Create Projects in Project Web App* dialog as shown in Figure 5 - 100. A message displays at the bottom of the page. In my case, the dialog informs me that the system created my project successfully. Click the *Close* button.

Figure 5 - 100: Create Projects in Project Web App dialog project successfully created

23. To verify project creation, navigate to your PWA home page and click the *Projects* link. The system displays the Project Center shown in Figure 5 - 101. Review the list of projects and find the new project you just created.

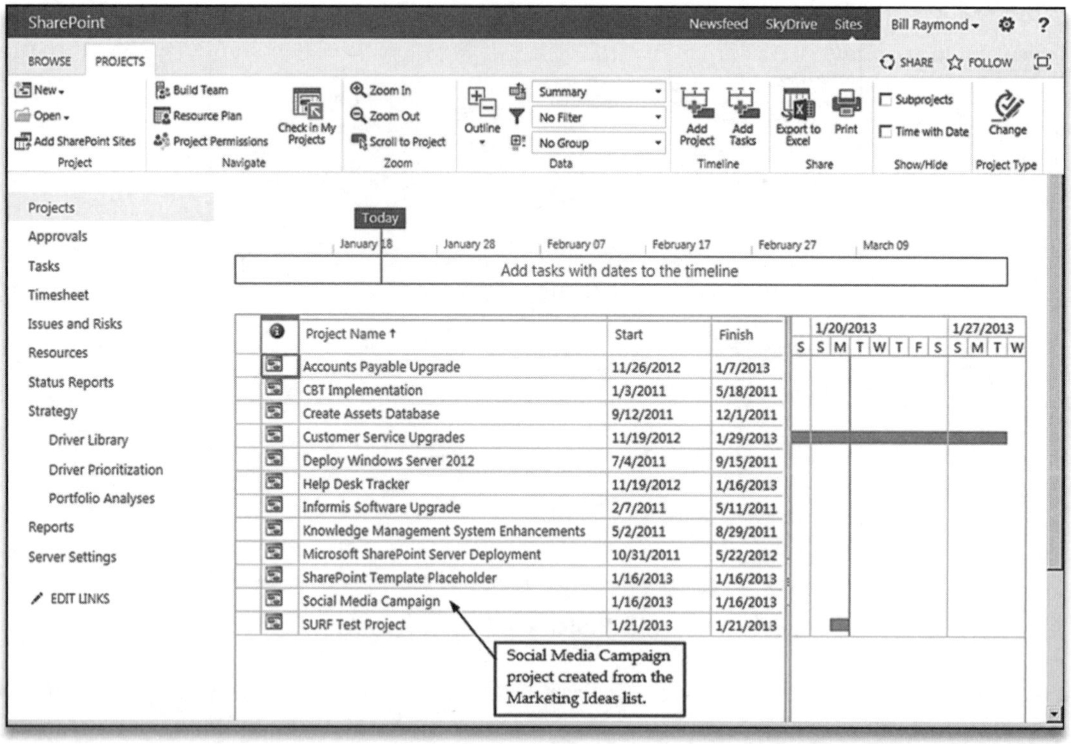
Social Media Campaign project created from the Marketing Ideas list.

Figure 5 - 101: Project Center

While you can create a list that enables demand management, the manual process of selecting list items and publishing them to Project Server 2013 may be tedious. For example, you may want the system to feed **any** new project that costs less than $5,000 to your PWA site automatically. You achieve this automation by running SharePoint Designer 2013 by creating a new list workflow.

Preparing Proposed Projects for Portfolio Analysis

Whether you build an onramp to your system such as a Demand Management site, or you choose to have your colleagues enter their proposals directly into Project Server, chances are these will follow a process where their proponents further develop the proposals by adding additional evidence such as estimates of benefits and costs.

Inasmuch as portfolio analysis uses cost, resource capacity, and demand as measures and strategic alignment and time as dimensions, it is imperative that you provide the system with data to fulfill these analysis criteria. The system does not limit you to the types of cost fields you can use for your analysis; however, resource capacity requires a sound resource pool model, and demand requires either a resource plan or a model embedded in the schedule. At the end of this section, I discuss the pros and cons of both approaches.

Creating a Resource Plan

In many if not most Project Server configurations used for portfolio analysis, early resource planning relies on *Resource Plans.* A *Resource Plan* is a way to "reserve" a resource for specific periods without assigning the resource to tasks. In the *SURF Workflow*, building a project team and assigning individual resources to tasks or building a resource plan happens during the *SURF Resources* stage of the *Underwrite* phase.

In a typical workflow, after you create a new proposal, and before portfolio selection, you need to commit resources to the proposal to show demand. To create a resource plan for a proposal, navigate to the Project Center page in Project Web App. Select your proposal by clicking the row header to the left of its name and then from the *Navigate* section of the *Project* ribbon, click the *Resource Plan* button. Project Server 2013 displays the *Resource Plan* page for the selected proposal shown in Figure 5 - 102.

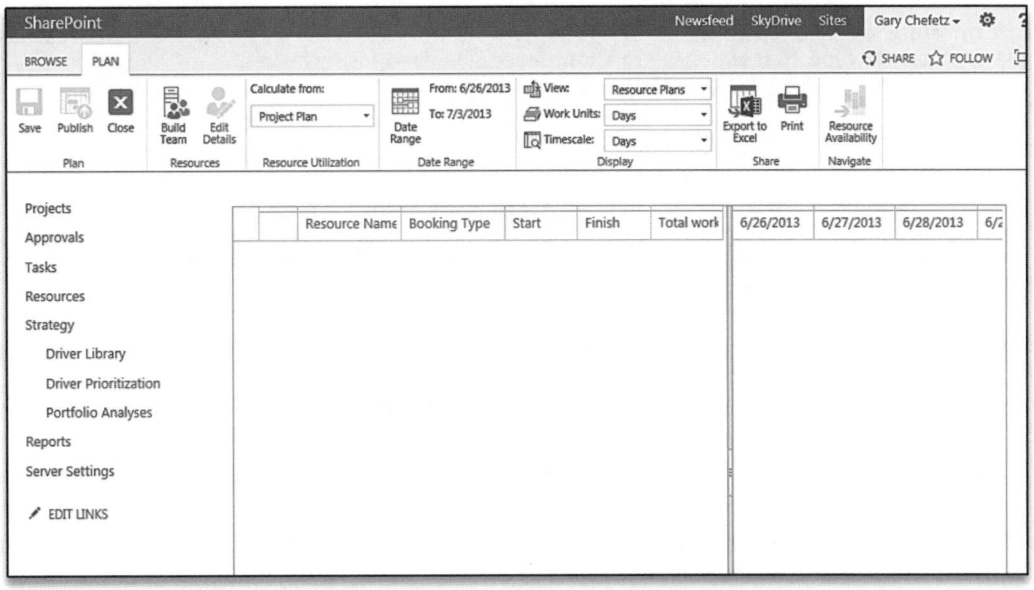

Figure 5 - 102: Resource Plan page for a proposal

Building a Team on a Resource Plan

The first step in creating a resource plan is to add resources. From the *Resources* section of the *Plan* ribbon, click the *Build Team* button. The system displays the *Build Resource Plan Team* page shown in Figure 5 - 103.

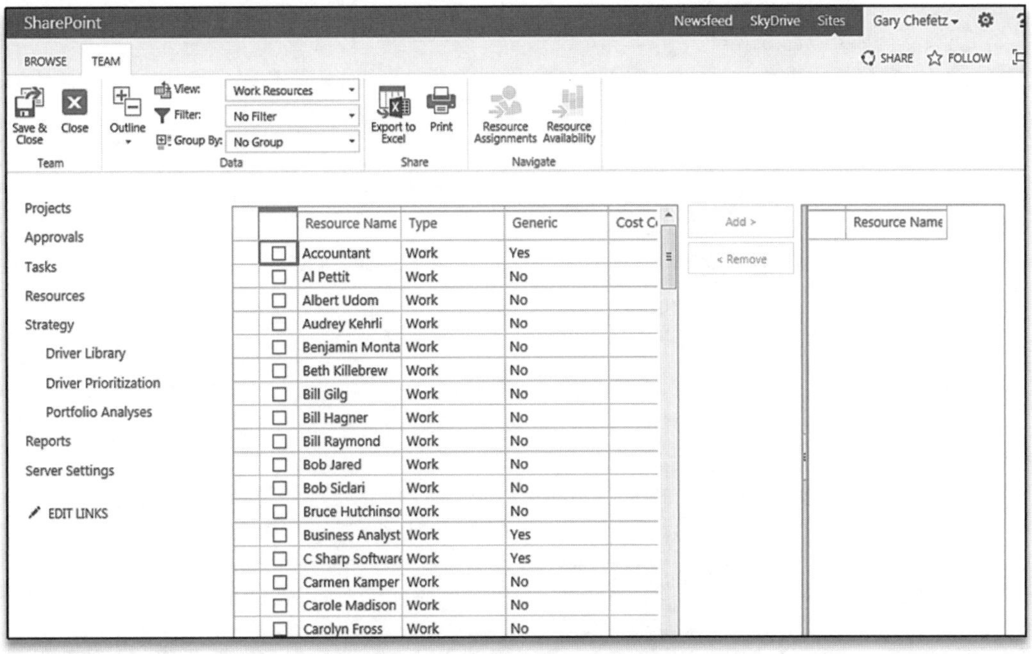

Figure 5 - 103: Build Resource Plan Team page

From the list of resources shown on the *Build Resource Plan Team* page, you must select the resources to serve on your project team. Begin by selecting the option checkbox to the left of each resource that may be a potential team member. You can select any type of resource using this page. In the *Data* section of the *Team* ribbon, use the *View* pick list to change views and select from various subsets of your resource pool. Most organizations are likely to use *Generic* resources to represent resource loading.

Information: Generic resources are a special type of work resource that you use to represent resources by role or capability type. You use these to show generic demand for resources.

Best Practice: MSProjectExperts recommends that you design your process using generic resources for early-phase resource demand modeling rather than actual resources. This allows you to differentiate between actual loading and proposed resource loading.

If you elect to use actual resources from your resource pool, Project Server 2013 offers you two ways to determine whether each resource is available to serve on your proposed team by using the *Resource Assignments* and *Resource Availability* buttons in the *Navigate* section of the *Team* ribbon. You can use these after selecting one or more resources. Because the expectation is that you are using generic resources exclusively at this point in the process, I do not cover these in this module. I describe these tools in detail in Module 15, *Working in the Resource Center*.

Adding Resources to the Team on a Resource Plan

To add generic resources to your plan, select the option checkboxes to the left of each resource name and then click the *Add* button. The system shows the list of selected resources in the upper right corner of the *Build Resource Plan Team* page shown in Figure 5 - 104.

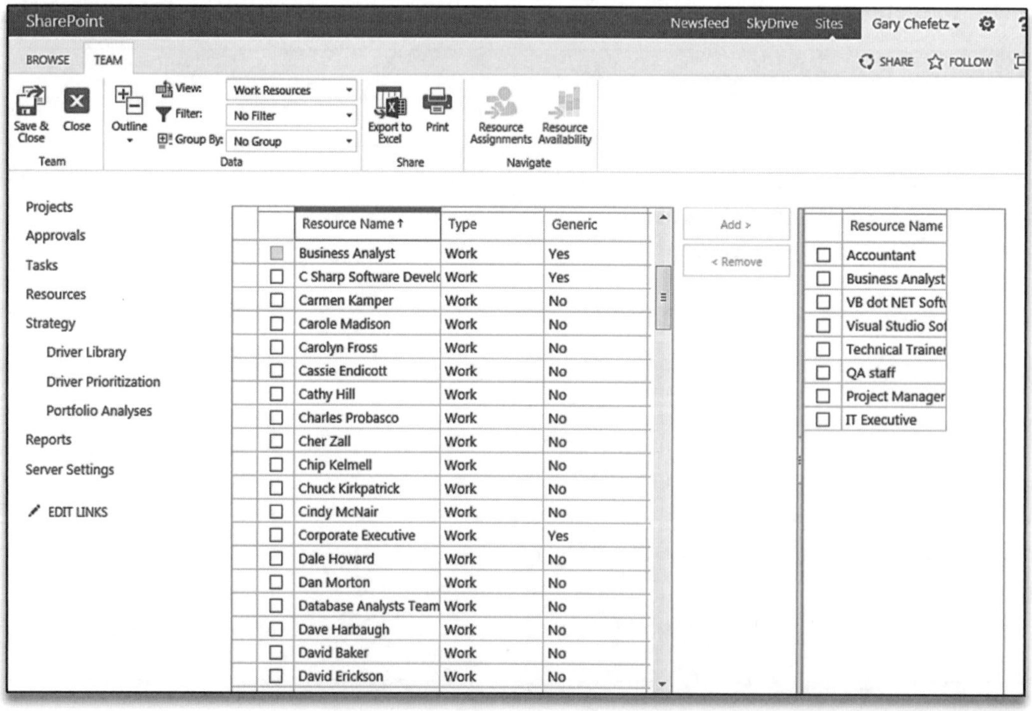

Figure 5 - 104: Build Resource Plan Team page with generic resources selected

In the *Team* section of the *Team* ribbon, click the *Save and Close* button to add the selected resources to the team for the proposal. Project Server 2013 redisplays the *Resource Plan* page with the new team members, as shown in Figure 5 - 105.

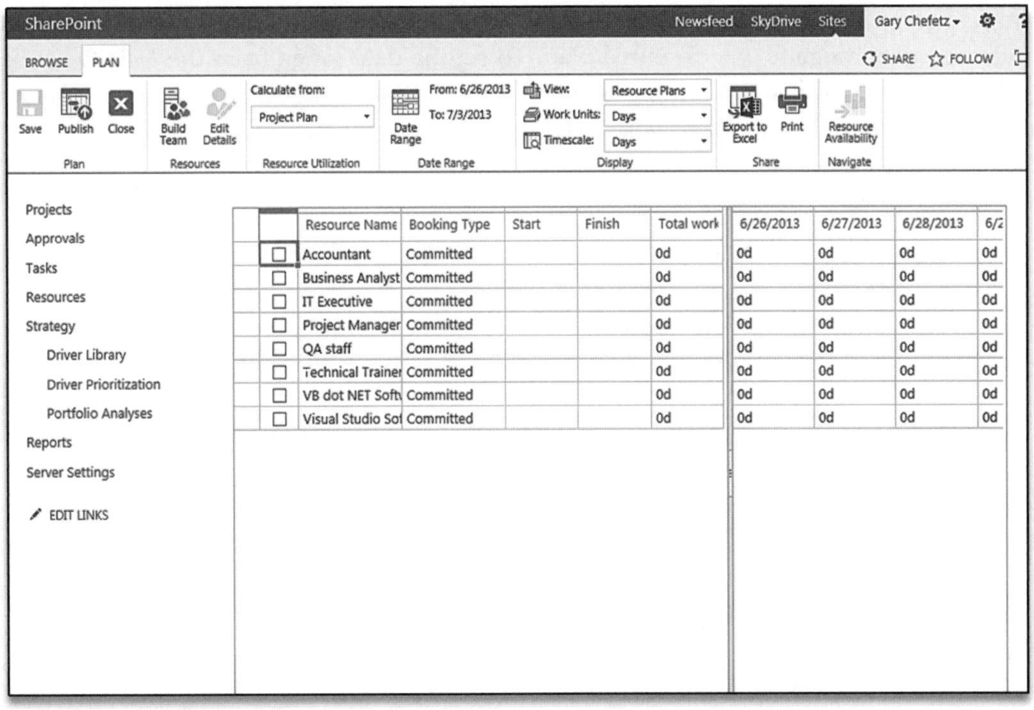

Figure 5 - 105: Resource Plan page with generic team members

Modeling Resource Demand in a Resource Plan

After you add resources to the proposal, you must designate the *Booking Type* for each resource and then "reserve" each resource for the periods for which you need them. Project Server 2013 offers two potential *Booking Type* values for a resource in a resource plan. Use the **Proposed** booking type to indicate a tentative resource booking when you are not certain that you will use the resource in the resource plan. Leave the default **Committed** booking type selected to indicate a firm resource commitment to the resource plan.

To set the *Booking Type* for a resource, click into the *Booking Type* field in the grid next to the resource name and change the value using the pick list as shown in Figure 5 - 106.

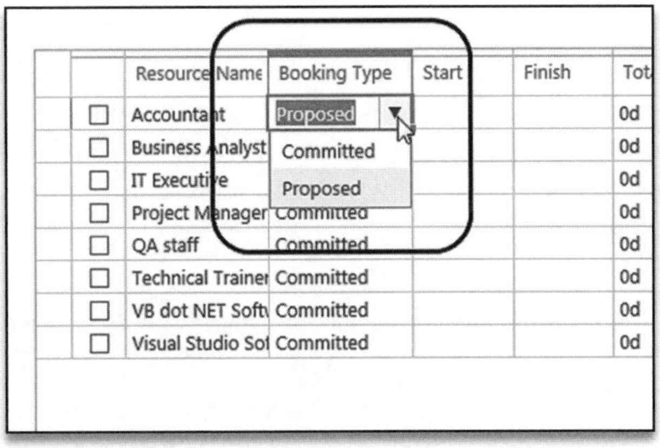

Figure 5 - 106: Edit Booking Type field

To change the *Booking Type* field value from *committed* to *proposed,* click the *Booking Type* pick list and select the *Proposed* value. In addition to changing the *Booking Type* field value, the system allows you to select a resource and edit it by clicking the *Edit Details* button in the *Resources* section of the *Plan* ribbon.

By default, Project Server 2013 displays the current date as the first available date in a *Resource Plan,* so you must manually specify the date range for the resource plan. To set the date range from the *Date Range* section of the *Plan* ribbon, click the *Date Range* button. The system opens the *Set Date Range* dialog shown in Figure 5 - 107. Enter dates in the *From* and *To* fields and then click the *OK* button to save your selections.

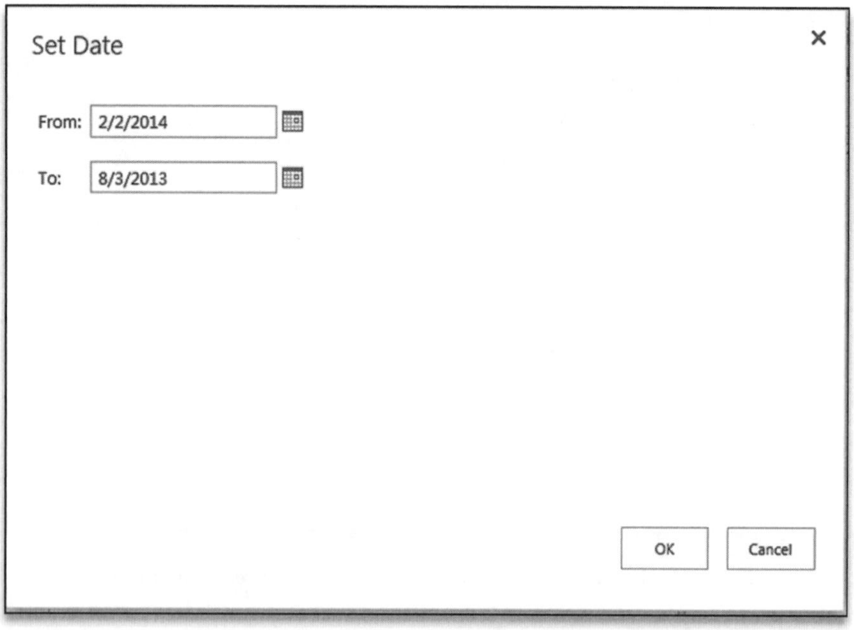

Figure 5 - 107: Set Date Range dialog

Click the *Timescale* pick list to set the timescale for resource planning. Typically, you want to select weeks or months, but for very long- duration projects, you also have the option of selecting quarters or years.

Best Practice: MSProjectExperts recommends that you enter the start date of your proposal in the *From* field and the estimated finish date in the *To* field. For simplicity's sake, MSProjectExperts also recommends that you set the *Timescale* value to *Weeks* or to *Months* rather than *Days*.

Click the *Work Units* pick list and select one of the three available options: *Hours, Days,* or *Full-time equivalent*. The default value is *Hours,* meaning that you reserve the resource's work in hours. Select the *Days* option if you want to reserve work in days, where each day represents 8 hours of work. If you select the *Full-time equivalent* option, you enter the work in full-time equivalents (FTE's), where 1.00 represents full-time work and .50 represents half-time work, for example.

Information: Using the *Full-time equivalent* option is an easy way to reserve full or part-time work for the resources in your resource plan; thus allowing the system to calculate the necessary number of hours.

Information: When you select the *Full-time equivalent* option, Project Server 2013 determines the number of hours of work in each period based on how your Project Server administrator configured your system. The system allows the Project Server administrator to define an FTE as either a specific number of hours per day (such as 8 hours/day), or according to the number of hours each day shown on each resource's calendar in the Enterprise Resource Pool.

For each resource on the team, enter time or FTE's in one or more periods to "reserve" the resource during each period. The information you enter shows your "forecast" of anticipated resource utilization over the life of the proposed project, even though you did not assign the resources to tasks.

If you enter work values or FTE's, you can display the total work reserved for each resource by selecting the *Hours* view from the *View* pick list. Figure 5 - 108 shows the resource plan with entries by FTE by month. Figure 5 - 109 shows the same information, after applying the *Hours* view and dragging the splitter bar to the right to show the *Total Work* column.

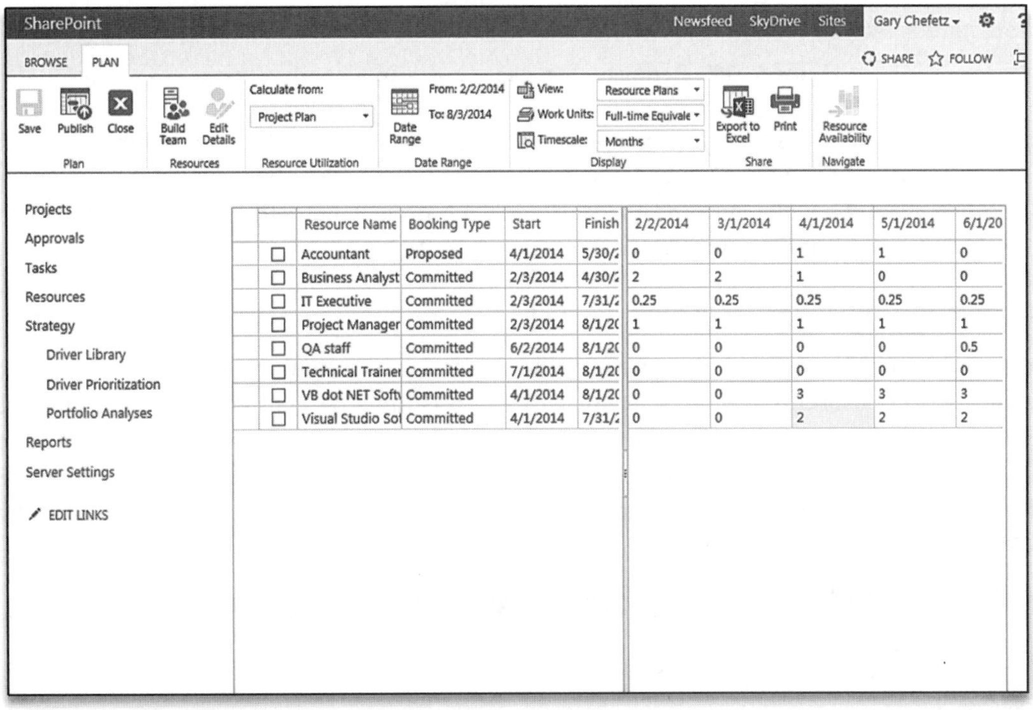

Figure 5 - 108: Resource Plan page shows monthly periods

For each resource on the team, enter time in one or more periods to "reserve" the resource during each period. The information you enter shows your "forecast" of anticipated resource utilization over the life of the proposed project, even though you did not assign the resources to tasks.

Figure 5 - 108 shows the FTE totals that I started entering into the monthly grid. Notice that my anticipated utilization of each resource varies by resource and that these can vary by period as well. Notice also the *Calculate from* pick list in the *Resource Utilization* section of the *Plan* ribbon. You must select the *Resource Plan* item to tell Project Server to use the resource plan rather than the project plan, which is the system default.

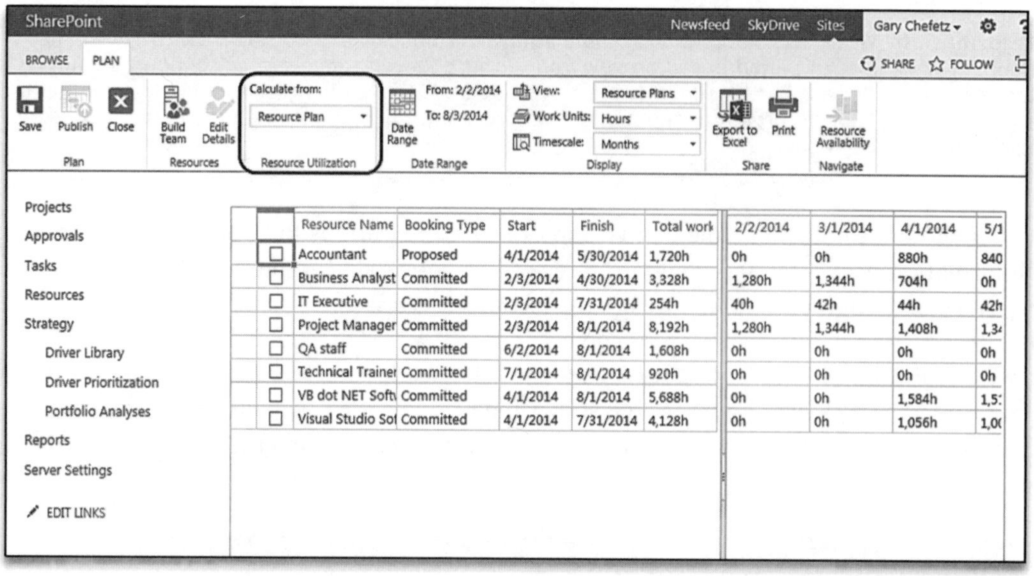

Figure 5 - 109: Resource Plan page shows Total work column

When you finish your resource plan for your proposal, from the *Plan* section of the *Plan* ribbon, click the *Save* button. Notice that you can also publish the resource plan. The demand for this project does not accrue until you publish the resource plan. After the system finishes saving the project, click the *Publish* or *Close* buttons respectively to publish and/or close the *Resource Plan* and return to the *Project Center* page.

Importing Resources from a Resource Plan

Typically, you apply a resource plan in order to enable the resource constraint analysis in a portfolio analysis. Once you move your proposal through the selection process, it is time to detail your plan with task assignments. Resources in a resource plan are not eligible for assignments in Project Pro 2013 unless you copy them from your resource plan into your project. To do this, I must open my project from the *Project Center* and use the *Build Team* tool. Select the row header for your project and from the *Navigate* section of the *Projects* ribbon, click the *Build Team* button. The system displays the *Build Team* page shown in Figure 5 - 110.

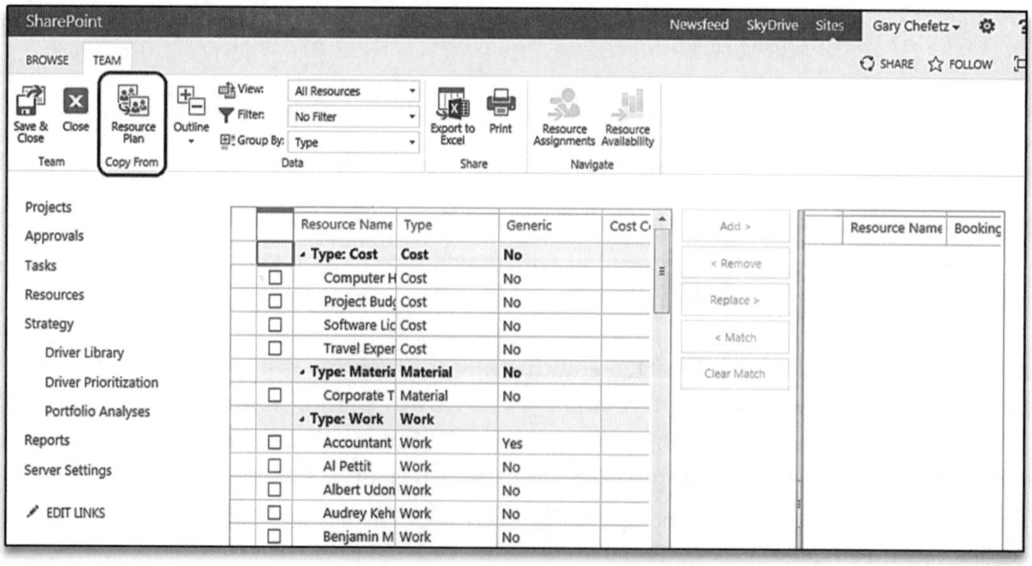

Figure 5 - 110: Build Team for a Project

This is essentially the same tool that you used to build your team for your *Resource Plan*. Notice that the *Team* ribbon now contains a *Copy From* section with a button labeled *Resource Plan* that allows you to copy the resources in your resource plan into your project. To copy the resource into your project, click the *Resource Plan* button and the system redisplays with the resources selected in the *Selected Resources* section on the right as shown in Figure 5 - 111.

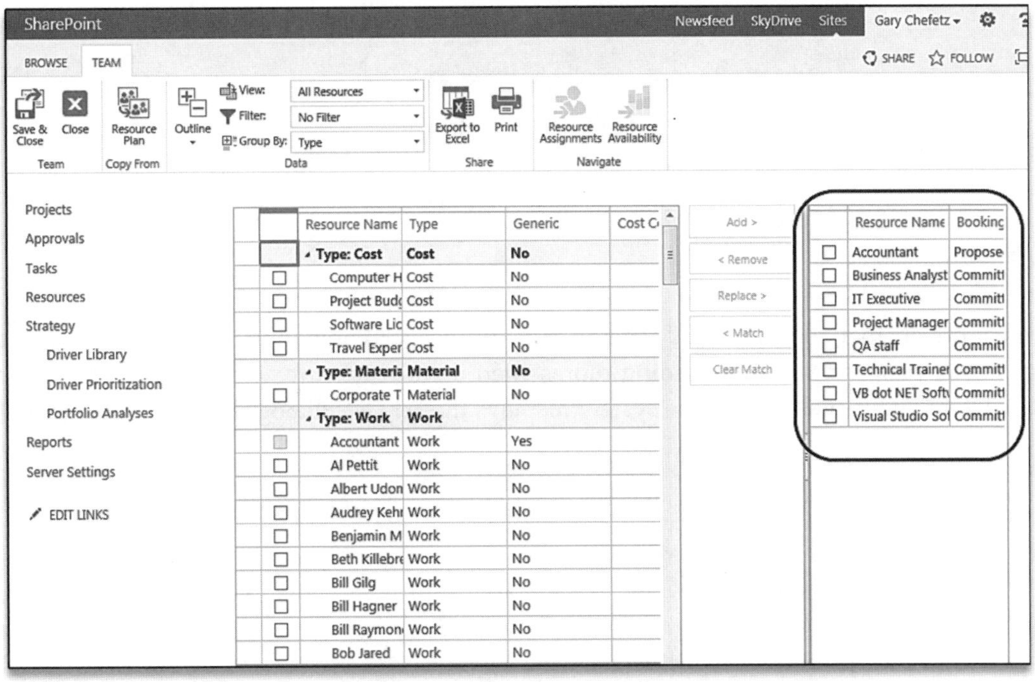

Figure 5 - 111: Build Team tool with Resources Copied from Plan

Now that you copied your resources from the *Resource Plan,* you use the *Build Team* tool the same way you did in the previous example. You can add or remove resources at this point and use the *Match* tool to replace your generic resources with human workers. Click the *Save and Close* button when you complete your resource selections. The system returns to your *Resource Plan* page.

Information: From the *Build Team* page, you can also determine the availability for one or more selected resources by clicking the *Resource Assignments* button or the *Resource Availability* button. Refer to Module 15, *Working in the Resource Center,* for complete information on how to use these two features.

Using a Resource Plan during Project Execution

As you can see, resource plans are very powerful for modeling resource demand during the proposal process allowing you to create a rich resource model at a high level with very little effort, and a more complex and contoured model with a moderate amount of effort. Resource plans are also very useful during project execution, particularly for projects with long durations or projects where detailed planning is possible for only a near-term horizon. On the *Resource Plan* page shown previously in Figure 5 - 109, notice in the *Resource Utilization* section of the *Plan* ribbon, the *Calculate From* pick list shown in focus in Figure 5 - 112.

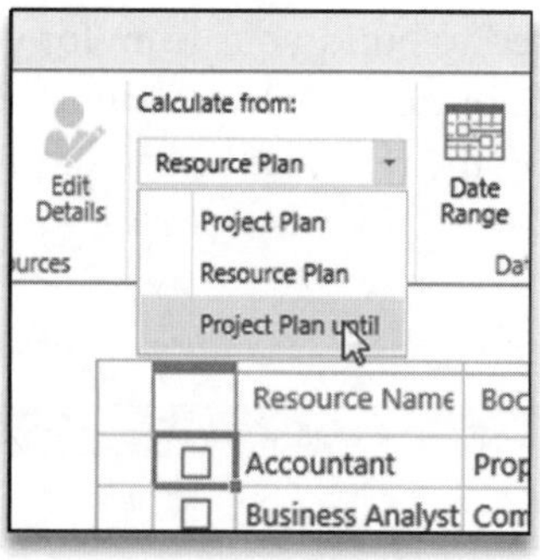

Figure 5 - 112: Calculate From pick list

As you execute a project that you cannot fully detail, you can use a combination of resources assigned to specific tasks in your project plan and resource loading represented in your resource plan. You do this by selecting the *Project Plan until* item on the pick list and the system displays the *Set Date* dialog shown in Figure 5 - 113.

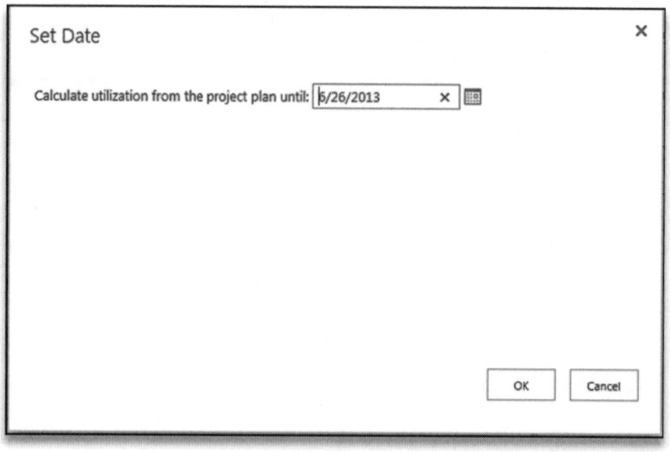

Figure 5 - 113: Set Date dialog

Selecting a date in the dialog tells the system to use the resources assigned to tasks in the project plan to determine utilization until the specified date; and thereafter, use the values in the resource plan allowing you to combine detailed bottom-up planning with high-level top-down planning to support this scenario.

Pros and Cons of using Resource Plans

Resource plans are most effective when you use them only as part of a proposal process. When you change the start date of a project within a portfolio analysis during a what-if planning session, the date change moves the resource demand represented in the resource plan accordingly. This is the pro. The problem is that if your proposed start date changes, then you must change the resource plan manually to reflect the change. This may be a minimal concern during a proposal process; however, it could end up being a major pain during execution. Resource plans do not respond to changes in the project schedule. They are not dynamic.

With slightly more effort, you can also model resource demand within the schedule using Project Pro 2013. Rather than using a WBS for this structure, you use tasks in the project to create a resource demand model for each resource or group of resources. If you build this correctly, whether the schedule moves forward or slips, the long-range resource demand moves with it.

Creating Project Dependencies

The final step in preparing a project for portfolio analyses is to identify programs and other project dependencies. Project Server 2013 portfolio analyses supports four types of project level dependencies that you can use to define relationships between projects:

- **Dependency:** If the primary project is selected, then all related projects must be selected.
- **Mutual Inclusion:** If any project in the group is selected, then all related projects must be selected.
- **Mutual Exclusion:** If one project in the set is selected, the all other projects in the set must be excluded.
- **Finish to Start:** The primary project must be completed before the successor starts.

The first three types of dependencies provide powerful constructs around inclusion and exclusion criteria. If we do this one, then we must also do these related projects. If we select this project, then we must select these projects, or if we select one from this set, the others in this set are excluded. This allows you to ensure that selecting a project automatically forces in or forces out related projects to your portfolio selection based on these relationship rules. The mutual inclusion criteria allows you to define a program of related projects where including any one of them forces in the others in your portfolio analysis. To create a new dependency, complete the following steps:

1. In the *Quick Launch* menu, click the *Portfolio Analyses* link.

2. From the *Navigate* section of the *Analyses* ribbon, click the *Project Dependencies* button. The system displays the *Project Dependencies* page shown in Figure 5 - 114.

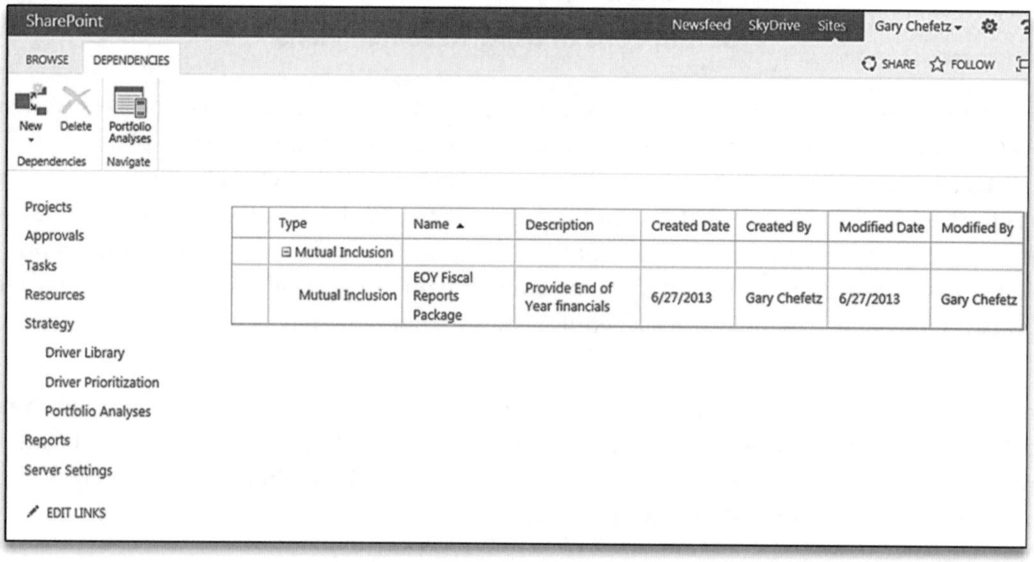

Figure 5 - 114: Project Dependencies page

3. From the *Dependencies* section of the *Dependencies* ribbon, click the *New* pick list and select a dependency. The system displays the *Add Dependency* page shown in Figure 5 - 115.

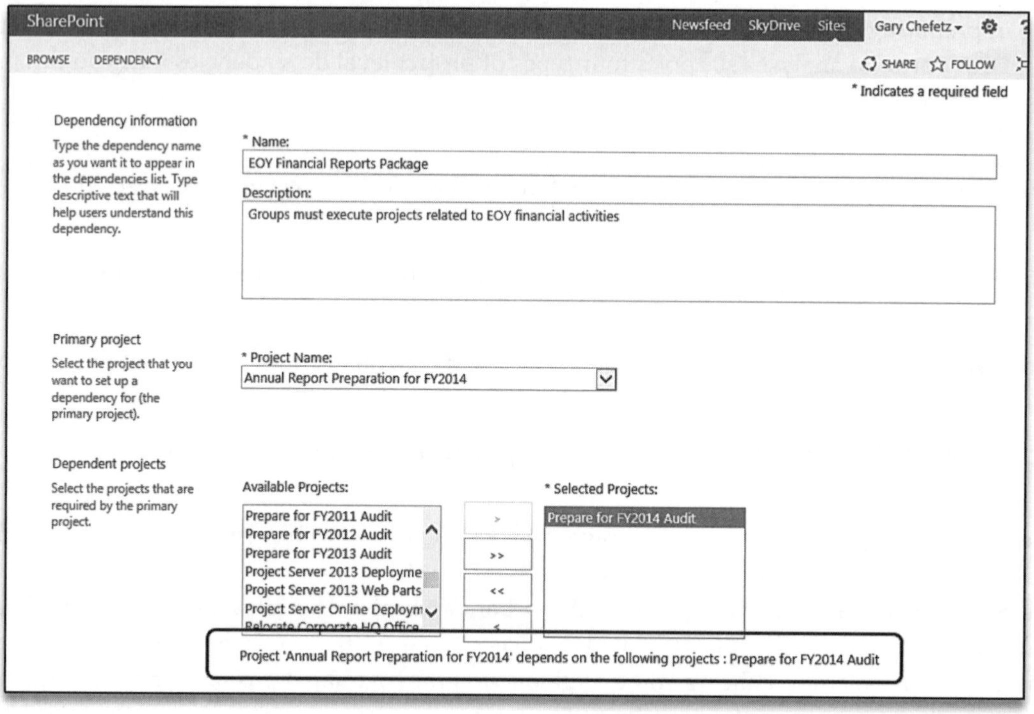

Figure 5 - 115: New Dependency

Notice in Figure 5 - 115 that I defined a dependency between the *Annual Report Preparation for FY2014* project and its corresponding *Prepare for FY2014 Audit* project. In Figure 5 - 116, I cast the same two projects together in a *Mutual Inclusion* dependency.

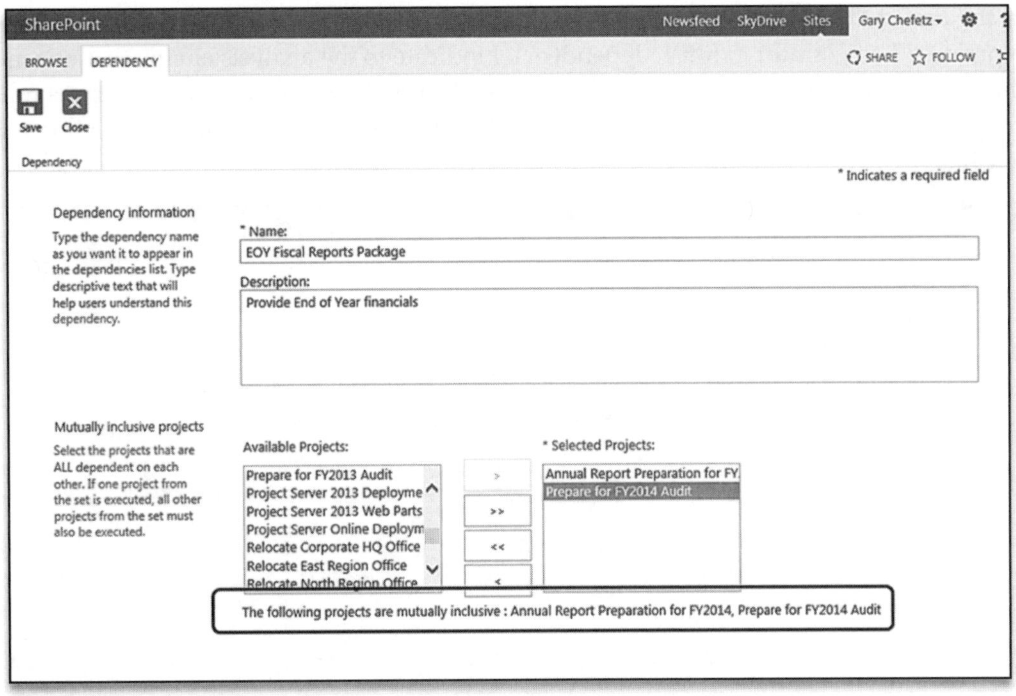

Figure 5 - 116: New Mutual Inclusion

Next, I go on to add a *Finish to Start* dependency to show that the *Annual Report Preparation for FY2014* project depends on the *Prepare for FY2014 Audit* project and must start after the latter completes as shown in Figure 5 - 117.

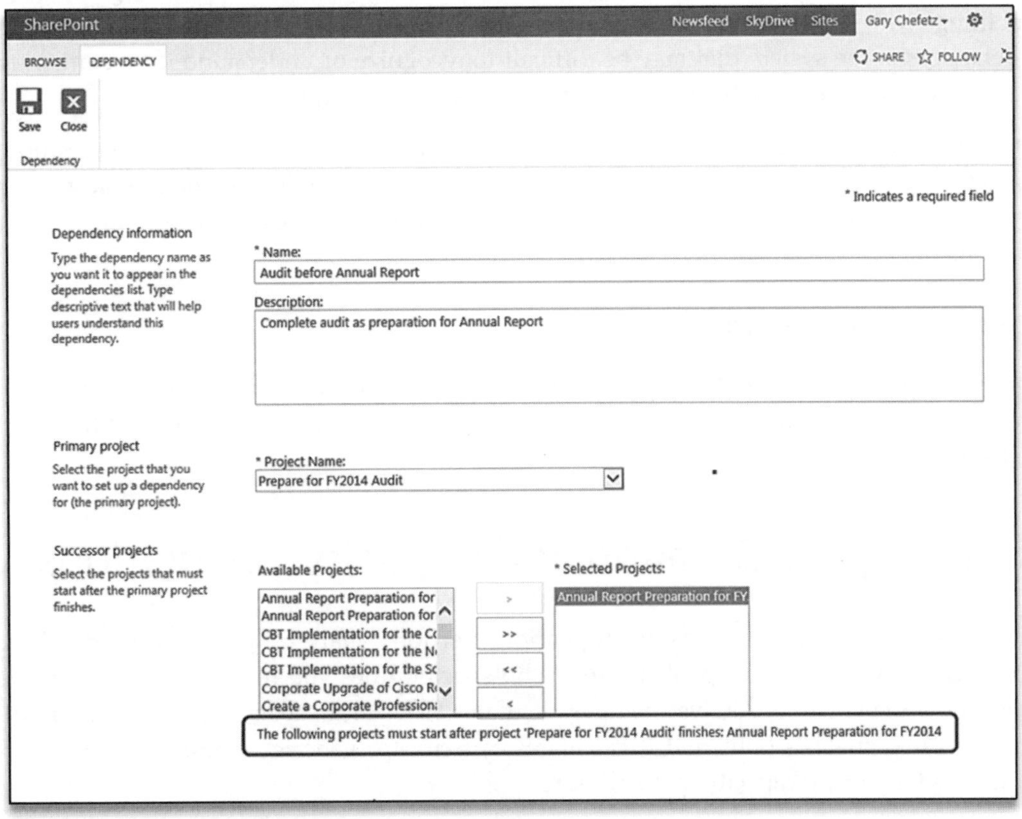

Figure 5 - 117: New Finish to Start dependency

Notice that in the *Project Dependencies* page shown in Figure 5 - 118 that I defined three dependencies involving the same two projects. Using a start to finish dependency I indicate to the analysis engine that one must complete before the other begins, and I indicate that the system should select both if it selects one using a mutually inclusive dependency and I indicate that it should exclude both if it excludes one of them by creating a mutually exclusive relationship.

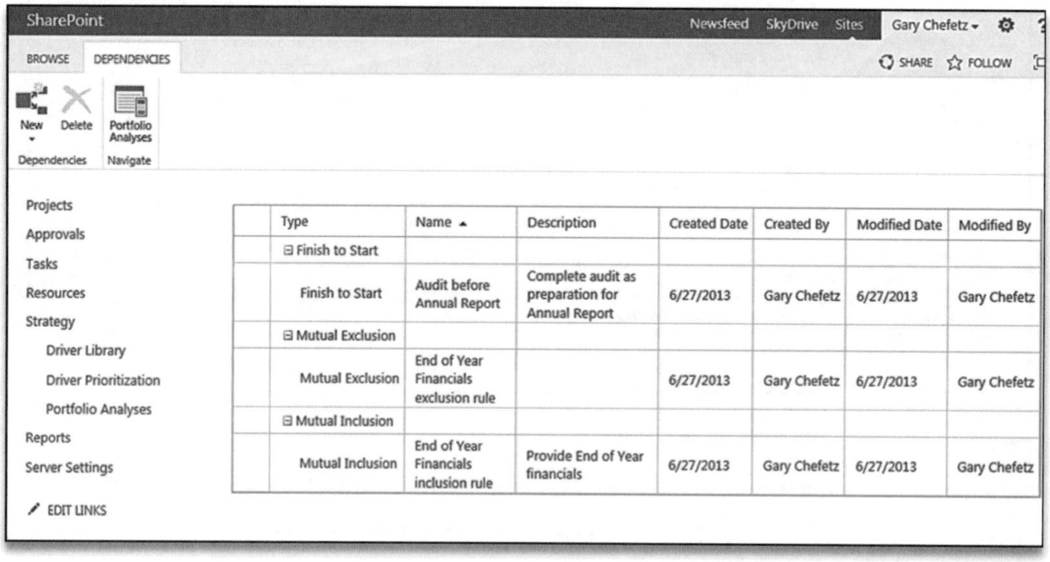

Figure 5 - 118: Project Dependencies page with entries

As you can see, these four simple project dependencies add a lot of depth to the modeling you can accomplish, but as with all things with Project Server 2013, you can go overboard with these. Remember that your web of logic will drive behaviors in the system that may be difficult to recognize or understand if they are overly complex, and remember that you are the one who has to understand the system output.

The project dependencies that you define apply to all portfolio analyses that you perform. Therefore, if you want to change project dependencies to run various scenarios, you must delete dependencies that you want to eliminate and create new ones that you want to apply. There is no way to undo these changes and return to a previous state without recreating the state manually.

Deleting Project Dependencies

To delete a project dependency, from the *Project Dependencies* page shown previously in Figure 5 - 118, select the header row for the dependency that you want to delete, and from the *Dependencies* section of the *Dependencies* ribbon, click the *Delete* button.

Understanding FTE Demand and Capacity Calculations

In order to use resource constraint analysis during various portfolio analyses, you must model demand in your projects and capacity in your resource pool. There are no specific rules you must follow, rather you need to be acutely aware of how the Portfolio Analysis engine calculates FTE's and capacity. Project Server 2013 calculates FTE values for portfolio analysis only, and it calculates capacity for generic resources differently for portfolio analyses than it does for general capacity in the resource pool.

FTE Demand Calculation Insight

When you enter full-time equivalents into a resource plan using a generic resource, the system includes the resources' *Max Units* value in the FTE calculation. For example, if you set the *Max Units* for a resource at 1000% (one thousand percent), and you assign that resource as three FTE's in a resource plan, the system calculates thirty (30) FTE's for that period.

Capacity Calculation Insight

Unlike capacity throughout the rest of the system, generic resources do not factor into modeled capacity in a portfolio analyses. This is important to know because you cannot use generic resources to model capacity. If you are adding portfolio analysis capability to your established Project Server implementation, you must examine your existing resource pool to make sure that your system administrator configured your resource pool suitably for generating clean capacity calculations in your portfolio analysis.

Demand and Capacity are Snapshots

Perhaps the most important thing to remember about demand and capacity calculated during the portfolio staging and analysis process represents a snapshot in time. The data recorded into your resource plan demand model does not recalculate unless you change the resource plan assignments. Changes that you make to your resource pool after you have created a resource plan do not update your existing resource plans. Similarly, when you create a new portfolio analysis, as I show you in the next section, the system calculates capacity at the time you create the analysis and these numbers do not change when you make changes to your resource pool capacity model. To consume updated capacity data, you must delete and recreate a portfolio analysis.

Working with Portfolio Analyses

Everything I covered in this module has led to configuring your system to perform portfolio analyses against a set of project proposals vetted through a structured governance process. From creating the elements of portfolio governance including phases, stages and PDP's, to creating a workflow with logical checkpoints to govern the proposal process, collectively these are the framework for your structured process. Next, I showed you how to create proposals, run them through the vetting process, and refine them for portfolio consideration. Now I show you how to run portfolio analyses using your project proposals as input.

Create a new Portfolio Analysis

Portfolio managers and administrators have permission to create new portfolio analyses in Project Server 2013. If you are using Project Server permissions mode, you can grant portfolio analyses permissions to other groups as well. To create a new portfolio analysis, in the *Strategy* section of the *Quick Launch* menu, click the *Portfolio Analyses* link to display the *Portfolio Analyses* page shown in Figure 5 - 119.

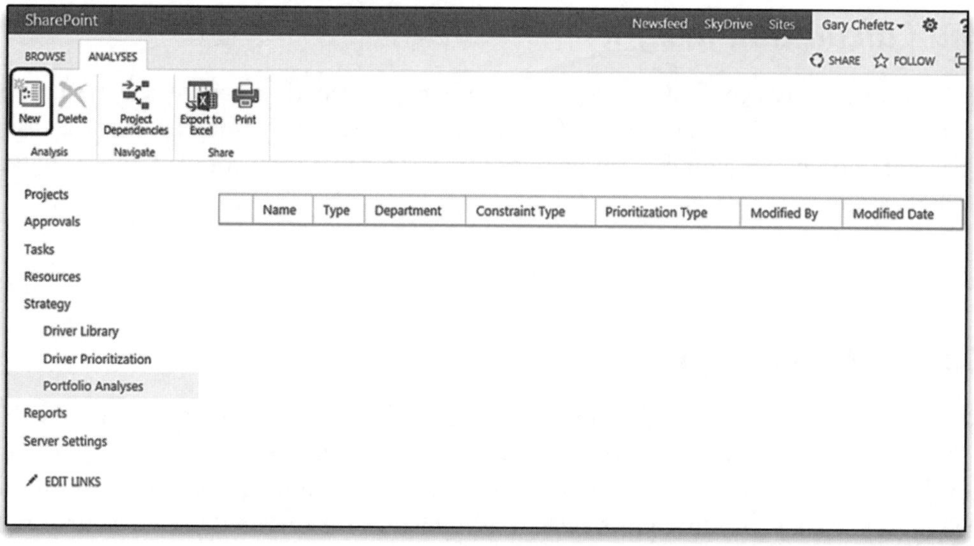

Figure 5 - 119: Portfolio Analyses page

From the *Analysis* section, click the *New* button. The system displays the *Define Properties* page shown in Figure 5 - 120 and Figure 5 - 122. This page begins a new portfolio analysis. In the *Name and Description* section, I give my portfolio analysis a name, *FY 2015 6-Month Authorization,* and I enter *First half of year spend* in the *Description* field. In the *Department* section, from the *Departments* pick list, I select the *Marketing* item. When I select the department, the system refreshes the *Prioritization Type* section to display the *Driver Prioritization* pick list with prioritizations belonging to that department. I select the *Executive Consensus for Marketing* prioritization.

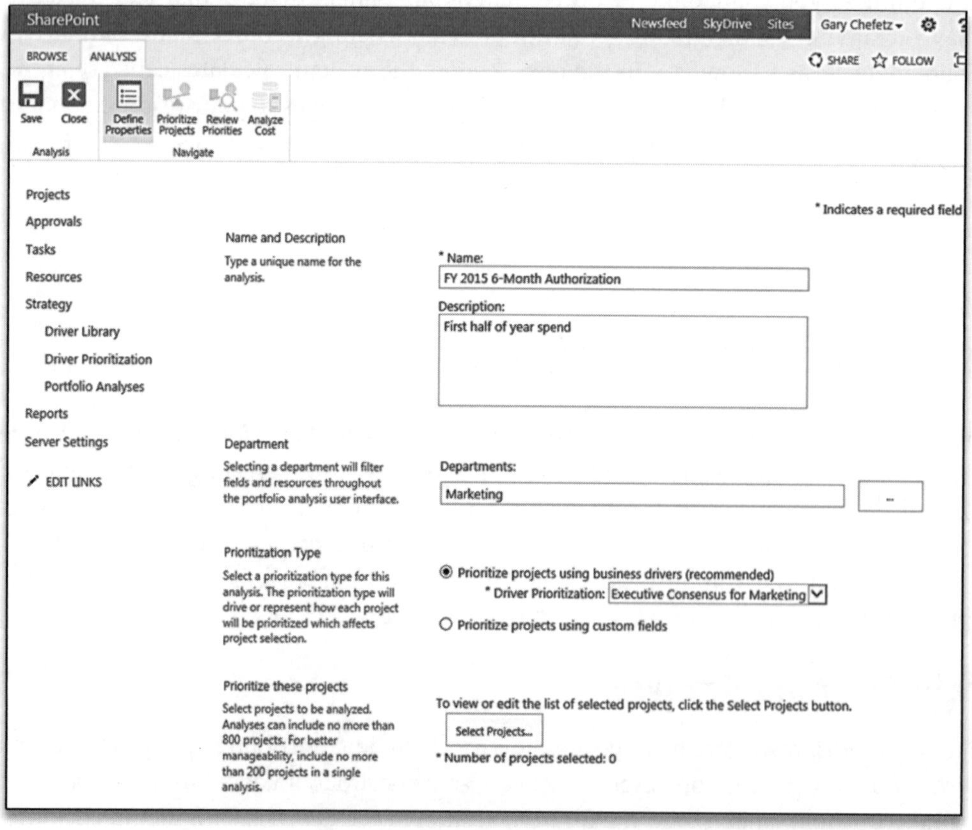

Figure 5 - 120: Define Properties page (for a new portfolio) top

The next step is to select the projects to analyze by clicking the *Select Projects…* button in the *Prioritize these projects* section. The system displays the *Select Projects* dialog shown in Figure 5 - 121.

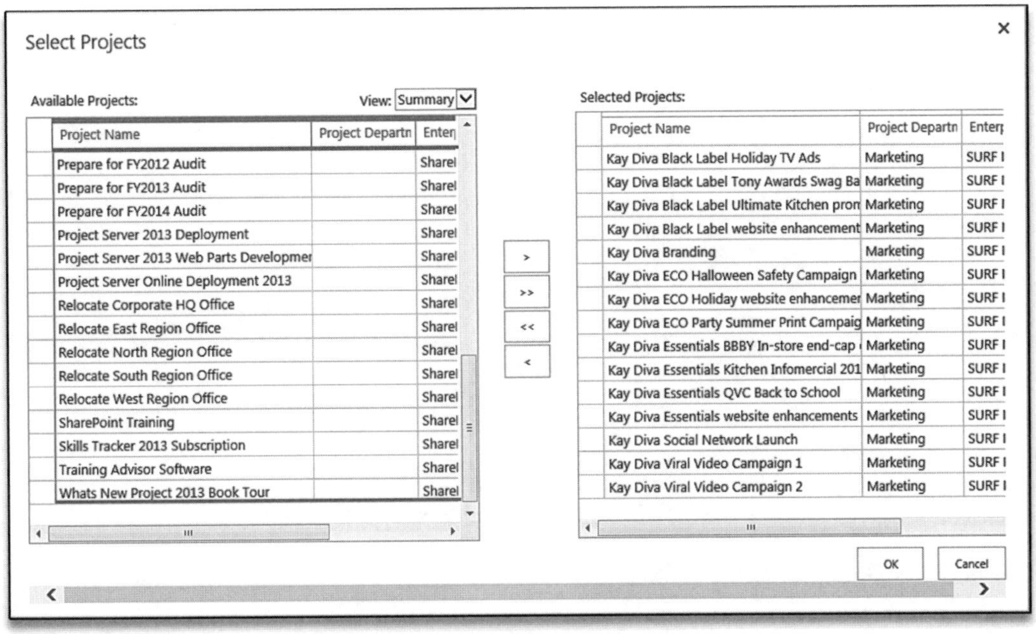

Figure 5 - 121: Select Projects dialog

Locate the projects that you want to include in your analysis and use the > button to move your projects to the *Selected Projects* section on the right. Click the *OK* button to complete your project selection. The system returns to the *Define Properties* page shown in Figure 5 - 122.

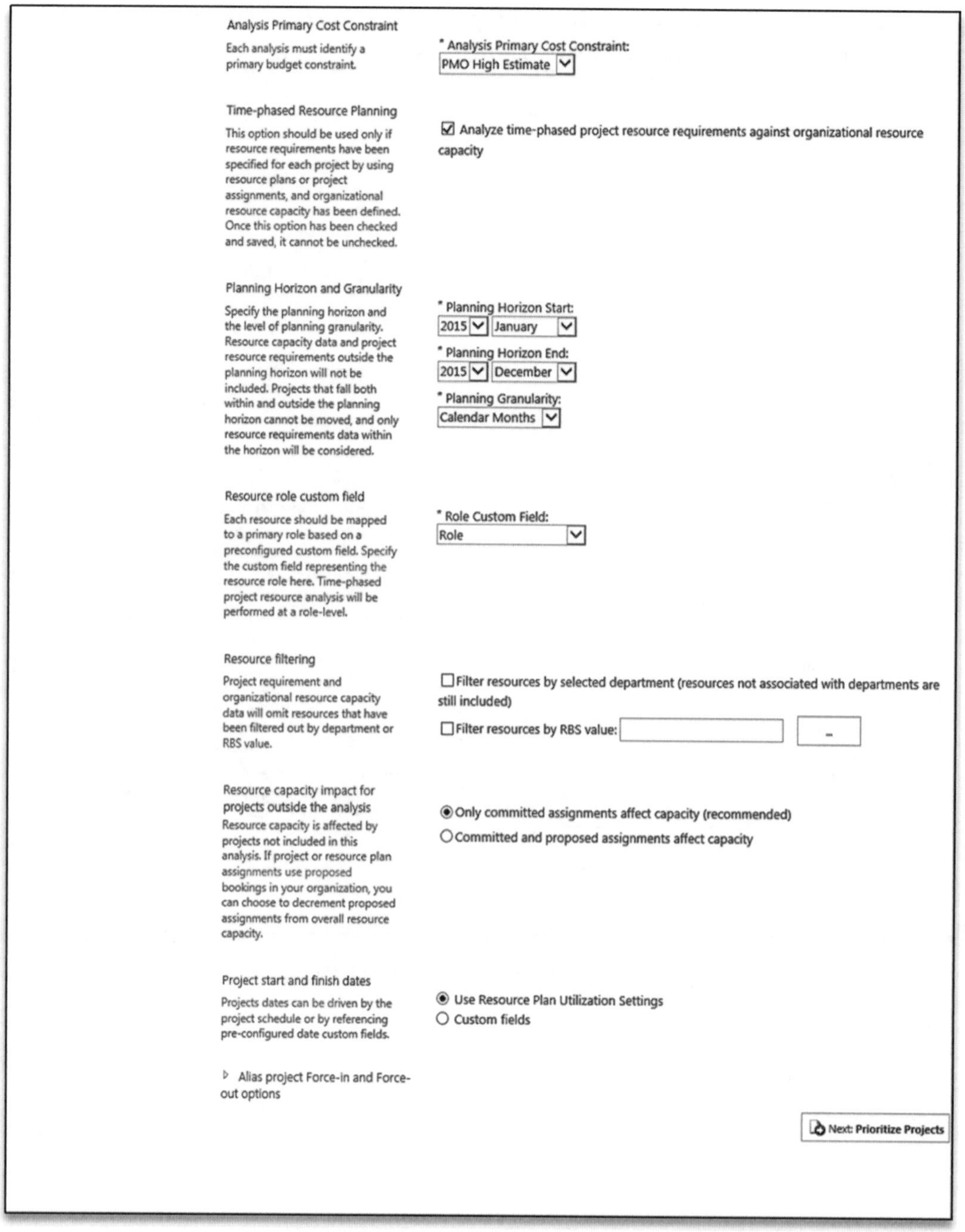
Analysis Primary Cost Constraint
Each analysis must identify a primary budget constraint.
* Analysis Primary Cost Constraint:
PMO High Estimate
Time-phased Resource Planning
This option should be used only if resource requirements have been specified for each project by using resource plans or project assignments, and organizational resource capacity has been defined. Once this option has been checked and saved, it cannot be unchecked.
Analyze time-phased project resource requirements against organizational resource capacity
Planning Horizon and Granularity
Specify the planning horizon and the level of planning granularity. Resource capacity data and project resource requirements outside the planning horizon will not be included. Projects that fall both within and outside the planning horizon cannot be moved, and only resource requirements data within the horizon will be considered.
* Planning Horizon Start:
2015 January
* Planning Horizon End:
2015 December
* Planning Granularity:
Calendar Months
Resource role custom field
Each resource should be mapped to a primary role based on a preconfigured custom field. Specify the custom field representing the resource role here. Time-phased project resource analysis will be performed at a role-level.
* Role Custom Field:
Role
Resource filtering
Project requirement and organizational resource capacity data will omit resources that have been filtered out by department or RBS value.
Filter resources by selected department (resources not associated with departments are still included)
Filter resources by RBS value:
Resource capacity impact for projects outside the analysis
Resource capacity is affected by projects not included in this analysis. If project or resource plan assignments use proposed bookings in your organization, you can choose to decrement proposed assignments from overall resource capacity.
Only committed assignments affect capacity (recommended)
Committed and proposed assignments affect capacity
Project start and finish dates
Projects dates can be driven by the project schedule or by referencing pre-configured date custom fields.
Use Resource Plan Utilization Settings
Custom fields
Alias project Force-in and Force-out options
Next: Prioritize Projects

Figure 5 - 122: Define Properties page (for a new portfolio) bottom

In the *Analysis Primary Cost Constraint* section, I select the *PMO High Estimate* custom field I created from the *Analysis Primary Cost Constraint* pick list. Next, I check the *Analyze time-phased project resource requirements against organizational resource capacity* checkbox, which refreshes the page displaying all of the sections you see below the checkbox in Figure 5 - 122. This allows me to set the *Role Custom Field* value, determine resource filtering, determine how the system behaves regarding committed and proposed assignments and whether to use custom files or resource plan utilization to represent project start and finish dates. Keep in mind that a simple project proposal without an associated schedule has no duration. It starts and ends on the same day. All of these selections affect the way the system determines capacity and demand and all of these are snapshot values. To change any of these parameters, you must start a new portfolio analysis. After you complete your property entries, click the *Next Pri-*

oritize Projects button at the bottom right. The system displays the *Prioritize Projects* page shown in Figure 5 - 123, which displays a summary of your selected projects along with their strategic alignment. This is your opportunity to adjust these impact statements within the portfolio analysis only, as any changes you make here do not affect the settings for the projects themselves. Click the *Next: Review Priorities* button at the lower right of the page or from the *Navigate* section of the ribbon, click the *Review Priorities* button.

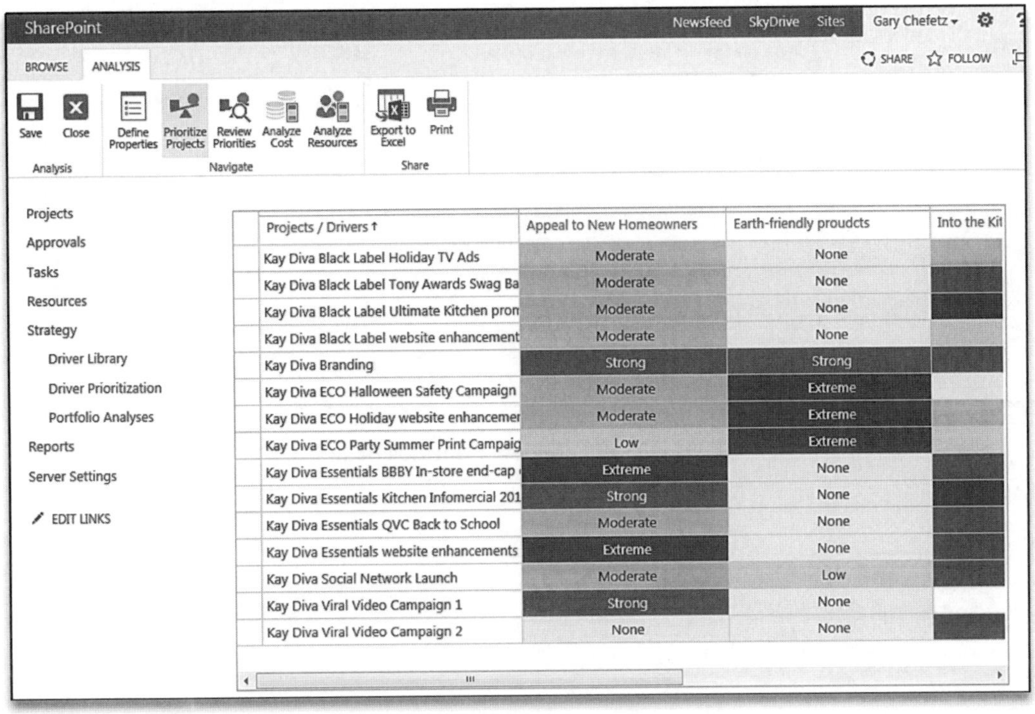

Figure 5 - 123: Prioritize Projects page

The system displays the *Review Priorities* page shown in Figure 5 - 124. Project Server 2013 displays the strategic alignment score of each project in your selection sorting them from highest priority to lowest. Click the *Next: Analyze Cost* button at the bottom right of the page.

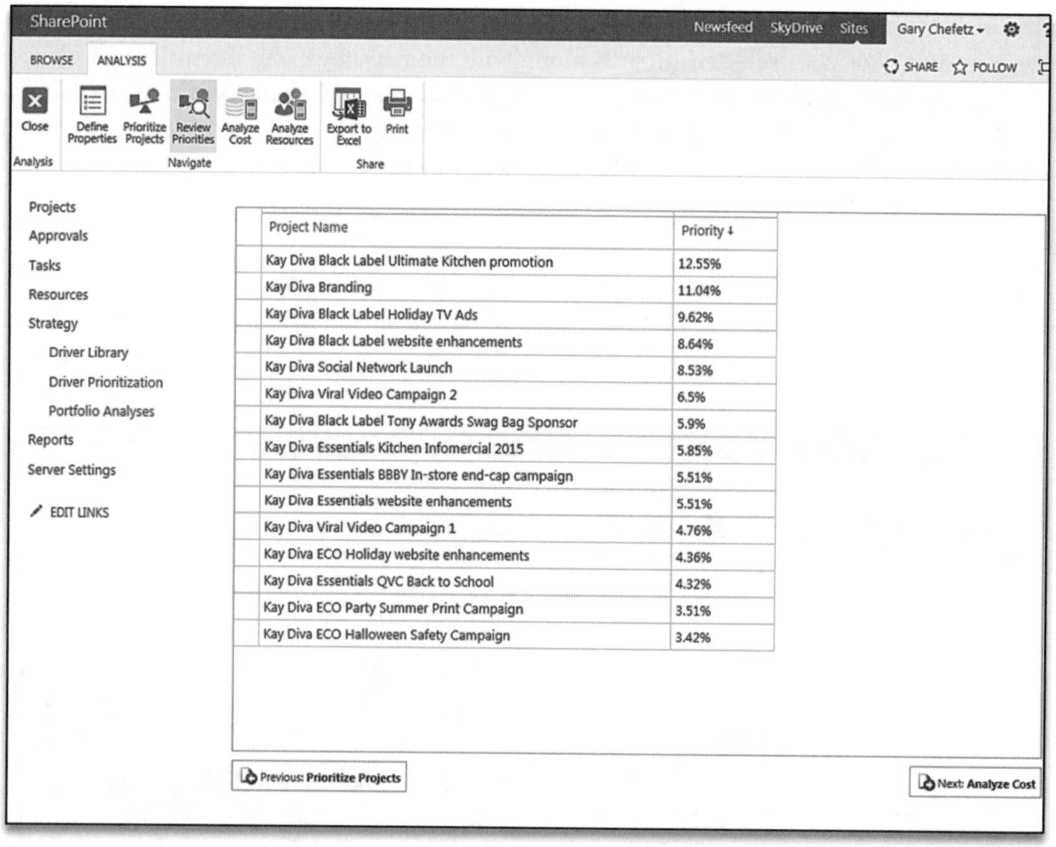

Figure 5 - 124: Review Priorities page

Analyzing Cost

Now that you have set and confirmed the settings, projects and parameters for your analysis, the next step is cost constraint analysis. When you click the *Next Analyze Cost* button at the bottom right or the *Analyze Cost* button on the ribbon, the system displays the *Analyze Cost* page shown in Figure 5 - 125. Beneath the *Analysis* ribbon, the page displays three sections, a *Metrics* section above a graphical display area for the *Efficient Frontier | Strategic Alignment* section, and a *Projects* section. Notice in the *Metrics* section that when you first land on this page, the system assumes that all projects are included and displays the total cost for the cost constraint field that you selected when you defined the analysis properties. In the example shown, I use the *PMO High Estimate* cost field. Notice also that the system summarizes the number of selected projects and the percentage of strategy realized in each selection scenario. Below the *Metrics* section, the figure shows the *Efficient Frontier* graph by default. The *Projects* grid displays all projects as selected by default and sorts on the *Priority* field.

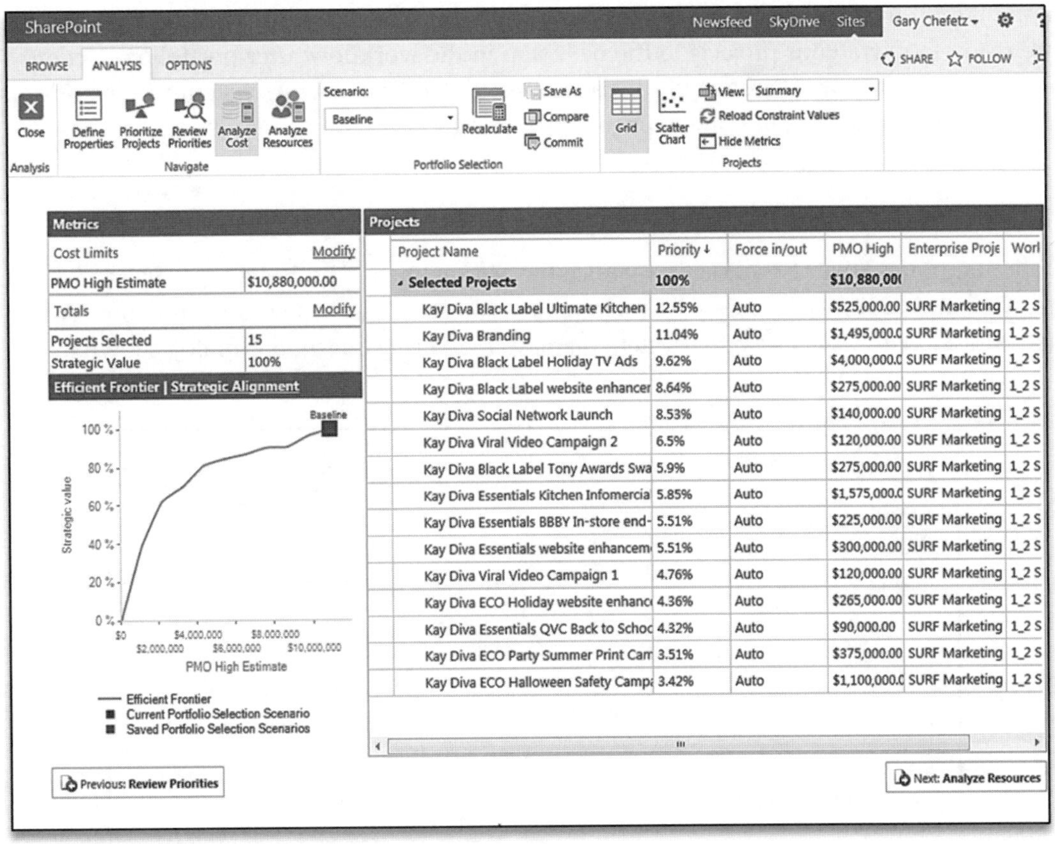

Figure 5 - 125: Analyze Cost page

To switch the graphical display to show strategic alignment, click the *Strategic Alignment* link above the graph. The system changes the display to the *Strategic Alignment* graph shown in Figure 5 - 126.

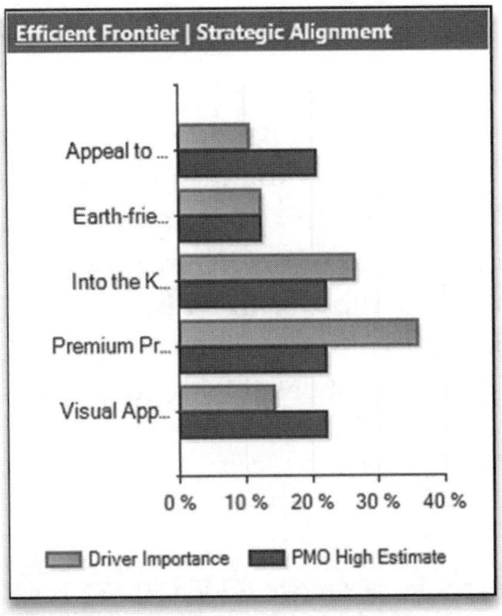

Figure 5 - 126: Strategic Alignment graph

The *Portfolio Selection* section of the *Analysis* ribbon shown previously in Figure 5 - 125, contains important tools that help you work with your analyses. The *Scenario* pick list allows you to switch between analysis scenarios that you save using the adjacent *Save As* button. Two additional buttons appear below this, *Compare* and *Commit*. You use the *Compare* button to compare scenarios and the *Commit* button to commit selected projects in the scenario when you are ready to move your projects to the next step in the workflow after portfolio selection. You use the prominent *Recalculate* button most frequently because this is what causes the system to reshuffle its selections when you change the constraint values on the page.

Returning your attention to the *Metrics* section, notice the *Modify* links in both the *Cost Limits* and *Totals* sections. *Cost Limit* is a **Constraint**. Not only does the system allow you to change constraints, it allows you to add them. When I click the *Cost Limits Modify* link, the system displays the *Modify Constraints* dialog shown in Figure 5 - 127.

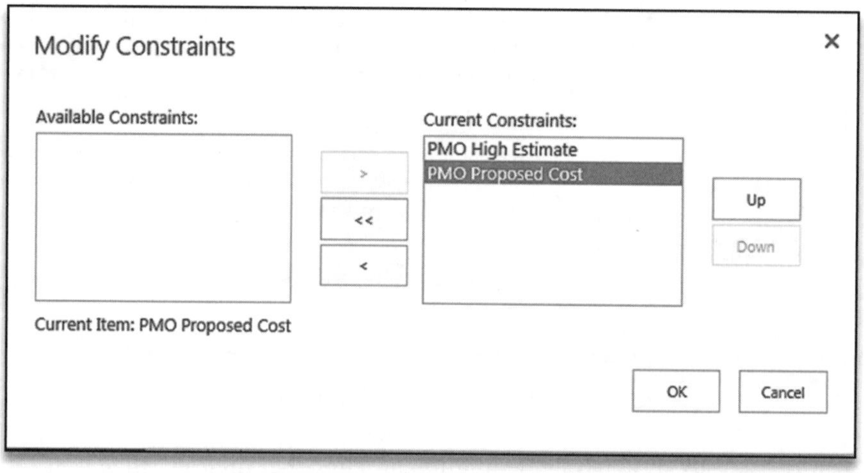

Figure 5 - 127: Modify Constraints dialog

Notice in the figure that I added the *PMO Proposed Cost* field to the *Current Constraints* area. Notice also that the system provides *Up* and *Down* buttons to change the ordering of constraints. This is because the system processes these from top to bottom. Keep in mind that the system respects all constraints that you set when moving projects in and out of the selected set. After you make your selections in the *Modify Constraints* dialog, click the *OK* button to close the dialog and accept your selections. The system redisplays the *Analyze Cost* page with the added constraints as shown in Figure 5 - 128. Notice that I also added the two fields to the *Totals* area. Adding totals is identical to the process of adding constraints, so I do not detail that process here.

Warning: A bug in the initial release of Project Server 2013 causes additional constraints to disappear from the analysis as you perform various functions that refresh the screen. You may need to add these multiple times during your session until Microsoft corrects the issue.

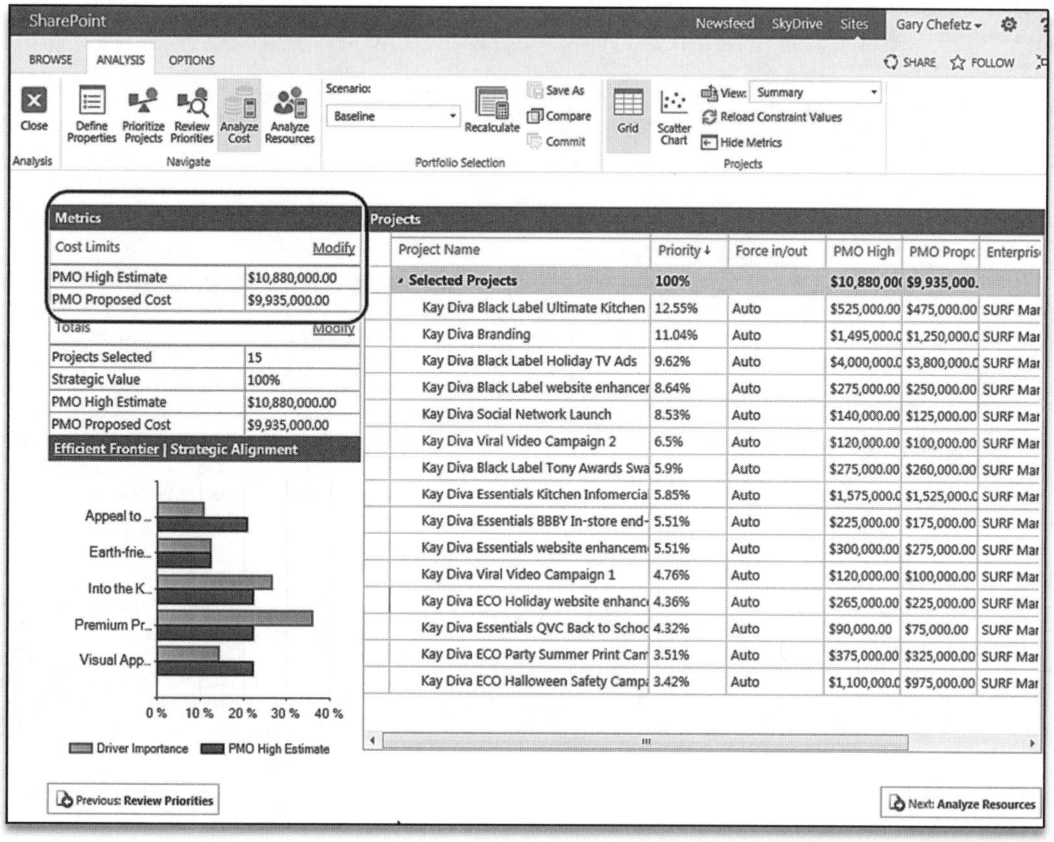

Figure 5 - 128: Analyze Cost page with additional constraints

Now that you understand the layout of the page information and tools, you should understand the scenario that I am analyzing in the example where my marketing department needs to determine which of its proposed projects to fund based on its available half-year budget for 2015. Notice now the values in the *Metrics* section. The marketing department has 15 proposed projects with a proposed cost just under $10 million and a high estimate of just under $11 million reflecting an average contingency allowance of around 10%. It is the fall of 2014 and marketing has an annual budget of $12 million for FY 2015. The goals of this analysis for marketing are:

- Allocate the first half-of the year budget
- Select projects that fit within the internal resource constraints
- Determine hiring needs for its contract labor force

The first thing I want to know is what can I get for half the budget, or $6 million, so I change the *High Estimate* field to $6,000,000. To see how my changes influence the strategic value of my portfolio, I click the *Analysis* tab, and then from the *Portfolio Selection* section, I click the *Recalculate* button. The system recalculates the portfolio scenario and redisplays the *Analyze Cost* page shown in Figure 5 - 129.

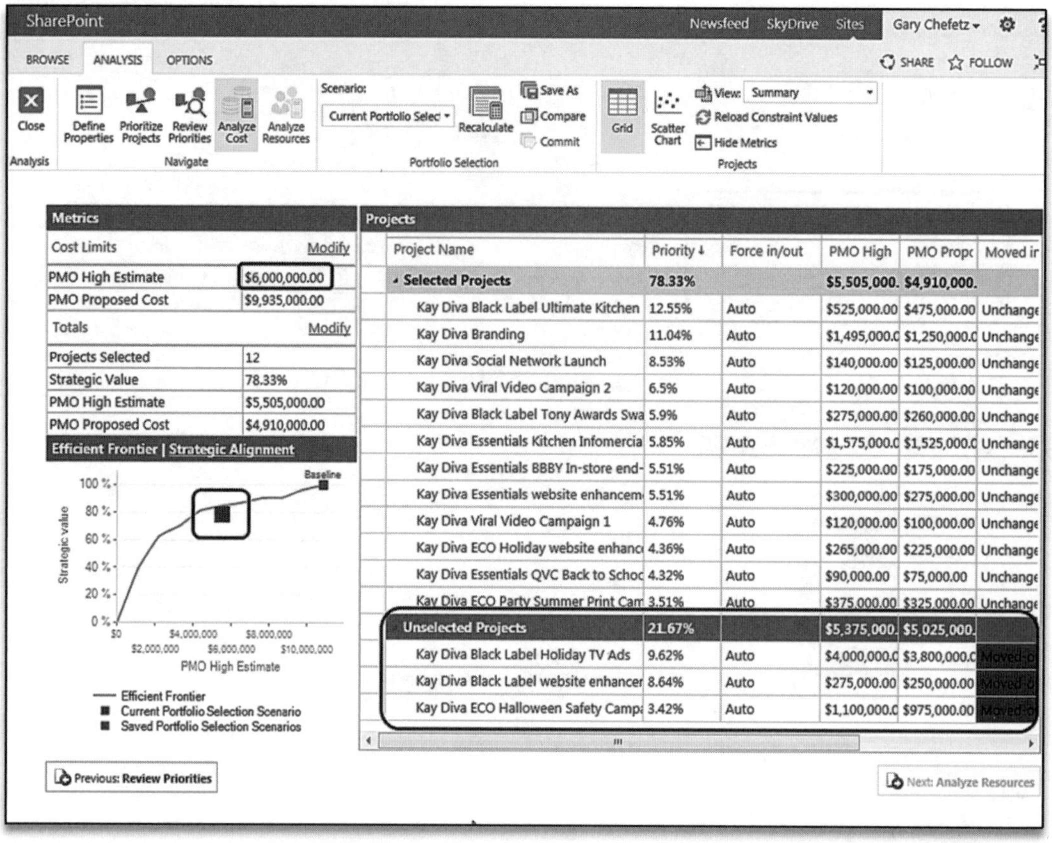

Figure 5 - 129: Analyze Costs $6 million scenario

The first thing to take note of in the redisplay is the appearance of the *Unselected Projects* group at the bottom of the data grid. Based on the cost constraint of $6 million dollars, the system deselected three projects. Because I added the additional total fields to the *Metrics* section, you can see that the high estimate cost of the selected projects is only $5.5 million, yet one of the projects the system moved out of the selection fits within the remaining budget. The $275,000.00 *Kay Diva Black label website enhancements* project is dependent on the *Kay Diva Black Label Holiday TV Ads* project. Because the system moved out that $4 million project, the system also moved out the dependent project. The marketing department set this dependency because they built the current version of the proposed project around sharing content with the larger project. Costs and resource usage will change for this project if the larger project fails to make the cut. The team will resubmit a revised version of the project in this event.

The good news is that the selected projects deliver 78% of the potential strategic value of the portfolio while spending only 54% of the total high estimated cost and an opportunity to achieve that strategic value for less than $5 million based on the proposed cost. That is a good measure of efficiency. The other good news is that marketing has enough money left in its budget to reclaim the 8.64% of strategic value it lost when the system moved out the dependent project when reconfigured as a stand-alone project. The bad news is that with a limited budget, the big TV ad promotion is just too costly to fund, especially considering the cost-to-strategic-value ratio. This explains the flattening of the *Efficient Frontier* curve as it approaches 80% of the portfolio value. The remaining cost in this portfolio adds dollars lacking in commensurate strategic value.

Information: Another way to view the flattening of the strategic *Efficient Frontier* curve is that the portfolio lacks enough good ideas to generate a straighter line. Having more good proposals with genuine potent impact on your business drivers, allows you to achieve higher efficiency in larger spends.

Saving a Scenario

Now that I have a working cost scenario, I need to save it so that I can continue with the process and analyze resources for the saved scenario. In the *Portfolio Selection* section of the *Analysis* ribbon, click the *Save As* button. The system displays the *Save Portfolio Selection Scenario* dialog shown in Figure 5 - 130.

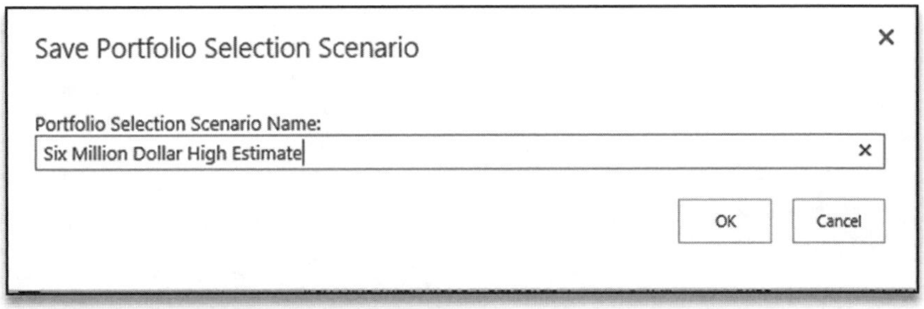

Figure 5 - 130: Save Portfolio Selection Scenario dialog

Enter a name for your scenario in the *Portfolio Selection Scenario Name* field and click the *OK* button to save your scenario. The system returns to the *Analyze Cost* page shown previously in Figure 5 - 129, however the *Portfolio* pick list in the ribbon now contains the name of your new scenario. Click the *Next: Analyze Resources* button to continue. The system displays the *Analyze Resources* page shown in Figure 5 - 131.

Analyzing Resources

Once you eliminate projects based on cost constraints, the system takes you to the next step, which is to determine which projects in the portfolio you can execute based on your resource constraints. As you can see in the figure, after comparing the resource demand in the marketing proposals against resource capacity in the database, the system moved all but three of the remaining projects to the *Not Selected* group. At this point, you might be thinking, "wow, the marketing department has a big budget but no resources." That is not the case at all.

The marketing department uses in-house resources for producers, copywriters, and copy editors. It also maintains an in-house staff of animators, graphic artists, web designers, and creative, but it supplements these roles with as much contract labor as required to execute its projects. Therefore, marketing uses this analysis step both to measure its ability to execute with it its in-house resource constraint, and for determining when and for how long to add contract labor. The marketing project proposals include budget for contract labor. The point is that you can use resource analysis for eliminating projects and/or for determining hiring needs.

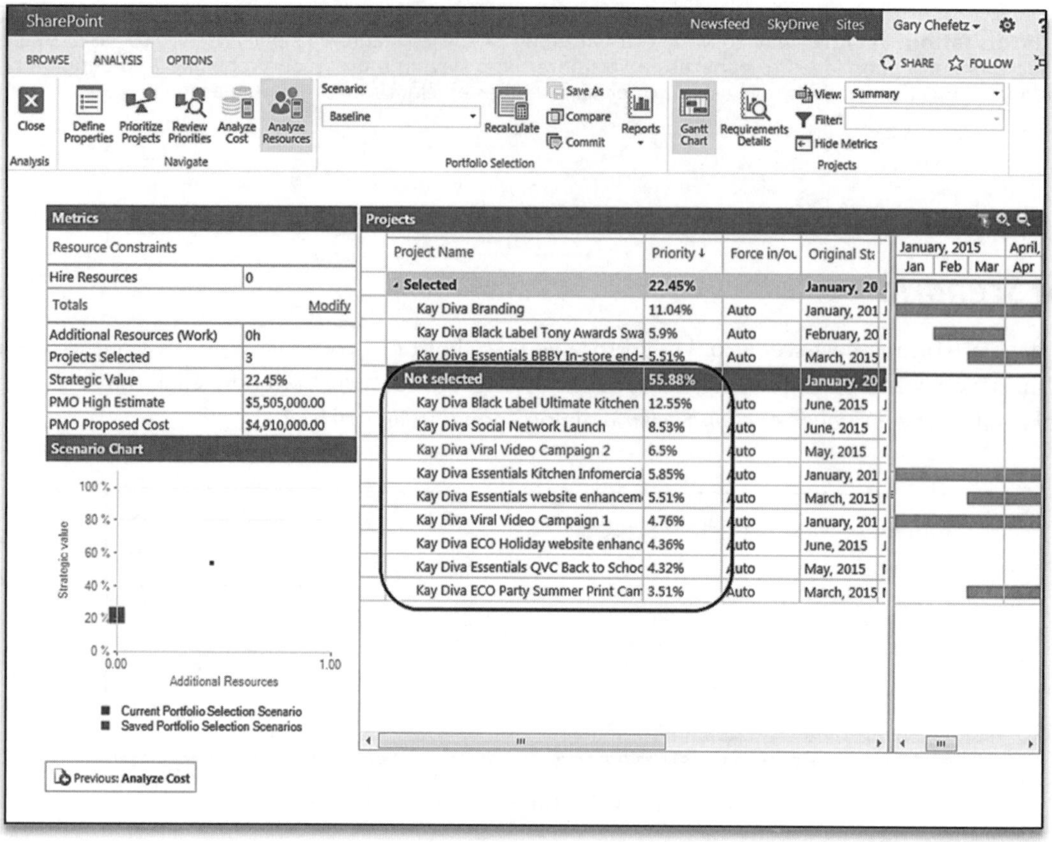

Figure 5 - 131: Analyze Resources page

Notice that the system defaults to the *Summary* view, which contains a Gantt chart. There are additional data columns that are important in this view. In the *Projects* section of the ribbon, you can use the *Hide Metrics* button to remove both the *Metrics* and *Scenario Chart* sections freeing up room for data display. Because the next logical step is to investigate the resource requirements that are causing the system to deselect the projects, from the *Projects* section of the ribbon, I click the *Requirements Details* button, and then I click the *Hide Metrics* button and the system displays the detailed resource requirements as shown in Figure 5 - 132.

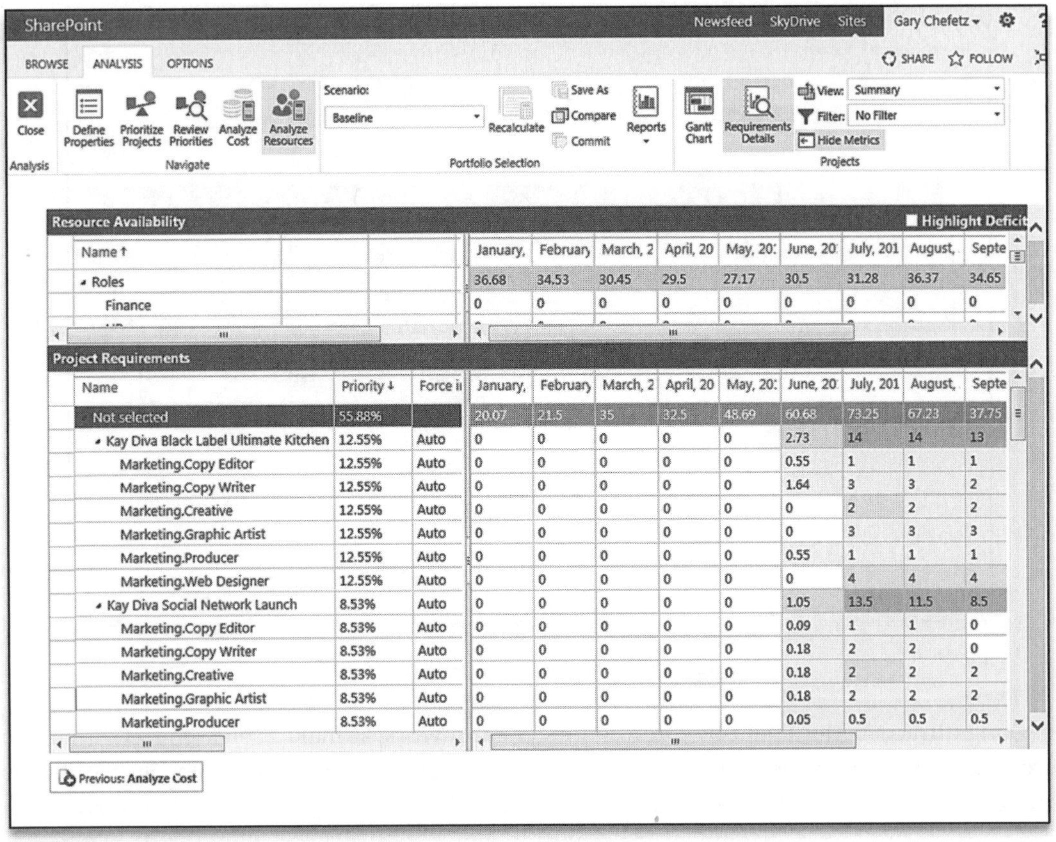

Figure 5 - 132: Resource Requirements Detail

The display is divided into quadrants with a summary of all resource availability in a split data grid at the top and the *Not selected* group of projects in a split data grid at the bottom showing the actual demand by project and role. You use this view to drill into resource demand detail.

Using the Deficit and Surplus Report

A better way to see the summary data is to use the *Deficit and Surplus* report. From the *Portfolio Selection* section of the ribbon, click the *Reports* pick list and select the *Deficit and Surplus* report. The system displays the deficit and surplus report shown in Figure 5 - 133. Notice that I highlighted the demand for web designers from May through September 2015. This is because all of the web projects focus heavily on back-to-school and holiday projects that contain "as late as possible" start dates in mind. The creative and animator roles reflect the same spike because projects tend to consume these skills together.

The report does not show any deficits for marketing's in-house staff roles indicating that there is enough producer, copywriter, and copy editor capacity to handle all of the projects, even the ones in the *Not Selected* group. The question the marketing department wants to answer is how to smooth out the demand bubble.

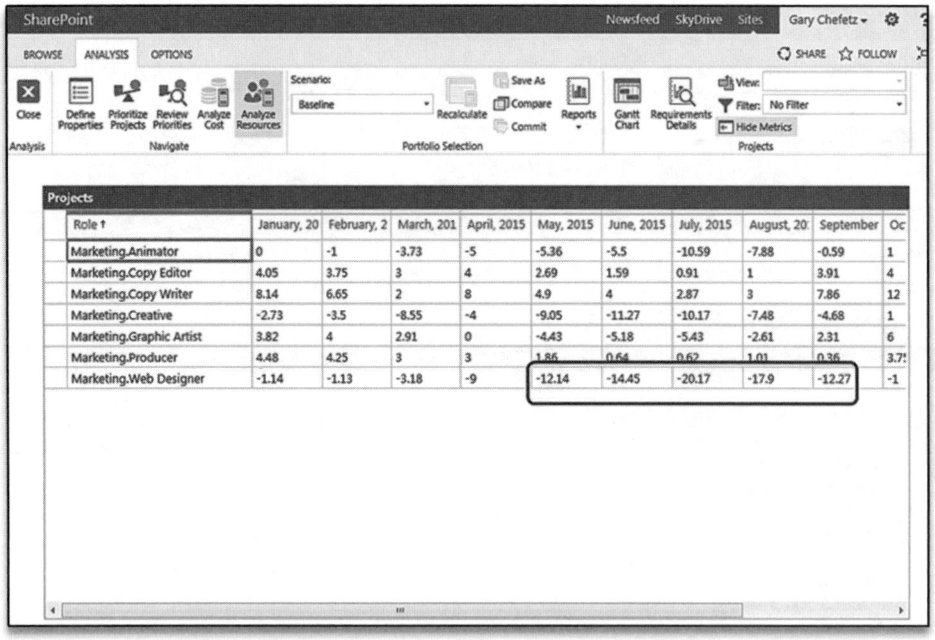

Figure 5 - 133: Deficit and Surplus report

Because marketing attracts better talent by offering longer-term work, it makes sense to flatten the demand bubble in the second and third quarters if possible. The reason marketing pushes these back is that they are dependent on obtaining product samples from product development. In order to pull a start date forward, it requires a firm commitment from product development for preproduction samples. From the *Projects* section of the ribbon, click the *Requirement Details* button to return to the view shown previously in Figure 5 - 132, then from the *Projects* section of the ribbon, click the *Filter* pick list and select the *Custom* item. The system displays the *Filters definition* page shown in Figure 5 - 134. Notice that the default filter state is to show all projects and all roles. Notice also, that I selected all of the roles in the *Selected Roles in Filter* section so that I can remove them and add back only a couple.

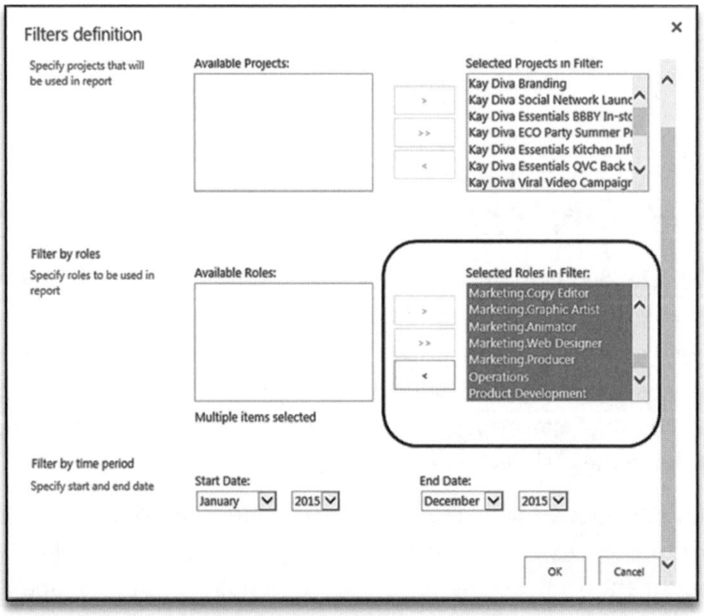

Figure 5 - 134: Filters definition page

Click the *OK* button to redisplay the *Resource Requirements Details* page as shown in Figure 5 - 135.

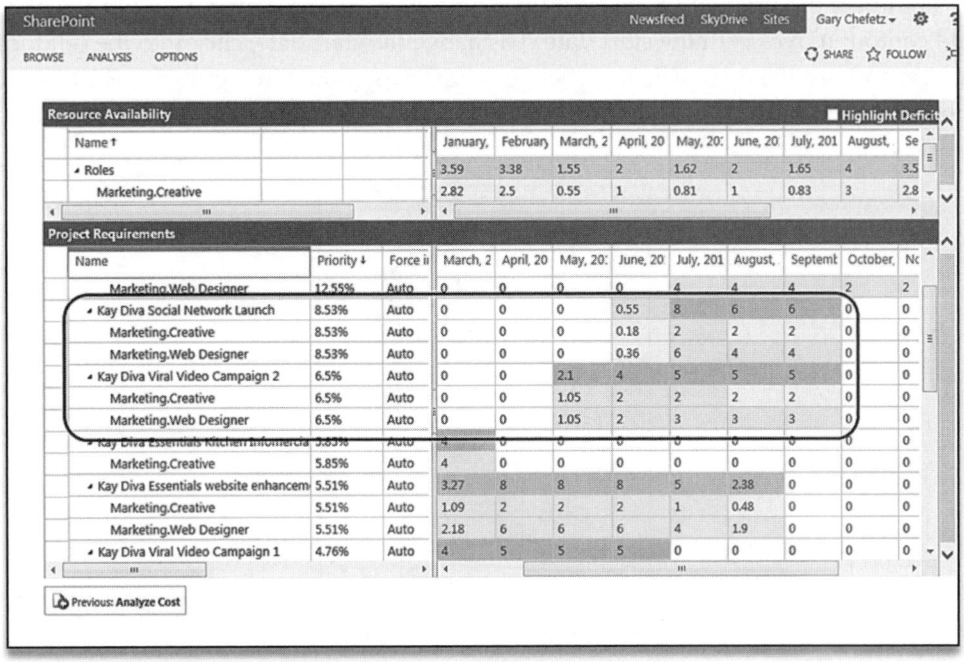

Figure 5 - 135: Resource Requirements Details with filter applied

Notice in the figure that I highlighted two projects, *Kay Diva Social Network Launch* and *Kay Diva Viral Video Campaign 2*. Marketing wants to answer the **What if** question, "what happens to demand for creative and web designers if we pull the *Kay Diva Viral Video Campaign 2* project forward to start in January with its sister project and push back the *Kay Diva Social Network Launch* project to December? To answer this question, from the *Projects* section of the ribbon, click the *Gantt Chart* button. The system displays the *Gantt Chart* display shown in Figure 5 - 136. Note that I pulled the splitter bar to the right of the *New Start* column.

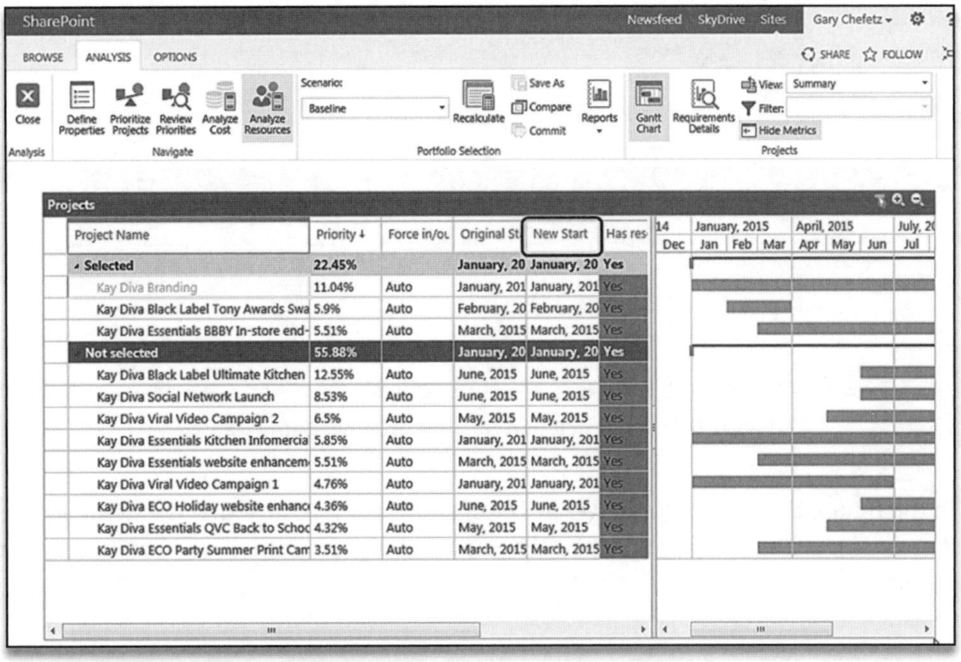

Figure 5 - 136: Gantt Chart with splitter bar pulled to right of New Start column

You use the *New Start* column to set new start dates for proposed projects within a portfolio analysis. The dates you set here do not affect the original proposal, rather only its resource demand within the analysis itself. The resource demand contour moves with the start date. To change the start date, click into the cell for the project that you want to change, and use the date picker to change the start as shown in Figure 5 - 137. Note that I am selecting January as the new start date for the *Kay Diva Viral Video Campaign 2* project.

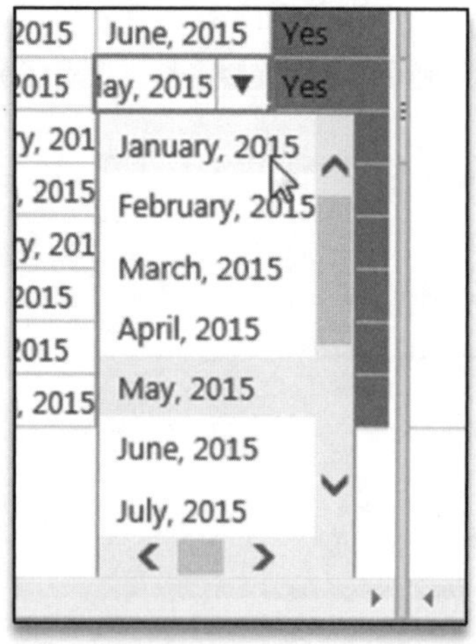

Figure 5 - 137: Change start date

After selecting new dates for your projects, you must recalculate the portfolio by clicking *Recalculate* button on the ribbon. After changing the start date on the *Kay Diva Social Network Launch* project, I recalculated the portfolio and then applied the *Deficit and Surplus* report as shown in Figure 5 - 138. Notice that the filter I set remains active until I change it in the session.

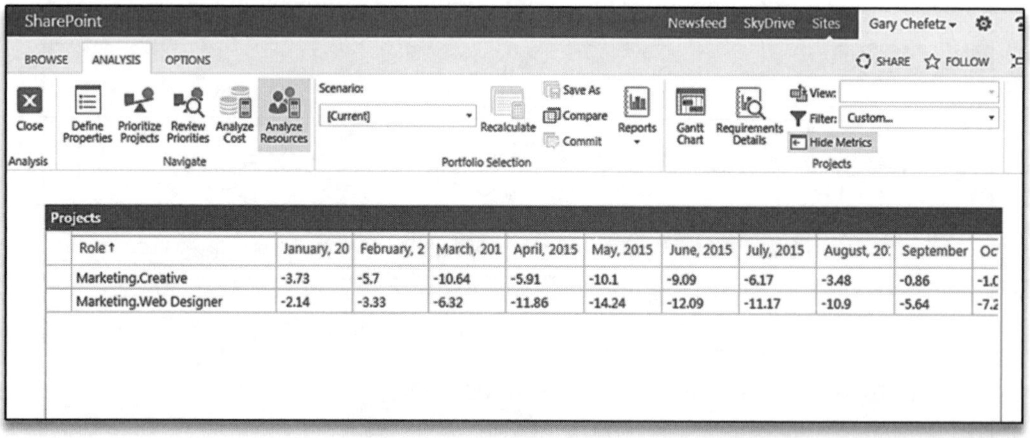

Figure 5 - 138: Deficit and Surplus after changing dates

As you can see in the figure, the answer to the **What-If** question is yes! Notice that the demand for web designers and creative resources is level where there previously was a bubble. Click the *Gant Chart* button on the ribbon to return to your analysis.

Forcing Projects In and Out

Now that I verified resource availability and leveled the contract labor demand to a manageable bell curve, I need to use the *Force in/out* feature to force the unselected projects in the portfolio analysis into the selected group. When you click into a cell in the *Force in/out* column, the system exposes a pick list icon as you can see to the right of the selected cell in Figure 5 - 139. Unfortunately, a production bug displays this pick list with a transparent background so its labels display over the data. If you look closely enough in the area I highlighted in the figure, you can just make out the two selections: *Forced-in* and *Forced-out.*

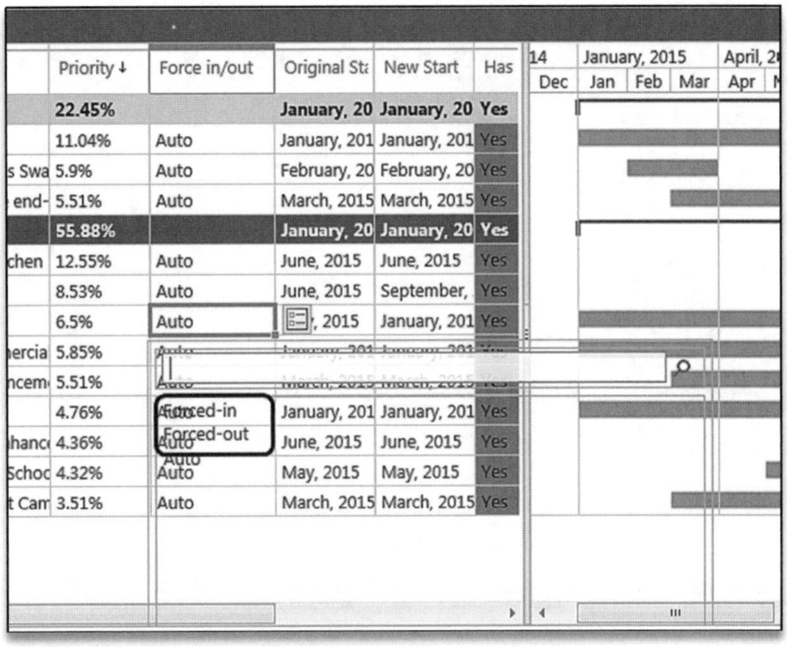

Figure 5 - 139: Using Force in/out

At the time of this writing, Microsoft was working on a fix for this display bug that affects other pick lists in the system.

Using the Hire Resources Field and Hired Resources Report

During resource analysis, the system accepts a *Hired Resources* parameter that allows you to specify a number of resources to hire and the system responds by moving projects into the *Selected* group. Figure 5 - 140 shows my analysis after hiring 53 resources. The system selects all projects when I specify this number and click the *Recalculate* button.

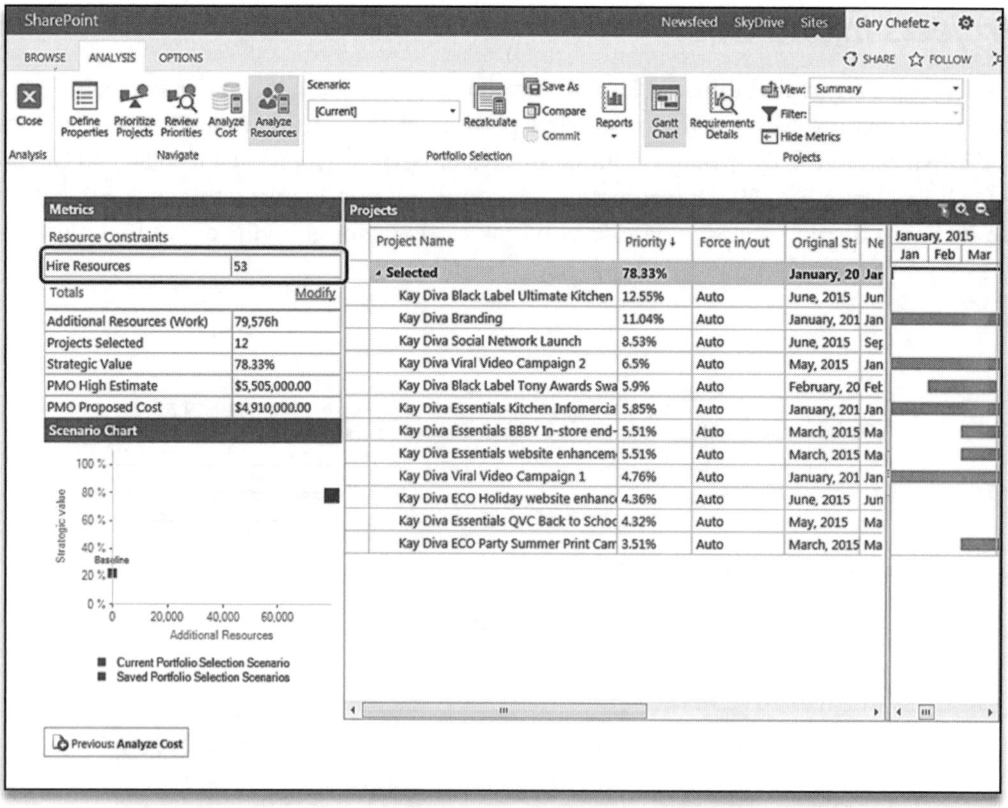

Figure 5 - 140: Analysis with 53 hired resources

To see the details about how the system calculated this number, click the *Reports* pick list and select the *Hired Resources* report. The system displays the *Hired Resources* report shown in Figure 5 - 141.

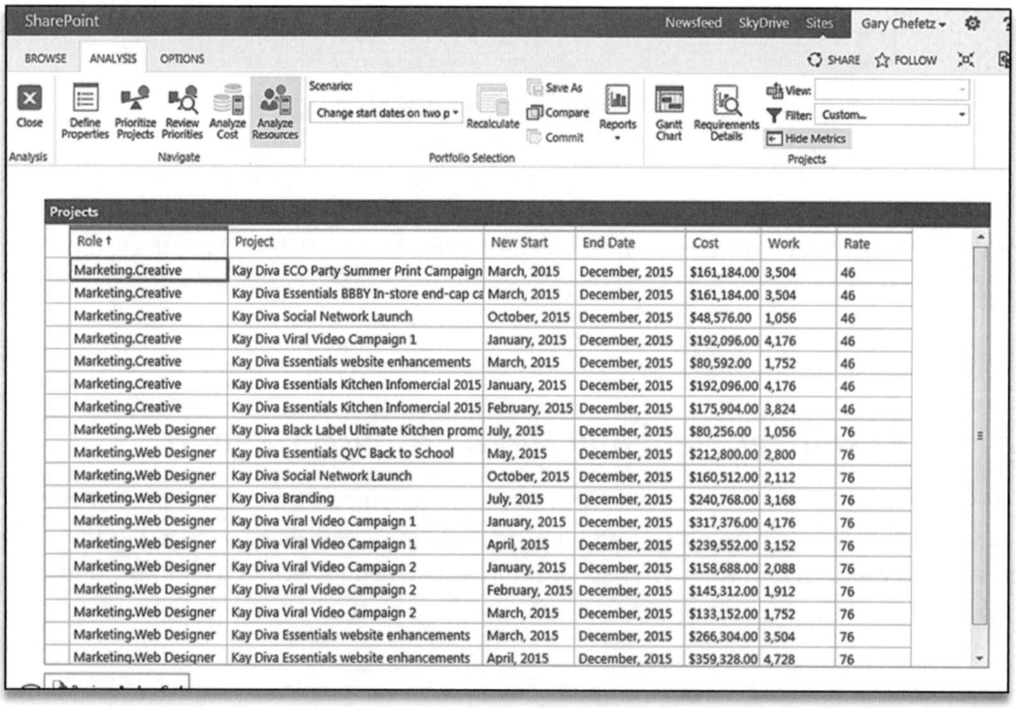

Figure 5 - 141: Hired Resources Report

By default, the report displays sorted by *Role* field and then by *Project* field. Notice that the system calculates the estimated cost for the resources. It is very likely that the rates you see in the *Rate* column do not reflect the base rates you set for generic resources; rather, the system averages the rate across resources it finds tagged with the *Role* field. To perform additional analysis on this data, like all pages containing data, you can click the *Options* ribbon and export the data to Excel. At this point, however, I am happy with my analysis and I save the scenario using the technique I showed you previously under the *Saving a Scenario* topical heading.

Comparing Analyses

Click the *Analysis* tab, and then from the *Portfolio Selection* section, click the *Compare* button. The system displays a comparison matrix between the two resource scenarios as shown in Figure 5 - 142. Note that I can export this data to Excel if I want to share these details with colleagues. Click the *Close* button.

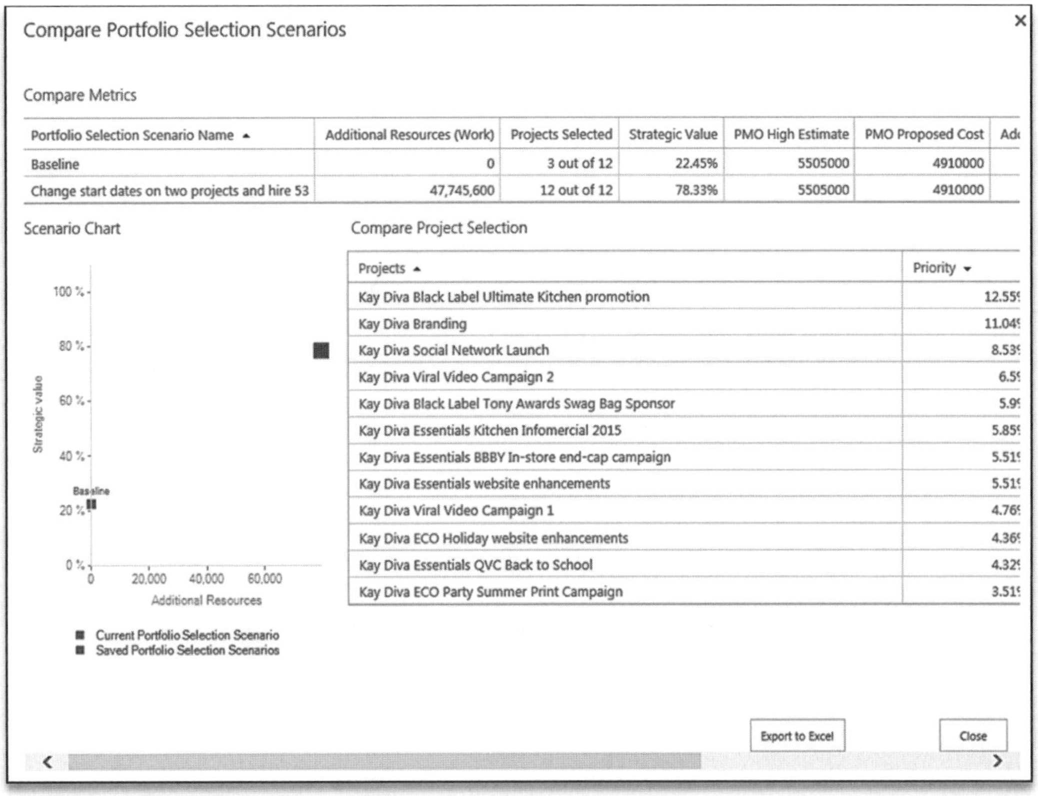

Figure 5 - 142: Compare Analyses

Portfolio Analysis Conclusion

Project Server 2013's portfolio analysis capabilities are very powerful. I only touch on some of the core features, which include comparing projects against strategic drivers and performing cost-based and resource-based what-if scenarios. It is important to note that nearly everything you do in the *Portfolio Analyses* area of PWA in no way impacts actual projects, meaning you do not have to worry about a scenario where moving a project out in a portfolio analysis actually changes a project manager's project plan.

Module 06

Creating Enterprise Projects

Learning Objectives

After completing this module, you will be able to:

- Create a new enterprise project using Project Pro 2013
- Create a new project from an enterprise template
- Define an enterprise project
- Set the task mode option
- Set options in the Project Options dialog
- Save a project
- Understand the local cache
- Open and close projects
- Delete or rename a project
- Work with offline projects
- Import a project into the enterprise

Inside Module 06

Creating an Enterprise Project Using Project Pro 2013

As I indicated previously in Module 05, you may create a new enterprise project as a proposed project from the *Project Center* page in Project Web App using the demand management process. You may also create a new enterprise project in Project Pro 2013 using either of the following methods:

- Import the project into the Project Server database using the *Import Project* wizard in the Project Pro 2013 client while connected to Project Server 2013.
- Create the project in the Project Pro 2013 client while connected to Project Server 2013 and save the project in the Project Server database.

Warning: Do not open a .mpp project file, click the *File* tab, click the *Save As* tab in the *Backstage*, and then save the project in the Project Server database. Saving a .mpp local project file directly into the Project Server database bypasses all of your organization's standards for setting project, resource, task, and calendar information in the project.

I discuss both of these methods for creating an enterprise project as separate topics in this module.

Importing a Local Project into Project Server 2013

If you have existing non-enterprise projects saved outside the Project Server system, you must bring them into the Project Server database by importing them. I recommend that you always use the *Import Project* wizard. Before you import either a project or a template into the system, close any open projects. If you have a project open, the system assumes that you want to import the open project.

1. Open the project file that you want to import.
2. Click the *File* tab and then click the *Save As* tab in the *Backstage.*
3. If necessary, select your instance of Project Web App and select the *Use Import Wizard* option located below the *Save* button highlighted in Figure 6 - 1.

Best Practice: MSProjectExperts recommends as a best practice to use the *Import Project* wizard for importing non-enterprise projects into the Project Server database. You must also close any open projects before beginning the import process. See the Warning below, concerning issues using the tool as of the writing of this book.

Warning: As of the writing of this book, with Project Server 2013 April CU 2013 applied in our installation, I had numerous problems with the projects that were imported using this tool. The behavior included missing assignments and resources, and scheduling engine calculations that were incorrect with what appeared to be "ghost assignments" that interfered with the calculations. It appeared as though many of the projects I imported using the wizard, with the purpose of writing this book, were now corrupt. Therefore, MSProjectExperts recommends not using the *Import Project* wizard in Project Pro 2013, at this time until we hear from Microsoft that the *Import Project* wizard is fixed. Another very annoying behavior is that on incomplete tasks with Actuals reported, the system will not replace a local resource with its equivalent enterprise resource, forcing the user to manually replace these resources using the Assign Resources dialog after the import process is complete, this is also true if you use *File➢Save As.*

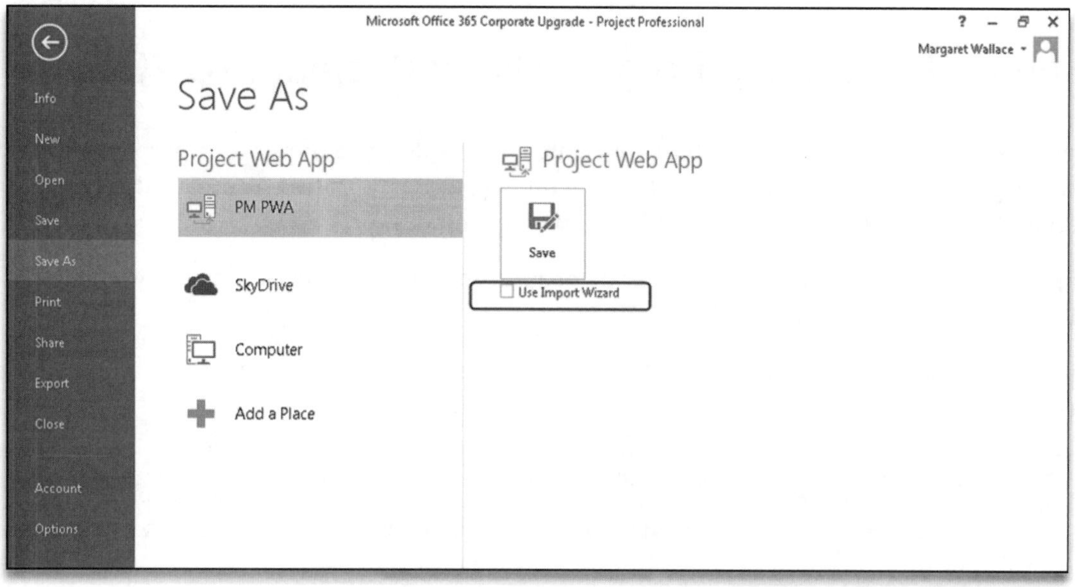

Figure 6 - 1: Save As page in Project Pro 2013

4. Click the *Save* button and Project Pro 2013 displays the *Import Project* wizard shown in Figure 6 - 2. The *Import Project* wizard assists you with the process of importing non-enterprise projects into the enterprise environment.

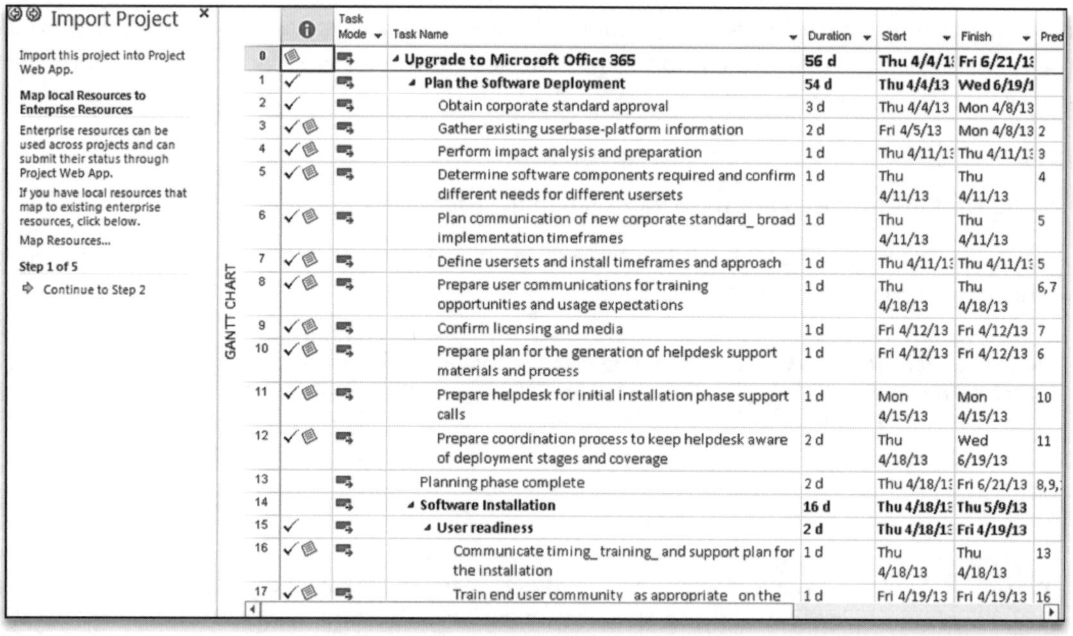

Figure 6 - 2: Import Project wizard

5. If your project contains resources, click the *Map Resources* link in the sidepane. The system displays the *Map Local to Enterprise Resources* dialog shown in Figure 6 - 3.

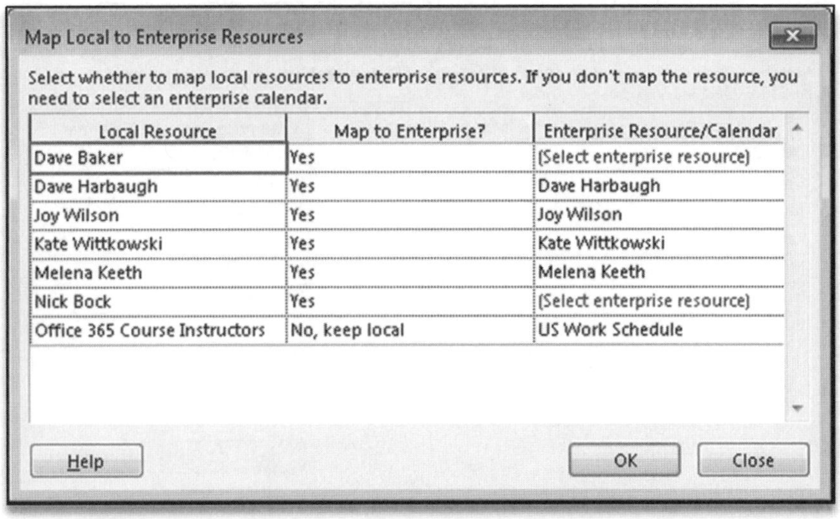

Figure 6 - 3: Map Local to Enterprise Resources dialog

Use the *Map Local to Enterprise Resources* dialog to match local resources in the project with enterprise resources in your organization's Enterprise Resource Pool (ERP). The default behavior of this dialog is as follows:

- If you use the exact same name for the local resource as the name of an enterprise resource, the system maps the local resource to the enterprise resource automatically. For example, notice in Figure 6 - 3 that the name of the local resource, Dave Harbaugh, exactly matches the name of the enterprise resource, Dave Harbaugh.

- If the name of the local resource does not match the name of any enterprise resource, then the system leaves the local resource unmatched by displaying *(Select enterprise resource)* in the *Enterprise Resource/Calendar* pick list. Notice in Figure 6 - 3 that local resources Dave Baker, Nick Bock, and Office 365 Course Instructors do not map to any enterprise resources in the ERP.

6. To map a resource, click the *Map to Resource?* pick list and select the *Yes* item on the list.

7. Click the *Enterprise Resource/Calendar* pick list and select the name of the enterprise resource in the ERP that represents the local resource.

You must repeat this process individually for every local resource in the project that does not match a corresponding enterprise resource in the ERP. The exception to this rule, however, concerns resources that you want to leave as local resources intentionally. For example, you can leave resources as local resources if they are contractors or consultants who are not in your ERP, or they are generic resources such as the Office 365 Course Instructors resource shown previously in Figure 6 - 3.

Notice in Figure 6 - 4 that I map the local resource Dave Baker to the enterprise resource David Baker, and I map the local resource Nike Bock to the enterprise resource Nicolas Bock. Notice also that the Office 365 Course Instructors generic resource is set to *No, keep local* for the *Map to Enterprise?* pick list, since this resource is a contractor that is not part of the organization's ERP.

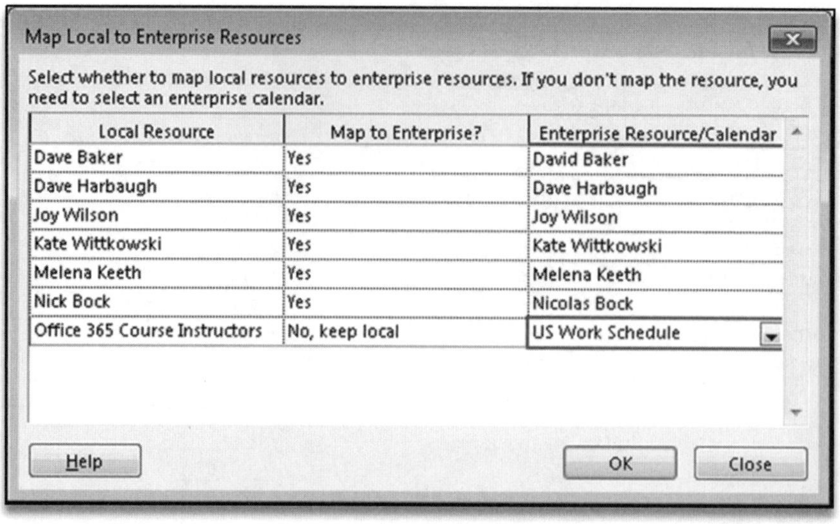

Figure 6 - 4: Match resources in the Map Local to Enterprise Resources dialog

8. When you finish mapping local resources with enterprise resources, click the *OK* button in the *Map Local to Enterprise Resources* dialog, and the system returns to the *Import Project* wizard sidepane.

9. Click the *Continue to Step 2* link in the sidepane. If you are not a Project Server administrator, the system may display a warning message indicating that you may not have permission to add the local resources to the ERP, and refers to any resources you left as local resources in the project. Furthermore, the message in this dialog means what it implies: because you are not a Project Server administrator, you do not have permission to add the local resources to the ERP.

If you see the warning message, click the *OK* button. Project Server 2013 displays the *Import Resources* page of the *Import Project* wizard sidepane as shown in Figure 6 - 5. This page lists the number of local resources in the project, along with the number of resource errors. The system might trigger a resource error if the Windows user account information for a resource no longer matches the same information on the network or is a duplicate of one in use in the ERP.

Information: If you see resource errors on the *Import Resources* page, cancel the process of importing the local project and contact your Project Server administrator immediately for assistance. Only someone who is a Project Server administrator can correct resource errors.

Best Practice: MSProjectExperts recommends that you spend time to clean up your stand-alone projects and templates before attempting to import them. Because the system allows you to map a resource only once, you should make sure that all resources in your stand-alone projects are consistently named and appear in only one form in each project.

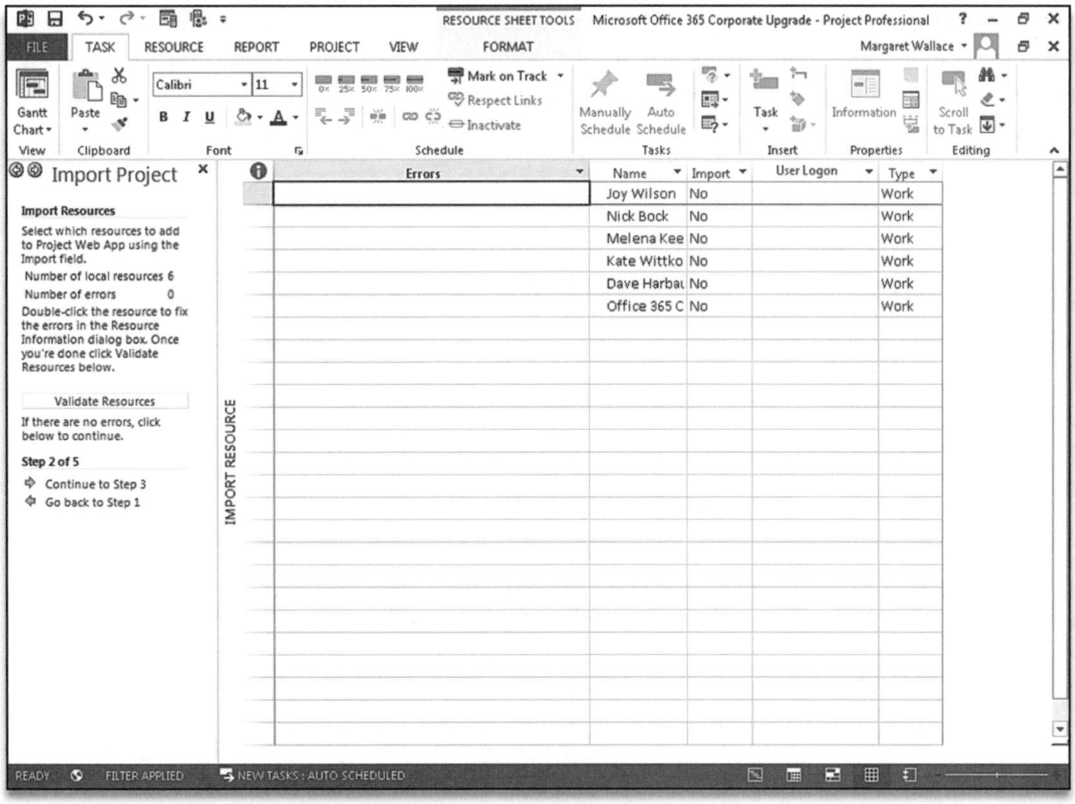

Figure 6 - 5: Import Resources page of the Import Project wizard sidepane

Notice in Figure 6 - 5 that the *Import Project* wizard shows six resources as local resources. The *Import* field on this page offers me the option to import these resources as new enterprise resources, which in this case, I do not want. In some cases, however, you might actually need to import a local resource as a new enterprise resource. To do this, set the *Import* field value to *Yes* and continue the import process. If you do not want to import the local resource as a new enterprise resource, make sure you set the *Import* field value to *No* as shown *in* Figure 6 - 5.

Warning: The default functionality in Project Server 2013 is to set a *No* value in the *Import* field for each local resource for which you selected the *No, keep local* option in the *Map Local to Enterprise Resource* dialog. If you complete the project import process with the *Yes* value selected, the system automatically imports all of the resources you designated as local resources, and converts them into enterprise resources (requires security group permission: *Edit Enterprise Resource Data*).

Warning: The default behavior of the *Import Project* wizard in Project Server 2013 is to leave local resources on in-progress tasks (tasks with Actual Work and Remaining Work > 0 hours), even when you match the local resource to an enterprise resource. The wizard correctly transfers completed tasks and not started tasks to the mapped enterprise resources. After importing the project, you must manually replace the local resources with enterprise resources using the *Replace* functionality in the *Assign Resources* dialog.

10. After correcting any resource errors, click the *Validate Resources* button in the *Import Project* wizard to confirm there are no longer any errors. Click the *Continue to Step 3* link in the sidepane when you complete the *Import Resources* page. Project Server 2013 displays the *Map Task Custom Fields* page in the *Import Project* wizard shown in Figure 6 - 6. If necessary, change the view to the *Gantt Chart* view.

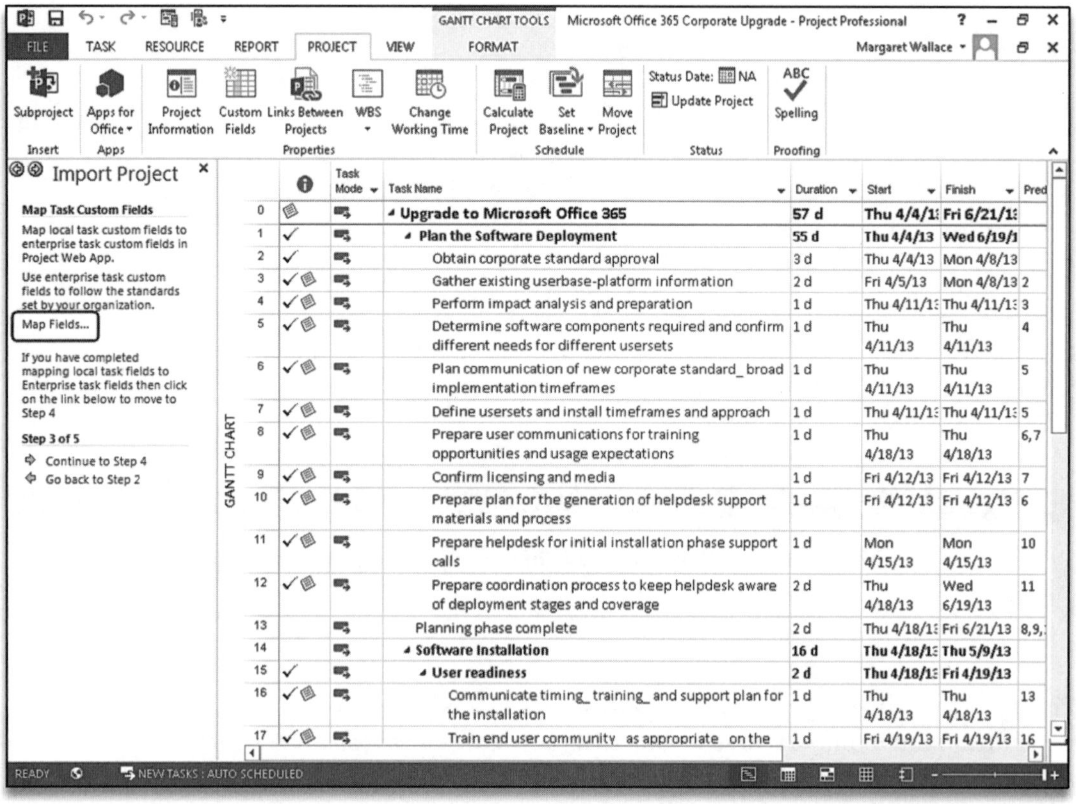

Figure 6 - 6: Map Task Custom Fields page in the Import Project wizard sidepane

Use the *Map Task Custom Fields* page to match any local custom task fields in your project with enterprise custom task fields in your Project Server 2013 system. If your project contains any local custom task fields, click the *Map Fields...* link in the *Import Project* wizard sidepane shown in Figure 6 - 6. The system displays the *Map Custom Fields* dialog shown in Figure 6 - 7.

> **Information**: If your project does not contain any local custom task fields, you can skip this step by clicking the *Continue to Step 4* link in the *Import Project* wizard sidepane.

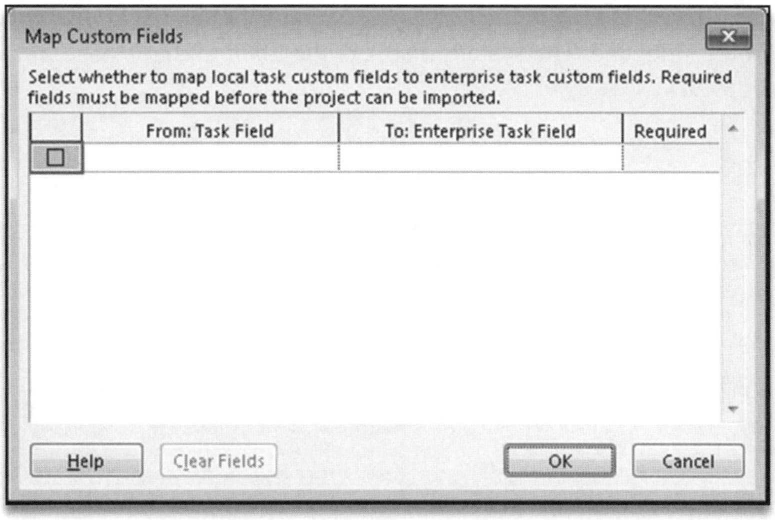
Map Custom Fields
Select whether to map local task custom fields to enterprise task custom fields. Required fields must be mapped before the project can be imported.
From: Task Field
To: Enterprise Task Field
Required
Help
Clear Fields
OK
Cancel

Figure 6 - 7: Map Custom Fields dialog

In the *Map Custom Fields* dialog, click the *From: Task Field* pick list and select a local custom task field. Click the *To: Enterprise Task Field* pick list and select the corresponding enterprise custom task field. Notice in Figure 6 - 8 that the *Is Key Milestone* local custom field maps to the *Major Milestone* enterprise custom field. Repeat this process for every local custom task field and then click the *OK* button when finished.

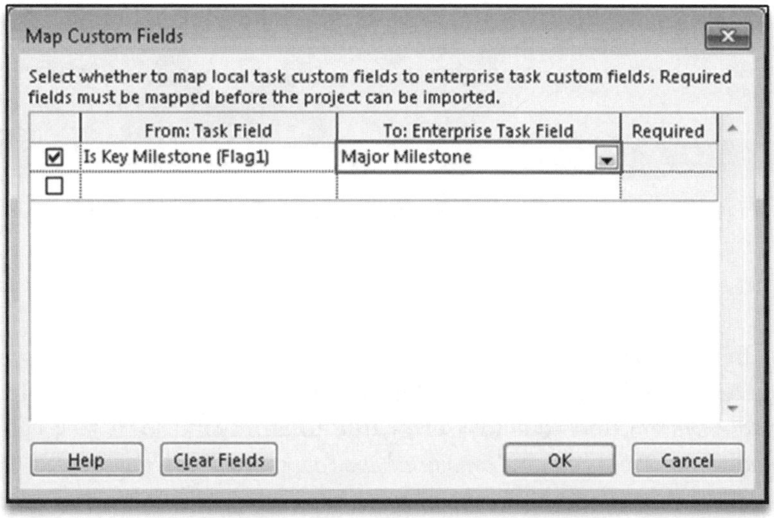
Map Custom Fields
Select whether to map local task custom fields to enterprise task custom fields. Required fields must be mapped before the project can be imported.
From: Task Field
To: Enterprise Task Field
Required
Is Key Milestone (Flag1)
Major Milestone
Help
Clear Fields
OK
Cancel

Figure 6 - 8: Map Custom Fields dialog
Is Key Milestone field mapped to Major Milestone field

Information: If you map custom local task fields with custom enterprise task fields using the *Map Custom Fields* dialog, the system copies the information from the local fields to the corresponding enterprise fields. The system **does not** remove your custom local task fields from your project. After importing your project, you can safely remove your local fields using the *Organizer* dialog or the *Custom Fields* dialog.

The system returns control to the *Map Task Custom Fields* page in the *Import Project* wizard sidepane. Click the *Continue to Step 4* link in the sidepane. The system displays the *Confirm Tasks* page in the *Import Project* wizard sidepane shown in Figure 6 - 9.

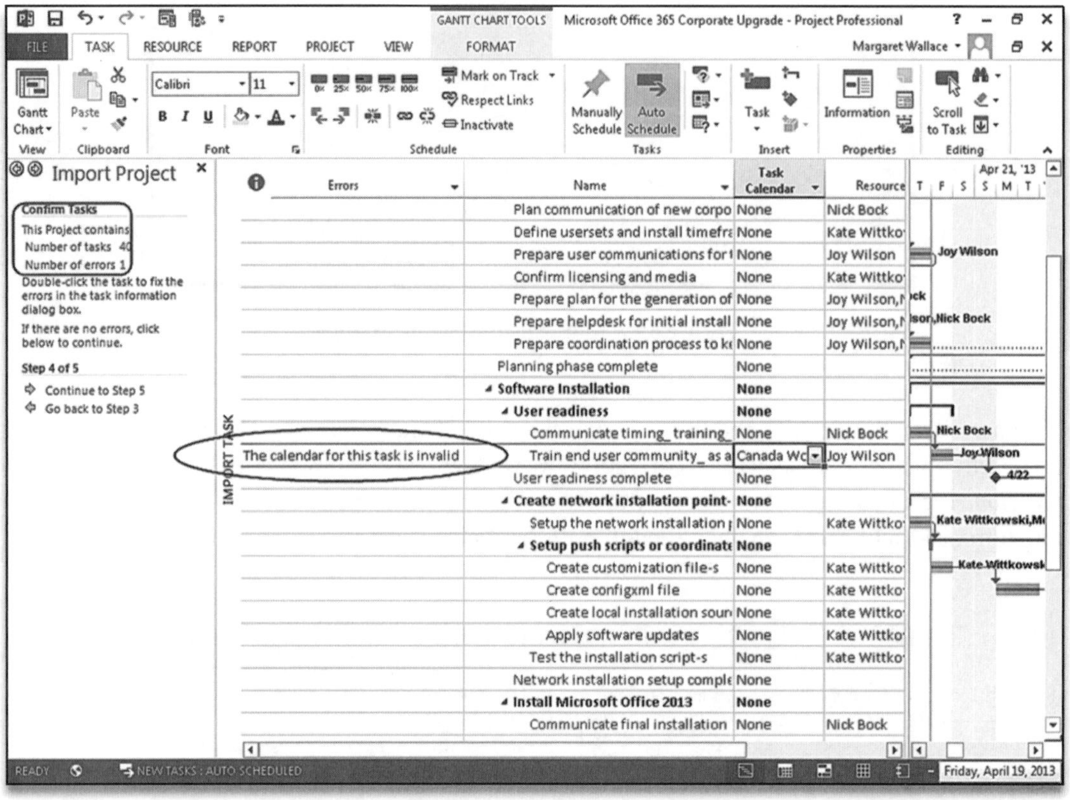

Figure 6 - 9: Confirm Tasks page in the Import Project wizard sidepane

If you see task errors on the *Confirm Tasks* page, you must correct the errors before the system allows you to continue. The *Errors* column tells you the nature of each task error and identifies the tasks triggering the errors. Notice in Figure 6 - 9 that the system finds one task error due to an invalid local task calendar (the *Canada Work Schedule* calendar) applied to the *Train end user community_ as appropriate_ on the software* task. Because the default settings in Project Server 2013 do not allow the use of local base calendars, this error needs correction before advancing to the next step. To correct this error, I must either remove the local task calendar from the task or replace it with an enterprise calendar.

As part of your error correction process, you can double-click the name of any task containing an error and examine information about the task in the *Task Information* dialog shown in Figure 6 - 10. Correct any task errors in the *Task Information* dialog and then click the *OK* button, such as changing the local calendar as highlighted in Figure 6 - 10.

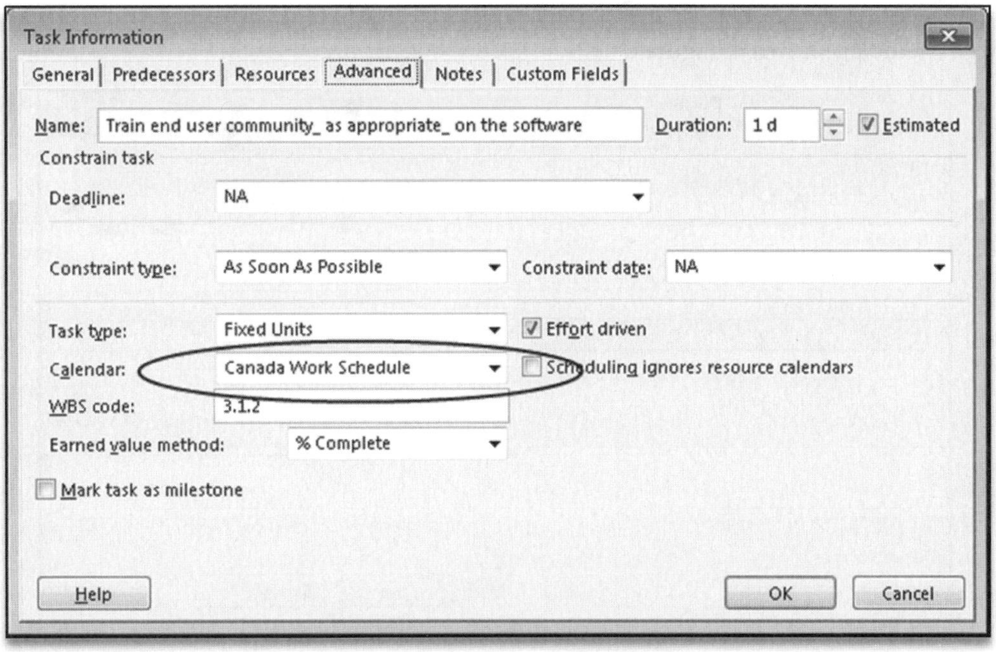

Figure 6 - 10: Task Information dialog

After you correct the task problems, the system redisplays the *Confirm Tasks* page in the *Import Project* wizard sidepane, without any errors listed in the *Errors* column. Click the *Continue to Step 5* link in the sidepane. Project Server 2013 displays the *Complete Import* page in the *Import Project* wizard sidepane shown in Figure 6 - 11.

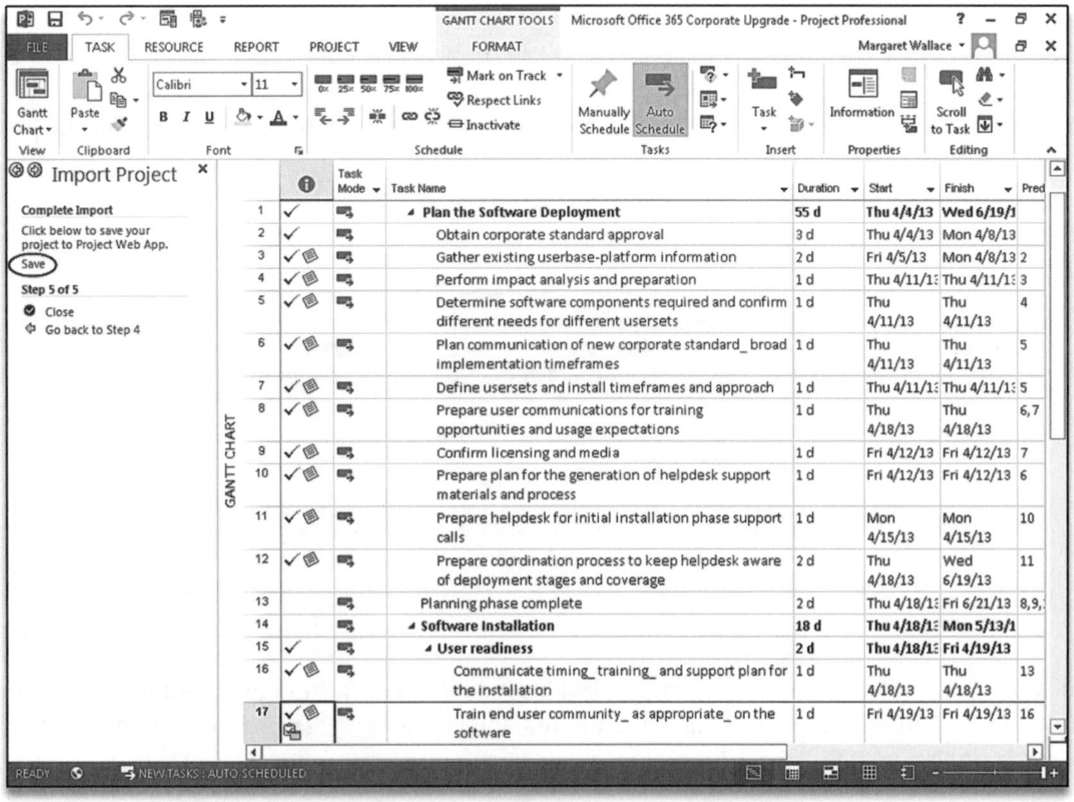

Figure 6 - 11: Complete Import page in the Import Project wizard sidepane

11. Click the *Save* link in the *Complete Import* page shown in Figure 6 - 11. The system displays the *Save to Project Web App* dialog shown in Figure 6 - 12.

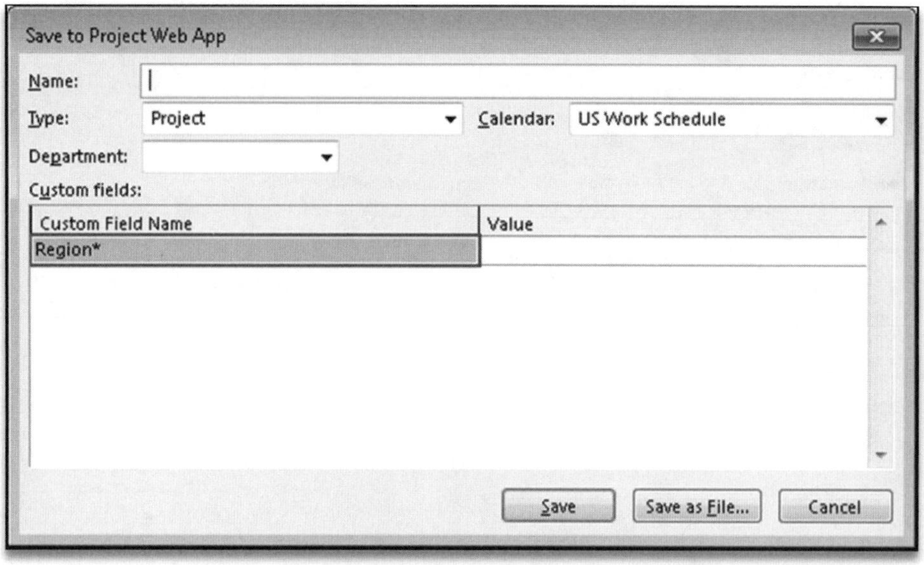

Figure 6 - 12: Save to Project Web App dialog

In the *Save to Project Web App* dialog, enter the following information:

- Using your organizational naming convention for enterprise projects, enter a name for the project in the *Name* field.
- Click the *Type* pick list and select the type of project (project or a template).
- Click the *Calendar* pick list and select a *Base* calendar to serve as the project calendar for the project, if different from the *Standard* calendar.
- Enter or select values for custom enterprise project fields in the *Custom fields* section.

Warning: When entering the name of your enterprise project, use only alphanumeric characters, spaces, and the underscore (_) character. Do not use any other special characters, such as ampersands (&), pound signs (#), dashes (-), or commas. Using special characters in the name of your enterprise project can lead to a corrupt project data.

Information: : If you want to import the project as an enterprise project template, remember to click the *Type* pick list and select the *Template* item in the *Save to Project Web App* dialog.

12. Click the *Save* button in the *Save to Project Web App* dialog shown in Figure 6 - 13. The system saves the project in the Project Server 2013 database and redisplays the *Import Project* wizard with a congratulations message, as shown in Figure 6 - 14.

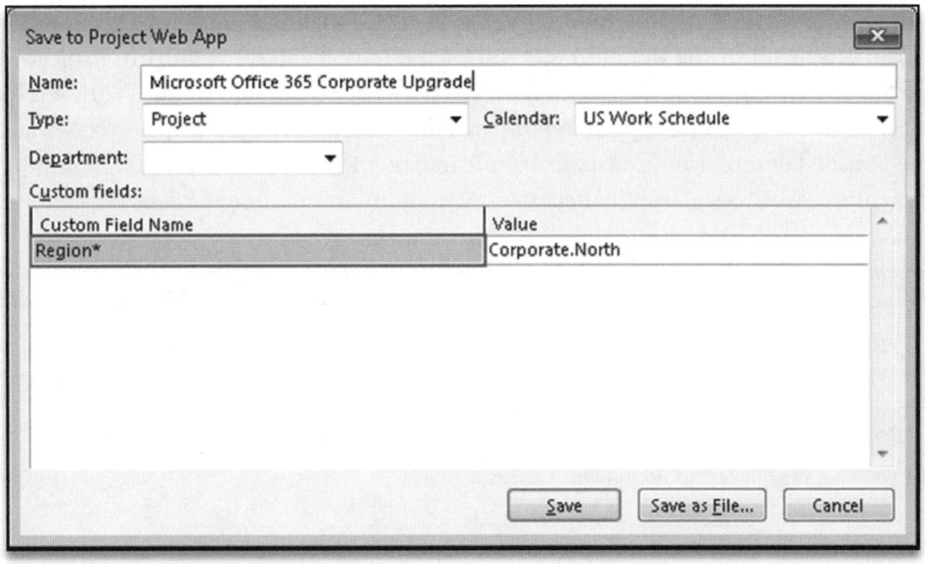

Figure 6 - 13: Save to Project Web App fields complete

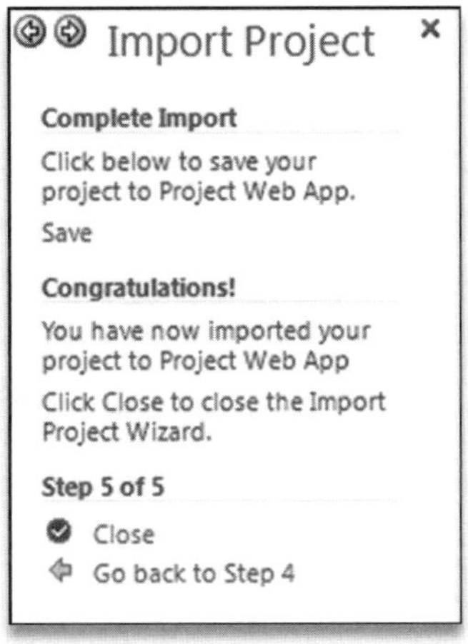

Figure 6 - 14: Import Project wizard with Congratulations! message

In the *Import Project* wizard sidepane shown previously in Figure 6 - 14, click the *Close* link to conclude the import process. The system closes the sidepane but leaves the project open for additional action. Close the project and then click the *Yes* button when prompted to check in the project.

Warning: The default behavior of the *Import Project* wizard in Project Server 2013 is to leave local resources on in-progress tasks (tasks with Actual Work and Remaining Work > 0 hours), even when you match the local resource to an enterprise resource. The wizard correctly transfers completed tasks and unstarted tasks to the mapped enterprise resources. After importing the project, you must manually replace the local resources with the enterprise resources using the *Assign Resources* dialog.

Before the system saves the project, it may optionally display the warning dialog regarding local resources shown in Figure 6 - 15. This is a result of the default behavior of the *Import Project* wizard in Project Server 2013 which leaves local resources on in-progress tasks (tasks with Actual Work and Remaining Work > 0 hours), even when you match the local resource to an enterprise resource. The wizard correctly transfers completed tasks and not started tasks to the mapped enterprise resources. After importing the project, you must manually replace the local resources with enterprise resources using the *Replace* functionality in the *Assign Resources* dialog.

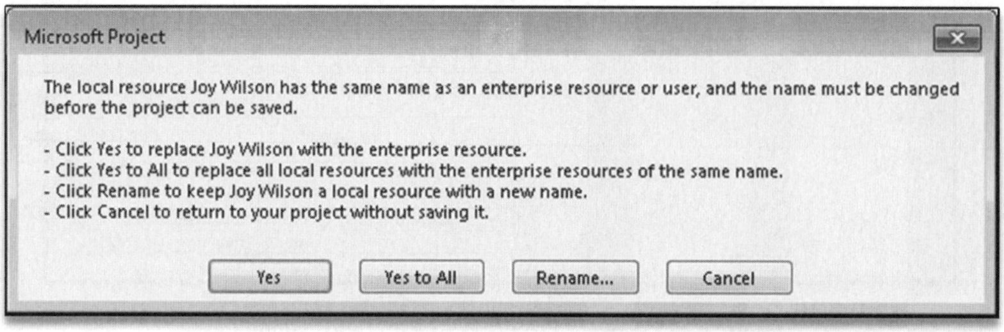
Microsoft Project
The local resource Joy Wilson has the same name as an enterprise resource or user, and the name must be changed before the project can be saved.
- Click Yes to replace Joy Wilson with the enterprise resource.
- Click Yes to All to replace all local resources with the enterprise resources of the same name.
- Click Rename to keep Joy Wilson a local resource with a new name.
- Click Cancel to return to your project without saving it.
Yes
Yes to All
Rename...
Cancel

Figure 6 - 15: Microsoft Project dialog, local resource message

Creating a New Project from an Enterprise Template

To create a new project in Project Pro 2013, click the *File* tab to display the *Backstage.* Click the *New* tab to display the *New* page shown in Figure 6 - 16. Notice that the *New* page includes the following template types:

- **Blank Project** – Use this template to create a new blank project that includes all of the options you specify in the *Project Options* dialog.

- **New from existing project** – Use this template to create a new project that is a copy of an existing project.

- **New from Excel workbook** – Use this template to create a new project from an Excel workbook using the *Import/Export* wizard.

- **New from SharePoint Tasks List** – Use this template to create a new project from a tasks list in a SharePoint site. To use this feature, someone must first create the tasks list in a SharePoint site.

In addition to the four types of templates listed previously, the *New* page also displays a selection of Project 2013 templates available in the *Office.com* website. Microsoft allows you to download and use any of these templates free of charge. Notice that each *Office.com* template button includes a preview picture of the file using that template type.

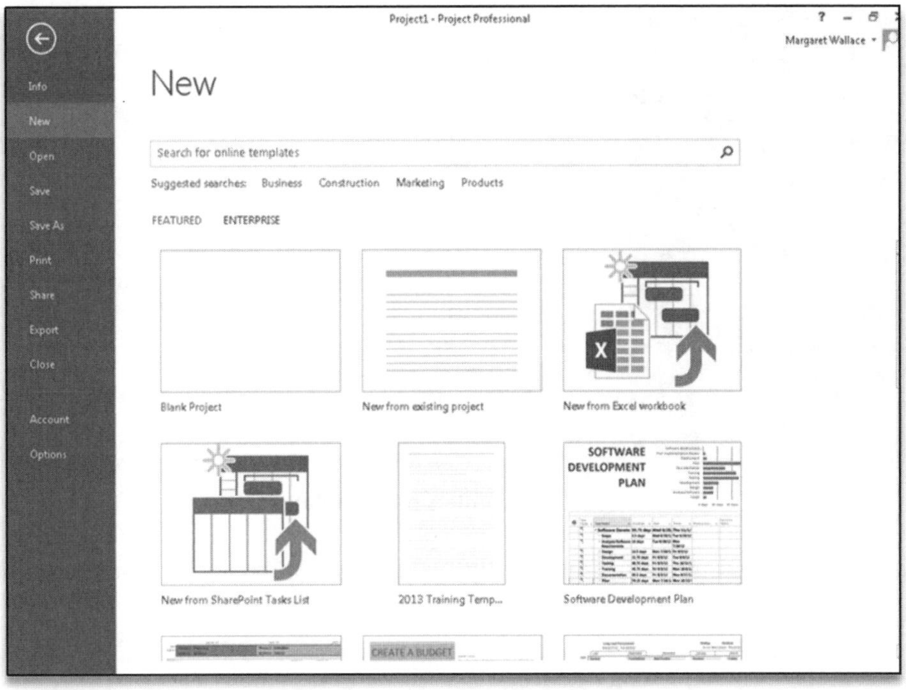

Figure 6 - 16: New page in the Backstage

To create a new project from a Project Server enterprise template, on the *New* page click the *ENTERPRISE* link as shown in Figure 6 - 17.

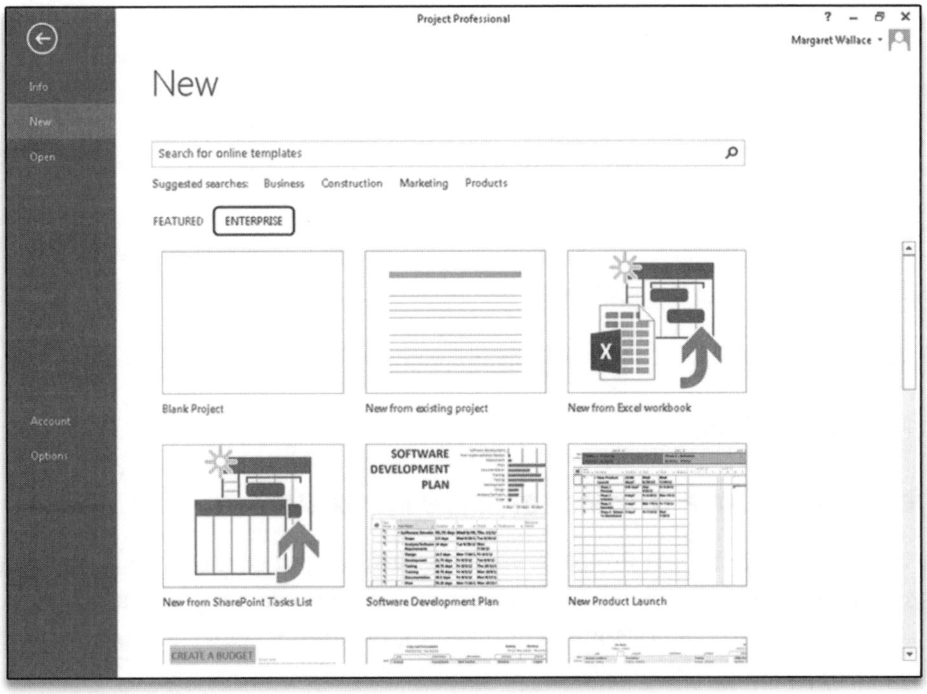

Figure 6 - 17: New page, ENTERPRISE link

The system displays the available enterprise templates for your organization. Notice that my organization currently offers two enterprise project templates as shown in Figure 6 - 18.

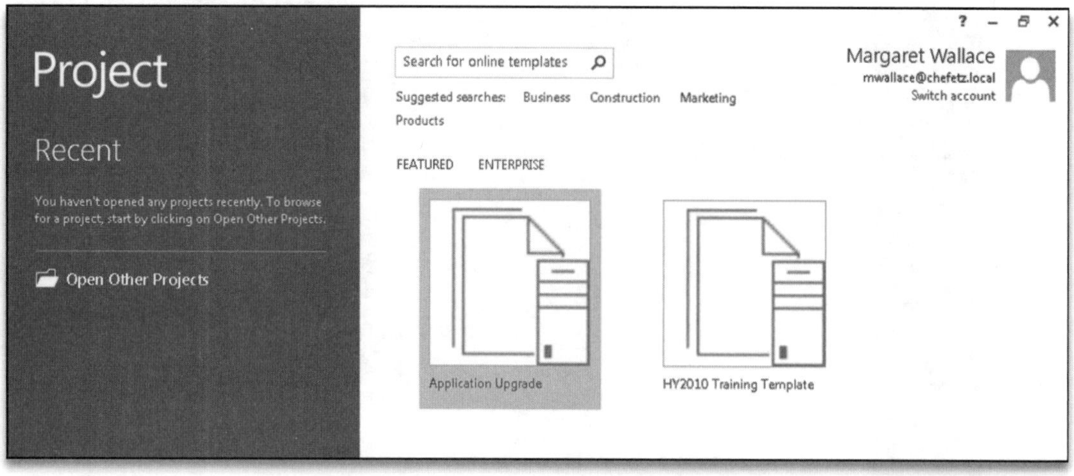

Figure 6 - 18: Enterprise templates

Select an enterprise template and then click the *OK* button. The system creates a new project using the template you select.

Defining an Enterprise Project

After you create a new enterprise project, either from scratch or from a template, you are ready to define the project in Project Pro 2013 using the six-step method recommended by MSProjectExperts. The six-step method includes the following:

1. Set the project *Start* date and enterprise field values.
2. Enter the project properties.
3. Display the Project Summary Task (aka Row 0 or Task 0).
4. Set the working schedule for the project using a calendar.
5. Set project options unique to this project.
6. Name and save the project using your organizational naming convention.

I discuss each of these steps individually.

Set the Project Start Date and Enterprise Field Values

When you define a new project in Project Pro 2013, you must set the *Start* date of the project. When you set a project's *Start* date, you allow the software to calculate an estimated *Finish* date basing the finish on the information you enter during the task, resource, and assignment planning process. To enter the *Start* date for a new project, complete the following steps:

1. Click the *Project* tab to display the *Project* ribbon.
2. In the *Properties* section of the *Project* ribbon, click the *Project Information* button. The system displays the *Project Information* dialog shown in Figure 6 - 19.

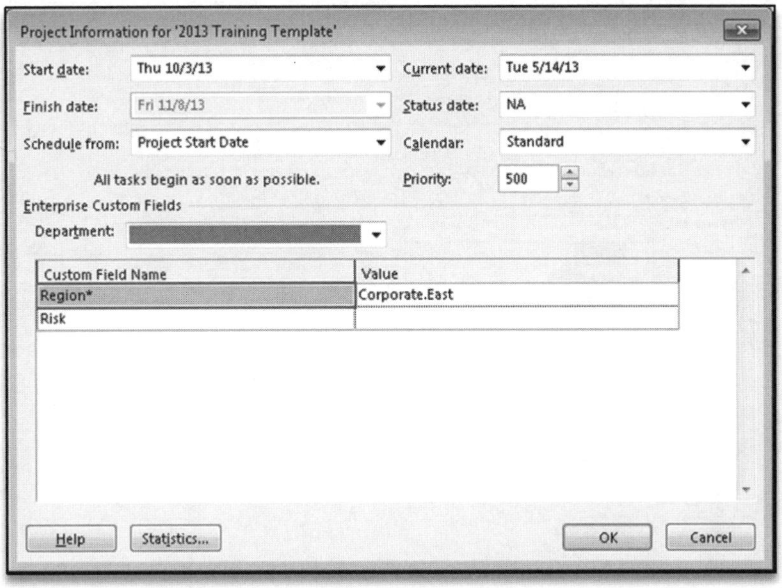

Figure 6 - 19: Project Information dialog

Information: As an alternative, in the *Schedule* section of the *Project* ribbon, click the *Move Project* button to display the *Move Project* dialog. This dialog allows you to move both the project *Start* date and any deadline dates within the project.

Best Practice: MSProjectExperts recommends that you use the *Move Project* dialog to move the *Start* date of a project when you need to move deadline dates. The *Move Project* dialog allows you to move deadline dates within the project automatically. This is useful when your organization uses a template and has special deadline dates for similar projects and the shifting of the *Start* date and its deadlines is necessary depending on the individual needs of a project.

3. Enter or select your desired project *Start* date in the S*tart date* field.

4. If your Project Server administrator defines *Departments* in your implementation, you can use the *Department* field pick list to display department-specific custom fields in the *Project Information* dialog.

Notice in Figure 6 - 20 that my organization includes ten departments: Accounting, Engineering, Human Resources, Information Technology, Legal, Marketing, Operations, Product Development, Publishing, and Sales departments.

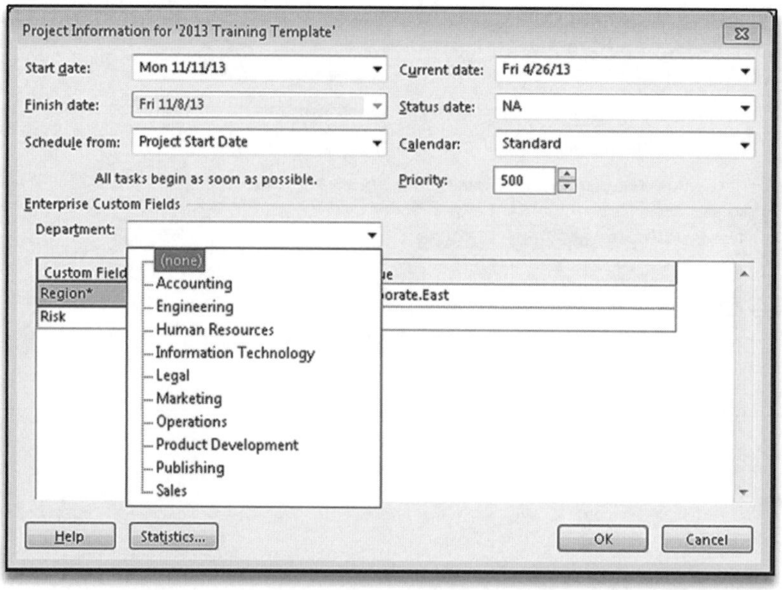

Figure 6 - 20: Project Information dialog, select a Department

If you select a value in the *Department* field, the system may refresh the *Enterprise Custom Fields* section of the *Project Information* dialog to include any department-specific custom fields. After selecting the *Marketing* item in the *Department* field pick list, notice in Figure 6 - 21 that the *Enterprise Custom Fields* section of the dialog now contains four additional fields: *SURF High Estimate, SURF Proposed Cost, SURF Supporting Business Units,* and *SURF Supporting Region* fields that are specific to the marketing department.

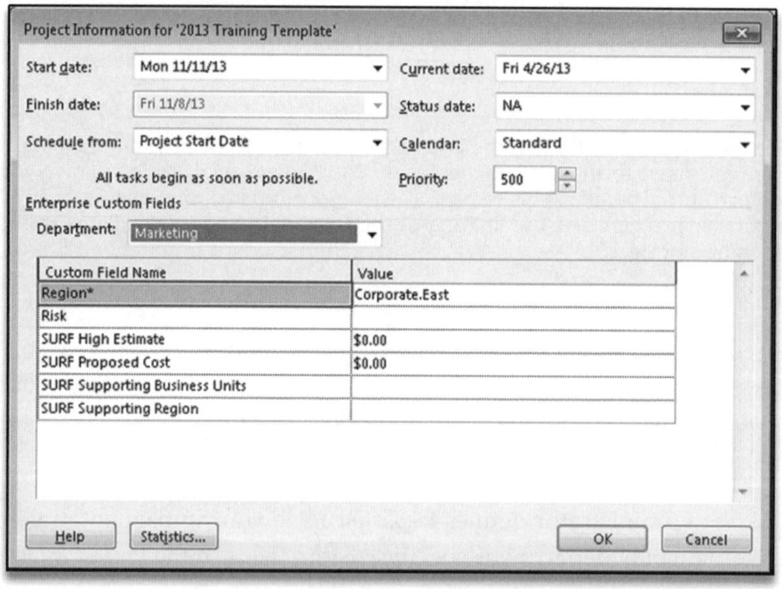

Figure 6 - 21: Project Information dialog
with additional department specific enterprise custom fields

5. Enter values in any required or optional enterprise custom fields in the *Enterprise Custom Fields* section of the dialog.

Notice in Figure 6 - 21, that one enterprise custom field, *Region*, shows an asterisk character (*) after the name of the field. The asterisk character indicates that this custom field requires a value set for the field prior to saving the project. This means that you must select or enter a value in this field before the system allows you to save the project in the Project Server database. Notice also that the *Risk* field does not include an asterisk character, indicating that this field does not require a value prior to saving the project.

> **Information**: In the *Enterprise Custom Fields* section of the dialog, note that you cannot enter or select a value in any field that contains a formula that generates a number.

6. After you enter a *Start* date and specify values in the enterprise custom fields, click the *OK* button.

Enter the Project Properties

Although you may be in the habit of skipping the file properties settings when creating a new Word document or Excel spreadsheet, you should set the properties for each new project you create in Project Pro 2013. This causes the software to display your properties information automatically in various places throughout the project such as in the headers and footers of printed views and reports. To set the properties information for a new project, complete the following steps:

1. Click the *File* tab and then click the *Info* tab in the *Backstage* to display the *Info* page for the current project. In the upper right corner of the *Info* page, click the *Project Information* pick list and select the *Advanced Properties* item. The system displays the *Properties* dialog for the new project, as shown in Figure 6 - 22.

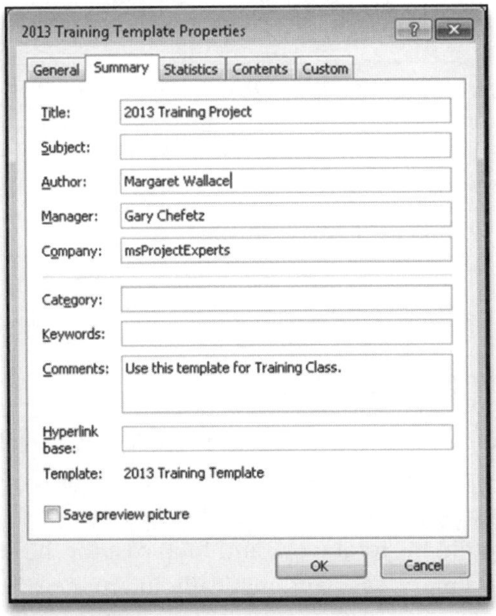

Figure 6 - 22: Properties dialog

2. Click the *Summary* tab, if necessary, and then enter values for each of the fields.
3. Click the *OK* button when finished.

Table 6 - 1 provides descriptions and recommendations for the use of properties fields in a Project Server 2013 environment.

Field Name	Description and Recommendations
Title	Displays as the task name in the Project Summary Task (Row 0), as the task name for subprojects inserted in a master project, and in the headers or footers of printed views and reports.
Subject	Not used with Project Server 2013.
Author	Enter the name of the person who manages the project. The system optionally displays the *Author* field in the headers or footers of printed views and reports.
Manager	Enter your name, or the name of the customer, or the name of your functional manager. The system optionally displays the *Manager* field in the headers or footers of printed views and reports.
Company	Enter the customer's company name, or the name of your own company. The system optionally displays the *Company* field in the headers or footers of printed views and reports.
Category	Not used with Project Server 2013.
Keywords	Not used with Project Server 2013.
Comments	The system displays the *Comment* information in the *Notes* field of the Project Summary Task (Row 0).
Hyperlink base	Not used with Project Server 2013.
Template	The system displays the name of the template you used to create the project file.
Save preview picture	Not used with Project Server 2013.

Table 6 - 1: Properties fields

Display the Project Summary Task

The Project Summary Task, also known as Row 0 or Task 0, is the highest-level summary task in your project. The Project Summary Task summarizes or "rolls up" all task values in the entire project. For example, the value in the *Duration* column for the Project Summary Task represents the duration of the entire project, while the values in the *Work* and the *Cost* columns represent the total work and total cost for the entire project. By default, Project Pro 2013 **does not** display the Project Summary Task automatically in any new blank project, so you must display it manually. To display the Project Summary Task in a project, complete the following steps:

1. Display the Project Summary Task by applying the *Gantt Chart* view and then clicking the *Format* tab to display the *Format* ribbon with the *Gantt Chart Tools* applied. In the *Show/Hide* section of the *Format* ribbon, select the *Project Summary Task* option. The system displays the Project Summary Task (Row 0) at the top of the current project, as shown in Figure 6 - 23.

	Indicators	Task Mode	Task Name	Duration
0			**2013 Training Project**	**27 d**
1			**PHASE I**	**17 d**
2			Determine Hardware Specifications	5 d
3			Design P1	5 d
4			Build P1	3 d
5			Test P1	2 d
6			Rebuild P1	2 d
7			Phase I Complete	0 d
8			**PHASE II**	**10 d**
9			Design P2	1 d
10			Build P2	4 d
11			Test P2	5 d
12			Phase II Complete	0 d
13			Design P3	1 d
14			Phase III Complete	1 d
15			PROJECT COMPLETE	1 d

Figure 6 - 23: Project Summary Task (Row 0)

2. Widen the *Task Name* column, if necessary, to "best fit" the task name of the Project Summary Task.

3. If you widen the *Task Name* column, drag the split bar to the right side of the *Duration* column, as needed.

When you display the Project Summary Task, Project Pro 2013 uses the text you enter in the *Title* field of the *Properties* dialog as the task name of the Project Summary Task. The system also uses the text you enter in the *Comments* field of the *Properties* dialog as the body of the note for the Project Summary Task.

Set the Project Working Schedule

Setting the project working schedule is an optional step, and is necessary if your project schedule does not follow the schedule using the enterprise *Standard* calendar. To determine which alternate calendar you may need to select, complete the following steps:

1. In the *Properties* section of the *Project* ribbon, click the *Change Working Time* button. Project Pro 2013 displays the *Change Working Time* dialog shown in Figure 6 - 24. Notice that the enterprise *Standard* calendar contains no company holidays, indicated by the blank data grid in the *Exceptions* section in the bottom half of the dialog.

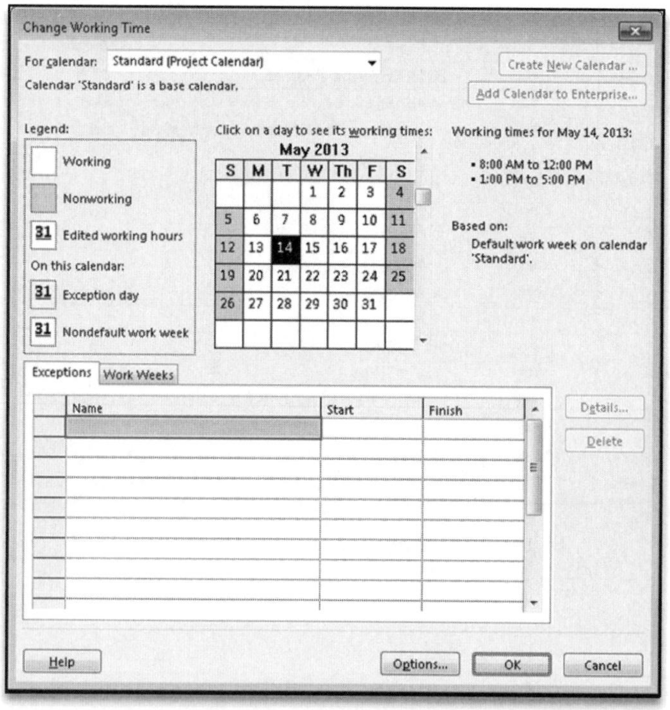

Figure 6 - 24: Change Working Time dialog; enterprise Standard calendar contains no company holidays

2. Click the *For calendar* pick list at the top of the *Change Working Time* dialog and select any calendar other than the enterprise *Standard* calendar. For example, Figure 6 - 25 shows the *US Work Schedule* enterprise calendar, which contains the company's holidays for offices in the United States.

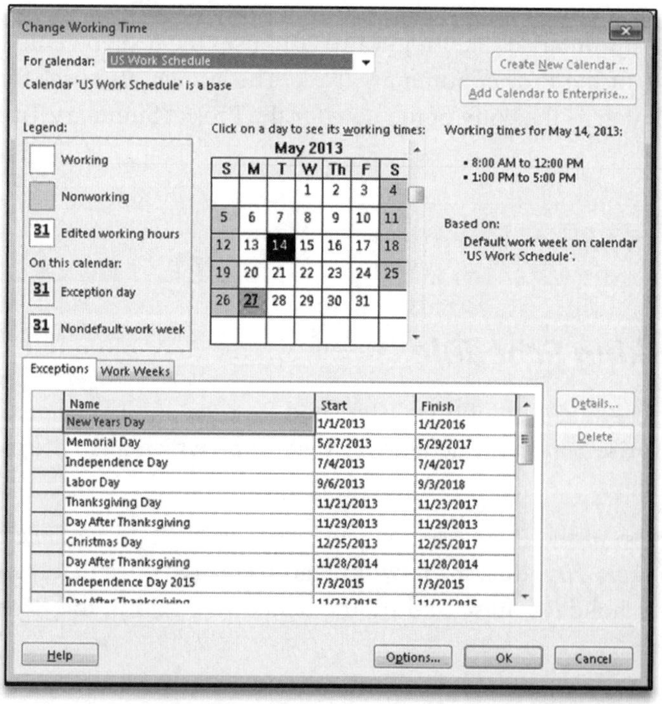

Figure 6 - 25: Change Working Time dialog; US Work Schedule enterprise calendar contains company holidays

3. After you determine which enterprise calendar you want to use, close the *Change Working Time* dialog by clicking either the *OK* button or the *Cancel* button.

> **Warning**: By default, project managers **do not** have permissions in Project Server 2013 to create or edit enterprise calendars. Because of this, the system disables the *Create New Calendar* button and does not allow you to create or edit holidays in the *Exceptions* grid at the bottom of the *Change Working Time* dialog. Administrators, however, by default do have the permissions in Project Server 2013 to create or edit enterprise calendars.

Setting the Project Calendar

In Project Pro 2013, the system allows you to specify two calendars for your project. When you select the *Project* calendar, the system uses this calendar to schedule all tasks in your project. Think of the *Project* calendar as the master schedule of the project. The system also allows you to specify the *Non-Working Time* calendar for the project. The system uses the *Non-Working Time* calendar for only one purpose: to display nonworking time as gray shaded vertical bands on the Gantt chart. If you select any calendar other than the enterprise *Standard* calendar as the *Project* calendar, you should select the same calendar as the *Non-Working Time* calendar as well.

If you need to specify a calendar other than the enterprise *Standard* calendar as the *Project* calendar, complete the following steps:

1. In the *Properties* section of the *Project* ribbon, click the *Project Information* button. The system displays the *Project Information* dialog shown previously in Figure 6 - 19.

2. In the *Project Information* dialog, click the *Calendar* pick list and select any calendar, as shown in Figure 6 - 26. Notice that I am selecting the same *US Work Schedule* enterprise calendar previously shown in Figure 6 - 25.

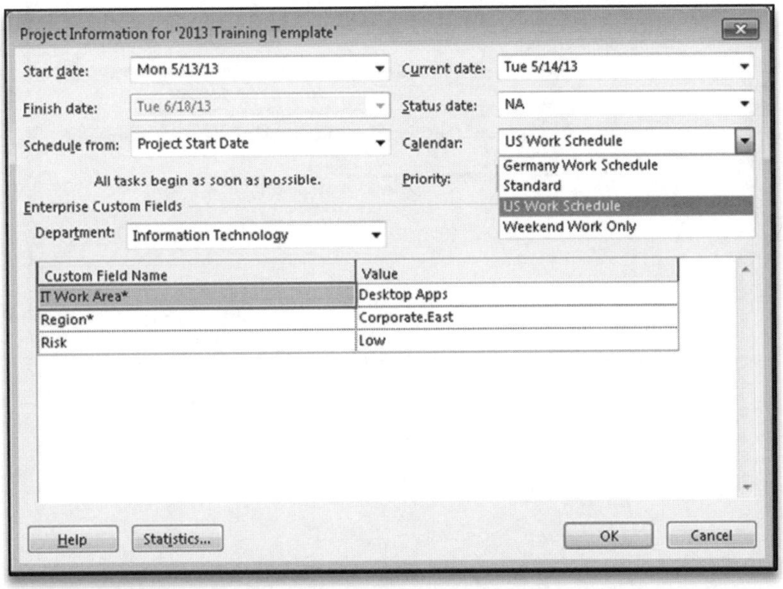

Figure 6 - 26: Project Information dialog; set the Project calendar

3. Click the *OK* button.

In the preceding steps, I set the *US Work Schedule* calendar as the *Project* calendar, which designates it as the master calendar for scheduling all tasks in the project. This means that Project Pro 2013 automatically schedules all tasks according to the working schedule shown on this calendar. If a task occurs on a US company holiday, the system automatically reschedules the task to the next working day.

Setting the Non-Working Time Calendar

After setting the *Project* calendar for the project, you must also set the *Non-Working Time* calendar. Remember that this calendar displays the nonworking time as gray shaded bands from the *Project* calendar in the Gantt chart. To set the *Non-Working Time* calendar, complete the following steps:

1. Double-click anywhere in the *Timescale* bar to display the *Timescale* dialog and then click the *Non-working time* tab.

> **Information**: The fastest way to display the *Timescale* dialog is to zoom the Gantt chart to *Weeks Over Days* and then double-click anywhere in a gray shaded vertical band, then select the *Non-working time* tab.

2. On the *Non-working time* page of the *Timescale* dialog, click the *Calendar* pick list and select the same calendar you specified previously as the *Project* calendar. For example, notice in Figure 6 - 27 that I am selecting the *US Work Schedule* enterprise calendar. Notice also that Project Pro 2013 designates this calendar as the *Project* calendar for the project.

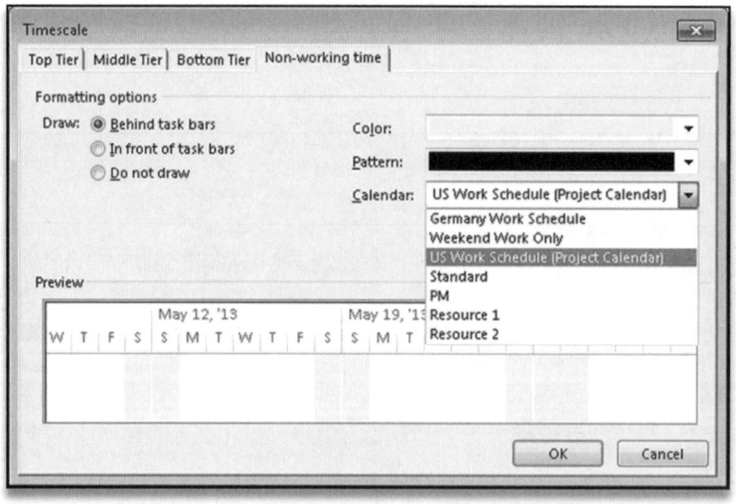

Figure 6 - 27: Timescale dialog, Non-working time page

3. Click the *OK* button.

> **Warning**: You must complete **both sets of steps** to set an alternate working schedule for your project. If you set the *Project* calendar but fail to select the *Non-Working Time* calendar, Project Pro 2013 schedules each task correctly; but you cannot confirm this schedule because you cannot see the holidays as gray shaded bands on the Gantt chart.

Set Options Unique to the Project

You need to specify two types of options for your new enterprise project. I discuss each of these types of options individually:

- Set the *Task Mode* option.
- Set options in the *Project Options* dialog.

Setting the Task Mode Option

Like its predecessor Project 2010, Microsoft continues with the default *Manually Scheduled* task mode setting for Project Pro 2013 and continues to allow you to specify tasks as either *Auto Scheduled* or *Manually Scheduled*. You can use this feature for tasks that you know you need to include in the project, but for which you may not have enough information to properly schedule, and you can use these for top-down planning exercises. Other potential purposes for this feature include more relaxed scheduling approaches that are preferable when modeling schedules for sprints in the SCRUM methodology.

The default *Task Mode* setting in Project Pro 2013 is the *Manually Scheduled* option, which specifies all new tasks as *Manually Scheduled* tasks. Every time you launch the software, you see this default *Task Mode* setting as a ScreenTip on the *Status* bar in the lower left corner of the application window, as shown in Figure 6 - 28.

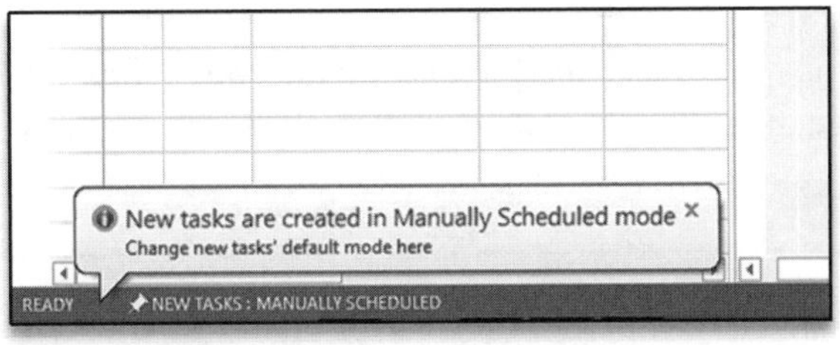

Figure 6 - 28: Task Mode option set to Manually Scheduled for all new tasks

To change the *Task Mode* setting and specify that all tasks must be *Auto Scheduled* in your new project, use either of the following methods:

- Click the *New Tasks* button on the *Status* bar and select the *Auto Scheduled* option.
- In the *Tasks* section of the *Task* ribbon, click the *Auto Schedule* button shown in Figure 6 - 29.

After selecting this option, when you create new tasks in your new project, Project Pro 2013 creates them as *Auto Scheduled* tasks. If you want to specify the default *Task Mode* setting for all new blank projects, you must specify this setting in the *Project Options* dialog. I discuss this setting in the next section of this module.

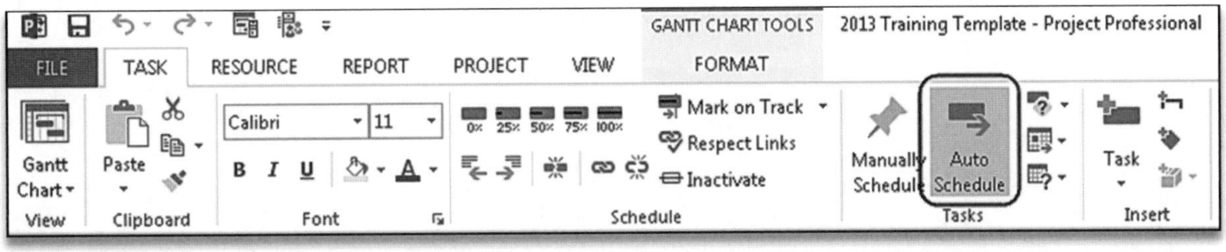

Figure 6 - 29: Auto Schedule button

Information: If you create a new enterprise project from a template, and the template author set the *Task Mode* option to *Auto Schedule*, then you do not need to specify a *Task Mode* option unless you want to change the option back to *Manually Schedule*.

Setting Options in the Project Options Dialog

After you specify the *Task Mode* setting for your new project, you are ready to specify options in the *Project Options* dialog. Project Pro 2013 allows you to specify three types of options settings in the *Project Options* dialog as follows:

- Application options that control how the software looks and works
- Options specific to any project currently open
- Options for all new projects created from a blank project

Information: Microsoft provides excellent *Help* articles for all of the options found in the *Project Options* dialog. I do not discuss each of these options individually; however, I focus on the new options found in Project Pro 2013, and other important options of which you should be aware. To access the *Project Help* page, press the **F1** function key or click the *Help* button (**?** button) in the upper right corner of the *Project Options* dialog to locate *Help* articles.

To specify all three types of options settings, click the *File* tab and then click the *Options* tab in the *Backstage*. The software displays the *General* page of the *Project Options* dialog shown in Figure 6 - 30.

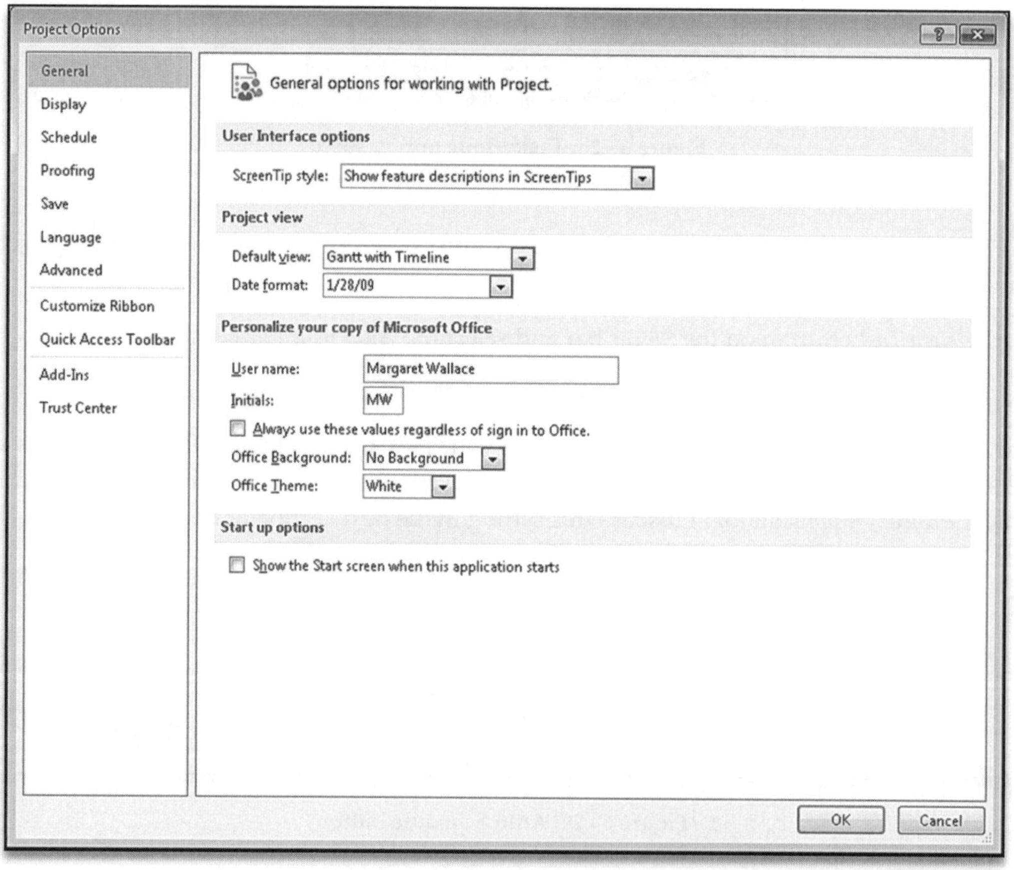

Figure 6 - 30: Project Options dialog, General page

Notice in Figure 6 - 30 that the *Project Options* dialog includes tabs for eleven pages of options: *General, Display, Schedule, Proofing, Save, Language, Advanced, Customize Ribbon, Quick Access Toolbar, Add-Ins,* and *Trust Center.*

Information: I do not discuss the *Customize Ribbon* and *Quick Access Toolbar* pages here, as these are in Module 02: *Project 2013 Overview* of our companion book *Ultimate Study Guide: Foundations Microsoft Project 2013*. I discuss all of the other pages in the following subtopical sections.

Setting General Options

The *General* page of the *Project Options* dialog, shown previously in Figure 6 - 30, contains application options only. Remember that these options control how the software looks, works, and displays every project you open. The *General* page includes several new options for Project Pro 2013.

The three new options for the *Personalize your copy of Microsoft Office* section that allow you to change the background pattern and background theme colors include:

- *Always use these values regardless of sign in to Office* selection
- *Office Background* pick list
- *Office Theme* pick list

The new *Start up options* section includes a single *Show the Start screen when this application starts* option, which is the default option in Project Pro 2013 and displays the *Start* page every time the software launches. If you disable this option, when Project Pro 2013 launches the software will instead:

- Open a new blank project
- Apply the *Gantt with Timeline* view

Table 6 - 2 shows the non-default options settings recommended by MSProjectExperts on the *General* page of the *Project Options* dialog.

Option	Setting
Date format	1/28/09
User name	Your name
Initials	Your initials

Table 6 - 2: Recommended options on the General page

Setting Display Options

Click the *Display* tab in the *Project Options* dialog to view the options on the *Display* page shown in Figure 6 - 31. As indicated at the top of the *Display* page, use the options on this page to control how Project Pro 2013 displays project data on the screen. Microsoft does not offer any new options on the *Display* page.

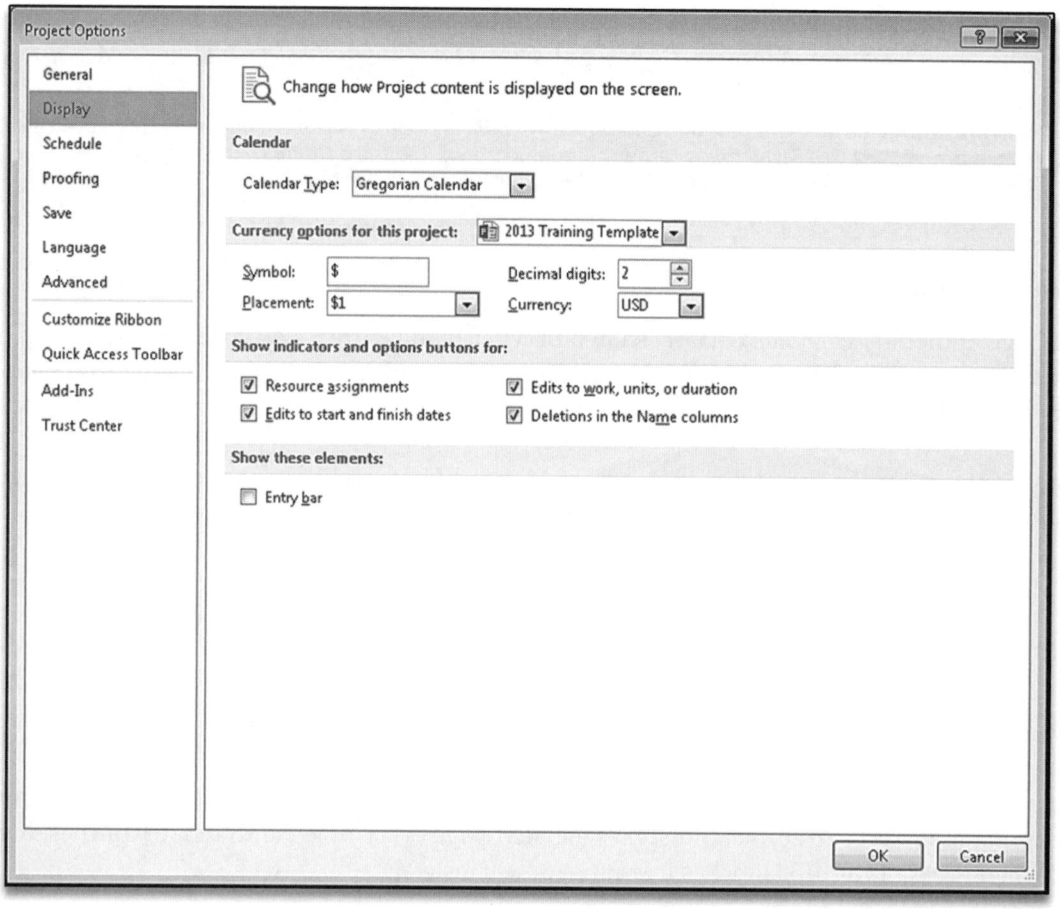

Figure 6 - 31: Project Options dialog, Display page

The *Display* page in Project Pro 2013 allows you to specify option settings for any project currently open, regardless of whether that project is the active project. You see this feature on the *Display* page in the *Currency options for this project* section. Click the *Currency options for this project* pick list to view a list of projects currently open. By default, the pick list pre-selects the active project, but you can choose any other open project and then specify the *Currency options for this project* setting for that project. This new functionality means that you can specify a unique set of options settings for each open project.

Information: MSProjectExperts recommends using the default settings on the *Display* page of the *Project Options* dialog.

Warning: You cannot change the information in any of the fields in the *Currency options for this project* section of the dialog if the Project Server administrator locked the currency settings on your organization's Project Server 2013 instance.

Setting Schedule Options

Click the *Schedule* tab in the *Project Options* dialog to view the options on the *Schedule* page shown in Figure 6 - 32 and Figure 6 - 33. As indicated at the top of the *Schedule* page in Figure 6 - 32, you use the options on this page to control scheduling, calendars, and calculations in Project Pro 2013. Notice in Figure 6 - 32 and Figure 6 - 33 that the *Schedule* page includes sections in which you may specify the following types of options: *Calendar options for this project*, *Scheduling options for this project*, and *Schedule Alerts options*, along with two sections for *Calculation* options. There are no new options on the *Schedule* page in Project Pro 2013.

Notice in Figure 6 - 32 and Figure 6 - 33 that four of the six sections on the *Schedule page* allow you to specify options for any project currently open. The pick lists on the *Schedule* page, however, differ slightly from the pick list shown on the *Display* page. For example, if you click the *Calendar options for this project* pick list, the list includes all projects currently open, plus an *All New Projects* item. If you select the *All New Projects* item, the system allows you to specify an options settings for all future projects created from a new blank project.

In the *Scheduling options for this project* section, you can use the *New tasks created* option to specify *Auto Scheduled* as the default *Task Mode* setting for all new projects. To do this, click the *Scheduling options for this project* pick list and select the *All New Projects* item. Next, click the *New tasks created* pick list and select the *Auto Scheduled* item. When you click the *OK* button to close the *Project Options* dialog, Project Pro 2013 sets the default *Task Mode* setting to *Auto Scheduled* for every new project you create from this point forward. The *New tasks created* option affects the default *Task Mode* setting for new tasks you add to your project.

On the *Auto scheduled tasks scheduled on* pick list, you can select the *Project Start Date* or *Current Date* options. The system creates *Auto Scheduled* tasks with dates in the *Start* and *Finish* fields and with a default duration value of *1 day* in the *Duration* field; the system creates all *Manually Scheduled* tasks with no values in the *Duration, Start,* and *Finish* fields.

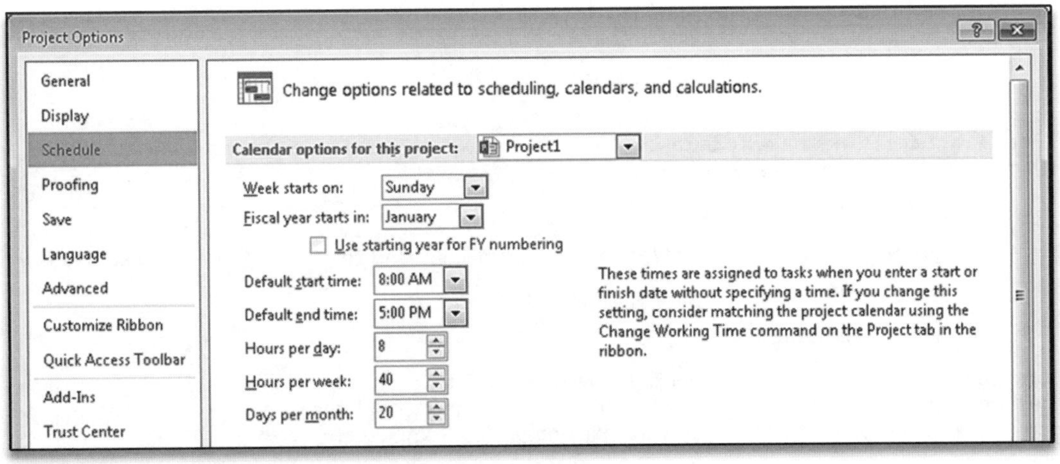

Figure 6 - 32: Project Options dialog, Schedule page (top half)

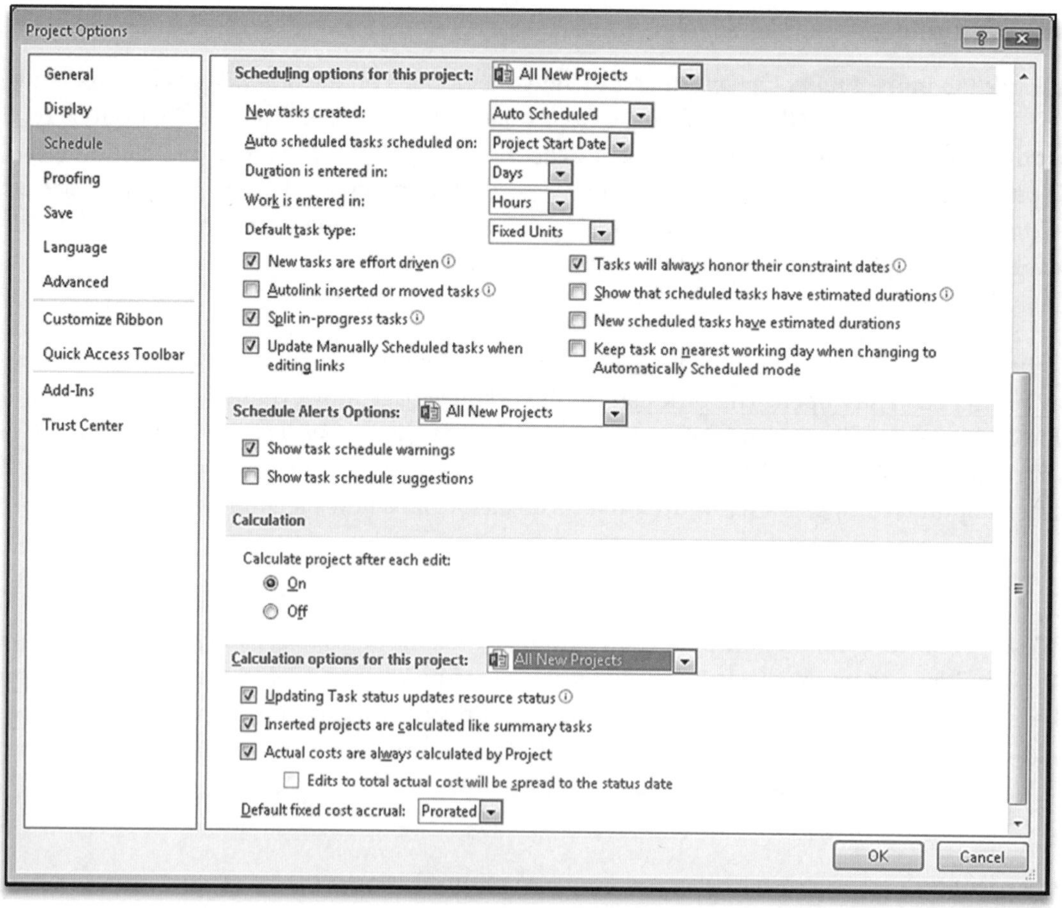

Figure 6 - 33: Project Options dialog, Schedule page (Bottom half)

Warning: Depending on the settings specified in your Project Server 2013 system by your Project Server administrator, you may not be able to change the *New Tasks Created* option for all new projects.

Best Practice: If the majority of tasks in your projects are Effort Driven tasks, MSProjectExperts recommends that you do the following early in your use of Project Pro 2013:

1. Create a new blank project.
2. Click the *Scheduling options for this project* pick list and select the *All New Projects* item.
3. Select the *New tasks are effort driven* option.
4. Click the *OK* button.

Completing the preceding steps sets the default value for all tasks to *Effort Driven* in all of the new blank projects you create from this point forward. If you use project templates to create new projects, you should also complete the above steps in each of your existing project templates.

Table 6 - 3 shows the non-default options settings recommended by MSProjectExperts on the *Schedule* page of the *Project Options* dialog. Furthermore, MSProjectExperts recommends you set these options for all open projects and for all new projects.

Option	Setting
New tasks created	Auto Scheduled
New tasks are effort driven	Selected
Show that scheduled tasks have estimated durations	Deselected
New scheduled tasks have estimated durations	Deselected
Show task schedule suggestions	Selected

Table 6 - 3: Recommended options on the Schedule page for all current and future project

Setting Proofing Options

Click the *Proofing* tab in the *Project Options* dialog to view the options on the *Proofing* page shown in Figure 6 - 34. As indicated at the top of the *Proofing* page, use the options on this page to control how Project Pro 2013 corrects and formats text in your projects. There are no new options on the *Proofing* page and MSProjectExperts recommends using the default settings.

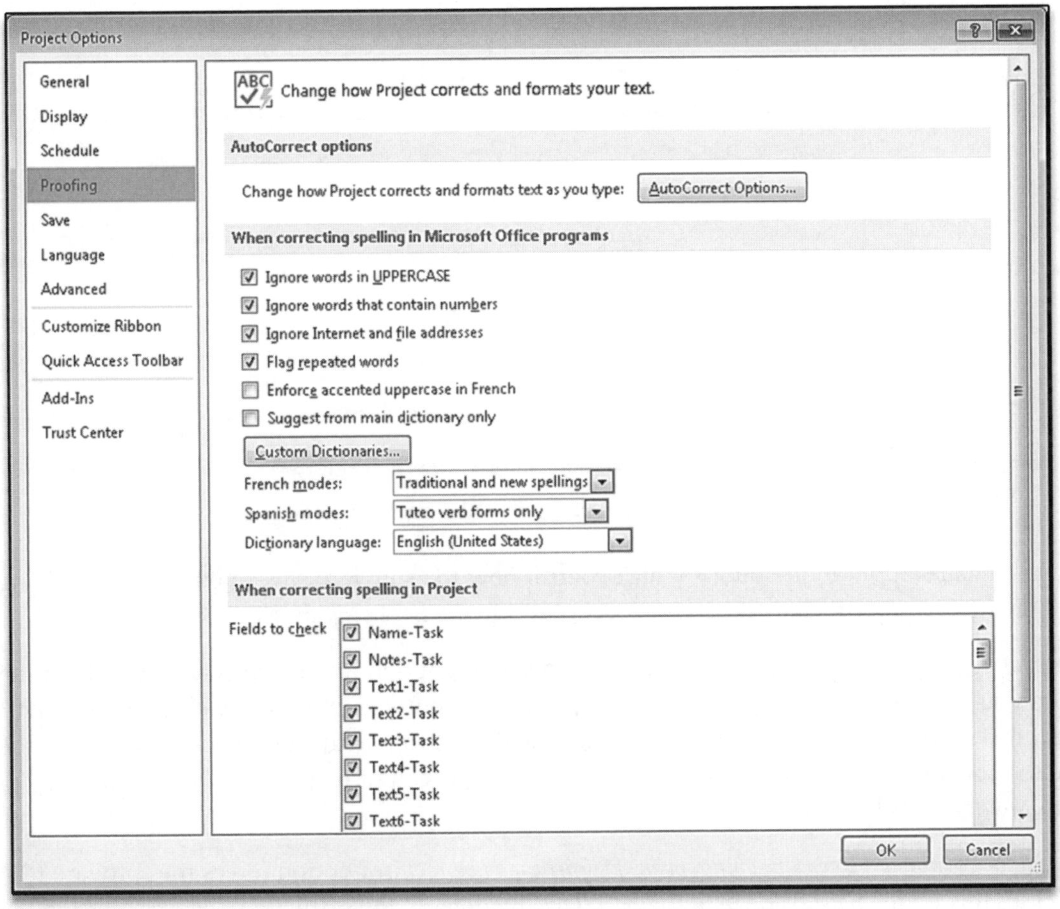

Figure 6 - 34: Project Options dialog, Proofing page

Warning: In the *AutoCorrect options* section of the *Project Options* dialog, click the *AutoCorrect Options* button to display the *AutoCorrect* dialog. Be careful with the settings in this dialog as the software may make corrections to your task names or resource names automatically. If you notice this behavior you may need to delete entries in the *AutoCorrect* dialog to prevent further corrections.

Setting Save Options

Click the *Save* tab in the *Project Options* dialog to view the options on the *Save* page shown in Figure 6 - 35. As indicated at the top of the *Save* page, use the options on this page to determine options for saving a project in Project Pro 2013.

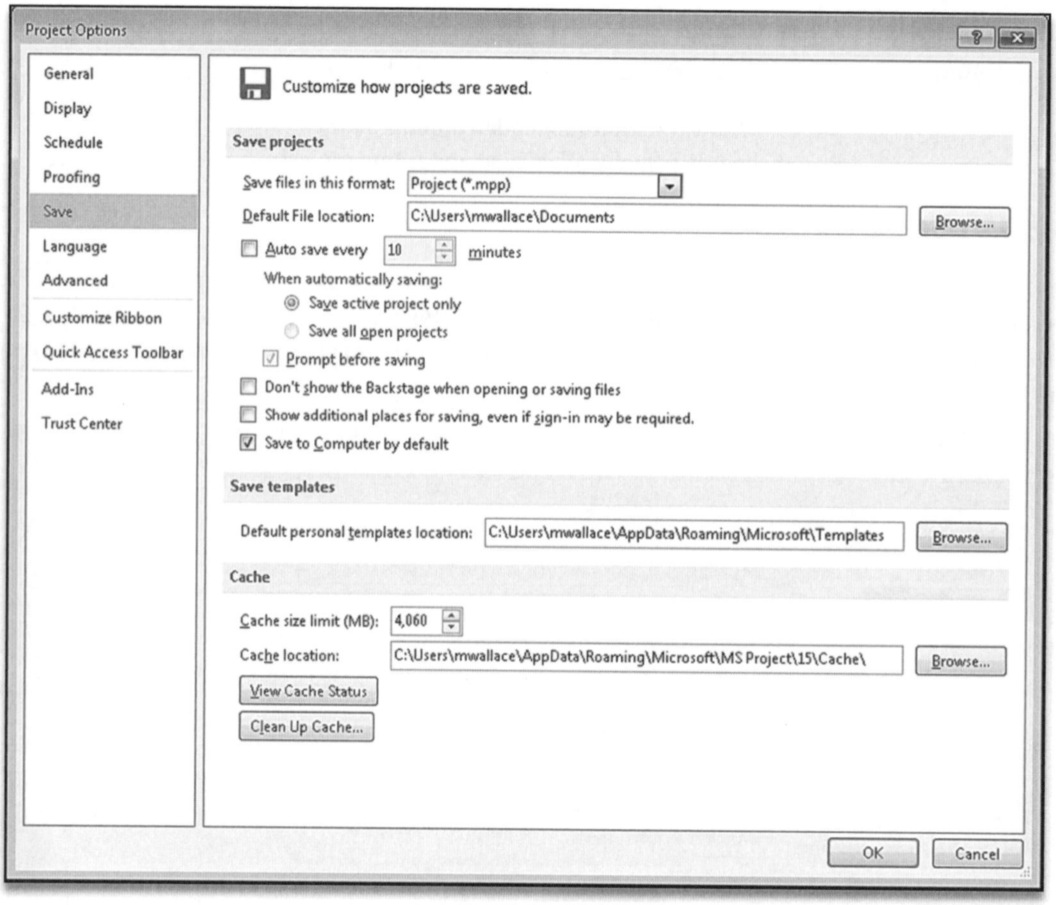

Figure 6 - 35: Project Options dialog, Save page

The *Save* page contains application options which control how the software saves your projects. Changes in Project Pro 2013 on the *Save* page include the three new options in the *Save projects* section:

- The *Don't show the Backstage when opening or saving files* option forces the software to hide the *Backstage* when you open or save a project using the *Open* or *Save* buttons on your *Quick Access Toolbar*. When you select this option and you click the *Open* button with no project currently open or you click the *Save* button, the software displays the *Open* or *Save As* dialog instead of displaying the *Backstage*. By default, the software deselects this option.

- The *Show additional places for saving, even if sign-in may be required* option forces the software to display the *SkyDrive* link on the *Save As* page in the *Backstage*. By default, the software selects this option.

- The *Save to Computer by default* option forces the software to select the *Computer* link on the *Save As* page every time you save a new project. By default, the software deselects this option.

> **Warning**: If you like to perform a "what if" analysis in your project, and you select the *Auto save every ___ minutes* option, be sure to leave the *Prompt before saving* option selected. Otherwise, you risk the possibility of overwriting your production project with the "what if" changes, with no recourse to use the *Undo* button since the save action clears the *Undo* cache.

Setting Language Options

Click the *Language* tab in the *Project Options* dialog to view and set options on the *Language* page shown in Figure 6 - 36. As indicated at the top of the *Language* page, use the options on this page to specify your language preference(s) for Project Pro 2013. The *Choose Editing Languages* section includes the new *Let me know when I should download additional proofing tools* option. By default, the software selects this option, which forces Project Pro 2013 to warn you when you open a project file created in a language different from your selected editing languages.

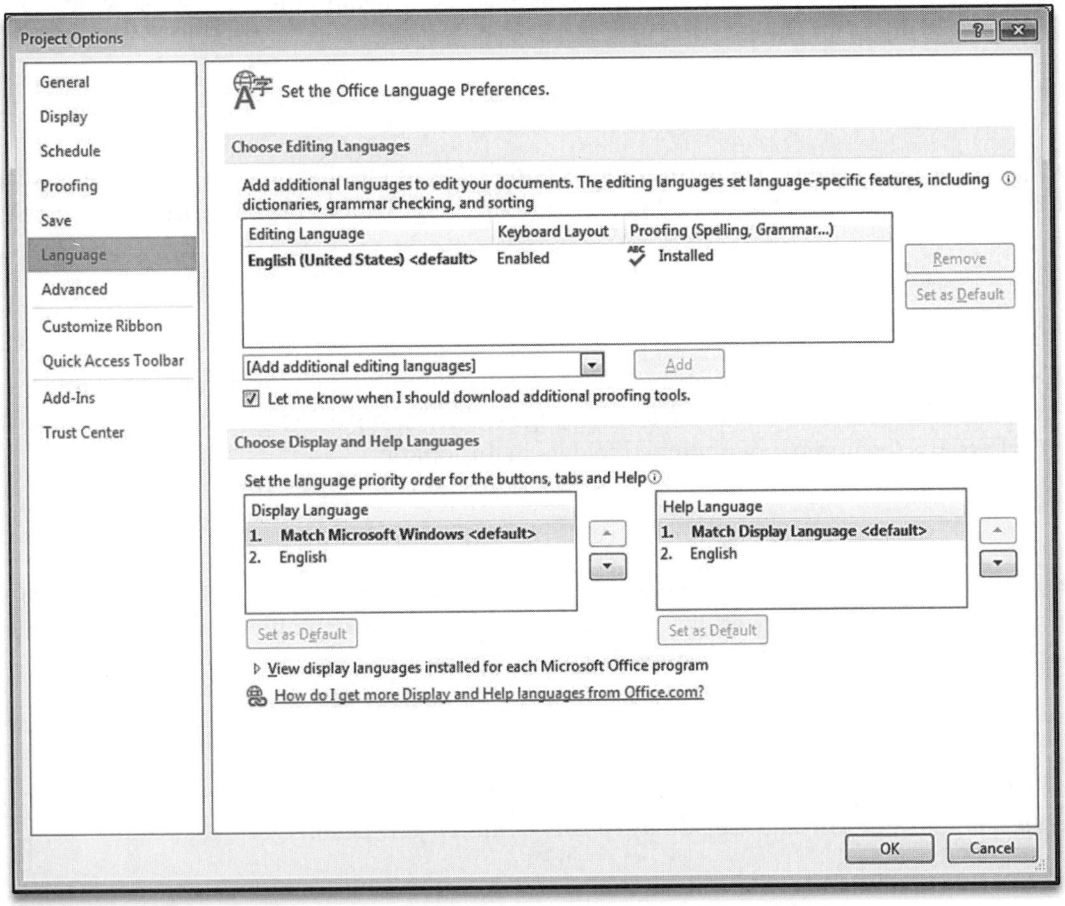

Figure 6 - 36: Project Options dialog, Language page

Before you can use the *Language* page, you must install one or more language packs for Office 2013 applications. After installing at least one language pack, you can specify the language you want to use for editing your projects, and choose the language the software uses to display your application and to display *Help* dialogs. If you do not install at least one language pack, the software limits you to the default options shown on the *Language* page.

Setting Advanced Options

Click the *Advanced* tab in the *Project Options* dialog to view the options on the *Advanced* page shown in Figure 6 - 37, Figure 6 - 38, and Figure 6 - 39. You use the options displayed at the top of the *Advanced* page in Figure 6 - 37 to specify advanced settings for Project Pro 2013 which include the *General, Project Web App, Planning Wizard, General options for this project,* and *Edit* options.

In the middle of the *Advanced* page you find the *Display* section shown in Figure 6 - 38 which contains four new options:

- The *Show this number of Recent Projects* option determines the number of recent projects to display in the *Recent Projects* section of the *Open* page in the *Backstage*. By default, the software specifies *25* projects for this option.

- The *Quickly access this number of Recent Projects* option determines the number of projects to display at the bottom of the sidepane on the left side of the *Backstage*. By default, the software does not select this option.

- The *Show this number of unpinned Recent Folders* option determines how many unpinned folders you see in the *Recent Folders* section of either the *Save As* page or the *Open* page in the *Backstage*. By default, the software selects *5* as the number of unpinned folders in this option.

- The *Disable hardware graphics acceleration* does what the name implies. By default, the software does not select this option. Depending on the graphics hardware in your computer, you may see this option as disabled (grayed out) so that you cannot change the option.

The bottom of the *Advanced* page shown in Figure 6 - 39 contains the *Cross project linking options for this project, Earned Value options for this project,* and *Calculation options for this project* sections.

Best Practice: Although not a new option, the *Show Project Summary Task* option offers a new setting state. To display the Project Summary Task in all new blank projects, click the *Display options for this project* pick list and select the *All New Projects* item, and then select the *Show Project Summary Task* option. In prior versions of Microsoft Project, the system required you to select this option for each project individually.

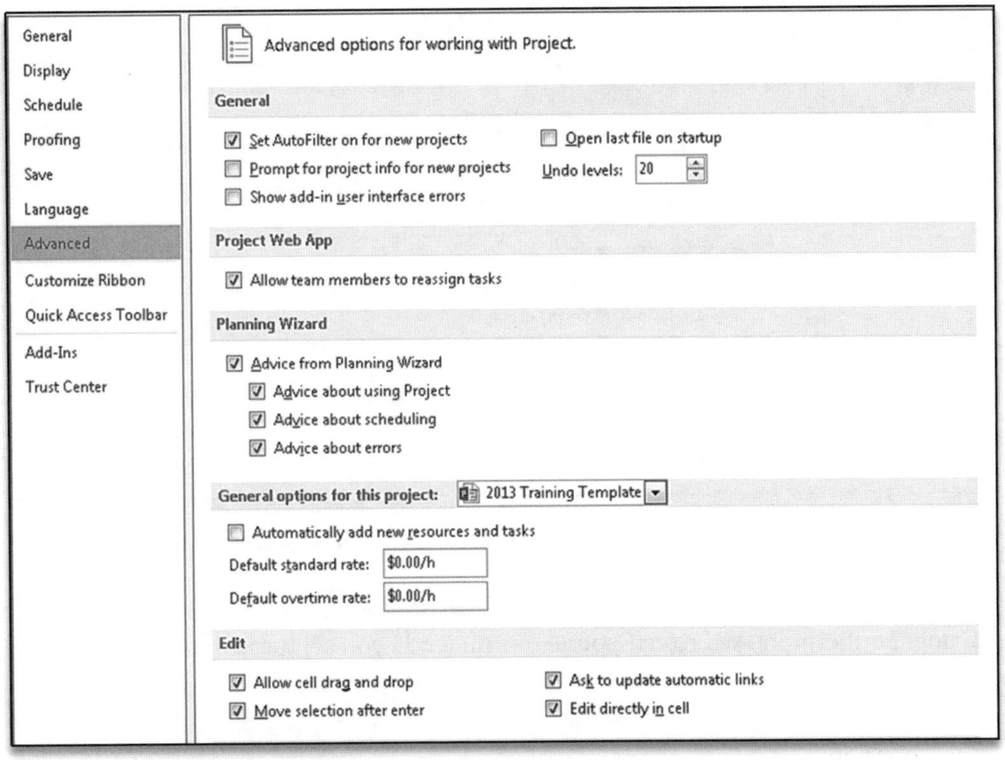

Figure 6 - 37: Project Options dialog, Advanced page (top)

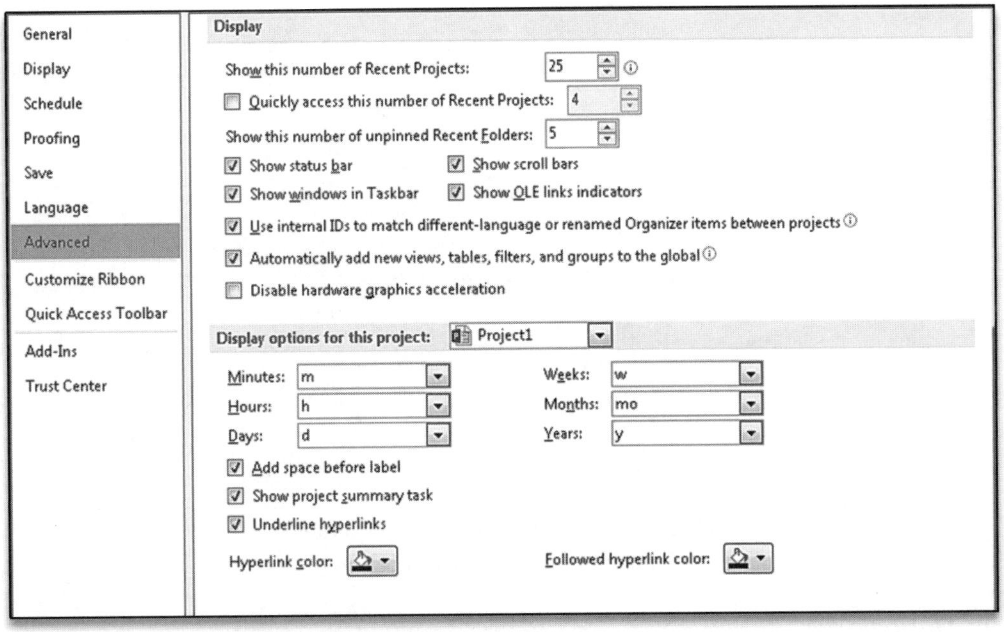

Figure 6 - 38: Project Options dialog, Advanced page (middle)

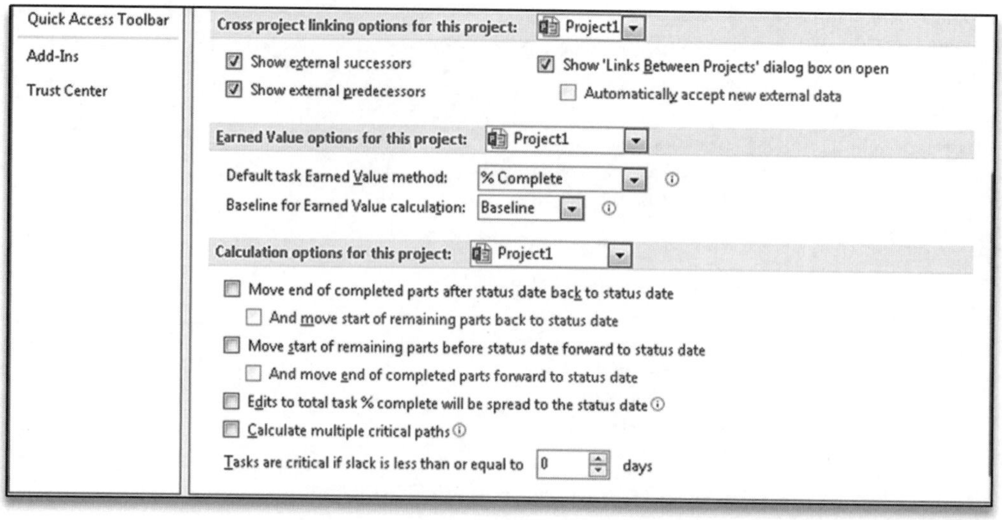

Figure 6 - 39: Project Options dialog, Advanced page (bottom)

Table 6 - 4 shows the non-default options settings recommended by MSProjectExperts on the *Advanced* page of the *Project Options* dialog. Furthermore, MSProjectExperts recommends you set these options for all open projects and for all new projects.

Option	Setting
Automatically add new resources and tasks	Deselected
Minutes	m
Hours	h
Days	d
Weeks	w
Months	mo
Years	y
Show project summary task	Selected

Table 6 - 4: Recommended options on the Advanced page for all current and future project

Setting Add-Ins Options

Click the *Add-Ins* tab in the *Project Options* dialog to view the options on the *Add-Ins* page shown in Figure 6 - 40. Use the options at the top of the *Add-Ins* page to view and manage COM Add-Ins for the applications in the Office 2013 suite of tools.

Information: As with the 2010 version, Project Pro 2013 **does not** include any of the pre-built macros found in the 2007 version and earlier. Note that the *Inactive Application Add-ins* section of the *Add-ins* page shown in Figure 6 - 40 includes the familiar macros from Project 2007. This is because I also have Project Pro 2007 installed on my computer. If you do not have Project Pro 2007 installed on your computer, you do not see the 2007 macros displayed in the *Inactive Application Add-ins* section of the page.

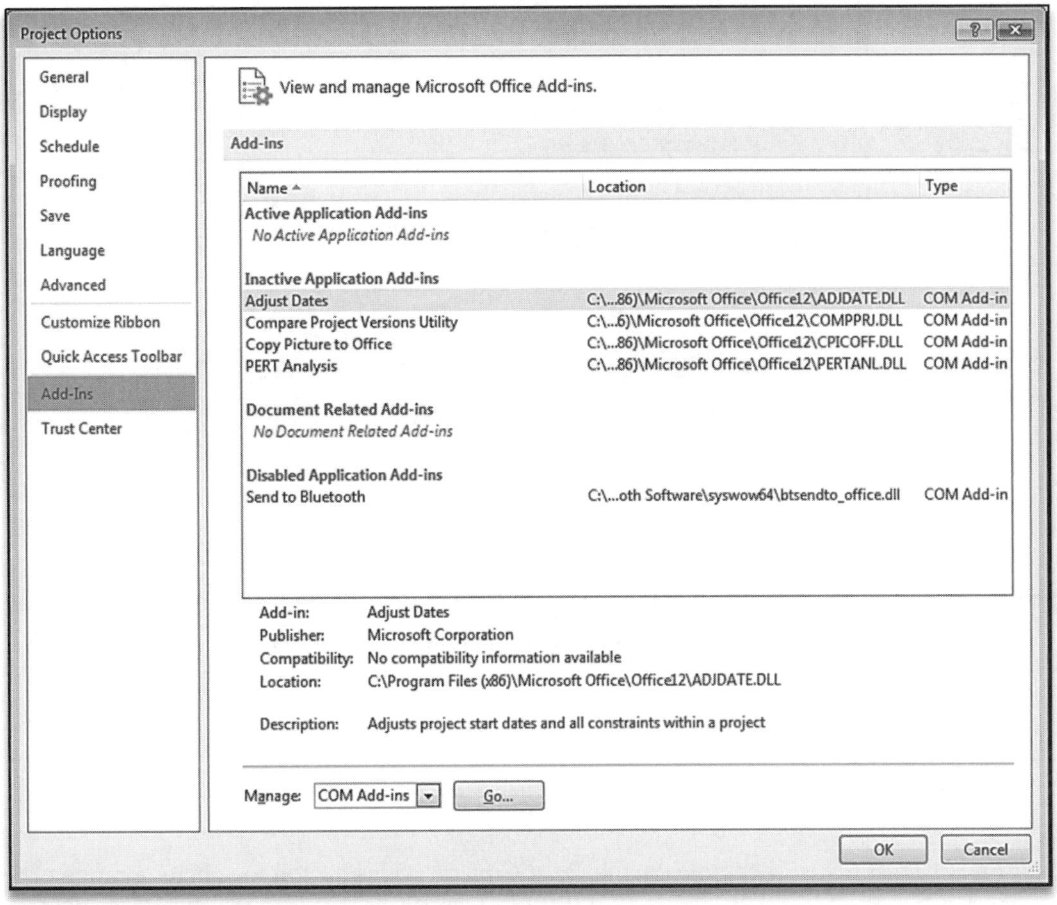

Figure 6 - 40: Project Options dialog Add-Ins page

Setting Trust Center Options

Click the *Trust Center* tab in the *Project Options* dialog to view the options on the *Trust Center* page shown in Figure 6 - 41. As indicated at the top of the *Trust Center* page, use the options on this page to provide security for your project and for your computer. The *Trust Center* page in the *Project Options* dialog provides three sections of security-related information. The *Protecting your privacy* section includes four links, the *Show the Microsoft Project privacy statement*, the *Office.com privacy statement*, the *Customer Experience Improvement Program*, and the *Microsoft Office Feedback "Send a Smile" Privacy Statement* links. I do not discuss these options, as they are self-explanatory. The *Security & more* section includes the *Microsoft Trustworthy Computing* link that displays the *Microsoft Trustworthy Computing* website. Again, I do not discuss this option, as it self-explanatory.

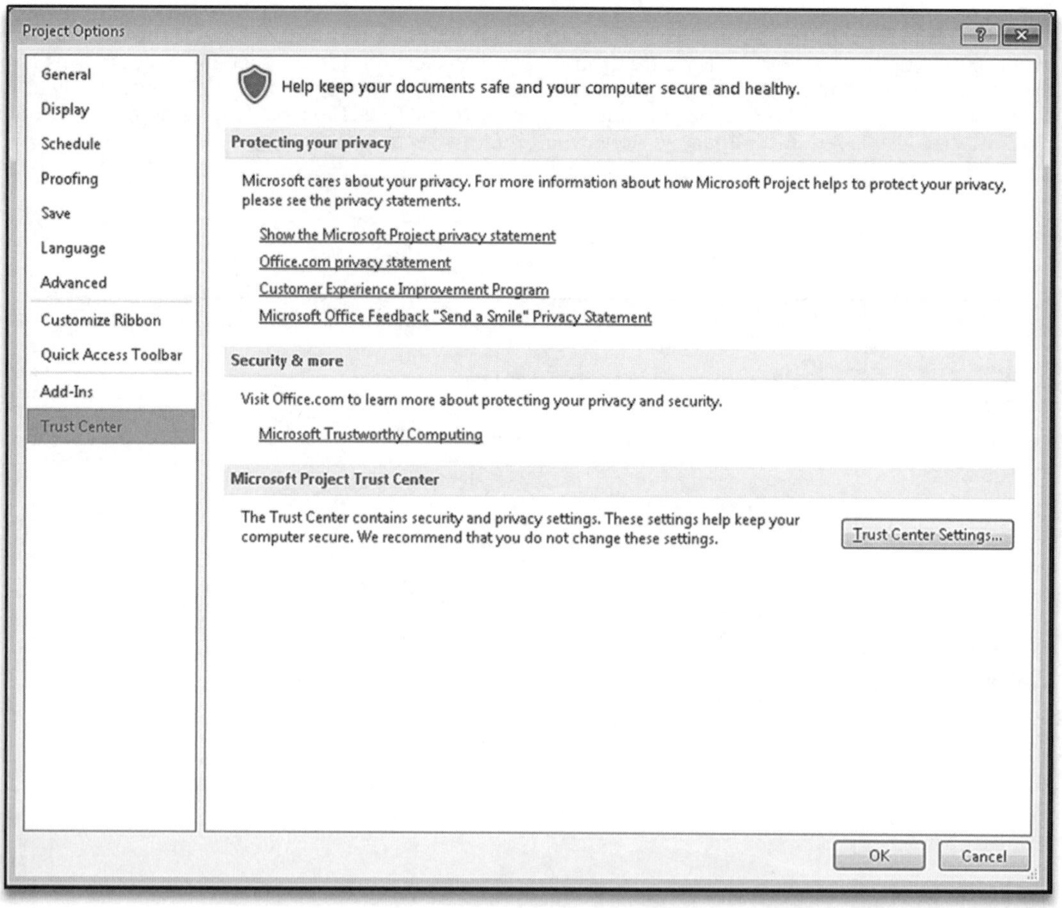

Figure 6 - 41: Project Options dialog, Trust Center page

In the *Microsoft Project Trust Center* section, click the *Trust Center Settings* button to specify a range of security settings. The system displays the *Macro Settings* page of the *Trust Center* dialog shown in Figure 6 - 42. Use the *Macro Settings* page to set your level of macro security. By default, Project Pro 2013 selects the *Disable all macros with notification* option, which prevents you from running macros in the application unless you authorize the macros to run. The software notifies you in a warning dialog about this limitation when you attempt to run a macro. To avoid the security warnings, select the *Disable all macros without notification* option. To specify a lower level of macro security, select either the *Disable all macros except digitally signed macros* option or the *Enable all macros* option to alter the security level. For enterprise projects, MSProjectExperts recommends using the *Disable all macros except digitally signed macros* option. Notice on the *Macro Settings* page that Microsoft does not recommend selecting the *Enable all macros* option. This is due to the possibility that a macro may contain a malicious virus.

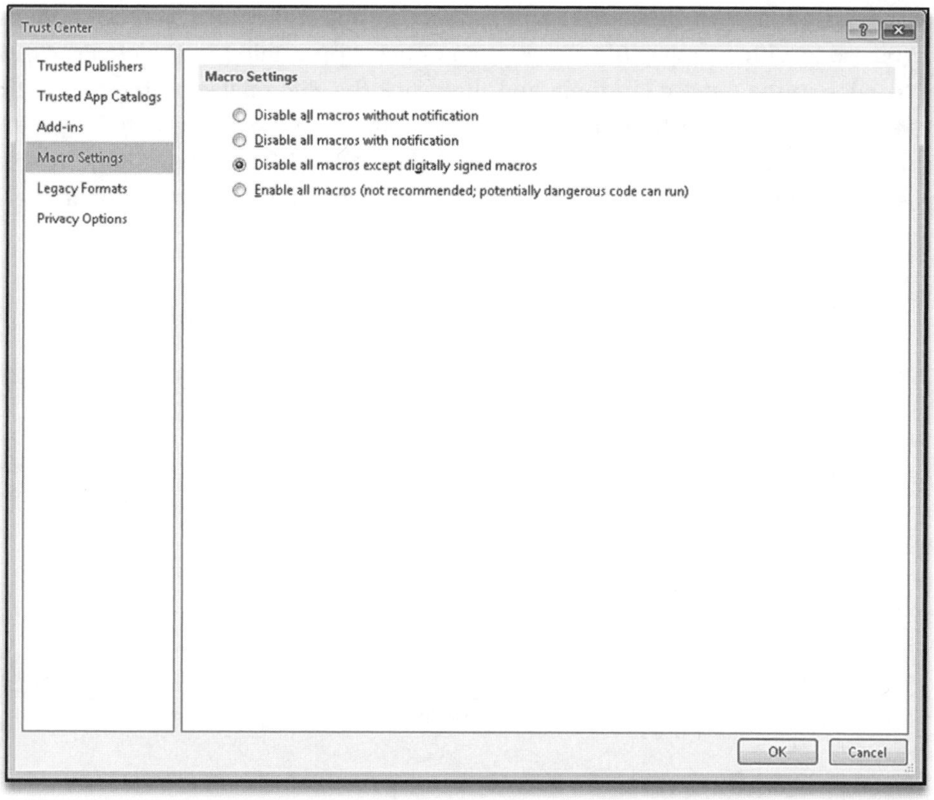

Figure 6 - 42: Trust Center dialog, Macro Settings page

Click the *Trusted Publishers* tab to display the *Trusted Publishers* page shown in Figure 6 - 43. The *Trusted Publishers* page shows macro authors whose VBA code you trust. Notice on the page that I do not currently have a formal macro trust relationship with any macro authors.

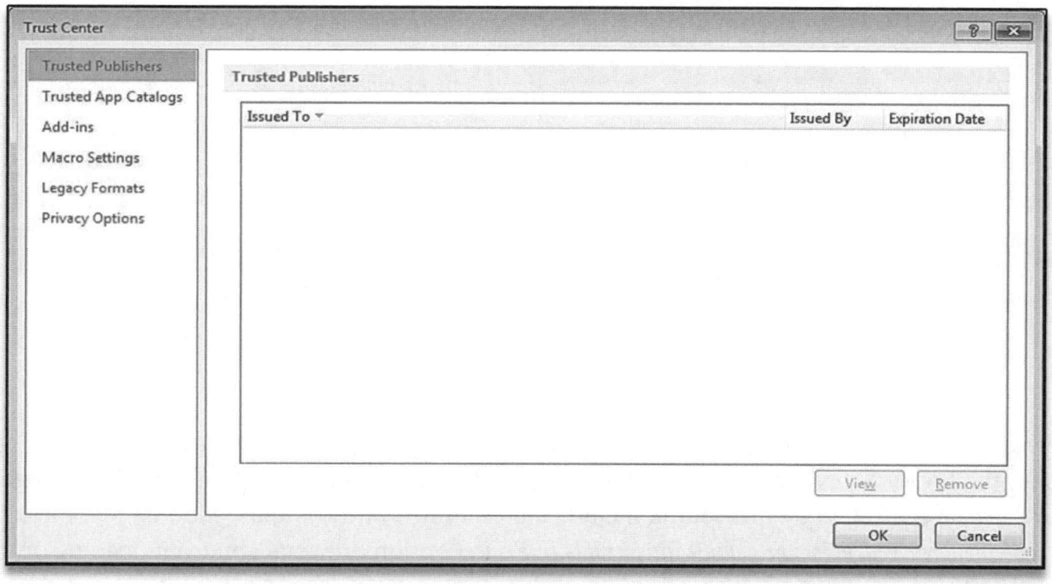

Figure 6 - 43: Trust Center dialog, Trusted Publishers page

Click the *Trusted App Catalogs* tab to display the new *Trusted App Catalogs* page shown in Figure 6 - 44. Use the options on this page to manage your Office Apps for all of the applications in the Office 2013 suite of tools. Office

Apps are web pages loaded inside an Office 2013 application. In Project Pro 2013, you can only use task pane Office Apps to help you work with a project file. To trust an Office App catalog in Project Pro 2013, enter the URL for the Office App catalog in the *Catalog Url* field, and then click the *Add catalog* button to add the Office App to the list in the *Trusted Catalogs Table* section of the dialog. To remove any existing Office App catalog, select the catalog, and then click the *Remove* button. In addition, you can disable Office App catalogs by selecting either the *Don't allow any apps to start* option or the *Don't allow apps from the Office Store to start* option in the *Trusted App Catalogs* section at the top of the page.

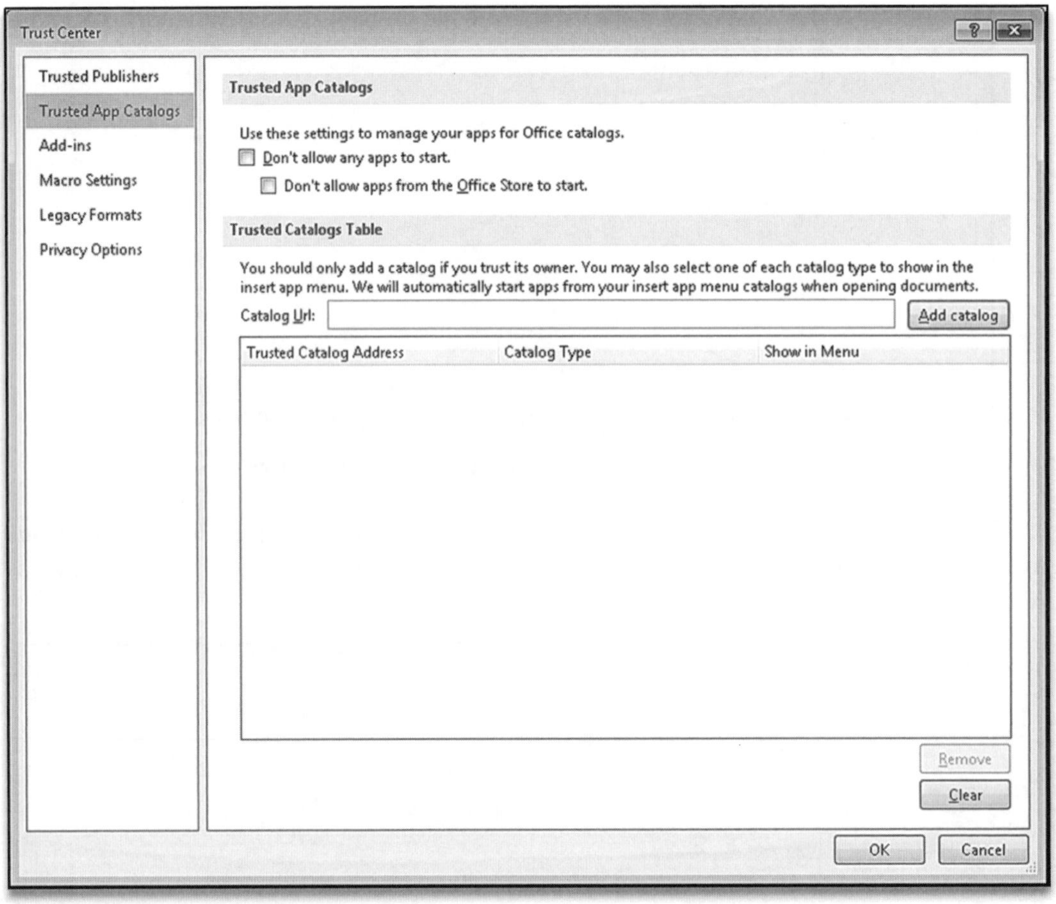

Figure 6 - 44: Trust Center dialog, Trusted App Catalogs page

Click the *Legacy Formats* tab to display the *Legacy Formats* page in the *Trust Center* dialog shown in Figure 6 - 45. The options on the *Legacy Formats* page control how Project Pro 2013 works with non-default and legacy file formats. Legacy formats controlled by this setting include tab-delimited and comma-delimited text files. The default *Do not open/save file with legacy or non-default file formats in Project* option prevents you from opening or closing files that are non-default or legacy format. If you need to work with non-default or legacy files, select either the *Prompt when loading files with legacy or non-default file format* option or the *Allow loading files with legacy or non-default file formats* option on the page.

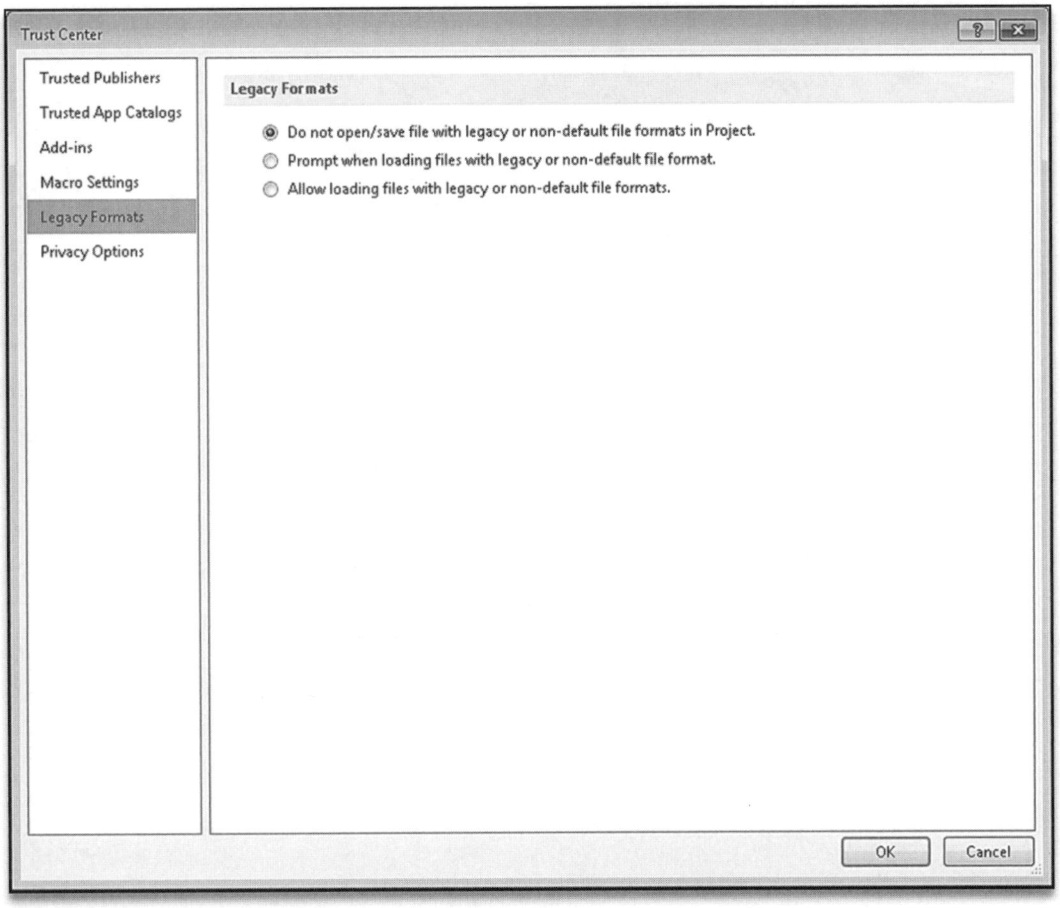

Figure 6 - 45: Trust Center dialog, Legacy Formats page

Warning: If you do not change the default option setting in the *Legacy Formats* page of the *Trust Center* dialog, the system prevents you from either importing or exporting with a legacy or non-default file format such as the Excel workbook format.

Click the *Privacy Options* tab to display the *Privacy Options* page in the *Trust Center* dialog shown in Figure 6 - 46. As the name of the page implies, use the settings on the *Privacy Options* page to control how much information Project Pro 2013 shares with Microsoft and other outside organizations. The *Privacy Options* page contains six application options and one project-specific option. The names of the six application options reveal their function, so I do not discuss them individually. If you select the *Remove personal information from file properties on save* option, the single project-specific option, the software clears the *Author, Manager, Company* and *Last Saved By* fields in the *Properties* dialog each time you save the project.

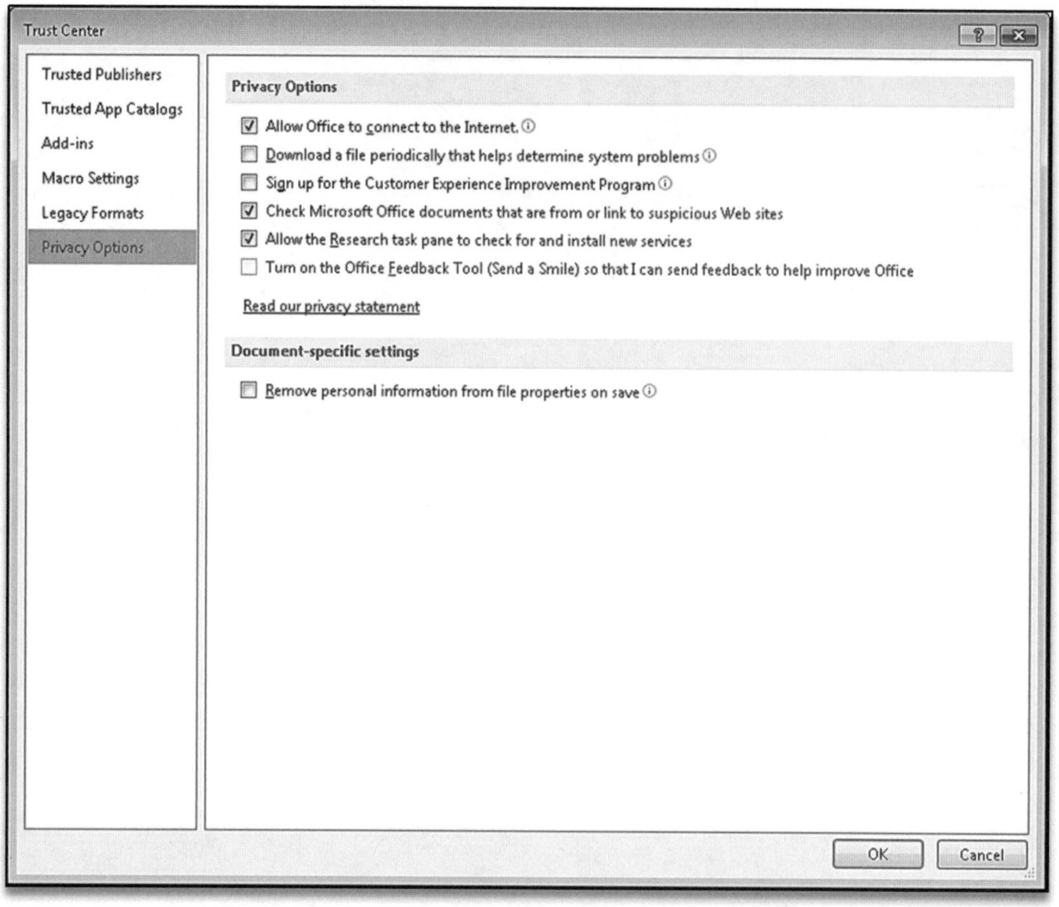

Figure 6 - 46: Trust Center dialog, Privacy Options page

After selecting your options in the *Trust Center* dialog, click the *OK* button to close the dialog, then click the *OK* button to close the *Project Options* dialog as well. Table 6 - 5 shows the non-default options settings recommended by MSProjectExperts on the *Trust Center* page of the *Project Options* dialog.

Option	Setting
Macro Settings	Disable all macros except digitally signed macros
Legacy Formats	Allow loading files with legacy or non-default file formats
Trusted App Catalogs	Add the URL for the Office Store catalog https://office.microsoft.com

Table 6 - 5: Recommended options for the Trust Center page

After selecting your options in the *Trust Center* dialog, click the *OK* button to close the dialog and then click the *OK* button to close the *Project Options* dialog.

Save the Project

The final step in the 6-step definition process is to save your project according to your organization's naming convention for enterprise projects. To save the project, complete the following steps:

1. In the *Save* section of the *Project* ribbon, click the *Save* button. The system displays the *Save to Project Web App* dialog shown in Figure 6 - 47.

> **Information**: You can also display the *Save to Project Web App* dialog by clicking the *Save* button on the *Quick Access Toolbar*, or by clicking the *File* tab and then clicking the *Save* or *Save As* items in the *Backstage*.

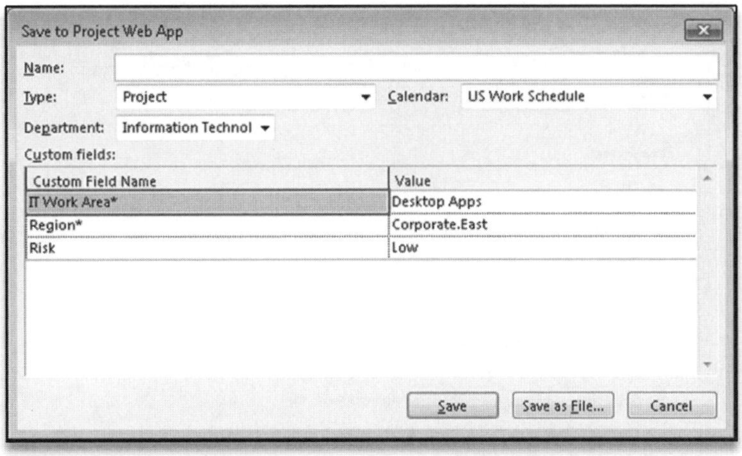

Figure 6 - 47: Save to Project Web App dialog

2. In the *Name* field, enter a name that meets your organization standards for naming an enterprise project.

> **Warning**: When entering the name of your enterprise project, use only alphanumeric characters, spaces, and the underscore (_) character. Do not use any other special characters, such as ampersands (&), pound signs (#), dashes (-), or commas. Using special characters in the name of your enterprise project can lead to a corrupted project.

3. Click the *Save* button in the *Save to Project Web App* dialog.

> **Information**: Notice in Figure 6 - 47 that the *Save to Project Web App* dialog contains a *Calendar* pick list and a *Custom fields* section, as seen previously in the *Project Information* dialog, this dialog provides one last chance to change any of these values prior to saving your project.

Understanding the Local Cache

When you save a new enterprise project to the Project Server database, the Project Server 2013 system saves a complete copy of your project file on your hard drive in a location known as the local project cache, and then "spools" the project information to the Project Server database. As you revise the project and save the changes, the system again saves a complete copy of your project in the cache, but "spools" only the changes to the Project Server database. When you open a project, the system opens the copy in your cache and then synchronizes this local copy with the enterprise project saved in the Project Server database. Because the cache works in the background, it makes the process of opening and saving enterprise projects much faster, even over a Wide Area Network (WAN) connection.

When you save a project in the Project Server database, you can see the status of the cache "spooling" operation on the *Status* bar at the bottom of your Project Pro 2013 application window. When the system completes the "spooling" operation, it displays a *Save completed successfully* message in the application *Status* bar.

Adjusting Local Cache Settings

To view and adjust the default settings for the cache, click the *File* tab and then click the *Options* tab in the *Backstage.* In the *Project Options* dialog, click the *Save* tab. Project Server 2013 displays the default settings for the cache in the *Cache* section of the *Save* page in the *Project Options* dialog, as shown in Figure 6 - 48.

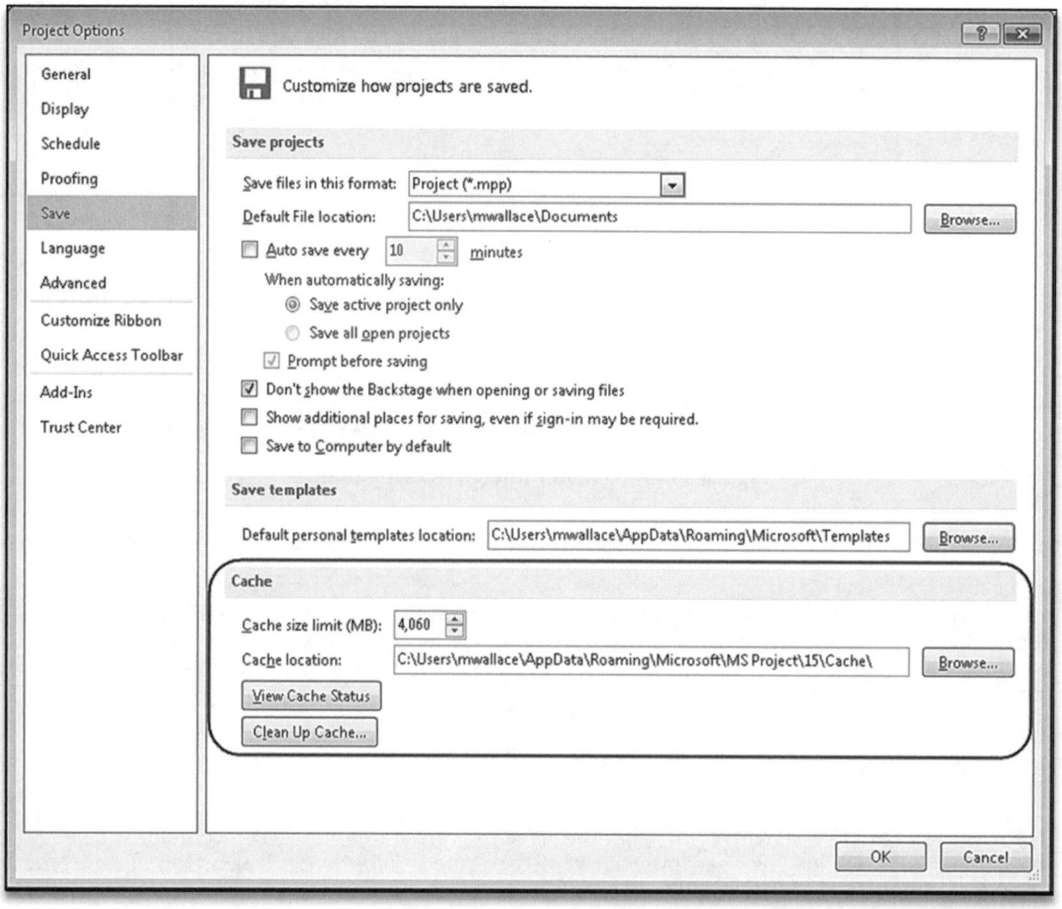

Figure 6 - 48: Cache settings in the Project Options dialog

The options in the *Cache* section of the *Project Options* dialog allow you to change two settings for the cache: the size limit and the location. To adjust the size limit of the cache, enter a new value in megabytes in the *Cache size limit (MB)* field. To change the location of the cache, click the *Browse* button to the right of the *Cache location* field and select a new file location. Click the *OK* button when finished.

Information: By default, Project Server 2013 stores the cache data in the following folder:

C:\Users\YourUserID\AppData\Roaming\Microsoft\MS Project\15\Cache

Warning: If your job requires you to travel, and you need to take enterprise projects with you while traveling, do not specify a cache location value that is outside your laptop's hard drive, such as on a network share. Project Server 2013 uses the cache for offline projects, which allows you to check out and modify enterprise projects while away from your corporate network.

Viewing Local Cache Contents

To view the contents of the cache, click the *File* tab and then the *Options* tab in the *Backstage*. In the *Project Options* dialog, click the *Save* tab. In the *Cache* section of the *Save* page in the *Project Options* dialog shown previously in Figure 6 - 48, click the *View Cache Status* button. The system displays the *Active Cache Status* dialog shown in Figure 6 - 49.

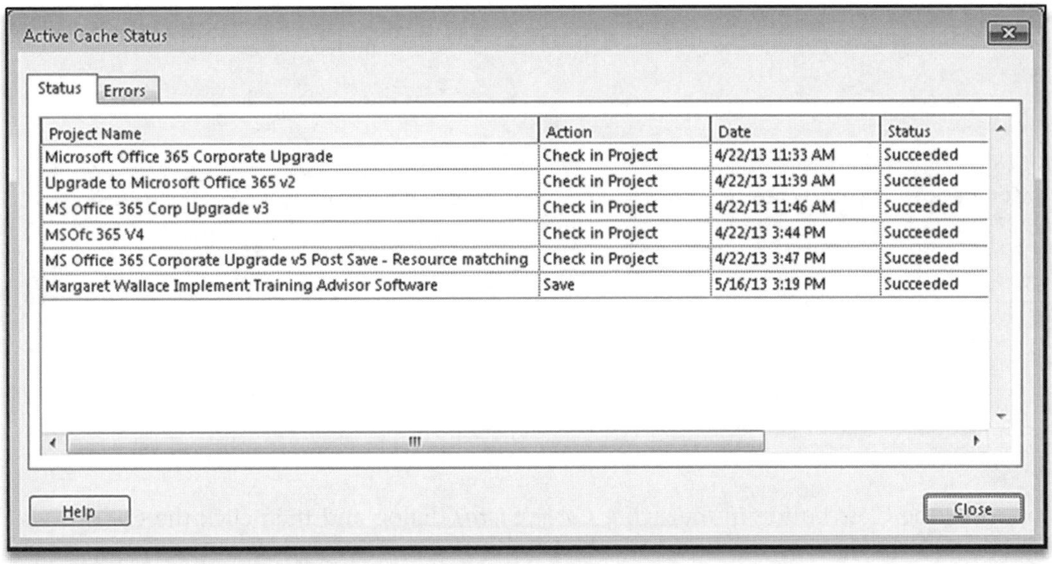

Figure 6 - 49: Active Cache Status dialog, Status page

The *Active Cache Status* dialog contains two pages: the *Status* and *Errors* pages. The *Status* page shows the status of recent cache activities, such as saving or publishing a project. Notice in Figure 6 - 49 that I successfully saved one enterprise project and checked in five other projects. Click the *Errors* tab to see errors that occurred during a save or publish operation. The system displays the *Errors* page shown in Figure 6 - 50. Notice that I see no errors on the *Errors* page in the *Active Cache Status* dialog.

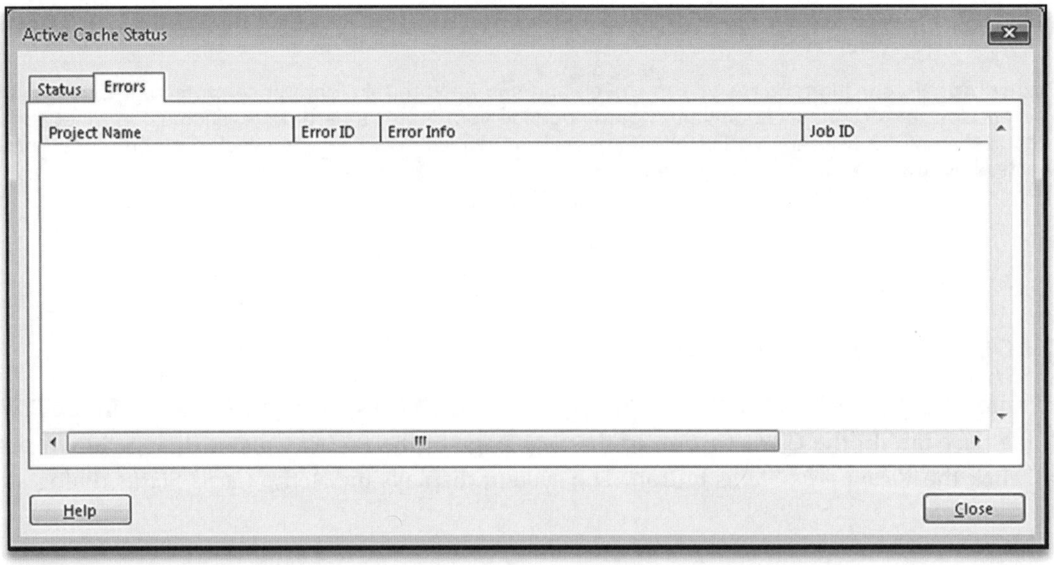

Figure 6 - 50: Active Cache Status dialog, Errors page

Information: If you see errors of any kind on the *Errors* page in the *Active Cache Status* dialog, contact your Project Server administrator immediately for help.

When finished, click the *Close* button in the *Active Cache Status* dialog and then click the *OK* or *Cancel* button to close the *Project Options* dialog.

Cleaning Up the Local Cache

At some point, you may want to clean up the cache to remove projects with which you no longer work, such as completed or cancelled projects, or to remove a project "stuck" in a checked-out state. To remove projects from the cache, click the *Cleanup Cache* button in the *Save* page of the *Project Options* dialog shown previously in Figure 6 - 48. Project Server 2013 displays the *Clean Up Cache* dialog shown in Figure 6 - 51.

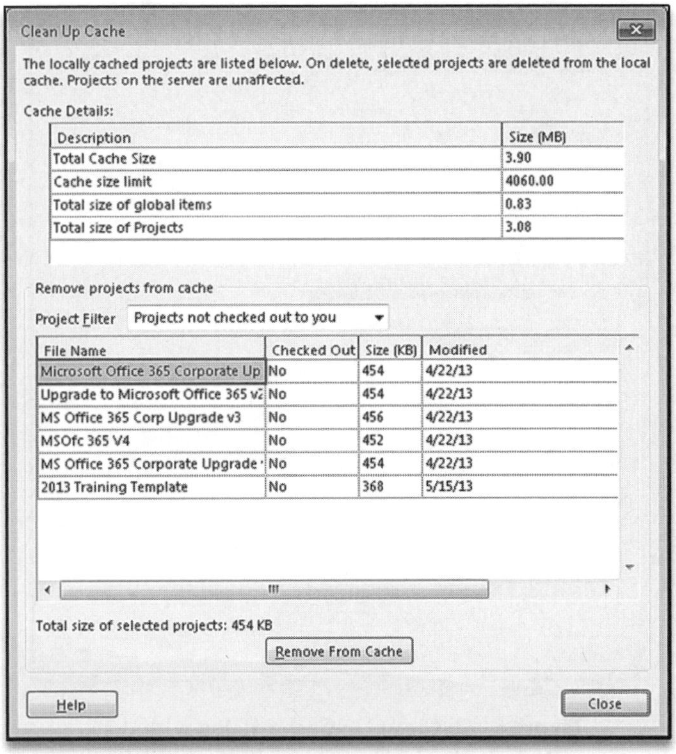

Figure 6 - 51: Clean Up Cache dialog with the Projects not checked out to you filter applied

Information: You can access the *Clean Up Cache* dialog by clicking the *File* tab and then clicking the *Options* tab in the *Backstage*. In the *Project Options* dialog, click the *Save* tab and then click the *Clean Up Cache* button in the *Cache* section of the dialog.

The *Clean Up Cache* dialog displays statistics about the cache in the *Cache Details* section at the top of the dialog. Using the *Project Filter* pick list, you can apply two filtering options: *Projects not checked out to you* and *Projects checked out to you*. The system applies the *Projects not checked out to you* filter by default. Notice in Figure 6 - 51 that the system lists six projects not checked out to me currently.

Figure 6 - 52 shows the *Clean Up Cache* dialog after applying the *Projects checked out to you* filter on the *Project Filter* pick list. Notice that the *Clean Up Cache* dialog shows no projects currently checked out to me.

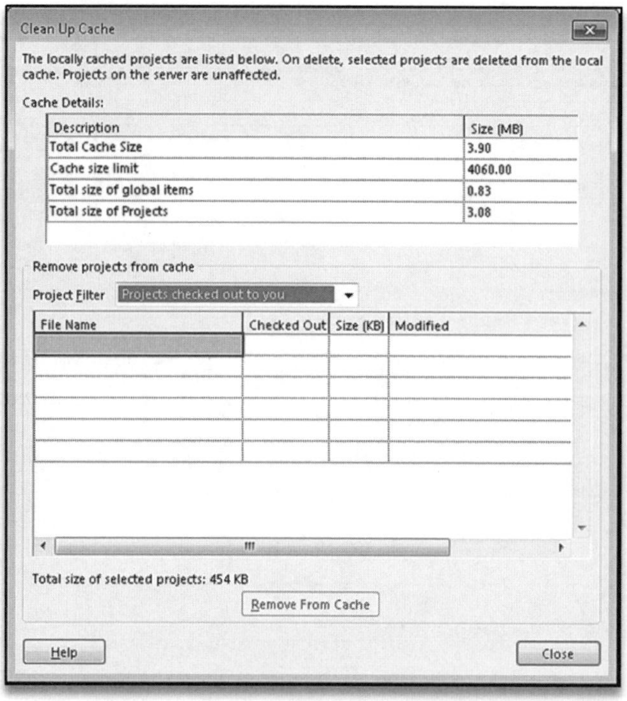

Figure 6 - 52: Clean Up Cache dialog with the Projects checked out to you filter applied

To remove a project from the cache, select the project in the *Remove projects from cache* list as shown in Figure 6 - 53 and then click the *Remove From Cache* button. If you select a project not checked out to you, the system simply removes the project from the cache. If you attempt to delete a project currently checked out to you, the system displays the warning dialog shown in Figure 6 - 54.

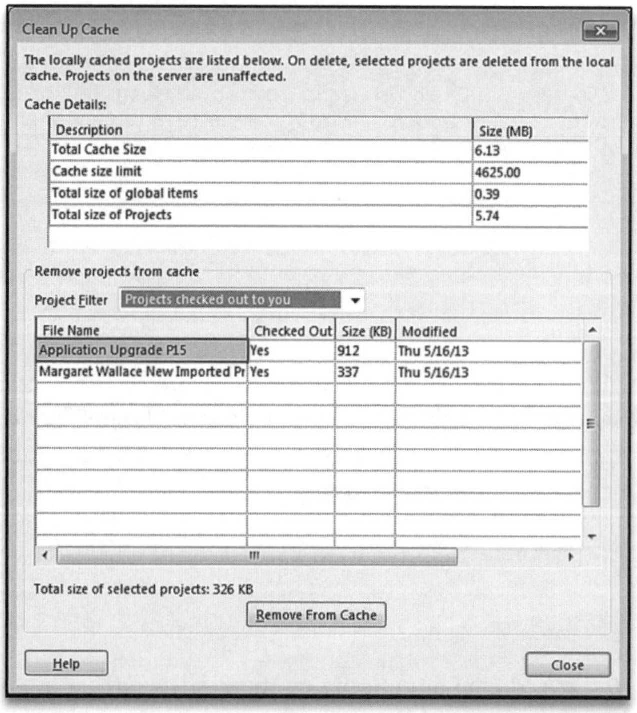

Figure 6 - 53: Clean Up Cache dialog, Remove From cache

If you are absolutely certain the project is "stuck" in a checked-out state, and not checked out because the project is in *Offline* mode, then click the *Yes* button to delete the project from the cache as shown in Figure 6 - 54. Click the *Close* button to close the *Clean Up Cache* dialog.

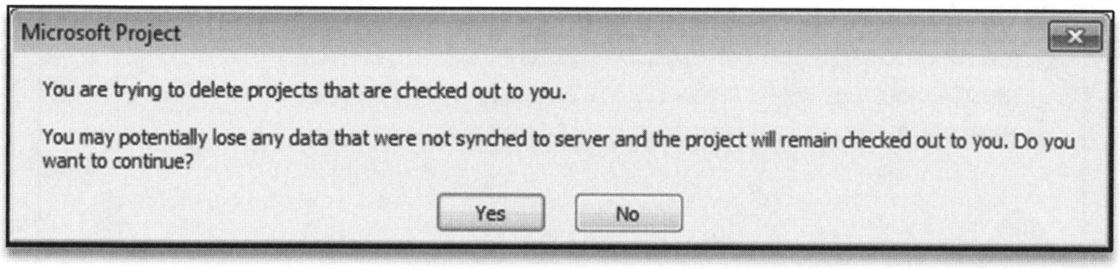
Microsoft Project
You are trying to delete projects that are checked out to you.
You may potentially lose any data that were not synched to server and the project will remain checked out to you. Do you want to continue?
Yes
No

Figure 6 - 54: Warning dialog before deleting checked-out project

Information: Deleting a project from the cache does not delete the project from the Project Server database; instead, the operation removes only the cached version of the project from your hard drive. The next time you open a project that you deleted from the cache, the system will take longer to open the project because it must load the entire project from the Project Server database.

Warning: If your Project Server administrator deletes a project from the Project Server database, and you are the owner or manager of the project, the system does not delete the project from your cache. Because the project continues to appear in the *Open* dialog, you should delete the project from your cache to avoid confusion and frustration.

Resolving Local Cache Corruption

Project Server 2013 can corrupt the cache, even with the major improvements to its functionality. If you see unusual behavior in your enterprise projects, and suspect that corrupt cache is the culprit, you can safely delete the cache files using the following steps:

1. Close Project Pro 2013.

2. Press the **Windows** key on your computer keyboard or click the *Start* button, and in the Windows 7 *Search* field, enter the following command:

```
%appdata%\Microsoft\MS Project\15\Cache
```

Windows filters the results in the *Search* window and displays the *Cache* folder location on your PC's hard drive.

3. Click the *Cache* folder icon to open the folder in a *Windows Explorer* application window as the system displays the cache folders shown in Figure 6 - 55.

4. To delete all of the folders and files in the *Cache* folder, select all of the folders, right-click using your mouse and select the *Delete* item in the pick list.

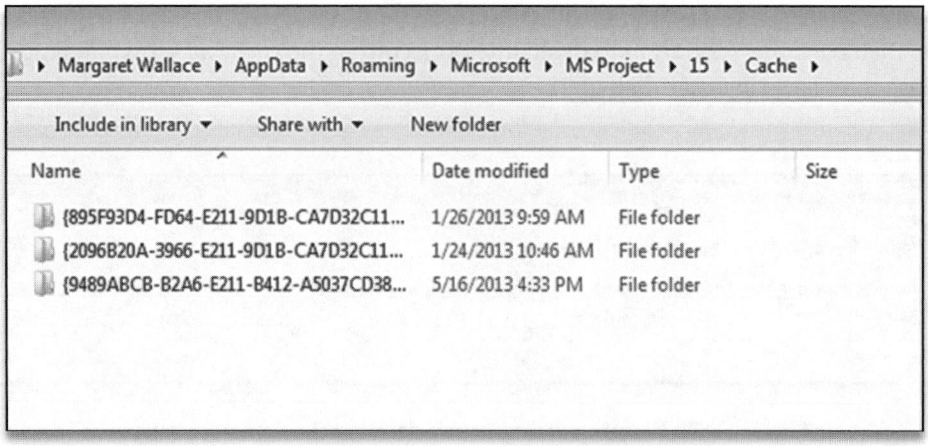

Figure 6 - 55: Cache folder showing the individual cache folders per project

The next time you attempt to open projects in the Project Server database, you must use the *Show me the list of all projects* option in the *Open* dialog.

Opening and Closing Projects

To open any project using Project Pro 2013, click the *File* tab and then click the *Open* tab in the *Backstage*. Project Server 2013 displays the *Open* page shown in Figure 6 - 56. Note that the software displays only projects you have permission to access in the Project Server database. By default, the system displays the following links:

- Project Web App account name
- Recent Projects
- SkyDrive
- Computer
- Add a Place

The Project Web App account name link provides access to projects in the Project Server database through the *Open* dialog and allows you to select the project to open. The *Recent Projects* list displays projects currently in your cache, and limits the number of projects displayed based on your previous configuration on the *Advanced* page in the *Project Options* dialog. The *SkyDrive* link provides access to files from your *SkyDrive* only, and does not provide access to projects in the Project Server database. The *Computer* link provides access to *Recent Folders* on your local PC where you already store project files that are not in the Project Server database but are local projects. The *Add a Place* link allows you to indicate an additional location to save or retrieve Office documents from the cloud; this option is for local projects only. An example for a location for *Add a Place* link would be a link to an additional *SkyDrive* location or *Office 365 SharePoint*.

To access enterprise projects in Project Server 2013, you need to use the *Recent Projects* link, or use the *Open* dialog that you access by selecting your Project Web App account name. These features vary slightly from the methods used to open projects in previous versions of Project Server in that by default, the projects open in *Read Only* mode, allowing the user to check out the project after it opens in Project Pro 2013.

Best Practice: MSProjectExperts recommends accessing your enterprise projects using the *Recent Projects* link method when possible in order to access the cache version of a project. The process of loading an enterprise project is much faster when using the local project cache. See the *Understanding the Local Cache* topical section discussed earlier in this module for a complete explanation.

Notice that on the *Open* page in the *Recent Projects* section shown in Figure 6 - 56, the system displays only eight projects, which are the only projects currently in my local cache.

Information: You can display the *Open* dialog in Project Pro 2013 by clicking the *File* tab, clicking the *Open* tab in the *Backstage*, and then double-clicking the Project Web App instance name.

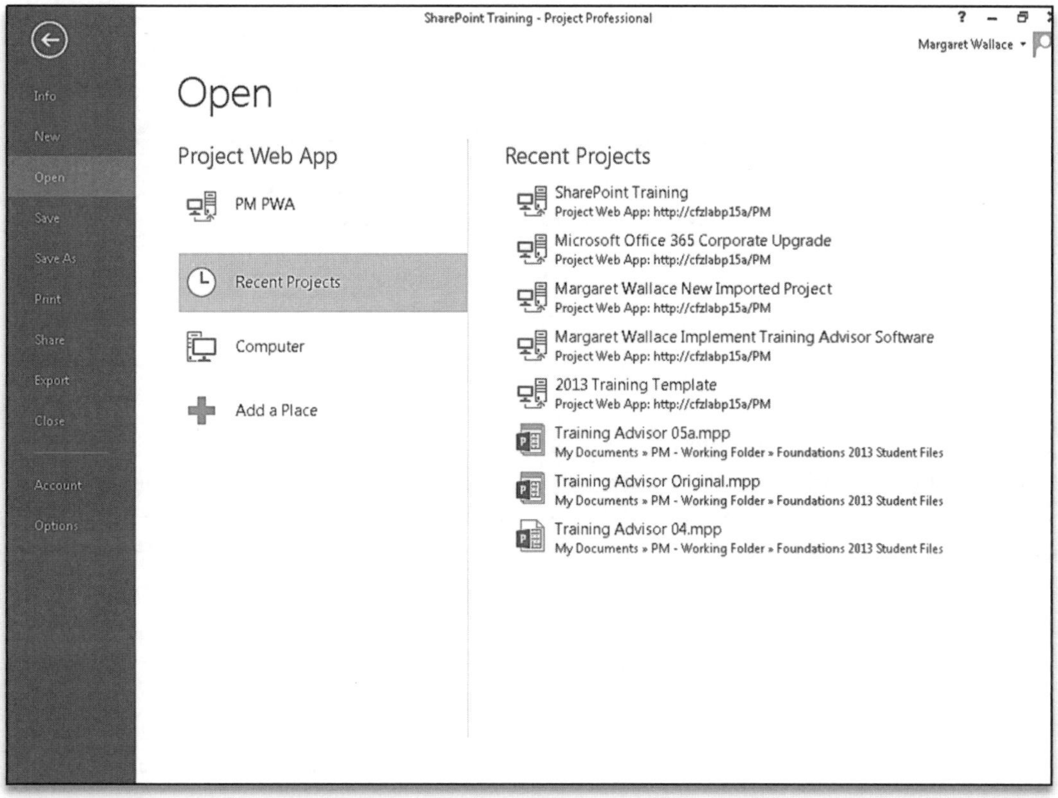

Figure 6 - 56: Open page showing Recent Projects

Notice in Figure 6 - 57, the *Open* dialog displays the same eight projects but also displays the *Cache Status* column indicating any projects in a currently *Checked Out* state.

Information: To access your cached project list as shown in Figure 6 - 57, from the *Open* page in the *Backstage* double click your Project Web App account to display your recently opened projects in the *Open dialog*. As an alternative, you may also double-click the *Browse* folder to display the recently opened projects list.

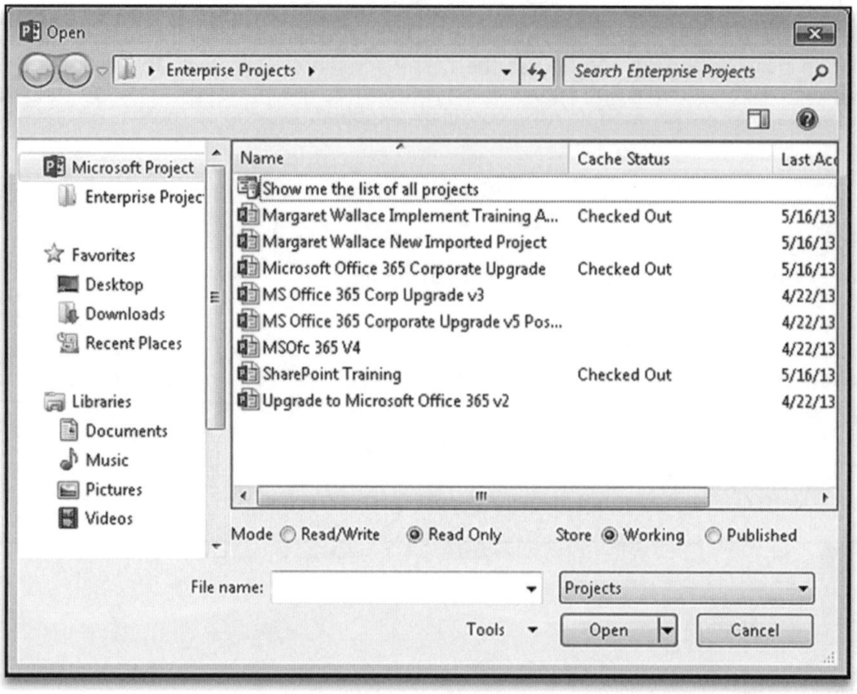

Figure 6 - 57: Open dialog shows all cache projects available to me in the Project Server 2013 database, with Cache Status

To display a complete list of all of the enterprise projects you have permission to access, double-click the Project Web App account name to display the *Open di*alog. Then, click the *Show me a list of all projects* link to display all projects to which you have access. The *Open* dialog refreshes with a list of all available projects in the Project Server database, as shown in Figure 6 - 58. Notice that the *Open* dialog now shows a number of additional projects that I have permission to access. I have also expanded this window to show the complete path name in the address bar.

Information: In Project Server 2010 to access all of the enterprise projects you have permission to access in the Project Server database, you clicked the *Retrieve the list of all projects from Project Server* link; however, in Project Server 2013 you must click the *Show me a list of all projects* link.

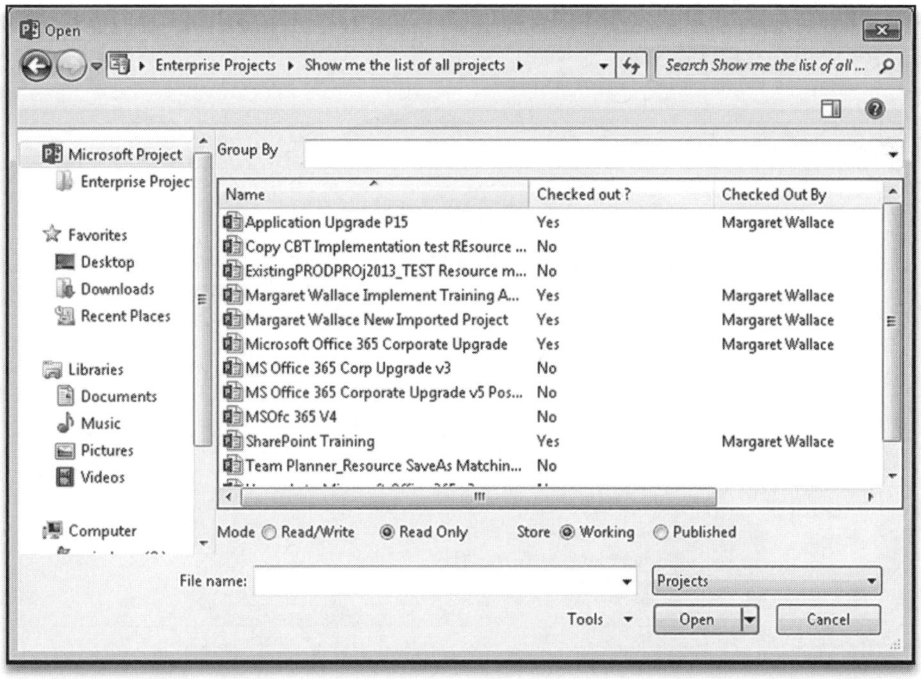

Figure 6 - 58: Open dialog, all enterprise projects and complete path description

When viewing the list of available projects in the Project Server database, the *Open* dialog includes a *Group By* pick list above the list of projects. This option is only available when you click the *Show me the list of all projects* link. The *Group By* pick list allows you to apply grouping to the projects listed in the dialog by any custom enterprise project field that contains a lookup table. If you want to group the projects listed, click the *Group By* pick list and select a custom enterprise field from the list, as shown in Figure 6 - 59.

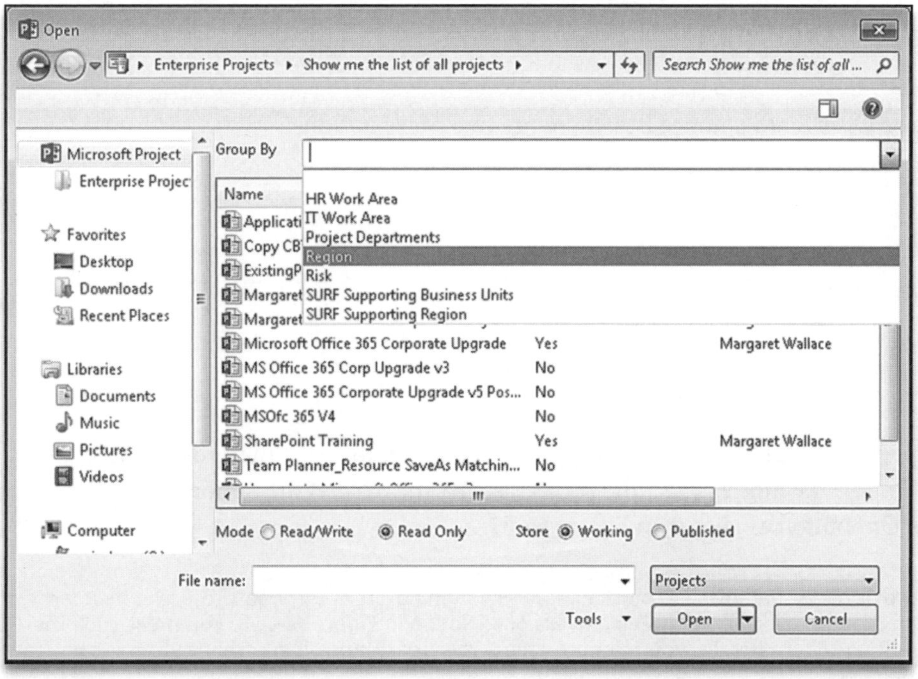

Figure 6 - 59: Open dialog, Group By pick list

Figure 6 - 60 shows the list of projects grouped by the *Region* custom field. This field allows a project manager to select a project for a particular region.

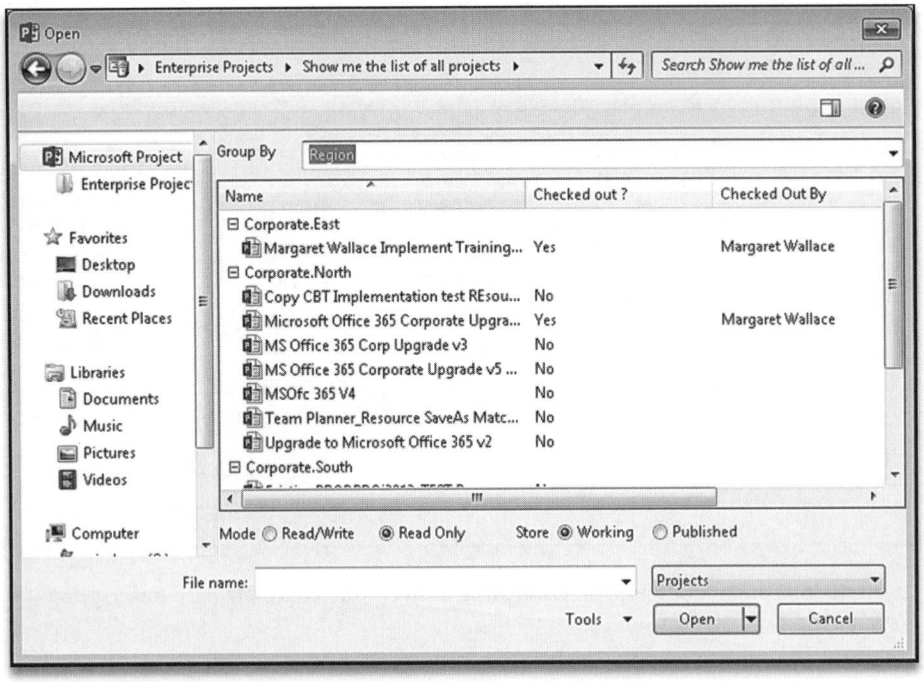

Figure 6 - 60: Open dialog, projects grouped by the Region field

Information: After you select an item in the *Group By* pick list in Project Pro 2013, the *Open* dialog sorts the project list in *Ascending* order as users might expect. This is a new feature in this version as previous versions sorted lists in *Descending* order. To sort the project list in *Descending* order, you must click once on the *Name* column header.

At the bottom of the *Open* dialog, notice that there are two *Mode* options:

- *Read/Write*
- *Read Only*

There are two *Store* options:

- *Working*
- *Published*

To open an enterprise project in *Read Only* mode, you need only to select the project and click the *Open* button. To open a project in *Read/Write* mode, select the project, select the *Read/Write* option, and then click the *Open* button, or select the *Check Out* button as shown in Figure 6 - 61.

Information: By default in Project Pro 2013, opening an enterprise project is in *Read Only* mode using the *Working* store version unlike previous versions. Notice in Figure 6 - 61, you must click the *Check Out* button to allow editing. Alternatively, you may pre-select the *Read/Write* mode that automatically checks out the project when opening.

Warning: When you see the following message in Project Server:

READ-ONLY This project was opened in read-only mode.

You must click the *Check Out* button, to check out the project to allow editing. In previous versions, there was no way to edit a project once it was in *Read Only* mode.

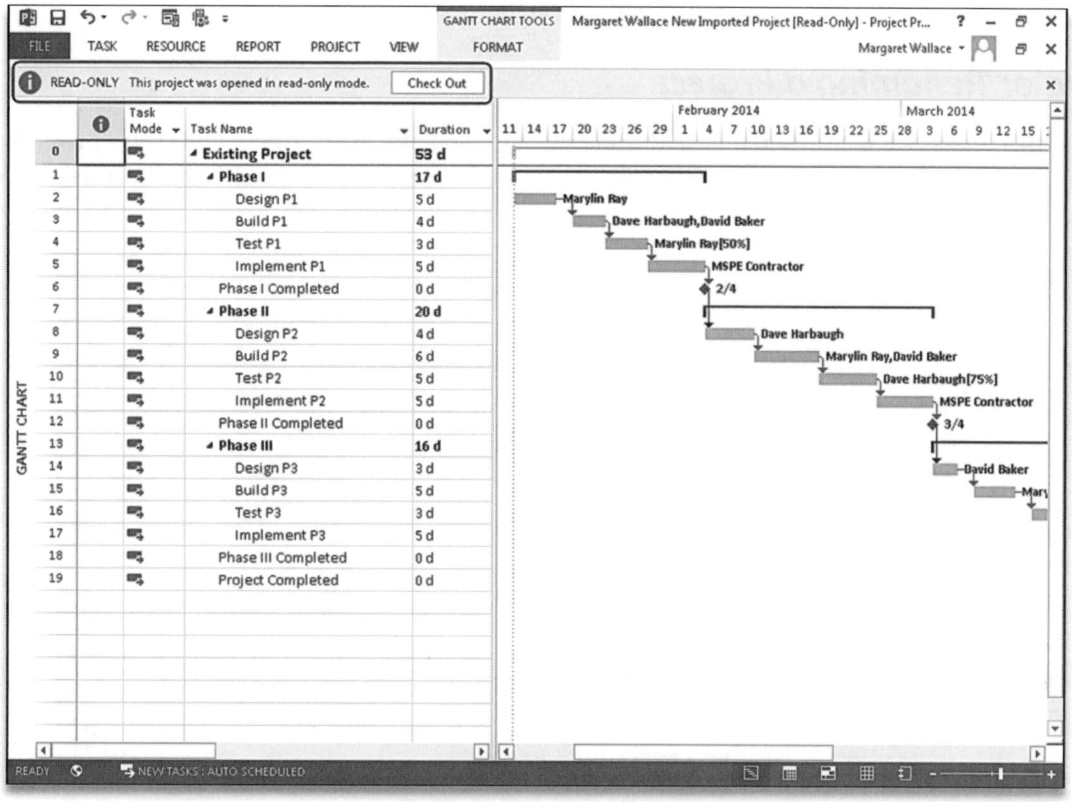

Figure 6 - 61: Open project in Read-Only mode requires Check Out to edit

To open a project from the *Working* store, you need only to select the project and click the *Open* button. However, by default the project is in *Read Only* mode when opening, allowing for the check-out to occur within Project Pro 2013 after opening the project. The *Working* version of the project contains all of the current information about the project. If you want to see the published information for a project, then you must select the *Published* option, the project name, and then click the *Open* button. The system opens the *Published* version of the project in *Read Only* mode, and does not allow you to save changes to the project.

Information: The *Working* version and *Published* version of a project may differ because you may edit an enterprise project and save the changes, but may not publish the changes to the Project Server database. Remember that only the *Published* version of the project is visible in the *Project Center* page in Project Web App.

If you attempt to open an enterprise project for which you only have permission to open in *Read Only* mode, Project Pro 2013 displays the warning dialog shown in Figure 6 - 62. Click the *Yes* button to open the project in *Read Only* mode.

Figure 6 - 62: Warning dialog when opening project with Read Only permissions

Deleting or Renaming a Project

Project Pro 2013 offers two features in the *Open* dialog when you have the list of all enterprise projects displayed. When you right-click the name of any enterprise project, the system displays the shortcut menu shown in Figure 6 - 63.

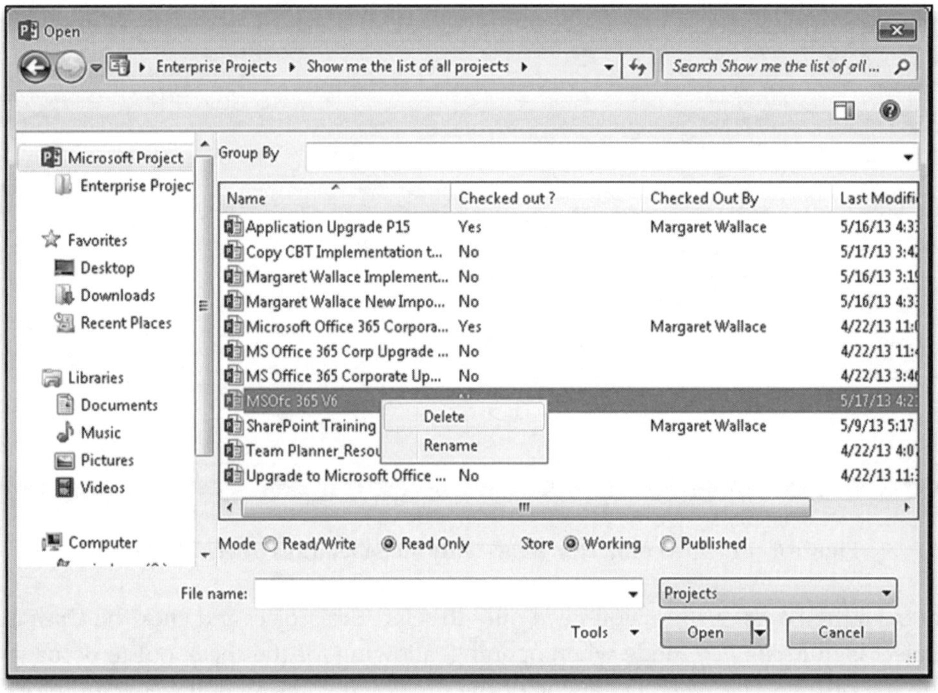

Figure 6 - 63: Delete or rename an enterprise project in the Open dialog

To delete an enterprise project, right-click the name of the project and then select the *Delete* item on the shortcut menu. The system displays the confirmation dialog shown in Figure 6 - 64. Click the *Yes* button in the dialog to complete the deletion process. When the system deletes your project, it will delete the project in both the *Draft* and *Published* databases, and will delete the Project Site associated with the project as well.

Information: The *Delete* option shown in Figure 6 - 63 for deleting an enterprise project requires a *Delete Project* category permission to allow the project deletion.

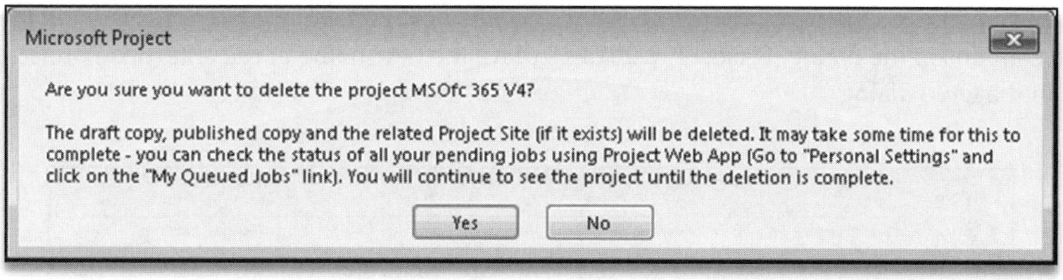

Figure 6 - 64: Confirmation dialog to delete an enterprise project

Warning: There is no *Undo* button to undo the deletion of an enterprise project. If you delete a project accidentally, contact your Project Server administrator immediately. Your administrator may be able to restore the project from the Archive database, if a backup of the project exists.

To rename an enterprise project, right-click the name of the project and then select the *Rename* item on the shortcut menu. The system highlights the name of the project in renaming mode as shown in Figure 6 - 65.

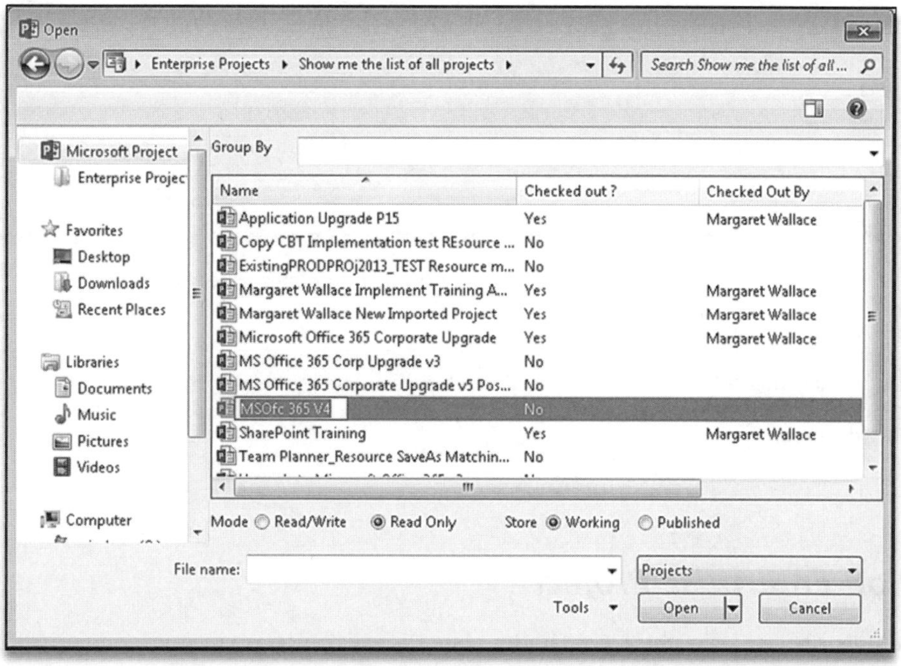

Figure 6 - 65: Open dialog, renaming an enterprise project

Edit the name of the project and press the **Enter** key on your computer keyboard. Project Pro 2013 displays the confirmation dialog shown in Figure 6 - 66.

Figure 6 - 66: Confirmation dialog for renaming a project

Click the *OK* button to close the confirmation dialog. To see the new name of the project, press the **F5** function key to refresh the contents of the dialog. Project Pro 2013 displays the new name of the enterprise project, as shown in Figure 6 - 67 in the *Open* dialog.

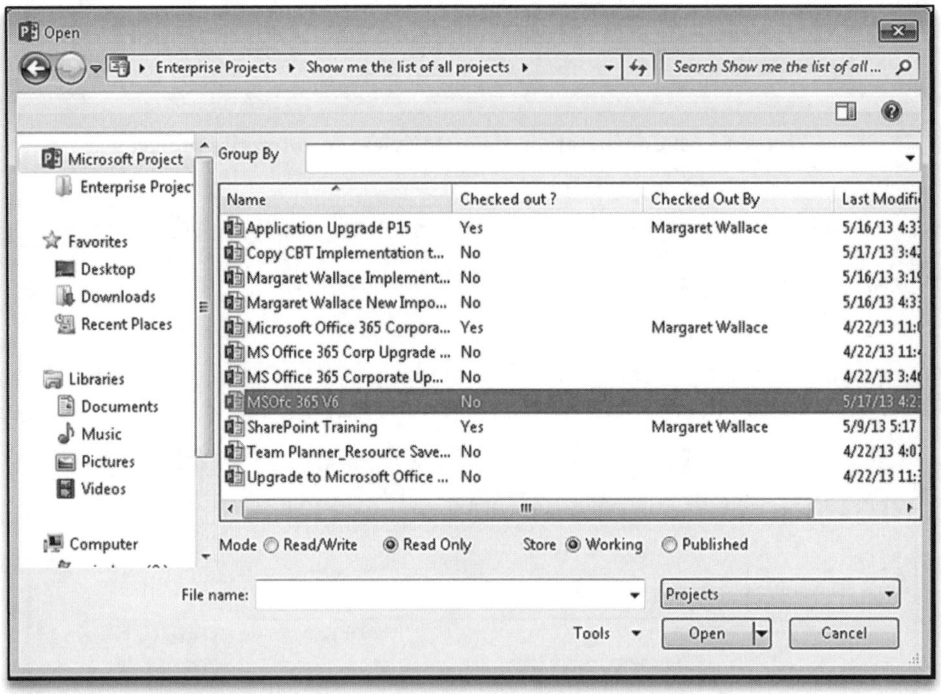

Figure 6 - 67: Rename enterprise project displaying new name

> **Warning**: Using this process to rename a project only changes the project name in the *Draft* database. If this project is a published project, you must also open the project and publish it to change the project name in the *Published* database.

Opening a Non-Enterprise Project

Beyond opening enterprise projects, the *Open* dialog also allows you to open non-enterprise projects (local projects) you store outside the Project Server database in other file formats. For example, click the *Computer* icon on the *Open* page to open projects in your *Recent Folders* location or use the *Browse* folder to locate a .mpp file to open.

Closing an Enterprise Project

When you open an enterprise project in *Read/Write* mode, the system automatically checks out the project to you. This allows you to edit the project exclusively, and limits all other users to opening the project in *Read Only* mode. To close an enterprise project properly, click the *File* tab and then the *Close* tab in the *Backstage*. When you close the project, the system prompts you to check in the project with the confirmation dialog shown in Figure 6 - 68. Click the *Yes* button to check in the project.

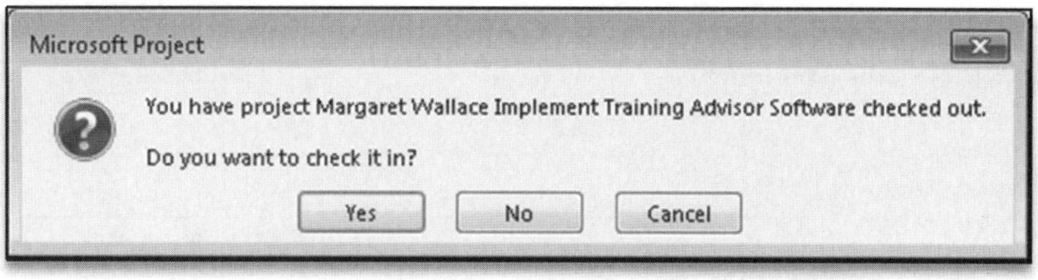
Microsoft Project
You have project Margaret Wallace Implement Training Advisor Software checked out.
Do you want to check it in?
Yes
No
Cancel

Figure 6 - 68: Check in enterprise project dialog

Warning: Do not close an enterprise project by clicking the *Close Window* button (lower X) or the *Close* button (upper X) in the upper right corner of the Project Pro 2013 application window. Using either of these buttons to close your enterprise project is the primary cause of projects getting "stuck" in a checked-out state in the cache.

Best Practice: To close an enterprise project, MSProjectExperts recommends that you click the *File* tab and then click the *Close* tab in the *Backstage*. To exit the application, click the *Close* button (upper X) in the upper right corner of the Project Pro 2013 application window. Make this a habit to avoid the possibility of an enterprise project becoming "stuck" in a checked-out state.

Working with Offline Projects

Project Pro 2013 and Project Server 2013 allow you to work on projects in *Offline* mode in situations where you must travel away from your company network. If you are a traveling project manager and need to take a project with you on the road, complete the following steps to save a project in *Offline* mode:

1. Before you disconnect from the corporate network, launch Project Pro 2013 and log in to Project Server.

2. Open in *Read/Write* mode the enterprise project you want to make an *Offline* project, and save the project one final time, if necessary.

3. Click the *File* tab and then click the *Close* tab. The system displays a confirmation dialog shown previously in Figure 6 - 68.

4. In the confirmation dialog that states, *Do you want to check it in?*, click the *No* button to close the project and do not allow the check-in.

5. Click the *File* tab and then click the *Close* button (upper *X*) in the upper right corner of the Project Pro 2013 application window to exit Project Pro 2013.

The first set of steps loads the latest version of the enterprise project into your cache as an *Offline* project, but leaves the project in *Read Only* mode so that no one can modify it while you are working with it in *Offline* mode, since the *Checked out?* status still displays as *Yes* as shown in Figure 6 - 69.

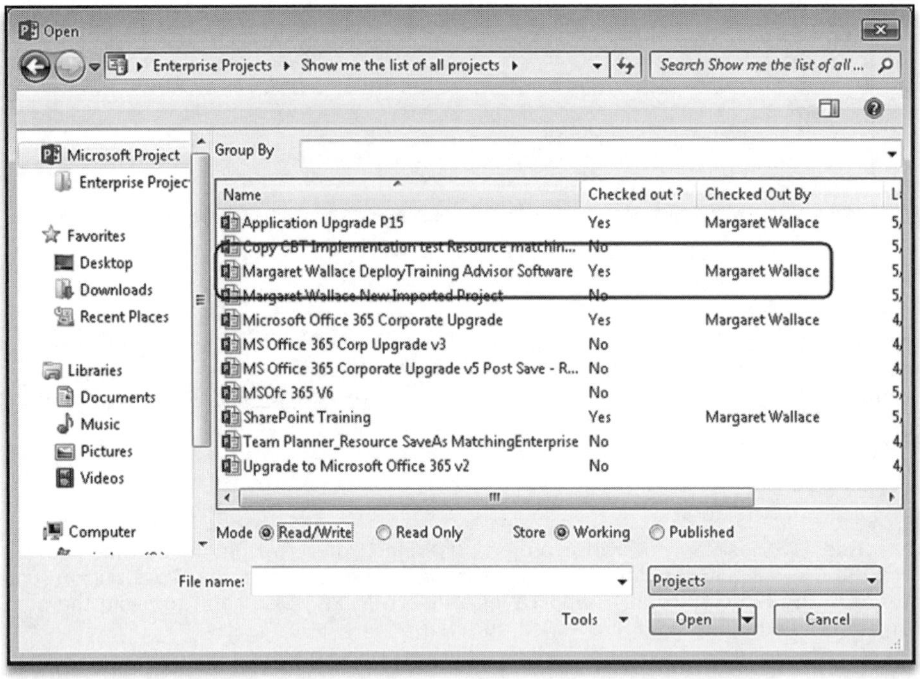

Figure 6 - 69: Open dialog, project Checked out?, Yes

While you are away from your corporate network, you can work with the *Offline* project by completing the following steps:

1. Launch Project Pro 2013. The system displays the *Login* dialog shown in Figure 6 - 70.

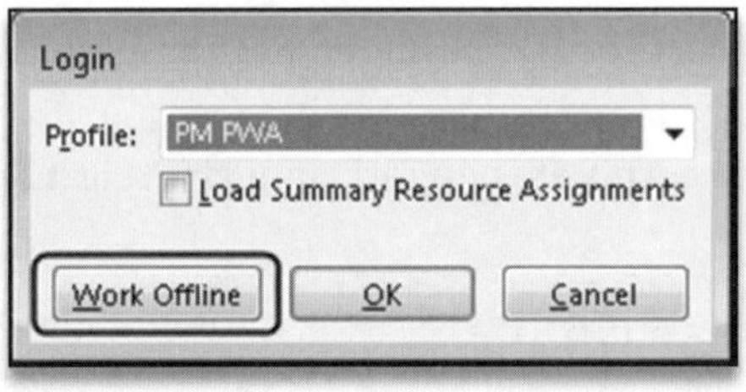

Figure 6 - 70: Login dialog

2. In the *Login* dialog, click the *Profile* pick list and select the Project Web App account for your production Project Server 2013 instance (**do not** select the *Computer* account from the *Profile* pick list).
3. Click the *Work Offline* button, as shown in Figure 6 - 70.

Project Pro 2013 launches in *Offline* mode without connecting to your Project Server system. The *Status* bar at the bottom of the application indicates that the software is in *Offline* mode, as shown in Figure 6 - 71.

Figure 6 - 71: Project Pro 2013 launched in Offline mode

4. Click the *File* tab and then click the *Open* tab in the *Backstage.*

5. Double-click the Project Web App account name to display a list of projects in your local project cache.

6. Select the *Read/Write* mode option to allow editing while working in *Offline* mode. Otherwise, the project will open in *Read Only* mode by default.

Information: Hover your mouse over the *Online Status* icon (globe), to reveal the text that displays *Working Offline* confirming the current status.

The system displays the *Open* dialog with a list of projects in your local project cache, as shown in Figure 6 - 72. Notice that the *Cache Status* column indicates that the *Margaret Wallace Deploy Training Advisor Software* project is currently in *Checked Out* status.

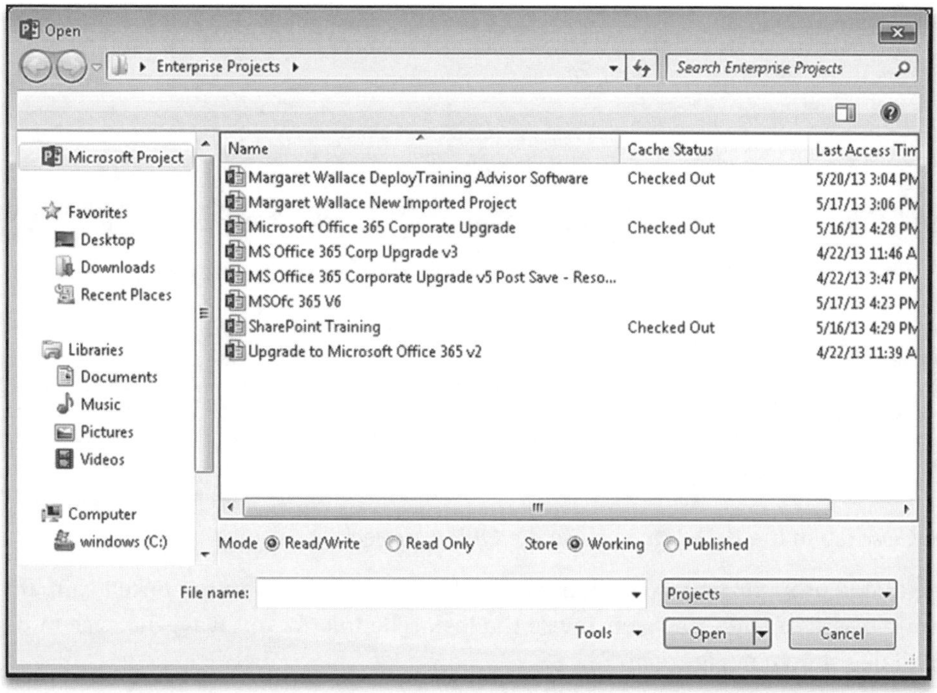

Figure 6 - 72: Open dialog shows projects in the cache

7. In the *Open* dialog, select your *Offline* project and click the *Open* button.

Information: While working with a project in *Offline* mode, you can perform many activities that you can do while working online, such as adding and editing tasks, setting task dependencies, etc. However, you cannot perform any activity in the project that requires a login connection to Project Server, such as using the *Build Team* dialog.

8. Edit your project, as necessary, and then click the *Save* button in the *Backstage* to save the *Offline* project in the cache. Notice in Figure 6 - 73, the message indicating the project is offline and that the data cannot synchronize to the server.

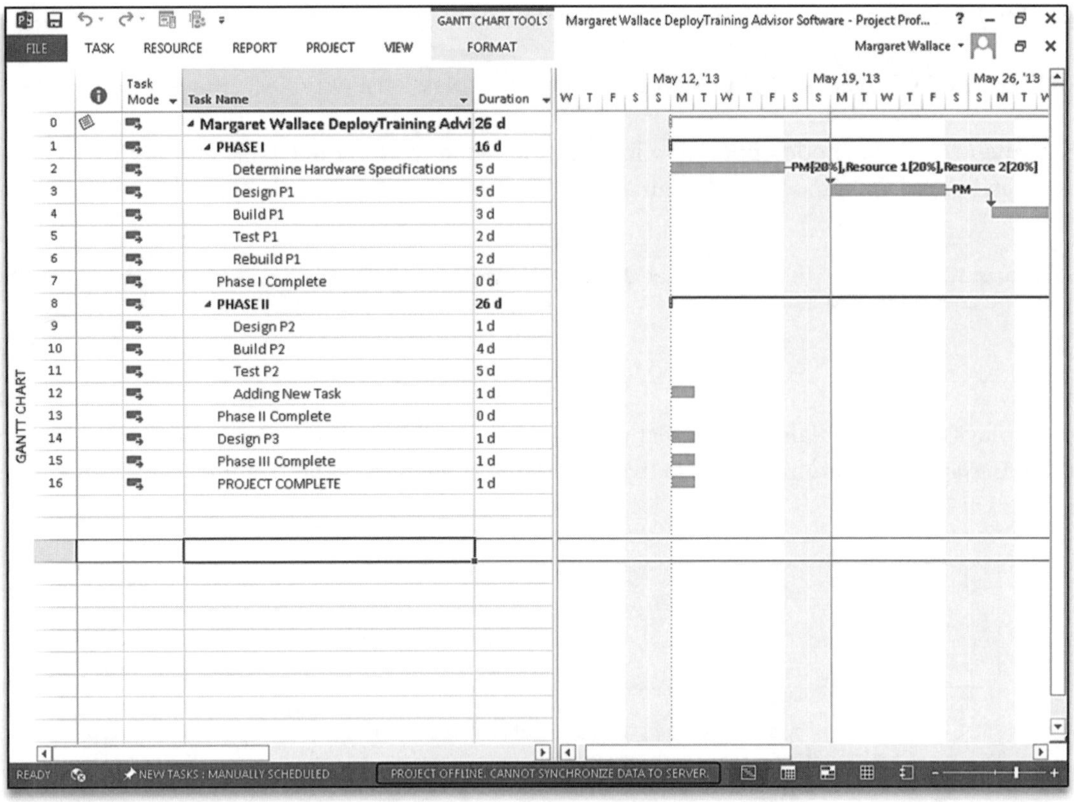

Figure 6 - 73: Project Offline. Cannot synchronize data to server.

Information: When you save your project while working in *Offline* mode, the system displays the message shown in Figure 6 - 73: *PROJECT OFFLINE. CANNOT SYNCRONIZE DATA TO SERVER.* The message displays in the right end of the *Status* bar at the bottom of the Project Pro 2013 application window. The save updates the local project cache version of the project until you save and synchronize the changes with the project in *Online* mode.

9. Click the *Close* tab in the *Backstage* to close the *Offline* project.
10. When the dialog prompts you to check in your project, click the *No* button once again. If your project contains resource assignments, and you revise the task schedule in any way, the system displays the informational dialog shown in Figure 6 - 74.

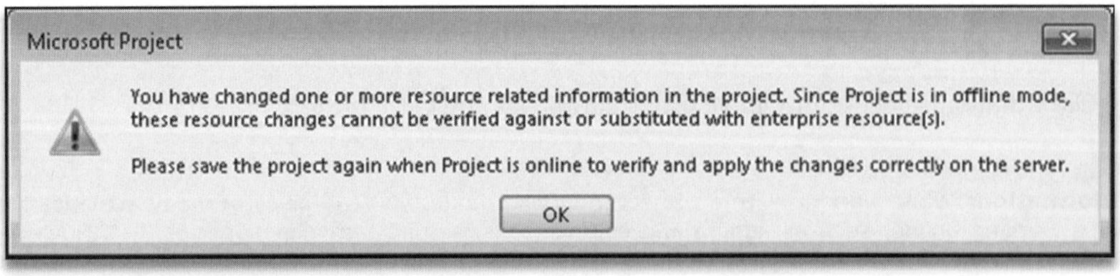

Figure 6 - 74: Information dialog about resource schedule changes

11. Click the *OK* button to close the informational dialog.
12. Press the **Alt + F4** key combination on your computer keyboard to exit Project Pro 2013.

When you return to your corporate network, complete the following steps to save the changes you made to the *Offline* project to the Project Server database:

1. Launch Project Pro 2013.
2. In the *Login* dialog, click the *Profile* pick list and select the Project Web App account for your production Project Server 2013 instance.
3. Click the *OK* button to connect to Project Server.
4. Click the *File* tab and then click the *Open* tab in the *Backstage*.
5. On the *Open* page, double-click the Project Web App account.
6. Select your *Offline* project in the cache list and click the *Open* button.
7. Click the *Save* button on the *Quick Access Toolbar* to synchronize your changes to the *Offline* project with the Project Server database.

Module 07

Resource and Assignment Planning

Learning Objectives

After completing this module, you will be able to:

- Understand enterprise resources
- Use the Build Team dialog to build a project team
- Use Proposed vs. Committed booking
- Set the published values for individual tasks
- Use local resources as project team members
- Assign resources to tasks
- Use Team Assignments for tasks
- Understand the Duration Equation
- Understand Task Types
- Understand Effort Driven scheduling
- Assign Cost, Budget Cost, and Expense Cost resources
- Use the Team Planner view
- Understand resource overallocation
- Use a leveling methodology and set leveling options
- Set Task Priority numbers
- Level resource overallocations in the Team Planner view and Task view

Inside Module 07

Understanding Enterprise Resources

The Enterprise Resource Pool in Project Server 2013 contains all of the enterprise resources needed to perform project work in your organization. In simple terms, resources are the people, equipment, and materials required to execute a project. In accounting terms, resources are the elements of project direct costs. Project Server 2013 defines enterprise resources in a variety of ways and organizes them in the Resource Organization Chart as shown Figure 7 - 1.

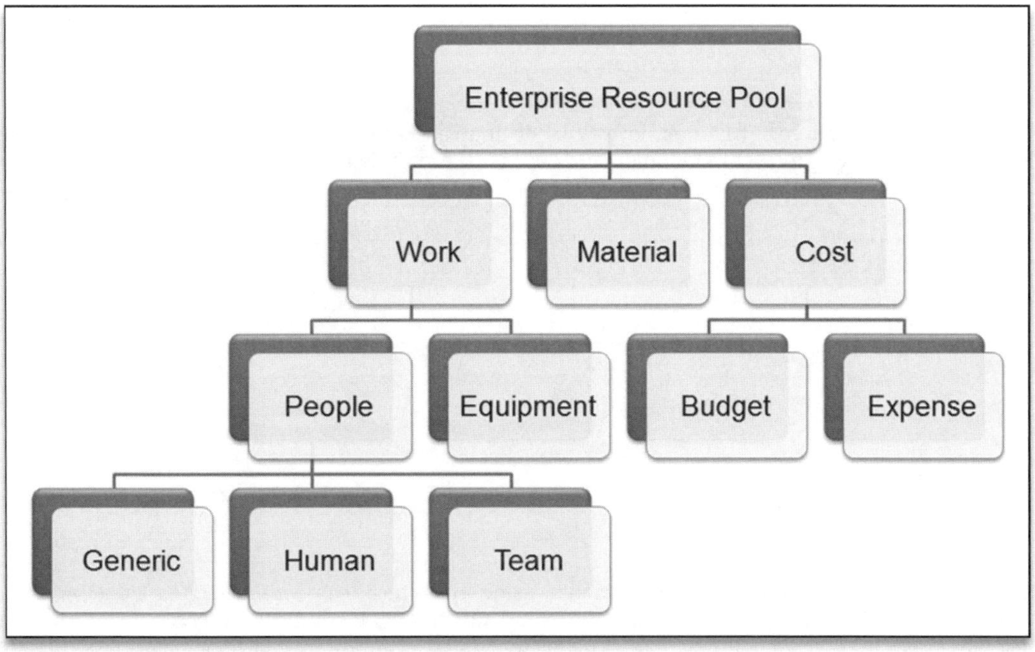

Figure 7 - 1: Resource Organization Chart

Project Server 2013 offers you three basic resource types: *Work, Material,* and *Cost*. You use *Work* resources to model people and equipment. You use *Material* resources to represent the supplies consumed during the project lifecycle. You use *Cost* resources to specify an overall budget and to track budget expenses unrelated to the *Work* resources assigned to tasks. *Work* resources affect both the schedule and the cost of the project, while *Material* and *Cost* resources affect only the project cost.

Project Server 2013 organizes *Work* resources into the following three groups:

- *Generic*
- *Non-Generic* (or *Human* resources)
- *Team* resources

A *Generic* resource is a skill-set placeholder for a resource, such as an SQL Server DBA. *Generic* resources allow you to specify the skills you require for a task assignment before you know which *Human* resources are available to work on the task. You can use skill-set matching to replace *Generic* resources with available *Human* resources who possess the same skills.

A *Non-Generic* or *Human* resource is a specific individual you can identify by name.

A *Team* resource is actually a special type of *Work* resource that represents a team of resources. You can only use *Team* resources if your organization uses dedicated project teams and the team members do not change from project to project. When you assign a *Team* resource to a task in a project and publish the project, any members of that team can self-assign the task, taking full ownership of the task, and can then report on the task in their Project Web App timesheets.

Warning: Project Server 2013 has no way to distinguish between *Work* resources that represent people and *Work* resources that represent equipment. Keep this fact in mind when you assign resources to tasks.

Best Practice: MSProjectExperts recommends using an enterprise custom field to identify the difference between the *Work* resources that are people, versus equipment. Using an enterprise custom field to distinguish this difference may be valuable to your organization since you may also use this information for reporting purposes, and for grouping and filtering *Work* resources in views.

Building a Project Team

After you define a new enterprise project and complete task planning, you are ready to begin the resource planning process by building your project team. The *Build Team* dialog in Project Pro 2013 provides you with tools for searching through the Enterprise Resource Pool to find the right resources for your project team. Start with a project already in the Project Server database. Using your Project Web App account, open the project in *Edit* mode using the *Check Out* button, if necessary. Next, click the *Resource* tab and in the *Insert* section of the *Resource* ribbon, click the *Add Resources* pick list button, and then select the *Build Team from Enterprise* item from the list to open the *Build Team* dialog as shown in Figure 7 - 2.

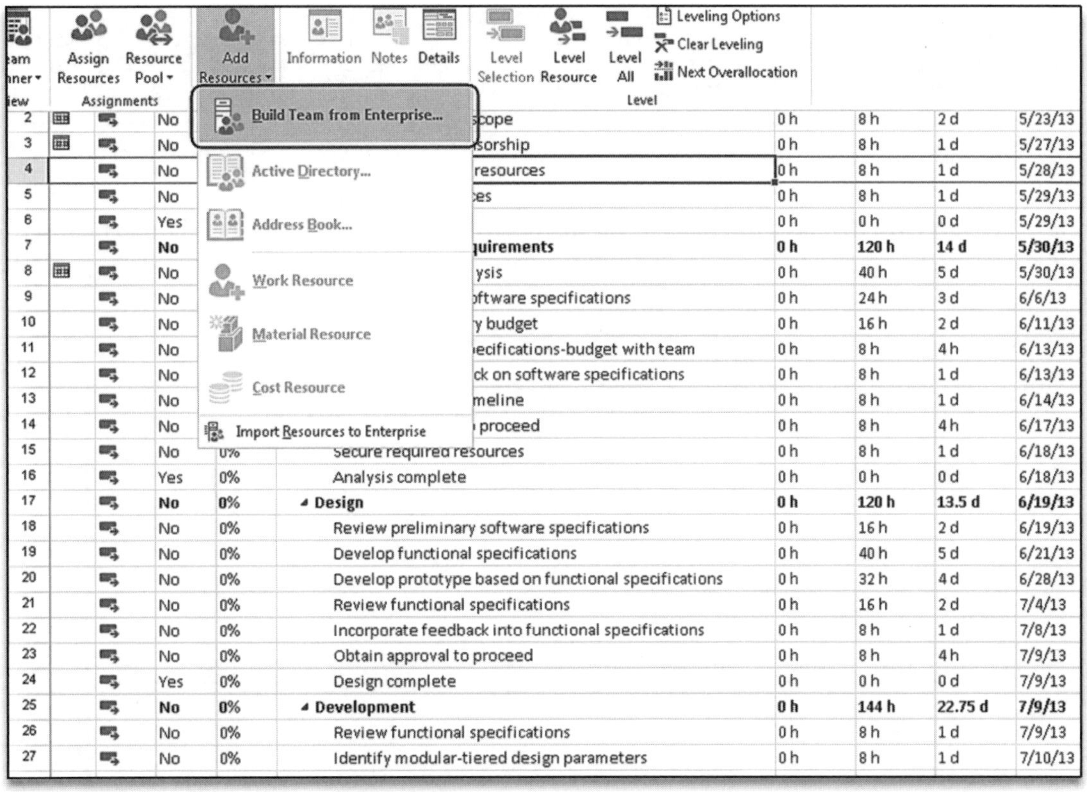

Figure 7 - 2: Add Resources, Build Team from Enterprise selection

The system displays the *Build Team* dialog shown in Figure 7 - 3.

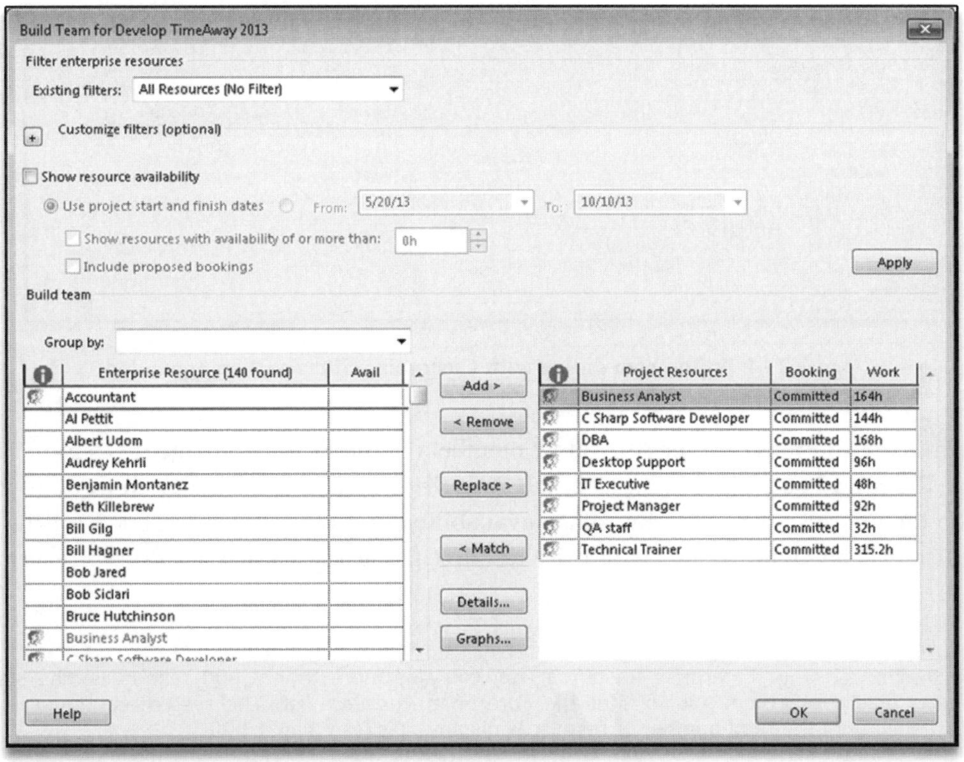

Figure 7 - 3: Build Team dialog

Information: You can also access the *Build Team* dialog by using a keyboard shortcut by pressing the **Ctrl +T** key combination on your computer keyboard. I highly recommend this method, as it is the quickest way to access the *Build Team* dialog in Project Pro 2013.

By default, Project Pro 2013 displays the *Build Team* dialog with the *Customize filters* section collapsed each time you access it. Click the *Expand (+)* button to the left of the *Customize Filters (optional)* section to expand it and show the complete dialog, as displayed in Figure 7 - 4.

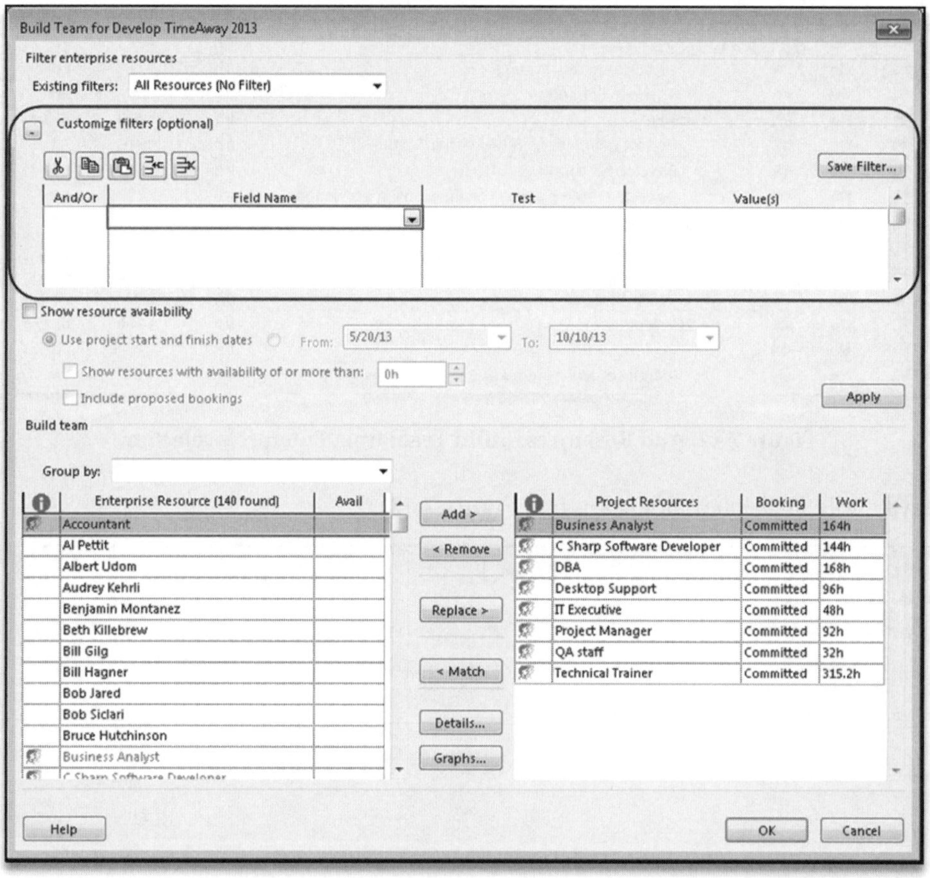

Figure 7 - 4: Build Team dialog with Customize filters section expanded

The default permissions in Project Server 2013 allow members of the Project Managers group to see all resources in the Enterprise Resource Pool. Using features in the *Build Team* dialog, you can search through your Enterprise Resource Pool to identify resources with the skills, availability, and other criteria needed for the job. The other criteria you can use depend on the custom enterprise resource fields created by your Project Server administrator.

Information: If your Enterprise Resource Pool contains more than 1,000 resources, the system displays a pre-filter dialog to prompt you to filter the *Enterprise Resource* list. The system continues to prompt you to filter the list until the total number of resources displayed is less than 1,000.

The *Build Team* dialog consists of two sections. The *Filter Enterprise Resources* section in the top half of the dialog contains filtering tools to restrict the list of enterprise resources to those that meet your filter criteria. The *Build Team* section in the bottom half of the dialog consists of two resource lists: the *Enterprise Resource* list on the left displays the list of resources from the Enterprise Resource Pool, while the *Project Resources* list on the right displays the current list of resources on your project team. Notice in Figure 7 - 4, shown previously, that my project team consists of eight *Generic* resources already in the project template and include assignments on tasks. The system provides a set of buttons for moving the resources between the two lists, such as the *Add, Remove, Replace,* and *Match* buttons as noted with the arrow buttons indicating the direction to move a resource from a list.

Notice in Figure 7 - 4 shown previously that the *Enterprise Resource* list on the left includes both *Human* resources and *Generic* resources – *Accountant, Business Analyst,* and *C Sharp Software Developer* display in the figure. The system displays *Generic* resources with a double-headed icon in the *Indicators* column.

Information: When applicable, the system displays additional indicators to the left of each name in the *Build Team* dialog, such as overallocation indicators and note indicators. Hover your mouse pointer over any indicator to display information about that indicator.

Filtering Resources

Because the default permissions in Project Server 2013 allow you to see all of the resources in the Enterprise Resource Pool, the *Build Team* dialog offers three methods to filter the list of resources:

- Use existing filter
- Create ad hoc custom filter
- Availability within a date range filter

To use an existing filter, click the *Existing filters* pick list at the top of the dialog and select a filter. The *Existing filters* pick list contains enterprise filters, standard filters, and your own personal filters. When you select a filter, the system applies it immediately and restricts the enterprise resources shown in the list on the left side of the dialog.

Information: Your Project Server administrator can build and save custom enterprise resource filters in the Enterprise Global file, which makes these enterprise filters available to all users. These filters are available using the *Existing filters* pick list.

To create your own ad hoc custom filter, use the data grid in the *Customize filters* section. The data grid consists of four columns: the *And/Or, Field Name, Test,* and *Value(s)* columns. In the *Field Name* column, you can select any resource field available in the system, including both standard and custom fields. Notice in Figure 7 - 5 that I am selecting the *Corporate Role (Enterprise)* field in the *Field Name* column.

Information: The (Enterprise) text to the right of the *Corporate Role* field name indicates that it is a custom enterprise resource field created by the Project Server administrator.

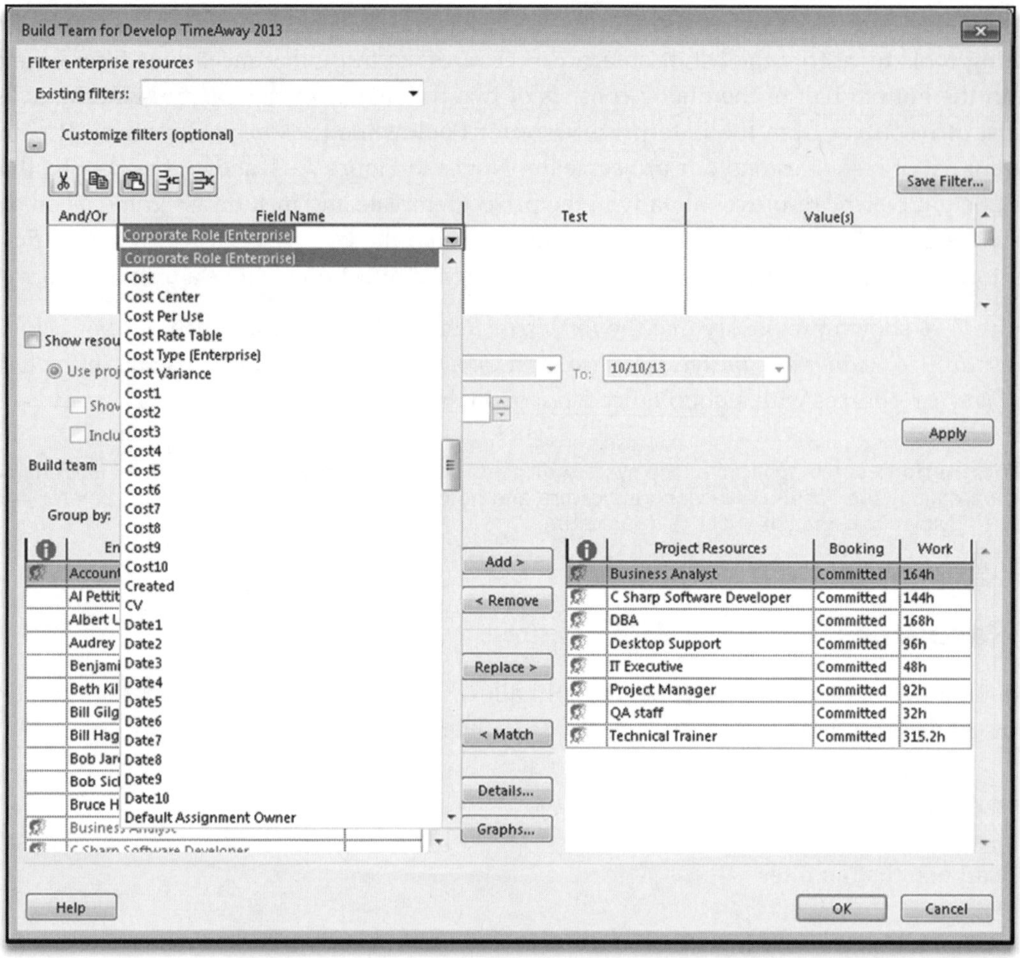

Figure 7 - 5: Select a field in the Field Name column

In the *Test* column, you must select the comparison test for your filter criteria. The available common Boolean test conditions in this column include *does not equal, equals, contains, does not contain, contains exactly*, etc.

After you select values in the *Field Name* and *Test* columns, you must select or enter a comparison value in the *Value(s)* column. In this column, you can select another field with which to compare, or select a value from the list of values found in the resource field you selected in the *Field Name* column. Notice in Figure 7 - 6 that I am selecting the *Accounting* value from the list of values available in the *Corporate Role* field.

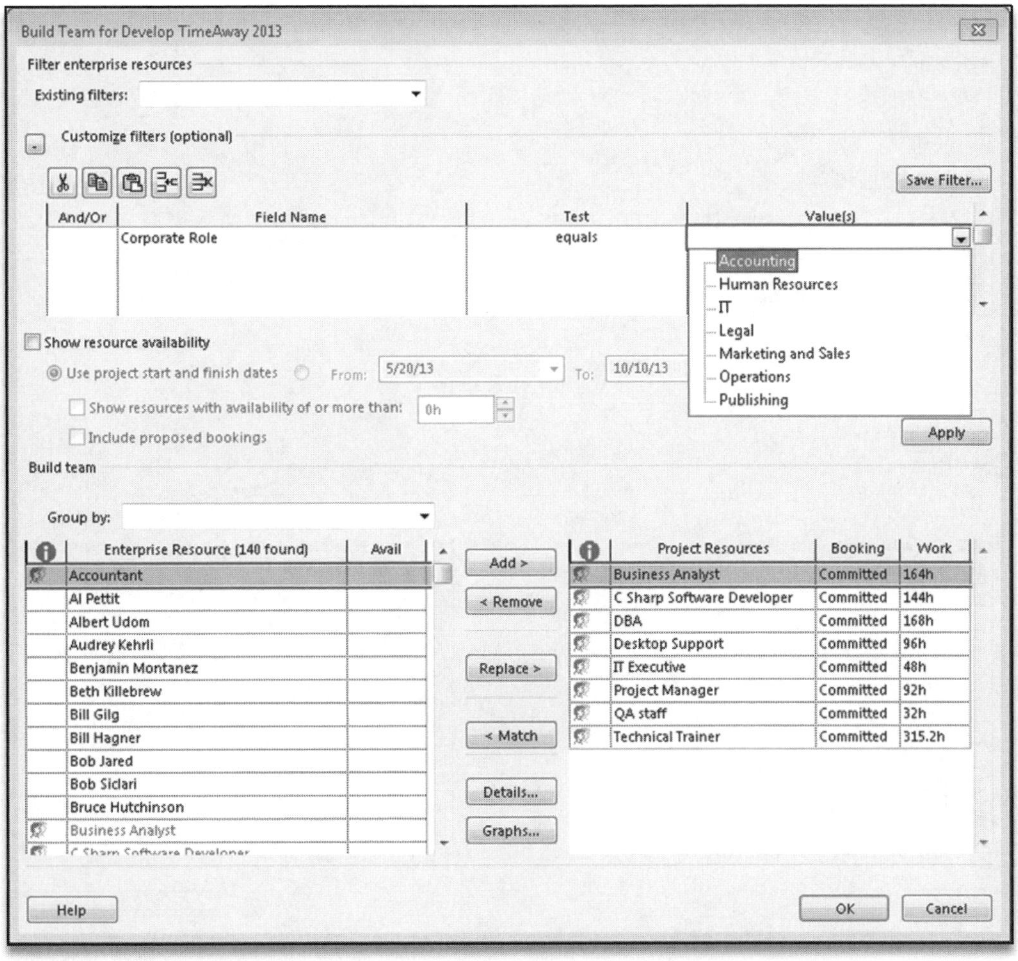

Figure 7 - 6: Select a field value in the Value(s) column

Information: If the field you select in the *Field Name* column contains a lookup table of values, the *Value(s)* column displays only the list of values available in the lookup table. If the field you select in the *Field Name* column is a standard field, such as the *Cost* field, then the *Value(s)* column contains a list of other field names.

The *Customize filters* data grid allows you to specify multiple criteria in your filter by using the *And/Or* column to add conditions to your custom filter using the Boolean *And* or *Or* functions. Notice in Figure 7 - 7 that I created a custom filter to locate resources whose *Corporate Role* field value is either *Accounting* or *Legal* using the *Or* option in the *And/Or* column.

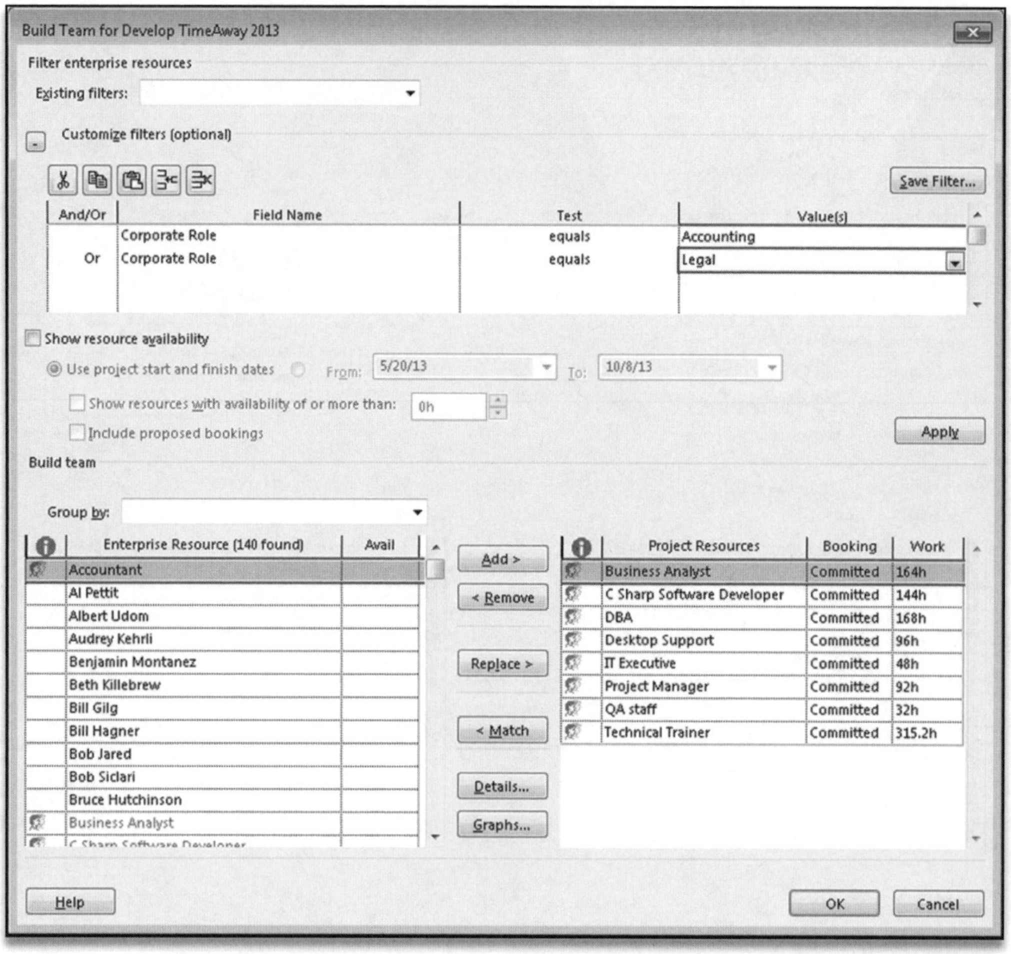

Figure 7 - 7: Custom filter with multiple filter criteria

When you complete your custom filter, click the *Apply* button to restrict the enterprise resources list using your filter. Figure 7 - 8 shows a filtered list of 12 enterprise resources that match my filter criteria: resources whose *Corporate Role* field value is either *Accounting* or *Legal.* Notice in Figure 7 - 8, that after filtering the list for *Accounting* and *Legal* staff the resulting *Enterprise Resource* list contains two *Generic* resources, , along with ten *Human* resources.

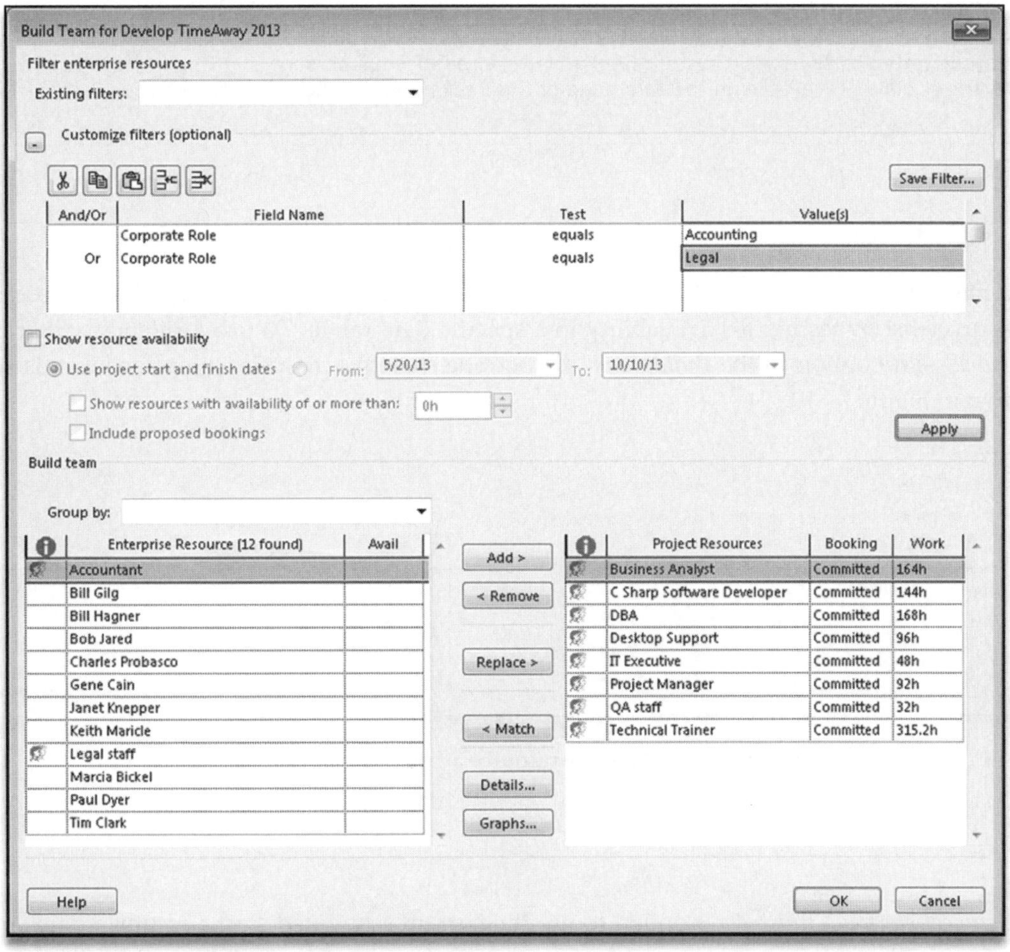

Figure 7 - 8: Filtering enterprise resources results show twelve enterprise resources in Accounting or Legal

After you create and test your custom filter, Project Server 2013 allows you to save it for future use by clicking the *Save Filter* button. The system displays the *Save Filter* dialog shown in Figure 7 - 9. Give your custom filter an original name and click the *OK* button to save it.

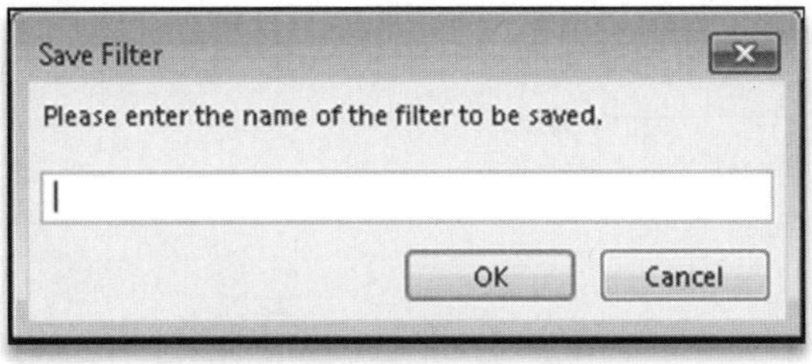

Figure 7 - 9: Save Filter dialog

Best Practice: MSProjectExperts recommends that you apply a naming convention to your personal custom filters so that you can easily distinguish them from both standard filters and enterprise custom filters. For example, you might preface the name of your filter with your initials. Using a naming convention, I might name the previous filter *_MRW Accounting and Legal Resources*. Using the underscore character at the beginning of the filter name forces the system to sort it to the top of the *Existing filters* pick list.

Warning: If you click the *Save Filter* button in the *Build Team* dialog, the system saves the filter in the **active project only**. To save your custom filter for use in all of your present and future projects, you must use the *Organizer* dialog (available on the *Info* page of the *Backstage*) to copy the filter to your Global.mpt file.

In addition to filtering resources using the *Existing filters* pick list and creating custom filters, you can restrict the enterprise resources list by testing for availability in a specific date range. To use availability filtering, select the *Show resource availability* option in the *Build Team* dialog. The system activates the options in this section of the dialog, as shown in Figure 7 - 10.

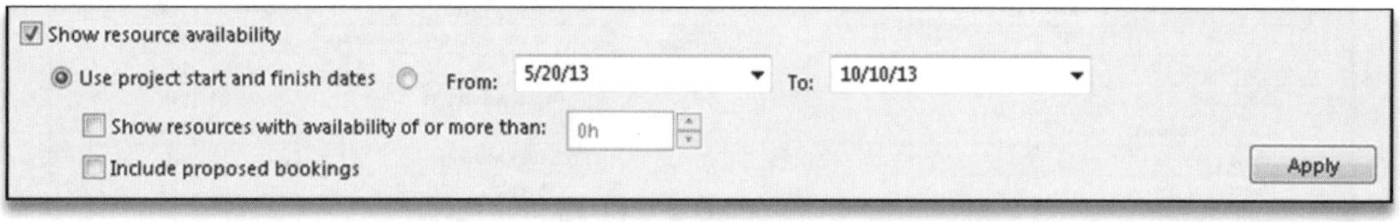

Figure 7 - 10: Show resource availability options

Select the *Use project start and finish dates* option to use the current scheduled start and finish dates in the project. Alternately, you can select the *From* option and enter a specific date range in the *From* and *To* fields.

Information: If you select the *From* option, the system sets the *From* date to the *Start* date of the project, and sets the *To* date to the current scheduled *Finish* date of the project. You can change either date to filter during a specific date range.

Click the *Apply* button. Project Server 2013 calculates the availability for each resource shown in the *Enterprise Resource* list on the left side of the dialog and displays this information in the *Avail* column, as shown in Figure 7 - 11. The system calculates the availability for each resource using the following formula for the specified date range:

Availability = Capacity - Work

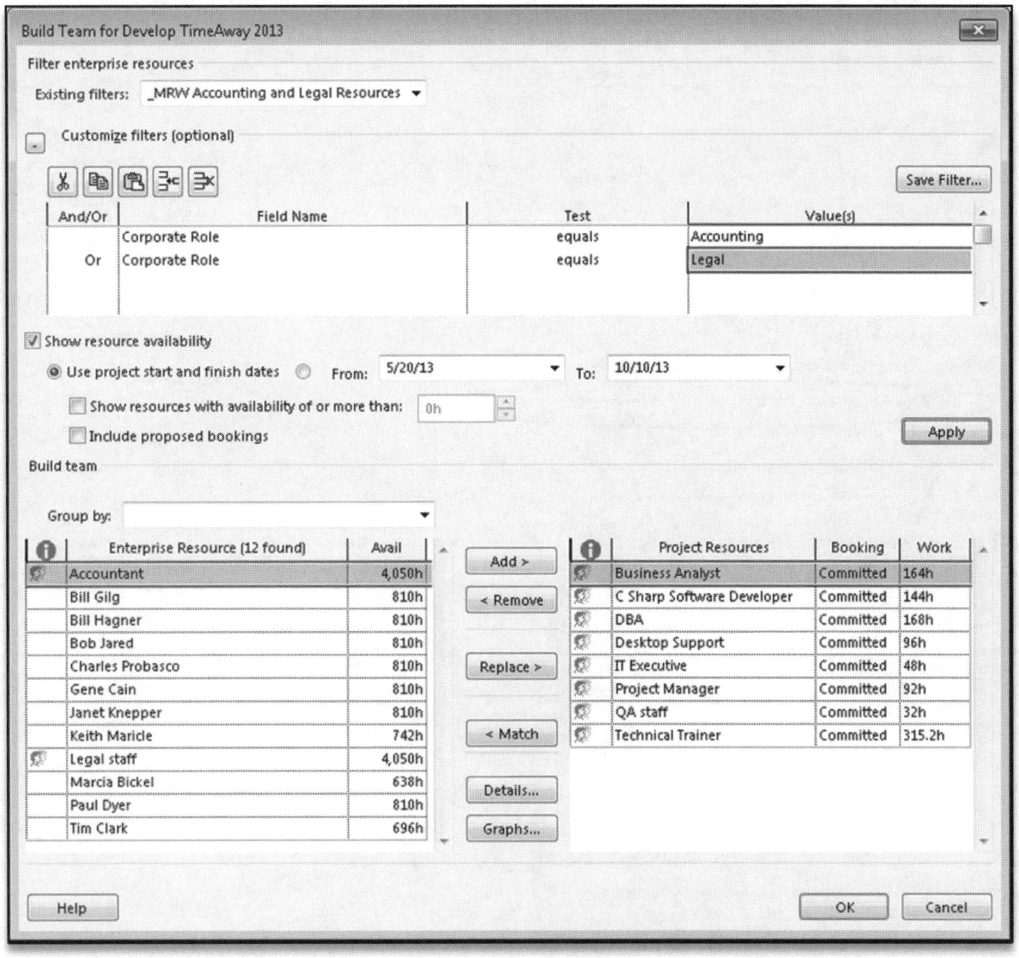

Figure 7 - 11: Availability calculation applied in the *Build Team* dialog

Notice in the *Enterprise Resource* list in Figure 7 - 11 that Keith Maricle has 742 hours of availability during the time span from 5/20/13 to 10/10/13. Notice also that Tim Clark and Marcia Bickel hours of availability are 696 and 638, respectively, during the same time span. This indicates these resources have assignments on other projects in the Project Server database. If you see a resource with 0 hours of availability, this means the resource is completely booked on other projects during the specific time span of your project, and is not available to work on your project.

Warning: Even if a resource has 0 hours of availability to work on your project, Project Server 2013 allows you to add the resource to your project team and to assign the unavailable resource to tasks in your project. Doing so is unwise as this action creates a cross-project overallocation of the resource.

To continue filtering by availability for a specific time period, select the *Show resources with availability of or more than* option and then enter the number of hours (810) in the corresponding field. Click the *Apply* button to show only those resources with the minimum amount of availability for your project. For example, I want to filter for accounting and legal resources that have full-time availability (810 hours) to work on my project as shown in Figure 7 - 12.

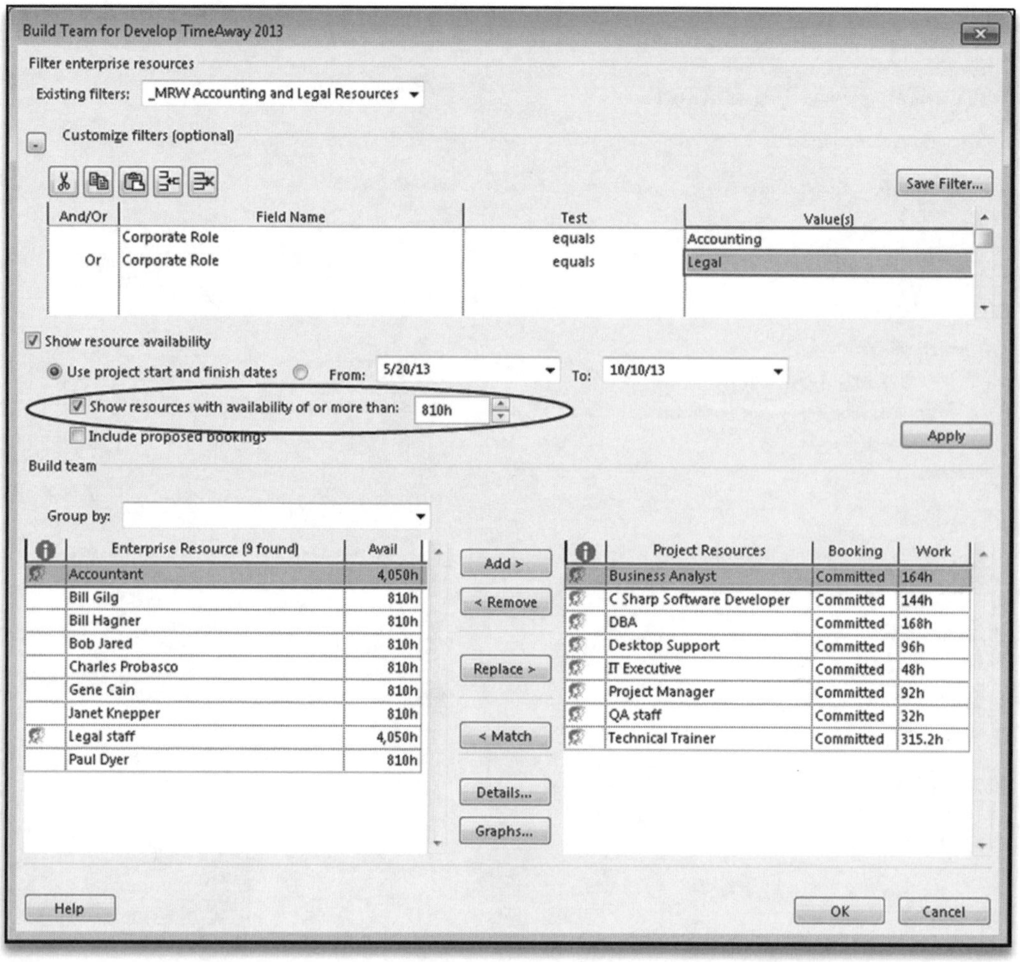

Figure 7 - 12: Filter for minimum availability in the Build Team dialog

When you filter for availability over a specific period, Project Server 2013 allows you to determine whether the system considers proposed bookings in the filtering process. A proposed booking indicates a tentative resource commitment to a project, while a committed booking (the default) indicates a firm commitment to a project. To include proposed bookings, select the *Include proposed bookings* option. To understand how this option works, consider the following example:

A fellow project manager books Mickey Cobb for 40 hours of work from October 14-18, 2013 as a proposed resource in an enterprise project. If you filter for availability and **select** the *Include proposed bookings* option, the system **subtracts** the 40 hours of proposed work from her availability. If you **do not** select the *Include proposed bookings* option, the system **does not subtract** the 40 hours of proposed work from her availability.

Information: To remove all filtering from the list of enterprise resources, click the *Existing filters* pick list and select the *All Resources (No Filter)* item.

Grouping Resources

The *Group by* pick list provides another way of refining your resource selections by applying grouping to the *Enterprise Resource* list on the left side of the dialog. Click the *Group by* pick list and then select any resource field available in the system, including both standard and custom fields. When you select a field from the list, the system immediately applies grouping to the *Enterprise Resource* list, with each group expanded to show all members of the group. As you review your resources groups, you can collapse or expand each group.

Figure 7 - 13 shows that I selected the *RBS* field from the *Group by* pick list. By the way, the *RBS* field defines the "pseudo org chart" for each resource in the Enterprise Resource Pool. Notice in Figure 7 - 13, that *Tim Clark* is the manager of the Accounting department, while *Bill Hagner, Charles Probasco, Gene Cain,* and *Keith Maricle* all report to *Tim Clark,* as defined by their hierarchical position below *Tim Clark* in the *RBS* field.

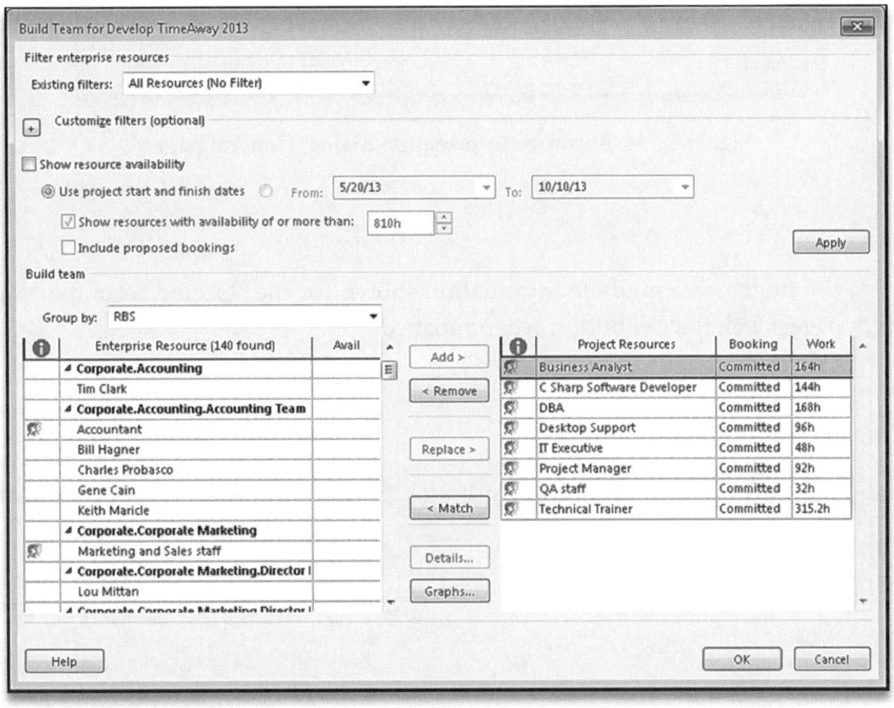

Figure 7 - 13: Apply Group by RBS to Enterprise Resource list

> **Information**: To remove grouping from the *Enterprise Resource* list, click the *Group by* pick list and select the blank field at the top of the pick list.

Viewing Resource Information

Select any resource in the list of resources on either the left side or right side of the *Build Team* dialog, and then click the *Details* button to display the *Resource Information* dialog for the selected resource. Figure 7 - 14 shows the *Resource Information* dialog for *Audrey Kehrli* on the *General* page.

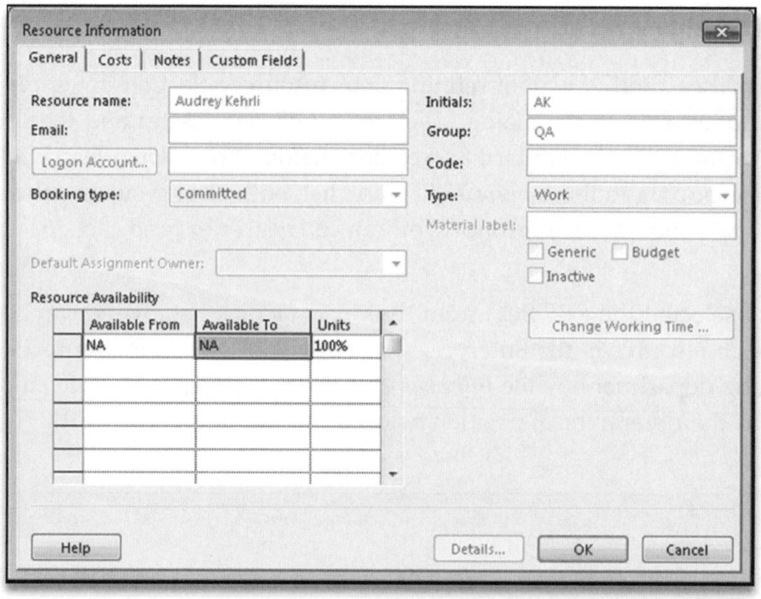

Figure 7 - 14: Resource Information dialog, General page

In the *Resource Information* dialog, examine the information shown for the selected resource on the *General, Costs, Notes,* or *Custom Fields* page. Click the *OK* button when finished.

Information: Only the Project Server administrator can edit enterprise resource information for any of the resources in the *Resource Information* dialog.

Viewing Resource Availability

The *Build Team* dialog also gives you direct access to resource availability information using resource graphs. Select one or more resources in the list of resources on the right or left side of the dialog, and then click the *Graphs* button. Project Server 2013 launches a new Internet Explorer application window, navigates to the *Resource Availability* page in Project Web App, and displays the availability information for the selected resources as shown in Figure 7 - 15. For example, notice in Figure 7 - 15 that the *Resource Availability* page shows availability information for *Audrey Kehrli,* and for the *C Sharp Software Developer* generic resource.

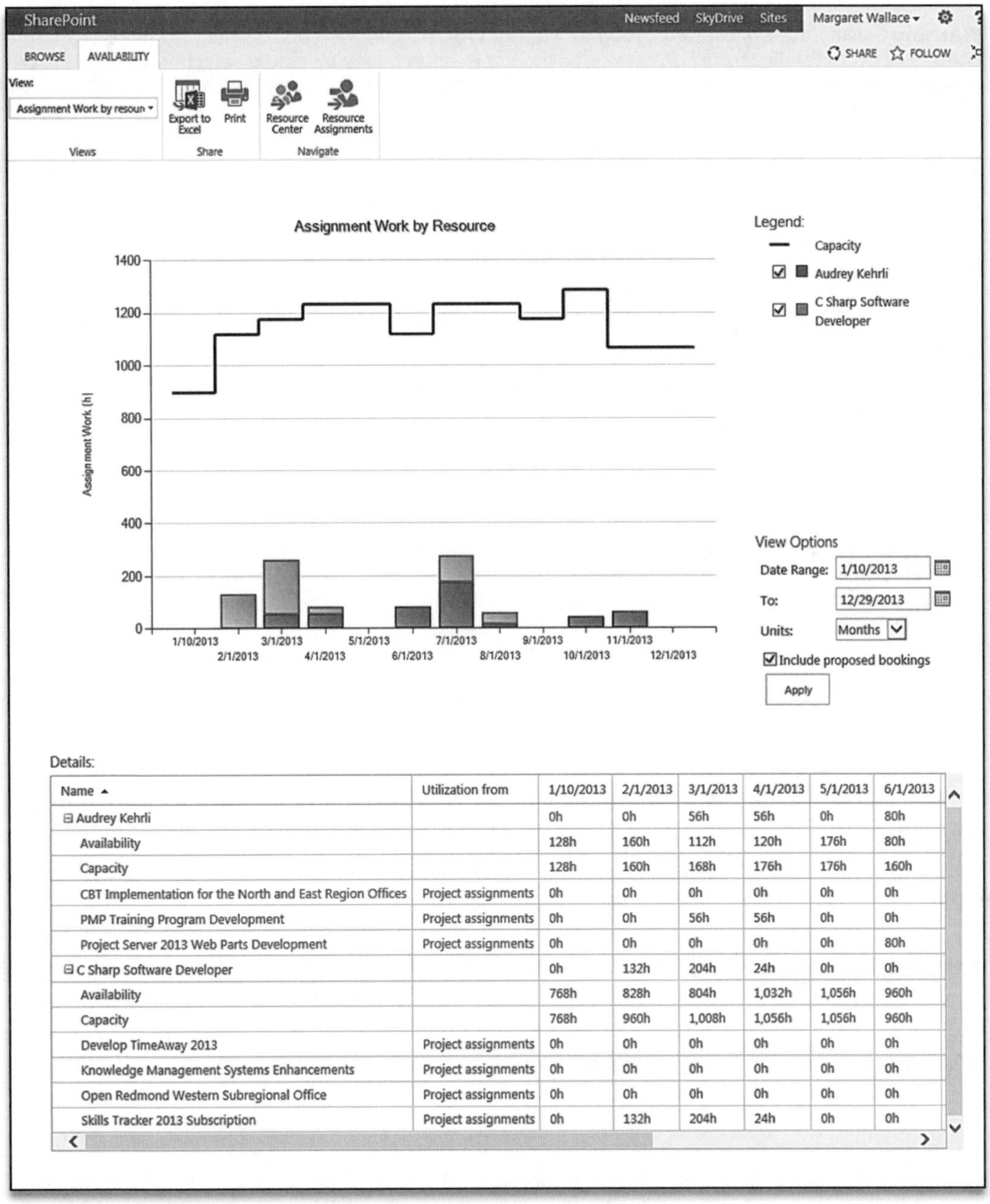

Name	Utilization from	1/10/2013	2/1/2013	3/1/2013	4/1/2013	5/1/2013	6/1/2013
⊟ Audrey Kehrli		0h	0h	56h	56h	0h	80h
Availability		128h	160h	112h	120h	176h	80h
Capacity		128h	160h	168h	176h	176h	160h
CBT Implementation for the North and East Region Offices	Project assignments	0h	0h	0h	0h	0h	0h
PMP Training Program Development	Project assignments	0h	0h	56h	56h	0h	0h
Project Server 2013 Web Parts Development	Project assignments	0h	0h	0h	0h	0h	80h
⊟ C Sharp Software Developer		0h	132h	204h	24h	0h	0h
Availability		768h	828h	804h	1,032h	1,056h	960h
Capacity		768h	960h	1,008h	1,056h	1,056h	960h
Develop TimeAway 2013	Project assignments	0h	0h	0h	0h	0h	0h
Knowledge Management Systems Enhancements	Project assignments	0h	0h	0h	0h	0h	0h
Open Redmond Western Subregional Office	Project assignments	0h	0h	0h	0h	0h	0h
Skills Tracker 2013 Subscription	Project assignments	0h	132h	204h	24h	0h	0h

Figure 7 - 15: Resource Availability page in PWA

Warning: Using the *Build Team* dialog in Project Pro 2013 allows you to select no more than 10 resources on either side from the *Enterprise Resource* or *Project Resource* lists by single selection using the **Ctrl** key on your computer keyboard. In Project Web App, the *Resource Availability* page displays up to 20 selected resources, when selected singly.

However, if you use the **Shift** key on your computer keyboard to multi-select resources, the system allows you to select more than 20 resources in the resources lists in the *Build Team* dialog, but the *Resource Availability* page in Project Web App limits the display to approximately 32 resources. When you select more than 32 resources, the system eliminates from the display resources that fall alphabetically in ascending order and are at the beginning of the *Enterprise Resource* list. For example, the system calculates the number of selected resources from both the *Enterprise Resource* and the *Project Resource* lists, reduces the number selected by sorting the *Enterprise Resource* list alphabetically in ascending order, and then eliminates from the display the first in the ascending order from the list. The system displays the remaining resources approximately 32-34, as I experienced varying results shown in the *Resource Availability* view.

The Build Team multi-select behavior changed after installing the Project Server 2013 April 2013 CU and this bug still exists. Hopefully, future hotfixes, or patches, may address this behavior.

Best Practice: MSProjectExperts recommends using the *Resource Availability* views in the *Resource Center* to view availability for more than 20 resources in place of using the *Build Team* dialog *Graphs* button. Accessing availability information using this method avoids the "missing" resources in your view, based on the system randomly eliminating resources from the view as discussed in the *Warning* dialog above.

In the *Legend* section of the *Resource Availability* page previously shown in Figure 7 - 15, select or deselect the checkboxes for the selected resources to view availability information for each resource individually.

In the *View Options* section of the page, select a date range and the time units (such as weeks) to view resource availability for a specific timeframe and units. If you want to include proposed work hours in the availability calculation, be sure to select the *Include proposed bookings* option. Click the *Apply* button to apply the changes to the view and to update the availability graph for the selected resources.

In the *Details* section of the page, the system displays a data grid with numerical information about the selected resources. The data grid also shows lines for *Capacity* and *Availability* data for each resource, as well as the *Work* assigned to each resource in every enterprise project as shown in the *Utilization from* column in the *Project assignments* rows. Close the Internet Explorer application window when you finish analyzing resource availability information.

Information: For the purpose of brevity, I provide only an overview presentation of the *Resource Availability* page in Project Web App. However, I provide an in-depth presentation of this page in Module 15: *Working in the Resource Center.*

Adding Resources to Your Project Team

To add resources to your project team, select one or more resources from the *Enterprise Resource* list on the left side of the *Build Team* dialog and then click the *Add* button. The system adds the selected resources to the *Project Resources* list on the right side of the dialog. To remove resources from your project team, select one or more resources from the *Project Resources* list on the right and then click the *Remove* button. In Figure 7 - 16, notice that I added two *Human* resources, *Audrey Kehrli* and *Bob Jared,* to the *Project Resources* list, and the system "grays out" both of these resources in the *Enterprise Resource* list on the left.

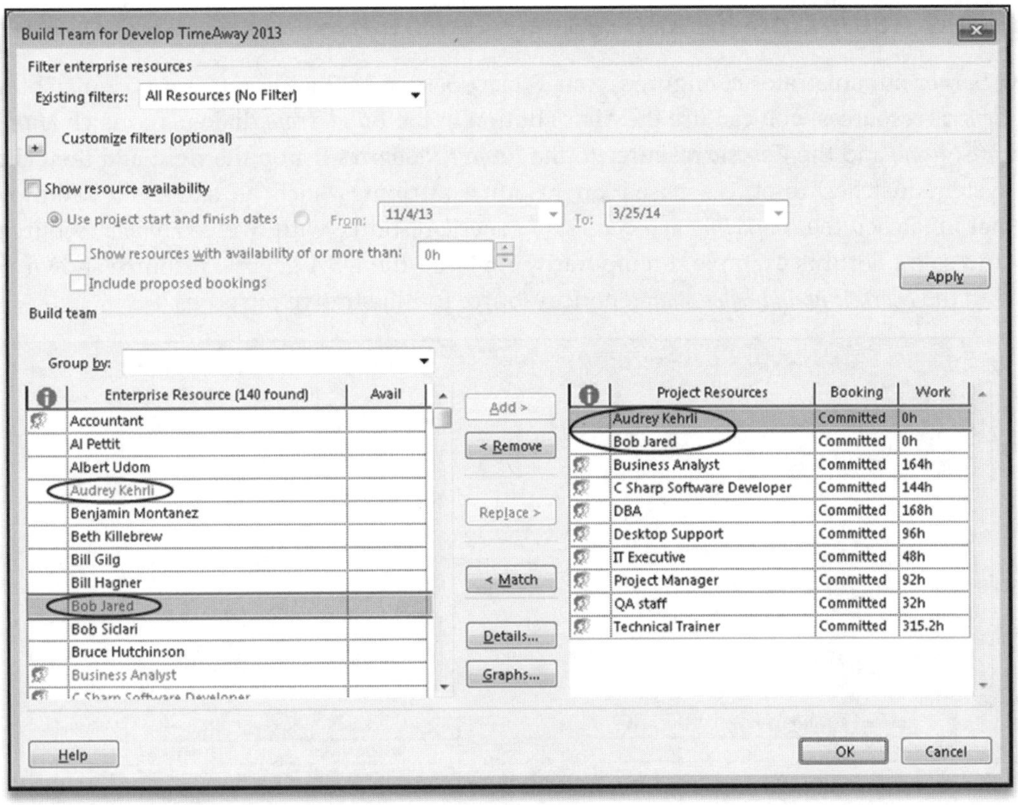

Figure 7 - 16: Two human resources added to Project Resources list

Using Team Resources

A *Team* resource is a special type of *Work* resource that represents a team of resources. If your Project Server 2013 system includes *Team* resources, you can add a *Team* resource to your project team and then assign the *Team* resource to tasks in your project. For example, suppose your Enterprise Resource Pool contains a *Team* resource named *Desktop Support Team* made up of three resources named *Bob Siclari, Larry McKain,* and *Susan Tartaglia.* You have a task in your schedule called *Install Microsoft Office 2013 Client Software* and any member of the team can perform this task, so long as it completes on time. You can add the *Desktop Support Team* resource to your project team and then assign the *Team* resource to this task.

When you publish this project, Project Server 2013 creates a *Team* task called *Install Microsoft Office 2013 Client Software* for all three of the team members (*Bob, Larry,* and *Susan*). These three team members can access this *Team* task using the *Insert Row* feature on the *Tasks* page in Project Web App. At any point, **one** of these team members can self-assign this task and take over **sole ownership** of it. Once a team member takes over sole ownership of the task, the system removes the task for the remaining team members assigning the task solely to the team member who self-assigned the task.

Team resources represent a way for you to assign a team to a task and to allow the team members to decide among themselves who should do the work on the task.

Matching and Replacing Resources

If your Project Server administrator configured your Project Server 2013 system to support matching *Human* resources with *Generic* resources, you can use the *Match* button in the *Build Team* dialog. To match *Human* resources with a *Generic* resource, add the *Generic* resource to the *Project Resources* list on the right and then click the *Match* button. The system matches resources based on resource attributes such as skills. For example, notice in Figure 7 - 17 that I matched the *Marketing and Sales staff* generic resource with twelve *Human* resources who work in marketing and sales. For this example, I temporarily replaced the *DBA* generic resource shown previously in Figure 7 - 16 with the *Marketing and Sales staff* generic resource for illustrative purposes.

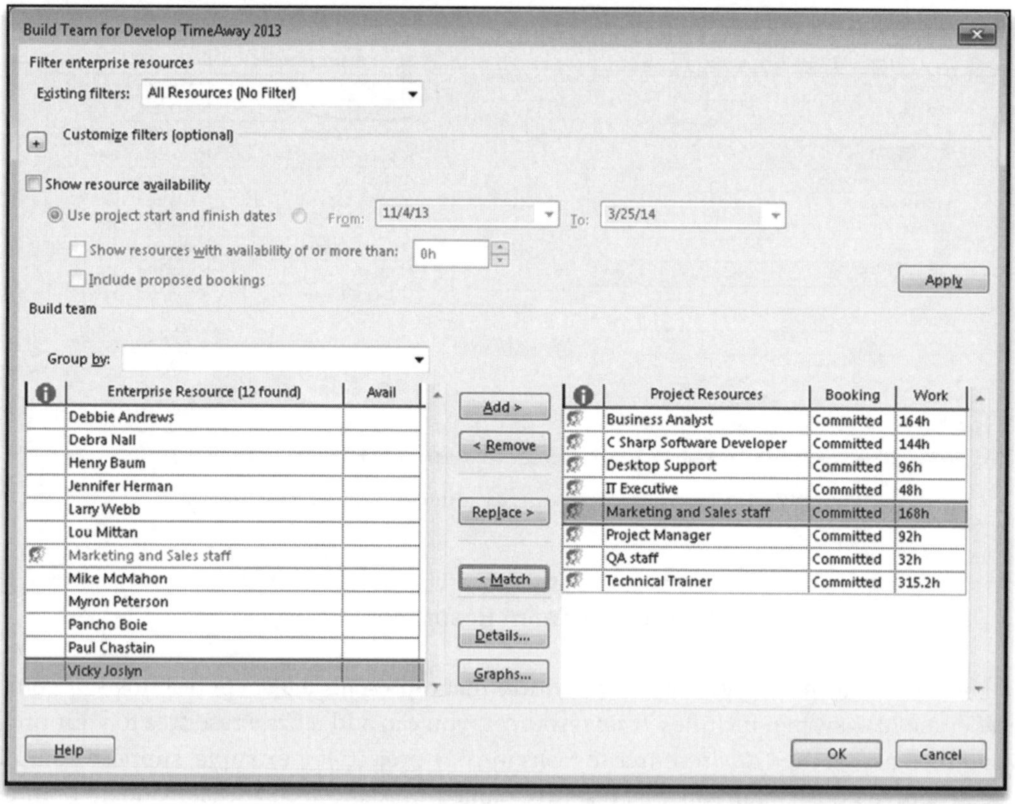

Figure 7 - 17: Match Human resources with Generic resources

When you use the *Match* feature in the *Build Team* dialog, the system applies a customized "contains" filter on the resources in the *Enterprise Resource* list using the matching attributes for the selected *Generic* resource. In our organization, the Project Server administrator configured the *Role* field for matching *Human* resources with *Generic* resources. Notice in the *Customize filters* grid shown in Figure 7 - 18 that the system created an ad hoc filter that displays any resource whose *Role* field contains the *Corporate.Marketing* value representing the marketing team.

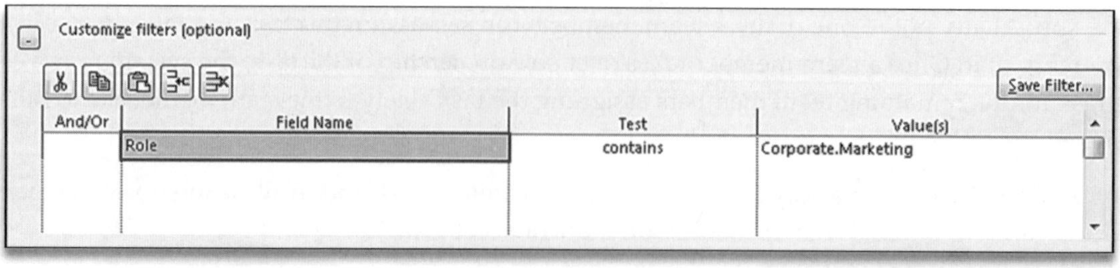

Figure 7 - 18: Customize filter data grid after a matching operation

Information: In most cases, you use the *Match* button to match specific skills between *Generic* resources and *Human* resources. However, because the system shows all matches for a selected resource, including both *Generic* and *Human* resources, you can use the matching feature to make human-to-human matches as well.

To replace a resource on the *Project Resources* list with one from the *Enterprise Resources* list, select a resource in each list, and then click the *Replace* button. The system replaces the former resource with the new resource on every task assignment in the entire project plan. If you use the *Replace* feature for a project team member who has actual progress in the project, the system displays the dialog shown in Figure 7 - 19.

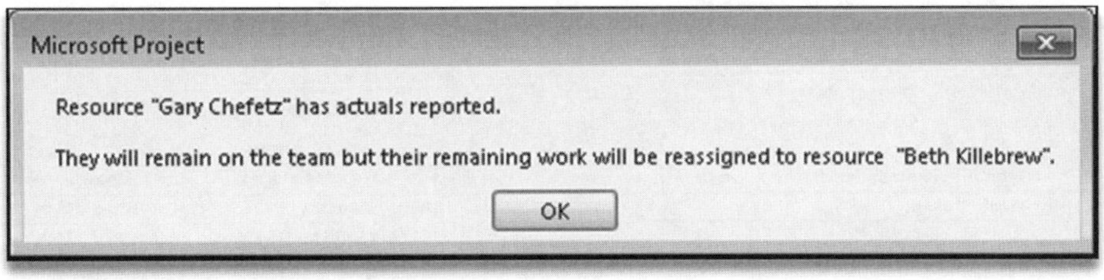
Microsoft Project
Resource "Gary Chefetz" has actuals reported.
They will remain on the team but their remaining work will be reassigned to resource "Beth Killebrew".
OK

Figure 7 - 19: Resource replacement warning dialog

Click the *OK* button in the dialog to complete the replacement. Project Server 2013 handles the resource replacement operation as follows:

- If the original resource reported no actual progress on a task, the system replaces the original resource with the new resource.
- If the original resource reported actual progress on a task, and the task is not complete, the system leaves the original resource on the task for historical purposes, and transfers all remaining work on the task to the new resource. This means that the system shows both the original resource and the new resource assigned to the task.
- If the original resource completed a task, the system leaves the original resource assigned and does not assign the new resource to the task.

Information: If you want to replace a *Generic* resource with a *Human* resource on completed tasks, you must use the *Replace* feature in the *Assign Resources* dialog for this purpose. I discuss the *Assign Resources* dialog in the next topical section of this module. As of the writing of this book, this is also true concerning local resources with the same name as an enterprise resource, even though the system recognizes that they have the same name and provides a confirmation dialog for you to accept to replace the resource. The system considers the replacement resource as a new resource and forces you to use the *Replace* feature to transfer any *Actual Work* already reported for the replaced resource on any tasks.

Using Proposed vs. Committed Booking

The *Booking* column in the *Project Resources* list on the right side of the *Build Team* dialog allows you to specify a booking type for each resource you add to your team. You may book team members as either *Proposed* or *Committed*. A *Proposed* booking indicates a tentative commitment for the resource, while a *Committed* booking indicates a firm commitment.

The default *Booking* value for each project team member is *Committed,* and varies depending on your configuration by the Project Server administrator for your resources in the Enterprise Resource Pool (ERP). To change the

Booking value for a project team member, click the *Booking* pick list for the resource and select the desired booking type. Notice in Figure 7 - 20 that I am setting the *Booking* value to *Proposed* for the resource *Cher Zall.*

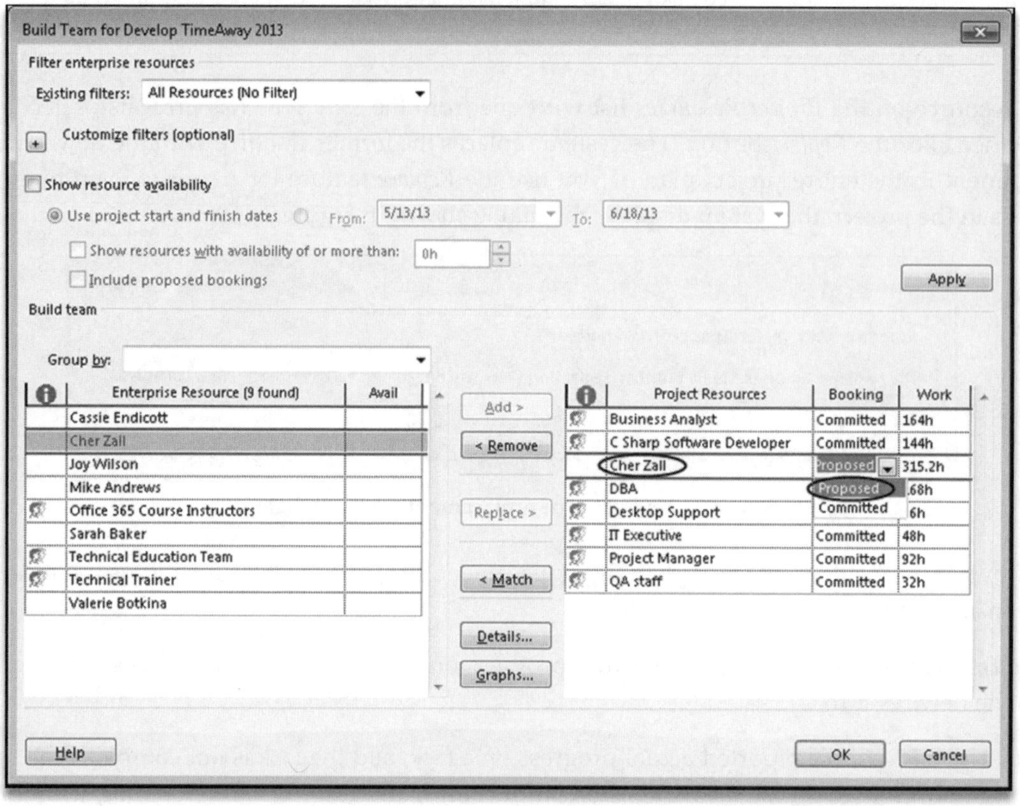

Figure 7 - 20: Change Booking to Proposed for a resource

When you book a team member as a proposed resource on a project, Project Server 2013 handles all task assignments in the project for the proposed resource as proposed assignments. The consequences of setting the *Booking* value to *Proposed* for a member of a project team are as follows:

- For proposed resources, published task assignments do not display on their *Tasks* page or their *Timesheet* page in Project Web App.
- On the *Resource Availability* page in PWA, you do not see projects assigned to a proposed resource. You must select the *Include proposed bookings* option on the page to view projects assigned to proposed resources. Refer to Figure 7 - 15, shown previously, to see the *Resource Availability* page.
- On the *Resource Assignments* page in PWA, you do not see proposed assignments..
- *Booking Type* is a dimension of the OLAP cube and is available to use in views on the *Business Intelligence Center* page in PWA.

Information: When you receive formal approval to begin the execution of your project, remember to change proposed bookings to committed bookings, or to replace proposed resources with committed resources.

Setting the published values for individual tasks

Project Pro 2013 uses the *Publish* field to indicate whether you published a task to Project Server with the remainder of the project. The field allows you to hide the unpublished tasks from team members' views, such as *Tasks* and *My Assignment* views, and from other stakeholders in PWA views. This allows flexibility in developing your project schedule allowing you to define a future phase or details of a new task or changes to tasks until a point in time when you are ready to share them with your team or project stakeholders. Once you complete the planning process for these unpublished tasks, you simply change the *Publish* field value to *Yes* for the task and then publish the project to Project Server. After you publish the project to Project Server, the newly published tasks become visible to team members and the stakeholders using PWA views. To set the *Publish* value for a task, complete the following steps in Project Pro 2013:

1. Click the *Task* tab and then in the *View* section of the *Task* ribbon, click the *Gantt Chart* button, to display the *Gantt Chart* view.

2. Right-click in the *Duration* column, and then in the resulting shortcut menu select the *Insert Column* item.

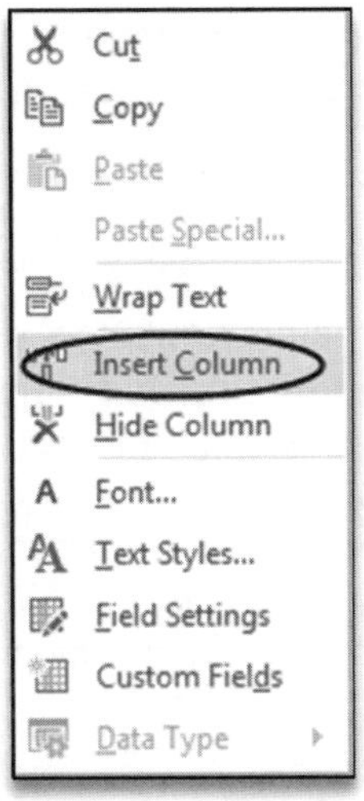

Figure 7 - 21: Select Insert Column item

3. In the resulting list, use the scroll bar to scroll down and then select the *Publish* item in the pick list, to display the *Publish* column.

Locate the task(s) in the project that you want to set the *Publish* value to *No*. In my example, I want to continue working on the *Deployment* phase in my project, and prevent the team members from seeing the tasks while I develop this portion of the schedule.

4. For the first task in the *Deployment* phase, *Determine final deployment strategy* I click in the *Publish* cell, and then click the dropdown arrow and select the *No* item in the pick list as shown in Figure 7 - 22.

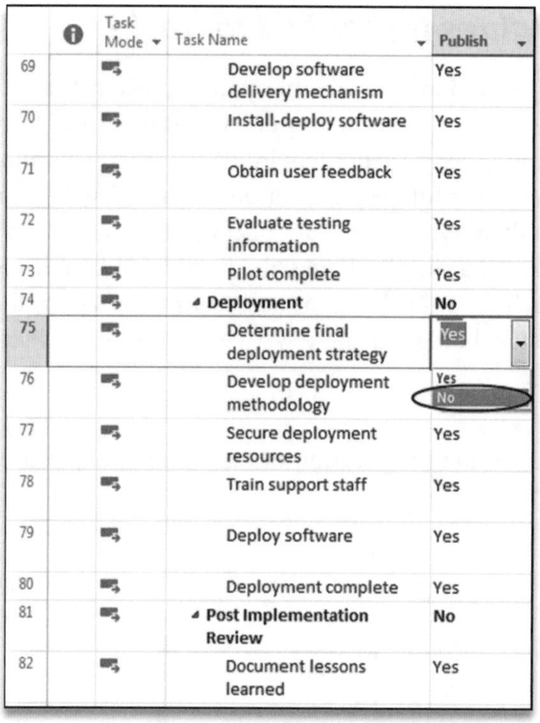

Figure 7 - 22: Set Publish value to No on a single task

5. From the *Publish* cell I just updated in the previous step, drag the *No* value down using the mouse cross-hair indicator for all of the cells I want to set the *Publish* value to *No* as shown in Figure 7 - 23. Alternatively, you may select each task and set the value for each task individually, this method is useful if you are not setting a value for the entire phase.

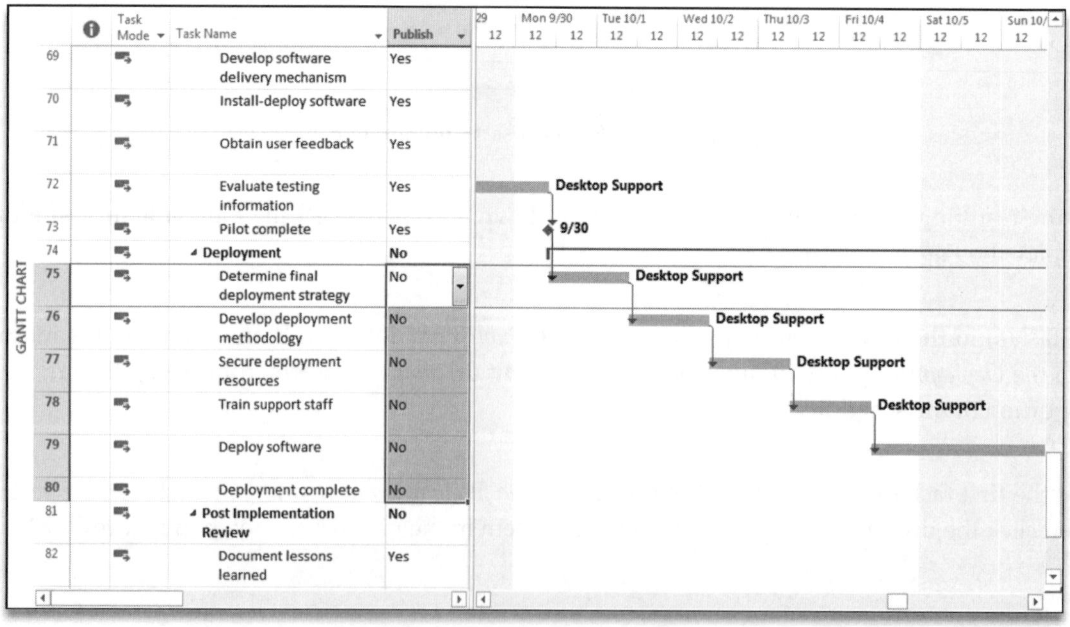

Figure 7 - 23: Drag down the Publish value to all tasks in a phase

After setting the *Publish* value for the task(s) in your project, save and publish the project to make the changes public to the team. In this case any task with the *Publish* value of *No* will no longer be visible to the project team after the project is published.

When you use *Publish* = *No*, tasks with the *No* value are:

- Not visible in *Task* views
- Not visible in *Resource Assignment* views
- Not visible in *Approval Center* views
- Do not automatically populate to new timesheets

For tasks that have actuals applied, the software simply hides the task from any of the PWA views, including the *Approval Center*. Once the task has a *Publish* value of *Yes*, the task is visible in any PWA views including the *Approval Center* with the task history.

Best Practice: MSProjectExperts recommends using the *Publish* field in Project Pro 2013 in a phase approach. Use this during the planning process, when the project manager is not ready for the resources to see an upcoming phase or assignments under development in a project already in the execution phase.

Using Local Resources in a Project Team

A local resource is any project resource not listed in the ERP. You can use local resources in an enterprise project to represent temporary resources, such as consultants or contractors, who do not use the Project Web App timesheet reporting system. To add a local resource to an enterprise project, complete these steps:

1. Click the *View* tab to display the *View* ribbon.
2. In the *Resource Views* section of the *View* ribbon, click the *Resource Sheet* pick list button and select the *Resource Sheet* view.
3. Type the name of the local resource and press the **Enter** key on your computer keyboard.
4. Enter general information for the local resource, as needed, such as information in the *Initials, Group, Max. Units*, or *Std. Rate, Ovt.*, and *Base Calendar* columns.

Project Pro 2013 displays the new local resource, as shown in Figure 7 - 24.

	ⓘ	Resource Name	Type	Material	Initials	Group	Max.	Std. Rate	Ovt.	Cost/Use	Accrue	Base
13		David Erickson	Work		DE	SoftDev	100%	$60.00/h	$90.00/h	$0.00	Prorated	Standard
14		Project Budget	Cost		PB$						Prorated	
15		Software Development Team	Work		SDT	SoftDev	100%	$60.00/h	$90.00/h	$0.00	Prorated	Standard
16		Audrey Kehrli	Work		AK	QA	100%	$40.00/h	$60.00/h	$0.00	Prorated	Standard
17		SoftDev Contractor	Work		SDC	Contractc	100%	$150.00/h	$225.00/h	$0.00	Prorated	US Work Schedule

Figure 7 - 24: Resource Sheet view, new resource

Notice the new indicator for Project Server 2013 in the *Indicator* column, for the resource shown in Figure 7 - 24. Use your mouse to hover over the indicator and the system displays a tooltip specifying that the new resource is a *Local Resource* in the project as shown in Figure 7 - 25.

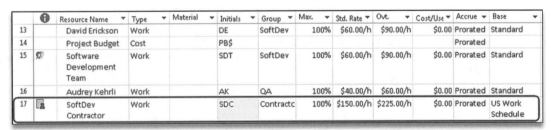

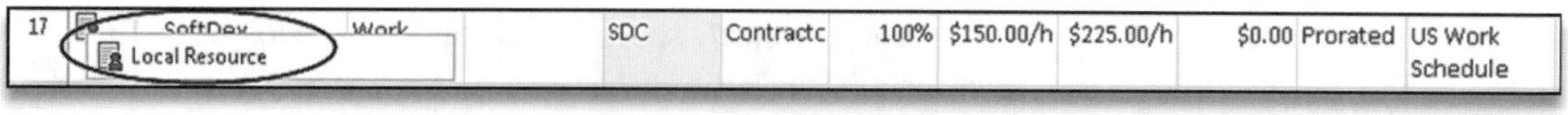

Figure 7 - 25: Resource Sheet view, Local Resource indicator

Assigning Resources to Tasks

After you build your project team in an enterprise project, you are ready to assign team members to tasks. Like the previous version of the tool, Project Pro 2013 offers three powerful tools for assigning resources to tasks, including:

- *Task Entry* view
- *Assign Resources* dialog
- *Team Planner* view

Warning: During the resource assignment process, **do not** assign resources to summary tasks, as this greatly increases the work hours and costs for your project. Instead, if you need to show a resource as the responsible person for a summary section of the project, use the built-in *Contact* field, or create a custom field and name it *Responsible Person*, or assign the resource to the milestone for the summary section of the project.

Assigning Resources Using the Task Entry View

The *Task Entry* view is the most powerful way to assign resources to tasks because it gives you total control over all of the attributes in the Project Pro 2013 scheduling engine. Using the *Task Entry* view, you can do all of the following in a single location:

- Assign multiple resources simultaneously, and specify different *Units* and *Work* values for each resource.
- Enter the *Duration* of the task.
- Set the *Task Type: Fixed Units, Fixed Work,* or *Fixed Duration* to determine which type to fix or "lock" for the task.
- Specify the *Effort Driven* status of the task to determine what happens when you add or remove resources on the task.
- Set the *Task Mode* for the task as either *Manually Scheduled* or *Auto Scheduled.*

Information: The disadvantage of using the *Task Entry* view is that you cannot assign resources to multiple tasks simultaneously. This means that you cannot use the *Task Entry* view to assign resources to a recurring task, for example.

To display the *Task Entry* view, complete the following steps:

1. Click the *View* tab and then in the *Task View* section click the *Gantt Chart* button.
2. In the *Split View* section of the *View* ribbon, select the *Details* option. Project Pro 2013 displays the *Task Entry* view, shown in Figure 7 - 26.

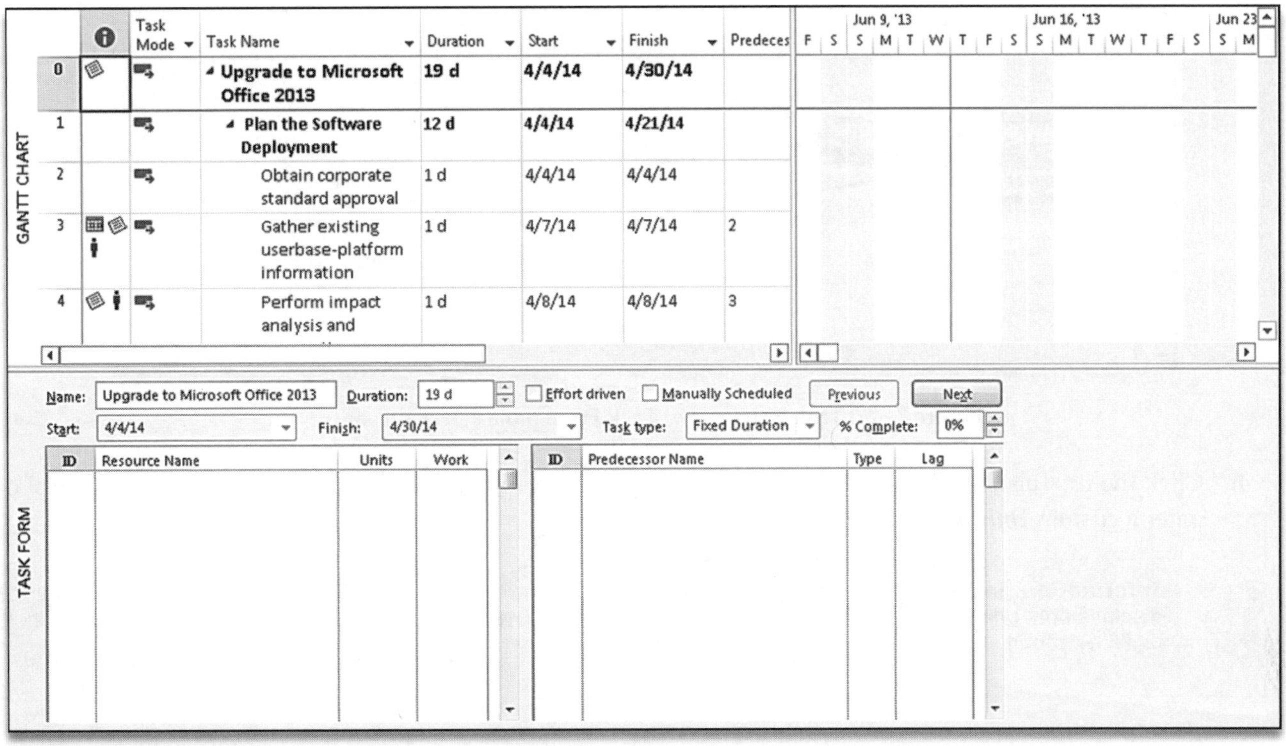

Figure 7 - 26: Task Entry view

Information: In the *Split View* section of the *View* ribbon, Project Pro 2013 will display either the *Timeline* or *Details* option at one time.

The *Task Entry* view is a combination view consisting of two views, which display in separate panes. The *Task Entry* view includes:

- *Gantt Chart* view in the top pane
- *Task Form* view in the bottom pane

To assign a resource to a task using the *Task Entry* view, complete the following steps:

1. Select a single task in the *Gantt Chart* pane.
2. In the *Task Form* pane, select the first blank cell in the *Resource Name* column and then click the pick list button. The software displays the list of resources that are already part of the project team, as shown in Figure 7 - 27.
3. Select the resource you would like to assign to the task. Notice in Figure 7 - 27 , I selected *Bob Siclari.*

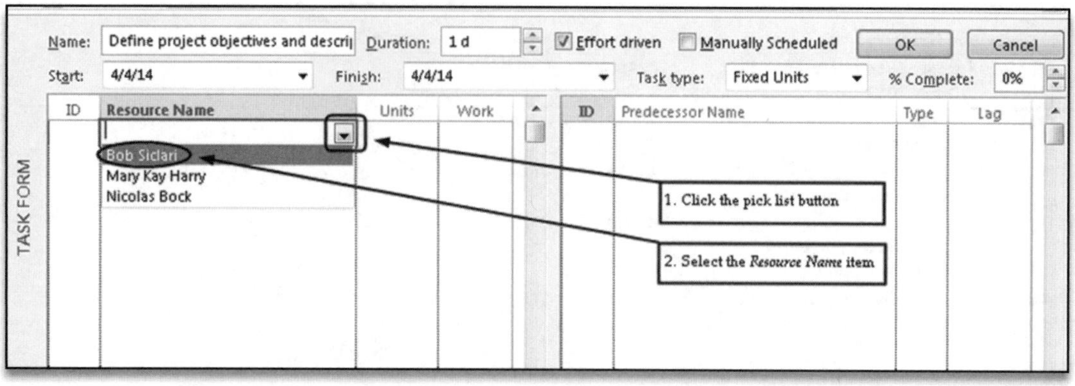

Figure 7 - 27: Task Entry view, Task Form pane select a resource

4. Click the first blank cell in the *Units* column and then select an increment value using the spin control or enter a custom *Units* value for the resource.

Information: In the *Units* column, you can use the spin control feature to select a value, but Project Pro 2013 displays only *Units* values in 50% increments (0%, 50%, 100%, etc.). For other increment *Units,* such as 25% or 75%, you must manually type the custom *Units* value.

5. Click in the first blank cell in the *Work* column and enter the estimated work hours for that resource.
6. Repeat steps #2-4 for each additional resource you wish to assign to the task.
7. Click the *OK* button.

Warning: Do not click the *OK* button in the *Task Form* pane until you finish selecting all of the resources you need and finish setting both the *Units* and *Work* values for each resource.

Project Pro 2013 assigns the resource to the task and then calculates the *Duration* value based on the *Units* and *Work* values you enter. Notice in Figure 7 - 28, *Bob Siclari's* assignment for the task is 50% *Units* and *16* hours of *Work* and based on these two numbers, the software recalculates a *Duration* value of *4 days* for the task. Notice also that the software changes the *OK* and *Cancel* buttons to the *Previous* and *Next* buttons, which allow you to navigate easily from task to task during the assignment process.

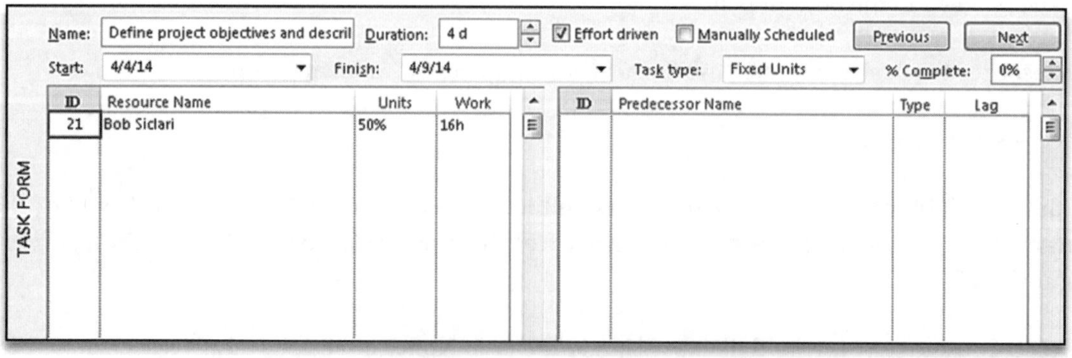

Figure 7 - 28: Task Entry view, Duration calculated after assigning a resource with Units and Work

In the *Gantt Chart* view of your enterprise project shown in Figure 7 - 29, the system sometimes displays a red "burning man" indicator. This indicates that Project Pro 2013 considers a resource overallocated for the task. I discuss how to resolve resource overallocations later in this module. After I assign *Bob Siclari* to the *Define project objectives and describe mission statement* task, notice that Project Pro 2013 displays a "burning man" indicator in the *Indicators* column to the left of the *Define project objectives and describe mission statement* task. The "burning man" indicator reveals that I accidentally overallocated *Bob Siclari* on this task.

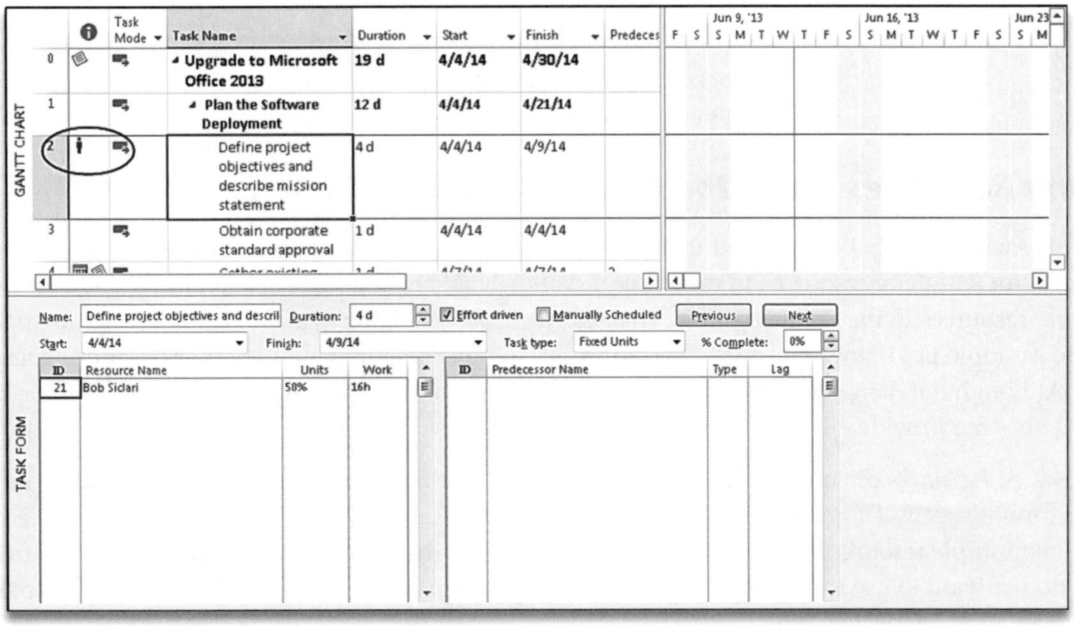

Figure 7 - 29: "Burning Man" indicator showing resource overallocation

8. Click the *Next* button to select the next task in the project and to continue assigning resources to tasks.

To assign resources to a task for which you already estimated a *Duration* value, complete the following steps:

1. In the *Gantt Chart* pane, select the task with the estimated *Duration* value.
2. In the *Task Form* pane, select the name of a resource from the list in the *Resource Name* column.
3. Enter a *Units* value for the resource in the *Units* column.
4. **Do not** enter a *Work* value.
5. Repeat steps #2-4 for each additional resource you want to assign to the task.
6. Click the *OK* button.

Project Pro 2013 calculates the *Work* value for each resource assigned to the task. Notice in Figure 7 - 30 that I assigned three resources to work full-time on the task with a *Duration* value of *10 days*, so the software calculated *80 hours* in the *Work* column for each resource.

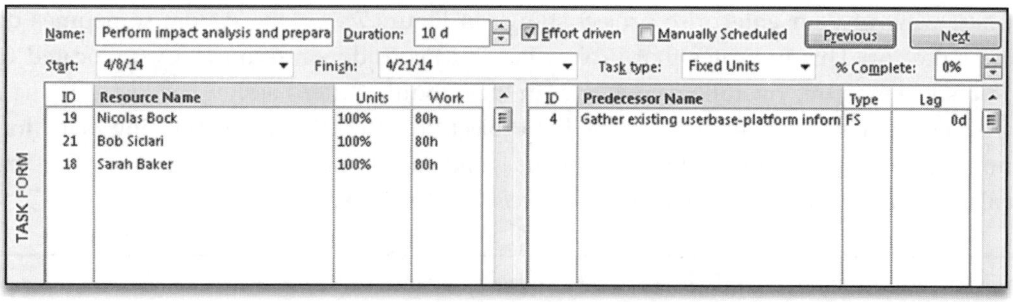

Figure 7 - 30: Task Entry view, Work calculated after assigning resources with Units and Duration

Assigning Resources Using the Assign Resources Dialog

The *Assign Resources* dialog is the second tool you can use during the assignment process. The *Assign Resources* dialog is ideal for assigning resources to recurring tasks, such as meetings, because it allows you to select and assign multiple resources to the recurring task. The *Assign Resources* dialog is also ideal for assigning one or more resources to multiple tasks simultaneously, and for replacing one resource with another on multiple tasks simultaneously. Although the *Assign Resources* dialog offers you a simple interface to assign resources to tasks, keep in mind that it does not provide all of the options available in the *Task Entry* view.

Using the *Assign Resources* dialog, you have no control over most of the attributes of the scheduling engine. This means you cannot specify *Duration, Task Type, Effort Driven* status, or the *Task Mode* for a task. Furthermore, you cannot assign multiple resources to a task and individually select different *Units* values for each resource. In most cases, you do not want to use the *Assign Resources* dialog to assign work. However, there is one exception I highlight in the following *Information* topic.

Information: A little known fact about the *Assign Resources* dialog is that you can enter work values in the *Units* field by adding a work value notation such as h, d, or m. For example, when you enter 5h in the *Units* field, the system accepts your input and then calculates % units based on the task duration. However, by doing so, the system does **not** recalculate the task duration. Instead, it creates an overallocation if you specify a work value that is greater than the working hours available for the resource during the specified period. The only time you might use this feature/quirk, is when you are working with fixed durations and known work values that you want to distribute across a specified duration. For example, if you want to assign a group of people to a single fixed-duration task, you could use this technique simply to calculate the *Units* value. The *Task Entry Form* remains a better choice, but entering work values in the *Assign Resources* dialog is also an option.

To display the *Assign Resources* dialog, use one of the following methods:

- Click the *Resource* tab and then in the *Assignment* section of the *Resource* ribbon click the *Assign Resources* button.
- Right-click any task and then select the *Assign Resources* item on the shortcut menu.
- Use the keyboard shortcut using the **Alt + F10** keys on your computer keyboard.

Project Pro 2013 displays the *Assign Resources* dialog shown in Figure 7 - 31.

Information: In the *Assign Resources* dialog, the system sorts the resources in ascending order by the *Resource Name* column, and not in the order they appear in the *Resource Sheet* view of your project.

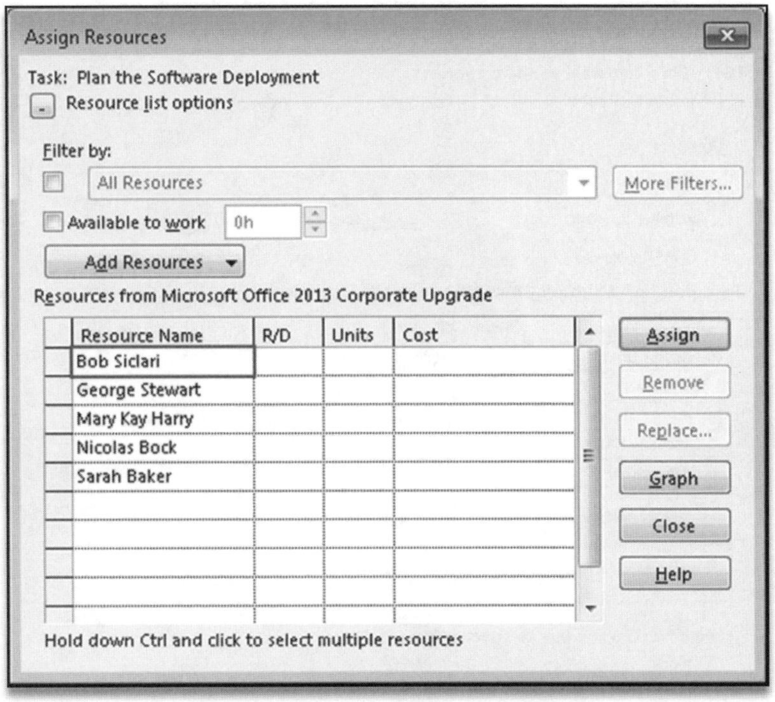

Figure 7 - 31: Assign Resources dialog

To assign a resource to tasks using the *Assign Resources* dialog, complete the following steps:

1. Select one or more tasks.

2. Select a single resource in the list of resources shown in the dialog.

3. Select or enter a *Units* value (if different from the default Max units for the resource).

4. Click the *Assign* button.

The *Assign Resources* dialog indicates a successful assignment to the tasks by moving the resource to the beginning of the list, and adding a checkmark indicator to the left of the resource's name. Notice in Figure 7 - 32, for example, that I assigned Nicolas Bock to work full time (*100%* units) on the selected task. If you previously entered cost rates for your resources in the *Std. Rate* column of the *Resource Sheet* view, Project Pro 2013 also calculates a cost value in the *Cost* column of the *Assign Resources* dialog for each assigned resource. Notice in Figure 7 - 32 that Nicolas Bock's assignment on the selected task costs the project *$800,* as indicated in the *Cost* column.

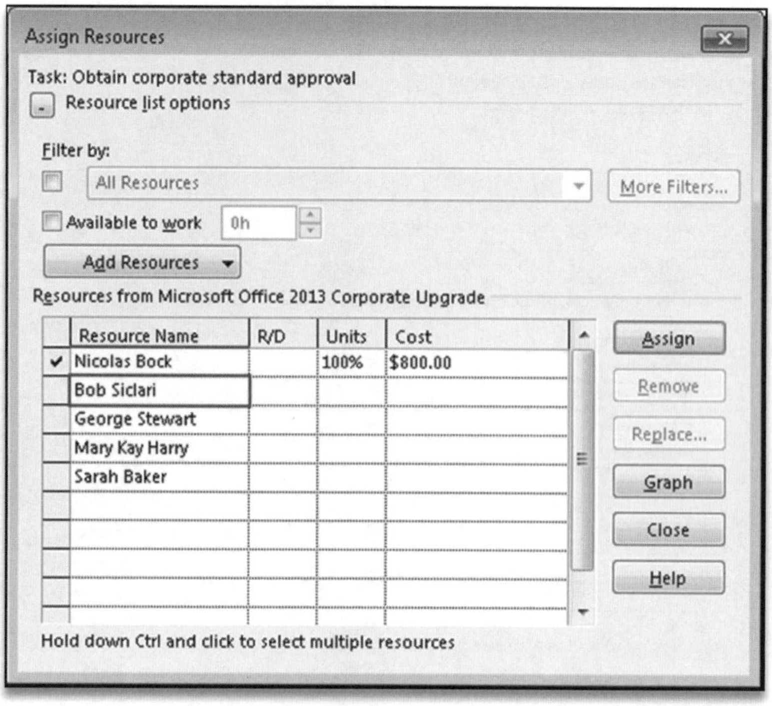

Figure 7 - 32: Assign Resources dialog with one resource assigned to a task

To assign multiple resources to tasks using the *Assign Resources* dialog, complete the following steps:

1. Select one or more tasks.

2. In the *Assign Resources* dialog, select multiple resources using either the **Control** key or the **Shift** key on your computer keyboard.

3. **Do not** set a *Units* value for any resource.

4. Click the *Assign* button.

If you do not enter a *Units* value when assigning a resource in the *Assign Resources* dialog, Project Pro 2013 enters the *Max. Units* value for the resource from the *Resource Sheet* view of your project. This means that if the *Max. Units* value for a resource is *50%*, and you do not supply a *Units* value when assigning this resource, the *Assign Resources* dialog assigns the resource with a *Units* value of *50%* automatically. The exception to this rule is for *Generic* resources that have a *Max. Units* value greater than 100%. In this case, if you do not supply a *Units* value for the *Generic* resource, the *Assign Resources* dialog assigns the *Generic* resource with a *Units* value of only *100%* automatically.

Warning: **Do not** use the *Assign Resources* dialog to assign multiple resources to a task that requires using a different *Units* value for each resource. The software assigns the first resource at the *Units* value you select and then adds each of the other resources as **helpers** on the task using Effort Driven scheduling, decreasing the *Duration* of the task accordingly. This behavior is one of the major reasons that new users find Project Pro 2013 so frustrating! Instead, use the *Task Entry* view when you need to assign multiple resources with different *Units* values.

Understanding Other Factors in Assignment Planning

During the assignment planning process, three factors affect how you assign resources in Project Pro 2013. These factors are:

- **Duration Equation** - The system uses the Duration Equation to calculate the *Duration, Work,* or *Units* value when you assign a resource to a task.
- **Task Type** - You use the *Task Type* option to fix or "lock" the *Duration, Work,* or *Units* value when you assign a resource to a task.
- **Effort Driven Scheduling** - You use *Effort Driven* scheduling to reduce the *Duration* value on a task by adding one or more helpers to the task.

I discuss each of these factors individually as subtopics in this section of the module.

Understanding the Duration Equation

When you assign a resource to a task using the *Task Entry* view, and you enter a *Units* value and a *Work* value for the resource, Project Pro 2013 calculates the *Duration* value for the task automatically. How does the software calculate duration? The software uses a simple formula known as the **Duration Equation**, written as follows:

$$\text{Duration} = \text{Work} \div (\text{Hours Per Day} \times \text{Units})$$

or

$$D = W \div (HPD \times U)$$

The default *Hours Per Day* value is 8 hours per day. You can locate this value by clicking *File ➢ Options* in the *Backstage*. In the *Project Options* dialog, click the *Schedule* tab to find the *Hours per day* option in the *Calendar options for this project* section, as shown in Figure 7 - 33.

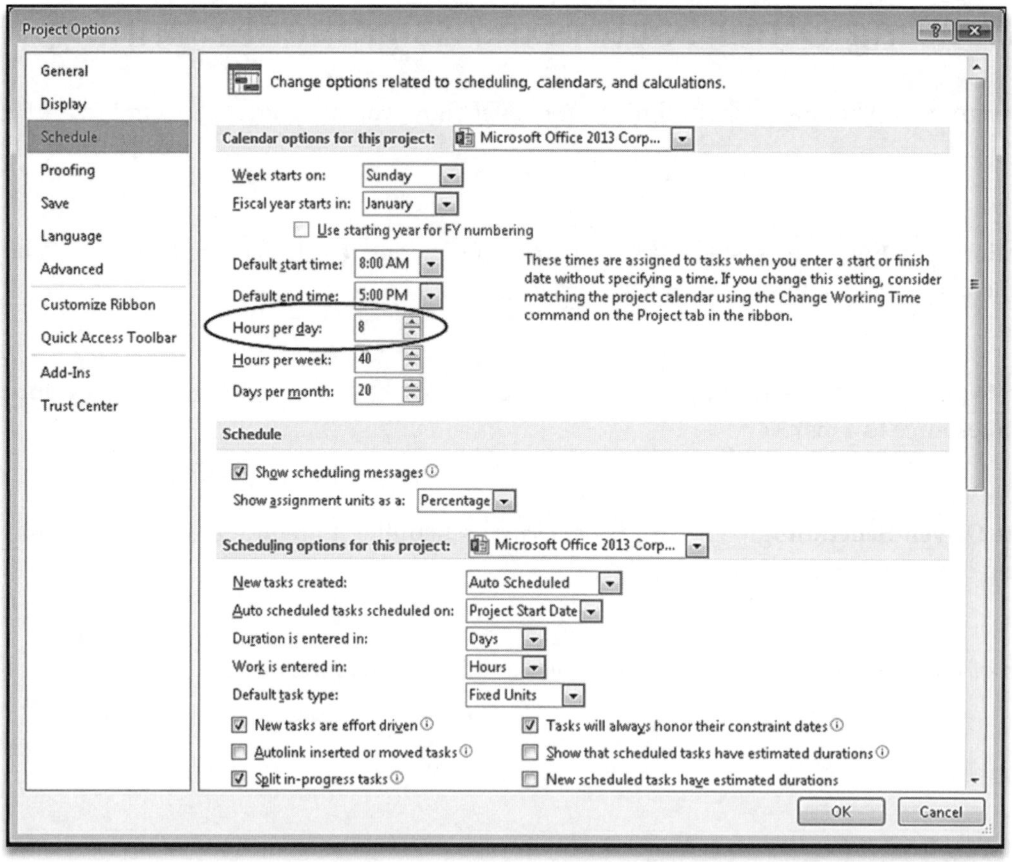

Figure 7 - 33: Project Options dialog, Schedule tab shows the Hours per day setting

To demonstrate how the Duration Equation works, I assign a resource to a task at *50% Units* and *40 hours* of *Work*. Using the Duration Equation, Project Pro 2013 calculates the *Duration* value at *10 days* as follows:

D = W ÷ (HPD × U)

D = 40 ÷ (8 × 50%)

D = 40 ÷ 4 = 10 days

When you assign a resource to a task and enter *Duration* and *Units* values (rather than *Units* and *Work* values), Project Pro 2013 calculates the *Work* value. How does the software calculate work? The software uses a modified version of the Duration Equation, rewritten to solve for the *Work* variable as follows:

Work = **D**uration × **H**ours **P**er **D**ay × **U**nits

or

W = D × HPD × U

For example, I assign a resource to work *50% Units* on a task with a *Duration* value of *10 days*, Project Pro 2013 calculates *40 hours* of *Work* as follows:

W = D × HPD × U

W = 10 × 8 × 50%

W = 10 × 4 = 40 hours

You can also rewrite the Duration Equation to solve for the *Units* variable as follows:

Units = **W**ork ÷ (**D**uration × **H**ours per **D**ay)

or

U = W ÷ (D × HPD)

For example, I assign a resource *40 hours* of *Work* on a task with a *Duration* value of *10 days*, Project Pro 2013 calculates a *Units* value of *50%* as follows:

U = W ÷ (D × HPD)

U = 40 ÷ (10 × 8)

U = 40 ÷ 80 = .5 or 50%

Understanding Task Types

You may specify the *Task Type* setting for any task to one of three types: *Fixed Units, Fixed Work,* or *Fixed Duration.* You can select **only one** *Task Type* setting for each task. The default *Task Type* setting for every task is *Fixed Units,* unless you specify otherwise in the *Project Options* dialog. To specify the *Task Type* setting for any task, select the task and then use one of the following methods:

- Apply the *Task Entry* view. In the *Task Form* pane, click the *Task Type* pick list and select the desired *Task Type* setting.
- Double-click the task and then click the *Advanced* tab in the *Task Information* dialog. Click the *Task Type* pick list and select the desired *Task Type* setting.
- In the *Properties* section of the *Task* ribbon, click the *Information* button and then click the *Advanced* tab in the *Task Information* dialog. Click the *Task Type* pick list and select the desired *Task Type* setting.
- Right-click the task, then select the *Information* item on the shortcut menu, and in the *Task Information* dialog, click the *Advanced* tab. Click the *Task Type* pick list and select the desired *Task Type* setting.

Information: You may also specify the *Task Type* setting for multiple tasks simultaneously by selecting a group of tasks first. In the *Properties* section of the *Task* ribbon, click the *Information* button and then click the *Advanced* tab in the *Multiple Task Information* dialog. Click the *Task Type* pick list and select the desired *Task Type* setting for the selected tasks.

Specify the *Task Type* setting for tasks using the following information as your guide:

- **Fixed Units** – Project Pro 2013 locks the *Units* value for all resources assigned to a *Fixed Units* task. Set the *Task Type* option to *Fixed Units* when a resource has a known availability to perform work on tasks in your project. For example, you assign a resource to work on a task at *50% Units* because the resource also works half time on the Help Desk. Use the *Fixed Units* task type on this task to guarantee that the software does not recalculate the *50% Units* value if you change either the *Work* or *Duration* values on the task.
- **Fixed Work** – The software locks the *Work* value for all resources assigned to a *Fixed Work* task. Set the *Task Type* option to *Fixed Work* when you are certain about the number of hours to complete a task. For example, you hire a consultant to work on a project task, and the work is set at 40 hours by contract. Use the *Fixed Work* task type on this task to guarantee that Project Pro 2013 does not recalculate the *40 hours* of *Work* if you change either the *Units* or *Duration* values on the task.

- **Fixed Duration** – The software locks the *Duration* value on a *Fixed Duration* task. Set the *Task Type* to *Fixed Duration* when you are certain of the *Duration* value for a task, such as when you have a known "window of opportunity" to complete the task. For example, you have a task called Shareholder Conference and the conference lasts 3 days. Use the *Fixed Duration* task type on this task to guarantee that the software does not recalculate the *Duration* value of *3 days* if you change either the *Units* or *Work* values on the task.

The *Task Type* setting you select fixes or "locks" one of the three variables in the Duration Equation for the selected task. When you change one of the two non-fixed variables, Project Pro 2013 calculates the other non-fixed variable automatically. Table 7 - 1 shows the behavior of all three *Task Types* when you change the non-fixed variable, and when you change the fixed variable.

Task Type	Fixed Value	You Change	Recalculated Value
Fixed Units	Units	Work	Duration
Fixed Units	Units	Duration	Work
Fixed Units	Units	Units	Duration
Fixed Work	Work	Units	Duration
Fixed Work	Work	Duration	Units
Fixed Work	Work	Work	Duration
Fixed Duration	Duration	Units	Work
Fixed Duration	Duration	Work	Units
Fixed Duration	Duration	Duration	Work

Table 7 - 1: Task Type behavior

The only exception to the *Task Type* behavior documented in Table 7 - 1 occurs when you initially assign a resource to a *Fixed Duration* task and enter a value in the *Work* field. In this situation, Project Pro 2013 does the following:

- In the *Units* field in the *Task Form* pane, the software enters the *Max. Units* value for the resource from the *Resource Sheet* view of your project.
- In the background, the software calculates the correct *Units* value, but does not display it in the *Units* field in the *Task Form* pane. Instead, the software stores this value in the *Peak* field, which you cannot see in the *Task Form* pane.
- The software assigns the resource using the correctly calculated *Units* value stored in the *Peak* field.

If you want to see the values in the *Units* and *Peak* fields, you can add the *Assignment Units* field and the *Peak* field to the *Task Usage* view of your project. At this point, however, do not despair. I provide an in-depth discussion of the behavior of the *Assignment Units* and *Peak* fields in the next section of this module.

When you change a non-fixed variable for any task type, Project Pro 2013 automatically recalculates the other non-fixed variable. When you change the **fixed** variable, however, the software invokes one of the programming decisions implemented by the software development team many years ago. For example, which variable should the software recalculate when you change the *Units* value on a *Fixed Units* task, you change the *Work* value on a *Fixed Work* task, or you change the *Duration* value on a *Fixed Duration* task?

We refer to the decisions made by the software development team as the programming biases. These programming biases are as follows:

- If you change the *Units* variable on a *Fixed Units* task, Project Pro 2013 **always** recalculates the *Duration* variable.

- If you change the *Work* variable on a *Fixed Work* task, Project Pro 2013 **always** recalculates the *Duration* variable.

- If you change the *Duration* variable on a *Fixed Duration* task, Project Pro 2013 **always** recalculates the *Work* variable.

As you can see, Project Pro 2013 has a bias to calculate changes in *Duration* rather than to *Work* or *Units*. If the software cannot change *Duration*, it has a bias to calculate changes in *Work* rather than *Units*.

Understanding the Peak and Assignment Units Fields

To gain a thorough understanding of the behavior of the *Assignment Units* and *Peak* fields, it helps to understand how the software works when you initially assign a resource to a task. Suppose that I assign resource *Henry Baum* to the *Design* task at a *Units* value of *100%* and *40 hours* of *Work*, as shown in Figure 7 - 34. Notice that Project Pro 2013 calculates a *Duration* value of *5 days* for this *Fixed Work* task.

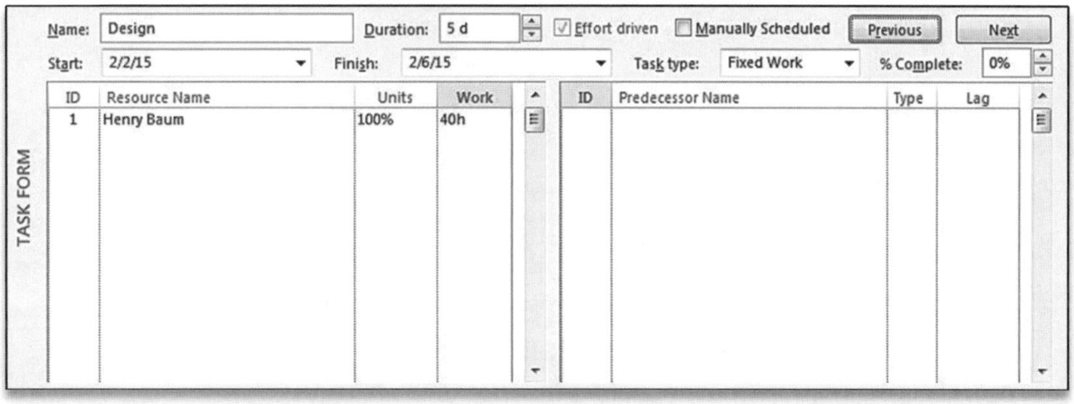

Figure 7 - 34: Resource assigned at 100% Units to the Design task

When I assign *Henry Baum* to the *Design* task, the software creates a resource assignment on the task and captures the original *Units* value of *100%*. You can see the resource assignment information in either the *Task Usage* view or *Resource Usage* view of a project. Figure 7 - 35 shows the initial assignment information in the *Task Usage* view for *Henry Baum's* resource assignment on the *Design* task. Notice that the software assigns the *40 hours* of *Work* using a flat pattern of 8 hours per day over the *Duration* of *5 days* for the task.

		Task Mode ▼	Task Name ▼	Work ▼	Details	Feb 1, '15 S	M	T	W	T	F	S
0		➤	⊿ **Understanding Units**	**40 h**	Work		8h	8h	8h	8h	8h	
1		➤	⊿ Design	40 h	Work		8h	8h	8h	8h	8h	
			Henry Baum	40 h	Work		8h	8h	8h	8h	8h	
					Work							
					Work							

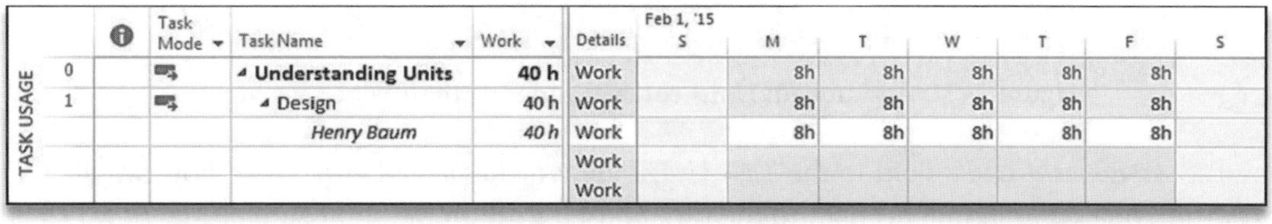

Figure 7 - 35: Task Usage view shows the resource assignment information

Although not displayed by default in either the *Task Usage* view or *Resource Usage* view, Project Pro 2013 offers several additional assignment fields you can use to understand how the software handles the original *Units* value on the resource assignment. These additional fields include:

- *Assignment Units* (an assignment field)
- *Peak* (an assignment field)
- *Percent Allocation* (a timephased assignment field)
- *Peak Units* (a timephased assignment field)

To add the *Assignment Units* field to the *Task Usage* view or the *Resource Usage* view, right-click the *Work* column header. The software displays the shortcut menu shown in Figure 7 - 36.

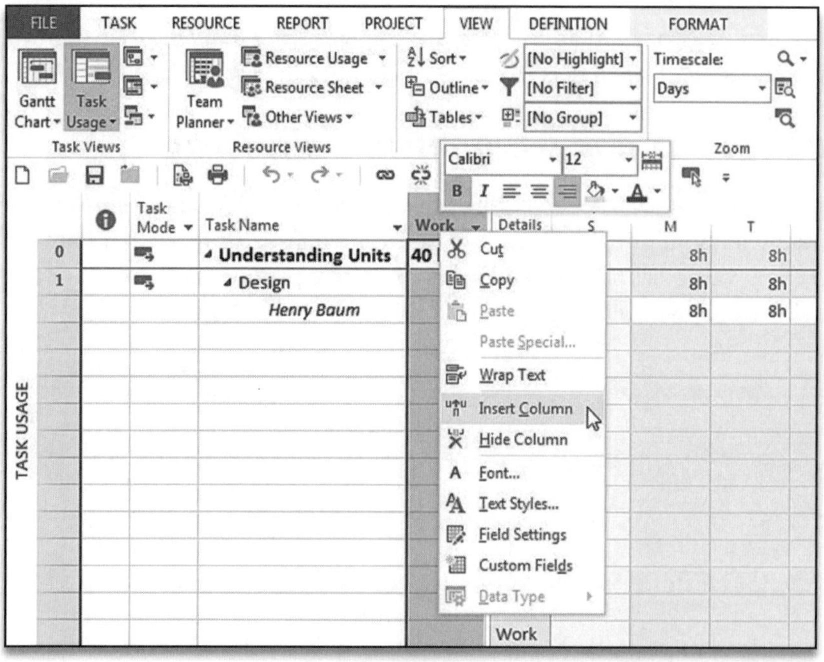

Figure 7 - 36: Shortcut menu to add a new field

Select the *Insert Column* item in the menu and then select the *Assignment Units* field from the pick list of available fields. Project Pro 2013 inserts the *Assignment Units* field to the left of the *Work* field, as shown in Figure 7 - 37.

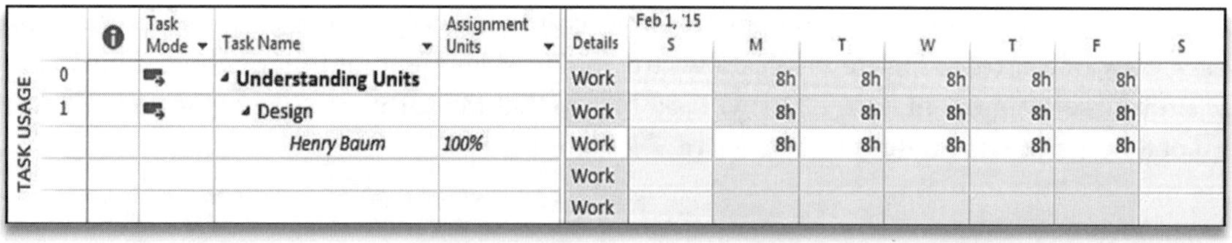

Figure 7 - 37: Assignment Units column added to the Task Usage view

After adding the *Assignment Units* field to the *Task Usage* view or *Resource Usage* view, you can also add the *Percent Allocation* (timephased assignment) field to the timephased grid on the right side of the view. To add the *Per-*

cent Allocation field, right-click anywhere in the timephased grid and select the *Detail Styles* item on the shortcut menu, as shown in Figure 7 - 38.

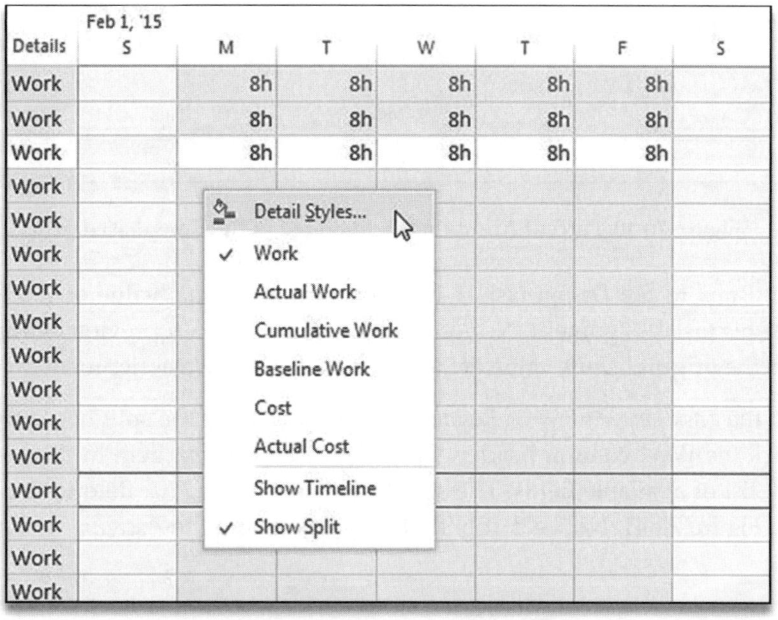

Figure 7 - 38: Shortcut menu to add a new timephased field to the timephased grid

The software displays the *Detail Styles* dialog shown in Figure 7 - 39. The *Detail Styles* dialog shows you the list of all available timephased fields in the *Available fields* list on the left side of the dialog.

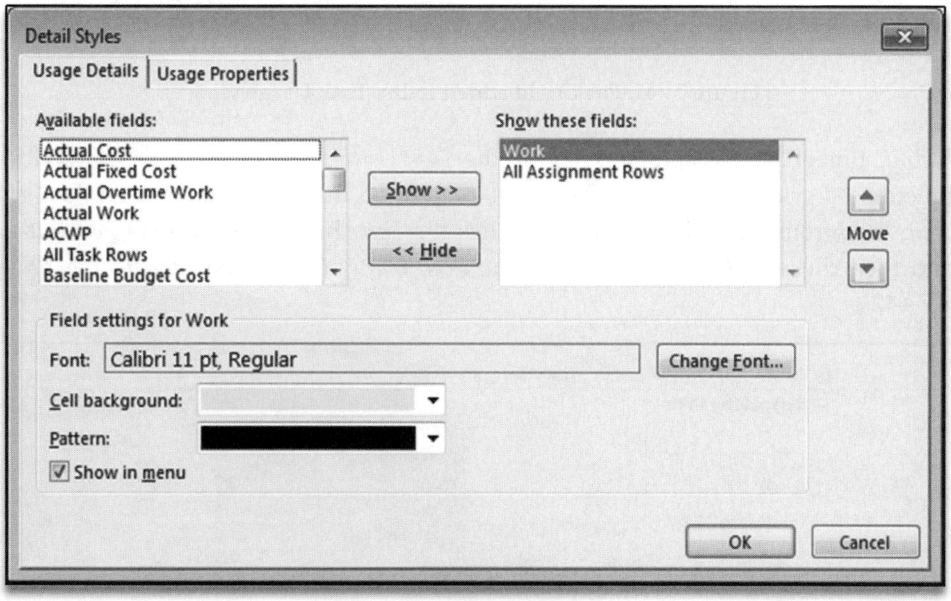

Figure 7 - 39: Detail Styles dialog

In the *Detail Styles* dialog, scroll to the bottom of the *Available fields* list and select the *Percent Allocation* field. Click the *Show* button to add the *Percent Allocation* field to the *Show these fields* list. Click the *OK* button to add the *Percent Allocation* timephased assignment field to the timephased grid, as shown in Figure 7 - 40.

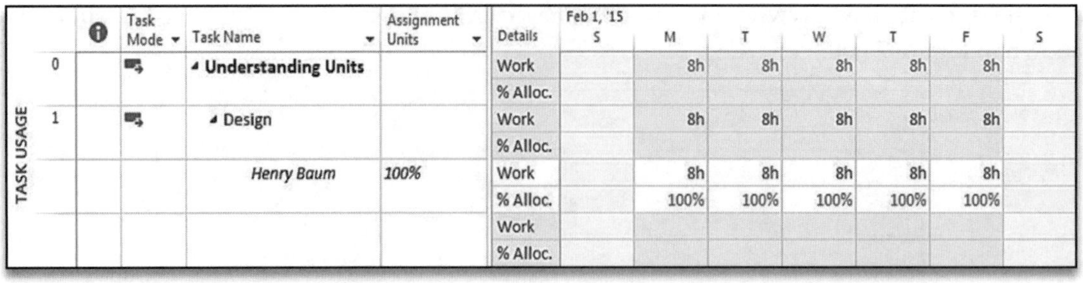

		Task Mode	Task Name	Assignment Units	Details	Feb 1, '15 S	M	T	W	T	F	S
0			◢ Understanding Units		Work		8h	8h	8h	8h	8h	
					% Alloc.							
1			◢ Design		Work		8h	8h	8h	8h	8h	
					% Alloc.							
			Henry Baum	*100%*	Work		8h	8h	8h	8h	8h	
					% Alloc.		100%	100%	100%	100%	100%	
					Work							
					% Alloc.							

Figure 7 - 40: Percent Allocation field added to the timephased grid

When I assigned *Henry Baum* to the *Design* task, I assigned him at a *Units* value of *100%*, which represents the **original** *Units* value for his task assignment. Notice in Figure 7 - 40 shown previously that the *Percent Allocation* timephased field shows the **original** *Units* value of *100%* for Henry Baum's assignment on the *Design* task.

To add the *Peak* field to the *Task Usage* view or *Resource Usage* view, drag the split bar to the right of the *Work* column and then right-click the *Work* column header. Click the *Insert Column* item in the menu and then select the *Peak* field from the pick list of available fields. The software displays the *Peak* field to the right of the *Assignment Units* field, as shown in Figure 7 - 41. Notice that both the *Peak* field and the *Assignment Units* field show the same *Units* value of 100%.

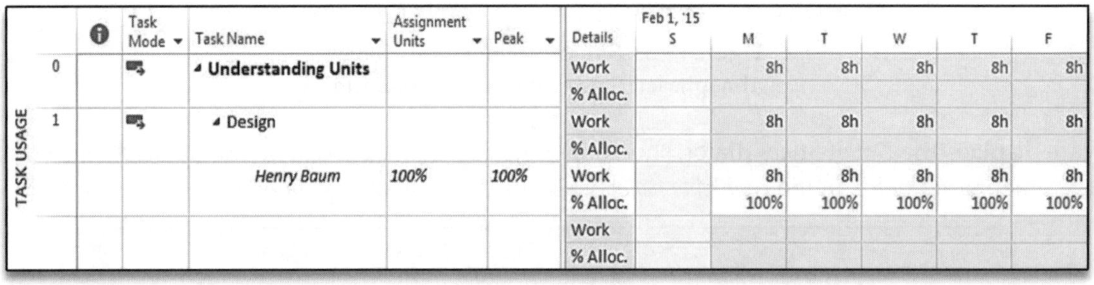

		Task Mode	Task Name	Assignment Units	Peak	Details	Feb 1, '15 S	M	T	W	T	F
0			◢ Understanding Units			Work		8h	8h	8h	8h	8h
						% Alloc.						
1			◢ Design			Work		8h	8h	8h	8h	8h
						% Alloc.						
			Henry Baum	*100%*	*100%*	Work		8h	8h	8h	8h	8h
						% Alloc.		100%	100%	100%	100%	100%
						Work						
						% Alloc.						

Figure 7 - 41: Peak field added to the Task Usage view

To add the *Peak Units* timephased assignment field to the *Task Usage* view or *Resource Usage* view, right-click anywhere in the timephased grid and select the *Detail Styles* item on the shortcut menu. In the *Detail Styles* dialog, select the *Peak Units* field from the *Available fields* list. Click the *Show* button to add the *Peak Units* field to the *Show these fields* list and then click the *OK* button to add the *Peak Units* timephased field to the timephased grid, as shown in Figure 7 - 42.

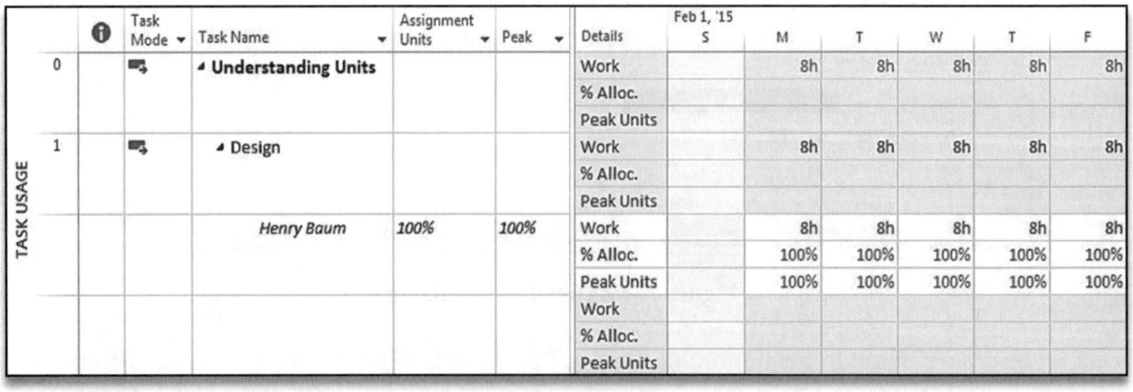

		Task Mode	Task Name	Assignment Units	Peak	Details	Feb 1, '15 S	M	T	W	T	F
0			◢ Understanding Units			Work		8h	8h	8h	8h	8h
						% Alloc.						
						Peak Units						
1			◢ Design			Work		8h	8h	8h	8h	8h
						% Alloc.						
						Peak Units						
			Henry Baum	*100%*	*100%*	Work		8h	8h	8h	8h	8h
						% Alloc.		100%	100%	100%	100%	100%
						Peak Units		100%	100%	100%	100%	100%
						Work						
						% Alloc.						
						Peak Units						

Figure 7 - 42: Peak Units field added to the timephased grid

When you make any change to the project that causes the Project Pro 2013 scheduling engine to recalculate the *Units* value on the assignment, such as when you change the *Duration* value on a *Fixed Work* task, or you change the *Work* value on a *Fixed Duration* task, the software responds as follows:

- The software displays the **original** *Units* value in the *Assignment Units* field.
- The software captures the **recalculated** *Units* value in the *Peak* field.
- Using the **recalculated** *Units* value in the *Peak* field, the software reschedules the timephased work accordingly in the timephased grid.

For example, I change the value in the *Duration* field to *10 days*, as shown in Figure 7 - 43. Notice that Project Pro 2013 **does not** show the recalculated *Units* value in the *Task Form* pane.

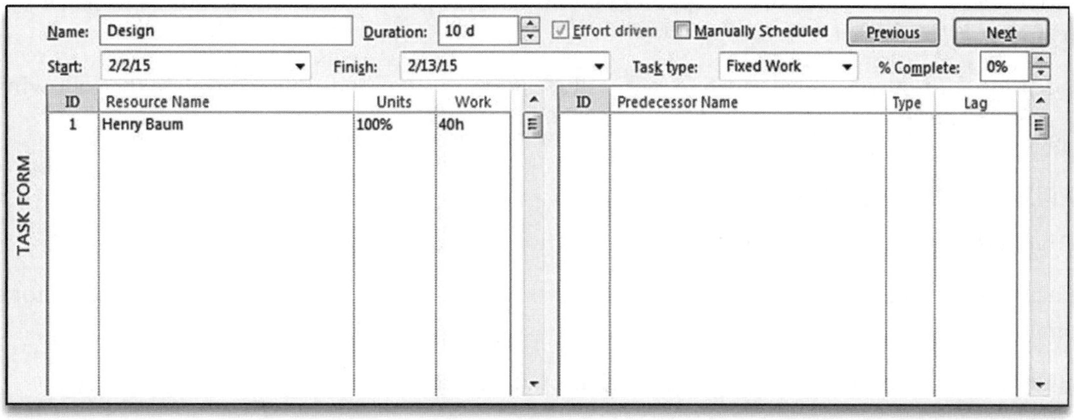

Figure 7 - 43: Change the Duration value to 10 days

Instead, Project Pro 2013 does the following in the *Task Usage* view shown in Figure 7 - 44:

- The software displays the **original** *Units* value of **100%** in the *Assignment Units* field.
- The software captures the **recalculated** *Units* value of **50%** in the *Peak* field.
- Using the new **50%** value in the *Peak* field, the software reschedules the timephased work at 4 hours per day in the timephased grid.

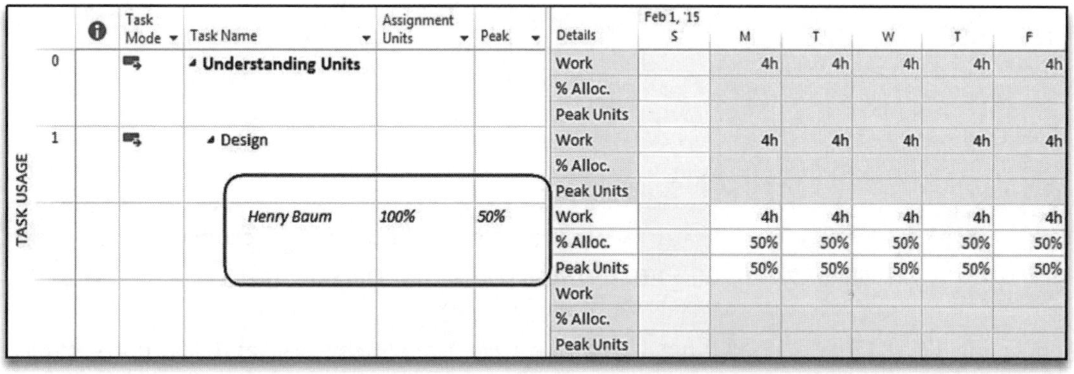

Figure 7 - 44: Peak field captures the recalculated Units value

Notice in Figure 7 - 44, shown previously, that the timephased *Percent Allocation* field shows the correct assignment *Units* value on Henry Baum's assignment in the timephased grid. Notice also that the software correctly schedules the timephased *Work* value for this task at 4 hours per day using the *50%* value.

> **Information**: Beyond the challenging behavior of the *Assignment Units* and *Peak* fields, as documented in this section of the module, you may see additional challenging behavior in Project Pro 2013 when you begin entering progress in your project. I provide thorough documentation about this additional new behavior in Module 08: *Project Execution*.

Understanding Effort Driven Scheduling

In Project Pro 2013, you can designate each task individually as either an *Effort Driven* task or a *non-Effort Driven* task. The *Effort Driven* status of any task determines how the software responds when you add or remove resources from a task to which you previously assigned one or more resources. The default setting for every task in Project Pro 2013 is *Effort Driven*.

To assign additional resources as helpers to a task using *Effort Driven* scheduling, complete the following steps:

1. Select a task to which you previously assigned at least one resource.
2. Apply the *Task Entry* view.
3. In the *Task Form* pane, select the *Effort driven* option, if not already selected.
4. Select one or more additional resources in the *Resource Name* column, and set a *Units* value for each additional resource.
5. **Do not** enter a *Work* value for any of the additional resources.
6. Click the *OK* button.

When you add a resource to an *Effort Driven* task, the software keeps the *Remaining Work* value constant and allocates the *Remaining Work* proportionately to each resource based on each resource's *Units* value. Consider the following examples of how Project Pro 2013 distributes the *Remaining Work* based on the *Units* values of each resource:

- I assign *Albert Udom* to the *Design* task at *100%* units and *80 hours* of work, and the software calculates the *Duration* for the task as *10 days*, as shown in Figure 7 - 45.

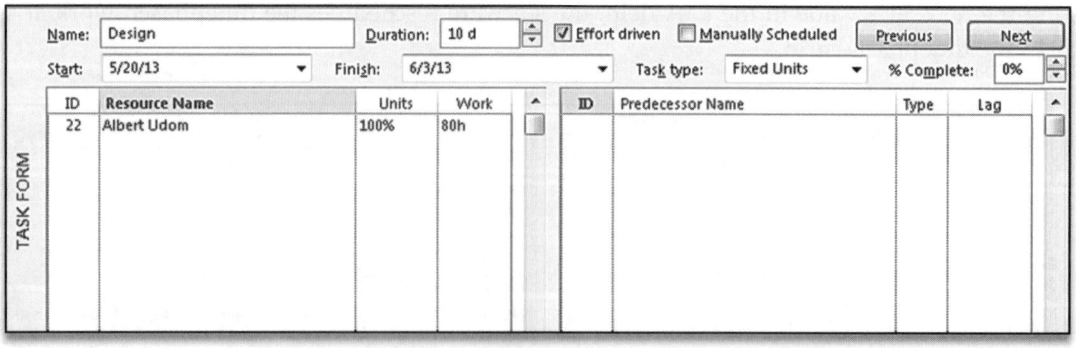

Figure 7 - 45: Using Effort Driven scheduling, Duration 10 days

- Then, using *Effort Driven* scheduling, I add *Kevin Holthaus* to the task at *100%* units. Project Pro 2013 shortens the *Duration* to *5 days* and allocates the *80 hours* of *Remaining Work* evenly between the two resources (*40 hours* each to *Albert Udom* and to *Kevin Holthaus*), as shown in Figure 7 - 46.

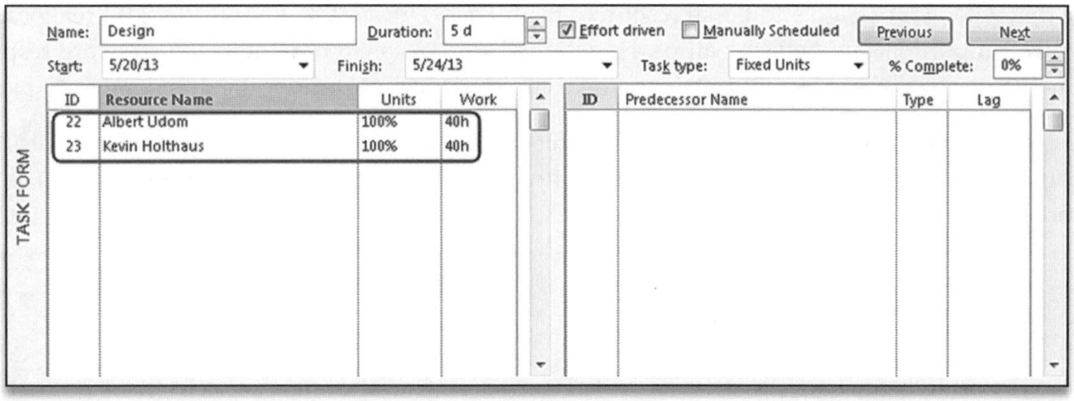

Figure 7 - 46: Using Effort Driven scheduling with identical Units values

- Next, I return to *Albert Udom's* assignment to the *Design* task at *100%* units and *80 hours* of work, and the *Duration* value of *10 days* for the task as shown previously in Figure 7 - 45. Using *Effort Driven* scheduling, I now add *Kevin Holthaus* to the task at **50% units**. In this situation, Project Pro 2013 shortens the duration to *6.67 days* and allocates the *80 hours* of *Remaining Work* **proportionately** between the two resources (*53.33 hours* to *Albert Udom* and *26.67 hours* to *Kevin Holthaus*), as shown in Figure 7 - 47.

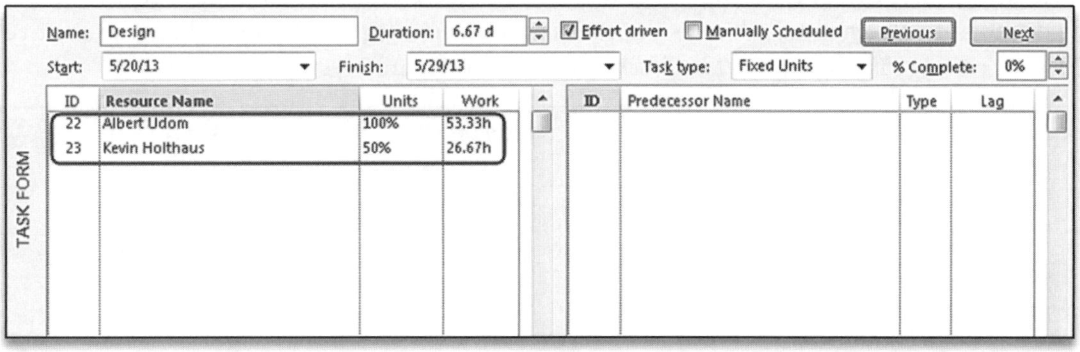

Figure 7 - 47: Effort Driven scheduling with different Units values

How does Project Pro 2013 actually determine the proportionate split of the original 80 hours of work? Albert Udom's *Units* value of *100%* is two-thirds of the total units of *150%* for both resources (100/150 = 2/3), so the system allocates Albert Udom two-thirds of the total work, which is 53.33 hours (80 x 2/3 – 53.33). Kevin Holthaus' *Units* value of *50%* is one-third of the total units value (50/150 = 1/3), so the system allocates Kevin Holthaus one-third of the total *Work*, which is 26.67 hours (80 x 1/3 = 26.67).

Best Practice: When you assign additional resources to an *Effort Driven* task, MSProjectExperts recommends that you also increase the *Work* hours for each resource in the range of 10% to 20% to account for the increased communications overhead between the resources.

Information: When you remove a resource from an *Effort Driven* task with multiple resources already assigned, Project Pro 2013 increases the *Duration* of the task and increases the *Remaining Work* value proportionately for each remaining resource. This behavior is due to *Effort Driven* scheduling, although most people do not realize this.

Remember that when you assign additional resources to an *Effort Driven* task, Project Pro 2013 reallocates the ***Remaining Work*** proportionately between all of the assigned resources. So how does the software respond when you add a helper to a task that already contains some completed work? Consider the following example:

- I assign *Bill Hagner* to the *Build* task at *100%* units and *80 hours* of work, and the software calculates a duration of *10 days* for the task. Brian completed *40 hours* of actual work, which leaves *40 hours* of remaining work as shown in Figure 7 - 48.

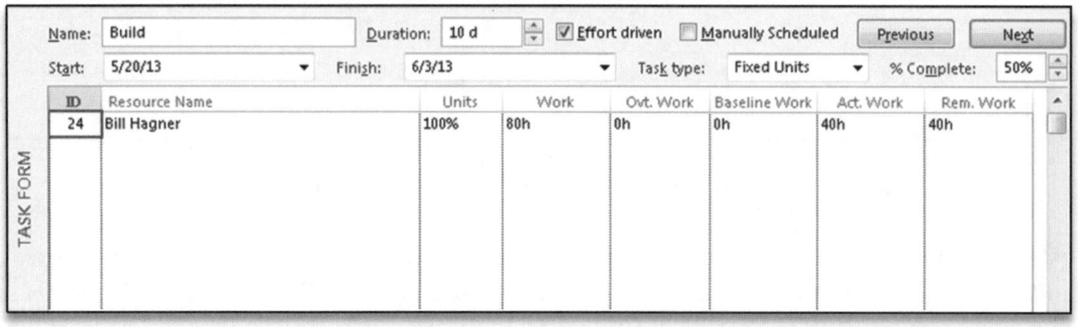

Figure 7 - 48: Effort Driven scheduling, with Actual Work 40 hours and Duration 10 days

- Then, using *Effort Driven* scheduling, I add *Lisa Brack* to the task at *100%* units. Project Pro 2013 shortens the duration to *7.5 days* and allocates the *40 hours* of **Remaining Work** evenly between the two resources (*20 hours* each to *Bill Hagner* and *Lisa Brack*), as shown in Figure 7 - 49.

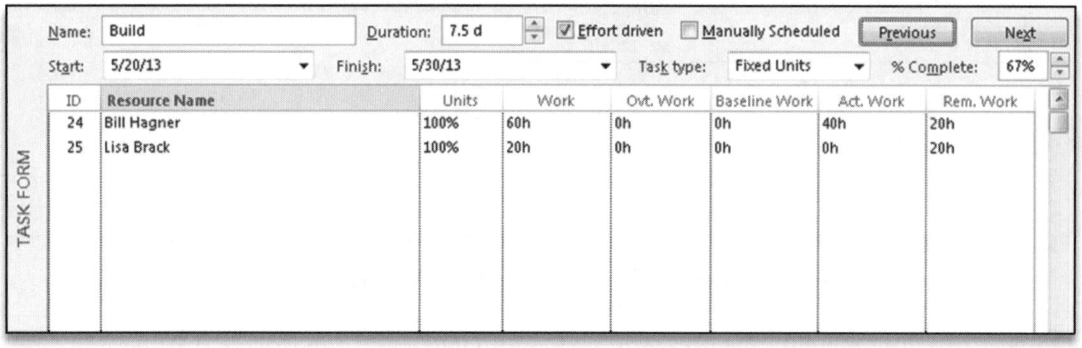

Figure 7 - 49: Using Effort Driven scheduling with completed work
Project Pro 2013 allocates Remaining Work

Figure 7 - 49 shows the *Task Form* view applying the *Work* details. To view the *Work* details, right-click anywhere in the *Task Form* pane and then select the *Work* item on the shortcut menu. Notice in Figure 7 - 49 that the software holds the *40 hours* of remaining work constant, which gives *Bill Hagner* 60 hours of total work (40 hours of actual work + 20 hours of remaining work) and gives *Lisa Brack* 20 hours of total work (0 hours of actual work + 20 hours of remaining work).

Information: For *Fixed Units* or *Fixed Work* tasks, when you assign additional resources using *Effort Driven* scheduling, Project Pro 2013 **shortens the Duration** of the task. Alternatively, for a *Fixed Duration* task, when you assign additional resources using *Effort Driven* scheduling Project Pro 2013, **decreases the Units** for each assigned resource.

Assigning Cost Resources

If your Project Server administrator included *Budget Cost* and *Expense Cost* resources in your Project Server 2013 system, it is important that you know how to assign each type of *Cost* resource. Because Microsoft does not include any type of standard view or table to use for assigning *Cost* resources, I teach you how to create a custom view you can use to assign each type of *Cost* resource.

Assigning a Budget Cost Resource

When you use a *Budget Cost* resource in a project, Project Pro 2013 allows you to assign the resource to **only** the Project Summary Task (Task 0). This allows you to set a budget for the overall project as a whole, but it does not allow you to set a budget on phases, deliverables, or individual tasks. To specify an overall budget for your project, complete the following steps:

1. Click the *View* tab and then in the *Task Views* section of the *View* ribbon, click the *Task Usage* button.

2. In your project, select the Project Summary Task (Task 0).

 Information: If you do not see the Project Summary Task in your project, click the *Format* tab to display the *Format* ribbon. In the *Show/Hide* section of the ribbon, select the *Project Summary Task* option to display the Project Summary Task.

3. Click the *Resource* tab and in the *Assignments* section of the *Resource* ribbon, click the *Assign Resources* button.

4. In the *Assign Resources* dialog, select your *Budget Cost* resource and click the *Assign* button.

5. Click the *Close* button to close the *Assign Resources* dialog.

Figure 7 - 50 shows that I assigned my *Budget Cost* resource to the Project Summary Task.

	Task Name	Budget Cost	Details	T	W	T	F	S
0	▲ **Relocate South Region Office to Larger Facilities**	$0.00	Work					
			Budget Cost	$0.00				
			Cost	$0.00				
			Actual Cost	$0.00				
	Project Budget	$0.00	Work					
			Budget Cost	$0.00				
			Cost					
			Actual Cost					
1	▲ **Office Move**		Work					
			Budget Cost					
			Cost	$0.00				
			Actual Cost	$0.00				
2	▲ **Two To Six Months Before Moving Day**		Work					
			Budget Cost					
			Cost					
			Actual Cost					
3	▲ Make list of key needs that must be met by new		Work					
			Budget Cost					
			Cost					
			Actual Cost					
	Dale Howard		Work					
			Budget Cost					
			Cost					
			Actual Cost					

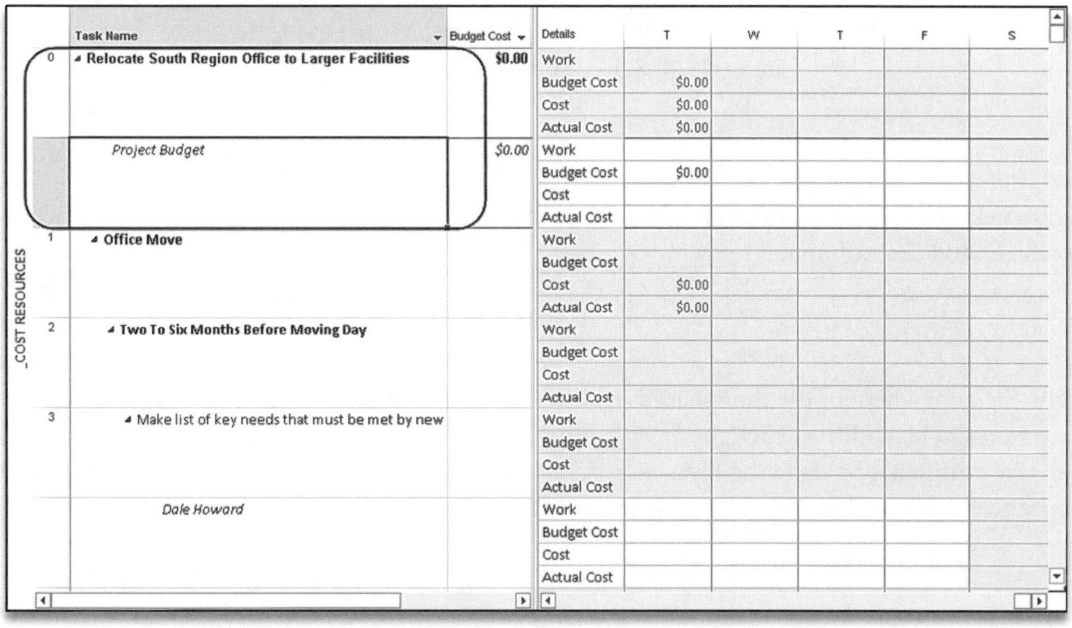

Figure 7 - 50: Budget Cost resource assigned to the Project Summary Task

6. Right-click the *Select All* button and select the *Cost* table on the shortcut menu as shown in Figure 7 - 51.

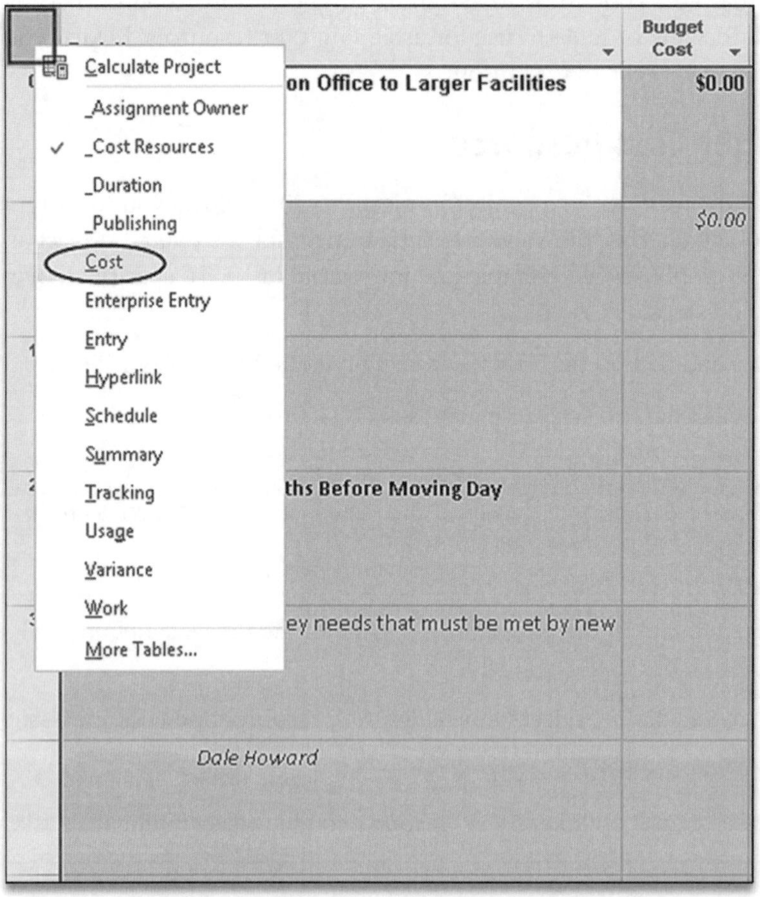

Figure 7 - 51: Select All button, Cost Table item

7. Right-click the *Fixed Cost* column header, select the *Insert Column* item on the shortcut menu, and then select the *Budget Cost* column.

8. Right-click anywhere in the timephased grid, select the *Detail Styles* item in the shortcut menu, select the *Budget Cost* field, and then click the *Show* button to add the field to the *Show these fields* list. Alternately, if there are additional fields in the *Show these fields* list select and remove them using the *Hide* button so that *Work* and *Budget Cost* are the only fields in the list.

Figure 7 - 52 shows the *Detail Styles* dialog with the *Budget Cost* field added to the *Show these fields* list.

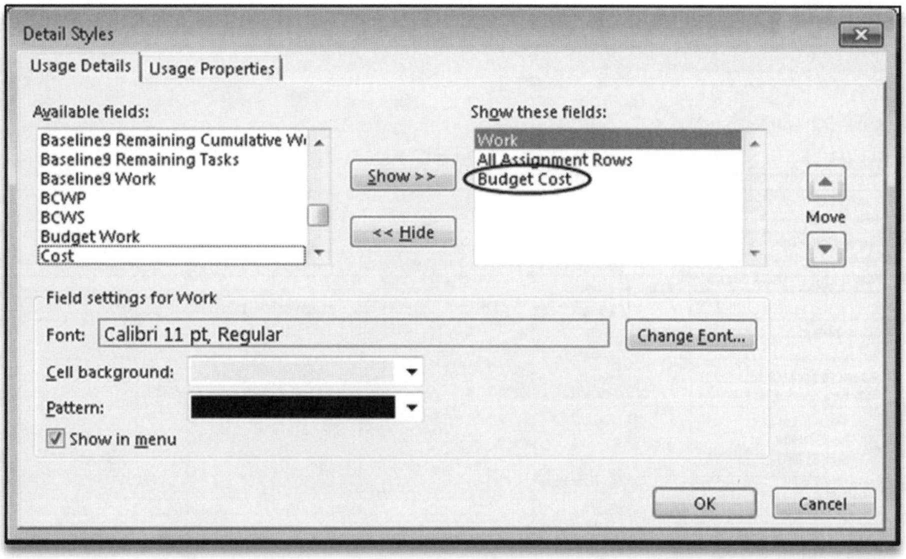

Figure 7 - 52: Detail Styles dialog, add Budget Cost field

9. Click the *OK* button to close the *Details Styles* dialog and to insert the *Budget Cost* timephased field.

10. In the timephased grid, double-click the right edge of the *Details* column header to "best fit" the column width.

Figure 7 - 53 shows the *Task Usage* view with the *Budget Cost* column displayed in the *Cost* table on the left and with the timephased *Budget Cost* field displayed in the timephased grid on the right.

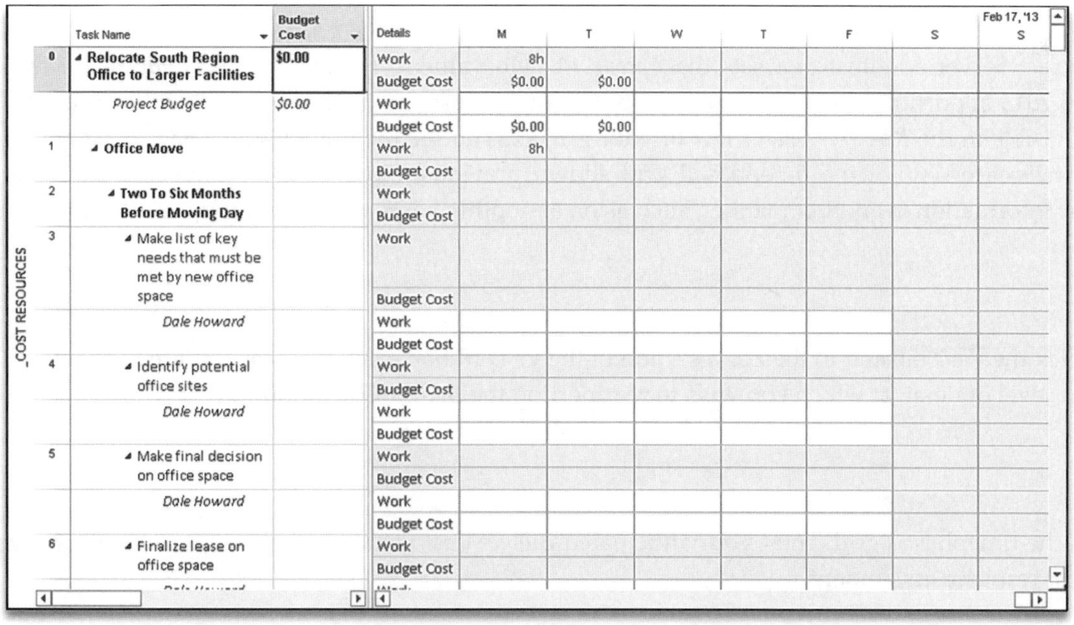

Figure 7 - 53: Task Usage view ready for project budget entry

11. In the *Budget Cost* column for the *Budget Cost* resource assignment on the Project Summary Task, enter your planned budget for the entire project and then press the **Enter** key on your computer keyboard.

Figure 7 - 54 shows the *Budget Cost* value for my *Project Budget* cost resource assigned to the Project Summary Task.

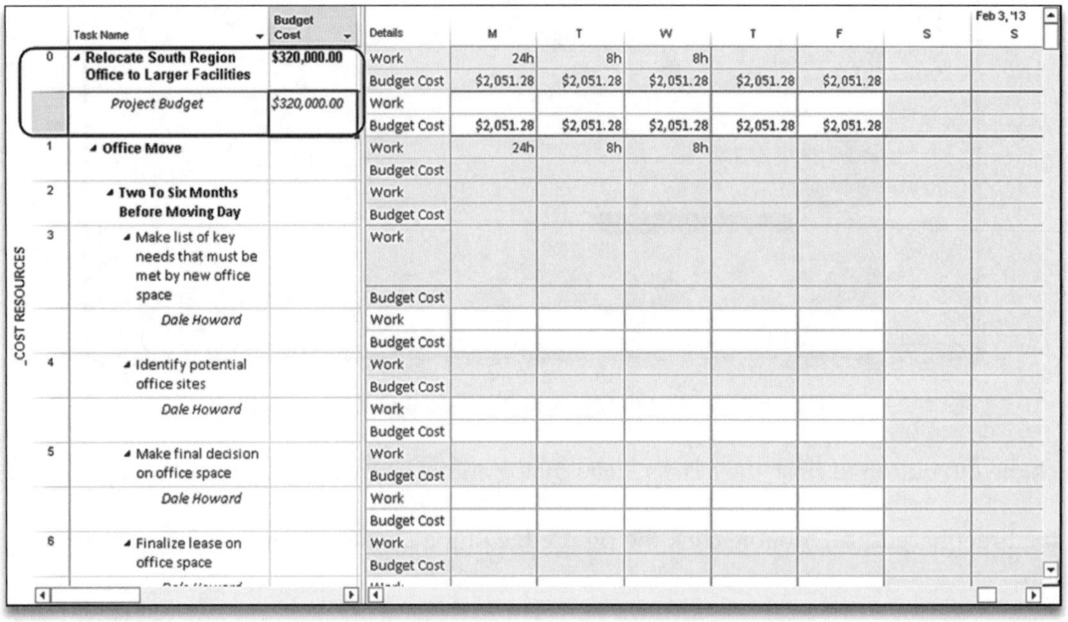

Figure 7 - 54: Budget Cost amount for entire project

If your Project Server administrator sets the *Accrue At* field value to *Prorated* for the *Budget Cost* resource, then Project Pro 2013 apportions the *Budget Cost* amount evenly across the time span of the entire project. The *Accrue At* field is visible in the *Resource Sheet* view of your project. You see the timephased *Budget Cost* amounts in each day ($2,051.28 each day) of the timephased grid shown previously in Figure 7 - 54. You may reapportion the *Budget Cost* information in another manner, such as on a monthly basis, by following these additional steps:

12. Click the *View* tab and in the *Zoom* section of the *View* ribbon, click the *Zoom* button. Zoom the *Timescale* to the level of detail at which you wish to reapportion the *Budget Cost* amount.

13. In the timephased grid, enter your anticipated *Budget Cost* values in the *Budget Cost* cells for your *Budget Cost* resource assignment.

In Figure 7 - 55, notice that I entered my *Budget Cost* values on a monthly basis for my *Project Budget* cost resource, roughly timephased to correspond with the planned work hours for each month.

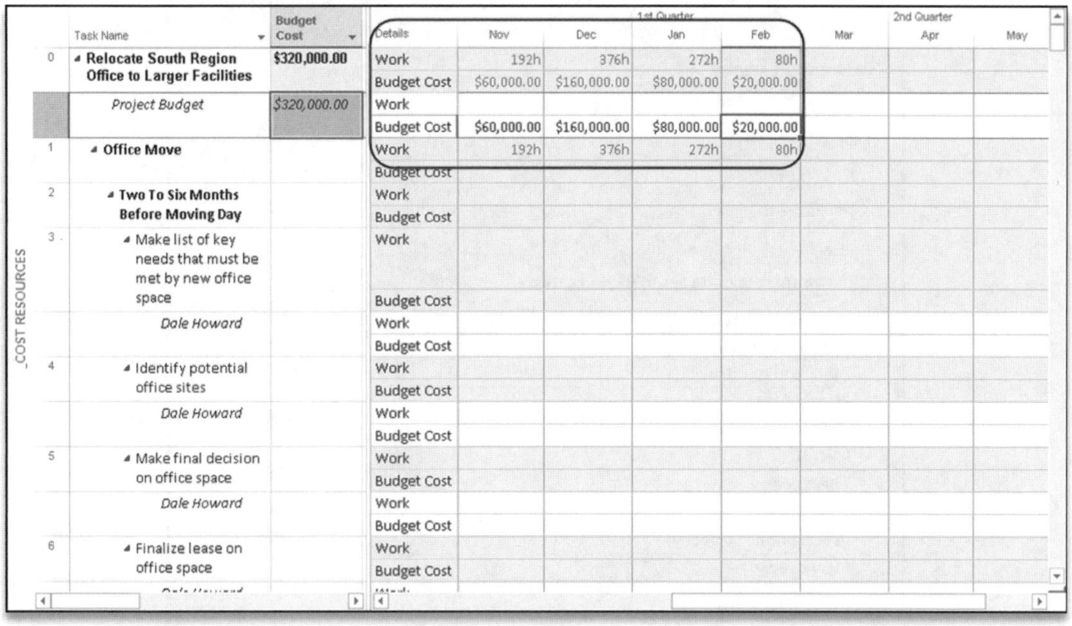

Figure 7 - 55: Budget Cost information, Project Budget entry timephased grid

Information: In addition to the *Budget Cost* field, Project Pro 2013 includes an additional budget field called *Budget Work*. This field allows you to specify an overall budget for working hours for your project in addition to specifying a monetary budget. Before you can use the *Budget Work* field, however, you must first create a *Budget Work* resource by creating a new *Work* resource and then selecting the *Budget* option in the *Resource Information* dialog for the new resource. After creating the new *Budget Work* resource, assign this resource to your Project Summary Task in the *Task Usage* view. Insert the *Budget Work* field in the *Details Styles* dialog and then enter your overall budget of working hours for the entire project in this field.

Assigning an Expense Cost Resource

After you enter your project's budget using a *Budget Cost* resource, you may assign *Expense Cost* resources to your project so that you can track additional project expenses. Project Pro 2013 allows you to assign *Expense Cost* resources to any type of task in the project, including summary tasks, subtasks, and milestone tasks. However, the software **does not** allow you to assign an *Expense Cost* resource to the Project Summary Task. To assign an *Expense Cost* resource to tasks in your project, complete the following steps:

1. Using the customized *Task Usage* view documented in the previous topical section, select any task in the project, including a regular task, a summary task, or a milestone task.

2. Click the *Resource* tab and then in the *Assignments* section of the *Resource* ribbon, click the *Assign Resources* button.

Note: You may need to add the *Expense Cost* resource named *Travel Expense* to your project as discussed previously in the *Adding Resources to Your Project Team* topical section.

3. In the *Assign Resources* dialog, select your *Expense Cost* resource and then click the *Assign* button.

Figure 7 - 56 shows the *Assign Resources* dialog after assigning an *Expense Cost* resource named *Travel Expense*. I want to use this resource to capture the travel expenses for my project so that I may report this amount as a line item expenditure.

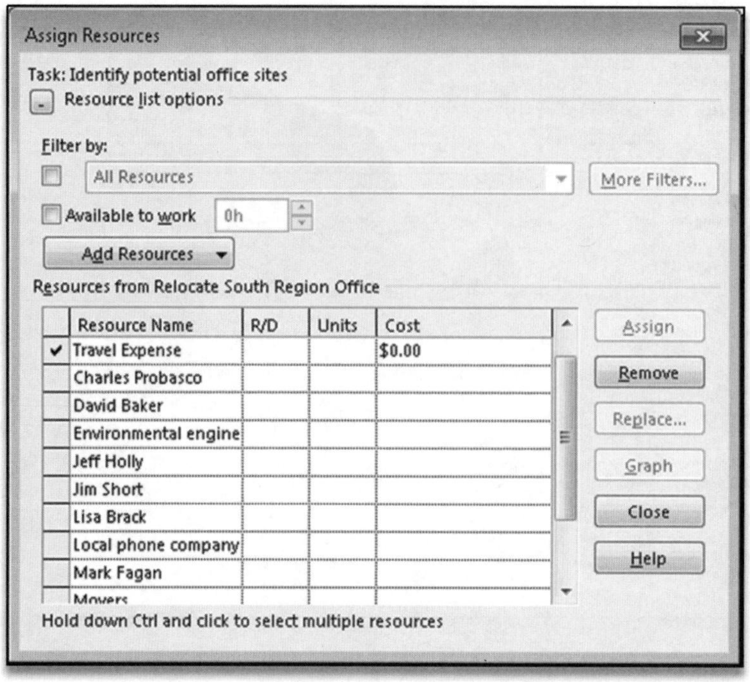

Figure 7 - 56: Assign Resources dialog after assigning Expense Cost resource

4. In the *Cost* column for the *Expense Cost* resource in the *Assign Resources* dialog, enter the amount of **anticipated expenditure** and then press the **Enter** key on your computer keyboard.

Figure 7 - 57 shows the *Assign Resources* dialog after entering my estimated expenditure for travel expenses on the selected task. Notice that I anticipate the travel expenses to be *$1,525* for this task.

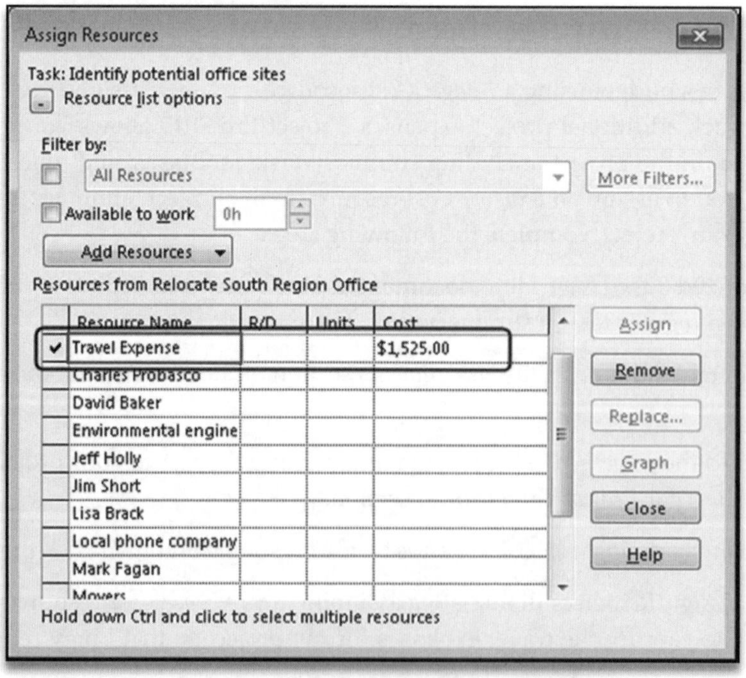

Figure 7 - 57: Assign Resources dialog after assigning Expense Cost resource with Cost

5. Continue selecting tasks, assigning the *Expense Cost* resources, and entering anticipated expenditures until you finish.
6. Click the *Close* button to close the *Assign Resources* dialog.

Recommendations for Using Cost Resources

Cost resources do have some limitations, so follow Microsoft's recommendations for using *Cost* resources effectively:

- Do not assign a *Cost* resource on the same task as a *Work* resource if the resource reports actual progress from Project Web App.
- Do not assign a *Task* calendar using 24-hour elapsed days (eDays) to a task assigned to a *Cost* resource.
- Do not disable the *Actual costs are always calculated by Microsoft Project* option in your project. You find this option in the *Calculation options for this project* section of the *Advanced* page in the *Project Options* dialog.
- Avoid using the *Undo* feature if you edit the *Remaining Duration* field for a task assigned to a *Cost* resource.

Using the Team Planner View

At any point during the assignment planning process, you may want to display the *Team Planner* view in Project Pro 2013. This view allows you to analyze the current state of resource assignments in your project using a friendly graphical display. To apply the *Team Planner* view, click the *Resource* tab and then in the *View* section of the *Resource* ribbon, click the *Team Planner* button. The system displays the *Team Planner* view for your project, as shown in Figure 7 - 58.

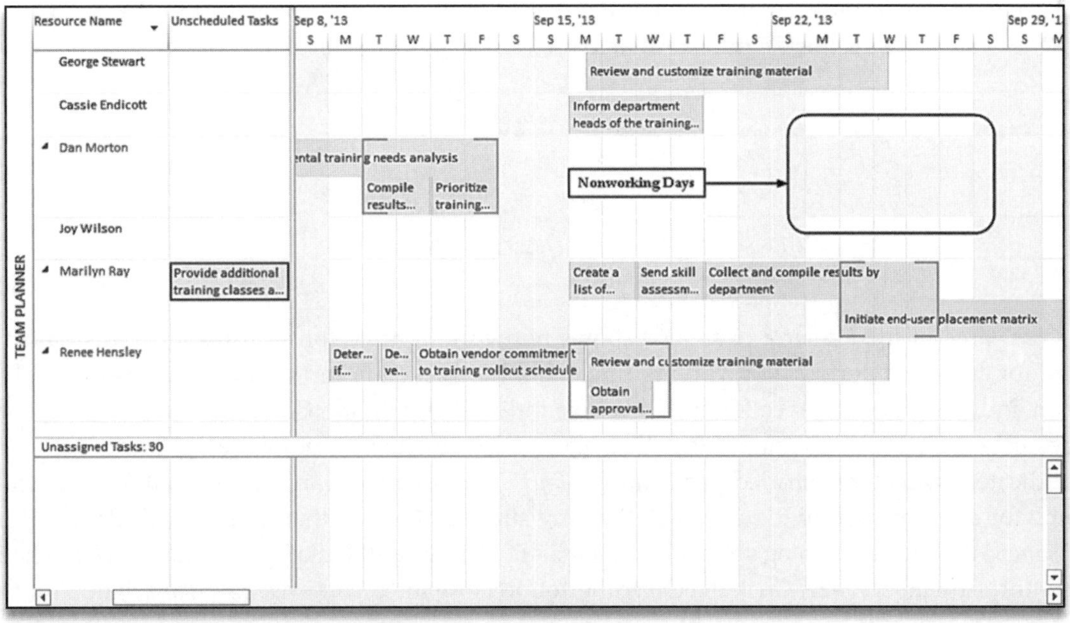

Figure 7 - 58: Team Planner view

> **Warning**: The first time you apply the *Team Planner* view in a project, the software always scrolls to the **current date** in the *Gantt Chart* area on the right side of the view. For projects that start in the future, you may not see any tasks in the *Unassigned Tasks* pane. To see tasks in the *Unassigned Tasks* pane, you must scroll the Gantt chart to the start date of your project.

The *Team Planner* view displays resources and their assignments in two panes across the top. The left side is the *Resource* pane and shows resources from the *Resource Sheet* view of your project, sorted by ID number. Assigned tasks for each resource appear to the right in the *Gantt Chart* area . Unlike the *Gantt Chart* view, however, the *Team Planner* view displays the Gantt bars arranged horizontally on a single line for each resource. *Unscheduled Tasks* (*Manually Scheduled* tasks with no *Duration, Start,* or *Finish* date) already assigned to a resource appear in the *Unscheduled Tasks* column to the right of the resource name.

The bottom pane of the *Team Planner* view is the *Unassigned Tasks* pane and shows the list of tasks not yet assigned to a resource, sorted by task ID number. The *Gantt Chart* area on the right side of the *Unassigned Tasks* pane shows the current schedule for each unassigned task, based on the schedule specified in the *Gantt Chart* view of the project. The system zooms the *Gantt Chart* area to the *Weeks Over Days* level of zoom by default.

The *Gantt Chart* area of the *Resource* pane also shows nonworking time for each resource, displayed as a gray shaded band for each time period. Nonworking time includes weekends and company holidays for all resources, plus vacation and planned sick leave for each resource individually. In the *Gantt Chart* area of the *Resource* pane shown previously in Figure 7 - 58, notice that *Dan Morton* has five days of nonworking time scheduled, September 23-27, indicated by the gray shaded band in the *Gantt Chart* area. To learn more about any individual's nonworking time for any time period, double-click the gray shaded band for that time period. Project Pro 2013 displays the *Change Working Time* dialog shown in Figure 7 - 59. Notice in the dialog that *Dan Morton* scheduled *Educational Leave* for September 23-27. Click the *Cancel* button to close the *Change Working Time* dialog for the selected resource.

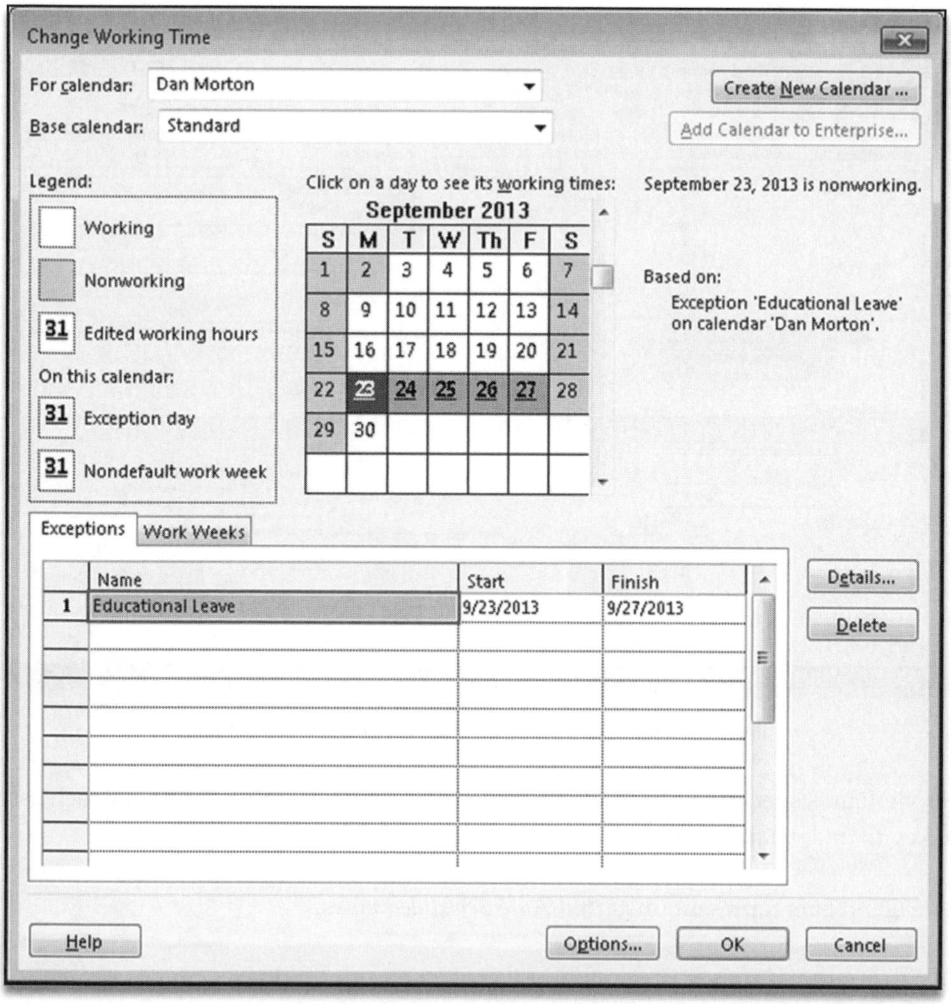

Figure 7 - 59: Change Working Time dialog, Dan Morton resource calendar

In the *Team Planner* view shown previously in Figure 7 - 58, notice that I already assigned tasks to each team member in the project, including one *Unscheduled Task* assigned to *Marilyn Ray*. To view additional information about any task, float your mouse pointer over the Gantt bar of the task. Project Pro 2013 displays a screen tip for the selected Gantt bar, as shown in Figure 7 - 60.

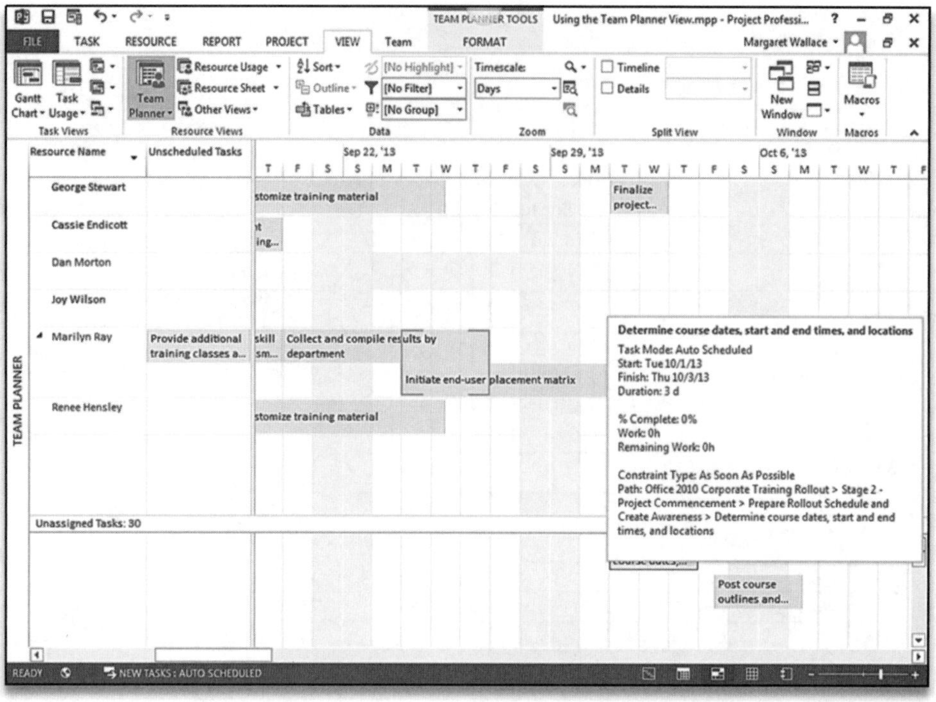

Figure 7 - 60: Schedule information for the selected task

The *Team Planner* view uses special colors and formatting to display task information for each assigned and unassigned task. The key to understanding the color formatting is as follows:

- Light Blue Gantt bars represent unstarted *Auto Scheduled* tasks.
- Light Teal (turquoise) Gantt bars represent *Manually Scheduled* tasks.
- Dark Blue Gantt bars represent task progress for both *Auto Scheduled* tasks and *Manually Scheduled* tasks.
- Light Gray Gantt bars represent external tasks in another project.
- Dark Gray Gantt bars with white text represent late tasks (tasks where the current *% Complete* progress does not extend to the *Status Date* of the project).
- *Resource Name* formatted in Red represents overallocated resource.
- Gantt bars formatted with Red borders represent the time periods of overallocation for a resource.

For example, in Figure 7 - 58 shown previously, the system formats *Dan Morton's* name in red, and displays red borders on three of his assigned tasks. This indicates that *Dan Morton* is overallocated on these tasks. In fact, he is overallocated specifically on September 10, 11, 12, and 13 on these three tasks. Similarly, notice that *Marilyn Ray's* name is formatted in red indicating she is also overallocated, she is overallocated on two tasks, noted with the red borders for the time period of September 24, 25, and 26. Finally, notice that *Renee Hensley's* name is also formatted in red indicating her overallocation and her overallocated time period of September 16, 17, and 18 on three tasks, formatted with red borders.

Dragging Tasks in the Team Planner View

You can use the "drag and drop" functionality of the *Team Planner* view to do any of the following:

- Drag an assigned task to a different time period to reschedule the task.
- Drag an assigned task to a different resource.
- Drag an unassigned task to a resource.

To reschedule a task to a different time period, simply drag the task's Gantt bar to the new time period. In Project Pro 2013, when you reschedule a task by dragging it to a new time period, Project Pro 2013 retains the resource *Units*, and *Work* hours set for the assignment. Keep in mind, however, when you reschedule a task by dragging it to a new time period, Project Pro 2013 sets a *Start No Earlier Than* (SNET) constraint on the task automatically. If you drag a task to the left to a prior time period and there is a predecessor link on the task, and moving the task would cause the assignment to break that link, the system displays the message shown in Figure 7 - 61. The system forces you to manually remove the link, or move the task to another time period that respects the link.

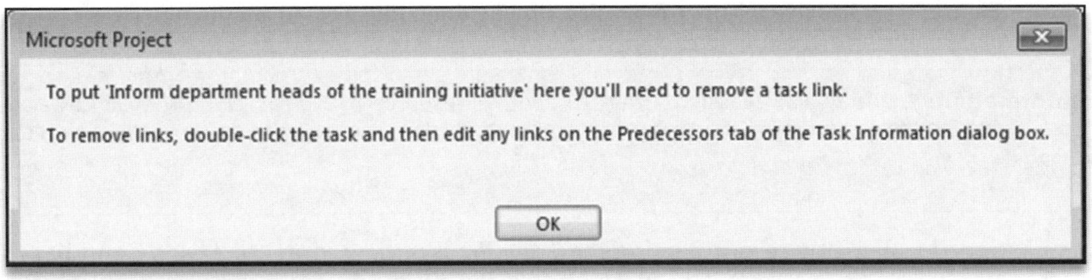
Microsoft Project
To put 'Inform department heads of the training initiative' here you'll need to remove a task link.
To remove links, double-click the task and then edit any links on the Predecessors tab of the Task Information dialog box.
OK

Figure 7 - 61: Team Planner view, remove task link message

If you drag a task beyond the right edge of the *Team Planner* view, the system automatically scrolls the view, so there is no need to release the mouse button and scroll manually.

Warning: The software's use of SNET constraints in the *Team Builder* view may be contrary to the best interests of your scheduling model if you want to maintain a fully dynamic model. SNET constraints prevent a task from moving to an earlier start date if an earlier start date becomes available. You can easily clear delays added by the built-in leveling tool with the press of a button, but you must manually remove constraints added by the *Team Planner*. I show you how to remove these constraints in an exercise later in this module.

Information: Note for rescheduling tasks that you drag to the same time period, the software **retains** the constraints as previously set for the task. MSProjectExperts recommends that you verify your constraints after using the *Team Planner* view to confirm that your project accurately reflects your scheduling decisions to maintain a fully dynamic model.

To reassign a task to another resource, simply drag the task's Gantt bar from the assigned resource to the new resource and drop it into the desired time period. For example, Figure 7 - 62 shows the *Team Planner* view after I used the drag and drop method to reassign two tasks from *Dan Morton* to *Cassie Endicott*. These two tasks were originally causing the resource overallocation for *Dan Morton* as shown previously in Figure 7 - 58.

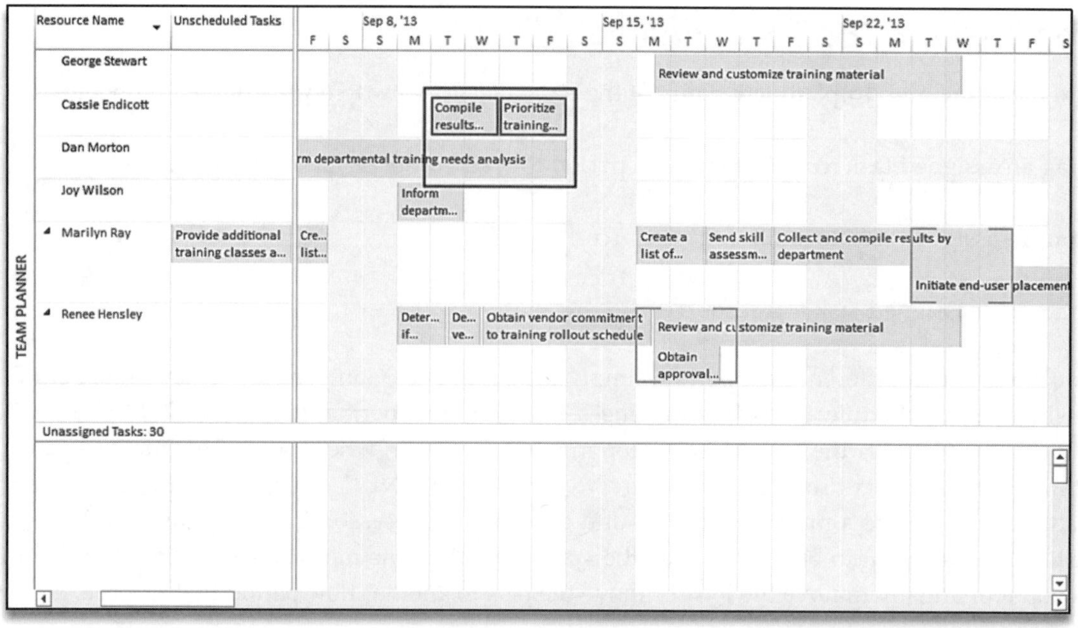

Figure 7 - 62: Resolve resource overallocation by dragging tasks to another resource

Information: You may also reassign a task to another resource by right-clicking the Gantt bar of the chosen task, selecting the *Reassign To* shortcut menu option, and then selecting the name of the new resource.

To assign an unassigned task to any resource using the *Team Planner* view, drag the task's Gantt bar from the *Unassigned Tasks* pane to the top pane and drop it in the time period you want to schedule the task for the selected resource. Keep in mind that when you assign a task to a resource using this method, Project Pro 2013 assigns the task to the resource at 100% *Units* automatically, indicating full-time work on the task.

Information: To reassign or reschedule multiple tasks simultaneously, press and hold the **Ctrl** key on your computer keyboard to select multiple tasks, and then drag and drop the group of selected tasks. However, in the *Team Planner* view, Project Pro 2013 **does not** allow you to simultaneously drag and drop multiple **unassigned** tasks.

Changing Schedule Information in the Team Planner View

As you analyze assignment information in the *Team Planner* view, at some point you may need to revise schedule information. Project Pro 2013 allows you to revise your project in the *Team Planner* view as follows:

- You can change the *Task Mode* option for a task by right-clicking the Gantt bar of the task and selecting the *Auto Schedule* or *Manually Schedule* item on the shortcut menu.
- You can set a task to *Inactive* status by right-clicking the Gantt bar for the task and selecting the *Inactivate Task* item on the shortcut menu.
- You can change information for any task (such as setting a constraint or applying a task calendar) by double-clicking the Gantt bar for the task and entering the information in the *Task Information* dialog. You may also right-click the Gantt bar for the task and choose the *Information* item on the shortcut menu.

- You can apply the *Task Details Form* in a split view arrangement with the *Team Planner* view by clicking the *Task* tab and then in the *Properties* section of the *Task* ribbon, click the *Display Task Details* button. When you select the Gantt bar for any assigned task in the top pane, the *Task Details Form* in the bottom pane displays relevant information about the task and its assigned resources. Notice in Figure 7 - 63 that the *Task Details Form* displays information about the *Perform departmental training needs analysis* task whose Gantt bar I selected in the top pane. To close the *Task Details Form*, click the *Display Task Details* button again in the *Task* ribbon.

Information: During the execution stage of your project, you can also enter progress against a task by right-clicking the task's Gantt bar in the *Team Planner* view and then selecting a *% Complete* value on the *Mini Toolbar* section of the shortcut menu. The *Mini Toolbar* offers you the *0%, 25%, 50%, 75%,* and *100%* buttons that you use to enter progress on a task quickly.

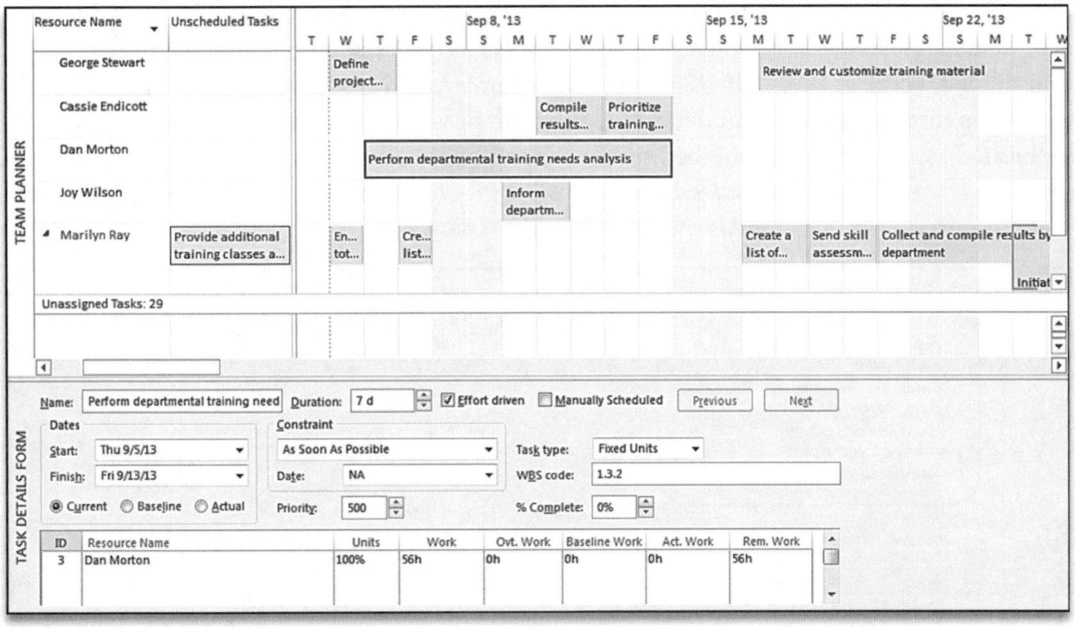

Figure 7 - 63: Team Planner view, Details Task Form applied in a split-screen

Understanding Resource Overallocation

During the resource assignment process, you may accidentally overallocate one or more resources in the project. An overallocation occurs when you assign more work to a resource than the resource can do during the working time available, resulting in a *Units* value that exceeds the *Max. Units* value for the resource. Each of the following situations results in an overallocated resource:

- You assign a resource to work 32 hours in a single day.
- You assign a resource to work 160 hours in a single week.
- You assign a resource to work 30 minutes in a 15-minute time period.

Leveling is the process you use to resolve resource overallocations so that your project resources are no longer overallocated. The third bullet point reveals an important truth about leveling overallocated resources:

Not all overallocations are worth leveling.

You should definitely level the overallocations I describe in the first two bulleted items above, because either situation would likely cause your project finish date to slip. The third situation is not worth leveling, however, as the amount of time spent leveling this overallocation is not worth the effort, and likely will not impact your project.

> **Information**: In addition to the three previous examples, you may also overallocate a resource by assigning the resource to a task at a *Units* value of *200%* when the *Max. Units* value for the resource is *100%*. You cannot resolve this type of overallocation using the built-in leveling tool in Project Pro 2013. Instead, you must manually resolve this type of overallocation by reducing the *Units* value for the resource's assignment on the task.

Locating Resource Overallocations

The easiest way to locate overallocated resources is to use the *Resource Usage* view. To apply this view, click the *Resource* tab to display the *Resource* ribbon, click the *Team Planner* pick list button, and then select the *Resource Usage* view from the list. Because Project Pro 2013 formats overallocated resources with the red font color, look for any resource names formatted in red. To determine the time periods during which resource is overallocated, select an overallocated resource and then in the *Level* section of the *Resource* ribbon, click the *Next Overallocation* button. When you click the *Next Overallocation* button, Project Pro 2013 scrolls the timephased grid and selects the start of the first resource overallocation, as shown in Figure 7 - 64.

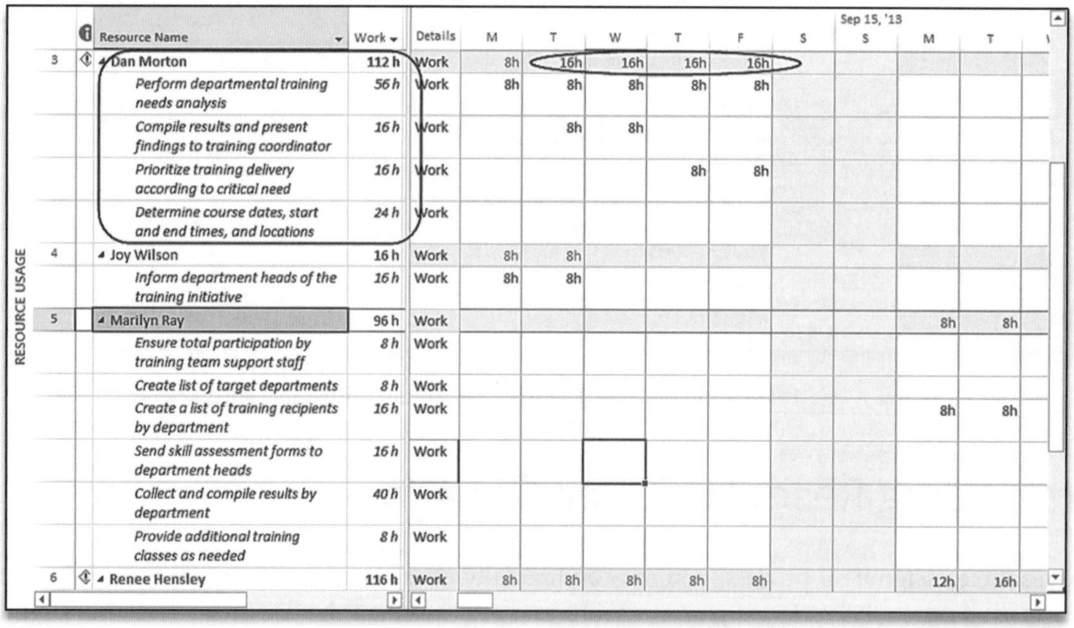

Figure 7 - 64: Resource Usage view shows first overallocation

> **Warning**: Due to an unfixed bug in the software, as of the writing of this book Project Pro 2013 does not display any time periods where a resource is overallocated using the *Next Overallocation* button for any of the *Resource* views. Instead, the software displays the dialog shown in Figure 7 - 65. Note, however, that the *Next Overallocation* button does function in other views such as the *Task Usage*, *Tracking Gantt*, or *Gantt Chart* views.

In Figure 7 - 64, notice that I assigned *Dan Morton* to work 16 hours each day in a four-day period during the week of September 8, 2013. I accidentally caused this overallocation when I assigned Dan to work on three overlapping tasks, each of which requires full-time work. In addition, I overallocated Renee Hensley. In Figure 7 - 64, you can see the start of two of her overallocations on the right side of the timephased grid.

As you continue to click the *Next Overallocation* button, Project Pro 2013 selects the start of each successive overallocation. When the software cannot locate any more resource overallocations, it displays the dialog shown in Figure 7 - 65.

Microsoft Project
There are no more overallocations starting after 9/3/2013 at 12:00 AM.
OK

Figure 7 - 65: No more resource overallocations

Leveling Overallocated Resources

As I previously stated, leveling is the process you use to resolve resource overallocations. There are many ways to level overallocated resources, including each of the following:

- Substitute an available resource for the overallocated resource.
- Increase the availability of overallocated resources.
- Schedule overtime for the overallocated resource.
- Manually delay tasks with overallocated resources.
- Delay the start of a resource assignment on a task.
- Adjust the project schedule using task constraints to eliminate resource assignment conflicts.
- Split tasks by interrupting the work on a task to make resources available for other assignments.
- Adjust dependencies and add *Lag* time.
- Add resources to an *Effort Driven* task to shorten the duration of the task.
- Look for potential overlapping work opportunities, such as Finish to Start dependencies that do not have a true "finish to start" relationship.
- Negotiate with your project sponsor or customer to delay the finish date of the project.
- Negotiate with your project sponsor or customer to reduce the feature set (scope) of the project.
- Use the built-in leveling tool in Project Pro 2013 with the *Resource Usage* or *Team Planner* view.

Notice that using the built-in leveling tool in Project Pro 2013 appears last on the preceding list! Each of the preceding leveling methods is powerful and useful for leveling overallocated resources; however, most users assume the only way to level is to use the built-in leveling tool found in Project Pro 2013. Given the complexity of using the software's leveling capabilities, the average user of Project Pro 2013 is far better off using any of the other manual leveling methods. The key to using any method for resource leveling is to remember that you must take **complete control** of all leveling decisions.

Using a Leveling Methodology

Many Project Pro 2013 users attempt to level all of their overallocated resources simultaneously in the *Gantt Chart* view using the built-in leveling tool. Although this approach can work in some situations, most often it leads to frustration. This approach does not give insight into how the software actually leveled the overallocations, and may lead to failure because you did not take control over the leveling process. A much better approach is to level overallocated resources using the following methodology:

1. Level each overallocated resource individually in the *Resource Usage* view.
2. Study the results of the leveling process in the *Leveling Gantt* view.
3. Clear unacceptable leveling results and then level the overallocated resource using any other method.
4. Repeat steps #1-3 for each overallocated resource.

Setting Leveling Options

Before you begin the process of leveling overallocated resources in the *Resource Usage* view, you should specify your leveling options by clicking the *Leveling Options* button in the *Level* section of the *Resource* ribbon. The system displays the *Resource Leveling* dialog shown in Figure 7 - 66.

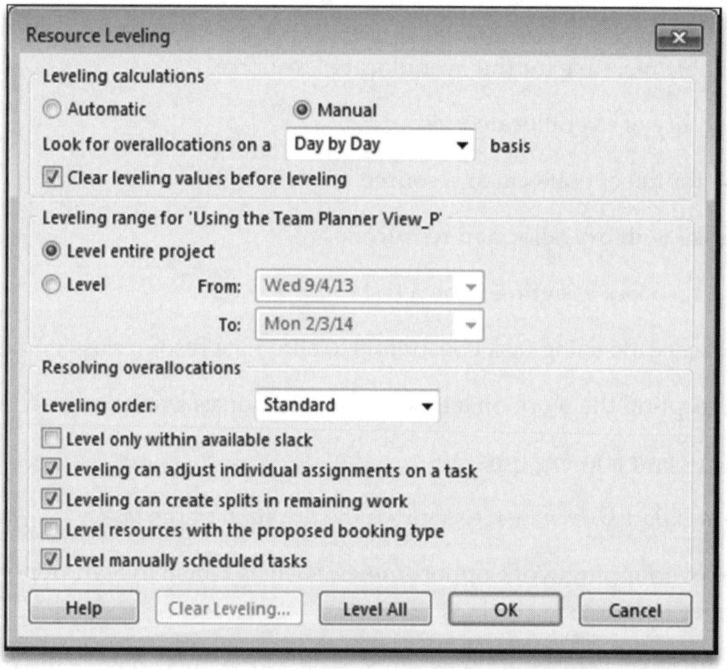

Figure 7 - 66: Resource Leveling dialog

In the *Leveling calculations* section of the *Resource Leveling* dialog, you find the *Look for overallocations on a ____ basis* option. This option controls the granularity used by Project Pro 2013 to determine whether resources are overallocated. The default setting is *Day by Day*, which means that the software only shows you overallocations where resources are overallocated in full day time periods. Click the *Look for overallocations on a ____ basis* pick list and select any other option, as needed. The finest level of granularity is the *Minute by Minute* setting and the coarsest level of granularity is the *Month by Month* setting. When Project Pro 2013 locates a resource overallocation at the granularity level you specify, the software formats the name of the resource in red, and displays a yellow indicator in the *Indicators* column to the left of the resource name. If you float your mouse pointer over the yellow indicator, the software simply displays a *This resource is overallocated* message in the tooltip.

> **Warning**: Be very cautious in using either the *Minute by Minute* or *Hour by Hour* settings on the *Look for overallocations on a _____ basis* pick list. Using either setting forces the software to show many overallocations that are not worth the time and effort to level, including overallocations in 15-minute time periods.

In the *Resource overallocations* section of the *Resource Leveling* dialog, there are several options that you may want to change from the default setting, including:

- Set the *Leveling order* option to the *Priority, Standard* value. By selecting this option, you force the software to consider first the *Priority* number of each task in the software's algorithm of five leveling factors. The additional leveling factors include predecessor task relationships, the start date of each task, the *Total Slack* value for each task, and whether the task has an inflexible constraint.

- Select the *Level only within available slack* option to guarantee that the leveling operation does not change the finish date of your project. Using this option, Project Pro 2013 levels overallocations until it reaches the point where it must delay the finish date of your project. At this point, the system discontinues the leveling process and displays a warning dialog. From this point forward, you must select an alternate method for leveling remaining overallocations.

- If your project contains *Manually Scheduled* tasks with overallocated resources, and you want to reschedule the tasks manually to resolve these overallocations, then you should **deselect** the *Level manually scheduled tasks* option. If you leave this option selected, Project Pro 2013 delays or splits any *Manually Scheduled* tasks with overallocated resources assigned to them.

> **Warning**: MSProjectExperts recommends that you never select the *Automatic* option in the *Leveling Calculations* section of the *Resource Leveling* dialog. When applied, the *Automatic* leveling option causes Project Pro 2013 to level all overallocated resources automatically in all open projects without asking your permission! This means you lose control over the leveling process.

After you select your leveling options in the *Resource Leveling* dialog, click the *OK* button. Project Pro 2013 saves your option selections in this dialog so that you do not need to reselect them every time you want to level resource overallocations.

> **Warning**: Do not click the *Level All* button in the *Resource Leveling* dialog. If you click the *Level All* button, you lose control over the leveling process because the software levels **all** of the overallocated resources in your project in a single operation.

> **Warning**: If you want to level an overallocated resource across multiple projects in the Project Server database, you must open each of these enterprise projects before you begin the leveling process.

Leveling an Overallocated Resource

Best Practice: Prior to leveling overallocated resources, MSProjectExperts recommends that you exit Project Pro 2013 and then re-launch the application. In the *Login* dialog, **deselect** the *Load Summary Resource Assignments* option and click the *OK* button. With this option deselected, the system focuses the leveling process on only those projects currently open and does not include assignments from other projects not currently open.

To start the process of leveling overallocated resources, select the most critical resource in the project. Your most critical resource is the one whose skills and availability are the most limited in your organization. After selecting this resource, in the *Level* section of the *Resource* ribbon, click the *Level Resource* button. Project Pro 2013 displays the *Level Resources* dialog shown in Figure 7 - 67.

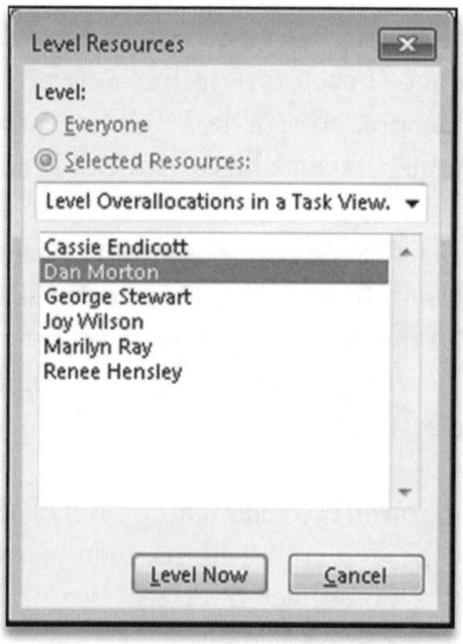

Figure 7 - 67: Level Resources dialog

The *Level Resources* dialog selects the same resource you selected in the *Resource Usage* view. Click the *Level Now* button in the dialog to level the overallocations for the first selected resource using the leveling options you set in the *Resource Leveling* dialog. When you use the built-in leveling tool to level an overallocated resource, Project Pro 2013 resolves the overallocation using one or both of the following methods:

- The software delays tasks or assignments.
- The software splits tasks or assignments.

To see the results of leveling the first overallocated resource, you must apply the *Leveling Gantt* view.

Viewing Leveling Results

The best way to apply the *Leveling Gantt* view is to open a new window containing this view by completing the following steps:

1. Click the *View* tab to display the *View* ribbon.
2. In the *Window* section of the *View* ribbon, click the *New Window* button. Project Pro 2013 displays the *New Window* dialog shown in Figure 7 - 68.

Figure 7 - 68: New Window dialog

3. Click the *View* pick list button and select the *Leveling Gantt* item on the list.
4. Click the *OK* button. The software displays the *Leveling Gantt* view shown in Figure 7 - 69.

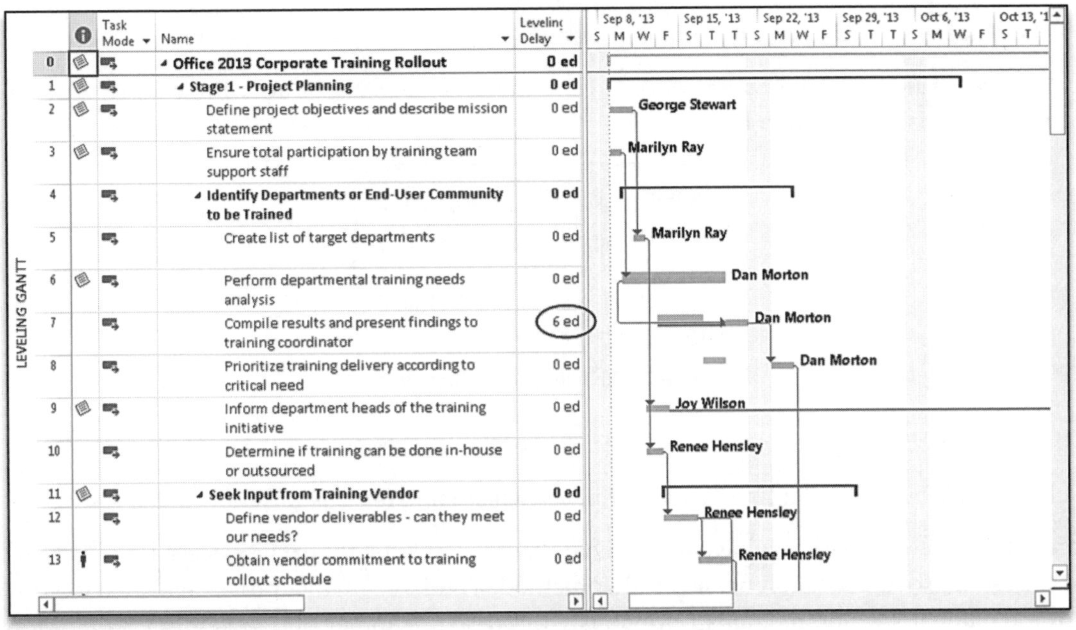

Figure 7 - 69: Leveling Gantt view

The *Leveling Gantt* view includes the *Delay* table on the left and the *Leveling Gantt* chart on the right. The symbols used in the *Leveling Gantt* view are as follows:

- The **Tan Gantt bars** represent the pre-leveled schedule for each task you assigned to the overallocated resource. Figure 7 - 69 shows that I created the resource overallocation for *Dan Morton* accidentally by assigning him to work full-time on three parallel tasks (task ID numbers #6, 7, and 8).
- The **Light Blue Gantt bars** represent the schedule of the tasks after the software levels the resource overallocation. Figure 7 - 69 shows that Project Pro 2013 delayed task ID #7 (which then delayed task ID #8 due to a Finish-to-Start dependency relationship with task ID #7), which resolved *Dan Morton* 's resource overallocation.

- The **Brown underscore** to the left of any Gantt bar represents the amount of delay applied to the task schedule to level the resource overallocation. Figure 7 - 69 shows the delay symbol to the left of the Gantt bar for task ID #7.
- The **Teal underscore** to the right of any Gantt bar represents the amount of time you can delay the task without delaying the finish date of the entire project.

The *Delay* table contains the *Leveling Delay* column to the right of the *Task Name* column. This column shows the amount of delay the software applies to a task to level a resource overallocation. By default, Project Pro 2013 measures the amount of *Leveling Delay* in **elapsed days** (displayed as **edays** or **ed**). Each elapsed day is a 24-hour calendar day that ignores nonworking time, such as weekends and holidays. In Figure 7 - 69, notice that the software delayed task ID #7 six elapsed days (6 ed).

Clearing Leveling Results

As you study the results of leveling an overallocated resource, you may find that Project Pro 2013 did not level the overallocation as you expected. In these situations, you must clear the unacceptable leveling result and then level using another method. To clear an unacceptable overallocation result, complete the following steps:

1. Click the *Resource* tab to display the *Resource* ribbon.
2. Select any tasks leveled in an unacceptable manner.
3. In the *Level* section of the *Resource* ribbon, click the *Clear Leveling* button. Project Pro 2013 displays the *Clear Leveling* dialog shown in Figure 7 - 70.

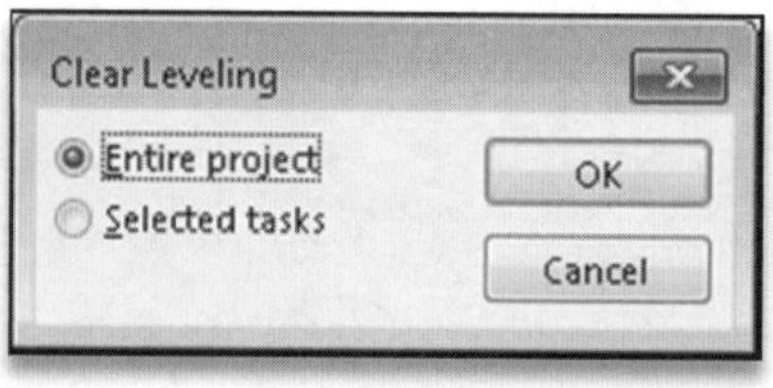

Figure 7 - 70: Clear Leveling dialog

4. In the *Clear Leveling* dialog, select the *Selected tasks* option and then click the *OK* button.
5. Click the *Undo* button in the *Quick Launch Toolbar*, when you are done previewing the results.

The software sets the *Leveling Delay* value back to the default value to *0d* for each selected task. At this point, you must level the resource overallocation using another method. You have many options available to you, including using one of the manual leveling methods I previously discussed. Another option is to set a *Priority* number on tasks showing the relative importance of each task, and then re-level the overallocations in the *Resource Usage* view.

Setting Task Priority Numbers

When you set task *Priority* numbers on tasks assigned to an overallocated resource, Project Pro 2013 levels the resource overallocation by factoring in task *Priority* numbers you assign. The software delays tasks with lower *Priority* numbers while maintaining the original schedule of the task with the highest *Priority* number. To set a *Priority* number on tasks with overallocated resources, complete the following steps:

1. In the *Task Usage* view, double-click a task assigned to an overallocated resource. Project Pro 2013 displays the *Task Information* dialog shown in Figure 7 - 71.

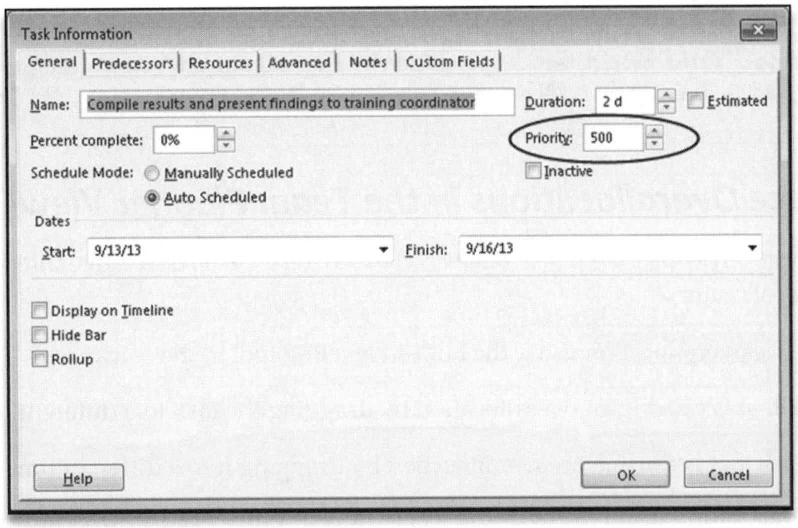

Figure 7 - 71: Task Information dialog, Set Priority number

2. Click the *General* tab, if necessary.

3. Set a value between 0 and 1000 in the *Priority* field.

Remember that 0 signifies the lowest priority and 1000 signifies the highest priority for any task. The default value is 500 and the system sets the value to 500 by default for all tasks to consider all tasks equally when leveling overallocations.

4. Click the *OK* button.

5. Repeat steps #1-4 for each task to which you assigned the overallocated resource.

When setting *Priority* numbers on multiple tasks, be sure to specify a **unique** priority number for each task. After setting task *Priority* numbers, return to the *Resource Usage* window and level the overallocated resource again.

Information: An alternate method for setting *Priority* numbers to tasks is to insert the *Priority* field temporarily in the *Leveling Gantt* view by completing the following steps:

1. Right-click the *Leveling Delay* column header, select the *Insert Column* item on the shortcut menu, and then in the pick list of available fields, select the *Priority* field.
2. Enter values in the *Priority* column for each task with an overallocated resource assigned.

Information: Not only can you set a *Priority* number at the task level, Project Pro 2013 also allows you to set a *Priority* number at the project level. To level across multiple projects, open each project, display the *Project Information* dialog, and specify a value in the *Priority* field for the project.

Leveling Resource Overallocations in the Team Planner View

Project Pro 2013 allows you to use the *Team Planner* view to resolve resource overallocations using different methods, including the following:

- Level the resource overallocation using the built-in leveling tool in the software.
- Reassign a task that is causing an overallocation by dragging the task to a different resource.
- Reschedule a task that is causing an overallocation by dragging it to a different time period.

To level a resource overallocation using the built-in leveling tool in Project Pro 2013, complete the following steps:

1. Select the name of an overallocated resource in the *Resource* pane.
2. In the *Level* section of the *Resource* ribbon, click the *Leveling Options* button. The system displays the *Resource Leveling* dialog shown previously in Figure 7 - 66.
3. In the *Resource Leveling* dialog, select the options you want to use for leveling the selected resource and then click the *OK* button.

Information: The system selects the *Level Manually Scheduled Tasks* option by default, and you must deselect it if you do not want the leveling operation to level *Manually Scheduled* tasks.

Warning: Do not click the *Level All* button in the *Resource Leveling* dialog. If you click the *Level All* button, you lose control over the leveling process because the software levels all of the overallocated resources in your project in a single operation.

4. In the *Level* section of the *Resource* ribbon, click the *Level Resource* button.

Remember that when you use the built-in leveling tool to level an overallocated resource, Project Pro 2013 resolves the overallocation using one or both of the following methods:

- The software delays tasks or assignments.
- The software splits tasks or assignments.

You may prevent resource overallocations in your project by clicking the *Format* tab and then clicking the *Prevent Overallocations* button in the *Format* ribbon. With this option selected, the software levels all existing overallocations in the project immediately, and levels any future resource overallocation when it occurs, such as when you drag a task or assign a task that causes a resource overallocation. In the *Team Planner* view, Project Pro 2013 indicates that you selected this option by highlighting the *Prevent Overallocations* button and by displaying a *Prevent Overallocations: On* indicator at the left end of the status bar at the bottom of the application window, as shown in Figure 7 - 72.

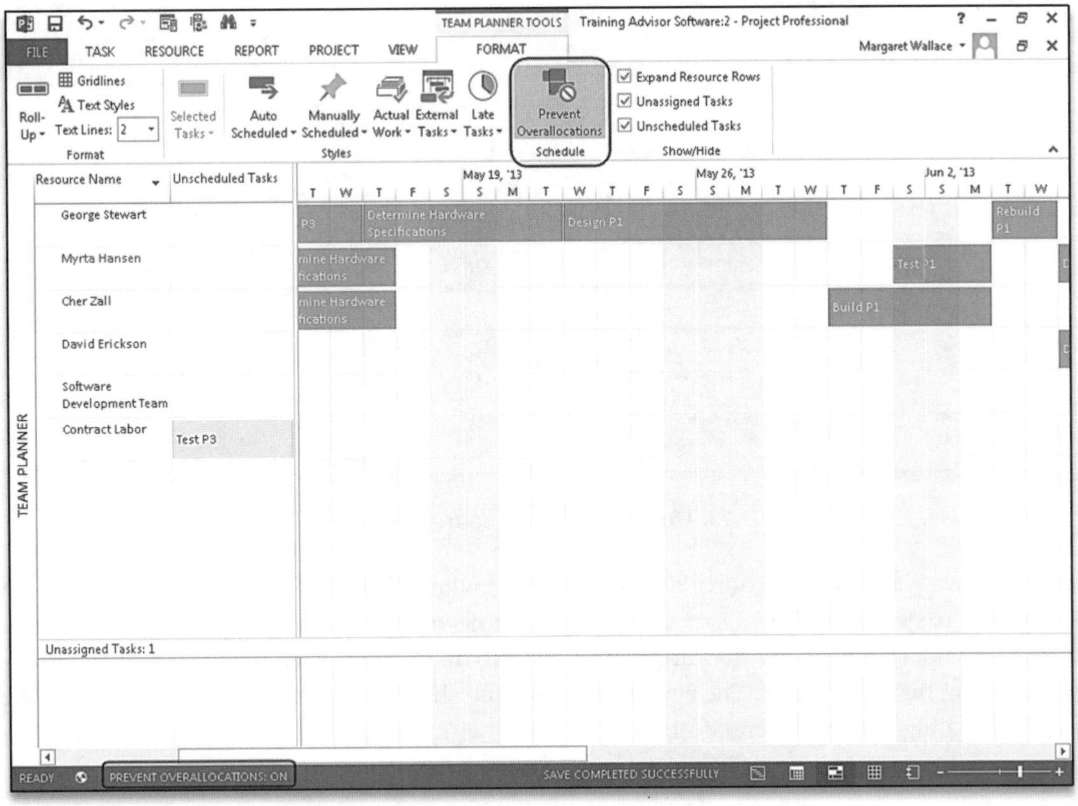

Figure 7 - 72: Prevent Overallocations option selected

Remember that if you prefer to use a manual approach to level a resource overallocation, Project Pro 2013 allows you to reschedule a task by dragging it to a different time period, or dragging a task to a different resource.

Leveling Resource Overallocations in a Task View

Another powerful feature in Project Pro 2013 helps you to locate and level resource overallocations on a task-by-task basis in any task view, such as the *Gantt Chart* view. To locate a resource overallocation in a task view, apply any task view, then look in the *Indicators* column for any task with a "burning man" indicator, which identifies the task as assigned to an overallocated resource. For example, Figure 7 - 73 shows the *Gantt Chart* view of my project. Notice the special indicator in the *Indicators* column for task IDs #6, #7, and #8, indicating that I have an overallocated resource assigned to these three tasks. In this situation, the overallocated resource is *Dan Morton*. The overallocation is a consequence of assigning *Dan Morton* at *100% Units* on three tasks that run in parallel. Because he cannot work full-time on three tasks simultaneously, the system shows that *Dan Morton* is an overallocated resource on these three tasks.

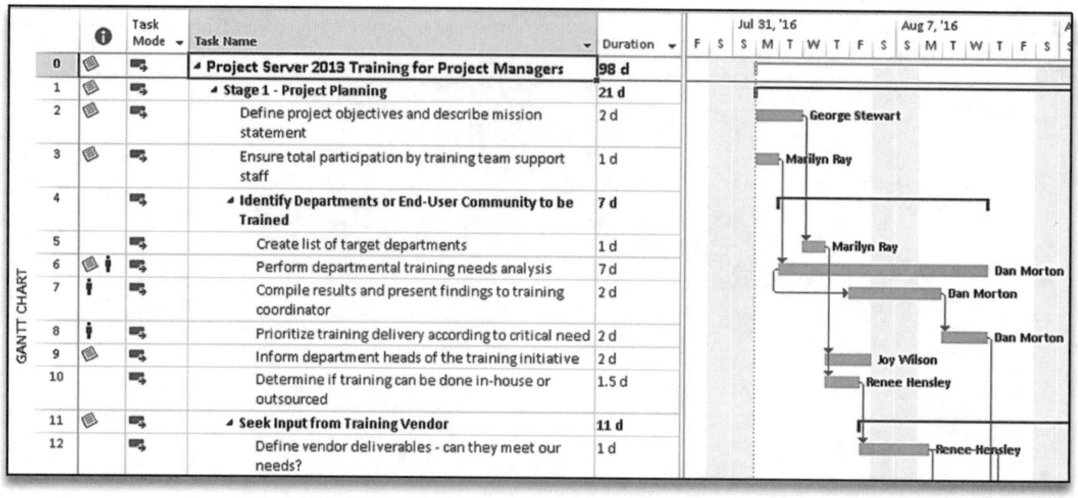

Figure 7 - 73: Three tasks with resource overallocations

Project Pro 2013 allows you to level resource overallocations on these three tasks by delaying the tasks individually, on a task-by-task basis in the *Gantt Chart* view. First, you need to decide which tasks you want to delay and which tasks you will not change. After deciding which tasks to delay, right-click the *Indicators* column on any cell containing a "burning man" indicator. The system displays the shortcut menu shown in Figure 7 - 74 and offers three methods for dealing with the overallocation.

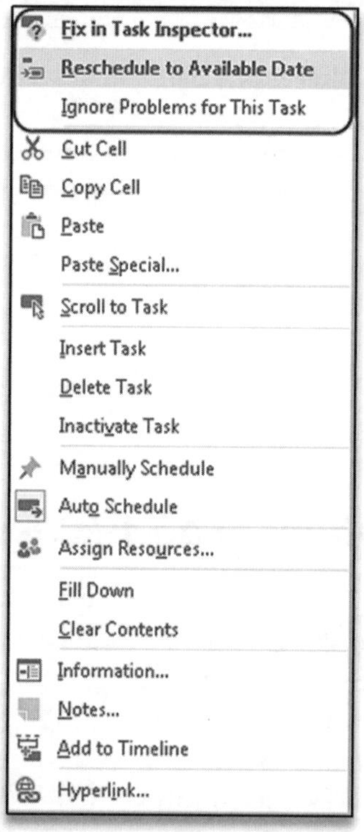

Figure 7 - 74: Shortcut menu for a task assigned to an overallocated resource

The first item in the shortcut menu is the *Fix in Task Inspector* option. If you select this option, the system opens the *Task Inspector* sidepane on the left side of the *Gantt Chart* view, as shown in Figure 7 - 75.

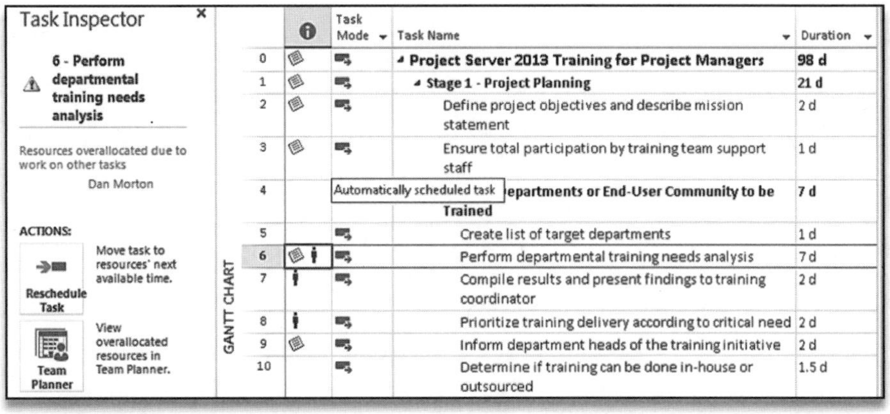

Figure 7 - 75: Task Inspector for a task assigned to an overallocated resource

The *Task Inspector* sidepane offers two options in the *Actions* section for resolving the resource overallocation. Click the *Reschedule Task* button to delay the task to the first available time period that resolves the overallocation. Click the *Team Planner* button to apply the *Team Planner* view, where you can level the resource using any of the methods I discussed in the previous section of this module.

The second item in the shortcut menu is the *Reschedule to Available Date* option. If you select this option, Project Pro 2013 delays the task to the first available time period that resolves the overallocation. Selecting this option is the same as clicking the *Reschedule* button in the *Task Inspector* sidepane.

The third option on the shortcut menu is the *Ignore Problems for This Task* option. If you select this option, the system hides the "burning man" indicator for that task in the *Indicators* column, but does nothing to resolve the resource overallocation.

Module 08

Project Execution

Learning Objectives

After completing this module, you will be able to:

- View the Critical Path
- Work with baselines
- Understand the results of publishing a project
- Set publishing options for a project
- Change the Status Manager for selected tasks in a published project
- Select an Assignment Owner
- Act as delegate for another project manager
- Delegate a project to another project manager
- Set custom permissions for a project
- Manage project deliverables

Inside Module 08

Analyzing the Critical Path

Project Pro 2013 defines the **Critical Path** as "The series of tasks that must be completed on schedule for a project to finish on schedule." Every task on the Critical Path is a **Critical task**. By default, all tasks on the Critical Path have a *Total Slack* value of 0 days, which means they cannot slip without delaying the project *Finish* date. If the *Finish* date of any Critical task slips by even 1 day, the project *Finish* date slips as well.

Project Pro 2013 defines a **non-Critical task** as any task that is 100% complete or any task with a *Total Slack* value greater than 0 days. A non-Critical task can slip by its amount of *Total Slack* before it affects the *Finish* date of the project. For example, if a task has 5 days of *Total Slack*, the task must finish more than 5 days late before the resulting slippage changes the project *Finish* date. To manage your project well, you should be aware of the non-Critical tasks in your project, but you should focus your energy on managing the tasks on the Critical Path.

> **Information**: Project Pro 2013 automatically calculates the *Total Slack* field value for each task to determine the Critical Path of the project. To view the *Total Slack* for any task, click the *View* tab to display the *View* ribbon. In the *Data* section of the *View* ribbon, click the *Tables* button, and then select the *Schedule* table. The *Total Slack* column is the last column on the right side of the *Schedule* table.

In Project Pro 2013, the Critical Path may run from the *Start* date to the *Finish* date of the project, or it may begin anywhere in the project and run to the *Finish* date of the project. This behavior is a key difference from the traditional Critical Path Method (CPM) definition of the Critical Path.

> **Information**: If you make changes to your project, either by entering actual progress or by making plan revisions, keep in mind that the Critical Path may change.

There are a number of ways to determine the Critical Path in any project in Project Pro 2013. The simplest method is to format the *Gantt Chart* view to display red Gantt bars for *Critical* tasks. To format the *Gantt Chart* view to show the Critical Path, complete the following steps:

1. Click the *View* tab and then in the *Task Views* section of the *View* ribbon, click the *Gantt Chart* button.

2. Click the *Format* tab to display the *Format* ribbon.

3. In the *Bar Styles* section of the *Format* ribbon, select the *Critical Tasks* checkbox.

4. Optionally select the *Slack* checkbox.

In the formatted *Gantt Chart* view shown in Figure 8 - 1, notice that Project Pro 2013 displays the following:

- **Red bars** represent Critical tasks on the Critical Path. These tasks have a *Total Slack* value of *0 days*.

- **Blue bars** represent non-Critical tasks. These tasks have a *Total Slack* value greater than *0 days*.

- A **black stripe** to the right of any Gantt bar represents the amount of *Total Slack* for the task.

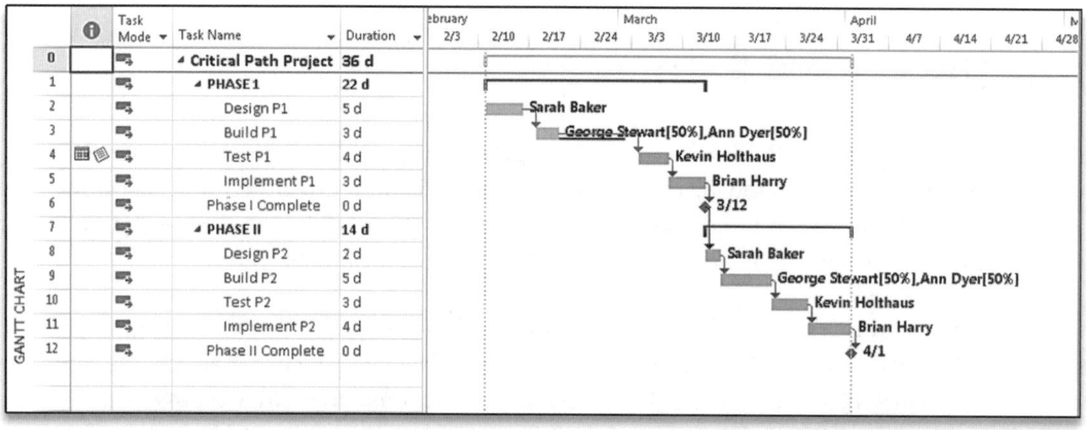

Figure 8 - 1: Gantt Chart view shows Critical Path and Total Slack

> **Information**: You can also view the Critical Path in any project by applying the *Tracking Gantt* view. Be aware, however, that the *Tracking Gantt* view displays Gantt bars for both the Critical Path and for the baseline schedule of the project. Remember that red Gantt bars show Critical tasks, blue Gantt bars show non-Critical tasks, and gray Gantt bars show the original baseline schedule of each task.

Viewing the "Nearly Critical" Path

In Project Pro 2013, you can change the software's definition of a Critical task by clicking the *File* tab and then clicking the *Options* tab in the *Backstage*. In the *Project Options* dialog, click the *Advanced* tab and then scroll down to the *Calculation options for this project* section of the dialog. To change the software's definition of a Critical task, change the *Tasks are critical if slack is less than or equal to* option to a value **greater than** *0 days*, and then click the *OK* button.

Using this technique is a helpful way to see the "nearly Critical tasks" in your project. "Nearly Critical tasks" are those tasks that are not on the true Critical Path, but are close enough to affect the *Finish* date of the project if they slip by an amount greater than their *Total Slack* value. For example, I have a task with only *1 day* of *Total Slack*, so this task is not a true Critical task since it has a *Total Slack* value greater than *0 days*. However, if this task slips by only 2 days, the *Finish* date of the project slips. Therefore, it is not a bad idea to identify the "nearly Critical tasks" in any enterprise project.

Working with Project Baselines

Prior to executing a project, you should save a baseline for your project. A baseline represents a snapshot of the work, cost, and schedule estimates as represented in your initial project plan. Your baseline should represent the schedule your stakeholders approved before you begin tracking progress. All of the variance measurements that Project Pro 2013 calculates for you are dependent on the existence of a baseline. Saving a project baseline provides you with a way to analyze project variance by comparing the current state of the project against the original planned state of the project (the baseline).

When you save a baseline in Project Pro 2013, the software captures the current values for five important task fields and two important resource fields, and then saves these values in a corresponding set of baseline fields. Table 8 - 1 shows the original fields and their corresponding baseline fields.

Data Type	Field	Baseline Field
Task	Duration	Baseline Duration
Task	Start	Baseline Start
Task	Finish	Baseline Finish
Task	Work	Baseline Work
Task	Cost	Baseline Cost
Resource	Work	Baseline Work
Resource	Cost	Baseline Cost

Table 8 - 1: Baseline information

In addition to the five important task fields captured in the baseline, Project Pro 2013 also captures some additional task information that includes:

- Extra task cost information in the *Fixed Cost* and *Fixed Cost Accrual* fields, saving this information in the *Baseline Fixed Cost* and *Baseline Fixed Cost Accrual* fields, respectively.
- Estimated task schedule information in the *Scheduled Duration, Scheduled Start,* and *Scheduled Finish* fields, saving this information in the *Baseline Estimated Duration, Baseline Estimated Start,* and *Baseline Estimated Finish* fields, respectively. Project Pro 2013 uses these estimated schedule fields primarily with the new *Manually Scheduled* tasks feature.
- Task and resource budget information in the *Budget Cost* and *Budget Work* fields, saving this information in the *Baseline Budget Cost* and *Baseline Budget Work* fields, respectively.
- Baseline information for the start and finish dates associated with deliverables in the *Baseline Deliverable Start* and *Baseline Deliverable Finish* fields.

Information: Project Pro 2013 also saves the timephased values for both tasks and resources in the timephased *Baseline Work* and *Baseline Cost* fields. You can view these timephased values in the timephased grid portion of either the *Task Usage* or *Resource Usage* views.

Protected Baselines

As in previous versions, Project Server 2013 offers functionality to use Protected Baselines, the use of these Protected Baselines allows an organization to manage who may set or clear these baselines. Protected Baselines are in the range of *Baseline 0–5* inclusive, whereas the unprotected baselines are in the range of *Baseline 6-10* inclusive.

In my experience, many organizations use a PMO user group or some other subset of users to manage the Protected Baselines, as they want to control who may set or clear the baseline and more importantly when the baseline is set. For example, it may occur during a Stage Gate in their project management process, and all projects must comply with the baseline being set at a specific lifecycle stage in the project. Using the Protected Baselines functionality requires the following Category Permissions:

- *Save Protected Baseline*
- *Save Project to Project Server*

Protected Baselines are available only in projects saved to Project Server, and are not available in a local project as the project must be an enterprise project published to the Project Server database. You may access the *Set Baseline* functionality to set a Protected Baseline in the *Schedule* section of the *Project* ribbon, and the options include:

- *Set Baseline*
- *Clear Baseline*

Follow the steps in the next subtopical section, *Saving a Project Baseline,* to set a Protected Baseline. Selecting *Baseline 0-5* requires that you have *Save Protected Baseline* and *Save Project to Project Server* category permissions. If you do not have the correct permissions to set a Protected Baseline, the message shown in Figure 8 - 2 displays.

Microsoft Project
Cannot Clear or Save Baseline.
You do not have the adequate permission to clear or save baselines to baselines 0 - 5.
OK

Figure 8 - 2: Protected Baseline, inadequate permissions

Saving a Project Baseline

To save a baseline for the entire project in Project Pro 2013, complete the following steps:

1. In Project Pro 2013, click the *Project* tab to display the *Project* ribbon.
2. In the *Schedule* section of the *Project* ribbon, click the *Set Baseline* pick list button and select the *Set Baseline* item on the list. The system displays the *Set Baseline* dialog shown in Figure 8 - 3.

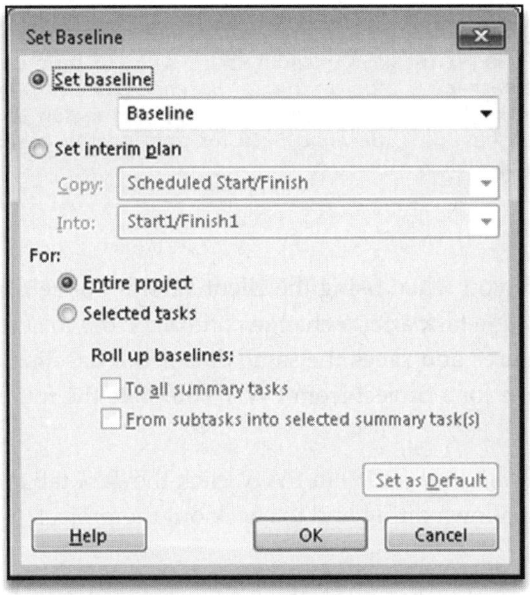

Figure 8 - 3: Set Baseline dialog

3. In the *Set Baseline* pick list, select the *Baseline* item.

4. In the *For:* section, leave the *Entire project* option selected.

5. Click the *OK* button.

Notice that *Baseline 0-10* are available in the pick list regardless of whether or not you have adequate permissions to set any baseline. Once you click the *OK* button, the system validates your permission level. If your permissions are inadequate to perform the action, the system displays the error message shown previously in Figure 8 - 2.

> **Information**: To view the task baseline information in any project, right-click the *Select All* button and select the *More Tables* item on the shortcut menu. In the *More Tables* dialog, select the *Baseline* table and then click the *Apply* button.

> **Best Practice**: MSProjectExperts recommends that you save an original baseline for the entire project only once during the life of a project. After a change control procedure that adds new tasks to your project, you may save a baseline for only the new tasks. This maintains the integrity of your original project baseline.

Setting a Baseline from PWA

The ability to set a baseline from PWA is a new functionality in Project Server 2013. In previous versions the functionality was only available using the client version of Project Pro. The options for setting baselines from PWA for the **entire** project include:

- Set Baseline 0-10
- Clear Baseline 0-10

Information: Your Project Server administrator may choose whether to allow users to save protected and/or unprotected baselines. If you do **not** have adequate permission to set a baseline you will receive an error message when you select the baseline number in the *Set Baseline* pick list in PWA on the *Schedule (PDP)* as shown in Figure 8 - 6 or Figure 8 - 7. Remember you may have permission to set *Baseline 0-10* for any baseline, *Baseline 0-5* for protected baselines, *Baseline 6-10* for unprotected baselines, or no baselines depending on your Project Server configuration.

There are more options available to you when using the client version for setting baselines, such as choosing the *Selected tasks* option to baseline a single task after a change control, or the *Roll up baselines* option. When you set a baseline in PWA, the software captures and saves the same data set of baseline data as if you set the baseline using Project Pro 2013. To set a baseline for a project from PWA, complete the following steps:

1. From the *Schedule Project Detail Page (PDP)* in PWA, click the *Task* tab and in the *Project* section of the ribbon, click the *Edit* button to allow editing and to check out the project.

2. In the *Editing* section of the *Task* ribbon, click the *Set Baseline* pick list shown in Figure 8 - 4 and select the *Set Baseline* item from the list.

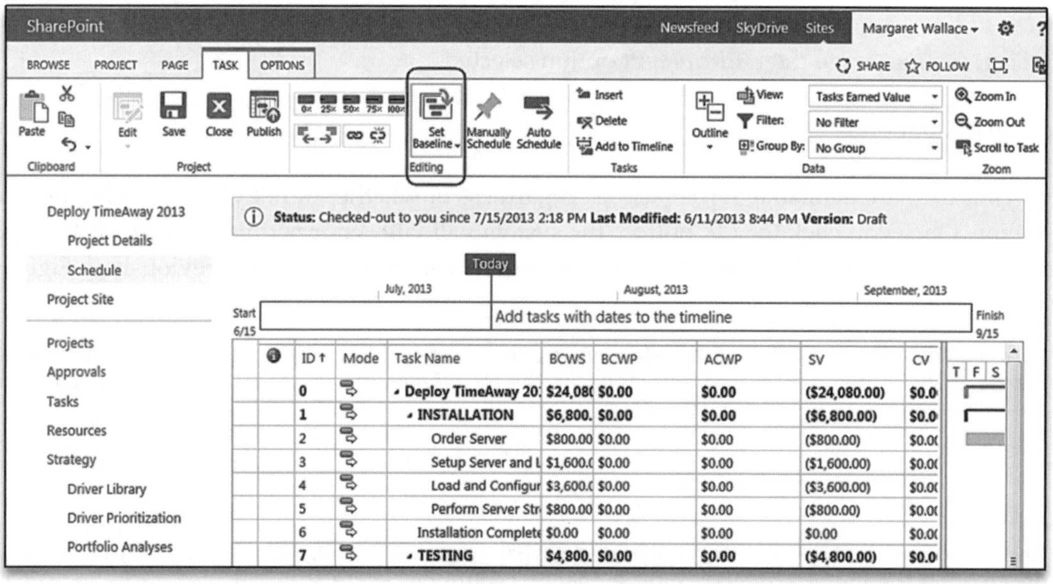

Figure 8 - 4: Schedule PDP, Set Baseline pick list button

3. In the fly out menu of the *Set Baseline* pick list, select the baseline you would like to save, which include *Baseline 0 – 10.*

Notice, in my case since *Baseline 0* does not have a date stamp, I select the *Baseline* item in the fly out menu to set a new baseline as shown in Figure 8 - 5.

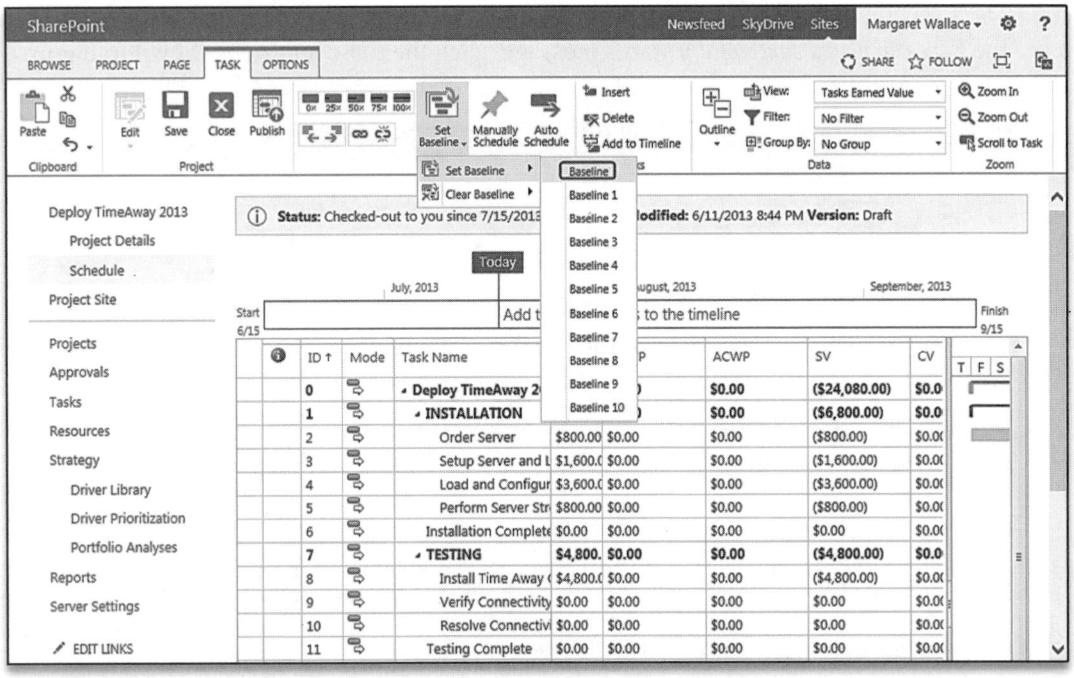

Figure 8 - 5: Schedule PDP, Set Baseline fly out menu

Once you select the *Baseline* item in the fly out menu, the system begins processing the request and you see the following messages in order: *Processing set Baseline…,* that quickly changes to *Baseline set successfully* once the baseline is set. If you do not have adequate permissions to perform the action, you may see one of the following messages shown in Figure 8 - 6 or Figure 8 - 7, indicating you *Cannot Clear or Save Baseline* (*Protected Baseline 0-5 or Unprotected Baseline 6-10*).

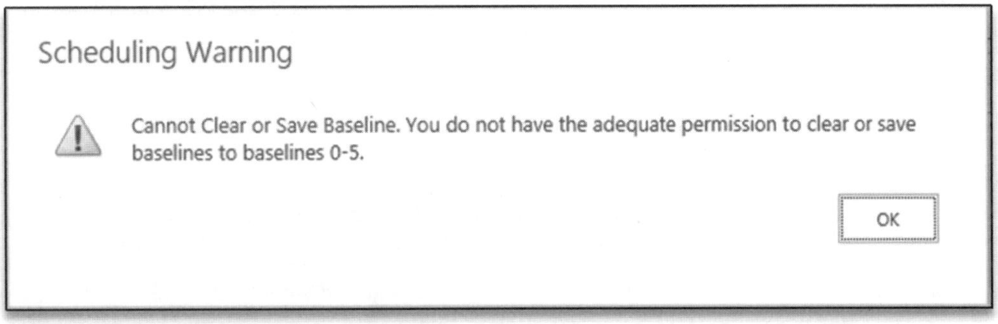

Figure 8 - 6 : Schedule Warning dialog, inadequate permissions for setting Protected Baseline

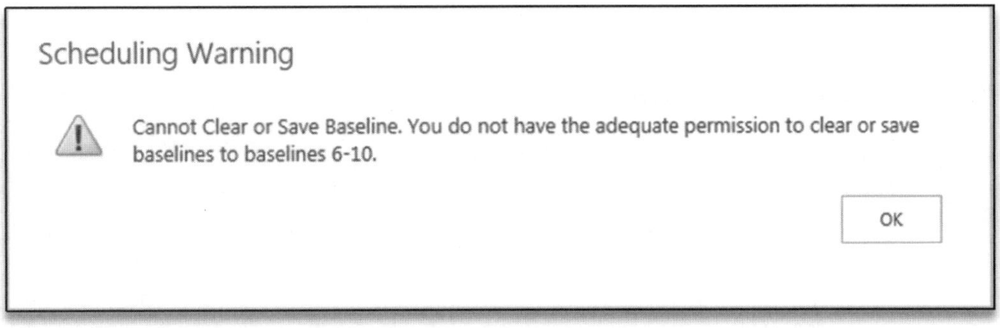

Figure 8 - 7: Schedule Warning dialog, inadequate permissions for setting Unprotected Baseline

4. In the *Project* section of the *Task* ribbon, click the *Save* button to save your enterprise project, then when you see the *Save completed successfully* status message, click the *Close* button as shown in Figure 8 - 8.

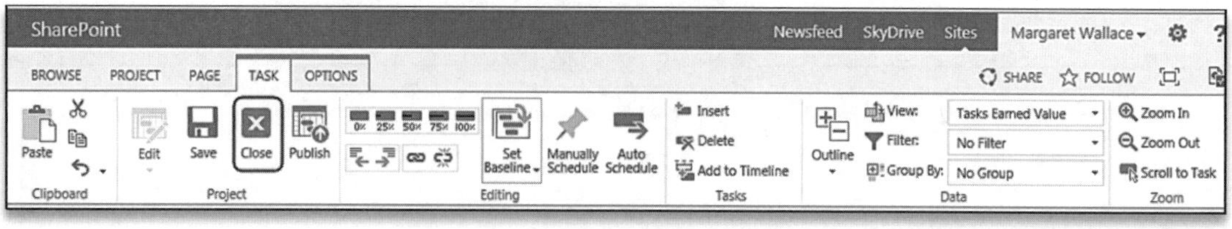

Figure 8 - 8: Task ribbon, Close button

5. In the resulting *Close* dialog, confirm that you want to check in the project by selecting the *Check it in* option and then click the *OK* button.

Information: In the *Project* section of the *Task* ribbon in PWA, Project Server 2013 now includes the *Close* button shown previously in Figure 8 - 8. This new feature allows easier access to check in your project, eliminating the need to navigate to another tab to check in the project unlike previous versions of Project Server that require multiple steps to check in projects in PWA.

Warning: There are limitations when setting baselines from PWA. The feature only allows setting a baseline for the entire project regardless of the type of baseline you set (Unprotected or Protected). If you select a task prior to selecting the *Set Baseline* pick list item, it is not immediately apparent that the baseline is set for the entire project. However, if you add any of the baseline fields to a project view, you can see that the baseline is set for the entire project. If you add a baseline field to a *Project* view by clicking *PWA Settings* ➢ *Manage Views* (which requires *Administrative Group* permission) such as, *Baseline 1 Start* if you set *Baseline 1*, the view shows that the baseline is set for the entire project.

Best Practice: MSProjectExperts recommends using this Project Server functionality for setting baselines from PWA when setting the *Protected Baseline 0* by a PMO user group or other user group who controls setting the original baseline. Setting the baseline from PWA can be a basic method for controlling the process ,of setting the original baseline, especially if no additional options are required when setting the baseline, and as an added bonus, Project Pro 2013 is not required to set a baseline in PWA.

Saving Over a Previous Baseline

To determine whether you previously saved an original baseline in a project, in the *Schedule* section of the *Project* ribbon, click the *Set Baseline* pick list button and select the *Set Baseline* item on the list. Project Pro 2013 indicates whether you previously saved a baseline displaying the date on which you saved it, as shown in Figure 8 - 9.

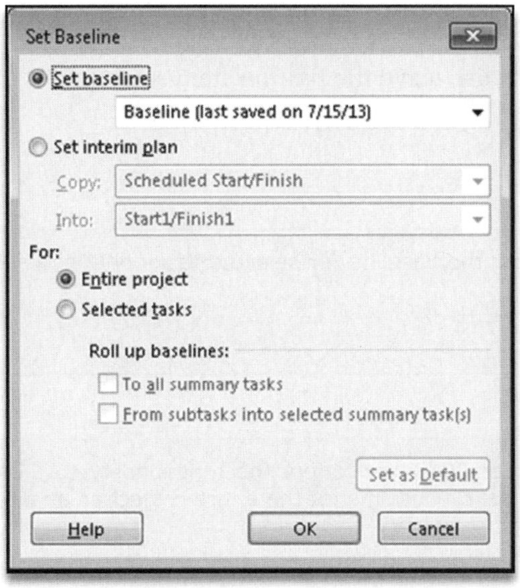

Figure 8 - 9: Last saved on date in the Set Baseline dialog

If you attempt to save baseline information over your original baseline, Project Pro 2013 warns you with the message in the dialog shown in Figure 8 - 10.

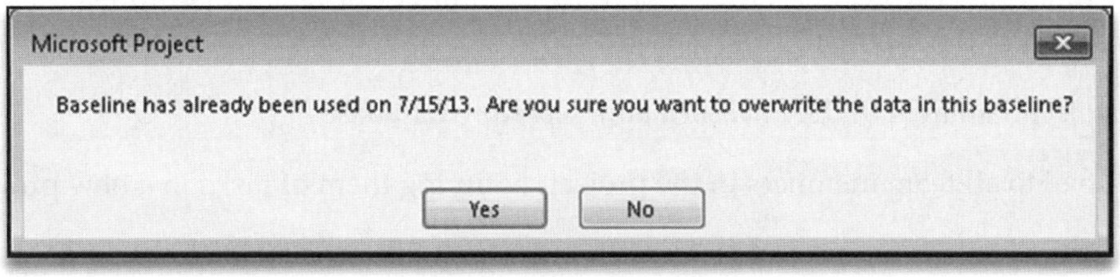

Figure 8 - 10: Warning dialog, Overwrite the data in this baseline

Clearing the Project Baseline

You may need to clear the baseline information for a project, such as when management decides to delay the start of your project indefinitely. In a situation like this, your baseline information is invalid when your executives finally determine a new project start date. To clear the baseline values for your project complete the following steps:

1. In the *Schedule* section of the *Project* ribbon, click the *Set Baseline* pick list button and select the *Clear Baseline* item on the list. Project Pro 2013 displays the *Clear Baseline* dialog shown in Figure 8 - 11.

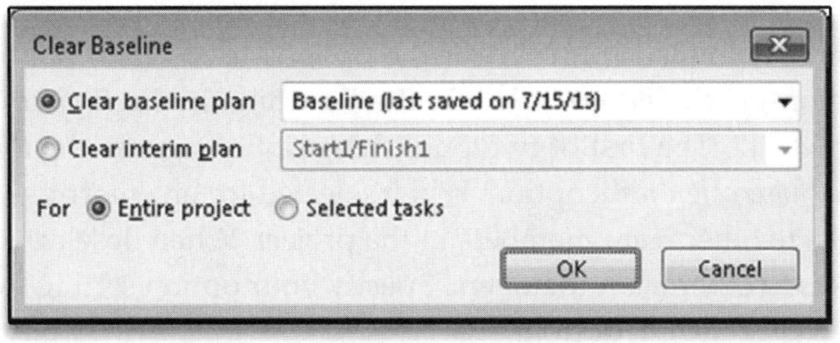

Figure 8 - 11: Clear Baseline dialog

2. Select the *Clear baseline plan* option.
3. On the *Clear baseline plan* pick list, leave the *Baseline* item selected.
4. Select the *Entire project* option.
5. Click the *OK* button.

Information: You can clear the baseline for selected tasks only by choosing the *Selected tasks* option in the *Clear Baseline* dialog.

Information: Project Server 2013 now offers the functionality to *Clear Baseline* from PWA, which offers a quick and easy method to clear a baseline for the entire project as an alternative method.

Understanding Publishing

When you are ready to "go live" with an enterprise project, you must publish the project. When you publish a project for the very first time, Project Server 2013 performs a number of major operations. In the simplest sense, the system performs each of the following:

- Saves the project data in both the *Published* and *Reporting* databases
- Sends an e-mail to all team members in the project, notifying them of tasks in a new project
- Creates a Project Site for the project in SharePoint, which allows all members of the project team to collaborate with the team on risks, issues, documents, and deliverables associated with the project

The result of the publishing operation is that all parties may now see information about the project in Project Web App. For example, executives see the project on the *Project Center* page in views, resource managers see resource assignment information on the *Resource Availability* page, and team members see their task assignments in both *My Work* and *Timesheet* views.

Publishing a project for the first time also determines who receives task updates from team members working on the project. Project Server 2013 designates the user who publishes the project initially as the *Status Manager* for every task in the project. The person designated as the *Status Manager* is the one who receives and approves task updates from team members for their task assignments. I discuss this feature a little later in this module.

Setting Publishing Options

Project Server 2013 gives you very limited control over the options used when publishing an enterprise project. To view these publishing options, click *File* ➤ *Options* in the *Backstage*. In the *Project Options* dialog, click the *Advanced* tab as shown in Figure 8 - 12. The first of two publishing options are in the *Project Web App* section of the dialog, the *Allow team members to reassign tasks* option. When selected for an enterprise project, this option allows a team member to delegate tasks to other team members in the project. When deselected, this option prevents team members from delegating tasks to other team members. Specify your option setting in the *Project Web App* section of the *Advanced* page, and then click the *OK* button.

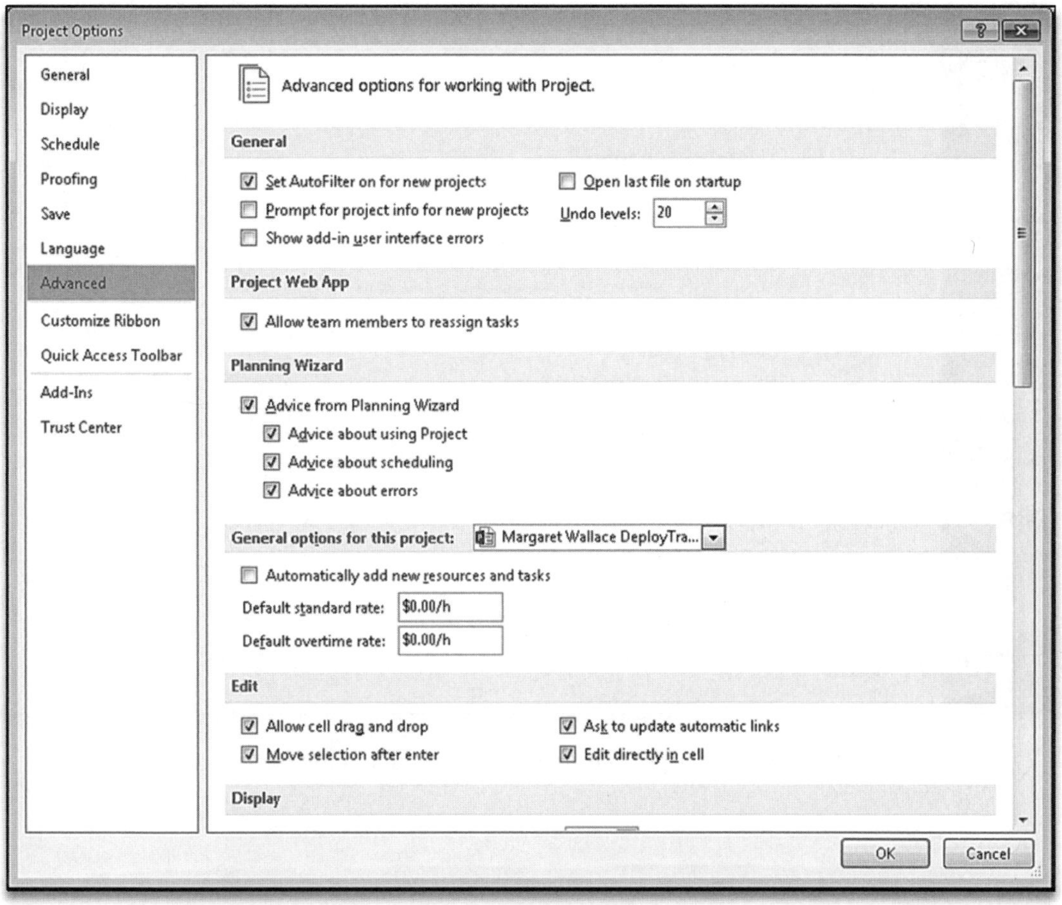

Figure 8 - 12: Advanced page in the Project Options dialog

To locate the other publishing option, click *File* ➤ *Info* in the *Backstage*. On the right side of the *Info* page in the *Backstage*, the system displays a *Tracking Method* pick list as shown in Figure 8 - 13. Project Server 2013 allows you to specify the default method of tracking for each enterprise project individually when you deselect the *Force project managers to use the progress reporting method specified above for all projects* option. You find this option on the *Task Settings and Display* page you reach by clicking the *Task Settings and Display* link in the *Time and Task Management* section of the PWA Settings page. Otherwise, you may select one of the items on the *Tracking Method* pick list. Select the *Actual/Remaining* method to track progress by capturing actual work and remaining work from team members. Select the *Percent Complete* method to track progress by capturing a percentage of completion value from team members. Select the *Specify Hours* option to capture actual work on a daily or weekly basis from team members. Otherwise, leave the *Server Default* item selected on the *Tracking Method* pick list to use the method specified for your organization by your Project Server administrator.

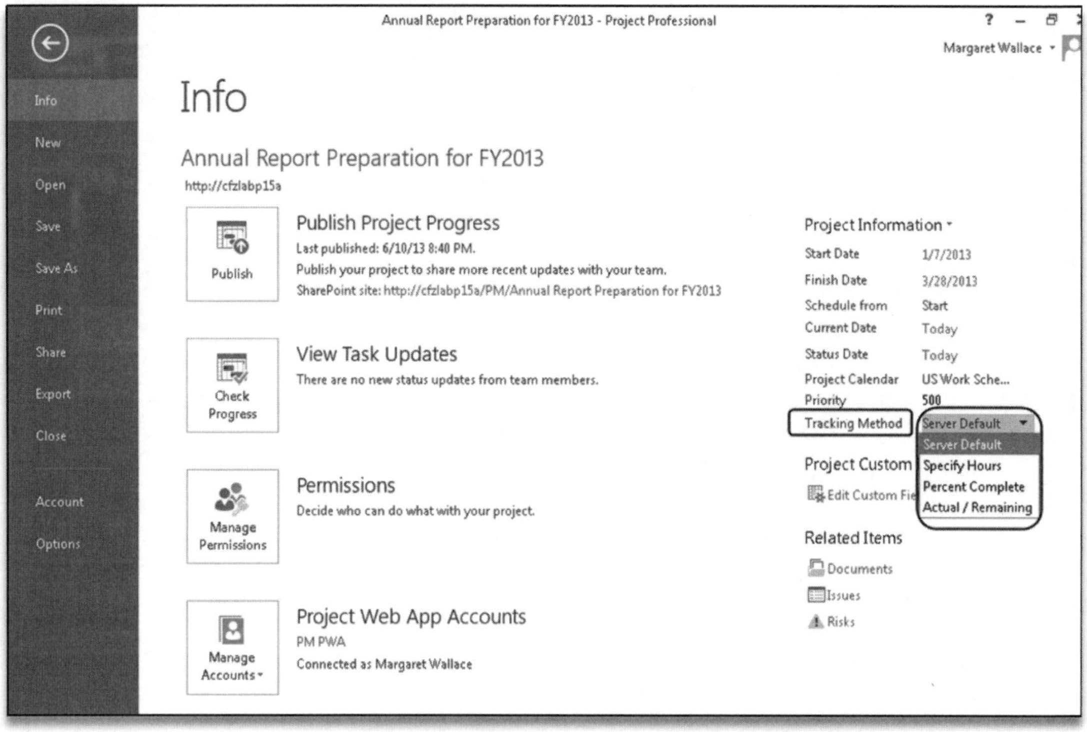

Figure 8 - 13: Info page, Tracking Method option in the Backstage

> **Information**: If your Project Server administrator locked the default method of tracking progress in Project Server 2013, then Project Pro 2013 locks the *Tracking Method* pick list on the *Info page* of the *Backstage*.

Publishing an Enterprise Project

To publish an enterprise project, click *File* ➤ *Info* in the *Backstage* and then click the *Publish* button as shown in Figure 8 - 14. Notice the message that describes the *Publish* status of the project indicating *This project has not been published to Project Web App.*

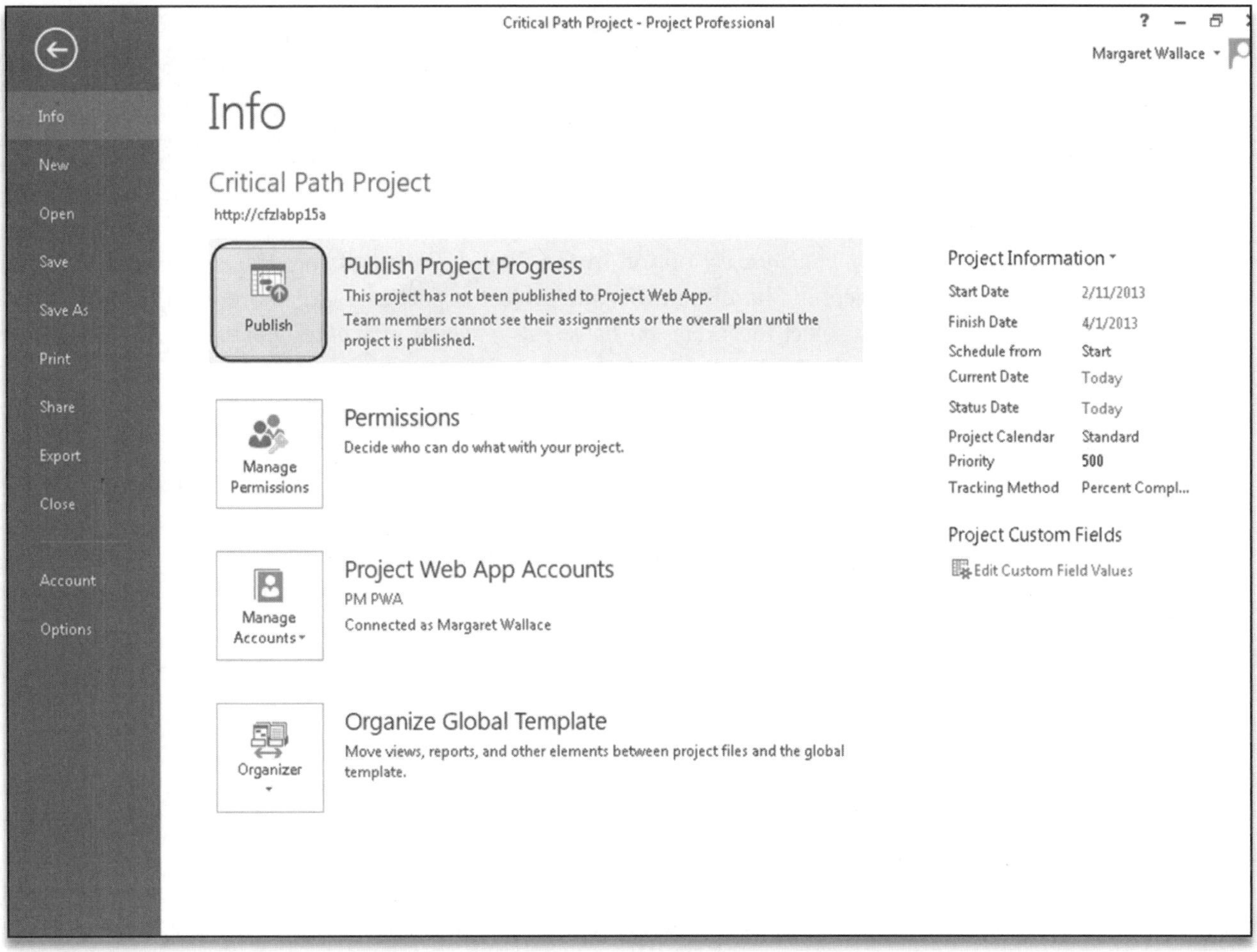

Figure 8 - 14: Backstage Info tab, Publish button

Project Pro 2013 displays the *Publish Project* dialog for the project shown in Figure 8 - 15. Notice the system grays out the new *Don't show this again for this project* option.

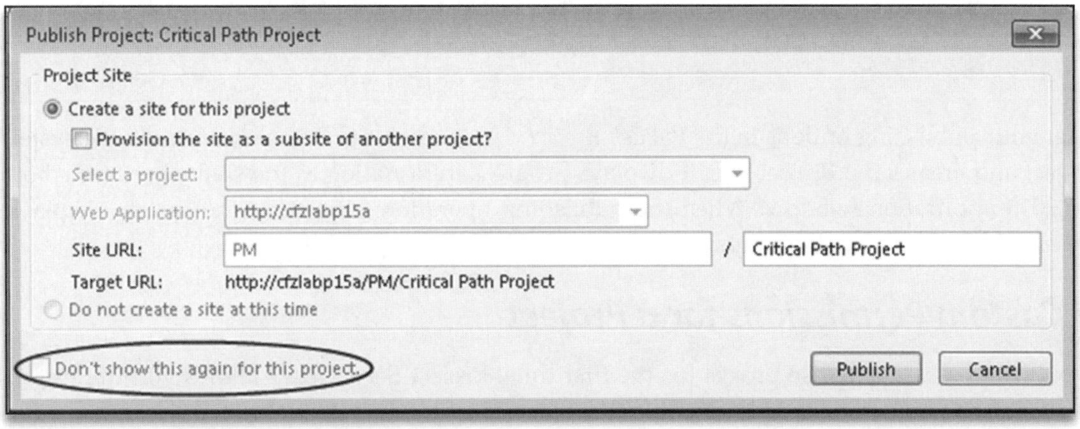

Figure 8 - 15: Publish Project dialog for a project, new option grayed out

Information: The *Publish Project* dialog includes a new option in Project Pro 2013, the *Don't show this again for this project* option, which is grayed out as shown previously in Figure 8 - 15. This option is **not available** if your administrator configures Project Server 2013 with the option that automatically creates a Project Site on the first publish. To enable this new option, you must first select the *Do not create a site at this time* option. Once selected, it prevents the *Publish Project* dialog from displaying each time you click the *Publish* button to publish your project. This is especially useful in an organization where creating a Project Site is optional and you want to prevent the *Publish Project* dialog from displaying.

If you select the default *Create a site for this project* option in the *Publish Project* dialog, the system automatically creates a new Project Site for the project in SharePoint. If your project is part of a larger program of projects that must share a single Project Site, then select the *Provision the site as a subsite of another project* option. The system activates the *Select a project* pick list in the *Publish Project* dialog as shown in Figure 8 - 16.

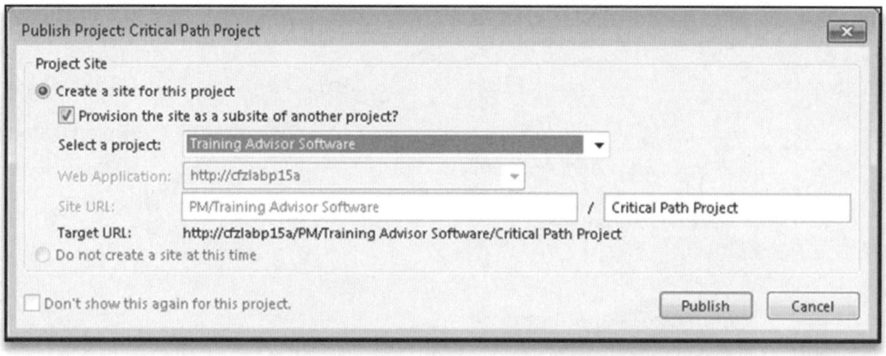

Figure 8 - 16: Publish Project dialog set to create a subsite of another project

Click the *Select a project* pick list and select the Project Site under which to create the new subsite. In my example shown previously in Figure 8 - 16, the *Critical Path Project,* Project Site is a subsite of the Project Site for *Training Advisor Software* project. Regardless of how you decide to create the Project Site, you may change the site display name for the project displayed in the *Site URL* field in the lower right corner of the dialog. Some organizations choose to shorten the *Site URL* field using an acronym for the project, thereby shortening the URL link they use for the project team.

Information: Notice in the two preceding figures that the system disables the *Do not create a site at this time* option in the lower left corner of the *Publish Project* dialog. This is because our organization's Project Server administrator selected an option requiring Project Server 2013 to create a Project Site when a manager initially publishes a project.

After you set your publishing options in the *Publish Project* dialog, click the *Publish* button. As the system publishes your project and creates the Project Site, it displays progress information in the status bar at the bottom of the Project Pro 2013 application window. When the publishing operation completes, the system displays a *Publish completed successfully* message in the status bar.

Setting Custom Permissions for a Project

After you publish a new enterprise project for the first time, Project Server 2013 allows you to designate special permissions for the project. For example, the default permissions in the system allow project managers to see and edit their own projects only, and do not allow project managers to see and edit projects they do not own or manage. Suppose that I need a fellow project manager named *Tom Godbold* to be able to see and edit a new enterprise project using Project Pro 2013, but I do not need him to see and edit the project in Project Web App. To set special permissions in Project Pro 2013, open and check out the enterprise project and complete the following steps:

1. Click *File* ➢ *Info* in the *Backstage*, and then click the *Manage Permissions* button as shown in Figure 8 - 17.

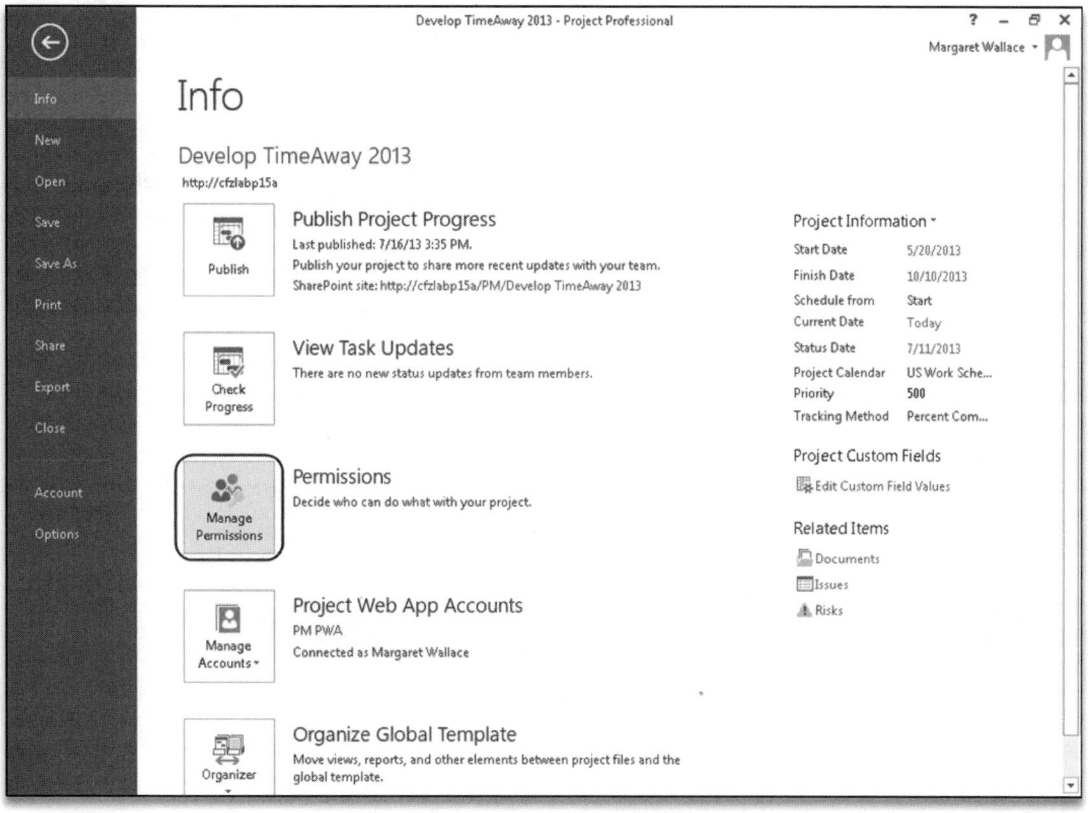

Figure 8 - 17: Set special permissions using the Manage Permissions button in the Backstage

Notice in Figure 8 - 18, the system displays the *Project Permissions* page for the enterprise project, and currently there are no special permissions set for this project.

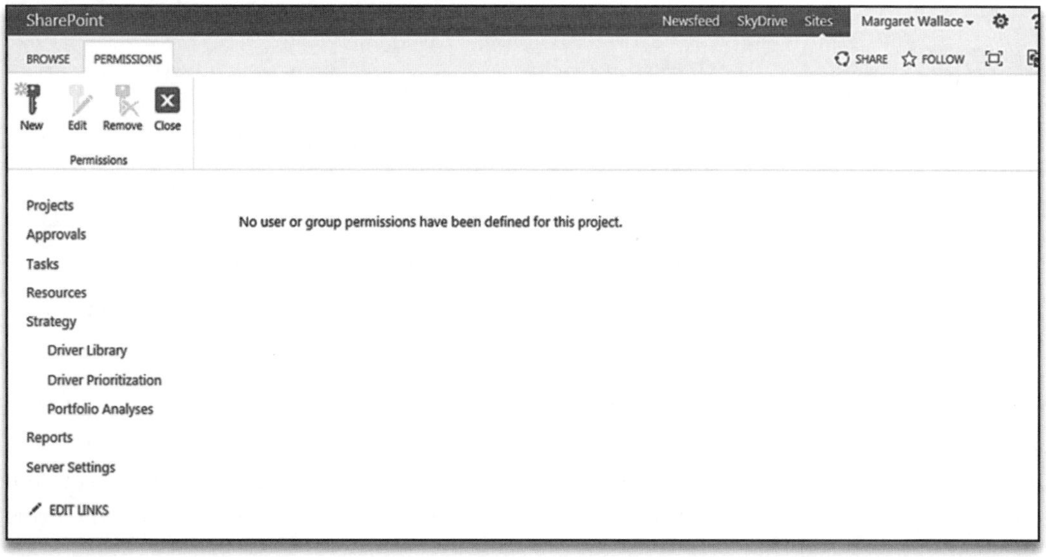

Figure 8 - 18: Project Permissions page for the Develop TimeAway 2013 project

Information: You may also access the *Project Permissions* page by navigating to the *Project Center* page in Project Web App. On the *Project Center* page, click the row header at the left end of the project name to select the project, and then in the *Navigate* section of the *Projects* ribbon, click the *Project Permissions* button.

2. On the *Project Permissions* page, click the *New* button on the *Permissions* ribbon to set new special permissions for the project. The system displays the *Edit Project Permissions* page for the enterprise project, as shown in Figure 8 - 19.

3. Select one or more users or groups in the *Available Users and Groups* list and then click the *Add* button to add the selected users and groups to the *Users and Groups with Permissions* list.

Notice in Figure 8 - 20 that I add *Tom Godbold* to the *Users and Groups with Permissions* list by clicking the *Add* button.

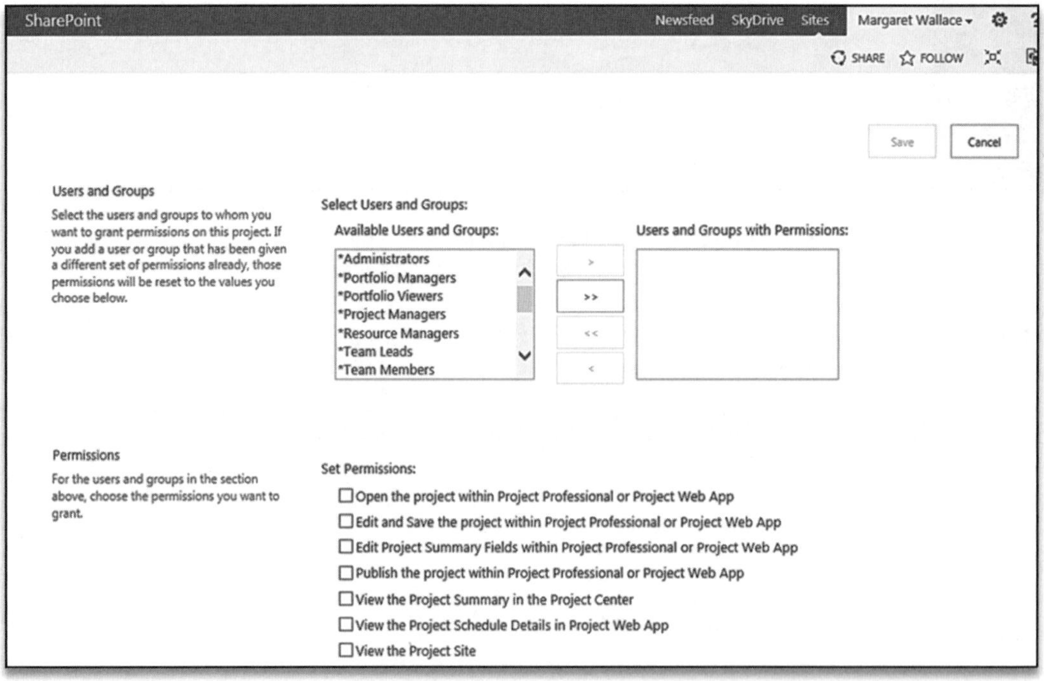

Figure 8 - 19: Edit Project Permissions page for the Develop TimeAway 2010 project

After selecting one or more users and groups, select the specific permissions you want to grant for the selected project in the *Permissions* section of the page. The available permissions allow a user to open, edit and save, publish, and edit project summary fields for an enterprise project in either Project Pro 2013 or Project Web App, view the project in either the *Project Center* page or *Project Details* page in Project Web App, or view the Project Site.

4. I select the following permissions **only,** to meet the special permissions needs for Tom Godbold as shown in Figure 8 - 20.

Set Permissions
Open the project within Project Professional or Project Web App
Edit and Save the project within Project Professional or Project Web App
Publish the project within Project Professional or Project Web App

Information: A user must be a member of the *Project Managers* security group for the following *Set Permissions* options to work properly: To open, edit and save, publish, or edit project summary fields for an enterprise project in either Project Pro 2013 or Project Web App. If a user cannot edit a project after granting them special permissions, check the security group permissions for the user.

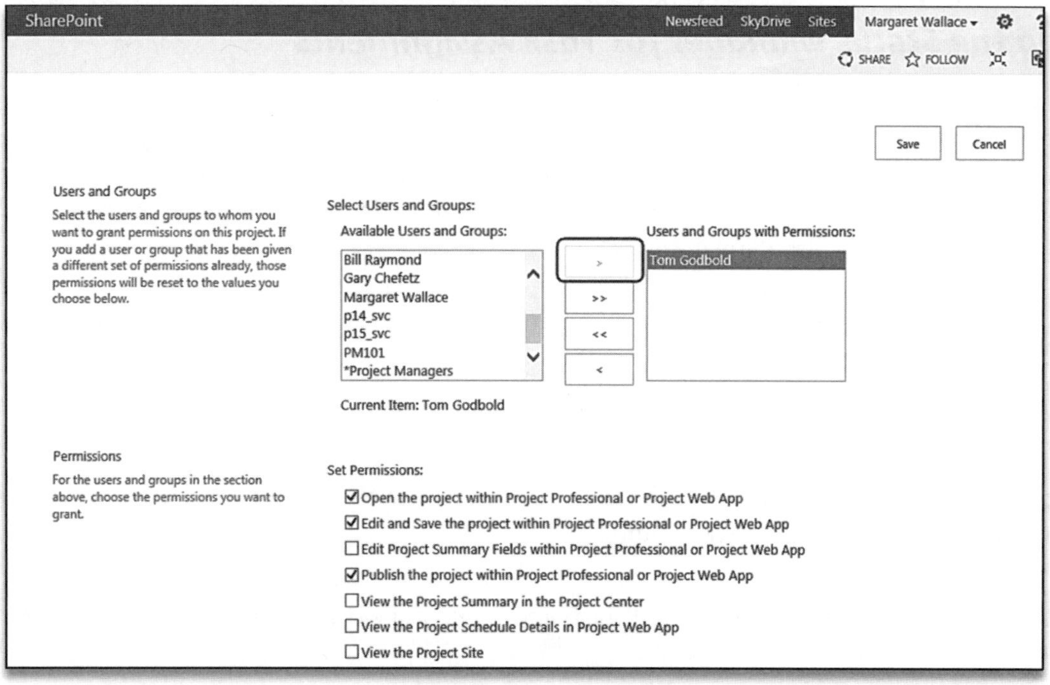

Figure 8 - 20: Edit Project Permissions page, Set Permissions for Tom Godbold

By selecting the preceding options, I allow Tom Godbold to open, edit, save, and publish the project in Project Pro 2013. Tom Godbold cannot edit the project using Project Web App, nor can he access the Project Site for the project because he cannot see the project in the *Project Center* page in Project Web App.

5. When you finish selecting special permissions for the selected users and groups, click the *Save* button. The system refreshes the *Project Permissions* page as shown in Figure 8 - 21.

Notice that the *Project Permissions* page shows the special permissions for Tom Godbold.

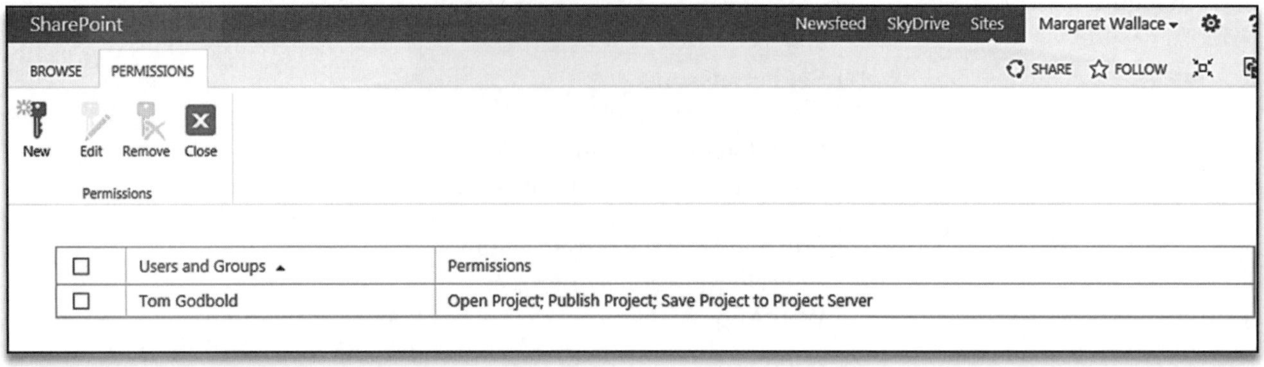

Figure 8 - 21: Project Permissions page for the Develop TimeAway 2013 project

Once you save the options you set on the *Project Permissions* page, you may edit, remove, or close the page, using the *Permissions* ribbon options. To edit the special permissions for a project, select the option for the special permissions and then on the *Permissions* ribbon, click the *Edit* button. To remove the special permissions for a project, select the option for the special permissions and then on the *Permissions* ribbon, click the *Remove* button. To navigate away from the *Project Permissions* page, in the *Permissions* ribbon, click the *Close* button. The system returns to the *Project Center* page shown previously in Figure 8 - 18.

Changing the Status Manager for Task Assignments

As I stated earlier, Project Server 2013 specifies the *Status Manager* on each task in an enterprise project as the manager who publishes the project initially. The system allows you to take over as the *Status Manager* of one or more tasks in another manager's project, either **temporarily** (such as when the other manager is on vacation) or **permanently** (such as when the other manager leaves the company). To take over as the *Status Manager* of another manager's project, complete the following steps:

1. Open the project in *Edit* mode, by checking out the enterprise project in question.

2. Apply any task view, such as the *Gantt Chart* view.

3. Right-click the column header to the right of the *Task Name* column and select the *Insert Column* item on the shortcut menu to insert a new column.

4. In the pick list of available fields, select the *Status Manager* field to insert it to the right of the *Task Name* field.

5. For each task that you manage, click the *Status Manager* pick list and select your name from the list.

The *Status Manager* pick list includes the names of all other *Status Managers* in the project, plus your own name when you open the project. If you are the second manager to open the project, for example, the *Status Manager* pick list includes the name of the first *Status Manager*, along with your name. Notice in Figure 8 - 22 that the system uses bold font for summary task rows and that *Margaret Wallace* displays in the *Status Manager* pick list.

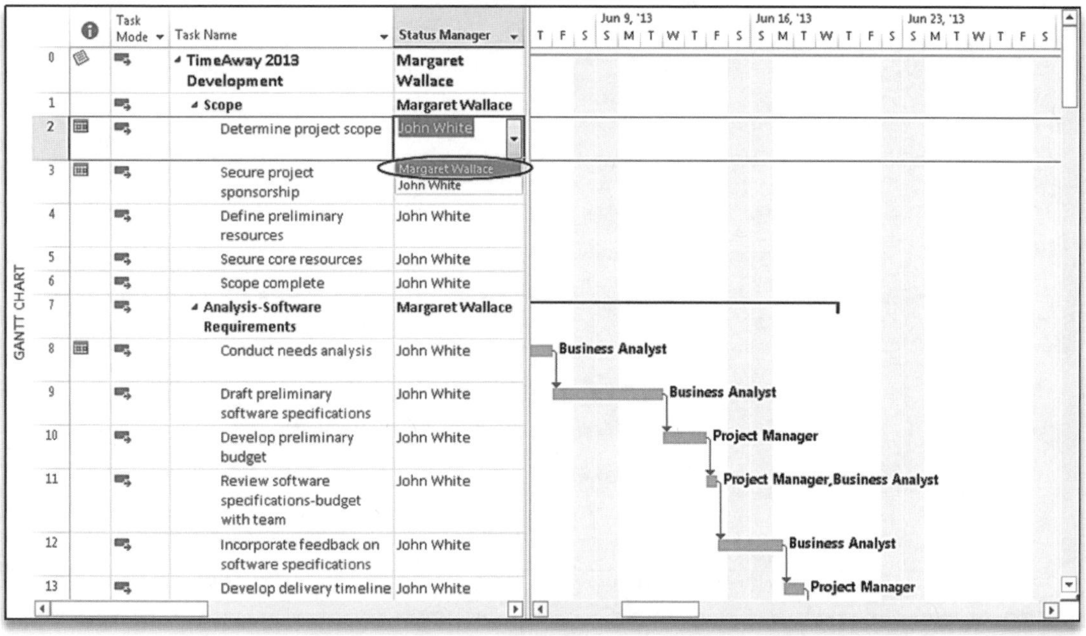

Figure 8 - 22: Select a Status Manager value in the Gantt Chart view of an enterprise project

Figure 8 - 22 shows an enterprise project managed by *John White* is currently opened by another manager, myself *Margaret Wallace*. I need to take over as the *Status Manager* for all of the tasks in the *Scope* and *Analysis-Software Requirements* sections of the project, since I need to accept status updates from resources on the tasks in these sections of the project. To accomplish this, I must select my name, *Margaret Wallace,* in the *Status Manager* column for every subtask in those two summary task sections of the project as shown in Figure 8 - 23.

Information: To speed up the entry process, select your name in the *Status Manager* column for a task and then use the Fill Handle in the selected cell to copy your name to other successive tasks in the project. You can also click the *Fill* pick list button in the *Editing* section of the *Task* ribbon and select the *Down* item on the pick list when making changes to the *Status Manager* for every task in the project. This tip for changing the *Status Manager* field quickly is useful when your organization has a process in place where the PMO controls the creation of the initial project. This method establishes the *Status Manager* on all tasks in the project to another user prior to turning the project over to the project manager during the execution phase.

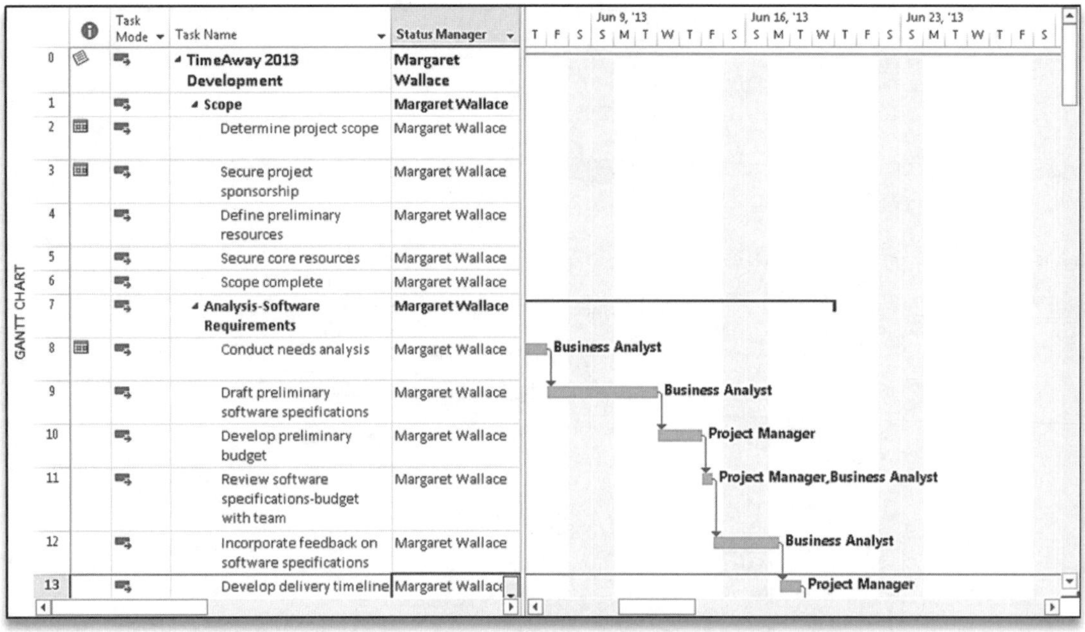

Figure 8 - 23: Status Manager updated for summary task sections

After setting yourself as the *Status Manager* for one or more tasks in an enterprise project, save and publish the project. As the new *Status Manager* for the selected tasks, Project Server 2013 redirects task updates for those tasks from the previous manager to you as the new *Status Manager*.

Information: As you create new tasks during a session, by default the name of the resource that opens the enterprise project becomes the *Status Manager* for any additional tasks. Any current *Status Manager* may change the values in this field.

Best Practice: MsProjectExperts recommends using multiple *Status Managers* for a project when different individuals are responsible for different phases in a project, allowing the task updates to flow to the manager responsible for the task. For example, a project manager may manage the core project while a project coordinator manages a single phase in the project.

Selecting an Assignment Owner

The *Assignment Owner* field value is the responsible person for entering their status in PWA for the current assignment, and is not necessarily the resource assigned to the task, and only the *Assignment Owner* can see the assignments in PWA. By default, all new work resources in the Enterprise Resource Pool (ERP) own their own assignments. In many organizations, however, there may be a single person responsible for reporting time for a team of individuals such as an administrative assistant that records time for the managers and executives in a particular department.

When the *Default Assignment Owner* field for a resource is blank in the ERP and the resource has an assignment in the project, the *Assignment Owner* field contains the name of the person who created the project plan. Project Server 2013 allows you to update the field to any work resource that is a part of the project team. Updating the field may be necessary when only the team lead is submitting time for all of the members of the team. The project manager may update the *Assignment Owner* field for this task for all resources and change the value of the field to the team lead to reflect this business rule. The project manager may need to update the *Assignment Owner* field for any of the following reasons for assignments:

- A team member other than the assigned work resource enters the status for the assignment.
- You assign multiple resources to a task, and only one of them is responsible for reporting status in Project Web App for the team.
- A resource does not have a default assignment owner, and needs to specify an assignment owner.
- A project manager needs to change the *Assignment Owner* field if a resource works remotely and does not have access to a computer to enter status updates.

To update the *Assignment Owner* field for a single resource assignment, complete the following steps:

1. Open your project in *Edit* mode, click the *View* tab, and then select the *Resource Usage* view.
2. In the *Resource Usage* view in the *Add New Column* pick list, select the *Assignment Owner* value to display in the field in the *Assignment Owner* column.
3. Double-click the *Task* name of the assignment where you want to change the *Assignment Owner* value to display the *Assignment Information* dialog.
4. In the *Assignment Information* dialog, click the *Assignment Owner* pick list and select the resource name to be the new *Assignment Owner* value and the person responsible for submitting status updates for this assignment.
5. Click the *OK* button.

Information: There is an alternative method for updating the *Assignment Owner* field in the *Resource Usage* view without using the *Resource Information* dialog. From the *Resource Usage* view in the *Assignment Owner* column, click the pick list for the assignment for which you want to update the *Assignment Owner* field and select the resource name.

To update the *Assignment Owner* field for multiple resources for a task, complete the following steps:

1. Open your project in *Edit* mode, and then click the *View* tab.
2. In the *Task Views* section of the *View* ribbon, click the *Gantt Chart* button to apply the *Gantt Chart* view.
3. In the *Gantt Chart* view, right-click the *Select All* button and select the *_Assignment Owner* table.
4. Double-click the *Task* name of the task whose *Assignment Owner* value you want to update to display the *Task Information* dialog.
5. In the *Task Information* dialog, click the *Resource* tab, and then in the *Assignment Owner* column, click the pick list and select the resource name you want to be the new *Assignment Owner* to be responsible for submitting status updates for the resource assigned to this task.
6. To update the *Assignment Owner* field for all resources assigned to the task, continue by repeating step 5 for each resource assigned to the task.
7. Click the *OK* button.
8. Complete the process by saving and publishing the project to update the assignments for the resources in the project and send the assignments to the new *Assignment Owner* for status updates.

Information: Apply the *Task Usage* or *Resource Usage* view when you need to review or update the names of individuals responsible for entering assignment status. Use the *Assignment Information* dialog to set the *Assignment Owner* value for an individual. Use the *Task Information* dialog for all resources assigned to a single task.

Warning: For enterprise projects, whoever initially publishes the project is the *Assignment Owner* for assignments where the field value is blank for a resource. This may be important in organizations where the PMO or another group manages the initial project publish in Project Server 2013, as the publisher becomes the *Assignment Owner* where the values are blank. In this situation, the project manager must review the *Assignment Owner* values for assignments in the project to verify the system identifies the correct individual to report status updates for the project.

Managing Project Deliverables

In project management terminology, a **deliverable** is the product of a completed project or an intermediate result within a project, such as at the end of each phase or deliverable section of the project. In the world of projects, deliverables can take the form of hardware, software, services, processes, documents, or even ideas.

Project Server 2013 offers you a formal method to indicate project deliverables, their negotiated delivery dates, and any external dependencies that may influence the delivery dates. There are three prerequisites that must be present to manage project deliverables in Project Server 2013 for an enterprise project that include the following:

- Project Web App connection
- Published project
- Project workspace site

Information: Your Project Server administrator may configure your environment allowing a project to publish without creating a project workspace site. However, managing deliverables requires the following: a published project, a Project Site, and a connection to PWA. If you select the *Don't show this again for this project* option shown previously in Figure 8 - 15, you will need to request your Project Server administrator to manually create a Project Site for you. This option hides the *Publish Project* dialog; and, subsequently, eliminates the choice to select the *Create a site for this project* option to create a project workspace site later, rather than during, the initial publish of your project.

Adding a New Deliverable in Project Pro 2013

Although it might make more sense to manage deliverables before you publish a project, Project Server 2013 does not allow you to create deliverables until **after** you publish an enterprise project. This is because your project must have an accompanying Project Site within which to manage project deliverables, and the initial publish creates the Project Site. After publishing your enterprise project, you may create deliverables in the project by completing the following steps:

1. Start by opening a previously published enterprise project in *Edit* mode, and then click the *Task* tab to display the *Task* ribbon.
2. In the *Insert* section of the *Task* ribbon, click the *Deliverables* pick list as shown in Figure 8 - 24, and then select the *Manage Deliverables* item on the list as shown in Figure 8 - 25.

Figure 8 - 24: Deliverables icon, no label

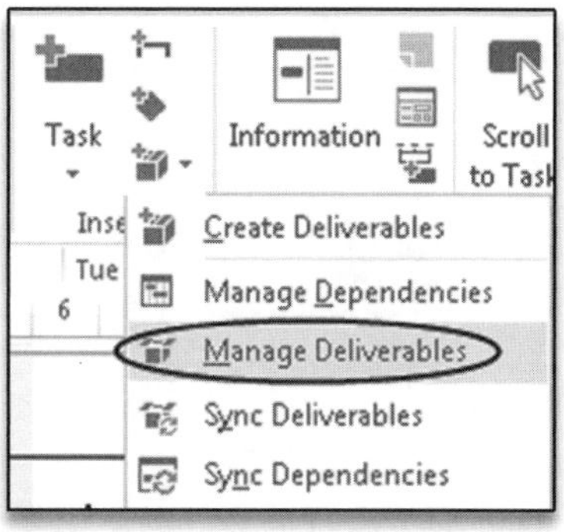

Figure 8 - 25: Manage Deliverables option

Notice that the *Deliverable* icon may display as an icon only, **without** a label as shown previously in Figure 8 - 24, or as icon **with** the *Deliverable* label as shown in Figure 8 - 26, depending on your monitor display and the application window size. Notice also, that when you hover your mouse over the *Deliverable* icon the system displays the description for the icon as shown in Figure 8 - 27.

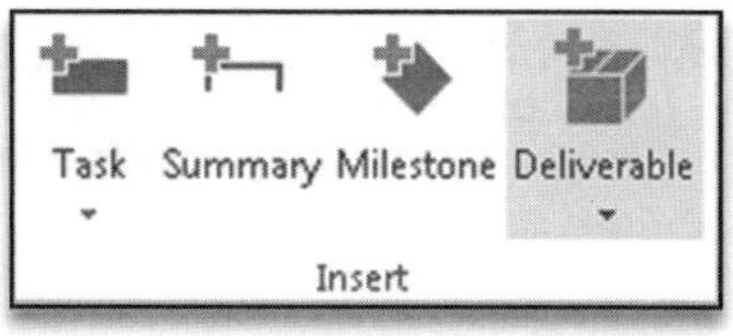

Figure 8 - 26: Task ribbon, Insert section showing Deliverable label highlighted

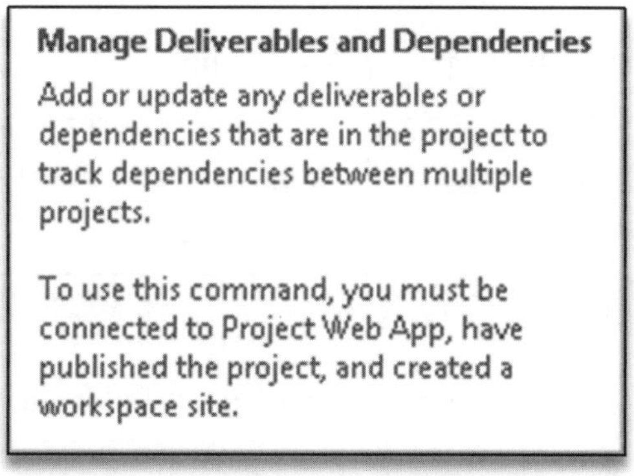

Manage Deliverables and Dependencies
Add or update any deliverables or dependencies that are in the project to track dependencies between multiple projects.
To use this command, you must be connected to Project Web App, have published the project, and created a workspace site.

Figure 8 - 27: Manage Deliverables and Dependencies description

3. Project Server 2013 opens the *Deliverables* sidepane in the Project Pro 2013 application window shown in Figure 8 - 28.

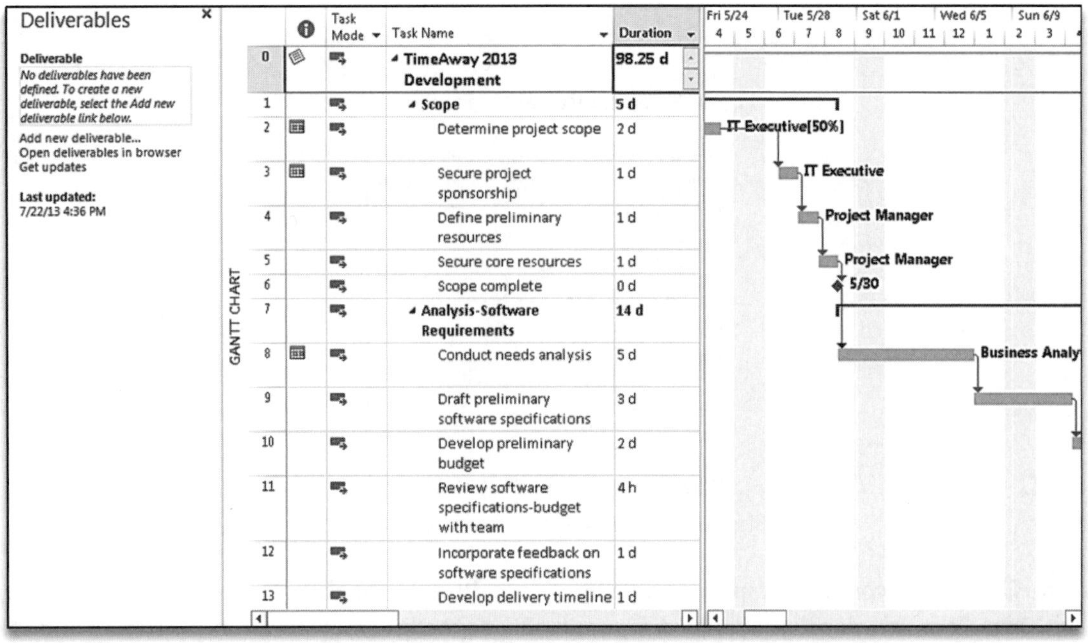

Figure 8 - 28: Deliverables sidepane in a published project

> **Information**: You may also display the *Deliverables* sidepane by clicking the *Task* tab to display the *Task* ribbon. In the *Insert* section of the *Task* ribbon, click the *Manage Deliverables and Dependencies* pick list and select the *Manage Deliverables* item or you can press the **Shift + M** keyboard combination shortcut.

Notice in Figure 8 - 28 that the system informs me there are no deliverables for the active project.

4. Select a task to which you want to link a deliverable, in my example I select the *Develop Functional Specifications* task.

5. In the *Deliverables* sidepane click the *Add new deliverable* link.

Project Server 2013 does not allow linking of a *Deliverable* to the Project Summary Task (row 0 or task 0). If you attempt to link a *Deliverable* using the *Link to selected task* option you receive the following message as shown in Figure 8 - 29.

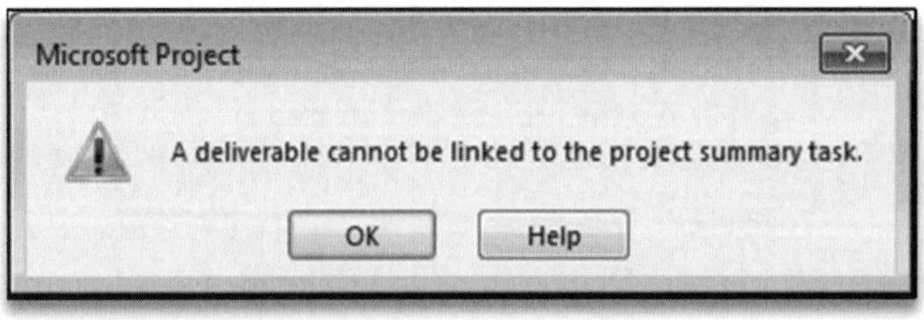
Microsoft Project
A deliverable cannot be linked to the project summary task.
OK
Help

Figure 8 - 29: Deliverable cannot be linked to Project Summary Task

> **Information**: If you attempt to link the Project Summary Task to a *Deliverable* using the *Link to selected task* option in Project Pro 2013, you receive the following message dialog: *A deliverable cannot be linked to the project summary task* as shown previously in Figure 8 - 29.

6. In the *Add Deliverable* sidepane, select the *Link to selected task* option. The system imports the task name into the *Title* field, imports the task's start date into the *Start* field, and imports the task's finish date into the *Finish* field in the *Deliverable Details* section of the *Add Deliverable* sidepane, as shown in Figure 8 - 30.

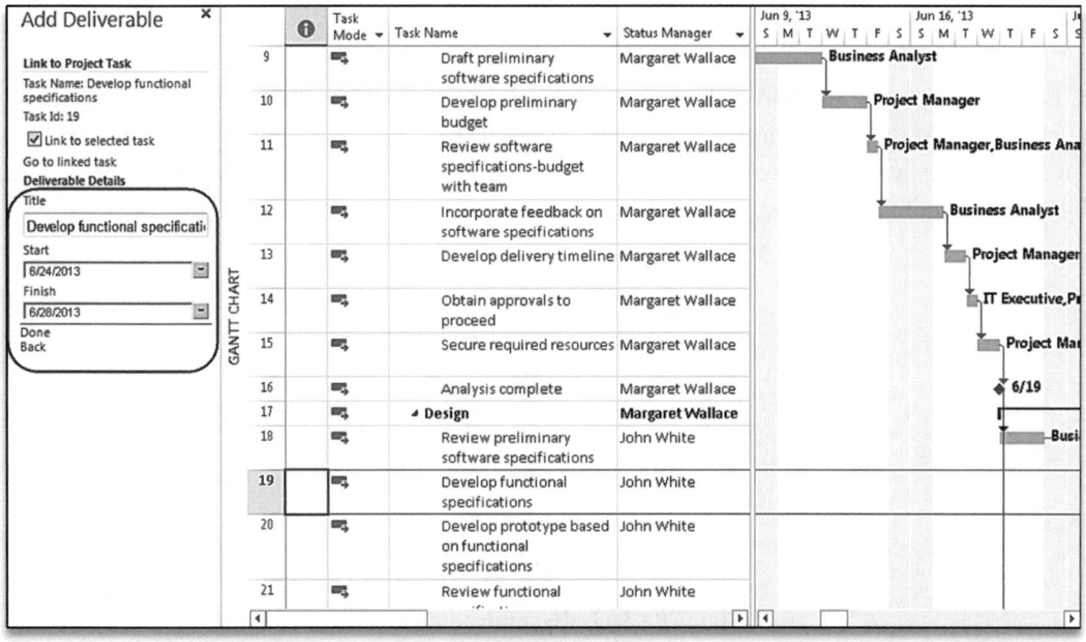

Figure 8 - 30: Deliverable information imported from a selected task

7. Edit the information in the *Title, Start,* and *Finish* fields of the *Add Deliverable* sidepane, as needed.

8. Below the *Finish* date field of the *Add Deliverable* sidepane, click the *Done* link. The system displays the new deliverable at the top of the *Deliverables* sidepane, as shown in Figure 8 - 31.

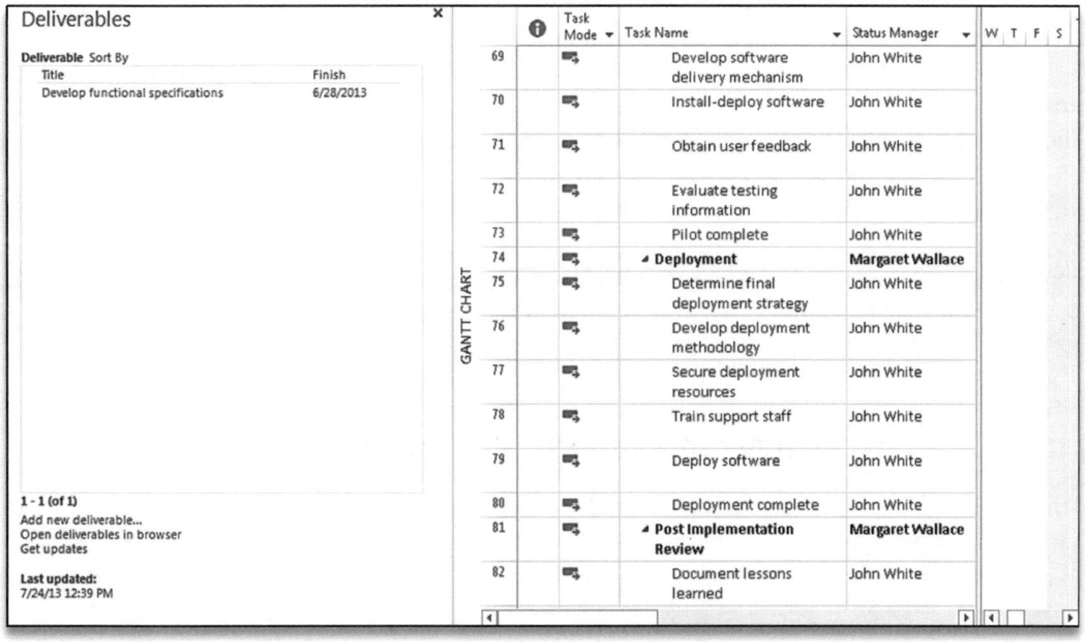

Figure 8 - 31: New Deliverable in the Deliverables sidepane

Information: To display the full name of the deliverable shown in the preceding figure, widen the *Deliverables* sidepane by clicking and holding the right edge of the sidepane to "grab" it, then moving the mouse pointer to the right, and releasing the mouse button.

By default, Project Pro 2013 sorts deliverables in ascending order by title in the *Deliverables* sidepane. To change the sorting, click the *Sort By* pick list in the upper left corner of the *Deliverables* sidepane and then select either the *Start Date* or *Finish Date* item on the pick list as shown in Figure 8 - 32. You may also change the sort order to descending by **deselecting** the *Ascending* item on the pick list.

Figure 8 - 32: Deliverables sidepane, default Sort By options

Warning: If you want to track variance on deliverable dates, **you must rebaseline your project** by clicking the *Set Baseline* pick list on the *Project* ribbon and selecting the *Set Baseline* item on the list. In the *Set Baseline* dialog, click the *OK* button to rebaseline the project. When prompted in a warning dialog, click the *Yes* button to update the baseline with the deliverable information. Project Server 2013 saves baseline information for each deliverable in the *Baseline Deliverable Start* and *Baseline Deliverable Finish* fields.

You may also create a new deliverable rapidly without using the *Deliverables* sidepane or changing the information in the *Title, Start,* or *Finish* fields. First, select the task you want to link to a deliverable, then in the *Insert* section of the *Task* ribbon, click the *Deliverables* pick list, and select the *Create Deliverables* item. The system creates the new deliverable for the selected task using the task name, start, and finish information from the task, without displaying the *Deliverables* sidepane.

Information: If you select the Project Summary Task (row 0 or task 0) for the task you want to add a deliverable, Project Pro 2013 grays out the *Create Deliverables* option. You cannot add a deliverable to the Project Summary Task.

Editing and Deleting Deliverables in Project Pro 2013

To edit a deliverable in Project Pro 2013, display the *Deliverables* sidepane and then float your mouse pointer over the name of the deliverable you want to edit. The system displays a tool tip to the right of the deliverable with information about the deliverable, and displays a pick list arrow button at the right side of the deliverable name, as shown in Figure 8 - 33.

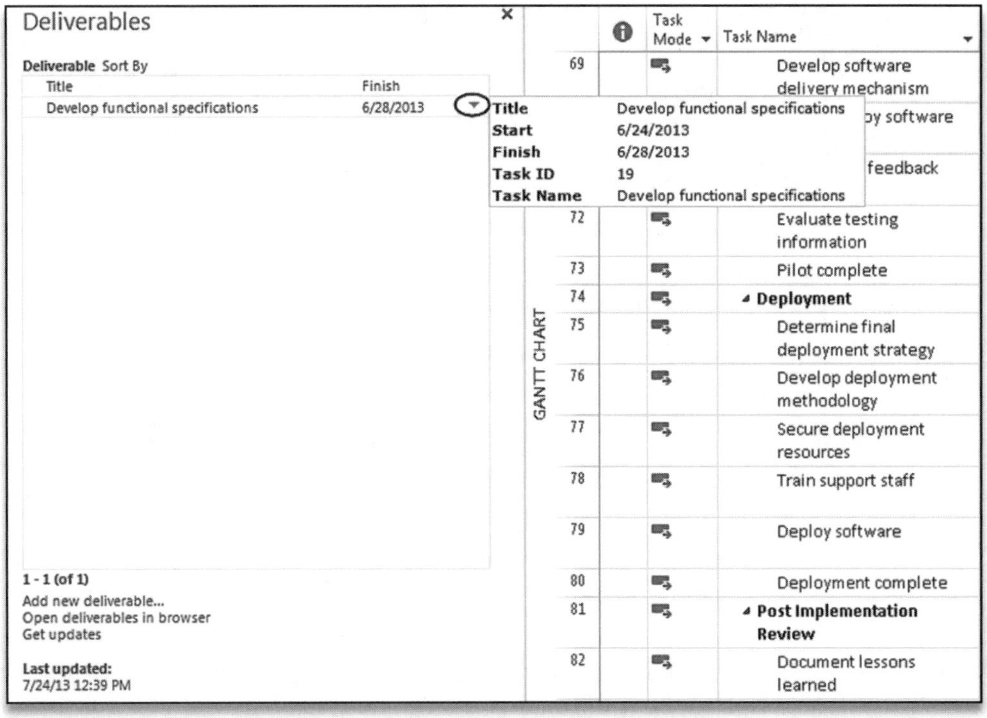

Figure 8 - 33: Prepare to edit a deliverable

Click anywhere on the deliverable name and the system displays a pick list menu of items, as shown in Figure 8 - 34. The items on the pick list allow the following:

- Edit the deliverable in Project Pro 2013
- Edit the deliverable in the Project Site using your Internet Explorer application
- Delete the deliverable
- Accept changes made to the deliverable on the Project Site

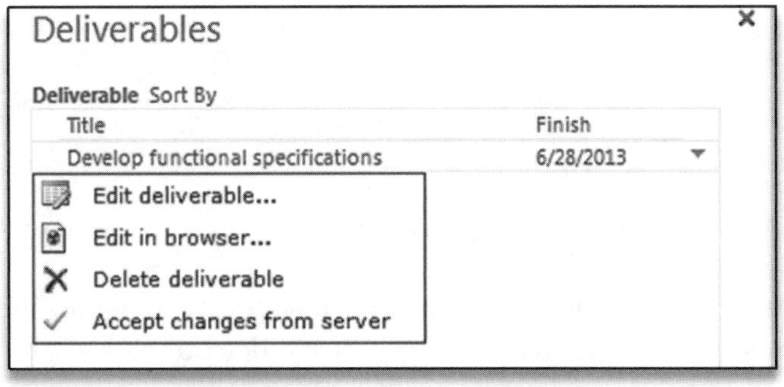

Figure 8 - 34: Deliverable edit menu

Select the *Edit deliverable* item on the pick list to edit the deliverable. The system displays the *Edit Deliverable* sidepane shown in Figure 8 - 35. In the *Edit Deliverable* sidepane, you have the option to link or unlink the deliverable with a specific task, or to edit the information in the *Title*, *Start*, and *Finish* fields. You may also click the *Go to linked task* link to select the task linked to the deliverable. When finished, click the *Done* link below the *View more properties* section of the sidepane.

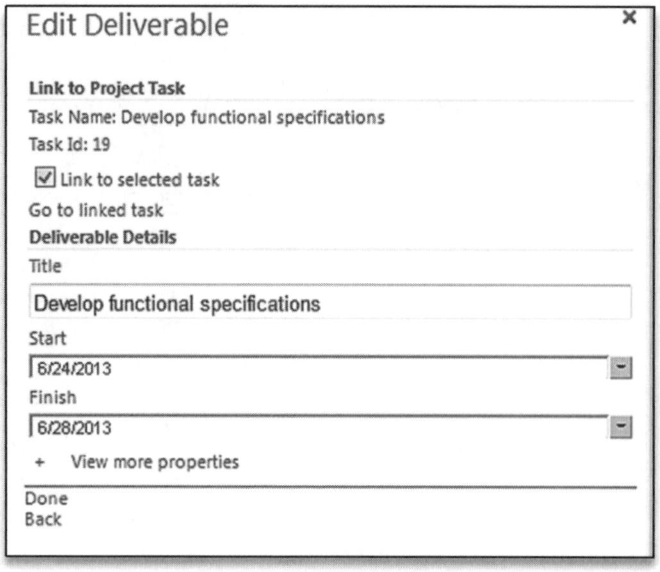

Figure 8 - 35: Edit Deliverable sidepane

To delete a deliverable, click anywhere on the deliverable name and, and then select the *Delete deliverable* item on the pick list menu. The system displays the confirmation dialog shown in Figure 8 - 36. Click the *OK* button to complete the deletion process.

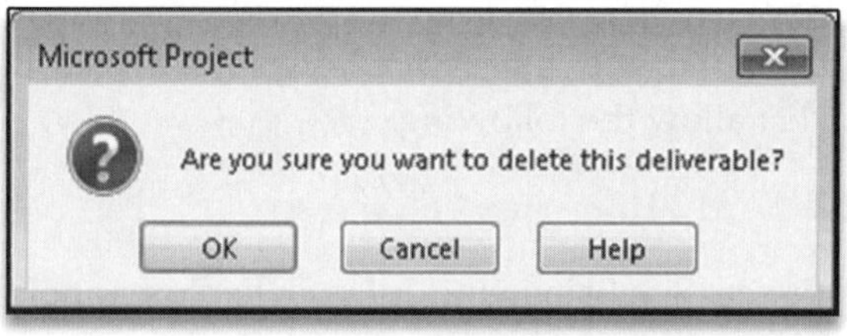

Figure 8 - 36: Delete deliverable confirmation dialog

Information: When you delete a deliverable in Project Pro 2013, the system moves the deliverable to the Recycle Bin on the Project Site for your enterprise project. The deliverable remains in the Recycle Bin for 30 days, after which the system deletes the deliverable permanently. At any time during the 30 days, you may navigate to the Recycle Bin on the Project Site and restore the deliverable.

Managing Deliverables in Project Web App

In addition to using the Project Pro 2013 client, you can also manage deliverables in Project Web App using the Project Site of the selected project. To view, create, edit, or delete deliverables in Project Web App, complete the following steps:

1. In the *Deliverables* sidepane in Project Pro 2013, click the *Open deliverables in browser* link at the bottom of the sidepane. The system launches a new Internet Explorer application window and displays the *Deliverables* page on the Project Site, as shown in Figure 8 - 37.

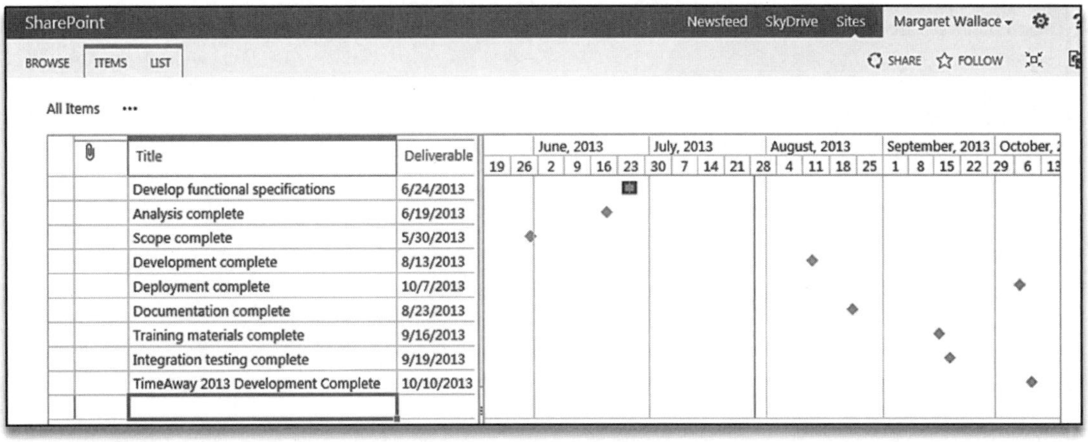

Figure 8 - 37: Deliverables page in the Project Site for Develop TimeAway 2013 project

Notice that the *Deliverables* page shown previously in Figure 8 - 37 shows the nine deliverables created so far for the selected project. The system represents each deliverable using either a milestone symbol or a Gantt bar in the *Gantt Chart* portion of the *Deliverables* page. The system uses a Gantt bar, when the *Deliverable Finish* date is later than the *Deliverable Start* date, such as when a deliverable has an "acceptable" date range for delivery of the product.

2. Widen the *Title, Deliverable Start,* or *Deliverable Finish* columns, as needed, and drag the split bar to the desired location on the page.

3. Click the *List* tab to display the *List* ribbon.

4. In the *Gantt View* section of the *List* ribbon, click the *Zoom Out* button until you see all of the deliverables for the project.

Information: The *Deliverables* page shown previously in Figure 8 - 37 reflects the changes I made to the page following steps #2-4 above.

Adding a New Deliverable in Project Web App

To create a new deliverable in Project Web App, navigate to the *Deliverables* page for your selected project, shown previously in Figure 8 - 37 then complete the following steps:

1. Click the *Items* tab to display the *Items* ribbon.

2. In the *New* section of the *Items* ribbon, click the *New Item* button. The system displays the *Deliverables - New Item* dialog shown in Figure 8 - 38.

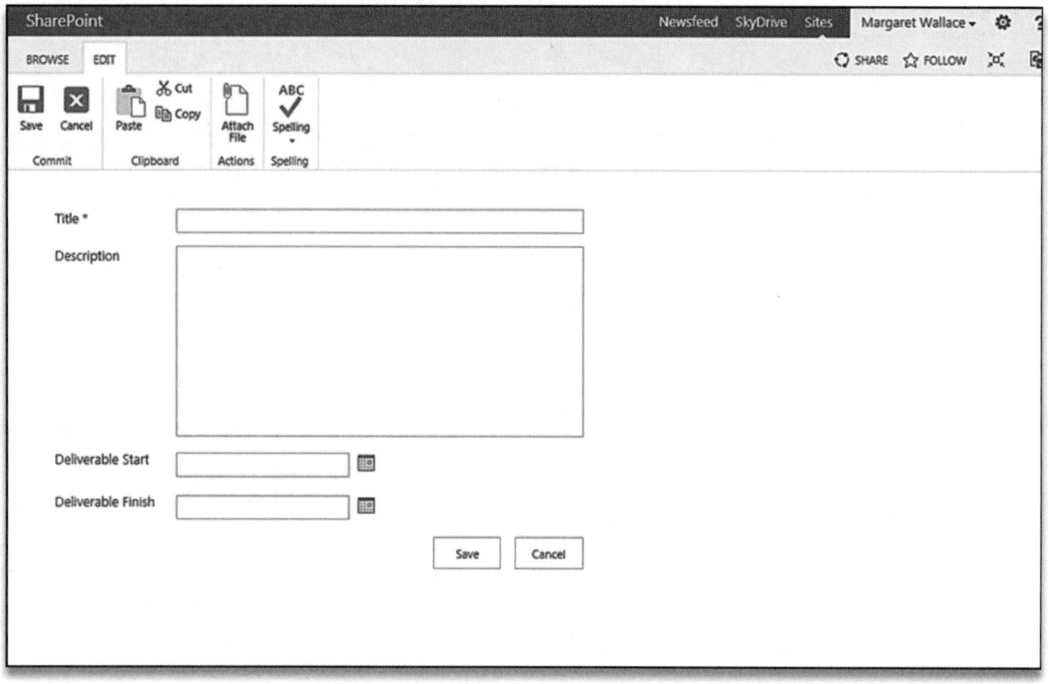

Figure 8 - 38: Deliverables - New Item dialog

3. Enter information in the *Title, Description, Deliverable Start,* and *Deliverable Finish* fields for the deliverable.
4. To attach a file to the deliverable, in the *Actions* section of the *Edit* ribbon, click the *Attach File* button. Project Server 2013 displays the *Deliverables: New Item* page with the *Name* field. Click the *Browse* button to locate an existing file to upload as an attachment, as shown in Figure 8 - 39.

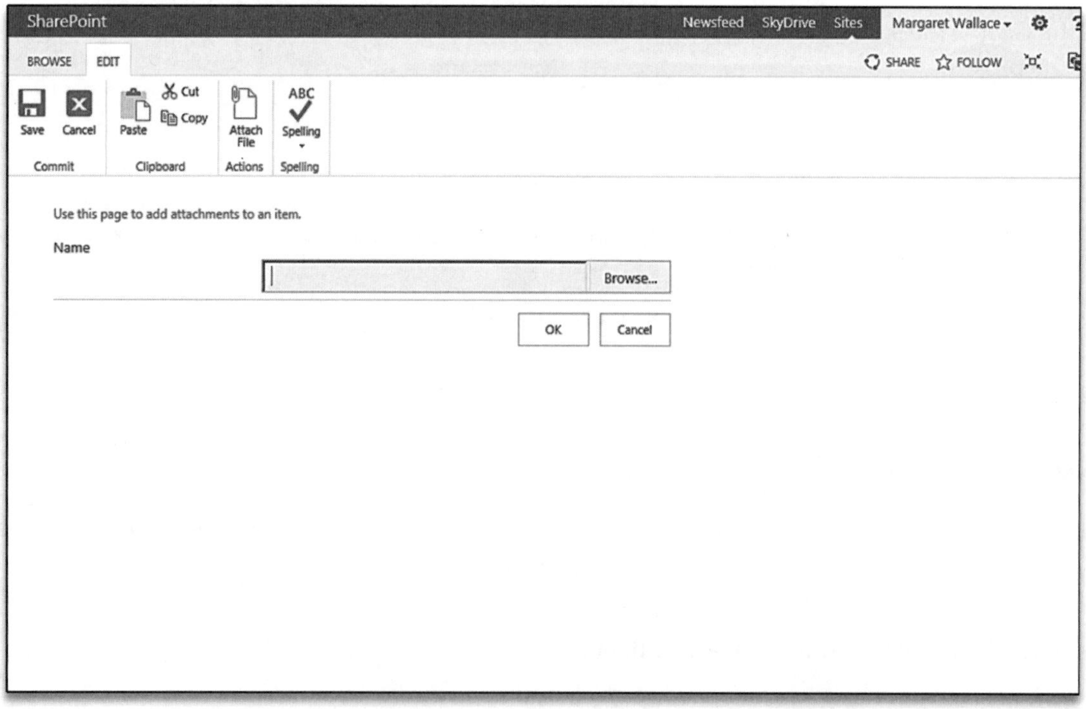

Figure 8 - 39: Attach a file in the Deliverables - New Item page

5. Navigate to the appropriate folder in the *Choose File to Upload* dialog, as shown in Figure 8 - 40, and then select a document and click the *Open* button.

Figure 8 - 40: Choose File to Upload dialog

6. When the system redisplays the *Deliverables: New Item* page for the document, click the *OK* button.

Notice the system redisplays the *Deliverables - New Item* page as shown in Figure 8 - 41 with the file path for the document you uploaded displayed in the *Attachments* section.

> **Information**: If you need to delete the attachment, click the *Delete* link to the right of the file name in the *Attachments* section at the bottom of the *Deliverables - New Item* page. You also have the option to upload more than one attachment for a deliverable, by using the *Attach File* button and selecting an additional file to upload.

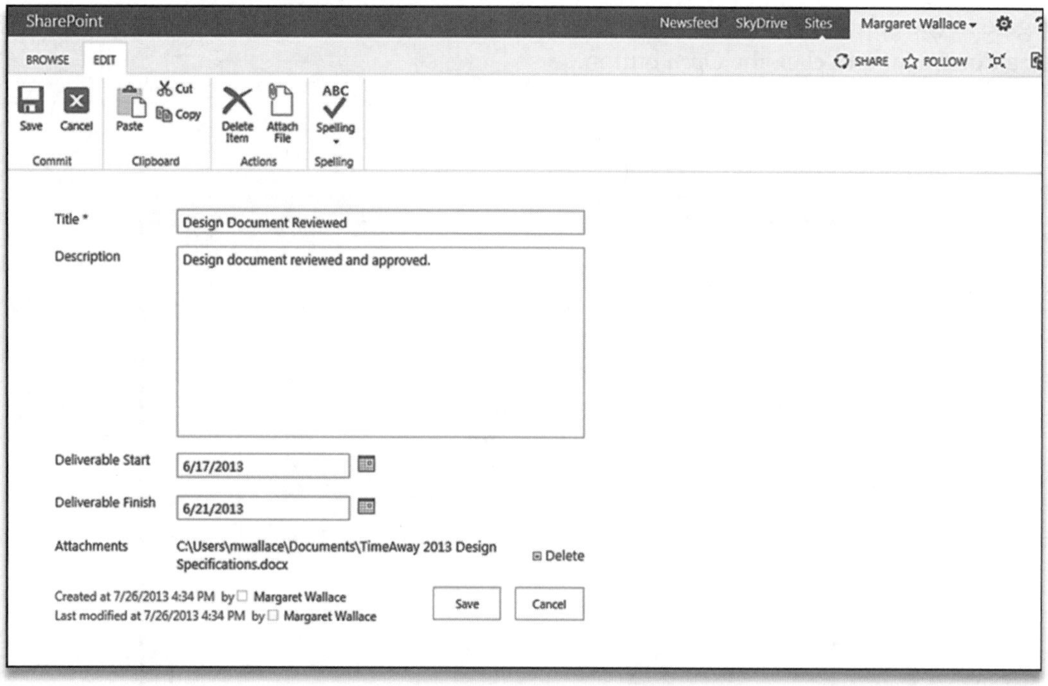

Figure 8 - 41: Deliverables - New Item page with the new Deliverable attached

7. In the *Commit* section of the *Edit* ribbon, click the *Save* button to save the new deliverable. Figure 8 - 42 shows the new deliverable on the *Deliverables* page of the Project Site for the selected project.

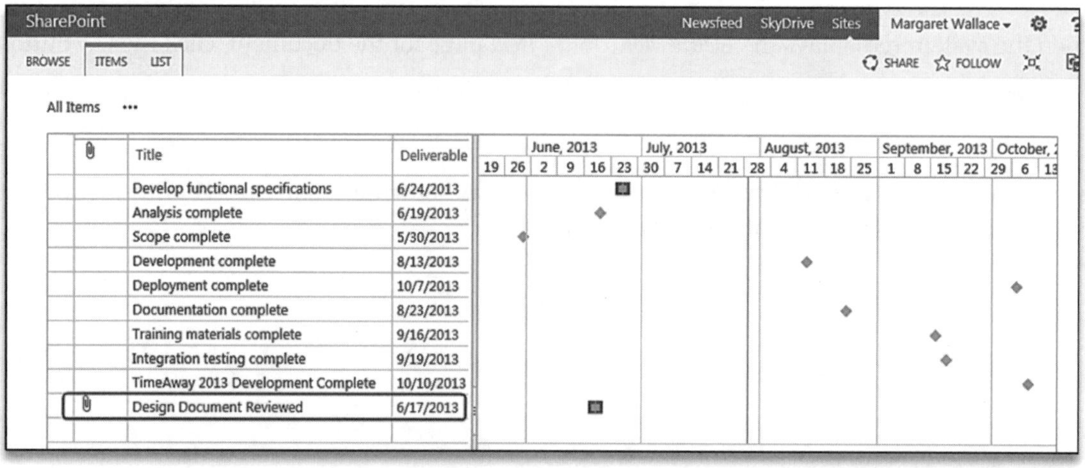

Figure 8 - 42: Deliverables page, new Deliverable with attachment

Warning: When you create a new deliverable from the Project Site using Internet Explorer, Project Server 2013 **does not** allow you to link the deliverable to a task in the project. Because of this limitation, you may want to create all deliverables in your enterprise projects using Project Pro 2013 instead.

Viewing Deliverable Information in Project Web App

Notice in Figure 8 - 42 shown previously, the system displays a paperclip icon to the left of the deliverable name, indicating that the deliverable has at least one file attachment. To view the information about any deliverable, select a deliverable, click the *Items* tab, and in the *Manage* section of the *Items* ribbon, click the *View Item* button. The system displays the deliverable information as shown in Figure 8 - 43 with the following options:

- *Edit Item* to edit the selected item
- *Shared With* to see everyone that has access to the list item
- *Delete Item* to delete the selected item
- *Alert Me* to receive email or mobile notifications when things change
- *Workflows* to start a workflow or view the status of a currently running workflow

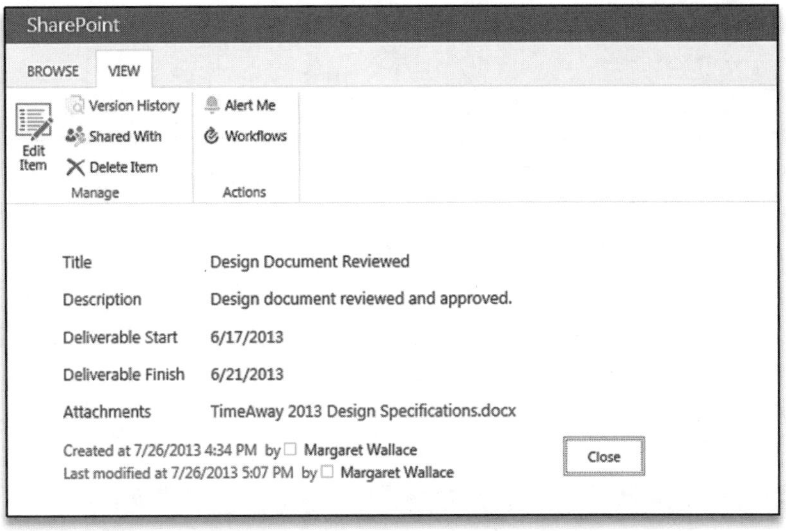

Figure 8 - 43: Deliverables page, View Item option selected

In the *Actions* section of the *View* ribbon on the *Deliverable – Design Document Reviewed* page shown previously in Figure 8 - 43, notice the *Alert Me* button. Click this button to set up e-mail alerts about changes made to the deliverable. Notice also that the *Attachments* section of the page shows the document I attached to this deliverable previously, as shown in Figure 8 - 38 through Figure 8 - 42. You may click the document name link to open the document in the application used to create it and in this case, the document opens in Microsoft Word.

In addition to the *View Item* options shown previously in Figure 8 - 43, notice the options available in the *Items* ribbon on the *Deliverables All Items* page shown in Figure 8 - 44. The options include:

- *New Item* to add a new deliverable to the current list
- *New Folder* to create a folder in the current list (if option is disabled you need special permissions)

- *Create Projects* to create a new Project Web App project based on the content of the list item. You can map column values to Project Web App custom fields.
- *View Item* to view the information for existing deliverable
- *Edit Item* to edit the information for existing deliverable
- *Delete Item* to delete an existing deliverable

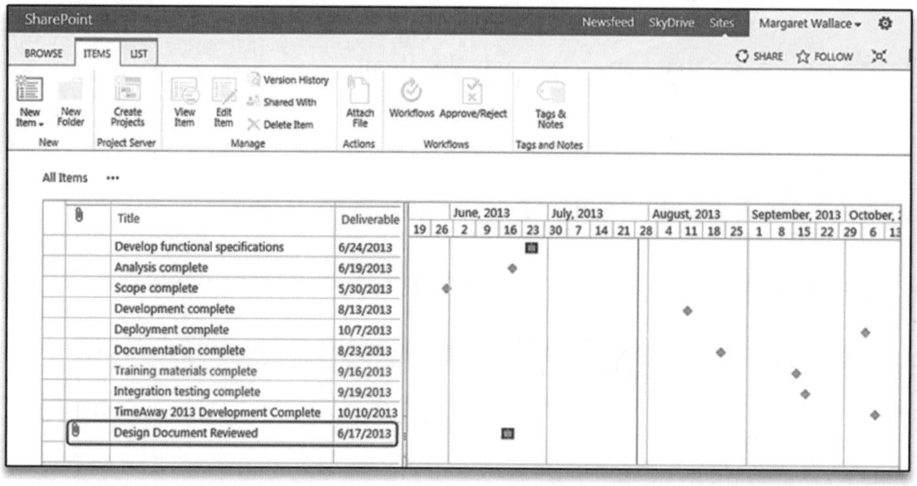

Figure 8 - 44: Deliverables All Items page, Items ribbon options

Editing and Deleting a Deliverable in Project Web App

To edit the selected deliverable, click the *Edit Item* button shown previously in Figure 8 - 44. The system opens the *Deliverables – Design Document Reviewed* page in *Edit* mode as shown in Figure 8 - 45. Edit the information in the *Title, Description, Deliverable Start*, and *Deliverable Finish* fields, as needed. On the *Edit* ribbon, click the *Attach File* button to attach an additional file to the deliverable, if needed. When you finish editing the deliverable, click the *Save* button in the *Edit* ribbon to save the changes.

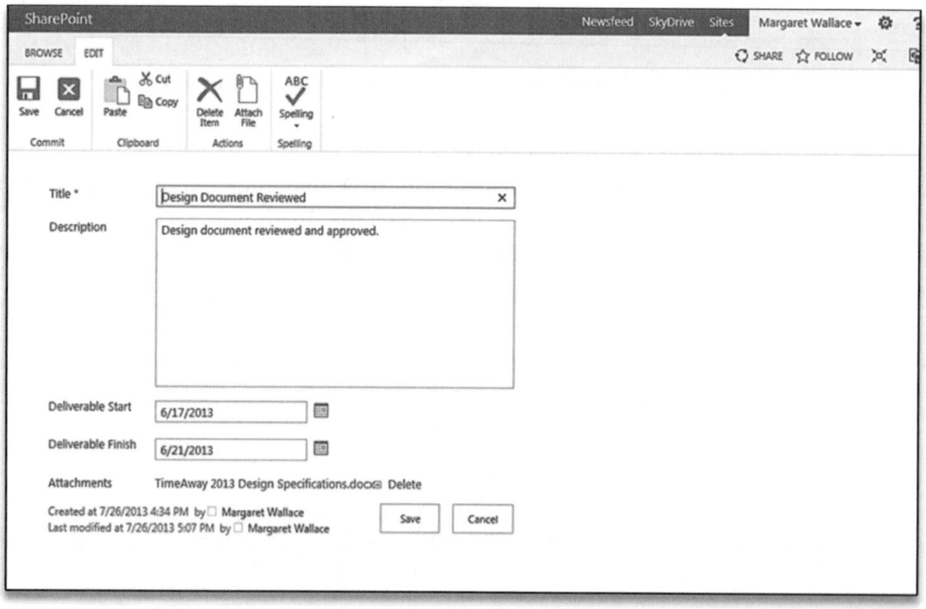

Figure 8 - 45: Deliverables Edit page, showing the Edit ribbon

To delete the selected deliverable, in the *Actions* section of the *Edit* ribbon, click the *Delete Item* button shown previously in Figure 8 - 45. The system displays the confirmation dialog shown in Figure 8 - 46. Click the *OK* button to complete the deletion and send the item to the Recycle Bin. In Project Web App when you delete a deliverable, the system moves the deliverable to the Recycle Bin for the Project Site, where it remains for 30 days. You can navigate to the Recycle Bin at any time during the 30 days after the deletion to restore the item to the *Deliverables* list for the project.

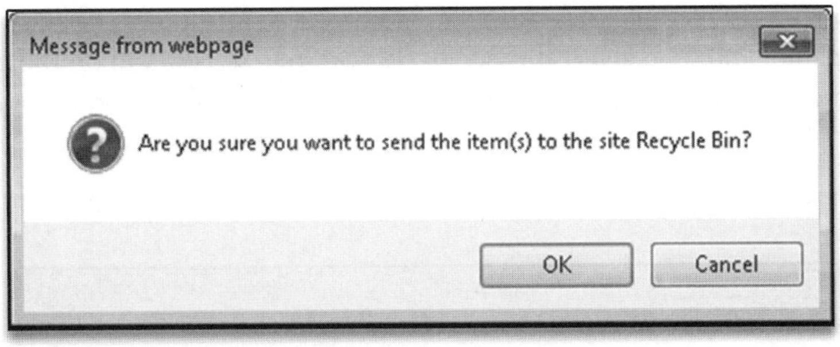

Figure 8 - 46: Confirmation dialog to delete a deliverable in Project Web App

Updating Deliverables in Project Pro 2013

If you create a new deliverable or edit an existing deliverable in Project Web App, and then reopen the enterprise project for these deliverables, Project Server 2013 **does not** automatically update the deliverable information in the project. Instead, Project Pro 2013 displays a red exclamation point icon to the left of the name of the new or changed deliverable in the *Deliverables* sidepane, as shown in Figure 8 - 47.

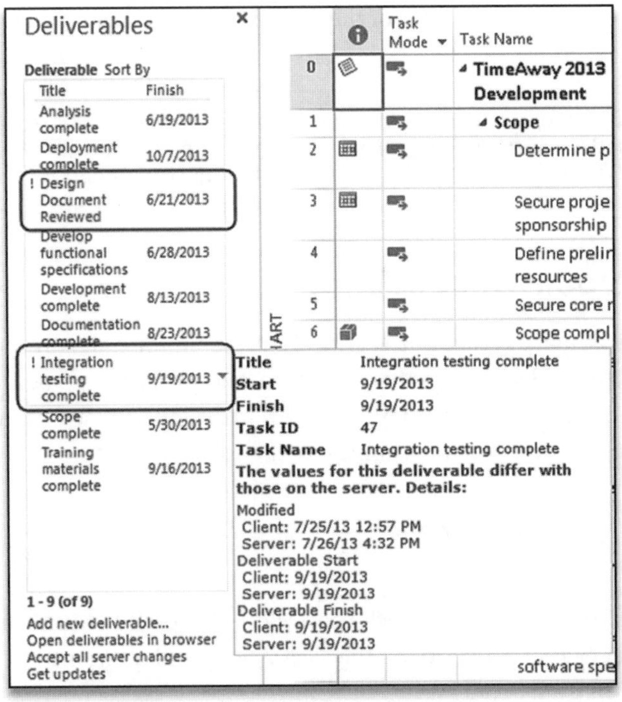

Figure 8 - 47: Deliverables sidepane displays new or changed deliverables

Notice in Figure 8 - 47 that the *Deliverables* sidepane shows two deliverables with a red exclamation point to the left of the deliverable name. To learn more about any new or changed deliverable, float your mouse pointer over the name of the deliverable. Notice in Figure 8 - 47 shown previously, that the system displays a tooltip for the *Integration testing complete* deliverable that indicates that the project is "out of sync" with the information in Project Web App.

To "sync" any new or changed deliverable individually, float your mouse pointer over the deliverable, click anywhere on the deliverable name, and then select the *Accept changes from server* item on the pick list menu. To "sync" all new and changed deliverables between the enterprise project and Project Web App, click the *Accept all server changes* link at the bottom of the *Deliverables* sidepane. Project Server 2013 displays the confirmation dialog shown in Figure 8 - 48.

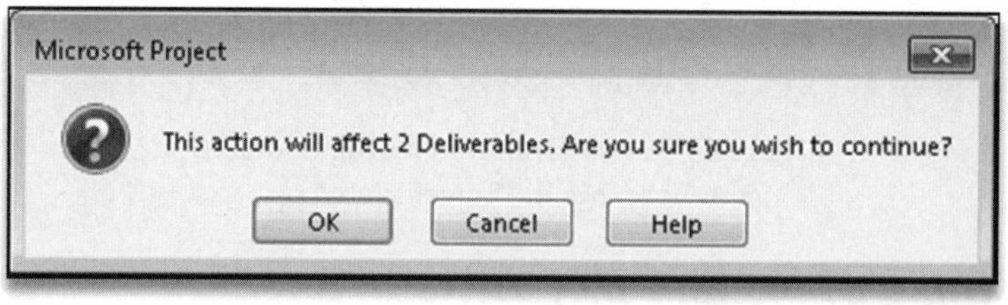
Microsoft Project
This action will affect 2 Deliverables. Are you sure you wish to continue?
OK
Cancel
Help

Figure 8 - 48: Confirmation dialog to "sync" Deliverables

The confirmation dialog tells you how many deliverables are "out of sync" and asks you to confirm the update. Click the *OK* button to update all deliverables. After you finish managing deliverables for your enterprise project, click the *Close* button (**X**) in the upper right corner of the *Deliverables* sidepane.

Information: To make sure you can see the current state of every deliverable, you may want to click the *Get updates* link at the bottom of the *Deliverables* sidepane before you click the *Accept all server changes* link. This guarantees that you see and accept all changes made in Project Web App.

Adding a New Deliverable Dependency

In the world of enterprise project management, it is entirely possible for dates in one project to be dependent on dates in one or more other projects. Because of this, a task in one project may be dependent on a deliverable in another project. To address this situation, you may specify a task dependency on an external deliverable in another project. To create a deliverable dependency, complete the following steps:

1. Click the *Task* tab to display the *Task* ribbon.

2. In the *Insert* section of the *Task* ribbon, click the *Deliverable* pick list and select the *Manage Dependencies* item on the list. Project Server 2013 opens the *Dependency* sidepane in the Project Pro 2013 application window shown in Figure 8 - 49.

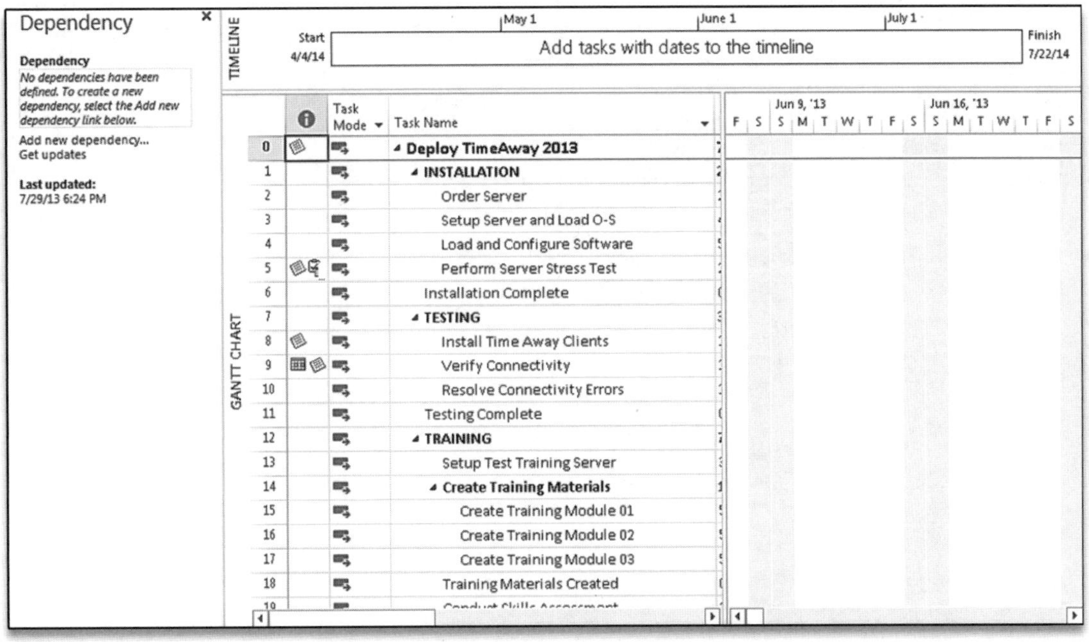

Figure 8 - 49: Dependency sidepane for an enterprise project

Figure 8 - 49 shows the *Dependency* sidepane for the Develop TimeAway 2013 project. The first task in this project, *Order Server*, is dependent on the final deliverable in the Develop TimeAway 2013 project, since we cannot deploy the software until the developers actually create it. Notice in Figure 8 - 49 that the system informs me I have not yet created any deliverable dependencies for the active project.

3. In the *Dependency* sidepane, click the *Add new dependency* link. The system displays the *Add Dependency* sidepane.

4. In the *Add Dependency* sidepane, click the *Select project* pick list and select a project on which the active project is dependent, as shown in Figure 8 - 50.

> **Information**: The *Select project* pick list shows all of the enterprise projects which you have permission to access, and which contain at least one deliverable.

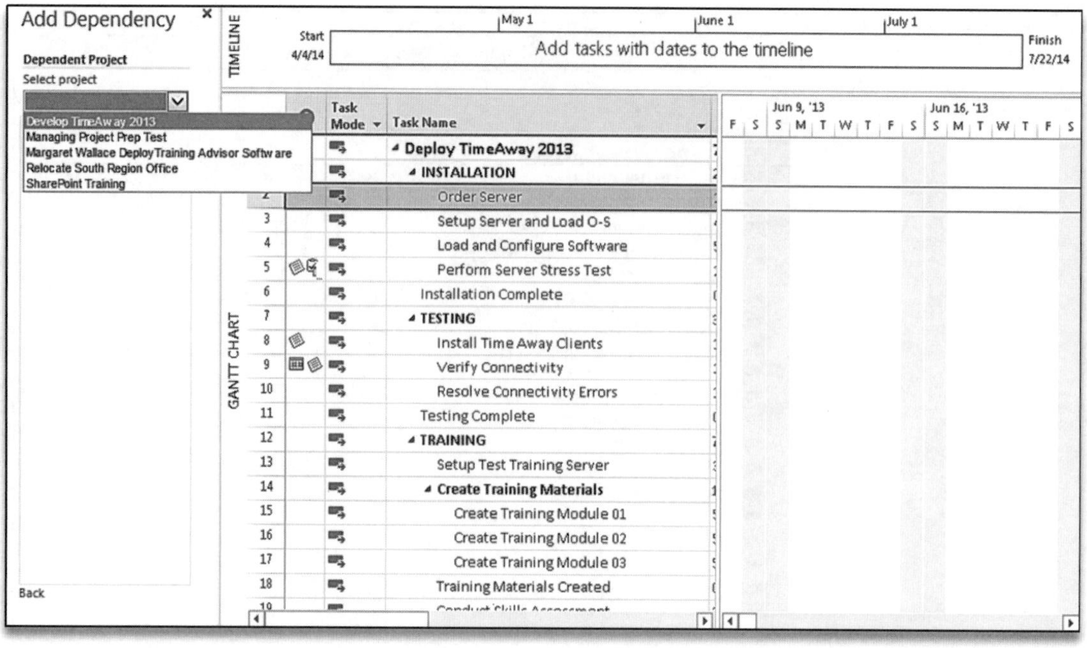

Figure 8 - 50: Select an enterprise project in the Select project pick list

Figure 8 - 51 shows the *Add Dependency* sidepane after I selected the Develop TimeAway 2013 project. Notice that the sidepane displays all of the deliverables in that enterprise project.

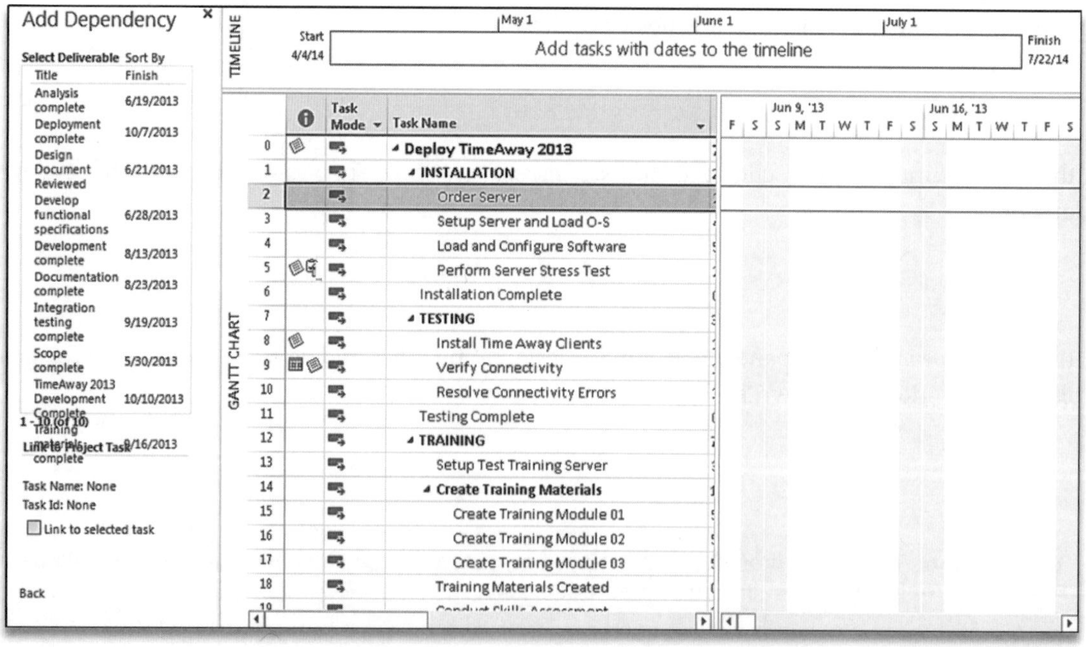

Figure 8 - 51: Add Dependency sidepane shows dependencies in the Develop TimeAway 2010 project

Warning: As of this writing, after you select the enterprise project in the *Add Dependency* sidepane as shown previously in Figure 8 - 51, notice the overlapping text in the *Select Deliverable* list. The default text in the sidepane overlaps the *Select Deliverable* list making it difficult to read the last deliverable in the list. As a work around, you may avoid the text overlap by increasing the width of the side pane. To widen the side pane, click and drag the right edge of the *Deliverables* sidepane toward the right until you see the deliverable *Title* and *Finish* date in a single row rather than the wrap text view.

5. Select a task in your enterprise project and then in the *Add Dependency* sidepane, click the *Link to selected task* option.

6. In the *Select Deliverable* list in the *Add Dependency* sidepane, select an external deliverable. In my example, I select the *Time Away 2013 Development Complete* deliverable as the dependency since the development needs to be complete prior to the *Order Server* task starting.

7. Click the *Done* link when finished. The system displays the external deliverable dependency in the *Dependency* sidepane as shown in Figure 8 - 52.

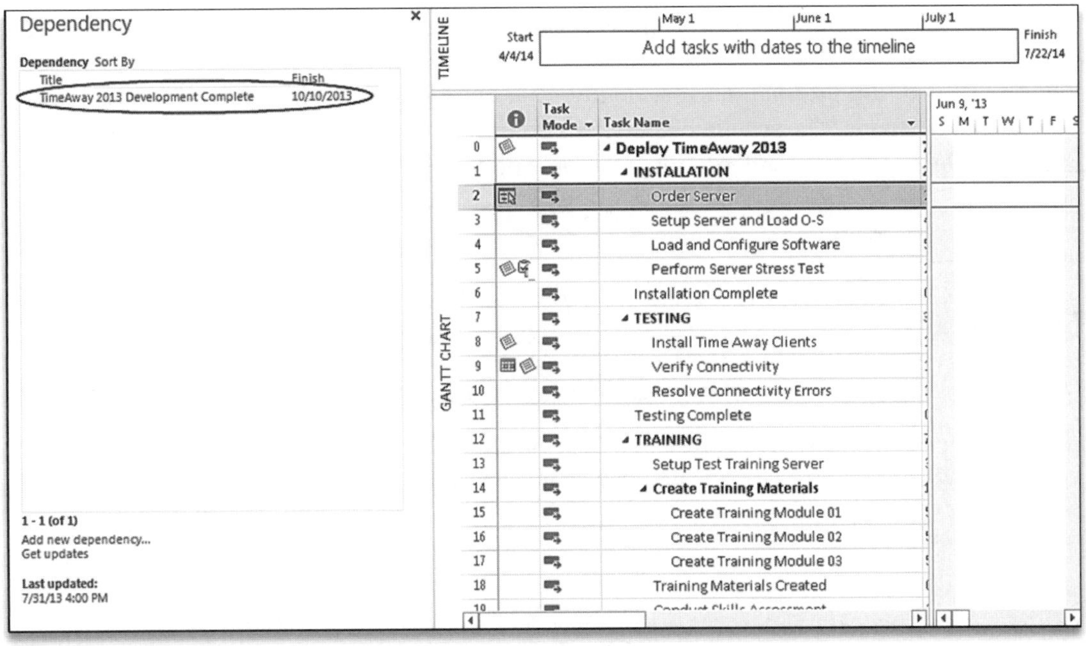

Figure 8 - 52: New deliverable dependency added in Dependency sidepane

8. Save and publish your enterprise project.

If the *Deliverable Start* date or *Deliverable Finish* date changes for the external deliverable, the system warns you with a red exclamation point to the left of the external deliverable in the *Dependency* sidepane. To view the changes to the external deliverable, float your mouse pointer over the external deliverable. The system displays a tooltip that provides information about the changes to the external deliverable, as shown in Figure 8 - 53. Notice that the tooltip indicates that both the *Deliverable Start* date and the *Deliverable Finish* date changed for the external deliverable.

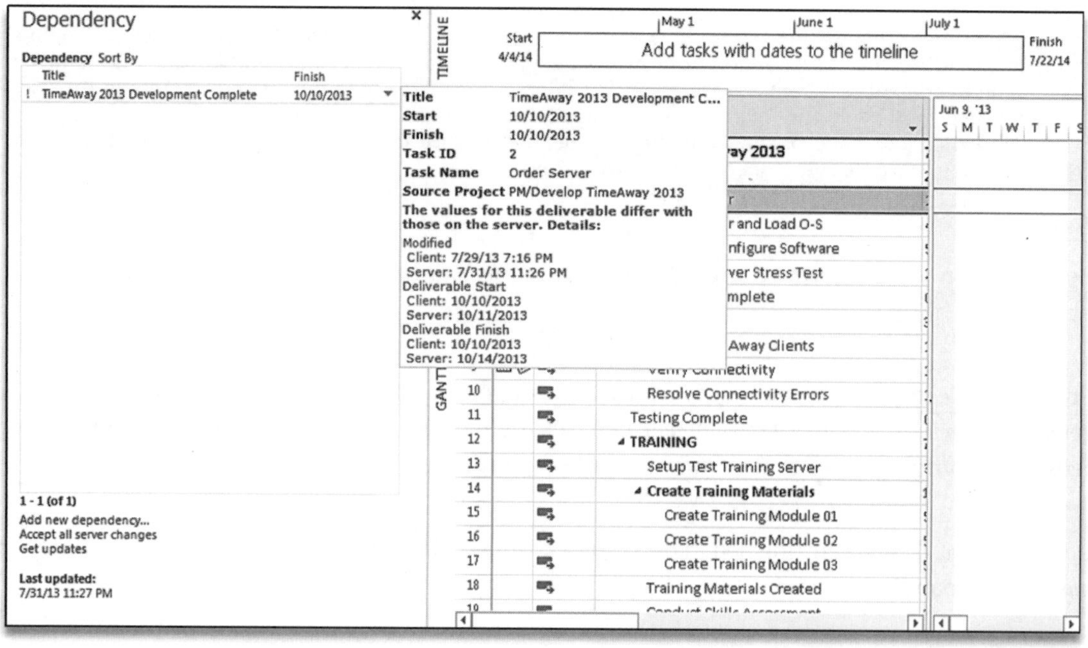

Figure 8 - 53: Schedule changes for an external deliverable

To update the project with the external deliverable information, click the *Accept all server changes* link at the bottom of the *Dependency* sidepane. The system displays the confirmation dialog shown in Figure 8 - 54. Click the *OK* button to update the deliverable dependency information, and then save and publish your enterprise project.

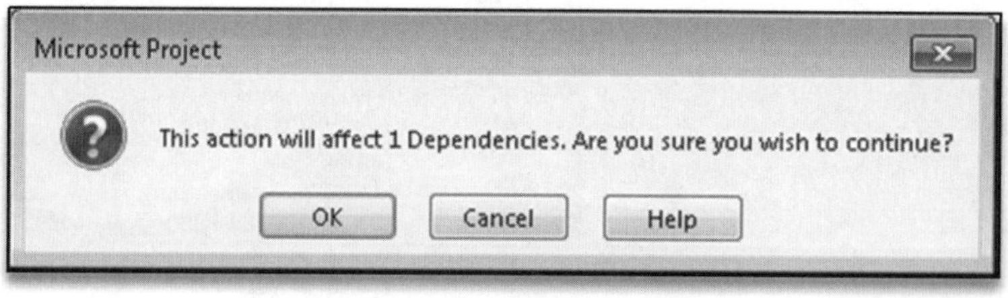

Figure 8 - 54: Confirmation dialog to update a deliverable dependency

Module 09

Tracking Time and Task Progress

Learning Objectives

After completing this module, you will be able to:

- Create a new timesheet
- Report time on the My Timesheet page
- Plan and submit administrative time
- Create a surrogate timesheet for another resource
- Report progress on the Tasks page
- Use the Task Center

Inside Module 09

Tracking Time in Project Web App

Project Server 2013 allows you to track both time and task progress using the Project Web App interface. Your organization can use a daily timesheet to track hours on all types of work, including both project and non-project work. Using the timesheet system, you can also track non-working time such as vacation or sick leave. The timesheet system in Project Server 2013 allows your organization to account for every hour of work every day for all of your resources.

Your organization can also track task progress in enterprise projects using the default method of tracking progress defined by your Project Server administrator. Table 9 - 1 outlines the potential uses of timesheets and tasks status tracking.

Function	Single Entry Mode	Double Entry Mode	Timesheet Stand Alone Mode	Tasks Stand Alone Mode
Timesheets	Timesheets track: • Billable hours • Non-billable hours • Administrative time • Project task progress Automatic data exchange with tasks	Timesheets track • Billable hours • Non-billable hours • Administrative time • Project task progress User initiated data exchange with tasks	Timesheets track • Administrative time No data exchange with tasks	Not used
Tasks	Work routing using Team tasks, Reassign task Management of Material resources	Tasks track of project task progress. User initiated data exchange with timesheets	Not used	Tasks track project task progress No data exchange with timesheets

Table 9 - 1: The Different Uses of Timesheets and Task Status Tracking

Single Entry Mode

Single Entry mode enables you to enter your time once and eliminates the duplicate effort of entering time and task progress separately. Organizations where tracking of project tasks and administrative time is important typically use the *Single Entry* mode as shown in Figure 9 - 1.

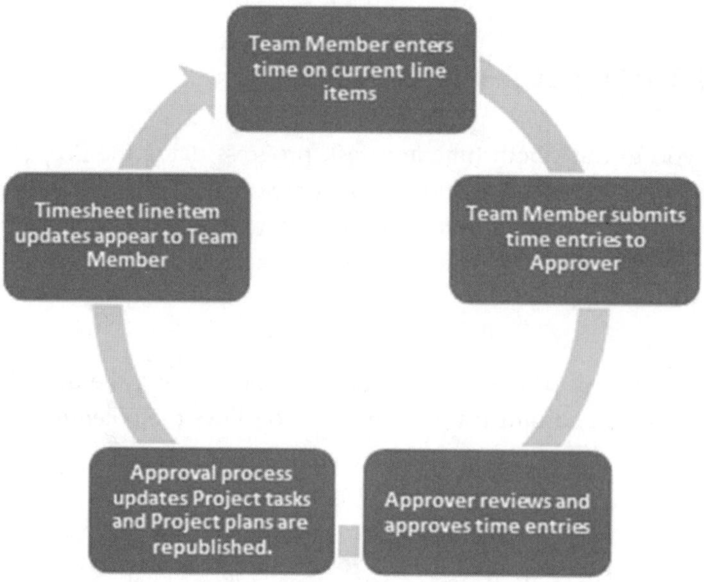
Team Member enters time on current line items
Team Member submits time entries to Approver
Approver reviews and approves time entries
Approval process updates Project tasks and Project plans are republished.
Timesheet line item updates appear to Team Member

Figure 9 - 1: Single Entry Mode Time Tracking Process Steps

Double Entry Mode

Double Entry mode enables you to separate task updates from timesheet entries. This capability is desirable in situations where customer billing uses timesheet data and task updates to keep the project plan up to date. For example, if you have a fixed bid contract, your billing must match a given number regardless of the actual number of hours invested in the project.

Standalone Modes

Standalone modes indicate that you are using either timesheets or tasks, but not using them together. Environments that have no billing need will likely not need timesheet capabilities. Environments that are only tracking time will not need task status capabilities.

The time tracking process is typically a repetitive process that happens on a regular schedule. Many organizations have weekly time tracking reporting periods. The needs of your organization determine your time tracking reporting period length.

Timesheet Items

Timesheets help organizations determine where it is investing its efforts and whether there is sufficient capacity to maintain those efforts. Timesheets capture three types of data to fulfill this information need.

Project Tasks

This timesheet item represents your planned activities for a given time period to support the outcomes of the associated project.

Administrative Time Categories

This timesheet item represents a capture mechanism to reflect the number of hours you spend on non-project work. The default Project Server configuration includes categories for *Administrative, Sick Time* and *Vacation*. Your Project Server administrator may add additional categories to meet your organization's specific needs.

Personal Tasks

Sometimes, your work does not fit in your project tasks or your administrative time categories. In this case, Project Server provides the ability to add personal tasks to your timesheet to capture this time.

> **Information**: Personal Tasks is an optional setting in PWA in *Server Settings ➢ Timesheet Settings and Defaults* located in the *Timesheet Policies* section. Your Project Server administrator may turn off this option to meet the needs of your organization and not allow users to enter personal tasks.

Accessing Your Timesheet

To navigate to your timesheet, use either of the following methods:

- In the *Quick Launch* menu, click the *Timesheet* link
- In the *Time and Task Management* section, click *Server Settings ➢ Manage Timesheets*

To navigate to your current period timesheet, in the *Quick Launch* menu, click the *Timesheet* link as shown in Figure 9 - 2 to display the *Timesheet* page. To see more of the content on the *Timesheet* page while hiding the *Quick Launch* menu, click the *Focus on Content* button in the upper right-hand corner of the page.

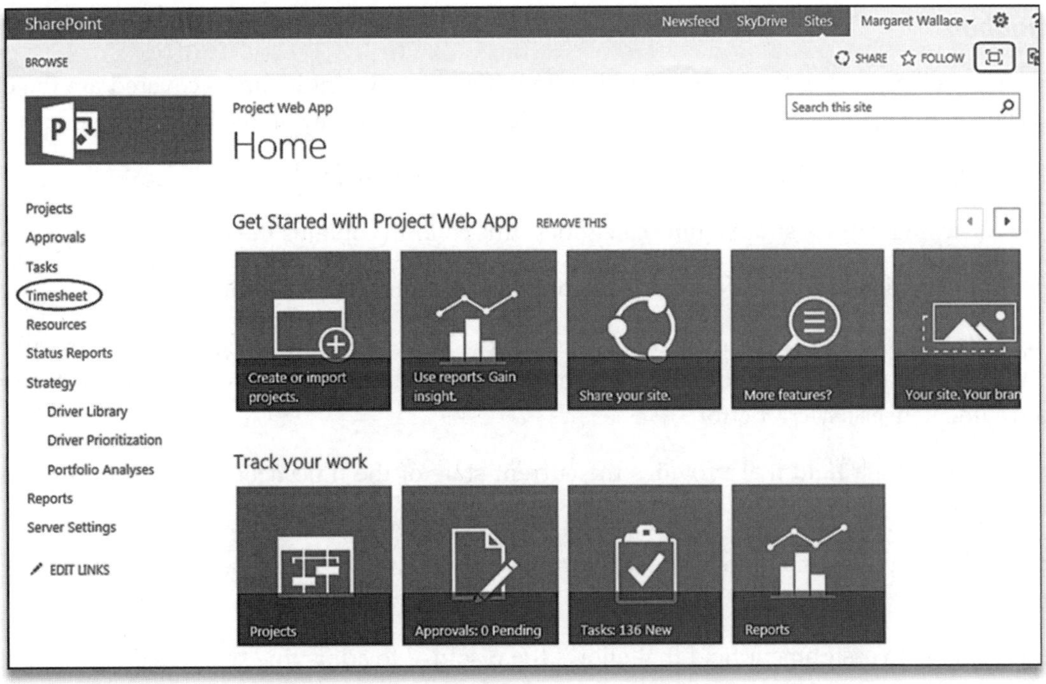

Figure 9 - 2: Project Web App Home Page
Timesheet link in Quick Launch and the Focus on Content button

Understanding the Timesheet Page

The *Timesheet* page enables you to capture your time spent on all planned and administrative activities for the current time reporting period. When you first click the *Timesheet* link, Project Server automatically creates your timesheet for the current time reporting period as shown in Figure 9 - 3.

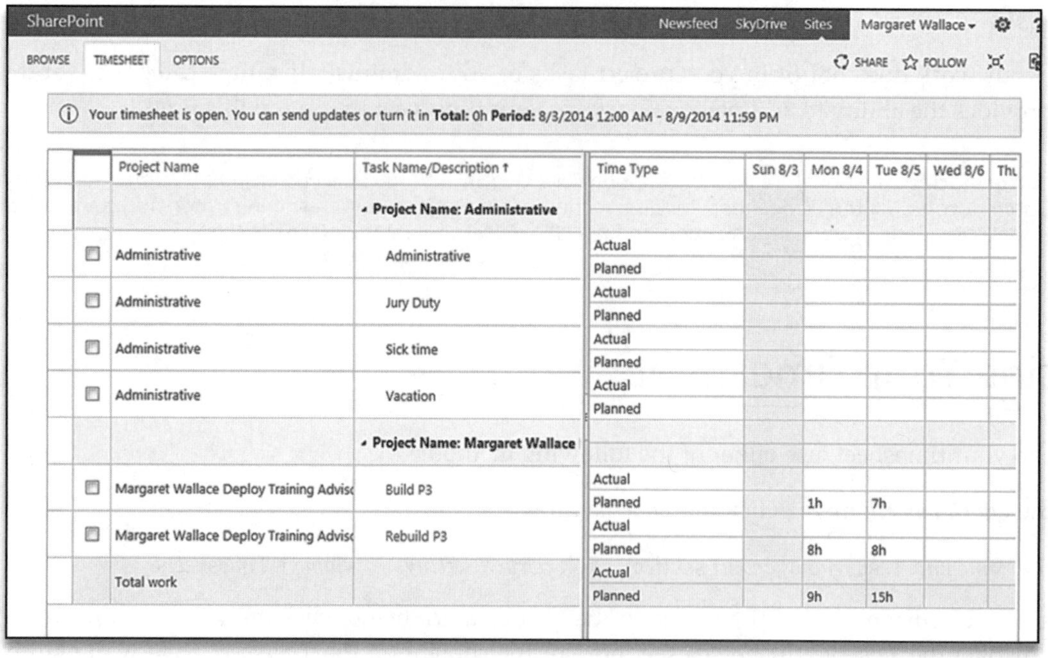

Figure 9 - 3: Project Server 2013 timesheet

Timesheet Ribbon

This module covers all aspects of the *Timesheet* ribbon functionality. The initial items covered are the display control options. The default display of the *Timesheet* page includes these columns in the *My Work* view:

- *Task Name/Description* - Descriptive name of the timesheet line item.
- *Project Name* - For administrative time categories, this column contains the term *Administrative.*
- *Comment* - Data field for you to add a comment related to this timesheet line item entry
- *Billing Category* - This optional field enables you to designate a billing category for a particular timesheet line item. For example, if the administrator set up a *Merger* billing category, you can set this value to designate a line item as a *Merger* effort.
- *Process Status* - Data field that provides the current state of the timesheet line item in regards to the approval cycle.
- *Start* – This is an assignment field that allows the resource to adjust the scheduled *Start* date for the assignment.
- *Finish* – This is an assignment field that allows the resource to adjust the scheduled *Finish* date for the assignment.
- *Remaining Work* – This is an assignment field that allows the resource to adjust the *Remaining Work* value for the assignment.
- *% Work Complete* – This is an assignment field that indicates the calculated value for *% Work Complete* for the assignment.
- *Work* – This is a *Read-Only* assignment field and displays the scheduled *Work* value for the task.

- *Actual Work* – This is an assignment field that indicates the calculated value for actual time the resource has worked on the assignment.

- *Duration* – This is a task field that allows the resource to adjust the duration for the task.

To the right of the *Duration* column, you also see a timesheet grid containing one week of daily cells for reporting your work.

> **Information**: The default settings in Project Server 2013 configure the *My Timesheet* page to allow the daily entry of work. Your Project Server administrator can change the configuration to allow users to enter an entire week of work for a seven-day period in a single cell.

Time Types

Each task in the timesheet by default includes two **time types**, which include *Actual* and *Planned*. You use the first line to enter actual work hours. The second line displays the planned or scheduled work hours for the task assignment. When you enter actual work hours for a task, Project Server 2013 assumes all hours are billable regular (non-overtime) work and it calculates the task cost using the *Standard Rate* value from the Enterprise Resource Pool. Some organizations, however, need to track overtime work in addition to regular work, and to differentiate between billable and non-billable work.

To add an additional time type to track overtime work for each project task, in the *Show/Hide* section of the *Options* ribbon, select the *Overtime* option as shown in Figure 9 - 4. For *Non-Billable* time, select the *Non-Billable* option. These time types appear in the timephased entry grid on the right. Notice that the *Overtime* and the *Non-Billable* time type only apply to project tasks as shown previously in Figure 9 - 4.

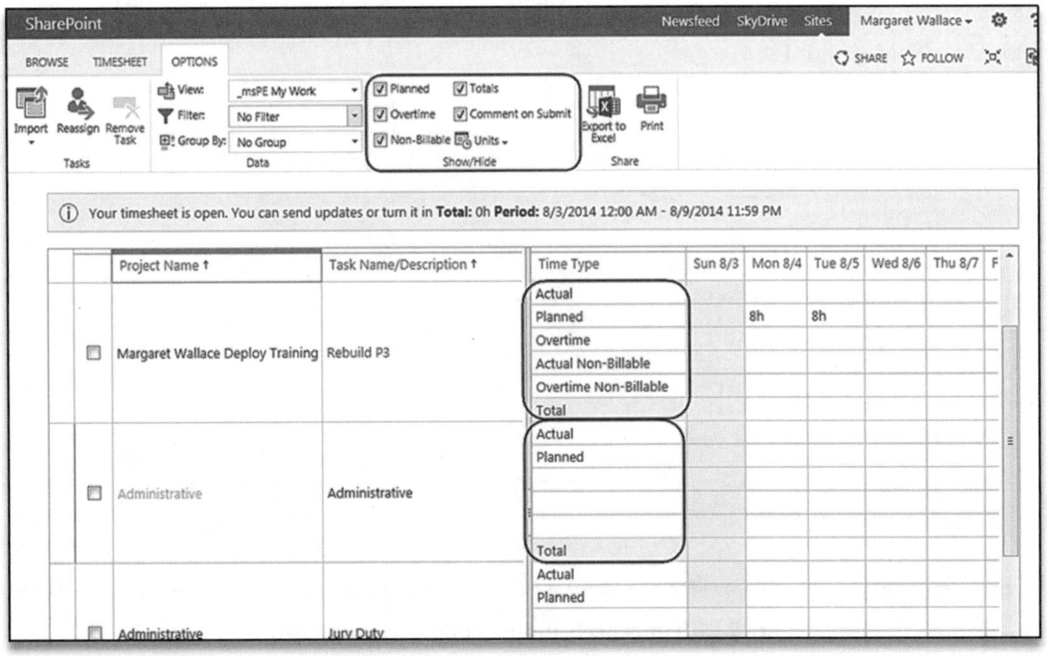

Figure 9 - 4: Show/Hide Line options

> **Information**: To remove the lines for overtime work and non-billable work, deselect the appropriate options in the *Show/Hide* section of the *Options* ribbon.

Other Show/Hide Options

The *Show/Hide* section of the *Options* ribbon contains two additional options. Selecting the *Comment on Submit* option provides a *Comment* dialog for you to enter timesheet level comments that appear when you turn in your timesheet for approval. While the system enables this option by default, you may change it by deselecting the option. The *Units* pick list enables you to decide the display formats of *Work, Duration* and *Date* fields on the page. For example, if you want to enter your updates as number of days, change the *Units* value for *Work* to *Days*.

> **Information**: In the *Show/*Hide section of the *Options ribbon,* the *Units* pick list controls the default unit of measure. For example, *Work* options include: *Minutes*, *Hours*, *Days*, and *Weeks* for entering time in the timephased grid.

Information Bar

The *Information* bar beneath the ribbon shows you information about the timesheet period, the total number of hours entered, and the current status of the timesheet. The bar turns *Yellow* when you make changes to the timesheet; thus, reminding you to save or turn in your timesheet.

Period Selectors

By default, the timesheet opens in the current time reporting period. However, you may need to switch to another time reporting period. In the *Period* section of the *Timesheet* ribbon, click the *Previous* and *Next* buttons to change the period or choose a specific period from the *Select Period* pick list as shown in Figure 9 - 5.

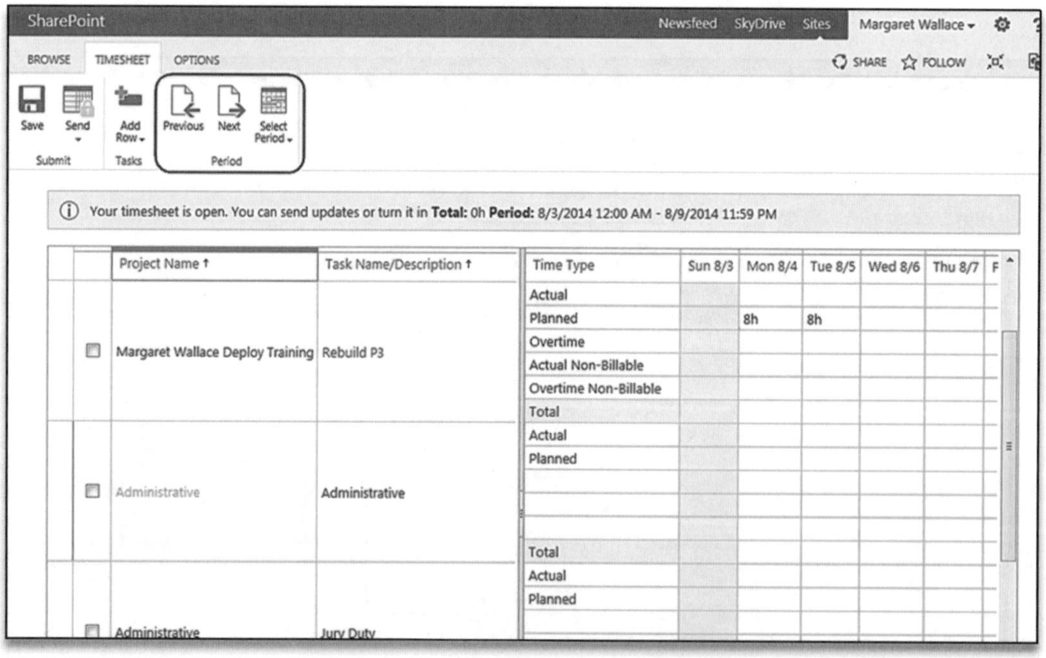

Figure 9 - 5: Timesheet ribbon, Period section buttons

Changing Views and Grouping

The *View* pick list shown in Figure 9 - 6 enables you to select the *Timesheet* view you want to use. Your Project Server administrator determines the views that appear in this list.

The *Filter* pick list shown previously in Figure 9 - 6, is only visible in *Single Entry Mode,* offers five filtering options for the timesheet period in the display and includes the following filtering options:

- *All Incomplete Tasks* option displays any task not *100% Complete,* plus the *Administrative* lines
- *Overdue Tasks* option displays any tasks that are overdue, plus the *Administrative* lines
- *Newly Assigned Tasks* option displays any new tasks, plus the *Administrative* lines
- *Completed Tasks* option displays any task that is *100% Complete,* plus *Administrative* lines
- *No Filter* option clears any previous filtering options and displays all tasks

The *Group By* pick list enables you to group your timesheet lines by the column name you select. For example, select *Process Status* grouping when you have a number of entries that are in progress or rejected so that you can see all of a given status together. Select *Project Name* grouping when you are entering time for a number of project-related tasks.

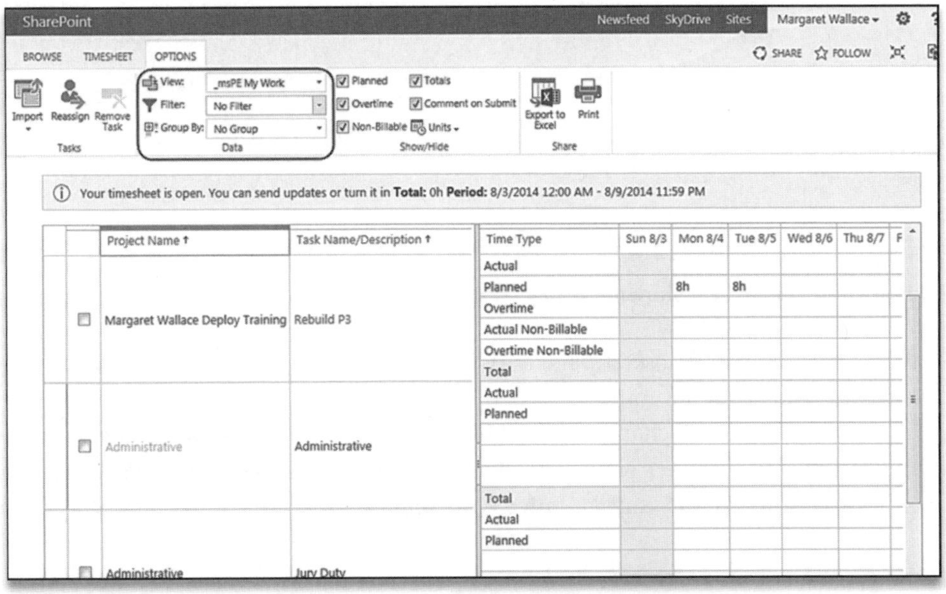

Figure 9 - 6: Data section, View/Filter/Group By options

Entering Time in the Timesheet

On the *Timesheet* page, you enter actual time spent on project and non-project work. There are a number of ways to enter time, including each of the following:

- Enter actual work manually in the daily timesheet grid for any of the items in the list.
- Add a new line to the timesheet to enter time on an item not in the list.
- Import the planned work as the actual work.
- If using *Double Entry* mode, you may import task progress from the *Tasks* page.

Entering actual work manually in the daily timesheet grid is simple. At the end of each day, enter the amount of time you spent that day on any task listed in the timesheet. In addition, you may want to add a comment in the *Comment* field for any task requiring additional information. After you enter your time each day, click the *Save* button to save the latest changes to your timesheet.

Figure 9 - 7 shows my timesheet for the week of October 20. Notice that I entered a combination of project task work, personal task work, and administrative time for the week. The *Information* bar shows that I entered a total of 40 hours for the week.

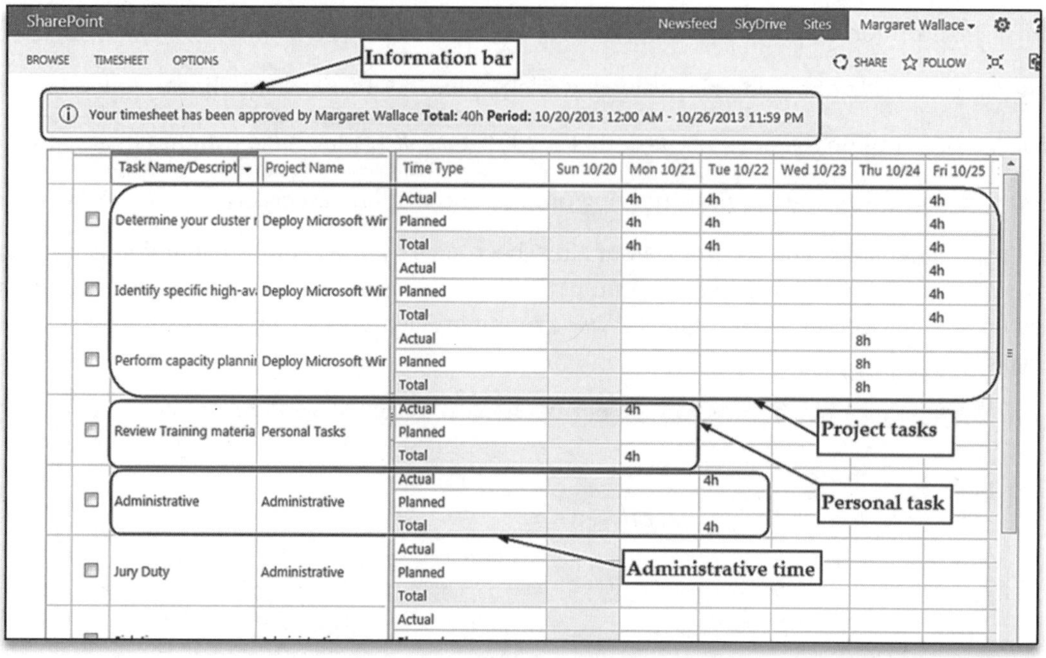

Figure 9 - 7: Timesheet showing project tasks, personal task, and Administrative time

A final step for entering time on the *Timesheet* page may include adjusting the *Remaining Work* value according to your organization's methodology for submitting time. By default, the *My Timesheet* view does not include the *Remaining Work* field. Instead, you should change to the *My Work* view to see this data column or have your administrator add this field to the *My Timesheet* view. The system displays the *Remaining Work* value according to the units you set as mentioned earlier in this section. Enter your remaining work for the task, if appropriate.

Adding a New Row to a Timesheet

You may occasionally work on an assignment that is either not on your timesheet or is of a category of work that needs special tracking. Figure 9 - 7 shown previously, shows the three kinds of work items that Project Server 2013 enables you to add to your timesheet including:

- **Project tasks** represents your planned activities for a given time period to support the outcomes of the associated project.
- **Administrative time** categories represent a capture mechanism to reflect the number of hours you spend on non-project work, by default includes *Administrative time,* Sick, and *Vacation*
- **Personal tasks** work that does not fit in your project tasks or your administrative time categories.

Let us review an example of how to add each work item and the reasons for the addition.

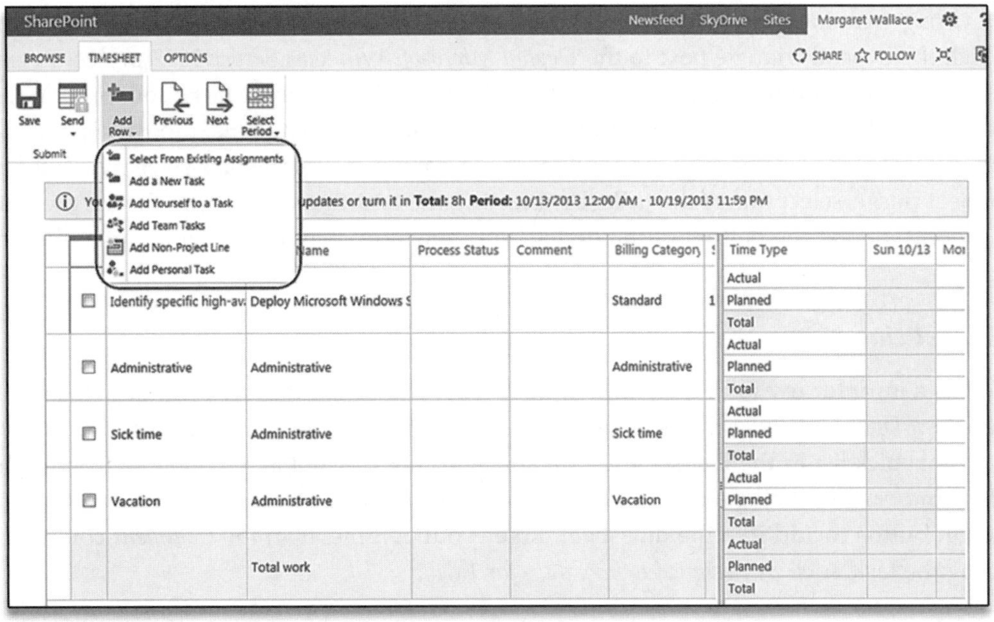

Figure 9 - 8: Timesheet Add Row

Add an Existing Assignment

For example, on Monday, October 14, I worked 2 hours on analyzing "Evaluate lessons learned" (not shown) on the *Deploy Microsoft Windows Server 2012* project, as I want to analyze some lessons from recent issues. My assignment for this task is not for the timesheet period. My organization requires resources to log all activities performed, therefore I need to capture this time by adding a new row on my timesheet. To add a new timesheet row, click the *Add Row* pick list, and then select the *Select from Existing Assignments* item as shown in Figure 9 - 8. Project Server 2013 displays the *Add an Existing Task* dialog shown in Figure 9 - 9.

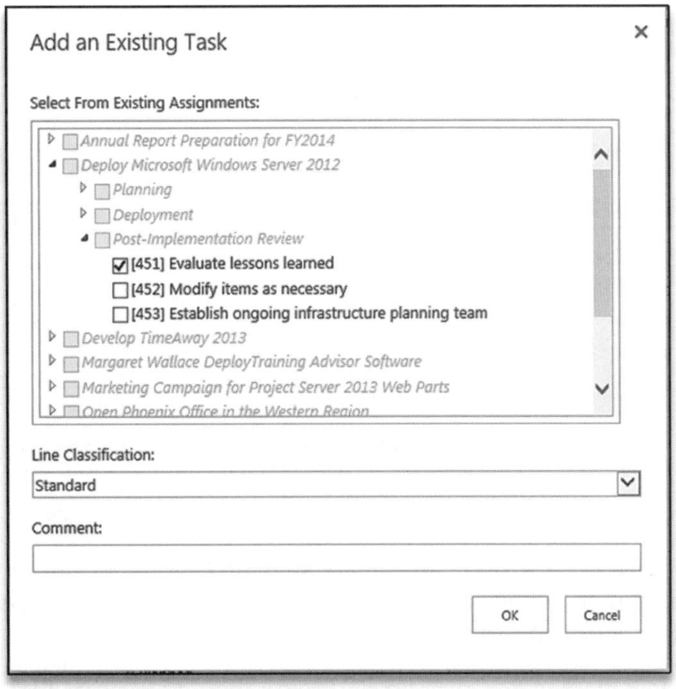

Figure 9 - 9: Add an Existing Task to your timesheet

In the *Add an Existing Task* dialog, you may select a task assignment from any project in which you have a current assignment. Click the expand triangle next to the *Deploy Microsoft Windows Server 2012* project to expand the task hierarchy for the task you want to select. The system displays all *Outline Level 1* tasks collapsed in the project plan as these top-level tasks typically denote project phases. Next, click the triangle next to the *Post Implementation Review* phase, this summary task expands the task hierarchy to narrow down the task selection. After expanding the appropriate project phase, select one of the tasks by selecting the task name option as shown previously in Figure 9 - 9. In the *Comment* field at the bottom of the dialog, you may add a comment explaining why you are adding the task.

Add a Non-Project Line

I was also listed as a juror for my local government this week, and called to duty for a day this week. My organization considers *Jury Duty* as *Administrative* time or *Non-Project* time; therefore, I add this time to my timesheet by clicking the *Add Row* pick list in the *Timesheet* ribbon and selecting the *Add Non-Project Line* item. The system displays the *Administrative Time* dialog shown in Figure 9 - 10. Click the *Category* pick list and select the *Jury Duty* item. Click the *OK* button to add it to the timesheet. Enter your comments in the *Comment* column describing the reason for adding the task, such as *Assigned to jury duty for 1 day.*

Warning: As of the writing of this book, using the *Description* field in the *Administrative Time* dialog results in updating the *Task Name/Description* in the timesheet, and this may be an unforeseen result. In the *Administrative Time* dialog, avoid using the *Description* field for your comments instead leave the default descriptor *Jury Duty* as shown previously in Figure 9 - 10. The *Jury Duty* name my organization uses provides consistency for our reporting needs, as we want to see all *Jury Duty* items using the same naming convention. *Instead* use the *Comment* column in the timesheet to document a specific reason for using an administrative line item.

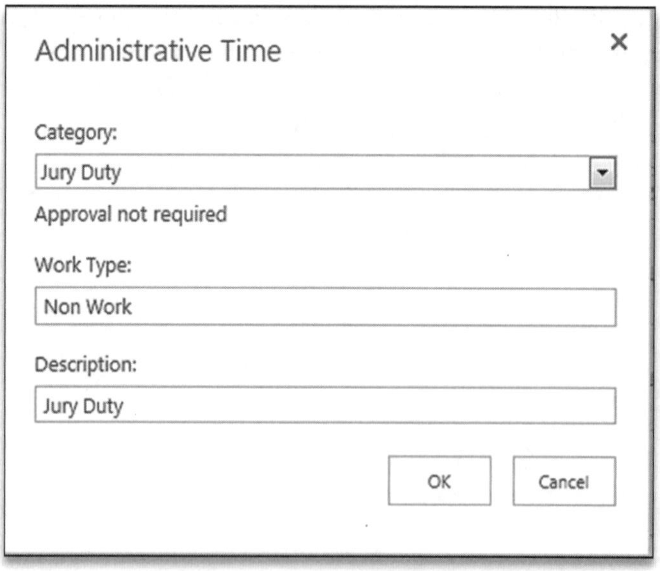

Figure 9 - 10: Add an Administrative Task to Your Timesheet

Add a Personal Task

I also participate on a *Merger System* selection team as my company recently acquired another company. For tax accounting reasons, my company tracks all merger activities. I attended a merger meeting for someone else and need to account for this time. A personal task fulfills this need.

From the *Timesheet* ribbon, click the *Add Row* pick list and select the *Add Personal Task* item from the list as shown in Figure 9 - 11. In the *Add New Personal Task* dialog, I enter a name in the *Type a Name for the New Timesheet Line* field; I click the *Line Classification* pick list and select the *Merger* category; and, finally, I enter a comment in the *Comment* field. Once I click the *OK* button, the line appears in my timesheet and I can enter time against this item.

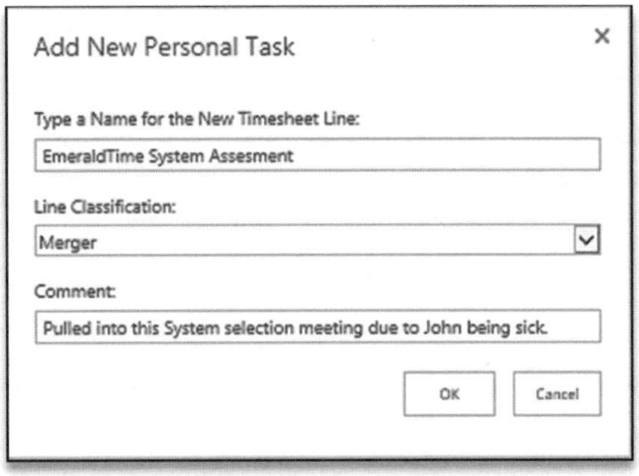

Figure 9 - 11: Add New Personal Task to Your Timesheet

Remove a Line

When you need to remove a timesheet line, click the *Options* tab to display the *Options* ribbon, select the checkbox to the left of the *Task Name/Description* column for the task you want to remove, and then click the *Remove Task* button. Project Server 2013 immediately removes the line from the timesheet and also removes the assignment in the project. When you remove a task from your timesheet, the task removal is subject to the approval of the project manager, and if the project manager rejects the removal of the task then the task becomes available to add in the *Add an Existing Task* dialog.

Information: The system does not prompt you prior to removing a timesheet line, so use this option carefully.

Warning: Removing tasks from your timesheet also removes the assignment from the project and is, therefore, subject to the approval of the project manager or *Status Manager* for the task. If the project manager **approves** the task removal you will not be able to add the task to a timesheet without communicating directly with the project manager to reassign the task. If the project manager **rejects** the task removal, the task displays the next time you open your timesheet for the same period displaying a *Rejected* value in the *Process Status* field. Use this option cautiously, as the ramification of removing tasks is more far-reaching than just removing a timesheet line from your timesheet.

Replacing Actual Work with Planned Work

Another method for entering time in your timesheet is to enter planned work as actual work for one or more selected tasks scheduled during the selected timesheet period. This feature enables you to enter your time rapidly on a large number of tasks. You then make manual adjustments only for those tasks where planned and actual values do not match.

Select a single or multiple tasks by selecting the checkbox(es) next to the task in the *Task Name/Description* column or select all tasks by clicking the cell to the left of the *Task Name/Description* column header and selecting the *Select All* item. Next, click the *Import* pick list and select the *Replace Actual with Planned* item on the list. Figure 9 - 12 shows the *Timesheet* page showing the planned work for two tasks scheduled the week of September 29.

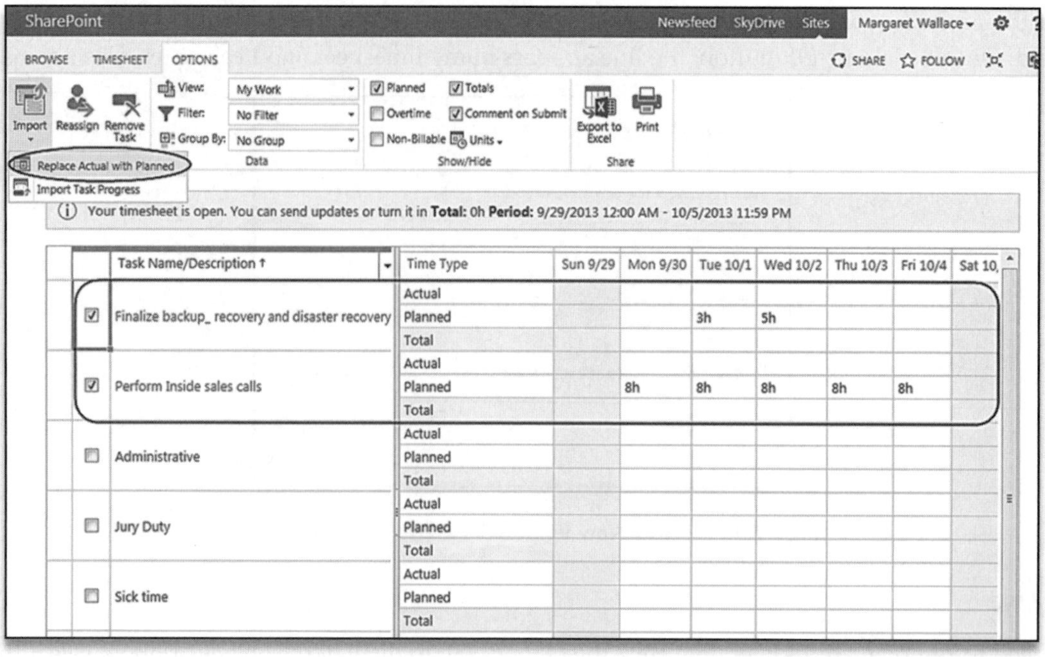

Figure 9 - 12: Timesheet shows Tasks Planned Work

The system updates the *Actual* work using the *Planned* work for each day, as shown in Figure 9 - 13. Note the *Information* bar appears *Yellow* after performing this option and the *Process Status* values change to *Not Submitted,* indicating that you have not yet submitted this information to the approver.

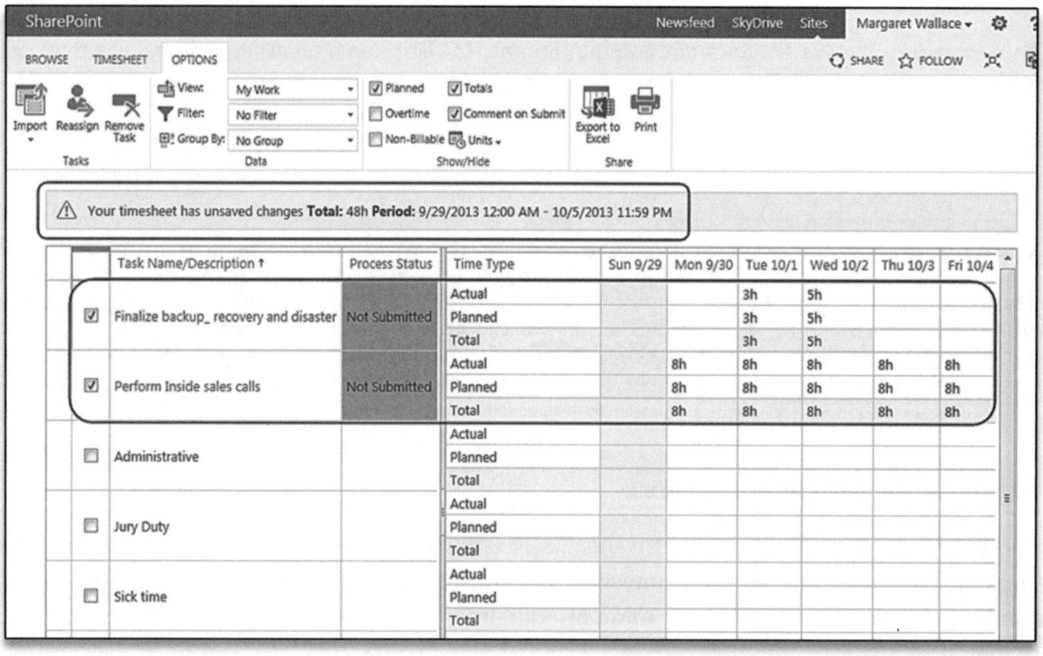

Figure 9 - 13: Replace actual work using planned work in the timesheet

After you replace the actual work using planned work, remember to save your timesheet by selecting the *Timesheet* tab and then in the *Submit* section of the *Timesheet* ribbon click the *Save* button to save your timesheet.

Warning: Updating actual work from planned work is a quick way to enter time in your timesheet, but it is not a good way to enter accurate information. In the real world, rarely does actual work ever match planned work for a task. This method requires reviewing the actual work and making adjustments where necessary for accurately reporting your work to your manager. In my example as shown previously in Figure 9 - 13, my total for the period is *48h* and does not meet my organization's business rule of *40 hours* per time period, so an adjustment is necessary to submit the actual work total at *40* hours.

Importing Task Progress

This section is only applicable if your organization uses *Double Entry* mode. If you already entered progress for a task on the *Tasks* page or the *Assignment Details* page, you may import the progress from either page to the *Timesheet* page.

For example, Figure 9 - 14 shows the *Tasks* page for my assignments during the week of November 11. Notice that I entered my daily *Actual* work in the timesheet grid for the *Design P1* task that week, and I saved the updates.

Information: The *Imported Task Progress* function only works for *Saved* or *Sent* time entries on the *Tasks* page.

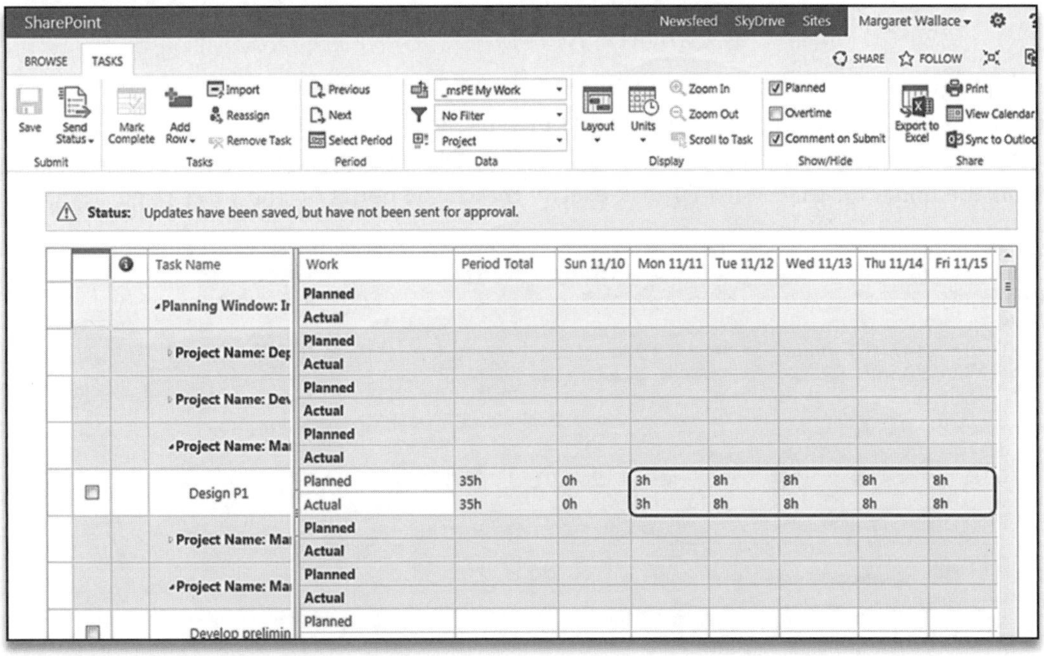

Figure 9 - 14: Tasks page, Actual Work entered and saved

Figure 9 - 15 shows my timesheet for the week of November 11. Notice that the *Planned* work shows *3h* for Monday and no *Actual* work in the Timesheet page for the *Design P1* task which differs from the *Planned work* and *Actual* work entered on the *Tasks* page.

Information: The *Import Task Progress* function only works on saved timesheet entries on the *Timesheet* page. Attempting to import task progress on a modified, but not saved timesheet entry, results in updated planning time but no change in actual time.

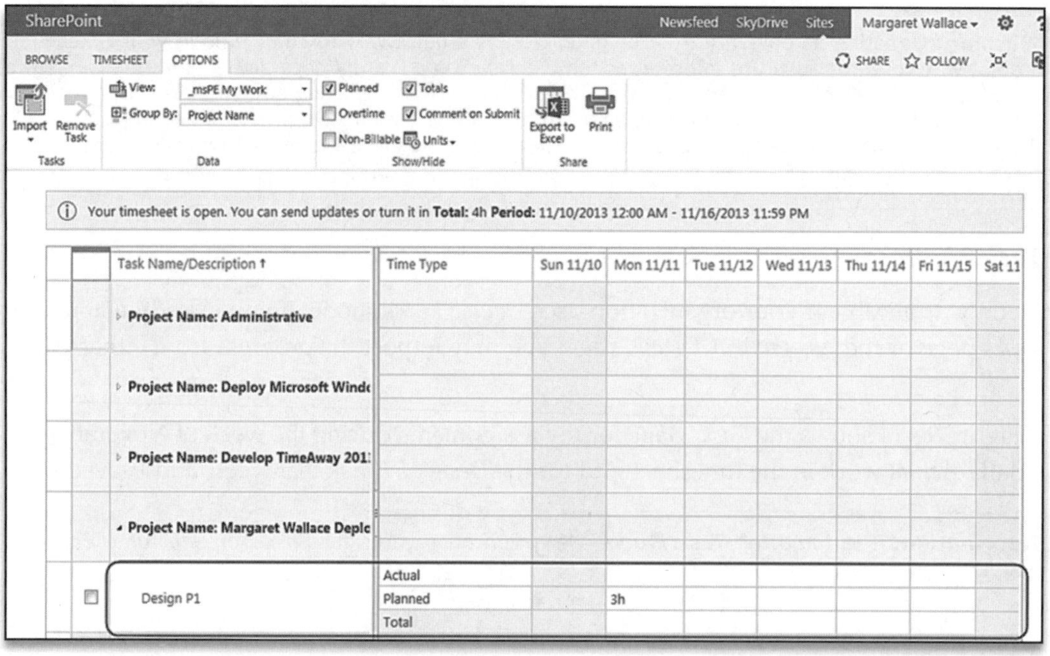

Figure 9 - 15: Timesheet Page shows task Planned work before Task Import

To import task progress from the *Tasks* page or the *Assignment Details* page, select the option checkbox to the left of the task name on the *Options* page, click the *Import* pick list and select the *Import Task Progress* item on the list. The system imports the time from the *Tasks* (or assignment details) page as shown in Figure 9 - 16. Notice that after the import the hours for the *Design P1* task exactly match the hours on the *Tasks* page shown previously in Figure 9 - 14.

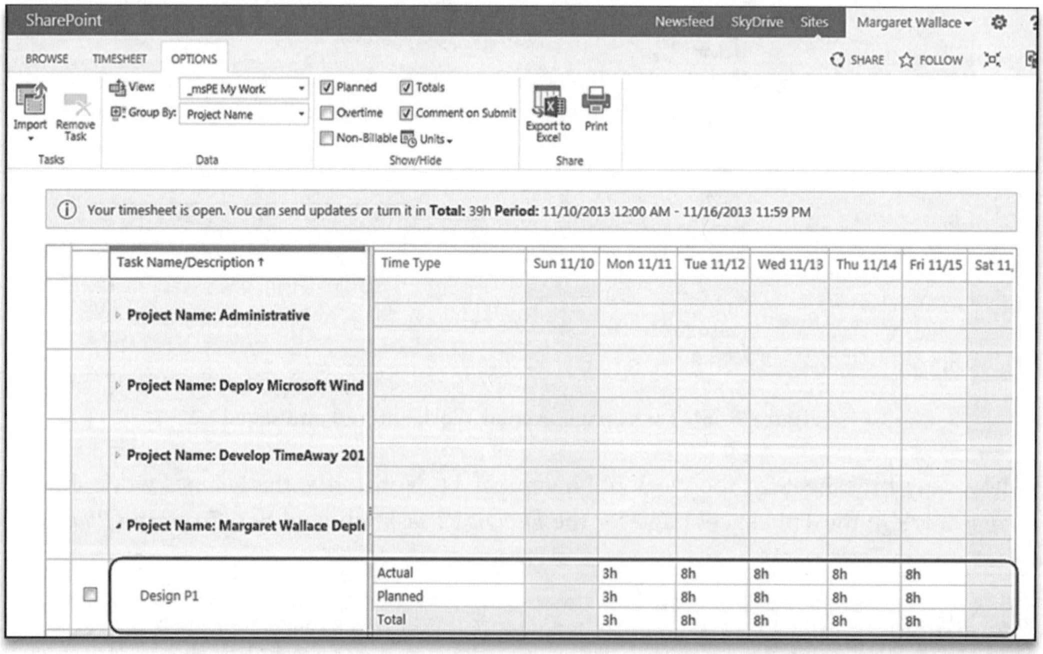

Figure 9 - 16: Timesheet Actual Work after Task Import

After you import task progress to your timesheet, remember to click the *Save* button to save your timesheet.

Managing Timesheets

The *Manage Timesheets* page shown in Figure 9 - 17 enables you to create new timesheets, review timesheet submission status, and delete your timesheets. The *Manage Timesheets* page shows the list of timesheets you already submitted, timesheets that are currently in-progress, and timesheets ready to create. I cover each of these functions in detail in later sections of this module.

> **Information**: The *Manage Timesheet* page lists timesheets in descending order by timesheet period. Therefore, your current timesheet always appears at the top of the page.

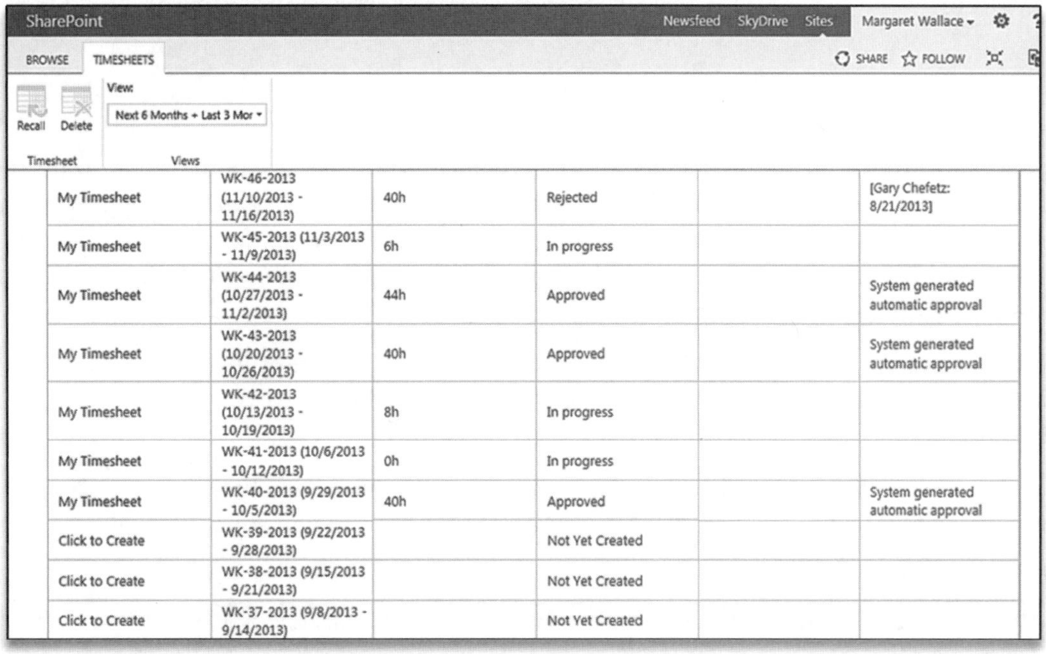

Figure 9 - 17: Manage Timesheets page

The *Manage Timesheets* page in the *Timesheets* ribbon includes a *View* pick list containing a list of views available for the page. The first time you access the *Manage Timesheets* page, the default view is *Current + Last Three Months*. If you click the *View* pick list, the system offers you the following views that control what timeframe the system uses to filter your list of timesheets:

- Current + Last 3 Months
- Next 6 Months + Last 3 Months
- Last 6 Months
- Last 12 Months
- Created and in progress
- All Timesheets

The view names explain each view, so further detail is not necessary. For most users, the default *Current + Last 3 Months* view suffices. The system reapplies this view if you navigate to another page in PWA and then return to the *Manage Timesheets* page.

The fastest way to create a new timesheet for a past or current time period is to click the *Click to Create* link to the left of the timesheet period in the grid. Project Server 2013 creates your new timesheet using the default information specified by your Project Server administrator, which is set to display all tasks scheduled during the selected time period, plus any administrative tasks required by your organization.

Entering Planned Administrative Time

The default settings in Project Server 2013 prevent resources from booking unapproved vacation time. Instead, the system imposes a formal process for submission and approval of vacation time. Note, your Project Server administrator may choose to extend this approval process requirement to other administrative time categories.

> **Best Practice**: You should plan for administrative time categories that require approval.

I decide to visit New York City from December 8 to December 14 to meet my brother and to do some holiday shopping. This requires me to request a week of vacation. To submit my vacation time request for approval by my timesheet manager, from the *Quick Launch* menu, I click the *Server Settings* link to display the *PWA Settings for* page. In the *Time and Task Management* section of the page, I click the *Manage Timesheets* link. The system displays a screen similar to Figure 9 - 17 shown previously.

My timesheet for December 8 is not visible. Therefore, in the *Views* section of the *Timesheets* ribbon, I click the *Views* pick list and select the *Next 6 Months + Last 3 Months* item from the list. Next, I click the *Click to Create* link to create the timesheet for the week of December 8 as shown in Figure 9 - 18.

Since the vacation time falls in a timesheet period for an uncreated timesheet, Project Server 2013 automatically sets the timesheet's status as *In Progress*. This status will not change until you submit actual time entries for that week.

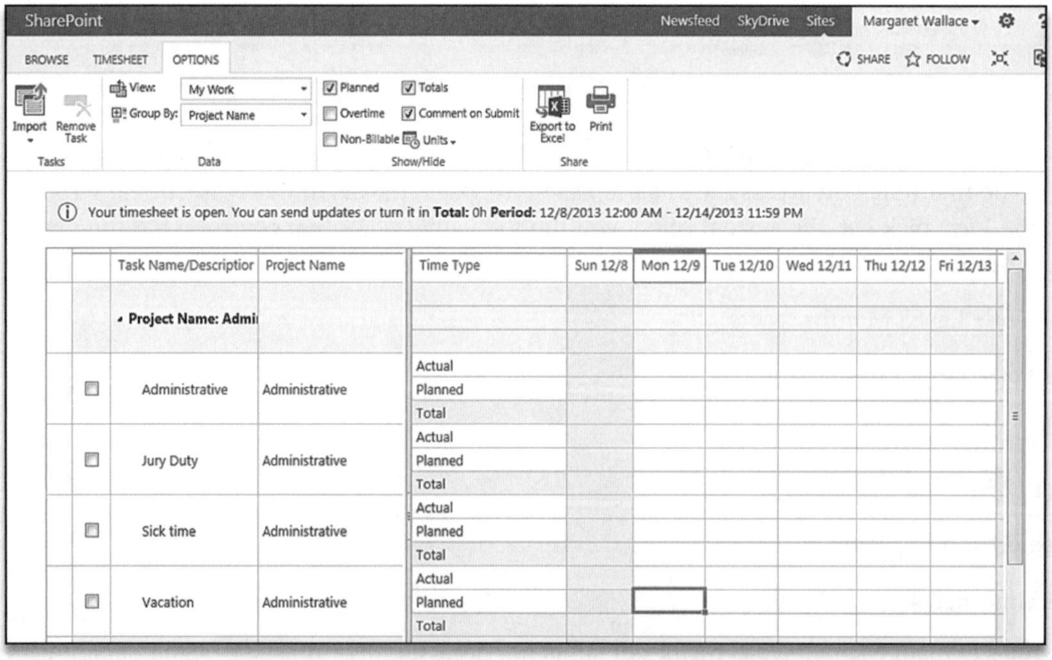

Figure 9 - 18: Create New Timesheet for Planning Period

Warning: Do not enter the planned vacation time on the *Actual* line. Doing so will mark this time as *Actual* work rather than *Planned* work.

I enter *8h* for each workday for the week as shown in Figure 9 - 19. I also enter "*Off to New York*" in the *Comment* column so that my timesheet approval manager knows why I am requesting this time. You may need to move the splitter bar to see this column in the left grid.

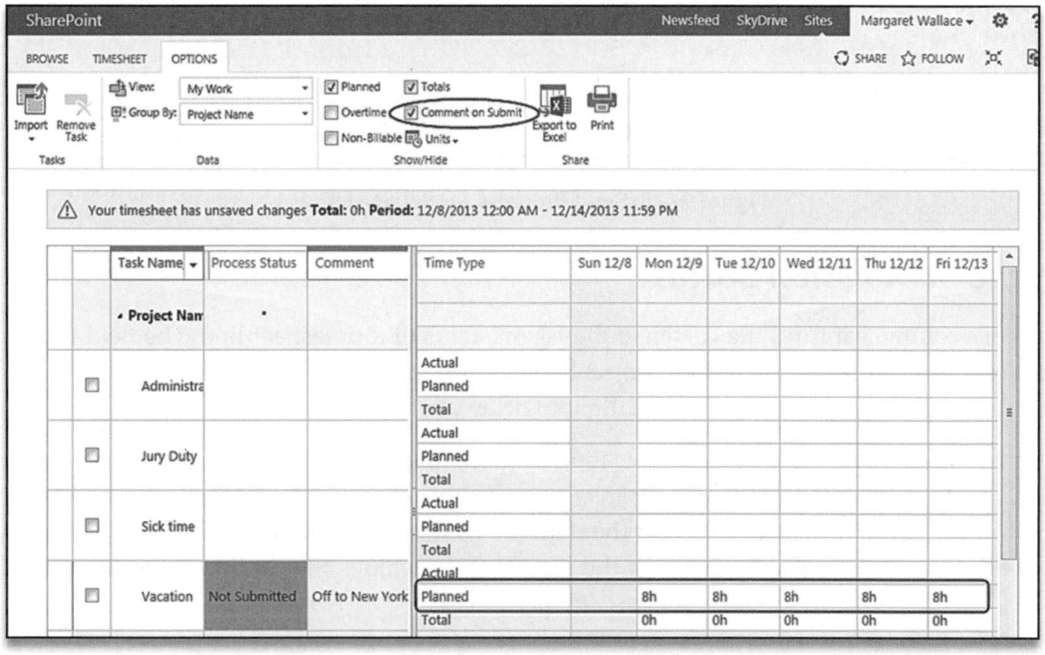

Figure 9 - 19: Enter Planned Vacation Time

The *Process Status* column shows the current state of the entry, as *Not Submitted,* which indicates that I have not sent the request to a manager yet. Select the checkbox to the left of the *Vacation* request, and then select the *Timesheet* tab to display the *Timesheet* ribbon. Then, in the *Submit* section of the ribbon click the *Send* pick list and select the *Send Progress for Selected Tasks* item on the list as shown in Figure 9 - 20. If you select the *Comment on Submit* option in the *Options* ribbon, you see the *Submit Timesheet Line* dialog prior to your final submission to enter additional comments. Click the *OK* button to send the vacation request to your timesheet approval manager for review and approval.

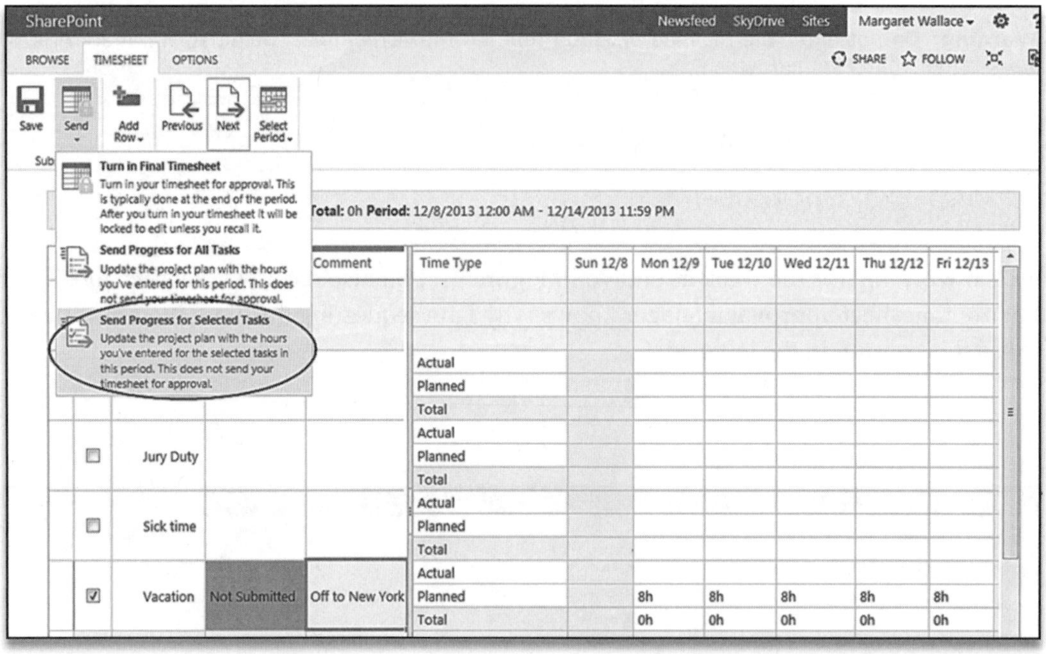
SharePoint
Newsfeed SkyDrive Sites
Margaret Wallace
BROWSE TIMESHEET OPTIONS
SHARE FOLLOW
Save Send Add Row Previous Next Select Period
Turn in Final Timesheet
Turn in your timesheet for approval. This is typically done at the end of the period. After you turn in your timesheet it will be locked to edit unless you recall it.
Send Progress for All Tasks
Update the project plan with the hours you've entered for this period. This does not send your timesheet for approval.
Send Progress for Selected Tasks
Update the project plan with the hours you've entered for the selected tasks in this period. This does not send your timesheet for approval.
Total: 0h Period: 12/8/2013 12:00 AM - 12/14/2013 11:59 PM
Comment
Time Type
Sun 12/8
Mon 12/9
Tue 12/10
Wed 12/11
Thu 12/12
Fri 12/13
Actual
Planned
Total
Jury Duty
Sick time
Vacation
Not Submitted
Off to New York
8h
0h

Figure 9 - 20: Send Progress for Selected Tasks

Viewing the Submission Status

The *Process Status* column captures the current submission status of a timesheet line. The field is blank when the current status requires no user action. When Project Server 2013 has a *Process Status* value that requires user attention, the system adds a text status and color highlight to draw your attention.

To view the current approval status of your vacation request, on the *Quick Launch* menu, click *Server Settings* ➤ *Manage Timesheets* to display the *Manage Timesheets* page. In the *Time and Task Management* section of the page, click the link for the future timesheet covering the dates of your vacation request. The system displays the timesheet for the selected period. Table 9 - 2 shows the *Process Status* values that indicate the current state of my request.

Process Status value	Color	What it means	User Action Required
[Blank]	None	Timesheet line is in an approved state.	None
Not Submitted	Red	You have not saved or submitted your change to this timesheet line.	Perform one of the following actions: Save Send Status Send Timesheet

Process Status value	Color	What it means	User Action Required
Awaiting Approval	Red	Submission of the line by you is complete but the approval manager has not acted upon the entry.	Prompt the approval manager for action if this state persists.
Rejected	Red	The approval manager rejected your update.	Make changes to the entry and resubmit. OR Accept the rejection and remove the line.
Manager Updated	Red	The task manager changed the task properties.	Review the task.

Table 9 - 2: Process Status values

Submitting a Timesheet for Approval

After you enter your time for the week, you must submit your timesheet for approval to the person designated as your timesheet approver. Before you submit your timesheet, however, remember that you use the timesheet to submit actual hours worked on tasks and on hours spent on administrative time.

Project Server 2013 does not prevent you from entering actual time for tasks that you did not plan for this period. Life sometimes has a way of interfering with your plans and Project Server provides flexibility in these cases. It is the duty of the timesheet approver to approve or reject your timesheet entry.

My car broke down on the way back to the office after a late lunch and I missed two hours of the workday. In Figure 9 - 21, I log two hours of vacation time on my timesheet although there is no planned time for this activity.

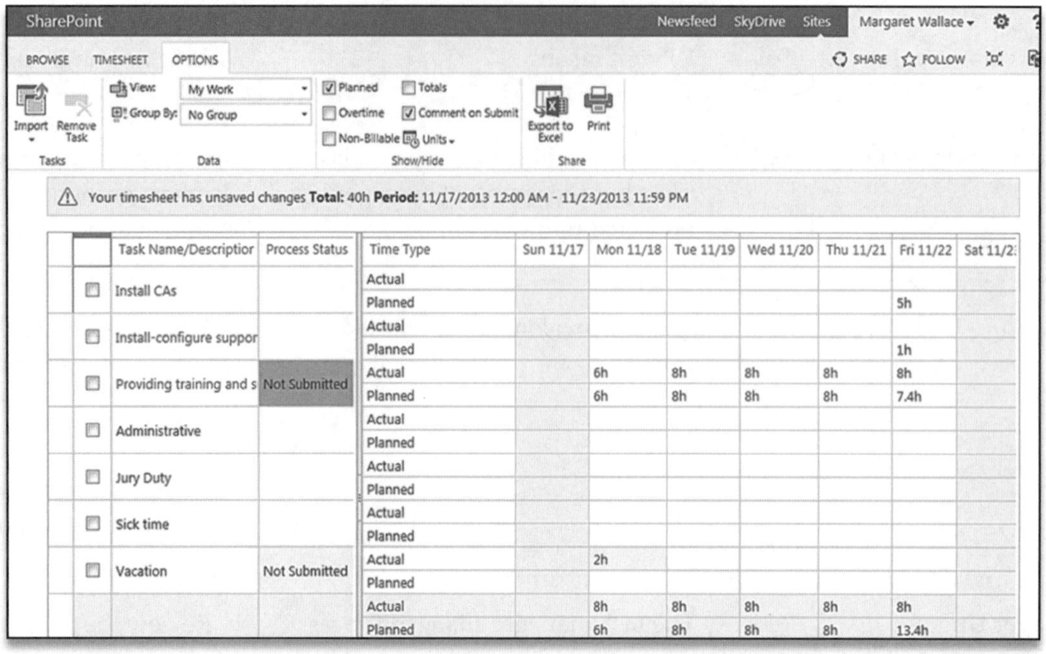

Figure 9 - 21: Unapproved Administrative Time Entry

Information: If your tracking routine includes importing time from your timesheet to the *My Tasks* page, import your time to the *My Tasks* page before you submit your timesheet.

To submit a timesheet, click the *Send* button, and then select the *Turn in Final Timesheet* item in the pick list. Project Server 2013 displays the *Send Timesheet* dialog shown in Figure 9 - 22. By default, the person shown in the *Send Timesheet to* field is the person designated as your timesheet manager by your organization's Project Server administrator.

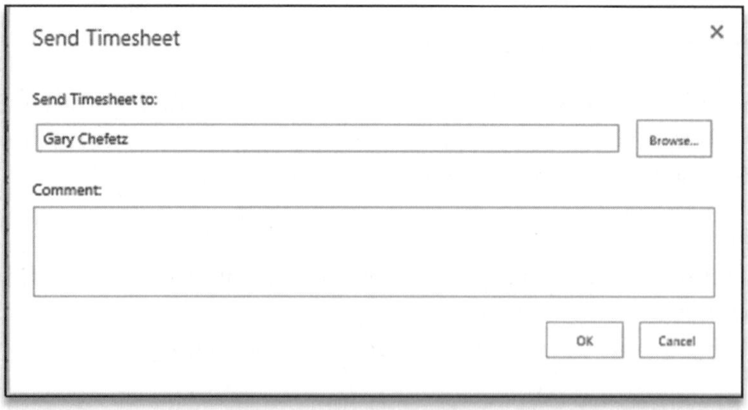

Figure 9 - 22: Send Timesheet dialog

Information: If your Project Server administrator specified you as your own timesheet manager, you do not see the *Send Timesheet to* field in the *Send Timesheet* dialog.

If the person shown in the *Send Timesheet to* field is not correct, click the *Browse* button. The system displays the *Pick Resource* dialog shown in Figure 9 - 23. This dialog contains the names of users who have permission to approve your timesheet.

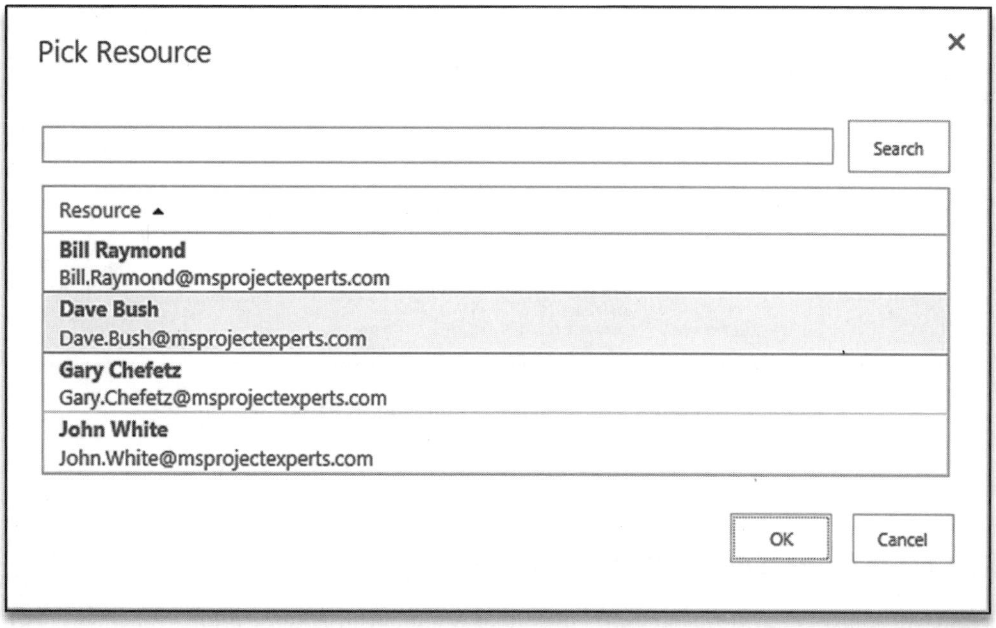

Figure 9 - 23: Pick Resource dialog

Information: The *Pick Resource* dialog displays only twenty names at a time in the dialog. If your organization has more than twenty users who can approve timesheets, use the *Search* field to filter the results by entering a portion of the user's name such as *Gary* to search for all approvers with *Gary* in their name. Then, click the *Search* button.

In the list of possible timesheet approvers, double-click the name of your timesheet approver. The system enters the selected user's name in the *Send Timesheet to* field in the *Send Timesheet* dialog. Enter any additional comments about the timesheet in the *Comments* field and then click the *OK* button to complete your timesheet submission.

To view the current approval status of a timesheet and any comments from the timesheet approver, on the *Quick Launch* menu, click the *Server Settings* link to display the *PWA Settings for* page. In the *Time and Task Management* section of the page, click the *Manage Timesheets* link to display the *Manage Timesheets* page shown in Figure 9 - 24. Refer back to Table 9 - 2 where I cover *Process Status* definitions.

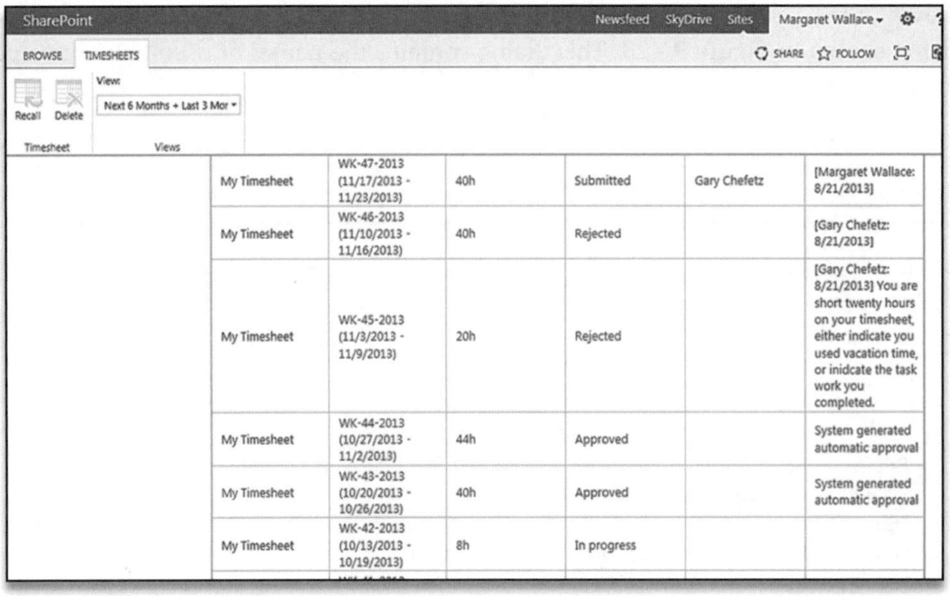

Figure 9 - 24: Manage Timesheets page

Responding to a Rejected Timesheet

In the normal flow of timesheet approvals, your timesheet manager approves your timesheets. However, a timesheet manager could reject a timesheet for a variety of reasons, such as:

- You submit a timesheet containing a factual error, such as when you enter the number 23 when you intended to type the number 3.

- You report work that totals greater than 24 hours in a single day.

- You create a new line of timesheet information to document time that does not fit into any of the tasks on your timesheet, but your timesheet manager needs you to add the time to the administrative task instead.

- You fail to report time on a day when you actually worked.

In situations like this, your timesheet manager may reject your timesheet and ask you to correct the troublesome information. For example, in the timesheet shown in Figure 9 - 25, I removed 20 hours of vacation time from my timesheet, but failed to enter any actual work in its place. My timesheet manager rejected my timesheet for the week of November 3, because my company requires resources to submit at least 40 hours of actual work each week.

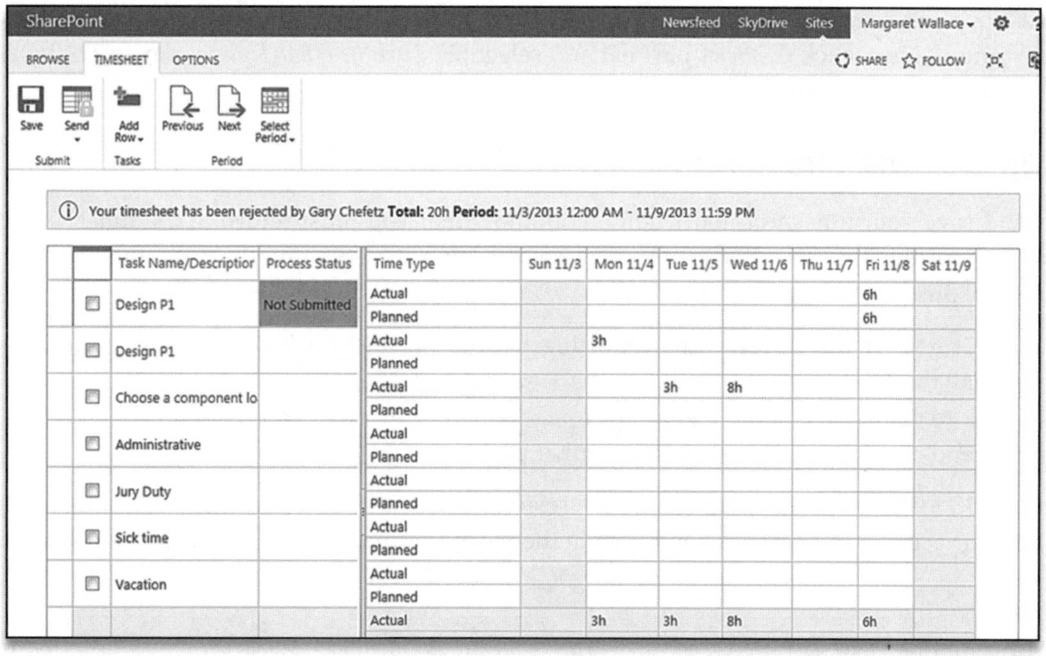

Figure 9 - 25: Timesheet Rejected due to missing time entries

When a timesheet manager rejects a timesheet, Project Server 2013 automatically sends an e-mail message to notify the resource of the rejection, once your Project Server administrator configures notifications in the system. The *Manage Timesheets* page shown in Figure 9 - 26 shows a *Rejected* timesheet status.

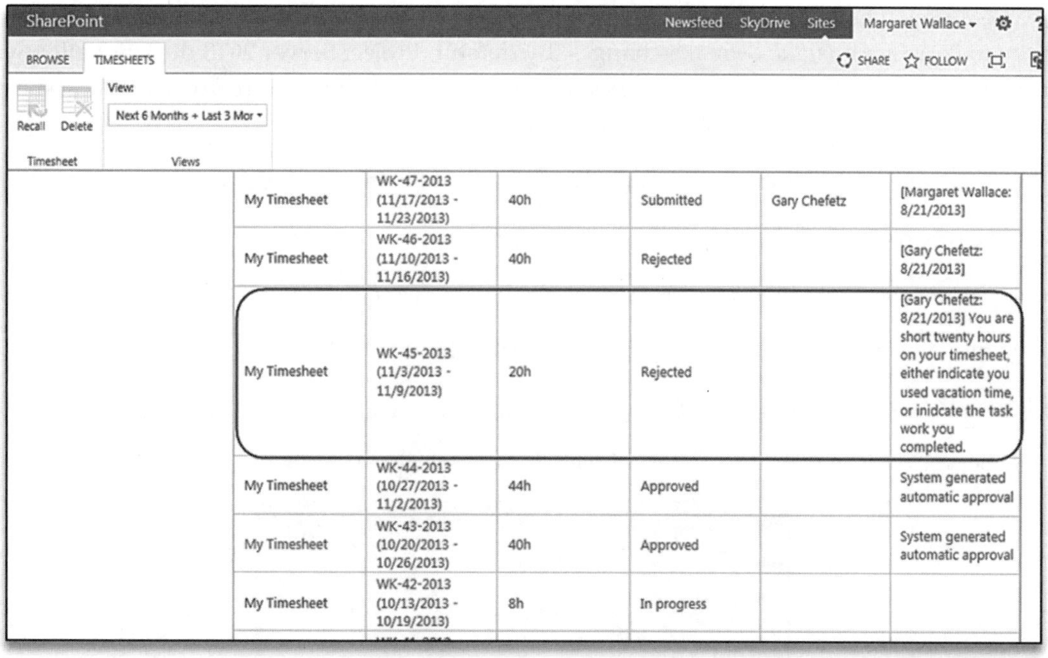

Figure 9 - 26: Rejected Timesheet

To respond to a rejected timesheet, on the *Manage Timesheets* page, click the *My Timesheet* link to the left of the rejected timesheet. The system opens the *Timesheet* page for the rejected timesheet. Make corrective action on the timesheet line that shows a *Rejected* process status to address the reason for the rejection, and any additional timesheet lines that need an adjustment. Once you complete your entries, in the *Submit* section of the *Timesheet* ribbon, click the *Save* button. Next, click the *Send* pick list and select the *Turn in Final Timesheet* item on the list to submit the timesheet for manager approval.

Editing an Existing Timesheet

If you enter and save your timesheet hours daily, you know that you must return to the timesheet today to add your actual work for the day. To edit the current time reporting period's timesheet, on the *Quick Launch* menu, click the *Timesheet* link.

If the timesheet is not for the current time reporting period, on the *Quick Launch* menu, click the *Server Settings* link to display the *PWA Settings for* page. In the *Time and Task Management* section of the page, click the *Manage Timesheets* link to display the *Manage Timesheets* page shown previously in Figure 9 - 26. Find the correct time reporting period and click the *My Timesheet* link for that period.

Project Server 2013 loads the *Timesheet* page for the selected timesheet. Use any of the methods discussed previously to enter your actual work for today and then in the *Submit* section of the *Timesheet* ribbon, click the *Save* button.

> **Information**: New to Project Server 2013: If your project manager publishes a new task that is assigned to you for the current period, the system automatically adds the new task to your timesheet.

Recalling a Submitted Timesheet

There may come a time when you need to edit information on a timesheet that you previously submitted for approval, such as to correct a mistake or make changes. By default, Project Server 2013 does not allow you to edit a submitted timesheet and locks all of the cells normally open for data entry. Before you can edit a submitted timesheet, you must recall it. To recall a timesheet, do the following:

- In the *Time and Task Management* section of the *PWA Settings for* page, click the *Manage Timesheets* link.
- Select the row of the timesheet period to recall.
- In the *Timesheet* section of the *Timesheets* ribbon, click the *Recall* button.
- The system displays the confirmation dialog shown in Figure 9 - 27.
- Click the *OK* button to recall the timesheet.
- Project Server 2013 displays the *Timesheet* page for the selected timesheet.

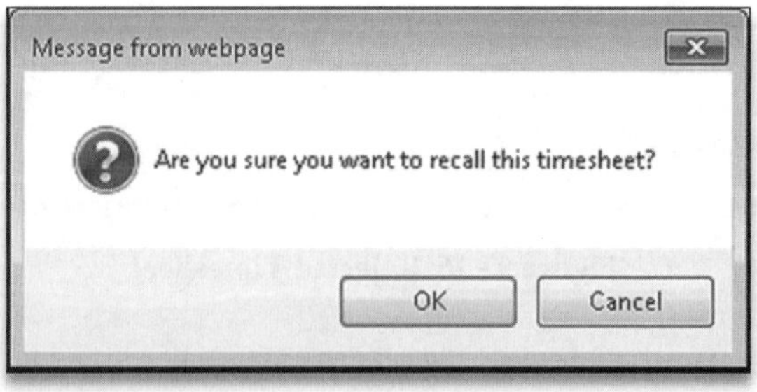
Message from webpage
Are you sure you want to recall this timesheet?
OK
Cancel

Figure 9 - 27: Recall Timesheet confirmation dialog

After recalling the timesheet, Project Server 2013 unlocks all data entry cells and resets the status of the timesheet to *In Progress*.

Information: You can recall timesheets with a *Submitted* or *Approved* status.

Warning: As of the writing of this book, once a timesheet displays a *Process Status* value of *Approved*, the system **allows** you to make changes to the timesheet without first recalling the timesheet. You can change the hours on the timesheet and then click the *Save* button without sending the timesheet for an additional approval. In fact, the system disables the ability to send the timesheet for approval. However, your adjustment displays the hours in the timesheet line where you make the change, and displays the new total hours on the *Manage Timesheets* page, while still displaying an *Approved* status.

Information: Recalling and resubmitting your timesheet has no effect on any task progress you may have reported through this timesheet period.

Deleting a Timesheet

There may come a time when you need to delete an entire timesheet and recreate it. This can result from a variety of situations, such as when you totally "mess up" a timesheet and want to start over. Complete the following to delete a timesheet:

- In the *Time and Task Management* section of the *PWA Settings for* page, click the *Manage Timesheets* link.
- Select the row of the timesheet you want to delete.
- In the *Timesheet* section of the *Timesheets* ribbon, click the *Delete* button.

The system displays the confirmation dialog shown in Figure 9 - 28.

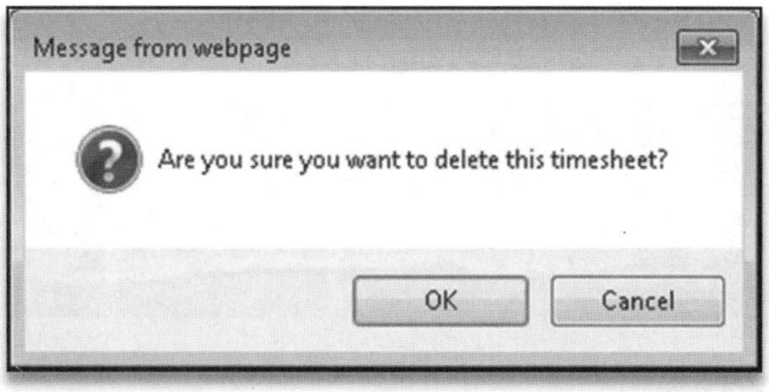
Message from webpage
Are you sure you want to delete this timesheet?
OK
Cancel

Figure 9 - 28: Confirmation dialog to delete a timesheet

- Click the *OK* button to delete the timesheet. Project Server 2013 deletes the timesheet and changes the timesheet name for that period to *Click to Create*.
- To recreate the timesheet, click the *Click to Create* link for the designated timesheet period.

Tracking Task Progress in Project Web App

In most organizations, the purpose for tracking time in Project Server 2013 is to track task progress. Task progress information directly affects the enterprise projects in your Project Server 2013 database. The system offers your organization four methods for tracking task progress. The difference between each tracking method is in the information that the system collects, as shown below:

- **Percent of Work Complete** allows resources to enter *% Work Complete* and a *Remaining Work* estimate on each task assignment.
- **Actual Work Done and Work Remaining** allows resources to enter the cumulative *Actual Work* value and to adjust the *Remaining Work* estimate on each task assignment.
- **Hours of Work Done per Period** allows resources to enter the hours of *Actual Work* completed for the current time period and to adjust the *Remaining Work* estimate on each task assignment.
- **Free Form** allows resources to enter their work using whichever of the previous three methods is most convenient and Project Server calculates the requisite values.

> **Information**: The *Percent of Work Complete* method is the system default for tracking progress unless your organization selects another method.

Understanding the Tasks Page

To begin the process of tracking task progress, launch your Internet Explorer application and navigate to your Project Web App Home page. As you see in Figure 9 - 29, I have 133 new tasks assigned to me.

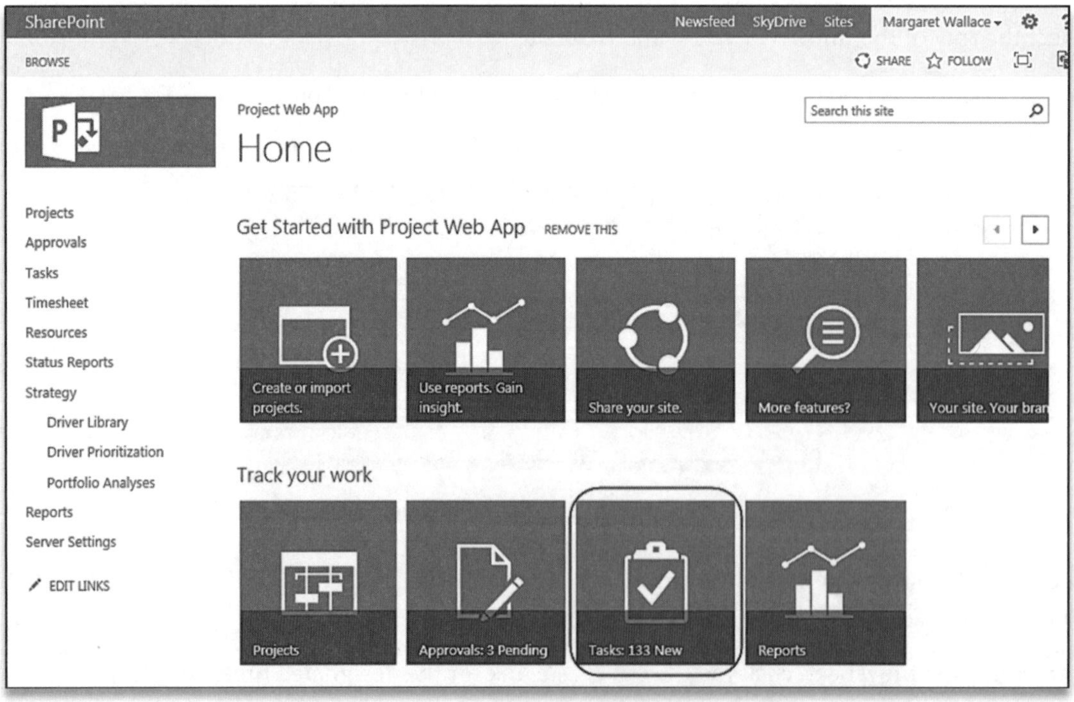

Figure 9 - 29: PWA Home Page Task Information

To navigate to the *Tasks* page, use any of the following methods:

- In the *Quick Launch* menu, click the *Tasks* link.
- In the *Track your work* section of the page, click the *Tasks* link.

Project Server 2013 displays the *Tasks* page, shown in Figure 9 - 30.

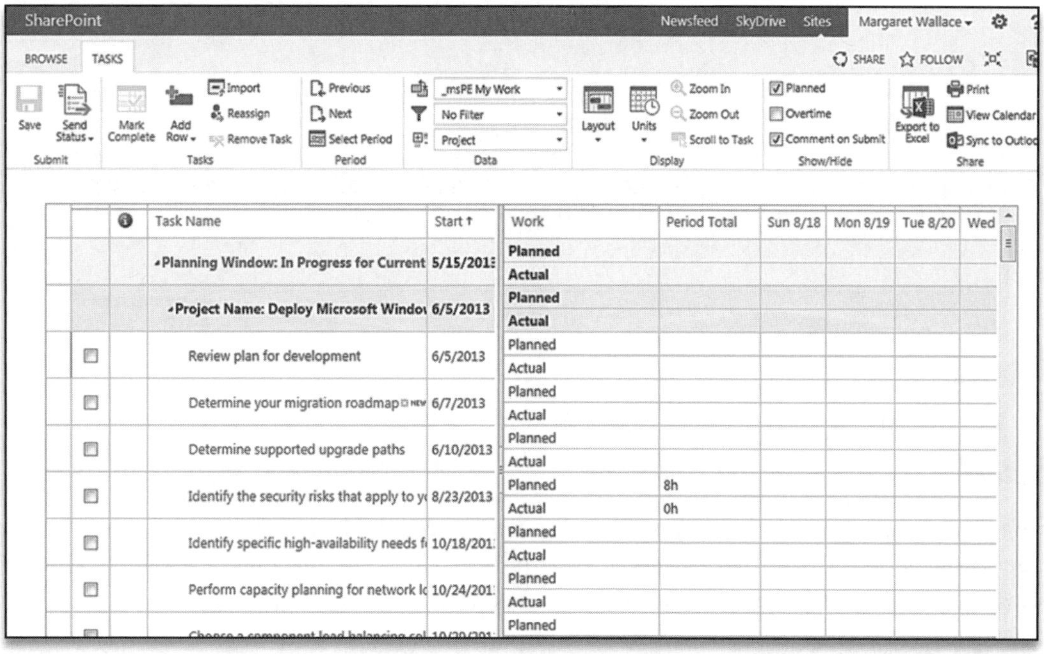

Figure 9 - 30: Tasks page

Tasks Ribbon

The *Tasks* ribbon is not new in Project Server 2013. This module covers all aspects of the *Tasks* ribbon functionality. The new functionality in the *Tasks* ribbon for Project Server 2013 is the *Sync to Outlook* button in the *Share* section of the ribbon.

Show/Hide Options

The *Show/Hide* section of the *Tasks* ribbon contains options that control the presentation of information. Selecting an option indicates you want to see that information.

The first two options relate to the *Time Types* the system displays. Each task includes two time types by default, *Actual* and *Planned*. You use the second line to enter actual work hours. The first line displays the planned or scheduled work hours for the task. This functionality is in reverse of the look and feel of the *Timesheet* page, where the *Actual* row is the first line, and the *Planned* row is second.

To add an additional time type to track overtime work for each project task, in the *Show/Hide* section of the *Tasks* ribbon, select the *Overtime* option as shown in Figure 9 - 31. All selected types now appear in the timephased entry grid on the right.

The *Comment on Submit* option determines whether a pop-up dialog displays to add a comment when you submit your timesheet for approval. You may change the default option that shows this dialog, by deselecting the option.

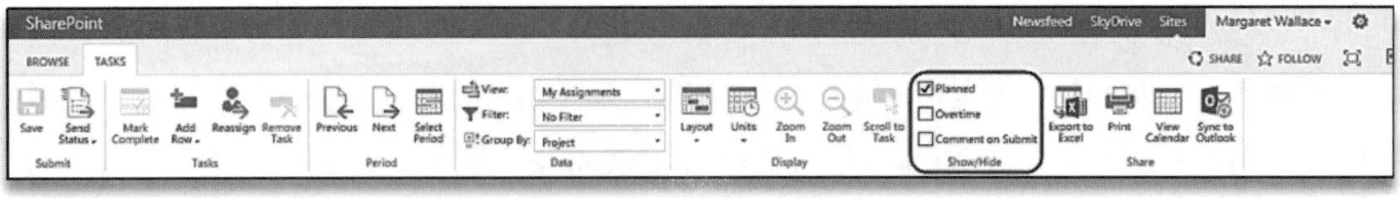

Figure 9 - 31: Tasks Show/Hide Options

Information: The *Units* pick list in the *Display* section of the *Tasks* ribbon, controls the default unit used for time (minutes, hours, days, weeks) entered in the timephased grid.

Period Selectors

By default, the *Tasks* page opens in the current time reporting period. However, you may need to navigate to another time reporting period. Click the *Previous* or *Next* buttons, as shown in Figure 9 - 32, to change periods or, you may choose a specific period from the *Select Period* pick list.

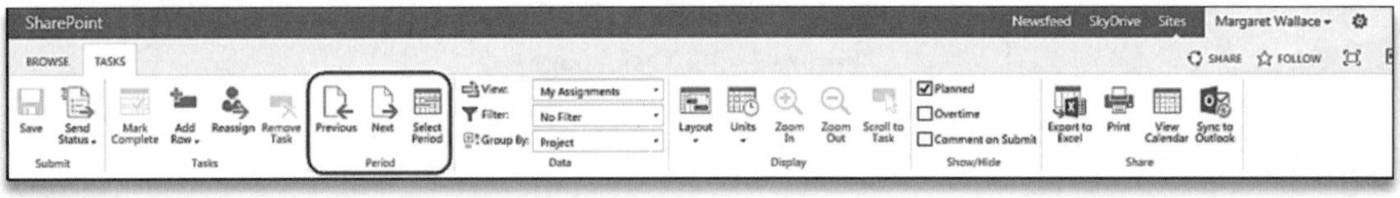

Figure 9 - 32: Period Selectors

View Calendar

The *View Calendar* option enables the user to see their tasks visualized as a calendar. Click the *View Calendar* button, as shown in Figure 9 - 33, to navigate to the *View Calendar* page shown in Figure 9 - 34.

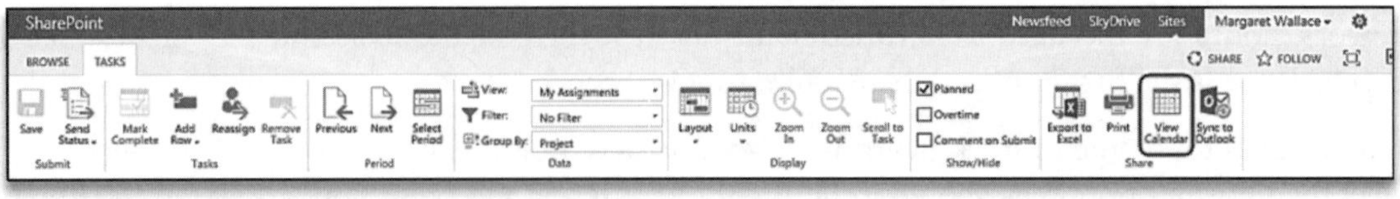

Figure 9 - 33: View Calendar button

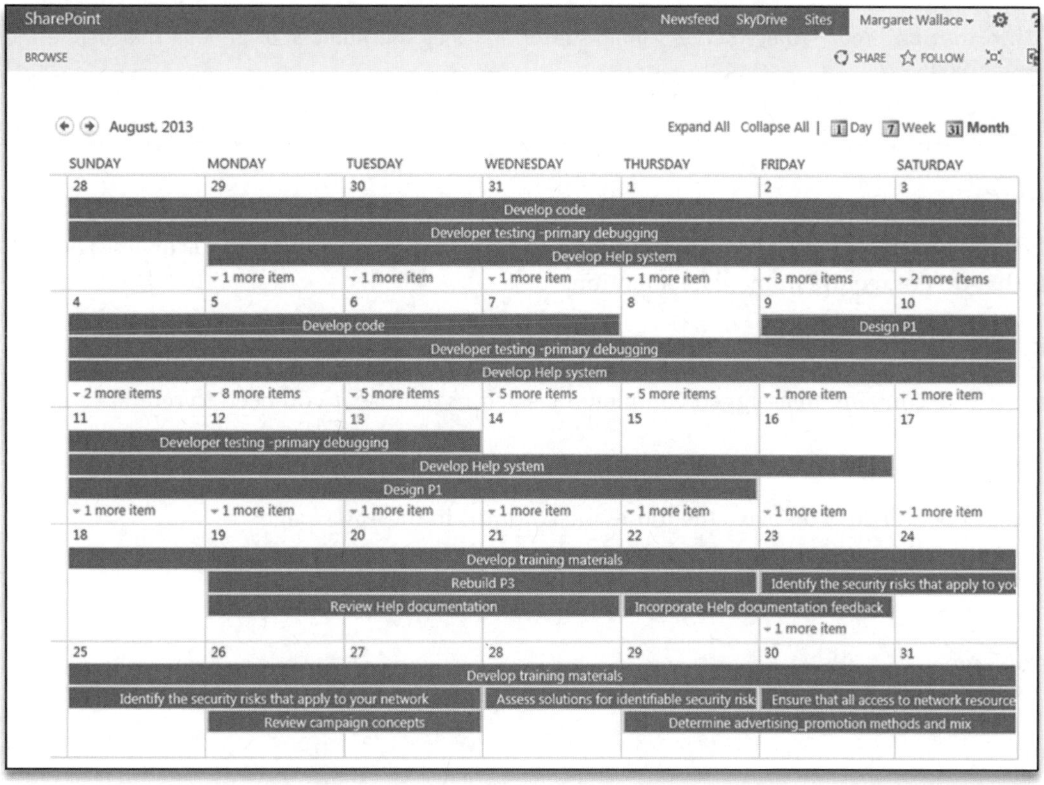

Figure 9 - 34: My Work page, View Calendar page

The display options for the calendar include day, week or month views. Clicking an individual task takes you to the *Assignment Details* page for that task.

Grouping and Views

By default, the system displays all tasks in the *Planning Window* grouping with tasks sorted by task start date. The *Planning Window* groups all of your tasks into four groups to facilitate your focus on the immediate tasks:

- In Progress for Current Period
- Near Future - Next x Periods
- Distant Future
- Completed

In Progress for Current Period

The *In Progress for Current Period* group includes all incomplete tasks which either have a task start date or task finish date less than or equal to the last day of the current period. The system no longer deems tasks as late; but rather as not currently complete. They appear at the top of the *Tasks* page to ensure they get proper attention.

Near Future – Next x Periods

The *Near Future – Next x Periods* group includes all tasks that have a task start date within the next x time reporting periods. Your Project Server administrator determines what number x will be in the configuration settings. By default, the *Near Future* period is *two*.

Information: Your Project Server administrator specifies the number of periods that define the *Near Future* task group.

Distant Future

The *Distant Future* group contains all tasks starting more than x time reporting periods away. These tasks are your assignments that do not require immediate attention.

Completed

The *Completed* group contains all assigned completed tasks for your use if you need to reference this information.

Fields

By default, Project Server 2013 displays the following columns in the *Tasks* page:

- Information
- Task Name
- Start
- Finish
- Remaining Work
- % Work Complete
- Work
- Actual Work
- Process Status

The *Information* column includes icons to denote task notes using a yellow note icon and a paperclip icon to denote linked issues, risks and documents.

Process Status

The *Process Status* column captures the current submission status of a *Task* line. The field is normally blank when the current status requires no user action. When Project Server 2013 has a *Process Status* that requires user attention, the system adds a text status and color highlight to draw your attention to the action required, as shown in Table 9 - 3.

Process Status Value	Color	What it means	User Action Required
[Blank]	None	Timesheet line is in an approved state.	None
Not Submitted	Red	You have not saved or submitted your change to this timesheet line.	Perform one of the following actions: • Save • Send Status • Send Timesheet
Awaiting Approval	Red	Submission of the line by you is complete but the approval manager has not acted upon the entry.	Prompt the approval manager for action if this state persists.
Rejected	Red	The approval manager rejected your update.	Make changes to the entry and resubmit. OR Accept the rejection and remove the line.
Manager Updated	Red	The task manager changed the task properties.	Review the task.
Save Needed	Green	You changed a task value but have not yet saved the change.	Save or exit without saving

Table 9 - 3: Process Status values

To rearrange the order of the fields, click and hold on the column header and drag the column to the desired location. The cursor changes to a four arrow cross to indicate the proper placement for dragging shown in Figure 9 - 35.

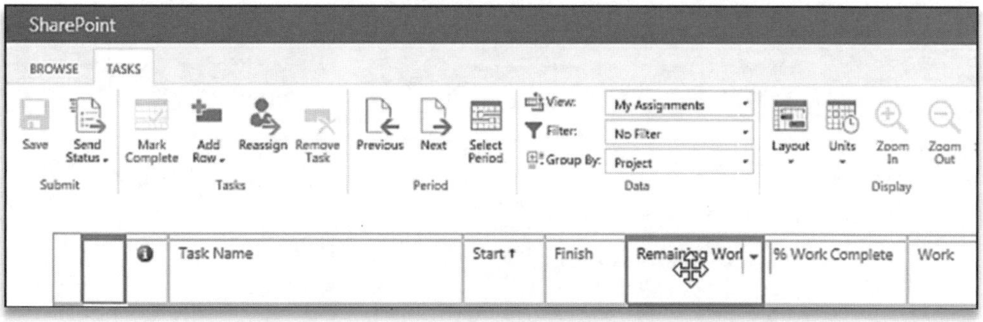

Figure 9 - 35: Example of Cursor Change for Column Rearrangement

Units

The *Units* pick list enables you to decide the display formats of *Work, Duration* and *Date* fields on the page as shown in Figure 9 - 36. For example, to enter your updates as number of days change the *Units* value for *Work* to *Days*.

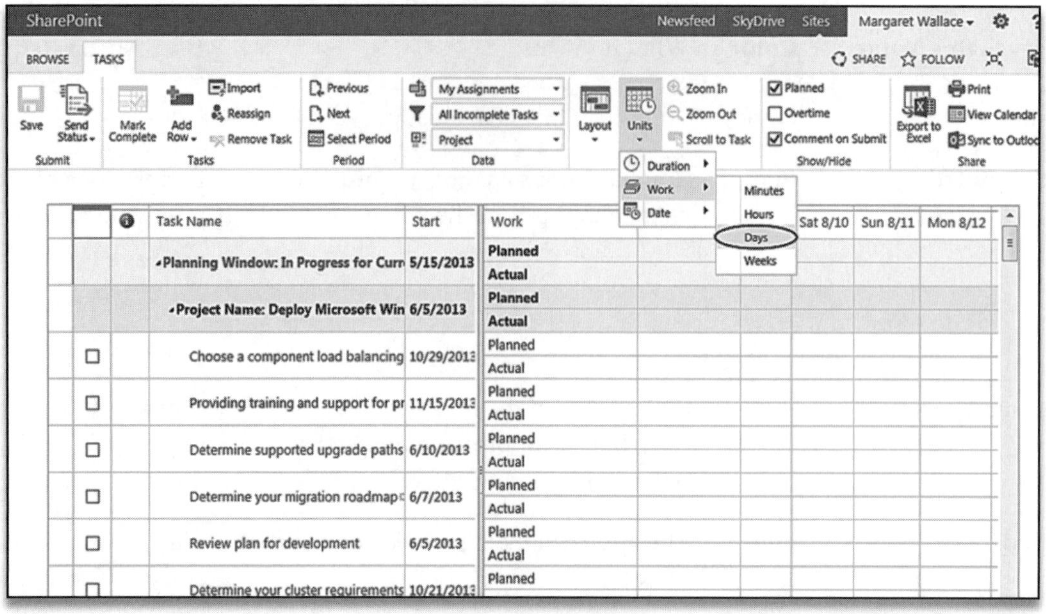

Figure 9 - 36: Units pick list

Information: The *Units* pick list in the *Task* ribbon controls the default unit used for time (minutes, hours, days, weeks) entered in the timephased grid.

Using the Timephased Data Layout

The *Tasks* page offers three screen layouts for your use. By default, the *Tasks* page displays the *Timephased Data* layout as shown in Figure 9 - 37. The right side of the page contains a data entry grid organized by day or week, where the user can enter actual and overtime data. This layout is best for hours per day or hours per week time entry.

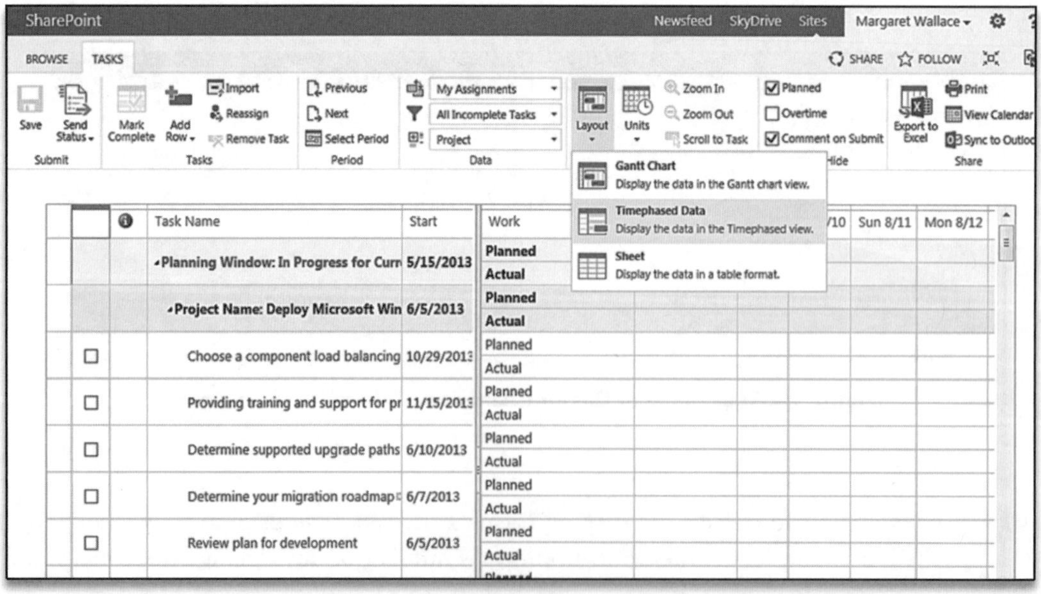

Figure 9 - 37: Timephased Data layout

Using the Gantt Chart Layout

The *Gantt Chart* layout, shown in Figure 9 - 38, provides the user with a way to visualize the relationships between their tasks. There are times where no graphics will show. Remember the current period is always the default so you may need to scroll to the appropriate place in the Gantt chart to see your tasks. The *Scroll to Task* button provides a quick way to do this. Highlight the row for the desired task, and then click the *Scroll to Task* button on the ribbon. The *Gantt Chart* graphics for that task come into view. The *Zoom In/Out* buttons also enable you to change the timescale used for the Gantt chart. By default, the view is at the day level; however, you can zoom out to view at the month level.

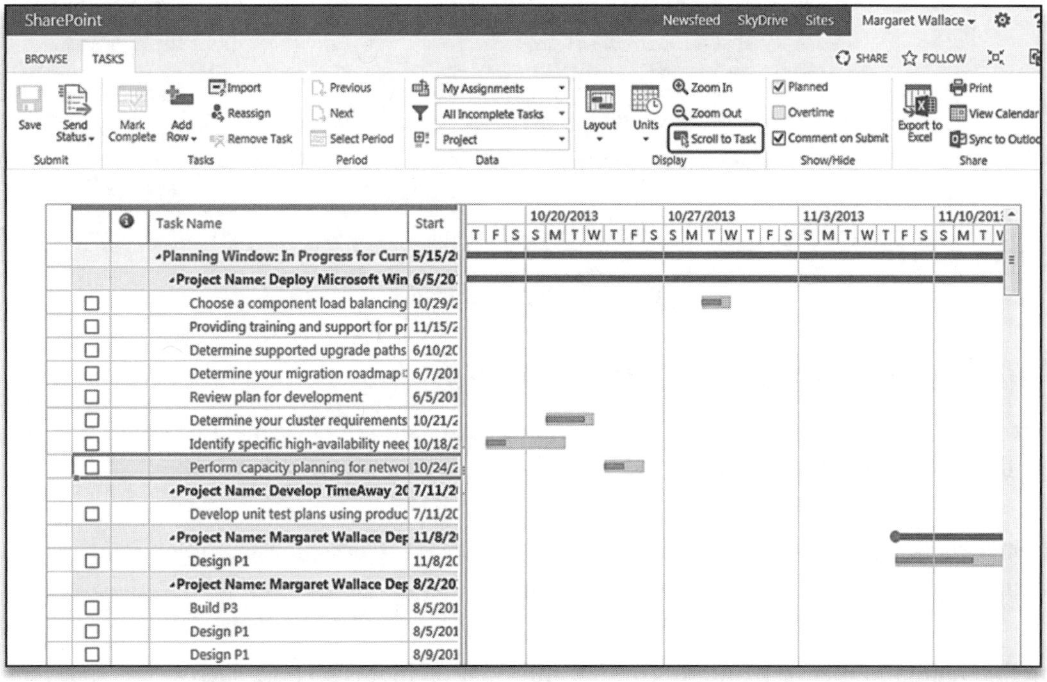

Figure 9 - 38: Gantt Chart layout, Scroll to Task

Using the Sheet Layout

The *Sheet* layout shown in Figure 9 - 39, provides a simple list view of your tasks by removing the right side timephased data entry grid. This layout best serves organizations that are using *% Complete* tracking and do not need the detail provided by the data entry grid.

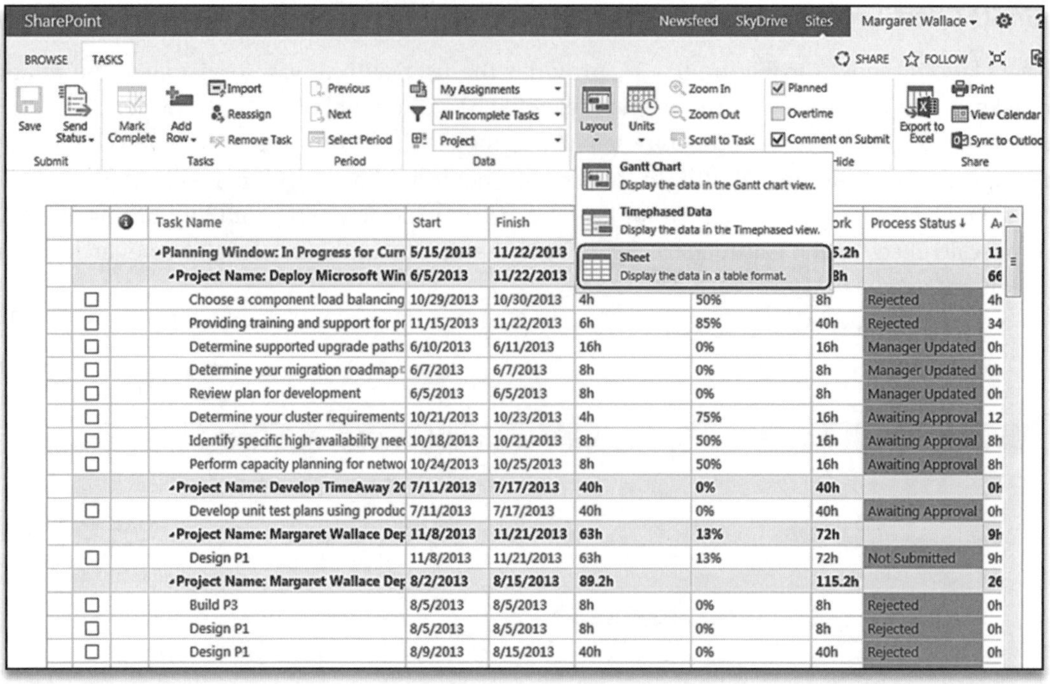

Figure 9 - 39: Sheet layout

Understanding the Assignment Details Page

To navigate to the *Assignment Details* page from the *Tasks* page, simply click the *Task Name* link. Project Server 2013 displays the *Assignment Details* page for the selected task.

The *Assignment Details* page, shown in Figure 9 - 40 and Figure 9 - 41, displays complete information for the selected task assignment and includes the following sections:

- **General Details** – Enter task progress update information in this section, such as the *Start* date, *Remaining Work*, or *Finish* date.

- **Recent Task Changes** – If your task spans more than the current time period, use this section to review the history of task changes, task updates, and comments that you or your project manager added.

- **Attachments** – From this section, you can view risks, issues, or documents associated with the task.

- **Contacts** – From this section you can see the names of your project manager, approval manager, and your fellow team members.

- **Related Assignments** –From this section you can see predecessor and successor tasks related to the selected task.

- **Notes** – From this section, you can add a note to the task.

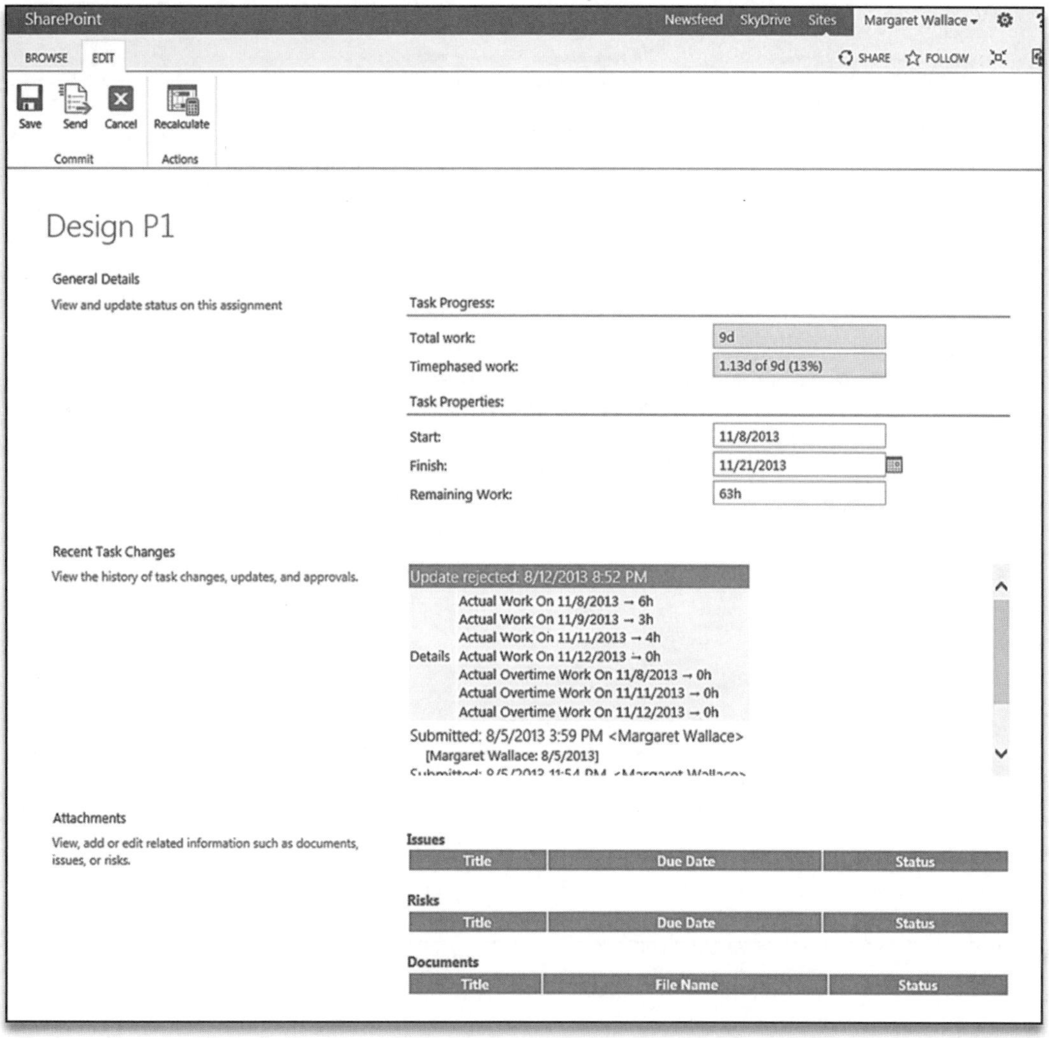

Figure 9 - 40: Assignment Details page (top)

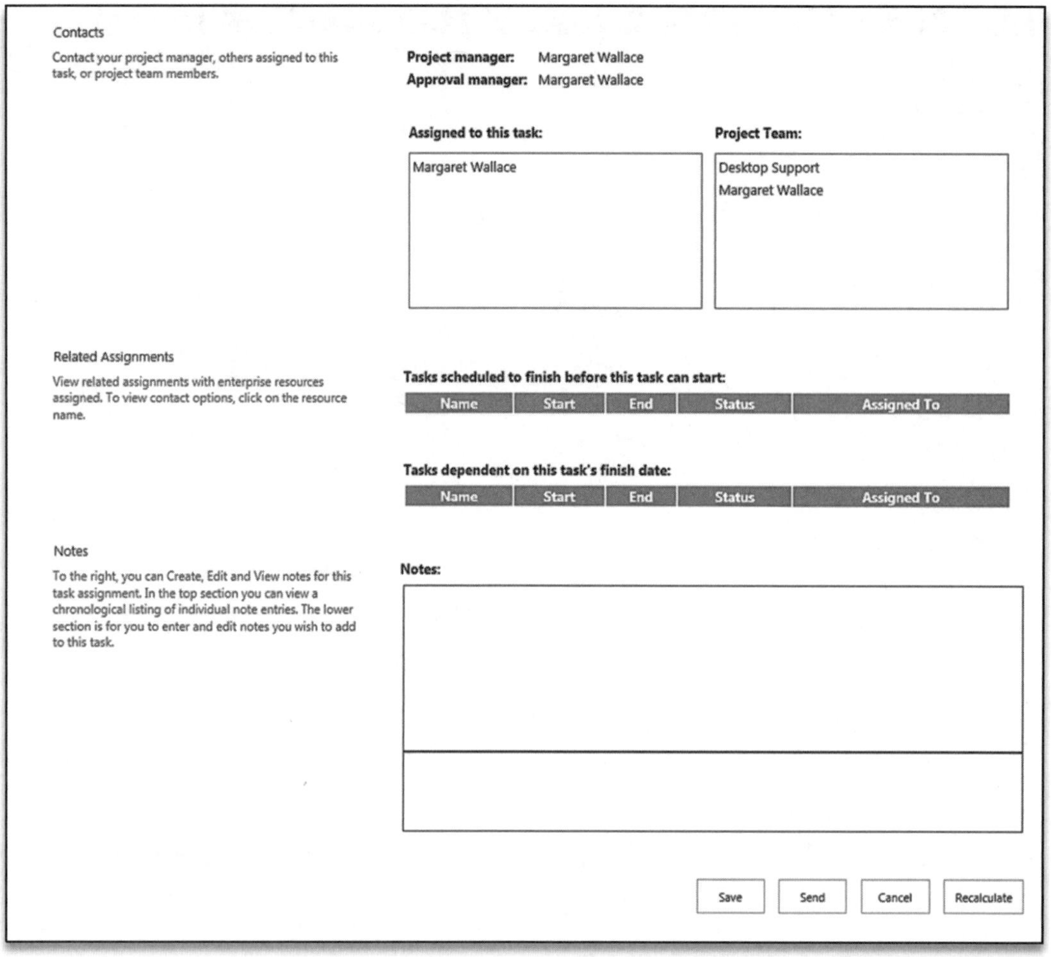
Contacts
Contact your project manager, others assigned to this task, or project team members.
Project manager: Margaret Wallace
Approval manager: Margaret Wallace
Assigned to this task:
Margaret Wallace
Project Team:
Desktop Support
Margaret Wallace
Related Assignments
View related assignments with enterprise resources assigned. To view contact options, click on the resource name.
Tasks scheduled to finish before this task can start:
Name
Start
End
Status
Assigned To
Tasks dependent on this task's finish date:
Name
Start
End
Status
Assigned To
Notes
To the right, you can Create, Edit and View notes for this task assignment. In the top section you can view a chronological listing of individual note entries. The lower section is for you to enter and edit notes you wish to add to this task.
Notes:
Save
Send
Cancel
Recalculate

Figure 9 - 41: Assignment Details page (bottom)

Reporting Progress from the Tasks Page

As I stated earlier, Project Server 2013 offers your organization four different methods for tracking progress. The information you enter on the *Tasks* page varies with the method of tracking your organization uses. Your organization may choose to use the default layout of the *Tasks* page, or use a modified layout recommended by MSProjectExperts. Because of this flexibility, I discuss each method of tracking progress, using both the default layout and the custom MSProjectExperts layout of the *Tasks* page.

Using Percent of Work Complete

Although you may report progress from the *Tasks* page using the *Percent of Work Complete* method of tracking progress, Project Server 2013 accepts only a limited amount of information with the default layout of the *Tasks* page. If your organization requires you to enter task progress from the *Tasks* page, use the following methodology to report progress on a task:

1. Click in the *% Work Complete* field and enter your estimate of the percentage of work completed to date on the task. The *Process Status* field value changes to *Save Needed* and the *Information* bar appears under the ribbon with the message: *Status: There are unsaved updates.*

Information: When you enter *100% complete* on a task, Project Server 2013 assumes that you started and finished the task as **originally scheduled**. The system has no way of knowing that you started or finished a task early or late compared to the original schedule.

2. To adjust the remaining work (also known as the ETC or Estimated Time to Completion) for the task, click in the *Remaining Work* field and enter your remaining work estimate.

3. To add a note to the task, click on the task name and scroll to the bottom of the *Assignment Details* page as shown in Figure 9 - 42. Enter your note and click the *Save* button.

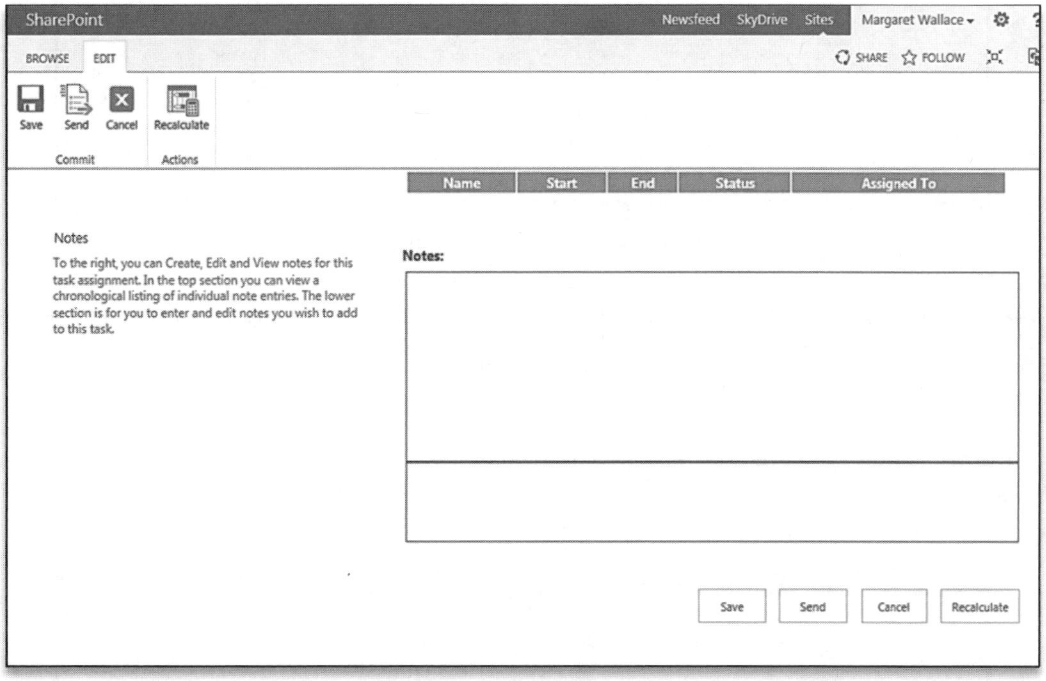
SharePoint
Newsfeed
SkyDrive
Sites
Margaret Wallace
BROWSE
EDIT
SHARE
FOLLOW
Save
Send
Cancel
Recalculate
Commit
Actions
Name
Start
End
Status
Assigned To
Notes
To the right, you can Create, Edit and View notes for this task assignment. In the top section you can view a chronological listing of individual note entries. The lower section is for you to enter and edit notes you wish to add to this task.
Notes:
Save
Send
Cancel
Recalculate

Figure 9 - 42: Add a Task Note

Information: If your project manager enters a note on a task in the actual Microsoft Project plan, the note text appears in the top half of the Project Web App *Assignment Notes* dialog. The top half of the dialog also contains notes that you previously submitted and which the project manager updated into the Microsoft Project plan.

Best Practice: MSProjectExperts recommends that you train team members to "date stamp" their notes text by adopting a standard convention for entering notes. Project Server 2013 "name stamps" each note to show who submitted the note, but does not "date stamp" the note to show when the team member submitted the note.

Project Server 2013 displays your attached note with an indicator to the left of the task name, as shown in Figure 9 - 43.

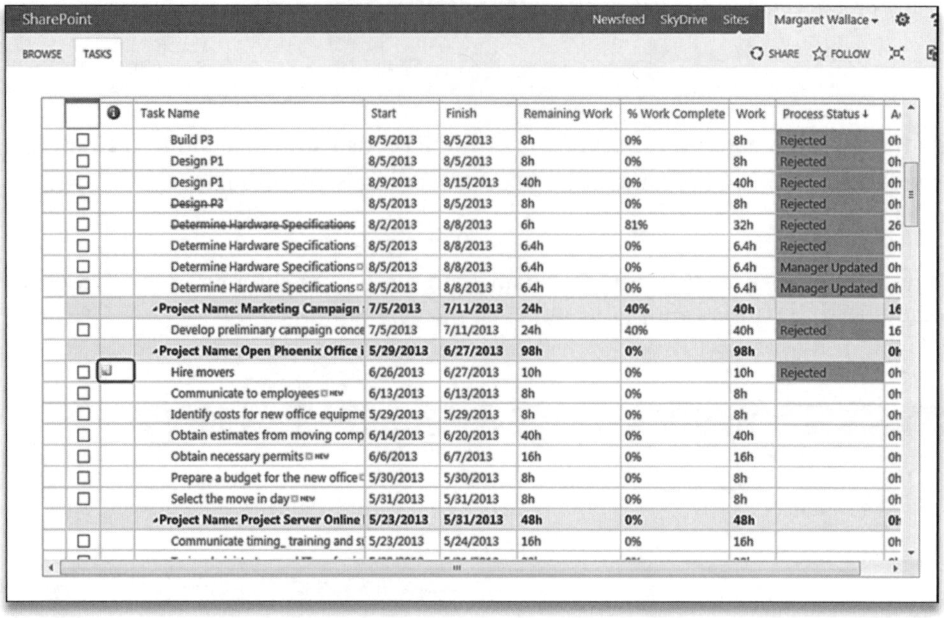

Figure 9 - 43: Task note indicators

> **Information**: To adjust the scheduled *Start* or *Finish* date for a future task, click the *Start* or *Finish* field and change the date on the calendar date picker. This alerts your project manager that the actual start or finish is different from the current schedule in the project plan.

4. Click the *Save* button to save your task progress changes if you are not ready to submit them to your project manager for approval. When you save the changes, Project Server 2013 changes the timesheet line *Process Status* value to *Not Submitted*, as shown in Figure 9 - 44.

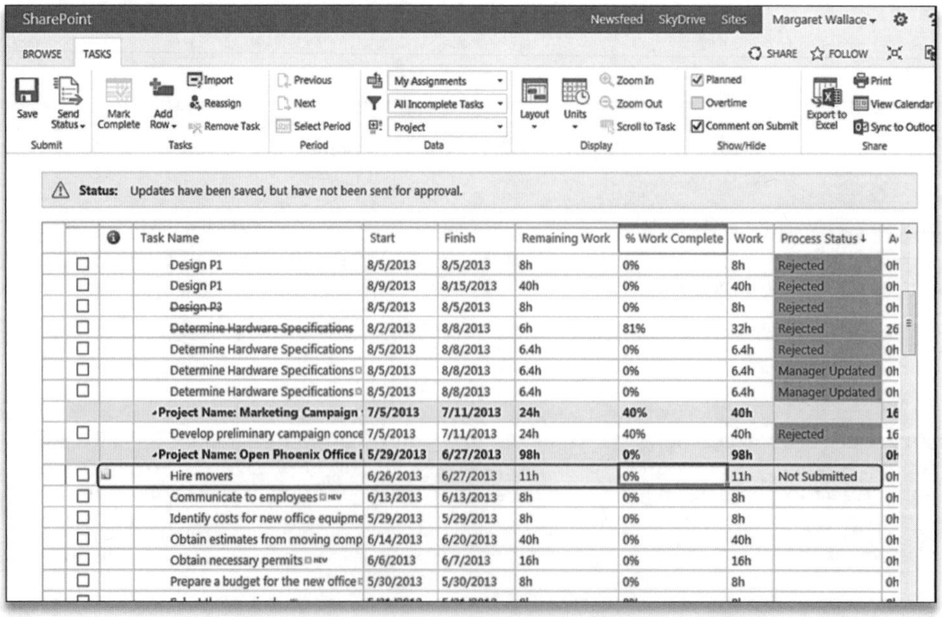

Figure 9 - 44: Saved Not Submitted Task

5. When you are ready to submit the task changes to your project manager, in the *Submit* section of the *TASKS* ribbon, click the *Send Status* pick list. The *All Tasks* option sends all changed tasks information for approval. The *Selected Tasks* option only sends the tasks that you selected in the list.
6. Project Server 2013 displays the *Submit Changes* dialog shown in Figure 9 - 45. Enter an optional comment about the update in the *Submit Changes* dialog and then click the *OK* button to submit the update to your project manager.

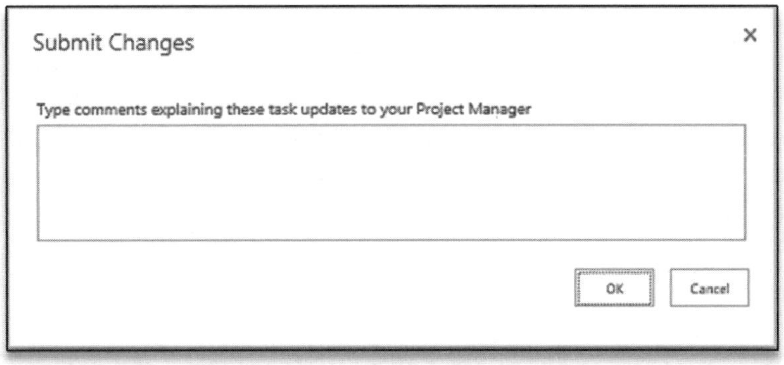

Figure 9 - 45: Submit Changes dialog

Information: In the *Show/Hide* section of the *TASKS* ribbon, Project Server 2013 selects by default the *Comment on Submit* option, which displays the *Submit Changes* dialog. To suppress the system prompt to add a comment each time you submit task progress, deselect the *Comment on Submit* option.

Project Server 2013 redisplays the *Tasks* page with a confirmation message in the *Information* bar indicating that the system submitted your updates for approval as shown in Figure 9 - 46.

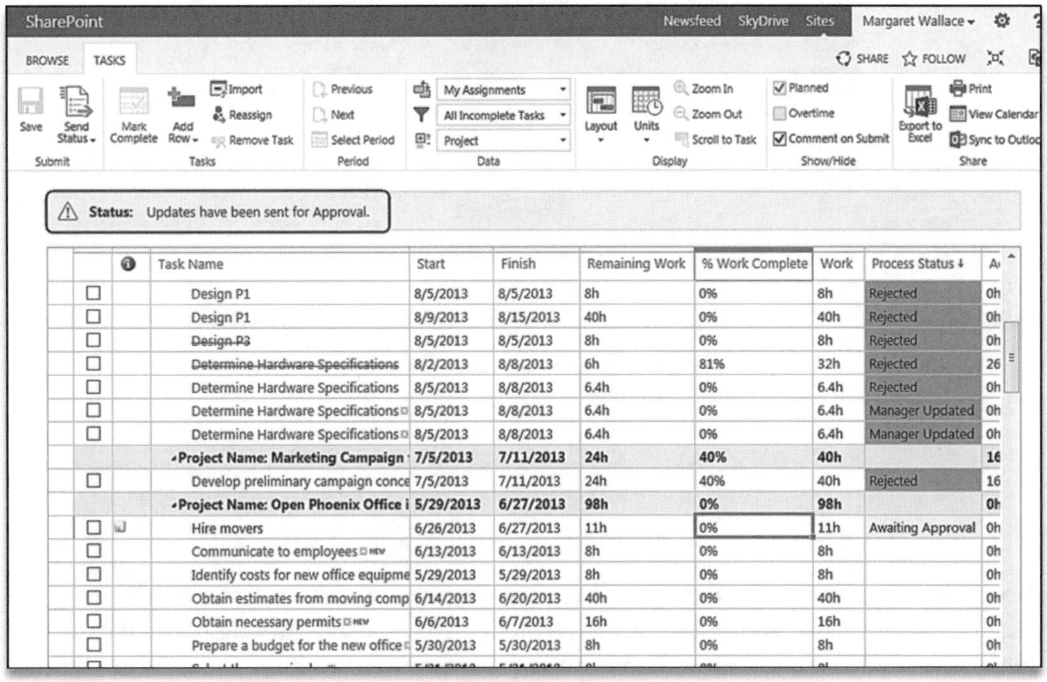

Figure 9 - 46: Submitted Tasks

Best Practice: Using Percent of Work Complete

MSProjectExperts recommends that your Project Server administrator create a custom view of the *Tasks* page to optimize your data entry experience. This view controls the data columns that are on the page. However, you may control other aspects such as grouping.

The custom view contains the following columns: *Project Name, Task Name, Process Status, Task Hierarchy, Health, Actual Start, % Work Complete, Remaining Work, Actual Finish,* and *Resource Name*. Optional fields are *Start, Finish, Work* and *Comments*. These fields enable you to see the original dates as well as any comments. I recommend the *Sheet* layout for this tracking method. The recommended grouping is by *Project*. Figure 9 - 47 shows the *Tasks* page with the custom view and MSProjectExperts recommended settings.

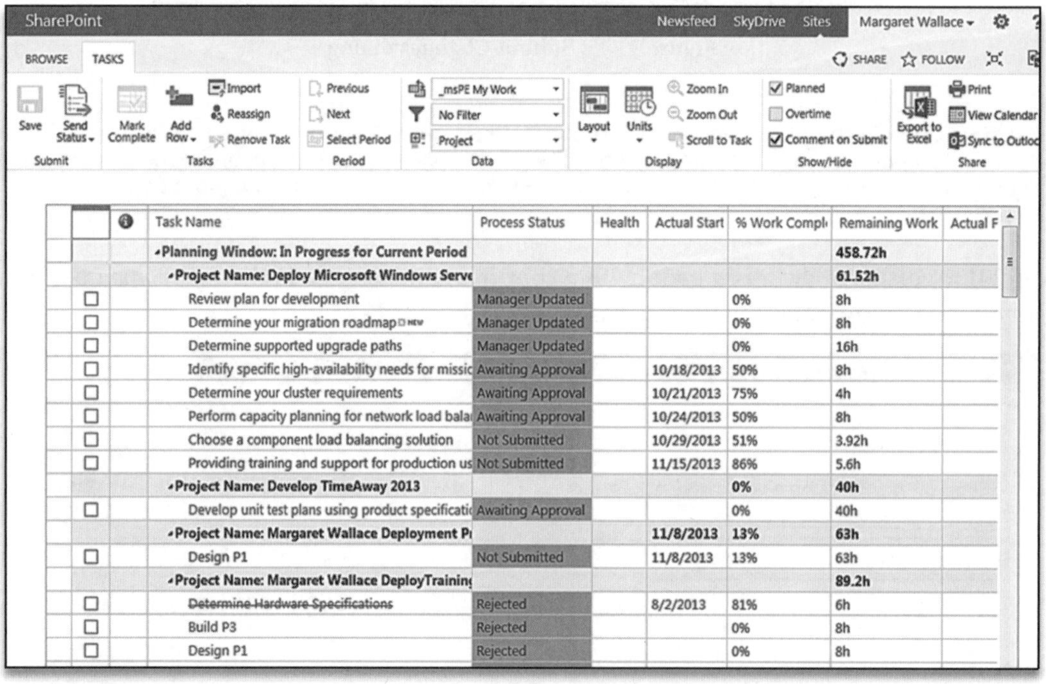

Figure 9 - 47: Recommended Percent Complete view

If you are managing assignments for other resources, I recommend an alternative custom grouping that segregates your personal assignments from those of the resources you manage. In this particular case, your custom grouping values are set to *Planning Window, Resource Name, Project Name,* yielding the view in Figure 9 - 48.

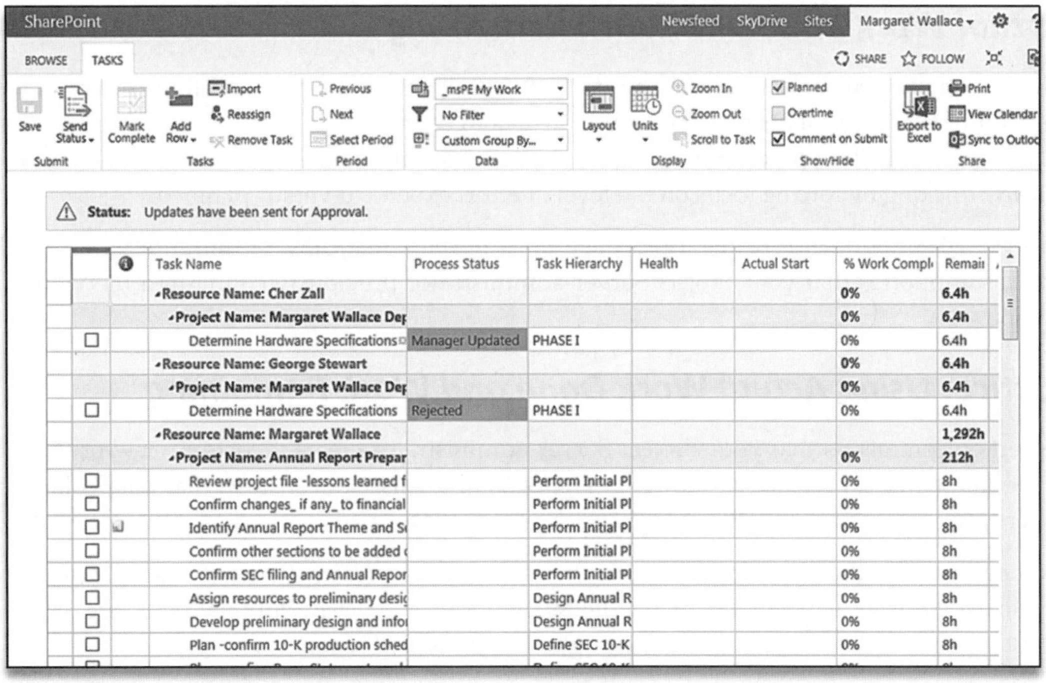

Figure 9 - 48: Tasks page Organized for Assignment Owners

To enter progress using the *Percent of Work Complete* method of tracking with this custom layout of the *Tasks* page, use the following methodology:

1. When you start a new task, click in the *Actual Start* field for the selected task and enter the date you began work on the task.
2. Click in the *%Work Complete* field and enter your estimate of the percentage of work completed to date on the task.
3. Enter your estimated amount of *Remaining Work* (or ETC) in the *Remaining Work* field.
4. When you complete a task, click in the *Actual Finish* field for the selected task and enter the date you finished work on the task.
5. To add a note to the task, click the name of the task and enter your note on the *Assignment Details* page, or use the *Comments* field to notate an explanation in the task view that includes the *Comments* column.
6. Click the *Save* button to save your task progress changes if you are not ready to send them to your project manager for approval.
7. When you are ready to send the task changes to your project manager, select the option to the left of each task that you want to send and in the *Submit* section of the *Task* ribbon, click the *Send Status* pick list and select the *Selected Tasks* item on the list. Alternately, you may also select the *All Tasks* item from the pick list to send all task changes automatically.

Information: Although this method of tracking requires a little more work on the part of team members, entering an *Actual Start* and *Actual Finish* date provides the project manager much more accurate scheduling information. This helps the project manager to better forecast schedule slippage due to a late *Actual Start* date or late *Actual Finish* date on a task and all successor tasks.

Using Actual Work Done and Work Remaining

In this tracking method, you are entering the amount of time spent on the task and the amount of work remaining. This method of time accrual enables you and your management to gauge progress toward the task outcome and the quality of the initial work estimate. This method also minimizes the somewhat subjective nature of *% Work Complete* tracking by forcing focus on the level of effort expended versus planned.

In Project Server 2013, the layout of the *Tasks* page does not automatically reconfigure based on the tracking method. The assumption is that your Project Server administrator previously configured the view based on the tracking method.

Best Practice: Using Actual Work Done and Work Remaining

MSProjectExperts recommends that your Project Server administrator create a custom view of the *Tasks* page to optimize your data entry experience as shown in Figure 9 - 49. This view ensures that data columns are on the page; however, you are in control of other aspects such as grouping.

The custom view contains the following columns: *Project Name, Task Name, Process Status, Task Hierarchy, Health, Actual Start, Actual Work, Remaining Work, Actual Finish,* and *Resource Name*. Optional fields are *Start, Finish, Work* and *Comments*. These fields enable you to see the original dates as well as any comments.

I recommend the *Sheet* layout for this tracking method. The recommended grouping is by *Project*.

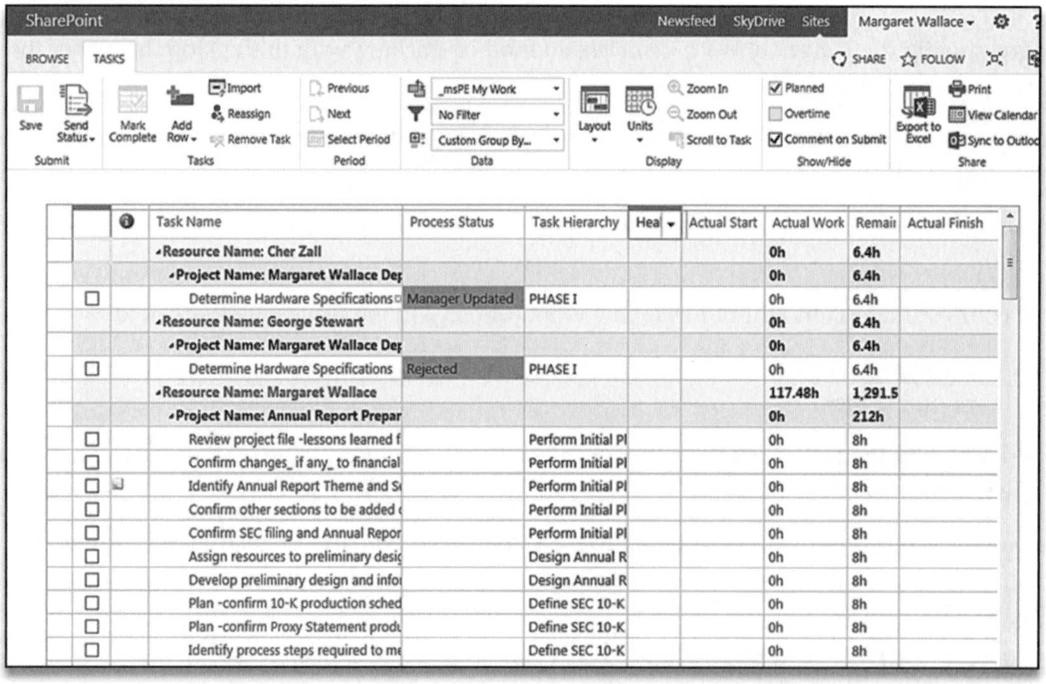

Figure 9 - 49: My Tasks for Actual Work Done tracking

> **Information**: As a courtesy, your Project Server administrator may also include the *Start* and *Finish* fields so that team members can see the scheduled dates for tasks to start and finish.

To enter progress using the *Actual Work Done* and *Work Remaining* method of tracking with the *Tasks* page custom layout, use the following methodology:

1. When you start a new task, click in the *Actual Start* field for the selected task and enter the date you began work on the task.

2. Click in the *Actual Work* field and enter the total amount of work completed to date (measured in hours) on the task.

Information: If you enter a total amount of work that equals the planned work on a task (indicating you completed the task), Project Server 2013 assumes that you started and finished the task as **originally scheduled**. The system has no way of knowing that you started or finished a task early or late compared to the original schedule.

3. Enter your estimated amount of *Remaining Work* (or *Estimated Time to Completion/ETC*) in the *Remaining Work* field.

4. When you complete a task, click in the *Finish* field for the selected task and enter the date you finished work on the task.

5. Click the *Save* button to save your task progress changes if you are not ready to submit them to your project manager for approval.

6. When you are ready to submit the task changes to your project manager, select the option to the left of each task that you want to submit, click the *Send Status* pick list and select the *Selected Tasks* item on the list. Alternately, you may also select the *All Tasks* item to send all task changes automatically.

Information: To adjust the scheduled *Start* or *Finish* date for a future task, click in the *Start* or *Finish* field and change the date on the calendar date picker. This alerts your project manager that the actual start or finish is different from the current schedule in the project plan.

7. If the *Submit Changes* dialog displays, enter an optional comment about the update and then click the *OK* button to send the update to your project manager.

Information: Although this method of tracking requires a little more work on the part of team members, entering an *Actual Start* and *Actual Finish* date gives the project manager much more accurate tracking information. This helps the project manager to better forecast schedule slippage due to a late *Actual Start* date or late *Actual Finish* date on a task and their successor tasks.

Using Hours of Work Done per Period

Organizations that use the *Hours of Work Done per Period* method of tracking progress need the finer level of detail, typically to meet billing requirements or the more rigorous requirements of a mature project management process. The *Tasks* page typically requires the timephased data entry grid for entries by day using this tracking method.

The *Tasks* page shown in Figure 9 - 50 includes a scroll bar at the bottom of the data grid. On lower screen resolutions, such as my current 1024 x 768 resolution, the data grid is too wide to fit on the page, and the system displays the scroll bar. At higher screen resolutions, such as at 1280 x 1024, the system displays the entire data grid without a scroll bar.

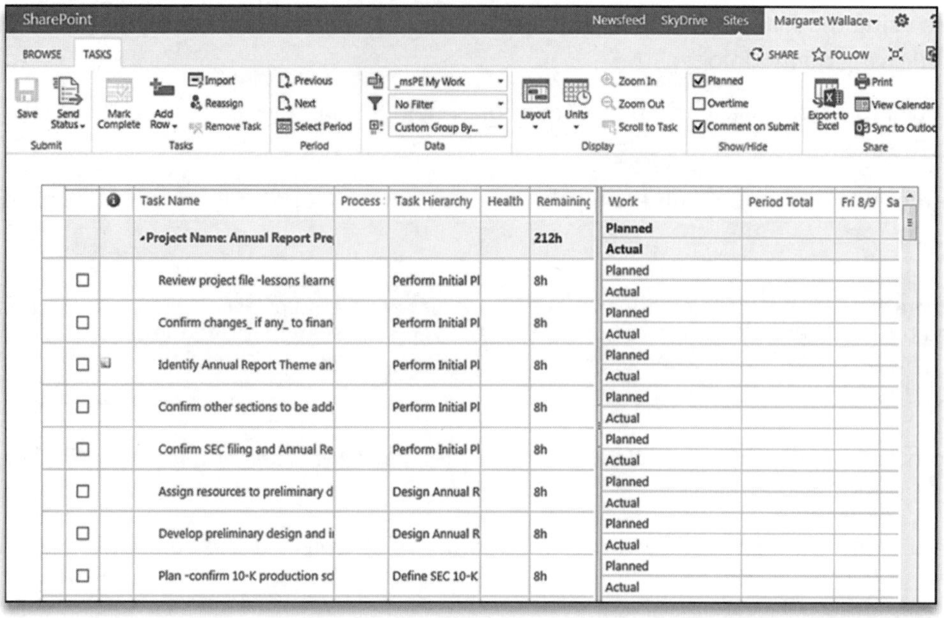

Figure 9 - 50: Tasks organized for Hours of Work Done Per Period tracking

Best Practice: Using Hours of Work Done per Period

MSProjectExperts recommends that your Project Server administrator create a custom view of the *Tasks* page to optimize your data entry experience as shown in Figure 9 - 51. This view ensures that data columns are on the page; however, you are in control of other aspects such as grouping.

The custom view contains the following columns: *Project Name, Task Name, Process Status, Task Hierarchy, Health, Remaining Work, Actual Finish,* and *Resource Name*. Optional fields are *Start, Finish, Work* and *Comments*. These fields enable you to see the original dates as well as any comments.

I recommend the *Timephased Data* layout for this tracking method. The recommended grouping is by *Project*.

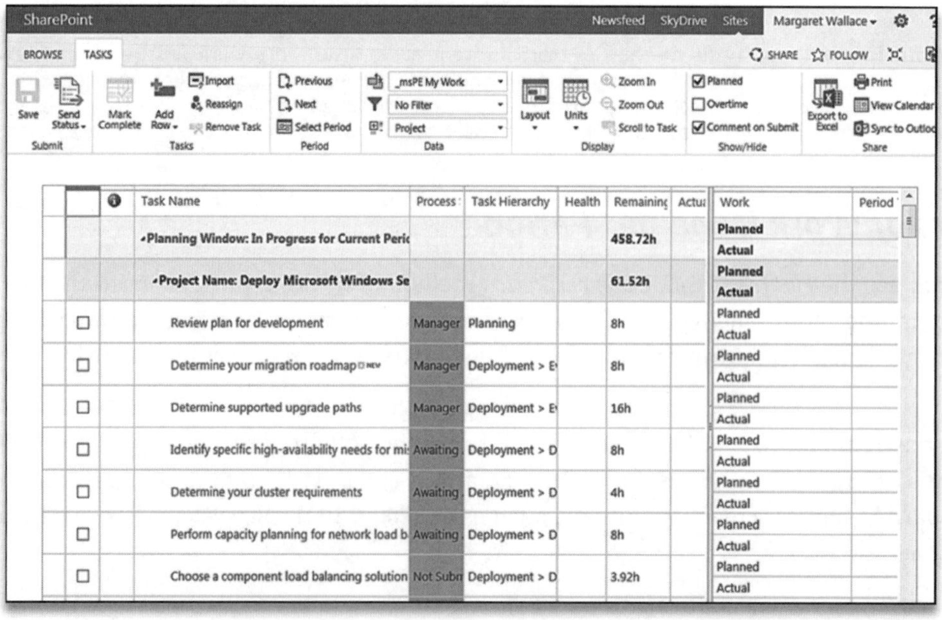

Figure 9 - 51: Tasks organized for Hours of Work Done tracking, with Planning Window grouping

To enter progress using the *Hours of Work Done per Period* method of tracking with the custom layout of the *Tasks* page, use the following methodology:

1. On a daily basis, enter the hours you worked on each task in the timesheet grid.

2. Add notes as needed for each task, by either entering your note in the *Comments* field, if it is present, or entering your note on the *Assignment Details* page.

> **Information**: To enter notes on the *Assignment Details* page, complete the following steps:
>
> 1. In the *Submit* section of the *Tasks* ribbon, click the *Save* button.
> 2. Click the *Task Name* link to navigate to the *Assignment Details* page.
> 3. Enter your note text at the bottom of the page.
> 4. Click the *OK* button.

3. Enter your progress daily and then in the *Submit* section of the *Task* ribbon, click the *Save* button to save your current progress at the end of each day.

4. On the last day of the reporting period, enter your estimated amount of *Remaining Work* (or *Estimated Time to Completion/ETC*) in the *Remaining Work* field for any tasks that require an adjustment.

5. Add a note to any task where you adjusted the *Remaining Work* value, using the *Comment* field in the view.

6. When you are ready to send the task changes to your project manager, select the option to the left of each task that you want to send, click the *Send Status* pick list and select the *Selected Tasks* item on the list. Alternately, you may also select the *All Tasks* item from the list to send all task changes automatically.

> **Information**: To adjust the scheduled *Start* or *Finish* date for a future task, click in the *Start* or *Finish* field and change the date on the calendar date picker. This alerts your project manager that the actual start or finish is different from the current schedule in the project plan.

7. If you see the *Submit Changes* dialog, enter an optional comment about the update and then click the *OK* button to send the update to your project manager.

> **Best Practice**: As a best practice, MSProjectExperts recommends that you enter actual progress on a daily basis and update progress to your project manager on a weekly basis.

Reporting Progress from the Assignment Details Page

An alternate method for entering task progress is to use the *Assignment Details* page. Because this page contains so much more information about each task than the *Tasks* page, using the *Assignment Details* page is helpful if your organization uses the default layout of the *Tasks* page. The *Assignment Details* page does not provide the same full update capabilities as the primary view. Depending on the tracking method, you may update the following values on the *Assignment Details* page as shown in Table 9 - 4.

Updatable Fields	% Complete	Actual Work / Remaining Work	Hours of Work Done
Completed Work		X	
Finish Date	X	X	X
Percent Complete	X		
Remaining Work	X	X	X
Start Date	X	X	X

Table 9 - 4: Updatable Fields on Assignment Details page

To access the *Assignment Details* page for any task, click the name of the task on the *Tasks* page. Figure 9 - 52 shows the layout of the *Assignment Details* page using the *Percent of Work Complete* method of tracking progress. Notice that the *Task Progress* section of the page includes the *Percent complete* field.

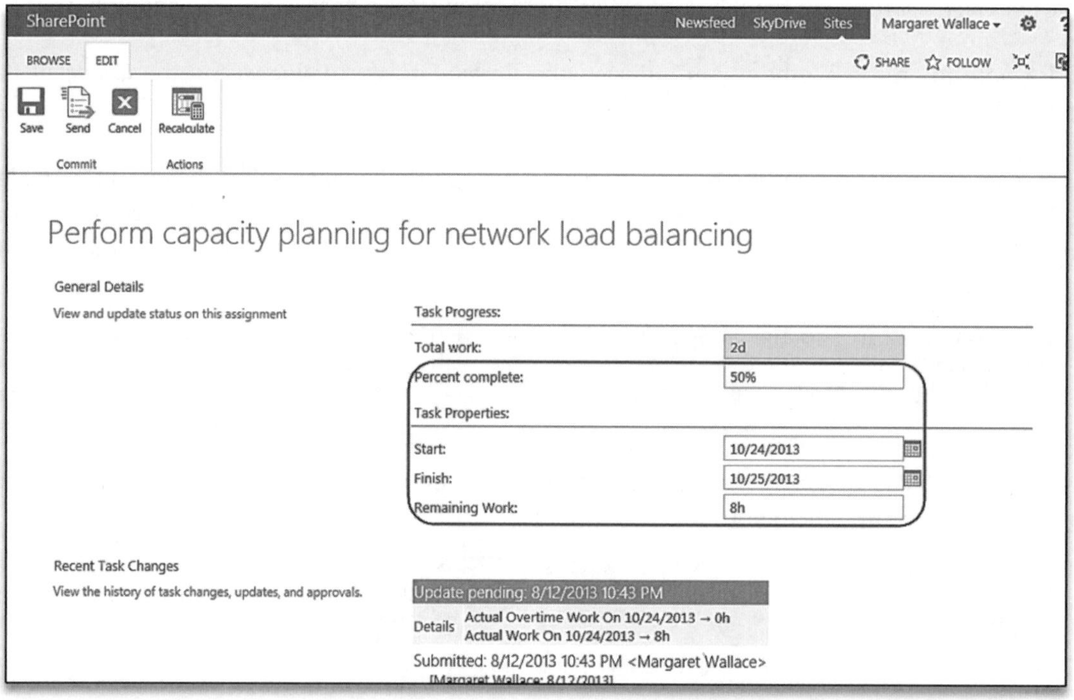

Figure 9 - 52: Assignment Details page using the % Work Complete method of tracking

Figure 9 - 53 shows the layout of the *Assignment Details* page using the *Actual Work Done* and *Work Remaining* method of tracking. Notice that the *Task Progress* section includes the *Completed work* field, measured in days.

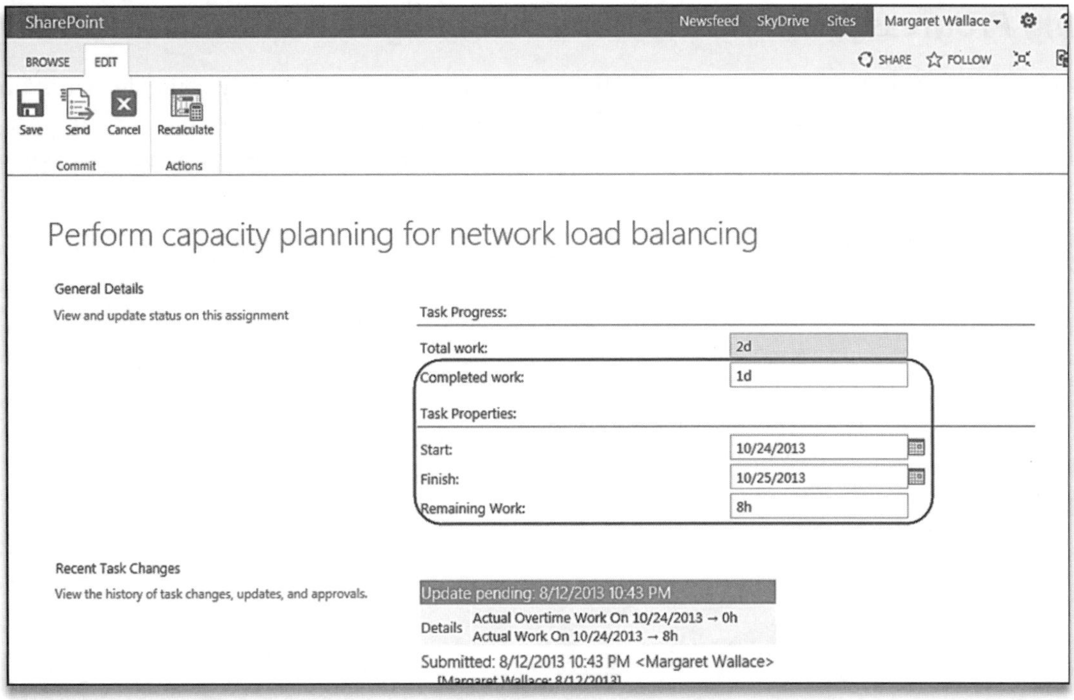

Figure 9 - 53: Assignment Details page using the Actual Work Done and Work Remaining method of tracking

Figure 9 - 54 shows the layout of the *Assignment Details* page using the *Hours of Work Done per Period* method of tracking. Note, in this tracking mode, you must use the primary *Tasks* view to enter time.

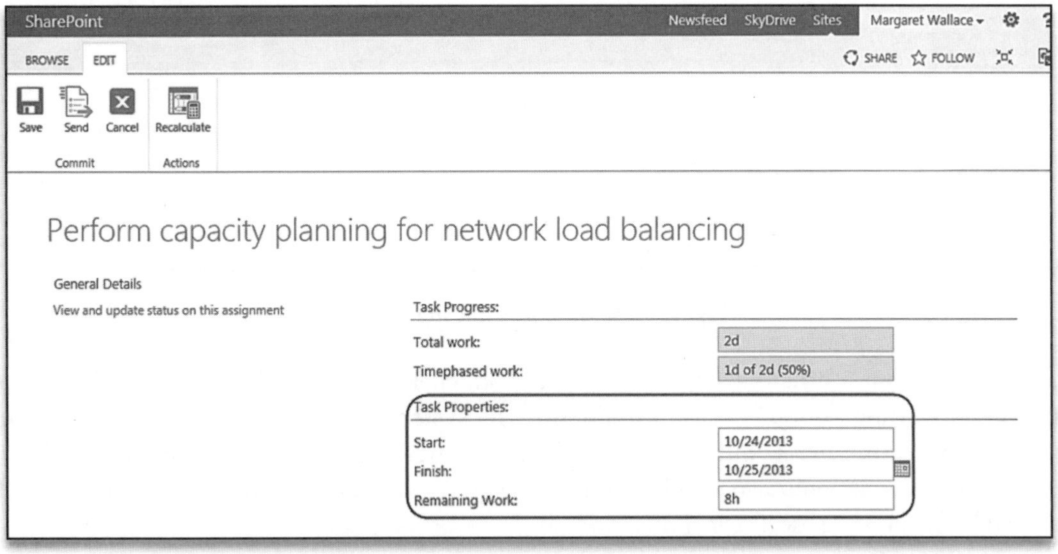

Figure 9 - 54: Assignment Details page using the Hours of Work Done per Period method of tracking

To report task progress from the *Assignment Details* page, use the same methodologies I presented earlier in this module for the method of tracking progress used by your organization. From this page, you may enter progress, adjust the *Remaining Work* value or add a note. When finished, click the *Save* button. From the *Tasks* page, send the update to your project manager by clicking the *Send Status* pick list and selecting either the *Selected Tasks* item or the *All Tasks* item on the list.

Importing Progress from the My Timesheet Page

Regardless of which hourly method your organization uses to track task progress, if you enter work hours in the *Timesheet* page, you can import the hours directly into the tasks shown on the *Tasks* page. To import timesheet hours, click the *Import* button on the *Tasks* page. Project Server 2013 displays the *Import Timesheet* page for the current time period, as shown in Figure 9 - 55.

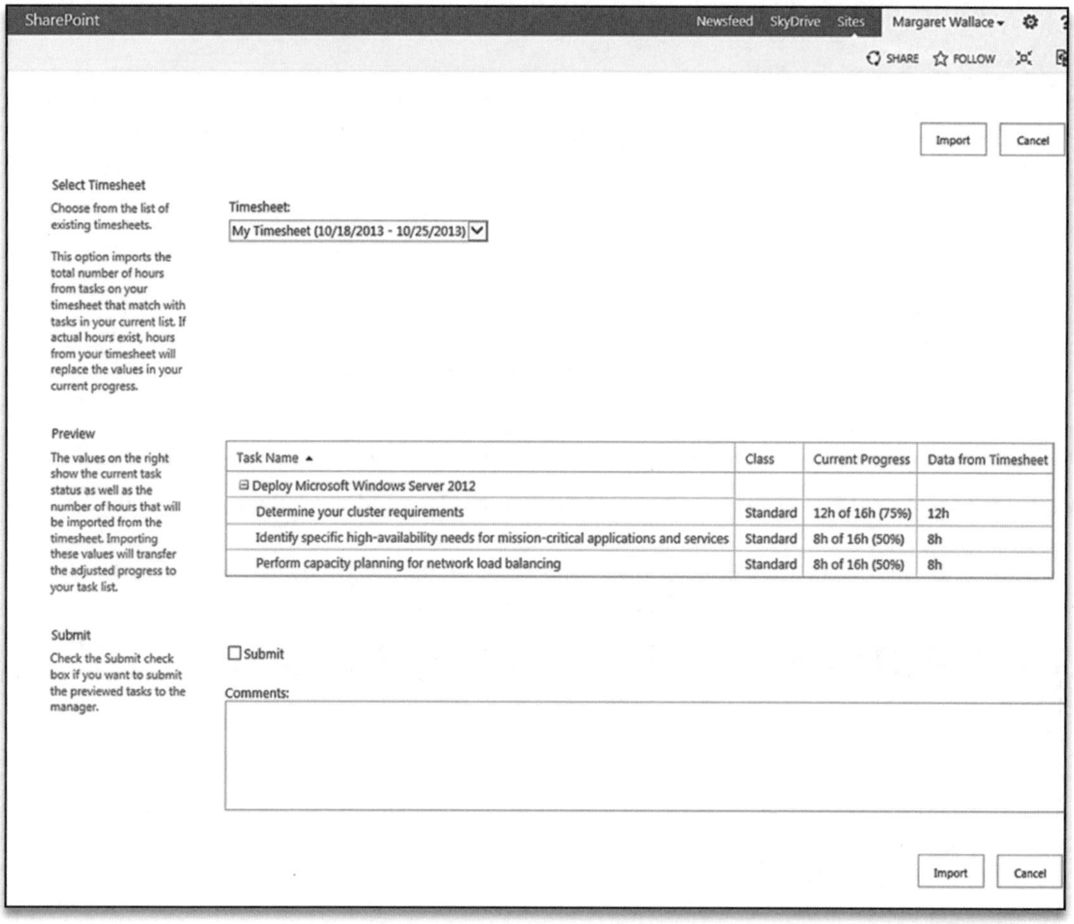
SharePoint
Newsfeed
SkyDrive
Sites
Margaret Wallace
SHARE
FOLLOW
Import
Cancel
Select Timesheet
Choose from the list of existing timesheets.
This option imports the total number of hours from tasks on your timesheet that match with tasks in your current list. If actual hours exist, hours from your timesheet will replace the values in your current progress.
Timesheet:
My Timesheet (10/18/2013 - 10/25/2013)
Preview
The values on the right show the current task status as well as the number of hours that will be imported from the timesheet. Importing these values will transfer the adjusted progress to your task list.
Task Name
Class
Current Progress
Data from Timesheet
Deploy Microsoft Windows Server 2012
Determine your cluster requirements
Standard
12h of 16h (75%)
12h
Identify specific high-availability needs for mission-critical applications and services
Standard
8h of 16h (50%)
8h
Perform capacity planning for network load balancing
Standard
8h of 16h (50%)
8h
Submit
Check the Submit check box if you want to submit the previewed tasks to the manager.
Submit
Comments:
Import
Cancel

Figure 9 - 55: Import Timesheet page

To import a timesheet from a different time reporting period, click the *Timesheet* pick list at the top of the page and select the time reporting period you want to import. The system refreshes the page to show an updated *Import Timesheet* page. Click the *Import* button to import the timesheet data to the tasks shown on the *Tasks* page. When finished, add task comments as needed, and then submit the update to your project manager, following the methods detailed in the previous sections of this module.

Managing Tasks

Along with reporting progress, other important task-related activities on the *Tasks* page include the following:

- Reassign work to someone else
- Add Team Tasks

- Add a New Task
- Add Yourself to a Task
- Propose to Remove a task

I cover each activity in detail in the sections that follow.

Reassign Work to Someone Else

After a project manager assigns you to a task, Project Server 2013 offers you the option to reassign the task to someone else. You might find this feature useful if you serve as a team leader to whom the project manager assigns tasks, and you are responsible for reassigning tasks to members of your team.

To reassign a task to someone else, navigate to the *Tasks* page, select one or more tasks to reassign and then click the *Reassign* button on the *Task* ribbon. Project Server 2013 displays the *Task Reassignment* page shown in Figure 9 - 56.

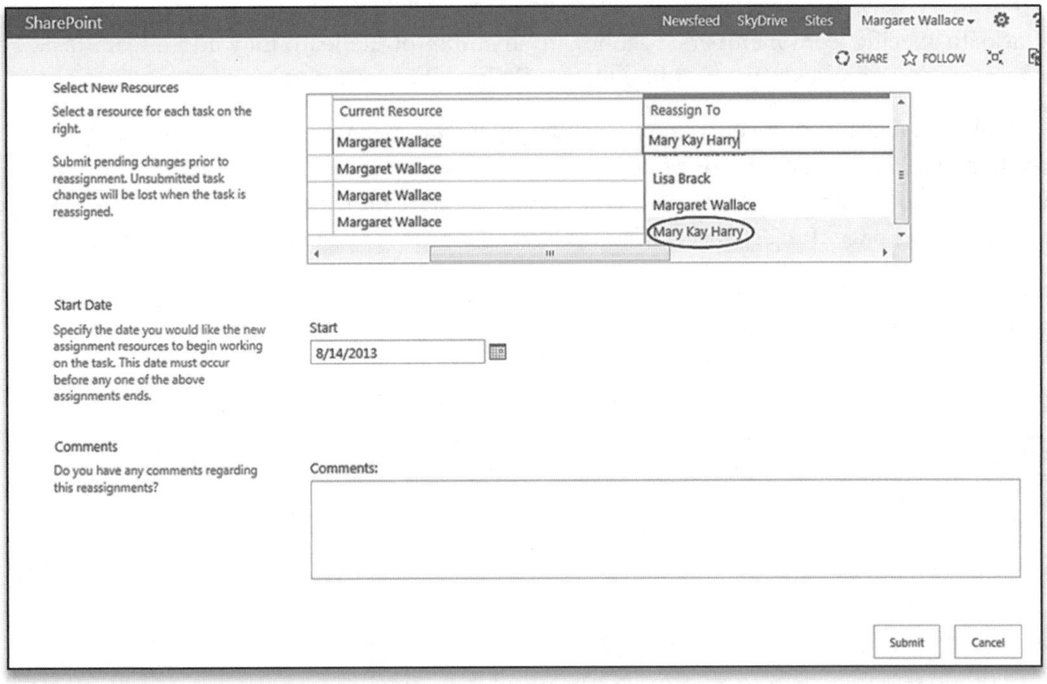
SharePoint
Newsfeed
SkyDrive
Sites
Margaret Wallace
SHARE
FOLLOW
Select New Resources
Select a resource for each task on the right.
Submit pending changes prior to reassignment. Unsubmitted task changes will be lost when the task is reassigned.
Current Resource
Reassign To
Margaret Wallace
Mary Kay Harry
Margaret Wallace
Margaret Wallace
Margaret Wallace
Lisa Brack
Margaret Wallace
Mary Kay Harry
Start Date
Specify the date you would like the new assignment resources to begin working on the task. This date must occur before any one of the above assignments ends.
Start
8/14/2013
Comments
Do you have any comments regarding this reassignments?
Comments:
Submit
Cancel

Figure 9 - 56: Task Reassignment page

The *Select New Resources* section of the *Task Reassignment* page shows you a list of all your selected task assignments from the *Tasks* page. The *Reassign To* column in the data grid allows you to select the resource to which you want to reassign a task. Click the pick list arrow for the *Reassign To* field for the task you want to reassign. The system displays the list of all resources of the project team.

Information: The default permissions in Project Server 2013 allow you to see only members of your project team. If you need to reassign a task to someone outside your project team, you must communicate with your project manager to first add the new resource to the project team in the project plan.

After you select the resources to which you want to reassign one or more tasks, in the *Start Date* section of the *Task Reassignment* page, click the *Start* pick list and select the date on which the system reassigns the selected tasks. The date in the *Start* field defaults to the current date. You must select a date that is before the *Finish* date of any selected tasks. Generally, you want the system to reassign the tasks immediately, which means you should keep the current date selected.

In the *Comments* field, enter any relevant comment text you want to add. When you complete your entries, click the *Submit* button. Project Server 2013 displays the *Tasks* page and removes the task(s) you reassigned.

The new resource can immediately enter time against the reassigned task. This enables team members to manage their own work to a certain extent in situations when the project manager is unavailable. However, the task reassignment is not final until the project manager approves the reassignment. When you click the *Submit* button, a task reassignment request automatically appears for the project manager to approve in the *Approval Center.*

Add Team Tasks

A team resource acts as an assignment proxy for all members of your team. This enables project managers to assign tasks to teams without knowing the specific resource to assign initially.

There are two primary ways to use team tasks. First, the team lead, if the system is properly configured, may reassign team tasks to specific team members. Second, any member of the team may add a team task. For example, if your team services work requests, then adding team tasks may be of interest.

If you are a member of a group of resources represented by a team resource, and the project manager assigns the team resource to a task, Project Server 2013 refers to the task as a team task. After the project manager publishes the enterprise project containing the team task, you may add the team task to yourself by clicking the *Add Team Tasks* button on the *Tasks* page. Project Server 2013 displays the *Team Tasks* page, as shown in Figure 9 - 57.

To add a team task, from the *Tasks* section of the *Tasks* ribbon, shown previously in Figure 9 - 51, click the *Add Row* pick list and select the *Add Team Tasks* option. The system displays the *Team Tasks* page in Figure 9 - 57. Select a task and click the *Assign to me* button on the ribbon. Project Server 2013 removes the task immediately from the *Team Tasks* page for all other resources. On the *Quick Launch* menu, click the *Tasks* link to return to the *Tasks* page.

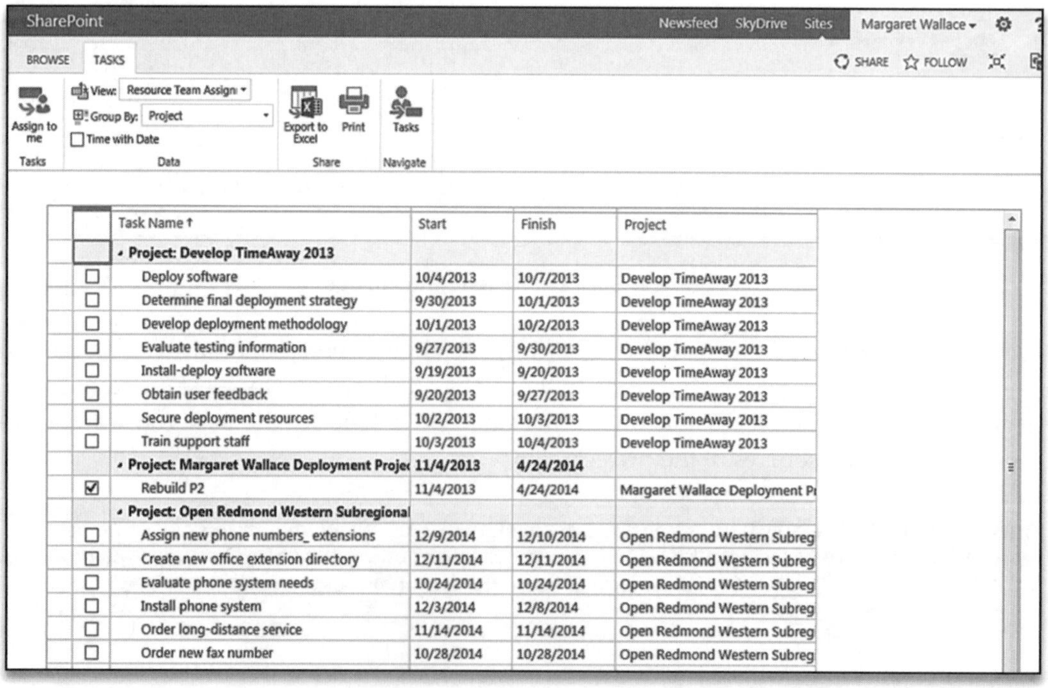

Figure 9 - 57: Team Tasks page

Information: When you add a team task, Project Server 2013 **does not** automatically approve the task reassignment. The system sends the project manager a *Status Update* for the task reassignment request for approval in the *Approval Center*. To locate the team task you may need to look in a different *Planning Window* (the *Distant Future* planning window, for example) depending on the time period the task falls. Click the *Add Row* pick list and select the *Select From Existing Assignments* option in the *Tasks* section of the *Timesheet* ribbon to add the task to your timesheet.

Add a New Task

In a collaborative project management environment, project team members may discover unplanned work and need to propose new tasks to their project manager. Proposed new tasks might include tasks related to tasks on which a resource is already working, but which were not included in the project plan, or future tasks that the team member anticipates.

To propose a new task, click the *Add Row* pick list and select the *Add a New Task* item on the list. Project Server 2013 displays the *New Task* page shown in Figure 9 - 58.

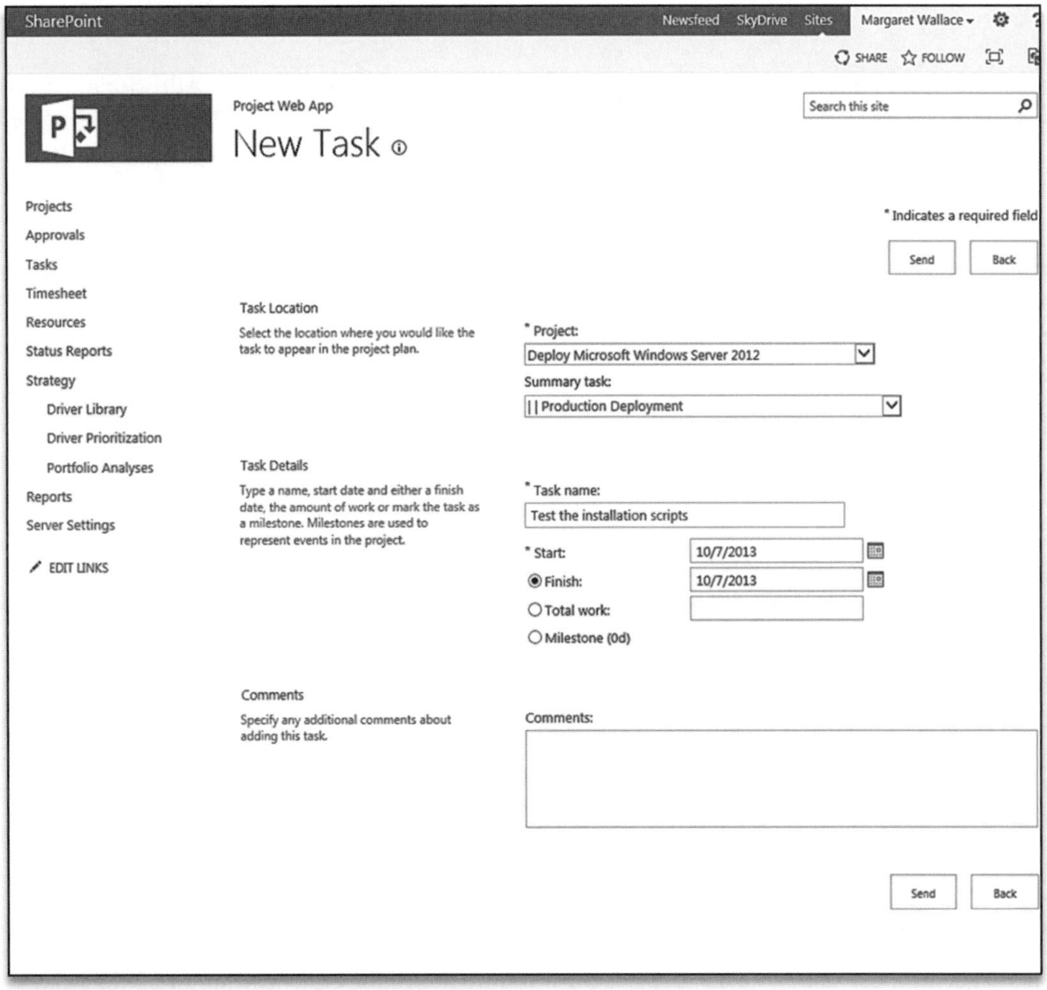

Figure 9 - 58: New Task page

To create the proposed task, begin by clicking the *Project* pick list and selecting the project in which to create the new task. The *Project* pick list contains only those projects in which you are a team member. Click the *Summary task* pick list and pick the level in the Work Breakdown Structure (WBS) at which to create the new task.

The first item on the *Subordinate to Summary task* pick list represents the highest level in the project. Selecting this item creates the new task at Outline Level 1, outside of any phase or deliverable sections in the project. The other items in the *Subordinate to Summary task* pick list include summary tasks that represent phase and deliverable sections in your project. Selecting one of these items creates the new task as a subtask of the selected phase or deliverable.

In the *Task Details* section of the *New Task* page, enter the new task name in *Task name* field. The *Start* field defaults to today's date but you should edit to reflect the actual anticipated start date. Lastly, either enter the anticipated finish date in the *Finish* field, the estimated work for the task in the *Total work* field, or mark the task as a milestone.

Information: After your project manager approves the new task request, Project Server 2013 adds the new task to the enterprise project and sets a Start No Earlier Than (SNET) constraint on the task using the date you enter in the *Start* field.

In the *Comments* field, add any additional documentation for your project manager. Additional comments might help your project manager to decide whether to approve the proposed task. Click the *Send* button when you finish. Project Server 2013 displays the *Tasks* page with the new proposed task added to the task list, as shown in Figure 9 - 59.

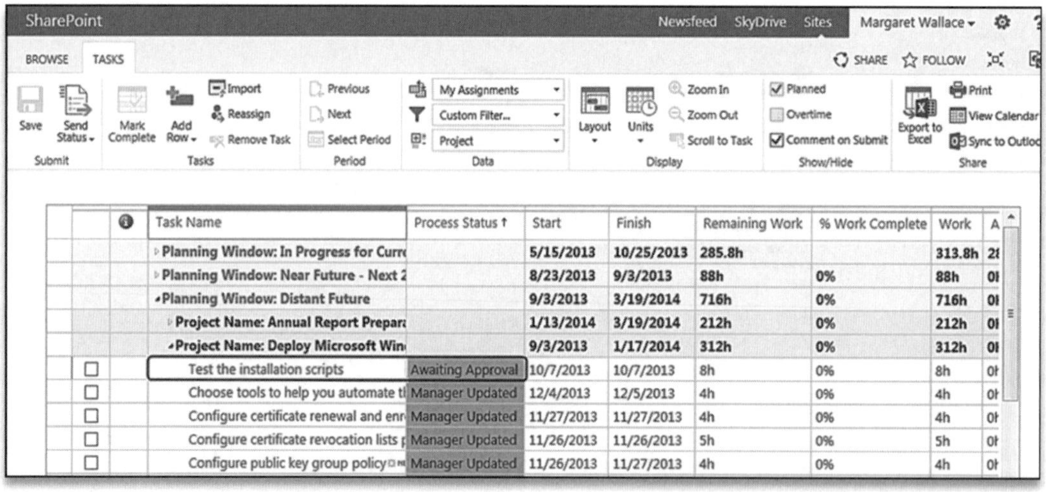

Figure 9 - 59: New Task Awaiting Approval

Add Yourself to a Task

Beyond the need for proposing new tasks, project team members might also need to add themselves to an existing task when enlisted by a fellow team member. Project Server 2013 allows a team member to add themselves to an existing task. To add yourself to a task, click the *Add Row* pick list and select the *Add Yourself to a Task* item on the list. Project Server 2013 displays the *Add Task* page shown in Figure 9 - 60.

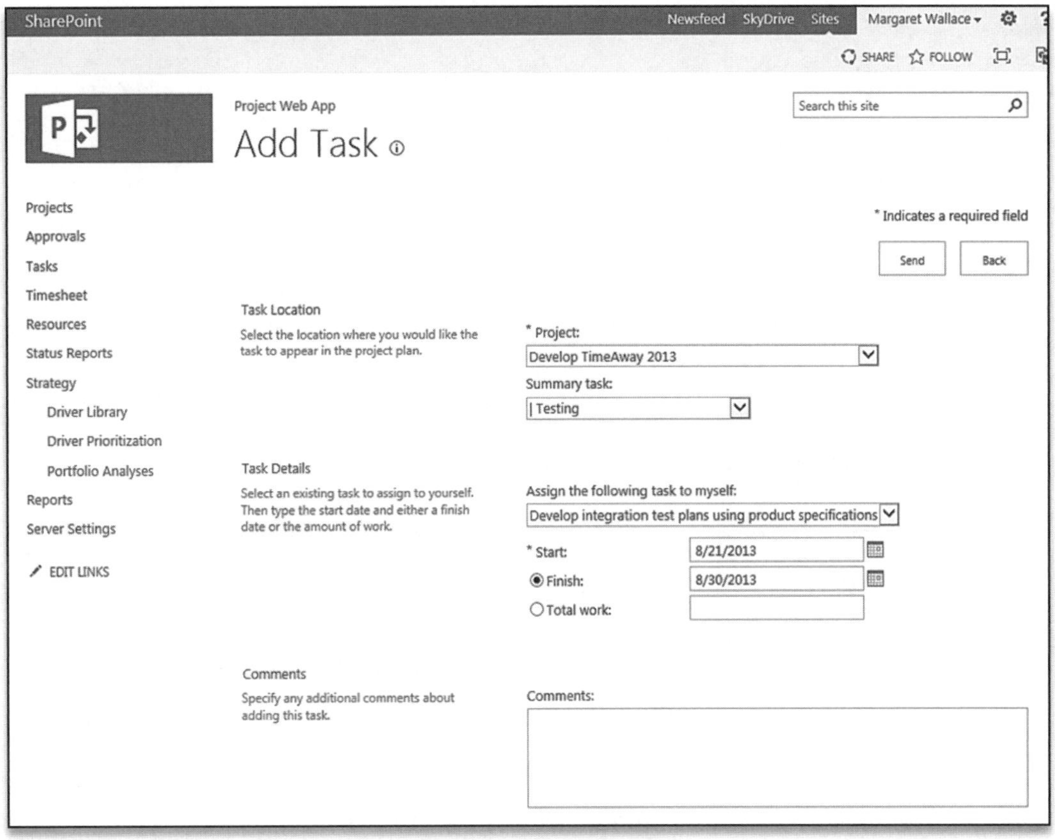

Figure 9 - 60: Add Task page

To begin, click the *Project* pick list and select the project containing the task you want to join. The *Project* pick list contains only those projects in which you are a team member. Click the *Summary task* pick list and pick the level in the Work Breakdown Structure (WBS) to which the task belongs. Lastly, click the *Assign the following task to myself* pick list and select the appropriate task.

Information: The *Assign the following task to myself* pick list contains only those tasks that are contained by the summary task you selected in the *Summary task* pick list.

In the *Task Details* section of the *Add Task* page, enter the anticipated start date of the new task in the *Start* field. Enter the anticipated finish date in the *Finish* field or enter the estimated work for the task in the *Total work* field. By default, the system sets dates in the *Start* and *Finish* fields to the current date.

Information: After your project manager approves the new task request, Project Server 2013 adds the new task to the enterprise project and sets a Start No Earlier Than (SNET) constraint on the task using the date you enter in the *Start* field.

In the *Comments* field, add any additional documentation for your project manager. Additional comments might help your project manager to decide whether to approve the proposed task.

Click the *Send* button when you finish. Project Server 2013 displays the *Tasks* page with the new proposed task added to the task list, as shown in Figure 9 - 61.

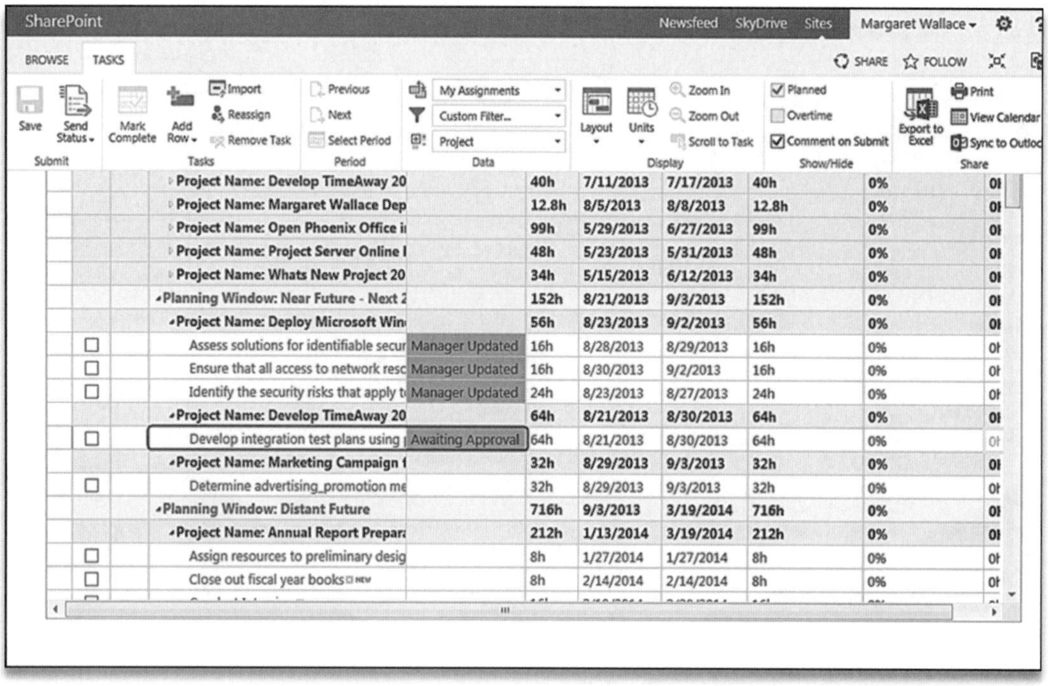

Figure 9 - 61: Added Task Awaiting Approval

When you click the *Send* button at the top right of the *Add Task* page, Project Server 2013 immediately submits a new task request to your project manager for approval. If the project manager approves the proposed task, the task remains on the *Tasks* page and you can enter and submit progress for the task. If your project manager rejects the proposed task, the system changes the *Process Status* value to *Rejected* as shown in Figure 9 - 62.

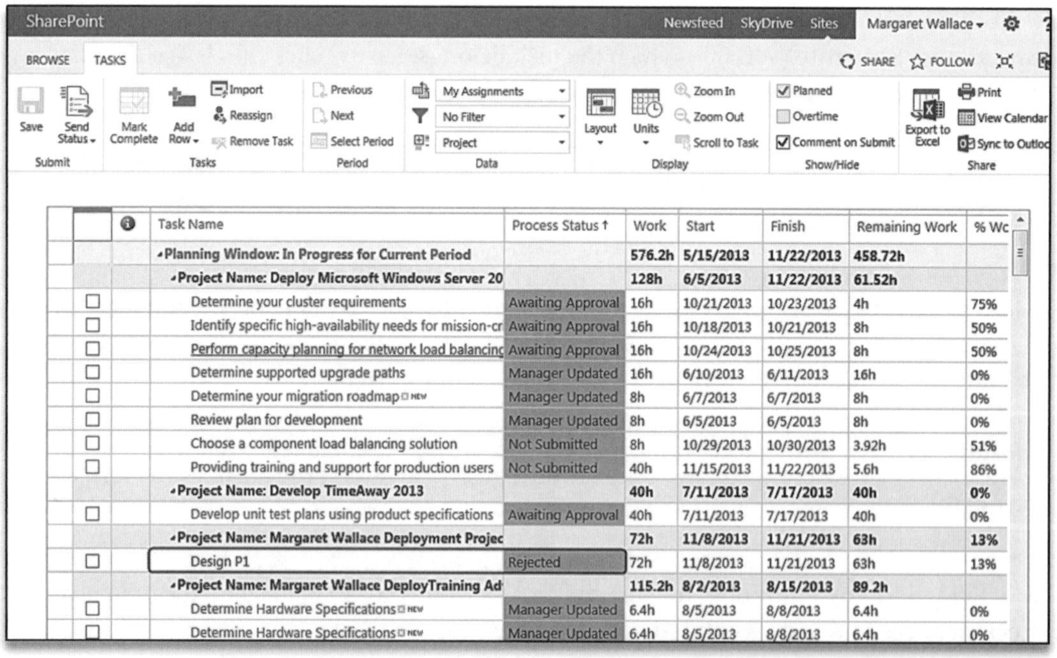

Figure 9 - 62: Tasks page shows rejected Add Task request

Information: If your project manager rejects your *Add Task* request, the system prevents you from entering progress against the task. Therefore, you should remove the rejected task from the *Tasks* page using the steps detailed below.

Removing Tasks

Project Server 2013 allows you to request removal of task assignments from the *Tasks* page. The *Remove* action creates a removal request that the project manager reviews and approves. Good targets for removal include rejected tasks, such as the rejected task shown previously in Figure 9 - 62.

Warning: Do not delete any other type of task from the *Tasks* page. If you attempt to delete a completed task, an in-progress task, or a future task, and your project manager accidentally approves your deletion request, the system removes you from the task in the Microsoft Project 2013 plan. You should delete future tasks only if your project manager gives you specific permission to do so, and intends to assign someone else to the tasks.

To remove tasks from the *Tasks* page, you and your project manager must follow a four-step process as follows:

1. You select and remove the tasks.
2. You submit the task removal request to your project manager.
3. Your project manager approves the task removal.
4. Your project manager publishes the changes in the project.

To begin the task removal process, select the option checkbox to the left of each task to remove and then click the *Remove Task* button. Project Server 2013 displays the confirmation dialog shown in Figure 9 - 63.

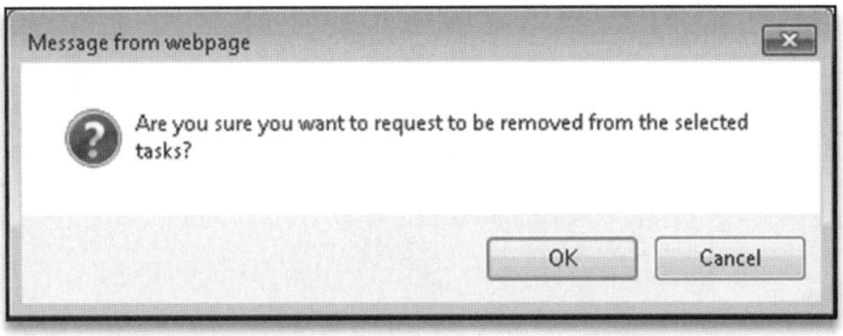
Message from webpage
Are you sure you want to request to be removed from the selected tasks?
OK
Cancel

Figure 9 - 63: Remove Task confirmation dialog

Click the *OK* button to complete the task removal process on the *Tasks* page. The system refreshes the *Tasks* page and does the following:

- Changes the task *Process Status* value to *Save Needed.*
- Strikes through the task name.
- Retains the selection status of the task

Notice in Figure 9 - 64 that the system formats the removed task with strikethrough text.

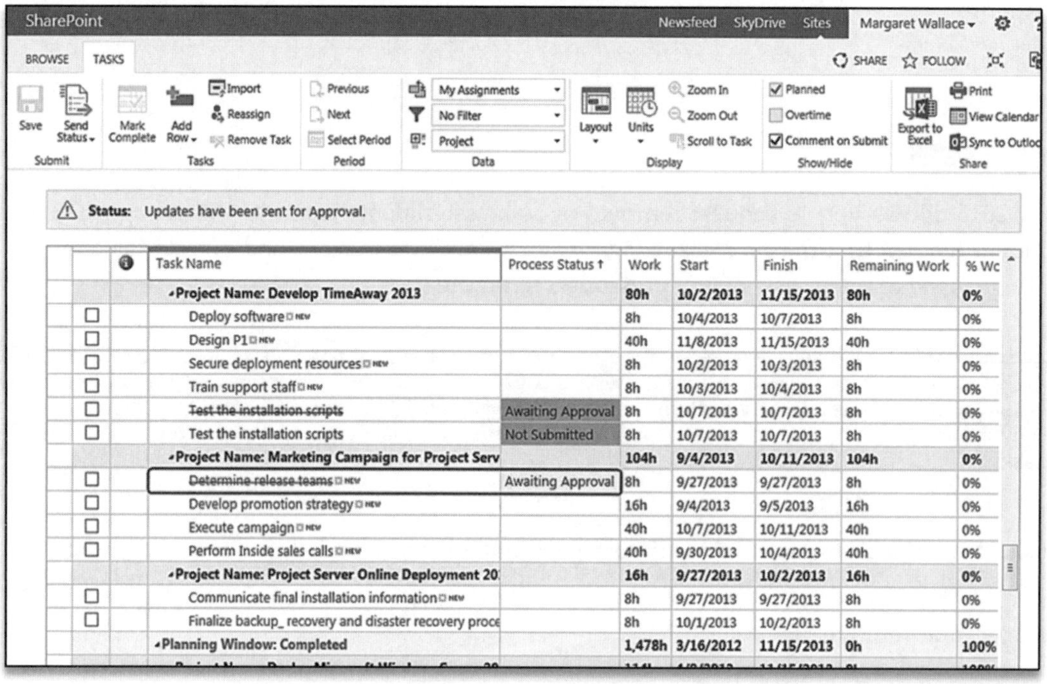

Figure 9 - 64: Tasks page showing Removed Task

Click the *Send Status* pick list and select the *Selected Tasks* or *All Tasks* item to submit the removal request to your project manager. Project Server 2013 sends your project manager a *Remove Assignment* request for each of the tasks you select. After your project manager approves the task removal and publishes the changes to the project, the task no longer appears on the project plan. However, the system does not remove the tasks from the *Tasks* page.

Module 10

Approving Time and Task Progress

Learning Objectives

After completing this module, you will be able to:

- View unsubmitted timesheets for resources
- View and adjust timesheets submitted by a resource
- Approve timesheets submitted by a resource
- Recall an approved timesheet
- Approve administrative time submitted by a resource
- Accept or reject task updates submitted by a resource
- Reschedule uncompleted work from the past into the current reporting period
- Set and run rules for automatically accepting updates from resources
- Manually update cost resource information

Inside Module 10

Approvals

Approvals are a key process if you are responsible for managing projects, timesheets, or time-off requests. Any changes to these items require your approval. As a project manager, you are the gatekeeper for task updates. Timesheet managers ensure that timesheet submissions contain correct data. Administrative time requests can affect project schedules; therefore, approvers need to be aware of dependencies.

The Approvals Center in Project Server 2013 combines all requests into one page. In many companies, a few people approve all requests for the various categories. Therefore, presenting you with all transactions requiring approval is easier to process. This module introduces the Approval Center and details the approval process for each transaction type.

Home Page

The Project Web App home page contains a synopsis of outstanding transactions that are pending your approval. Figure 10 - 1 shows the *Track your work* carousel, *Approvals Pending* live tile that appears on the PWA home page, and displays the number of pending approvals. Click the *Approvals Pending* live tile to see the transactions.

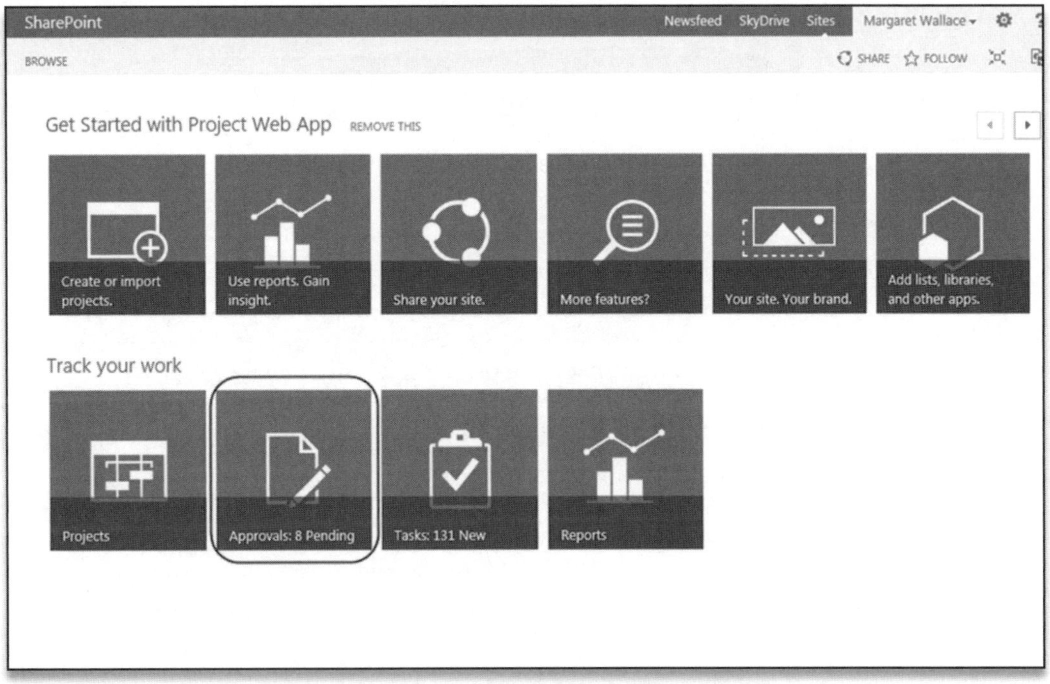

Figure 10 - 1: Home Page Approvals Pending

Approval Center

Figure 10 - 2 shows the *Approval Center* page that is your focal point for all approval related information and activity. You can see all task, timesheet, and administrative time submissions in one list. You access the *Approval Center* page by clicking the *Approvals* link on the *Quick Launch* menu.

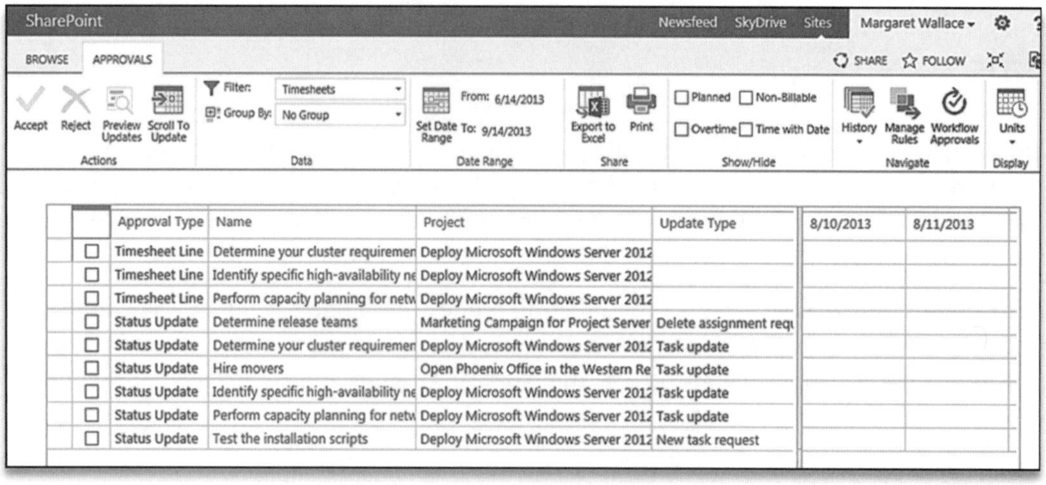

Figure 10 - 2: Approval Center page

Approval Center Information

The *Approval Center* page contains the following data columns. You may customize the page to meet your particular needs by dragging columns into the order in which you want to see them and by applying custom grouping and filtering. You may perform up to three levels of grouping using the fields outlined in Table 10 - 1.

Field	Definition
Approval Type	This value indicates the transaction type of the line. - Status Update is a task transaction - Timesheet Line is a timesheet transaction - Administrative time is an administrative time transaction
Name	Name of the task, timesheet line or administrative time category
Project	For Status Update and Timesheet Line transactions, this is the name of the project. Value is blank for all other transactions.
Update Type	For tasks, indicates the nature of the transaction. - *New Task Request* indicates a new task request by a team member - *Task Reassignment request* indicates a change to the assigned resource - *New Reassignment* indicates a team task assignment - *Task Update* indicates a change to task data - *Delete assignment* indicates resource request to remove a task This column is blank for timesheet and administrative time transactions.
Resource	Name of the resource to which the transaction applies

Field	Definition
Owner	Assignment owner of the resource, and is blank for timesheet and administrative time transactions.
Transaction Comment	Comment entered by resource to provide more context to the transaction.
Sent Date	Date of the transaction submission, and is blank for timesheet and administrative time transactions.
Start	Start date of the transaction.
Finish	Finish date of the transaction.
Total	Total hours entered for the transaction. This applies if the transaction updates hours worked or remaining work otherwise will be zero.
% Complete	Task completion percentage, this is blank for timesheet and administrative time transactions.
Remaining Work	Task remaining work, this is blank for timesheet and administrative time transactions.
Task Hierarchy	This is the flattened task hierarchy for the task. The task hierarchy provides a breadcrumb trail of where the task is within the project plan. This is blank for timesheet and administrative time transactions.

Table 10 - 1: List of Approval Page data fields

By default, the system displays *Actual* work for each transaction. The *Show/Hide* section of the *Approval Center* ribbon has options that you may select to show *Planned* work, *Overtime* work, *Non-Billable* work and *Time with Date.* Displaying *Planned, Overtime* and *Non-Billable* work increases the height of each row and reduces the number of rows appearing on the page.

By default, the system shows all transaction types. Click the *Filter* pick list on the ribbon to restrict visible transactions to a specific type. Available filters are *Administrative Time, Status Updates, Timesheet Lines,* and *Timesheets.*

The system does not group transactions by default. Click the *Group By* pick list to group by any field in the view. The *Custom Group...* option enables you to group the list by up to three levels using different fields available in the view.

The system also enables you to set a date range for viewed transactions. To change the date range, in the *Date Range* section of the *Approvals* ribbon, click the *Set Date Range* button. Figure 10 - 3 shows the dialog that appears where you may select the *From* and *To* dates of transactions to appear.

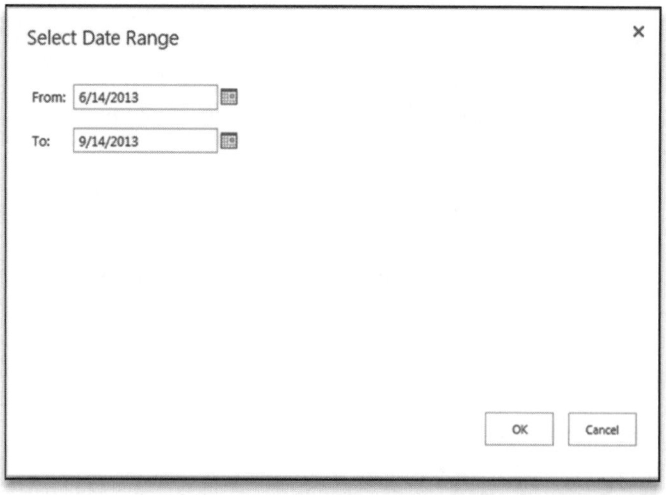

Figure 10 - 3: Select Date Range dialog

Approving timesheets

Project Server 2013 offers you two methods for approving or rejecting submitted timesheets:

- Approve/reject high-level timesheet information on the *Approval Center* page.
- Approve/reject detailed timesheet information for individual timesheet lines on the *Review Timesheet Details* page.

The difference between the two methods is the amount of timesheet data you must view and approve. The first method is much quicker, but may not be as accurate. The second method takes more time, but allows you to review the time submitted for all lines in every timesheet.

> **Best Practice:** MSProjectExperts recommends that you develop a standard process for approving timesheets and then train each resource manager how to follow this process.

Approving a timesheet using Summary Data

If you wish to approve each timesheet using only the high-level data shown on the *Approval Center* page, do the following:

- Apply the *Timesheets* filter, as shown in Figure 10 - 4.
- Select the option checkbox to the left of each timesheet you want to approve.
- Click the *Accept* button when you are ready to approve the selected timesheets.
- Enter documentation in the *Confirmation* dialog as you determine necessary when prompted, and click the *OK* button.

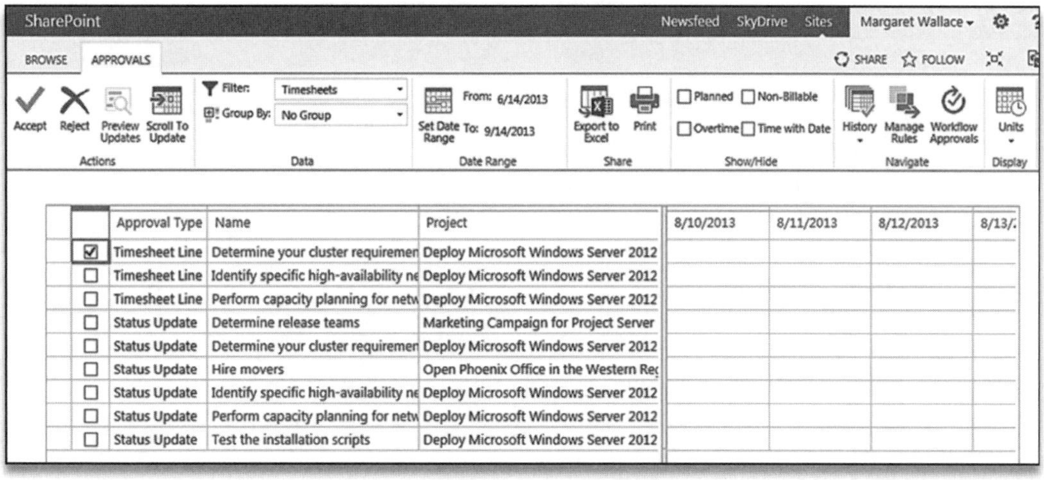

Figure 10 - 4: Approve High Level timesheet

Rejecting a timesheet using Summary Data

In some situations, such as when a resource enters erroneous information on the timesheet, you may need to reject a submitted timesheet. To reject timesheets, select the option checkbox to the left of each timesheet you want to reject, and then click the *Reject* button. Project Server 2013 sends the resource an e-mail message about the timesheet rejection and marks the *Status* field to *Rejected* for the rejected timesheet on the resource's *Manage Timesheets* page. On the *Timesheet* page, the information bar on the rejected timesheet will show a *Your timesheet has been rejected by* (timesheet approver's name) status. The resource must correct the timesheet errors and then resubmit the timesheet to you for approval.

Approve Timesheet Lines using Detailed Data

To approve detailed timesheet information, click the *Timesheet* name link. The system displays the *Review Timesheet Details* page grouped by project shown in Figure 10 - 5. Examine the data submitted for each timesheet line, and then click the *Approve* button.

Information: The *Approve* button approves the entire timesheet. You cannot select specific line items and only approve those items.

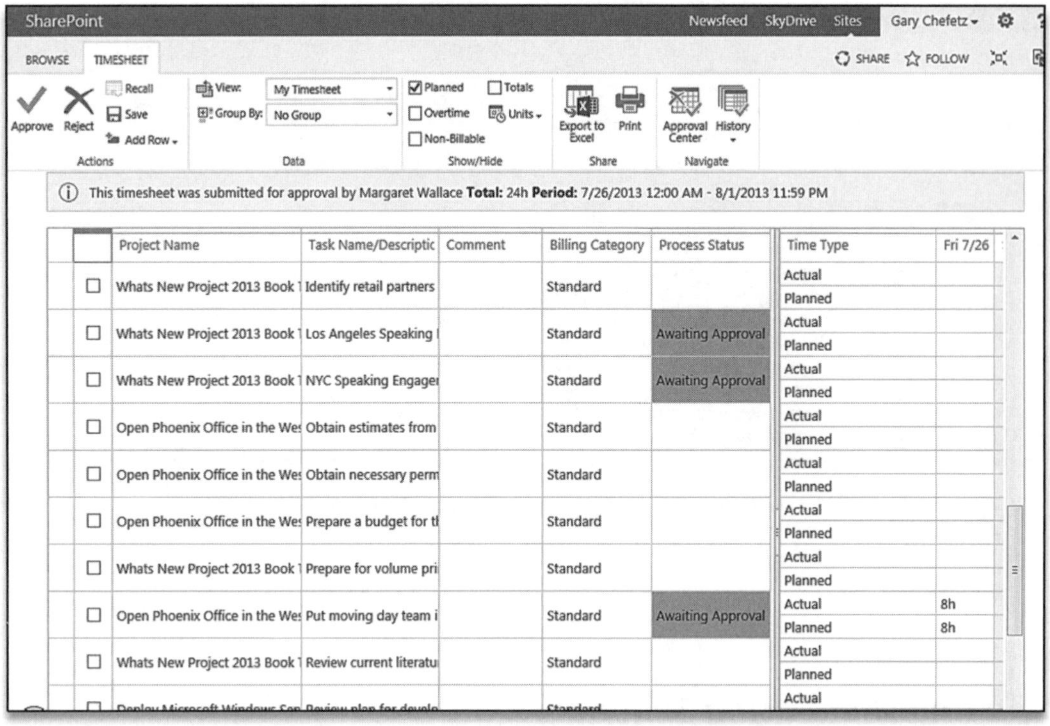

Figure 10 - 5: Review Timesheet Details page

Enter additional information in the *Comment* field and then click the *OK* button. The *Approval Center* page appears and the timesheet no longer appears in the list.

Reject Timesheet Lines using Detailed Data

To reject a timesheet, examine the data submitted for each timesheet line as shown in Figure 10 - 5, and then click the *Reject* button. Project Server 2013 displays the *Submit Timesheet* dialog. Enter additional information in the *Comment* field and then click the *OK* button. The *Approval Center* page appears and the timesheet no longer appears in the list. Project Server 2013 sends the resource an e-mail message about the timesheet rejection and marks the *Status* field to *Rejected* for the timesheet on the resource's *Manage Timesheets* page. On the *Timesheet* page, the information bar on the rejected timesheet will show *Your timesheet has been rejected by* (timesheet approver's name) *Total:* (xx)*h Period:* (indicates timesheet period) status. The resource must correct the timesheet errors and then resubmit the timesheet to you for approval.

Recalling an Approved Timesheet

From time to time, you may accidentally approve or reject a timesheet. To address this situation, you must recall the timesheet and then take the intended action. To recall a previously approved timesheet, do the following:

1. Navigate to the *Approval Center* page.
2. In the *Navigate* section of the *Approval Center* ribbon, click the *History* pick list and select the *Timesheets* item from the list. The system displays the *Timesheet Approval History* page.
3. In the *Data* section of the *Timesheets* ribbon, select the *Approved By Me* option and then click the *Apply* button.
4. The system displays the history of your approved timesheets.

5. Select the desired timesheet by clicking in the *Resource name* cell to select the row.
6. In the *Actions* section of the *Timesheets* ribbon, click the *Recall* button.

Project Server 2013 returns the timesheet to your *Approval Center* page. Follow the procedures discussed previously to take the appropriate action for an approval or rejection.

Viewing Unsubmitted Timesheets

It is a good practice to determine which resources have not submitted their current timesheet to you. Project Server 2013 provides two options out of the box that provide information about unsubmitted timesheets, one option uses the Approval Center's *Timesheet Approval History* page , and the second option uses the built-in reports in Project Web App.

To view the unsubmitted timesheets for your resources as shown in Figure 10 - 6, do the following:

- On the *Quick Launch* menu, click the *Approvals* link to display the *Approval Center* page.
- Click the *History* pick list and select the *Timesheet* item on the list to display the *Timesheet Approval History* page.
- In the *Data* section of the *Timesheets* ribbon, click the *Filters* pick list, select the *My Resources Unsubmitted Timesheets* item and click the *Apply* button.

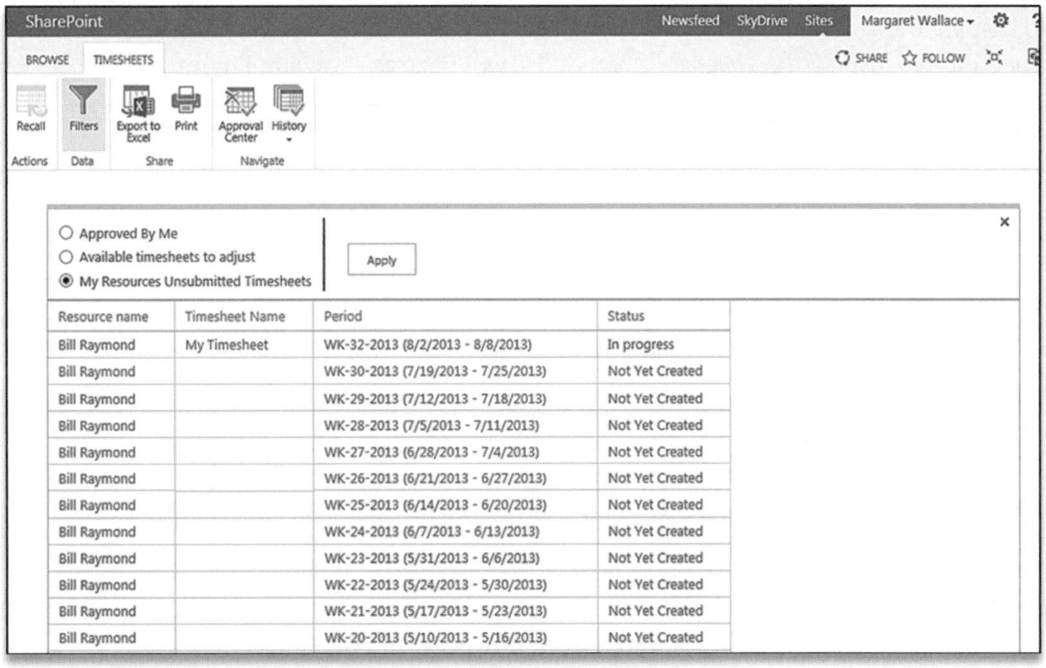

Figure 10 - 6: Timesheet Approval History page, unsubmitted timesheets

By default, the system displays unsubmitted timesheets sorted in descending order by timesheet period.

Notice in Figure 10 - 6 that the entries have a *Not Yet Created* status. *Not Yet Created* status happens for many reasons. Sometimes resources are out of town or away from the corporate network, and cannot create their own timesheets. Other causes can be resource forgetfulness or a simple neglect of the organization's time reporting obligation to create and submit timesheets in a timely manner.

Project Server 2013 also provides the *Timesheet Actuals* sample report that enables you to see what time you have reported and where it is in the approval process. In Module 18, *Working with Business Intelligence and Reporting*, I discuss how you can customize built-in reports to meet your organization's specific needs.

Best Practice: During the early stages of a Project Server 2013 implementation, resources routinely forget to create and submit timesheets because they are simply not yet in the habit of doing it. MsProjectExperts recommends that you use positive encouragement and feedback to help your resources establish good reporting habits with the system.

Best Practice: MsProjectExperts recommends that you develop a standard process for timesheet creation and submittal. This presents a training and performance issue for your resources. Train them how to create and submit timesheets and then hold them accountable for this performance. Deal appropriately with any resource who continually fails to submit timesheets.

Viewing and Adjusting Submitted Timesheets

To view submitted timesheets from your resources, on the *Quick Launch* menu, click *Approvals* link to display the *Approval Center* page. In the *Navigate* section of the *Approvals* ribbon, click the *History* pick list and select the *Timesheets* item to display the *Timesheet Approval History* page. Next, select the *Available timesheets to adjust* option and click the *Apply* button to display the *Timesheet Approval History* page as shown in Figure 10 - 7.

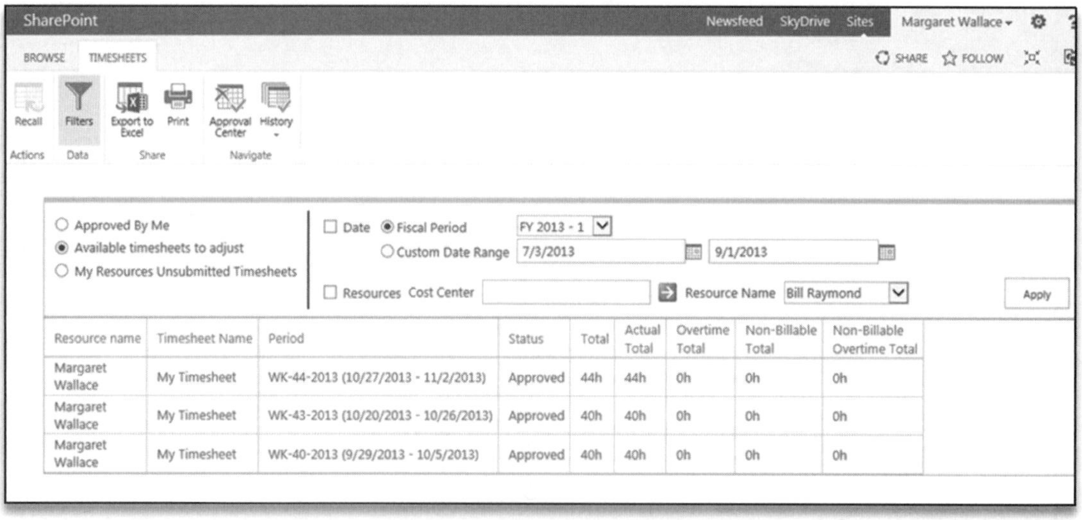

Figure 10 - 7: Timesheet Approval History page with submitted timesheets

The *Timesheet Approval History* page contains a section at the top that allows you to display different types of timesheets and to filter the list of timesheets shown on the page. For example, you may select each of the following types of timesheet lists by selecting the appropriate option at the top:

- Approved By Me
- Available timesheets to adjust
- My Resources Unsubmitted Timesheets

To change the timesheets shown on the page, select one of the three options and click the *Apply* button. Select the *Approved By Me* option to see your past history of timesheet approvals. Select the *Available timesheets to adjust* option to see timesheets for which you have permission to edit the submitted actuals. Select the *My Resources Unsubmitted Timesheets* option to view timesheets that are due but which your resources have not yet submitted to you for approval.

Warning: By default, members of the *Resource Managers* group do not have the *Adjust Timesheet* permission. If you need this capability, ask your Project Server administrator to allow this permission for the *My Direct Reports* category in the *Resource Managers* group. In addition, if fixed approval routing is not enabled, a timesheet user may select from the list of managers that are on the *Managers* list on the *Specify Timesheet Managers* page, located in the *Time and Task Management* section of the *Timesheet Managers* page.

The *Timesheet Approval History* page contains a filter pane that allows you to filter the list of timesheets shown on the selected page, such as when the page displays a very large list of timesheets and you need to locate the timesheets for one particular resource. To filter the list of timesheets, select one or more filter options in the filter pane and then click the *Apply* button. Select the *Date* option to filter by date. Select the *Fiscal Period* option and choose a period from the *Fiscal Period* pick list, or select the *Custom Date Range* option and then set a date range. Select the *Resources* option and then enter a cost center number or select a resource name from the *Resource Name* pick list. For example, Figure 10 - 8 shows the *Timesheet Approvals* page filtered for a resource named *Bill Raymond*.

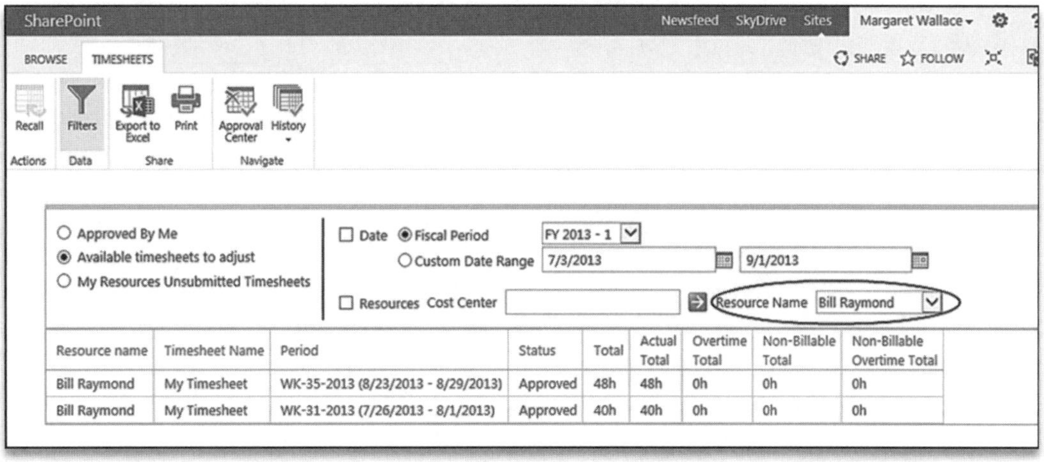

Figure 10 - 8: Timesheet Approval History page filtered for Bill Raymond

Information: If you do not see the filter pane at the top of the *Timesheet Approval History* page, click the *Filter* button on the *Timesheets* ribbon.

Information: To view all timesheets again, deselect the *Date* and *Resource* options and then click the *Apply* button.

By default, the *Timesheet Approvals* page contains the following columns:

- Resource name
- Timesheet Name
- Period
- Status
- Total
- Actual Total
- Overtime Total
- Non-Billable Total
- Non-Billable Overtime Total

Depending on your organization's timesheet reporting method, the last four columns may or may not contain information. For example, if you do not track *Overtime* work, then the *Overtime Total* column is irrelevant.

> **Information**: Your Project Server administrator must set timesheet approvers in Project Server 2013 by designating the *Timesheet Manager* value for each resource in the Enterprise Resource Pool (ERP). For example, for each of the resources who report to Marilyn Ray, the Project Server administrator specified Marilyn Ray in their *Timesheet Manager* field. Todd Chia is the timesheet manager for Marilyn Ray and the value is set accordingly.

To view the complete timesheet for a resource, click the *My Timesheet* link to the right of the resource's name for the desired reporting period. Project Server 2013 displays the *Review Timesheet Details* page shown in Figure 10 - 9.

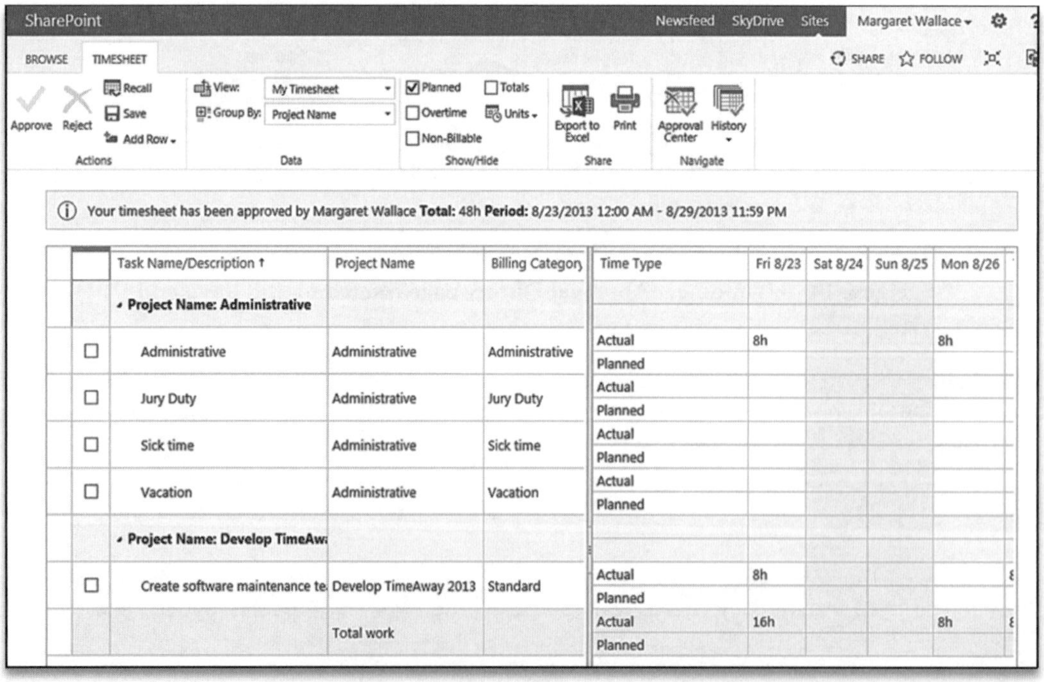

Figure 10 - 9: Review Timesheet Details page

Adjusting Timesheet Updates

Occasionally, team members make a mistake entering data in the timesheet grid. For example, in Figure 10 - 10, Bill Raymond accidentally entered 23 hours of administrative time for Oct 10. Because you realize that Bill Raymond did not work 23 hours that day, you contact him and find out that he only worked 3 hours on that task. Therefore, you must adjust the timesheet to show the correct value. To adjust the timesheet entry, click in the cell containing the mistake; then enter the correct value and click the *Approve* button to save the changes.

Information: Remember that members of the *Resource Managers* group do not have the *Adjust Timesheet* permission. If you need this capability, ask your Project Server administrator to allow this permission for the *My Direct Reports* category in the *Resource Managers* group.

Information: If you want your resources to make their own corrections, select the option checkbox to the left of the timesheet line containing the mistake and then click the *Reject* button. The system automatically sends the resource an e-mail message requesting that the resource correct the rejected timesheet line.

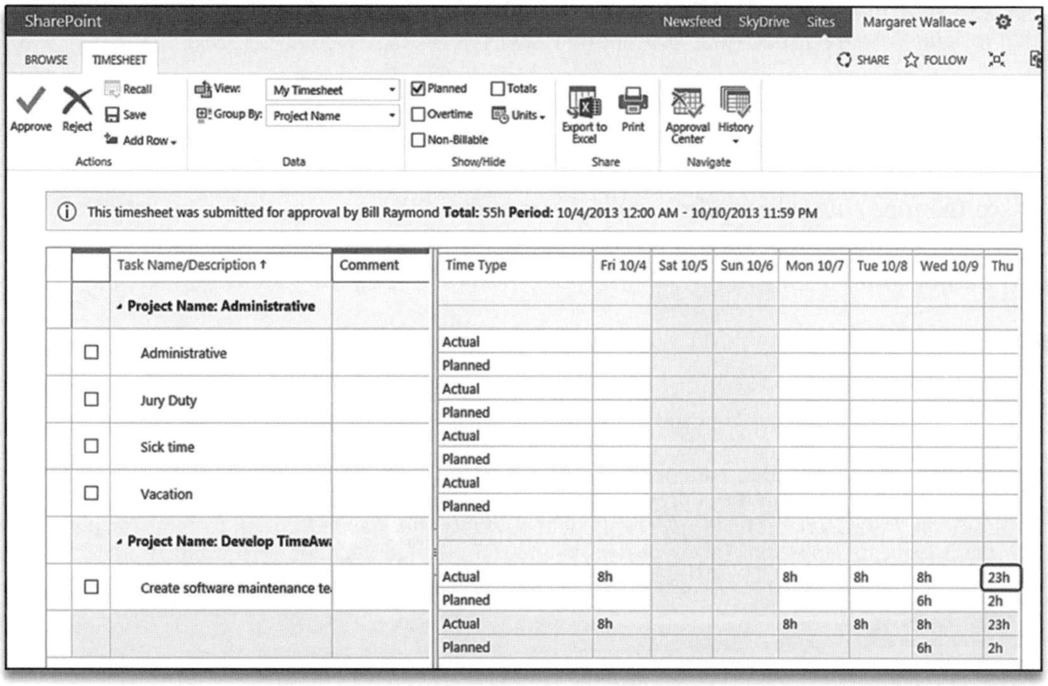

Figure 10 - 10: Timesheet Detail with entry error

Managing Administrative Time Requests

Project Server 2013 provides a formal approval process for administrative time requests such as vacation or educational leave. Your Project Server administrator must configure the system to determine the types of administrative time subject to approval. If your organization requires you to approve administrative time requests from your resources, you may use the *Approval Center* to manage those requests.

On the *Quick Launch* menu, click the *Approvals* link. The system displays the *Approval Center* page shown previously in Figure 10 - 2.

Warning: As of the writing of this book, when you access the *Approval Center* page as shown previously in Figure 10 - 2, and you want to approve administrative requests, the *Administrative Time* filter does not display any results. Using the *Timesheets* filter does not help because the display does not indicate Administrative requests. To approve administrative time, select the timesheet name link to view the timesheet on the *Review Timesheet Details* page, and then you may view the administrative timesheet line and approve the administrative request.

Information: As a work around, you may use the out-of-box *TimesheetActuals* report to identify timeperiods with administrative time requests. To access this report, navigate to the *Business Intelligence Center* and in the *Quick Launch* menu, click the *Reports* link and then click the *English (United States)* folder link to locate the *TimesheetActuals* report. This report allows you to filter for administrative requests so you know which *Timesheet (Approval Type)* item contains administrative time. You may also use a report filter for timesheets that include the *Administrative* project name.

If you do not see the time entered for administrative time immediately, select the row selector to the left of the request and click the *Scroll to Update* button on the ribbon. The system displays the first instance of related hours for the selected transaction.

Warning: As of the writing of this book, the administrative time approvals features, such as the *Scroll to Update* function, only relates to administrative time, which you submit as *Actual* hours. When using the administrative lines to document future vacation planning, this function does not work when submitting *Planned* hours. In the *Show/Hide* section of the *Approvals* ribbon, select the *Planned* option to filter for planned time that resources submit for approval. In my case, I submitted planned vacation in the future that requires approval of my manager.

Approve Administrative Time Requests

To approve administrative time requests, select the option checkbox to the left of each request you want to approve and then in the *Actions* section of the *Approvals* ribbon, click the *Accept* button. Enter any approval comments, if prompted. The system redisplays the *Approval Center* page and removes the approved requests from the page. The approved administrative time shows up on the resource's timesheet as planned work for vacation line for the designated period as shown in Figure 10 - 11.

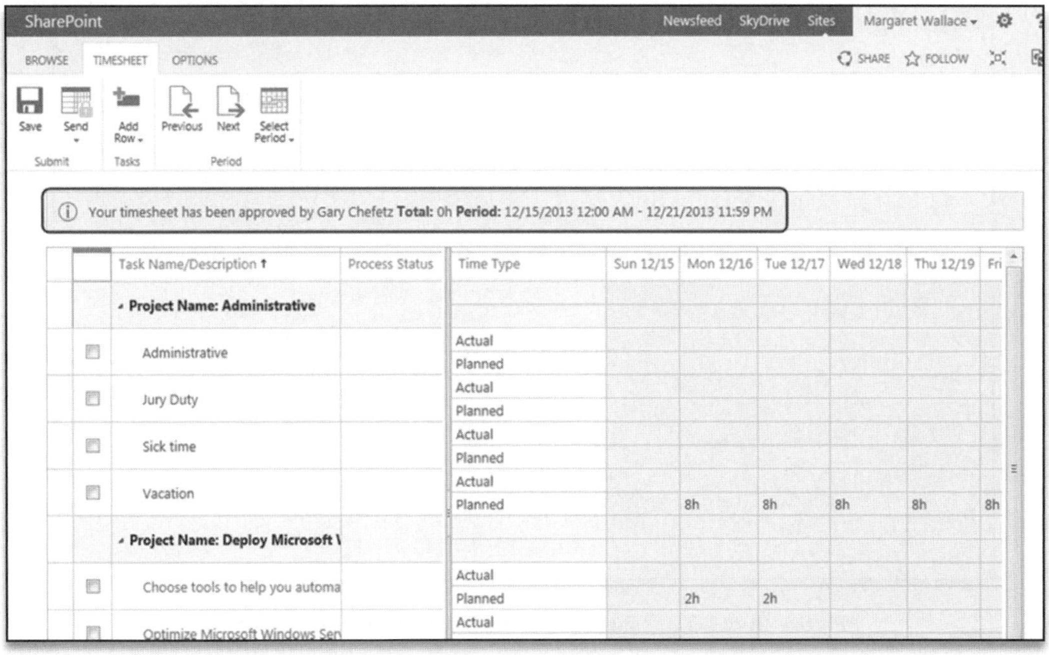

Figure 10 - 11: Timesheet page, Planned Administrative time approved

Rejecting Administrative Time Requests

To reject an administrative time request, select the requests to reject, and then click the *Reject* button. The system removes the administrative time request from the *Approval Center* page and notifies the resource of the rejection with an e-mail message. Project Server 2013 displays the *Rejected* status in the *Information* bar beneath the ribbon as shown in Figure 10 - 12.

Information: Unlike the *Timesheet Approvals* page, Project Server 2013 does not show you a history of approved and rejected administrative time requests. The *Process Status* column does not display a status for administrative time requests; therefore, the *Information* bar is the only location indicating the status of the request.

Best Practice: MSProjectExperts recommends using the comments section for administrative requests to document the date of approval or rejection so the resource is clear about the manager's intentions.

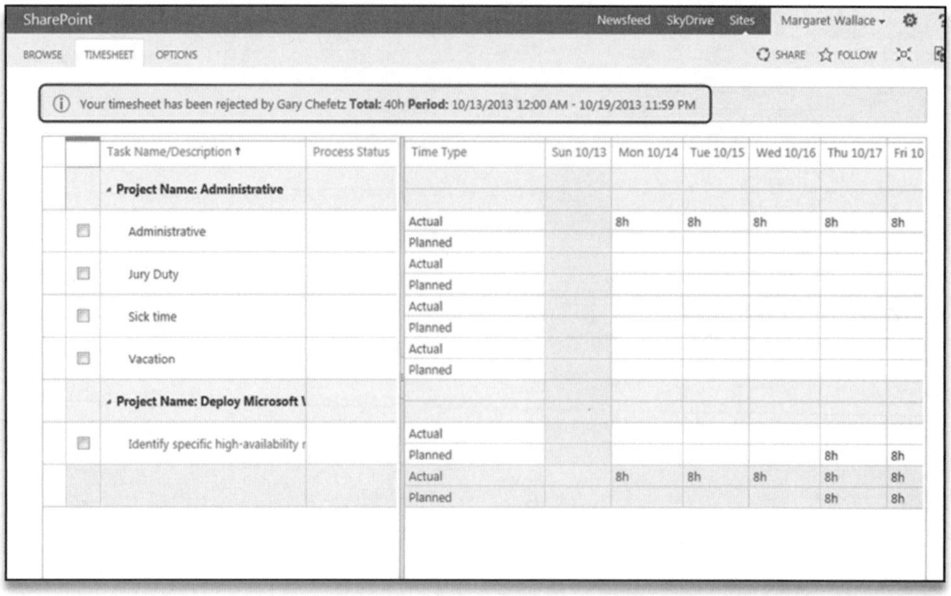

Figure 10 - 12: Timesheet page, Administrative time Rejected

Viewing Task Updates

As project manager, you must approve or reject task updates from your resources, in addition to approving timesheets and administrative time. Project Server 2013 indicates the number of task updates pending your approval on the *Approvals* tile of the Project Web App Home page. For example, Figure 10 - 13 shows that I have *6 Pending* task updates from my resources.

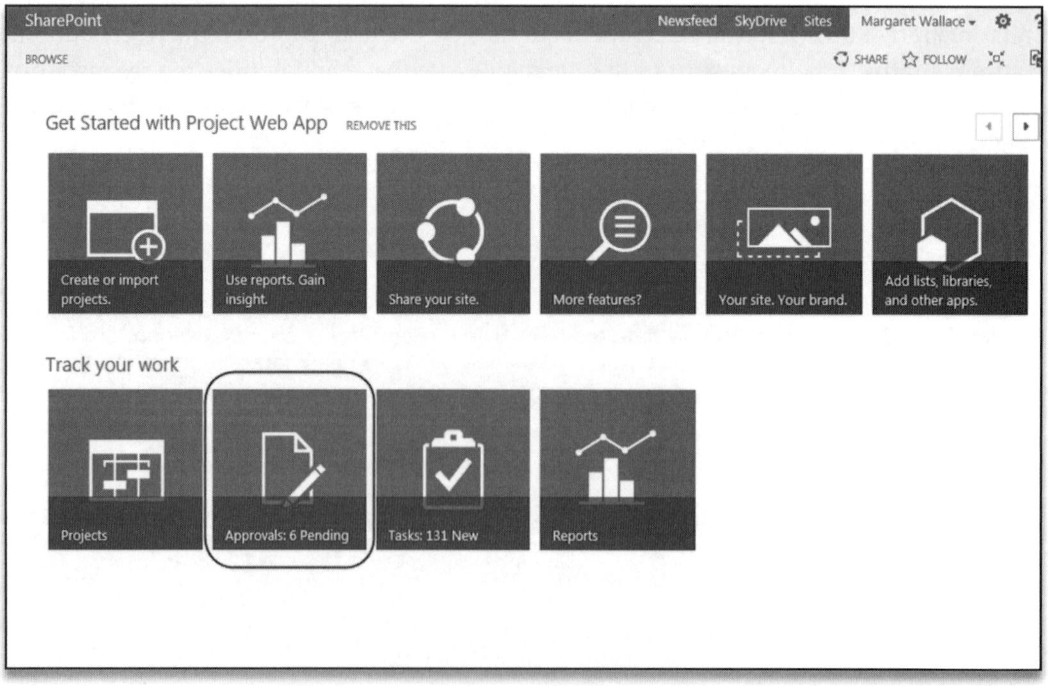

Figure 10 - 13: Project Web App Home page shows task updates awaiting approval

To view the task updates awaiting your approval, click the *Approvals* tile in the *Track your work* carousel. The system displays the *Approval Center* page shown in Figure 10 - 14. Optionally, you may use the *Filter* option value of *Status Updates* to filter the results for task updates.

Information: The display of planned and overtime work influences the row height of each update. Later, I discuss how to enable or disable these settings.

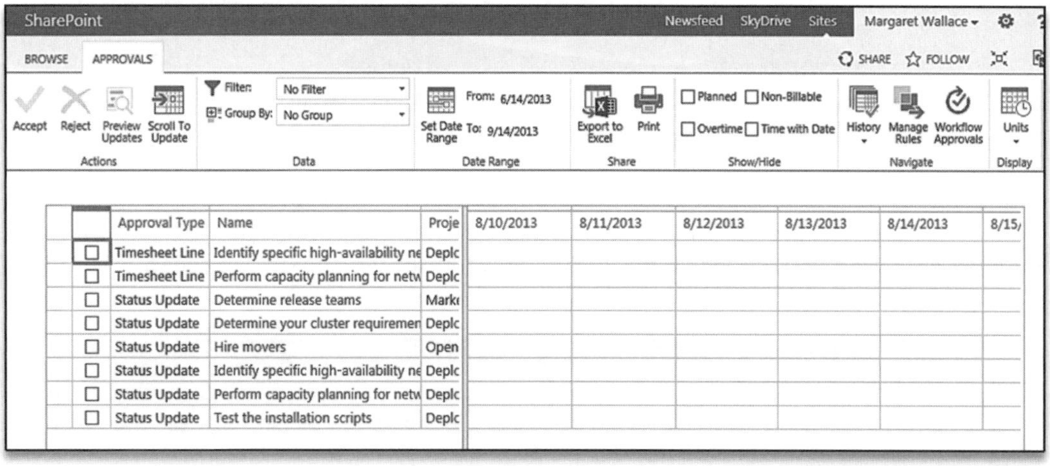

Figure 10 - 14: Approval Center page, with six Status Update items

Best Practice: For best results using the *Approval Center* page for *Status Update approval types*, MSProjectExperts recommends that you select the *Planned* option in the *Show/Hide* section of the *Approvals* ribbon to display planned work. This option allows you to compare the planned work with the actual work for each task update.

If you click the hyperlink for any update in the *Name* field, Project Server 2013 displays a summary of the update information in the *Task Details* dialog, as shown in Figure 10 - 15. The *Task Details* dialog does not offer any additional information beyond that presented and is not modifiable.

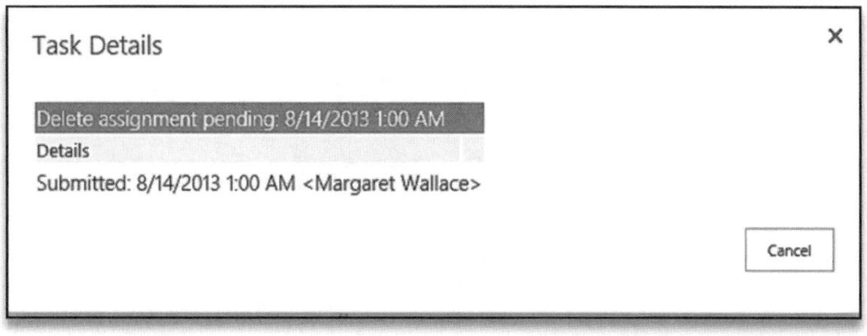

Figure 10 - 15: Task Details dialog for a selected task update

Task Update Processing

Successfully processing task updates requires the process steps shown in Figure 10 - 16. You must repeat this process for each reporting cycle.

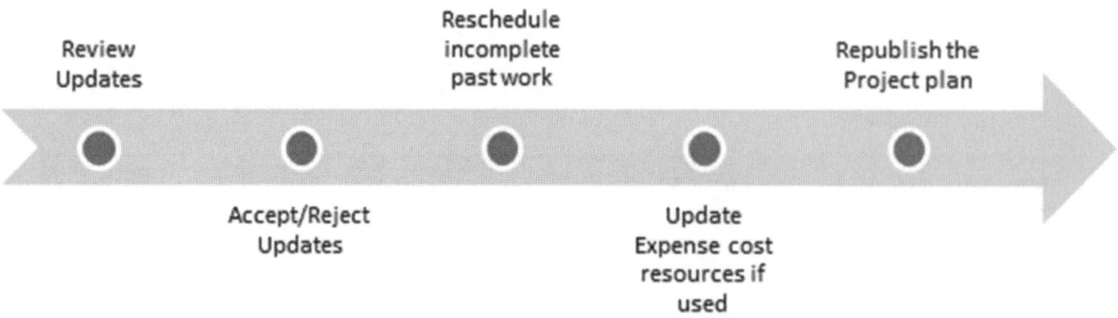

Figure 10 - 16: Task Update processing steps

The *Approval Center page* displays up to six types of updates, four of which you can see in Figure 10 - 17 and Figure 10 - 18.

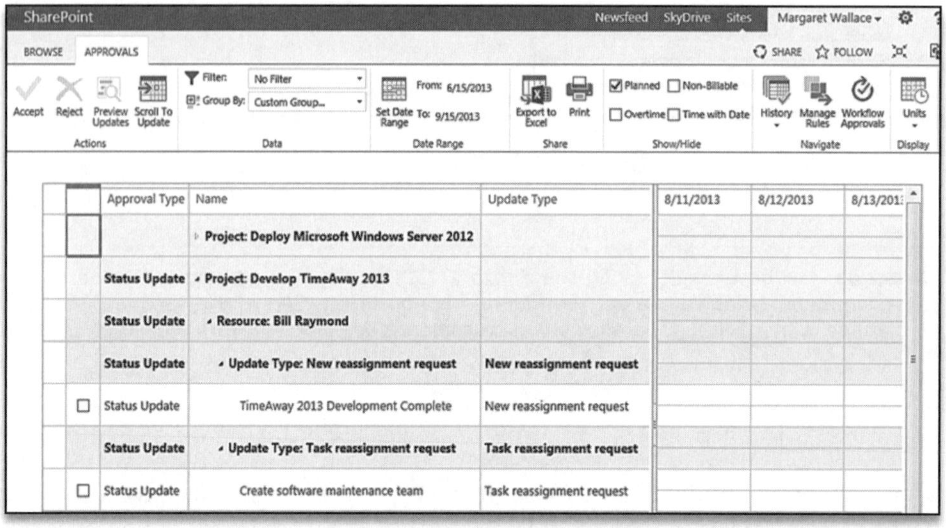

Figure 10 - 17: Examples of different Update types, Custom grouping applied (Top)

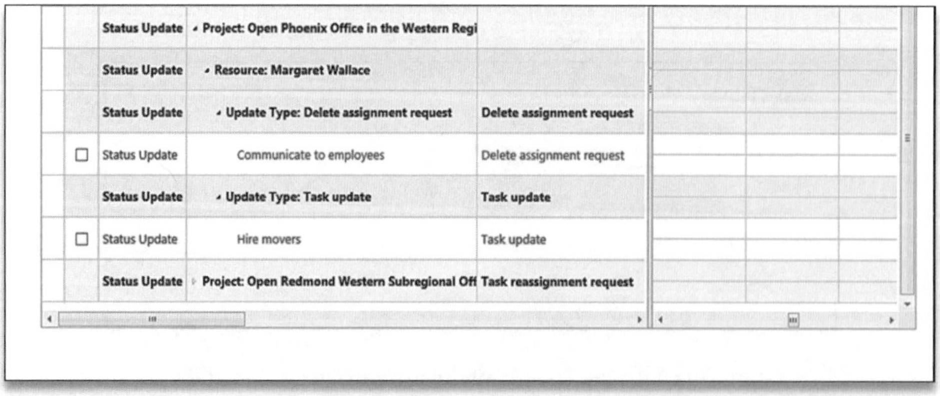

Figure 10 - 18: Examples of different Update types, Custom grouping applied (Bottom)

The custom grouping of *Project, Resource,* and *Update Type* enables the illustrated view. Table 10 - 2 illustrates each *Update* type, with the action that creates it and what happens when you approve the transaction.

Action by Team Member	Resulting Update Type	What Does It Mean?
Updated task status	*Task update*	If approved, reported progress applies to the project plan
Updated task status and changed information such as Remaining Work	*Task update* with changed information shown in red, if present	If approved, reported progress and other changes apply to the project plan
Add self to an existing task	*New reassignment request*	If approved, the system creates a new assignment on the task for the requesting resource, enabling them to log time against the task
Resource reassigned their assignment to another resource	*Task reassignment request*	If approved, the system transfers remaining work of the assignment to the new resource
Resource requests removal from a task.	*Delete assignment request*	If approved, the system removes the resource from the assignment
Resource requests a new task	*New Task Assignment* (not shown)	If approved, the system adds the new task and assignment to the project plan.

Table 10 - 2: Task Update types

Warning: MSProjectExperts recommends that you never accept a *Delete Assignment* request from a resource because this action automatically removes the resource from the task in the Project Pro 2013 plan. A better approach is to reject the *Delete Assignment* request and to communicate with the resource to delegate the task to another team member. If this is not possible, then reject the request and then manually replace the resource on the task in the Project Pro 2013 project.

Review Task Updates

It is your responsibility as project manager to accept or reject all updates submitted by your resources. Accepting a task update automatically transfers the updated task information into the appropriate project plan. Rejecting a task update triggers an automatic e-mail message to the resource and may require the resource to take the appropriate action in response to your rejection. This process guarantees that you, the project manager, always serve as the "gatekeeper" between updates from your project team members and the actual Project Pro 2013 project.

Information: Project Server 2013 does not allow the system to bypass you and automatically update task progress from your team members into the Project Pro 2013 project. Because the system requires your participation in the update process, you must provide minimal oversight to all updates, preventing the system from updating "dirty data" into your Project Pro 2013 project.

Before you process updates, pay special attention to any task update that includes a note in the *Comment* column. You may also click the *Name* link to view the details of the transaction as shown in Figure 10 - 19. A note attached to a task update usually indicates that your team members are trying to give you additional information about their task updates. In this case, the team member is "overbooked to complete the assignment" and suggests reassigning the task to Mary Kay.

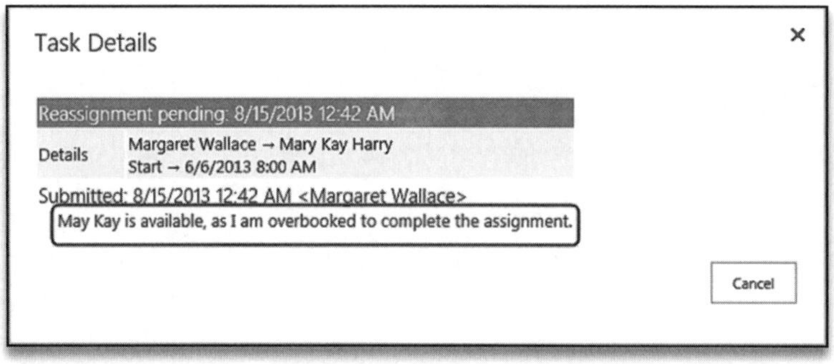

Figure 10 - 19: Task Details dialog with submission note

After reviewing the note, click the *Cancel* button to close the dialog and return to the *Approval Center* page.

Best Practice: MSProjectExperts strongly recommends that you take the time to read all notes included with task updates. If your team member took the time to write a note, you need to take the time to read the note!

Reject Task Updates

This process assumes you are not accepting some of the updates as you review your approvals. To begin the process of rejecting task updates, select the option checkbox to the left of each update to reject and then click the *Reject* button. Project Server 2013 displays the confirmation dialog into which you should enter rejection notes, as shown in Figure 10 - 20. Project Server 2013 removes the update from the *Approval Center* page.

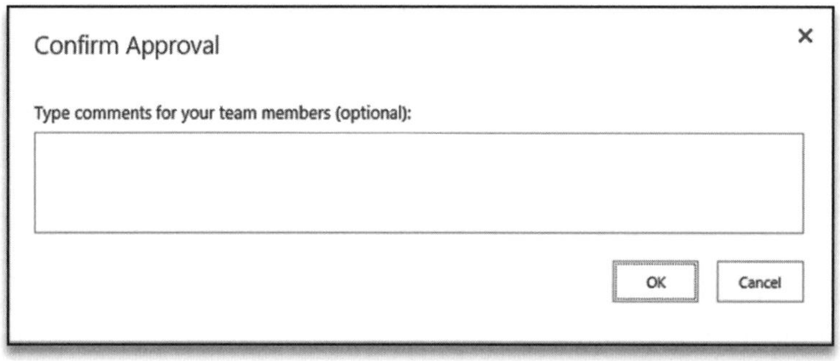

Figure 10 - 20: Confirmation dialog to enter notes regarding selected action

You might reject a task update when a resource accidentally types an incorrect *Actual* work value, forgets to update *Remaining* work, or fails to annotate a new task request. You might also reject a *Task Assignment* request or a *Task Reassignment* request that is not appropriate. As indicated previously, you should always reject a *Delete Assignment* request.

> **Information**: If your organization uses single entry mode for time tracking, *Rejected* tasks show only on the *Tasks* page with a *Rejected* value. The *Timesheet* page only shows current approved tasks.

> **Information**: If you reject a task update because the resource made a data entry error, the resource must complete the following steps to see your rejection comments:
>
> 1. Click the name of the rejected task on the *Tasks* page.
> 2. On the *Task Details* page, view the *Notes*.

Approve Task Updates

> **Warning**: Before accepting task updates in Project Web App, close and check in your project in Project Pro 2013. If you have an enterprise project open while accepting task updates, you prevent Project Server 2013 from applying the updates to the open project. You must check in the project before the system can apply the approved updates to your enterprise project.

To begin the process of approving task updates, select the option checkbox to the left of each update to approve. If all task updates are from the same project, you may want to click the *Select All* button to select all of the updates. If you want to preview the impact of the updates on the selected project, click the *Preview Updates* button. Project Server 2013 opens a separate Internet Explorer window and displays the *Approval Preview* page, shown in Figure 10 - 21.

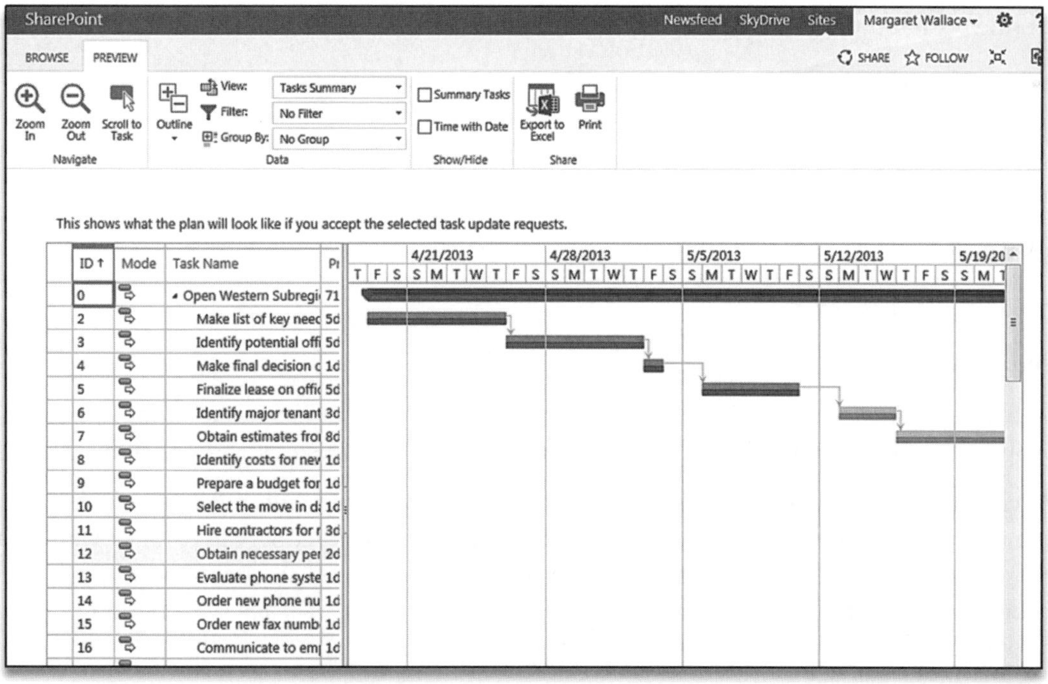

Figure 10 - 21: Approval Preview page

The system indicates your selected task updates by displaying a hyperlink in the *Task Name* column. The *Approval Preview* page displays the *Tasks Summary* view for the project, and shows the post-approval state of the project before you actually approve the task updates. The information shown in the *Approval Preview* page looks similar to the *Tracking Gantt* view available in Project Pro 2013.

The Gantt Chart portion of the view shown in the *Approval Preview* page allows you to compare current task progress against the original baseline schedule for each task. The system displays this information as follows:

- The **gray Gantt Bar** represents the previous schedule of each task.
- The **blue Gantt Bar** represents the new schedule of each task after updates.
- The **filled part of each Gantt bar** represents the % Complete (current progress) on each task.
- The **gray diamond** represents the previous schedule for each milestone task.
- The **black diamond** represents the new schedule for each milestone task after task updates.

The table portion of the view shown in the *Approval Preview* page contains columns you can use to assess the current schedule. The default columns in the *Approval Preview* page include the following:

- ID
- Mode
- Task Name
- Previous Duration (the pre-approval duration)
- Duration (the post-approval duration)
- Previous Start (the pre-approval start date)
- Start (the post-approval start date)
- Previous Finish (the pre-approval finish date)
- Finish (the post-approval finish date)
- Previous % Complete
- % Complete
- Work
- Resource Names

When you see a task *Duration* value that is greater than the *Previous Duration* value, it indicates that the task is slipping. If you see a task *Finish* date later than the *Previous Finish* date, it also indicates that the task is slipping.

In the *Approval Preview* page ribbon, click the *View* pick list to see a list of views available in the *Approval Preview* page. The list includes default detailed project views available with Project Server 2013, as well as any custom views created by your Project Server administrator. From the *View* pick list, choose and apply any additional views you want to use for the project in its pre-approval state. Click the *Window Close* button in the upper right corner of the window to close the window when finished.

After you examine the project in the *Approval Preview* page, click the *Accept* button to approve your selected updates. The system displays the confirmation dialog shown previously in Figure 10 - 20.

Enter any additional information in the confirmation dialog and then click the *OK* button. Project Server 2013 transfers the updated information into the project and then removes the updates from the *Approval Center page.*

Once you complete processing your updates, **publish the project plan** to update to the latest information state for all involved parties.

> **Best Practice**: MSProjectExperts recommends that you accept task updates for only one project at a time. This allows you to study the impact of the updates in the enterprise project, reschedule uncompleted work, make plan revisions, and publish schedule changes before you process updates for the next project.

Updating schedules with protected user updates

Your Project Server administrator may configure the software to protect user updates by selecting the *Only allow task updates via Tasks and Timesheets* option on the *Task Settings and Display* page. To enable this option, click the *Server Settings* link to display the *PWA Settings for* page then in the *Time and Task Management* section of the page, click the *Task Settings and Display*. In the *Protect User Updates* section of the *Task Settings and* Display page, select the *Only allow task updates via Tasks and Timesheets* option. If your business requirements include preventing your project managers from manually entering actual progress in their enterprise projects in Project Pro 2013, then protecting user updates is a way to configure this requirement in the system. Project managers should always check for pending actual work updates prior to deleting or changing assignments to ensure proper handling of actual work data. Important considerations when using protected user updates include the following:

Dos:

- Use *Physical Complete* as an indicator of a task being complete
- Mark *Milestones* with *Percent Complete*

Don'ts:

- Enter *Actual Work* for an enterprise resource
- Enter a *Percent Complete* for a work resource

Project managers may use *Physical Complete* to indicate a work resource's task is complete. However, if you use *Percent Complete* to indicate the work resource task is complete, the scheduling engine attempts to calculate the *Actual Work* value required for the resource to complete the work. Since updates made directly in the project for *Actual Work* values are not acceptable, no changes save in the project concerning *Percent Complete* values or *Actual Work* values. Notice in Figure 10 - 22, if you change an *Actual Work* value in your project, the resulting warning dialog indicates Project Web App only allows *Actual Work* updates by team members. However, you may use a *Percent Complete* value to indicate that a *Milestone* is complete and save your changes to the project.

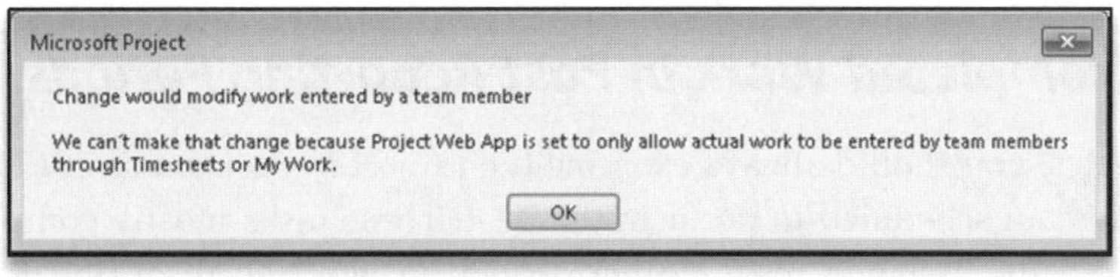
Microsoft Project
Change would modify work entered by a team member
We can't make that change because Project Web App is set to only allow actual work to be entered by team members through Timesheets or My Work.
OK

Figure 10 - 22: Change would modify work entered by team member

Information: If you make changes to a *Percent Complete* value and save your project, and the values are missing the next time you open the project, you should check with your Project Server administrator. Likely, your system's configuration includes user-protected actuals, which does not allow the project manager to make this type of update. Note that the *Actual Work* field is editable in Project Pro 2013 allowing for "what if" analyses, but not allowing you to save a value to the field.

Best Practice: MSProjectExperts recommends that you train resources not to reassign or self-assign tasks. As these types of assignments should go through the project manager or resource manager and resources should communicate directly with the appropriate manager to reassign or add themselves to a task. The Project Server administrator may also configure the system by not allowing resources to reassign or add themselves to a task.

Best Practice: MSProjectExperts recommends applying updates to your project prior to deleting or changing assignments when using protect user updates to avoid losing user-entered data. On opening your project, you may see a message about new updates and the dialog shown in Figure 10 - 23, asking if you would like to apply the updates to the project, you should select the *Yes* button to proceed with applying the updates.

Approving Task Updates in Project Pro 2013

In addition to using the *Approval Center page* in Project Web App, Project Server 2013 also allows you to process task updates within the Project Pro 2013 client. When you open an enterprise project in Project Pro 2013 and the project has pending unapproved task updates, the system displays the dialog shown in Figure 10 - 23.

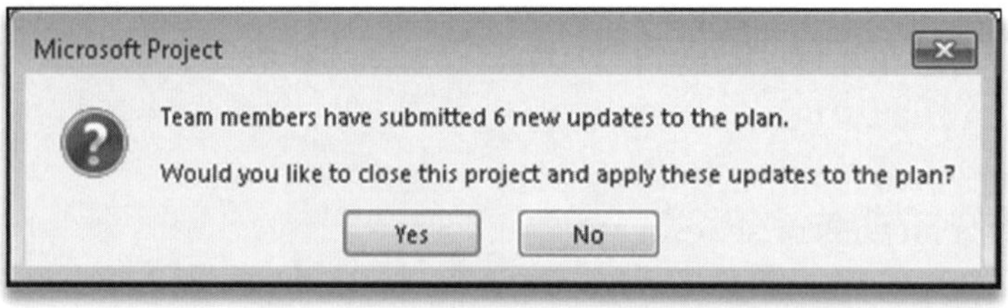
Microsoft Project
Team members have submitted 6 new updates to the plan.
Would you like to close this project and apply these updates to the plan?
Yes
No

Figure 10 - 23: Enterprise project has outstanding task updates

Your choice is either to process outstanding updates now or later. Clicking the *Yes* button opens the *Approval Center* page for you to process task updates, as covered previously. Clicking the *No* button opens the project plan for editing.

Information: Be cognizant of changing the schedule when there are pending updates. If you anticipate schedule or work change, it is better to accept the updates so that the plan is at a known agreed state between you and the team members prior to making subsequent changes.

Rescheduling Uncompleted Work in Past Reporting Periods

After accepting task updates, you should always examine the project in Project Pro 2013 to locate and reschedule uncompleted tasks that remain scheduled to occur in the past. These tasks mostly comprise unstarted tasks and in-progress tasks for which the assigned resource performed no work at all during the last reporting period. When a resource reports progress on a task, and you subsequently update the progress into the plan, the system automatically reschedules the incomplete work to begin after the update status date. The system **does not** automatically reschedule work on current tasks not updated by resources, as the system takes no action on them.

Figure 10 - 24 shows a project that contains uncompleted work that I scheduled to occur prior to the *Project Status Date*. The *Project Status Date,* found on the *Project* tab, defaults to today unless the project manager manually changes this date.

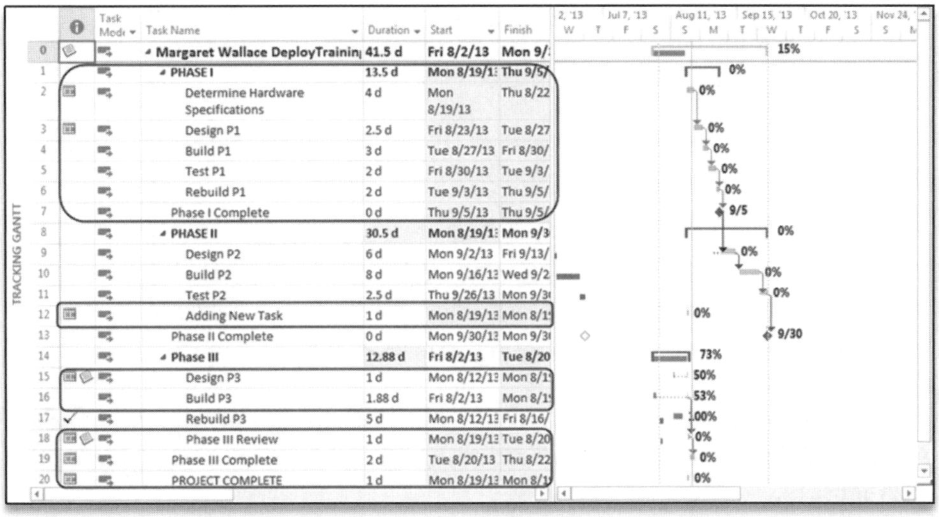

Figure 10 - 24: Enterprise project with uncompleted work in the past

To reschedule uncompleted work from a past reporting period into the current reporting period, complete the following steps:

1. Click the *Project* tab to display the *Project* ribbon.
2. In the *Status* section of the *Project* ribbon, click the *Status Date* button, and then in the *Status Date* dialog enter the status date of your project in the *Status date* field, and then click the *OK* button.

> **Information**: The status date for your project should be the last day of last week's reporting period. The status date represents the date by which you expect your team members to enter their task progress for last week.

3. In the *Status* section of the *Project* ribbon, click the *Update Project* button.
4. Project Pro 2013 displays the *Update Project* dialog. The *Update work as complete through* setting is the default setting.
5. Change the settings as follows:
   - Select the *Reschedule uncompleted work to start after* option.
   - Click the *Reschedule uncompleted work to start after* pick list and select a date at least one day **before** the work must resume on the uncompleted tasks (defaults to the status date you enter in Step 2).
   - Select the *Selected tasks* option if you selected tasks; otherwise, leave the *Entire Project* option selected.
6. Figure 10 - 25 illustrates the proper dialog settings. Review your settings and continue to the next step.
7. Click the *OK* button.
8. The dialog closes and the uncompleted work moves to begin on the date selected in **Step 2**.

9. The software highlights tasks where the uncompleted work moves to begin after the *Status Date.*

> **Information**: If you select the *Entire project* option in the *Update Project* dialog, Project Pro 2013 reschedules any task with uncompleted work in the past. This option is very useful for large projects with hundreds or thousands of tasks.

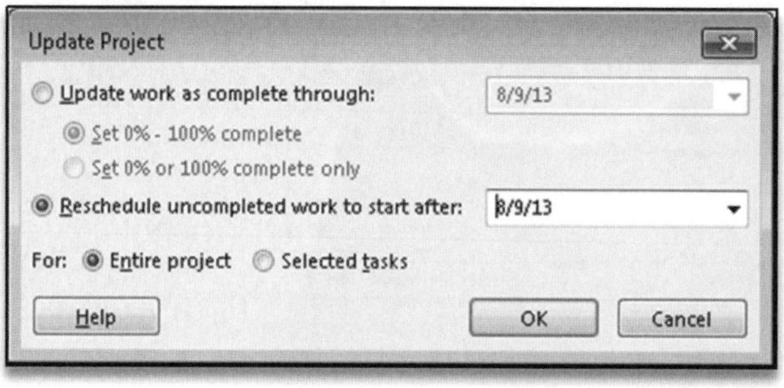

Figure 10 - 25: Update Project dialog set to reschedule uncompleted work

Figure 10 - 25 shows the *Update Project* dialog set to reschedule tasks to start on Monday, August 12. Notice that I selected Friday, August 9, 2013 as the date in the *Reschedule uncompleted work to start after* option, forcing the selected tasks to start August 12.

Figure 10 - 26 shows how Project Pro 2013 reschedules tasks with unstarted and uncompleted work from past reporting periods into the current reporting period by setting a Start No Earlier Than (SNET) constraint on the selected tasks. If the task is in-progress, Project Pro 2013 splits the task and moves only the uncompleted portion to the current reporting period.

Because the *Design P1* task is a predecessor task to *Build P1* task of the project, delaying this task affects the schedule of a chain of other dependent tasks. Notice that the *Change Highlighting* feature shows every task impacted by the rescheduled task.

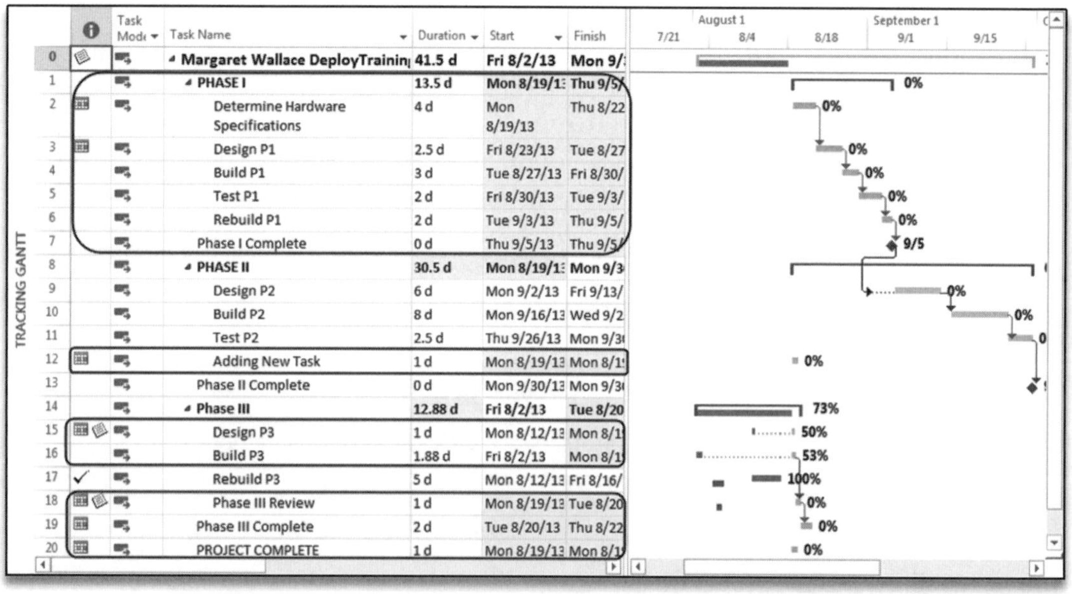

Figure 10 - 26: Uncompleted work rescheduled after date given

Updating Expense Cost Resource Information

After you reschedule uncompleted work in past time periods, you may need to update project expenditures for *Expense Cost* resources. Project Server 2013 offers two methods to update *Expense Cost* resource information:

- Programmatically update the *Expense Cost* resources from a third-party financial system.
- Manually enter the *Expense Cost* information.

If you use the programmatic approach, you do not need to take any action since the system automatically updates the *Expense Cost* resource information from your financial system.

To update the *Expense Cost* resource information manually, complete the following steps:

1. In Project Pro 2013, from the *View* tab of the *Task* ribbon, click the *Task Usage* button.
2. Click the *Tables* pick list and select the *Cost* item to apply the *Cost* table.
3. Pull the split bar to the right of the *Remaining Cost* column and compare your screen to Figure 10 - 27.
4. Enter the cost in the *Actual Cost* column for the *Expense Cost* resource assignment you want to expense.
5. Reduce the *Remaining Cost* value to $0.00, if necessary.

Figure 10 - 27 shows that I assigned the *Computer Hardware* resource to the *Design P2* task in the second phase of my project. This is because I intend to track this expense in that project phase. The view is already set up to enable you to enter *Actual Cost* values for the *Computer Hardware* resource.

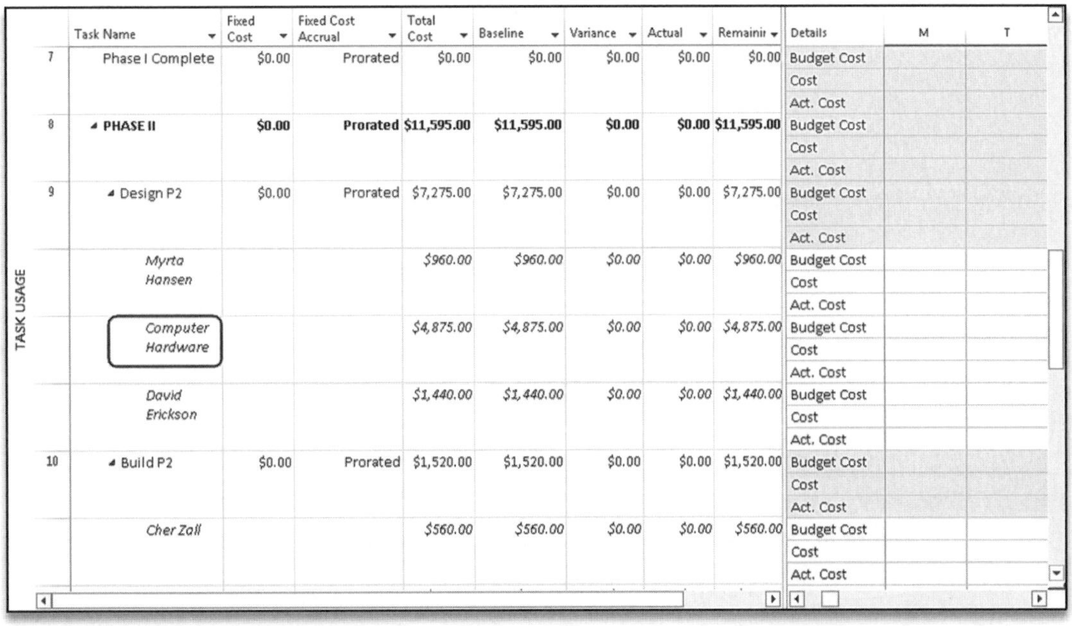

	Task Name	Fixed Cost	Fixed Cost Accrual	Total Cost	Baseline	Variance	Actual	Remaining	Details	M	T
7	Phase I Complete	$0.00	Prorated	$0.00	$0.00	$0.00	$0.00	$0.00	Budget Cost		
									Cost		
									Act. Cost		
8	**PHASE II**	**$0.00**	**Prorated**	**$11,595.00**	**$11,595.00**	**$0.00**	**$0.00**	**$11,595.00**	Budget Cost		
									Cost		
									Act. Cost		
9	Design P2	$0.00	Prorated	$7,275.00	$7,275.00	$0.00	$0.00	$7,275.00	Budget Cost		
									Cost		
									Act. Cost		
	Myrta Hansen			*$960.00*	*$960.00*	*$0.00*	*$0.00*	*$960.00*	Budget Cost		
									Cost		
									Act. Cost		
	Computer Hardware			*$4,875.00*	*$4,875.00*	*$0.00*	*$0.00*	*$4,875.00*	Budget Cost		
									Cost		
									Act. Cost		
	David Erickson			*$1,440.00*	*$1,440.00*	*$0.00*	*$0.00*	*$1,440.00*	Budget Cost		
									Cost		
									Act. Cost		
10	Build P2	$0.00	Prorated	$1,520.00	$1,520.00	$0.00	$0.00	$1,520.00	Budget Cost		
									Cost		
									Act. Cost		
	Cher Zall			*$560.00*	*$560.00*	*$0.00*	*$0.00*	*$560.00*	Budget Cost		
									Cost		
									Act. Cost		

Figure 10 - 27: Computer Hardware resource assigned to task in the second phase

Figure 10 - 28 shows the *Task Usage* view with the timephased grid set up to enter *Actual Cost* information for the *Computer Hardware* expense cost resource. Notice that the *Task Usage* view shows $812.50 of *Actual Cost* for the *Computer Hardware* expense cost resource, timephased across the 6 days of the *Design P2* task.

Project Pro 2013 distributes the *Actual Cost* value evenly across the duration of the task in the timephased grid. In reality, the expense likely accrued on a specific day due to payment of an invoice or the filing of an expense report. To reallocate the *Actual Cost* value to a specific day or days, complete the following additional steps:

1. Pull the split bar back to the edge of the *Fixed Cost* column to expose the timephased grid (gray timesheet on the right side of the view).

2. If costs are not visible, right-click anywhere in the timephased grid and select the *Cost* item, right-click again, select the *Actual Cost* item and then right-click one more time, and deselect the *Work* item.

3. Edit the *Actual Cost* information in the timephased grid.

Warning: Enter 0 for any days that scheduled expenses will no longer occur. Otherwise, Project Server 2013 attempts to reschedule the existing timephased cost, which can lead to double counting. The total cost column can indicate if your entries are correct.

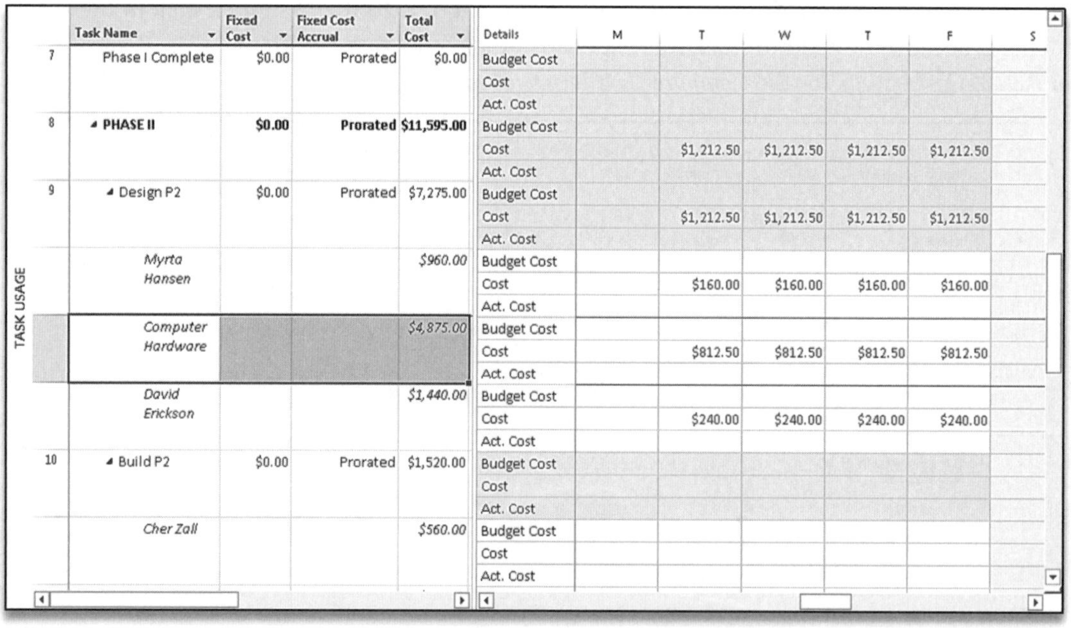

TASK USAGE
Task Name
Fixed Cost
Fixed Cost Accrual
Total Cost
Details
M T W T F S
7 Phase I Complete $0.00 Prorated $0.00 Budget Cost Cost Act. Cost
8 PHASE II $0.00 Prorated $11,595.00 Budget Cost Cost Act. Cost
$1,212.50 $1,212.50 $1,212.50 $1,212.50
9 Design P2 $0.00 Prorated $7,275.00 Budget Cost Cost Act. Cost
$1,212.50 $1,212.50 $1,212.50 $1,212.50
Myrta Hansen $960.00 Budget Cost Cost Act. Cost
$160.00 $160.00 $160.00 $160.00
Computer Hardware $4,875.00 Budget Cost Cost Act. Cost
$812.50 $812.50 $812.50 $812.50
David Erickson $1,440.00 Budget Cost Cost Act. Cost
$240.00 $240.00 $240.00 $240.00
10 Build P2 $0.00 Prorated $1,520.00 Budget Cost Cost Act. Cost
Cher Zoll $560.00 Budget Cost Cost Act. Cost

Figure 10 - 28: Task Usage view set up to view Actual Cost information

Notice in Figure 10 - 29 that I entered all of the $4875.00 of *Actual Cost* for the *Computer Hardware* expense cost resource on Friday as the receipt of the computer hardware occurred on that day. Notice also that the total cost appears as $8937.50. If you advance to the following week using the right arrow key on your computer keyboard, you will notice that there are values in the *Cost* field that you should have updated to zero values. This reflects that the *Actual Cost* occurs only on the date indicated and the scheduled expenses will no longer occur the following week.

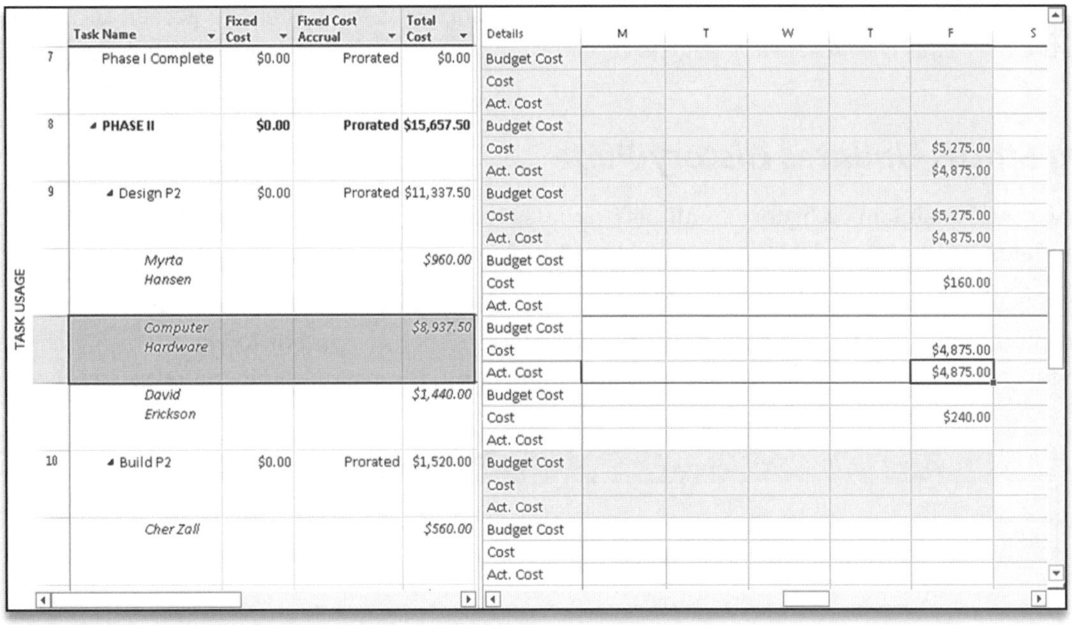

Figure 10 - 29: Task Usage view shows all $4875.00 of Actual Cost on Friday

Publishing the Latest Schedule Changes

After you update task progress into your project, reschedule uncompleted work, and update *Cost* resource information, you must **always** save the project and then publish the latest schedule changes. This step is extremely important, as it updates the latest schedule information on the *Tasks* page of each team member in the project. To publish the latest schedule changes, click *File* ➤ *Info* in the *Backstage*, and then click the *Publish* button. The system updates the Project Server 2013 database with the current information for the project, making the current schedule visible everywhere in Project Web App.

Warning: If you fail to publish the latest schedule changes after updating a project, your project becomes "out of sync" between the Project Pro 2013 plan and Project Web App. "Out of sync" project information adversely affects your project team members, as they cannot see the current task schedule on the *Tasks* page. Remember that you must **always** publish your enterprise project after updating it with task progress.

Best Practice: MSProjectExperts recommends that you make project and task publishing a training and performance issue. Teach your project managers to publish their enterprise project after every process of task updates, and then hold them accountable for this performance.

Using Status Updates History Page and Approval Rules

The next topical sections relate to the *Status Updates History* page and automatic approval rule setup. You use these two functions together to make the management of projects that track processes or ad hoc tasks easier. For example, you use a project plan as a way of allocating resources to a repetitive process, like customer setup. The template assigns the standard tasks to team generic resources. Team leads then reassign the work to actual work resources. The status of each task is paramount to the actual schedule as customer setup is a known process with well-known timelines. Automatic approval rules allow you to direct the system to accept all updates to these plans. You use the *Status Updates History* page to monitor for new updates and to republish the project plan on the server.

Viewing Status Updates History Page

Project Server 2013 maintains a history of all task updates that you accept and reject. To view the history of in-progress updates, on the *Approval Center* page, click the *History* pick list and select the *Status Updates* item. The system displays the *Status Updates History* page shown in Figure 10 - 30.

The *Action* column indicates the transaction approval status as either *Accepted* or *Rejected*. The *Status* column indicates the publish state of the transaction as *Published, Unpublished, Error,* or *Pending* if a project is checked out and the change cannot be applied yet.

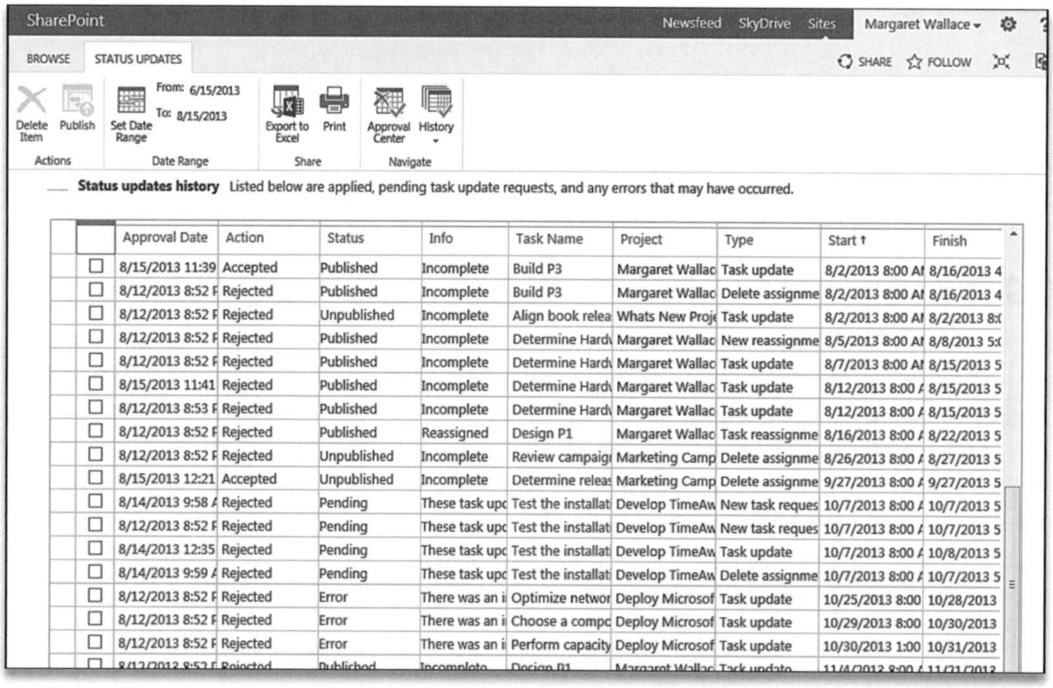

Figure 10 - 30: Status Updates History page

If you attempt to accept or reject task updates in a project checked out to someone else, Project Server 2013 cannot complete the update process, and displays them as *Unpublished* or *Pending* on the *Status Updates History* page. If you navigate to this page and find any task updates with an *Unpublished* or *Pending* status, close the enterprise project indicated in the *Project* column so that Project Server 2013 can complete the update process. After completing the updates, the system changes the status to *Published.*

To update transactions on the *Status Updates History* page, do one of the following three actions:

1. From the Project Center, check in any project that has transactions with a *Pending* or *Unpublished* status. This enables the system to apply outstanding changes.

2. Publish the project. Select any transaction from a project and then click the *Publish* button to process all outstanding transactions for that project.

3. Delete a transaction by selecting the transaction that you want to delete and then in the *Actions* section of the *Status Updates* ribbon, click the *Delete Item* button. Note that you may only delete published transactions.

> **Warning**: The *Delete* function does **not** give you a confirmation prompt before executing the deletion. Therefore, ensure this is really what you want to do prior to performing the deletion. Use the *Delete* functionality carefully as you are deleting published data. You should republish the project after a deletion to ensure that the system synchronizes the project plan and the server data.

Managing Rules for Accepting Task Updates

The *Rules* feature in Project Server 2013 allows you to create logical rules for quickly approving task updates into your projects. When you apply a rule, the system approves only those task changes that meet the criteria defined in the rule. You may configure rules to execute automatically; however, rules now have an option to publish automatically the updates for which transactions are accepted or rejected.

Access the *Rules* feature from the *Approval Center* page. In the *Navigate* section of the *Approvals* ribbon, click the *Manage Rules* button to display the *Rules* page shown in Figure 10 - 31.

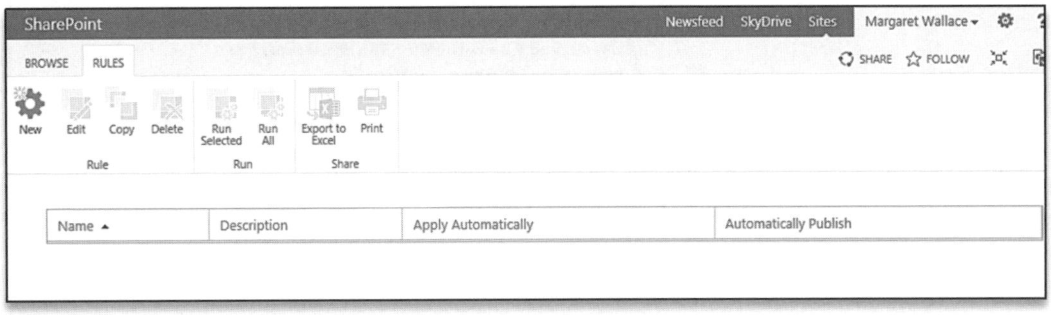

Figure 10 - 31: Automatic Approval Rules page

Create a New Rule

In the *Rule* section of the *RULES* ribbon, click the *New* button to begin the process of creating the new rule. The system displays the *Edit/Create Rule* page shown in Figure 10 - 32.

In the *Name* section of the *Edit/Create Rule* page, enter a name for the new rule in the *Name* field and enter an optional description in the *Description and Comments for Team Members* field.

In the *Automatic updates* section of the page, select the *Automatically run this rule* option if you want Project Server 2013 to run the rule automatically or when you click the *Run All Rules* button on the *Rules* page. Leave the option deselected if you want to run the rule manually. If you run the rule automatically, you may monitor the transactions resulting from the rule execution on the *Status Updates History* page. Select the *Automatically publish the updates* option to automatically publish the updates. If the project is checked out to someone else, the updates are published after the project is checked in and another update comes through or after you publish the project.

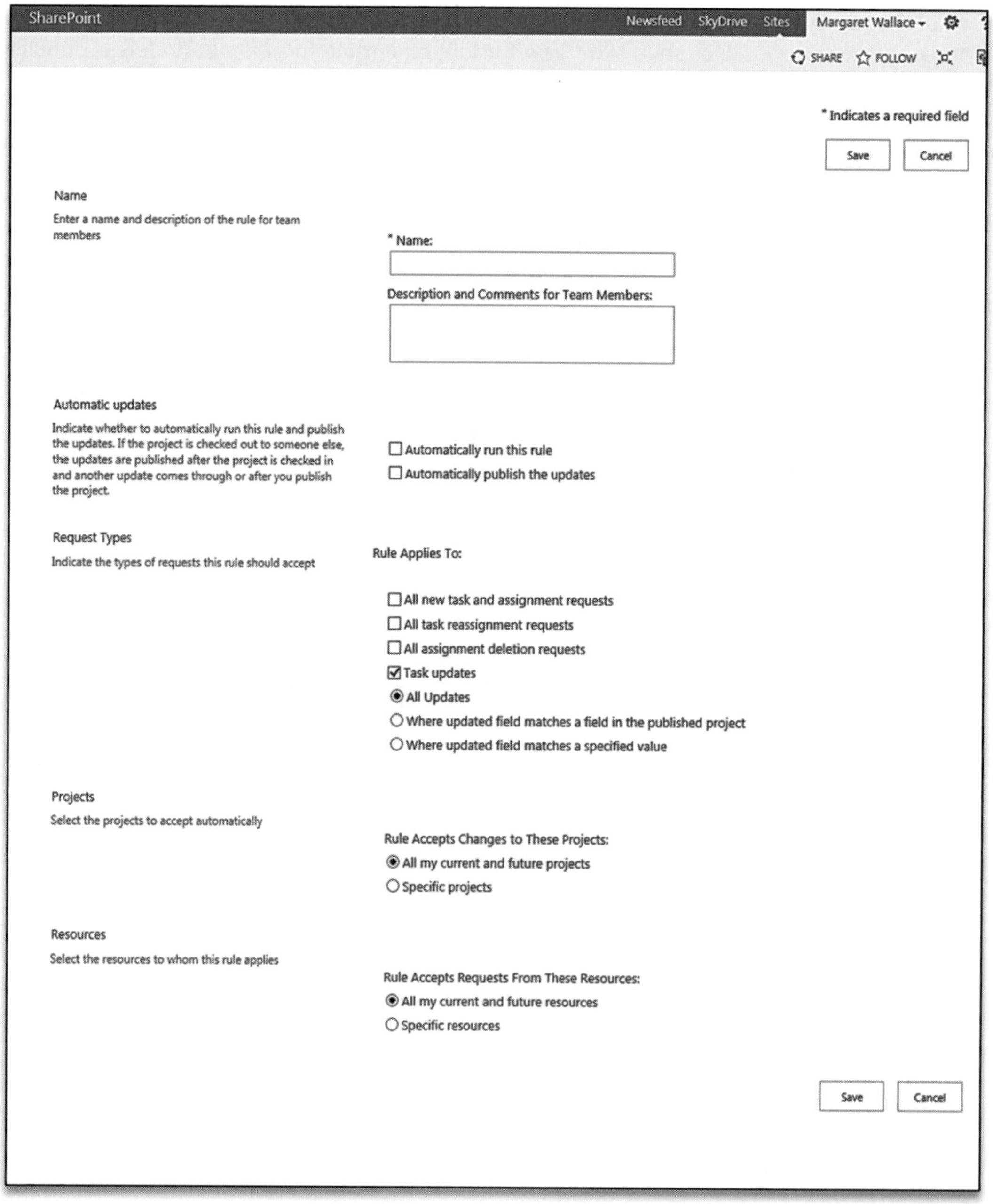

Figure 10 - 32: Edit/Create Rule page

In the *Request Types* section, select the type of updates you want to process with the rule as shown in Table 10 - 3.

Setting	Action
All new task and assignment requests	Select the option to process updates for which a resource proposes a new task or assigns himself to an existing task.
All task reassignment requests	Select the option to process updates for which a resource delegates a task to another team member, or assigns himself to a task previously assigned to a team resource.

Setting	Action
All assignment deletion requests	Select the option to process updates for resource rejected task assignments.
Task updates	Select the option to process task progress updates from your resources.

Table 10 - 3: List of Request Types

If you select the *Task updates* option as shown previously in Figure 10 - 32, you must select one of the three following options:

- All Updates
- Where updated field matches a field in the published project
- Where updated field matches a specified value

Select the *All Updates* option to process all progress updates from your resources. If you select the *Where updated field matches a field in the published project* option, Project Server 2013 expands the *Request Types* section with additional options, as shown in Figure 10 - 33. In the expanded *Request Types* section, create a custom filter by specifying values from the *Updated Field, Operator,* and *Published Field* pick lists. For example, you can enable automatic approval of updates where *Assignment Actual Work* is equal to *Assignment Baseline Work.*

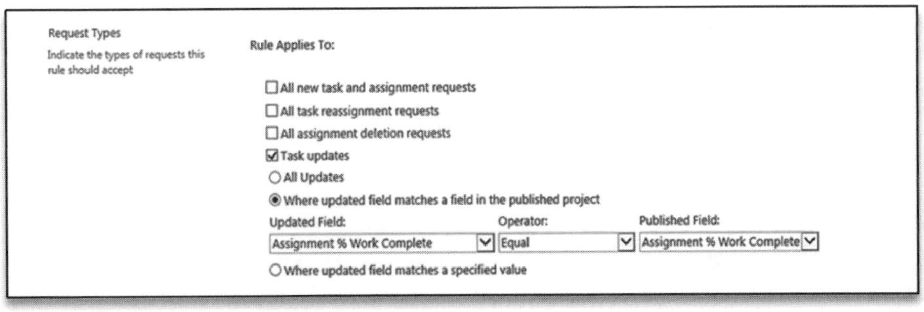

Figure 10 - 33: Request Type custom filter based on field value match

If you select the *Where updated field matches a specific value* option, Project Server 2013 expands the *Request Types* section with additional options, as shown in Figure 10 - 34. In the expanded *Request Types* section, create a custom filter by specifying values from the *Updated Field* and *Operator* pick lists, and enter a value in the *Value* field. For example, you can enable automatic approvals for all updates where the assignment *% Work Complete* value is equal to *100.*

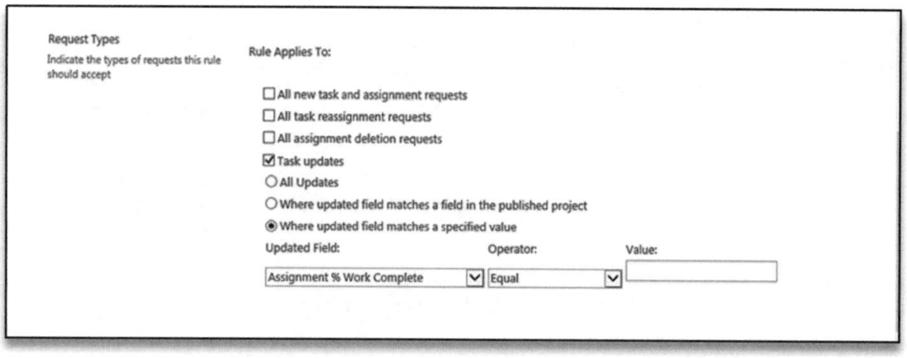

Figure 10 - 34: Request Type custom filter based on specific value match

In the *Projects* section of the page, select an option to determine to which projects the rule must apply. Select the *All my current and future projects* option to apply the rule to all current and future projects. If you select the *Specific projects* option, the system expands the *Projects* section, as shown in Figure 10 - 35.

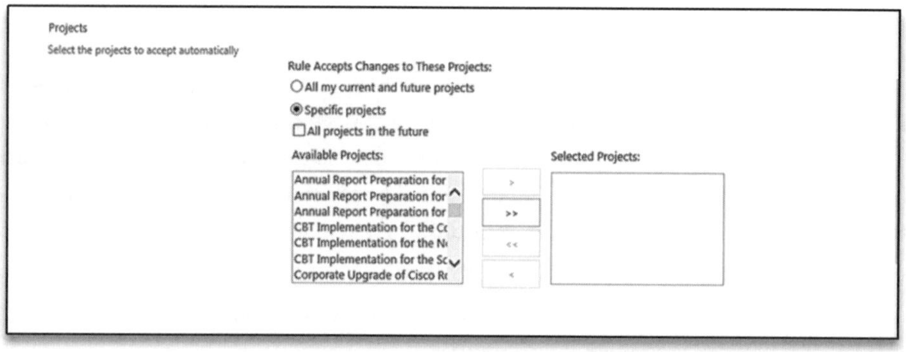

Figure 10 - 35: Expanded Projects section allows selection of specific projects

From the *Available Projects* list, select one or more projects and then click the *Add* button (>>) to add your selections to the *Selected Projects* list. If you want the rule to process future projects in addition to the selected projects, select the *All projects in the future* checkbox option as well.

In the *Resources* section, select an option to determine the resources to which the rule applies. Select the *All my current and future resources* option to apply the rule to updates from all current and future resources. If you select the *Specific resources* option, the system expands the *Resources* section, as shown in Figure 10 - 36.

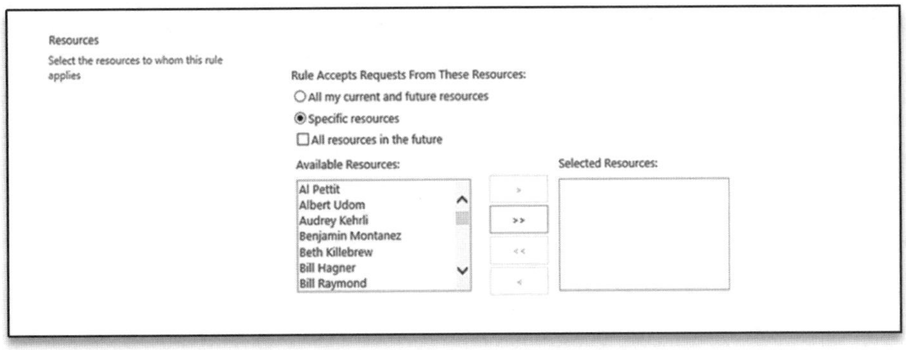

Figure 10 - 36: Expanded Resources section allows selection of specific resources

From the *Available Resources* list, select one or more resources and then click the *Add* button (>>) to add them to the *Selected Resources* list. If you want the rule to process updates from future resources in addition to the selected resources, select the *All resources in the future* checkbox option.

Information: If you select the *All task reassignment requests* option in the *Request Types* section of the page, the system adds two additional options in the *Resources* section. These options allow you to select the specific resources for task reassignment.

Figure 10 - 37 shows my completed rule that automatically approves progress updates from all resources for all projects when the task assignment is not completed. The new rule ignores all task updates that complete a task assignment, requiring the project manager to approve such updates manually. The rule also ignores all other types of updates.

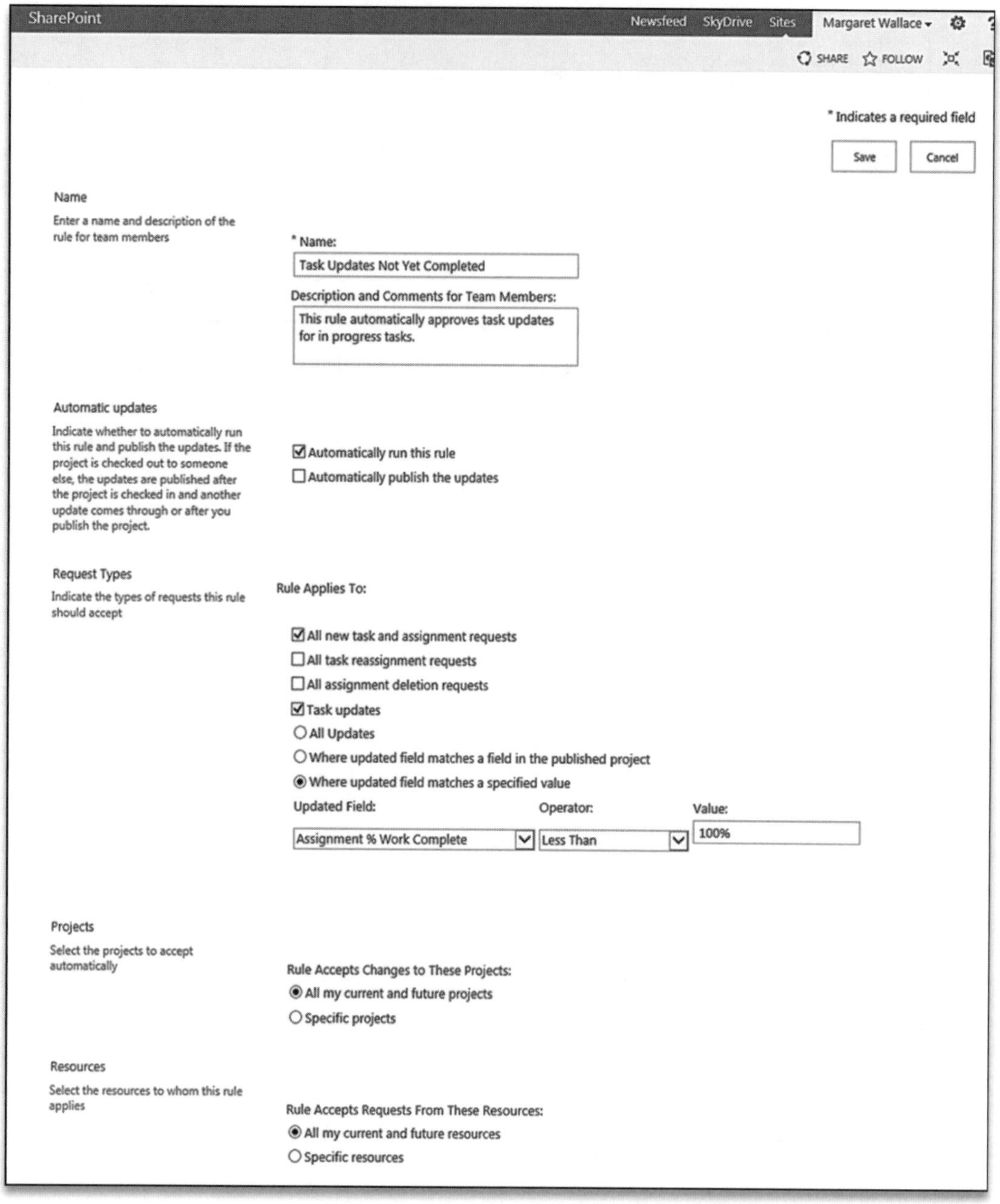

Figure 10 - 37: New rule created to approve task updates

Click the *Save* button to save the new rule. Figure 10 - 38 shows three rules on the *Rules* page in Project Web App. These rules are as follows:

- **Any Update from PMO Team Members** automatically approves any type of update in any project from a resource in the PMO.
- **Task Reassignment Updates from Team Leaders** automatically approves task reassignment requests from resources designated as a team leader.
- **Task Updates Not Yet Completed** automatically approves task updates for in-progress assignments, but ignores updates that complete work on a task assignment.

Use these three rules as examples for creating your own rules.

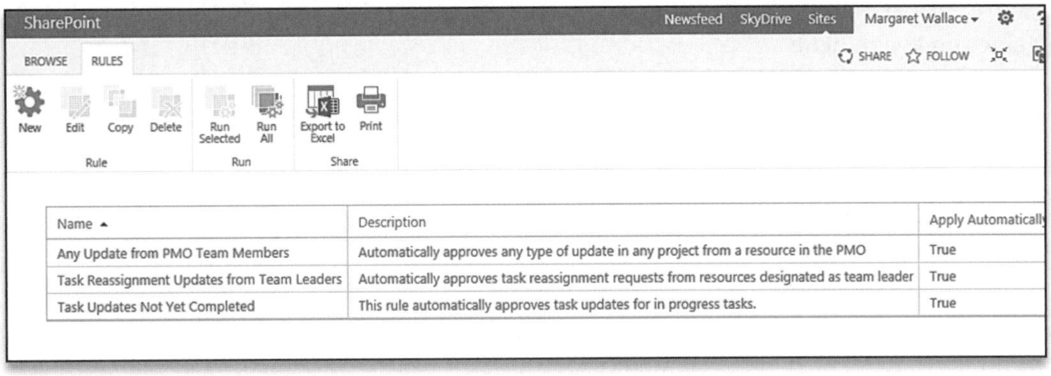

Figure 10 - 38: New rule on the Rules page

In Figure 10 - 38, notice the buttons on the *RULES* ribbon. When you select a rule in the data grid, these buttons give you the option to edit, copy, delete, or run the rule individually. Click the *Edit* button to modify the selected rule. Click the *Copy* button to create a new rule based on a copy of the selected rule. After copying a rule, you must then edit the copy, including naming the rule. Click the *Delete* button to remove the selected rule.

Select a rule in the data grid and then click the *Run Selected* button in the *Run* section of the ribbon to run only the selected rule. To run all rules in a single operation, click the *Run All* button. Project Server 2013 approves all updates indicated in the rules for which the *Apply Automatically* option is set to *True*. If the *Apply Automatically* option is set to *False*, then you must run the rule individually by selecting it and clicking the *Run Selected* button.

Axioms for Success with Tracking Progress

To be successful in tracking project progress using Project Server 2013, your organization should keep the following in mind:

- Everyone in your organization who is responsible for reporting progress should enter their time and send their updates on a standard day and time whether this is daily, weekly, semi-weekly or other predictable and appropriate reporting standard.
- Project managers should process task updates on a standard day each reporting period.
- Managers should deal appropriately with anyone who is responsible for reporting progress, but who fails to cooperate or participate fully in the process. You must take all necessary steps to ensure the full participation of everyone in your organization in order to validate the project data in the system.
- Your organization should track and manage the absence of resources during each update cycle. If necessary, you can create delegates to manage timesheets for absent resources.
- Your organization should also track and manage the absence of managers during each update cycle. For updating purposes, other managers can delegate (take over tasks) owned by absent managers and process the updates.
- Stay current with progress reporting and updates to make sure that you are managing your projects with current data.

- If using the protect user updates option, resources should communicate directly with the project manager or resource manager for task assignments that include reassigning or adding self to a task, to preserve *Actual* values on assignments.

Module 11

Variance Analysis, Plan Revision, and Reporting

Learning Objectives

After completing this module, you will be able to:

- Understand the different types of project variance
- Define plan revision and change control
- Revise a project plan to bring it back on schedule
- Use change control procedures to add a new task to a project
- Baseline a project after adding new tasks
- Use the Timeline view with the Gantt Chart view
- Use Visual Reports with Excel and Visio

Inside Module 11

Understanding Variance

At the end of every reporting period, you should analyze project variance by comparing actual progress and remaining estimates against the original project baseline. This is the way you determine schedule slippage and overruns, as well as identifying existing and/or potential problems with your project schedule. Analyzing variance is the first step in revising the project plan to bring it back on track with its original goals and objectives.

Understanding Variance Types

In Module 08, *Project Execution,* I stated that when you save a baseline in Project Pro 2013, the software baselines the current values for five important task fields. These fields include the *Duration, Start, Finish, Work,* and *Cost* fields. Because the system saves five task values in a project baseline, the system calculates five types of task variance:

- Duration variance
- Start variance
- Finish variance
- Work variance
- Cost variance

About Those Extra Task Baseline Fields

In Module 08, I noted that in addition to the five important task fields captured in the baseline, Project Pro 2013 also captures extra baseline information in several other task fields. The software captures the extra baseline information in the following fields: *Baseline Fixed Cost, Baseline Fixed Cost Accrual, Baseline Estimated Duration, Baseline Estimated Start, Baseline Estimated Finish, Baseline Budget Cost* and *Baseline Budget Work* fields.

Even though Project Pro 2013 captures the extra task baseline information in these seven fields, the software **does not** include any corresponding variance fields for them. This means that if you want to analyze *Fixed Cost* variance, for example, there is no default field called *Fixed Cost Variance.* If you want to analyze *Fixed Cost* variance, you must create a custom task field containing a formula to calculate this variance. The same is true for the other six extra baseline fields as well.

Calculating Variance

To calculate variance, Project Pro 2013 uses the following formula:

Variance = (Actual Progress + Remaining Estimates) - Baseline

In Project Pro 2013, a positive variance is unfavorable to the project, and means that the project schedule is late, or that work and/or cost are over budget. Negative variance is favorable to the project, and means that the project is ahead of schedule, or that work and/or cost are under budget.

For example, suppose that the actual work for a task is 60 hours, the remaining work estimate is 40 hours, and the baseline work for the task is 80 hours. Using the formula above, Project Pro 2013 calculates the work variance as:

Work Variance = (Actual Work + Remaining Work) – Baseline Work

Work Variance = (60 hours + 40 hours) – 80 hours

Work Variance = 100 hours - 80 hours

Work Variance = 20 hours

The resulting 20-hour work variance is unfavorable to the project because the total work hours exceed the original baseline work budget.

Analyzing Project Variance

Project Pro 2013 offers you the following locations from which to analyze project variance:

- *Tracking Gantt* view
- *Variance* table
- *Work* table
- *Cost* table

The *Tracking Gantt* view and the *Variance* table allow you to analyze start and finish variance for tasks. The *Work* and *Cost* tables allow you to analyze work and cost variance, respectively.

Information: Project Pro 2013 does not offer a default table from which to analyze *Duration* variance. If you want to see *Duration* variance, you must create your own custom table for this purpose. Later in this module, I teach you how to use the custom duration slippage view included in the Project Server 2013 system used with this course.

Analyzing Date Variance

Date variance is a major concern for every project manager because many projects have an inflexible project finish date. You may analyze *Date* variance graphically by applying the *Tracking Gantt* view. To apply the *Tracking Gantt* view, use one of the following methods:

- On the *Task* ribbon, click the *Gantt Chart* pick list button and select the *Tracking Gantt* view from the list.
- On the *Resource* ribbon, click the *Team Planner* pick list button and select the *Tracking Gantt* view from the list.
- On the *View* ribbon, click the *Gantt Chart* pick list button and select the *Tracking Gantt* view from the list.

Project Pro 2013 applies the *Tracking Gantt* view shown in Figure 11 - 1.

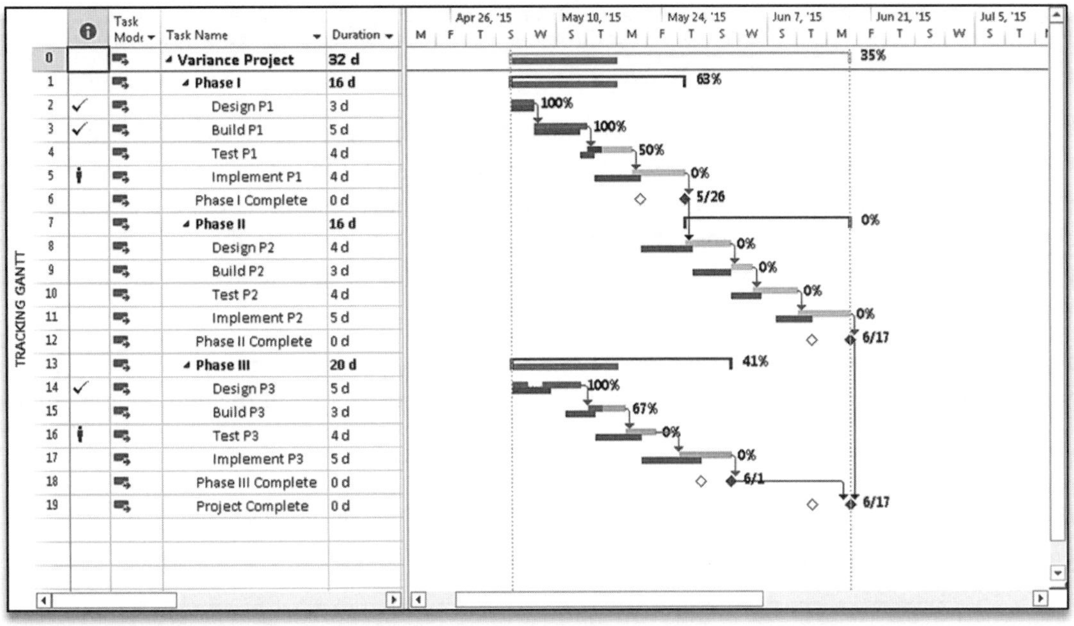

Figure 11 - 1: Tracking Gantt view

Following is a description of the symbols shown in the *Gantt Chart* screen on the right side of the *Tracking Gantt* view:

- Light red Gantt bars represent planned work for tasks on the Critical Path.
- Light blue Gantt bars represent planned work for tasks not on the Critical Path.
- Light teal Gantt bars represent planned work for *Manually Scheduled* tasks not on the Critical Path.
- Dark red Gantt bars represent completed work for tasks on the Critical Path.
- Dark blue Gantt bars represent completed work for tasks not on the Critical Path.
- Dark teal Gantt bars represent completed work for *Manually Scheduled* tasks not on the Critical Path.
- Gray Gantt bars represent the baseline schedule for each task.
- Black solid diamonds represent the current schedule for each milestone task.
- Teal solid diamonds represent the current schedule for *Manually Scheduled* milestone tasks.
- Hollow diamonds represent the baseline schedule for each milestone task.
- The percentage value at the right end of each Gantt bar represents the *% Complete* field value for each task.
- The tan bar on the bottom half of each summary task Gantt bar represents the cumulative *% Complete* field value for all of the subtasks for the summary task.

> **Information**: To see every possible symbol that Project Pro 2013 can display in the *Tracking Gantt* view, double-click anywhere in the white part of the Gantt Chart screen on the right side of the view. The system displays the *Bar Styles* dialog, which shows you the definition for every symbol used in the *Tracking Gantt* view.

The *Tracking Gantt* view allows you to see slippage graphically in your project by comparing blue, red, and teal Gantt bars with their accompanying gray Gantt bars (the baseline schedule for each task). If a blue, red, or teal Gantt bar slips to the right of its gray Gantt bar, then the task is slipping. Additionally, if a black or teal diamond slips to the right of its hollow diamond, then the milestone task is slipping. Using the *Tracking Gantt* view to analyze date variance makes it easy to see the slippage in all phases of the project, as well as the overall slippage for the final project finish date.

Use the *Variance* table to view the *Date* variance in a numerical format, such as in days. To apply the *Variance* table, display any task view (such as the *Tracking Gantt* view) and then use either of the following methods:

- Right-click the *Select All* button and then select the *Variance* table in the shortcut menu.
- In the *View* ribbon, click the *Tables* pick list and select the *Variance* table in the list.

Project Pro 2013 displays the *Variance* table shown in Figure 11 - 2.

	Task Mode	Task Name	Start	Finish	Baseline Start	Baseline Finish	Start Var.	Finish Var.
0		**Variance Project**	**5/4/15**	**6/17/15**	**5/4/15**	**6/12/15**	**0 d**	**3 d**
1		**Phase I**	**5/4/15**	**5/26/15**	**5/4/15**	**5/20/15**	**0 d**	**3 d**
2		Design P1	5/4/15	5/6/15	5/4/15	5/6/15	0 d	0 d
3		Build P1	5/7/15	5/13/15	5/7/15	5/12/15	0 d	1 d
4		Test P1	5/14/15	5/19/15	5/13/15	5/14/15	1 d	3 d
5		Implement P1	5/20/15	5/26/15	5/15/15	5/20/15	3 d	3 d
6		Phase I Complete	5/26/15	5/26/15	5/20/15	5/20/15	3 d	3 d
7		**Phase II**	**5/27/15**	**6/17/15**	**5/21/15**	**6/12/15**	**3 d**	**3 d**
8		Design P2	5/27/15	6/1/15	5/21/15	5/27/15	3 d	3 d
9		Build P2	6/2/15	6/4/15	5/28/15	6/1/15	3 d	3 d
10		Test P2	6/5/15	6/10/15	6/2/15	6/5/15	3 d	3 d
11		Implement P2	6/11/15	6/17/15	6/8/15	6/12/15	3 d	3 d
12		Phase II Complete	6/17/15	6/17/15	6/12/15	6/12/15	3 d	3 d
13		**Phase III**	**5/4/15**	**6/1/15**	**5/4/15**	**5/28/15**	**0 d**	**2 d**
14		Design P3	5/4/15	5/12/15	5/4/15	5/8/15	0 d	2 d
15		Build P3	5/14/15	5/18/15	5/11/15	5/14/15	3 d	2 d
16		Test P3	5/19/15	5/22/15	5/15/15	5/20/15	2 d	2 d
17		Implement P3	5/26/15	6/1/15	5/21/15	5/28/15	2 d	2 d
18		Phase III Complete	6/1/15	6/1/15	5/28/15	5/28/15	2 d	2 d
19		Project Complete	6/17/15	6/17/15	6/12/15	6/12/15	3 d	3 d

Figure 11 - 2: Variance table applied in the Tracking Gantt view

To analyze *Date* variance, examine each value in the *Start Variance* and *Finish Variance* columns. Figure 11 - 2 shows that the *Finish Variance* value for the Project Summary Task (Row 0) equals *3 days*, revealing that this project is 3 days late on its finish date, caused by the late finish for the tasks in Phase I. Because of the 3 days of *Finish Variance* in Phase I, all of the tasks in Phase II are 3 days late as well. Notice also that the tasks in Phase III are each 2 days late on their finish date due to the late finish of the *Design P3* task.

Analyzing Work Variance

Use the *Work* table to analyze *Work* variance and to determine when project work exceeds its original planned work budget. To apply the *Work* table, display any task view (such as the *Tracking Gantt* view) and then use either of the following methods:

- Right-click the *Select All* button and then select the *Work* table in the shortcut menu.
- In the *View* ribbon, click the *Tables* pick list and select the *Work* table in the list.

Project Pro 2013 displays the *Work* table shown in Figure 11 - 3.

	Task Name	Work	Baseline	Variance	Actual	Remaining	% W. Comp.
0	**Variance Project**	**488 h**	**464 h**	**24 h**	**176 h**	**312 h**	**36%**
1	**Phase I**	**168 h**	**136 h**	**32 h**	**120 h**	**48 h**	**71%**
2	Design P1	24 h	24 h	0 h	24 h	0 h	100%
3	Build P1	80 h	64 h	16 h	80 h	0 h	100%
4	Test P1	32 h	16 h	16 h	16 h	16 h	50%
5	Implement P1	32 h	32 h	0 h	0 h	32 h	0%
6	Phase I Complete	0 h	0 h	0 h	0 h	0 h	0%
7	**Phase II**	**152 h**	**152 h**	**0 h**	**0 h**	**152 h**	**0%**
8	Design P2	32 h	32 h	0 h	0 h	32 h	0%
9	Build P2	48 h	48 h	0 h	0 h	48 h	0%
10	Test P2	32 h	32 h	0 h	0 h	32 h	0%
11	Implement P2	40 h	40 h	0 h	0 h	40 h	0%
12	Phase II Complete	0 h	0 h	0 h	0 h	0 h	0%
13	**Phase III**	**168 h**	**176 h**	**-8 h**	**56 h**	**112 h**	**33%**
14	Design P3	40 h	40 h	0 h	40 h	0 h	100%
15	Build P3	24 h	32 h	-8 h	16 h	8 h	67%
16	Test P3	64 h	64 h	0 h	0 h	64 h	0%
17	Implement P3	40 h	40 h	0 h	0 h	40 h	0%
18	Phase III Complete	0 h	0 h	0 h	0 h	0 h	0%
19	Project Complete	0 h	0 h	0 h	0 h	0 h	0%

Figure 11 - 3: Work table applied in the Tracking Gantt view

To analyze work variance, examine each value in the *Variance* column. In Figure 11 - 3, the *Variance* value for the Project Summary Task (Row 0) reveals that this project is currently 24 hours over budget. Phase I is currently 32 hours over its work budget. The *Build P1* task is 16 hours over budget, and the task is complete; therefore, the *Build P1* task shows actual variance. The *Test P1* task is also 16 hours over budget, but the task is only 50% complete; therefore, the *Test P1* task shows estimated variance. Phase III is 8 hours **under** its work budget, indicated by the negative value in the *Variance* column.

Information: In the *Work* table, the real name of the *Variance* column is *Work Variance*. Microsoft uses the shorter name as the title of this column for display purposes only. You can see the real name of the column by floating your mouse pointer over the *Variance* column header. The system displays a tooltip that shows the title of the column, followed by the real name of the column in parentheses.

Analyzing Cost Variance

Use the *Cost* table to analyze *Cost* variance and to determine when project costs exceed its original planned cost budget. To apply the *Cost* table, display any task view (such as the *Tracking Gantt* view) and then use either of the following methods:

- Right-click the *Select All* button and then select the *Cost* table in the shortcut menu.
- In the *View* ribbon, click the *Tables* pick list and select the *Cost* table in the list.

Project Pro 2013 displays the *Cost* table shown in Figure 11 - 4.

	Task Name	Fixed Cost	Fixed Cost Accrual	Total Cost	Baseline	Variance	Actual	Remaining
0	▲ **Variance Project**	**$0.00**	**Prorated**	**$26,900.00**	**$23,200.00**	**$3,700.00**	**$11,300.00**	**$15,600.00**
1	▲ **Phase I**	**$0.00**	**Prorated**	**$10,900.00**	**$6,800.00**	**$4,100.00**	**$8,500.00**	**$2,400.00**
2	Design P1	$0.00	Prorated	$1,200.00	$1,200.00	$0.00	$1,200.00	$0.00
3	Build P1	$2,500.00	Prorated	$6,500.00	$3,200.00	$3,300.00	$6,500.00	$0.00
4	Test P1	$0.00	Prorated	$1,600.00	$800.00	$800.00	$800.00	$800.00
5	Implement P1	$0.00	Prorated	$1,600.00	$1,600.00	$0.00	$0.00	$1,600.00
6	Phase I Complete	$0.00	Prorated	$0.00	$0.00	$0.00	$0.00	$0.00
7	▲ **Phase II**	**$0.00**	**Prorated**	**$7,600.00**	**$7,600.00**	**$0.00**	**$0.00**	**$7,600.00**
8	Design P2	$0.00	Prorated	$1,600.00	$1,600.00	$0.00	$0.00	$1,600.00
9	Build P2	$0.00	Prorated	$2,400.00	$2,400.00	$0.00	$0.00	$2,400.00
10	Test P2	$0.00	Prorated	$1,600.00	$1,600.00	$0.00	$0.00	$1,600.00
11	Implement P2	$0.00	Prorated	$2,000.00	$2,000.00	$0.00	$0.00	$2,000.00
12	Phase II Complete	$0.00	Prorated	$0.00	$0.00	$0.00	$0.00	$0.00
13	▲ **Phase III**	**$0.00**	**Prorated**	**$8,400.00**	**$8,800.00**	**($400.00)**	**$2,800.00**	**$5,600.00**
14	Design P3	$0.00	Prorated	$2,000.00	$2,000.00	$0.00	$2,000.00	$0.00
15	Build P3	$0.00	Prorated	$1,200.00	$1,600.00	($400.00)	$800.00	$400.00
16	Test P3	$0.00	Prorated	$3,200.00	$3,200.00	$0.00	$0.00	$3,200.00
17	Implement P3	$0.00	Prorated	$2,000.00	$2,000.00	$0.00	$0.00	$2,000.00
18	Phase III Complete	$0.00	Prorated	$0.00	$0.00	$0.00	$0.00	$0.00
19	Project Complete	$0.00	Prorated	$0.00	$0.00	$0.00	$0.00	$0.00

Figure 11 - 4: Cost table applied in the Tracking Gantt view

To analyze cost variance, examine each value in the *Variance* column. In Figure 11 - 4, the *Variance* value for the Project Summary Task (Row 0) reveals that the project is currently $3,700 over budget. This variance is because Phase I is currently $4,100 over budget while Phase III is currently $400 **under** budget. Notice that a significant part of the *Cost* variance in Phase I arises from the $2,500 in the *Fixed Cost* column for the *Build P1* task. Remember that you can use the *Fixed Cost* column to track unanticipated task costs.

 Information: In the *Cost* table, the real name of the *Variance* column is *Cost Variance*. Microsoft uses the shorter name as the title of this column for display purposes only. You can see the real name of the column by floating your mouse pointer over the *Variance* column header. The system displays a tooltip that shows the title of the column, followed by the real name of the column in parentheses.

Revising a Project Plan

After completing variance analysis, you may need to revise your project plan to bring it "back on track" against its original goals, objectives, and schedule. There are a number of strategies for revising a project plan, but each one requires careful consideration before you make the revision. You should perform a "what-if" analysis before making plan revisions, especially if you need formal approval to make the revisions.

Project Pro 2013 offers a number of methods for revising a project plan. These methods include:

- Add resources to *Effort Driven* tasks.

- Ask project team members to work overtime or on weekends.

- Increase project team availability for your project.

- Modify mandatory dependencies, including reducing or removing *Lag* time, or adding *Lead* time.

- Reduce the scope of the project.

- Renegotiate the project finish date.

Potential Problems with Revising a Plan

Prior to employing any of the preceding techniques, you should be aware of potential problems that may arise when you implement the revisions. Some of the potential problems include:

- Adding resources to an *Effort Driven* task can increase the total work on the task due to increased communication needs between the team members.
- Asking team members to work overtime on a regular basis may increase your employee turnover rate.
- Increasing team member availability for your project reduces their availability for projects managed by other project managers, causing those projects to slip.
- Reducing *Lag* time on task dependencies can create an overly optimistic project schedule.
- Adding *Lead* time on task dependencies can create a scheduling crisis when the predecessor task must finish completely, thus negating the intent of adding the *Lead* time.
- The scope of your project may be non-negotiable.
- The finish date of your project may be non-negotiable.

Using a Change Control Process

Change control is the process of managing requested changes in your project. Change requests can arise from a variety of sources, including your customer, your project sponsor, your project stakeholders, your company's executives, your fellow project managers, and even from your project team members. Because each change can result in schedule slippage and cost overruns, it is important that you manage all changes in your project. Remember the old project management saying, "Either you manage change, or change manages you!"

Your change control process should identify and maximize the benefits of change, and should avoid all changes that offer no benefit to the project or that affect the project negatively. Document your change management process in both the Statement of Work document and in the "rules of engagement" with your project sponsor and/or client. The following is an example of a change management process:

- Use a paper or electronic change request form to initiate the change request.
- Perform an impact analysis to assess the impact of the change on the project. Determine who is responsible to complete the impact analysis and how they report the results.
- Calculate the cost of the impact analysis and determine who is responsible for paying for it. Remember that an impact analysis is never free!
- Enlist the support of an executive in your organization with the authority to accept or reject the change request.
- Apply a procedure for implementing an approved change request.
- In your project plan, indicate the tasks you changed or added because of the change request.

Inserting New Tasks in a Project

The most common change request is to add new tasks to a project. When you insert a new task between two dependent tasks, the *Autolink* feature of Project Pro 2013 determines whether the software automatically adds dependency links to the new task. If you disabled the *Autolink* feature in the *Project Options* dialog, per my directions in Module 06, *Creating Enterprise Projects*, the software **does not** automatically link the new task to the existing tasks in the project. However, if you did not disable the *Autolink* feature, then Project Pro 2013 handles the task linking operation as follows:

- If the dependent tasks have a Finish-to-Start (FS) dependency, the software automatically links the new task to the existing tasks using the FS dependency.
- If the dependent tasks have any other type of dependency (SS, FF, or SF), then Project Pro 2013 **does not** automatically link the new task to the existing tasks. Instead, the software leaves the new task unlinked.

Best Practice: Because you should always make task dependency decisions, and not the software, MsProjectExperts recommends that either you disable the *Autolink* feature in the *Project Options* dialog, or you break the task dependency links between tasks in the section where you intend to insert new tasks. After inserting the new tasks, establish appropriate task dependencies for tasks in that section of your project.

Information: To disable the *Autolink* feature of Project Pro 2013, click *File* ➤ *Options* in the *Backstage*. In the *Project Options* dialog, click the *Schedule* tab. In the *Scheduling options for this project* section, deselect the *Autolink inserted or moved tasks* option, and then click the *OK* button.

Best Practice: When you add new tasks to a project through a change control process, MsProjectExperts recommends that you format the new tasks with a unique color. You may format the font, the cell background color, and/or the Gantt bar color, as needed. Keep in mind that you can see these formatting changes only in the view in which you apply the formatting.

Rebaselining Your Project

After you add new tasks to your project through change control, you must rebaseline your project. Although there are several methodologies for rebaselining a project, I recommend you use one of following two methods:

- Back up your current baseline into one of the ten additional sets of baseline fields, and then baseline only the new tasks in the project using the default *Baseline* set of fields.
- Rebaseline all tasks in the project using one of the ten additional sets of baseline fields (the *Baseline 1* through *Baseline 10* sets of fields). If you want to use this technique, you must change the baseline that Project Pro 2013 uses to calculate variance. You must also change how the system displays the baseline schedule, shown by gray Gantt bars, in the *Tracking Gantt* view of your project.

I discuss each of these rebaselining methodologies separately.

Information: The default *Baseline* set of fields includes the following: *Baseline Start, Baseline Finish, Baseline Duration, Baseline Work,* and *Baseline Cost.* The ten additional sets of baselines, named *Baseline 1* through *Baseline 10*, include a corresponding set of fields. For example, the *Baseline1* set of fields includes the following: *Baseline 1 Start, Baseline 1 Finish, Baseline 1 Duration, Baseline 1 Work,* and *Baseline 1 Cost.*

Backing up an Original Baseline

Before you rebaseline your project after a change control procedure, it is wise to back up the current baseline data stored in the default *Baseline* set of fields. This is true, regardless of how you rebaseline your project. As you know by now, Project Pro 2013 offers you 11 sets of fields in which to save baseline data. These sets of fields include the default *Baseline* set of fields, plus the *Baseline 1* through *Baseline 10* sets. You can use any of these ten sets of alternate baseline fields to back up the current baseline before you rebaseline your project. To back up your current baseline values, use the *Interim Plan* feature of Project Pro 2013 by completing the following steps:

1. Click the *Project* tab to display the *Project* ribbon.

2. In the *Schedule* section of the *Project* ribbon, click the *Set Baseline* pick list button and then select the *Set Baseline* item on the menu. Project Pro 2013 displays the *Set Baseline* dialog shown in Figure 11 - 5.

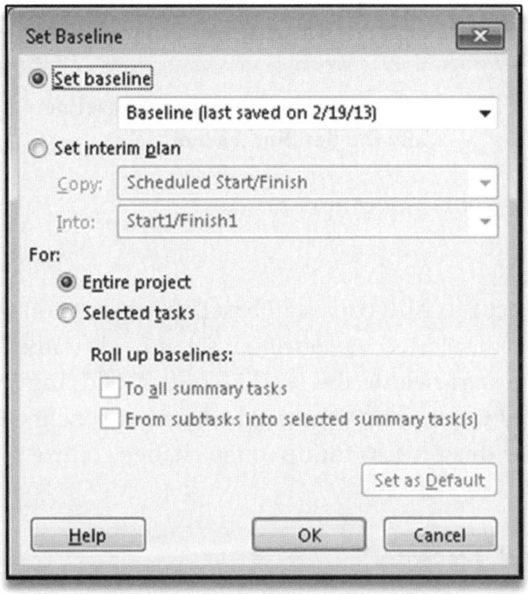

Figure 11 - 5: Set Baseline dialog

3. In the *Set Baseline* dialog, select the *Set interim plan* option.

4. Click the *Copy* pick list and select the *Baseline* item.

5. Click the *Into* pick list and select the next available set of baseline fields into which you want to back up the current baseline of the project, as shown in Figure 11 - 6.

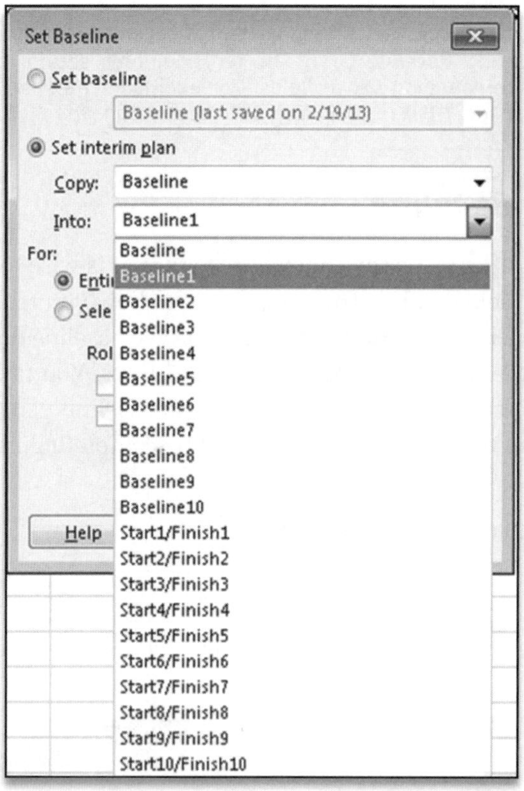

Figure 11 - 6: Back up the current baseline into the Baseline 1 set of fields

6. In the *For:* section, select the *Entire project* option.
7. Click the *OK* button.

When you use this procedure, Project Pro 2013 copies all baseline information from the *Baseline* set of fields to the set of fields for the alternate baseline. I selected the *Baseline 1* set of fields in the *Into* pick list, the system copies the values for every task in the *Baseline Start* field to the *Baseline 1 Start* field, the *Baseline Finish* field to the *Baseline 1 Finish* field, etc. This is a useful way to preserve your original project baseline for historical purposes before you rebaseline your project. You can use this process for up to ten change control procedures, at which point you run out of alternate sets of baseline fields.

Baselining Only Selected Tasks

An ideal method for rebaselining a project after adding new tasks through a change control procedure is to baseline **only** the new tasks you added to the project. Project Pro 2013 offers you two methods for baselining only selected tasks:

- Baseline only the selected tasks, but do not roll up the baseline values to any summary tasks in the project. Using this technique, new tasks show as variance against the original project baseline.
- Baseline only the selected tasks, but roll up the baseline values to all summary tasks in the project. When you choose this option, the baseline data rolls up to all summary tasks for which the selected tasks are subtasks, including the Project Summary Task (Row 0). Using this technique, new tasks do not show as variance against the original project baseline.

To baseline only selected tasks, complete the following steps:

1. Select the tasks you want to baseline.

2. Click the *Project* tab to display the *Project* ribbon.

3. In the *Schedule* section of the *Project* ribbon, click the *Set Baseline* pick list button and then select the *Set Baseline* item on the menu. Project Pro 2013 displays the *Set Baseline* dialog.

4. Select the *Set baseline* option, then click the *Set baseline* pick list and select the *Baseline* value.

5. In the *For:* section, select the *Selected tasks* option, as shown in Figure 11 - 7.

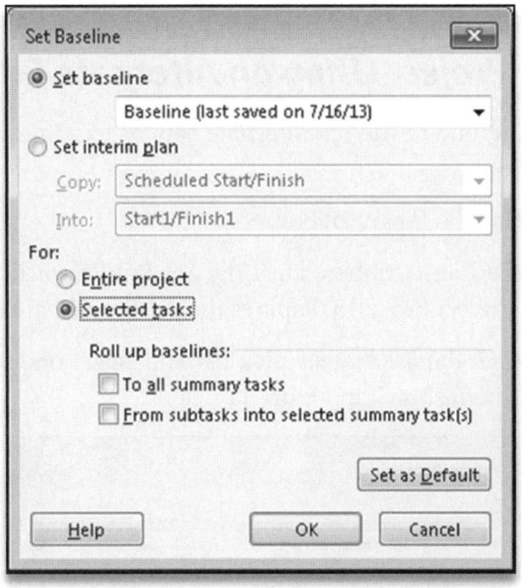

Figure 11 - 7: Set Baseline dialog to baseline the selected tasks

6. To roll up the baseline values to summary tasks, choose one of the following options in the *Roll up baselines* section:

- Select the *To all summary tasks* option if you want the software to roll up the baseline values to all summary tasks for which the selected tasks are subtasks and to the Project Summary Task as well.

- Select the *From subtasks into selected summary tasks* option if you want the software to roll up the baseline values to only the summary tasks currently selected (you must select these summary tasks before you begin the baselining process).

Information: If you do not want to roll up the baseline values to any summary tasks, do not select either of the options in the *Roll up baselines* section of the dialog. This means that the selected tasks continue to show as variance against the current project baseline.

7. To save the current options in the *Roll up baselines* section of the dialog, click the *Set as Default* button.

8. Click the *OK* button. Project Pro 2013 warns you about overwriting the baseline data in the warning dialog shown in Figure 11 - 8.

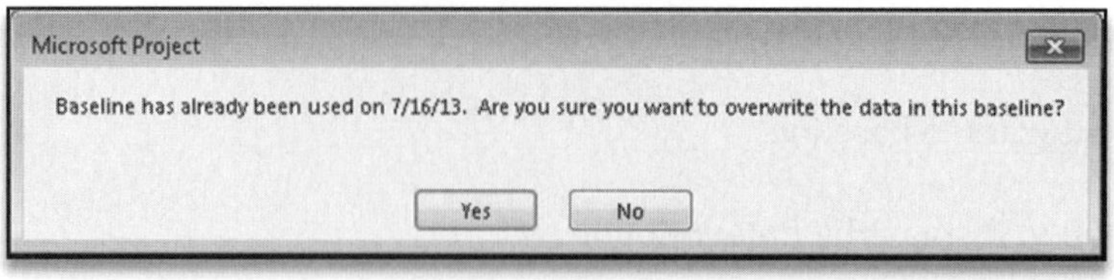

Figure 11 - 8: Warning dialog about overwriting baseline data

9. When warned about overwriting the original baseline, click the *Yes* button in the warning dialog.

Information: In spite of the warning in the dialog, using this procedure does not actually "overwrite" the data in your original baseline. Instead, this procedure "appends" the baseline data from the new tasks to the current project baseline.

Rebaselining the Entire Project Using an Alternate Baseline

To rebaseline an entire project using one of the ten alternate sets of baseline fields, such as the *Baseline 1* set of fields, complete the following steps:

1. Click the *Project* tab to display the *Project* ribbon.
2. In the *Schedule* section of the *Project* ribbon, click the *Set Baseline* pick list button and then select the *Set Baseline* item on the menu. Project Pro 2013 displays the *Set Baseline* dialog.
3. In the *Set Baseline* dialog, click the *Set baseline* pick list and select one of the ten alternate sets of baseline fields, such as the *Baseline 2* item shown in Figure 11 - 9.

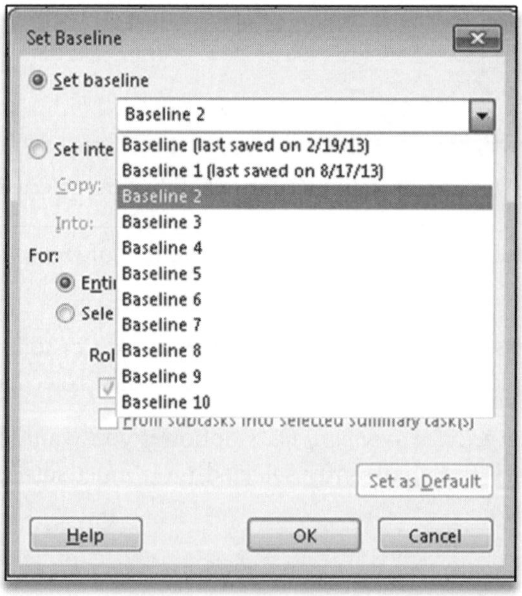

Figure 11 - 9: Set Baseline dialog, select the Baseline 2 set of fields

4. In the *For:* section, select the *Entire project* option.
5. Click the *OK* button.

After you rebaseline your project using one of alternate sets of baseline fields, you must change the baseline Project Pro 2013 uses to calculate variance. To make this change, complete the following steps:

1. Click *File* ➢ *Options* in the *Backstage.*
2. In the *Project Options* dialog, click the *Advanced* tab.
3. In the *Earned Value options for this project* section of the dialog, click the *Baseline for Earned Value Calculation* pick list and select the alternate set of baselines used during the rebaselining process, as shown in Figure 11 - 10.
4. Click the *OK* button.

When you change the *Baseline for Earned Value Calculation* option in the *Project Options* dialog, you change how Project Pro 2013 calculates variance in your project. When you change this option, the system now uses the new set of baseline fields to calculate all variance in the project. This affects the *Start Variance, Finish Variance, Duration Variance, Work Variance,* and *Cost Variance* fields, and you see the results in the task *Work, Cost,* and *Variance* tables. For example, if you selected the *Baseline 2* set of fields in step #3 above, the system calculates the values in the *Work Variance* field for every task using the following formula:

Work Variance = Work – Baseline 2 Work.

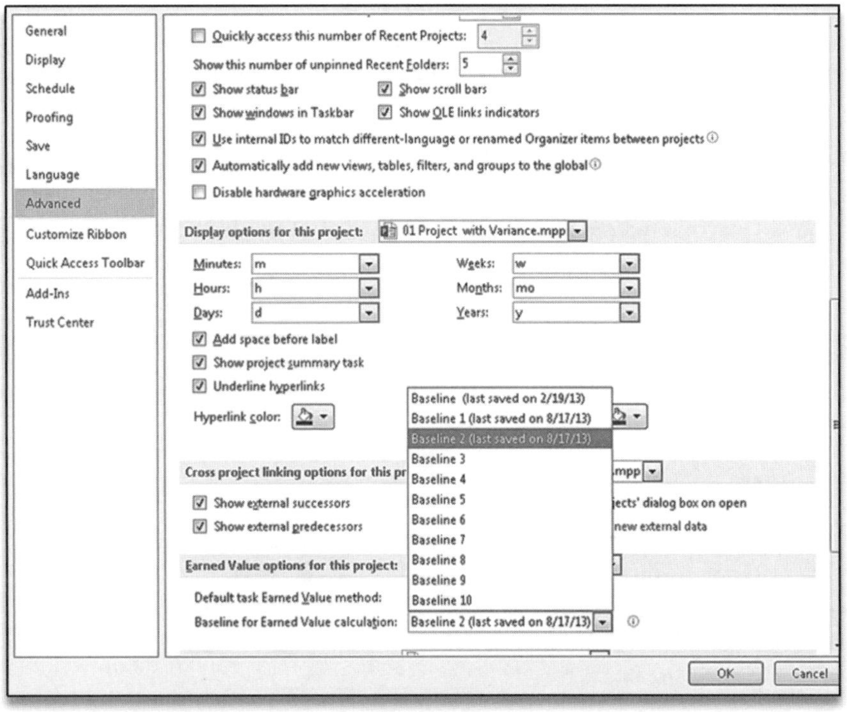

Figure 11 - 10: Select an alternate set of baseline fields

In addition to changing the set of baseline fields used to calculate variance in Project Pro 2013, you must also change the baseline schedule shown in the *Tracking Gantt* view. To change this view, complete the following additional set of steps:

1. Using the *Gantt Chart* pick list button on either the *Task* ribbon or the *View* ribbon, select the *Tracking Gantt* view.
2. Click the *Format* tab to display the *Format* ribbon.

3. In the *Bar Styles* section of the *Format* ribbon, click the *Baseline* pick list button, and then select the alternate set of baseline fields, as shown in Figure 11 - 11.

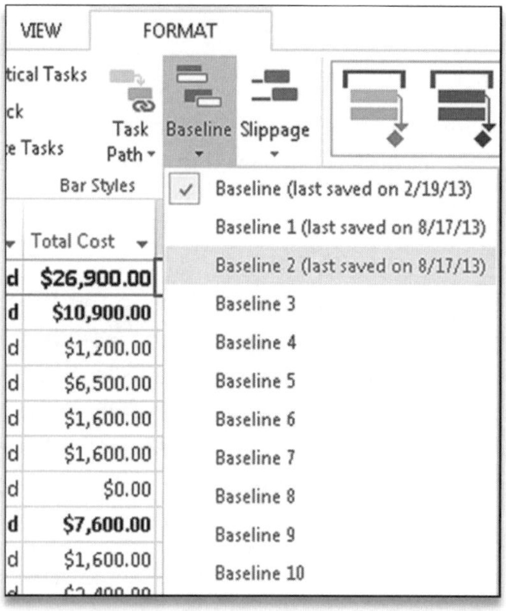

Figure 11 - 11: Select the alternate set of baseline fields for the Tracking Gantt view

For example, Figure 11 - 12 shows the default *Tracking Gantt* view for a project after a change control procedure added a new task to the project, and after the project manager rebaselined the project using the *Baseline 1* set of fields. Because the *Tracking Gantt* view uses the default *Baseline* set of fields to create the gray Gantt bars, the baseline schedule shown with the gray Gantt bars is not correct.

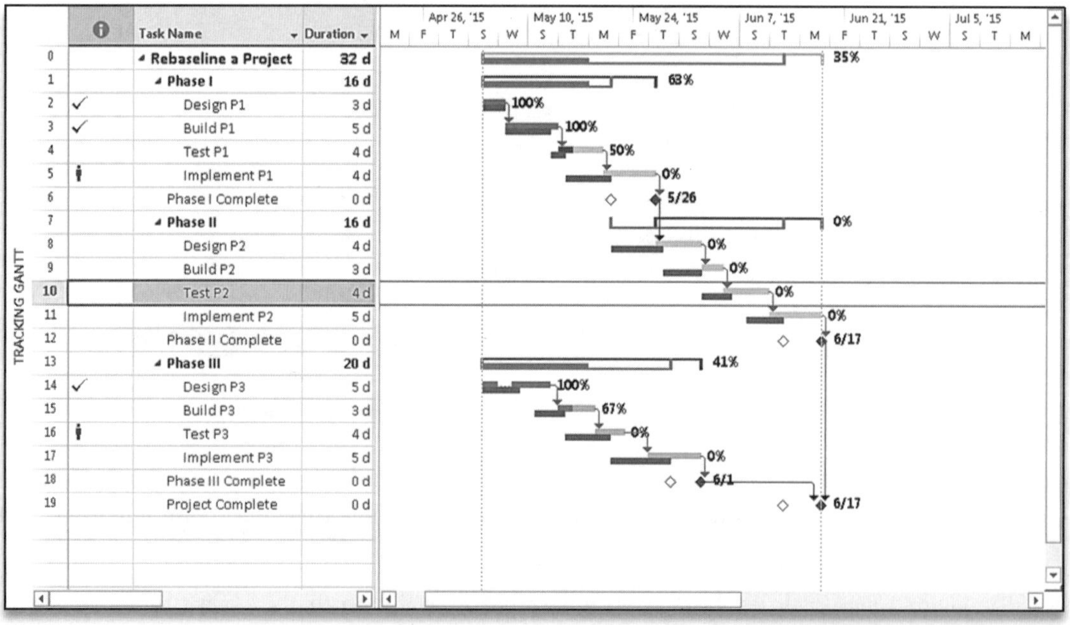

Figure 11 - 12: Tracking Gantt view using the Baseline schedule

Figure 11 - 13 shows the *Tracking Gantt* view after the project manager selected the *Baseline 1* set of fields in the *Baseline* pick list on the *Format* ribbon. The *Tracking Gantt* view now uses the *Baseline 1* set of fields to show the baseline schedule, which results in an accurate baseline schedule.

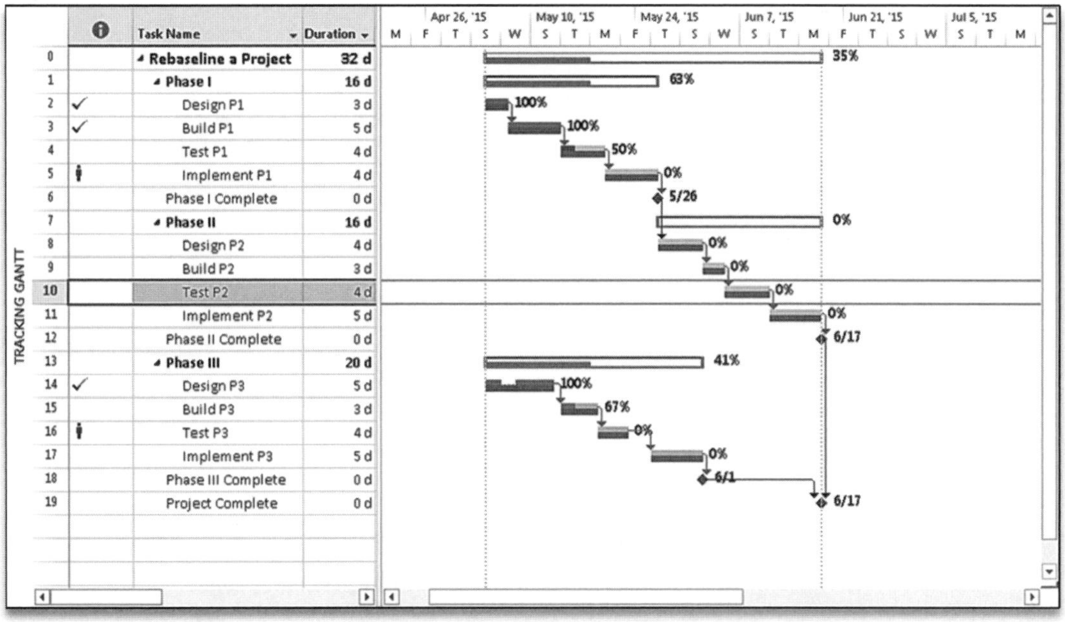

Figure 11 - 13: Tracking Gantt view using the Baseline 1 schedule

Warning: If you want to use this methodology for rebaselining a project after a change control procedure, you **must always** complete the steps to change the baseline used to calculate variance **and** the set of steps to show the correct baseline schedule in the *Tracking Gantt* view. If you fail to complete these two extra sets of steps, you cannot analyze project variance accurately, and you do not see the accurate baseline schedule in the *Tracking Gantt* view.

Using the Gantt with Timeline View

During project execution, you must report project progress to one or more stakeholder groups. These typically include your project sponsor, your customer, your company executives, and even your project team. Although Project Pro 2013 offers you a number of ways to report about your project, the *Timeline* view offers you a powerful new means of reporting on your projects.

Project Pro 2013 includes one default *Timeline* view that displays the current project schedule using a timeline presentation similar to what you see in Microsoft Visio or in any other timeline software application. You can modify the default *Timeline* view to show your current project schedule according to your reporting requirements. You may also export any *Timeline* view to other Microsoft Office applications, such as Microsoft PowerPoint.

The *Gantt with Timeline* view is the default view for every new project you create in Project Pro 2013. In fact, you see this view every time you launch the software, because the software always creates a new blank project on application launch. The *Gantt with Timeline* view is a split view that shows the *Timeline* view in the top pane and the *Gantt Chart* view in the bottom pane. Figure 11 - 14 shows the *Gantt with Timeline* view applied to an in-progress project.

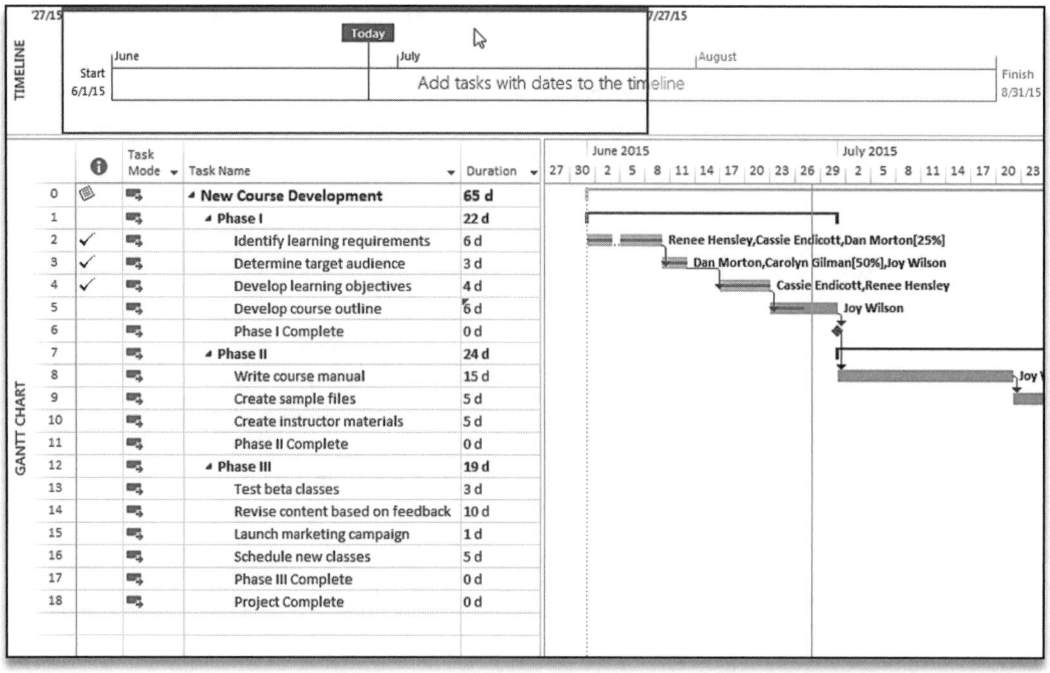

Figure 11 - 14 Gantt with Timeline view for an in-progress project

Information: If you do not see the *Gantt with Timeline* view when you open a project, apply the *Gantt Chart* view and then click the *View* tab. In the *Split View* section of the *View* ribbon, select the *Timeline* option.

Depending on the level of zoom applied in your project, the *Timeline* view shows the following information by default:

- The white *Timeline* bar represents the time span of the entire project, with the project *Start* date on the left end of the bar and the project *Finish* date on the right end of the bar. Notice in Figure 11 - 14 shown previously, that the project runs from 6/1/15 to 8/31/15, indicated by the dates to the left and right of the white *Timeline* bar.
- The software divides the *Timeline* bar into date segments consistent with the level of zoom you have currently applied in the *Gantt Chart* pane. In Figure 11 - 14 shown previously, Project Pro 2013 displays tick marks for months across the top of the *Timeline.*
- The software indicates the current date with the word *Today* formatted with green text above the *Timeline* bar and with a green line in the *Timeline* bar.
- The software uses two green vertical lines to show the time span of the project currently visible in the *Gantt Chart* view. These green vertical lines show the beginning and ending dates of this time span. If you float your mouse pointer anywhere between the two green vertical lines, Project Pro 2013 displays a green border around the entire time span such as you see in Figure 11 - 14 shown previously. The software refers to the thick green border at the top of the *Timeline* view as the *Pan & Zoom* bar.
- The software uses faint shading for the portion of the *Timeline* bar not visible in the *Gantt Chart* view. Figure 11 - 14 shown previously, indicates that project information is not visible past 7/27/15 in the *Gantt Chart* view, indicated by the faint shading in the *Timeline* bar after that date.

Information: As you scroll right or left in the *Gantt Chart* view, the *Pan & Zoom* bar scrolls with you to indicate the portion of the timeline currently visible in the *Gantt Chart* view.

Adding a Task to the Timeline

To add any task to the *Timeline* view, in the *Task Sheet* part of the *Gantt Chart* view, right-click the name of the task and then select the *Add to Timeline* item on the shortcut menu. To add multiple tasks to the *Timeline* view, select a block of tasks, right-click anywhere in the selected block of tasks, and then select the *Add to Timeline* item on the shortcut menu. Project Pro 2013 adds the selected tasks to the *Timeline* view as shown in Figure 11 - 15. Notice that I added the *Phase I, Phase II,* and *Phase III* tasks to the *Timeline* view, along with the first three subtasks in the *Phase II* section of the project. By default, the software formats each bar you add to the *Timeline* view using a light blue cell background color.

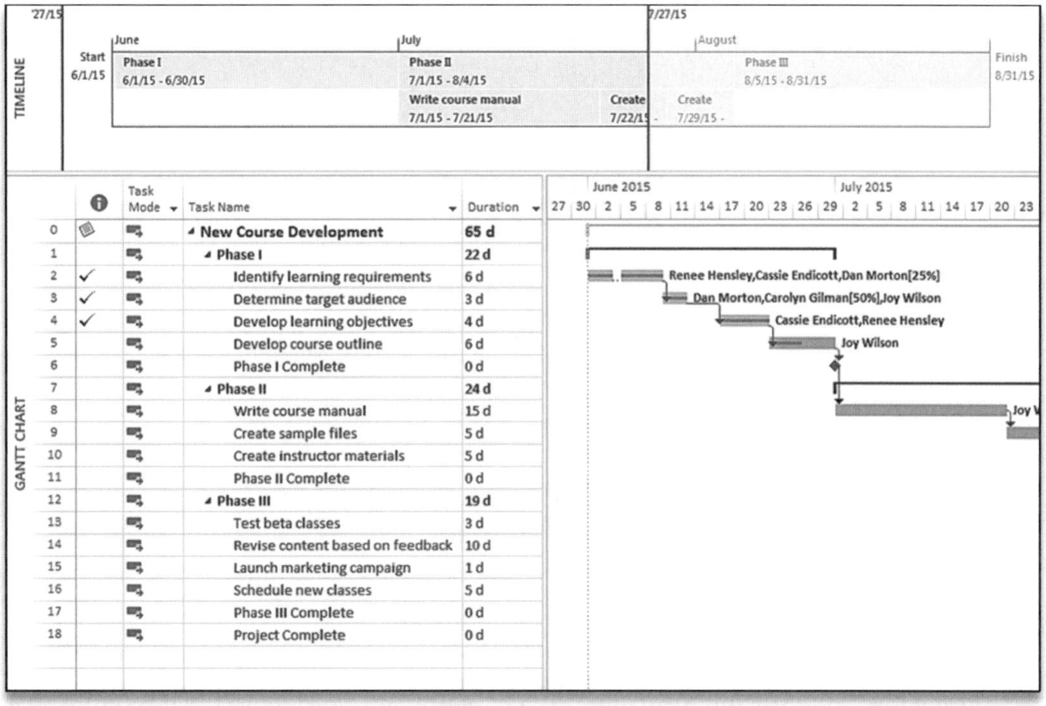

Figure 11 - 15: Tasks added to the Timeline view

Information: You can also add a task to the *Timeline* view by double-clicking the task to display the *Task Information* dialog. On the *General* page of dialog, select the *Display on Timeline* option. If you select multiple tasks, you can add a task to the *Timeline* view by navigating to the *Properties* section of the *Task* ribbon and clicking the *Information* button. On the *General* page of the *Multiple Task Information* dialog, select the *Display on Timeline* option and then click the *OK* button.

After you add tasks to the *Timeline* view, you can rearrange the tasks on the *Timeline* bar using any of the following techniques:

- Drag a task to a new row above or below its current position in the *Timeline* bar.
- Drag a task above or below the *Timeline* bar to display the task as a callout.

- Drag a block of tasks by selecting them while pressing and holding the **Control** key on your computer keyboard, and then dragging the block of the selected tasks to a new position.
- Right-click any task in the *Timeline* bar and select the *Display as Callout* item on the shortcut menu.
- Drag a new callout from the top of the *Timeline* bar to a position below the *Timeline* bar.
- Right-click any callout and then select the *Display as Bar* item on the shortcut menu to convert the callout to a task bar.

When you drag tasks into a new position on the *Timeline* bar, or create callouts above or below the *Timeline* bar, Project Pro 2013 adjusts the height of the *Timeline* view automatically to accommodate the new information. For example, Figure 11 - 16 shows my *Timeline* view after I created two callouts and dragged the *Phase II* task and its subtask to a new row in the *Timeline* bar.

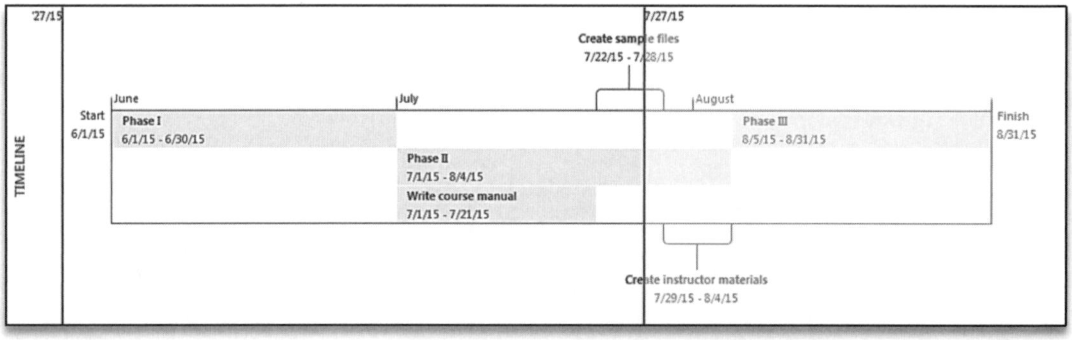

Figure 11 - 16: Rearranged tasks in the Timeline view

Information: To remove a task or callout from the *Timeline* view, right-click the task bar or callout and then select the *Remove from Timeline* item on the shortcut menu.

Project Pro 2013 also allows you to scroll to any task in the *Gantt Chart* pane by right-clicking the task bar or task callout in the *Timeline* pane, and selecting the *Scroll to Selected Task* item on the shortcut menu. The software selects the task in the *Gantt Chart* pane and then scrolls the Gantt chart to the beginning of the selected task, in a manner similar to the functionality of the *Scroll to Task* button on the *Task* ribbon.

Formatting the Timeline View

To format the *Timeline* view, click anywhere in the *Timeline* pane to activate the pane, and then click the *Format* tab. Project Pro 2013 displays the contextual *Format* ribbon with the *Timeline Tools* applied, shown in Figure 11 - 17.Using the features on the *Format* ribbon, the software offers you many ways to format the *Timeline* view.

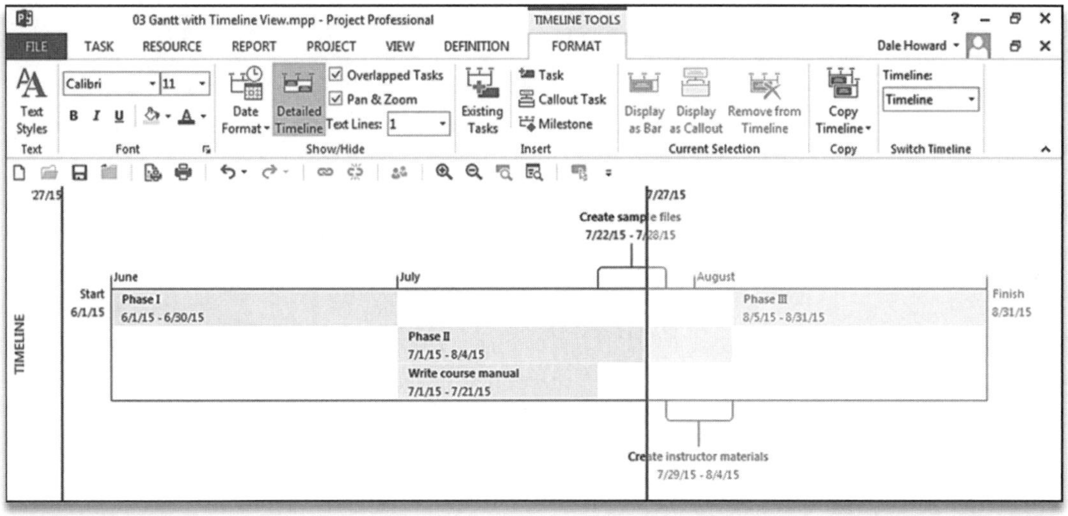

Figure 11 - 17: Format ribbon with the Timeline Tools applied

Using the Text Tools

To format the text for a specific set of objects shown in the *Timeline* view, such as all milestone dates, in the *Text* section of the contextual *Format* ribbon, click the *Text Styles* button. Project Pro 2013 displays the *Text Styles* dialog shown in Figure 11 - 18. Select any type of object on the *Item to Change* pick list, such as the *Milestone Date* item. Change the formatting options in the *Font, Font styles, Size,* and *Color* fields. Optionally select the *Underline* or *Strikethrough* options, as needed, and then click the *OK* button. Project Pro 2013 applies the specified text formatting to all objects of the type you selected.

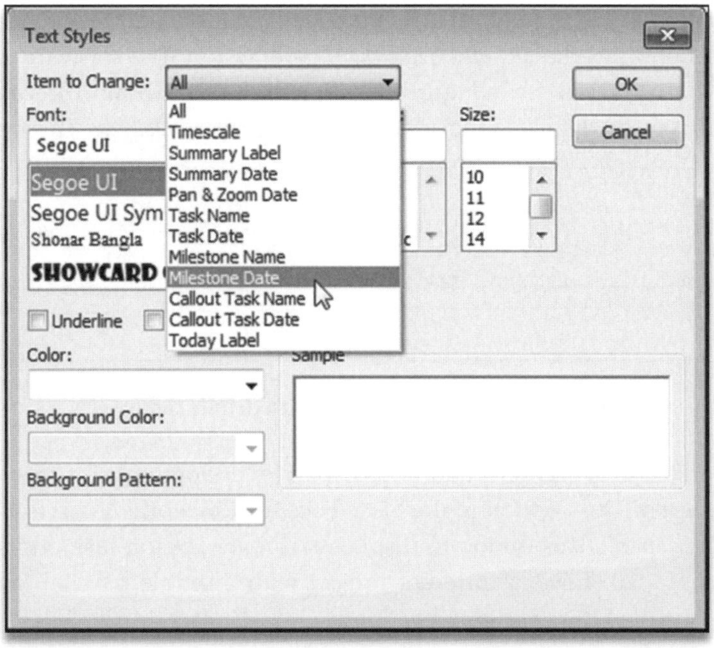

Figure 11 - 18: Text Styles dialog, Item to Change pick list

Information: Notice in Figure 11 - 18 shown previously, that Project Pro 2013 **does not** allow you to change the *Background Color* or *Background Pattern* options in the *Text Styles* dialog for the *Timeline* view, the software limits you to changing only text formatting options such as the *Font* and *Color* items.

Information: You may also display the *Text Styles* dialog by right-clicking anywhere in the white part of the *Timeline* view and then selecting the *Text Styles* item on the shortcut menu.

Using Font Tools

To change the font or the cell background color of an individual object in the *Timeline* view, select the object and then change the formatting using the options in the *Font* section of the contextual *Format* ribbon. To display the *Font* dialog, click the *Font* dialog launcher icon in the lower right corner of the *Font* section of the ribbon. To change the background color of a task bar, for example, select the bar and choose a new color on the *Background Color* pick list.

Using Show/Hide Tools

To change the date format of the dates shown in the *Timeline* view, in the *Show/Hide* section, click the *Date Format* pick list button and select a new date format. By default, the *Timeline* view uses the date format specified in the *Date Format* field on the *General* page of the *Project Options* dialog. On the *Date Format* pick list, Project Pro 2013 also allows you to hide some of the dates shown by default on the *Timeline* view. To hide the dates shown for each task, click the *Date Format* pick list and **deselect** the *Task Dates* option. To hide the current date, **deselect** the *Current Date* option on the *Date Format* pick list. To hide the dates shown above the *Timeline* bar, **deselect** the *Timescale* option on the *Date Format* pick list

To remove the details from the *Timeline* view, such as the names of tasks and task dates, in the *Show/Hide* section of the contextual *Format* ribbon, click the *Detailed Timeline* toggle button. The software completely removes all details from the *Timeline* view. As you can see in Figure 11 - 19, without the details, the *Timeline* view is probably not very useful to you. To redisplay the details in the *Timeline* view, click the *Detailed Timeline* toggle button again.

Figure 11 - 19: Timeline view with details removed

If your project contains parallel task sections, and you display overlapping tasks from these parallel sections in the *Timeline* view, the *Overlapped Tasks* option in the *Show/Hide* section works to your advantage. By default, Project Pro 2013 selects the *Overlapped Tasks* option to display each overlapping task on its own row in the *Timeline* view. For example, Figure 11 - 20 shows a different project with multiple parallel task sections and with each summary task section displayed on the *Timeline* view. Notice how Project Pro 2013 displays each overlapping section on its own task row in the *Timeline* view.

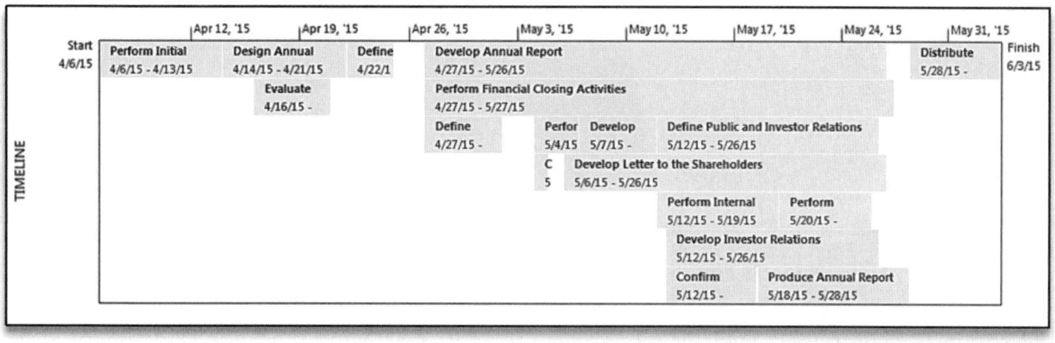

Figure 11 - 20: Timeline with Overlapped Tasks option selected

Figure 11 - 21 shows the same *Timeline* view with the *Overlapped Tasks* option deselected. Notice how the software displays all tasks on a single task row in the *Timeline* view, rendering the information all but impossible to read. For this reason, I recommend you leave the *Overlapped Tasks* option selected for the *Timeline* view.

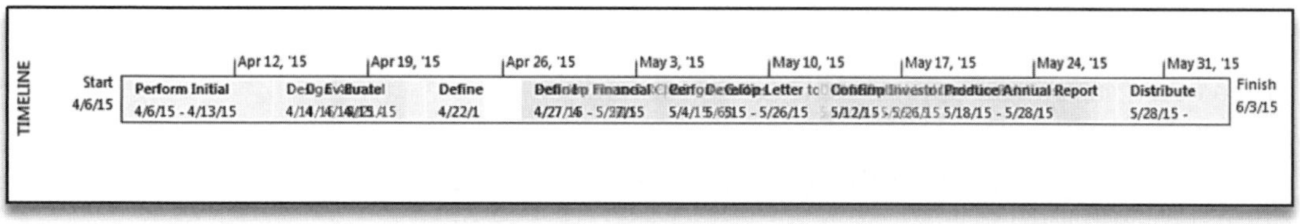

Figure 11 - 21: Timeline with Overlapped Tasks option deselected

In the *Show/Hide* section of the contextual *Format* ribbon, the *Pan & Zoom* option allows you to display or hide the two green vertical lines in the *Timeline* that show the time span of the project currently visible in the *Gantt Chart* view. If you select the *Pan & Zoom* option, the software displays the *Pan & Zoom* bar (the two green vertical lines); if you deselect this option, the software hides the *Pan & Zoom* bar.

The final option in the *Show/Hide* section is the *Text Lines* option, which allows you to determine how many lines of text to display for every task shown in the *Timeline* view. By default, the software sets the *Text Lines* value to *1 line*, as shown in Figure 11 - 22. Because of this, the software truncates long task names when displayed in the *Timeline* view. For example, in the *Timeline* view shown in Figure 11 - 15 notice how the software truncates the names of two of the three subtasks shown in the *Phase II* section with the *Text Lines* value set to the default *1 line* value.

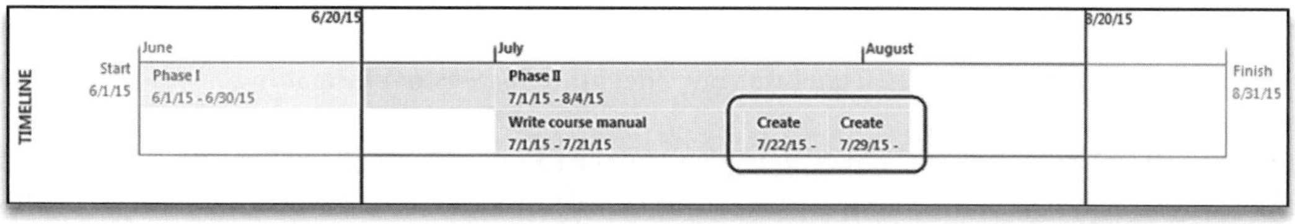

Figure 11 - 22: Timeline view with the Text Lines option set to 1 line

Figure 11 - 23 shows the same *Timeline* view with the *Text Lines* value set to *3 lines*. Notice that you can now read the full name of all three subtasks in the *Phase II* section.

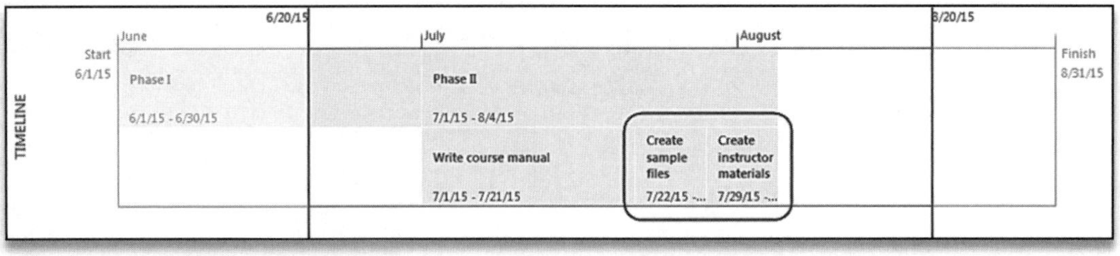

Figure 11 - 23: Timeline view with the Text Lines option set to 3 lines

Figure 11 - 24 shows the completed *Timeline* view after I formatted it using methods I documented in this section of the module. To format the *Timeline* view, I did the following:

- I added the *Phase III* summary task and the *Project Complete* milestone task to the *Timeline* view.
- I changed the two tasks to callouts in the *Phase II* section.
- I dragged the *Create instructor materials* callout to a position below the *Timeline* bar.
- I changed the *Date Format* option to the *Jan 28* format.
- I changed the *Background Color* setting for each task individually.
- I changed the *Font Color* setting to *White* for the *Phase III* bar and the *Write course manual* bar.
- Using the *Text Styles* dialog, I changed the *Font Color* setting to *Red* for the dates of every callout.
- I changed the *Text Lines* value to 2 to display two lines of text in each bar.
- I deselected the *Pan & Zoom* option to hide the *Pan & Zoom* bar.

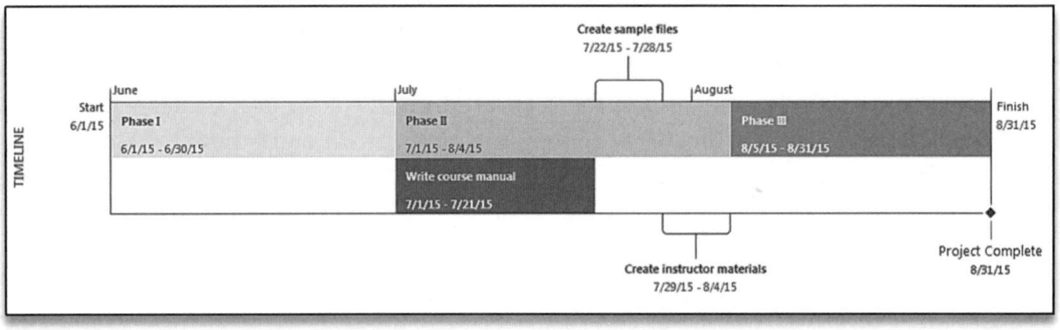

Figure 11 - 24: Timeline view after applying custom formatting

To change the type of object displayed in the *Timeline* view, or to remove an object from the *Timeline* view, use the buttons in the *Current Selection* section of the contextual *Format* ribbon. For example, to change a callout to a task bar, right-click the callout and then select the *Display as Bar* item on the shortcut menu. To change a task bar to a callout, right-click the task bar and then select the *Display as Callout* item on the shortcut menu. To remove a task or a callout from the *Timeline* view, right-click the task or callout and then select the *Remote from Timeline* item on the shortcut menu.

Information: While you have the *Timeline* pane activated, be careful not to click the *Zoom* button in the *Zoom* section of the *View* ribbon and then select either the *Zoom In* or *Zoom Out* option. If you zoom in or zoom out with the *Timeline* pane activated, you cannot use the *Zoom In* or *Zoom Out* options to return to the default level of zoom applied to the *Timeline* view. To return to the default level of zoom, in the *Zoom* section of the *View* ribbon, you must click the *Zoom Entire Project* button. You can also right-click anywhere in the *Timeline* pane and select the *Zoom to Screen* item on the shortcut menu.

Adding Tasks Using the Contextual Format Ribbon

In addition to the formatting options available on the contextual *Format* ribbon with the *Timeline Tools* applied, this ribbon also offers options for adding or removing tasks in the *Timeline* view. In the *Insert* section of the *Format* ribbon, Project Pro 2013 includes four buttons that allow you to add new tasks to the *Timeline* view. To add a new existing task to the *Timeline* view, click the *Existing Tasks* button. The software displays the *Add Tasks to Timeline* dialog shown in Figure 11 - 25. To add a task to the *Timeline* view, select the checkbox to the left of the task name, and then click the *OK* button.

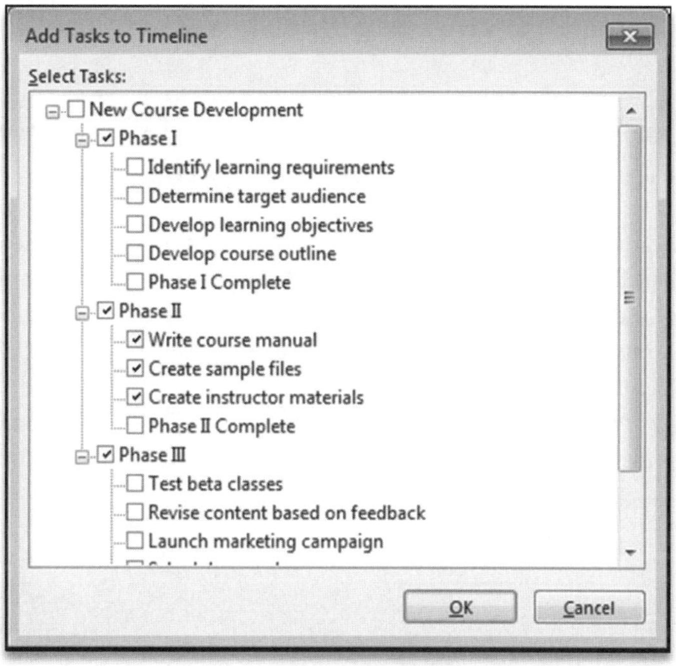

Figure 11 - 25: Add Tasks to Timeline dialog

The software adds the selected task(s) to the *Timeline* view. For example, notice in Figure 11 - 26 that I added the *Phase I Complete* milestone task to the *Timeline* view.

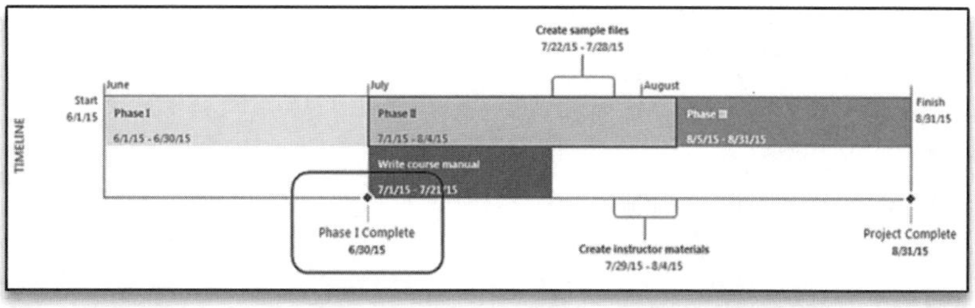

Figure 11 - 26: Milestone task added to the Timeline view

To add a completely new task to your project and simultaneously add the new task to the *Timeline* view, in the *Insert* section of the contextual *Format* ribbon, click the *Task* button, the *Callout Task* button, or the *Milestone* button. Project Pro 2013 displays the *Task Information* dialog shown in Figure 11 - 27.

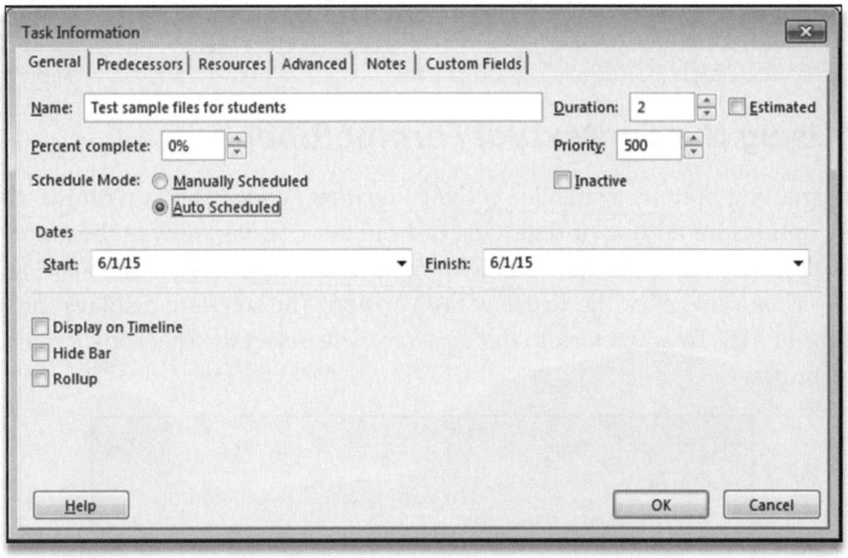

Figure 11 - 27: Task Information dialog

In the *Task Information* dialog, enter complete information about the new task, including information in the *Name* and *Duration* fields, and select the desired *Schedule Mode* option. Assuming you want to display the new task in the *Timeline* view, be sure to select the *Display on Timeline* option. If necessary, select predecessor tasks on the *Predecessors* page and assign resources to the new task on the *Resources* page. Click the *OK* button to add the new task to the project and to the *Timeline* view. Project Pro 2013 creates the new task as the last task in the task list, and adds the new task to the *Timeline* view. Figure 11 - 28 shows the new *Test student sample files* task. After creating the new task, you must drag the task to the correct place in the project and set additional dependencies as needed.

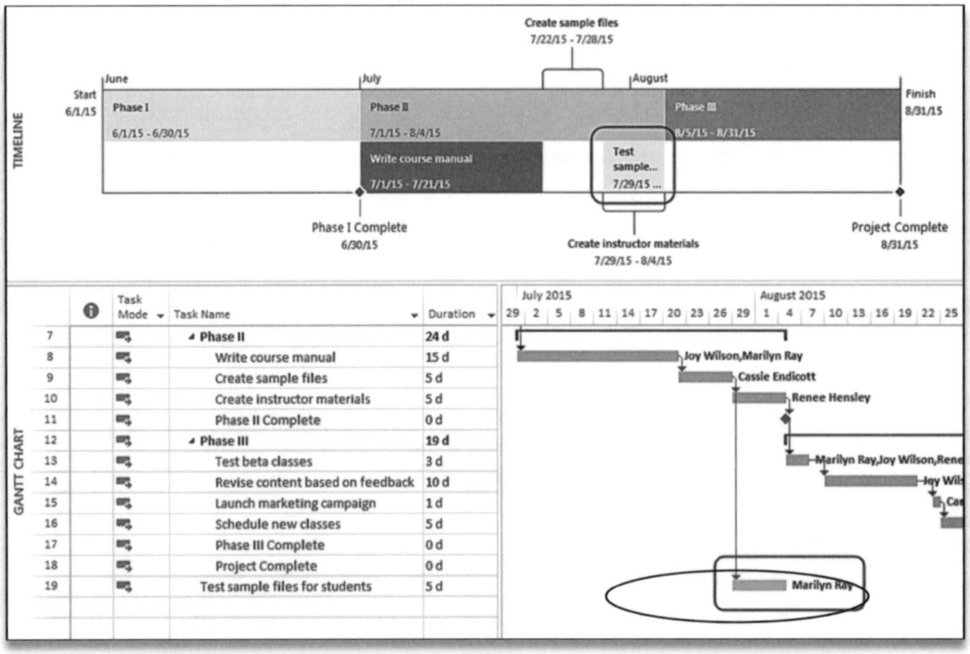

Figure 11 - 28: New task added to the project and to the Timeline view

Information: You may also insert a new task in the project and add it to the *Timeline* view by right-clicking anywhere in the white part of the *Timeline* view, selecting the *Insert Task* menu item, and then selecting the *Callout Task, Task*, or *Milestone* item on the flyout menu.

Exporting the Timeline View

Project Pro 2013 allows you to export the entire *Timeline* view to any Office application, such as PowerPoint or Word. To copy the *Timeline* view, in the *Copy* section of the contextual *Format* ribbon, click the *Copy Timeline* pick list button. The *Copy Timeline* pick list contains three choices, including *For E-Mail, For Presentation,* and *Full Size.*

If you select the *Full Size* item on the *Copy Timeline* pick list, Project Pro 2013 copies the full-size image of the current *Timeline* view to your Windows clipboard. If you select the *For Presentation* item, the software optimizes the image for use in PowerPoint by reducing the image size to approximately 90% of full size. If you select the *For E-Mail* item, the software optimizes the image for use in Microsoft Outlook by reducing the image size to approximately 60% of full size.

After copying the *Timeline* view to your clipboard, paste the image in one of the Office applications. If you use an application that has image editing capabilities, such as Word or PowerPoint, you can continue to refine your *Timeline* view presentation. For example, Figure 11 - 29 shows the *Timeline* view after I pasted the image into a PowerPoint presentation and applied additional formatting. Notice that I used the *Bevel* feature to give the tasks a 3-D appearance, and I used the *Glow* feature to alter the appearance of the *Project Complete* milestone task.

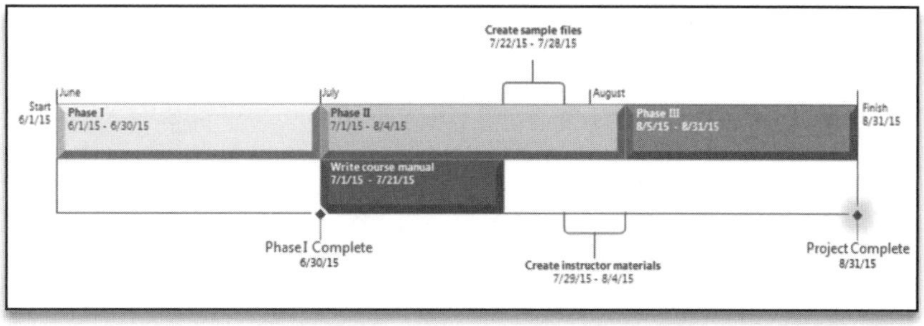

Figure 11 - 29: Timeline view formatted in Microsoft PowerPoint

Information: You may also copy the *Timeline* view by right-clicking anywhere in the white part of the *Timeline* view, selecting the *Copy Timeline* item from the shortcut menu, and then selecting the *For E-Mail, For Presentation*, or *Full Size* item on the flyout menu.

Using Visual Reports

Microsoft introduced visual reports as a new feature in Project Pro 2007, and continues to offer improved visual report functionality in Project Pro 2013. Visual reports allow you to see your project data in a *PivotChart* and *PivotTable* in Excel or in a *PivotDiagram* in Visio. The software creates the visual report by building a local OLAP (On Line Analytical Programming) cube directly on your computer's hard drive. The local OLAP cube provides a multi-dimensional summary of task and resource data in your project.

Information: You may use the Excel visual reports with Excel 2007, 2010, or 2013. To use the Visio visual reports, however, you must have the **Professional** version of Visio 2007, 2010, or 2013. If you use the Standard version of Visio, you do not see the Visio visual report templates at all in the *Visual Reports – Create Report* dialog.

To access visual reports, click the *Report* tab to display the *Report* ribbon. In the *Export* section of the *Report* ribbon, click the *Visual Reports* button. Project Pro 2013 displays the *Visual Reports – Create Report* dialog shown in Figure 11 - 30.

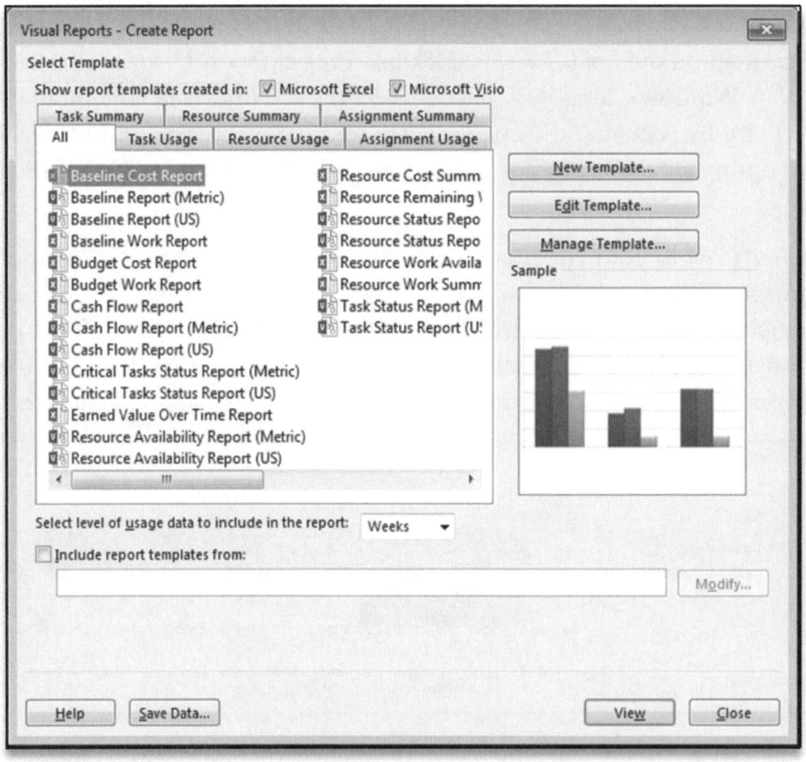

Figure 11 - 30: Visual Reports – Create Report dialog

The *Visual Reports – Create Report* dialog provides you with six categories of default visual reports. The *Task Usage, Resource Usage,* and *Assignment Usage* categories display timephased task, resource, and assignment data, respectively. The *Task Summary, Resource Summary,* and *Assignment Summary* categories display task, resource, and assignment data without timephased data. The next six tables describe the 16 default visual reports in Table 11 - 1 through Table 11 - 6.

Task Usage		
Report Name	**Type**	**Description**
Cash Flow	Excel	Combination column chart/line chart shows *Cost* (columns) and *Cumulative Cost* (line) over time.

Table 11 - 1: Task Usage visual reports

Task Summary		
Report Name	**Type**	**Description**
Critical Tasks Status	Visio	Diagram shows *Work, Remaining Work,* and *% Work Complete* for both critical and non-critical tasks at *Outline Level 1*, with a progress bar representing the *% Work Complete* for each summary task.

Table 11 - 2: Task Summary visual reports

Resource Usage		
Report Name	**Type**	**Description**
Cash Flow	Visio	Diagram shows *Cost* and *Actual Cost* over time, broken down by resource type (*Work, Material,* and *Cost* resources). Diagram shows an orange triangle symbol when the *Cost* exceeds the *Baseline Cost*.
Resource Availability	Visio	Diagram shows *Work* and *Remaining Availability* for each resource, broken down by resource type (*Work, Material,* and *Cost* resources).
Resource Cost Summary	Excel	2-D pie chart shows project costs, filtered by the *Weekly Calendar* dimension. By default, this report does not display the resource types; therefore, you must add the *Type* dimension to the *Axis Fields* drop area to use this report.
Resource Work Availability	Excel	Column chart shows *Work Availability, Work,* and *Remaining Availability* for all resources over time.
Resource Work Summary	Excel	Column chart shows *Work Availability, Work, Remaining Availability,* and *Actual Work,* filtered by the *Weekly Calendar* dimension. By default, this report does not display any resources; therefore, you must add the *Resources* dimension to the *Axis Fields* drop area to use this report.

Table 11 - 3: Resource Usage visual reports

Resource Summary		
Report Name	**Type**	**Description**
Resource Remaining Work	Excel	Stacked column chart shows *Actual Work* and *Remaining Work*. By default, this report does not display any resources; therefore, you must add the *Resources* dimension to the *Axis Fields* drop area to use this report.

Table 11 - 4: Resource Summary visual reports

Assignment Usage		
Report Name	**Type**	**Description**
Baseline Cost	Excel	Column chart shows *Baseline Cost, Cost,* and *Actual Cost*. By default, this report does not display any tasks or resources; therefore, you must add the *Tasks* and/or *Resources* dimensions to the *Axis Fields* drop area to use this report.
Baseline	Visio	Diagram compares *Work* and *Cost* with *Baseline Work* and *Baseline Cost* over time for all tasks at *Outline Level 1*. The report displays a red stoplight when *Work* exceeds *Baseline Work,* and displays a yellow flag when *Cost* exceeds *Baseline Cost.*
Baseline Work	Excel	Column chart shows *Baseline Work, Work,* and *Actual Work* for all tasks. By default, this report does not display any tasks; therefore, you must add the *Tasks* dimension to the *Axis Fields* drop area to use this report.
Budget Cost	Excel	Column chart shows *Budget Cost, Baseline Cost, Cost,* and *Actual Cost* over time.
Budget Work	Excel	Column chart shows *Budget Work, Baseline Work, Work,* and *Actual Work* over time.
Earned Value Over Time	Excel	Line chart shows *Earned Value, Planned Value,* and *Actual Cost* over time through the *Status Date* of the project.

Table 11 - 5: Assignment Usage visual reports

Assignment Summary		
Report Name	**Type**	**Description**
Resource Status	Visio	Diagram shows *Cost* and *Work* for each resource with color shading in each box, representing *% Work Complete*. The shading gets lighter as the *% Work Complete* value nears *100%*, ranging from dark purple shading where the *% Work Complete* value is *0%* to white shading where the *% Work Complete* value is *100%*.
Task Status	Visio	Diagram displays *Cost* and *Work* for all tasks at *Outline Level 1*, and displays an orange progress bar representing *% Work Complete* for each task. Diagram shows a yellow "unhappy face" when *Work* exceeds *Baseline Work*, shows a yellow "neutral face" when *Work* is equal to *Baseline Work*, and shows a "happy face" when *Work* is less than *Baseline Work*.

Table 11 - 6: Assignment Summary visual reports

Information: Project Pro 2013 offers two types of Visio visual reports: *Metric* and *US*. The differences between these two types of visual reports are minor. In the *Metric* visual reports for Visio, the software measures the *Ruler* bar in **millimeters** and the default paper size is **A4** (210 mm x 297 mm). In the *US* visual reports for Visio, the software measures the *Ruler* bar in **inches** and the default paper size is **Letter** (8.5 inches x 11 inches).

Viewing a Visual Report

To view a visual report, complete the following steps:

1. In the *Export* section of the *Reports* ribbon, click the *Visual Reports* button.
2. In the *Visual Reports – Create Report* dialog, select the tab containing the type of visual report you want to view.
3. On the selected report page of the dialog, select a visual report.
4. Click the *Select level of usage data to include in this report* pick list and select the data granularity you want to use in the report, as shown in Figure 11 - 31.

Information: Based on the size of your project, Project Pro 2013 sets a recommended value in the *Select level of usage data to include in this report* pick list. For most projects, the recommended value is *Weeks*. For very large projects, the recommended value might be *Months, Quarters*, or even *Years*. Project Pro 2013 then generates the data in the local OLAP cubes using the granularity you select and then transfers the data to the visual report.

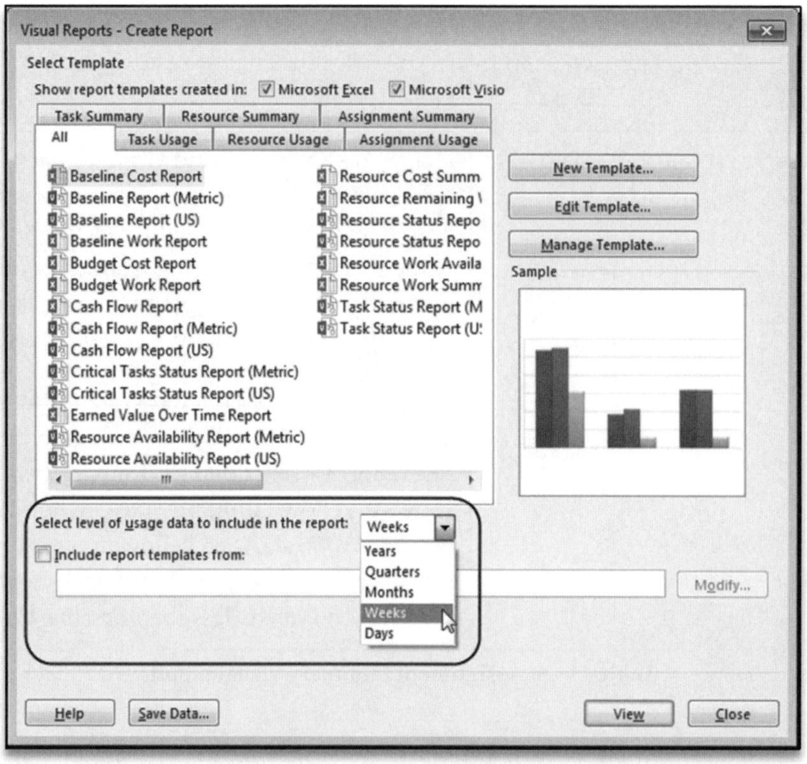

Figure 11 - 31: Visual Reports – Create Report dialog, select the granularity for the Baseline Cost Report

5. If you want to supplement the standard list of task and resource details included with the local OLAP cube, click the *Edit Template* button.

Project Pro 2013 displays the *Visual Reports – Field Picker* dialog shown in Figure 11 - 32. In the *Selected Fields* list on the right side of the dialog, you see the default list of standard detail fields added to the local OLAP cube automatically. This list includes fields like *Cost, Baseline Cost,* and *Actual Cost.* If you want to supplement this list with additional standard fields, select one or more fields in the *Available Fields* list and click the *Add* button.

The *Available Custom Fields* list shows the list of custom fields available for inclusion in the local OLAP cube, and includes any custom fields you created in the project. For example, notice in Figure 11 - 32 that the list includes two custom fields I created in this project: the *Accountable Person Task (dimension)* field and the *Cost Center ID Task (dimension)* field. To add any custom field to the local OLAP cube, select one or more fields in the *Available Custom Fields* list and click the *Add* button. Click the *Edit Template* button when finished.

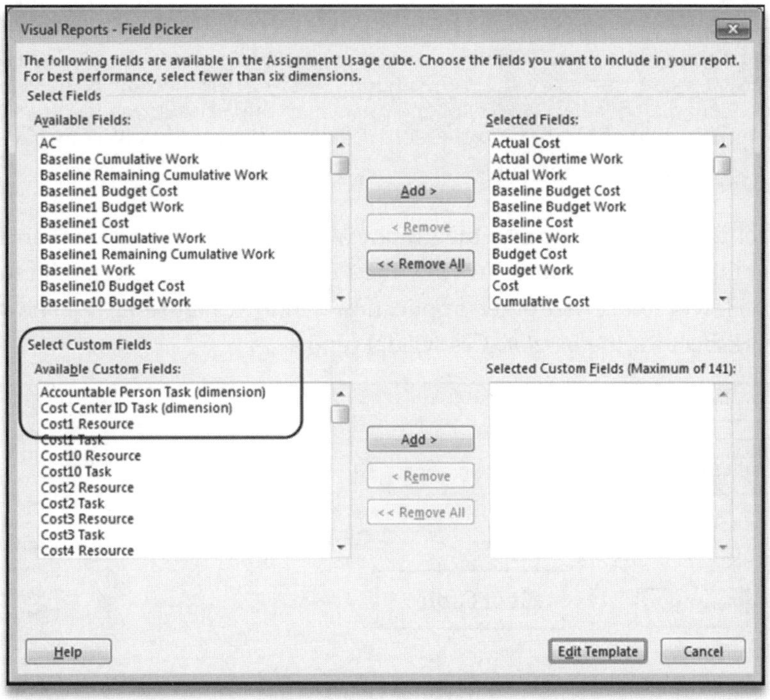

Figure 11 - 32: Visual Reports – Field Picker dialog

6. If you did not need to use step #5 and add custom fields to your visual report, click the *View* button in the *Visual Reports – Create Report* dialog to create the visual report.

Project Pro 2013 displays a progress indicator at the bottom of the dialog in which it indicates that it is gathering data for the report, building the local OLAP cube, and then opening the visual report template for viewing. Figure 11 - 33 shows the completed *Baseline Cost* visual report in Excel. Notice that the legend at the top of the chart explains the meaning of each column color.

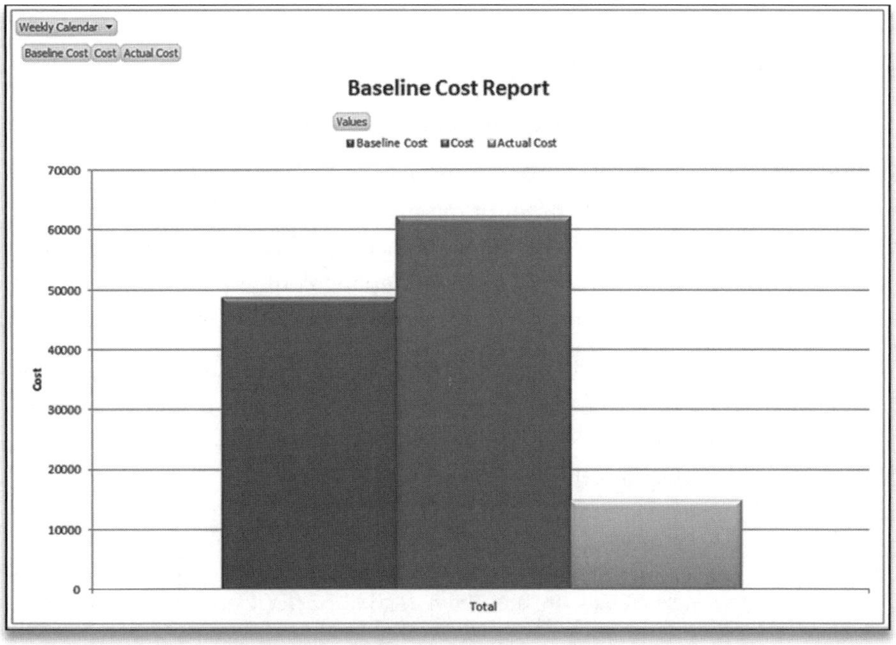

Figure 11 - 33: Baseline Cost visual report

Information: The Excel application sets the default level of zoom to *125%* for each visual report. Depending on your monitor size and screen resolution, you may need to zoom out for every visual report you view. In Excel, click the *View* tab to display the *View* ribbon. In the *Zoom* section of the *View* ribbon, click the *Zoom* button. In the *Zoom* dialog, select a level of zoom, such as the *Fit selection* level, and then click the *OK* button. You can also set the level of zoom using the *Zoom Slider* in the lower right corner of the Excel application window.

The visual report in Excel consists of two parts: the graphical *PivotChart*, shown previously in Figure 11 - 33, and the *PivotTable* containing the underlying data. To view the *PivotTable* data, click the tab further to the right of the two worksheet tabs in the lower left corner of the application window. Figure 11 - 34 shows the *PivotTable* data on the *Assignment Usage* worksheet for the *Baseline Cost* visual report.

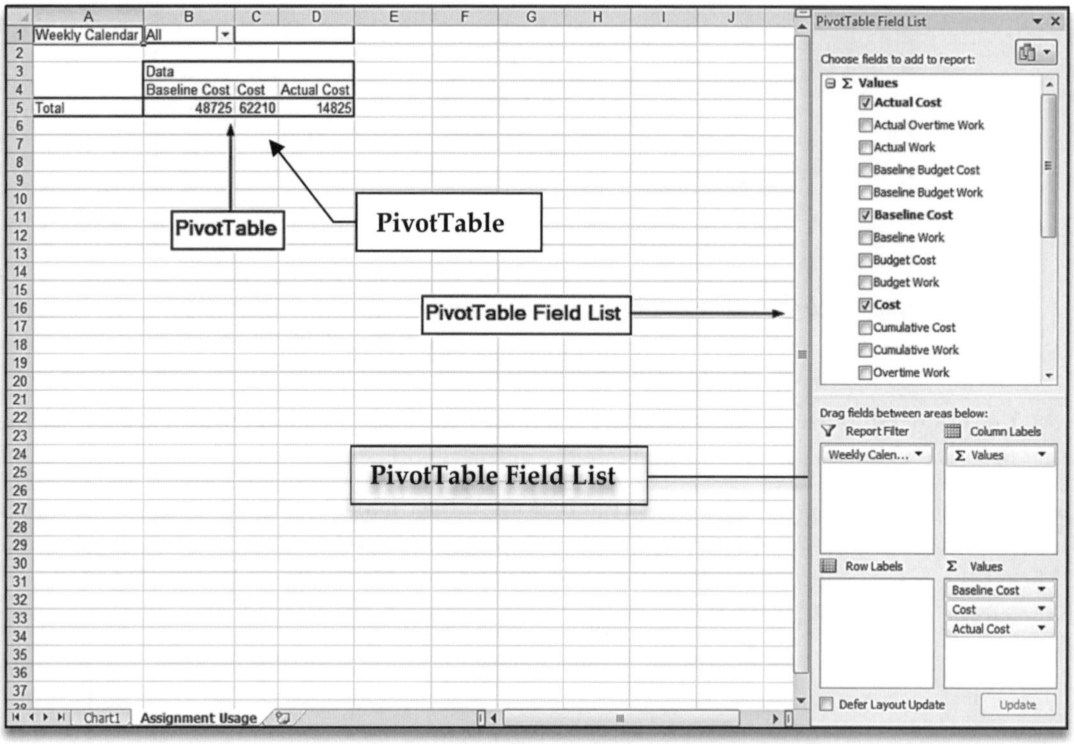

Figure 11 - 34: PivotTable data for the Baseline Cost visual report

Notice that the *Assignment Usage* worksheet shown previously in Figure 11 - 34 consists of two parts. The worksheet displays the *PivotTable* in the upper left corner of the page. The *PivotTable* includes data areas for row fields, column fields, project filter fields, and total fields. The worksheet displays the *PivotTable Field List* sidepane on the right side of the page. The top of the *PivotTable Field List* sidepane contains the list of fields that you can use in your report, while the bottom includes drop areas to which you can add the fields in your report.

Figure 11 - 35 shows the *Task Status* visual report in Visio. Notice that a visual report in Visio consists of the *PivotDiagram* and the *PivotDiagram* sidepane on the left side of the screen. If you work with Visio Professional 2007, the software displays a *PivotDiagram* toolbar at the top of the visual report page. If you work with Visio Professional 2010 or 2013, the software displays the *PivotDiagram* ribbon instead

Warning: Because the Visio application sets the default zoom level to display the width of all the data shown in the *PivotDiagram*, you probably need to zoom in to see your visual report data clearly. In Visio, click the *View* tab to display the *View* ribbon. In the *Zoom* section of the *View* ribbon, click the *Zoom* button. In the *Zoom* dialog, select a level of zoom, such as *100%*, and then click the *OK* button. You can also set the level of zoom using the *Zoom Slider* in the lower right corner of the Visio application window.

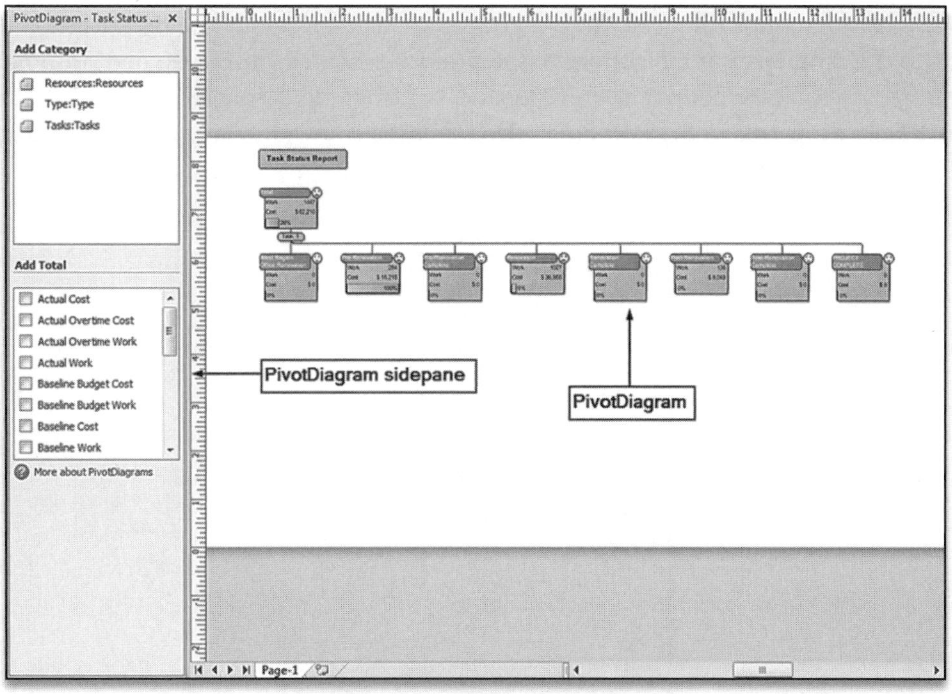

Figure 11 - 35: Task Status visual report

Customizing an Excel Visual Report

You can customize any Excel visual report by changing the data in the *PivotTable*. For example, you can use any of the following methods to customize the *PivotTable* data in the *Baseline Cost* visual report:

- In the *PivotTable Field List* sidepane, deselect any fields you do not want to display, and select the fields you do want to display. The software adds the newly selected field(s) to the appropriate area in the sidepane. For example, notice in Figure 11 - 36 that I **deselected** the *Actual Cost* field in the *PivotTable Field List* sidepane, removing this field from both the *PivotTable* and the *PivotChart* consequently. Though not visible in Figure 11 - 36, I also selected the *Tasks* field for inclusion in the Excel visual report.

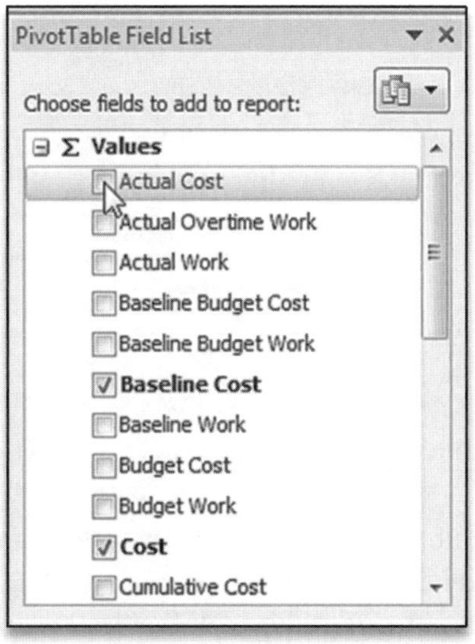

Figure 11 - 36: Deselect the Actual Cost field

- In the *PivotTable Field List* sidepane, drag and drop fields between the field list section at the top of the sidepane to the drop areas at the bottom of the sidepane. You can also drag and drop fields between the different drop areas at the bottom of the sidepane. For example, I dragged the *Weekly Calendar* field from the *Report Filter* drop area to the *Row Labels* drop area, as shown in Figure 11 - 37. You can see the *Tasks* field in the *Row Labels* area.

Figure 11 - 37: Move the Weekly Calendar field to the Row Labels area

- In the *PivotTable,* click the *Expand* (+) or *Collapse* (-) buttons in any section on the left side to show the level of details you want to see in the visual report. Notice in Figure 11 - 38 that I expanded the *Year* section to show *Quarters,* and I expanded the *West Region Office Renovation* task to show first-level tasks in the *Task 1* section.

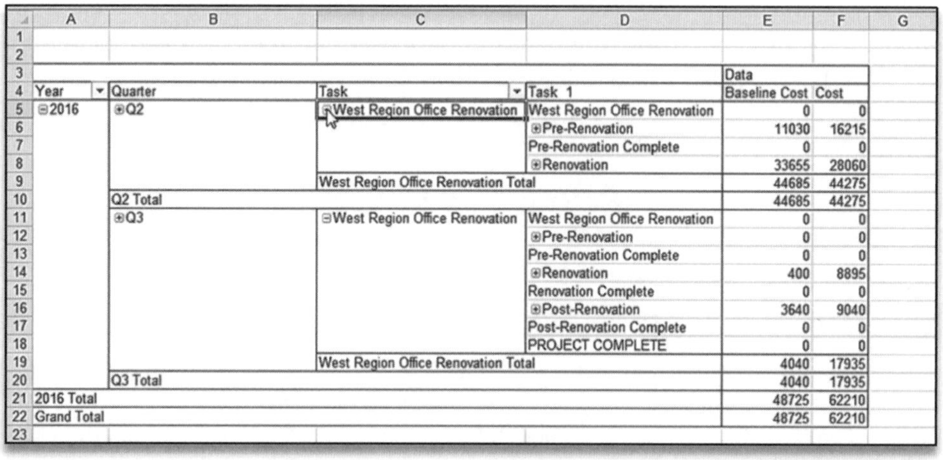

	A	B	C	D	E	F	G
1							
2							
3					Data		
4	Year	Quarter	Task	Task 1	Baseline Cost	Cost	
5	⊟2016	⊞Q2	⊟West Region Office Renovation	West Region Office Renovation	0	0	
6				⊞Pre-Renovation	11030	16215	
7				Pre-Renovation Complete	0	0	
8				⊞Renovation	33655	28060	
9			West Region Office Renovation Total		44685	44275	
10		Q2 Total			44685	44275	
11		⊞Q3	⊟West Region Office Renovation	West Region Office Renovation	0	0	
12				⊞Pre-Renovation	0	0	
13				Pre-Renovation Complete	0	0	
14				⊞Renovation	400	8895	
15				Renovation Complete	0	0	
16				⊞Post-Renovation	3640	9040	
17				Post-Renovation Complete	0	0	
18				PROJECT COMPLETE	0	0	
19			West Region Office Renovation Total		4040	17935	
20		Q3 Total			4040	17935	
21	2016 Total				48725	62210	
22	Grand Total				48725	62210	
23							

Figure 11 - 38: PivotTable with Year and Task sections expanded

- Select the details you want to see for any field in the *Row Labels* area by clicking the pick list arrow button in the column header for that field. For example, to edit the details for the *Task* field, click the *Task* pick list. The software displays the *Select field* dialog. Notice in the *Select field* dialog shown in Figure 11 - 39 that I expanded the Project Summary Task so that I can now see all first-level tasks, including summary tasks and milestone tasks. Using this dialog, I select the checkboxes for only the task items I want to see in the *PivotTable,* such as first-level summary tasks that represent phases of the project, and deselect the checkboxes for items I do not want to see, such as the first-level milestone tasks.

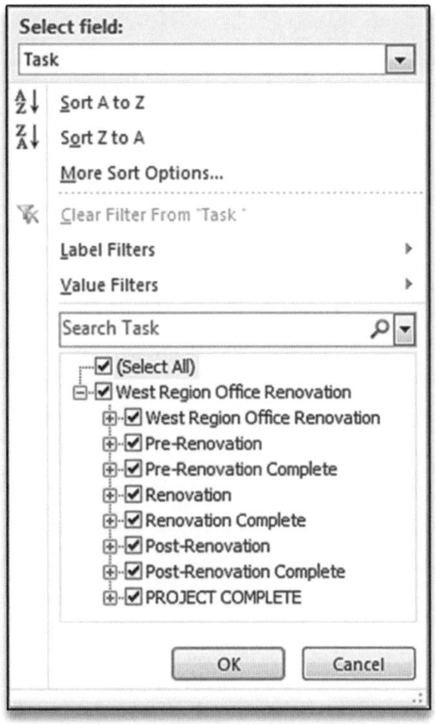

Figure 11 - 39: Select field dialog

Information: You can also use the *Select field* dialog to apply sorting or filtering to the data in the selected column of the *PivotTable*. Select the *Sort A to Z*, *Sort Z to A*, or *More Sort Options* item to apply sorting. Select the *Label Filters* or *Value Filters* items to apply filtering.

- Display properties fields in the *PivotTable,* if needed. If you add the *Task* field or the *Resource* field to the *Row Labels* area in a visual report, right-click the *Task* or *Resource* field, and in the shortcut menu, select the *Show Properties in Report* menu item. Then use the fly out menu to select the additional details you want to see in the report, as shown in Figure 11 - 40.

Information: For this example, I do not include any properties fields in the *PivotTable*. In your own projects, take a conservative approach when adding properties fields to your visual reports. Keep in mind that Excel limits how much number formatting you can apply to properties fields, or prevents number formatting entirely. Beyond this, adding properties fields to your *PivotTable* can negatively affect the appearance of your *PivotChart*.

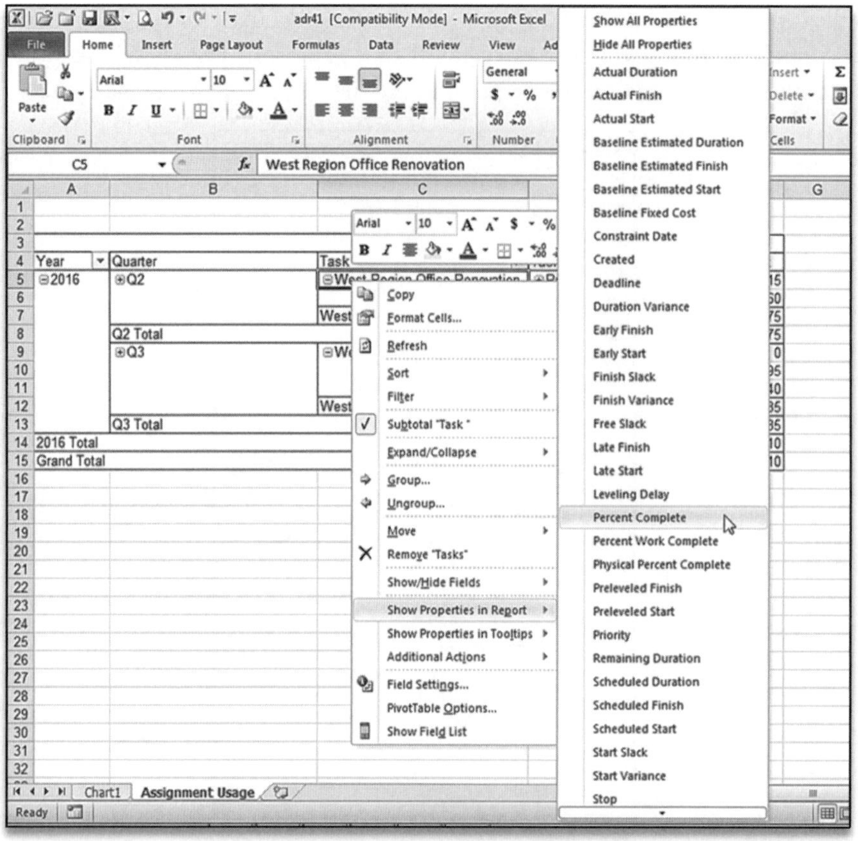

Figure 11 - 40: Add the Percent Complete details to the PivotTable

- Apply numeric formatting to the numbers in the *PivotTable*. For example, in Figure 11 - 41, I applied the *Accounting Number Format* numeric formatting to the data shown in the *PivotTable,* and then I used the *Decrease Decimal* button to reduce to *zero* the number of digits to the right of the decimal.

	A	B	C	D	E	F	G
1							
2							
3					Data		
4	Year	Quarter	Task	Task 1	Baseline Cost	Cost	
5	⊟2016	⊞Q2	⊟West Region Office Renovation	⊞Pre-Renovation	$ 11,030	$ 16,215	
6				⊞Renovation	$ 33,655	$ 28,060	
7			West Region Office Renovation Total		$ 44,685	$ 44,275	
8		Q2 Total			$ 44,685	$ 44,275	
9		⊞Q3	⊟West Region Office Renovation	⊞Pre-Renovation	$ -	$ -	
10				⊞Renovation	$ 400	$ 8,895	
11				⊞Post-Renovation	$ 3,640	$ 9,040	
12			West Region Office Renovation Total		$ 4,040	$ 17,935	
13		Q3 Total			$ 4,040	$ 17,935	
14	2016 Total				$ 48,725	$ 62,210	
15	Grand Total				$ 48,725	$ 62,210	
16							

Figure 11 - 41: PivotTable with numeric formatting applied

When you make changes to the data shown in the *PivotTable,* Excel updates the changes immediately in the *PivotChart*. Figure 11 - 42 shows the updated *PivotChart* after making changes to the underlying data in the *PivotTable.* If you compare this updated *Baseline Cost* report with the original *Baseline Cost* report shown previously in Figure 11 - 33, you see dramatic changes in appearance after making only a few simple changes in the *PivotTable.*

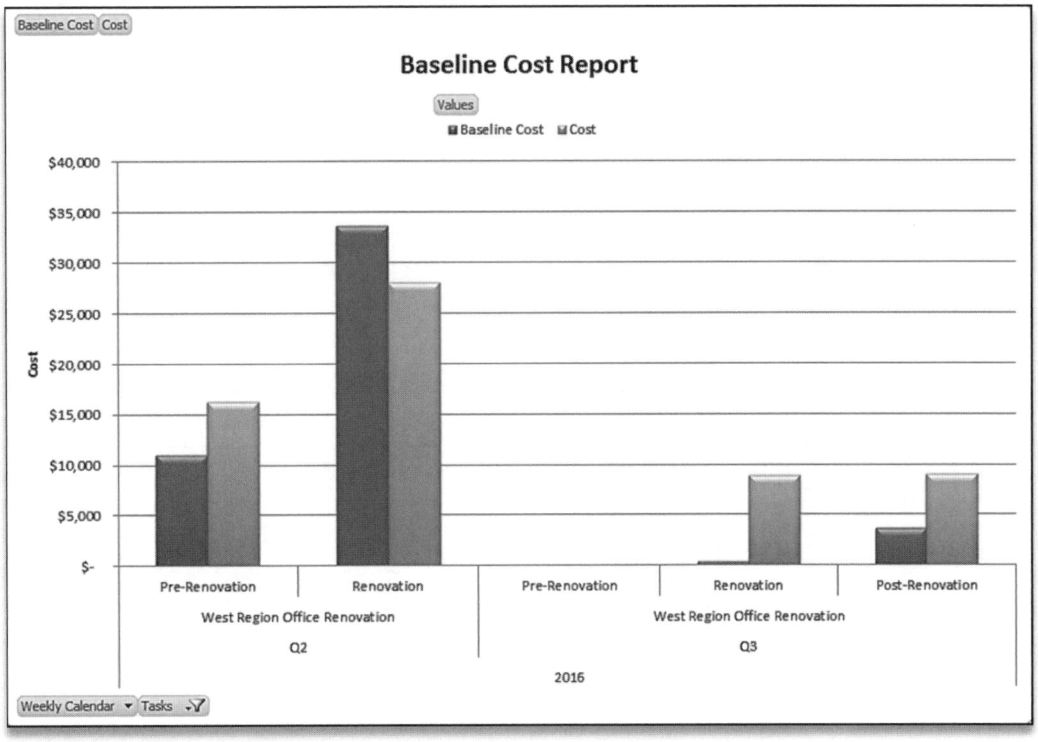

Figure 11 - 42: Updated Baseline Cost visual report

You may also modify the *PivotChart* by right-clicking anywhere in the chart area you want to change. For example, when you right-click in the *Plot Area* of the *PivotChart*, Excel displays the shortcut menu shown in Figure 11 - 43. Using the options on this shortcut menu, you can use any of the built-in chart formatting capabilities available in Excel, such as changing the chart type.

Information: In Excel 2007, 2010, and 2013 you can also double-click anywhere in the PivotChart. The software displays the appropriate *Format* dialog for the data you double-clicked. For example, if you double-click in the *Plot Area*, Excel displays the *Format Plot Area* dialog. In addition, Excel 2010 and 2013 also display the contextual *Design* ribbon with the *PivotChart Tools* applied. Using the features in the *Format* dialog and on the *Design* ribbon, you can apply many different types of formatting to the PivotChart.

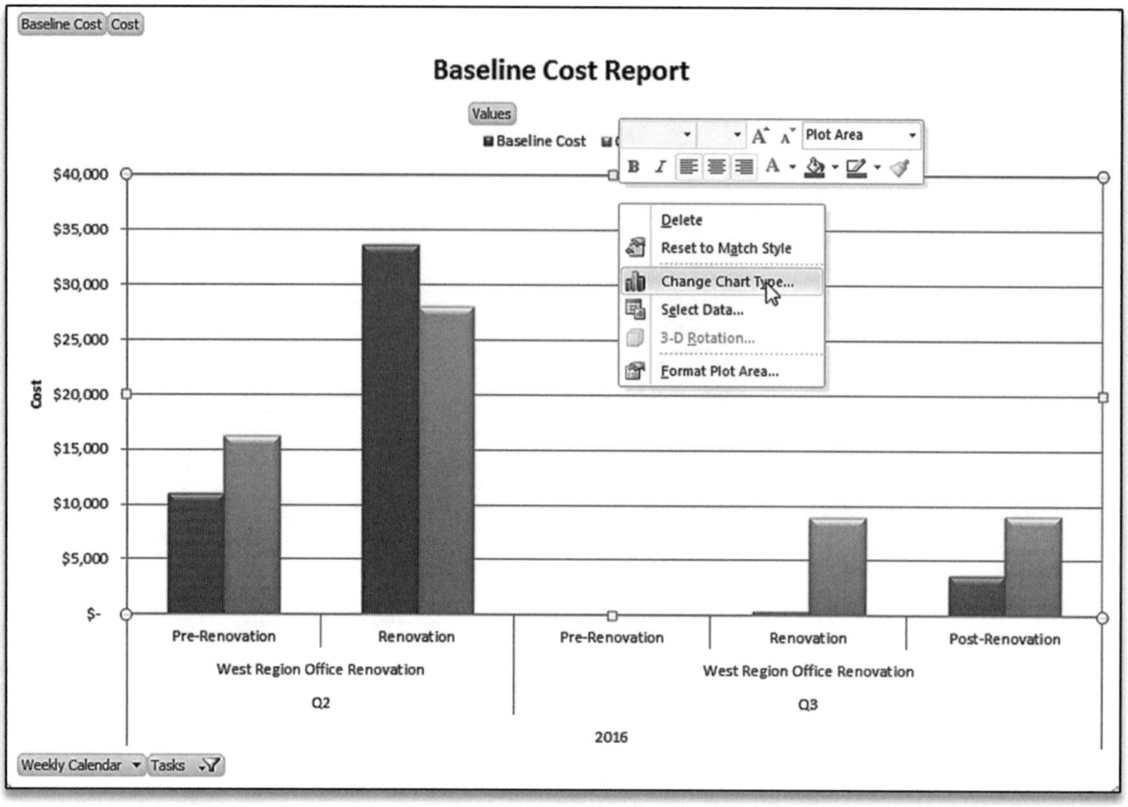

Figure 11 - 43: Right-click in the PivotChart to display the shortcut menu

If you select the *Change Chart Type* item on the shortcut menu, Excel displays the *Change Chart Type* dialog shown in Figure 11 - 44. Select an alternate chart type in this dialog and then click the *OK* button.

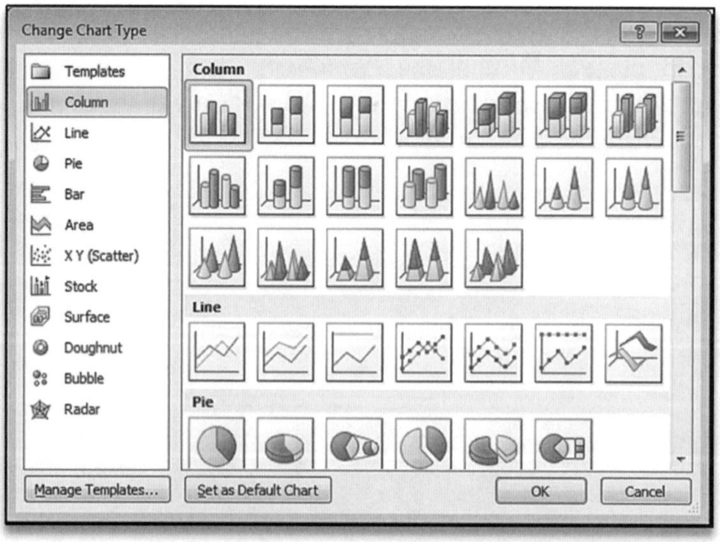

Figure 11 - 44: Change Chart Type dialog

Figure 11 - 45 shows the *PivotChart* after I applied the *Clustered Cylinder* chart type in the *Change Chart Type* dialog.

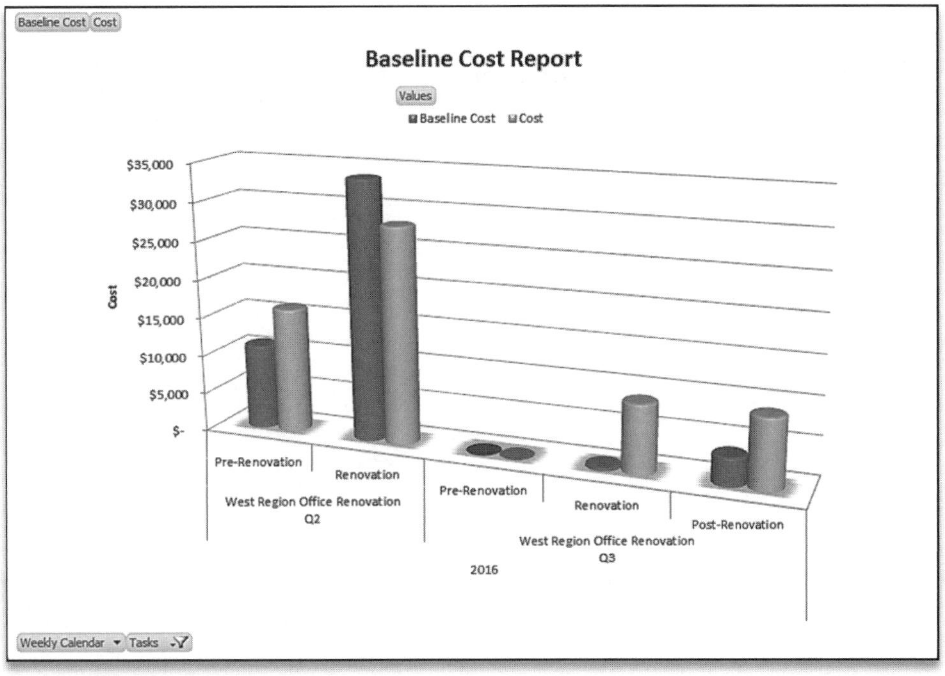

Figure 11 - 45: PivotChart formatted using the Clustered Cylinder chart type

> **Information**: Because this is not a course on Excel, I do not provide an exhaustive discussion about how to format either the PivotTable or the PivotChart in an Excel visual report.

After viewing and formatting an Excel visual report, you may print, or save the visual report, as needed.

Customizing a Microsoft Visio Visual Report

You can customize a Visio visual report by using any of the following methods:

Select one or more shapes in the *PivotDiagram* and then change the options in the *Add Category* section of the *PivotDiagram* sidepane. Notice in the *Task Status* visual report, shown previously in Figure 11 - 35, that the report displays only the first-level tasks representing the phases in the project. In this visual report, I want to show the second-level summary tasks for the *Renovation* phase to view the deliverables for that phase. To accomplish this, click the *Renovation* shape to select it in the *PivotDiagram*. In the *Add Category* section of the *PivotDiagram* sidepane, click the *Tasks* pick list, and then select the *Task 2* item, as shown in Figure 11 - 46 . After completing these steps, Figure 11 - 47 shows the *Task Status* visual report after adding the second-level task shapes to the report, and notice that the *PivotDiagram* now shows the *Construction* and *Furnish* summary tasks, but it also shows the *Construction Complete* and *Furnish Complete* milestone tasks.

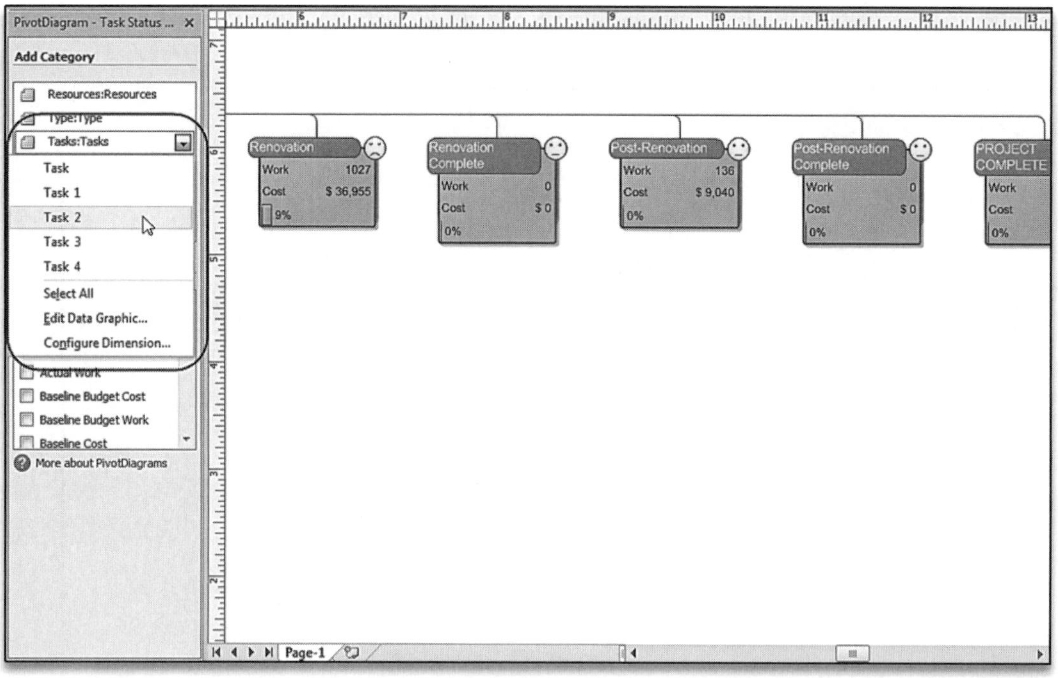

Figure 11 - 46: Tasks menu in the PivotDiagram sidepane

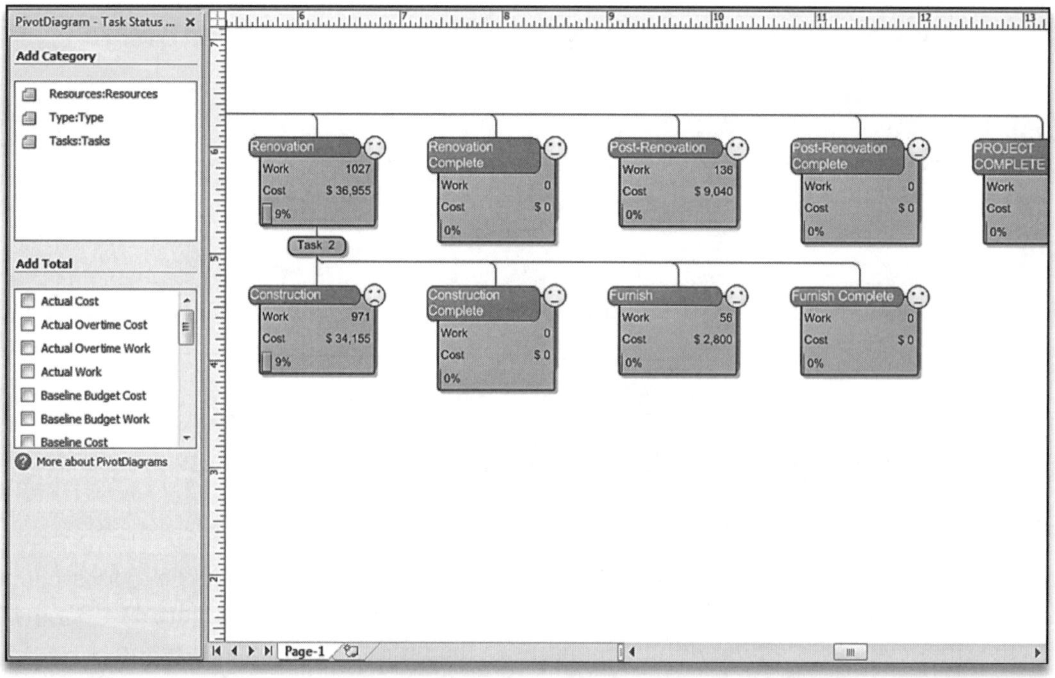

Figure 11 - 47: Task Status visual report with second-level summary tasks for the Renovation phase

- Change the fields displayed in the *PivotDiagram* by selecting or deselecting the fields in the *Add Total* section of the *PivotDiagram* sidepane. For example, Figure 11 - 48 shows the *Task Status* visual report after I selected the *Baseline Work* and *Baseline Cost* fields.

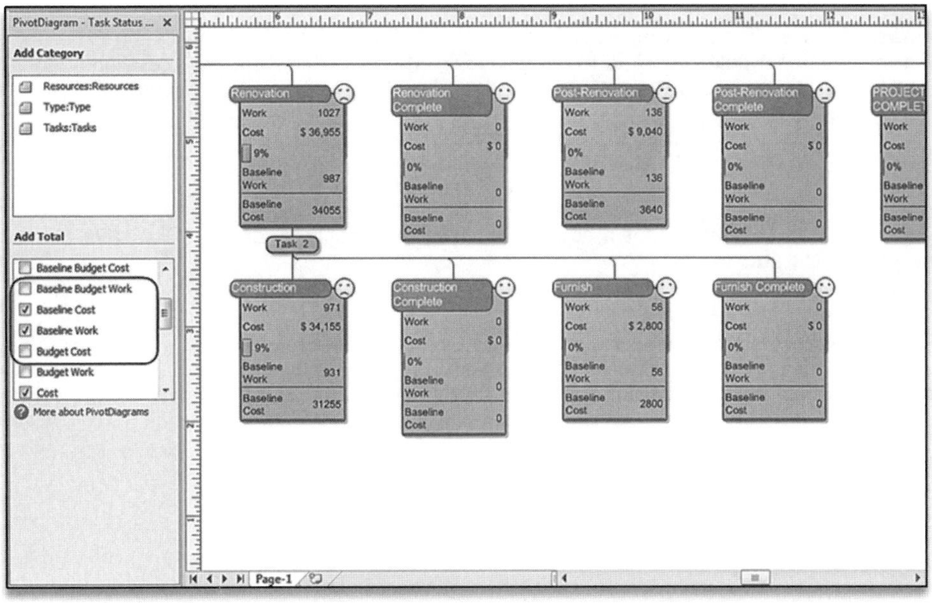

Figure 11 - 48: Task Status visual report after changing displayed fields

- Manually delete objects in the *PivotDiagram*. In the *Task Status* visual report shown previously in Figure 11 - 46 through Figure 11 - 48, I want to remove the shapes representing the Project Summary Task and all of the milestone tasks. To delete a shape in the *PivotDiagram*, click the shape to select it, and then press the **Delete** key on your computer keyboard.
- Rearrange the layout of shapes in the *PivotDiagram*. To change the layout of the shapes, in the *Layout* section of the *PivotDiagram* ribbon, click the *Re-Layout All* button. You can also manually drag and drop shapes anywhere on the *PivotDiagram*. Figure 11 - 49 shows the *Task Status* visual report after changing the layout of the *PivotDiagram* shapes using the *Re-Layout All* button.

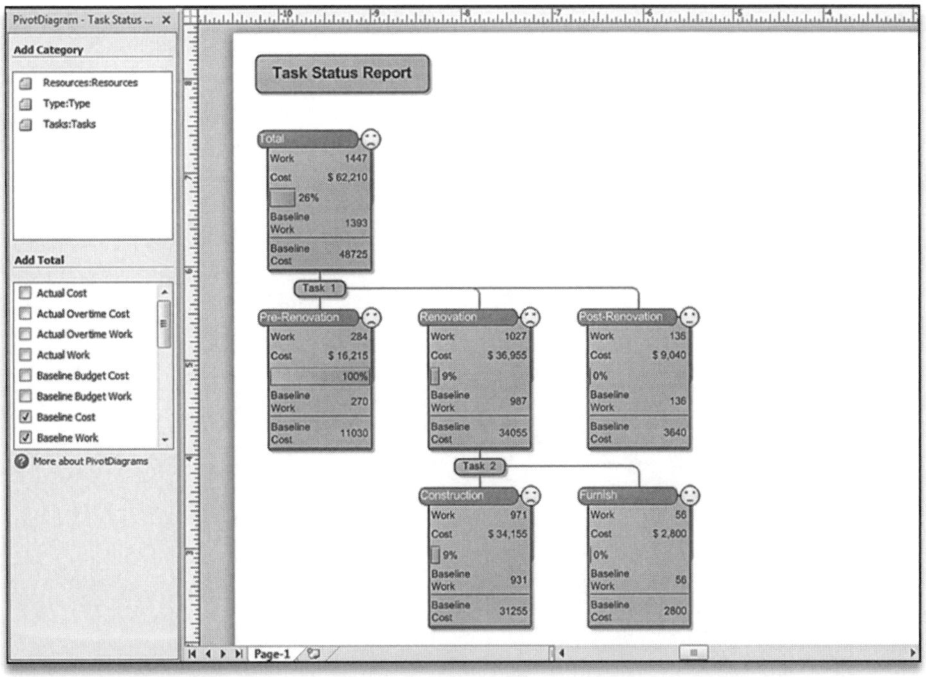

Figure 11 - 49: Task Status visual report after changing the layout

Information: In addition to the preceding four procedures, you may also change the display order and formatting for additional fields you add to the shapes in the *PivotDiagram*. For these additional formatting options refer to Module 11, *Advanced Reporting* in our *Ultimate Study Guide: Foundations, Microsoft Project 2013*.

Information: Because this is not a course on Visio, I do not provide an exhaustive discussion about how to format a PivotDiagram.

After viewing and formatting a Visio visual report, you can print the visual report or save the visual report, as needed.

Module 12

Managing Personal Settings

Learning Objectives

After completing this module, you will be able to:

- Set e-mail Alerts and Reminders for yourself
- Set e-mail Alerts and Reminders for resources that you manage
- Manage queued jobs
- Set delegations for yourself
- Act as a delegate

Inside Module 12

Personal Settings Overview

Depending on your permissions within the system, Project Server 2013 provides you with a number of personal settings that you can modify to suit your needs. Click the *Gear* icon and select the *PWA Settings* item. The *Personal Settings* group displays in the upper left-hand corner of the page as shown in Figure 12 - 1.

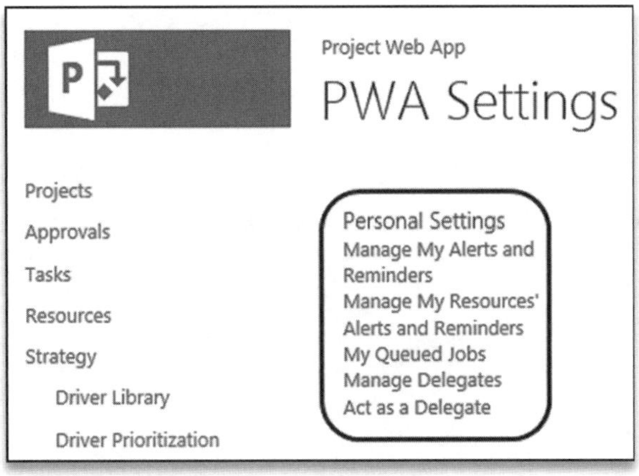

Figure 12 - 1: Personal Settings page in Project Web App

Depending on your permissions in Project Server 2013 and your method of authentication, the *Personal Settings* page may offer you some or all the following options:

- Manage My Alerts and Reminders
- Manage My Resource's Alerts and Reminders
- My Queued Jobs
- Manage Delegates
- Act as a Delegate

I discuss each of these options individually.

Warning: If your system is set to SharePoint permissions mode *Manage Delegates* and *Act as a Delegate* links do not display. The software does not support delegation in this mode.

Warning: As of this writing, *Manage My Alerts and Reminders* is not available for Project Online users. A user in a Project Online tenant running in SharePoint permissions mode will see the *My Queued Jobs* link only.

Managing Alerts and Reminders for Yourself

Project Web App allows you to set up a subscription to receive e-mail Alerts and Reminders from Project Server 2013. An Alert is an e-mail message that the system sends immediately when an event occurs, such as when the project manager publishes a new project in which you are a team member. A Reminder is an e-mail message that the system sends on a periodic cycle, usually once a day at midnight, to remind you of upcoming or overdue responsibilities, such as an overdue status report.

To manage your subscription for Alerts and Reminders, click the *Manage My Alerts and Reminders* link on the *Personal Settings* page. Project Server 2013 displays the *Manage My Alerts and Reminders* page shown in Figure 12 - 2.

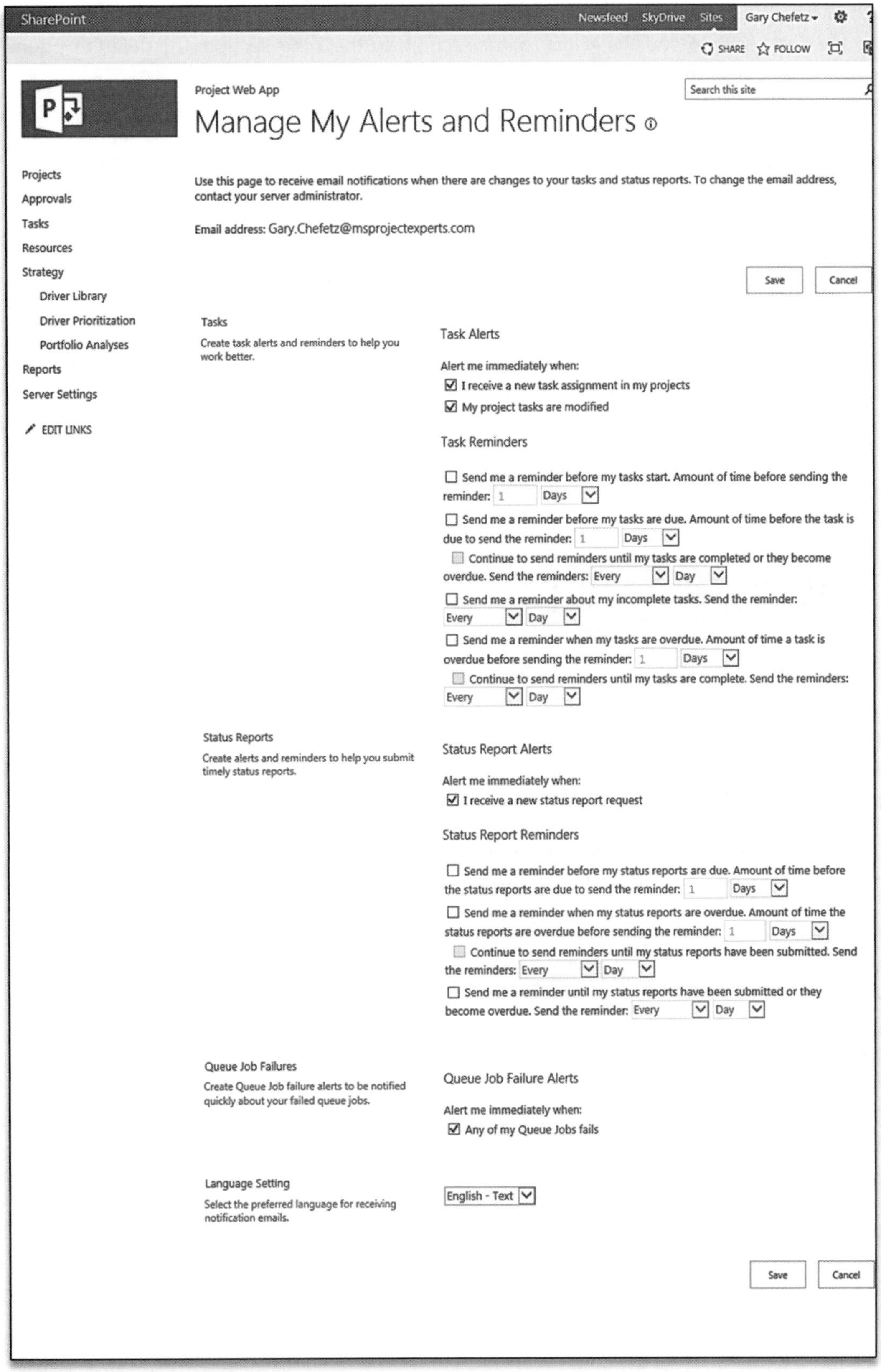
SharePoint
Newsfeed SkyDrive Sites Gary Chefetz
SHARE FOLLOW
Project Web App
Manage My Alerts and Reminders
Search this site
Projects
Approvals
Tasks
Resources
Strategy
Driver Library
Driver Prioritization
Portfolio Analyses
Reports
Server Settings
EDIT LINKS
Use this page to receive email notifications when there are changes to your tasks and status reports. To change the email address, contact your server administrator.
Email address: Gary.Chefetz@msprojectexperts.com
Save
Cancel
Tasks
Create task alerts and reminders to help you work better.
Task Alerts
Alert me immediately when:
I receive a new task assignment in my projects
My project tasks are modified
Task Reminders
Send me a reminder before my tasks start. Amount of time before sending the reminder: 1 Days
Send me a reminder before my tasks are due. Amount of time before the task is due to send the reminder: 1 Days
Continue to send reminders until my tasks are completed or they become overdue. Send the reminders: Every Day
Send me a reminder about my incomplete tasks. Send the reminder: Every Day
Send me a reminder when my tasks are overdue. Amount of time a task is overdue before sending the reminder: 1 Days
Continue to send reminders until my tasks are complete. Send the reminders: Every Day
Status Reports
Create alerts and reminders to help you submit timely status reports.
Status Report Alerts
Alert me immediately when:
I receive a new status report request
Status Report Reminders
Send me a reminder before my status reports are due. Amount of time before the status reports are due to send the reminder: 1 Days
Send me a reminder when my status reports are overdue. Amount of time the status reports are overdue before sending the reminder: 1 Days
Continue to send reminders until my status reports have been submitted. Send the reminders: Every Day
Send me a reminder until my status reports have been submitted or they become overdue. Send the reminder: Every Day
Queue Job Failures
Create Queue Job failure alerts to be notified quickly about your failed queue jobs.
Queue Job Failure Alerts
Alert me immediately when:
Any of my Queue Jobs fails
Language Setting
Select the preferred language for receiving notification emails.
English - Text
Save
Cancel

Figure 12 - 2: Manage My Alerts and Reminders page

Notice that the *Manage My Alerts and Reminders* page includes options in four sections. You set your Alerts and Reminders in the *Tasks* section and the *status reports* section. In the *Tasks* section, the default options trigger the system to send you an e-mail message whenever the following occurs:

- A project manager publishes a new project containing a task assigned to you, or the project manager assigns you to a new task in an existing project and then publishes the project.

- The schedule changes for one or more of your task assignments in an existing project.

Between the two default e-mail subscriptions for Alerts on tasks, the first is most valuable because you should always notify team members about new task assignments. The second e-mail subscription is problematic, however, because it can lead to a large number of e-mail messages sent to team members every time the project schedule changes. If team members receive too many e-mail messages from Project Server 2013, they may treat these messages as "spam" and create an Outlook rule to filter out all messages originating with Project Server.

Best Practice: To reduce the number of e-mail messages that users receive from Project Server 2013, MSProjectExperts recommends that all project managers and team members deselect the *My project tasks are modified* option on the *Manage My Alerts and Reminders* page.

The second set of options in the *Tasks* section allows you to subscribe to e-mail reminders related to specific task criteria for project work. Each night the system tests your criteria and generates an email message containing the task reminders for your subscriptions. You receive an email only if you set reminder criteria and the system finds an appropriate match between your tasks in the system and your specified criteria. Think of these criteria as triggering conditions, which include each of the following:

- Before a task starts

- Before a task is due

- Until a task is complete or becomes overdue

- When you have an incomplete task

- When you have an overdue task

- Until an overdue task is complete

Notice in Figure 12 - 2 that the default settings include none of these options. If you select any of these options, you should also specify the frequency, as you do not have to receive these messages every day unless you prefer daily delivery.

The options in the *Status Reports* section are similar to those in the *Tasks* section. The default permission for Alerts on status reports causes the system to send you an e-mail message immediately when a manager includes you in a new status report request. The second set of options allows you to subscribe to reminders for status reports.

The *Queue Job Failures* section of the *Manage My Alerts and Reminders* page includes only a single option. This option causes Project Server 2013 to send you an e-mail message immediately if any job you send to the queue fails in the queuing process. For example, if you submit a timesheet or a task update, each of these constitutes a job sent to the queue for processing. If the job fails, the system immediately sends you an e-mail message.

The *Language Setting* section contains a single option that allows you to set your language preference for e-mail messages sent to you by Project Server 2013. Select the language you want, if necessary, and then click the *Save* button to save the selections you specify.

Managing Alerts and Reminders for Your Resources

In addition to managing e-mail subscriptions for Alerts and Reminders for yourself, Project Server 2013 also allows you to manage e-mail subscriptions for your team members and your resources. The system defines "your team members" as those resources who are a team member in your projects and assigned to at least one task. The system defines "your resources" as any resource included in a status report request. To set e-mail subscriptions for your team members and resources, click the *Manage My Resource's Alerts and Reminders* link on the *Personal Settings* page. Project Server 2013 displays the *Manage My Resource's Alerts and Reminders* page shown in Figure 12 - 3.

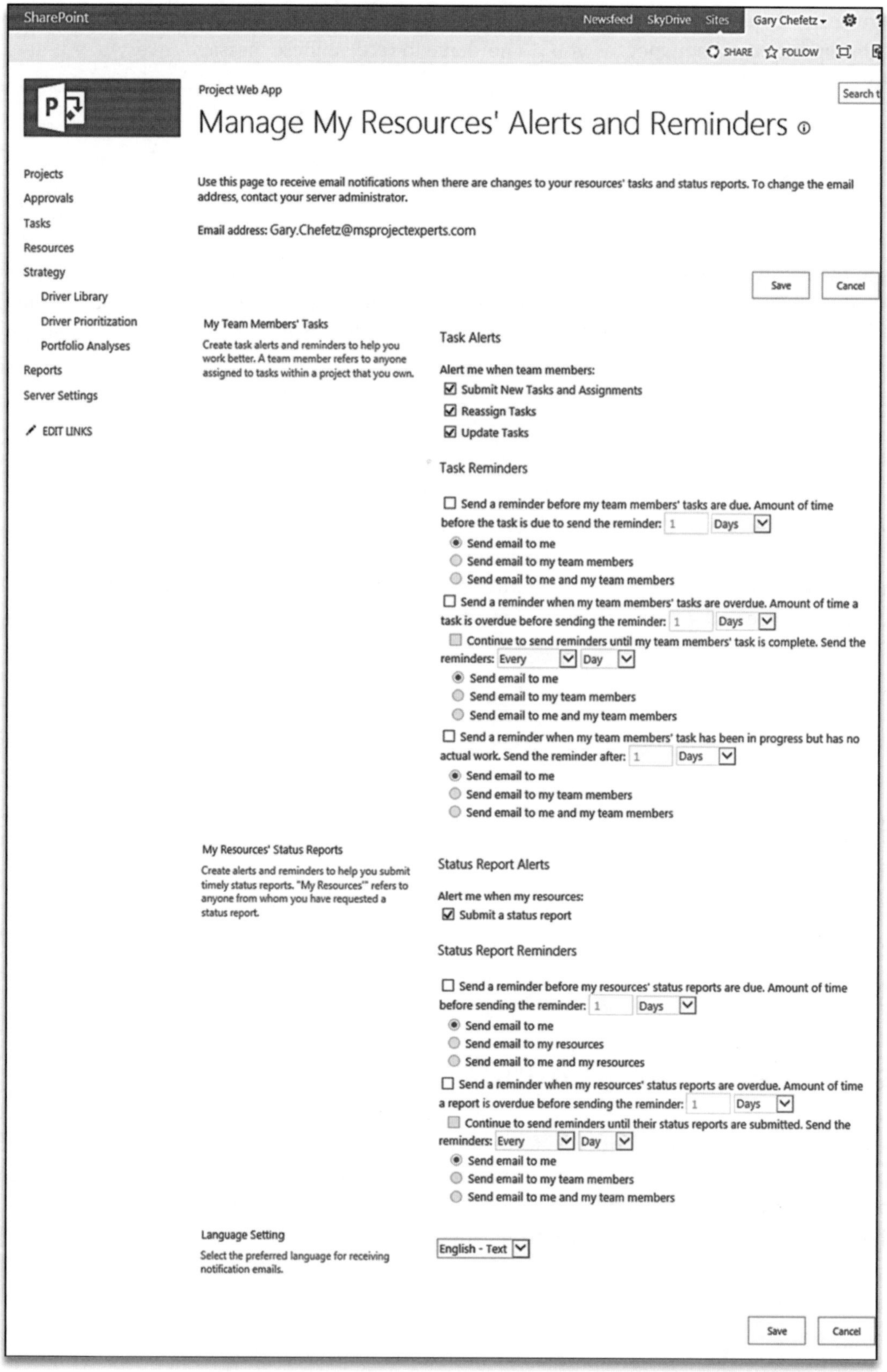
SharePoint
Newsfeed
SkyDrive
Sites
Gary Chefetz
SHARE
FOLLOW
Project Web App
Manage My Resources' Alerts and Reminders
Projects
Approvals
Tasks
Resources
Strategy
Driver Library
Driver Prioritization
Portfolio Analyses
Reports
Server Settings
EDIT LINKS
Use this page to receive email notifications when there are changes to your resources' tasks and status reports. To change the email address, contact your server administrator.
Email address: Gary.Chefetz@msprojectexperts.com
Save
Cancel
My Team Members' Tasks
Create task alerts and reminders to help you work better. A team member refers to anyone assigned to tasks within a project that you own.
Task Alerts
Alert me when team members:
Submit New Tasks and Assignments
Reassign Tasks
Update Tasks
Task Reminders
Send a reminder before my team members' tasks are due. Amount of time before the task is due to send the reminder: 1 Days
Send email to me
Send email to my team members
Send email to me and my team members
Send a reminder when my team members' tasks are overdue. Amount of time a task is overdue before sending the reminder: 1 Days
Continue to send reminders until my team members' task is complete. Send the reminders: Every Day
Send email to me
Send email to my team members
Send email to me and my team members
Send a reminder when my team members' task has been in progress but has no actual work. Send the reminder after: 1 Days
Send email to me
Send email to my team members
Send email to me and my team members
My Resources' Status Reports
Create alerts and reminders to help you submit timely status reports. "My Resources" refers to anyone from whom you have requested a status report.
Status Report Alerts
Alert me when my resources:
Submit a status report
Status Report Reminders
Send a reminder before my resources' status reports are due. Amount of time before sending the reminder: 1 Days
Send email to me
Send email to my resources
Send email to me and my resources
Send a reminder when my resources' status reports are overdue. Amount of time a report is overdue before sending the reminder: 1 Days
Continue to send reminders until their status reports are submitted. Send the reminders: Every Day
Send email to me
Send email to my team members
Send email to me and my team members
Language Setting
Select the preferred language for receiving notification emails.
English - Text
Save
Cancel

Figure 12 - 3: Manage My Resources' Alerts and Reminders page

Notice in Figure 12 - 3 that the *Manage My Resource's Alerts and Reminders* page layout is similar to the *Manage My Alerts and Reminders* page. In this case, the page consists of only three sections, including *My Team Member's Tasks*, *My Resource's Status Reports*, and *Language Settings*. Notice also that the default options in the *Task Alerts* section of the page cause Project Server 2013 to send you an e-mail alert immediately when one of the following triggering events occurs:

- A team member submits a *New Task* request or a *New Assignment* request to you.
- A team member reassigns (delegates) a task to another team member.
- A team member submits task progress to you.

Because these three default options can lead to a high volume of e-mail messages sent to you by Project Server 2013, you may wish to deselect one or more of these options. Of the three, the *Update Tasks* option causes the system to send the most e-mail messages.

The *Task Reminders* section of the page allows you to set up subscriptions for e-mail reminders for your team members about their project work. When you set up reminder subscriptions for your team members, you may choose to have the reminder sent to you only, to the team members only, or to both you and your team members. Set the reminders for your team members and specify who receives the e-mail reminders.

The *Status Report Alerts* section contains only a single option, selected by default. This option causes Project Server 2013 to send you an e-mail alert immediately when a resource submits a status report to you. Again, because this option can lead to a flurry of e-mail messages, you may want to deselect it.

The *Status Report Reminders* section allows you to set up subscriptions for e-mail reminders for those resources assigned to *Status Report* requests you create. Again, you may choose to have the reminders sent to you only, to the resources only, or to both you and your resources.

Information: If one of your team members or resources deselects a *Reminder* option on the *Manage My Alerts and Reminders* page, and you select the same reminder option for your team members or resources on the *Manage My Resource's Alerts and Reminders* page, your selection overrides the user's selection and sets the reminder.

In the *Language Setting* section, specify your language preference and then click the *Save* button to save your settings.

Managing My Queued Jobs

Every time you stand in line at a fast food restaurant, you are waiting in a "queue." In Project Server 2013, the queue is a waiting line that is necessary whenever the number of service requests to the system is greater than the system's optimum serving capacity. When you save and submit a timesheet or a task update, the system places your job in the queue for processing.

Project Server 2013 allows you to view the jobs in the queue by clicking the *My Queued Jobs* link on the *Personal Settings* page. The system displays the *My Queued Jobs* page shown in Figure 12 - 4.

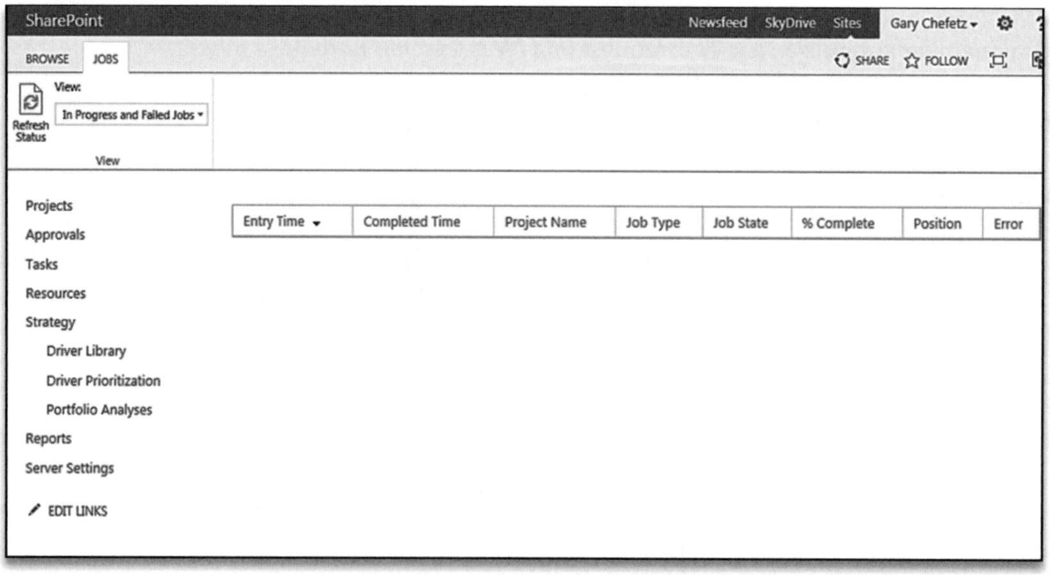

Figure 12 - 4: My Queued Jobs page

The *My Queued Jobs* page should normally appear blank, as shown previously in Figure 12 - 4. A blank page means, "no news is good news." This indicates that Project Server 2013 is running without errors. If you see a queue job on the *My Queued Jobs* page, you can watch the job's progress in the system by clicking the *Refresh Status* button occasionally.

In addition to being able to view jobs currently processing in the queue, Project Server 2013 allows you to view the history of processed jobs. Click the *View* pick list in the *View* ribbon and select one of the following views:

- In Progress and Failed Jobs in the Past Week (the default view)
- All In Progress and Failed Jobs
- Successful Jobs in the Past Week
- All Successful Jobs
- All Jobs in the Past Week
- All Jobs

For example, Figure 12 - 5 shows the *My Queued Jobs* page with the *Successful Jobs in the Past Week* view selected. Notice that the page shows a number of different job types.

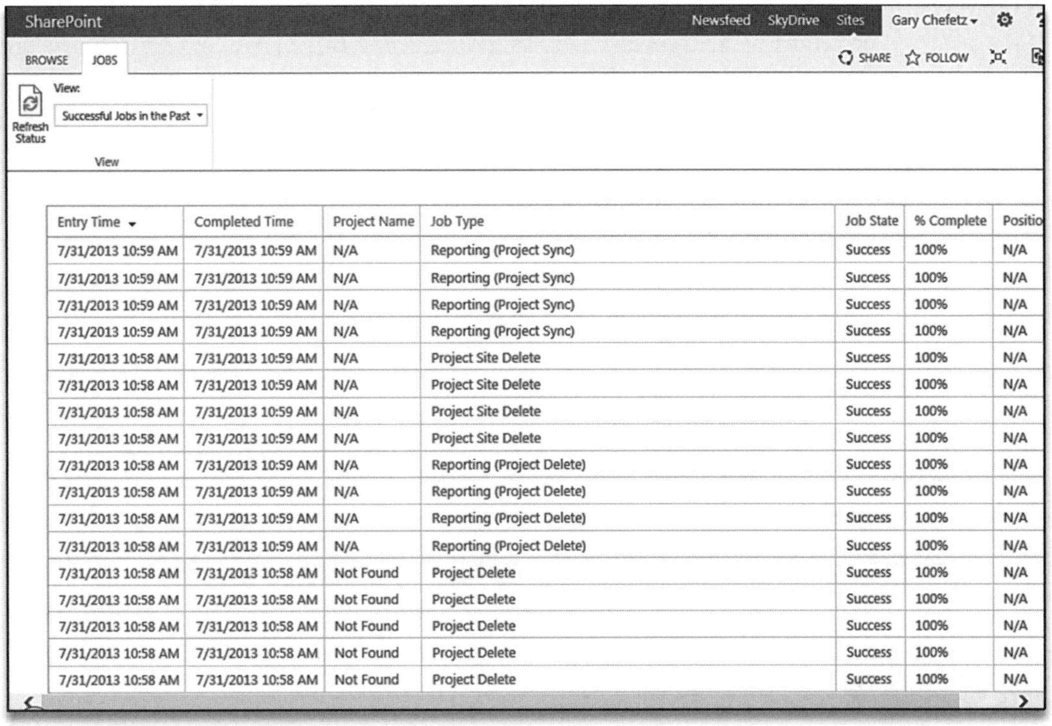

Entry Time	Completed Time	Project Name	Job Type	Job State	% Complete	Positio
7/31/2013 10:59 AM	7/31/2013 10:59 AM	N/A	Reporting (Project Sync)	Success	100%	N/A
7/31/2013 10:59 AM	7/31/2013 10:59 AM	N/A	Reporting (Project Sync)	Success	100%	N/A
7/31/2013 10:59 AM	7/31/2013 10:59 AM	N/A	Reporting (Project Sync)	Success	100%	N/A
7/31/2013 10:59 AM	7/31/2013 10:59 AM	N/A	Reporting (Project Sync)	Success	100%	N/A
7/31/2013 10:58 AM	7/31/2013 10:59 AM	N/A	Project Site Delete	Success	100%	N/A
7/31/2013 10:58 AM	7/31/2013 10:59 AM	N/A	Project Site Delete	Success	100%	N/A
7/31/2013 10:58 AM	7/31/2013 10:59 AM	N/A	Project Site Delete	Success	100%	N/A
7/31/2013 10:58 AM	7/31/2013 10:59 AM	N/A	Project Site Delete	Success	100%	N/A
7/31/2013 10:58 AM	7/31/2013 10:59 AM	N/A	Reporting (Project Delete)	Success	100%	N/A
7/31/2013 10:58 AM	7/31/2013 10:59 AM	N/A	Reporting (Project Delete)	Success	100%	N/A
7/31/2013 10:58 AM	7/31/2013 10:59 AM	N/A	Reporting (Project Delete)	Success	100%	N/A
7/31/2013 10:58 AM	7/31/2013 10:59 AM	N/A	Reporting (Project Delete)	Success	100%	N/A
7/31/2013 10:58 AM	7/31/2013 10:58 AM	Not Found	Project Delete	Success	100%	N/A
7/31/2013 10:58 AM	7/31/2013 10:58 AM	Not Found	Project Delete	Success	100%	N/A
7/31/2013 10:58 AM	7/31/2013 10:58 AM	Not Found	Project Delete	Success	100%	N/A
7/31/2013 10:58 AM	7/31/2013 10:58 AM	Not Found	Project Delete	Success	100%	N/A
7/31/2013 10:58 AM	7/31/2013 10:58 AM	Not Found	Project Delete	Success	100%	N/A

Figure 12 - 5: My Queued Jobs page shows the Successful Jobs in the Past Week view

If you notice a job that the system simply does not process, or a job that failed, you should contact your Project Server administrator immediately for assistance. To help the Project Server administrator, click the *Click to view the error details* link in the *Error* column. The *Queue Job Error Details* dialog contains valuable information to help your Project Server administrator diagnose and solve the queue errors. To share the error information with your Project Server administrator, click the *Copy to Clipboard* button and paste the error contents into an email message.

Manage Delegates

Project Server 2013 allows you to designate delegates who can act on your behalf in the system, such as when you know you will be away when timesheets are due. Using delegation in Project Server allows you to appoint a coworker to submit your timesheet for you. Click the *Manage Delegates* link on the *Personal Settings* page and the system opens the *Manage Delegates* page shown in Figure 12 - 6.

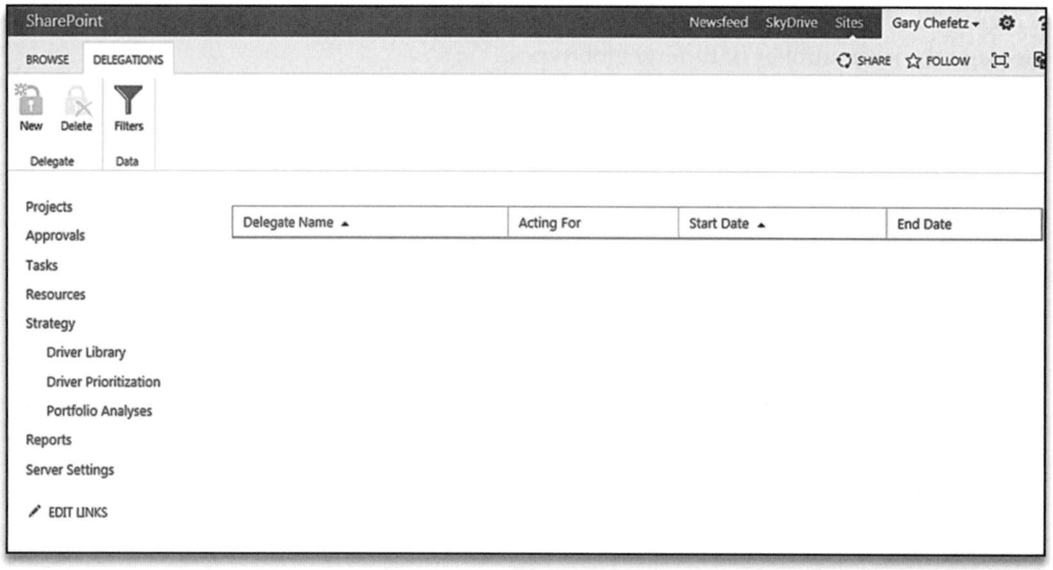

Figure 12 - 6: Manage Delegates page

To create a new delegation, in the *Delegate* section of the *Delegations* ribbon, click the *New* button. The system displays the *Add Delegation* page shown in Figure 12 - 7.

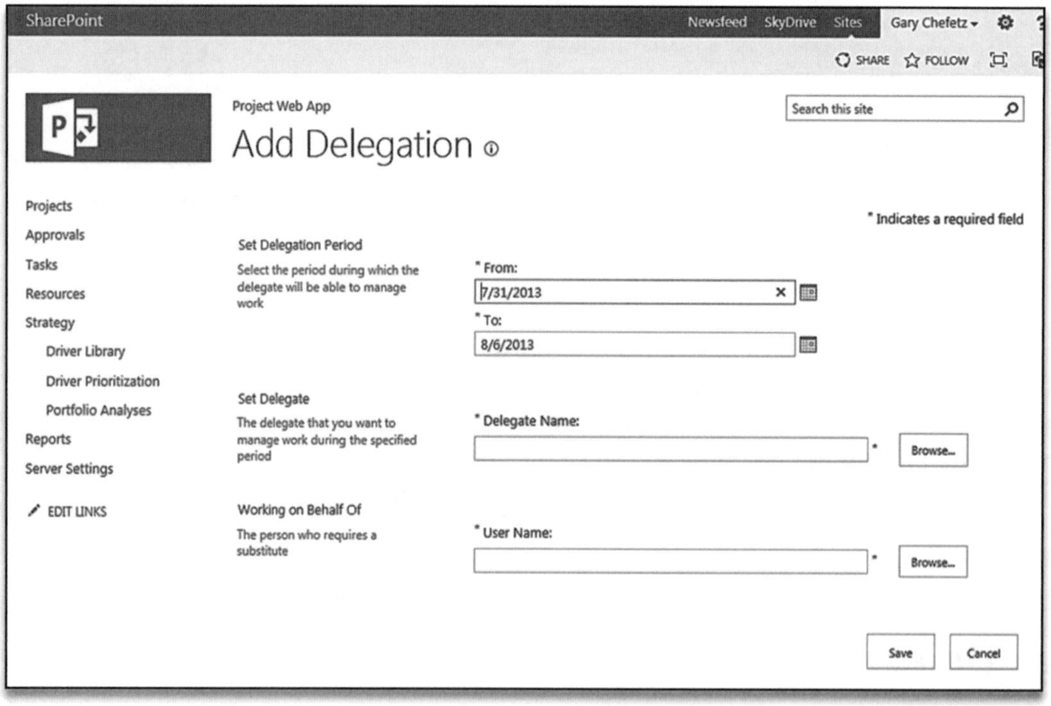

Figure 12 - 7: Add Delegation page

To add a new delegation, begin by setting a date range during which the delegation is effective using the *From* and *To* fields. Next, select the person who you would like to act as your delegate by clicking the *Browse* button and selecting the username from the list. Finally, click the *Browse* button in the *Working on Behalf of* section to select yourself from the list. Click the *Save* button when you complete your entries.

Information: Administrators and others who have *Manage Resources' Delegates* permission can create delegations for themselves and anyone else who has the *Act as Delegate* permission. Non-administrators may only create delegations for themselves unless a Project Server administrator gives them additional permissions.

Act as Delegate

When another user selects you as a delegate by creating a delegation, you can act on behalf of that person to perform most functions within Project Web App. To act as a delegate, click the *Act as a Delegate* link from the *Personal Settings* page. The system displays the *Act as a Delegate* page shown in Figure 12 - 8.

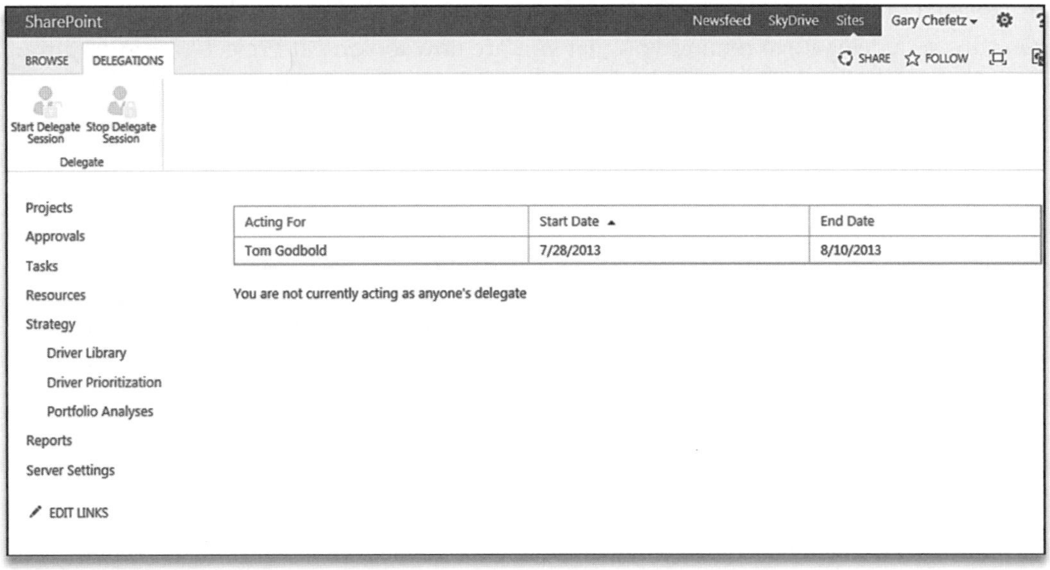

Figure 12 - 8: Act as a Delegate page

If another user or administrator created a delegation for you to act on behalf of another user, the *Act as a Delegate* page displays those delegations. Notice in Figure 12 - 8 that I have a delegation from Tom Godbold effective July 28 through August 10, 2013. To start a delegate session, select the delegation you want to use by highlighting the row, and from the *Delegate* section of the *Delegations* ribbon, click the *Start Delegate Session* button. The page changes to indicate that the delegation session is active as shown in Figure 12 - 9.

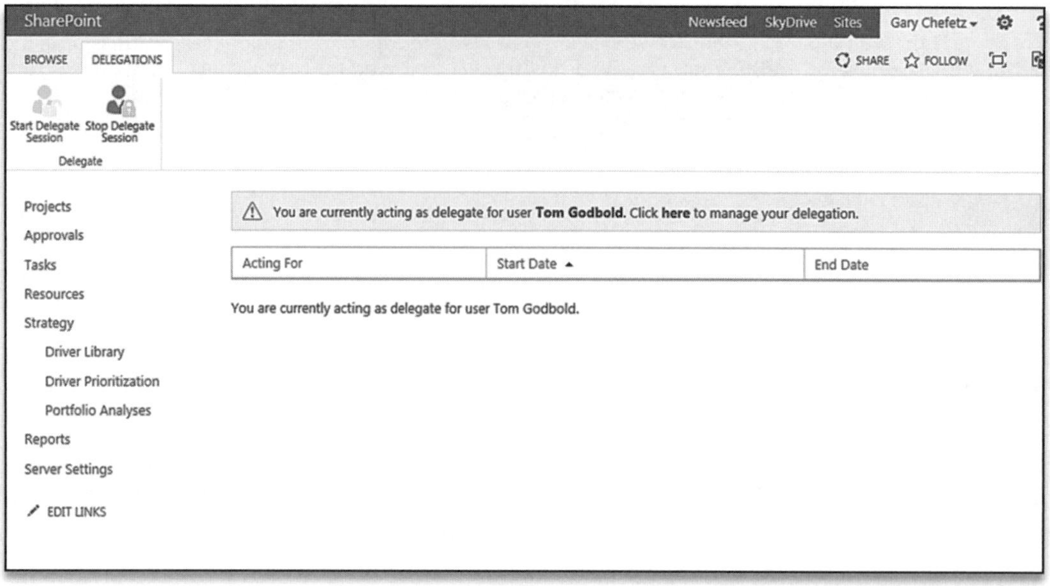

Figure 12 - 9: Act as Delegate page with delegation session in progress

Notice in Figure 12 - 9 that the screen changes by displaying a band across the page just beneath the ribbon indicating that the delegation session is active. This warning band remains across every page in Project Web App while you are acting as a delegate to remind you that you are now looking at Project Web App through someone else's eyes. After you complete your work on behalf of the other user, you end your delegate session by returning to the *Act as Delegate* page by clicking on the *Click here* link in the information band, or by navigating to the page from the *Personal Settings* page. From the *Delegate* section of the *Delegations* ribbon, click the *Stop Delegate Session* button. The system exits the delegate session and the page displays *You are not currently acting as anyone's delegate* in the message section.

Warning: Delegation does not apply to all features. For instance, features supported by SharePoint only, such as Project Sites and the BI Center, are not included in delegation. Delegation does not apply to Project Pro 2013 or editing project schedules with Project Pro 2013.

Module 13

Managing Risks and Issues

Learning Objectives

After completing this module, you will be able to:

- Track and manage project risks
- Track and manage project issues

Inside Module 13

Tracking Project Risks

The Project Management Institute defines a risk as "an uncertain event or condition that, if it occurs, has a positive or negative effect on a project objective." Risks have both causes and consequences. If a risk occurs, the consequence can be either negative or positive. Your organization's risk management methodologies may dictate that you log and document anticipated risks to your project work.

Creating a New Risk

To create a new risk in the Project Site, on the *Quick Launch* menu, click the *Risks* link. Project Server 2013 displays the *Risks* list page for the project shown in Figure 13 - 1.

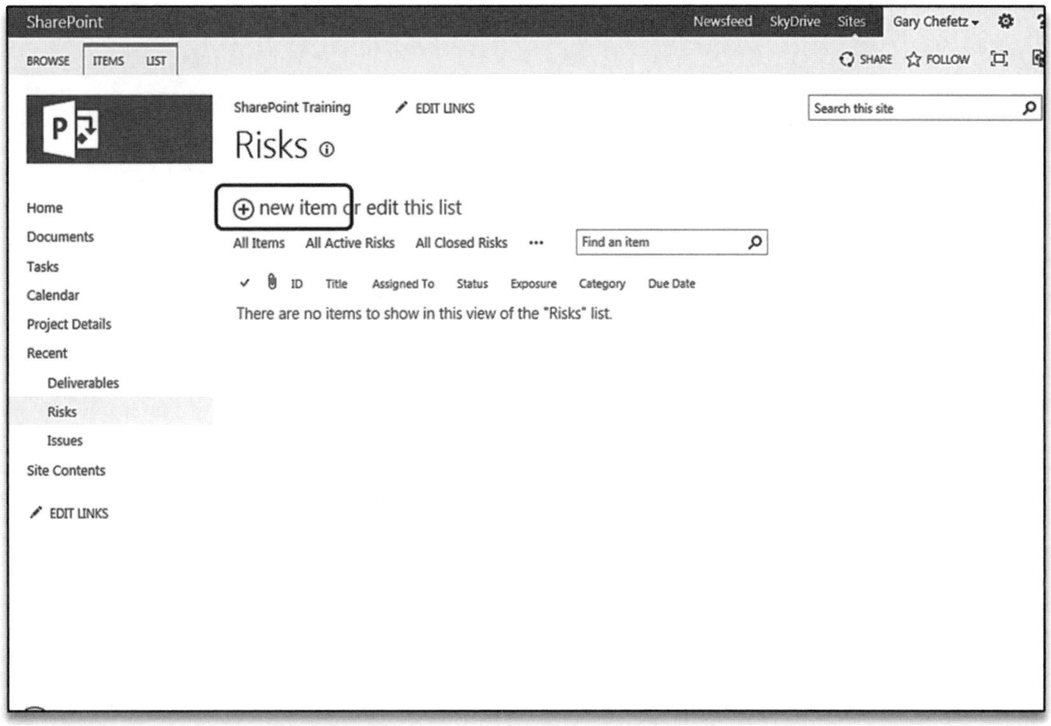

Figure 13 - 1: Risks page for the SharePoint Training project

Click the + *new item* link on the page. The system displays the *New Item* page for risks shown in Figure 13 - 2.

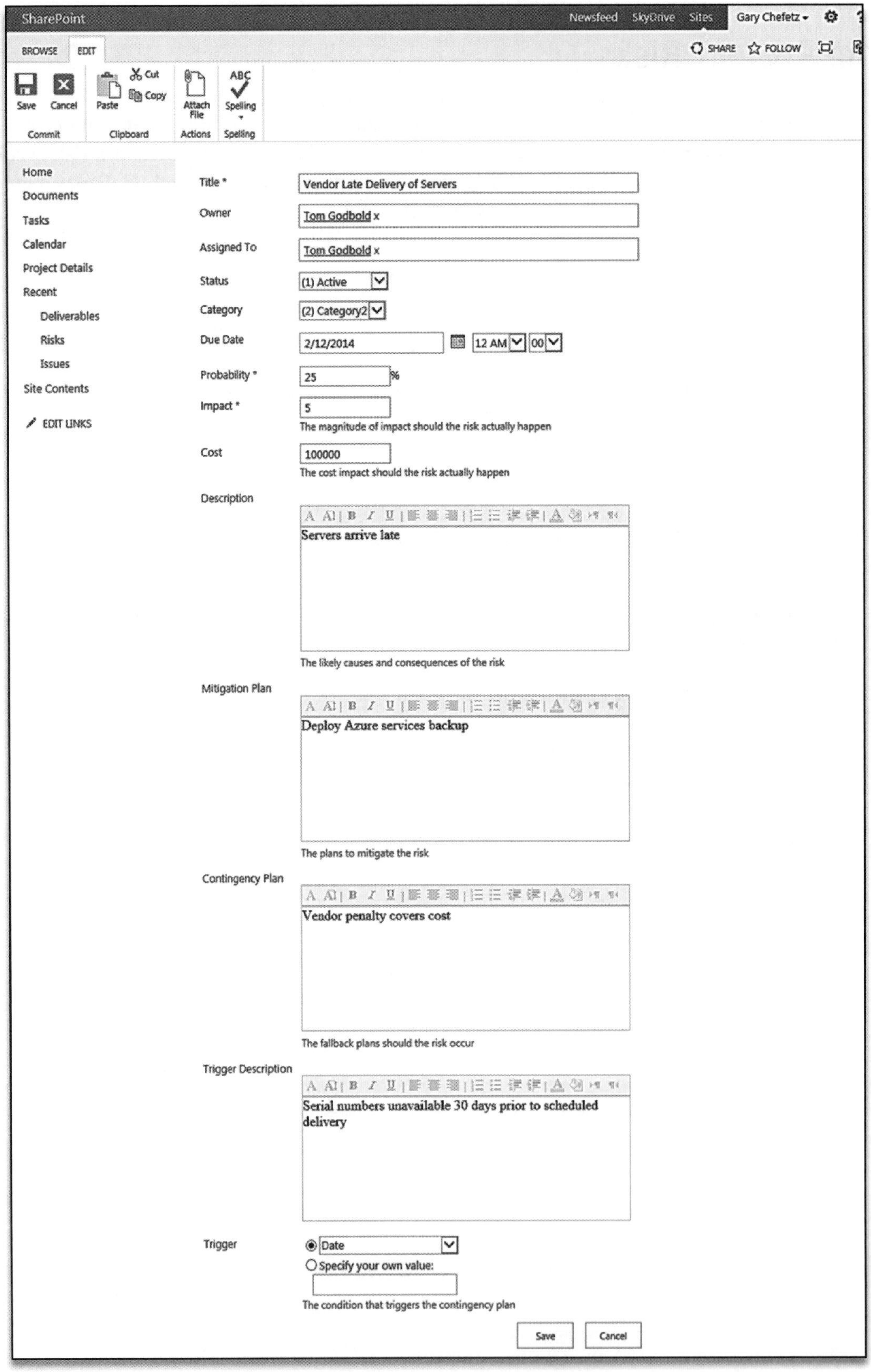

Figure 13 - 2: New Item page for risks

The *New Item* page for risks contains fields into which you can enter relevant information about the risk. The system requires you to enter information into only four fields: *Title, Status, Probability,* and *Impact*. Notice that the *Status* field defaults to *Active* status. This field determines the status of the risk for display in your reminders on the homepage, the Project Server reminder email, and on the *Issues and Risks* page. Project Server 2013 requires probability and impact entries to determine the *Exposure* value for the risk, which it calculates by multiplying the two numbers.

Information: Project Server 2013 displays the *Exposure* field on the *Risks* page. You can use the *Exposure* value to rank risks in descending order by severity. For example, your organization might establish a risk management methodology that requires you to create a risk management plan for the top four risks ranked by exposure.

Warning: Do not change the values for the *Status* field or you break some of the integration with Project Server 2013.

In the *Title* field, enter a brief description. In the *Owner* field, enter the name of the individual who owns the new risk. Start typing the name or email address and the system automatically starts searching as shown in Figure 13 - 3. Enter a full or partial name in the *Owner* or *Assigned To* fields to activate this feature. Use your mouse or **Down Arrow** and **Enter** keys on your computer keyboard to select the user from the list.

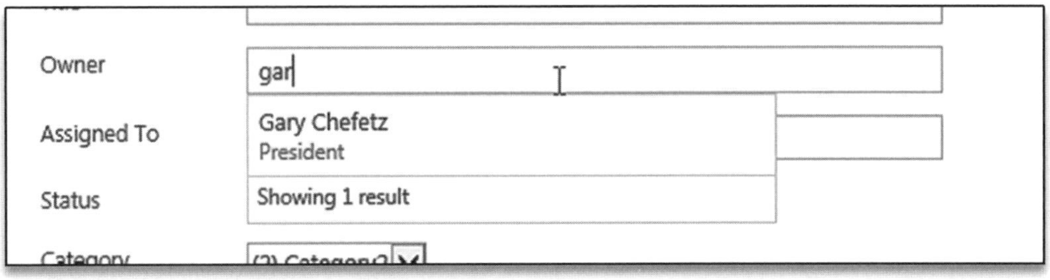

Figure 13 - 3: Select People and Groups Webpage dialog

In the *Assigned To* field, select the name of the person responsible for managing the risk. This is the person assigned to monitor risk conditions and enact a backup plan if the risk occurs.

Click the *Status* pick list and select the status. Options include *Active, Postponed,* and *Closed,* and *Active* status is the default for new risks. The *Category* field is a field your organization should edit to display risk management information specific to your organization or your particular project. The default values in this field do not contain relevant identifiers, so unless you or your Project Server administrator modifies these values, you may ignore this field.

In the *Due Date* field, enter either the date on which you anticipate the risk may occur, or the date on which the *Assigned To* person must complete the risk management plan. Because this field is optional, your organization may use it any way you deem appropriate. You may also select a date and time for the *Due Date* field using the *Calendar* button and the *Time* pick lists to the right of the field.

In the *Probability* field, enter a percentage value between 0 and 100, representing the likelihood that the risk may actually occur. In the *Impact* field, enter a number between 1 and 10 to describe the magnitude of the consequences in the project should the risk occur. Remember that Project Server 2013 multiplies these two numbers to determine the *Exposure* value for the risk. In the *Cost* field, enter any additional cost incurred to the project if the risk occurs.

> **Information**: Entering a value of *0%* in the *Probability* field makes no sense. If there is no chance of risk, there is no risk. Entering a value of *100%* makes no sense either. If the risk is absolutely certain, it is not a risk, it is an issue.

Click into the *Description* field to activate the text editing buttons at the top of the field. Enter additional information about the risk, such as causes of the risk and consequences to the project, should the risk occur. Format the text using the formatting buttons at the top of the field.

Click into the *Mitigation Plan* field and enter your plan for reducing the likelihood of the risk occurring, or to reduce the impact of the risk should it occur. Click in the *Contingency Plan* field and enter your backup plan for action should the risk actualize.

Click into the *Trigger Description* field and enter the description of what triggers the risk and determines whether it is about to occur, is currently occurring, or has already occurred. If you want to enter additional trigger information, click the *Trigger* pick list button and select an item from the list. Alternately, you may also select the *Specify your own value* option and enter text in the accompanying field.

Working with Existing Risks

While working with existing risks, the system allows you to do the following:

- Add related items
- Apply a view to the *Risks* page
- Sort the risks by the data in any column
- View a risk
- Edit a risk
- Delete a risk
- Subscribe to e-mail alerts about changes to a risk

I cover each of these topics individually. Figure 13 - 4 shows the *Risks* page for the *SharePoint Training* project. Notice the active risk associated with the project.

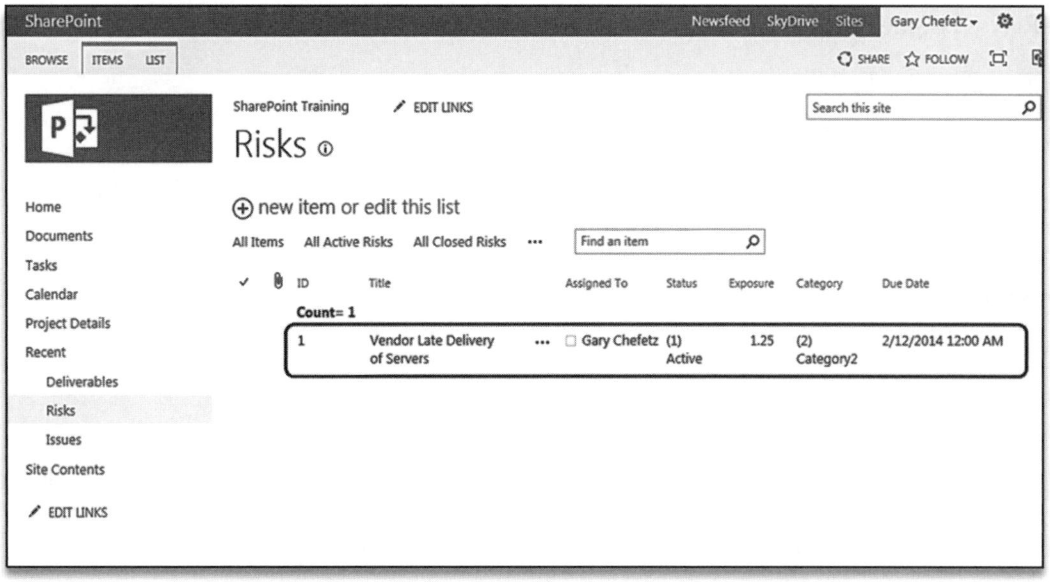

Figure 13 - 4: Risks page for the SharePoint Training project

Working with Risk List Views

To apply a view to the *Risks* page, click the *List* tab, and from the *Manage Views* section, click the *Current View* pick list button and then select an available view as shown in the expanded pick list in Figure 13 - 5.

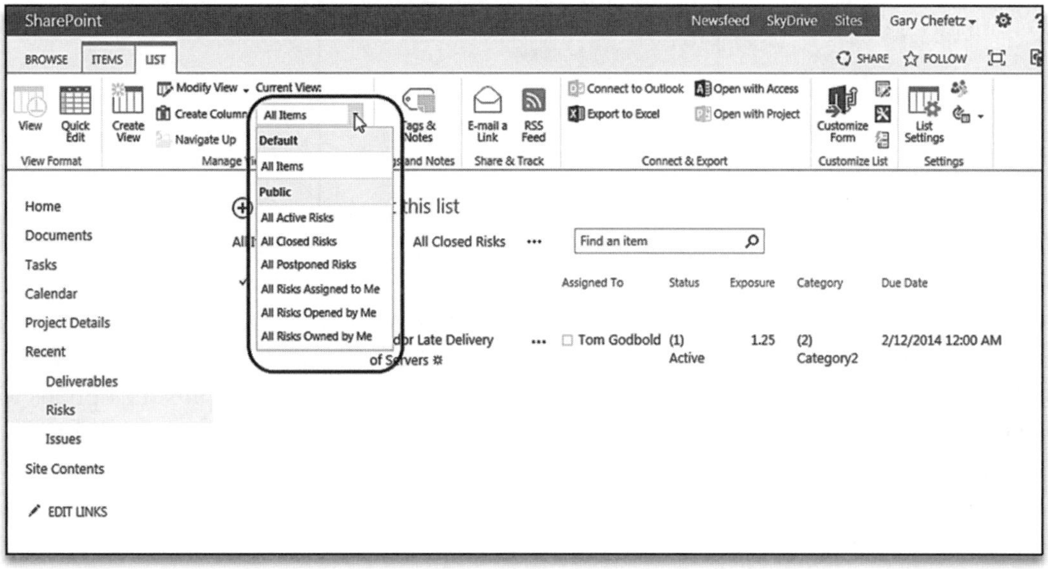

Figure 13 - 5: Current View pick list shows available views

The *Current View* pick list for the *Risks* page offers seven pre-defined *Public* views, including the following:

- All Items (the default view)
- All Active Risks
- All Closed Risks
- All Postponed Risks

- All Risks Assigned to Me
- All Risks Opened by Me
- All Risks Owned by Me

Remember, Project Server 2013 also allows you to modify views and to create new views. After you apply a view from the *Current View* pick list, the system filters the list of risks as suggested in the view name.

> **Information**: You use the *Configure Views for This Location* selection in the *Other* section when you use the *Locations* feature in SharePoint. For more information on this topic, see Microsoft's TechNet site.

To sort the risks in any view, click the name of the column header on which to sort the data. The system applies default sorting on the ID number column, sorted in the order users created the risks. For example, Figure 13 - 6 shows that you can change the sort order by floating your mouse pointer over the column header to reveal the pick list control, then select either the *Ascending* or *Descending* item from the pick list.

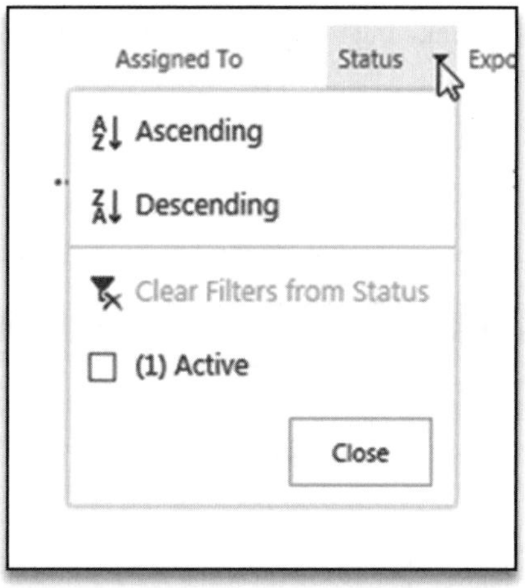

Figure 13 - 6: Selecting a sort order

Notice the downward-pointing arrow indicator to the right of the *Status* column name, indicating sorting in descending order in Figure 13 - 7. You can also see the list of *AutoFilter* options. Notice that the pick list for the *Status* column, shown previously in Figure 13 - 6, contains every value in the column, plus the options to sort in *Ascending* (Smallest on Top) or *Descending* (Largest on Top) order. Select an item from the pick list to AutoFilter the risks based on data contained in that column.

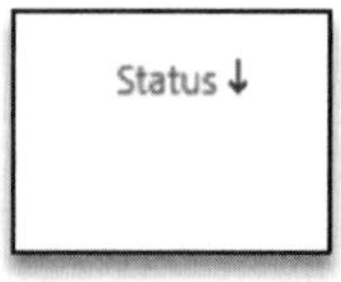

Figure 13 - 7: Sort order for the Status column

> **Information**: When you apply AutoFiltering to a column, Project Server 2013 indicates the AutoFiltered column by displaying a funnel indicator to the right of the column name. To remove AutoFiltering from a column, click the pick list button and select the *Clear Filters from _____* item on the list. Where I put a blank line you see the name of the column.

Viewing and Editing Existing Risks

To work with an existing risk, such as to view or edit it, you can click the name of the risk or click the ellipsis (…) and Project Server 2013 displays the pick list shown in Figure 13 - 8.

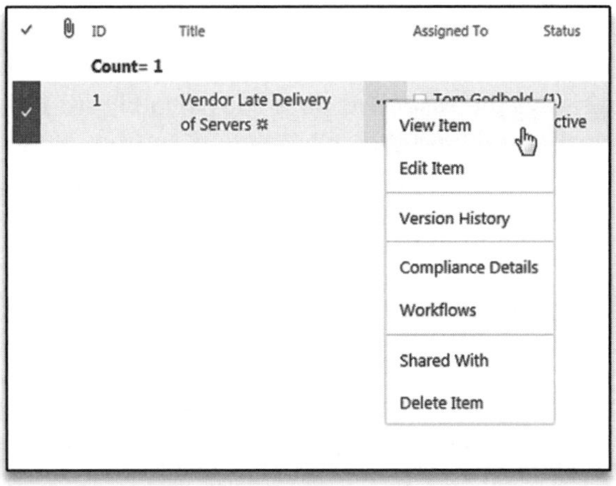

Figure 13 - 8: Pick list button and pick list for an existing risk

Notice that the menu allows you to select from *View Item, Edit Item, Compliance Details, Workflows, Shared With* or *Delete Item,* and view the *Version History* for the list if you enabled version control. These concepts apply when using both the *Risks* list and the *Issues* list, and any other SharePoint list you work with. The *Compliance Details* feature is something you use when your system employs advanced types of SharePoint document management features including, among others, records compliance, content retention policies, and content validation. These features are beyond the scope of this book.

Click *View Item* on the pick list to open a risk in *View-Only* mode, as shown in Figure 13 - 9.

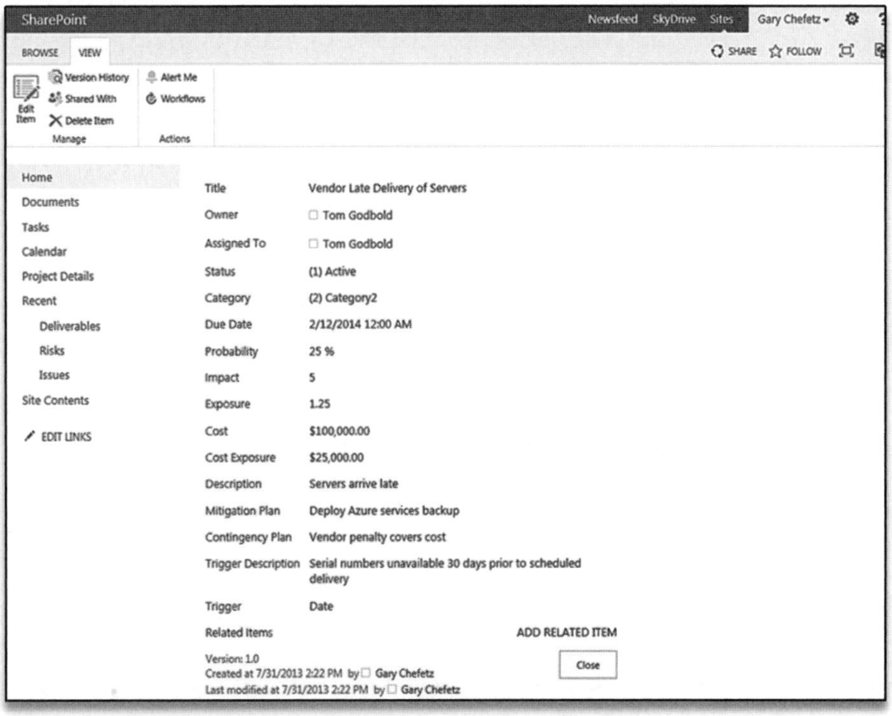

Figure 13 - 9: Risks page for the selected risk in view-only mode

Information: You can also display a risk in *View-Only* mode by clicking the name of the risk in the *Title* field.

To subscribe to e-mail alerts about changes to a risk or other list type item, click the *View* tab to display the *View* ribbon and from the *Actions* section of the ribbon, click the *Alert me* button. If you choose to receive e-mail messages about the risk, the system displays the *New Alert* page shown in Figure 13 - 10. On the *New Alert* page, specify your options in each section of the page and then click the *OK* button. Notice that the *New Alert* page allows you to determine what type of change triggers the system to send an e-mail message to you, and that you can determine this change when the system sends the message.

Warning: You must configure your SharePoint server for email to use the *Alerts* feature in SharePoint.

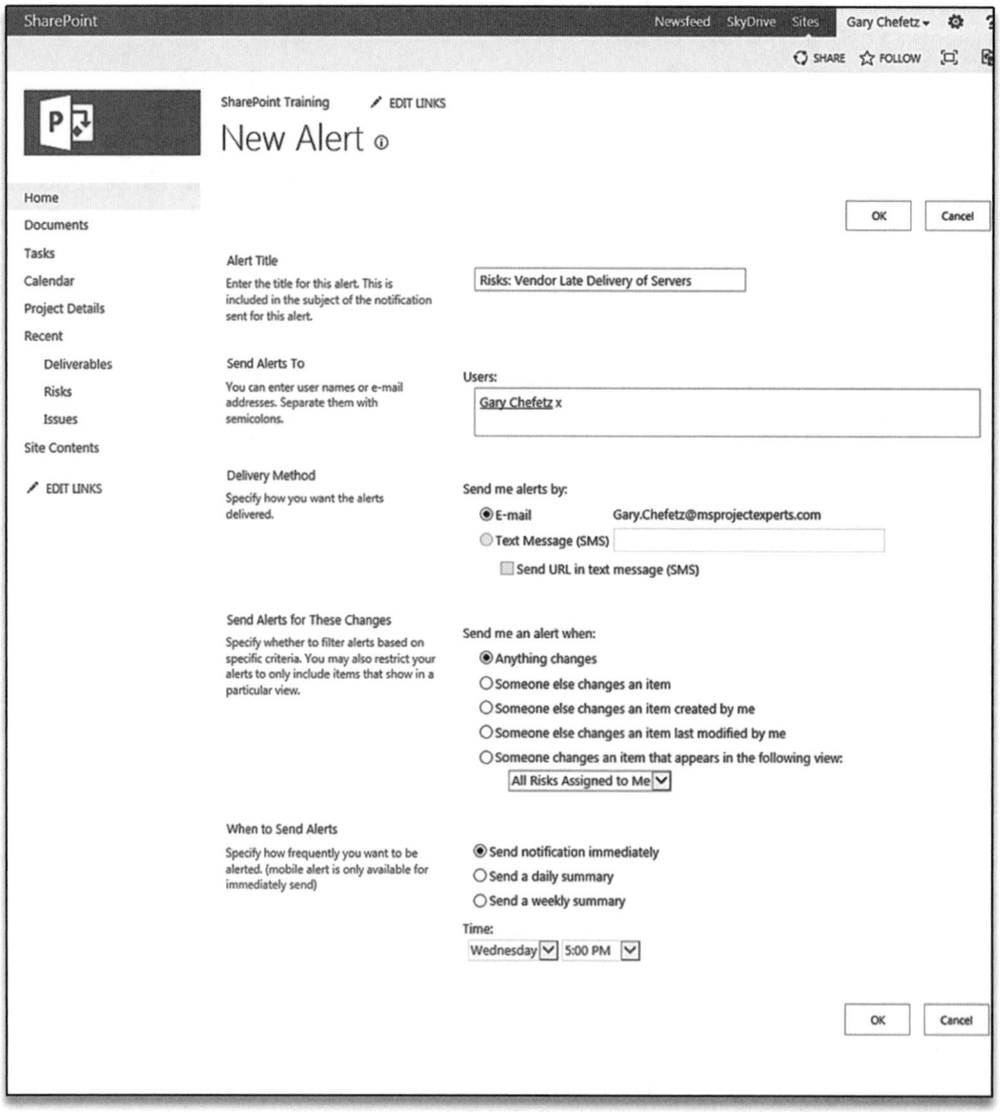

Figure 13 - 10: New Alert dialog

To edit the selected risk, from the *Manage* section of the *View* ribbon, click the *Edit Item* button or select the *Edit Item* option from the pick list menu shown previously in Figure 13 - 8. The system opens the risk for editing in the *Risk* dialog as shown previously in Figure 13 - 2.

Adding Related Items

The process for linking risks and other objects to tasks changes dramatically in Project Server 2013 to more closely follow the SharePoint model. If you want to link the new risk to one or more project objects, with the risk open in *Read Only* mode, scroll to the bottom of the page. To link the new risk to an existing file, click the *ADD RELATED ITEM* link as shown in Figure 13 - 11.

> **Information**: The *ADD RELATED ITEM* link displays only when the item is open to view, not when it is open for editing.

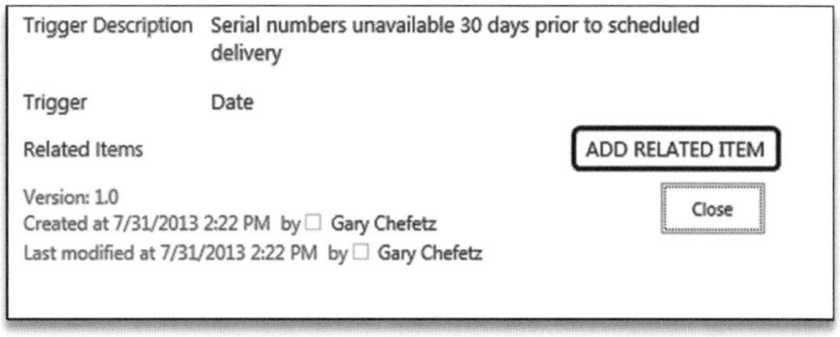

Figure 13 - 11: Add Related Item link

Click the *ADD RELATED ITEM* link and the system displays the *Select an Asset* dialog shown in Figure 13 - 12.

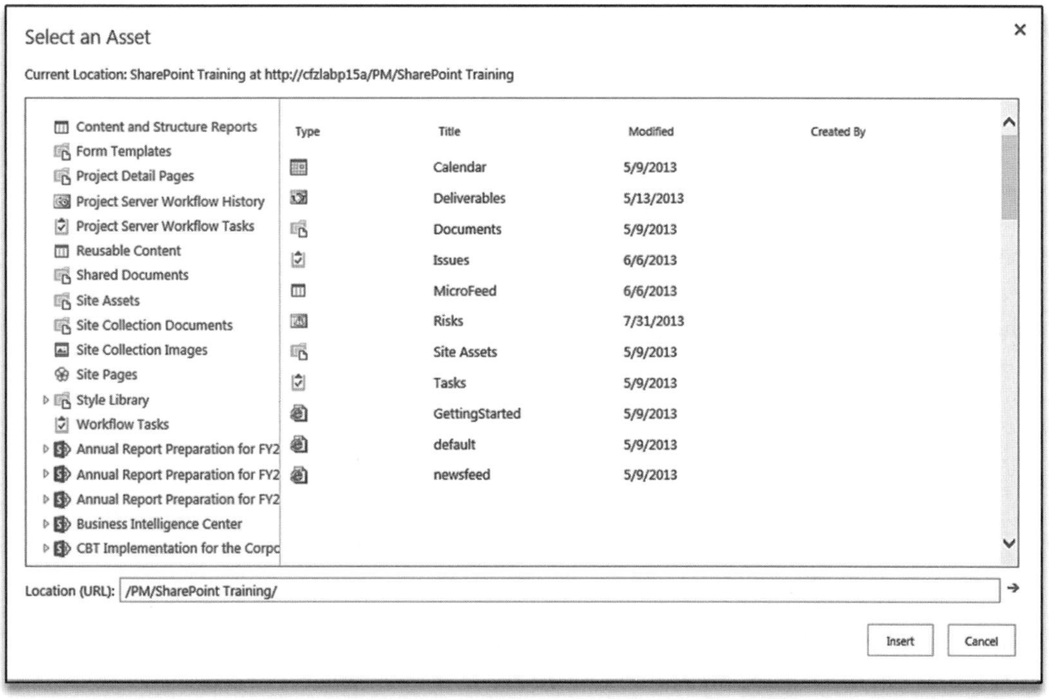

Figure 13 - 12: Select an Asset dialog

Notice in Figure 13 - 12 shown previously, the collapsed tree structure on the left and a main content area on the right. By default, the current Project Site contents display in the main content area. The function of this screen is a bit odd as it only sports one scroll bar. The open folder, in this case, is well down the list of Project Sites displayed on the left so you cannot see it unless you scroll down causing the contents in the content pane to disappear from view. Keep in mind that if you scroll to view more objects on the left, after selecting one, you may need to scroll back to the top of the dialog to see the contents. To link a new [object/issue/risk?] to tasks, for instance, double-click the *Tasks* item in the main content area. The system displays the task list, as shown in Figure 13 - 13.

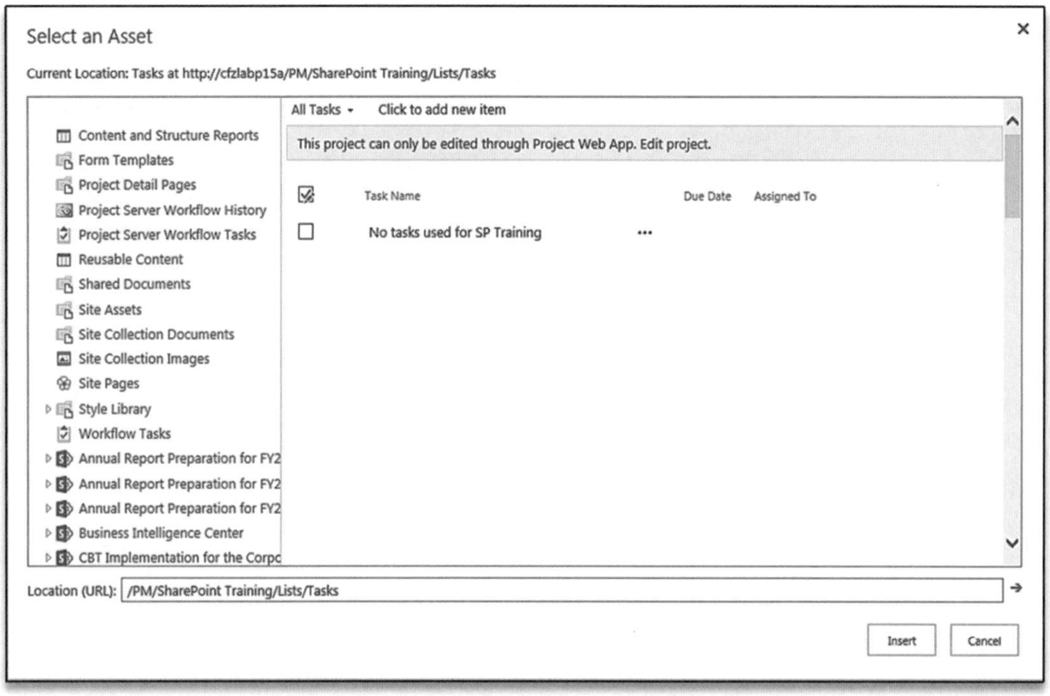

Figure 13 - 13: Select an Asset showing tasks

The *No tasks used for SP Training* item is the name of the only task in the schedule indicating that there are no tasks in the schedule other than this dummy item. To link the risk to this or any other task, select the item by clicking on it, which highlights the task in light green. Note that the checkbox does not display a check when you select the task as you might expect. Notice also that it does write the URL in the *Location (URL):* entry field. Click the *Insert* button to save the new link. The system redisplays the *Risks* page with the new related item information displayed at the bottom as shown in Figure 13 - 14.

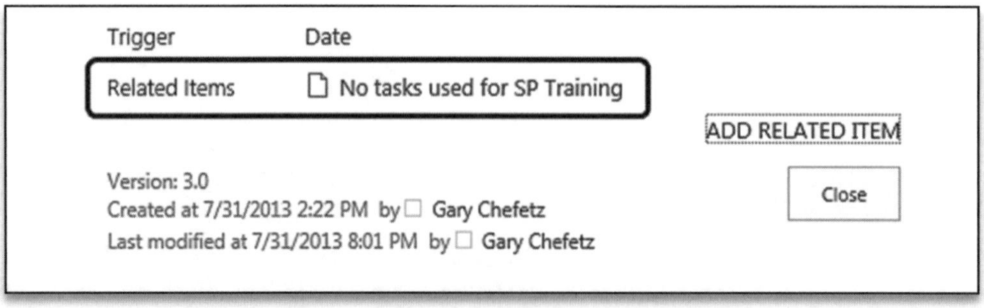

Figure 13 - 14: Related item displayed on Risks page

Deleting a Risk

To delete a risk, from the *Risks* page select the risk you want to delete and click the *Items* tab to display the *Items* ribbon. You can click the *Delete Item* button as shown in Figure 13 - 15, or you may select the *Delete Item* option from the pick list menu shown previously in Figure 13 - 8.

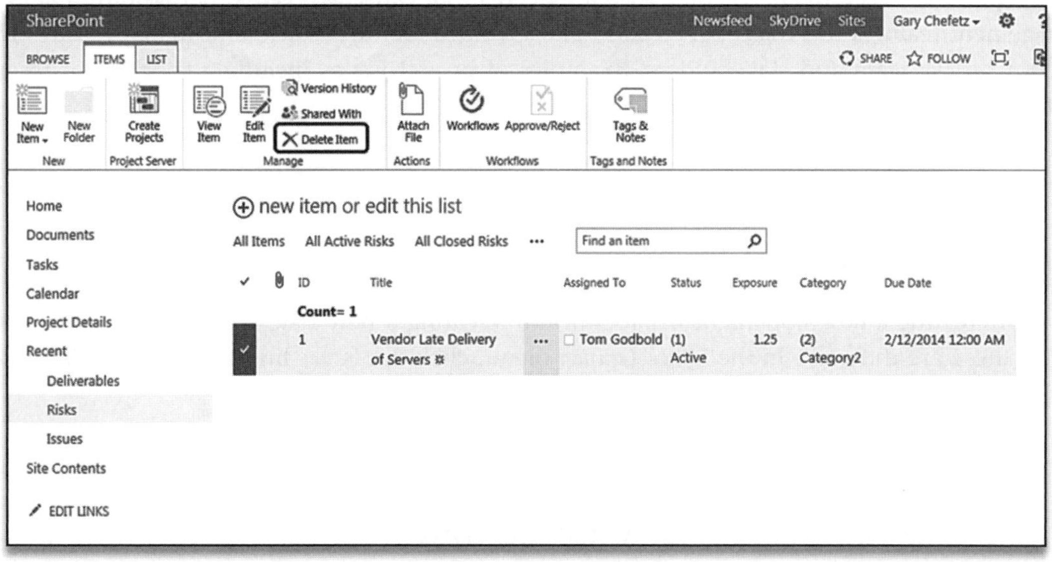

Figure 13 - 15: Delete Risk

If you choose to delete a risk, Project Server 2013 displays the confirmation dialog shown in Figure 13 - 16. Click the *OK* button to delete the risk and send it to the Recycle Bin for the Project Site.

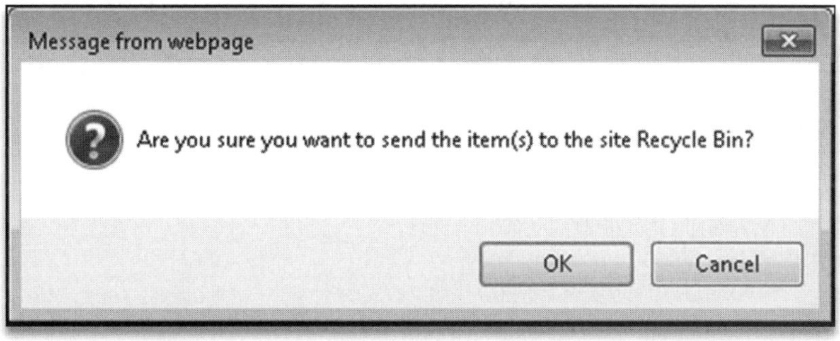

Figure 13 - 16: Confirmation dialog to delete a risk

Restoring a Deleted Risk from the Recycle Bin

When you delete a risk, Project Server 2013 transfers the record to the Recycle Bin for the Project Site. If you accidentally delete a risk, Project Server 2013 allows you to restore it easily. In the *Quick Launch* menu, click the *Recycle Bin* link to begin the restoration process. On the *Recycle Bin* page, select the option checkbox to the left of the item you want to restore, such as the deleted risk, and then click the *Restore Selection* link above the content area.

Information: SharePoint systems also have an administrative Recycle Bin that captures all deletions in the system. Therefore, it may be possible for your system administrator to restore items that you permanently delete from the user Recycle Bin depending upon the retention policies enforced by your organization.

Managing Project Issues

An issue is any type of problem or concern you might experience and need to manage during the life of the project. Another way to think of an issue is to consider it a realized risk. Whether or not you predicted their occurrence through proactive risk management, issues are events that cause problems that require management. The issues management features in Project Server 2013 allow you to identify, track, and manage issues in collaboration with your project team and stakeholders. Examples of project issues include a shortage of resources or an unanticipated hardware upgrade requirement.

Creating a New Issue

The process for creating a new issue is nearly identical to creating a new risk, although the fields in the custom web parts for these are different. In the *Quick Launch* menu, click the *Issues* link of your Project Site and Project Server 2013 displays the *Issues* page, as shown in Figure 13 - 17.

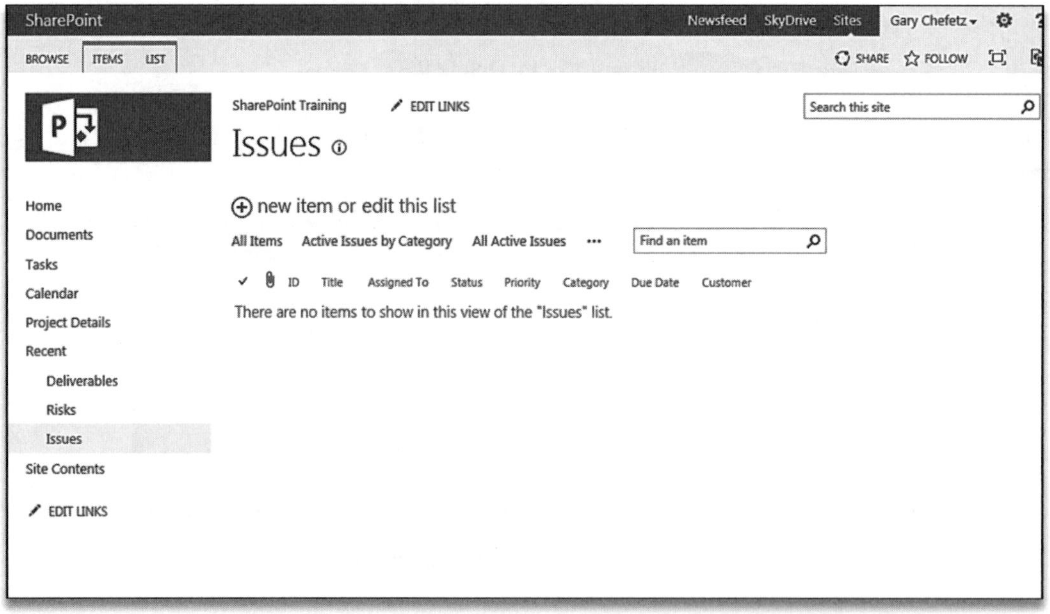

Figure 13 - 17: Issues page for the SharePoint Training project

Click the *New Item* link on the page. The system displays the *New Item* page for issues shown partially in Figure 13 - 18.

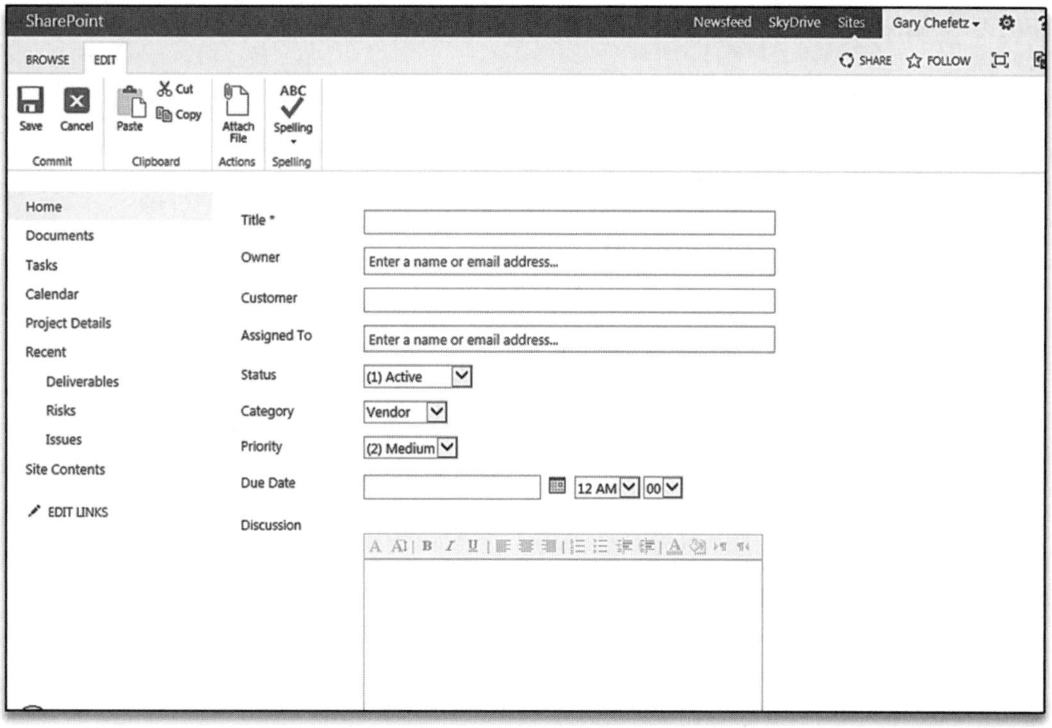

Figure 13 - 18: New Item page for issues (partial)

The *New Item* page for issues contains only two required fields, the *Title* field and the *Status* field. Enter a descriptive name for the issue in the *Title* field. Note that Figure 13 - 18 reflects customizations that I made to the site when writing Module 02, *Task lists, Project Sites and News Feed*. The same caution about the *Status* field for risks applies to the *Status* field for issues. You must not alter the values in this field or you break the display of issue status in Project Web App. Use the same process described in the *Creating a New Risk* topical section of this module to enter data in the *Owner, Assigned To, Status,* and *Category* fields.

Click the *Priority* pick list and select an item from the list. Notice that the system allows you to set the priority of an issue as *High, Medium,* or *Low*. Enter a date in the *Due Date* field. In the *Discussion* field, enter preliminary discussion details to describe the issue, including potential resolutions for the issue. Do not enter any information in the *Resolution* field, unless you already have an idea about ways to resolve the issue. You use the same process described in the *Creating a New Risk* topical section to link your new issue to a file or to other issues, tasks, risks, and documents. Click the *Save* button to save and complete your new issue.

Viewing and Editing Existing Issues

Figure 13 - 19 shows the *Issues* page for my *Deploy Training Advisor Software* project. Notice that there are three active issues associated with the project. Notice also that I customized the values for the *Category* field.

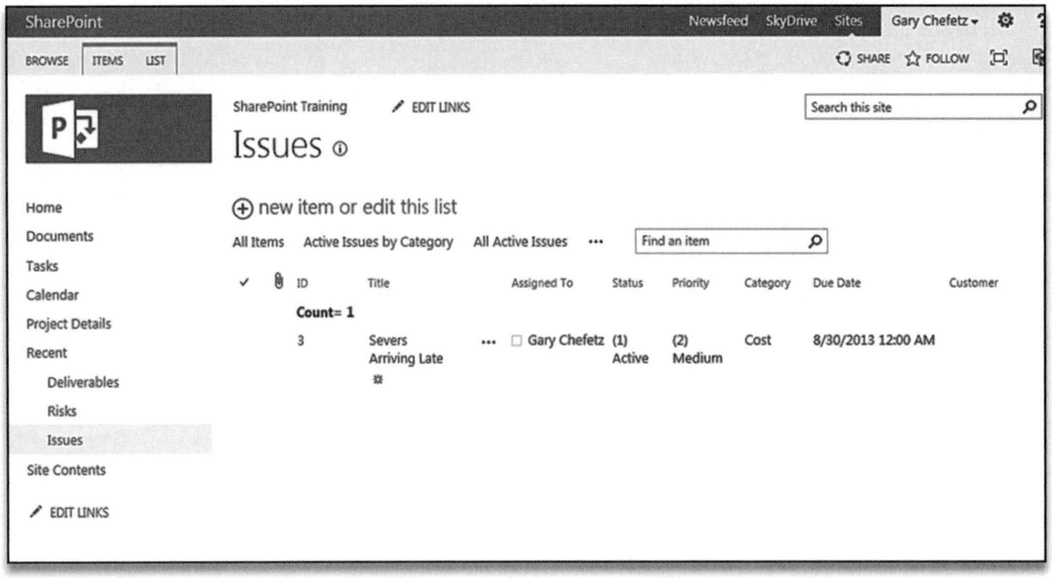

Figure 13 - 19: Issues page for the SharePoint Training project

Similar to risks, the system allows you to do the following with existing issues:

- Apply a view to the *Issues* page
- Sort the issues by the data in any column
- AutoFilter the issues using the data in any column
- View an issue
- Edit an issue
- Delete an issue
- Subscribe to e-mail alerts about changes to an issue

Because I described how to do each of these in the *Working with Existing Risks* topical section of this module, I do not repeat this information here except for editing an existing issue, because you need to know how to close an issue when it is resolved. I also cover viewing issue version history because I did not cover that in the risk topics. To edit an existing issue, click the title of the issue and the system opens the issue in *Read-Only* mode as shown in Figure 13 - 20.

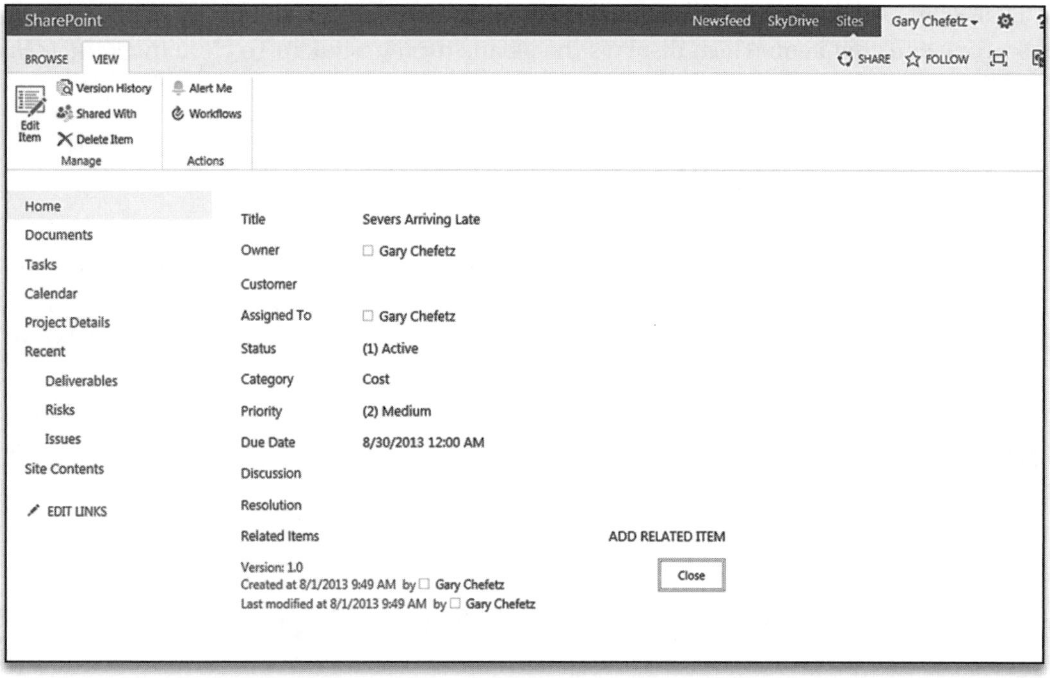

Figure 13 - 20: Issues dialog for a selected issue

In the *Manage* section of the *View* ribbon, click the *Edit Item* button. The system redisplays the page in *Edit* mode. To close the issue, click the *Status* pick list button and then select the *Closed* item from the list. In the *Resolution* field, enter text to describe how you resolved the issue. Click the *Save* button to finish.

Working with Version History

If your issues list, or any SharePoint list you may work with, has version control enabled, the system automatically creates a new version of list items each time someone edits them. To view the item history for a list item, click the ellipsis (…) next to the title and select the *Version History* item. The system displays the *Version History* dialog shown in Figure 13 - 21.

Figure 13 - 21: Version History dialog for a list item

Notice that the system creates a version record when you first create the item and then creates a version record every time someone edits the item, which displays the details for the version. To close the *Version History* dialog, click the *Close* (**X**) button.

Viewing Your Assigned Issues and Risks

Project Server 2013 offers you a quick way to view and manage the risks and issues assigned to you. Navigate to any page in Project Web App that displays the *Quick Launch* menu, and then click the *Issues and Risks* link. The system displays the *Issues and Risks* page, shown in Figure 13 - 22. The page displays issues and risks assigned to me.

Warning: The *Issues and Risks* page does not display on the *Quick Launch* menu by default. You or a Project Server administrator must set this item to display.

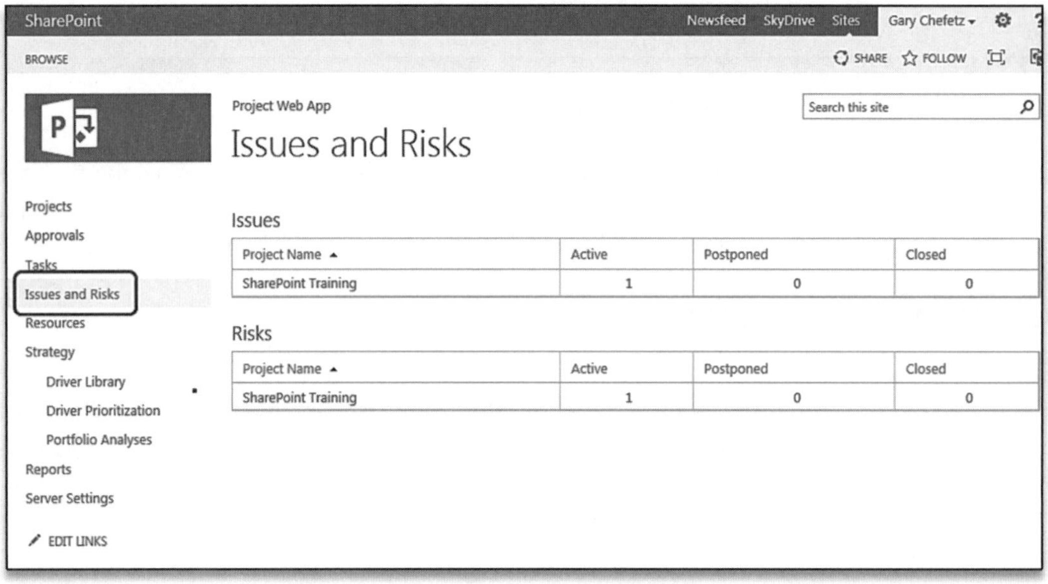

Figure 13 - 22: Issues and Risks page

To access either the *Risks* page or the *Issues* page for one of the listed projects, click the project name in the *Issues* or *Risks* section of the page. Project Server 2013 displays the *Risks* or *Issues* page for the selected project applying the *All Risks Assigned to Me* view.

Module 14

Working with Status Reports

Learning Objectives

After completing this module, you will be able to:

- Create and send a new status report request
- Edit and delete a status report
- Respond to a status report request
- Submit an unrequested status report
- View the status report archive
- View status report responses
- View unrequested status reports

Inside Module 14

Requesting a Status Report

Not only does Project Server 2013 provide time and task tracking, the system also allows managers to capture text-based information from resources using status reports. You can use the status reports feature to create periodic status reports due on a regular basis from specific resources or to request a one-time status report. To create a new *Status Report* request, click the *Status Reports* link in either the *Quick Launch* menu or the main content area of the *Home* page in Project Web App. The system displays the *Status Reports* page shown in Figure 14 - 1.

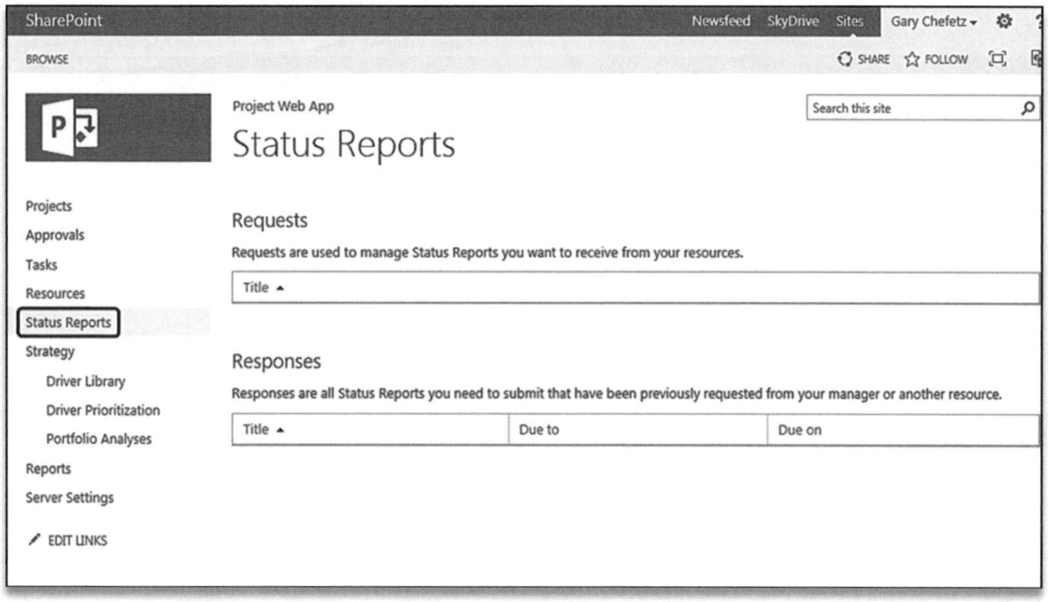

Figure 14 - 1: Status Reports page

Information: The *Request a Status Report* feature is dependent on permissions granted in groups in Project Web App. By default, this feature is available only to members of the following groups: Executives, Portfolio Managers, Project Managers, Resource Managers, Team Leads, and Administrators.

The *Status Reports* page includes two sections. Use the options in the *Requests* section to create and manage *Status Report* requests. Use the options in the *Responses* section to view and work with *Status Report* responses from your resources.

Warning: The *Status Reports* link does not display on the *Quick Launch* menu by default. Either you or a Project Server administrator must display the link before you can use it.

To create a new *Status Report* request, click into the data area in the *Requests* section to display the *Status Report Requests* ribbon shown in Figure 14 - 2.

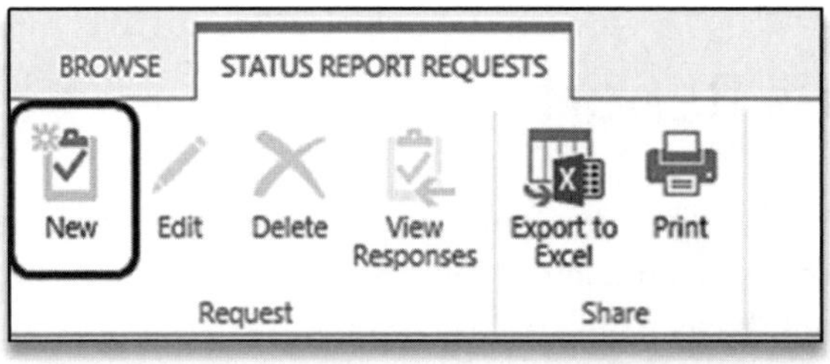

Figure 14 - 2: Status Report Requests ribbon

In the *Request* section, click the *New* button. Project Server 2013 displays the *Status Report Request* page shown in Figure 14 - 3.

Figure 14 - 3: Status Report Request page

On the *Status Report Request* page, enter a descriptive name for the *Status Report* request in the *Title* field. In the *Frequency* section, select the appropriate options to set the recurrence for the *Status Report* request. The system offers you a wide variety of options for setting a recurrence pattern, such as weekly, monthly, and yearly. Using the available options in the *Frequency* section, you can even create recurrences such as bi-weekly or quarterly. Click the *Start* pick list and select the *Start* date for the first reporting period.

Warning: Project Server 2013 does not allow you to select a *Start* date earlier than the current date. This means that you cannot create a monthly report in the middle of the month and set the *Start* date to the first day of the month!

In the *Available Resources* list, select the resources that must respond to your *Status Report* request and then click the *Add* button. Next, you set up the topical sections for the status report in the *Sections* part of the page. By default, the system offers three standard topical sections: *Major Accomplishments, Objectives for the Next Period*, and *Hot Issues*. You can delete, reorder, rename, add additional topical sections, add descriptions, or simply accept the default topical sections listed on the *Status Report Request* page.

When you complete your new *Status Report* request, click the *Send* button. Project Server 2013 sends an e-mail message to each resource, notifying them of the new *Status Report* request. The system displays your new *Status Report* request in the *Requests* section of the *Status Reports* page. Notice in Figure 14 - 4 that I created a monthly *Status Report Request* for members of the Training team. Notice also that I included myself, *Gary Chefetz*, in the respondents list, so this new *Status Report* request displays in the *Responses* section as well.

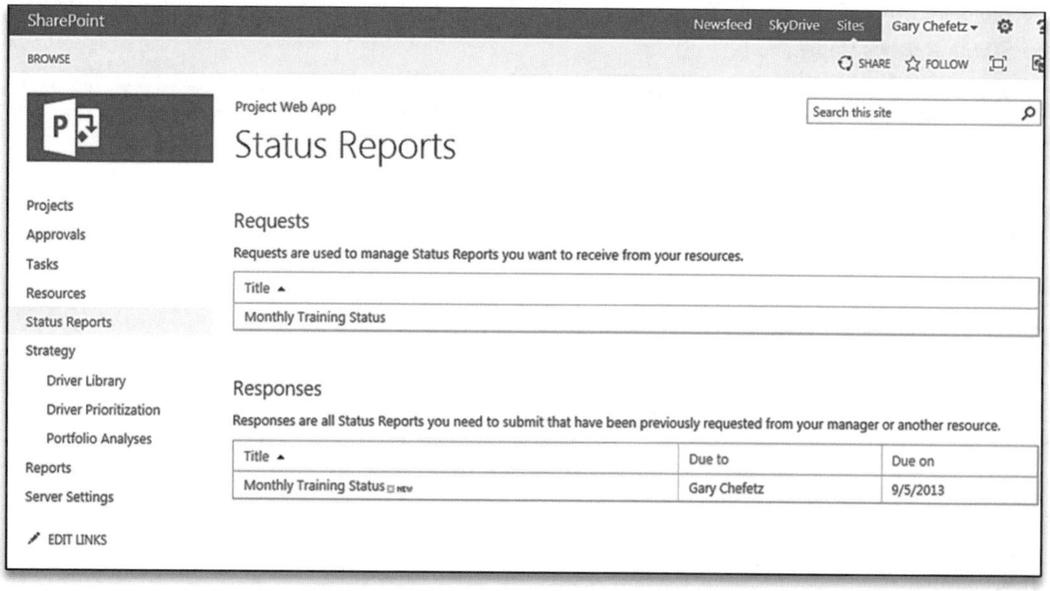

Figure 14 - 4: New Status Report request on the Status Reports page

Editing and Deleting Status Reports

To edit an existing status report, navigate to the *Status Reports* page. Click the row for the *Status Report* request that you want to edit without clicking the title link and then from the *Request* section of the ribbon, shown previously in Figure 14 - 2, click the *Edit* button. The system displays the *Status Report Request* page shown previously in Figure 14 - 3. Edit the information as you determine necessary and then click the *Send* button.

To delete a *Status Report* request, click the row for the *Status Report* request you want to delete and then from the *Request* section of the ribbon, click the *Delete* button. Project Server 2013 displays the confirmation dialog shown in Figure 14 - 5. In the confirmation dialog, click the *OK* button to complete the deletion.

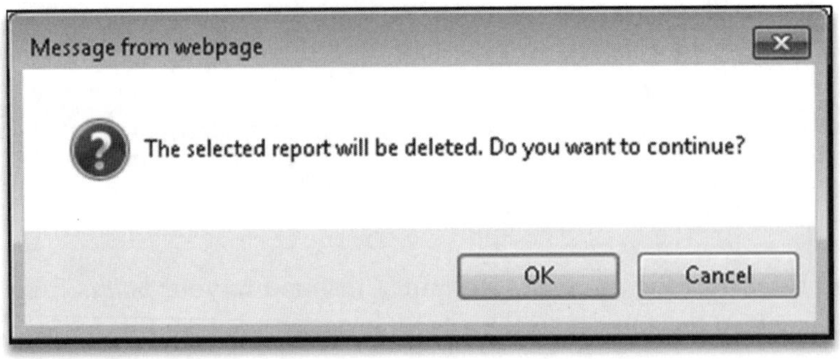

Figure 14 - 5: Delete a Status Report request confirmation

Responding to a Status Report Request

As I mentioned earlier in this module, when a manager sends a *Status Report* request, Project Server 2013 sends an e-mail message to each resource included in the *Status Report* request. Resources can see the *Status Report* request by clicking the *Status Reports* link in either the *Quick Launch* menu. The system displays the new *Status Report* request in the *Responses* area of the *Status Reports* page. For example, Figure 14 - 6 shows the *Monthly Training* status report on the *Status Reports* page.

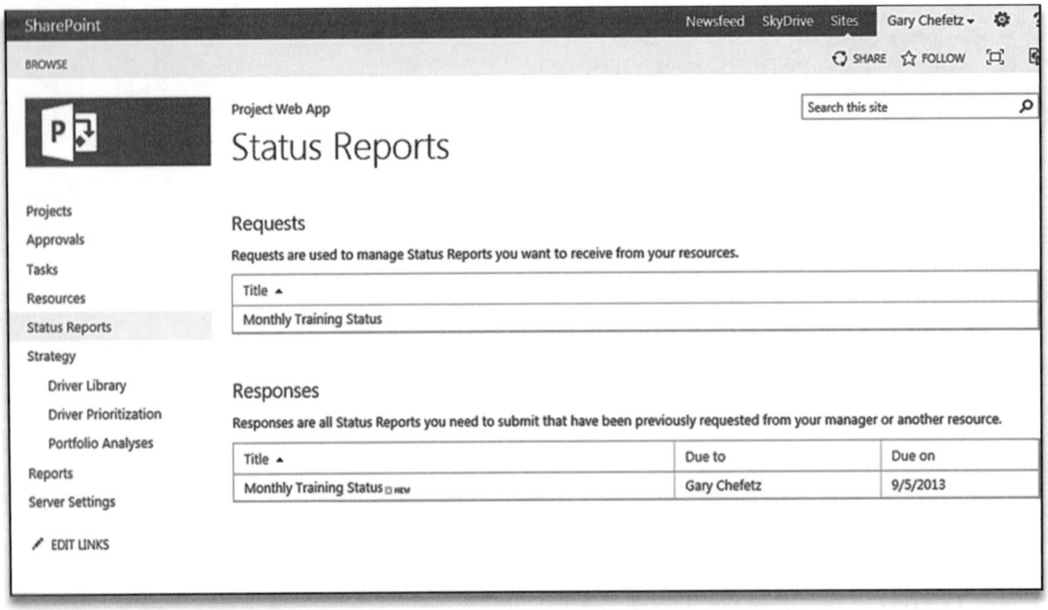

Figure 14 - 6: Status Reports page shows a new Status Report request

On the *Status Reports* page, resources may see multiple *Status Report* requests created by different managers. To respond to a *Status Report* request; click the link for the status report to which you want to respond. Project Server 2013 displays the *Status Report Response* page shown in Figure 14 - 7.

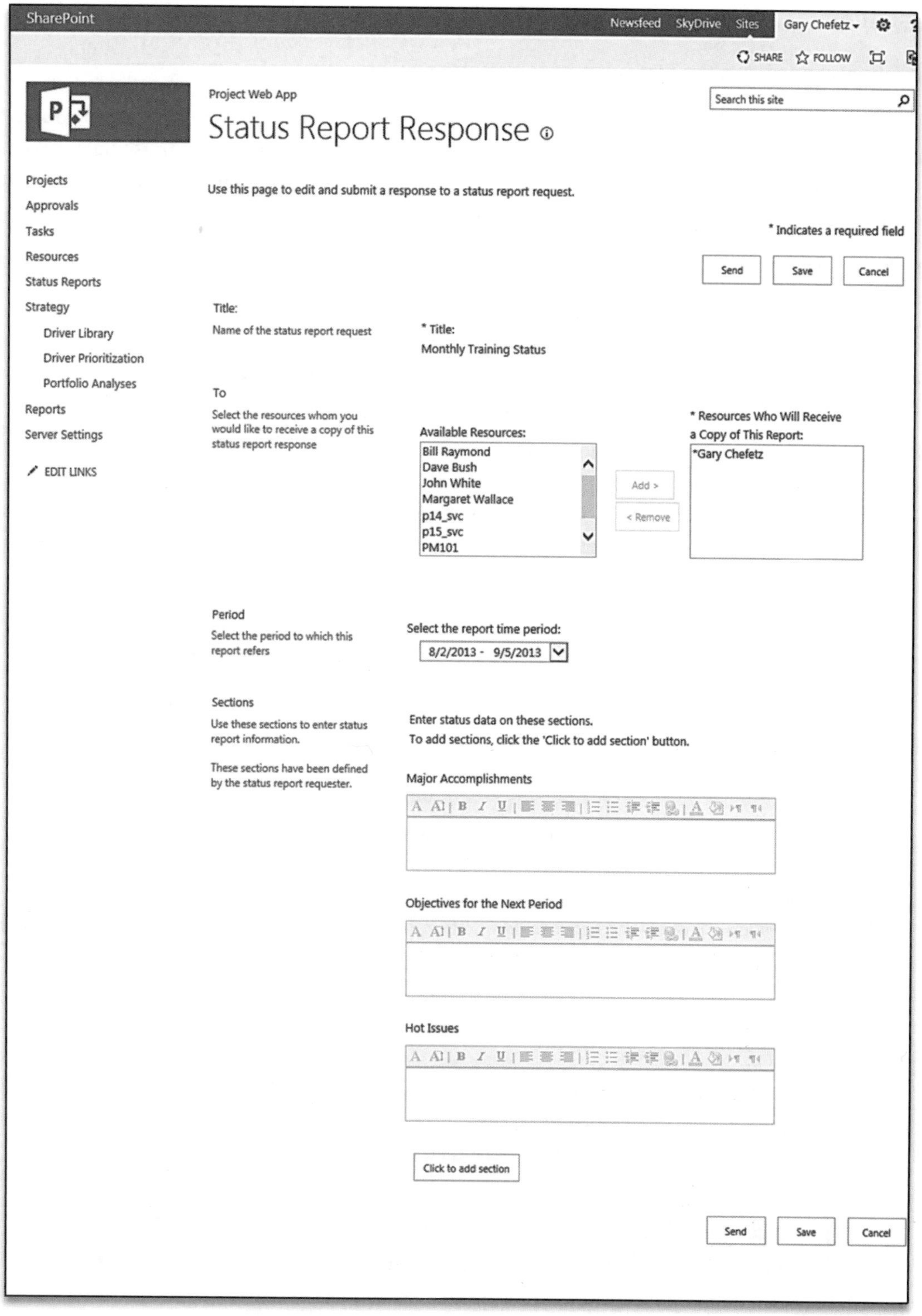

Figure 14 - 7: Status Report Response page

The *Status Report Response* page includes four information sections:

- The *Title* section shows the *Status Report* request name.
- The *To* section shows the *Available Resources* field where you select the name(s) of the resource(s) who you want to respond to the *Status Report* request. You click the *Add* button to add these names to the *Resources Who Will Receive a Copy of This Report* field. This field also shows the name of the *Status Report* requestor, as indicated by an asterisk character (*) to the left of the manager's name.
- The *Period* section allows you to select the period to which the report refers. Click the *Select the report time period* pick list and select the time period to which you want to respond.
- The *Sections* section contains the topical sections chosen by the manager who created the *Status Report* request. Notice in Figure 14 - 7 shown previously that the *Status Report* request image shows: *Major Accomplishments, Objectives for the Next Period,* and *Hot Issues.*

To enter information into any of the topical sections, click anywhere in the text field for the topic. Project Server 2013 activates the toolbar at the top of the text field giving you extensive formatting capabilities. For example, Figure 14 - 8 shows the activated toolbar for the *Major Accomplishments* field. Notice that the toolbar gives you text-formatting options such as font size, font style, alignment, and numbered or bulleted lists.

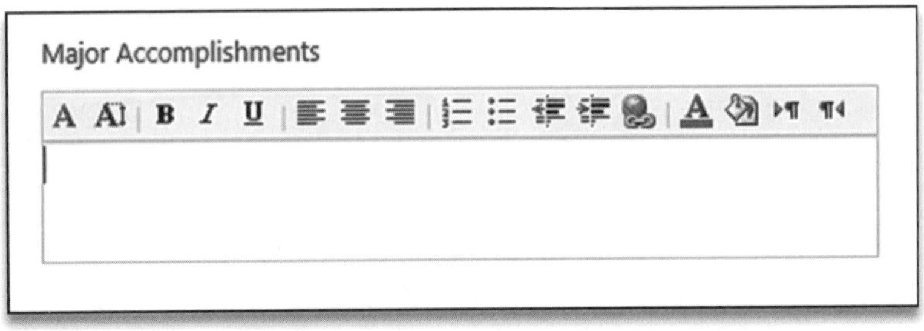
Major Accomplishments

Figure 14 - 8: Activated toolbar for Major Accomplishments field

In each of the topical sections, enter information required to complete the *Status Report* response. If you need to add an additional topical section, click the *Click to add section* button at the bottom of the page as shown previously in Figure 14 - 7. The system displays the *Section Name* dialog shown in Figure 14 - 9.

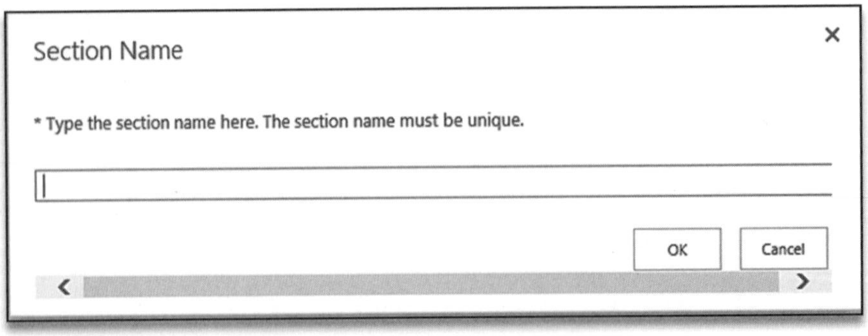
Section Name
* Type the section name here. The section name must be unique.
OK
Cancel

Figure 14 - 9: Section Name dialog

In the dialog, enter a unique name for the new section in the text field and then click the *OK* button. Enter additional information in the new topical section, as you require.

Information: If you create a topical section that you no longer need, click the *Delete this section* button in the upper right corner of the section. You can delete any section that you add; however, you cannot delete a section added by the requestor.

When you finish entering information in the topical sections, Project Server 2013 offers you two options:

- *Save the Status Report* response for additional editing and later submission.
- *Send the Status Report* response immediately.

If you are working on an in-progress *Status Report* response and are not ready to send it to your manager, click the *Save* button. The system saves the *Status Report* response in your *Status Report Archive,* where you can edit it and send it at a later time. Project Server 2013 displays the *Status Report Archive* page with the saved *Status Report* response. For example, Figure 14 - 10 shows a *Status Report* response saved on August 1.

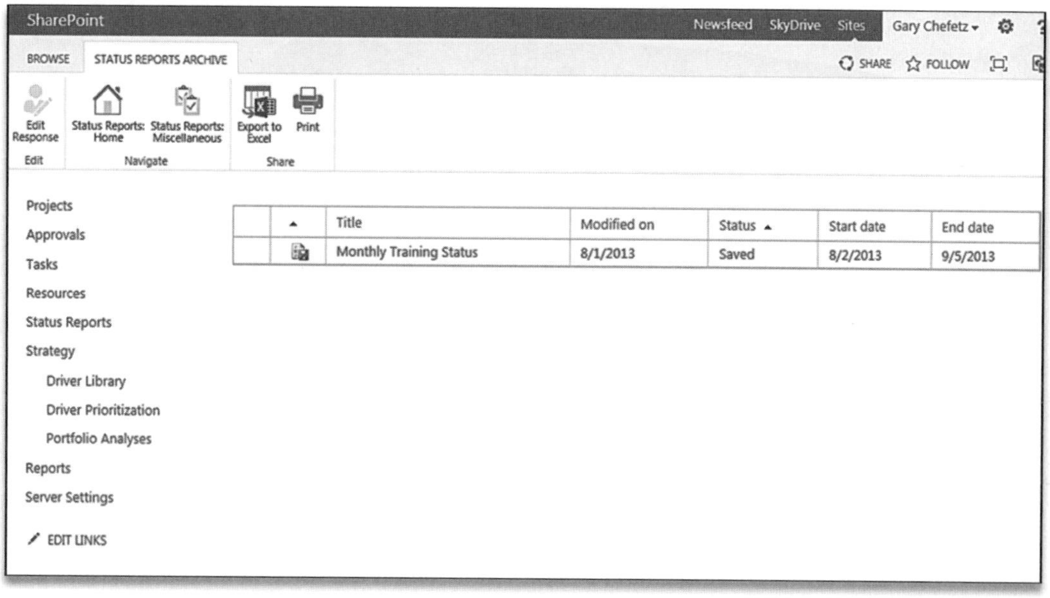

Figure 14 - 10: Status Report Archive page with saved Status Report response

Information: To update an in-progress *Status Report* response, navigate to the *Status Reports* page, click into the *Response* data area and in the *Navigate* section, click the *Status Reports Archive* button. Click the name of the *Status Report* response you want to update, and then update it, save it, or send it.

If you are ready to submit the *Status Report* response to your manager, click the *Send* button. The system saves the *Status Report* response in your *Status Report Archive* and sends your manager an e-mail message notifying her of your *Status Report* response.

Submitting an Unrequested Status Report

You can create and send an ad hoc status report without a manager request. To submit an unrequested status report, navigate to the *Status Reports* page, click into the *Responses* section, and from the *Submit* section of the ribbon, click the *Unrequested Report* button. Project Server 2013 displays the *Unrequested Status Report* page shown in Figure 14 - 11.

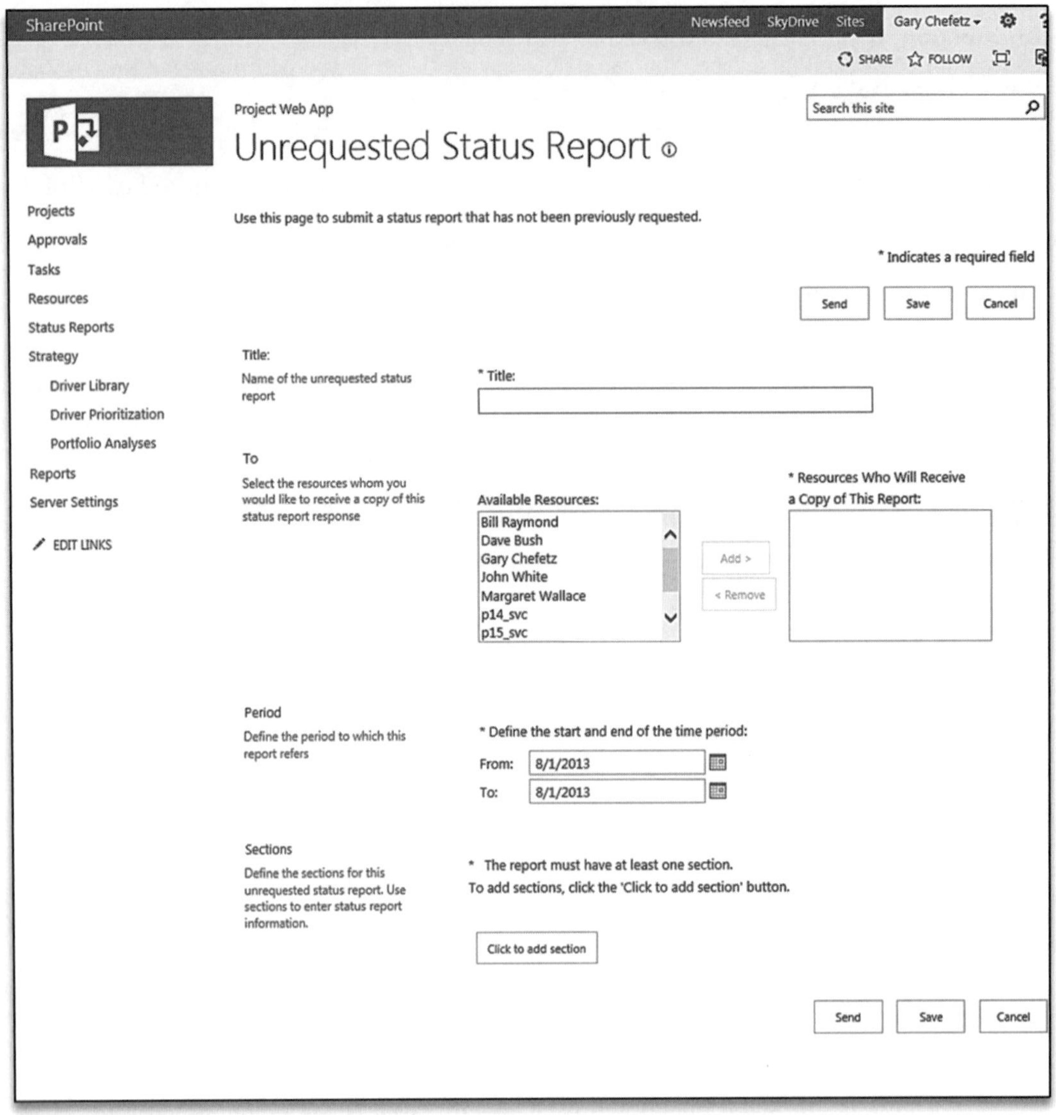

Figure 14 - 11: Unrequested Status Report page

To create the unrequested status report, enter the name of your status report in the *Title* field. In the *Available Resources* list, select the resources to which you want to send the unrequested status report and then click the *Add* button. In the *Period* section of the page, enter dates in the *From* and *To* fields to indicate the period for your report. Click the *Click to add section* button, enter a name for the topical section in the dialog, and then click the *OK* button. Enter data in the topical section and add additional topical sections until you complete your report and then click the *Send* button. The system adds your new unrequested status report to the *Status Report Archive*.

Viewing the Status Report Archive

The *Status Report Archive* page gives you access to your saved status reports and any previously submitted status reports. To access the *Status Report Archive* page, navigate to the *Status Reports* page, click into the *Response* data area, and from the *Navigate* section of the ribbon, click the button in the *Responses* section, and then click the *Status Reports: Archive* button. Project Server 2013 displays the *Status Reports Archive* page shown in Figure 14 - 12.

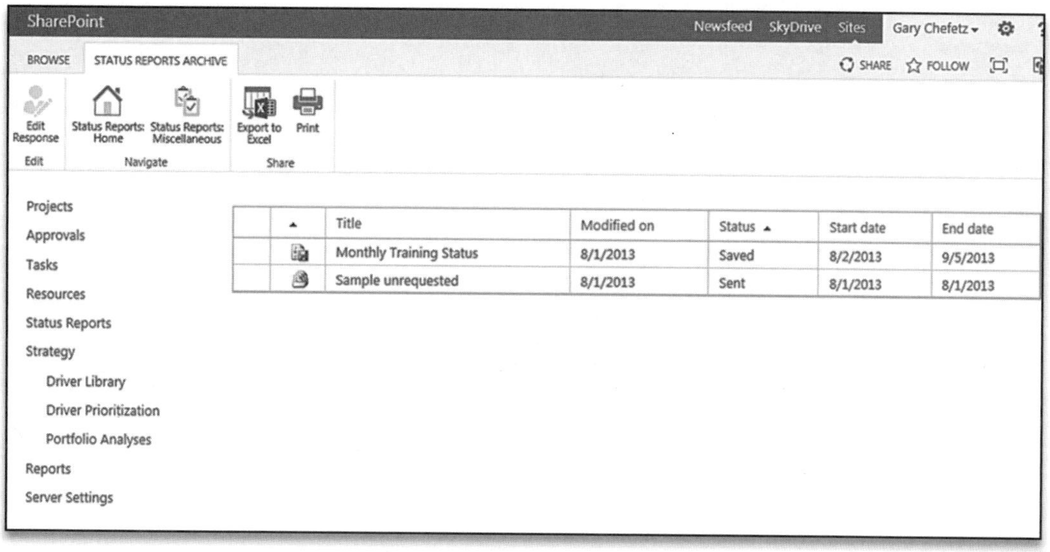

Figure 14 - 12: Status Report Archive page

Notice in Figure 14 - 12 that I submitted a monthly status report and one *Unrequested* status report. To edit an in-progress or previously submitted *Status Report* response, click the title of the status report you want to edit. Project Server 2013 displays the *Unrequested Status Report* page because I selected an unrequested status report in the archive as shown in Figure 14 - 13.

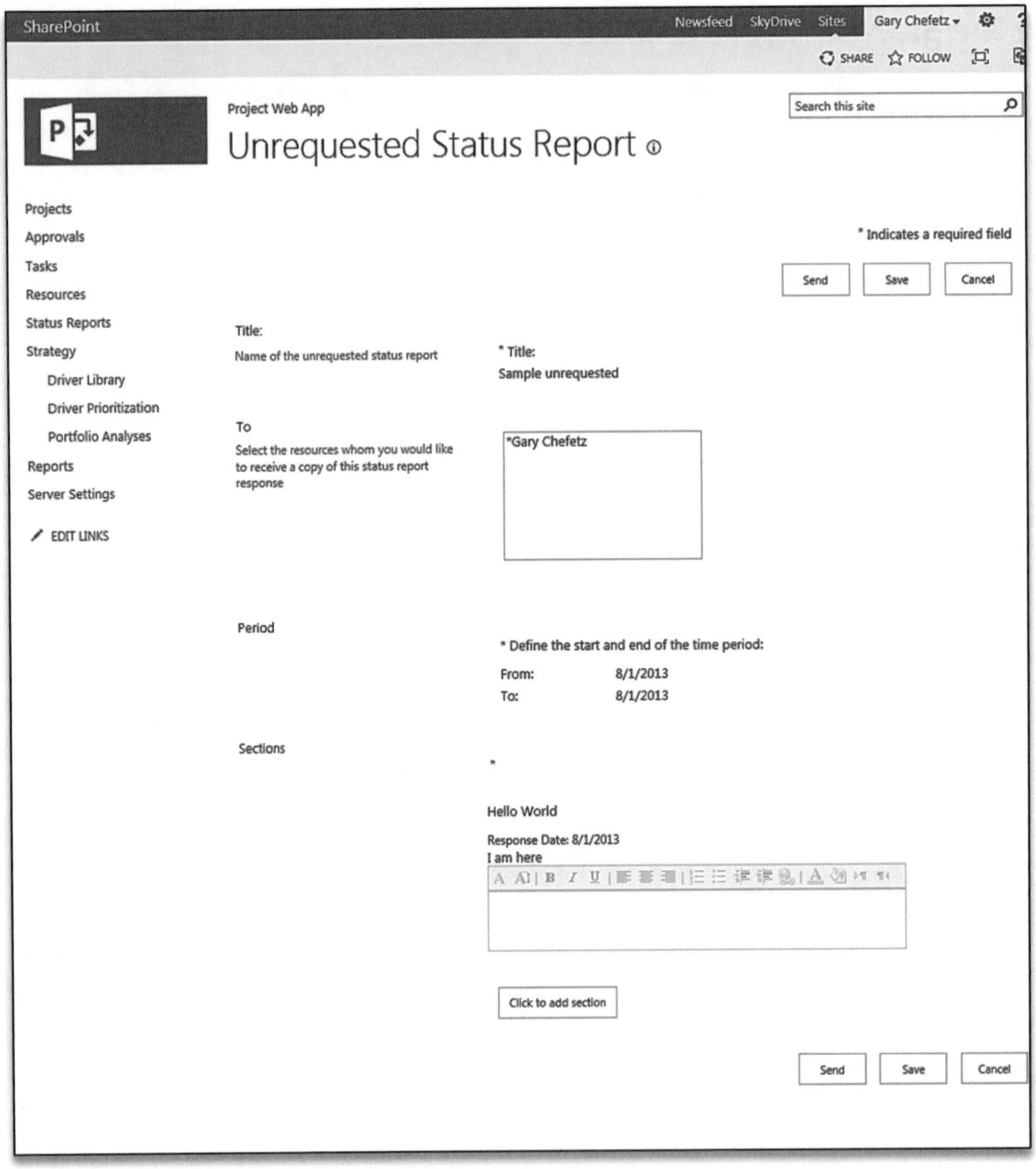

Figure 14 - 13: Unrequested Status Report page ready for editing

Because I previously submitted this *Unrequested Status Report* response shown in Figure 14 - 13, notice how the system makes read-only the information in the *To* and *Period* sections, as well as the text previously entered in each of the topical sections. Enter additional information in any of the topical sections and then click the *Send* button to send the *Status Report* response to your manager.

Viewing Status Report Responses

When a resource sends you a *Status Report* response, Project Server 2013 automatically alerts you with an e-mail message. To view the *Status Report* responses from your resources, navigate to the *Status Reports* page and in the *Requests* section of the page, click the name of the status report you want to view. The system displays the *View Responses* page for the selected status report. Figure 14 - 14 shows the *View Responses* page for my *Monthly Training Status* report.

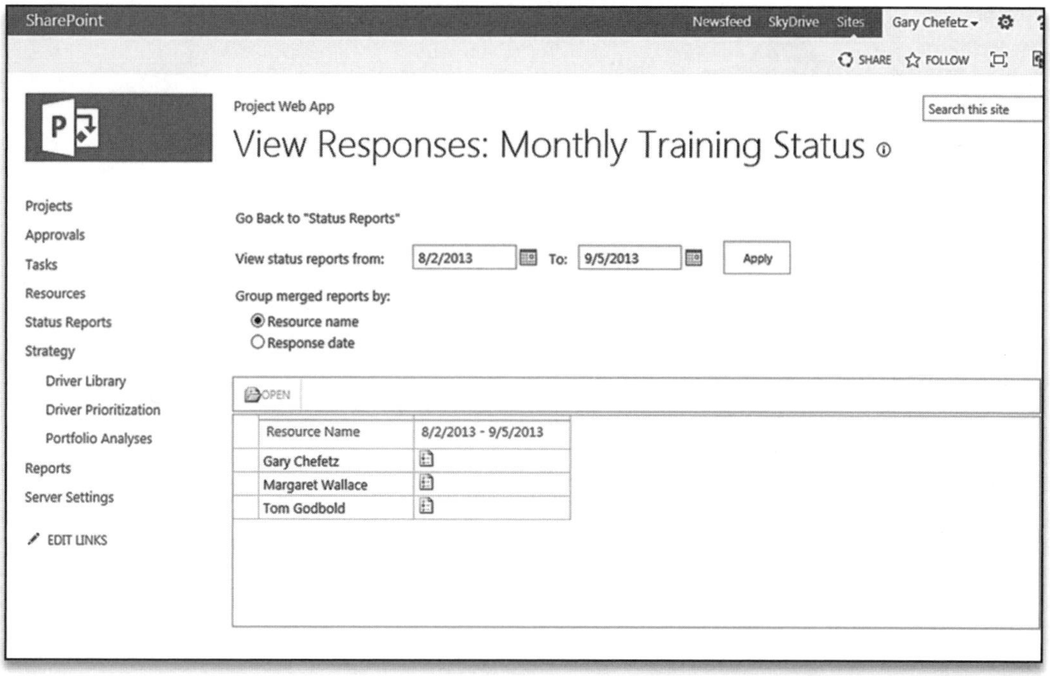

Figure 14 - 14: View Responses page for the Monthly Training Status report

The options at the top of the *View Responses* page allow you to view *Status Report* responses for specific reporting periods and to group the responses into a merged report. By default, the *View Responses* page shows the *Status Report* responses for each reporting period, with columns representing the current reporting period and all past periods. To display status responses for specific reporting periods, select the date range you want in the *From* and *To* fields and then click the *Apply* button.

If you select all of the cells, Project Server 2013 merges all selected *Status Report* responses into a merged team status report for each reporting period. The *Group merged reports by* option allows you to group by *Resource name* or *Response date.* Select the *Resource name* option to display the responses grouped by the name of each resource. Select the *Response date* option to display the responses grouped by the date each resource sent the response.

To view an individual *Status Report* response, click the cell to the left of the name of the person whose response you want to see and then click the *Open* button. To view the merged team *Status Report* response, select the names of all response cells and then click the *Open* button. The system displays the *Status Report Responses* page for the selected status report. Figure 14 - 15 shows the *Status Report Responses* page for the *Monthly Training Status* report, grouped by resource name.

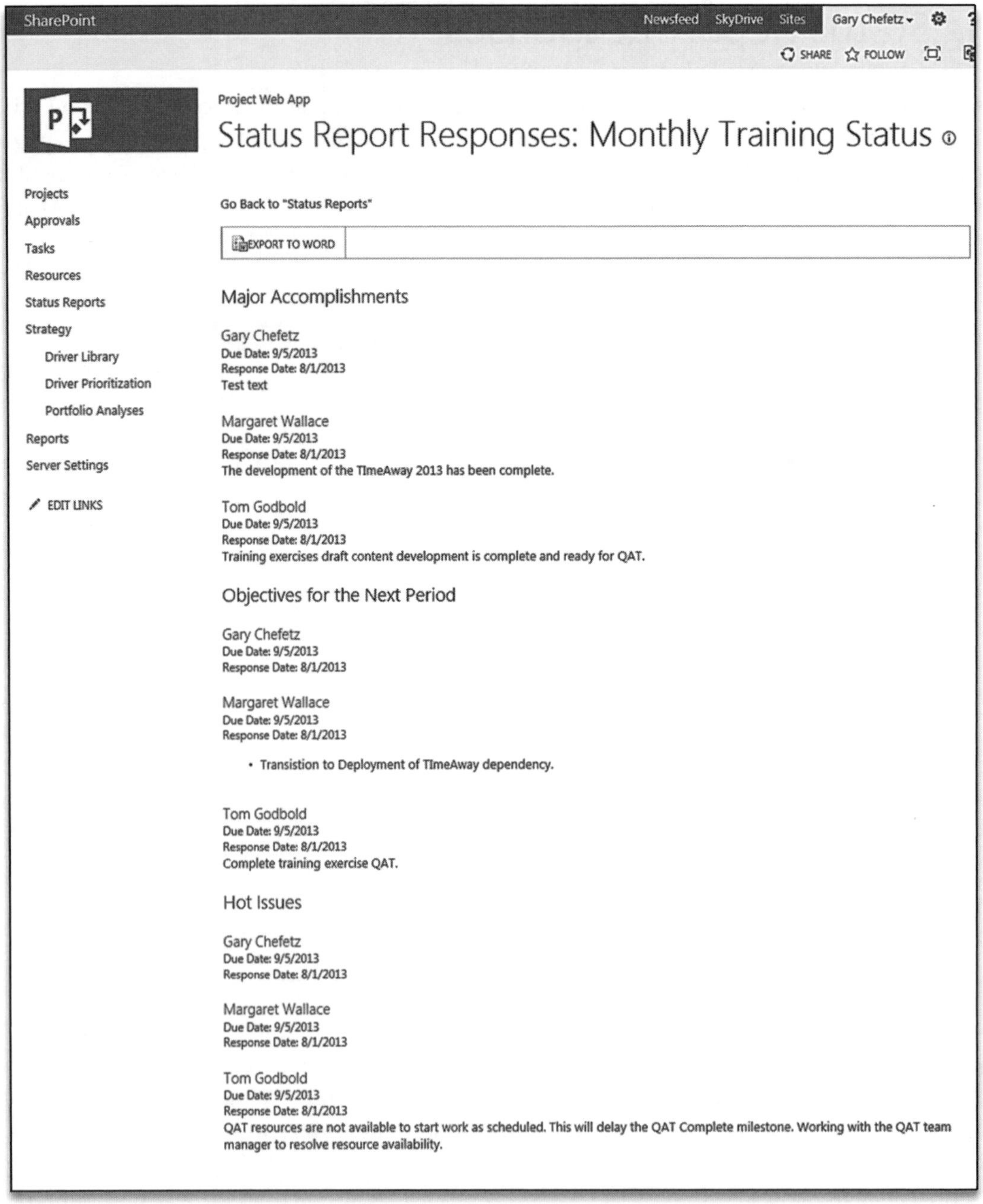

Figure 14 - 15: Status Report Responses page grouped by resource name

Beyond reading the responses on the *Status Report Responses* page, Project Server 2013 offers you one additional option; you can export the merged team status report to Microsoft Word. Click the *Export to Word* button shown previously in Figure 14 - 15 and the system displays the *File Download* warning dialog shown in Figure 14 - 16.

Best Practice: If the merged team status report is associated with a particular project, MsProjectExperts recommends that you upload the saved copy of the merged team status report to the document library for that project. This allows you to share the status reports with the team and with other stakeholders.

Figure 14 - 16: File Download warning

Click the *Save* button to save the Word document on your local computer or click the *Open* button in the dialog and the system opens Microsoft Word with the merged team status report in a new document. Figure 14 - 17 shows the Microsoft Word application with the top part of the merged team status report.

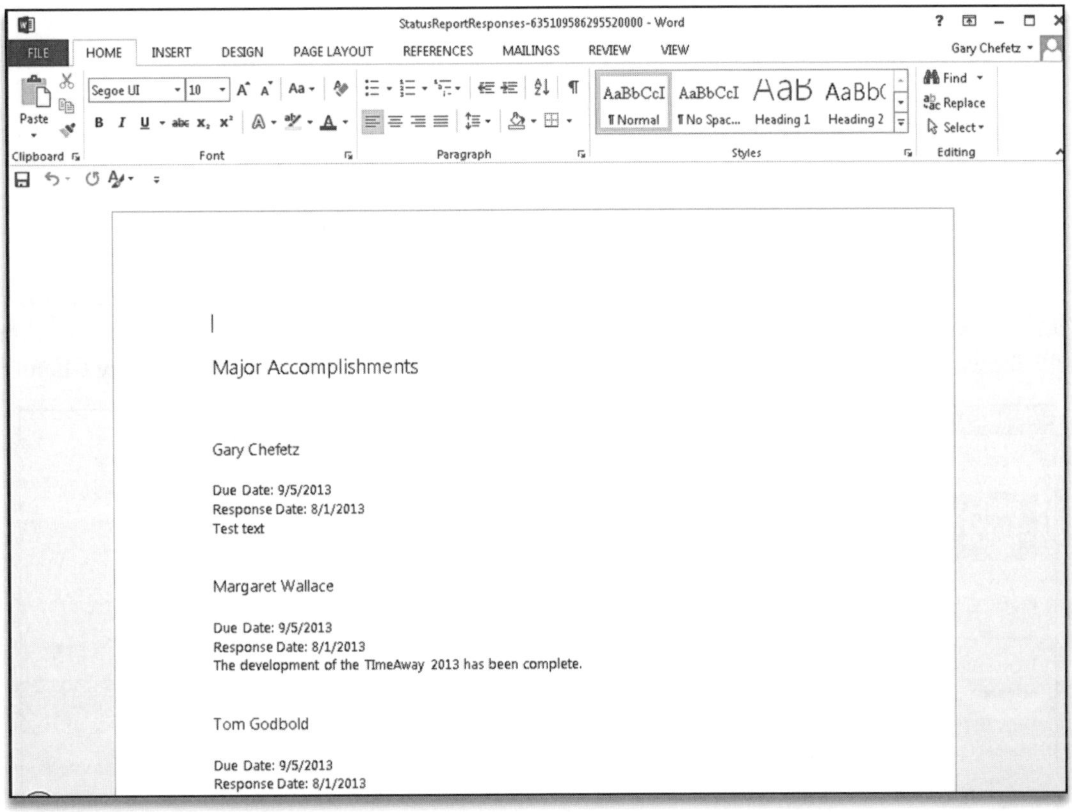

Figure 14 - 17: Merged team status report in Microsoft Word 2010

From the Microsoft Word application, you can edit the merged team status report document and then save it. After saving it, you can e-mail the document to your manager or upload the document to the document library of a related project for further sharing.

Viewing Unrequested Status Reports

Resources may occasionally send you an unrequested status report, or may include you as an additional recipient of a *Status Report* response to another manager. To view either of these types of status reports, navigate to the *Status Reports* page, click into the *Responses* data area to display the ribbon, and from the *Navigate* section, click the *Status Reports: Miscellaneous* button. Project Server 2013 displays the *Miscellaneous Status Reports* page shown in Figure 14 - 18.

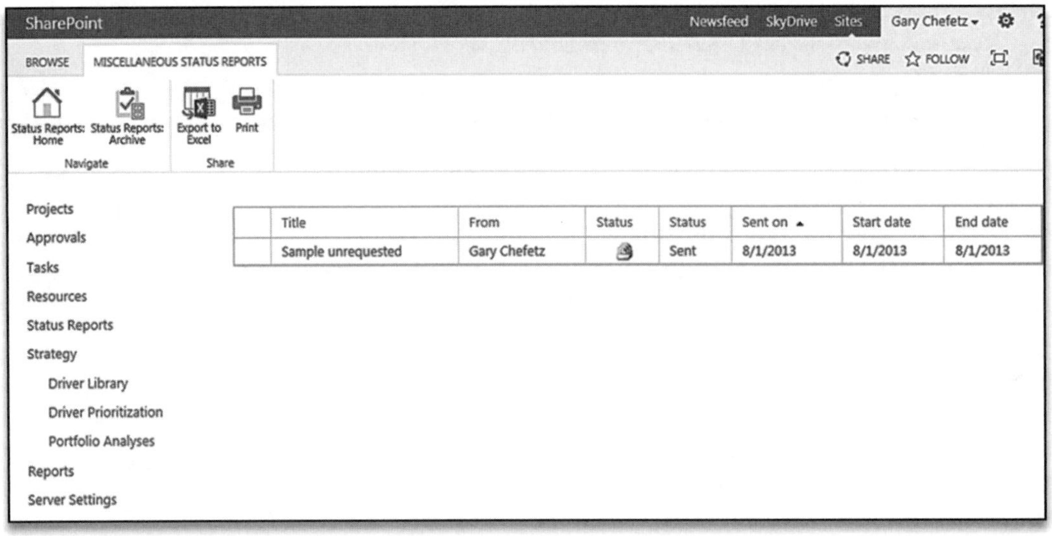

Figure 14 - 18: Miscellaneous Status Reports page

To view an *Unrequested* status report or a copy of a *Status Report* response, click the name of the status report you want to view. Project Server 2013 displays the *Status Report Responses* page for the selected status report. Figure 14 - 19 shows the *Status Report Responses* page for the *Hello World* status report from Gary Chefetz.

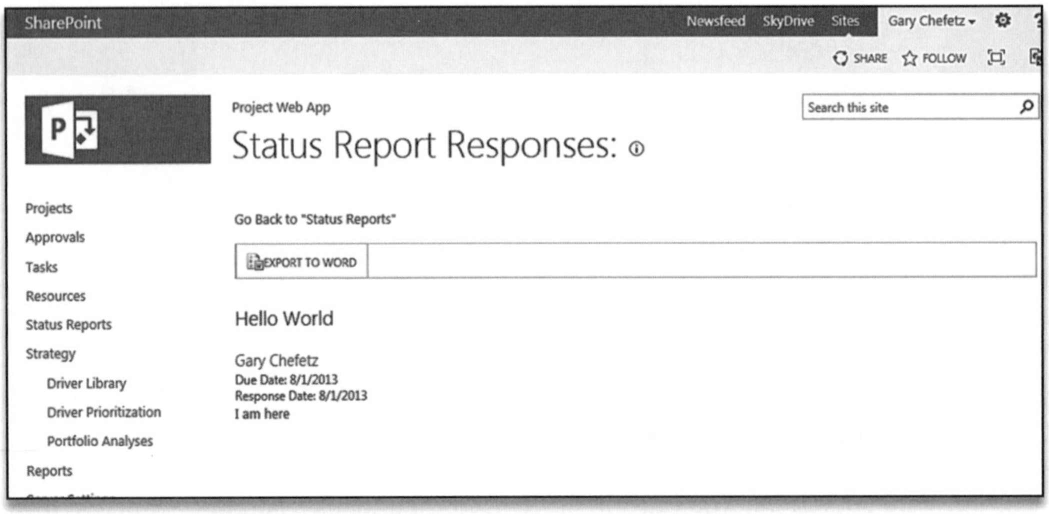

Figure 14 - 19: Status Report Responses page from Gary Chefetz

As with individual or merged team status reports, you can export the status report to Microsoft Word by clicking the *Export to Word* button shown previously in Figure 14 - 19. Click the *Go Back to "Status Reports"* link to return to the *Status Reports* page.

Warning: When you click the *Go Back to "Status Reports"* link, the system returns to the *Status Reports* page rather than the *Miscellaneous Status Reports* page. The only way to return directly to the *Miscellaneous Status Reports* page is to click the *Back* button in your Internet Explorer application.

Module 15

Working in the Resource Center

Learning Objectives

After completing this module, you will be able to:

- Apply Resource Center views
- View resource availability
- View resource assignment information
- Edit resource details for a group of resources
- Edit resource details individually for a group of resources
- Open a group of resources for editing in Project Pro 2013

Inside Module 15

Using the Resource Center

When you click the *Resources* link in the *Quick Launch* menu, Project Server 2013 displays the *Resource Center* page shown in Figure 15 - 1. The *Resource Center* page contains a data grid that displays all of the resources your security permissions allow you to see in the Enterprise Resource Pool. By default, the system applies the *All Resources* view when you display the *Resource Center* page the first time. This view displays all resources, grouped by resource type (*Work, Material,* and *Cost*).

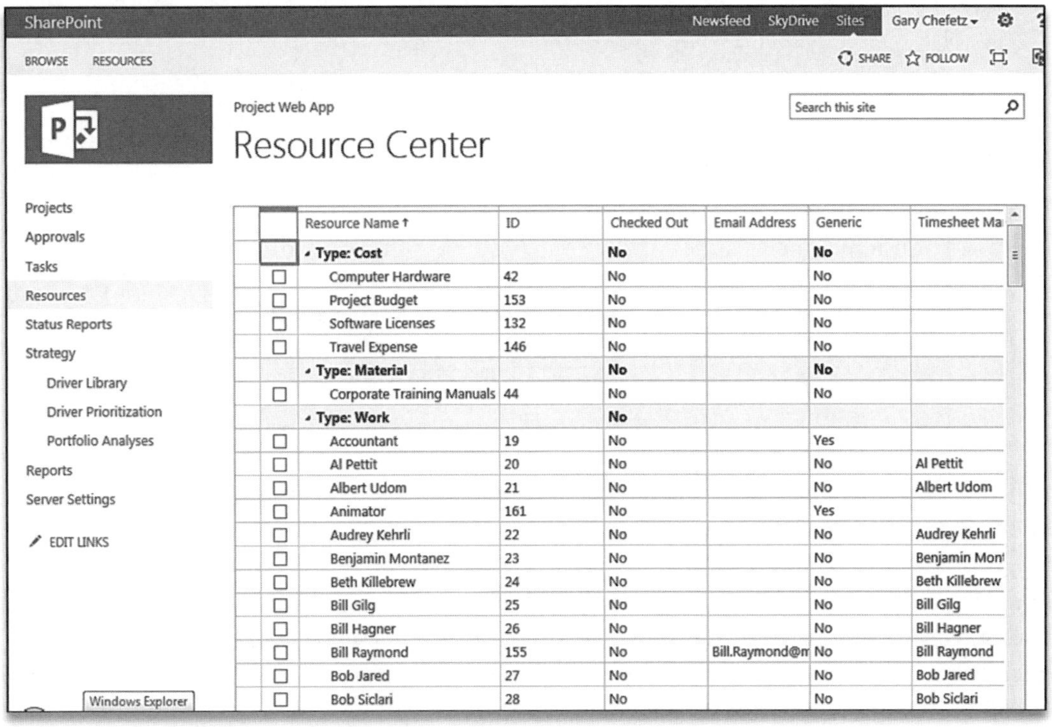

Figure 15 - 1: Resource Center page

The *Resource Center* page provides a central location from which you can manage all aspects of enterprise resources that you have permission to manage. From this page, you can do each of the following:

- View resource assignments across all enterprise projects
- View resource availability across all enterprise projects
- Edit resource information, if you have the necessary security permissions

Before you begin working with resources in the *Resource Center* page, click the *Resources* tab to display the *Resources* ribbon and notice the options available to you in the *Data* section of the ribbon. Use the *Settings* buttons and pick lists shown in Figure 15 - 2 to quickly filter, group, or search through the resources shown in the *Resource Center* page.

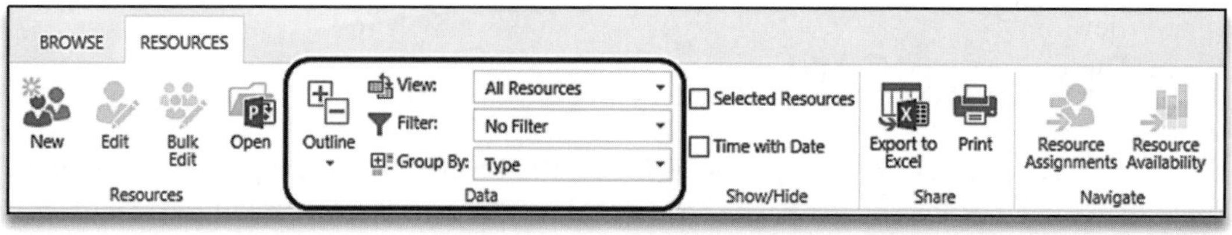

Figure 15 - 2: Resources ribbon with Data Section circled

> **Information**: The Resource Center displays only enterprise resources. It does not display local resources.

To filter for resources that meet certain criteria, click the *Filter* pick list and select the *Custom Filter* item. Project Server 2013 displays the *Custom Filter* dialog shown in Figure 15 - 3.

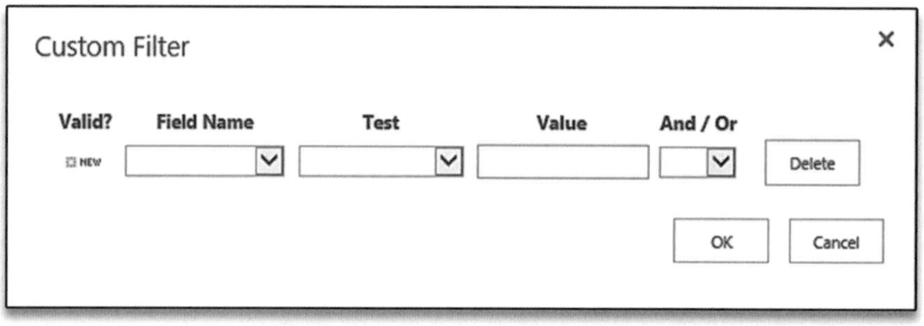

Figure 15 - 3: Custom Filter dialog

Using the *Grouping* pick list, you can group by any field in the view. You can also sort any field by hovering over any field heading, clicking the pick list and selecting either the *Ascending* or *Descending* item from the menu. Use the *Outline* pick list to show any level in your grouping. For example, select the *Outline Level 1* option from this menu to show all grouping collapsed or expanded.

Applying Resource Center Views

To apply a view in the *Resource Center* page, in the *Data* section of the *Resources* ribbon, click the *View* pick list as shown in Figure 15 - 4. The pick list includes all standard and custom views that your permissions allow you to see. Project Server 2013 includes five default views, including *All Resources, Material Resources, Work Resources, Resources by Team,* and *Cost Resources*. The *Work Resources for Grouping* view is a custom view I created to display fields by which my stakeholders like to group resources on the fly.

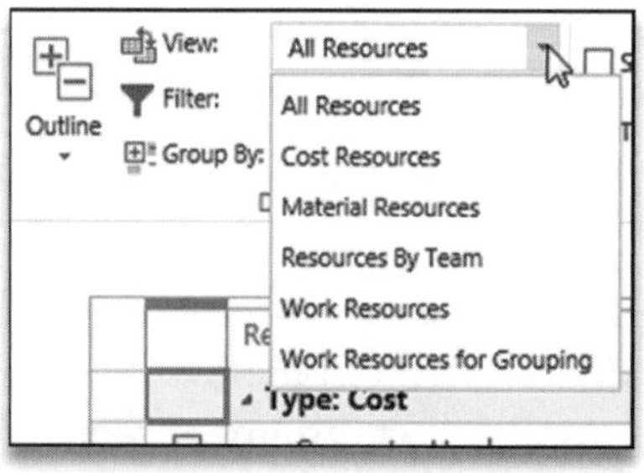

Figure 15 - 4: View pick list

The *All Resources* view displays all resources, grouped by resource type. The *Material Resources* view displays only material resources, while the *Work Resources* view displays only work resources. The *Resources by Team* view displays team resources grouped by team. The *Cost Resources* view, shown in Figure 15 - 5, displays only budget cost and expense cost resources.

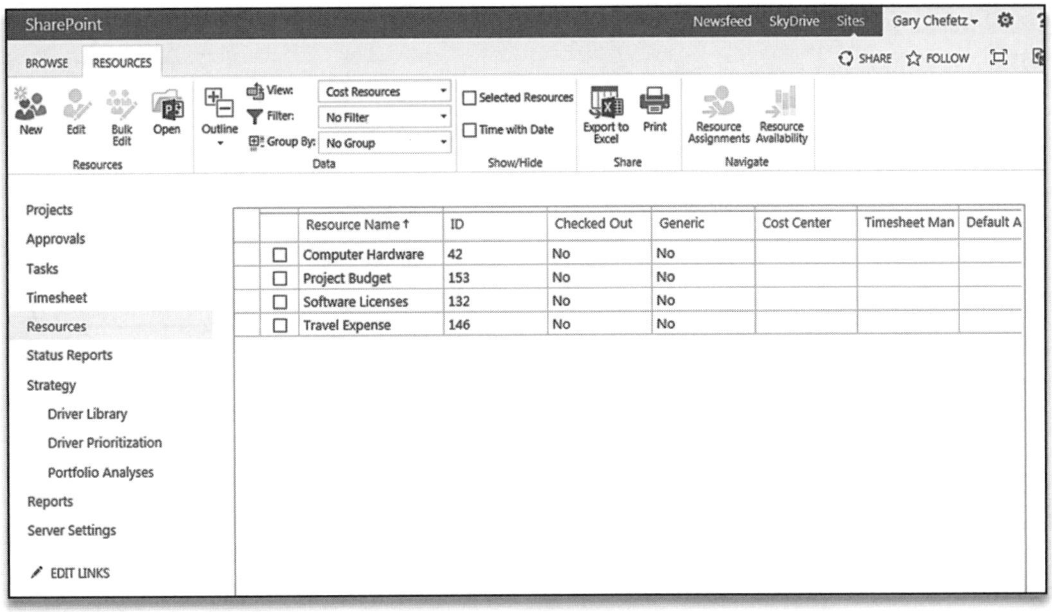

Figure 15 - 5: Cost Resources view in the Resource Center

Information: Your Project Server administrator controls the views available to you in the Resource Center. If you need a custom view, contact your Project Server administrator for assistance.

Selecting and Deselecting Resources

After applying a view, you must select one or more resources before activating other features available in the *Resource Center* page. To select a resource, click the option checkbox to the left of the resource's name. To quickly select all resources or to quickly clear your resource selections, float your mouse pointer over the checkbox header column to reveal the pick list menu arrow. Select the *Select All* or *Clear All* item on the menu as shown in Figure 15 - 6.

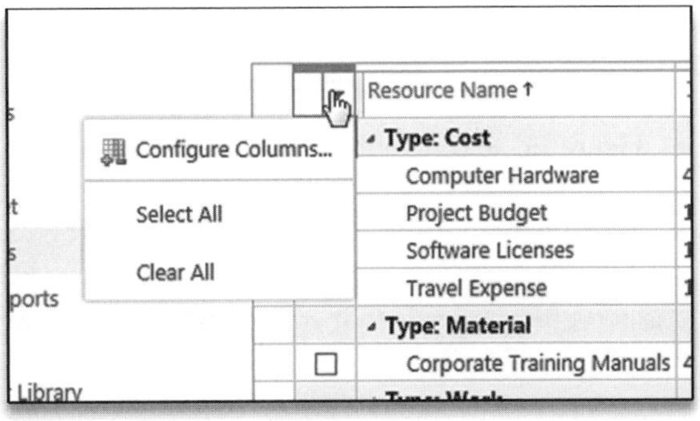

Figure 15 - 6: Select All or Clear All

After selecting resources, you can view availability or assignment information for the selected resources, or edit the details for the selected resources. To show the list of selected resources, in the *Show/Hide* section of the *Resources* ribbon, select the *Selected Resources* option. The system dynamically displays the list on the right side of the page as shown in Figure 15 - 7.

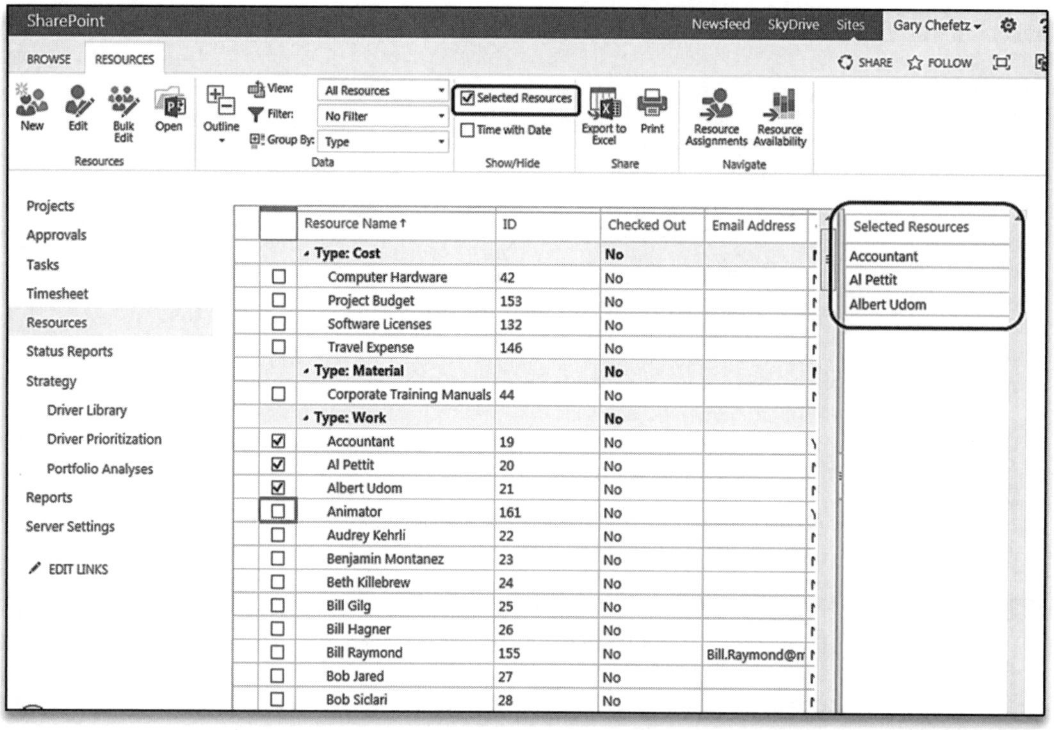

Figure 15 - 7: Resource Center with selected resources panel

Notice that the *Selected Resources* panel appears to the right of the grid. Deselect the *Selected Resources* option to hide the *Selected Resources* panel. In the *Show/Hide* section of the ribbon, select the *Time with Date* option to add the timestamp to any date field displayed in the grid as shown in the *Last Modified* field in Figure 15 - 8.

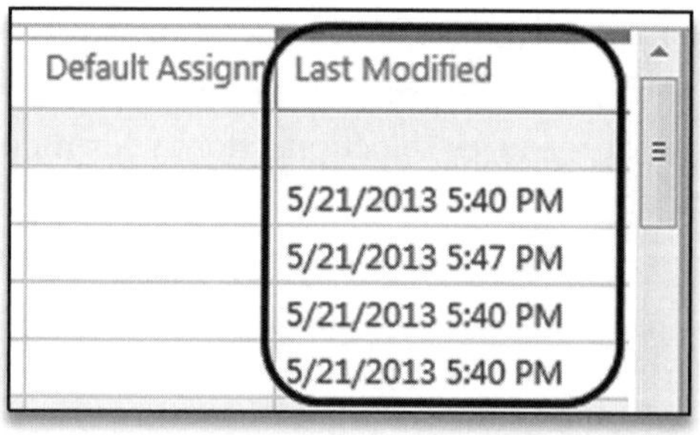

Figure 15 - 8: Date with Timestamp example

Project Web App also allows you to print the grid, or to export it to Microsoft Excel.

Best Practice: MSProjectExperts recommends that you export to Excel before printing as the print functionality is limited in Project Web App.

Viewing Resource Availability

You can use the Resource Center to analyze availability for one or more resources across all projects in the Project Server database. Begin by selecting the resources in the data grid and then from the *Navigate* section of the *Resources* ribbon, click the *Resource Availability* button. Project Server 2013 displays the *Resource Availability* page shown in Figure 15 - 9.

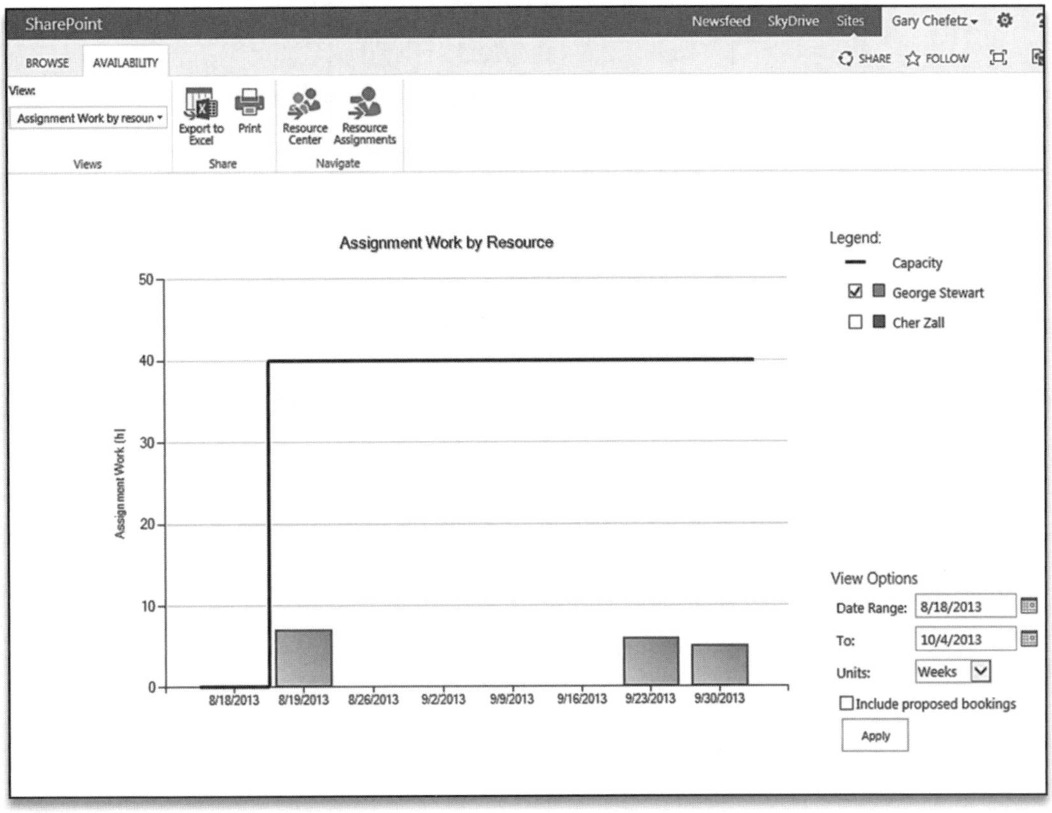

Figure 15 - 9: Resource Availability page

The *Resource Availability* page contains two sections: a chart at the top and a *Details* section with a timesheet grid at the bottom. For each selected resource, the timesheet grid displays the following information:

- Availability
- Capacity
- Assignment work for each project in which the resource is a team member
- Work entered in the resource's *My Timesheet* page

The chart displays a graphic representation of the data displayed in the timesheet grid. The *Resource Availability* page uses Project Server 2013 terminology that may be new to you. **Capacity** is the amount of time a resource has available to work after calendar exceptions. **Remaining Capacity** is **Capacity** less **Assignment Work**.

By default, the chart and the timesheet show a 2-week period beginning in the current week. To change the date range as I did, in the *View Options* section in the middle of the page to the right of the chart, select a start date in the *Date Range* field and a period end date in the *To* field as shown in Figure 15 - 10. Click the *Apply* button to apply your selection.

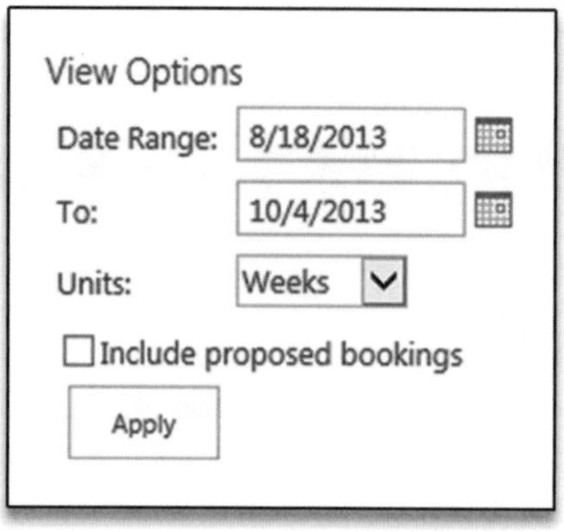

Figure 15 - 10: View Options

In the upper left corner of the page, the *View* pick list allows you to select one of four available views:

- Assignment Work by Resource
- Assignment Work by Project
- Remaining Availability
- Work

Each of these four views controls the presentation of data shown in the chart. The *Assignment Work by Resource* view shows a stacked bar chart of the assignment work for each selected resource, along with a line chart of the total capacity for all selected resources. In the *Legend* area of the page, select or deselect the option checkboxes to the left of each resource name to dynamically include or exclude the resource's information in the chart.

The *Assignment Work by Project* view shows a stacked bar chart for all of the projects for the selected resources and a line chart for the total capacity for all selected resources, along with bars for timesheet information and optional availability information. Figure 15 - 11 shows the *Resource Availability* page with the *Assignment Work by Project* view applied.

Information: If you select the *Availability* checkbox option, Project Server 2013 shows you the total Availability (Remaining Availability) for all selected resources with a stacked bar chart.

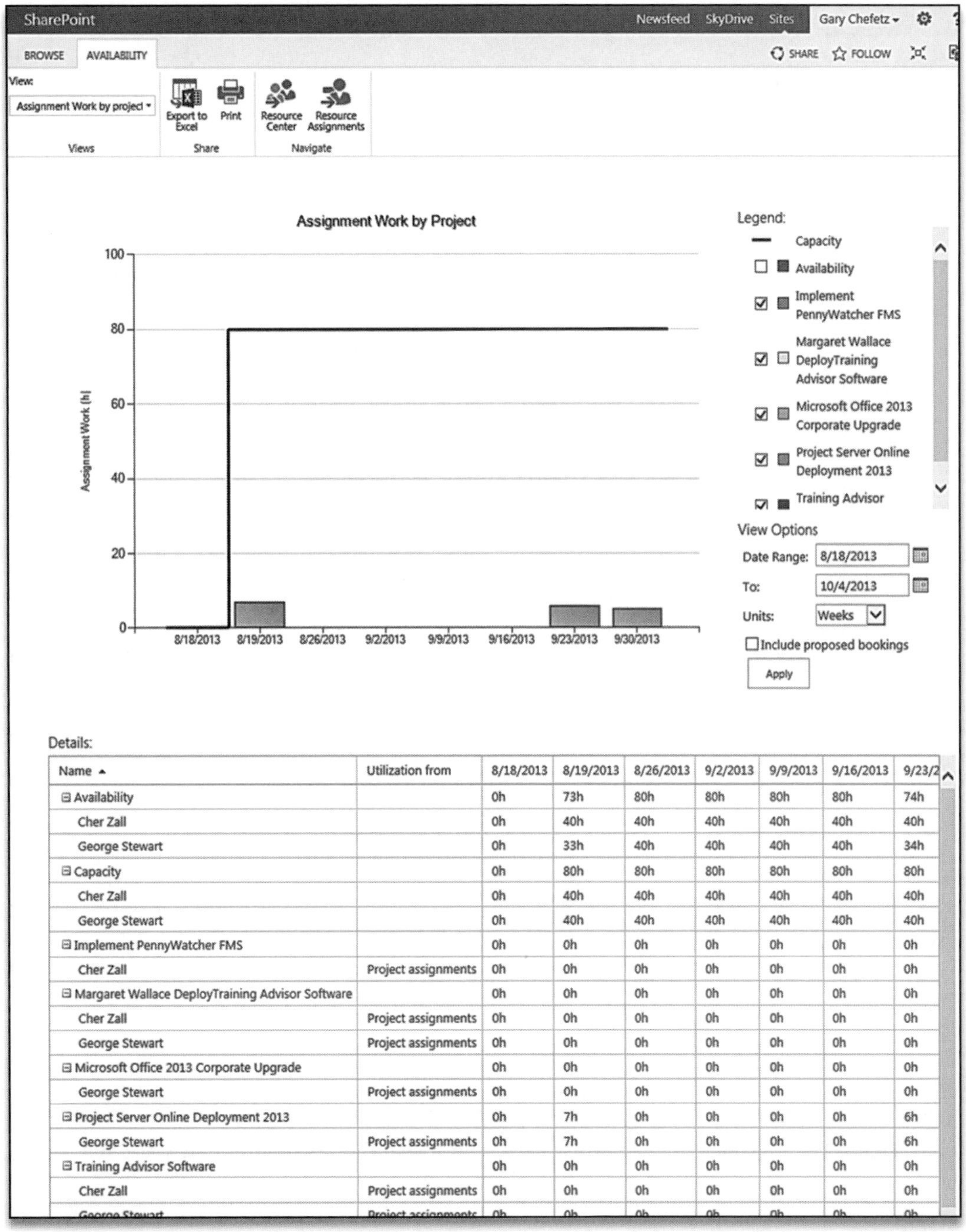

Figure 15 - 11: Resource Availability with the Assignment Work by Project view applied

The *Remaining Availability* view displays a bar chart showing the remaining availability for each selected resource. With multiple resources selected, this view is difficult to use; therefore, you should select resources individually to see their remaining availability. Figure 15 - 12 shows the *Resource Availability* page with the *Remaining Availability* view applied with one resource selected.

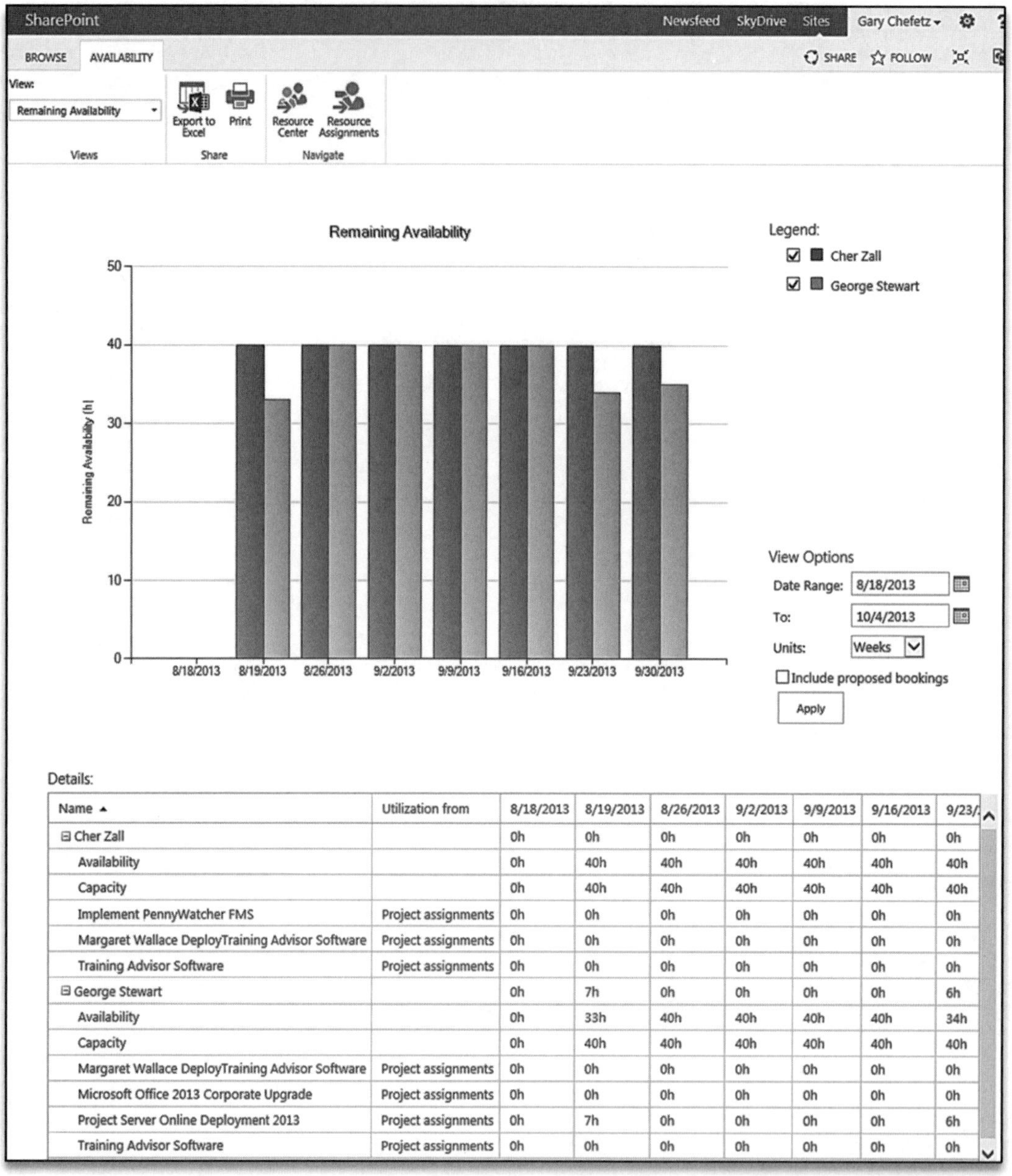

Name	Utilization from	8/18/2013	8/19/2013	8/26/2013	9/2/2013	9/9/2013	9/16/2013	9/23/
⊟ Cher Zall		0h	0h	0h	0h	0h	0h	0h
Availability		0h	40h	40h	40h	40h	40h	40h
Capacity		0h	40h	40h	40h	40h	40h	40h
Implement PennyWatcher FMS	Project assignments	0h	0h	0h	0h	0h	0h	0h
Margaret Wallace DeployTraining Advisor Software	Project assignments	0h	0h	0h	0h	0h	0h	0h
Training Advisor Software	Project assignments	0h	0h	0h	0h	0h	0h	0h
⊟ George Stewart		0h	7h	0h	0h	0h	0h	6h
Availability		0h	33h	40h	40h	40h	40h	34h
Capacity		0h	40h	40h	40h	40h	40h	40h
Margaret Wallace DeployTraining Advisor Software	Project assignments	0h	0h	0h	0h	0h	0h	0h
Microsoft Office 2013 Corporate Upgrade	Project assignments	0h	0h	0h	0h	0h	0h	0h
Project Server Online Deployment 2013	Project assignments	0h	7h	0h	0h	0h	0h	6h
Training Advisor Software	Project assignments	0h	0h	0h	0h	0h	0h	0h

Figure 15 - 12: Resource Availability page with Remaining Availability view applied

The *Work* view displays a bar chart showing the total assigned work for each selected resource. With multiple resources selected, this view is difficult to use; therefore, you should select resources individually to see their assigned work. Figure 15 - 13 shows the *Resource Availability* page with the *Work* view applied with one resource selected.

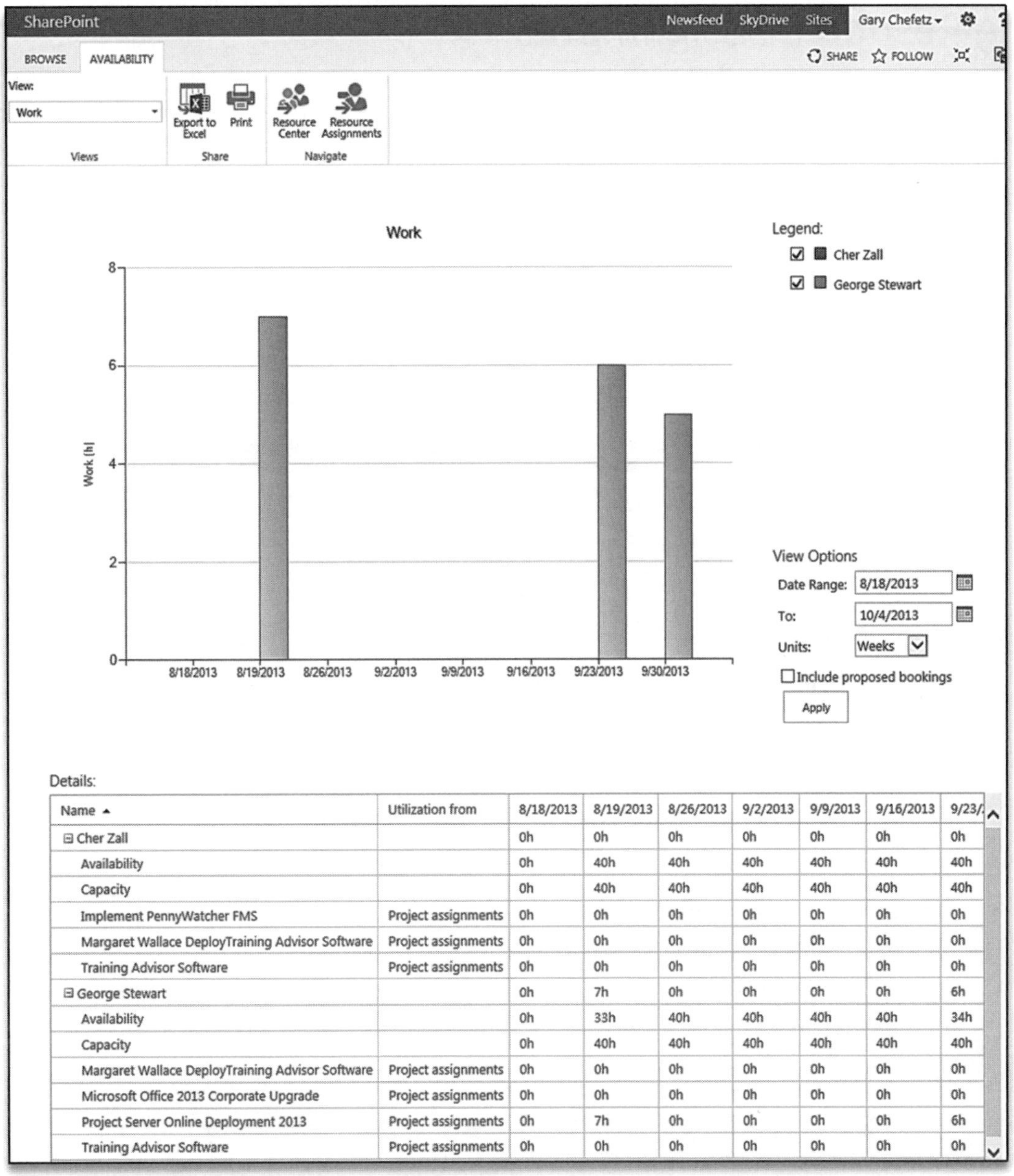

Figure 15 - 13: Resource Availability page with the Work view applied

The next time you return to the *Resource Availability* page, Project Server 2013 maintains your selected *Date Range* settings and selected view. To return to the *Resource Center* page, in the *Navigate* section of the *Resources* ribbon, click the *Resource Center* button.

Viewing Resource Assignments

After selecting one or more resources on the *Resource Center* page, in the *Navigate* section of the *Resources* ribbon, click the *Resource Assignments* button to view all project work currently assigned to the selected resource(s). The system displays the *Resource Assignments* page shown in Figure 15 - 14. Using the *Resource Assignments* page, you can determine the total amount of task work assigned to each selected resource and determine the specific times during which each resource has scheduled work.

> **Warning**: To access the *Resource Assignments* page, you must select no more than 100 resources.

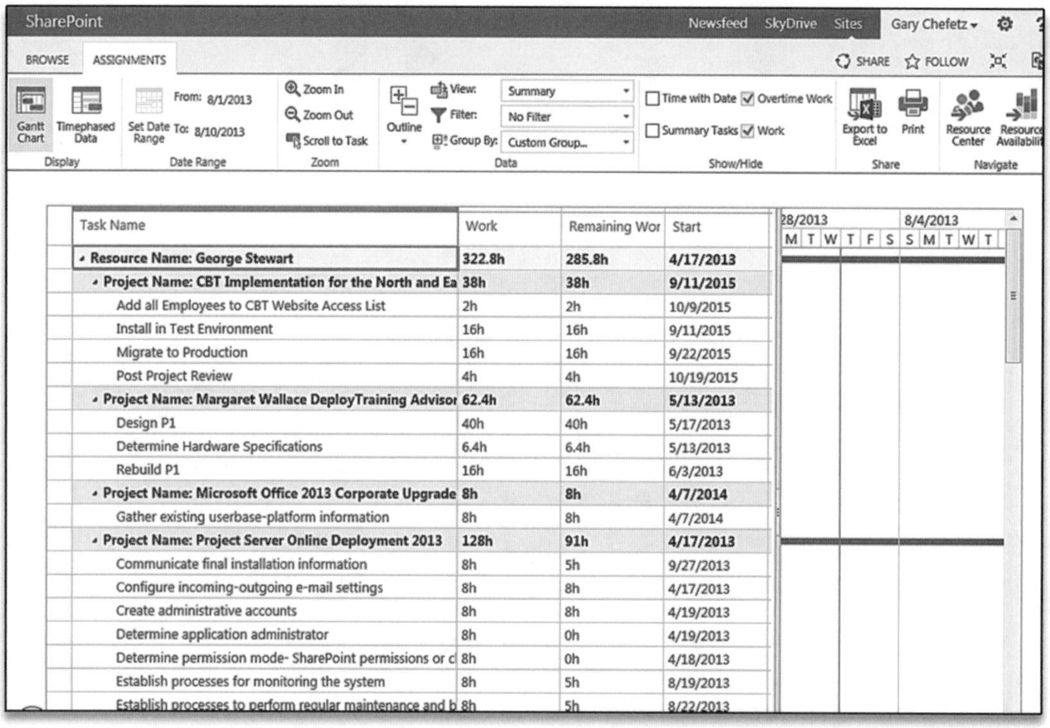

Figure 15 - 14: Resource Assignments page

The *Resource Assignments* page includes a table on the left that lists resource assignments, with either a Gantt chart on the right or a time-phased grid on the right that depicts the periods for each resource assignment. In the *Display* section of the *Assignments* ribbon, click either the *Gantt Chart* button or the *Timephased Data* button to switch between these two views. From the *Date Range* section of the *Assignments* ribbon, click the *Set Date Range* button to set a date range for the timephased data. By default, Project Server 2013 groups the resource assignment information by resource name and then by project name.

In the *Show/Hide* section of the *Assignments* ribbon, select the *Summary Tasks* option to include summary tasks in the display. Select the *Time with Date* option to display dates with times, and deselect the *Overtime Work* option to hide the *Overtime* item in the timephased display or deselect the *Work* option to hide the *Planned* item in the timephased grid.

In the *Zoom* section of the *Assignments* ribbon, use the *Zoom In, Zoom Out,* and *Scroll to Task* buttons to navigate in the Gantt chart. In the *Data* section of the ribbon, the *Summary* view is the only available selection on the *View* pick list by default, unless your Project Server administrator creates additional views for your organization. The table in the *Summary* view includes the following fields:

- Task Name
- Work
- Remaining Work
- Start
- Finish
- % Work Complete
- Comments
- Resource Name
- Project Name

To return to the *Resource Center* page, in the *Navigate* section of the *Assignments* ribbon, click the *Resource Center* button.

Editing Resource Details

If you are a member of the *Administrators* group or the *Resource Managers* group, and the *Resource Managers* group has the correct permissions, you can edit resource information from the *Resource Center* page. Begin by selecting the option checkbox for the resource(s) you want to edit. Project Server 2013 allows you to edit resource information several ways, including:

- Edit the details for a group of resources simultaneously in Project Web App (Bulk Edit).
- Edit the details for one or more resources individually in Project Web App (Single or Batch Edit).
- Edit additional resource information in Project Pro 2013.

To edit the details for a group of resources simultaneously, in the *Editing* section of the *Resources* ribbon, click the *Bulk Edit* button. Project Server 2013 displays the *Bulk Edit* page for the selected resources as shown in Figure 15 - 15. Notice in the figure that I selected two resources for bulk editing and that the system displays the resource names in the page header.

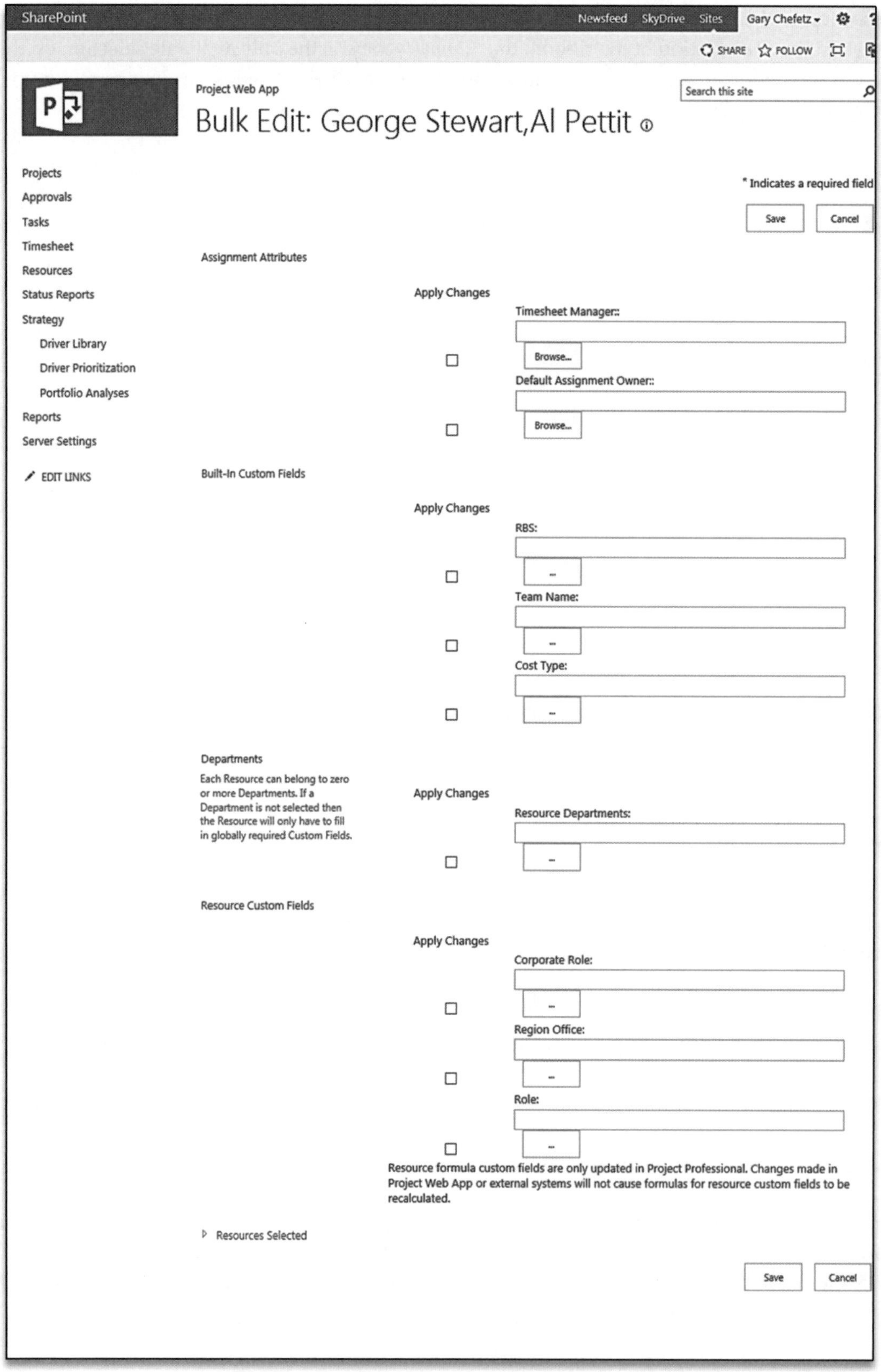

Figure 15 - 15: Bulk Edit page for two selected resources

The *Bulk Edit* page contains four sections in which you can edit resource details that apply to all selected resources. The *Assignment Attributes* section contains two important fields: the *Timesheet Manager* and *Default Assignment Owner* fields. The *Timesheet Manager* field must contain the name of the manager who approves timesheets for the selected resources. The system uses the *Default Assignment Owner* field value to determine on whose *Tasks* page to display task assignments when a manager publishes a project. If your organization uses team leaders who are responsible for reporting progress on behalf of their team members, then enter the team leader's name in this field. If each selected resource must see assigned tasks on his/her own *Tasks* page, then you cannot use the *Bulk Edit* page when editing values in this field. Instead, you must edit each resource individually.

To select a value in either the *Timesheet Manager* field or the *Default Assignment Owner* field, click the *Browse* button for that field. The system displays the *Pick Resource* dialog shown in Figure 15 - 16. In the *Pick Resource* dialog, double-click the name of the resource you want to select. The system closes the *Pick Resource* dialog and enters the selected name in the field automatically.

Figure 15 - 16: Pick Resource dialog

The *Built-In Custom Fields* section contains the three built-in custom enterprise resource fields that ship with Project Server 2013: *RBS*, *Team Name*, and *Cost Type* fields. The *Departments* section contains one field: the *Resource Departments* field. You use this field to attribute resources to departments for master filtering. If you do not select a department, the resource has only to fill in globally required custom fields. The *Resource Custom Fields* section contains any custom enterprise resource fields specifically created for your organization. Notice in Figure 15 - 15 shown previously, that the *Resource Custom Fields* section contains three custom enterprise fields, the *Corporate Role*, *Region Office*, and *Role* fields. The system collapses the *Resources Selected* section by default, as this section does not contain any editable fields.

To select a value for a field in the *Built-In Custom Fields, Departments,* or *Resource Custom Fields* sections, click the ellipsis button (...) located below the field and select a value from the pick list. For example, Figure 15 - 17 shows the pick list for the *RBS* field.

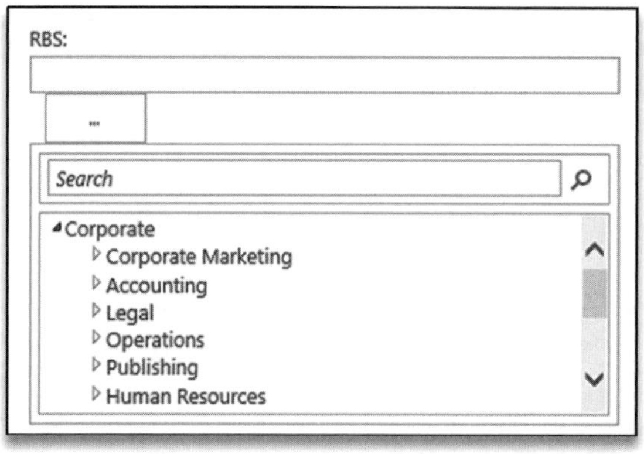

Figure 15 - 17: RBS pick list items

If you edit any field on the *Bulk Edit* page, you must select the *Apply Changes* option checkbox to the left of the field name. Figure 15 - 18 shows the *Bulk Edit* page after I set the *Timesheet Manager* field value to *Margaret Wallace* and the *RBS* field value to *Corporate.Publishing.PublishingTeam* for the two selected resources. Notice that I selected the *Apply Changes* option checkbox for these two fields as well. Click the *Save* button and Project Server 2013 applies the field changes to each of the resources you selected.

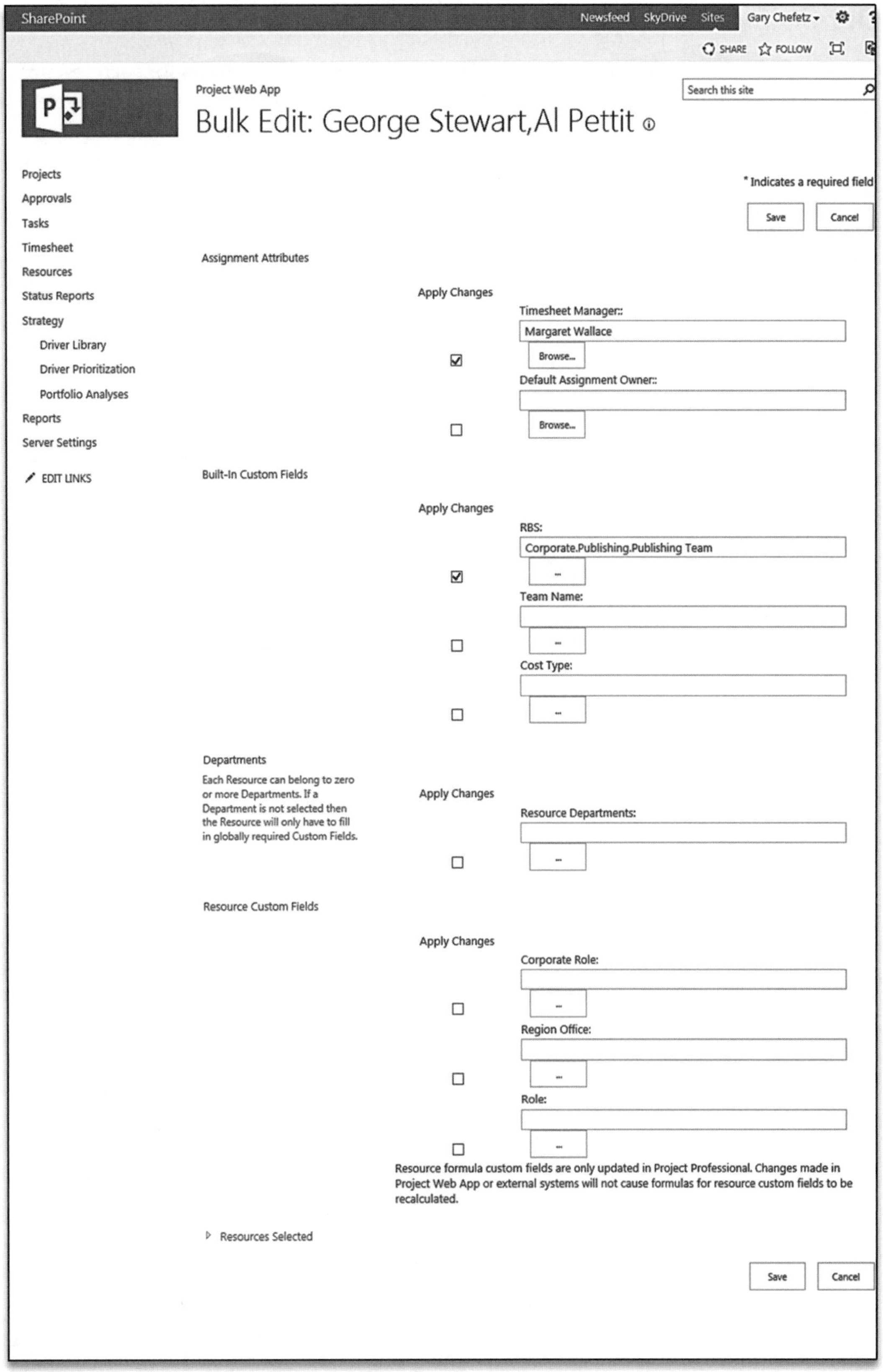

Figure 15 - 18: Bulk Edit page after editing two fields

Editing Details Individually for a Group of Resources

At times, you may need to edit a group of resources, but you need to specify values for each resource individually. For example, I need to set the *Default Assignment Owner* field for each of the two resources I selected in the last example. Select the option checkbox to the left of each resource name and then from the *Resources* section of the *Resources* ribbon, click the *Edit* button. Project Server 2013 displays the *Edit Resource* page for the first selected resource shown in Figure 15 - 19 and Figure 15 - 20. Notice that the *Edit Resource* page contains three buttons at the top and bottom of the page that you use to navigate through each of the selected resources.

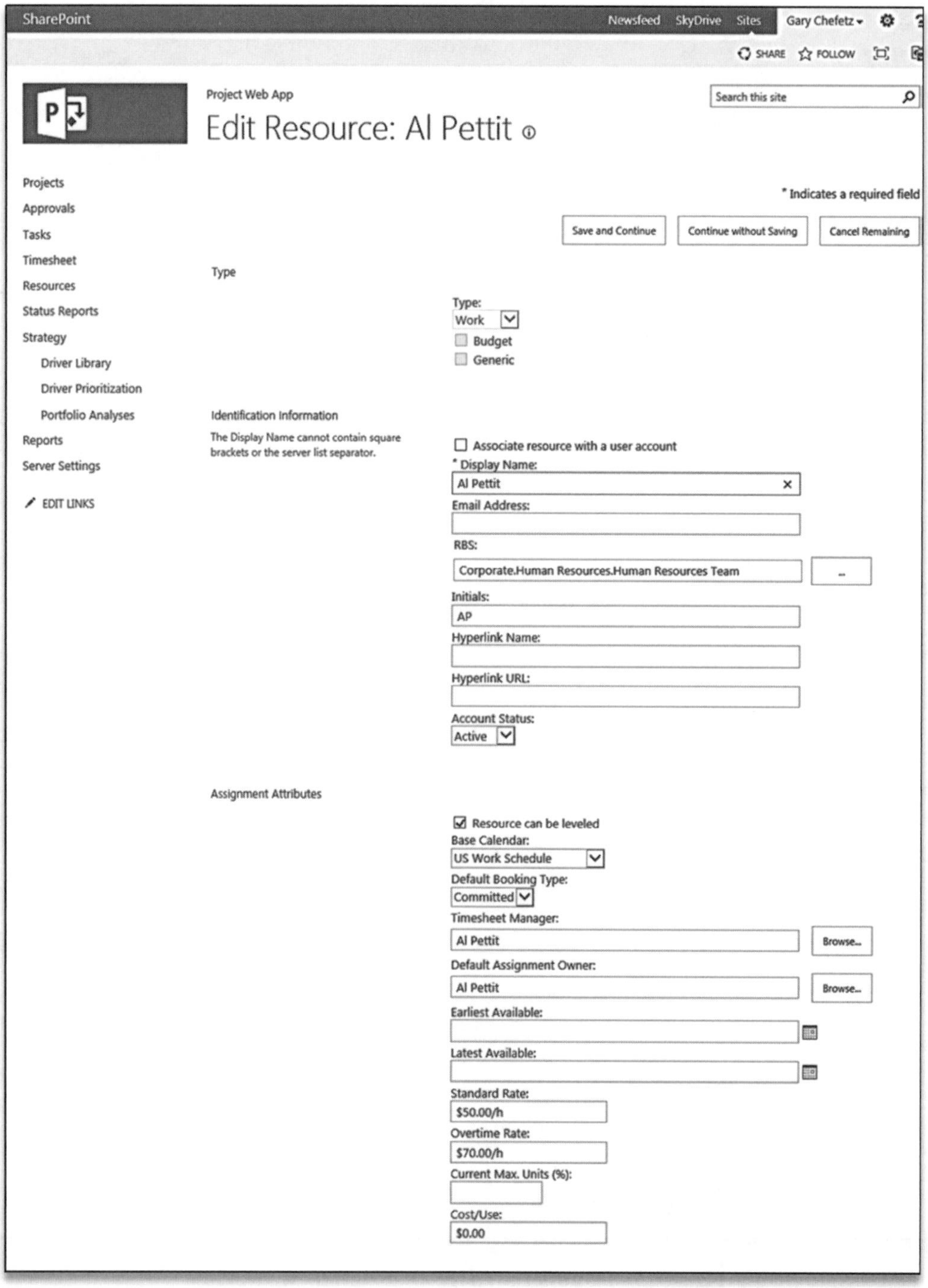

Figure 15 - 19: Edit Resource page for first selected resource top half

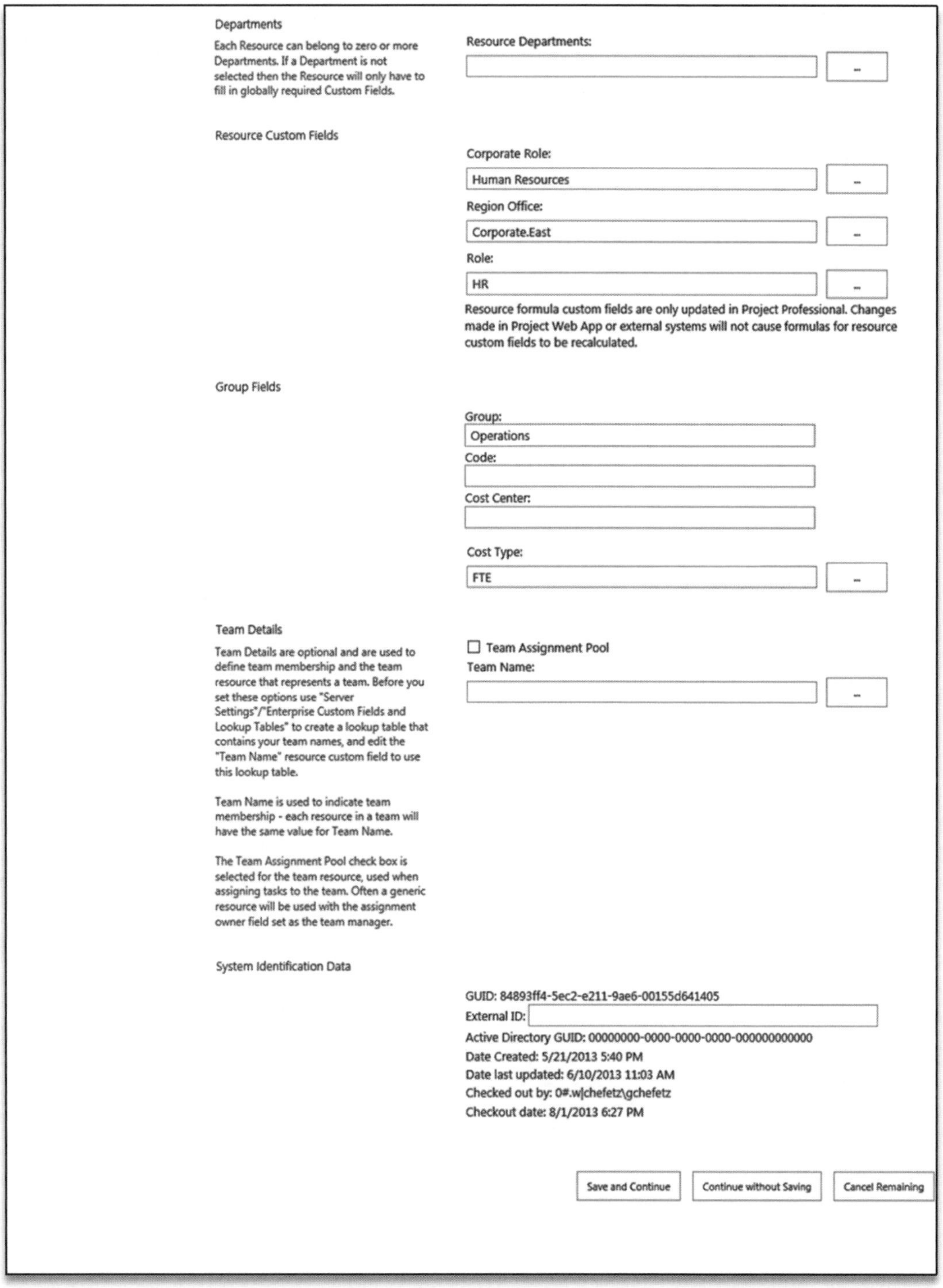
Departments
Each Resource can belong to zero or more Departments. If a Department is not selected then the Resource will only have to fill in globally required Custom Fields.
Resource Departments:
Resource Custom Fields
Corporate Role:
Human Resources
Region Office:
Corporate.East
Role:
HR
Resource formula custom fields are only updated in Project Professional. Changes made in Project Web App or external systems will not cause formulas for resource custom fields to be recalculated.
Group Fields
Group:
Operations
Code:
Cost Center:
Cost Type:
FTE
Team Details
Team Details are optional and are used to define team membership and the team resource that represents a team. Before you set these options use "Server Settings"/"Enterprise Custom Fields and Lookup Tables" to create a lookup table that contains your team names, and edit the "Team Name" resource custom field to use this lookup table.
Team Name is used to indicate team membership - each resource in a team will have the same value for Team Name.
The Team Assignment Pool check box is selected for the team resource, used when assigning tasks to the team. Often a generic resource will be used with the assignment owner field set as the team manager.
Team Assignment Pool
Team Name:
System Identification Data
GUID: 84893ff4-5ec2-e211-9ae6-00155d641405
External ID:
Active Directory GUID: 00000000-0000-0000-0000-000000000000
Date Created: 5/21/2013 5:40 PM
Date last updated: 6/10/2013 11:03 AM
Checked out by: 0#.w|chefetz\gchefetz
Checkout date: 8/1/2013 6:27 PM
Save and Continue
Continue without Saving
Cancel Remaining

Figure 15 - 20: Edit Resource page for first selected resource bottom half

On the *Edit Resource* page for the first selected resource, change the values in any of the individual fields as needed. When you finish editing the first resource, click the *Save and Continue* button. The system displays the *Edit Resource* page for the next selected resource. Continue editing each selected resource, and click the *Save and Continue* button on each page. When you finish editing the last selected resource on the *Edit Resource* page, you only have two options: the *Save* and *Cancel* buttons. Click the *Save* button to save your changes or click the *Cancel* button to return to the *Resource Center* page. Should you decide to skip any of the selected resources during your editing, click the *Continue without Saving* button. To cancel at any time without continuing, click the *Cancel Remaining* button.

Module 16

Working in the Project Center

Learning Objectives

After completing this module, you will be able to:

- Work with features in the Project Center
- Work with Project Center views
- Work with detailed Project views
- Access Project Workspace features from the Project Center
- Open projects from the Project Center page
- Check in a project
- Close enterprise projects to update
- Edit project details and open a project in the Project Center

Inside Module 16

Using the Project Center

In Project Server 2013, the Project Center is the central location for project and portfolio information, a launching point for new projects and the gateway to editing projects on the web. To navigate to the *Project Center* page, click the *Projects* link in the *Quick Launch* menu. Figure 16 - 1 shows the *Project Center* page with the *Summary* view applied and interface elements removed. The *Project Center* page displays a timeline view and a data grid with a project list on the left and a Gantt chart on the right. The timeline element is new for Project Server 2013. The project list displays a single line of information about each project and proposed project, with multiple columns of information about each item. The Gantt chart displays one or two Gantt bars representing the life span of the project. When the system displays two Gantt bars, one represents the baseline schedule while the other represents the current schedule of the project.

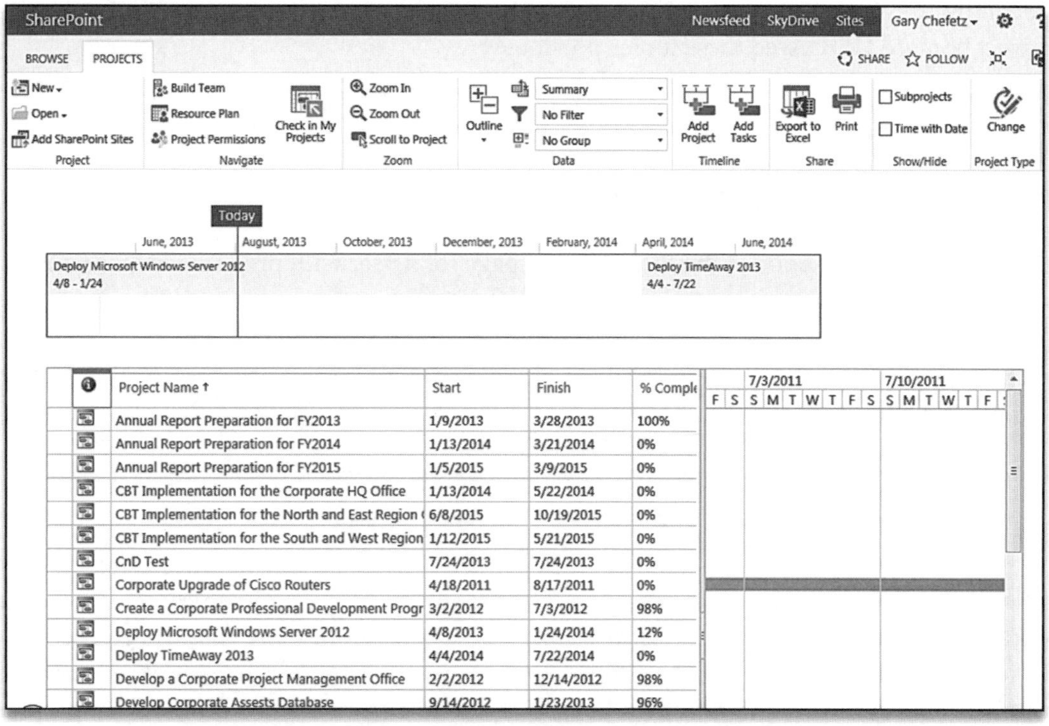

Figure 16 - 1: Project Center page with custom view applied

The *Project Center* page allows you to do each of the following:

- View the portfolio of active and proposed enterprise projects.
- View master projects and subprojects.
- Navigate to the Project Detail Pages for a project, the Project Site for a project, or navigate directly to the *Risks, Issues,* or *Documents* page for the project.
- Create new enterprise projects and proposed projects.
- Edit the properties for an enterprise project or proposed project.
- Drill down to a detailed *Project* view to view or edit the project.

- Build a team or create a resource plan for any project.
- Open a single project or a group of projects in Project Pro 2013.
- Set individual permissions for a project.
- Check in a project stuck in a checked-out state.

In this module, I discuss all of the above topics except for how to create a new enterprise project plan or proposed enterprise project because I discussed these topics previously.

Using the Projects Ribbon in the Project Center

Figure 16 - 2 shows the *Project* ribbon of the *Project Center* page for a user with project manager permissions.

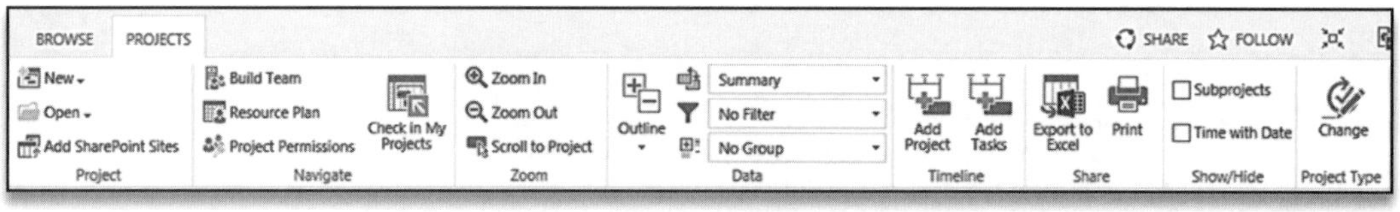

Figure 16 - 2: Project Center page Projects ribbon

The *Projects* ribbon has one context-sensitive tab, the *Projects* tab. The *Projects* ribbon contains menu selections in eight sections: *Project, Navigate, Zoom, Data, Timeline, Share, Show/Hide* and *Project Type*. If you used prior versions of Project Server, you can see right away that Project Web App has a much richer set of available functionality than ever before. From here, you can drill down to projects for editing in the browser or open projects in Project Pro 2013, and you can synchronize data between projects and SharePoint lists and add SharePoint lists as visibility projects.

The *Navigate* section provides familiar functions carried forward from previous versions including *Build Team, Resource Plan, Project Permissions* and *Check in My Projects* buttons. You use the tools in the *Zoom* section to zoom the timescale of the Gantt chart and scroll to projects in the Gantt chart. From the *Data* section you can collapse outline levels in views that contain multi-level grouping, select and apply views, and apply ad-hoc filters and grouping to your views. The new *Timeline* section provides buttons for adding projects or tasks to the timeline. Use the *Share* section to export your view to Microsoft Excel or to send it to a printer. The *Show/Hide* section provides two toggle options, the first displays subprojects along with master projects and the second determines whether the system displays the time in date fields. Finally, the *Project Type* section contains one selection, *Change.* You use this to change the *Project Type* of a proposed or existing project.

Using Project Center Views

The *Project Center* page displays only the projects and proposed projects that you have permission to see, including projects and proposed projects that you own. Unless you have additional privileges in the system, these may be the only projects that you see. The first time you access the *Project Center* page, the system displays the default *Summary* view, unless your Project Server administrator removed that view. The system provides five standard views that you can select from the pick list in the *Data* section of the page:

- Summary
- Tracking
- Cost
- Earned Value
- Work

The *Summary* view, shown in Figure 16 - 3, displays the "vital statistics" for each project, with columns showing the project's *Start* date, *Finish* date, *% Complete, Work, Duration*, and *Owner*. The *Summary* view includes a Gantt chart with a single Gantt bar for each project and a black stripe indicating project progress. Notice in Figure 16 - 3 that the *Deploy Microsoft Windows Server 2012* project contains a black stripe within the blue Gantt bar, indicating the current progress for that project.

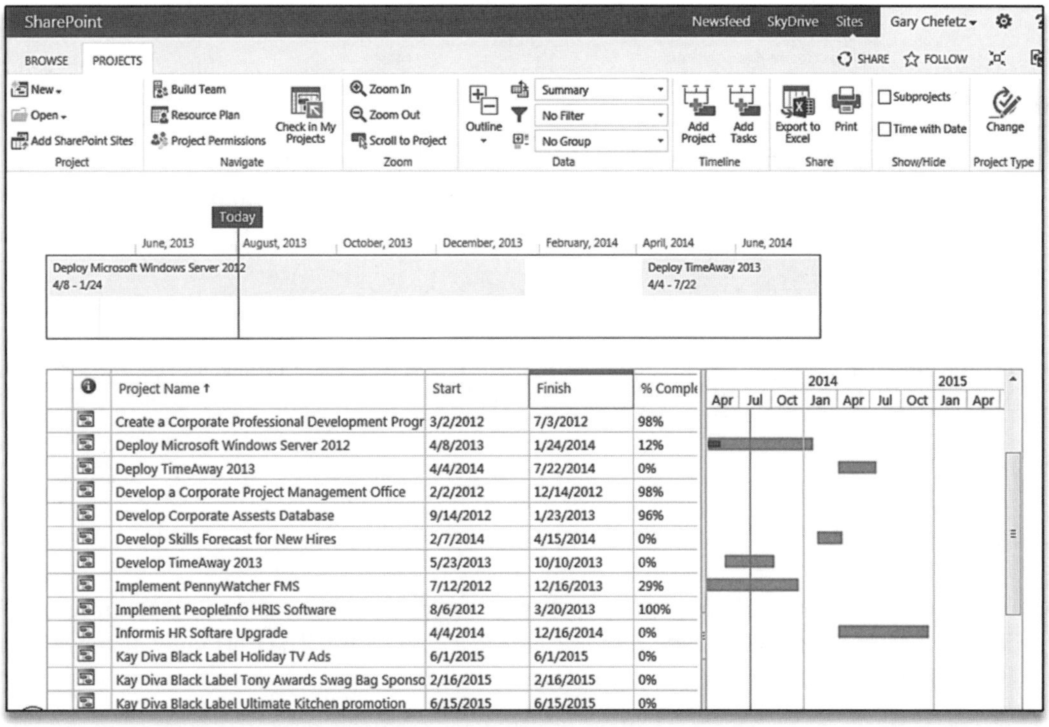

Figure 16 - 3: Summary view in Project Center

The *Tracking* view displays variance information about each project using the following fields: *% Complete, Actual Cost, Actual Duration, Actual Finish, Actual Start, Actual Work, Baseline Finish, Baseline Start, Duration, Remaining Duration, Finish,* and *Start*. The *Tracking* view, shown in Figure 16 - 4, displays a *Tracking* Gantt chart with two Gantt bars for each project. The top Gantt bar represents the current schedule for each project, while the bottom Gantt bar represents the baseline schedule for each project. The black stripe in the top Gantt bar indicates project progress.

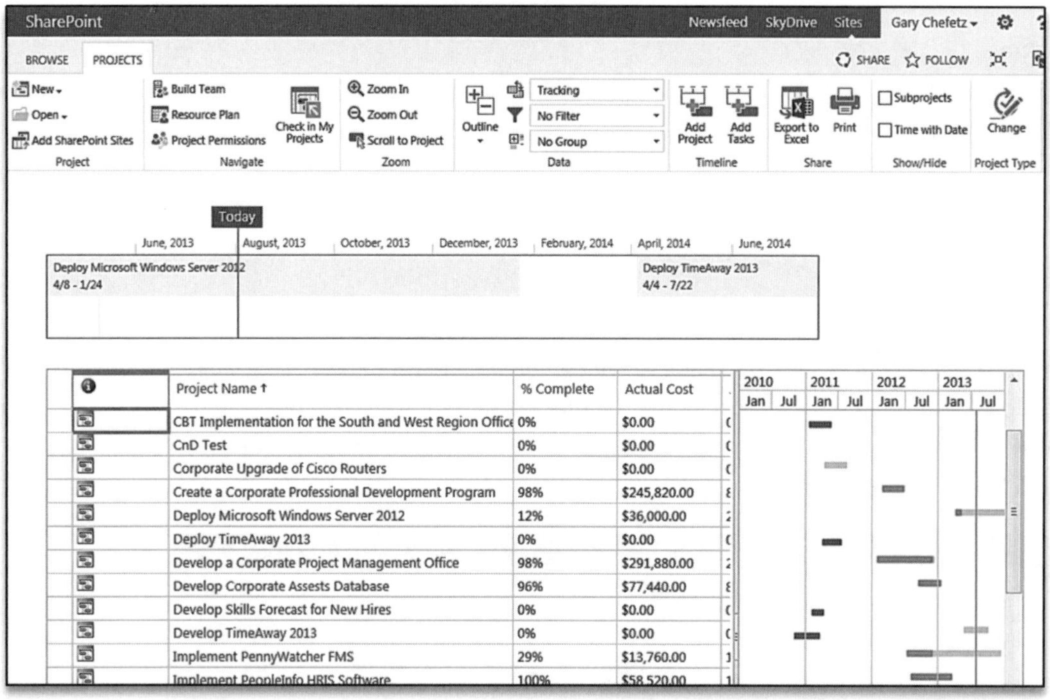

Figure 16 - 4: Project Center page with the Tracking view applied

Information: If you do not see the lower of the two Gantt bars for a project in the *Tracking* view, this indicates that you did not set a baseline for the project before you published it.

The *Cost* view shown in Figure 16 - 5 displays information about project costs, including columns for *Finish, Start, Cost, Baseline Cost, Actual Cost, Fixed Cost, Cost Variance,* and *Remaining Cost*. The *Cost* view also displays a *Tracking* Gantt chart identical to the one shown in the *Tracking* view.

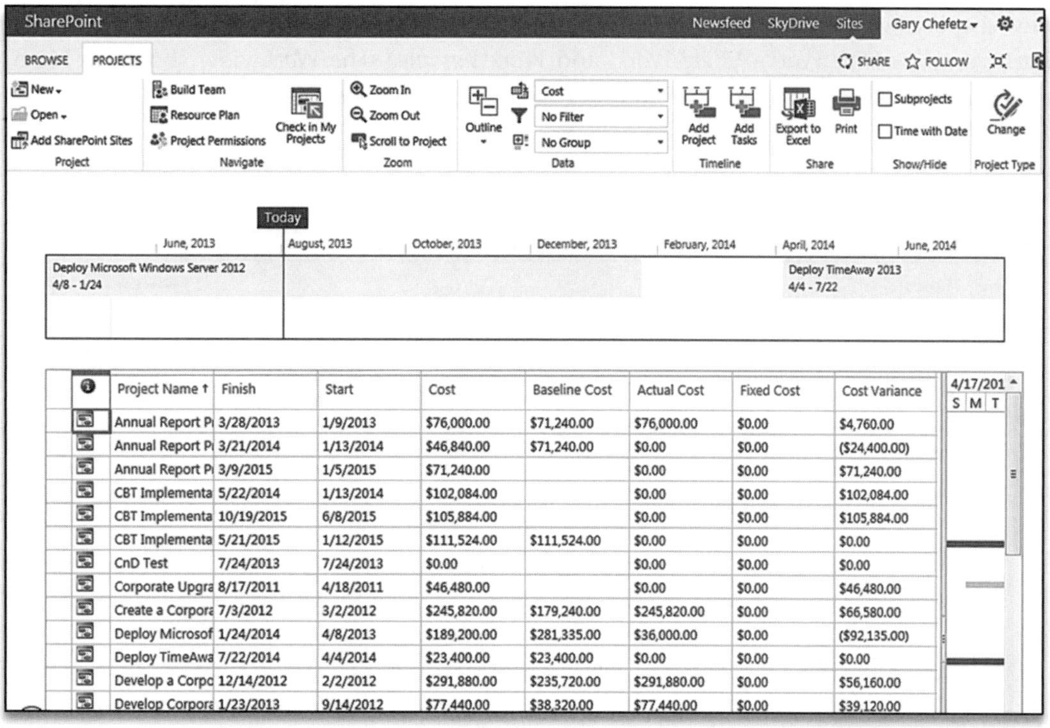

Figure 16 - 5: Project Center page with the Cost view applied

The *Earned Value* view displays the calculated earned value at the project level for each project. This view includes columns for *Finish, Start, Cost, Baseline Cost, BCWP, BCWS, SV, CV, ACWP,* and *VAC*. The *Earned Value* view shown in Figure 16 - 6 includes the same *Tracking* Gantt chart as the *Tracking* and *Cost* views.

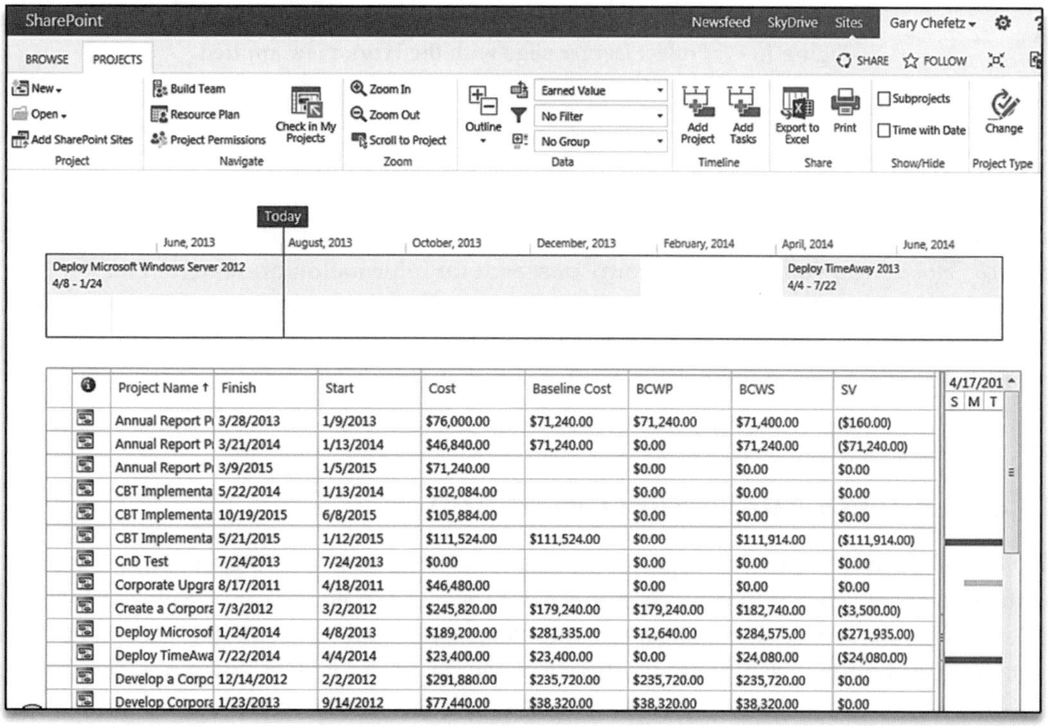

Figure 16 - 6: Project Center page with the Earned Value view applied

The *Work* view displays information about project work hours with columns for *% Work Complete, Finish, Remaining Work, Start, Work, Baseline Work, Actual Work,* and *Work Variance*. The *Work* view shown in Figure 16 - 7 displays the same *Tracking* Gantt chart found in all other *Project Center* views.

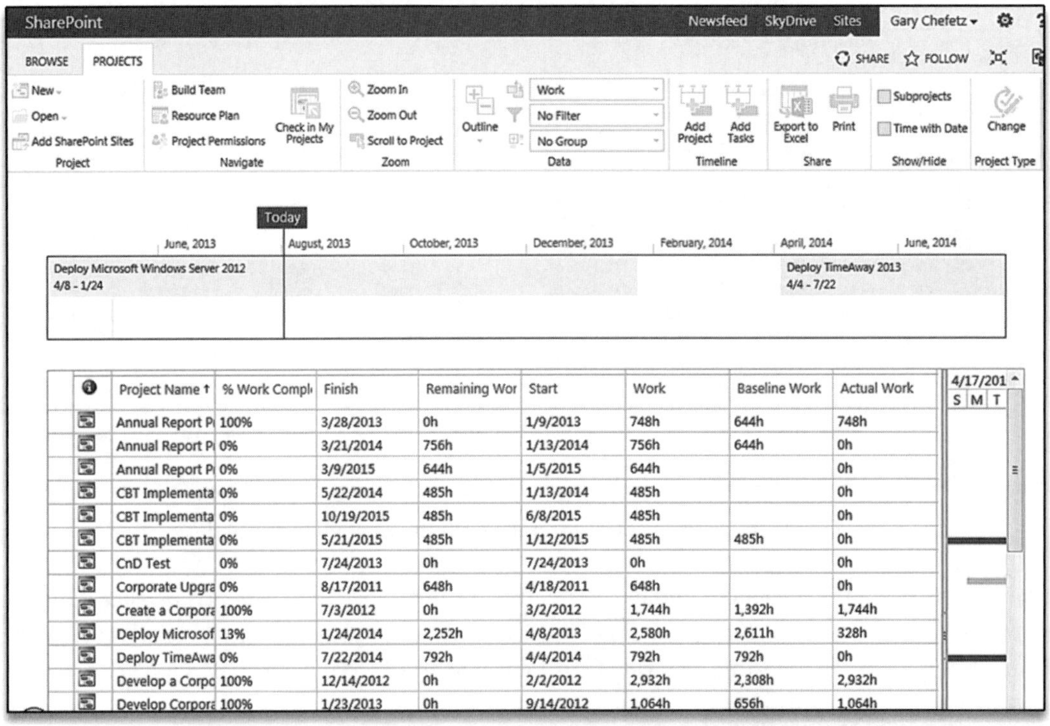

Figure 16 - 7: Project Center page with the Work view applied

In addition to the five standard views, the *View* pick list may also include custom views created by your Project Server administrator. The Project Center is a great forum for the use of graphical indicators in custom views. As with the *Resource Center* page, you can filter, group, or search for information presented in the *Project Center* page. Use the *Zoom In* and *Zoom Out* buttons to change the timescale of the Gantt chart. You can change the timescale to periods as small as 15-minute intervals or as large as half years. Use the *Scroll to Task* button to scroll the Gantt chart to the start date of the selected project.

Checking In a Project from Project Web App

Occasionally you will leave a project in a checked-out state caused by a network problem or a workstation crash. Fortunately, the system allows you to check in your own projects without seeking administrative help. To check in a project, navigate to the *Project Center* page, click the *Projects* tab, and from *Navigate* section of the ribbon, click the *Check in my projects* button. Project Server 2013 displays the *Force Check-in Enterprise Objects* page shown in Figure 16 - 8.

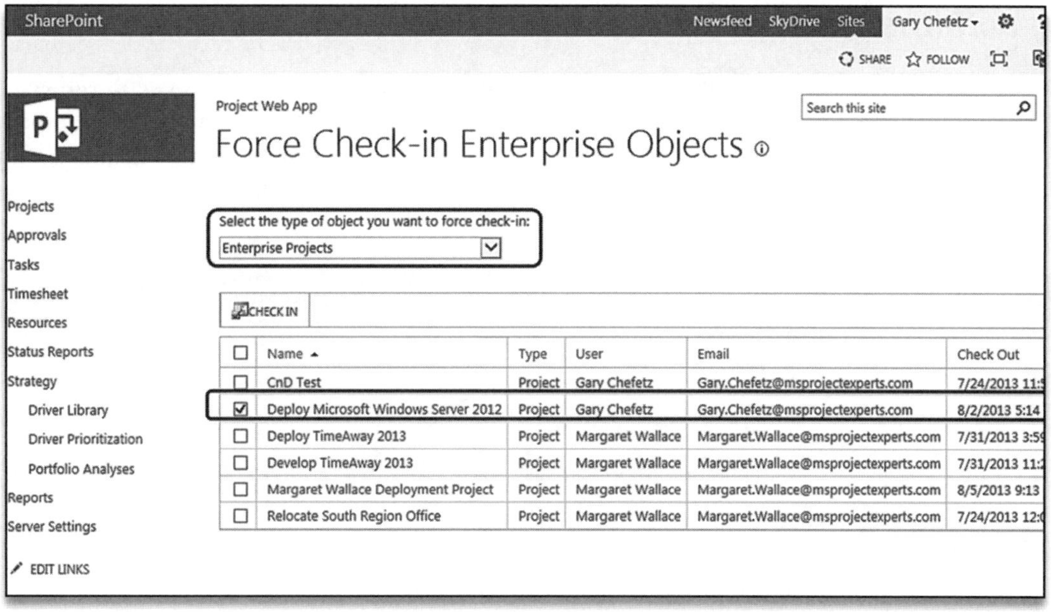

Figure 16 - 8: Force Check-in Enterprise Objects page

The *Force Check-in Enterprise Objects* page lists all projects currently checked out to you, and any additional projects to which you have administrative access. For instance, I am acting as a delegate for Margaret Wallace, so the system displays Margaret's projects as well as my own, including projects that are stuck in a checked-out state and projects that you currently have open in Project Pro 2013. Notice that Figure 16 - 8 displays six projects.

To check in a project, select the option checkbox to the left of one or more projects you want to check in and then click the *Check-In* button on the toolbar (not shown). The system displays the confirmation dialog shown in Figure 16 - 9. When you click the *OK* button, the system redisplays the *Force Check-in Enterprise Objects* page with the projects that you selected removed from the view.

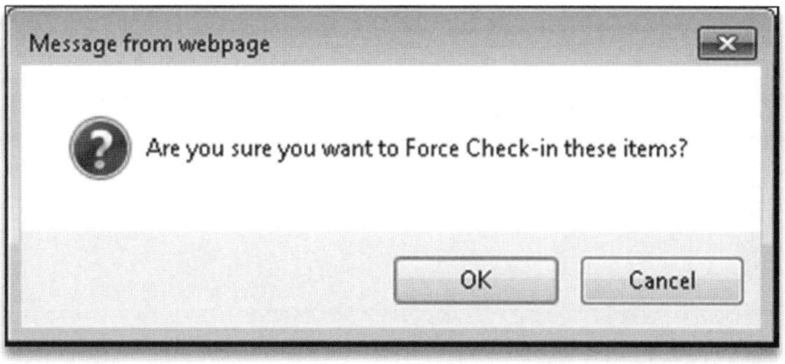

Figure 16 - 9: Confirmation dialog for Force Check-in

Information: If you have administrative rights to force check-in projects in the system, you see more than your own projects in the *Force Check-in Enterprise Objects* page.

Working with the Timeline

The timeline web part in the Project Center is not view specific like it is in the Project client, rather it provides a singular presentation shared among all Project Center views. The changes that you make to the timeline are visible to all users. Figure 16 - 7 shows the default ribbon state of the Project Center page with the data grid active. When you click on to the timeline itself, the system changes the ribbon display to reveal a *Timeline* ribbon as shown in Figure 16 - 10.

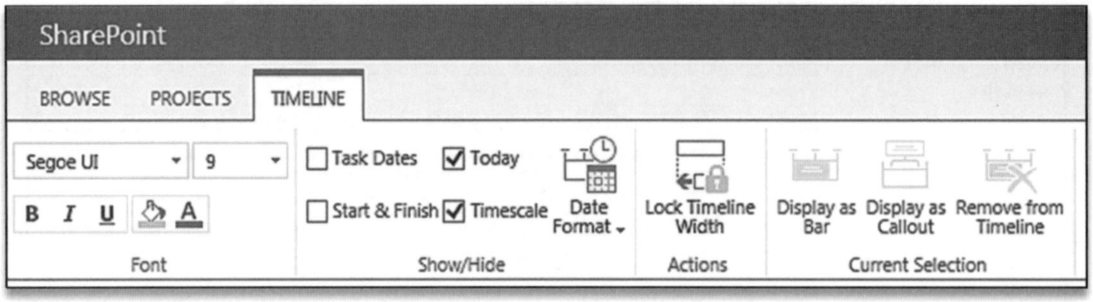

Figure 16 - 10: Timeline ribbon

You determine the content displayed in the timeline using the *Projects* ribbon. You style it using the options and tools on the *Timeline* ribbon. Note that the system allows you to select the *Projects* ribbon, but it will remain grayed out until you click into the data grid area. The *Timeline* section of the *Projects* ribbon, shown previously in Figure 16 - 7, contains two buttons: *Add Project* and *Add Tasks*.

To add a project to the timeline, select the row header for the project and click the *Add Project* button. The system immediately adds the project to the timeline. By default, this creates a bar reflecting the duration of the project on the timeline. You can also add tasks or milestones to the *Timeline* view. To do so, select the header row for a project and then click the *Add Tasks* button to display the *Select Tasks for Timeline* dialog shown in Figure 16 - 11.

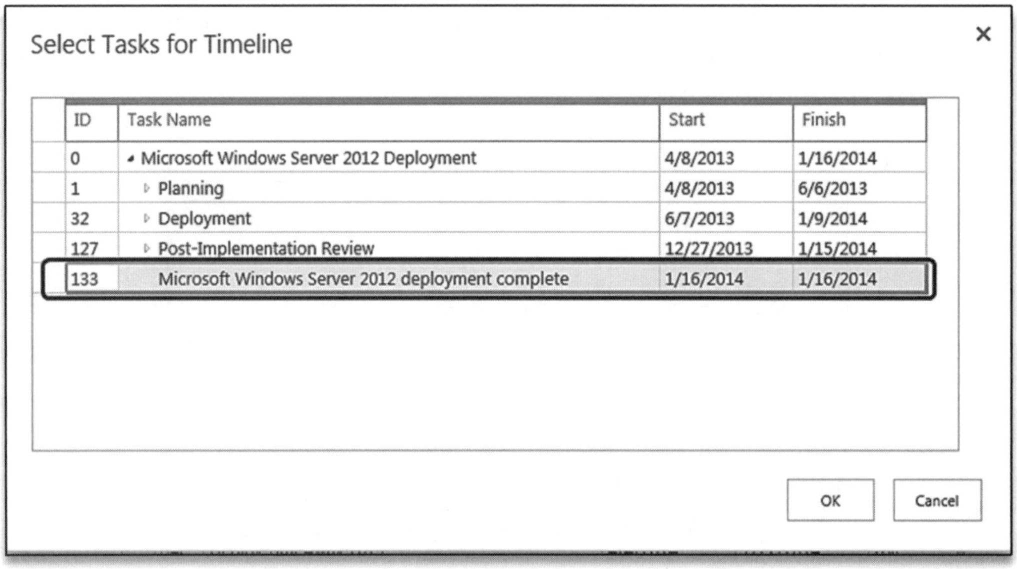

Figure 16 - 11: Select Tasks for Timeline dialog

Notice that I selected the project completion milestone. Surfacing milestones from projects is the most likely use of this feature in a multi-project timeline view. It certainly serves as a visual enhancement as shown in Figure 16 - 12.

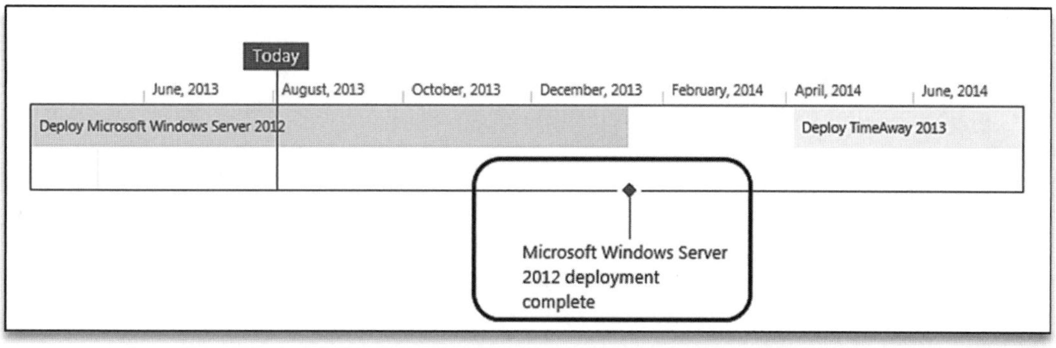

Figure 16 - 12: Project Milestone added to timeline

Notice that the system adds milestones to the timeline as callouts. Besides adding tasks and projects to the timeline, you can style each timeline object individually as well as set global options for the timeline display. When you click into a task or project on the timeline, the system displays the popup shown in Figure 16 - 13.

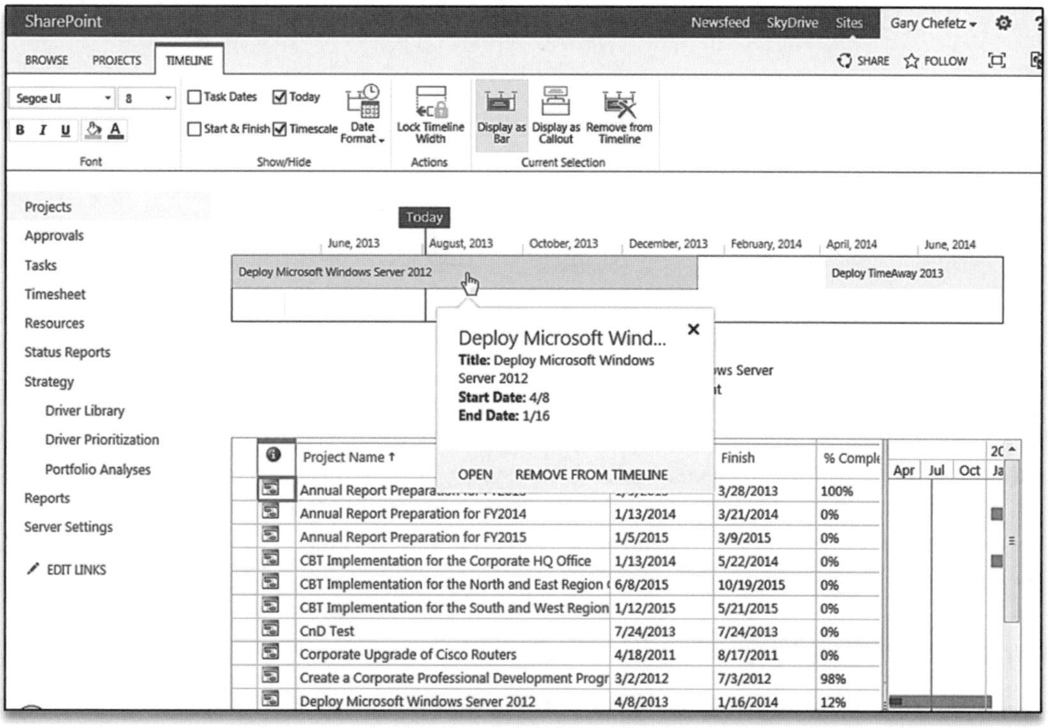

Figure 16 - 13: Clicking on a timeline object activates a popup

Notice the links in the gray area at the bottom of the popup that allow you to open the project from the timeline or remove the object from the timeline. When you select a timeline object, the buttons in the *Current Selection* section of the ribbon activate. Here you find buttons to switch between displaying the object as a bar or as a callout. Notice in the figure that the *Display as Bar* button highlights to indicate it is the current selection. You can also remove projects or tasks from the timeline using the *Remove from Timeline* button.

Options you set in the *Font* section of the ribbon act upon the object you select, allowing you to style each element uniquely. For brevity sake, I assume you know how to use these common controls. By default, the *Show/Hide* section has the *Today* and *Timescale* options selected. Figure 16 - 14 indicates each of these elements on the timeline. Use the *Date format* pick list to set the format for the date display in the timeline. The system provides the standard selections for your language and region settings.

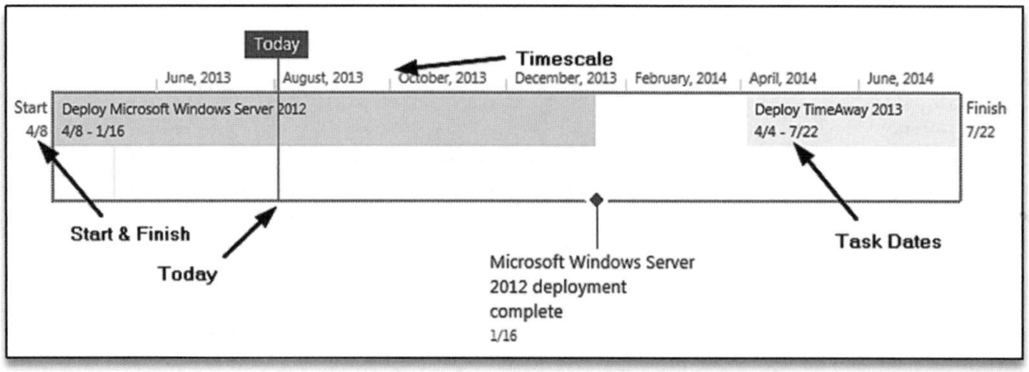

Figure 16 - 14: Timeline options

Understanding Show/Hide Options

The *Show/Hide* section of the *Projects* ribbon, shown in Figure 16 - 15 contains two options: *Subprojects* and *Time with Date.* When you select the checkbox for *Time with Date,* the system redisplays the page with a time in every date field.

Figure 16 - 15: Show/Hide options

Selecting the *Subprojects* checkbox produces a more subtle change to the page. When this option is deselected, the default, and there are master projects in the system, you do not see the individual plans that are part of the master projects in the individual rows for projects. Instead, the system hides these from view and you must select the master project to drill down into the subprojects. When you select the *Subprojects* checkbox, the system displays the subprojects as individual project records and it displays the master project. Select the options that best fit your needs for any work session.

Understanding Indicators

Notice the *Indicators* column identified with the icon in the column header (not shown) in the *Project Center* page shown in Figure 16 - 16.

Relocate South Region Office	7/9/2012	2
Relocate West Region Office	1/9/2012	7
SharePoint Training	5/9/2013	5
Skills Tracker 2013 Subscription	2/4/2013	4
Training Advisor Software	5/13/2013	6

Figure 16 - 16: Project Center page shows indicators in the Indicators column

You can quickly see the meaning of the indicators by floating your mouse over any icon in the *Indicators* column for any project. The resulting tooltip displays the type of project and the number of Risks, Issues, and Documents associated with the project. Table 16 - 1 displays the indicators you may see in the *Indicators* column.

Indicator	Meaning
	Enterprise project
	Master Project
	Risks
	Issues
	Documents

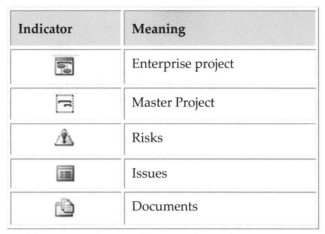

Table 16 - 1: Indicators shown on the Project Center page

To access the *Risks, Issues, Documents*, or *Deliverables* page for any project, click the *Risks, Issues*, or *Documents* indicator in the *Indicators* column to the left of the project. Project Server 2013 opens a new Internet Explorer window and displays the Project Site for the selected project.

Opening Projects in Project Pro 2013 from the Project Center

The filtering and grouping capabilities in the Project Center make it an ideal location from which to open one or more enterprise projects, particularly if you have many projects in your Project Server data store. While the *Open* dialog in Project Pro 2013 allows you to group projects on custom enterprise fields, you cannot use multiple views the way you can in the Project Center, and you cannot create ad-hoc filters the way you can on the *Project Center* page.

To open an individual project in Project Pro 2013 from the *Project Center* page, select the header row for a project in a *Project Center* view and click the *Open* pick list. The system displays the pick list show in Figure 16 - 17.

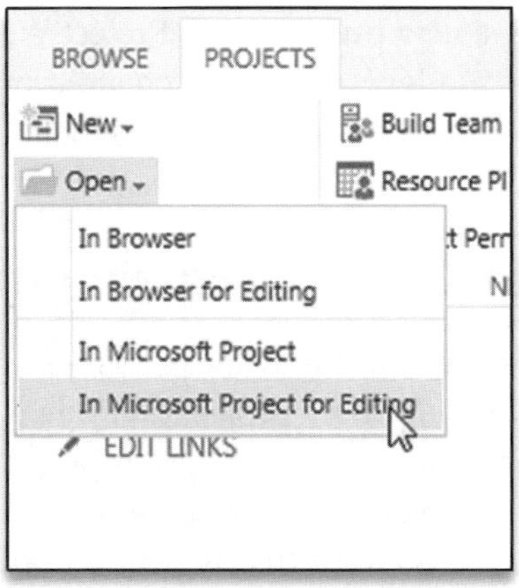

Figure 16 - 17: Open pick list

Notice that you have four selections, one for read/write and one for read-only for both Project Pro 2013 and Project Web App. When you select either *In Project Professional (Read Only)* or *In Project Professional for Editing,* the system launches Project Pro 2013 (if you have not already launched it), and then checks out and opens the selected project. You can edit and save your project once it is open.

Warning: Before attempting to open a project from the *Project Center* page, you must confirm that the URL you entered for your login account in Project Pro 2013 **matches exactly** the URL you use to access Project Web App. If these two URL's do not match exactly and you attempt to open a project from the *Project Center* page, Project Server 2013 displays an error message indicating that the required version of Project is not installed and the system fails to open the project.

Creating Programs

The first time you publish a project to Project Server 2013, the system prompts you with the *Publish Project* dialog shown in Figure 16 - 18. In order to create a Project Site as a subsite of another site, such as you might want for a program of related projects, you must first create the program-level site so that the creators of the member projects can select the program site in the *Publish Project* dialog.

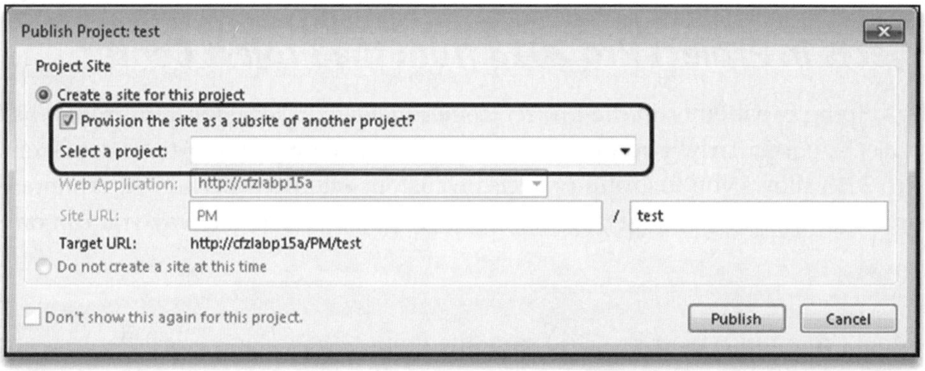

Figure 16 - 18: Publish Project dialog

You can create a program site by creating a new project using Project Web App or Project Pro 2013. You can later insert the member projects into the program-level project to create a master project, or you can surface critical milestones in the program-level project using cross-project dependencies.

Opening Multiple Projects to Create a Master Project

To open multiple projects simultaneously to create a new master project or temporary master project, use the **Ctrl** key on your computer keyboard to select two or more projects, and then click the *Open* pick list. Instead of opening each selected project individually, the system creates a master project in Project Pro 2013 with each of the selected projects as subprojects of the master project. You can use a master project to set cross-project dependencies between tasks in the selected projects, or to analyze trends in the portfolio of selected projects. Figure 16 - 19 shows a master project consisting of three subprojects.

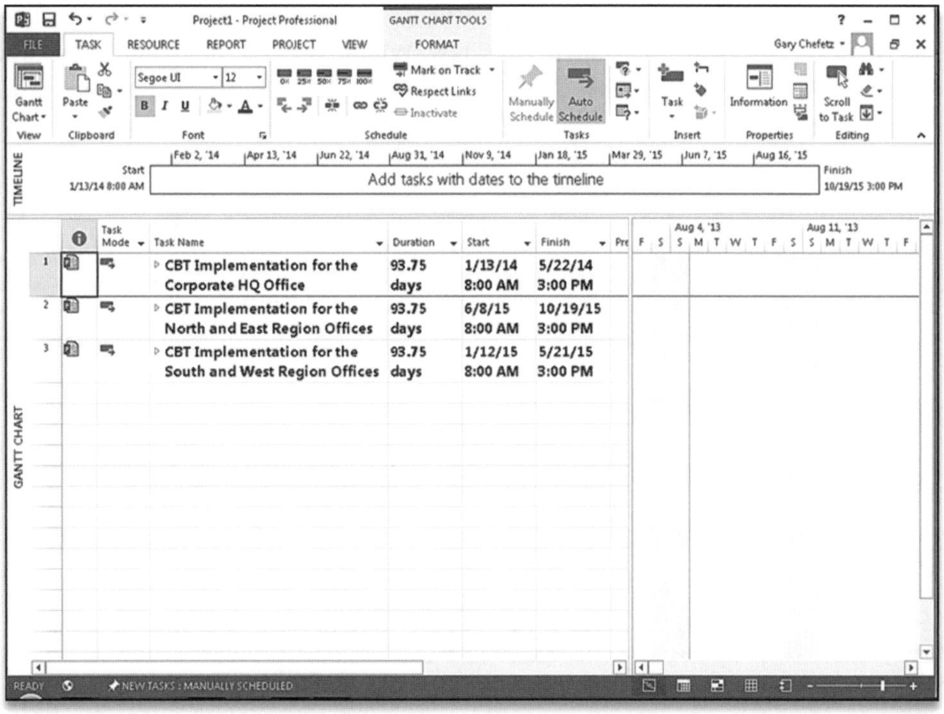

Figure 16 - 19: Master project includes three subprojects

After you create the master project, expand each of the subprojects by clicking the *Expand/Collapse* indicator (▸) to the left of each project name. To limit the amount of scrolling you must do to open each subproject, begin with the last subproject, and work your way toward the top. Edit each subproject as per your requirements, including setting cross-project dependencies between the various subprojects. If you save and publish a master project in Project Server 2013, the master project appears as a regular project in the *Project Center* page except that it has a unique icon indicating that it is a master project as shown in Figure 16 - 20.

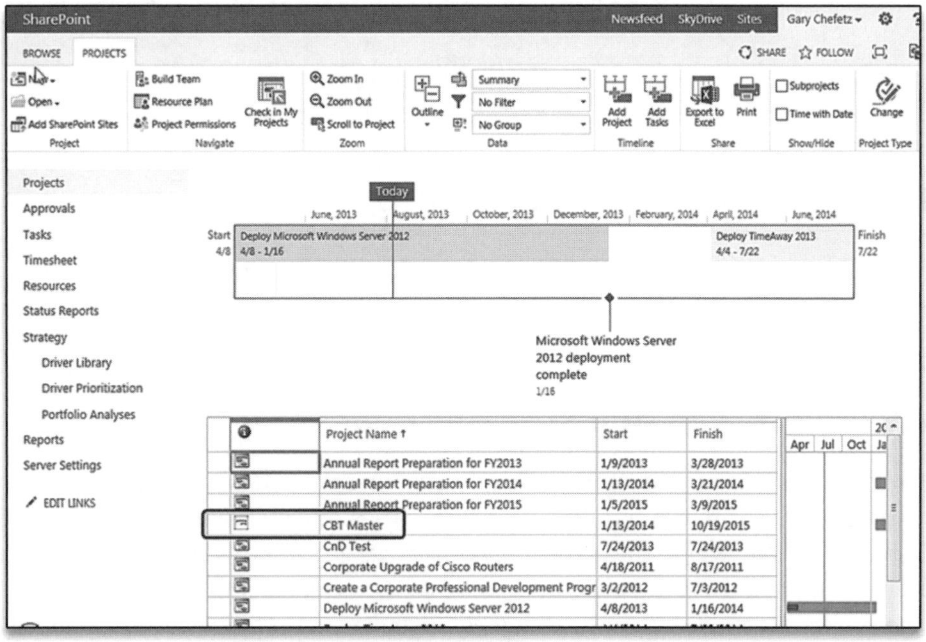

Figure 16 - 20: Master Project in Project Center

Notice that the three CBT projects no longer show in the Project Center. To view subprojects, from the *Show/Hide* section of the *Projects* ribbon, select the *Subprojects* checkbox. When you click the name of a master project in the *Project Center* page and then select the *Schedule* page, the system displays a detailed master project view that allows you to expand the details in each subproject. Figure 16 - 21 shows the *Schedule* page for the master project with one of the subprojects expanded to show the project details.

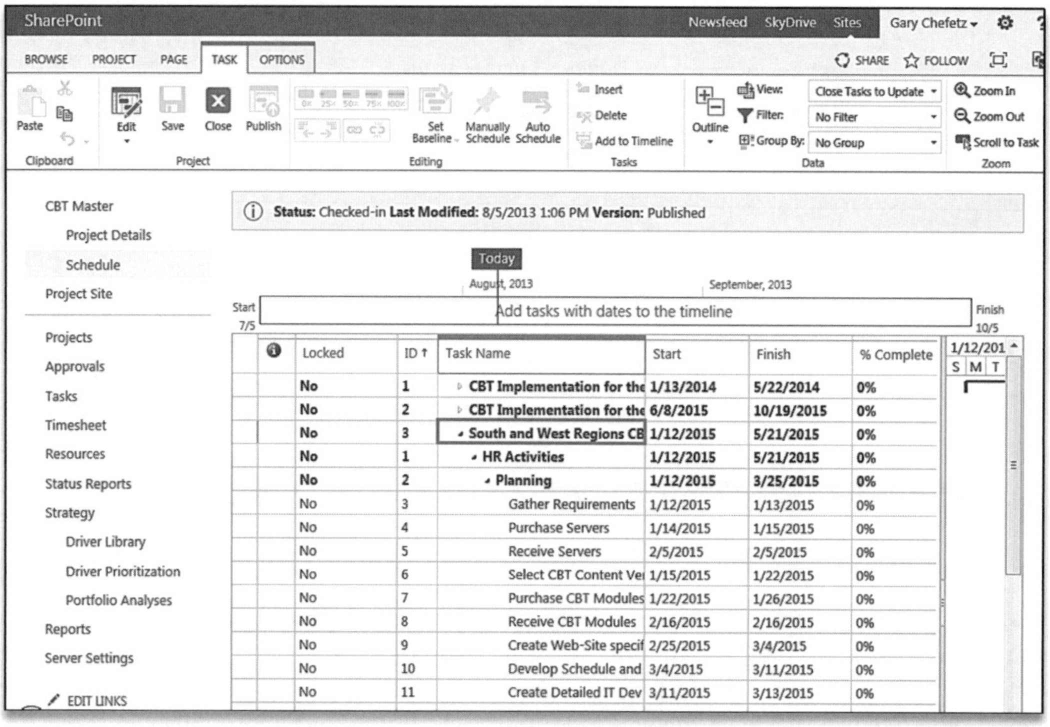

Figure 16 - 21: Project Details page for a master project

Warning: You cannot edit a Master Project in Project Web App. Instead, you must use Project Pro 2013.

Editing Projects in Project Web App

Not only can you view information in project detail views, you can also edit projects using these views. You can open a project for editing within Project Web App or open a project for editing in Project Pro 2013 from the *Project Center* page in Project Web App.

Working with Project Web App Schedule Page

You navigate to the *Project Detail Pages* for a project by clicking on the name of a project in the *Project Center* page. The *Project Detail* pages, visible for each individual project, varies by enterprise project type. You learned these concepts in Module 05, *Working with Portfolio and Project Governance,* where you not only learned to work with *Project Detail* pages, you learned to create them. In Module 05, you created an Enterprise Project Type (EPT) with a workflow, but the project shown in Figure 16 - 22 does not have a workflow evident by the absence of a *Workflow Status* page.

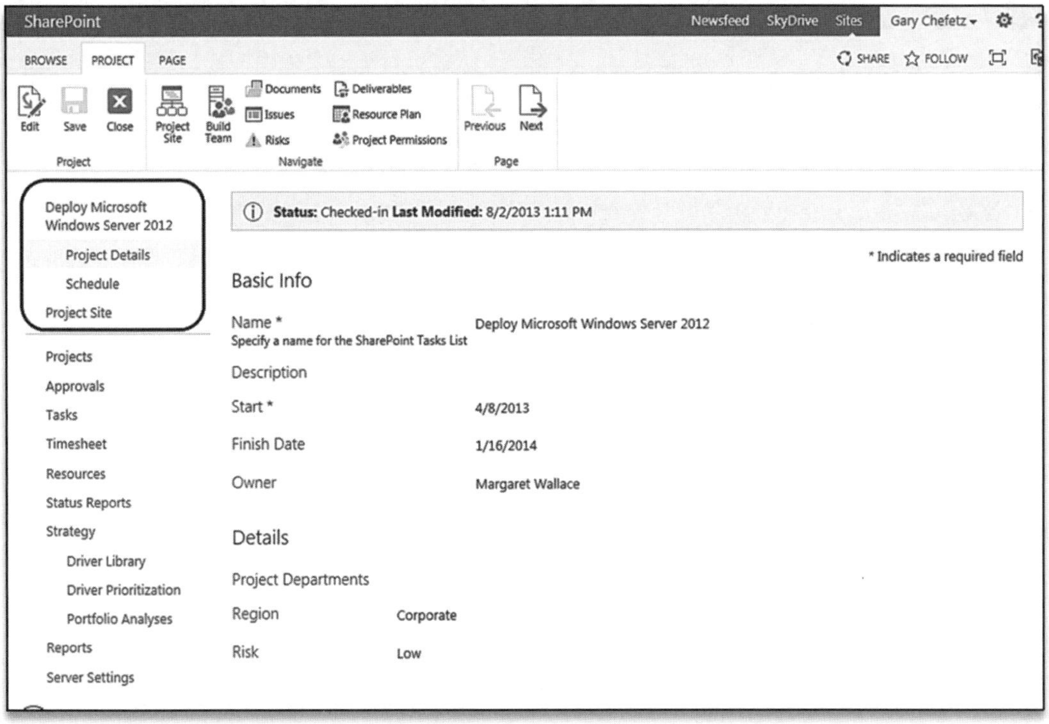

Figure 16 - 22: PDP collection for a project without workflow

EPT's without workflow display all *Project Detail* pages assigned to it at all times. Remember that you need a workflow to use stages, and stages give you control over PDP display. In this case, the EPT also does not display a *Strategic Impact* page. If your organization does not use the portfolio analysis features of Project Server 2013, this presentation is more likely your norm.

Information: When you open a project that is in a stage of a workflow that occurs prior to allowing users to edit the schedule, you may not be able to access the *Schedule* page for the project. Instead, the system displays the set of Project Detail Pages that the creator of the workflow determined that you should see at the current stage.

The *Project Details* page displays the current values for fields exposed on the page. Notice in Figure 16 - 23, the gray information band across the top displaying the *Checked-in* state of the project and the *Last Modified* date. By default, projects open in *Read-Only* mode in Project Web App unless you already have the project open in your current session. In the *Project* section of the *Project* ribbon, use the *Edit, Save* and *Close* buttons to perform basic file operations.

Warning: It is very easy to leave a project open and checked out when closing your browser sessions. When you forget to close and check in a project, you may need to use the *Check in My Projects* button found in the *Navigate* section of the *Projects* ribbon in the Project Center shown previously in Figure 16 - 6.

Before you can edit project details or the project schedule, you must click the *Edit* button on the *Project* ribbon, or activate the *Task* ribbon visible on the *Schedule* page as shown in Figure 16 - 23. Notice the familiar gray status bar across the page that indicates the project is open as does the fact that the system does not gray out the various buttons in the *Editing* section of the ribbon.

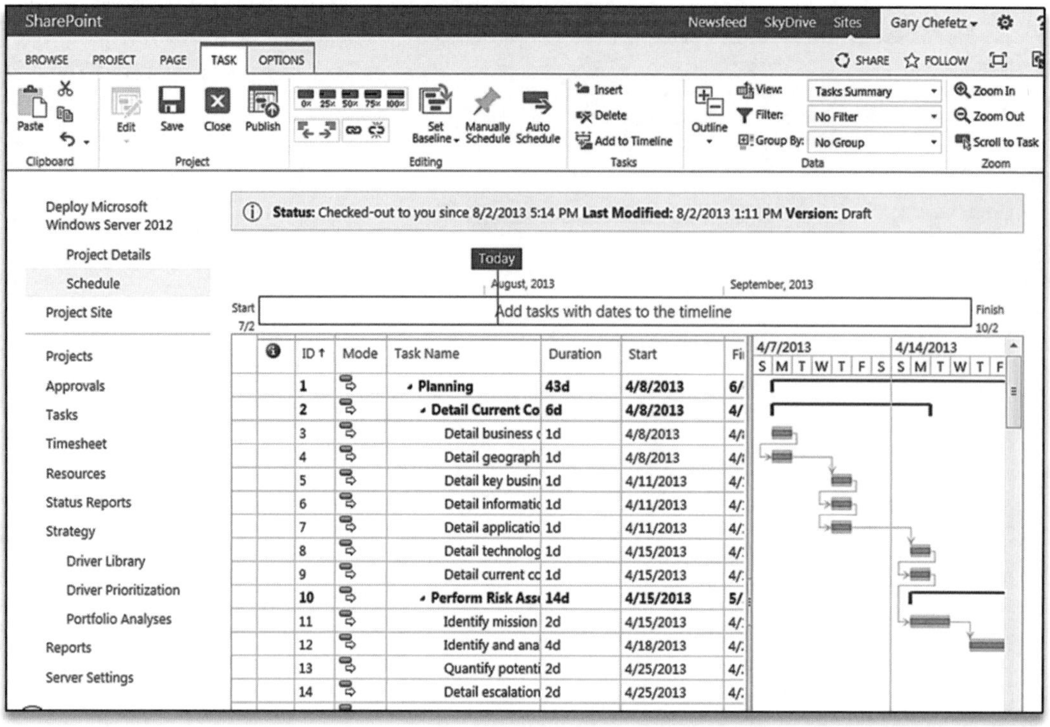

Figure 16 - 23: Schedule page with Task ribbon active

Regardless of whether you open and edit your project in Project Web App or use Project Pro 2013, you are always working on a draft. The changes that you make to the schedule in your draft copy do not appear in the system until you publish them. However, project summary data and custom fields do become available when you save those changes. The *Schedule* page contains both a *Project* and a *Task* tab because you need access to both project-level and task-level functions on this page. In Figure 16 - 24, I zoom in on the critical editing features on the ribbon.

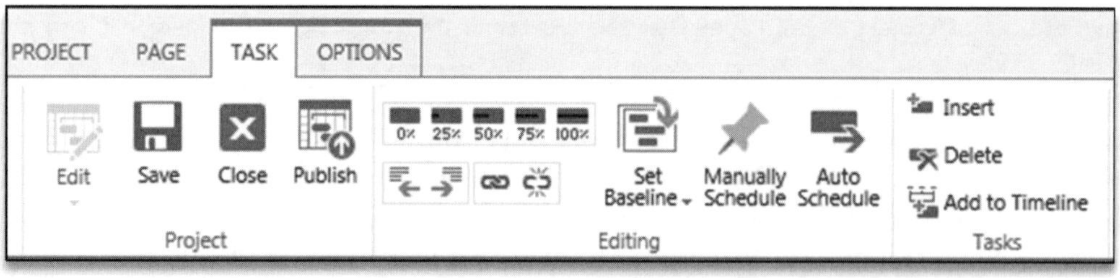

Figure 16 - 24: Project Details page with the Task ribbon selected

In the partial *Task* ribbon shown in Figure 16 - 24, notice the *Project, Editing* and *Tasks* sections. These three sections contain the web-based project editing tools available in Project Server 2013 using familiar functionality similar to what you find in Project Pro 2013. Project Web App's editing capability supports much stronger project management collaboration, allowing numerous users to participate in project schedule development, or even to manage simple projects from end to end, including project tracking, without using Project Pro 2013. The now familiar *Data* and *Zoom* sections that I do not show provide you with tools to manipulate the data display and Gantt chart displays, respectively.

Information: The project editing tools available in the Project Web App interface are a "simple" subset of the editing capabilities you find in Project Pro 2013, and are limited in their functionality. For example, you cannot save an interim plan using the *Set Baseline* feature in Project Web App.

Set a Baseline

New for Project Web App with the 2013 release is the ability to set or clear a baseline, something that required the Project Pro client software in previous versions. To set a baseline for your project, click the *Set Baseline* pick list to reveal the menu selections shown in Figure 16 - 25. Notice that you can set or clear a baseline for any of the baselines to which you have access.

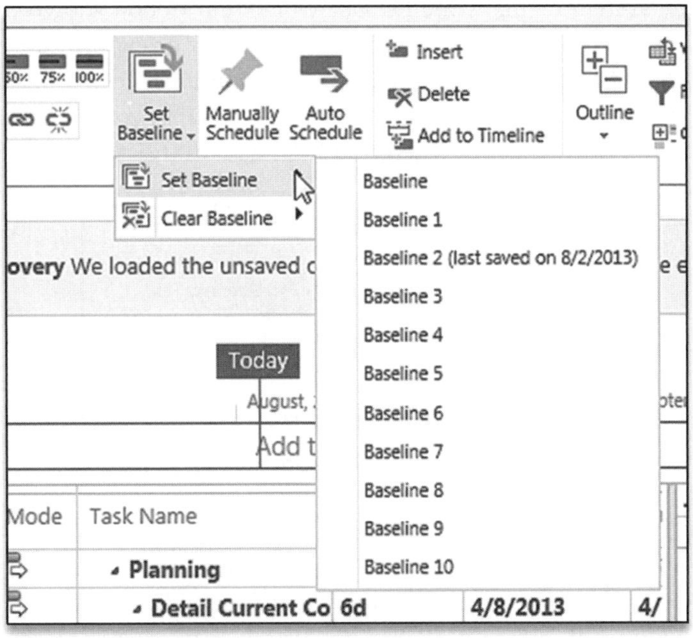

Figure 16 - 25: Set Baseline fly out menu

Using the Timeline on the Schedule Page

The *Tasks* section of the *Task* ribbon contains an *Add to Timeline* button. Because this page strictly deals with tasks, the ribbon does not give you the option to add projects. If you are creating a timeline for a master project, the system sees all lines as tasks. Using the timeline on the *Schedule* page is identical to using the timeline on the *Project Center* page so I do not rehash it here.

Using the Project Ribbon

If you click the *Project* tab, the system displays the *Project* ribbon shown in Figure 16 - 26. This ribbon provides redundant *Edit, Save,* and *Close* buttons. The *Navigate* section provides navigation to the *Project Site* page using the *Project Site* button or to any of the four primary *Project Site* features using the *Documents, Issues, Risks* and *Deliverables* buttons. You also find *Build Team* and *Resource Plan* buttons to activate these two features and the *Project Permissions* button that allows you to set project-level permissions specific to your selected project. Finally, the *Previous* and *Next* buttons found in the *Page* section of the ribbon, allow you to switch between schedule pages and the *Project Fields* page where you can edit the *Project Name, Project Start Date* and *Project Owner* fields as well as any enterprise custom fields applicable to the specific project. Note in the figure that the system grays out the *Edit* button because the project is open for editing.

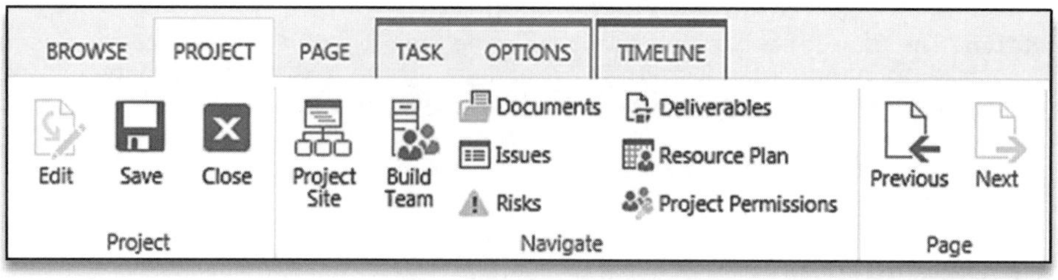

Figure 16 - 26: Project ribbon

Using the Options Ribbon

Click the *Options* tab and the system displays the *Options* contextual ribbon shown in Figure 16 - 27. Using the *Share* section of the *Options* ribbon, you can choose to print the project or export it to Excel. In the *Show/Hide* section, select the *Project Summary Task* option to display the project summary task in the current view and select the *Time with Date* option to change the date/time format. The *Link To* section contains the *Related Items* button to access the linking functionality you learned about when creating issues and risks.

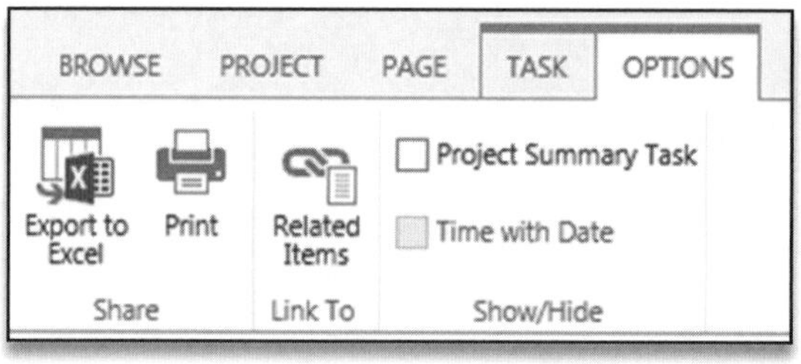

Figure 16 - 27: Options ribbon

To edit the project, from the *Project* section of the *Task* ribbon, click the *Edit* pick list and select the *In Project Web App* item. The system opens the project for editing, refreshes the page, updates the status bar below the ribbon to indicate the project is checked out, and makes all but the *Edit* button on the ribbon available as the project is now open for editing as shown in Figure 16 - 28.

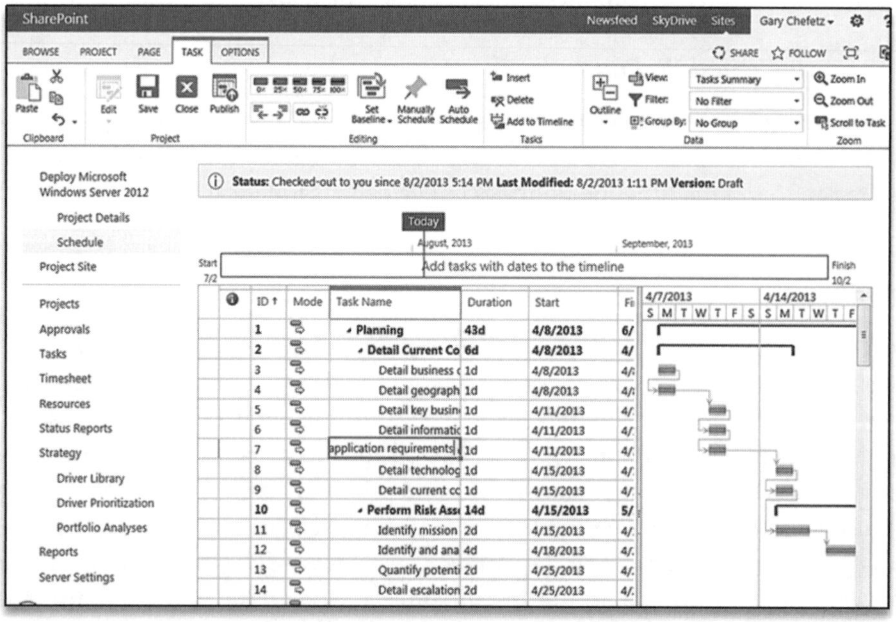

Figure 16 - 28: Project Open for Editing

Editing the Project Schedule in Project Web App

With your project open for editing and the *Schedule* page displayed in Project Web App, you can edit your project schedule in a variety of ways. You can create, edit, and delete tasks and you can link tasks using Project Web App. You can add resources to tasks, but the controls available to you make complex assignments difficult to execute. For instance, the *Assign Resources* dialog in Project Pro 2013 allows you to reassign remaining work on a task that has already started. You cannot do this using any approach in Project Web App. For the most part, the system limits you to editing only what you can see, and what you can do with what you see, in a simple web data grid. Therefore, you must create one or more detail views suited to perform the type of editing you want to do. Figure 16 - 29 shows the *Units* column added to the *Assignments Detail* view in Project Web App allowing me to set the units value for the resource on an assignment; however, this view does not allow me to create or remove an assignment.

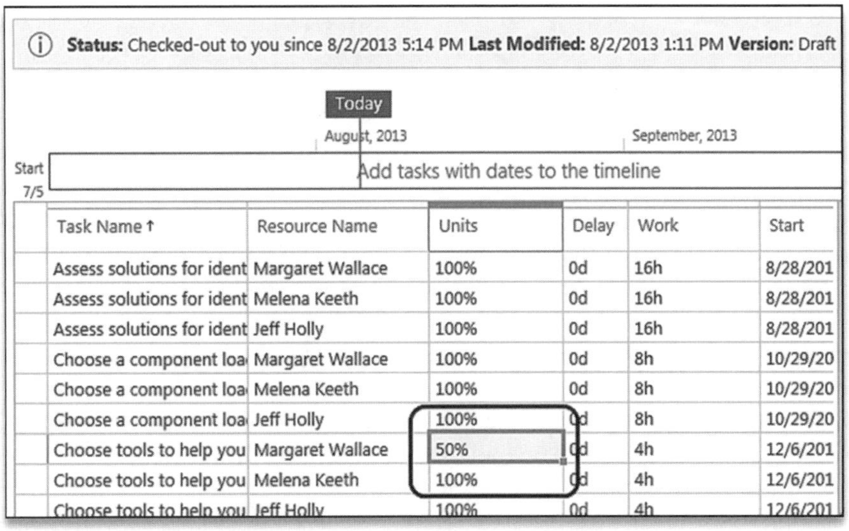

Figure 16 - 29: Units field added to Assignments Detail view

Best Practice: MSProjectExperts recommends that you create views specifically for editing projects as the product team designed all of the default views for viewing and not editing. By creating views specifically for this purpose, you can expose the information you need to edit and exclude information that you do not want edited in Project Web App.

To create a resource assignment you must use a task view. When you click the pick list in the *Resource Names* column, the system displays a list of all resources on the project team as shown in Figure 16 - 30.

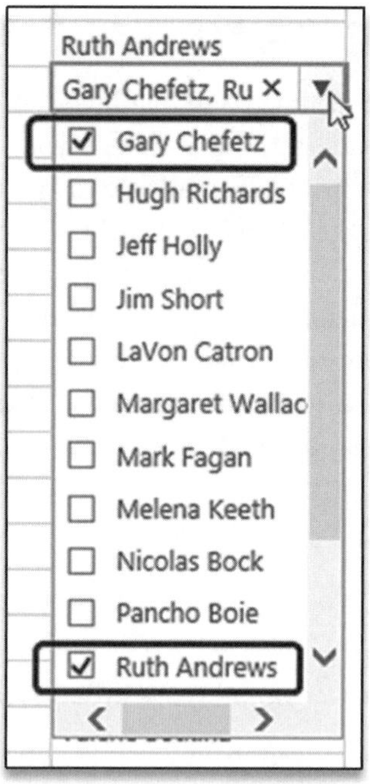

Figure 16 - 30: Resource Names column

Notice that the pick list allows you to select multiple resources, but it does not allow you to specify or edit the assignment *Units* value, you must switch to a custom assignment view to edit assignment units. You also cannot specify the task type. Project Web App uses the default task type specified for the project.

Limitations when Editing Projects in Project Web App

There are a number of features not supported when you edit projects in Project Web App. The most important limitations are those that cause your project to be ineligible for editing as follows:

- Blank task lines or blank rows in a project schedule cause a project to open read-only and the system does not allow you to edit the schedule. Project in a stand-alone environment can handle blank lines, but realize that when you save your schedules to Project Server, you are saving to a database. Databases do not handle blank records very well. Besides making your schedule ineligible for editing in Project Web App, these can cause unexpected problems elsewhere in the system.

- Other than using Project Web App to help you create master projects, you cannot edit master projects in Project Web App. These will always open read-only.

- Project Web App does not support editing projects with task calendars applied. If you include these in your project schedules, they will open read-only in Project Web App.

Beyond those items that render your project read-only in Project Web App, you should be aware of functional limitations you face when editing a project on the web as follows:

- You cannot make a task inactive using Project Web App.

- Cross-project links require that you use Project Pro 2013.

- You cannot make an assignment on summary tasks using Project Web App. Although there are some advanced scheduling techniques where assignments on summary tasks are useful, these are generally a bad idea and can cause unexpected results if you do not understand the ramifications.

- *Cost* and *Material* resource assignments are out of reach in Project Web App. You must use the Project Pro 2013 client to support these.

- Not surprisingly, you cannot set a *Task* type in Project Web App.

- You cannot edit a subproject, or create or edit master projects using Project Web App, except for the technique I showed you earlier in this module.

- You must set deadlines for tasks using Project Pro 2013, as nothing in Project Web App allows you to do this.

- You must edit WBS fields using Project Pro 2013 as Project Web App does not support setting or editing these.

- The web interface does not support *effort-driven* scheduling; therefore, you must address effort-driven tasks using Project Pro 2013. Notice that the system deselects the *effort-driven* option by default in Project Pro 2013.

Tips for Editing Projects in Project Web App

Perhaps the most significant new experience for Project Web App is that it now recalculates the schedule for you with every entry the way Project Pro 2013 does when you have the *Calculation* option set to *Automatic.* Opening and closing the file also invokes the scheduling engine similar to Project Pro 2013.

When you edit projects in Project Web App, it is very easy to forget to save and check in your projects. Unlike the Project client that persists on your desktop until you close it, it is very easy to wander off to other tasks without saving your changes or checking in your project. You must be constantly mindful of this or you are likely to cause frustration for yourself and others by forgetting these important steps. If you are trying to edit a project in Project Web App and you cannot, ask yourself whether you remembered to open it for editing. Remember that the status bar that appears just below the ribbon when you open a project for editing contains important information regarding the current state of your project.

Renaming a Project using Project Web App

To rename a project, edit the name in the *Name* field as shown in Figure 16 - 31. When you edit the name of the project, this action renames the project in the Project Server 2013 database. Changing the name in the *Owner* field allows the new owner to see and open the project in Project Pro 2013, if they do not otherwise have permission to access the project. In addition to editing the *Name* and *Owner* fields, you can also edit the values in any custom enterprise *Project* fields.

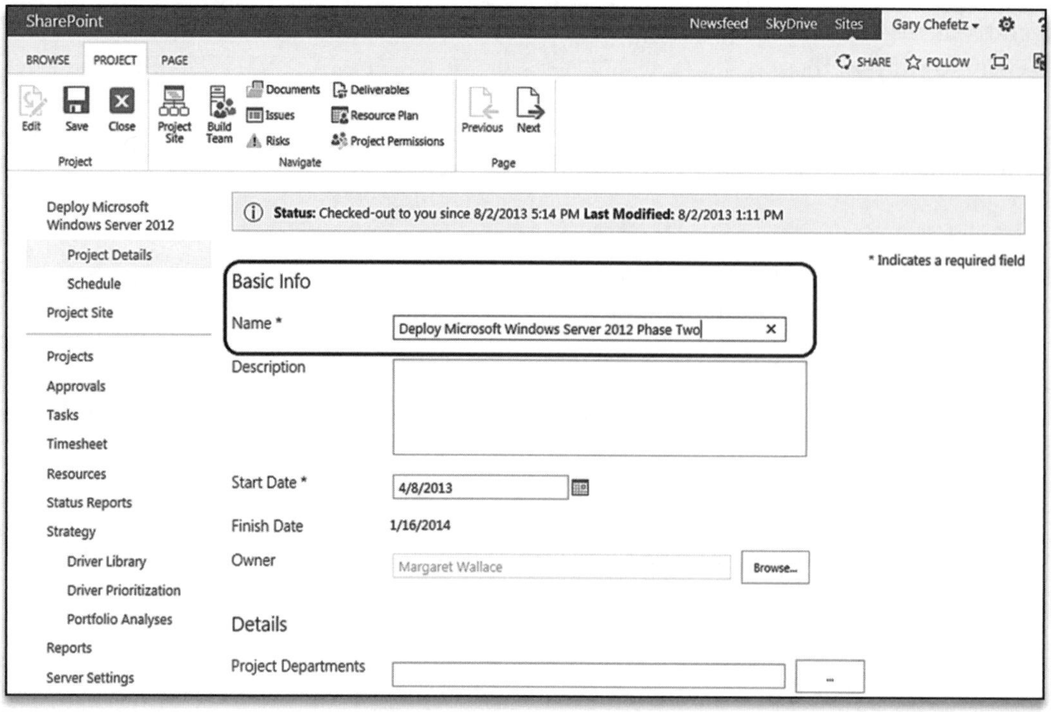

Figure 16 - 31: Edit Project Name field

After you make your changes on the *Project Details* page, from the *Project* section of the *Project* ribbon, click the *Save* button to save the changes in the *Draft* database. While the system saves the changes, it displays progress information in the upper right corner of the page.

Warning: To rename the project, you must both save and publish the project. When you save the project, the system changes the project name in the *Draft* database. When you publish the project, the system changes the project name in the *Published* database and in the Project Site associated with the project.

If you want to publish the changes to the *Published* database, from the *Quick Launch* menu, click the *Schedule* link or the *Project Name* link. The system displays the *Schedule* page. From the *Project* section of the *Task* ribbon, click the *Publish* button. While the system publishes the changes, it displays progress information in the upper right corner of the page. When finished, click the *Project* tab to display the *Project* ribbon and then click the *Close* button. The system displays the *Close* dialog shown in Figure 16 - 32.

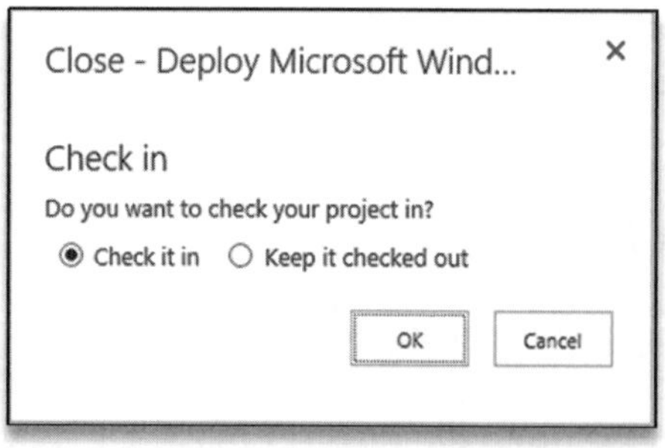

Figure 16 - 32: Close dialog

The *Close* dialog gives you the option to check in your project by selecting the *Check it in* option or you can select the *Keep it checked out* option. Click the *Cancel* button if you want to cancel your action. Clicking the *OK* button closes the project in the state you selected.

Rename a Project Using Project Pro 2013

You can also rename a project using Project Pro 2013 by completing the following steps:

1. Click *File* ➢ *Open* in the *Backstage*.
2. In the *Open* dialog, double-click the *Retrieve the list of all projects from Project Server* item.
3. Right-click the name of the project and select the *Rename* item on the shortcut menu.
4. Enter the new name for the enterprise project and then press the **Enter** key on your computer keyboard.
5. In the confirmation dialog, click the *OK* button.
6. Open the project from the *Open* dialog.
7. Publish the project again.

Working with Project Detail Views

The *View* pick list offers twenty default views for the *Project Details* page along with any custom views created by your Project Server administrator. Project Detail views include three types of views: *Task* views, *Assignment* views, and *Resource* views. Table 16 - 2 lists the available views for each type.

Information: The system remembers which detailed project view you select each time you display the *Project Details* page, and returns to that view when you select another project from the *Project Center* page.

Task Views	Assignment Views	Resource Views
Tasks Cost	Assignments Cost	Resources Cost
Tasks Detail	Assignments Detail	
Tasks Earned Value	Assignments Earned Value	Resources Earned Value
Tasks Leveling		
Tasks Schedule		
Tasks Summary	Assignments Summary	Resources Summary
Tasks Top-Level		
Tasks Tracking	Assignments Tracking	

Task Views	Assignment Views	Resource Views
Tasks Work	Assignments Work	Resources Work
Close Tasks to Update		

Table 16 - 2: Available Views on the Project Details page

Like *Project Center* views, you can apply grouping and filtering to any detailed project view. Use the *Zoom In* and *Zoom Out* buttons to change the Gantt chart timescale from periods as small as 15-minute intervals to as large as years. Use the *Scroll to Task* button to scroll the Gantt chart to the start date of the selected task.

Closing Tasks to Updates

For Project Server 2013, you close tasks to updates using a task view rather than a menu item, as was the case for Project Server 2010. When you complete an enterprise project, or when you complete part of a project, you can close tasks in the project to prevent team members from entering additional progress on completed tasks. To close tasks to further updates, from the *Data* section of the *Task* ribbon, click the *View* pick list and select the *Close Tasks to Updates* item as shown in Figure 16 - 33.

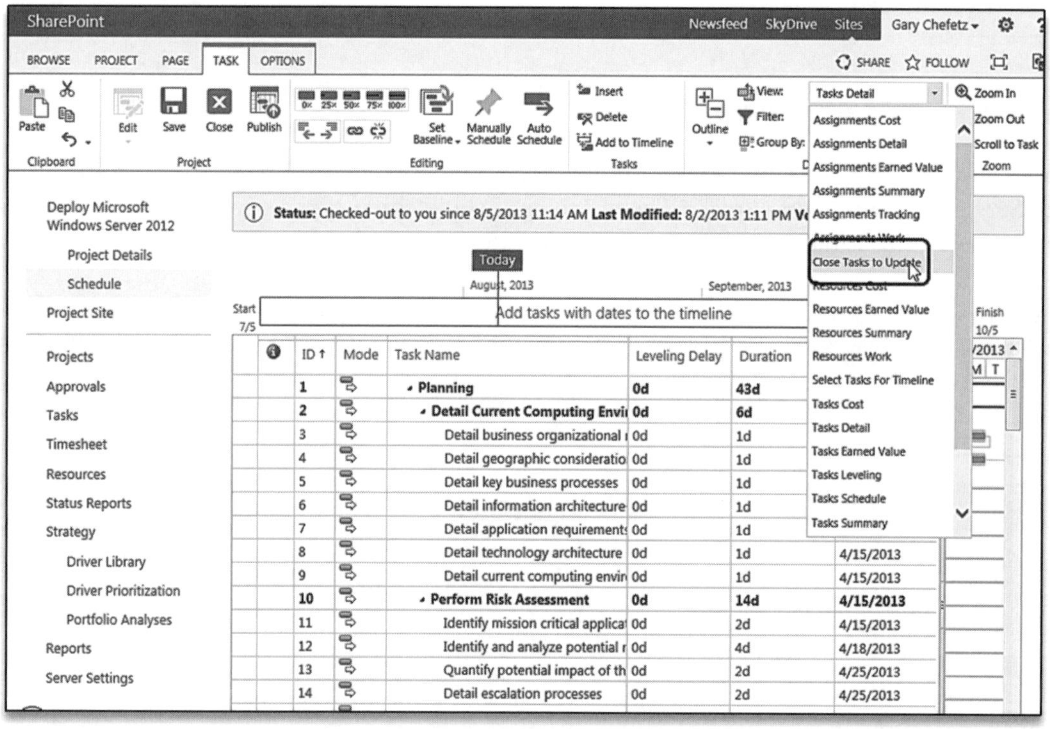

Figure 16 - 33: Close Tasks to Update view

The system applies the *Close Tasks to Update* view containing the *Locked* column shown in Figure 16 - 34. Click the pick list in the *Locked* column and select the *Yes* value to lock the task, thus preventing team members from entering and submitting progress against them, or leave the default *No* value to allow team members to continue entering and submitting progress. Next, click the *Submit* button to submit your changes and publish them later, or click the *Publish* button to finalize the action immediately. After publishing your project, the system locks the selected tasks with the *Yes* value to prevent team members from entering and submitting progress against them.

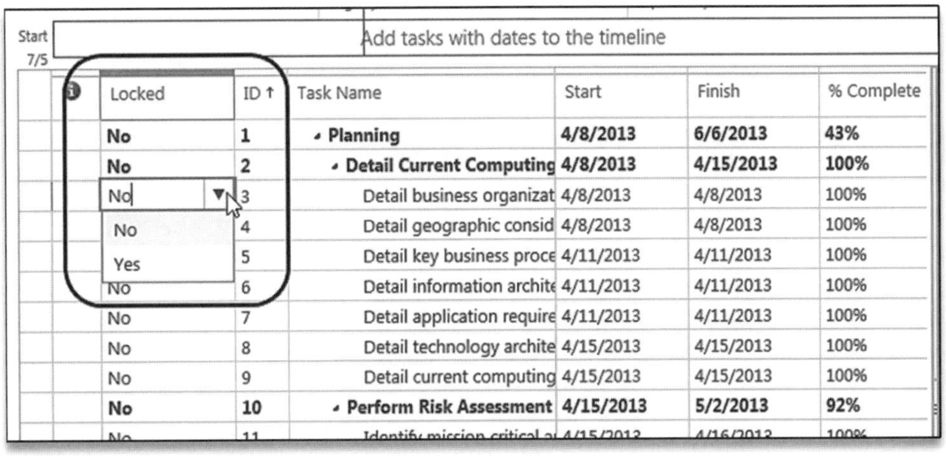

Figure 16 - 34: Close Tasks to Update view, Locked column

Warning: By default, Project Server 2013 applies sorting on the *ID* column, displaying the tasks in natural sequence order. Click any column header to re-sort the tasks by values in that column.

Warning: When you change from the default SharePoint permissions mode, to Project Server permissions mode, a bug causes the system to omit category membership for the *Close Tasks to Update* view. You must add the *My Organization* and the *My Projects* categories to the view; otherwise, it is not visible to any users.

Setting Project Permissions

Project Server 2013 allows project owners to set special permissions for users on the project. Without administrator rights a project manager can grant permissions so that Project Web App users, who cannot otherwise access the project, can perform specific actions on the project. Project managers/owners can grant the following permissions using this new feature:

- Open the project within Project Pro 2013 or Project Web App
- Edit and save the project within Project Pro 2013 or Project Web App
- Edit Project Summary Fields within Project Pro 2013 or Project Web App
- Publish the project within Project Pro 2013 or Project Web App
- View the Project Summary in the Project Center
- View the Project Schedule Details in Project Web App
- View the Project Site

Information: In order for a project manager to use this feature, the project manager must have the *Manage Basic Project Security* category permission enabled.

To access the *Project Permissions* feature with your project open in Project Web App, from the *Navigate* section of the *Project* ribbon, click the *Project Permissions* button. The system displays the *Project Permissions* page shown in Figure 16 - 35.

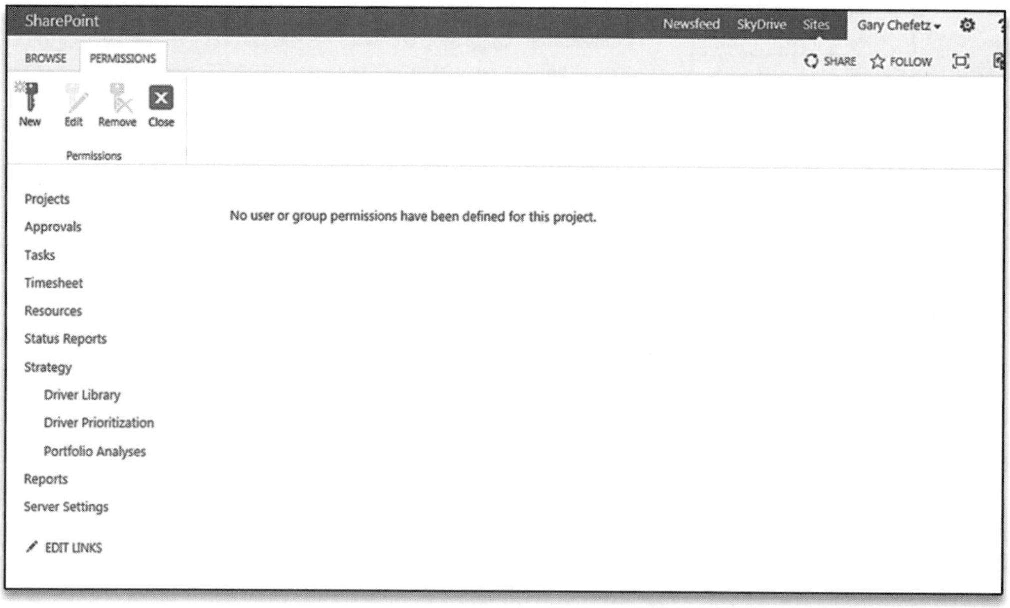

Figure 16 - 35: Project Permissions page

To create new permissions, from the *Permissions* section of the *Permissions* ribbon, click the *New* button. The system displays the *Edit Project Permissions* page shown in Figure 16 - 36.

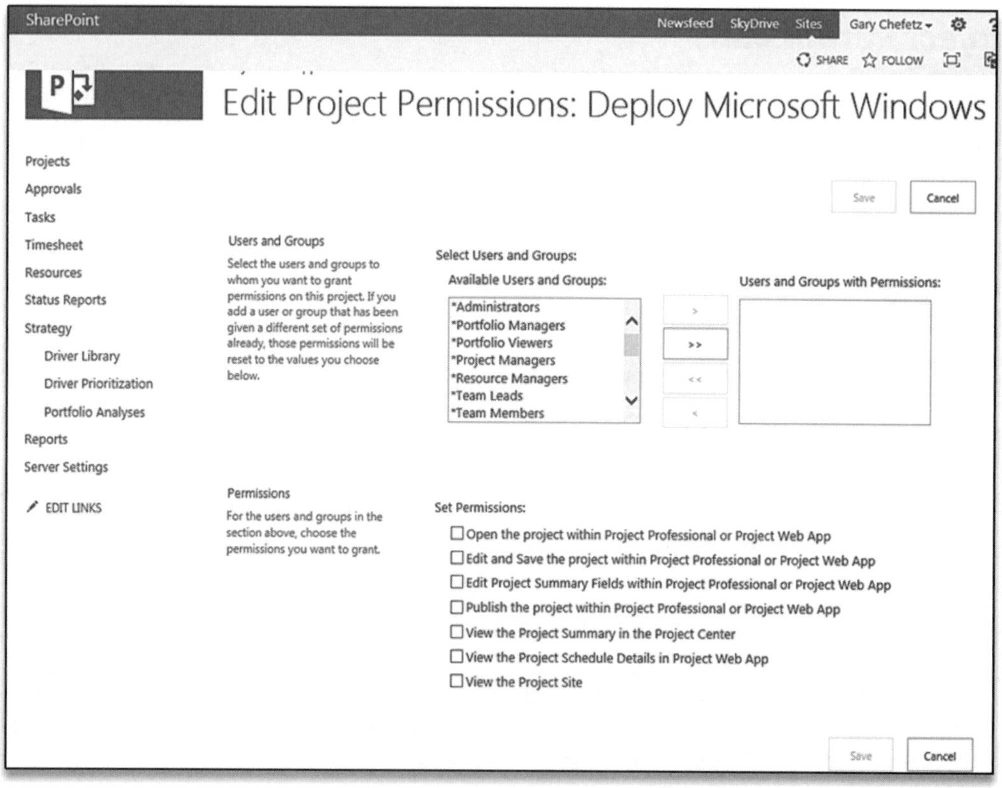

Figure 16 - 36: Edit Project Permissions page

Notice in the *Users and Groups* section of the page that you can specify permissions for entire security groups in Project Server 2013 as well as for individual users. Select a user or group from the *Available Users and Groups* list on the left and click the *Add* button to move them to the *Users and Groups with Permissions* list on the right. To select multiple users or groups, hold the **Ctrl** key on your computer keyboard to multi-select. Next, select the permissions that you want to grant to the selected user(s) and click the *Save* button to activate your changes. The system redisplays the *Project Permissions* page with the added permissions set as shown in Figure 16 - 37.

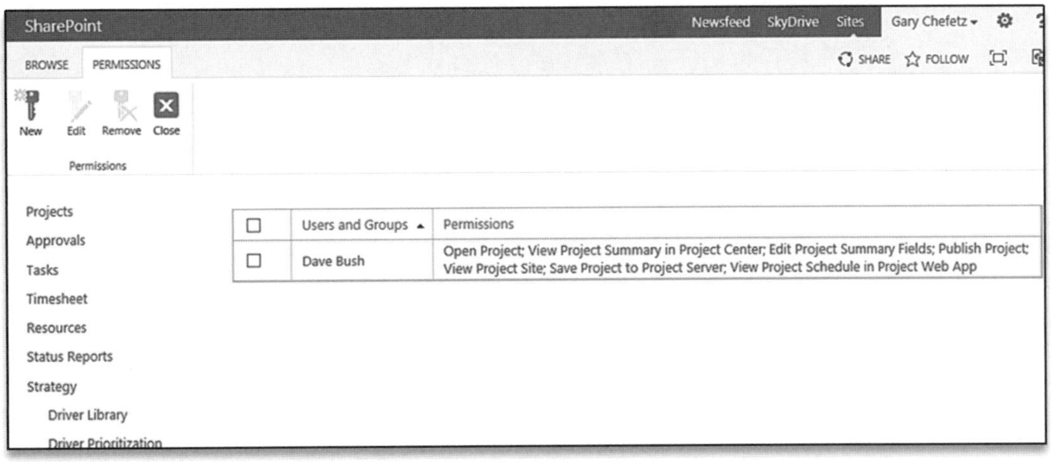

Figure 16 - 37: Project Permissions page with a permission set displayed

Notice that I gave *Dave Bush* all permissions available for this project. To edit the permission set after creating it, simply select the checkbox next to the permission set you want to edit and click the *Edit* button. To remove a permission set completely, click the *Remove* button after selecting it from the grid. Click the *Close* button to return to your previous screen.

Navigating to the Project Site

You use the *Project Detail* view to access Project Sites for projects or to navigate directly to the *Risks, Issues, Documents,* or *Deliverables* page for a project. To navigate to the Project Site, from the *Navigate* section of the *Projects* ribbon, click the *Project Site* button. Project Server 2013 opens a new Internet Explorer tab or window and displays the Project Site for your selected project.

Project Center Summary

Since you created your first proposal in Module 03, *Understanding the Project Web App 2013 Interface,* you continuously return to the Project Center to launch most of the day-to-day tasks that you perform in Project Web App. The Project Center is the hub of most activity and the source for the latest information about your entire project portfolio.

Module 17

Creating and Managing Views

Learning Objectives

After completing this module, you will be able to:

- Create and manage Gantt chart formats
- Create and manage grouping formats
- Create and modify Project Web App views
- Create custom enterprise Task and Resource views in Project Pro 2013

Inside Module 17

Understanding Views

One of the most common tasks for maintaining Project Server 2013 is creating and maintaining views. With both project data and resource data in the Project Server database, the next step is to create the custom views your system users need. You likely need to create two types of views:

- Views visible in Project Web App
- Views visible in Project Pro 2013

Information: It is not possible to create a view that is visible in both Project Web App and Project Pro 2013. If you need to display the same information in both applications, you must create two separate views. In this module, I teach you how to create both types of views.

View Types

Project Server 2013 includes eleven types of Project Web App views:

- **Project Center** views are portfolio-level views that display *Project Summary Task* information across the portfolio of projects, with a single line of information for each project.
- **Project** views display information for a single project. You access these by clicking the name of a project on the *Project Center* page. In Project Server 2013, these are not simply views; they also provide editing access to the projects they display. These views are further complemented by Project Detail Pages (PDP's) that you learned about in Module 05, *Working with Portfolio and Project Governance,* which provide *Read/Write* access to additional project information.
- **Resource Assignments** views display task assignment information for selected resources across all projects in the Project Server database.
- **Resource Center** views display information about the resources in the Enterprise Resource Pool.
- **My Work** views show project team members their task assignment information on the *Tasks* page and the *Assignment Details* page.
- **Resource Plan** views display *Resource Plan* information for proposals and enterprise projects.
- **Team Task** views display tasks assigned to *Team* resources. Accessed from the *Tasks* page by clicking the *Insert Task* button, *Team Task* views allow team members to take responsibility for tasks assigned to the *Team* resource.
- **Team Builder** views allow managers to build a team on an enterprise project from Project Web App.
- **Timesheet** views show project team members their assignment or project information on the *Timesheet* page using the *My Timesheet* or *My Work* views.
- **Portfolio Analysis Project Selection** views display workflow information for all projects and display in the project selection process of creating a portfolio analysis.
- **Portfolio Analyses** views display during the analysis process when performing a portfolio analysis.

Before you create any of these types of custom views for Project Web App, you may also need to create custom *Gantt Chart* formats and custom *Grouping* formats to apply to your custom views.

Creating Gantt Chart Formats

Before you begin creating Project Web App views, you should be aware of supporting customizations that can greatly enhance the visual appearance of the views you create. You must apply a *Gantt Chart* format to views that contain a Gantt chart, and you can optionally apply a *Grouping* format to most views in the system. For both of these elements you can use an existing format in the system or one that you customize using the built-in tools. Project Server 2013 displays Gantt charts in *Project Center, Project,* and *Assignment* views in Project Web App, along with the *Approval Preview* window available from the *Approvals* page. *Resource Center* views do not include a Gantt chart.

To create or modify *Gantt Chart* formats, log in to Project Web App with administrator permissions, click the *Gear* icon, and then click the *PWA Settings* link. In the *Look and Feel* section of the *PWA Settings* page, click the *Gantt Chart Formats* link. The system displays the *Gantt Chart Formats* page partially shown in Figure 17 - 1.

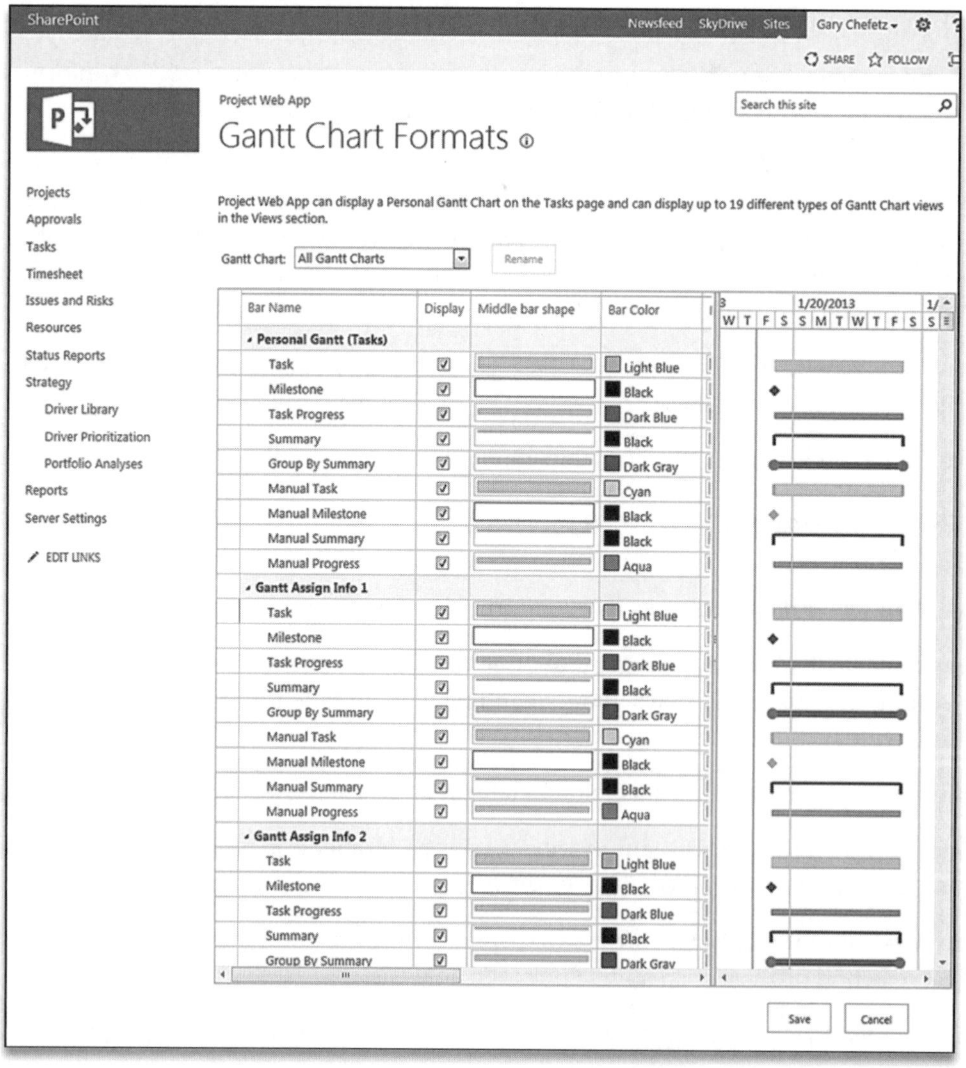

Figure 17 - 1: Gantt Chart Formats page

From the *Gantt Chart Formats* page, you can define up to 23 Gantt formats for use in Project Web App views. These formats are as follows:

- Personal Gantt (Tasks)
- Gantt Assign Info 1-4
- Approvals Gantt
- Gantt Chart (Project Center)
- Tracking (Project Center)
- Gantt Chart (Views)
- Detail Gantt (Views)
- Leveling Gantt
- Tracking Gantt
- Gantt 1–11

The *Personal Gantt (Tasks), Approvals Gantt,* and *Gantt Assign Info 1-4* formats apply to *Assignment* views only. You may apply the remaining Gantt formats to *Project Center* views and *Project* views. The *Personal Gantt (Tasks), Approvals Gantt,* and *Gantt Assign Info 1-4* formats offer graphical symbols for each of the following types of tasks:

- Normal Task
- Delegated Task
- Milestone
- Summary Task
- Group By Summary
- Progress
- Old Task (Approvals Gantt only)
- Old Summary (Approvals Gantt only)
- Old Milestone (Approvals Gantt only)

Project Center views and *Project* formats offer graphical symbols for the following types of tasks:

- Normal Task
- Critical Task
- External Task
- Milestone
- Summary Task
- Project Summary
- Group By Summary

- Progress
- Summary Progress
- Baseline Task
- Baseline Summary
- Baseline Milestone
- Preleveled Task
- Preleveled Summary
- Preleveled Milestone
- Deadline
- Slippage
- Delay
- Custom Duration 1–10
- Early Schedule
- Late Schedule
- External Milestone

From the preceding list of *Gantt Chart* format symbols, detailed task information does not apply to *Project Center* views. In other words, when you apply a *Gantt Chart* format that includes graphical symbols for detailed task information to a *Project Center* view, the system ignores task-level formatting because *Project Center* views do not display detailed task information.

For each symbol you select in the *Gantt Chart* format, you can determine whether the system displays the element, and if it does, you can select the start and end shapes, the middle bar shape, and the bar color and pattern for each shape. Project Server 2013 provides you a selection of 11 bar patterns, 17 colors, 22 start and end shapes, and 7 middle bar shapes. Using these options, you can create a distinctive look to emphasize specific information.

To create a custom *Gantt Chart* format, click the *Gantt Chart* pick list and select one of the custom *Gantt Chart* formats from the list. For example, notice in Figure 17 - 2 that I am about to select the *Gantt 1* format from the *Gantt Chart* pick list.

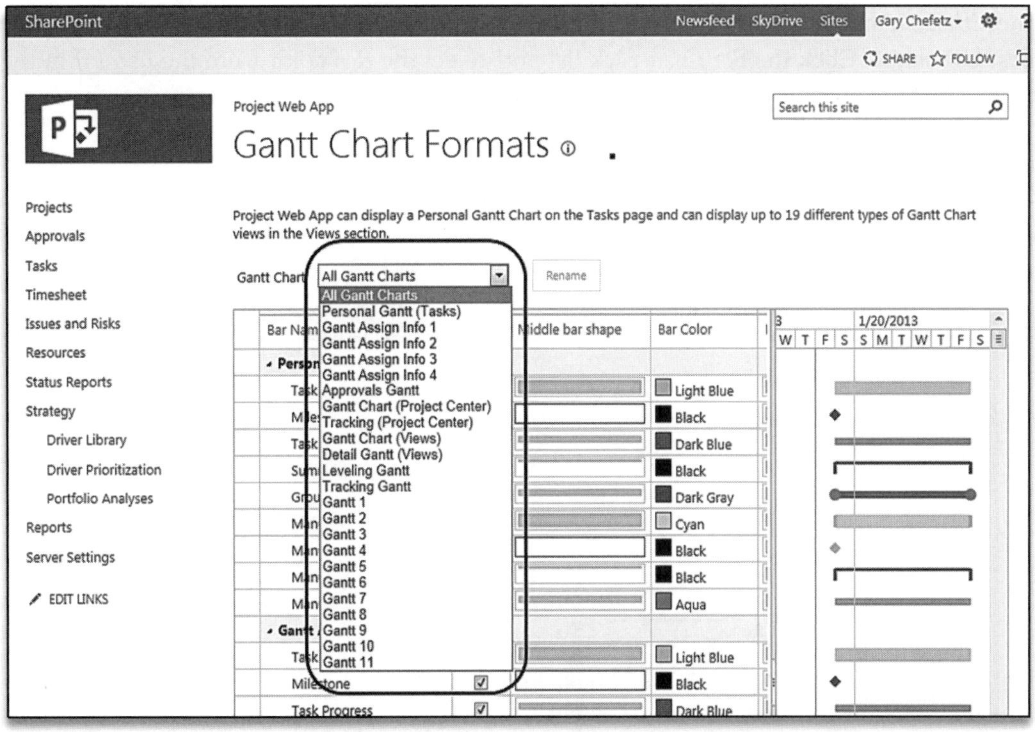

Figure 17 - 2: Select the Gantt 1 format from the Gantt Chart pick list

I want to create a custom *Gantt Chart* format using the *Gantt 1* format to show the critical path in detailed project views. In this custom *Gantt Chart* format, I want the system to format critical tasks in red and non-critical tasks in green, and I do not want to display external tasks. To create this custom *Gantt Chart* format, I must complete the following steps:

1. Select the *Gantt 1* format from the *Gantt Chart* pick list, click the *Rename* button, name the format *Critical Path Gantt*, and then click the *OK* button as shown in Figure 17 - 3.

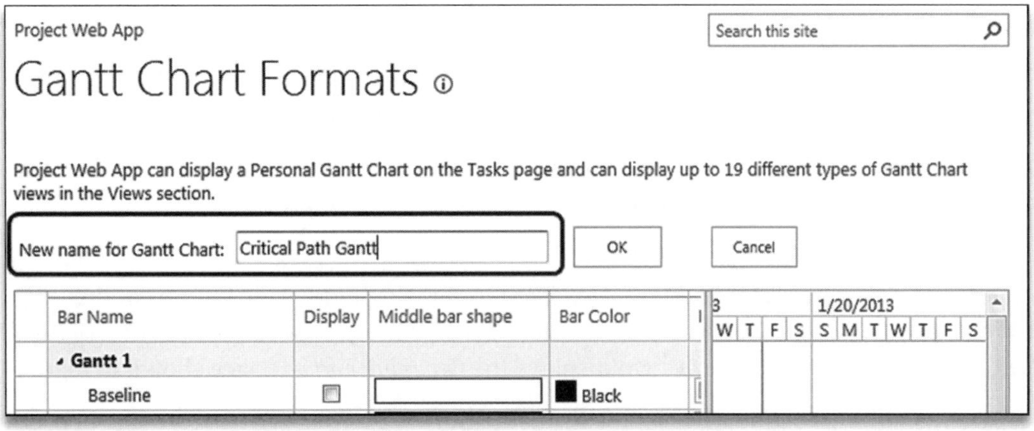

Figure 17 - 3: Renaming Gantt 1 to Critical Path Gantt

2. For the *Task* element, click the *Bar Color* pick list and select the *Green* color from the list. Click the *Bar Pattern* pick list and select the *Medium Fill* bar pattern (fourth item on the list).

3. For the *Critical* element, select the checkbox in the *Display* column. Click the *Middle Bar* pick list and select the first bar shape. Click the *Bar Color* pick list and select the *Red* color from the list. From the *Bar Pattern* pick list, select the *Medium Fill* bar pattern (fourth item on the list).
4. For the *External Task* element, deselect the *Display* checkbox option.

Figure 17 - 4 shows the completed custom *Critical Path Gantt* format definition. After you create a new custom *Gantt Chart* format, it becomes an available option for any related custom views you create for Project Web App. Click the *Cancel* button to exit the *Gantt Chart Formats* page to return to the *PWA Settings* page.

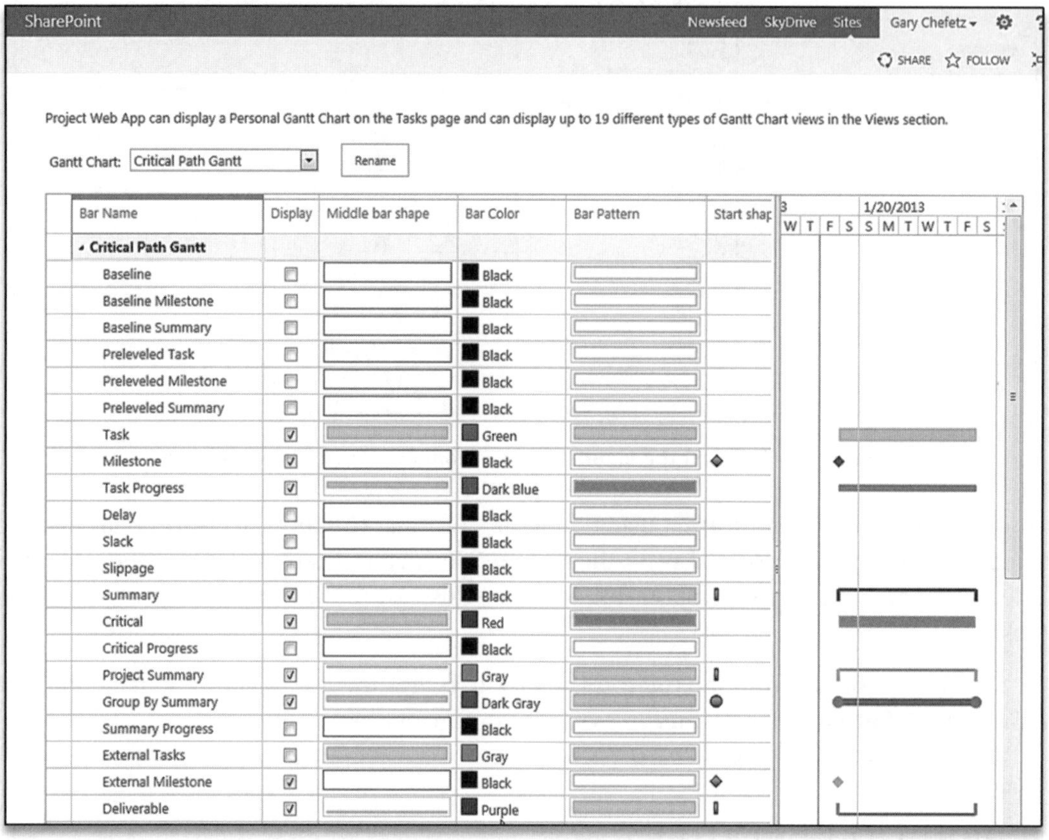

Figure 17 - 4: Completed custom Critical Path Gantt format

Creating Grouping Formats

Project Server 2013 allows you to create custom *Grouping* formats that apply colorful formatting to grouping levels in Project Web App views. To create a custom *Grouping* format, in the *Look and Feel* section of the *PWA Settings* page, click the *Grouping Formats* link. The system displays the *Grouping Formats* page shown in Figure 17 - 5.

Project Server 2013 includes two default *Grouping* formats, the *Timesheet* and *Views* formats, and also includes a *Generic* format plus nine additional *Grouping* formats that you can customize. The twelve available *Grouping* formats are as follows:

- Timesheet
- Views

- Generic
- Grouping 1–9

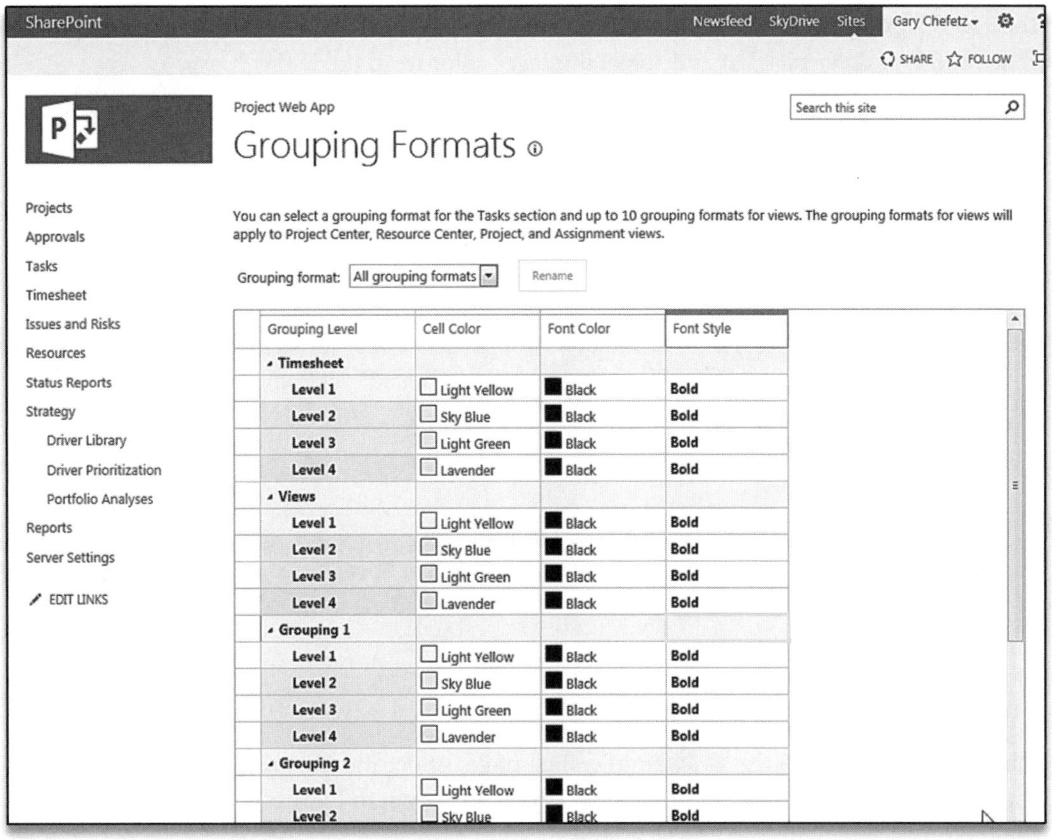

Figure 17 - 5: Grouping Formats page

You may determine the style of each *Grouping* format by selecting the following criteria for each of the four available grouping levels:

- Cell Color
- Font Color
- Font Style

Your color choices for cell colors and font colors for grouping formats are also limited to 16 colors like the *Gantt Chart* formats; however, the color assortment introduces lighter colors that are more applicable to use for backgrounds. Because grouping styles apply to the text as well as cell background formatting for rows in views, you also have the option to select from text font styles *Regular, Italic, Bold,* and *Bold Italic* for your custom *Grouping* format.

To create a custom *Grouping* format, click the *Grouping format* pick list and select one of the nine custom formats from the list. For example, I selected the *Grouping 1* format because I want to create a custom grouping format using my company's official colors. These colors are primarily blue and yellow with some gray. To create this custom *Grouping* format, complete the following steps:

1. Click the *Rename* button, name the format *Company Colors,* and then click the *OK* button. The system re-displays the *Grouping Formats* page. Reselect your renamed *Grouping* format, *Company Colors,* from the pick list.
2. For the *Level 1* grouping, click the *Cell Color* pick list and select the *Light Yellow* color from the list, and then click the *Font Color* pick list and select the *Black* color from the list.
3. For the *Level 2* grouping, click the *Cell Color* pick list and select the *Aqua* color from the list, then click the *Font Color* pick list and select the *Black* color from the list.
4. For the *Level 3* grouping, click the *Cell Color* pick list and select the *Light Gray* color from the list, click the *Font Color* pick list and select the *Black* color from the list, and then click the *Font Color* pick list and select the *Black* color from the list.

Warning: Although Project Server 2013 allows you to define four levels of grouping, the system allows users to apply only three levels of grouping in Project Web App views. Therefore, there is no point in defining the fourth level of grouping for any custom *Grouping* format.

Best Practice: MSProjectExperts recommends that you use font colors that contrast with the cell colors you select for each grouping level. This makes it easier for users to read the grouping level text in views that use your custom *Grouping* formats.

5. Click the *Save* button. The system returns to the *PWA Settings* page.

To view my changes, I navigate to the *Grouping Formats* page, select the *Company Colors* item from the *Grouping Format* pick list and the system displays the *Grouping* format as shown in Figure 17 - 6.

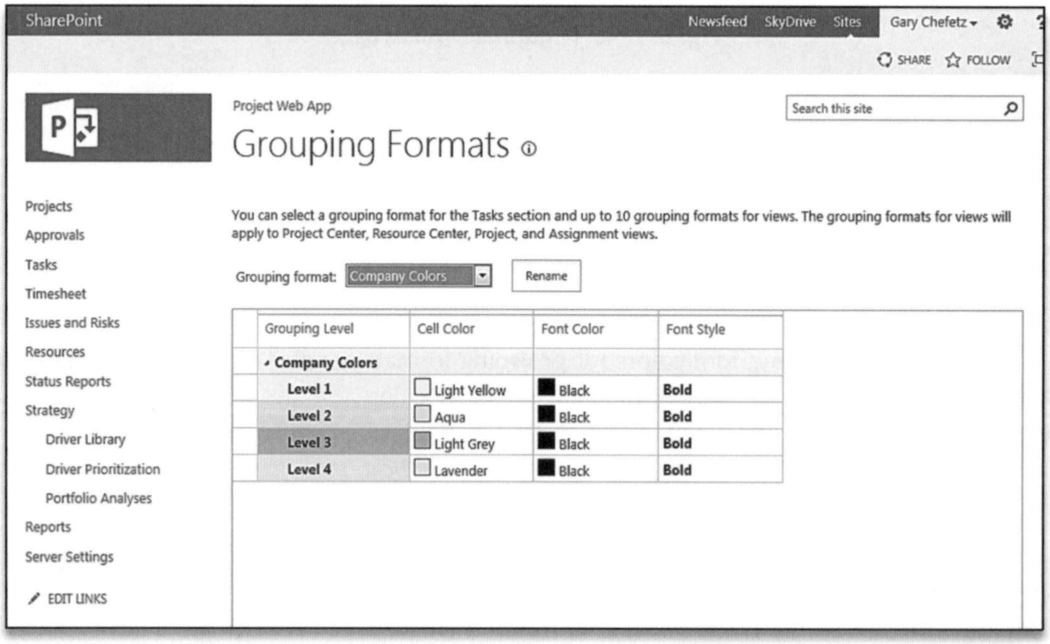

Figure 17 - 6: Company Colors custom Grouping format

Managing Project Web App Views

To create or modify Project Web App views, in the *Look and Feel* section of the *PWA Settings* page, click the *Manage Views* link. The system displays the *Manage Views* page shown in Figure 17 - 7 and Figure 17 - 8. As you prepare to create custom views in Project Server 2013, the *Manage Views* page shows all default views that ship with the system, grouped by view type. The system offers eleven types of views:

- Project
- Project Center
- Resource Assignments
- Resource Center
- My Work
- Resource Plans
- Team Tasks
- Team Builder
- Timesheet
- Portfolio Analyses
- Portfolio Analysis Project Selection

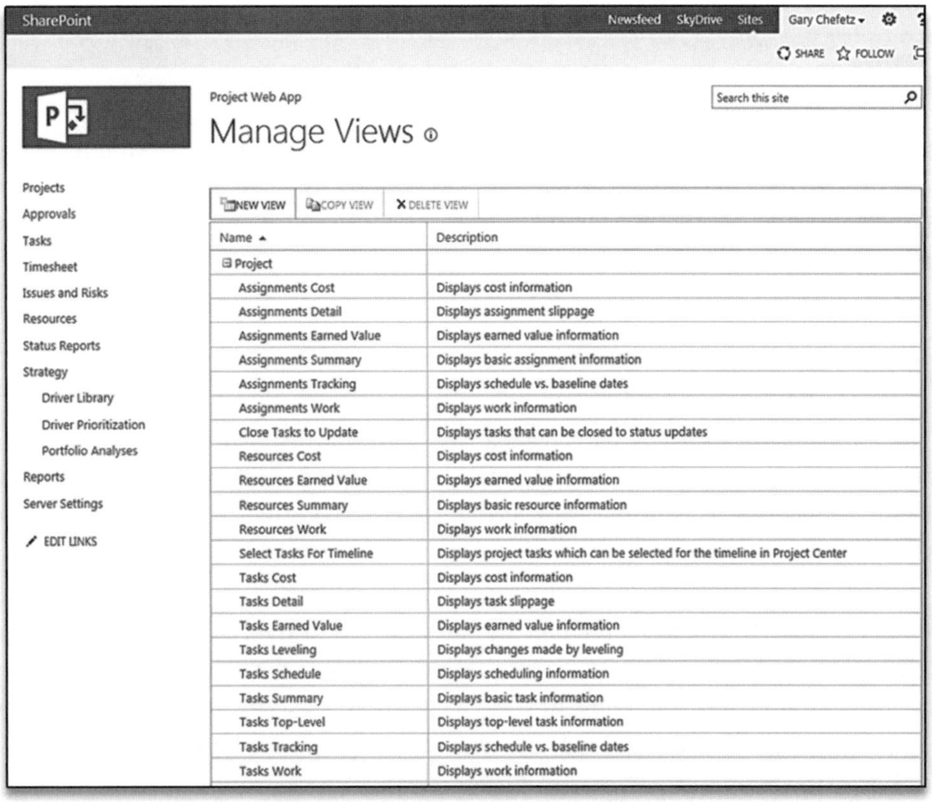

Figure 17 - 7: Manage Views page (top)

⊟ Project Center	
Cost	Displays cost information
Earned Value	Displays earned value information
Summary	Displays basic project information
Tracking	Displays schedule vs. baseline dates
Work	Displays work information
⊟ Resource Assignments	
Summary	Displays basic assignment information
⊟ Resource Center	
All Resources	Displays basic resource information for all resources
Cost Resources	Displays basic resource information for cost resources
Material Resources	Displays basic resource information for material resources
Resources By Team	Displays basic resource information for resources who are part of a team assignment pool
Work Resources	Displays basic resource information for work resources
⊟ My Work	
Details	Assignment Details Page
My Assignments	Tasks assigned to the current user
⊟ Resource Plans	
Resource Plans	Displays basic information for every resource in a resource plan
⊟ Team Tasks	
Resource Team Assignments	Displays assignments for the team resources
⊟ Team Builder	
All Resources	Displays basic information for all resources in team builder
Cost Resources	Displays basic information for cost resources in team builder
Material Resources	Displays basic information for material resources in team builder
Work Resources	Displays basic information for work resources in team builder
⊟ Timesheet	
My Timesheet	Timesheet for the current user
My Work	My Work for the current user
⊟ Portfolio Analyses	
Summary	Displays workflow information for all projects
⊟ Portfolio Analysis Project Selection	
Summary	Displays workflow information for all projects

Figure 17 - 8: Manage Views page (bottom)

The *Manage Views* page provides three buttons at the top of the page to assist you with managing views: the *New View*, *Copy View*, and *Delete View* buttons. Click the *New View* button to create a new view from scratch. Click the *Copy View* button to create a new view by copying an existing view and then modifying it. Click the *Delete View* button to delete an existing view.

Copying and Modifying Views

Using the *Copy View* button is the fastest way to create a new view, particularly if an existing view is close to what you want. You can also use the *Copy View* button to make a backup of a default view if you need to modify the default view. Backing up the default view allows you to recover the original view configuration if your customization fails to provide the desired results.

To make a copy of an existing view, select anywhere in the *Name* cell or the *Description* cell for the view you want to copy. **Do not** click the name of the view, however, because this action displays the *Edit View* page for the selected view. After selecting the view you want to copy, click the *Copy View* button. In the example, I select the *Tasks Cost* view. Project Server 2013 displays the *Copy View* dialog shown in Figure 17 - 9.

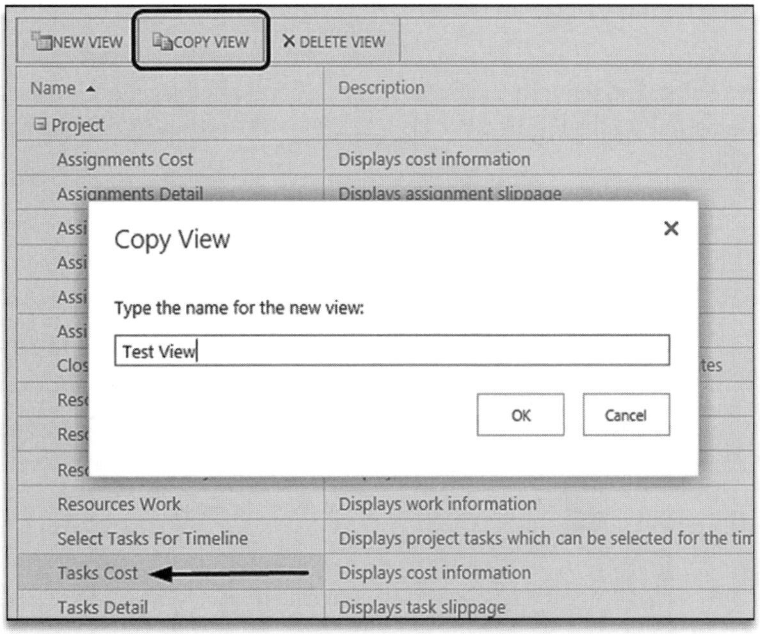

Figure 17 - 9: Copy View dialog

In the *Name* field, enter a new name for the new custom view according to your organization's naming convention as I demonstrated in the preceding figure. Click the *OK* button to complete the action. The system adds the new view to the data grid in the *Manage View* page as shown in Figure 17 - 10. Notice that I created a new *Test View* view to use in the project drilldowns.

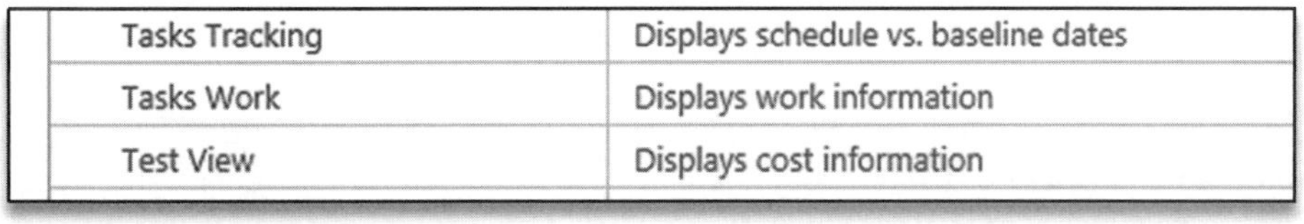

Figure 17 - 10: Manage View page, Test View view added

Information: You can add a leading underscore to the name, as in *_Test View*, which positions the view to the top of the view list in Project Web App.

Best Practice: MSProjectExperts recommends that your organization establish a standard naming convention for all custom views in both Project Web App and Project Pro 2013.

After copying an existing view, you must modify the copied view to create your new view according to your specifications. To modify your newly-copied view, click the name of the view in the data grid. Project Server 2013 displays the *Edit View* page for the selected view, ready for modification. Because the steps you use to edit views are nearly identical to the steps you use to create new views from scratch, I discuss all of the necessary steps in the next major section of this module.

Deleting Views

To delete an existing view, select the view in the data grid and then click the *Delete View* button. The system displays the confirmation dialog shown in Figure 17 - 11. Click the *OK* button to delete the view or click the *Cancel* button to cancel the deletion.

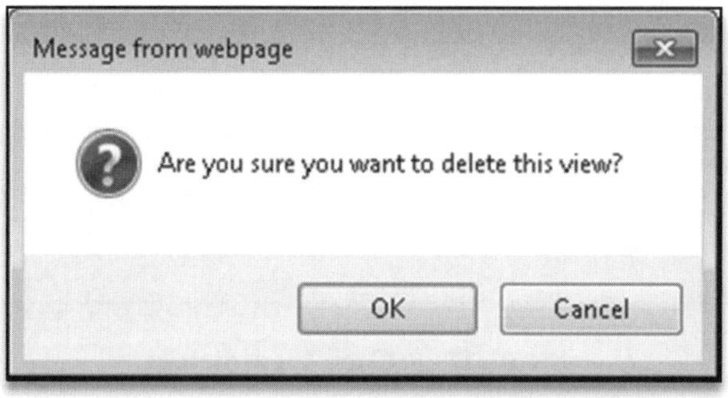
Message from webpage
Are you sure you want to delete this view?
OK
Cancel

Figure 17 - 11: Deletion confirmation dialog

Warning: If you do not back up the default Project Web App views using the system's *Administrative Backup* tool, and then you delete a default view, there is no way to undo the deletion. Therefore, think twice before you delete any default Project Web App view.

Creating Custom Views in Project Web App

To create a completely new custom view in Project Web App, at the top of the data grid on the *Manage Views* page, click the *New View* button. The system displays the *New View* page shown in Figure 17 - 12. Notice that the system selects the *Project Center* value in the *View Type* field by default. This is because I had a *Project Center* view description selected in the *Manage Views* page before I clicked the *New View* button.

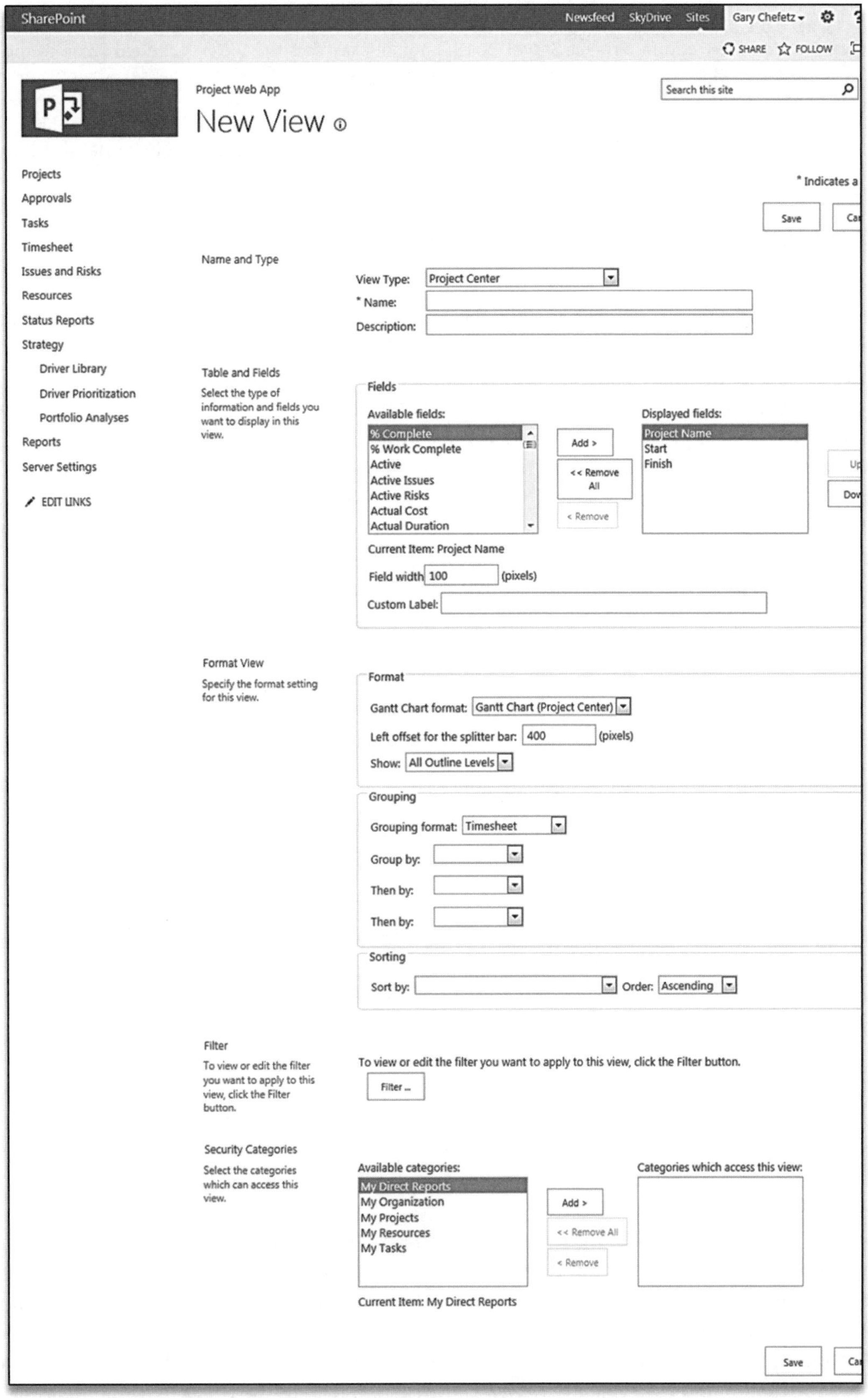

Figure 17 - 12: New View page for a custom Project Center view

Information: If you select the *Name* cell or *Description* cell for any view on the *Manage Views* page and then click the *New View* button, Project Server 2013 automatically sets the *View Type* field value to the type of view currently selected in the data grid.

In the *Name and Type* section of the *New View* page, click the *View Type* pick list and select one of the eleven available *View* types. The system refreshes the *New View* page with options appropriate to the type of view you select.

Creating a Custom Project Center View

Project Web App views are the ideal location to display your custom fields and to use custom fields to shape, filter, and sort your project data. To create a custom *Project Center* view, click the *View Type* pick list and select the *Project Center* item from the list, if it is not already selected. The system displays the *New View* page shown previously in Figure 17 - 12. In the *Name and Type* section, enter a name for your new view and in the *Table and Fields* section, select the fields you want to display in your new view. Figure 17 - 13 shows that I am creating a new *Project Center* view called *Projects by Region* and I added three built-in cost fields, *Baseline Cost, Cost,* and *Cost Variance* as well as my *Percent Cost Variance* custom calculated field and my custom *Region Office* field. Notice in the figure that I selected the *Percent Cost Variance* custom field after I moved it to the *Displayed fields* section, and I specified 75 pixels in the *Field width* field. I could also enter an optional custom label for each field that I select in the *Custom Label* field. When you specify a value in this field, the system uses it instead of the standard label. You can do this for your custom fields and for system standard fields.

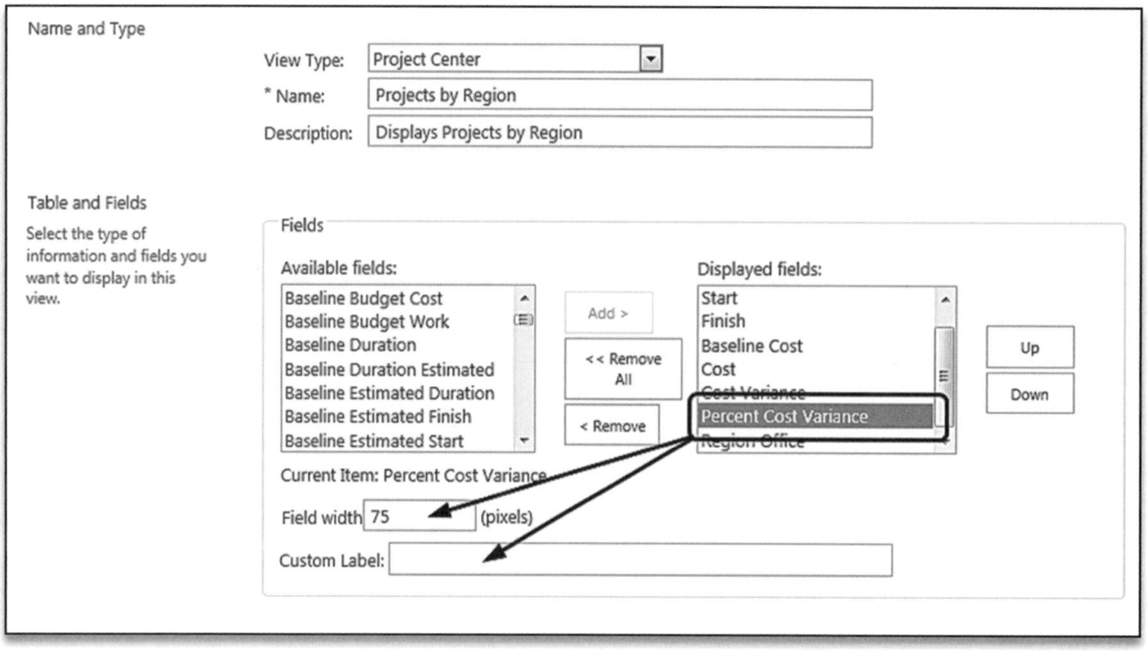

Figure 17 - 13: Naming and adding fields to a new view

What the figure does not show is that I also specified a 250 pixel width for the *Name* field and I created a custom label for the built-in *Cost* field renaming it *Cost at Completion.* My organization understands what project calculates as current projected cost, as "Cost at completion." Renaming the field eliminates confusion for my users. Now that I selected and applied formatting to individual fields, I must apply formatting to the view. Figure 17 - 14 shows that in the *Format View* section *Grouping* options area, I selected the *Company Colors* grouping format I created previously and I selected my *Region Office* custom field as the *Group by* value.

Information: In order to use a field to group a view, you must add it to the view. Because the field displays in the grouping, you may want to suppress its display in the view itself as you cannot prevent it from displaying. Two techniques you can apply are setting the *Field Width* value to a small number and moving the field to the end of the display list.

Note that I can optionally select a different *Gantt Chart* format or accept the default. I can determine the offset for the splitter bar to move its default position to the left or the right. I can also create multiple grouping levels and sort the view on any visible field.

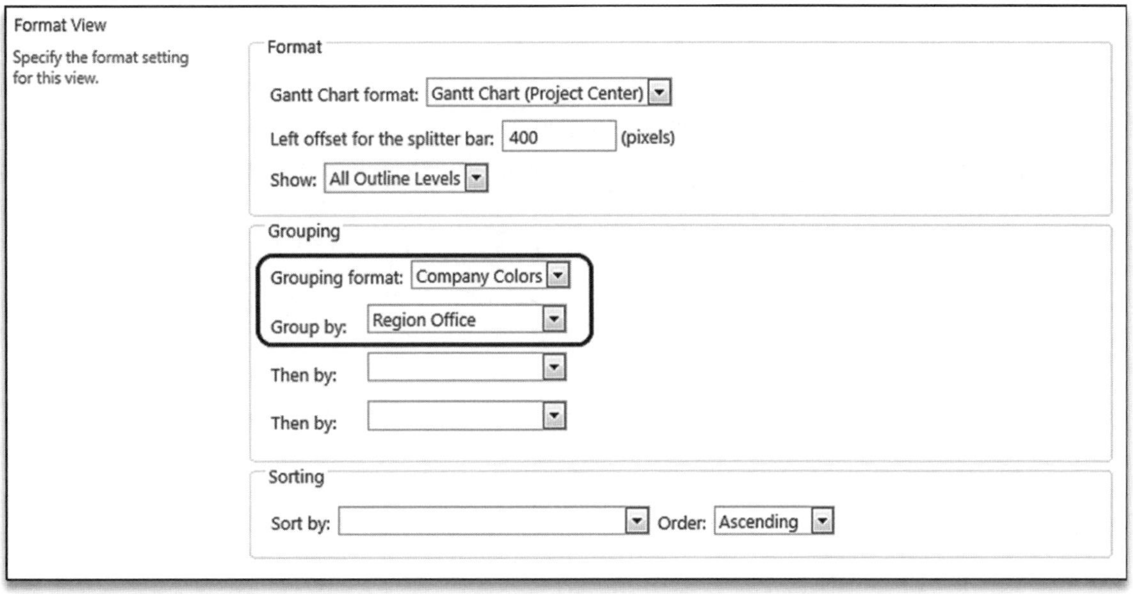

Figure 17 - 14: Formatting a new view using grouping

In a large organization I might need to create an individual view for each regional office. If this were the case, then I would use the *Region Office* field as a filter rather than for grouping the view. The *Filter* section of the *New View* page, shown in Figure 17 - 15, allows you to set a filter on any field contained in the view. In the *Security Categories* section, select one or more categories in the *Available Categories* list and click the *Add* button to add them to the *Categories which access this view* list. The categories you select determine which users can see the custom view in Project Web App. For example, if you want the *Executives* group to see the custom view, add the *My Organization* category to the *Categories which access this view* list. If you want the *Project Managers* group to see the custom view, then add the *My Projects* category to the *Categories which access this view* list. Click the *Save* button on the *New View* page to save your custom view. Without a category assignment, no user in the system can see the view, even you the administrator. In my case, I add it to the *My Organization* category. Click the *Save* button to save the changes to your new view.

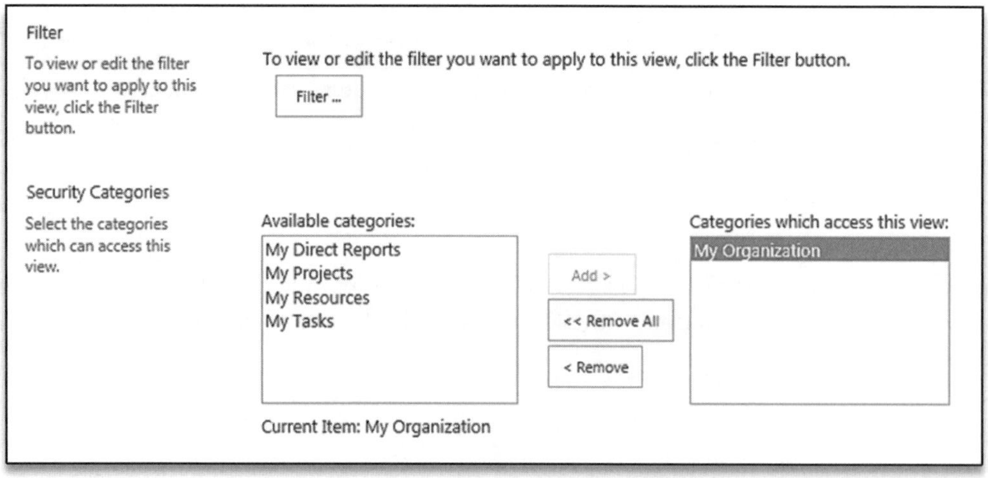

Figure 17 - 15: Add a new view to a category

Figure 17 - 16 shows my new view applied in the Project Center. Given the fact that I added only *Cost* fields, perhaps I should have called my view "Project Costs by Region."

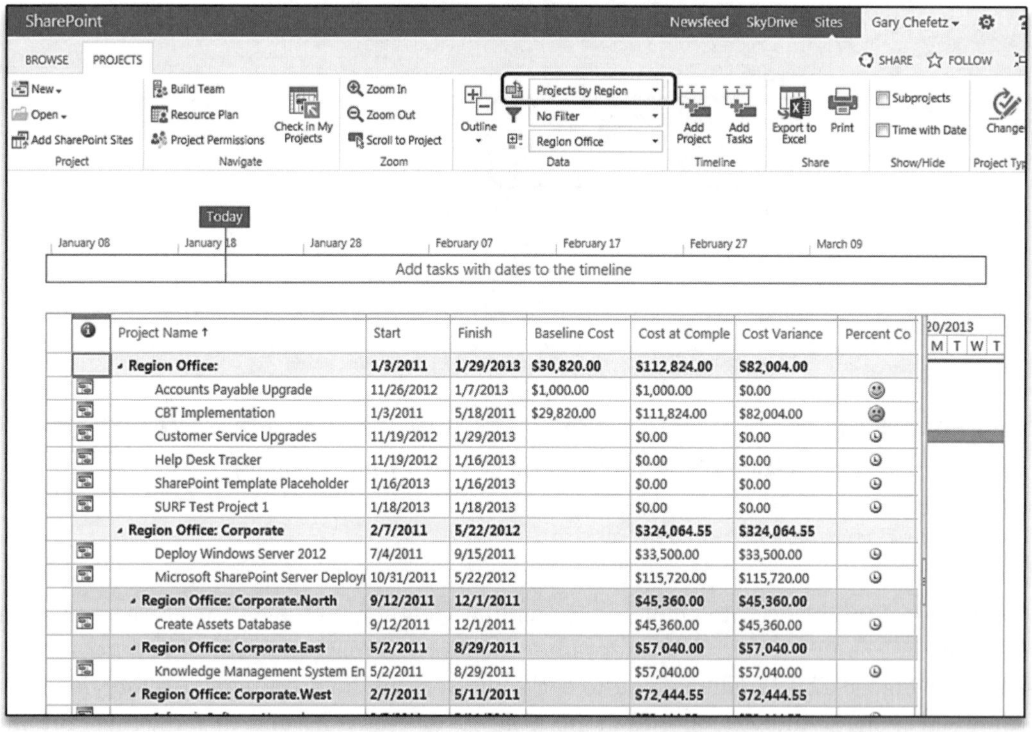

Figure 17 - 16: Completed Project Center view

Creating a Custom Project View

Creating a custom project view is nearly identical to creating a *Project Center* view, except that when you create a project view, in the *Table* section you must choose an option to display *Task, Resource* or *Assignment* data in the view. Remember that project tasks can contain multiple resource assignments, so a task view displays the rolled up value for all assignments on a task, while an assignment view displays the task detail broken down to the assignment level. Selecting the *Resource* option allows you to display work and cost data for resources in the project.

Whereas a task view is a rollup of all assignments, a resource view is also a rollup of all assignments for each resource rather than each task. In the *Table and Fields* section, first select a *Table* option and then select the fields you want to display. Notice that the figure shows that I selected the *Task* option and the system added the *Task Name, Start, Finish,* and *Resource Names* fields to the view by default. Select the *Table* option before entering any other information as changing this information causes a page refresh. In the *Name and Type* section of the page, enter a name for your new view in the *Name* field and then add an optional description in the *Description* field as shown in Figure 17 - 17.

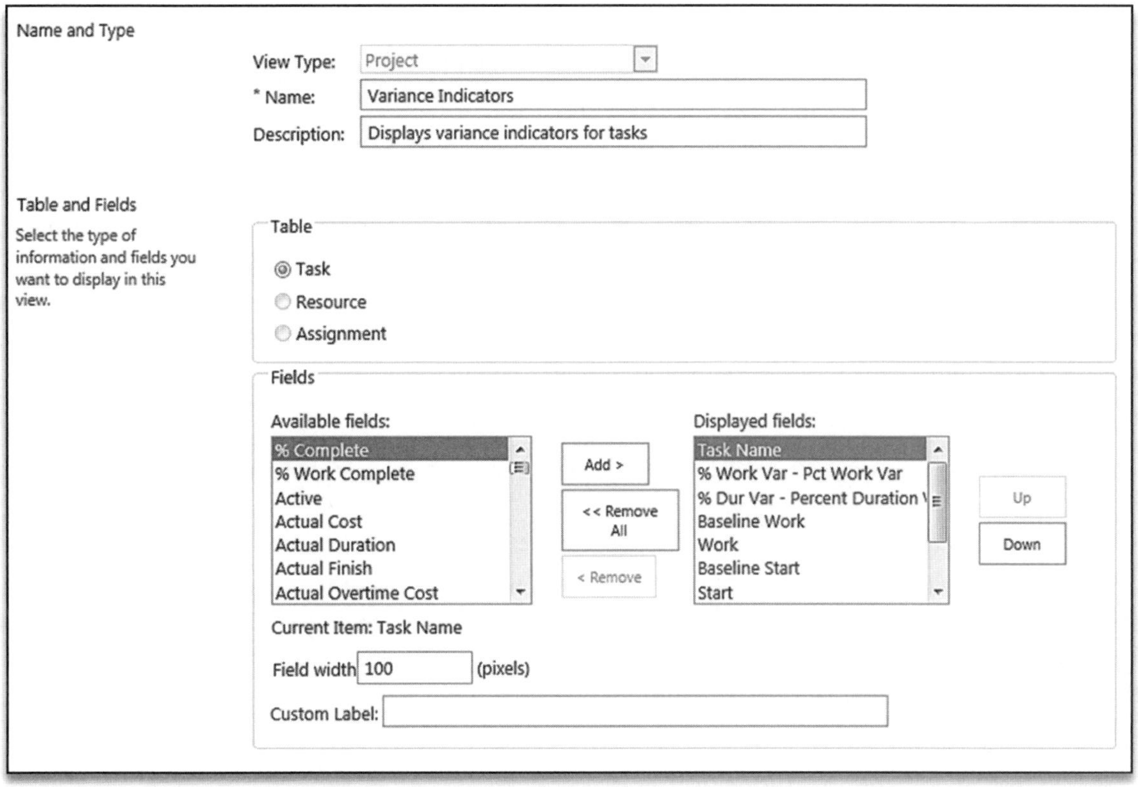

Figure 17 - 17: Name and Type, and Table and Fields sections of New View page

If you select the *Task* option in this section, the system adds the *Task Name, Start, Finish,* and *Resource Names* fields to the *Displayed fields* list by default. If you select the *Resource* option, the system adds the *Unique ID* and *Resource Name* fields to the *Displayed fields* list by default. If you select the *Assignment* option in this section, the system adds the *Task Name, Start,* and *Finish* fields to the *Displayed fields* list by default. These fields are mandatory in any *Project* view, and the system does not allow you to remove any of these default fields from the *Displayed fields* list. In the *Available fields* list, select the fields you want to display in your new view, and then click the *Add* button to move the selected fields to the *Displayed fields* list. To move fields up or down in this list, select one field and then click either the *Up* or *Down* button.

Warning: Project Server 2013 does not allow you to select a block of fields and then move the fields as a group. Therefore, you can only move fields one at a time.

There are two options at the bottom of the *Table and Fields* section that control how Project Server 2013 displays the fields in the view. For each field in the *Displayed fields* list, you may select one of two options:

- Select the *Field width ____ (pixels)* option and specify a fixed width in pixels for the column.
- Set the *Custom Label* option to change the display title for the field in this particular view. Enter an alternate name for the field in the *Custom Label* column. You can enter a shorter name (or "nickname") for any field that has a long name. For example, you might enter *% W Comp* as a nickname for the *% Work Complete* field.

> **Information**: You can use the *Field width ____ (pixels)* option to almost hide any default field that you do not want visible in your new view. Set the pixel value to 1 to almost hide a field. This trick shrinks the actual display to around 50 pixels.

In the *Format View* section of the *New View* page, select the options to format your custom view display. If you selected the *Task* or *Assignment* option in the *Tables and Fields* section, the *Format View* section includes a *Gantt Chart format* pick list and a *Left offset for the splitter bar* field. When you select the *Resource* option, the system omits both of these fields. Click the *Gantt Chart format* pick list and select one of the available *Gantt Chart* formats. The default *Gantt Chart* format value is *Gantt Chart (Views)*.

> **Information**: If you customize one of the other nine *Gantt Chart* formats, such as the *Critical Path Gantt* format I created earlier in this module, then you can select the custom format from the *Gantt Chart Format* pick list.

In the *Left offset for the splitter bar* field, specify the number of pixels to offset the vertical split bar from the left side of the page. The default offset value is *400 pixels*. Because this value and the *Field Width* values are difficult to set precisely without being able to see the results immediately, you may need to finish creating the view, and then navigate back and forth between your new custom *Project* view and the *Edit Views* page to fine-tune these values precisely.

> **Information**: To position the splitter bar on the far right side of the view to hide the Gantt chart portion of the view, set the value in the *Left offset for the splitter bar* field to at least 1200 pixels.

Click the *Show* pick list and select the number of *Outline Levels* to display. The default setting for this field is *All Outline Levels*. If you want to see all tasks in the view, be sure to select the *All Outline Levels* option. Click the *Grouping format* pick list and select one of the available *Grouping* formats. The default *Grouping* format is the *Timesheet* format.

> **Information**: If you customize one of the nine *Grouping* formats, such as the *Company Colors* format I created earlier in this module, you can select the custom *Grouping* format from the *Grouping format* pick list.

To apply grouping to the fields in your custom view, click the *Group by* pick list and the *Then by* pick lists, and then select the fields that you want the system to use for grouping. Each of these pick lists contains only those fields in the *Displayed fields* list.

To apply sorting to the rows displayed in the custom view, click the *Sort by* pick list and select a field, and then click the *Order* pick list and select either the *Ascending* or *Descending* item from the pick list. The *Sort by* pick list contains only those fields in the *Displayed fields* list. By default, Project Server 2013 does not apply grouping or sorting in any custom view.

In the *Filter* section, the system allows you to build a custom filter to apply to the data in your custom view. To build a filter, click the *Filter* button. The system displays the *Custom Filter* dialog shown in Figure 17 - 18. Notice that I entered valid filter criteria to select only milestone tasks.

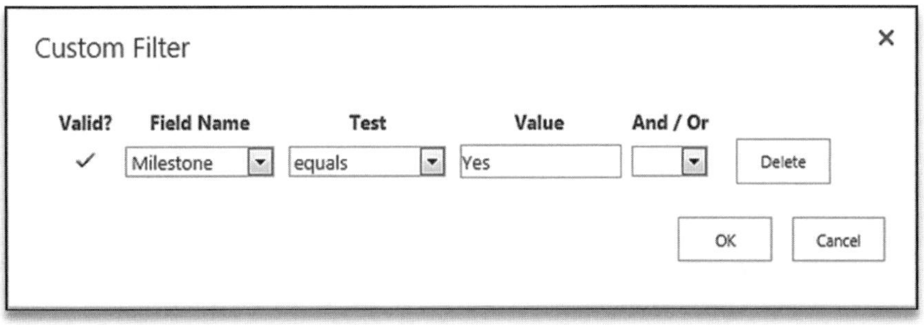

Figure 17 - 18: Custom Filter dialog

Click the *Field Name* pick list and select the first field on which you want to filter. The *Field Name* pick list contains a field set based on your selection of the *Task, Resource,* or *Assignment* option in the *Table and Fields* section of the dialog. Click the *Test* pick list and select the type of test used in the filter. Manually enter a value in the *Value* field. If you want to create a compound filter, click the *And/Or* pick list, select an item from the pick list, and then add additional lines to the test. If you enter invalid test criteria, the system displays a red X character in the *Valid* column as shown in Figure 17 - 19.

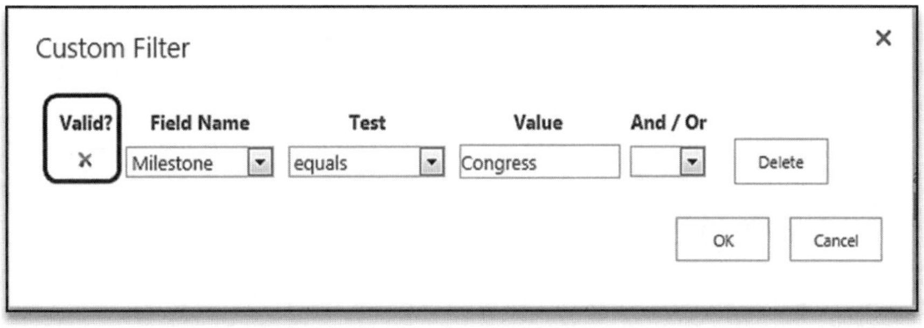

Figure 17 - 19: Invalid Filter Criteria

If your filter contains an error of any type, you see the error indicator in the *Valid* column; when you try to save it, the system will prompt you with the warning dialog shown in Figure 17 - 20.

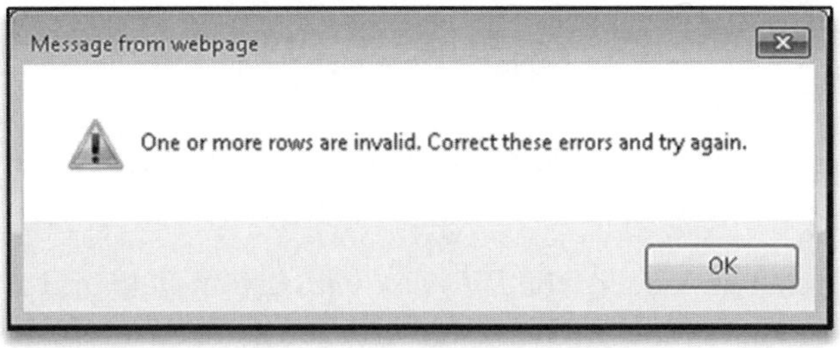

Figure 17 - 20: Invalid row warning

Figure 17 - 21 shows the *Custom Filter* dialog with the custom filter I created for my *Project* view. I want this filter to display only regular tasks, but not summary tasks or milestones. After you create a valid filter, click the *OK* button to close the *Custom Filter* dialog.

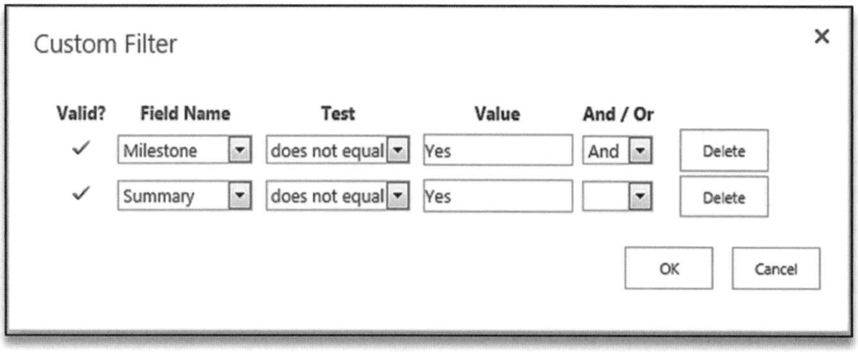

Figure 17 - 21: Custom Filter dialog containing a valid filter

After you create your filter, Project Server 2013 does not display any information about it in the *Filter* section of the *New View* page that indicates that the view contains a filter. To determine whether a view contains a filter, you must always click the *Filter* button and examine the *Custom Filter* dialog.

Information: To delete the filter criteria line in the *Custom Filter* dialog, click the *Delete* button to the right of the criteria line you want to delete.

In the *Security Categories* section, select one or more categories in the *Available Categories* list and click the *Add* button to add them to the *Categories which access this view* list. The categories you select determine which users can see the custom view in Project Web App. For example, if you want the *Executives* group to see the custom view, add the *My Organization* category to the *Categories which access this view* list. If you want the *Project Managers* group to see the custom view, then add the *My Projects* category to the *Categories which access this view* list. Click the *Save* button on the *New View* page to save your custom view.

Warning: If you fail to add any categories to the *Categories which access this view* list, no one in your organization can see the new custom view, including you!

Figure 17 - 22 shows the *Edit View* page for my new custom *Project* view. I created this *Variance Indicators* view to show both schedule and cost indicators in a *Project Detail* view that my project managers can use to quickly identify problems with schedule or cost overruns in the project. To create this custom view, I completed the following steps:

- I added the *Pct Work Var* and *Percent Duration Variance* custom fields to the *Displayed fields* list and then moved the fields into the correct order.
- I applied a *% Work Var* custom label to the *Pct Work Var* custom field and a *% Dur Var* custom label to the *Percent Duration Variance* custom field. The system indicates the custom label on the *Pct Work Var* field, for example, using the text string *"% Work Var – Pct Work Var"* in the *Displayed Fields* list.
- I set the *Field Width* value to *75 pixels* on the indicator fields to maximize them for the view and changed the width of the *Task Name* field to 200 pixels to accommodate longer task names.

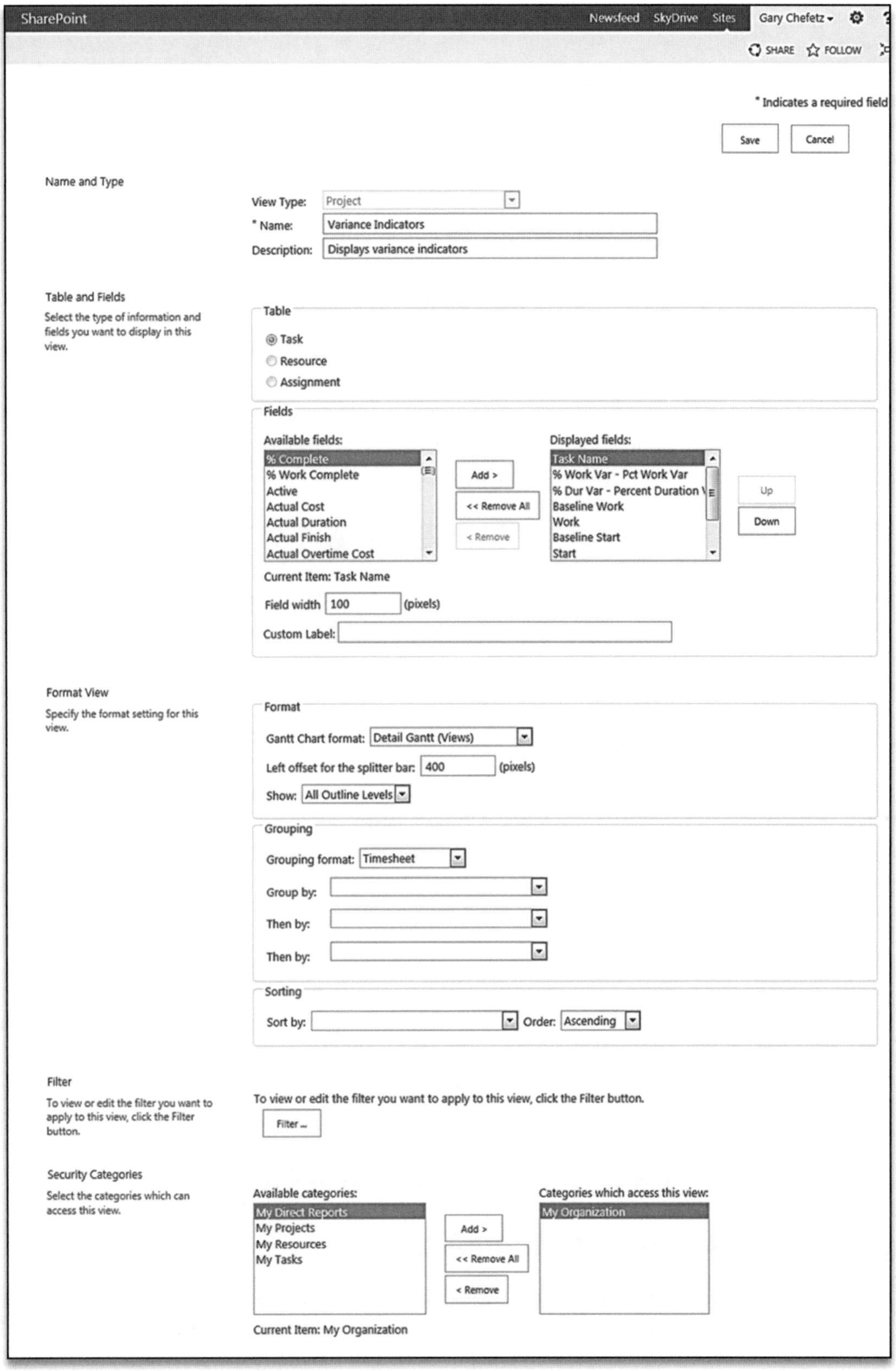

Figure 17 - 22: Edit View page for custom view

- I set the *Left offset for the splitter bar* field value to *600* pixels to move the splitter bar to the right of its default setting.
- In the *Show* pick list, I selected the *All Outline Levels* option.
- I left the default *Timesheet* grouping format because the view does not use grouping.
- I created a filter to display only regular tasks, but not summary tasks or milestones.
- I added the *My Organization* and *My Tasks* categories to the *Categories which access this view* list.

When you finish defining your custom view, click the *Save* button. The system adds the new custom view to the *Project* section of the *Manage Views* page. To access this new *Project* view, users must navigate to the *Project Center* page and click the name of any enterprise project. The system displays the *Project Details* page for the selected project. Users must then navigate to the *Schedule* page, click the *View* pick list, and select the custom view. Figure 17 - 23 shows the new custom view applied to an enterprise project on the *Schedule* page.

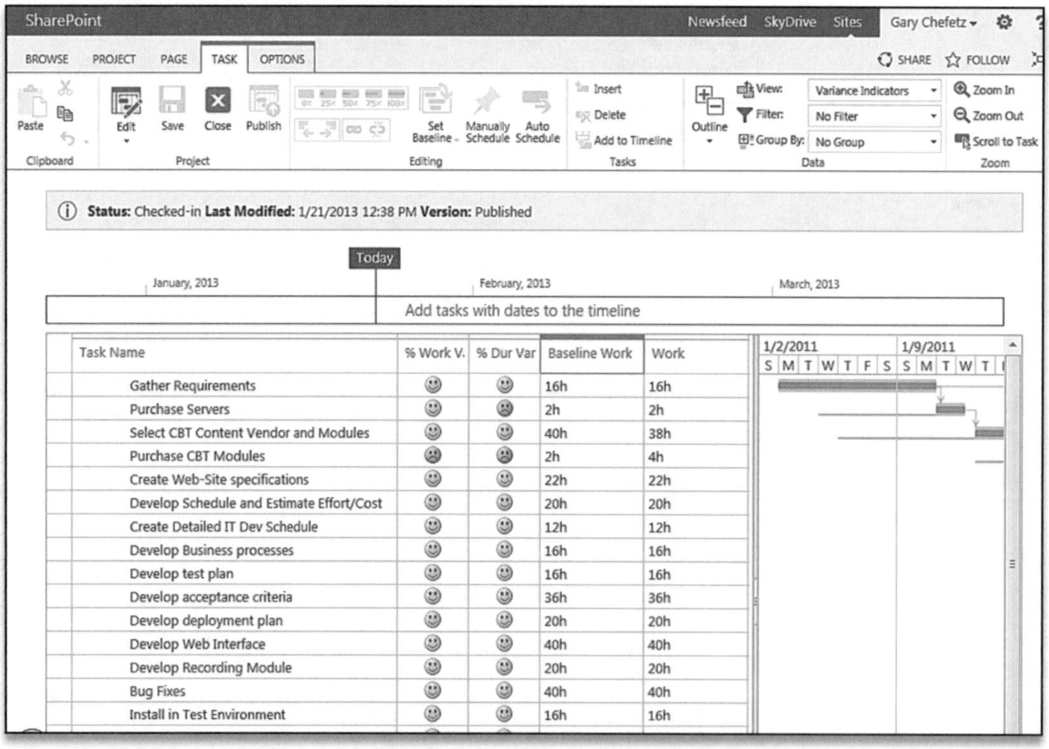

Figure 17 - 23: _Schedule Status custom view applied

Creating a Custom Resource Assignments View

Resource Assignments views help managers determine the tasks to which selected resources are assigned across all projects in the Project Server 2013 database. To create a new *Resource Assignments* view, on the *Manage Views* page, click the *New View* button. Click the *View Type* pick list and then select the *Resource Assignments* item. The system refreshes the *New View* page as shown in Figure 17 - 24.

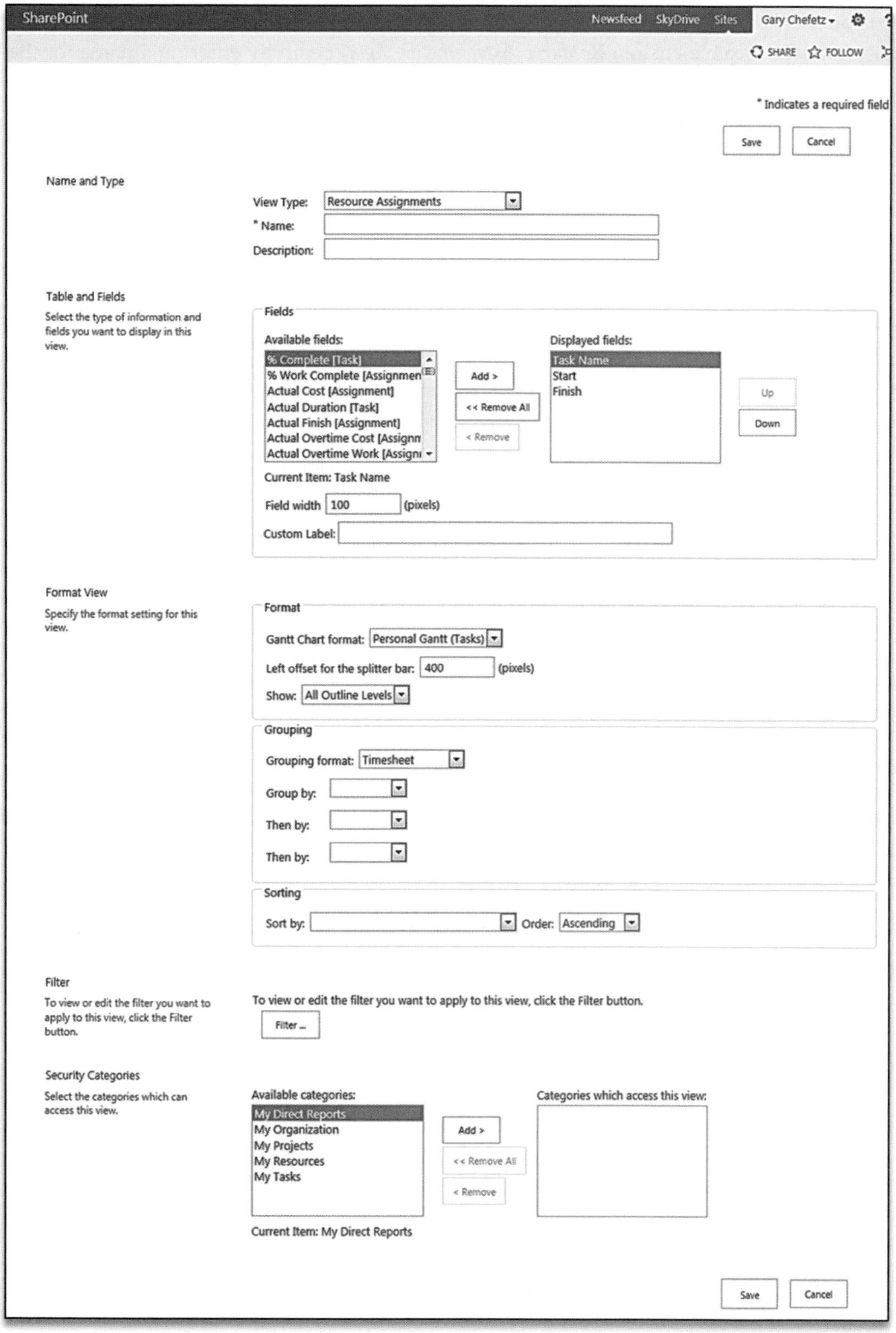

Figure 17 - 24: New View page for a custom Resource Assignments view

Creating a custom *Resource Assignments* view in Project Web App is similar to the process for creating *Project* and *Project Center* views. To create a custom *Resource Assignments* view, begin by entering a name for the view in the *Name* field and an optional description in the *Description* field.

In the *Table and Fields* section of the page, the *Available fields* list contains both standard and custom task fields and resource fields. By default, the system includes the *Task Name, Start,* and *Finish* fields in the *Displayed fields* list. In addition to the three default fields, you **must** also add the following fields to the *Displayed fields* list:

- Resource Name
- Project Name

Because a *Resource Assignments* view shows task assignments, grouped by resource and then by project, you **must** include the *Project Name, Task Name,* and *Resource Name* fields in your custom *Resource Assignments* view. Add any other fields you want to the *Displayed fields* list, and then move the fields into the correct display order. Enter a *Custom Label* value for any field with a long name, if you like.

In the *Format View* section, select the items you need in the *Gantt Chart format, Show,* and *Grouping format* pick lists. Remember to enter a value greater than 0 in the *Left offset for the splitter bar* field. Because a *Resource Assignments* view shows task assignments, grouped by resource and then by project, you **must** set the *Group by* value to *Resource Name* and set the *Then by* value to *Project Name.*

In the *Security Categories* section, remember to add at least one category to the *Categories which access this view* list. Figure 17 - 25 shows the definition for a custom *Resource Assignments* view.

I created the custom *Assignment Owner* view shown in Figure 17 - 25 to display the name of the person who reports task progress on the *Tasks* page for each task assignment, whether it be the resource him/herself, or a "proxy" who reports progress on behalf of the resource. To create this custom *Resource Assignments* view, I completed the following steps:

- I added the *Assignment Owner, Baseline Work, Work, Actual Work, Remaining Work, Project Name,* and *Resource Name* fields to the *Displayed fields* list, and then moved these fields into the correct order.
- I set the *Left offset for the splitter bar* value to *800* pixels.
- In the *Show* pick list, I selected the *All Outline Levels* option.
- In the *Group by* pick list, I selected the *Resource Name* field, and in the *Then by* pick list, I selected the *Project Name* field.
- In the *Sort by* pick list, I selected the *Resource Name* field.
- I positioned the *Resource Name* field and the *Project Name* field at the end of the list and set them to *1 pixel* width in order to hide them as much as possible as they display in the grouping.
- I selected the *Task Name* field and increased the pixel width to 350 to better display the name of the task and the values in the grouping fields.
- I added the *My Organization, My Projects,* and *My Resources* categories to the *Categories which access this view* list.

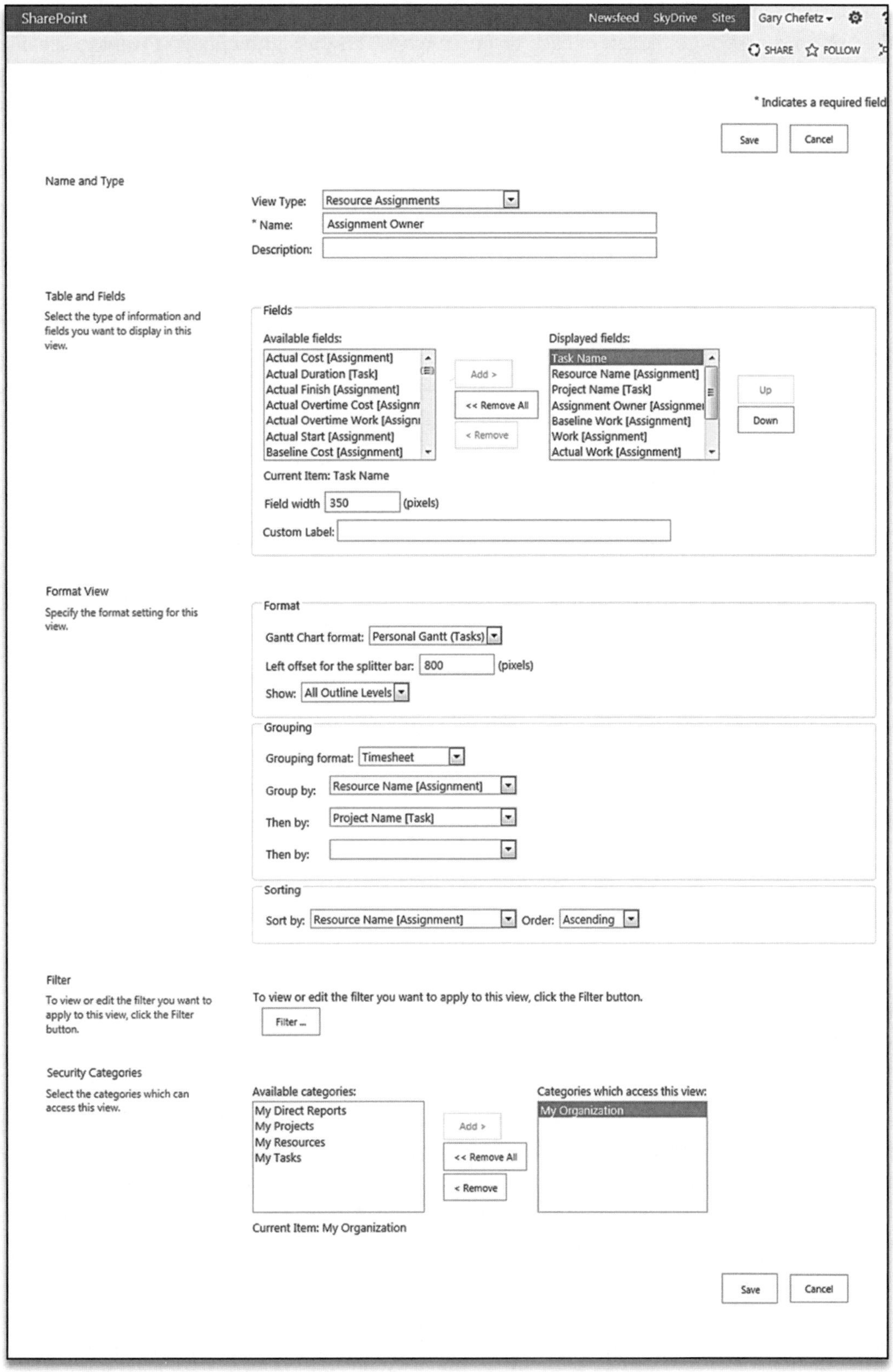

Figure 17 - 25: Assignment Owner view definition

Click the *Save* button when finished. To access a *Resource Assignments* view, navigate to the *Resource Center* page and select the option checkbox to the left of each resource whose task assignments you want to see. From the *Navigate* section of the *Resources* ribbon, click the *Resource Assignments* button. On the *Resource Assignments* page, click the *View* pick list and select the custom view. Figure 17 - 26 shows the new custom *Resource Assignments* view named *_Assignment Owner*.

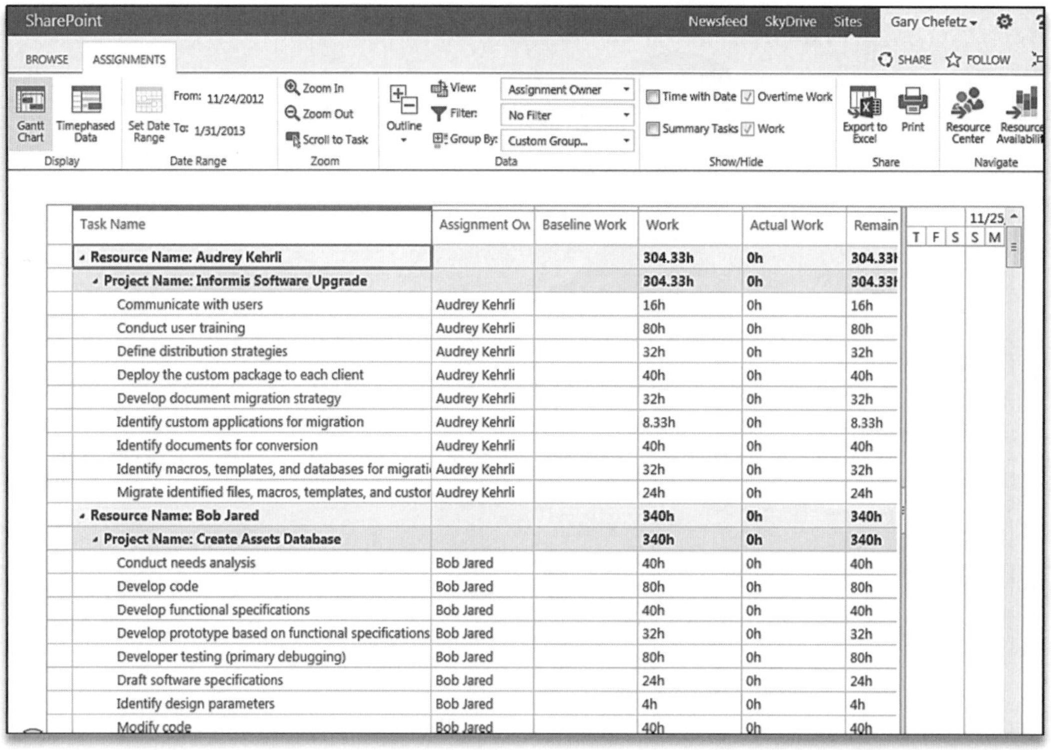

Figure 17 - 26: Assignment Owner custom Resource Assignments view

Creating a Custom Resource Center View

The *Resource Center* page provides an interface for resource managers and Project Server administrators to manage enterprise resources. If you defined custom enterprise resource fields in your Project Server 2013 system, then *Resource Center* views are the ideal location in which to display these custom fields. To create a new *Resource Center* view, on the *Manage Views* page, click the *New View* button. Click the *View Type* pick list and then select the *Resource Center* item on the list. The system refreshes the *New View* page as shown in Figure 17 - 27.

Creating a custom *Resource Center* view in Project Web App is very similar to creating *Project, Project Center*, and *Resource Assignments* views. To create a custom *Resource Center* view, begin by entering a name for the view in the *Name* field and an optional description in the *Description* field. In the *Table and Fields* section of the page, the *Available fields* list contains both standard and custom resource fields. The only required field in the *Displayed fields* list is the *Resource Name* field. Add additional fields to the *Displayed fields* list and format each field, as needed. Select the options you want in both the *Format View* and *Filter* sections of the page.

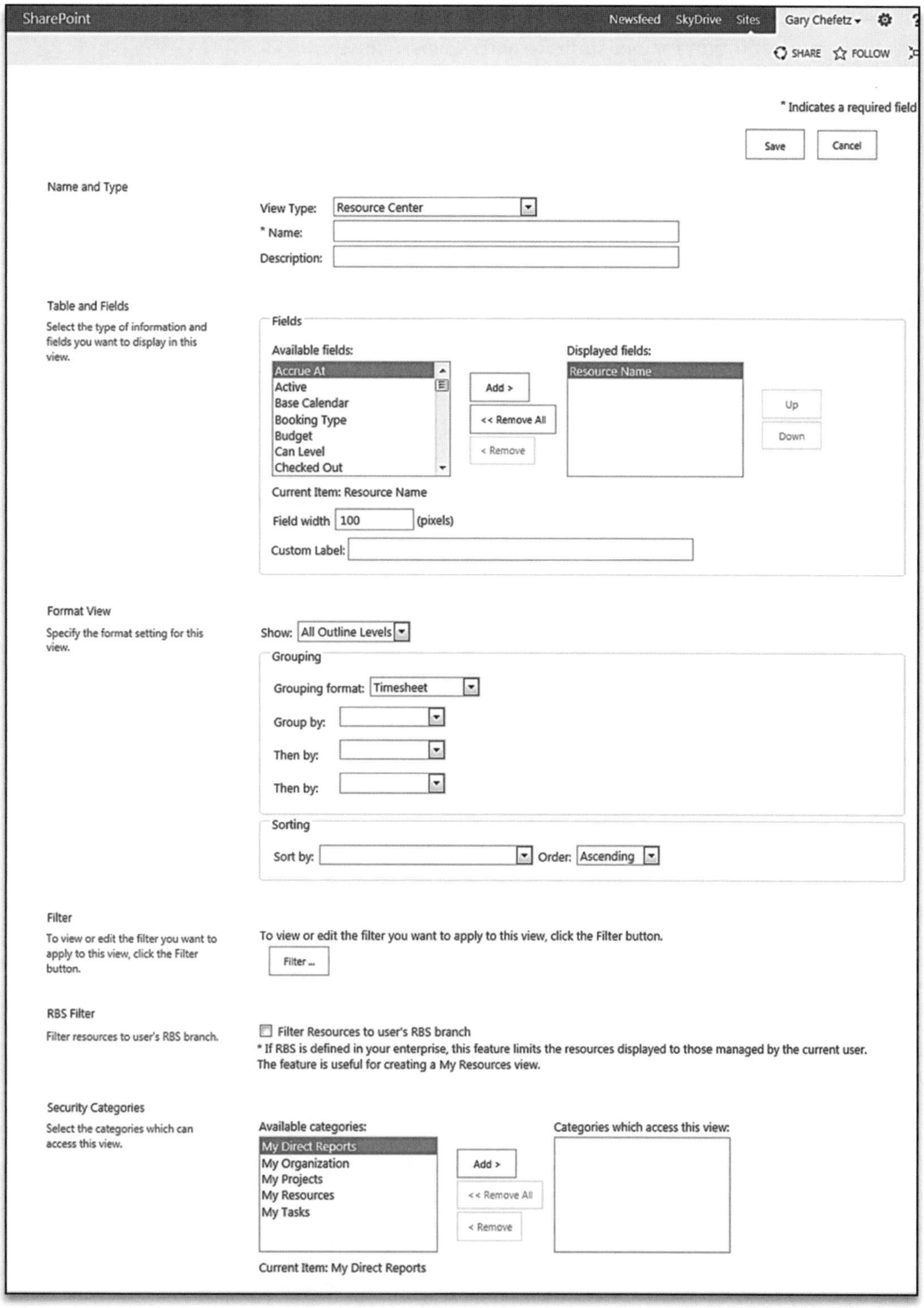

Figure 17 - 27: New View page for a custom Resource Center view

Notice the *RBS Filter* section near the bottom of the *New View* page shown in Figure 17 - 27. In this section, select the *Filter Resources to user's RBS branch* option to limit the resources displayed in the view to only those managed by the current user who is accessing the *Resource Center* view. This option is useful only if you populated the lookup table in the *RBS* field and specified an *RBS* value for each resource in the Enterprise Resource Pool. In the

Security Categories section, remember to add at least one category to the *Categories which access this* list. Figure 17 - 28 shows the definition for a custom *Resource Center* view.

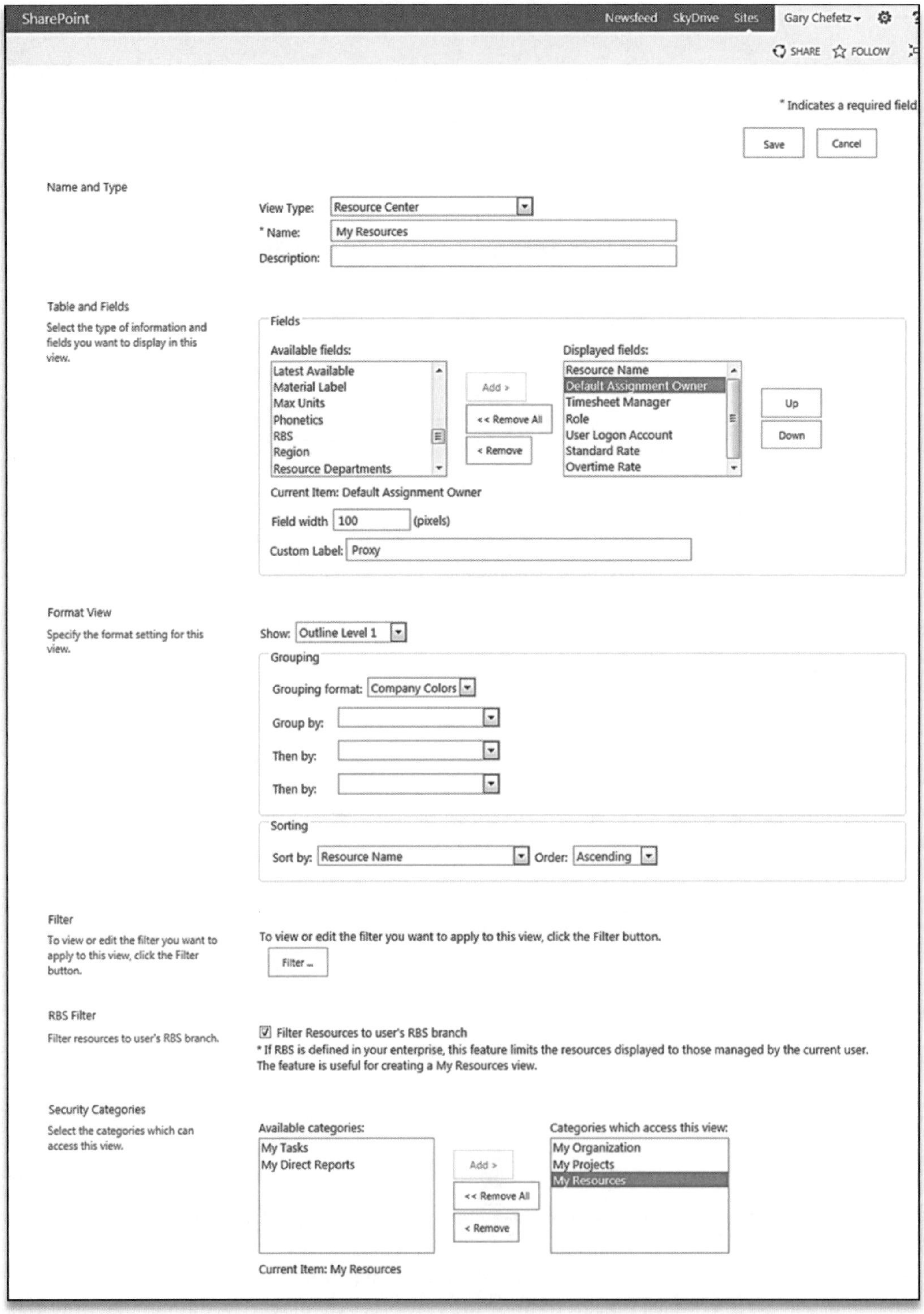

Figure 17 - 28: My Resources view definition

I created the custom *My Resources* view shown in Figure 17 - 28 for resource managers to display the standard and custom fields for the resources that report to them. To create this custom *Resource Center* view, I did the following:

- I added the *Default Assignment Owner, Timesheet Manager, Role, User Logon Account, Standard Rate,* and *Overtime Rate* fields to the *Displayed fields* list.
- I applied the *Proxy* custom label to the *Default Assignment Owner* to narrow the width of the column.
- On the *Resource Name* field, I applied *Ascending* sorting.
- I selected the *Filter Resources to user's RBS branch* option to limit the resources displayed in the view to only those managed by the current user who is accessing the *Resource Center* view.
- I added the *My Organization, My Projects,* and *My Resources* categories to the *Categories which access this view* list.
- I added a filter to show only *Active* resources.

Click the *Save* button when finished. To access a custom *Resource Center* view, navigate to the *Resource Center* page. Click the *View* pick list and select the custom view. Figure 17 - 29 shows the *_My Resources* custom *Resource Center* view.

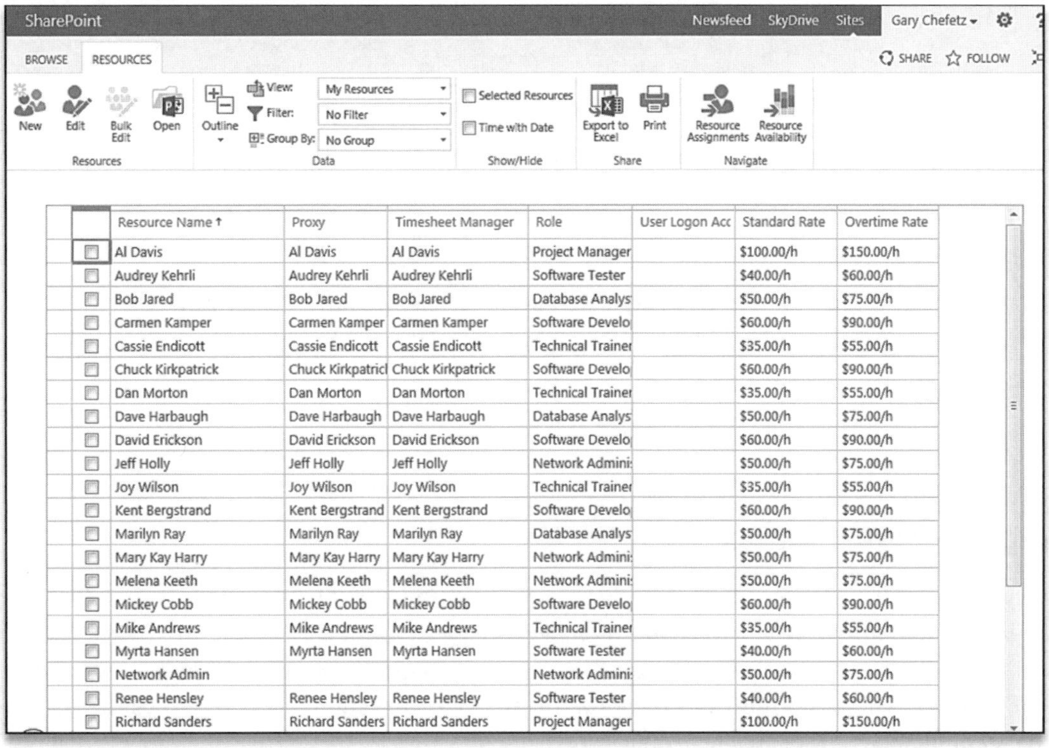

Resource Name ↑	Proxy	Timesheet Manager	Role	User Logon Acc	Standard Rate	Overtime Rate
Al Davis	Al Davis	Al Davis	Project Manager		$100.00/h	$150.00/h
Audrey Kehrli	Audrey Kehrli	Audrey Kehrli	Software Tester		$40.00/h	$60.00/h
Bob Jared	Bob Jared	Bob Jared	Database Analys		$50.00/h	$75.00/h
Carmen Kamper	Carmen Kamper	Carmen Kamper	Software Develo		$60.00/h	$90.00/h
Cassie Endicott	Cassie Endicott	Cassie Endicott	Technical Trainer		$35.00/h	$55.00/h
Chuck Kirkpatrick	Chuck Kirkpatricl	Chuck Kirkpatrick	Software Develo		$60.00/h	$90.00/h
Dan Morton	Dan Morton	Dan Morton	Technical Trainer		$35.00/h	$55.00/h
Dave Harbaugh	Dave Harbaugh	Dave Harbaugh	Database Analys		$50.00/h	$75.00/h
David Erickson	David Erickson	David Erickson	Software Develo		$60.00/h	$90.00/h
Jeff Holly	Jeff Holly	Jeff Holly	Network Admini		$50.00/h	$75.00/h
Joy Wilson	Joy Wilson	Joy Wilson	Technical Trainer		$35.00/h	$55.00/h
Kent Bergstrand	Kent Bergstrand	Kent Bergstrand	Software Develo		$60.00/h	$90.00/h
Marilyn Ray	Marilyn Ray	Marilyn Ray	Database Analys		$50.00/h	$75.00/h
Mary Kay Harry	Mary Kay Harry	Mary Kay Harry	Network Admini		$50.00/h	$75.00/h
Melena Keeth	Melena Keeth	Melena Keeth	Network Admini		$50.00/h	$75.00/h
Mickey Cobb	Mickey Cobb	Mickey Cobb	Software Develo		$60.00/h	$90.00/h
Mike Andrews	Mike Andrews	Mike Andrews	Technical Trainer		$35.00/h	$55.00/h
Myrta Hansen	Myrta Hansen	Myrta Hansen	Software Tester		$40.00/h	$60.00/h
Network Admin			Network Admini		$50.00/h	$75.00/h
Renee Hensley	Renee Hensley	Renee Hensley	Software Tester		$40.00/h	$60.00/h
Richard Sanders	Richard Sanders	Richard Sanders	Project Manager		$100.00/h	$150.00/h

Figure 17 - 29: My Resources custom Resource Center view

Earlier in this module, I demonstrated how to create a new custom view by copying an existing view. In the following example, I create a custom *Resource Center* view that displays only *Generic* resources. In the *Resource Center* section of the *Manage Views* page, I copied the *All Resources* view and renamed it *All Generic Resources*. To edit the *All Generic Resources* view, I click the name of the view in the *Manage Views* page. The system displays an *Edit View* page that is identical in every way to the *New View* page, except the system locks the *Resource Center* item on the

View Type pick list. While editing this new view, I remove irrelevant fields from the *Displayed fields* list and add relevant fields. Then I create a custom filter that uses the following criteria: **Generic = Yes**. Figure 17 - 30 shows the resulting *All Generic Resources* view in the *Resource Center* page.

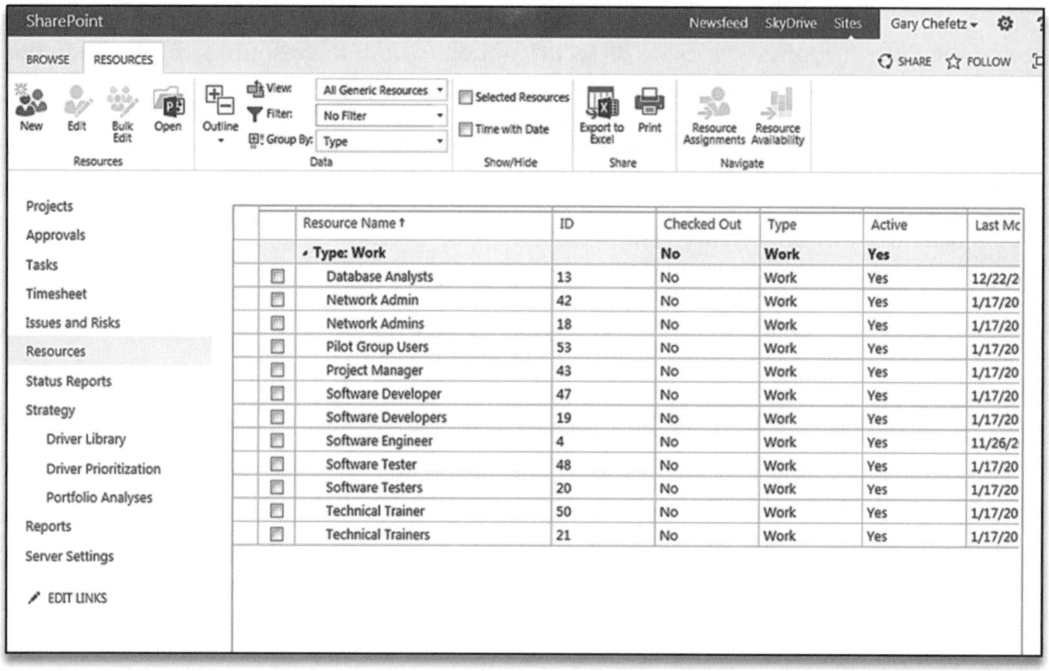

Figure 17 - 30: All Generic Resources custom Resource Center view

Modifying My Work Views

The *My Work* section of the *Manage Views* page lists two default views: *My Assignments* and *Details*. The *My Assignments* view is the default view when a team member navigates to the *Tasks* page in Project Web App. When a team member clicks the name of a task on the *Tasks* page, the system displays the *Details* view on the *Assignment Details* page. Figure 17 - 31 shows the *Tasks* page for a team member. Figure 17 - 32 shows the *Assignment Details* page after the team member clicks on a task on the *Tasks* page.

Although Project Server 2013 allows you to create additional *My Work* views, I strongly recommend that you **do not** create any additional views of this type. Adding extra views to the *Tasks* page can confuse team members who must remember to select the correct view on this page. Instead, I recommend that you edit the default *My Assignments* view to reflect your organization's method of tracking progress, and edit the *Details* view if your requirements call for it.

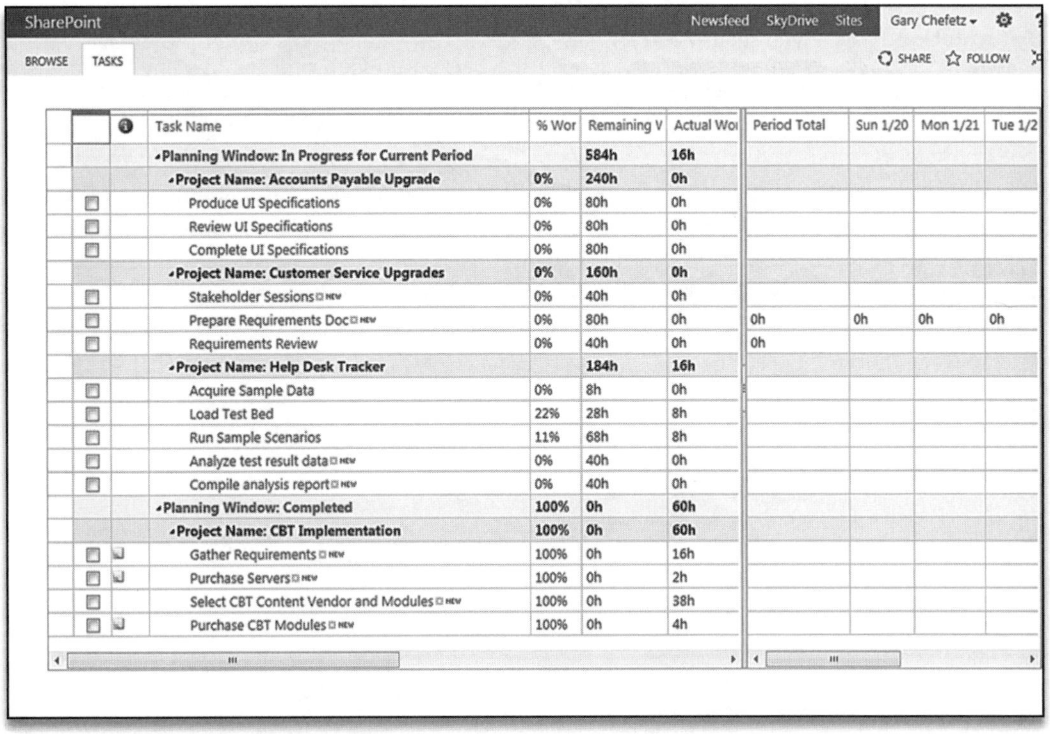

Figure 17 - 31: Tasks page displays the My Assignments view

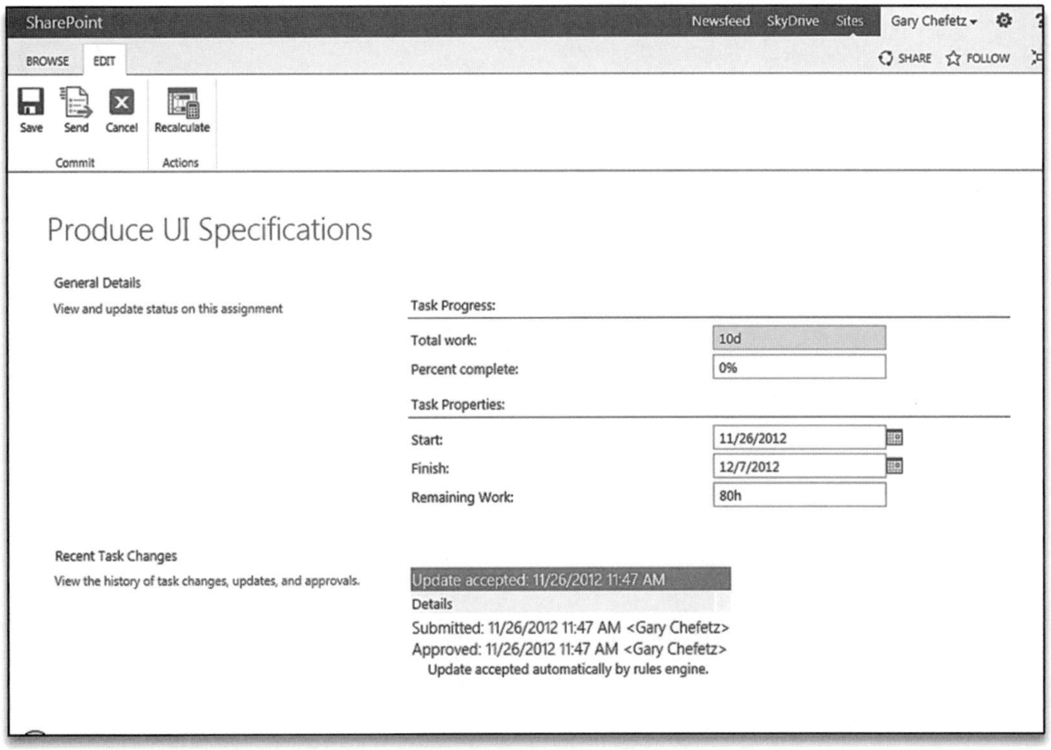

Figure 17 - 32: Assignment Details page displays the Details view

> **Information**: Before you modify the *My Assignments* view, make a backup of the default view and rename it something like *My Assignments Backup*. Modify the backed up view and remove any categories from the view so that the view is no longer visible in Project Web App. Making a backup of the *My Assignments* view allows you to recover the original view if your edits to the original view fail to produce the desired results.

To modify the *My Assignments* view, in the *My Work* section of the *Manage Views* page, click the *My Assignments* link. Project Server 2013 displays the *Edit View* page for the *My Assignments* view, shown in Figure 17 - 33.

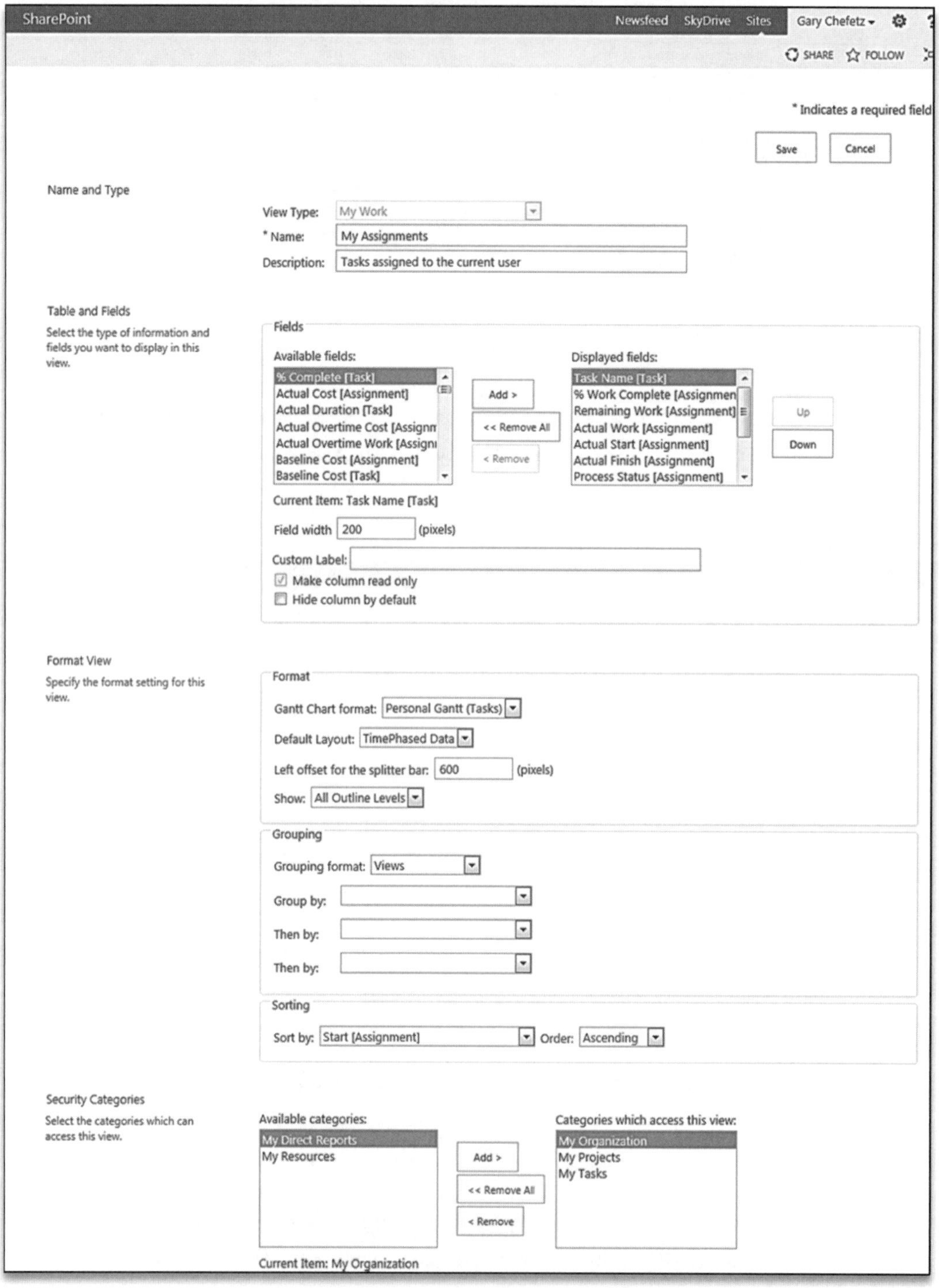

Figure 17 - 33: Edit View page for the My Assignments view

The *Edit View* page for the *My Assignments* view contains four sections with which you are already familiar: the *Name and Type, Table and Fields, Format View,* and *Security Categories* sections. To edit this view, begin by modifying the fields shown in the *Displayed fields* list in the *Table and Fields* section. By default, Project Server 2013 includes the following fields in the *Displayed fields* list: *Task Name [Task], % Work Complete [Assignment], Start [Assignment], Finish [Assignment], Remaining Work [Assignment], Actual Work [Assignment], Work [Assignment], Process Status,* and *Resource Name [Assignment].* Remove the fields you do not want to display in the view and then add any other fields you want to display. The fields you select in the *Displayed fields* list should conform to the default method of tracking progress you selected for your Project Server instance.

The *Make column read only* option is a very important feature in the *Table and Fields* section of the page. Use this feature to lock any field so that the user cannot change any values in the field. For example, Project Server 2013 does not lock the *Start* and *Finish* fields by default, which means that users can manually change the start or finish date of their task assignments. If you select the *Start* field and then select the *Make column read only* option, you lock the field and make it read-only for users to prevent them from changing the start date of their task assignments.

Specify a *Column Label* value for any field with a long name. For example, you might enter *% W Comp* in the *Column Label* field to shorten the display name of the *% Work Complete* field. Click the *Save* button when finished.

You may also want to edit the *Details* page to include the same fields used in the *My Assignments* view. Unfortunately, Project Server 2013 does not allow you to copy the *Details* view, so you must modify the original view. To modify the *Details* view, in the *My Work* section of the *Manage Views* page, click the *Details* link. Project Server 2013 displays the *Edit View* page for the *Details* view, shown in Figure 17 - 34.

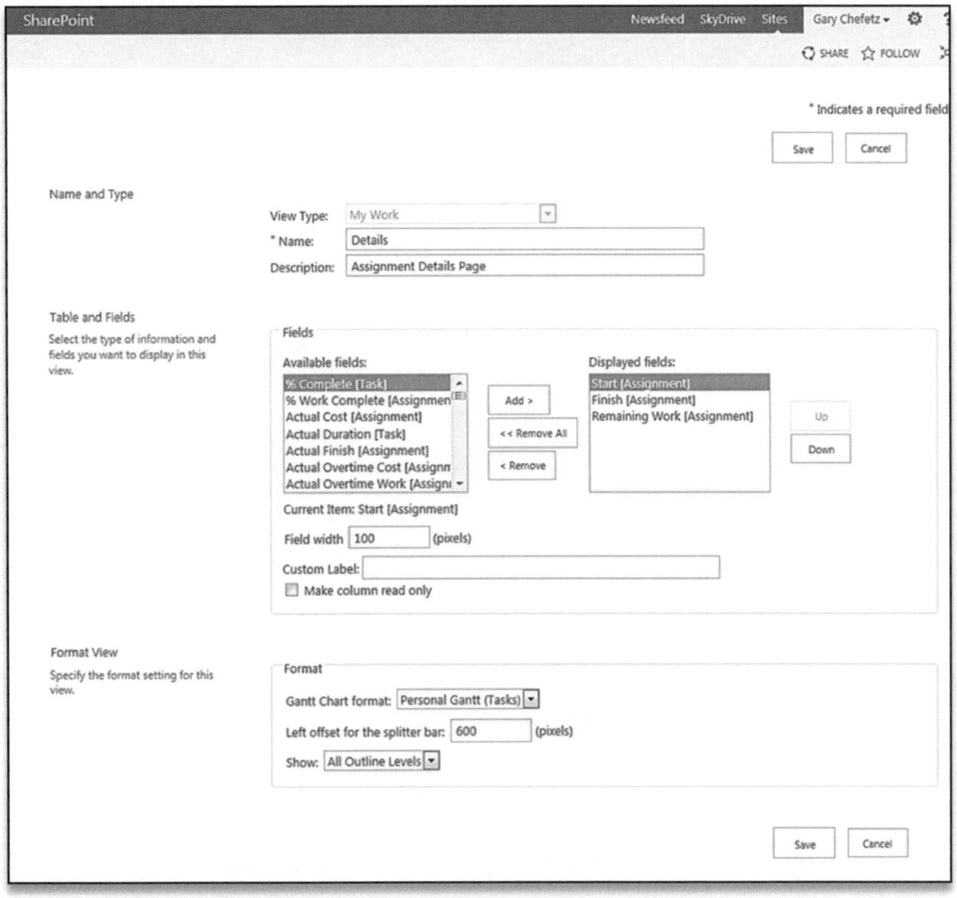

Figure 17 - 34: Edit View page for the Details view

By default, Project Server 2013 includes the following fields in the *Displayed fields* list for the *Details* view: *Start [Assignment], Finish [Assignment],* and *Remaining Work [Assignment]*. Remove the fields you do not want to display in the *Details* view and then add the fields you do want to display. Click the *Save* button when finished.

Information: If your organization does not want to allow team members to adjust the *Remaining Work* value, remove the *Remaining Work [Assignment]* field from the *Displayed Felds* list or lock the field by selecting the *Make column read only* option.

Creating a Custom Resource Plan View

Project managers and resource managers use resource plans to define resource requirements for enterprise projects when they do not know the precise resource requirements yet. For example, a project manager creates a resource plan in a proposed project to show that she needs a specific resource role to work full-time during the first two months and work half-time during the remaining three months of the project. The project manager can then set the resource plan to create the demand for resources in the system. Using a *Resource Plan* view, the project manager can define these general requirements for each resource role required to execute the project. *Resource Plan* views are an ideal place to feature your custom enterprise resource fields.

To create a new *Resource Plan* view, on the *Manage Views* page, click the *New View* button. Click the *View Type* pick list and then select the *Resource Plan* item on the list. The system refreshes the *New View* page as shown in Figure 17 - 35.

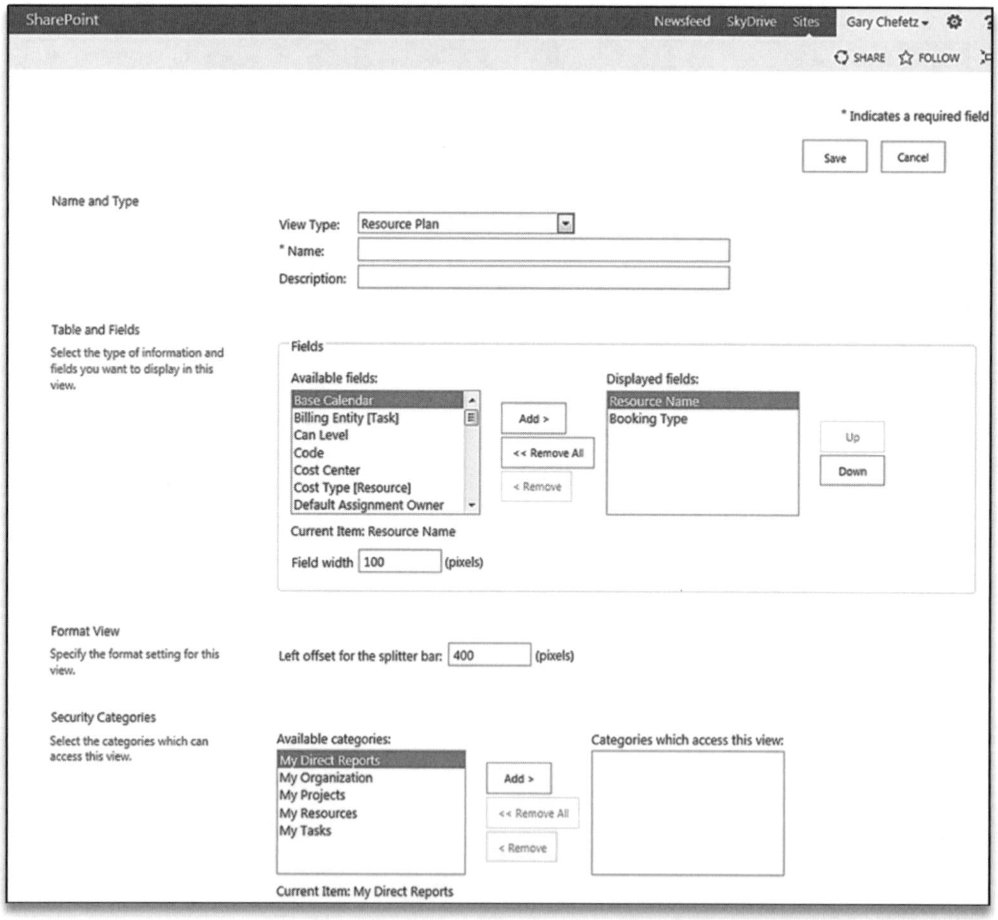

Figure 17 - 35: New View page for a custom Resource Plan view

Creating a custom *Resource Plan* view in Project Web App is very similar to creating *Project, Project Center, Resource Assignments,* and *Resource Center* views. To create a custom *Resource Plan* view, begin by entering a name for the view in the *Name* field and an optional description in the *Description* field. In the *Table and Fields* section of the page, the *Available fields* list contains both standard and custom resource fields, plus built-in and custom enterprise task fields. The only required field in the *Displayed fields* list is the *Resource Name* field. Add additional fields to the *Displayed fields* list as you require. In the *Security Categories* section, remember to add at least one category to the *Categories which access this view* list. Figure 17 - 36 shows the definition for a custom *Resource Plan* view.

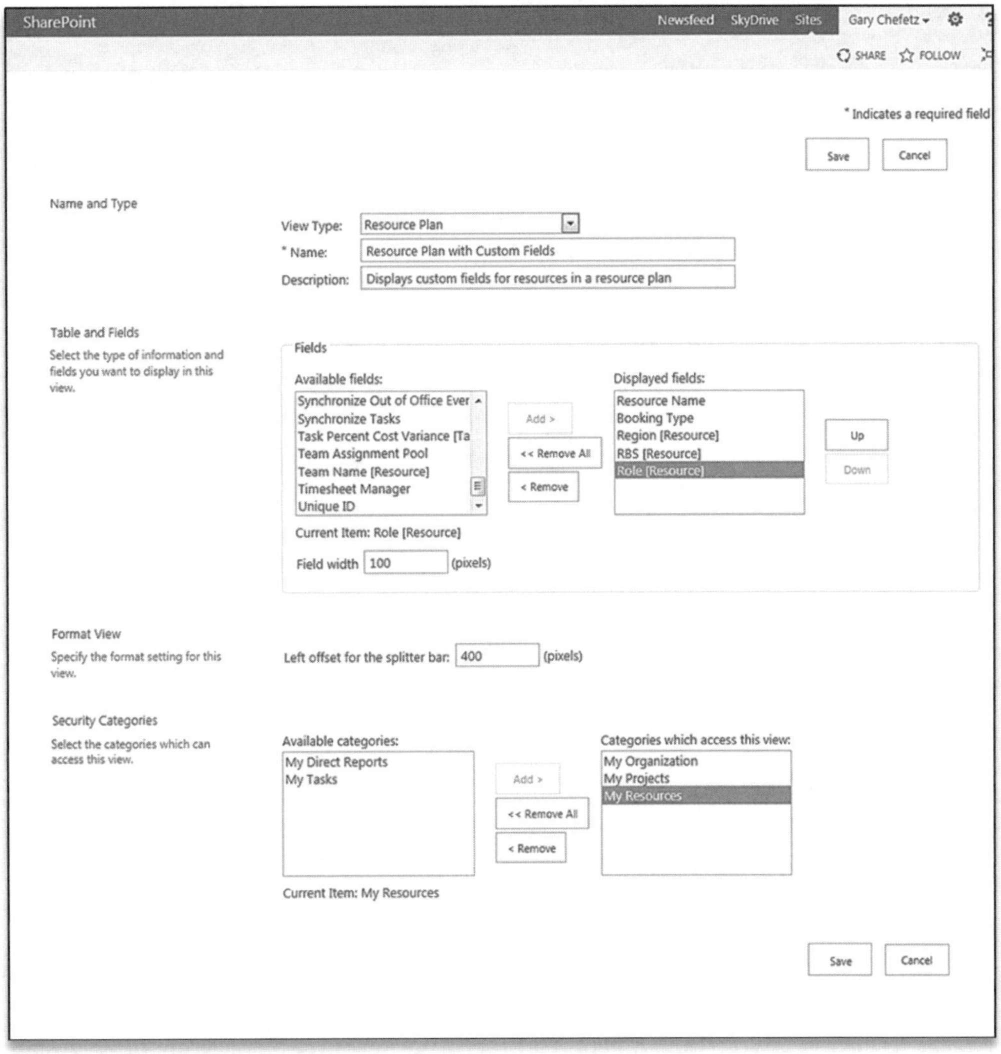

Figure 17 - 36: Resource Plan with Custom Fields view definition

I created the custom *Resource Plan with Custom Fields* view shown in Figure 17 - 36 to display our organization's custom enterprise resource fields to assist a project manager with creating a resource plan for an enterprise project or proposed project. I added the underscore before the name of my custom view so that it displays first when I look at my list of views. To create this custom *Resource Plan* view, I did the following:

- I added the *Region (Resource), RBS (Resource),* and *Role (Resource)* fields to the *Displayed fields* list.
- I added the *My Organization, My Projects,* and *My Resources* categories to the *Categories which access this view* list.

Click the *Save* button to save your configuration. To access a custom *Resource Plan* view, navigate to the *Project Center* page. Select an enterprise project, and then on the *Project* ribbon, click the *Resource Plan* button. The system displays the *Resource Plan* page for the selected project. Click the *View* pick list and select the new custom view.

Figure 17 - 37 shows the custom *Resource Plan* view called *Resource Plan with Custom Fields* applied to a proposed project. Notice that the custom view shows the *Region, RBS,* and *Role* fields.

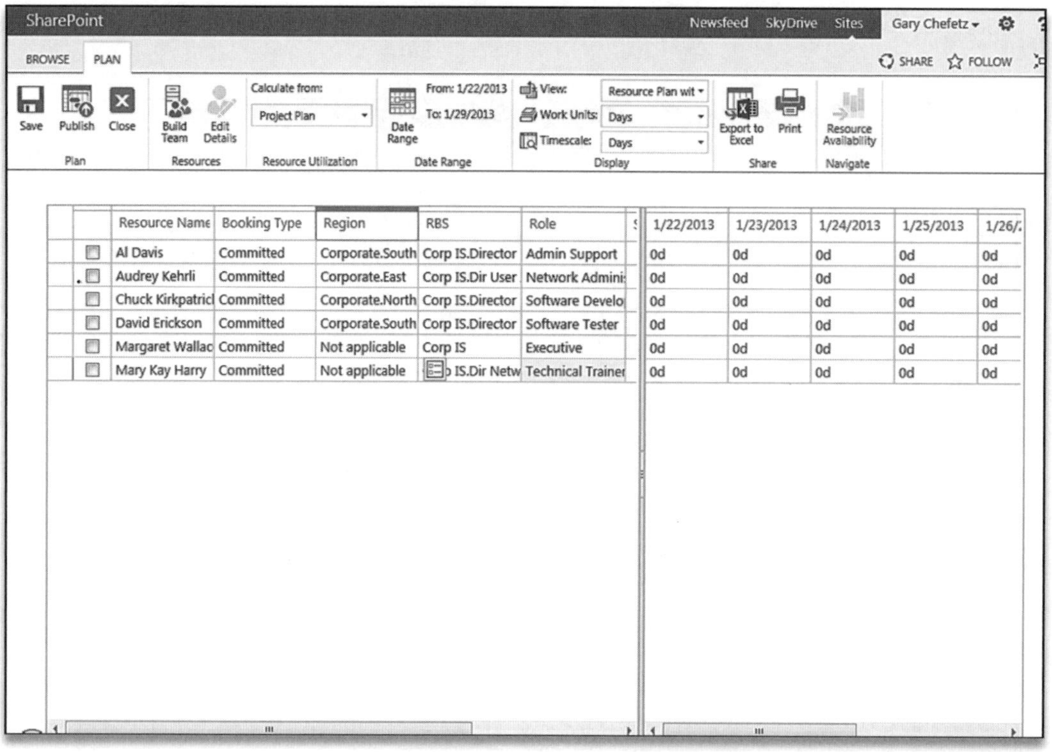

Figure 17 - 37: Custom Resource Plan view

Information: I applied the custom *Resource Plan* view to a resource plan already containing resources on the team. On a new resource plan, users must click the *Build Team* button on the *Resource Plan* page to build the team for the resource plan.

Modifying a Team Tasks View

If you created *Team* resources in your organization's Enterprise Resource Pool, your project managers can use *Team* resources in enterprise projects and proposed projects to assign a group of resources to a task. After the project manager publishes the enterprise project, resources represented by the *Team* resource can view the team assignment pool on the *Team Tasks* page and self-assign these tasks to themselves.

Although Project Server 2013 allows you to create additional *Team Tasks* views, I strongly recommend that you **do not** create any additional views of this type. Adding extra views to the *Team Tasks* page can confuse team members who must remember to select the correct view on this page. Instead, edit the default *Resource Team Assignments* view to include the fields your resources require.

Information: Before you modify the *Resource Team Assignments* view, make a backup of the default view and rename it something like *Resource Team Assignments Backup*. Modify the backed up view by removing any categories from the view so that it is no longer visible in Project Web App. Making a backup of the *Resource Team Assignments* view allows you to restore the original view if your edits fail to produce the desired results.

To modify the *Resource Team Assignments* view, in the *Team Tasks* section of the *Manage Views* page, click the *Resource Team Assignments* link. Project Server 2013 displays the *Edit View* page for the *Resource Team Assignments* view, shown in Figure 17 - 38.

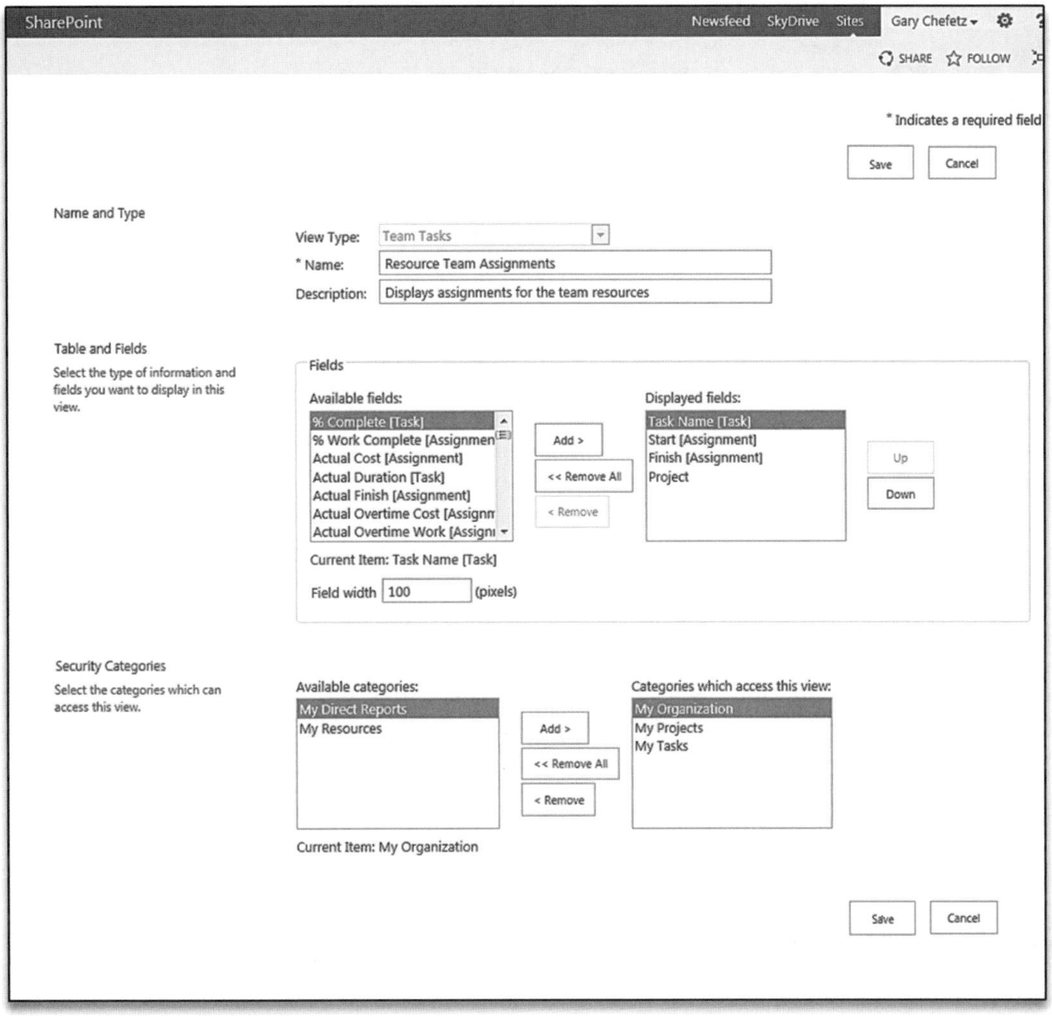

Figure 17 - 38: Edit View page for the Resource Team Assignments view

The *Edit View* page for the *Resource Team Assignments* view contains three sections with which you should already be familiar: the *Name and Type, Table and Fields,* and *Security Categories* sections. To edit this view, modify the fields shown in the *Displayed fields* list in the *Table and Fields* section. By default, Project Server 2013 includes only the following fields in the *Displayed fields* list: *Task Name, Start, Finish,* and *Project*. Remove the fields you do not want to display in the view and then add the fields you do want to display. Move your selected fields into position and click the *Save* button when you complete your configuration.

To access team assignments, team members must first navigate to the *Tasks* page in Project Web App, click the *Add Row* pick list button, and then select the *Add Team Tasks* item on the pick list as shown in Figure 17 - 39.

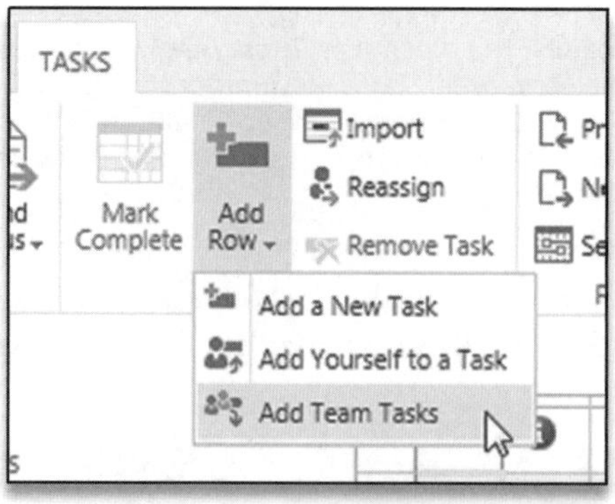

Figure 17 - 39: Add Team Tasks

The system displays the *Team Tasks* page and applies the modified *Resource Team Assignments* view. For example, Figure 17 - 40 shows the *Team Tasks* page with no assignments.

Figure 17 - 40: Team Tasks page

On the *Team Tasks* page, a resource must select the checkbox for one or more *Team* tasks and then click the *Assign to me* button. Project Server 2013 removes the *Team* task from the *Team Tasks* page and moves it to the resource's *Tasks* page. Only one resource can self-assign a *Team* task. Once one resource self-assigns a task, the task is no longer available to the rest of the team.

Creating a Custom Team Builder View

Resource managers who do not use Project Pro 2013 can build a team for enterprise projects using the *Build Team* tool in Project Web App. Project managers or resource managers must also use the *Build Team* tool to build a team in a proposed project. While using the *Build Team* tool, managers can apply *Team Builder* views to help find and select the correct resources for the team. If you defined any custom enterprise resource fields in your Project Server 2013 system, *Team Builder* views are an ideal location in which to display these custom fields. Project Server 2013 ships with four *Team Builder* views: *All Resources, Cost Resources, Work Resources,* and *Material Resources.* You can create new views, or modify the built-in views.

To create a new *Team Builder* view, on the *Manage Views* page, click the *New View* button. Click the *View Type* pick list and then select the *Team Builder* item on the list. The system refreshes the *New View* page as shown in Figure 17 - 41.

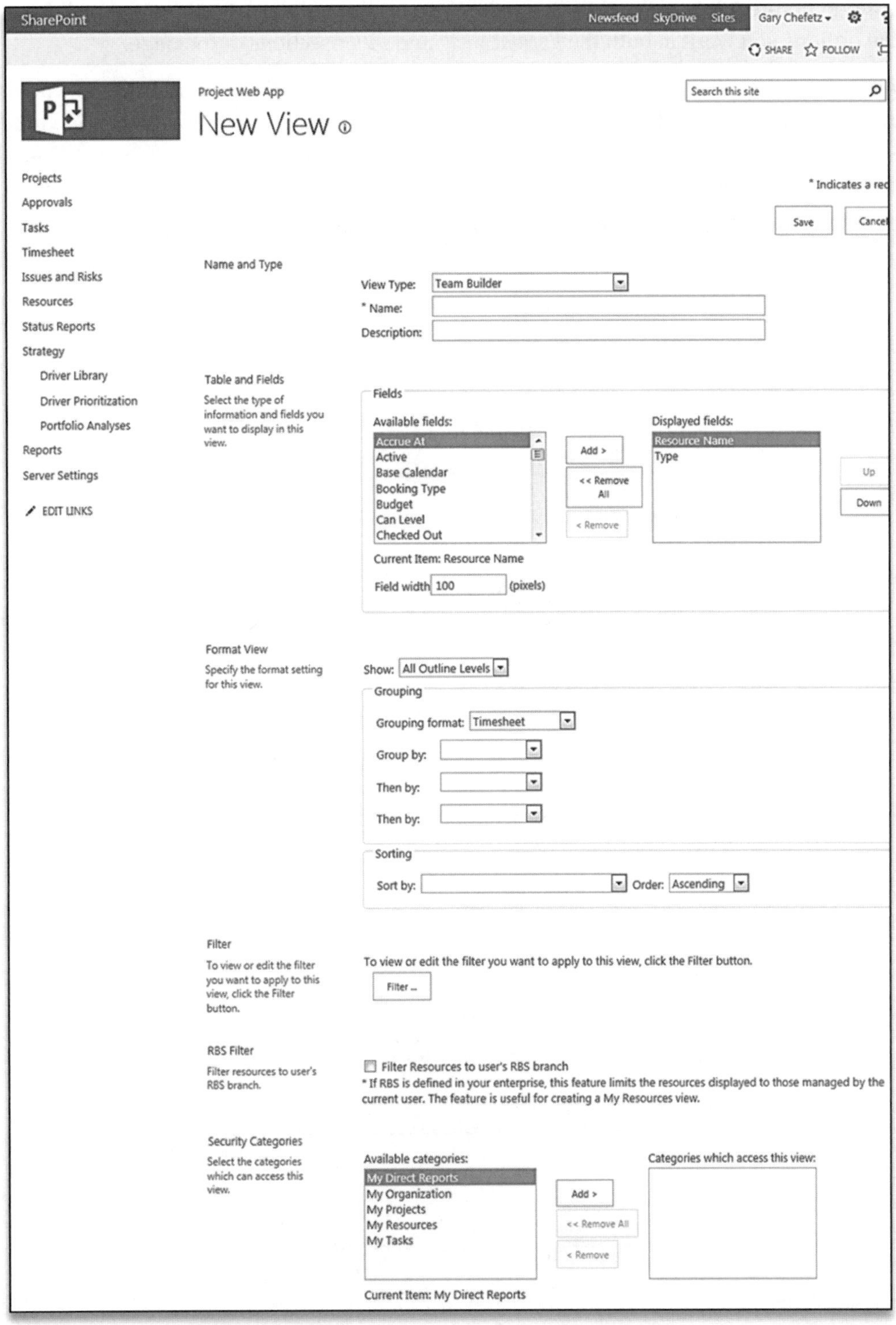

Figure 17 - 41: New View page for a Team Builder view

To create a custom *Team Builder* view, begin by entering a name for the view in the *Name* field and an optional description in the *Description* field. In the *Table and Fields* section of the page, the *Available fields* list contains both standard and custom resource fields. By default, the *Displayed fields* list contains one required field, the *Resource*

Name field, and one non-required field, the *Type* field. Add additional fields to the *Displayed fields* list as you require. Select the options you want in both the *Format View* and *Filter* sections of the page.

In the *RBS Filter* section, select the *Filter Resources to user's RBS branch* option to limit the resources displayed in the view to only those managed by the current user accessing the *Team Builder* view. In the *Security Categories* section, remember to add at least one category to the *Categories which access this view* list. Figure 17 - 42 shows the definition for a custom *Team Builder* view.

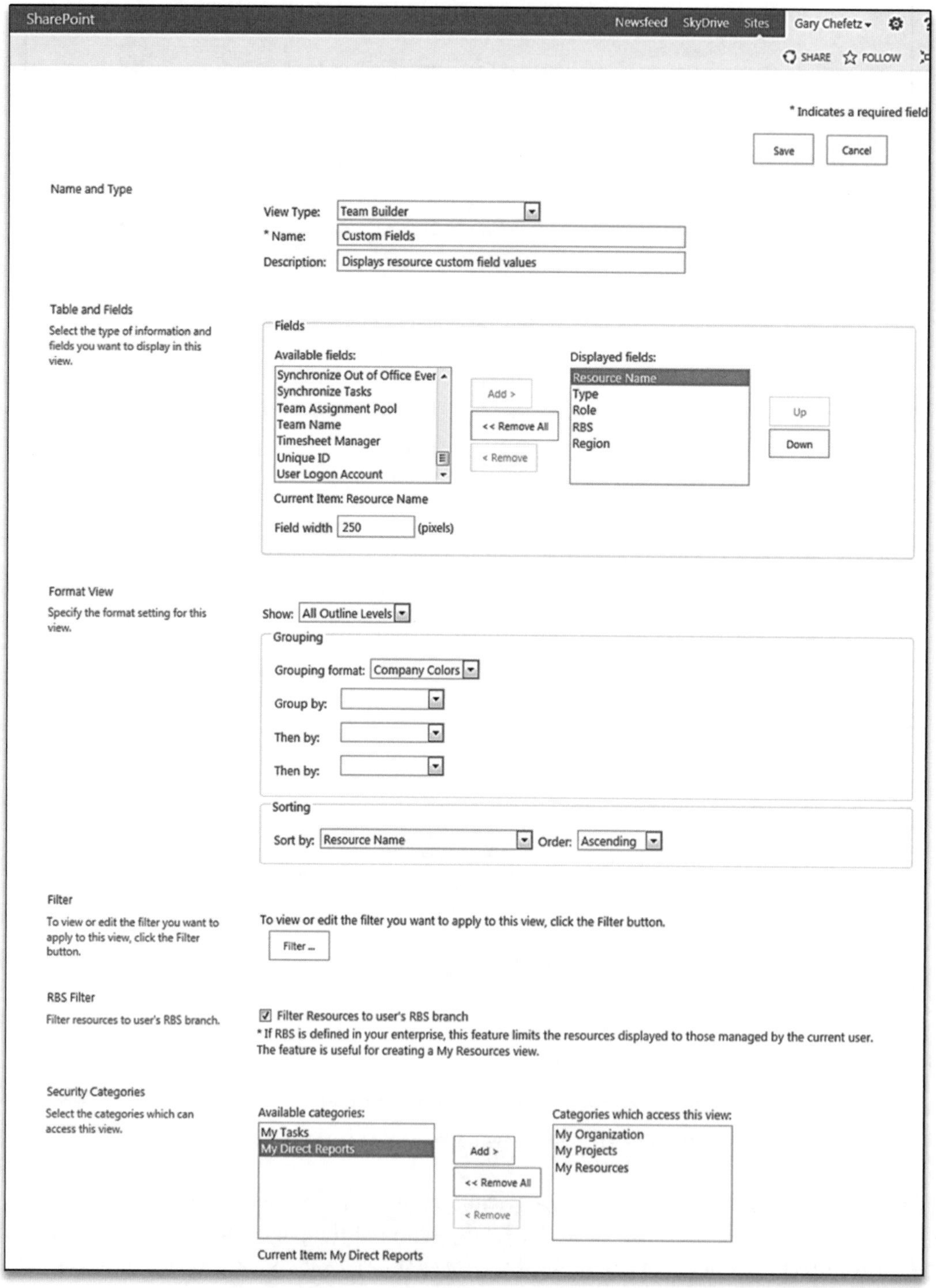

Figure 17 - 42: Custom Fields Team Builder view definition

I created the custom *Custom Fields* view shown in Figure 17 - 42 to display my organization's custom enterprise resource fields to assist a project manager with adding resources to a team in an enterprise project or proposed project. To create this custom *Team Builder* view, I did the following:

- I added the *Role, Region,* and *RBS* fields to the *Displayed fields* list.
- On the *Resource Name* field, I applied *Ascending* sorting.
- I selected the *Filter Resources to user's RBS branch* option to limit the resources displayed in the view to only those managed by the current user who is accessing the *Team Builder* view.
- I added the *My Organization, My Projects,* and *My Resources* categories to the *Categories which access this view* list and clicked the *Save* button to finish.

To apply a *Team Builder* view in Project Web App, resource managers and project managers can use either of the following methods:

- To build a team directly on a project, navigate to the *Project Center* page, select an enterprise project or proposed project, and then from the *Navigate* section of the *Projects* ribbon, click the *Build Team* button.
- To build a team for a project from a resource plan, navigate to the *Project Center* page, select an enterprise project or proposed project and from the *Navigate* section of the *Projects* menu, click the *Resource Plan* button and then from the *Resources* section of the *Plan* ribbon, click the *Build Team* button to create the *Resource Plan* team.

After accessing the *Build Team* page using any of the preceding methods, click the *View* pick list and select a standard or custom *Team Builder* view. For example, Figure 17 - 43 shows my custom *Team Builder* view on the *Build Team* page.

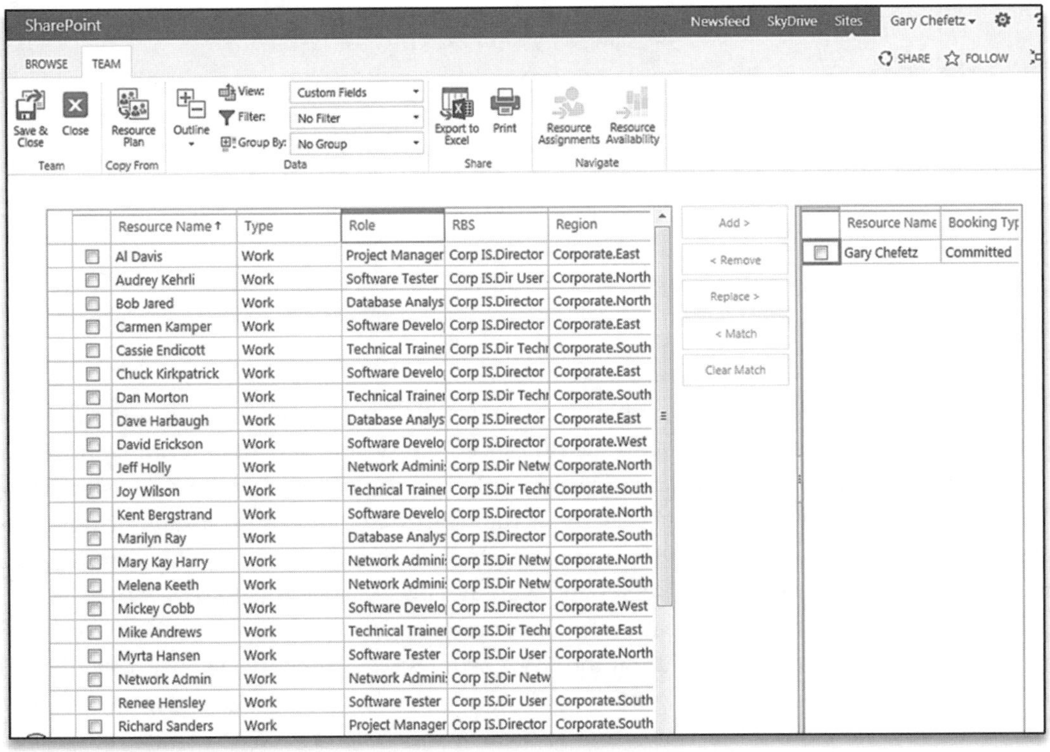

Figure 17 - 43: Custom Team Builder view applied in the Build Team page

Customizing the Timesheet Page

By default, the *Timesheet* page in Project Server 2013 includes two views, *My Timesheet* and *My Work*. The *My Work* view contains the following default fields: (Note: The *My Timesheet* view contains only the first five fields on the list.)

- Task Name
- Project Name
- Comment
- Billing Category
- Process Status
- Start
- Finish
- Remaining Work
- % Work Complete
- Work
- Actual Work
- Duration

If you are tracking time in weekly buckets rather than daily time tracking and you use the *Single Entry Mode* method, when a resource updates a task through the timesheet, the system cannot determine the actual start date and actual finish date for a task. This isn't a problem for daily time reporting because the system recognizes that the first date a user reports time against a task is the actual start date, and the last date of time reporting that causes the task to become 100% complete is the actual finish date. In the case of weekly reporting buckets, you need to capture this information from your users if you want the project schedule to reflect these dates accurately. You can modify both timesheet views or create your own views for this purpose. To modify one of the existing timesheet views, from the *Look and Feel* section of the *PWA Settings page,* click the *Manage Views* link. The system displays the *Manage Views* page shown in Figure 17 - 44 and Figure 17 - 45. Notice in Figure 17 - 45 that I highlighted two sections, one containing the views that appear in the *Timesheet* page and the other containing the views for the *Tasks* page, which I cover next. I also cover creating and managing views in more depth in Module 17, *Creating and Managing Views*.

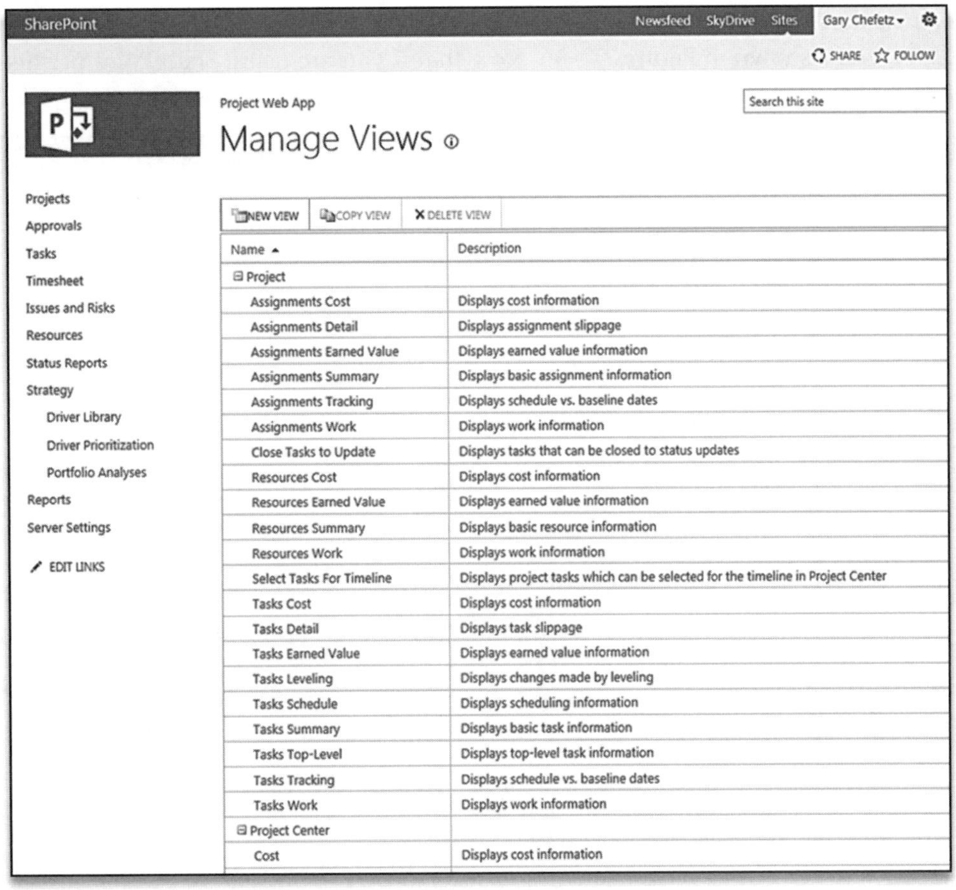

Figure 17 - 44: Manage Views page (part one)

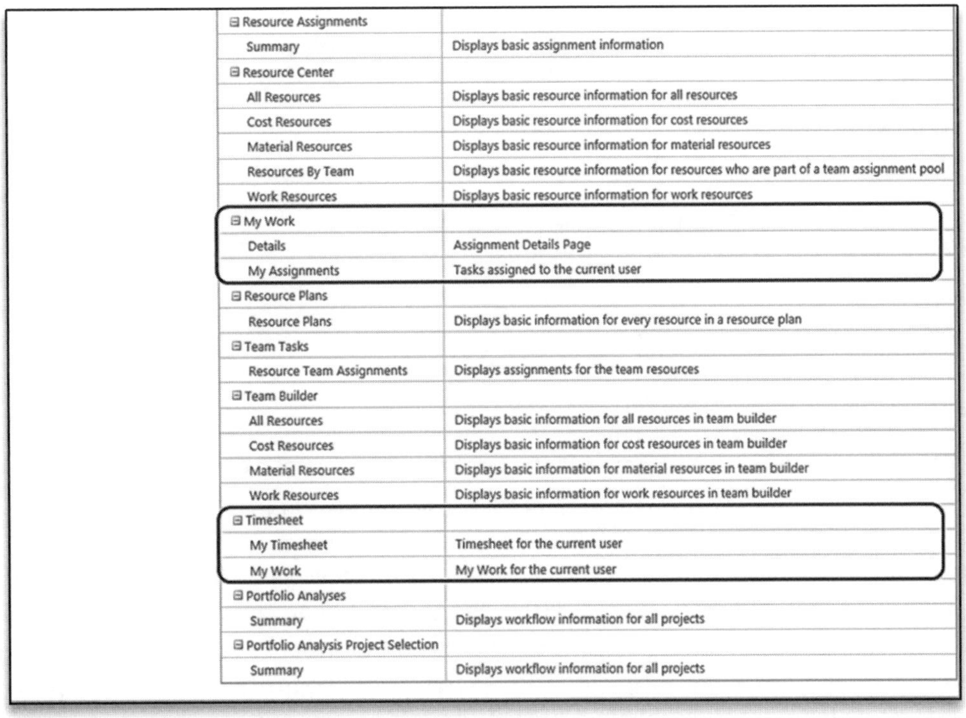

Figure 17 - 45: Manage View page (part two)

From the *Timesheet* section, click the *My Work* view to open it for modification. The system displays the *Edit View* page for the *My Work* view shown in Figure 17 - 46. Note that if you are using SharePoint permissions mode, the system does not display the *Security Categories* section you see in the figure.

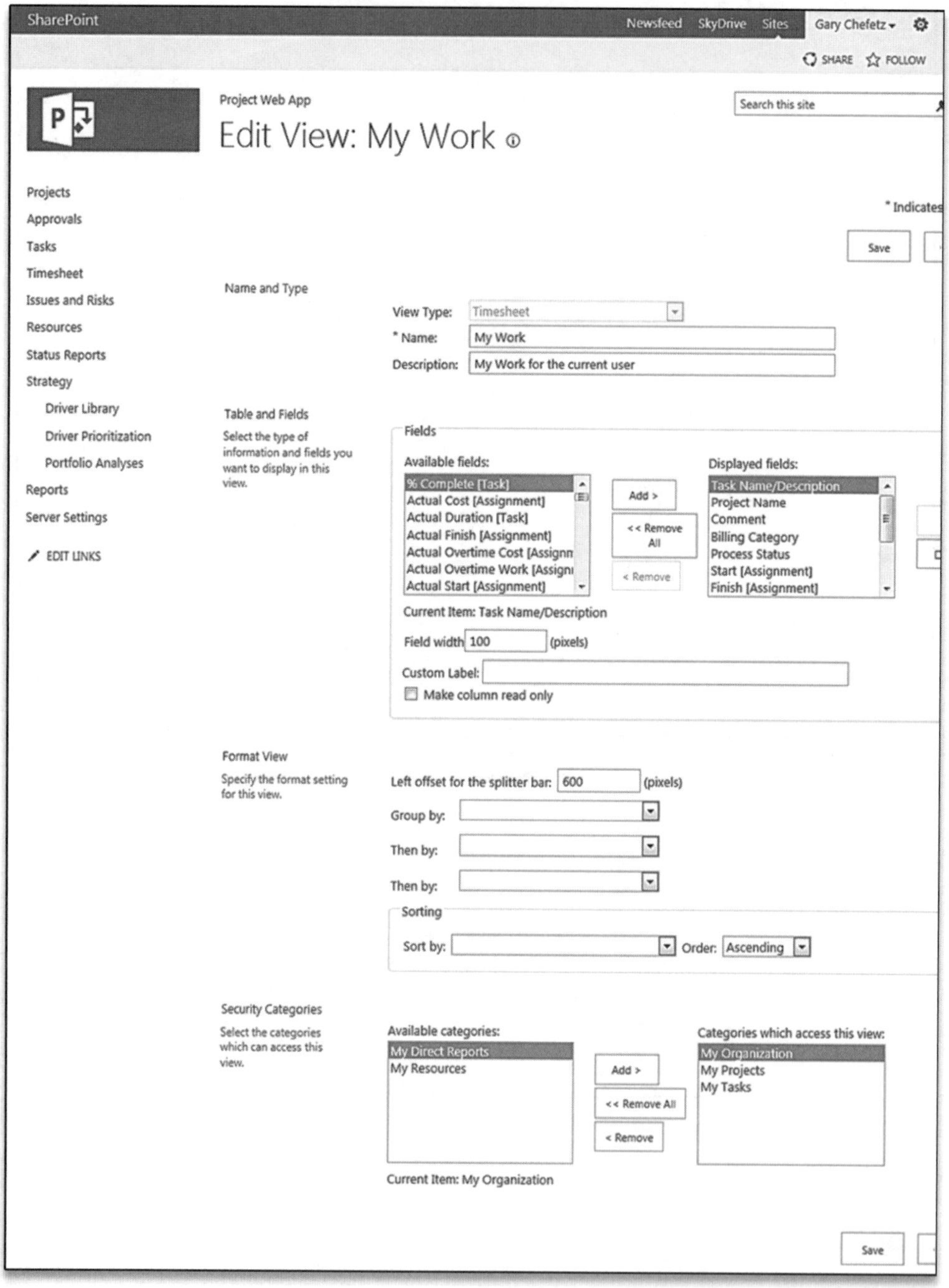

Figure 17 - 46: Edit View page for My Work

To add the *Actual Start* and *Actual Finish* dates to the view, in the *Table and Fields* section, locate and select the fields in the *Available fields* list on the left and click the *Add* button to add them to the *Displayed fields* list on the right. Use the *Up* and *Down* buttons to move the fields to the position where you want them to appear. Notice the controls below the field selectors in the *Table and Fields* section. You can further tailor the display of fields by selecting a *Displayed field* on the right and changing three attributes:

1. **Field Width** in pixels: Allows you to set the field width in the display.
2. **Custom Label**: Allows you to change the label for the field in the column header display.
3. **Make column read only**: Allows you to lock the field for editing in the view.

By default, a user can edit any field in the view except for the *Project Name* and *Task Name/Description* fields and the fields that the system locks based on the tracking method options you select. You can prevent users from editing other fields by selecting the *Make column read only* option. Use this feature, for instance, if you do not want to allow your users to change planned start or finish dates. Do not change any values in the *Security Categories* section until you understand the impacts of these actions.

Project Server 2013 adds a new *Format View* section to the page that allows you to group and sort the view as well as to offset the splitter bar. I cover these options thoroughly in Module 17, *Creating and Managing Views*.

> **Information**: You can follow the same steps to customize the *My Timesheet* view as you used to customize the *My Work* view.

Customizing the Tasks Page

As I stated earlier, Project Server 2013 offers your organization four methods for tracking task progress. Because the default layout of the *My Assignments* view for the *Tasks* page is static, MSProjectExperts recommends that you create a custom layout of this view based on your tracking method. The key action is to modify the *Tasks* page layout to capture the most relevant information about task progress for each project manager. This is particularly important if you are not using timesheets in Project Server 2013, or if you use the manual import from timesheets to populate progress in the *Tasks* page, and you require additional input from your users regarding the status of tasks. The *My Assignments* view contains the following default fields:

- Task Name
- Start
- Finish
- Remaining Work
- % Work Complete
- Actual Work
- Process Status

Using Percent of Work Complete

To capture the most relevant information about task progress using the *Percent Work Complete* method of tracking, MSProjectExperts recommends that you modify the *My Assignments* view layout by completing the following steps:

1. Log in to Project Web App with administrator permissions.
2. In the *Quick Launch* menu, click the *Server Settings* link.
3. In the *Look and Feel* section of the *PWA Settings* page, click the *Manage Views* link.
4. In the *My Work* section of the *Manage Views* page, click the *My Assignments* link to open the *My Assignments* view for editing, as shown in Figure 17 - 47.

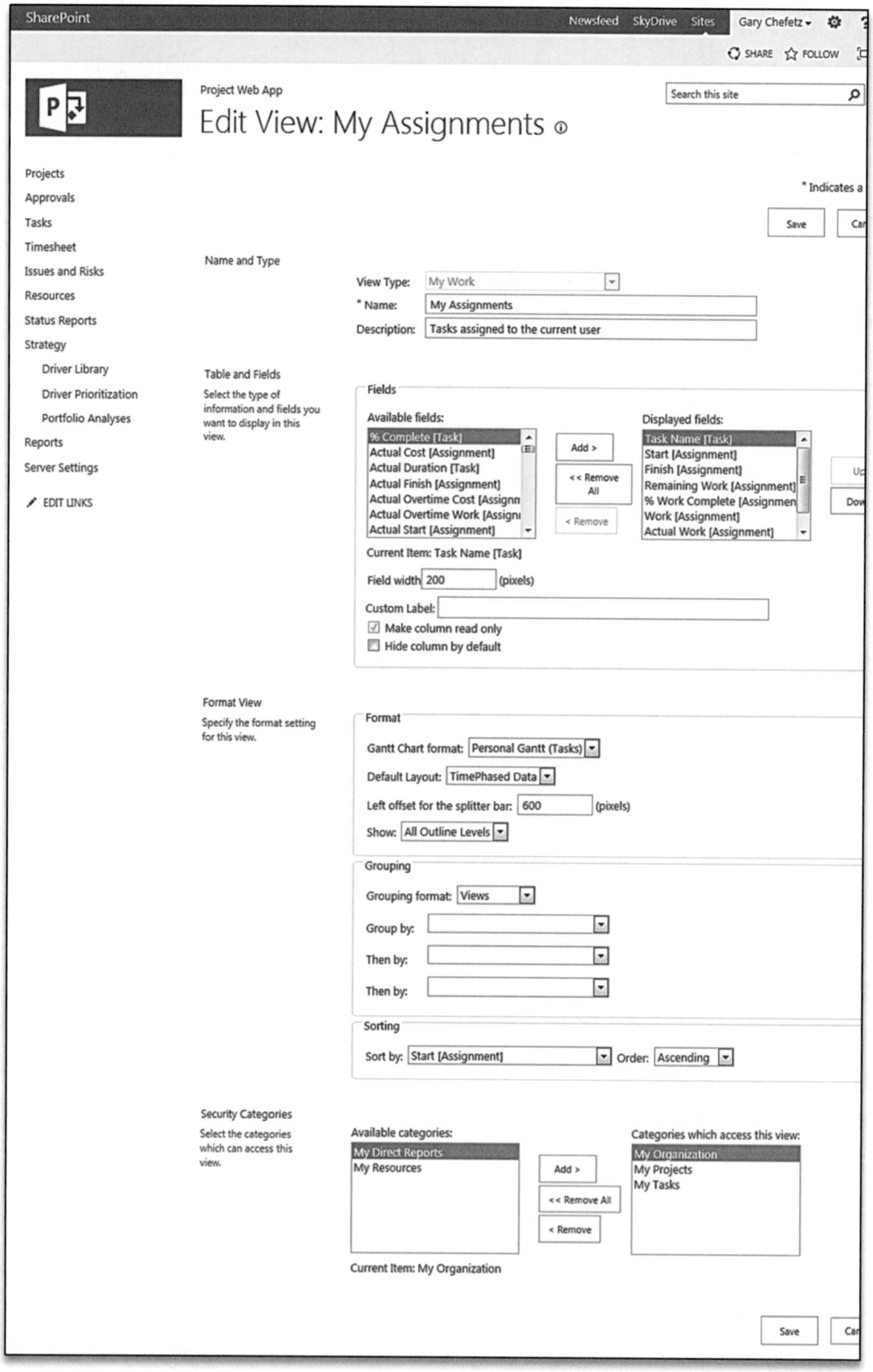

Figure 17 - 47: Edit View page for the My Assignments view

5. Select the *Start [Assignment]* field and *Finish [Assignment]* field in the *Displayed fields* list on the right and click the < *Remove* button.
6. Select the following fields in the *Available fields* list and then click the *Add* > button to add them to the *Displayed fields* list:
    - Actual Finish [Assignment]
    - Actual Start [Assignment]
    - Actual Work [Assignment]
    - Work [Assignment]
    - Resource Name [Assignment]
    - Task Hierarchy
7. Use the *Up* and *Down* buttons to move the fields in the *Displayed fields* list into the following order:
    - Task Name [Task]
    - Actual Start [Assignment]
    - % Work Complete [Assignment]
    - Remaining Work [Assignment]
    - Actual Finish [Assignment]
    - Resource Name [Assignment]
    - Process Status
    - Task Hierarchy
    - Start [Assignment]
    - Finish [Assignment]

Information: Note that this is a suggested layout. You can choose to keep fields that I suggest removing, or you can add additional fields if you require additional input from your users.

Best Practice: MSProjectExperts recommends that you include the *Start* and *Finish* fields for sorting the view, whether you set the sort order in the view specifications or you provide this for user convenience. If you do not want users to submit changes to planned start and finish dates, then you should set these fields to *Read-Only* mode in the view.

The *Task Hierarchy* field allows you or your users to show the summary task hierarchy for each task. If you do not pre-group your view by this field, I recommend that you add this field to the *My Assignments* view for the convenience of your users, who can use this to group the view in order to see the plan structure around their assignments. Figure 17 - 48 shows the recommended order of the fields in the *My Assignments* view. The fields you select for this view appear on the *Tasks* page for each resource in Project Web App.

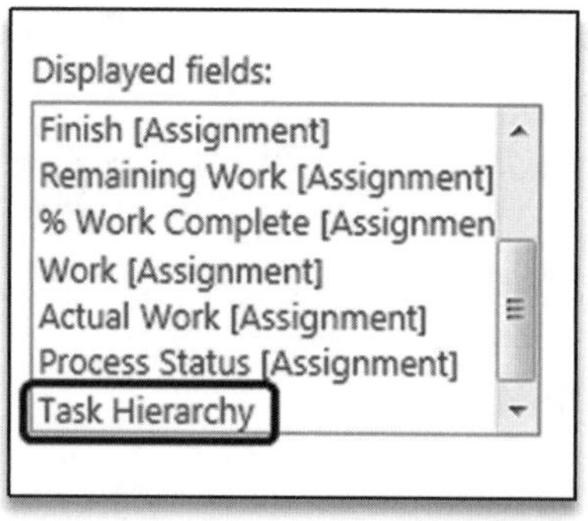

Figure 17 - 48: Displayed fields list for the My Assignments view using Percent of Work Complete

8. Click the *Save* button to complete the changes. Figure 17 - 49 shows a user's *Tasks* page with the custom layout applied.

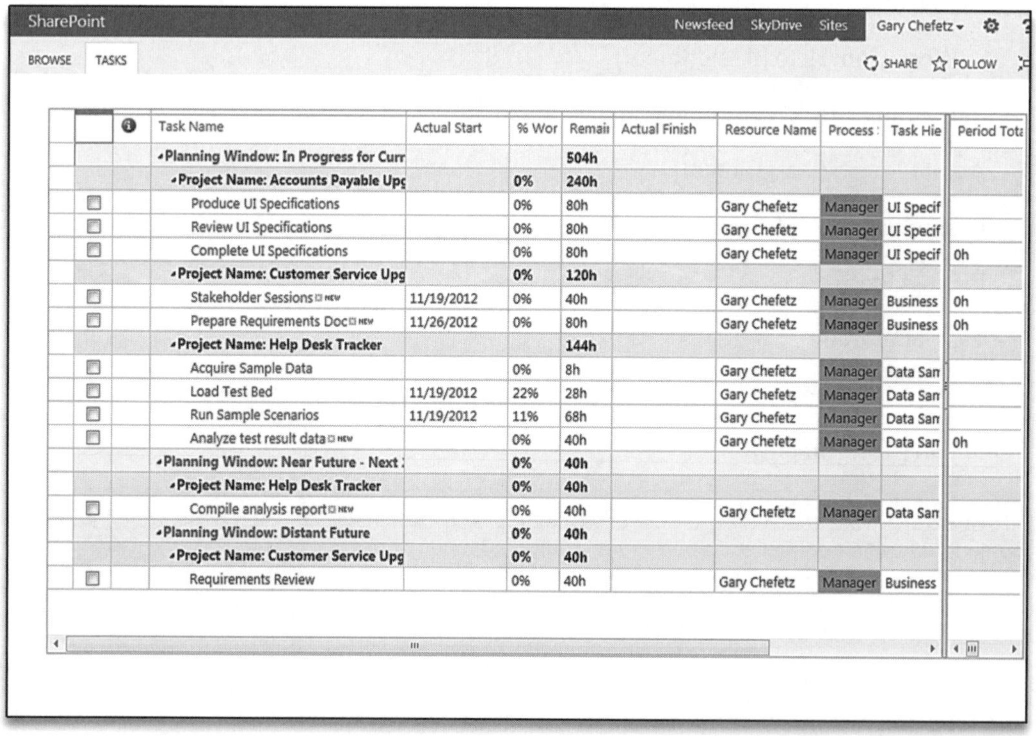

Figure 17 - 49: Tasks page with custom Percent of Work Complete layout

Users with Project Server 2007 experience will be delighted that the grouping options for both the *Tasks* and *Timesheet* views are back for Project Server 2013 after being absent in 2010. In order to use the *Task Hierarchy* field to change the display of the *Tasks* page, each user must apply the grouping manually or you can build this grouping into the default display. Figure 17 - 50 shows the same view as Figure 17 - 49 with custom grouping applied by the user in the view. I expanded the *Task Name* view to better show the task hierarchy display.

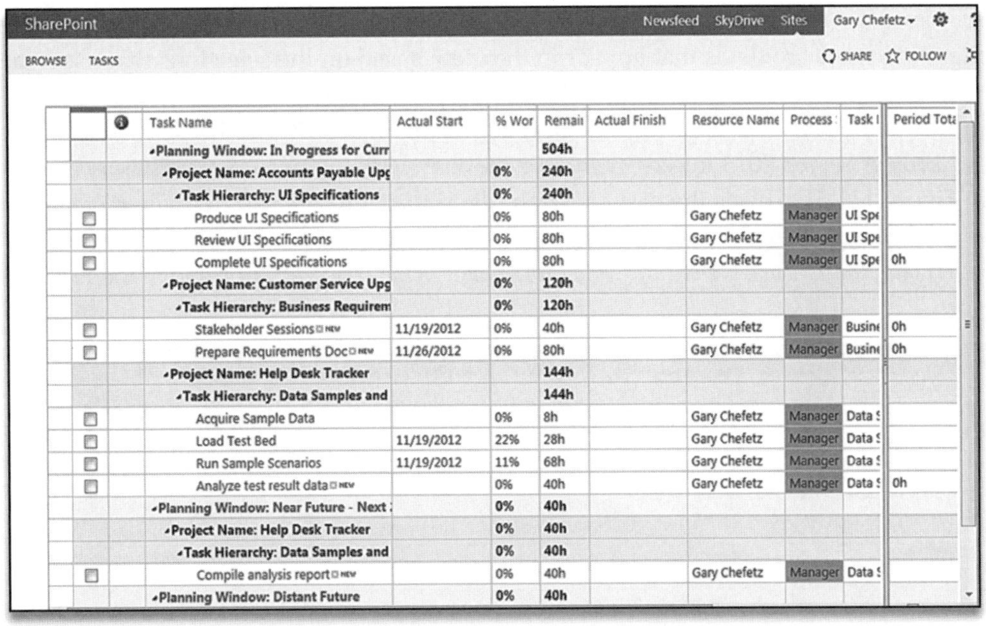

Figure 17 - 50: Tasks page with custom grouping applied

Creating a Portfolio Analyses View

A *Portfolio Analyses* view is one of two types of views in Project Server 2013 that support the *Portfolio Analyses* features. The system includes one default *Portfolio Analyses* view, the *Summary* view, but you can create other *Portfolio Analyses* views as your organization requires. *Portfolio Analyses* views appear when you display the *Analysis* ribbon when you analyze cost or resources as shown in Figure 17 - 51. You can modify the existing *Summary* view, or you can create additional views for your users.

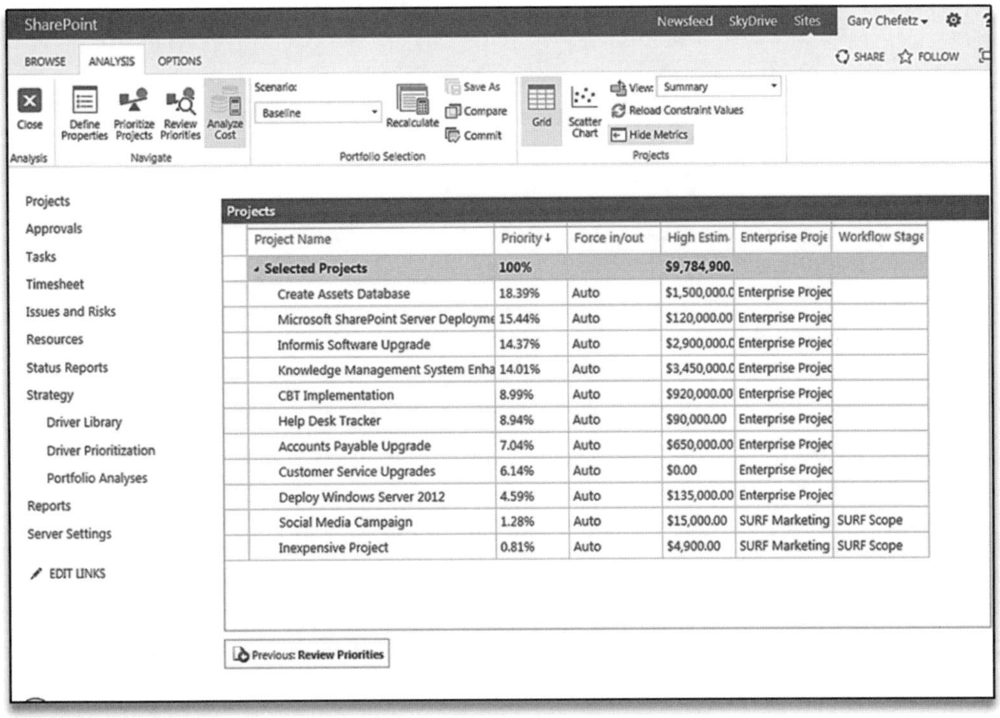

Figure 17 - 51: Portfolio Analyses view

Portfolio Analyses views are unique in that there are fields that appear in these views that you cannot control from the *Edit View* page, and there are fields that appear in the view based on the selections that users make when they create a new portfolio analysis. Notice in Figure 17 - 51 that the view displays the *Priority* and *Force in/out* fields. These do not appear in the *Edit View* page for this view shown in Figure 17 - 52. These two fields are default fields for the view and Project Server 2013 injects them into the view. This is not user-definable. Notice also the *High Estimate* field in Figure 17 - 51. This is the cost constraint field that the user selected when creating this particular portfolio analysis. More importantly, notice in Figure 17 - 52 that the only fields defined in the *Edit View* page are *Project Name, Enterprise Project Type Name,* and *Workflow Stage Name.* You cannot remove the *Project Name* field.

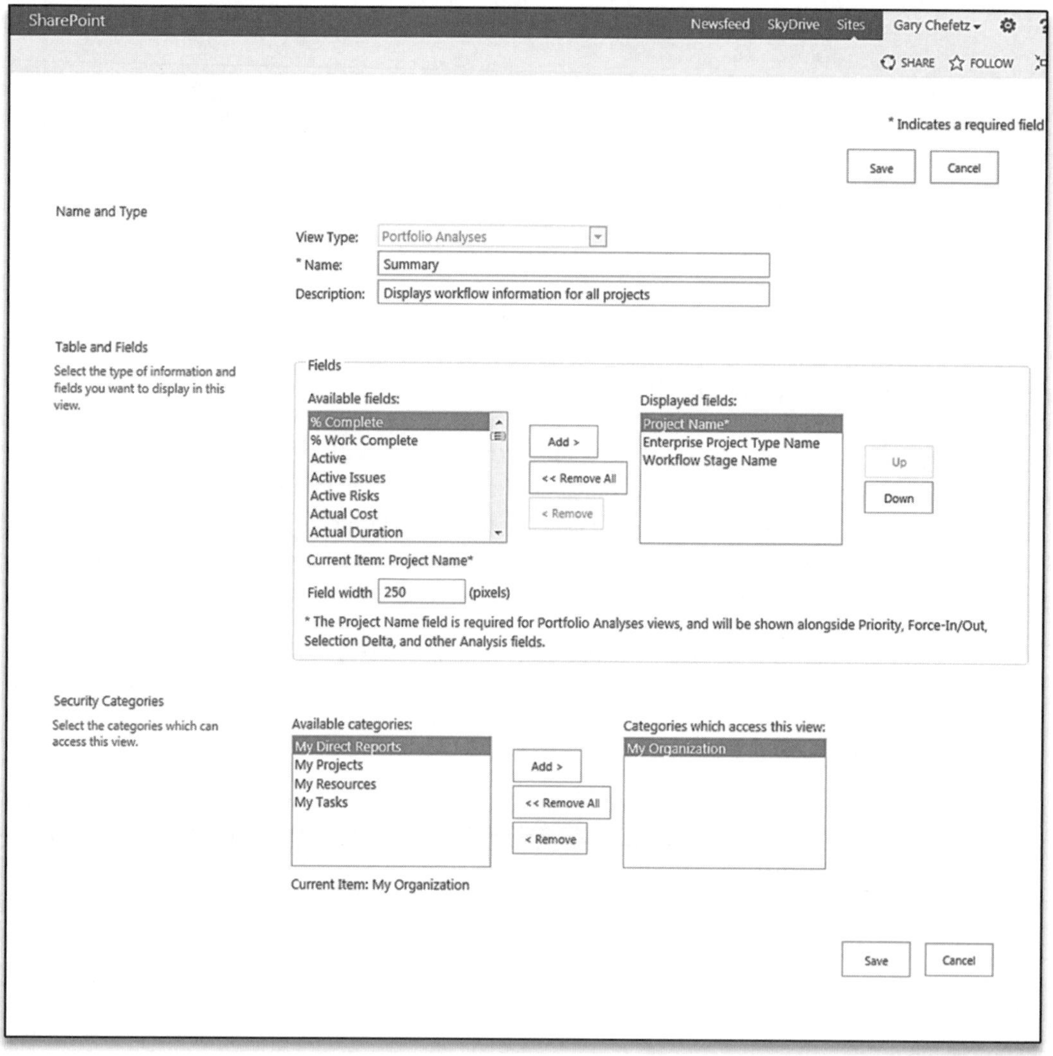

Figure 17 - 52: Edit View page for Portfolio Analyses Summary view

When you display the same *Summary* view in the *Analyze Resources* screen, the system adds three fields: *Original Start, New Start,* and *Has Resource* fields. Project Server 2013 injects these fields into the view. The system bases the *Original Start* field value on the project start date. You use the *New Start* field to move projects within a portfolio analysis exercise, but it does not appear anywhere else in the system as this is a functional field specifically for this purpose.

To create a new *Portfolio Analyses* view, on the *Manage Views* page, click the *New View* button. Click the *View Type* pick list and then select the *Portfolio Analyses* item on the list. The system refreshes the *New View* page as shown in Figure 17 - 53.

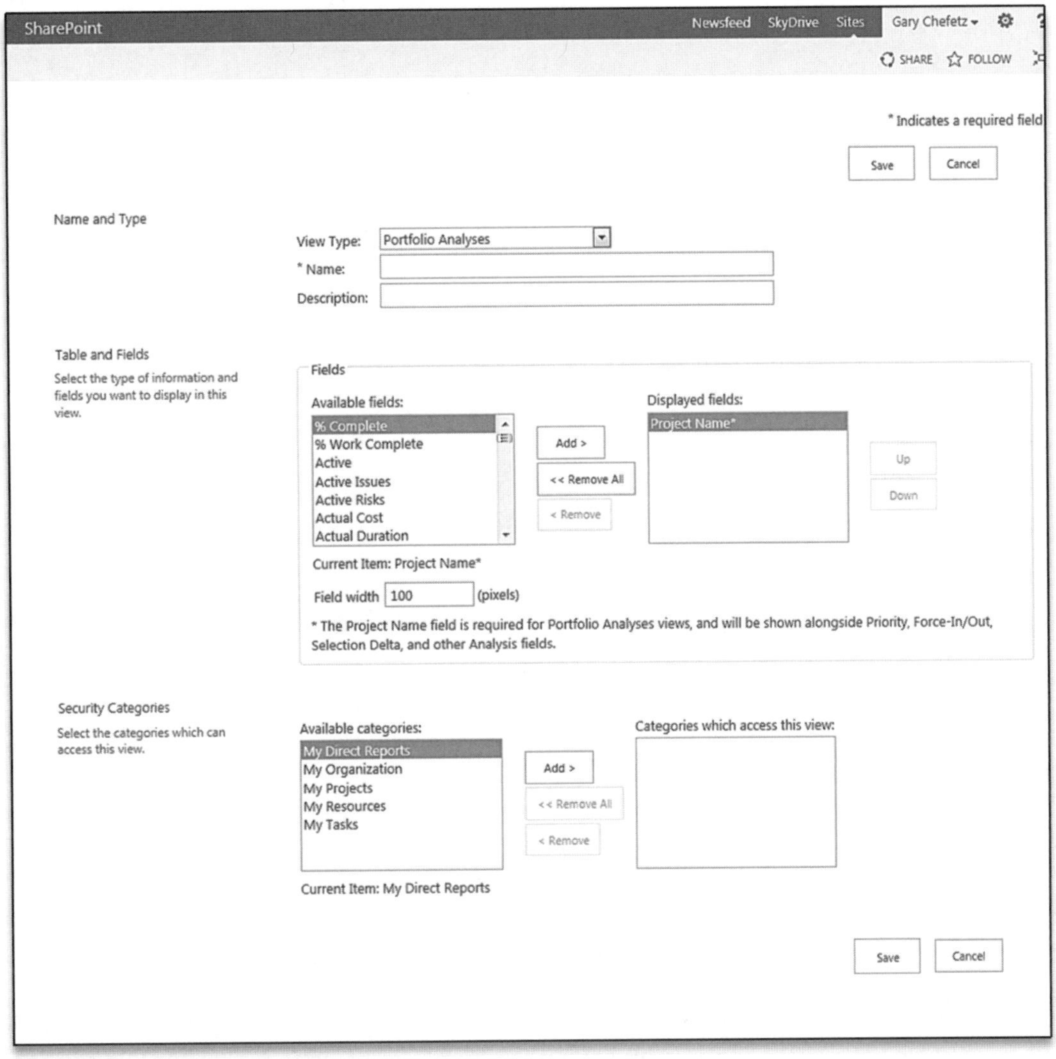

Figure 17 - 53: New View page for a custom Portfolio Analyses view

To create a custom *Portfolio Analyses* view, begin by entering a name for the view in the *Name* field and an optional description in the *Description* field. In the *Table and Fields* section of the page, the *Available fields* list contains both standard and custom project fields, fields reflecting important information in the Project Site for the project (such as the *Active Issues* and *Active Risks* fields), and fields used in the workflow process (such as the *Workflow Stage Name* and *Workflow State* fields). By default, the *Displayed fields* list contains one required field, the *Project Name* field. Add additional fields to the *Displayed fields* list as you require.

In the *Security Categories* section, remember to add at least one category to the *Categories which access this view* list. Figure 17 - 54 shows the definition for a custom *Portfolio Analyses* view.

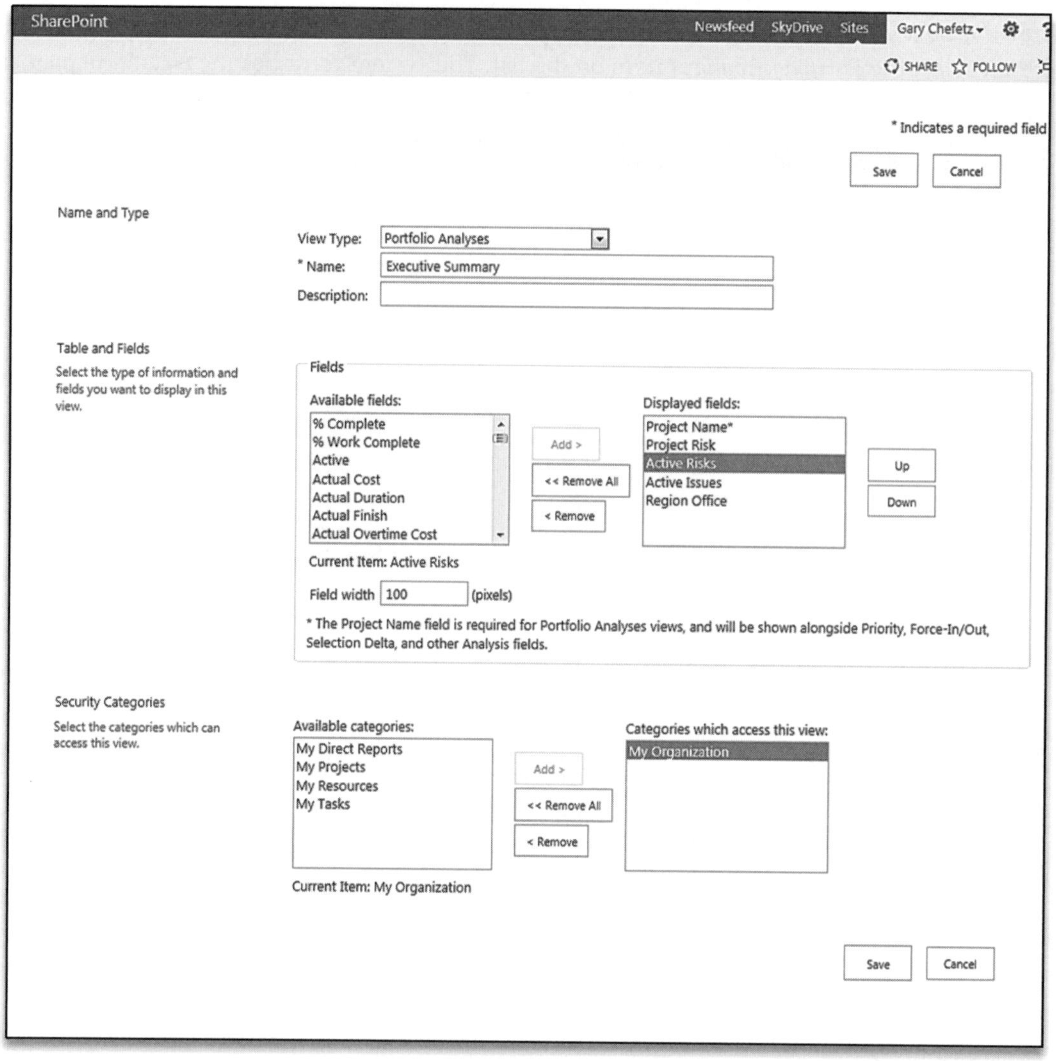

Figure 17 - 54: Executive Summary Portfolio Analyses view definition

I created the custom *Executive Summary* view shown in Figure 17 - 54 to display the project information fields that can assist our executives with analyzing our organization's portfolio of project requests. To create this custom *Portfolio Analyses* view, I did the following:

- I added the *Project Risk, Active Issues, Active Risks,* and *Region Office* fields to the *Displayed fields* list.
- I added the *My Organization* category to the *Categories which access this view* list.

Creating a Portfolio Analysis Project Selection View

A *Portfolio Analysis Project Selection* view is the second type of view specific to the portfolio analyses capabilities in Project Server 2013. The system includes one default *Portfolio Analysis Project Selection* view, the *Summary* view, but you can create other *Portfolio Analysis Project Selection* views that your users may require. *Portfolio Analysis Project Selection* views appear in the *Select Projects* dialog shown in Figure 17 - 55. These views appear in the *Select Projects* dialog that appears when a user clicks the *Selected Projects* button on the *New Portfolio Analysis* page when a user creates a new portfolio analysis, or when a user clicks the *Define Properties* button from an existing analysis and the system displays the *Edit Portfolio Analysis* page.

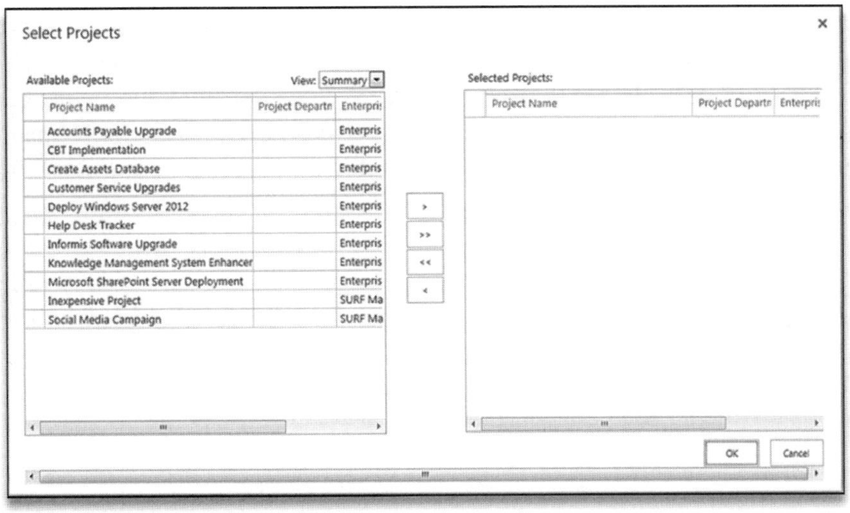

Figure 17 - 55: Select Project dialog showing a Portfolio Analysis Project Selection view

To create a new *Portfolio Analysis Project Selection* view, on the *Manage Views* page, click the *New View* button. Click the *View Type* pick list and then select the *Portfolio Analysis Project Selection* item on the list. The system refreshes the *New View* page as shown in Figure 17 - 56.

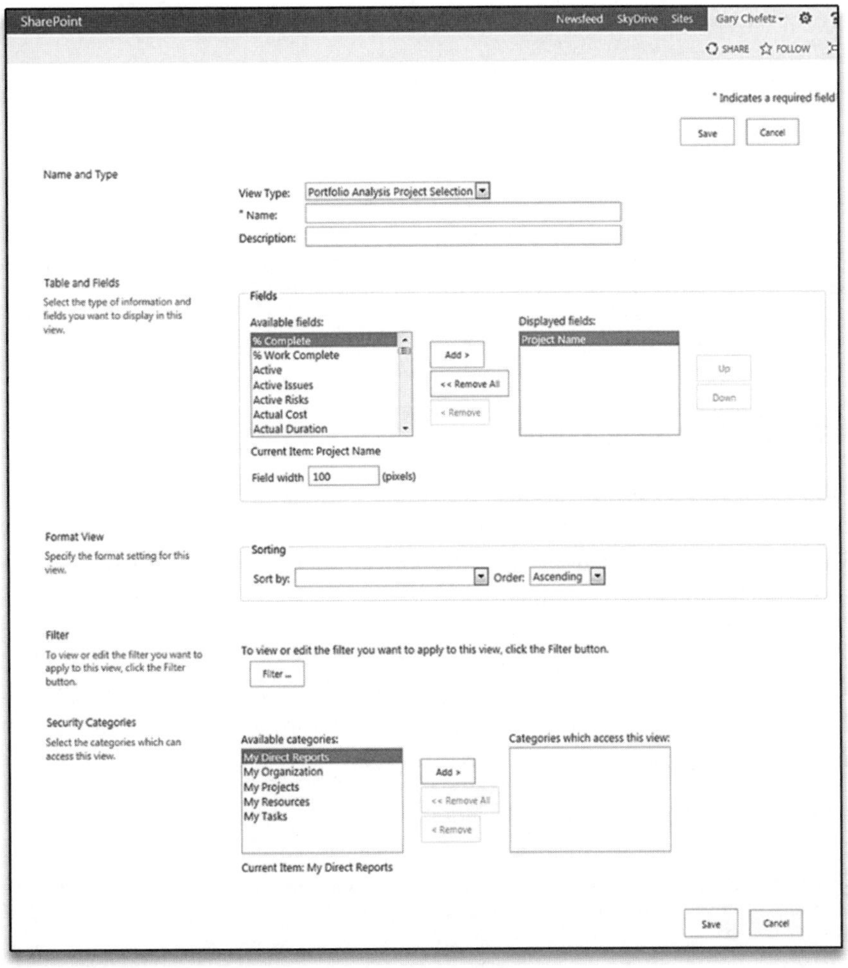

Figure 17 - 56: New View page for a custom Portfolio Analysis Project Selection view

To create a custom *Portfolio Analyses* view, begin by entering a name for the view in the *Name* field and an optional description in the *Description* field. In the *Table and Fields* section of the page, the *Available fields* list contains both standard and custom project fields, fields used in the Project Site (such as the *Active Issues* and *Active Risks* fields), and fields used in the workflow approval process (such as the *Workflow Stage Name* and *Workflow State* fields). By default, the *Displayed fields* list contains one required field, the *Project Name* field. Add additional fields to the *Displayed fields* list as you require.

Understanding Enterprise Views in Project Pro 2013

Many Project Pro 2013 users define a view as a "way of looking at our project data." In that regard, they are right. However, the software generally defines a view as follows:

View = Table + Filter + Group + Screen

In order to extract meaningful information from projects, you may need to create custom enterprise views so that your project managers can open a project and apply a view which allows them to:

- See the columns of data that they require (the Table).
- See only specific data rows (the Filter).
- See the data grouped by a specific attribute (the Group).
- See their project data using a specific layout (the Screen).

After you create custom enterprise views for your project managers, they can click the *View* menu in Project Pro 2013 and select the custom enterprise view.

Information: The *Screen* option that you select determines what appears on the right side of the view. The screen can display a Gantt chart of some type (such as in the *Gantt Chart* or *Tracking Gantt* views), a timephased grid (such as in the *Task Usage* or *Resource Usage* view), or nothing on the right side of the view (such as in the *Task Sheet* view). The screen you select is very important to the effectiveness of each view you create; therefore, give careful thought to the screen needed by users in each view.

Working with the Enterprise Global

The *Enterprise Global* is your organization's "library" of custom enterprise objects, including views, tables, filters, groups, reports, etc. Every time a project manager launches Project Pro 2013 and connects to Project Server 2013, the system opens a copy of the *Enterprise Global* in the background. This gives your project managers access to all custom objects you create, including custom enterprise views.

Before creating a custom enterprise view, table, filter, or group, most Project Server administrators assume that they must first open the *Enterprise Global* and then create the objects directly in the *Enterprise Global*. Instead, I strongly recommend that you **do not** open the *Enterprise Global* before you build your custom view. Instead, use the following approach for creating all custom enterprise objects:

1. Open an existing enterprise project in *Read-Only* mode.

Information: To open a project in *Read-Only* mode, click *File* ➤ *Open* in the *Backstage*. In the *Open* dialog, select the project, select the *Read Only* option at the bottom of the dialog, and then click the *Open* button.

2. In the enterprise project you opened in *Read-Only* mode, create the custom view, table, filter, and group.
3. Test the new custom view in the enterprise project to confirm that the view works as you intended.
4. To open the *Enterprise Global* for editing, click the *File* ➢ *Info* in the *Backstage*. In the *Organize Global Template* section of the *Backstage,* click the *Organizer* button and select the *Open Enterprise Global* item from the pick list.
5. Use the organizer tool to copy the new custom enterprise view, table, filter, and group from the enterprise project to the *Enterprise Global*.
6. Close the enterprise project without saving it.
7. Save and close the *Enterprise Global*.
8. Exit and re-launch Project Pro 2013 and reconnect to Project Server 2013 to gain access to the new custom enterprise view, table, filter, and group.

Best Practice: MsProjectExperts recommends that you always use the above steps to create custom enterprise views. Using these steps prevents accidental "pollution" of the *Enterprise Global* caused by the typical experimentation you tend to do while creating the custom view, table, filter, and group.

Adding Custom Views to the Enterprise Global

After creating and testing your new view in the *Read-Only* enterprise project, you are ready to copy the new view and its components to the *Enterprise Global*. To open the *Enterprise Global*, click *File* ➢ *Info* in the *Backstage*. In the *Organize Global Template* section of the *Backstage,* click the *Manage Global Template* button and select the *Open Enterprise Global* item from the pick list. The system opens and checks out the *Enterprise Global* for editing displaying the *Gantt Chart* view of what appears to be a blank project as shown in Figure 17 - 57.

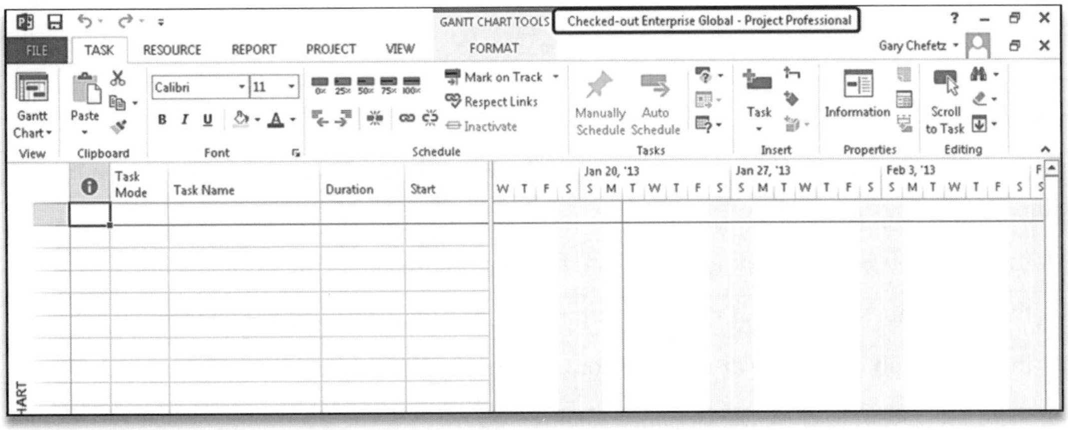

Figure 17 - 57: System shows Checked-out Enterprise Global

To add the new view, table, and filter to the *Enterprise Global*, you must use the *Organizer* tool. Click *File* ➢ *Info* in the *Backstage*. In the *Organize Global Template* section of the *Backstage,* click the *Organizer* button and select the *Organizer* item from the pick list to display the *Organizer* dialog shown in Figure 17 - 58.

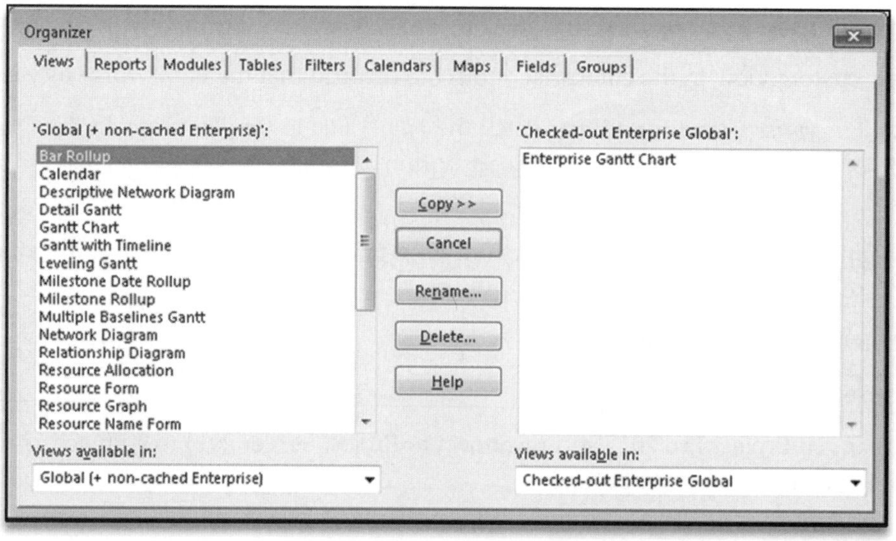

Figure 17 - 58: Organizer dialog

In Project Pro 2013, you use the *Organizer* dialog to manage any of the custom enterprise objects that you create. The *Organizer* dialog includes pages for each of the following types of objects: views, reports, modules, tables, filters, calendars, maps, fields, and groups.

Information: You can use the *Fields* page of the *Organizer* dialog to manage only local task and resource fields. You cannot use this page to manage enterprise fields.

The right side of the dialog lists the enterprise objects currently found in the *Enterprise Global*. To copy the new custom view from the *Read-Only* enterprise project to the *Enterprise Global*, complete the following steps:

1. Click the *Views* tab.
2. In the lower left corner of the *Organizer* dialog, click the *Views available in* pick list and select the *Read-Only* enterprise project.
3. In the list of views on the left side of the dialog, select one or more custom views and then click the *Copy* button.
4. Click the *Tables* tab, select one or more custom tables, and then click the *Copy* button.
5. Click the *Filters* tab, select one or more custom filters, and then click the *Copy* button.
6. Click the *Groups* tab, select one or more custom groups, and then click the *Copy* button.
7. Click the *Close* button to close the *Organizer* dialog.

Warning: When you use the *Organizer* dialog to copy a new custom view to the *Enterprise Global*, remember to copy **all** new tables, filters, or groups you created to support your custom view. If you neglect to copy all objects included in the new custom view, Project Pro 2013 displays an error message when a user attempts to apply the new enterprise view to a project.

After copying the new custom views, custom tables, custom filters, and custom groups to the *Enterprise Global*, save and close the *Enterprise Global*, and then close the *Read-Only* enterprise file as well. Exit Project Pro 2013, then re-launch the software and reconnect to Project Server 2013. You must exit and re-launch Project Pro 2013 to "refresh" your copy of the *Enterprise Global* and to gain access to the new custom view. In addition, after you add a new view to the *Enterprise Global*, all of your project managers must exit and re-launch Project Pro 2013 to obtain the new view.

Removing Pollution from the Enterprise Global

A common mistake of many self-taught Project Server administrators is to create custom views, tables, filters, and/or groups while they have the *Enterprise Global* open. During this process, Project Pro 2013 often copies non-enterprise objects into the *Enterprise Global*. Because the *Enterprise Global* must contain **only** enterprise objects, the presence of these non-enterprise objects "pollutes" the file. This is why I recommend that you create custom views in a *Read-Only* enterprise project, and then copy the views to the *Enterprise Global*. This process prevents the accidental "pollution" of the *Enterprise Global*.

When the *Enterprise Global* becomes polluted with non-enterprise objects, the most likely non-enterprise "culprits" are the *Gantt Chart* view and the task *Entry* table. The accidental pollution always happens when you create a new view or table by copying an existing view or table, such as the *Gantt Chart* view or task *Entry* table. The pollution happens when you apply any non-enterprise view while you have the *Enterprise Global* open. For instance, examine Figure 17 - 58, shown previously. Notice that the only view on the right side, the *Checked-out Enterprise Global*, is the *Enterprise Gantt Chart* view. Now look at the *Organizer* dialog in Figure 17 - 59.

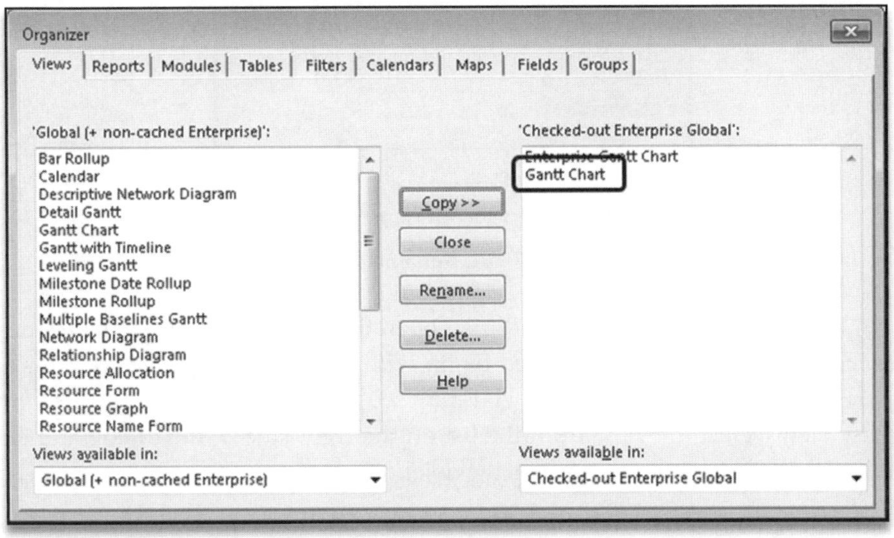

Figure 17 - 59: Enterprise Global containing non-enterprise object

Notice that *Gantt Chart* view is now in the *Checked-out Enterprise Global*. In order to make this happen, all I did was apply the *Gantt Chart* view in the current project. The system then automatically copied this into the *Enterprise Global*. This is the way the software behaves. It is treating the *Enterprise Global* just as it does any other open file. When you apply a view for the first time in a new project, the system copies that view to the current project, and the project then retains that copy of the view until you remove it. That is how the system remembers the formatting you apply to a view. It simply keeps its own copy of it in each project file. When you accidentally pollute the *Enterprise Global* with non-enterprise objects, the system warns Project Pro 2013 users about duplicate views or tables in their projects **every time** they open a project. For example, Figure 17 - 60 shows a Project Pro 2013 warning dialog about a duplicate *Gantt Chart* view in the *Enterprise Global*. I created this error by saving the *Enterprise Global* after creating the pollution shown in Figure 17 - 59.

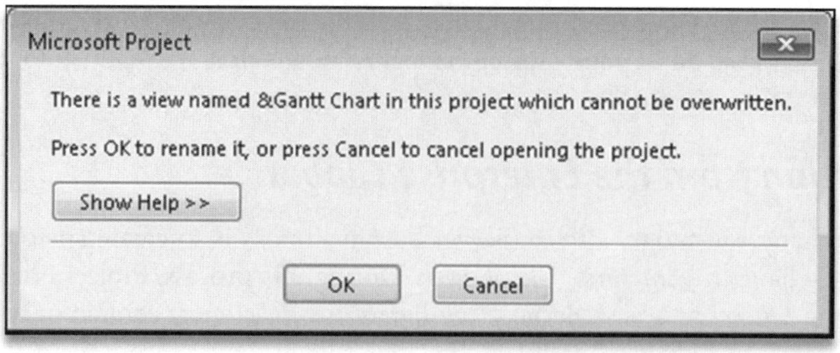
Microsoft Project
There is a view named &Gantt Chart in this project which cannot be overwritten.
Press OK to rename it, or press Cancel to cancel opening the project.
Show Help >>
OK
Cancel

Figure 17 - 60: Warning dialog about a duplicate view

If your users begin to receive warning messages such as the one shown in Figure 17 - 60, it means that you polluted your *Enterprise Global* with non-enterprise objects, and that you must rid the file of any non-enterprise objects. In the example above, the system complains about the *Gantt Chart* view. In this case, it will also complain about the *Entry* table, which gets copied along with the *Gantt Chart* view. The easiest way around this mess is to rename these objects temporarily. When you see the warning dialog shown previously in Figure 17 - 60, click the *OK* button and the system displays the *Rename* dialog shown in Figure 17 - 61.

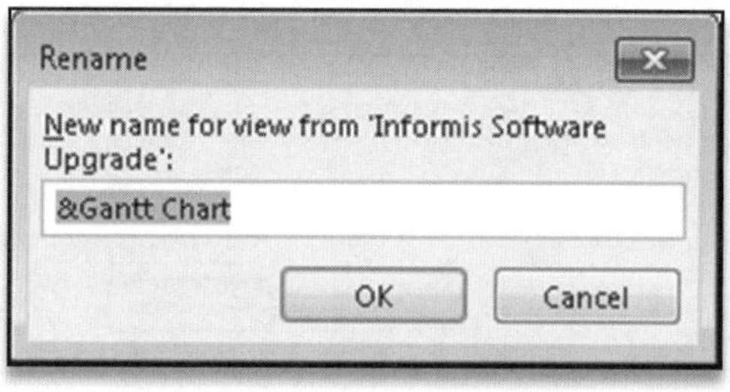
Rename
New name for view from 'Informis Software Upgrade':
&Gantt Chart
OK
Cancel

Figure 17 - 61: Rename dialog

To clean up the mess, open the *Enterprise Global* and then open the *Organizer* dialog. Make sure that you have an *Enterprise* view selected before you proceed further. Begin with the *Views* page and look for any view that is a non-enterprise view. Typical non-enterprise views you may see are the *Gantt Chart* and *Resource Sheet* views. To delete a non-enterprise view, select the view from the list on the right side of the dialog and click the *Delete* button. When prompted, click the *Yes* button to confirm the deletion.

After deleting any non-enterprise views, click the *Tables* tab and make sure the *Task* option is selected in the upper left corner of the *Tables* page. Examine the list of task tables shown on the right side of the dialog. Again, look for any non-enterprise tables such as the *Entry* table. Select and delete any non-enterprise task tables. Select the *Resource* option in the upper left corner of the *Tables* page to look for non-enterprise resource tables. Select and delete any non-enterprise resource tables.

Click the *Filters* tab. The only non-enterprise filters allowable in the *Enterprise Global* are the *[No Filter], Confirmed, Unconfirmed,* and *Update Needed* filters. The system does not allow you to delete the *[No Filter]* filter, but you can delete the other three filters if you like. If you see any other non-enterprise filters, select them and delete them.

Click the *Groups* tab. The only non-enterprise groups allowable in the *Enterprise Global* are the *[No Group]* and *Team Status Pending* groups. The system does not allow you to delete the *[No Group]* group, but you can delete the other group. If you see any other non-enterprise groups, select them and delete them. When finished, click the *Close* button, then save and close the *Enterprise Global*. Exit and re-launch Project Pro 2013.

Information: In addition to copying and deleting enterprise objects in projects and in the *Enterprise Global*, the *Organizer* dialog allows you to rename objects as well. To rename an object, select it and then click the *Rename* button. Enter a new name for the object and then click the *OK* button.

Using the 4-Step Method to Create a New View

You create a custom enterprise view by following a 4-step method based on the definition of a view detailed previously. These four steps are:

1. Select or create a table.
2. Select or create a filter.
3. Select or create a group (most of the time this step is optional).
4. Create a new view using the desired table, filter, group, and screen.

Select or Create a Table

The first step is to select an existing table or to create a new table if no existing table meets your reporting needs. By definition, a table is a collection of fields or columns. A key question to ask before attempting to create a table is, "What columns of data do users need to see in my new table?" The answer to this question leads you either to select an existing table or to create a new custom table.

Best Practice: A quick way to create a new table is to copy an existing table and then to modify the copy. MsProjectExperts recommends that you never modify the default tables in Project Pro 2013. Instead, create new tables for your reporting needs.

Select or Create a Filter

The second step is to select an existing filter, or to create a new filter if no existing filter meets your reporting needs. The filter extracts the particular rows of data your users see.

Select or Create a Group

The third step is to select an existing group, or to create a new group if no existing group meets your reporting needs. In Project Pro 2013, groups are a way of categorizing, sorting, and summarizing the data in a view. Because very few default groups exist in the software, it is very likely that you will need to create a new group as part of creating any new table that has a grouping requirement.

Create the New Custom View

The final step is to create a new custom view by selecting your table, filter, group, and screen for the view. The screen is a very important part of any custom view because it controls how the software arranges the project data. Some of the common screens from which you might choose are the *Gantt Chart, Task Sheet, Task Usage,* and *Resource Usage* screens.

Notice that the screen choices I just listed are the same as many of the common views found in Project Pro 2013. When creating a new task view, your screen choice allows you to decide whether to include the Gantt chart on the right of your new view (as with the *Gantt Chart* view), or whether to display the task sheet without a Gantt chart (as with the *Task Sheet* view).

Warning: Carefully select the *Screen* option before you complete the new view, as you cannot change this selection when editing the view at a later time.

Creating Useful Enterprise Views

Part of your job as the Project Server implementer or administrator is to determine what views your project managers need for communication and reporting in Project Pro 2013. You should meet with your project managers to determine these needs, and then create the necessary custom views. You should also periodically review these requirements to ensure that your system continues to meet your user's needs. It is very likely that your stakeholder requirements demand custom views for reporting project variance, such as cost variance or date variance. You should also consider creating three special views: one to help you administer the system, one to help your project managers publish their projects, and one to help your project managers analyze schedule variance. These useful views in Project Pro 2013 include the following:

- A custom enterprise *Task* view that allows project managers to analyze duration variance for each task in a project.
- A custom *Enterprise Task Usage* view to allow your project managers better access to important parameters when publishing a project.
- A custom *Enterprise Resource Sheet* view that allows you to edit your organization's custom enterprise resource fields for the resources in your Enterprise Resource Pool.

In the remainder of this module, I teach you how to create each of these types of views. I begin first by creating a variance view used to track task duration variance. Next I show you how to create the *Enterprise Publishing* view in the form of an *Enterprise Task Usage* view. After that I teach you how to create a custom *Enterprise Resource Sheet* view used for editing the Enterprise Resource Pool.

Creating an Enterprise Duration Variance View

Project Pro 2013 allows users to analyze four types of task variance: start and finish variance (date variance), work variance, cost variance, and duration variance. Users can analyze date variance using the *Tracking Gantt* view and the task *Variance* table. Users can analyze work variance using the task work table or analyze cost variance using the task cost table, Oddly enough, Project Pro 2013 **does not** offer any default view or table that allows a user to analyze duration variance.

Duration variance is the difference between the current duration of a task and the original baseline duration of the task, which the system measures in days, by default. For example, if the current duration of a task is 8 days, while the baseline duration of the task is 5 days, the duration variance for this task is 3 days (8 days – 5 days). Project managers need to be able to analyze duration variance in their projects, so you should create a custom view for this purpose. You create this view using the four-step process detailed previously.

Information: Remember to open an enterprise project in *Read-Only* mode before you create the custom view. After you create and test the view in the project, you can open the *Enterprise Global* and copy the new view from the project to the *Enterprise Global*.

Select or Create a Table

Before creating a new table, it is always wise to determine if an existing table meets your reporting needs. Because Project Pro 2013 does not include a default duration table, you must create a custom table. The easiest way to create a new table is to copy an existing table, and then modify the copy.

Although the task *Work* table contains work fields, such as work and baseline work, each work field has a corresponding duration field, such as duration and baseline duration. Therefore, you can copy the *Work* table and replace each work field with its corresponding duration field. This makes quick work out of an otherwise tedious process you might go through to determine which duration fields to show in your new *Duration* table.

To create the *Duration* table, apply the *Gantt Chart* view and then in the *Data* section of the *View* ribbon, click the *Tables* button. Select the *More Tables* item from the pick list, and the system displays the *More Tables* dialog shown in Figure 17 - 62.

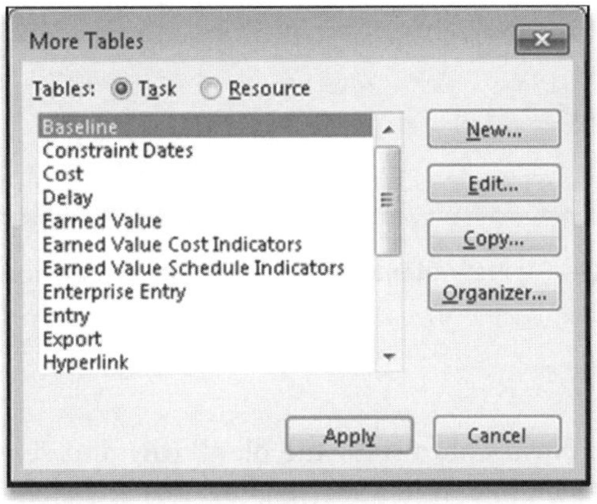

Figure 17 - 62: More Tables dialog

Select the *Work* table and click the *Copy* button. The system displays the *Table Definition* dialog shown in Figure 17 - 63.

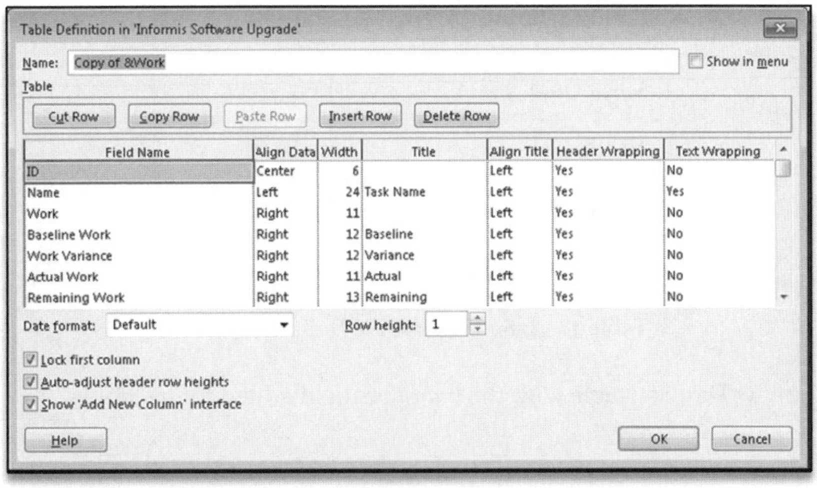

Figure 17 - 63: Table Definition dialog for Copy of Work table

In the *Name* field at the top of the dialog, enter a name for the new table according to your organization's naming convention, and then select the *Show in menu* option. After copying the *Work* table to create the *Duration* table, this new table does not include the *Indicators* field. To insert the *Indicators* field, select the *Name* field and then click the *Insert Row* button. The system adds a new blank row above the *Name* field, as shown in Figure 17 - 64.

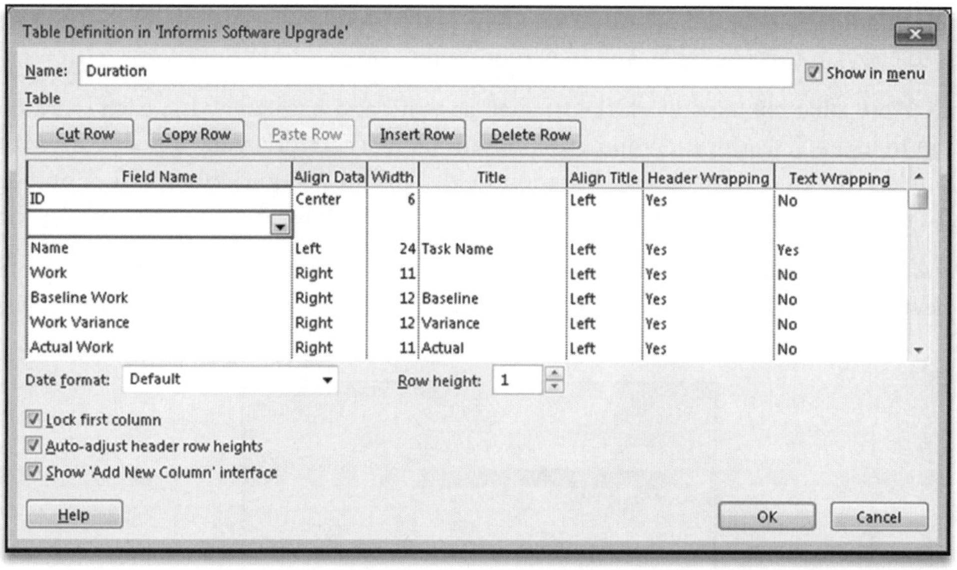

Figure 17 - 64: New blank row in the Table Definition dialog

Click the pick list button in the *Field Name* column for the blank row and select the *Indicators* field from the pick list. For the *Indicators* field, specify the values shown in Table 17 - 1.

Column Name	Value
Align Data	Left
Width	8
Align Title	Left
Header Wrapping	Yes

Table 17 - 1: Settings for the Indicators field

Figure 17 - 65 shows the new *Duration* table with the *Indicators* field added to the table.

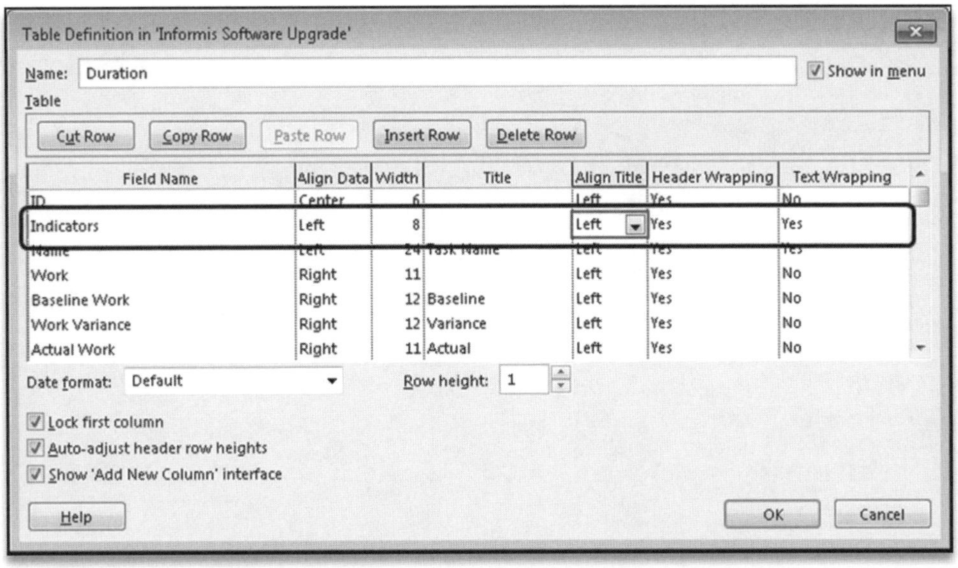

Figure 17 - 65: Duration table includes the Indicators field

After adding the *Indicators* field to the *Duration* table, replace each *Work* field with its corresponding *Duration* field. For example, to replace the *Work* field with the *Duration* field, click the pick list in the *Work* field and select the *Duration* field. Replace each of the *Work* fields with the corresponding *Duration* fields shown in Table 17 - 2.

Work Field	Duration Field
Work	Duration
Baseline Work	Baseline Duration
Work Variance	Duration Variance
Actual Work	Actual Duration
Remaining Work	Remaining Duration
% Work Complete	% Complete

Table 17 - 2: Replace Work fields with corresponding Duration fields

Information: In Table 17 - 2, notice that I replace the *% Work Complete* field with the *% Complete* field. Most people do not realize that the *% Complete* field actually represents the **% Duration Complete** for a task, and shows the percentage of the *Duration* window "used" over the life of the task.

In the *Table Definition* dialog, remove the value in the *Title* column for every *Duration* field. Click in the *Title* column for each *Duration* field and then press the **Backspace** key on your computer keyboard to delete the information. **Do not** use the **Delete** key, which removes the entire field.

Because the *Duration Variance* field contains the information most relevant to our project managers, I want to move this field to the immediate right of the *Task Name* field. To move the *Duration Variance* field to a new location, select the field and then click the *Cut Row* button. Select the *Duration* field and then click the *Paste Row* button. Figure 17 - 66 shows the completed definition for the *_Duration* table in the *Table Definition* dialog.

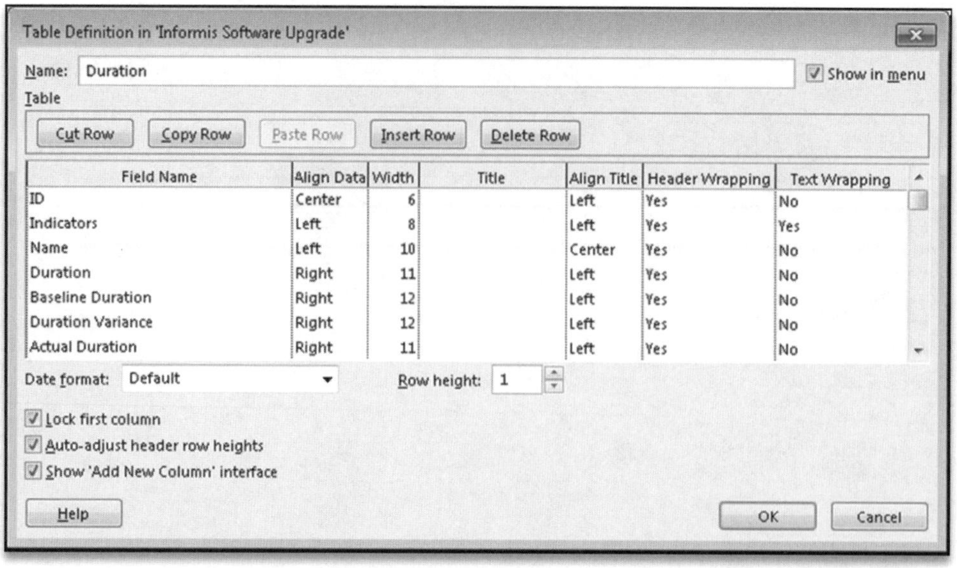

Figure 17 - 66: Completed Duration definition in the Table Definition dialog

Click the *OK* button. Project Pro 2013 shows the new *Duration* table on the list in the *More Tables* dialog shown in Figure 17 - 67.

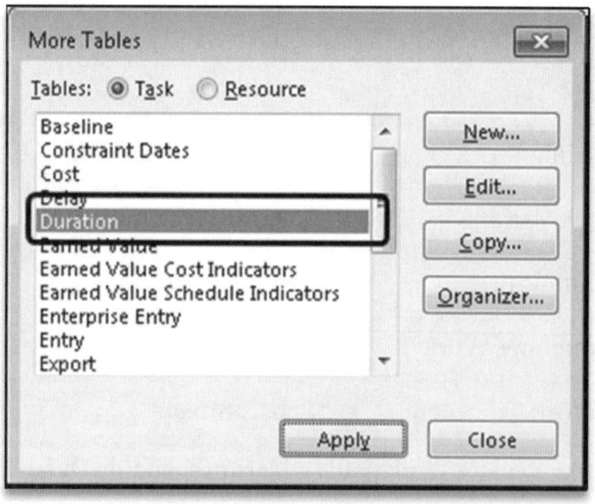

Figure 17 - 67: More Tables dialog showing new table

In the *More Tables* dialog, click the *Close* button. To view and test the new table, click the *Tables* button on the ribbon and select the new *Duration* table. Pull the split bar to the right to see all of the columns in the new table. Figure 17 - 68 shows the new *Duration* table for a project that is currently in-progress. Notice that the *Duration Variance* column shows several tasks with duration variance greater than 0 days, in this case indicating that the duration is taking less time than planned.

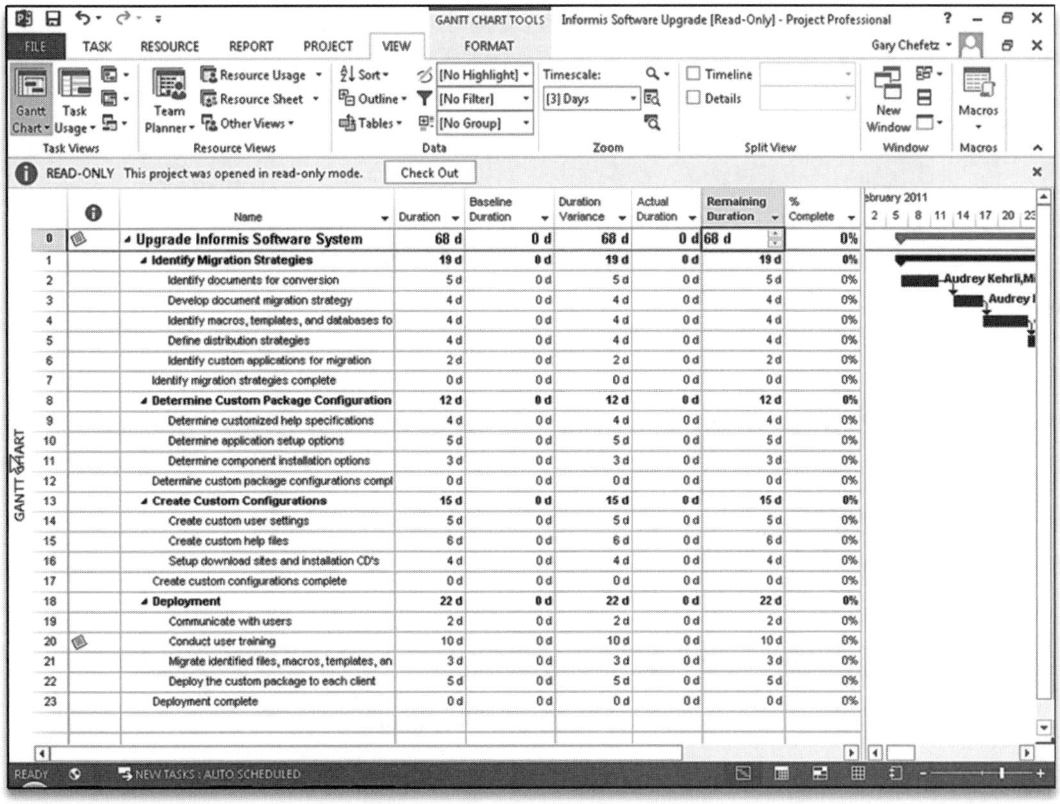

Figure 17 - 68: Duration table applied

Select or Create a Filter

After you create your new custom table, you turn your attention to the filter you need for the view. The filter extracts the rows of information your project managers need to see. If an existing filter meets your criteria, you can use the existing filter; otherwise, create a new filter. To see the list of available filters, click the *Filter* pick list in the *View* ribbon as shown in Figure 17 - 69.

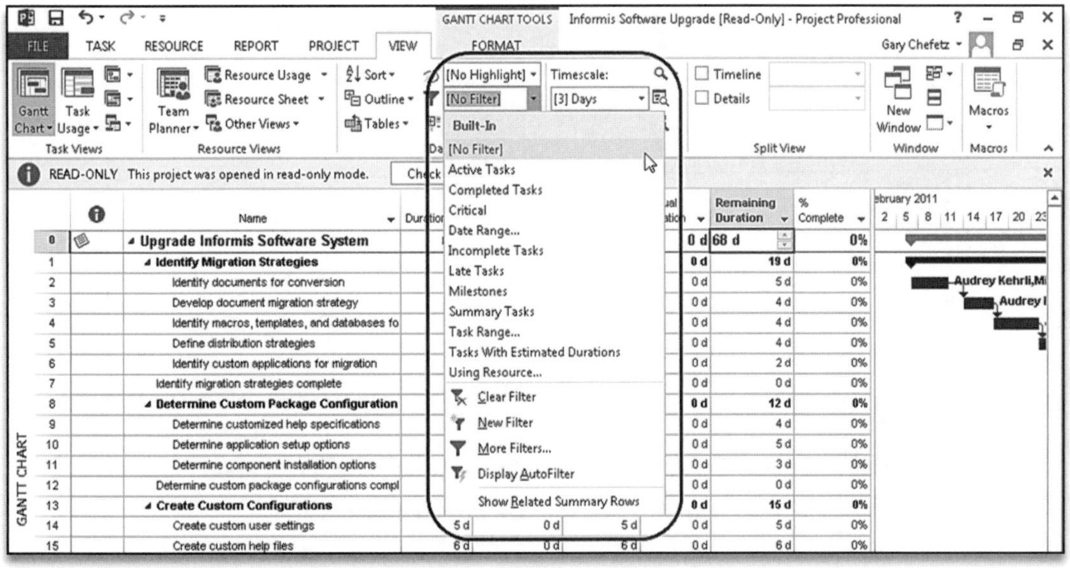

Figure 17 - 69: Accessing the Filters list in Project

Select the *More Filters* item from the pick list. Project Pro 2013 displays the *More Filters* dialog shown in Figure 17 - 70.

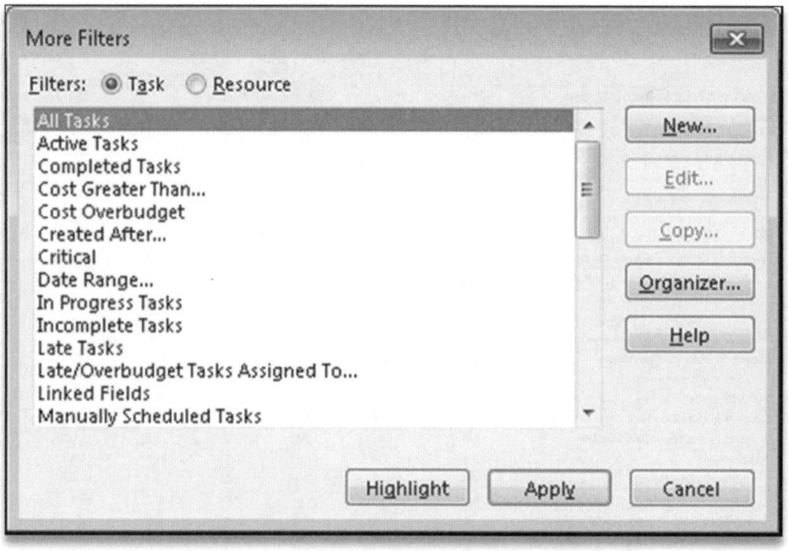

Figure 17 - 70: More Filters dialog

Based on the view requirements, I need to apply a filter that shows tasks with a duration variance greater than 0 days. After examining the list of available filters in Project Pro 2013, I quickly determine that there is no default filter that meets my reporting needs. Therefore, I must create a new custom filter for this purpose. To create a new filter, click the *New* button in the *More Filters* dialog. The system displays the *Filter Definition* dialog shown in Figure 17 - 71.

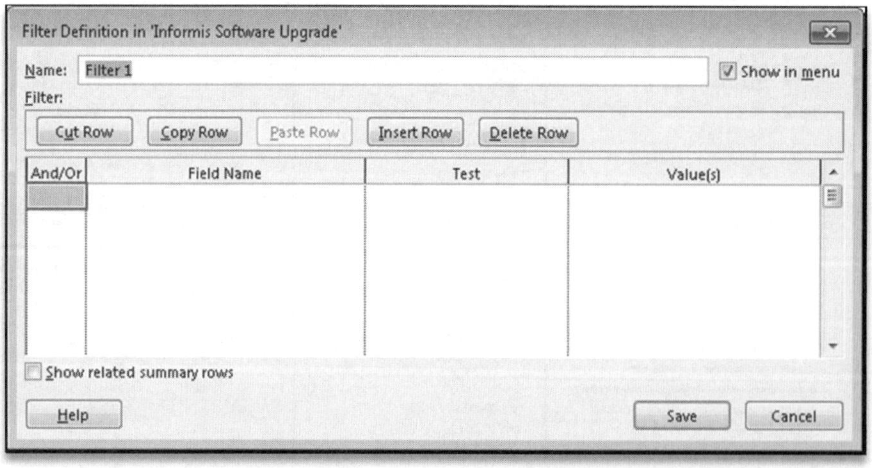

Figure 17 - 71: Filter Definition dialog

In the *Filter Definition* dialog, enter the filter criteria shown in Table 17 - 3.

Name	Duration Variance > 0d		
Show in menu	Selected		
And/Or	**Field Name**	**Test**	**Value(s)**
	Duration Variance	is greater than	0
Show related summary rows	Selected		

Table 17 - 3: Filter Criteria for the Duration Variance > 0d filter

> **Information**: To create a filter with multiple criteria, add additional criteria on each line in the data grid and select a value in the *And/Or* field for each additional line.

> **Information**: When you select the *Show related summary rows* option in the *Filter Definition* dialog, it guarantees that the filter displays the Work Breakdown Structure (WBS) of summary tasks that represent phases and deliverables in your project, even if the summary tasks do not meet the filter criteria.

Click the *Save* button to complete your filter configuration. The system displays the new *Duration Variance > 0d* filter at the top of the list in the *More Filters* dialog and selects the new filter. Click the *Apply* button to test the new custom filter.

Figure 17 - 72 shows the project with the custom *Duration Variance > 0d* filter applied. Notice that the filter displays only those tasks with a duration variance value greater than 0 days, indicating all tasks where current duration value is greater than their original *Baseline Duration* value. Notice also that when you do not set a baseline, everything is variance!

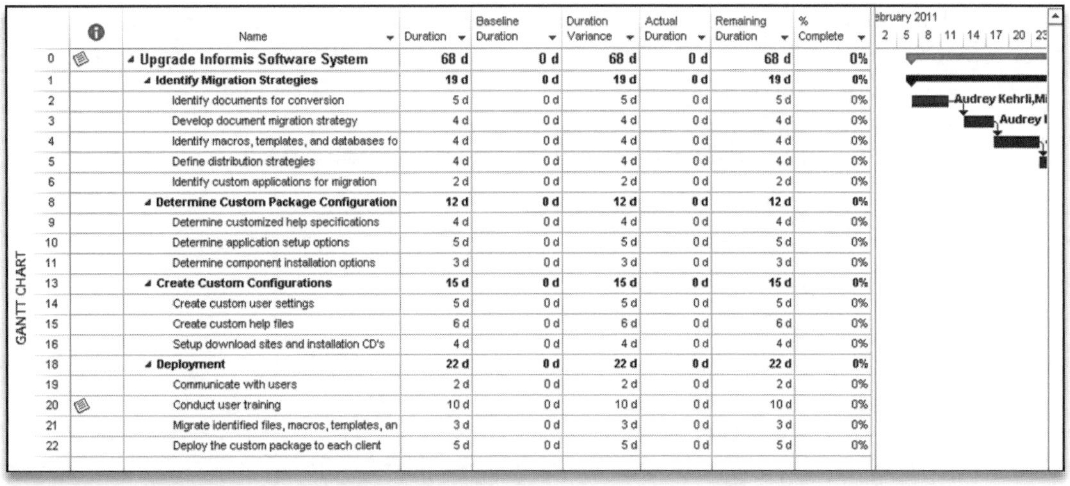

	Name	Duration	Baseline Duration	Duration Variance	Actual Duration	Remaining Duration	% Complete
0	**Upgrade Informis Software System**	**68 d**	**0 d**	**68 d**	**0 d**	**68 d**	**0%**
1	**Identify Migration Strategies**	**19 d**	**0 d**	**19 d**	**0 d**	**19 d**	**0%**
2	Identify documents for conversion	5 d	0 d	5 d	0 d	5 d	0%
3	Develop document migration strategy	4 d	0 d	4 d	0 d	4 d	0%
4	Identify macros, templates, and databases fo	4 d	0 d	4 d	0 d	4 d	0%
5	Define distribution strategies	4 d	0 d	4 d	0 d	4 d	0%
6	Identify custom applications for migration	2 d	0 d	2 d	0 d	2 d	0%
8	**Determine Custom Package Configuration**	**12 d**	**0 d**	**12 d**	**0 d**	**12 d**	**0%**
9	Determine customized help specifications	4 d	0 d	4 d	0 d	4 d	0%
10	Determine application setup options	5 d	0 d	5 d	0 d	5 d	0%
11	Determine component installation options	3 d	0 d	3 d	0 d	3 d	0%
13	**Create Custom Configurations**	**15 d**	**0 d**	**15 d**	**0 d**	**15 d**	**0%**
14	Create custom user settings	5 d	0 d	5 d	0 d	5 d	0%
15	Create custom help files	6 d	0 d	6 d	0 d	6 d	0%
16	Setup download sites and installation CD's	4 d	0 d	4 d	0 d	4 d	0%
18	**Deployment**	**22 d**	**0 d**	**22 d**	**0 d**	**22 d**	**0%**
19	Communicate with users	2 d	0 d	2 d	0 d	2 d	0%
20	Conduct user training	10 d	0 d	10 d	0 d	10 d	0%
21	Migrate identified files, macros, templates, an	3 d	0 d	3 d	0 d	3 d	0%
22	Deploy the custom package to each client	5 d	0 d	5 d	0 d	5 d	0%

Figure 17 - 72: Duration table with the Duration Variance > 0d filter applied

After testing your filter to confirm that it works, press the **F3** function key on your computer keyboard to reapply the *[No Filter]* filter and display all tasks in the project.

Select or Create a Group

Because my organization does not want to apply grouping in the new custom enterprise duration variance view, I do not need to create a new custom group for this view. Later in this module, however, I show you how to create a custom group when you create a custom enterprise *Resource Sheet* view.

Create the New View

Before creating a new task view, it is wise to restore the default *Gantt Chart* view. Therefore, if you have a filter currently applied, press the **F3** function key on your computer keyboard to reapply the *[No Filter]* filter. From the *Data* section of the *View* ribbon, click the *Tables* pick list and reapply the default *Entry* table. Once done, you are ready to create a new view.

To create the new enterprise *Duration Variance* view, from the *Task Views* section of the *Views* ribbon, click the *View* pick list or from the *Views* section of the *Task* ribbon, click the *View* pick list and select the *More Views* item. The system displays the *More Views* dialog shown in Figure 17 - 73.

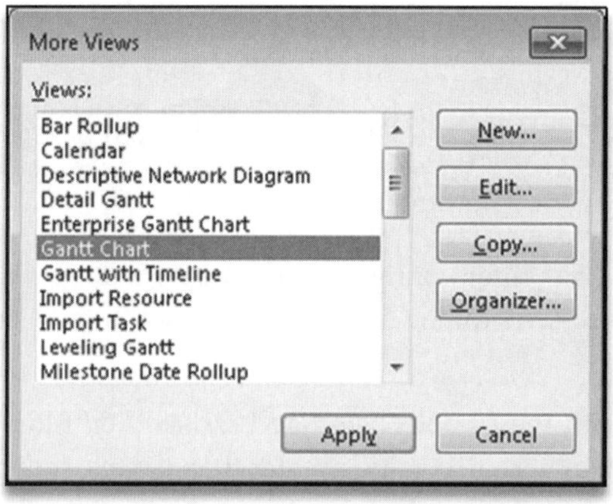

Figure 17 - 73: More Views dialog

In my new *Duration Variance* view, I want to include the *Tracking Gantt* chart on the right side of the view. To accomplish this, I copy the existing *Tracking Gantt* view by selecting it and clicking the *Copy* button. The system displays the *View Definition* dialog shown in Figure 17 - 74.

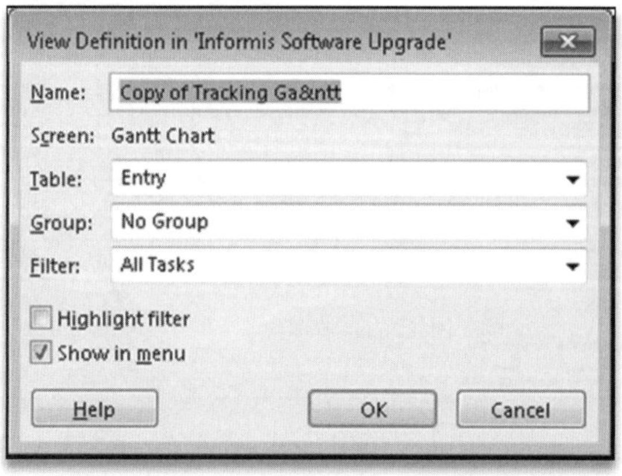

Figure 17 - 74: View Definition dialog

In the *View Definition* dialog, name your new view according to your organization's naming convention for custom views. In addition, enter or select the options shown in Table 17 - 4.

Field Name	Value
Name	Duration Variance
Table	Duration
Group	[No Group]
Filter	Duration Variance > 0d
Highlight filter	Selected
Show in menu	Selected

Table 17 - 4: Options for the new Duration Variance view

Information: Select the *Highlight Filter* option to apply your selected filter as a highlight filter. When applied, a highlight filter displays all tasks, and highlights all tasks that meet the filter criteria using yellow cell background formatting.

Click the *OK* button to return to the *More Views* dialog, and then click the *Apply* button to apply the new custom view. The system displays the *Duration Variance* view, shown in Figure 17 - 75.

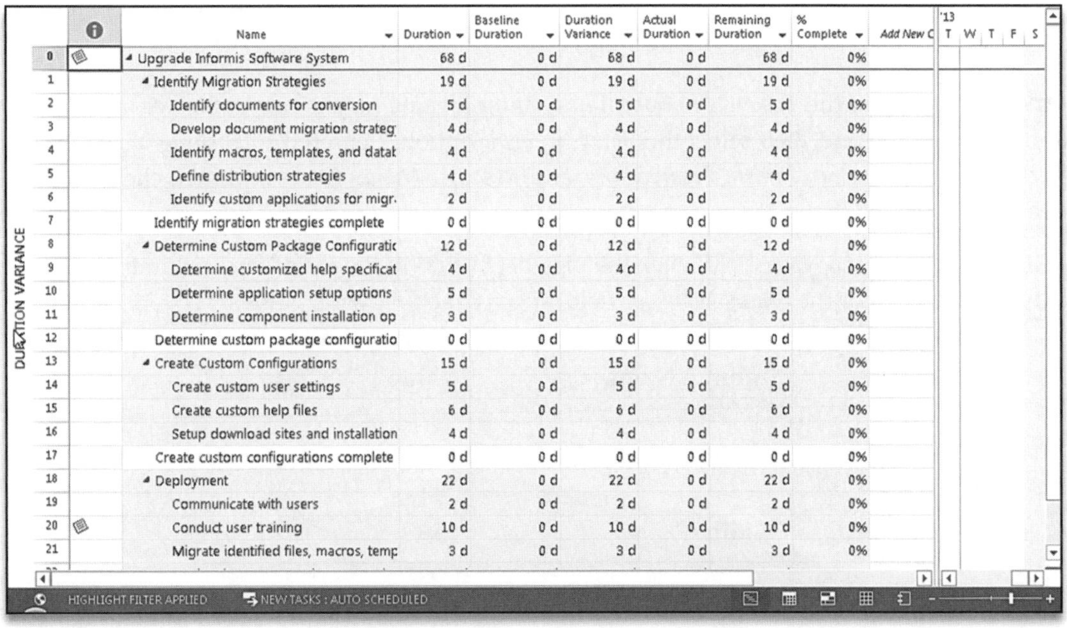

	Name	Duration	Baseline Duration	Duration Variance	Actual Duration	Remaining Duration	% Complete	Add New C
0	Upgrade Informis Software System	68 d	0 d	68 d	0 d	68 d	0%	
1	Identify Migration Strategies	19 d	0 d	19 d	0 d	19 d	0%	
2	Identify documents for conversion	5 d	0 d	5 d	0 d	5 d	0%	
3	Develop document migration strateg	4 d	0 d	4 d	0 d	4 d	0%	
4	Identify macros, templates, and datal	4 d	0 d	4 d	0 d	4 d	0%	
5	Define distribution strategies	4 d	0 d	4 d	0 d	4 d	0%	
6	Identify custom applications for migr.	2 d	0 d	2 d	0 d	2 d	0%	
7	Identify migration strategies complete	0 d	0 d	0 d	0 d	0 d	0%	
8	Determine Custom Package Configuratic	12 d	0 d	12 d	0 d	12 d	0%	
9	Determine customized help specificat	4 d	0 d	4 d	0 d	4 d	0%	
10	Determine application setup options	5 d	0 d	5 d	0 d	5 d	0%	
11	Determine component installation op	3 d	0 d	3 d	0 d	3 d	0%	
12	Determine custom package configuratio	0 d	0 d	0 d	0 d	0 d	0%	
13	Create Custom Configurations	15 d	0 d	15 d	0 d	15 d	0%	
14	Create custom user settings	5 d	0 d	5 d	0 d	5 d	0%	
15	Create custom help files	6 d	0 d	6 d	0 d	6 d	0%	
16	Setup download sites and installation	4 d	0 d	4 d	0 d	4 d	0%	
17	Create custom configurations complete	0 d	0 d	0 d	0 d	0 d	0%	
18	Deployment	22 d	0 d	22 d	0 d	22 d	0%	
19	Communicate with users	2 d	0 d	2 d	0 d	2 d	0%	
20	Conduct user training	10 d	0 d	10 d	0 d	10 d	0%	
21	Migrate identified files, macros, temp	3 d	0 d	3 d	0 d	3 d	0%	

Figure 17 - 75: Duration Variance view

When you apply a filter as a highlight filter, the system highlights the tasks using the cell background formatting functionality in Project Pro 2013, highlighting the tasks using yellow cell background formatting, which makes the highlighted tasks very visible. After you complete this custom view, open the *Enterprise Global* and use the *Organizer* dialog to copy the new view, filter, and new table to the *Enterprise Global*.

Creating an Enterprise Publishing View

One very important view you should create for your Project Pro 2013 users is one to assist them with publishing a project. During project publishing, users need to control three factors: the manager of each task, whether to publish each task, and the assignment owner of each task assignment. To create this custom enterprise view, begin by opening any enterprise project in *Read-Only* mode. Because you need to see tasks and resource assignments (the resources assigned to each task), initially apply the *Task Usage* view for testing purposes by selecting it from the *Task Views* section of the *View* ribbon. Then follow the four-step method to create the view.

Select or Create a Table

Because no default table contains the columns we need to see in the table, you must create a custom table. The columns that users need to see in the table are as follows:

- ID
- Indicators
- Task Name
- Status Manager
- Publish
- Assignment Owner

Because the task *Entry* table contains three of the required columns, create a new custom table by copying the task *Entry* table. In the *Data* section of the *View* ribbon, click the *Tables* button. Select the *More Tables* item from the pick list and the system displays the *More Tables* dialog. In the *More Tables* dialog, select the *Entry* table and click the *Copy* button.

In the *Name* field at the top of the *Table Definition* dialog, enter a name for the new table according to your organization's naming convention and then select the *Show in menu* option. I entered *Publishing* in the *Name* field. Individually select the *Duration, Start, Finish, Predecessors,* and *Resource Names* fields and then click the *Delete Row* button to remove each of these fields.

In the first blank row below the *Name* field, click the pick list button in the *Field Name* column and select the *Status Manager* field from the list. For the *Status Manager* field, specify the following values:

Column Name	Value
Align Data	Left
Width	15
Align Title	Left
Header Wrapping	Yes

In the blank row below the *Status Manager* field, click the pick list button in the *Field Name* column and select the *Publish* field from the list. For the *Publish* field, specify the following values:

Column Name	Value
Align Data	Center
Width	10
Align Title	Center
Header Wrapping	Yes

In the blank row below the *Publish* field, click the pick list button in the *Field Name* column and select the *Assignment Owner* field from the list. For the *Assignment Owner* field, specify the following values:

Column Name	Value
Align Data	Left
Width	20
Align Title	Left
Header Wrapping	Yes

When you complete your entries, select the *Show in menu* option and click the *OK* button to close the *Table Definition* dialog. In the *More Tables* dialog, click the *Apply* button to view and test the new custom table. Figure 17 - 76 shows the *Publishing* table displayed in the *Task Usage* view in a new enterprise project. Notice that the *Task Usage* view shows each task in the project, as well as the resource assignments for each task.

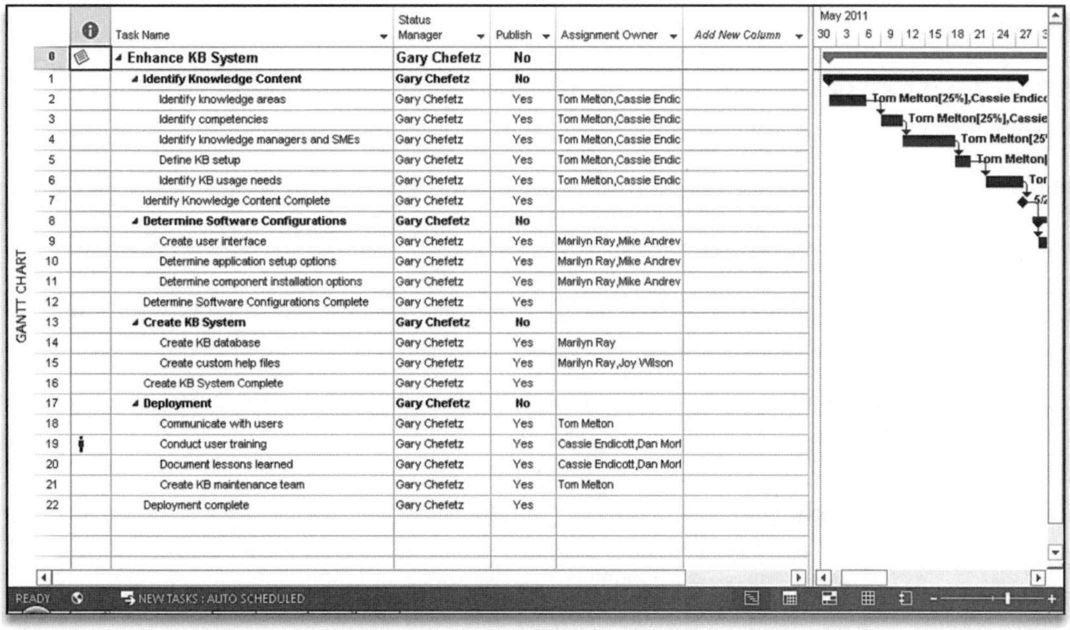

Figure 17 - 76: Publishing table applied in the Task Usage view

Notice in Figure 17 - 76 that the system designates my login as the status manager for every task. This is because I imported and published the project initially. The person named in the *Status Manager* field is the person to whom

Project Server 2013 directs task updates from the resource(s) assigned to the task. Project managers can use the *Status Manager* field to take over ownership of selected tasks or an entire project, either temporarily or permanently.

Notice also in Figure 17 - 76 that the system sets the default value in the *Publish* field to *Yes*. The value in this field determines whether Project Server 2013 publishes the information for each task on the *Tasks* page in Project Web App for the assigned resource(s). If a project manager is not ready to publish all tasks in a project, such as when they may have completely planned one phase but the other phases are only in skeleton form, then by setting the *Publish* field value to *Yes* in the first phase, and to *No* for all tasks in the other phases, a project manager can selectively publish only the information ready for public consumption.

Lastly, notice in Figure 17 - 76 shown previously that the system sets each assigned resource as the owner of each resource assignment in the *Assignment Owner* field. The person designated in the *Assignment Owner* field for an assignment is the person who sees the assignment on their *Tasks* page in Project Web App and is the person responsible for submitting task progress on that assignment. If your organization uses a proxy to update task assignments, such as team leads that may have the responsibility to perform this duty, you can specify the team lead in the *Assignment Owner* field for the manager's tasks. As you can clearly see, this custom table becomes extremely valuable to your Project Pro 2013 users in controlling their publishing operations.

Information: Before you can choose any other resource (such as an administrative assistant or team lead serving as a proxy) in the *Assignment Owner* field for an assignment, you must add that resource to the project team using the *Build Team from Enterprise* dialog.

Select or Create a Filter

Because your users need to see all tasks in every project, you do not need to create a custom filter. Instead, use the default *[No Filter]* filter in your custom view.

Select or Create a Group

Because your users do not need to apply grouping in this view, you do not need to create a custom group. Instead, use the default *[No Group]* group in your custom view.

Create the New View

Before creating a new task view, reapply the default *Entry* table by clicking the *Tables* pick list from the *View* ribbon and selecting the *Entry* item. To create the new enterprise publishing view, select the *More Views* item from the *Views* pick list. In the *More Views* dialog, click the *New* button and then click the *OK* button in the *Define New View* dialog, leaving the default item, *Single View,* selected.

In the *View Definition* dialog, name your new view according to your organization's naming convention for custom views. In addition, enter or select the following options in this dialog:

Field Name	Value
Name	Publishing
Screen	Task Usage
Table	Publishing

Field Name	Value
Group	[No Group]
Filter	[No Filter]
Highlight filter	Not Selected
Show in menu	Selected

When you are done configuring your view, the *View Definition* dialog should look like the one shown in Figure 17 - 77.

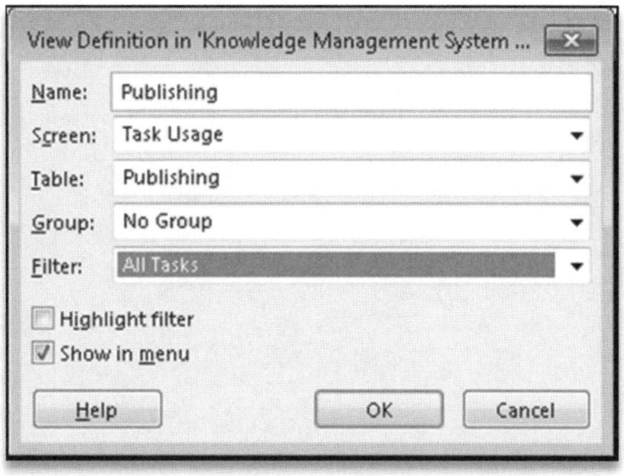

Figure 17 - 77: View Definition dialog for Publishing view

Click the *OK* button to return to the *More Views* dialog. Click the *OK* button in the *More Views* dialog to close this dialog as well. To apply the new custom enterprise view, select it from the *View* pick list. After you complete this custom view, open the *Enterprise Global* and use the *Organizer* dialog to copy the new view and new table to the *Enterprise Global*. Your completed view should look something like the one shown in Figure 17 - 78, which is a new enterprise task usage view.

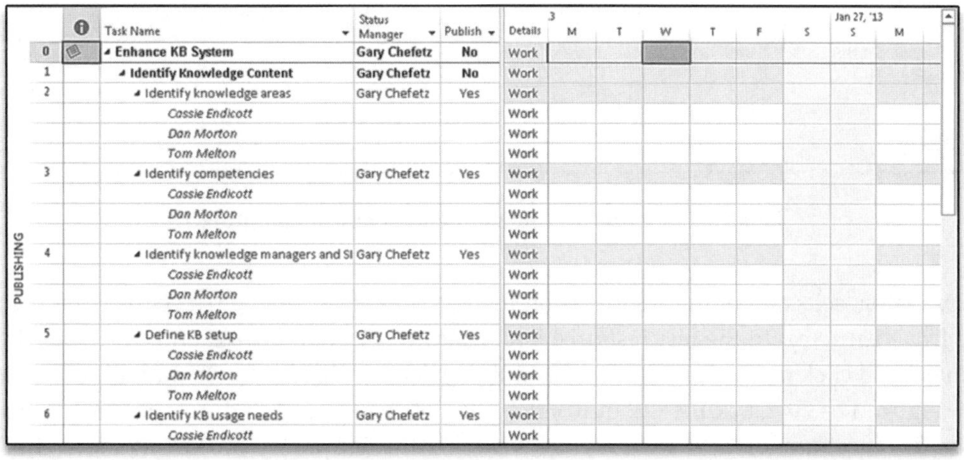

Figure 17 - 78: Publishing view applied

Creating an Enterprise Resource Sheet View

To simplify your work with managing your organization's resources in the Enterprise Resource Pool, you should create a custom *Resource Sheet* view containing your organization's custom enterprise resource fields. You can use this view to speed up the process of adding new resources or editing the custom information about existing resources in the Enterprise Resource Pool.

Before you create this new custom view, I recommend that you create a temporary blank project by clicking *File* ➤ *New* in the *Backstage.* Then double-click the *Blank Project* item. In this temporary project, add some or all of the resources in the Enterprise Resource Pool to your project team to create what looks and functions like a temporary resource pool for testing purposes. From the *Insert* section of the *Resources* ribbon, click the *Add Resources* pick list and select the *Build Team from Enterprise* item. Project Pro 2013 displays the *Build Team* dialog shown in Figure 17 - 79.

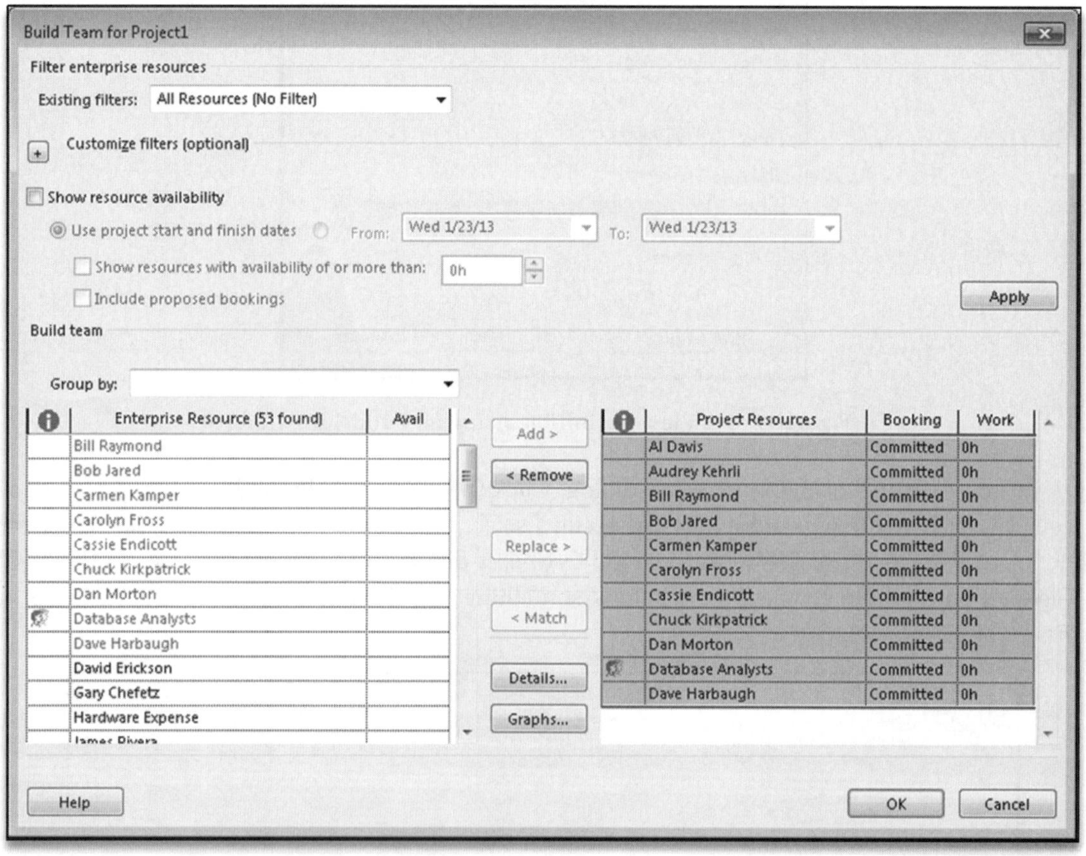

Figure 17 - 79: Build Team dialog for a new blank project

In the *Build Team* dialog, select all of the resources on the left side of the dialog (select the first resource you want to select on the list, then scroll to the last resource you want to select and press and hold the **Shift** key on your computer keyboard and click on the last resource) and then click the *Add* button to add all resources to the project team as I did in Figure 17 - 79. Click the *OK* button to complete the team-building operation. Click the *View* pick list and select the *Resource Sheet* view to see the project team in the temporary project, as shown in Figure 17 - 80.

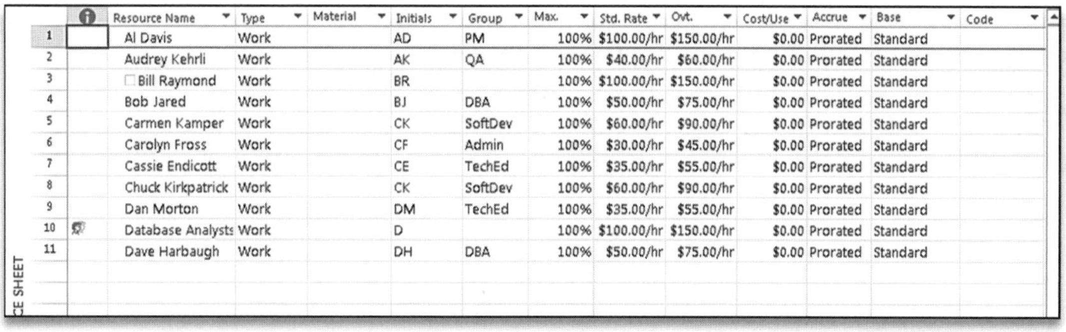

ⓘ	Resource Name	Type	Material	Initials	Group	Max.	Std. Rate	Ovt.	Cost/Use	Accrue	Base	Code
1		Al Davis	Work		AD	PM	100%	$100.00/hr	$150.00/hr	$0.00	Prorated	Standard	
2		Audrey Kehrli	Work		AK	QA	100%	$40.00/hr	$60.00/hr	$0.00	Prorated	Standard	
3		☐ Bill Raymond	Work		BR		100%	$100.00/hr	$150.00/hr	$0.00	Prorated	Standard	
4		Bob Jared	Work		BJ	DBA	100%	$50.00/hr	$75.00/hr	$0.00	Prorated	Standard	
5		Carmen Kamper	Work		CK	SoftDev	100%	$60.00/hr	$90.00/hr	$0.00	Prorated	Standard	
6		Carolyn Fross	Work		CF	Admin	100%	$30.00/hr	$45.00/hr	$0.00	Prorated	Standard	
7		Cassie Endicott	Work		CE	TechEd	100%	$35.00/hr	$55.00/hr	$0.00	Prorated	Standard	
8		Chuck Kirkpatrick	Work		CK	SoftDev	100%	$60.00/hr	$90.00/hr	$0.00	Prorated	Standard	
9		Dan Morton	Work		DM	TechEd	100%	$35.00/hr	$55.00/hr	$0.00	Prorated	Standard	
10	📝	Database Analysts	Work		D		100%	$100.00/hr	$150.00/hr	$0.00	Prorated	Standard	
11		Dave Harbaugh	Work		DH	DBA	100%	$50.00/hr	$75.00/hr	$0.00	Prorated	Standard	

Figure 17 - 80: Resource Sheet view applied to temporary Resource Pool project

You use this temporary resource pool project to simulate the "look and feel" of the actual Enterprise Resource Pool displayed in the *Resource Sheet* view. To create the new custom enterprise *Resource Sheet* view, you again use the four-step method.

Select or Create a Table

In Project Pro 2013, no default table contains your organization's custom enterprise resource fields, but the *Entry* table does contain some of the columns your project managers need to see. Therefore, you should create a new custom enterprise table by copying the *Entry* table. From the *View* ribbon, select the *Tables* pick list and select the *More Tables* item. In the *More Tables* dialog, select the *Resource* option at the top of the dialog, then select the *Entry* table and click the *Copy* button. The system displays the *Table Definition* dialog shown in Figure 17 - 81.

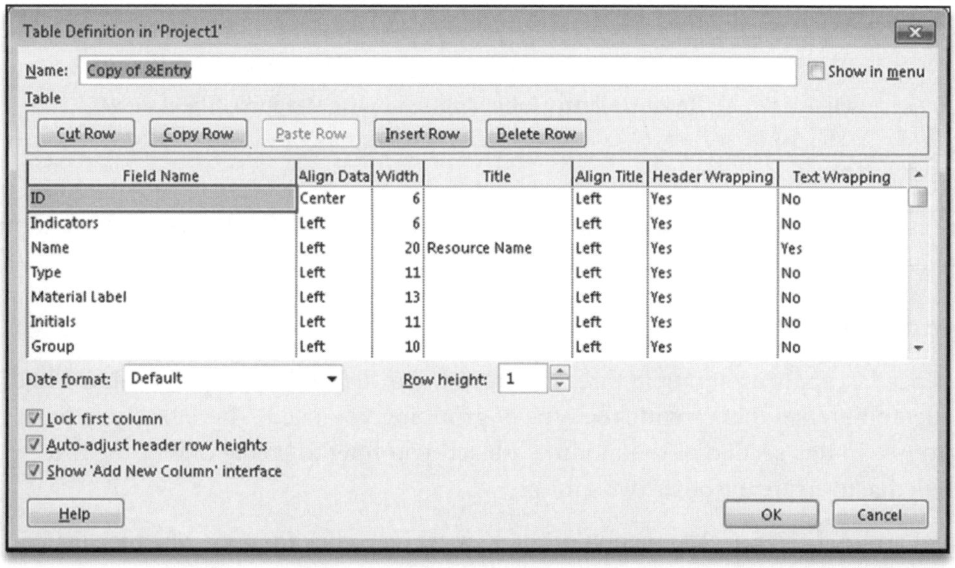

Figure 17 - 81: Table Definition dialog

To manage the custom field values for the resources in the Enterprise Resource Pool, the project managers in my organization need to see the following fields displayed in the following order:

- ID
- Indicators
- Resource Name
- Type
- Material Label
- Role
- Region
- RBS

In the *Table Definition* dialog, name your custom table according to your organization's naming convention, and then select the *Show in menu* option. I named this table the *Resource Entry* table. Using the skills gained in the last three major sections of this module, delete the rows you do not need and add additional rows in the data grid to show all of your organization's custom enterprise resource fields. For each field you add, set your preferred values for the *Align Data, Width, Title, Align Title,* and *Header Wrapping* columns. When you finish, click the *OK* button. In the *More Tables* dialog, click the *Apply* button to view your new table. Figure 17 - 82 shows the new *Resource Entry* table applied in the *Resource Sheet* view.

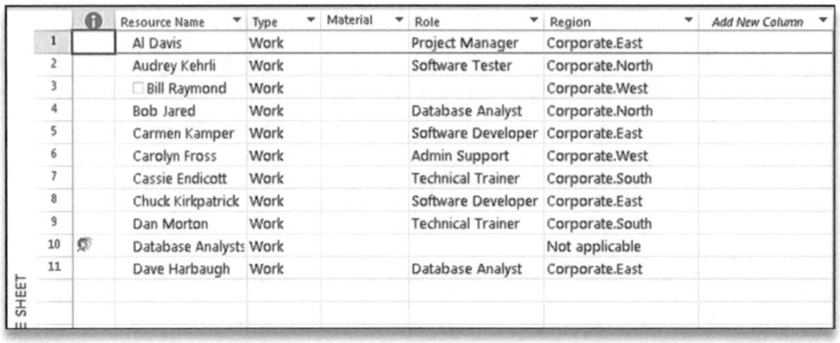

		Resource Name	Type	Material	Role	Region	Add New Column
1		Al Davis	Work		Project Manager	Corporate.East	
2		Audrey Kehrli	Work		Software Tester	Corporate.North	
3		Bill Raymond	Work			Corporate.West	
4		Bob Jared	Work		Database Analyst	Corporate.North	
5		Carmen Kamper	Work		Software Developer	Corporate.East	
6		Carolyn Fross	Work		Admin Support	Corporate.West	
7		Cassie Endicott	Work		Technical Trainer	Corporate.South	
8		Chuck Kirkpatrick	Work		Software Developer	Corporate.East	
9		Dan Morton	Work		Technical Trainer	Corporate.South	
10		Database Analysts	Work			Not applicable	
11		Dave Harbaugh	Work		Database Analyst	Corporate.East	

Figure 17 - 82: Resource Entry table applied in the Resource Sheet view

Select or Create a Filter

Because your users need to see all of the resources in the Enterprise Resource Pool, you do not need to create a custom filter. Instead, use the default *All Resources* filter in your custom view.

Select or Create a Group

Project managers need to apply grouping in three different ways: *Role, Region,* or *RBS* value. Project Pro 2013 does not include any default groups that provide the type of grouping you need. Therefore, you must create three different custom groups. In this section of the module, I teach you how to create one of the three groups, and you can use this knowledge to create the other two groups.

To create a custom group, from the *Data* section of the *View* ribbon, click the *Group by* pick list and select the *More Groups* item. Project Pro 2013 displays the *More Groups* dialog shown in Figure 17 - 83.

Figure 17 - 83: More Groups dialog

In the *More Groups* dialog, click the *New* button. The system displays the *Group Definition* dialog shown in Figure 17 - 84.

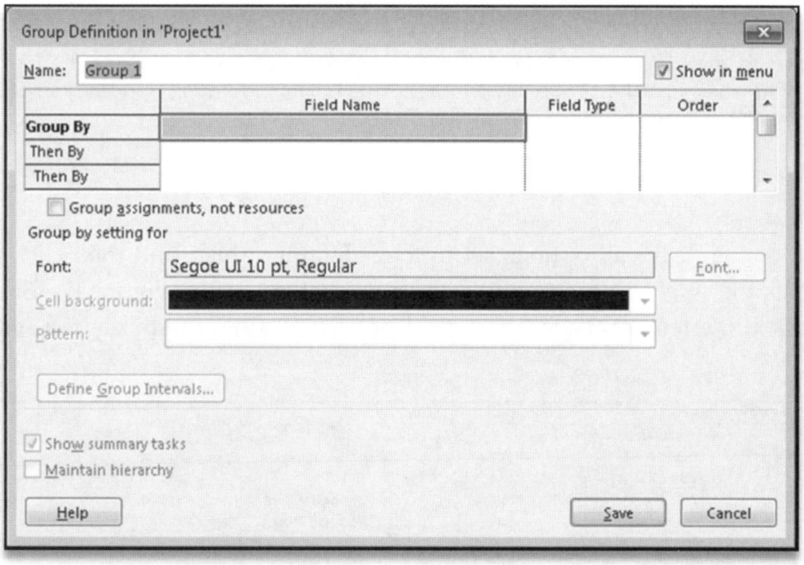

Figure 17 - 84: Group Definition dialog

In the *Group Definition* dialog, name your custom group according to your organization's naming convention and then select the *Show in menu* option. I named this group the *Role* group. Click the pick list button for the *Group By* line in the *Field Name* column, and select the first field you want to group by. In my case, I selected the *Role* field. Figure 17 - 85 shows the completed *Group Definition* dialog for the *Role* group.

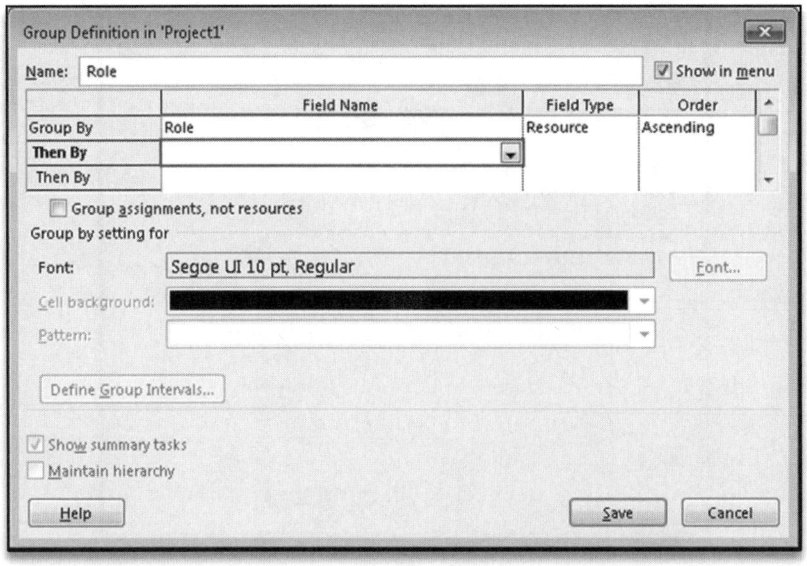

Figure 17 - 85: Group Definition dialog for the Role group

Information: Notice in the *Group Definition* dialog that Project Pro 2013 allows you to create multiple levels of grouping by selecting other fields on the *Then By* lines in the data grid.

Information: In the *Group Definition* dialog, you can create a group specifically intended for use in the *Resource Usage* view. Select the *Group assignments, not resources* option and then select the *Assignment* item in the *Field Type* pick list.

In the *Group Definition* dialog, leave all options set to their default values, and then click the *OK* button. In the *More Groups* dialog, click the *Apply* button to apply the new custom group. Figure 17 - 86 shows the *Role* group applied to the resources in the temporary resource pool project. Notice how nicely the system groups resources by role.

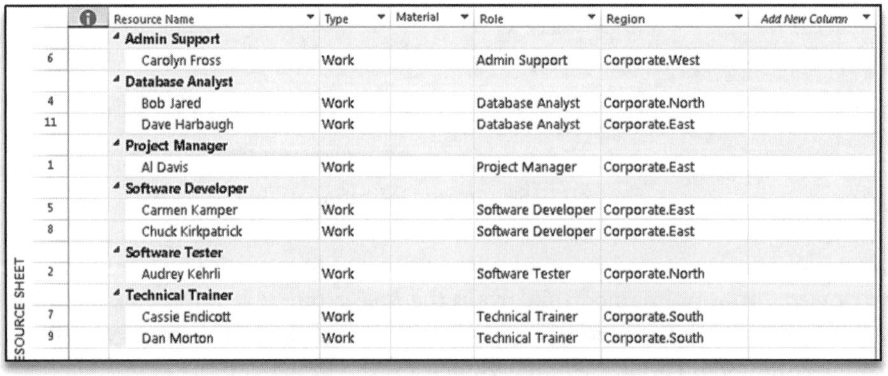

	Resource Name	Type	Material	Role	Region	Add New Column
	Admin Support					
6	Carolyn Fross	Work		Admin Support	Corporate.West	
	Database Analyst					
4	Bob Jared	Work		Database Analyst	Corporate.North	
11	Dave Harbaugh	Work		Database Analyst	Corporate.East	
	Project Manager					
1	Al Davis	Work		Project Manager	Corporate.East	
	Software Developer					
5	Carmen Kamper	Work		Software Developer	Corporate.East	
8	Chuck Kirkpatrick	Work		Software Developer	Corporate.East	
	Software Tester					
2	Audrey Kehrli	Work		Software Tester	Corporate.North	
	Technical Trainer					
7	Cassie Endicott	Work		Technical Trainer	Corporate.South	
9	Dan Morton	Work		Technical Trainer	Corporate.South	

Figure 17 - 86: Role group applied to temporary Resource Pool file

Information: Notice that the system uses the literal values from the *IT Skill* field as grouping labels. If you enter information in the *Description* field when you set up your lookup table, the system uses these values for the grouping labels instead.

Using the skills you gained in this section of the module, create all other groups required by your Project Server administrators. For my organization, I also created groups based on the *RBS* and *Region* custom field.

Create the New View

Before creating a new *Resource* view, restore the default *Resource Sheet* view by selecting the *[No Group]* item from the *Group by* pick list to remove grouping from the list of resources. Select the *Entry* table from the *Tables* pick list as well. To create the new enterprise *Resource Sheet* view, select the *More Views* item from the *Views* pick list. In the *More Views* dialog, click the *New* button and then click the *OK* button in the *Define New View* dialog. In the dialog, name your new view according to your organization's naming convention for custom views. In addition, enter or select the following options in this dialog:

Field Name	Value
Name	Enterprise Resource Sheet
Screen	Resource Sheet
Table	Resource Entry
Group	Role
Filter	All Resources
Highlight filter	Not Selected
Show in menu	Selected

Click the *OK* button to return to the *More Views* dialog. Click the *Apply* button to apply the new view. After you complete and test this custom view, open the *Enterprise Global* and use the *Organizer* dialog to copy the new view, new table, and the new groups from the temporary resource pool file to the *Enterprise Global*. Close the temporary resource pool file and do not save the changes. Exit Project Pro 2013 and re-launch the software to see and use all of your new views, tables, filters, and groups.

Module 18

Working with Business Intelligence and Reporting

Learning Objectives

After completing this module, you will be able to:

- Understand Business Intelligence concepts and apply them to Project Server
- Understand the Business Intelligence Center and the Project Server reporting architecture
- Use the built-in Excel assets for Project Server reporting
- Build custom Excel reports using the built-in Excel assets
- Control access to the Business Intelligence Center

Inside Module 18

Understanding Project Server 2013 Business Intelligence

What is BI (Business Intelligence)?

Business Intelligence (BI) is a set of processes, tools, and techniques for gathering, organizing, and analyzing large volumes of complex data in an effort to develop an accurate understanding of business dynamics. You use it to improve strategic and tactical business decision-making. In other words, the purpose of BI is to capture large amounts of data, make some sense out of it, and use it to make sound business decisions. The ultimate goal is to develop the ability to spot problems and trends, and to make informed decisions to mitigate risks, improve efficiencies, and identify opportunities.

You may be more familiar with the term **reporting** which references the data visualization aspects of the BI process. Project Server 2013 Business Intelligence differs from the Project Professional reporting capabilities in that you are able to do analysis and reporting across multiple projects and resources across the organization. This enhanced scope enables you to see beyond your project plan and understand the organizational impacts to your plan.

Levels of BI

BI requirements focus on three major groups as shown in Figure 18 - 1.

Figure 18 - 1: Levels of Business Intelligence

Enterprise Business Intelligence

Enterprise BI enables better information sharing and decision-making. Enterprise Business Intelligence typically focuses on long term needs. An example of Enterprise Business Intelligence is a timesheet adherence report across all resources. Finance would use such a report as an input to capture billing milestones or capitalize costs for tax purposes.

Collaborative BI

Collaborative BI enables better information sharing and decision-making within an interested group of people where other methods of collaboration (email, face-to-face, etc.) can no longer meet the group's information needs effectively. Typically, this type of BI addresses information needs of the Project Team, Project Stakeholders, Work Team, or Department and addresses both short-term and long-term information needs of the group. An example of Collaborative BI is a *Project Status* dashboard, which allows stakeholders to see current status, issues, risks, and milestones.

Personal BI

Personal BI enables the person consuming the information to accomplish their work in a more effective manner through better decision making. This type of BI can include personal, ad hoc, and single use reports that you use to address short-term situations or gain insight to specific questions. Personal BI tends to be tactical in nature. An example of Personal BI is a *Project Last Status Update* report used by the project manager to ensure timely status updates from each project team member.

Common Business Intelligence Needs

A project effort is similar to managing a car trip in many ways. You can categorize the project manager's BI needs, similar to the driver, as follows:

Analysis and Planning

The project manager's analysis and planning must focus on the work that must occur to accomplish planned project goals and assumptions. When there is deviation from the original plan, this analysis and planning must also encompass the generation of alternatives to meet the plan. Lastly, there is an ongoing need to validate the plan against changing business conditions and project risks as to alert the project manager to potential issues.

Think of this as similar to a driver determining where to go and the best possible route to get there based on trip requirements. (Let's take this route so we can see the world's largest ball of string!). The driver plans a destination (outcome), stops along the way (milestones), and makes adjustments to achieve progress as weather and road conditions affect the plan (risk management). Project BI systems make it easier to fill these needs just as GPS-based navigation systems make it much easier for drivers to meet similar needs through automatic route generation and points of interest.

Status Reporting

Status reporting focuses on communicating the current state of the effort and health of the plan to the project team and stakeholders. The current-state report ensures that all interested parties receive consistent information for decision-making and planning. Similarly, the current position of a driver can be the most valuable information delivered by a navigation system. By knowing where you are, you can plan a path to a specific destination.

Progress Monitoring

Project managers monitor progress so that they can clearly communicate short-term plans and ensure that the team is expending the effort required to meet the plan objectives. Variations of effort at this level can translate to larger progress issues over time. Similarly, a navigation system calculates the average speed of the driver and time to goal. If the driver decides to make a large number of stops, gets caught in traffic, or decides to take a scenic detour, the navigation system shows the impact accordingly.

Reporting and Business Intelligence Overview

Organizations spend time and money implementing Project Server 2013 to capture work data, make sense out of it, and use it to make decisions such as:

- **Spotting problems and trends** - Is the project running late or over budget?
- **Mitigating risks** - What can we do to avoid missing our launch deadline?
- **Improving efficiencies** - Who is the best-qualified person to perform the work?
- **Identifying opportunities** - What if we design the database and the user interface at the same time?

A well-designed BI system should do the following:

- Extract large amounts of complex data from one or more sources, such as CRM, supply chain management, ERP, and PPM systems
- Centralize, organize, and standardize information in repositories such as data warehouses or data marts
- Provide analytical tools through multiple delivery methods that allow business and technical specialists to run queries against the data and to perform analyses to uncover patterns and diagnose problems
- Present the right information, at the right time, in the right format in order to make the right decisions and take the right actions to achieve the right performance

Project Server 2013 helps to do these things already. It aggregates different types of complex work data from different locations into a central set of databases and OLAP cubes, or BI data store, such as those shown in Figure 18 - 2.

Figure 18 - 2: Aggregating Project Server Data into the BI Data Store

When used in conjunction with SharePoint Server 2013 and SQL Server 2012, Project Server 2013 provides a set of rich analytical tools to build reports and visuals for data analysis. The list below and Figure 18 - 3 represent the available tools.

- Project Professional Visual Reports
- Visio Diagrams
- Excel Tabular and Pivot-Style Reports
- PowerPivot Models
- Power View Dashboards
- SQL Server Reporting
- Key Performance Indicators
- PerformancePoint Balanced Scorecards
- Interactive Dashboards

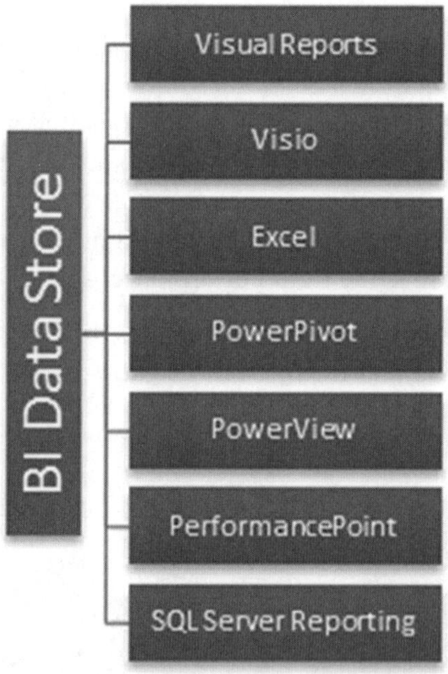

Figure 18 - 3: Reporting on Data in the BI Data Store

Business Intelligence is much more than operational and status reporting, such as extracting work hours for billing purposes, issuing logs for firefighting, or simply determining "what is my team working on today?" BI tools assist you in performing different types of analyses:

- Historical analyses, such as what, when, who, and how much as events occurred in the past
- Predictive analyses, such as forecasting, profiling, trend analysis of why and what-if scenarios as events might happen in the future

A few examples of analyses that people typically perform with a BI system include demographic trends, product line profitability, group or office profitability, profit margins, billing volumes, utilization, billing lags, payment lags, product trends, measurement of goals, cross-departmental data. A few examples of questions that Project Server 2013 work analyses might answer include:

- Which departments have availability to work on IT projects?
- How much time have project managers spent performing administrative work?
- Have we been spending more time on operational work or project work?
- What types of projects have more risks or issues, and what are the types of risks or issues?
- If we hire more engineers, can we complete more projects this year?
- Can we improve deliverable quality if people work less?

Understanding Available Data

Project Server 2013 generates data about the current state of projects, resources, timesheets, and the interactions between them. All Business Intelligence data for Project Server 2013 is contained within two data stores. The first is the BI relational data store, commonly referred to in previous versions as either the Reporting Database or RDB. As Project Server 2013 has only one database, calling the BI relational data store the **RDB**, is a misnomer.

The BI relational data store is always available, assuming your Project Server administrator provided you with the appropriate security access. The other data store, available for on-premise installations, contains one or more optional OLAP databases. As a Project Server 2013 administrator, you can create as many OLAP databases as your organization requires. All OLAP analytical data derives from the BI relational data store.

Project Server 2013 utilizes a cloud-friendly database design, in that all data resides within a single database. What were separate databases in Project Server 2010 are now different database schemas within a single database. A database schema refers to the structure of the data within a database; much like a floor plan refers to the layout of space within a house.

In both releases, the naming convention is Database.Schema.Table. The upgrade process maps the old database name to a new schema name in the new consolidated 2013 database. For example, ProjectServer_Published.dbo.MSP_TASKS in Project Server 2010 becomes ProjectService.pub.MSP_TASKS in Project Server 2013 as outlined in Table 18 - 1.

Project Server 2010 Database (database tables)	Project Server 2013 Database Schema (database views)
Draft	draft.
Published	pub.
Reporting	dbo.
Archive	ver.

Table 18 - 1: Mapping of the Project Server 2010 databases to the new Project Server 2013 views

It is important to note the flow and the timing of data through Project Server 2013's BI data store. The source data for all projects originates in the tables that are part of the Project Server Draft schema within the Project database.

The system copies the data to the tables in the Project Server Pub schema within the Project database when project managers publish their schedules. As a part of the publishing process, the system also transforms the project data and copies it to the tables within the Project Server dbo schema within the Project database, making it immediately available for reporting in the form of tables and views. Finally, on a schedule specified by the Project Server or SharePoint administrator, the system ships the data to SQL Server Analysis Services, which then re-organizes the data, tallies it by business dimensions, and stores it in an OLAP database, making it available for reporting in the form of multi-dimensional cubes as illustrated in Figure 18 - 4.

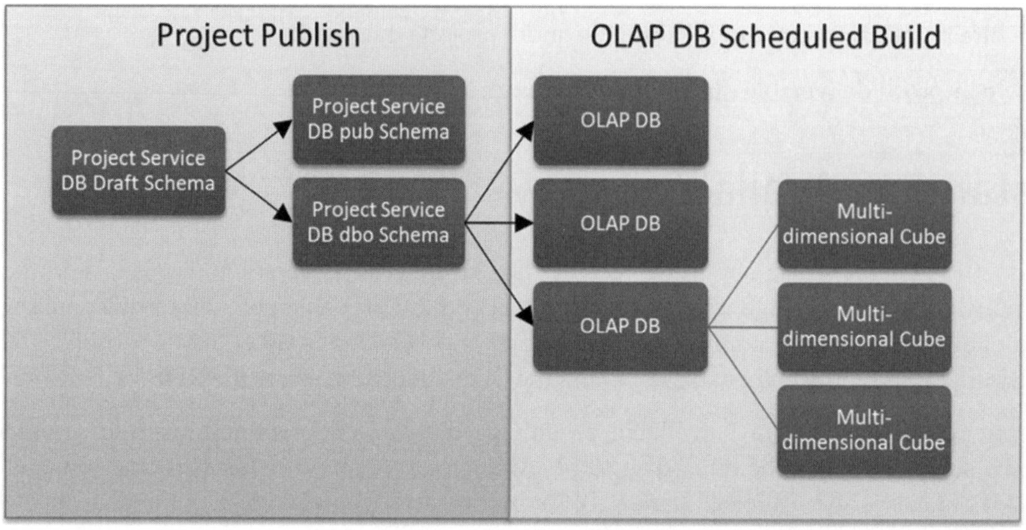

Figure 18 - 4: Data flow through Project Server BI Data Stores

Accessing the Data

Project Server 2013 supports three methods of accessing data for reporting on premises and Project Online as outlined in Table 18 - 2. The first method uses direct relational database access to retrieve the data. The second method, new to Project Server 2013, uses OData access to retrieve information. The third method uses shared data connections to access the OLAP cube.

Direct database access uses OLEDB between the Excel client and the SQL Server database to retrieve the data schema and data for developing reports in Excel. Viewing the report within SharePoint uses Excel Services web service calls to retrieve the data and render the report as a web page.

OData is a web-based open standards protocol for querying data via HTTP protocol over port 80 or port 443 (SSL). To the user, it appears as a long URL. The advantages of OData are direct database access is not required to author reports and this data access method services both report authors and report viewers.

Information: The OLAP database provides a robust mechanism to quickly access large amounts of data. All OLAP data is a copy of data stored in the BI relational data store.

Access Method	Supported Online?	Supported On-premises?
Direct SQL access to the BI relational data store using OLEDB	No	Yes
OData access to the BI data store using HTTP or HTTPS	Yes	Yes
Shared data access to the OLAP cube	No (OLAP cubes are not available)	Yes

Table 18 - 2: Access Methods

Which Data Source Should I Use?

You should base your choice of data source on two primary factors, the timeliness of the data you need and the type of intelligence you require. Table 18 - 3 shows examples of needs and the appropriate data source for each need. The data in the BI relational data store is most appropriate for factual intelligence needs that require near real time accuracy. The system places the data in the BI relational data store at nearly the same time that Project Server 2013 publishes and other save operations occur. Therefore, the BI relational data store best serves your short term or near term information need such as situations where lists of information are necessary.

OLAP data, on the other hand, is best suited for analytical intelligence needs. The system structures OLAP data in such a fashion as to optimize it for aggregating and summarizing data. However, the freshness of the data is only as good as the last time you refreshed the OLAP data. OLAP data is typically a snapshot from the prior day, but in some cases, this data can be several days old. Therefore, OLAP data is better suited to longer-term data analysis.

Example Question	Best Suited to OLAP Data?	Best Suited to BI Relational Data?
What is the utilization of all the resources in the resource pool?	X	
What projects will complete this month?		X
Have all timesheets been processed for the prior period?		X
How does the level of administrative time this quarter compare to that of past quarters?	X	

Table 18 - 3: Examples of BI needs and appropriate data to fit that need

Relational Data Overview

You access data within the BI relational data store using SQL views that end with "UserView." Project Server 2010 offered seventeen views. Project Server 2013 expands this list to thirty-eight and introduces some new tables as well as some additional fields to the existing tables. For example, there are now views that contain cumulative cost and work fields, and additional portfolio views.

Table 18 - 4 outlines the SQL views currently available in the BI relational data store. I do not list all views as many end with the suffix **CF**, which stands for *Custom Fields*.

Entity	View Name	Description
Assignments	MSP_EpmAssignment_UserView	Assignment details across all projects and resources
Assignment Cumulative Baselines By Day	MSP_EpmAssignmentBaselineCumulativeByDay_UserView	Assignment baseline cumulative totals by day for every existing baseline across all projects and resources
Assignments By Day	MSP_EpmAssignmentByDay_UserView	Assignment details by day across all projects and resources
Assignments Cumulative By Day	MSP_EpmAssignmentCumulativeByDay_UserView	Assignment cumulative totals by day across all projects and resources
Business Driver	MSP_EpmBusinessDriver_UserView	Business driver details and impact descriptions
Business Drivers by Department	MSP_EpmBusinessDriverDepartment_UserView	Cross-reference of business drivers associated to specific departments
Portfolio Analysis Summary	MSP_EpmPortfolioAnalysis_UserView	Describes all of the core properties and characteristics of the Portfolio Analysis
Portfolio Analysis Details by Project	MSP_EpmPortfolioAnalysisProject_UserView	Project specific information for a Portfolio Analysis such as priority and schedule constraints
Optimizer Scenario Details by Project	MSP_EpmPortfolioCostConstraintProject_UserView	Project specific information for an Optimizer model, such as Project Force Status

Entity	View Name	Description
Scenario Summary	MSP_EpmPortfolioCostConstraintScenario_UserView	Scenario summary information from the Optimizer for a given Analysis
Resource Planner Details by Project	MSP_EpmPortfolioResourceConstraintProject_UserView	Project specific information for a Resource Planner model
Resource Planner Scenario Summary	MSP_EpmPortfolioResourceConstraintScenario_UserView	Resource planner properties for a given scenario
Prioritization Session Summary	MSP_EpmPrioritization_UserView	Prioritization session properties
Business Drivers by Prioritization	MSP_EpmPrioritizationDriver_UserView	Business driver details and impact descriptions for a given prioritization
Business Driver Rank by Prioritization	MSP_EpmPrioritizationDriverRelation_UserView	Pair-wise comparison data between business drivers
Projects	MSP_EpmProject_UserView	Project summary information
Project Decisions	MSP_EpmProjectDecision_UserView	Information related to finalized Optimizer and Planner solutions
Resources	MSP_EpmResource_UserView	Resource summary
Resource by Day	MSP_EpmResourceByDay_UserView	Resource capacity and work by day
Tasks	MSP_EpmTask_UserView	Task details across all projects
Task Baselines Cumulative By Day	MSP_EpmTaskBaselineCumulativeByDay_UserView	Task baseline cumulative totals by day for every existing baseline across all projects and resources
Tasks by Day	MSP_EpmTaskByDay_UserView	Task details by day across all projects
Tasks Cumulative By Day	MSP_EpmTaskCumulativeByDay_UserView	Task cumulative totals by day across all projects and resources

Entity	View Name	Description
Timesheet Classes by Department	MSP_TimesheetClass_UserView	Cross-reference of Timesheet classes by Department
Timesheets	MSP_TimesheetLine_UserView	Timesheet summary information across all time reporting periods
Deliverable to Project Links	MSP_WssDeliverableToProjectLinks_UserView	Deliverable details and their associated project
Deliverable to Task Links	MSP_WssDeliverableToTaskLinks_UserView	Deliverable details and their associated project task
Documents to Issues Links	MSP_WssDocumentToIssueLinks_UserView	Document details and link to associated projects issue
Documents to Risk Links	MSP_WssDocumentToRiskLinks_UserView	Document details and link to associated projects risk
Documents to Tasks	MSP_WssDocumentToTaskLinks_UserView	Document details and link to associated project task
Issues to Task Associations	MSP_WssIssueTaskAssociation_UserView	Summary of project tasks that have links to associated issues
Issue to Issue Links	MSP_WssIssueToIssueLinks_UserView	Project issue details including links to associated issues
Issue to Risk Links	MSP_WssIssueToRiskLinks_UserView	Project issue details including links to associated risks
Issue to Task Links	MSP_WssIssueToTaskLinks_UserView	Project issue details including links to associated tasks
Risk to Task Association	MSP_WssRiskTaskAssociation_UserView	Summary of project tasks that have links to associated issues

Entity	View Name	Description
Risk to Issue Links	MSP_WssRiskToIssueLinks_UserView	Project risk details including links to associated issues
Risk to Risk Links	MSP_WssRiskToRiskLinks_UserView	Project risk detail including links to associated risks
Risk to Task Links	MSP_WssRiskToTaskLinks_UserView	Project risk details including links to associated tasks

Table 18 - 4: Currently documented Project Server 2013 SQL views

Microsoft includes the database schema in their SDK (Software Development Kit). Here are some links (subject to change) where you should gain access to the database schema and other valuable information:

- **Microsoft SDK** - http://www.microsoft.com/en-us/download/details.aspx?id=30435
- **Microsoft Programmability Blogs (latest schema as of this writing):** http://blogs.msdn.com/b/project_programmability/
- If the last two links are no longer accessible, go to the http://microsoft.com website and search for **Project2013Reporting.exe** or **Project 2013 SDK** using your favorite Internet search engine.

Microsoft's published database scheme shows the relationships between fields and views. Figure 18 - 5 through Figure 18 - 9 help you visualize these views and their relationships. I do not list every possible relationship but give you an overview of how to relate information to build custom data queries.

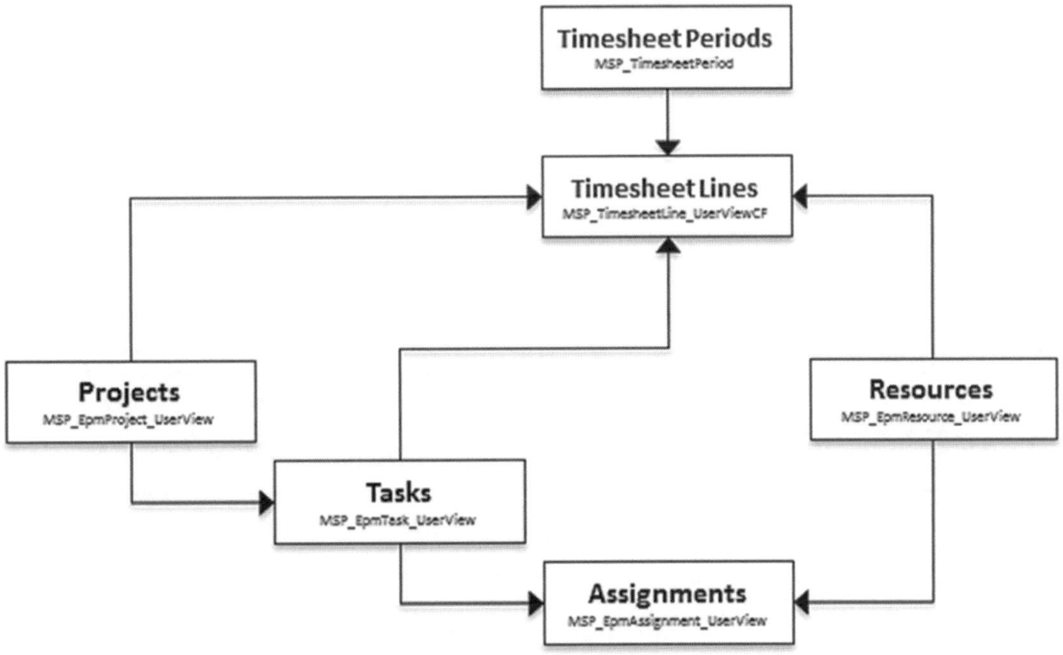

Figure 18 - 5: Conceptual relationship diagram to access timesheet data

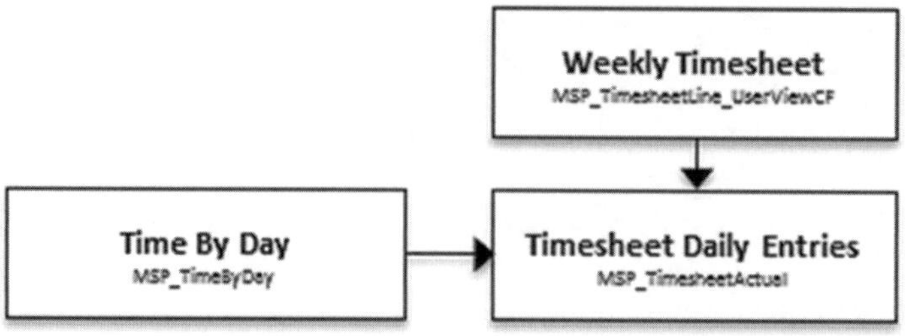

Figure 18 - 6: Conceptual relationship diagram to access detailed timesheet data

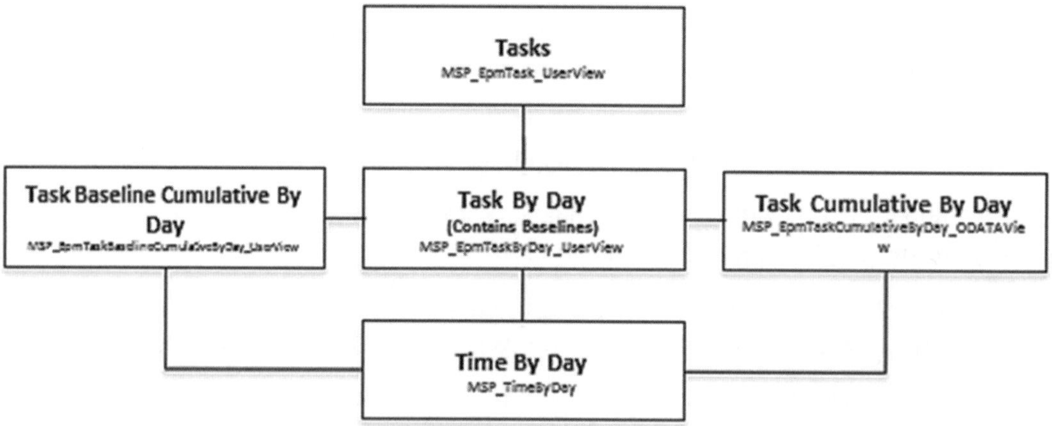

Figure 18 - 7: Conceptual relationship diagram to access task data

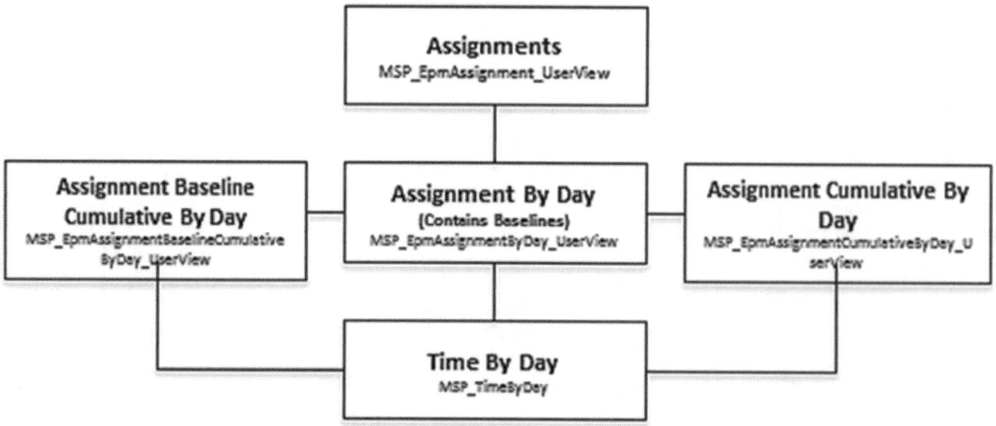

Figure 18 - 8: Conceptual relationship diagram to access task assignment data

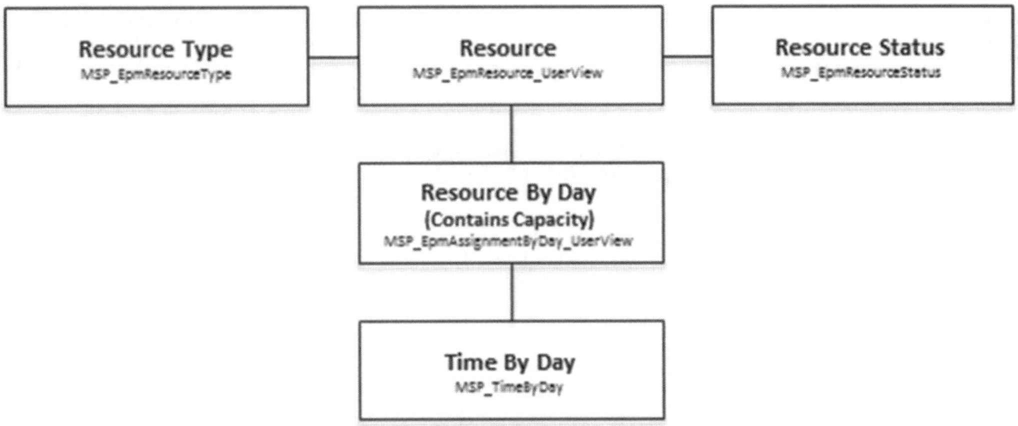

Figure 18 - 9: Conceptual relationship diagram to access resource data

OLAP Overview

An OLAP, or Online Analytical Processing, database differs from a traditional database in several ways. Fundamentally, traditional database tables store data in a flat two-dimensional format. In order to derive data totals from a relational database, such as **sales for the month**, users must execute a query. OLAP databases, on the other hand, consist of data cubes that store pre-processed data in a multi-dimensional format, allowing users to work with factual data that the system has already totaled along various business dimensions for detailed data mining and analytics.

What is OLAP?

The Online Analytical Processing (OLAP) technology relies on a multidimensional view of project, resource, and task data. The relational database structure that underpins most transactional applications is two-dimensional. OLAP leverages data cubes based on relational fact sources, which contain preprocessed three-dimensional data, typically time-phased and aggregated by business dimension. The advantages of employing OLAP technologies for business analytics include the performance advantages of using preprocessed data and, more important, the transparent enforcement of standardized analytical formulas.

If you are familiar with using PivotTables in Excel, you will be very comfortable working with the OLAP cube. Figure 18 - 10 shows an example of an Excel 2013 PivotTable connected to a Project Server 2013 OLAP cube.

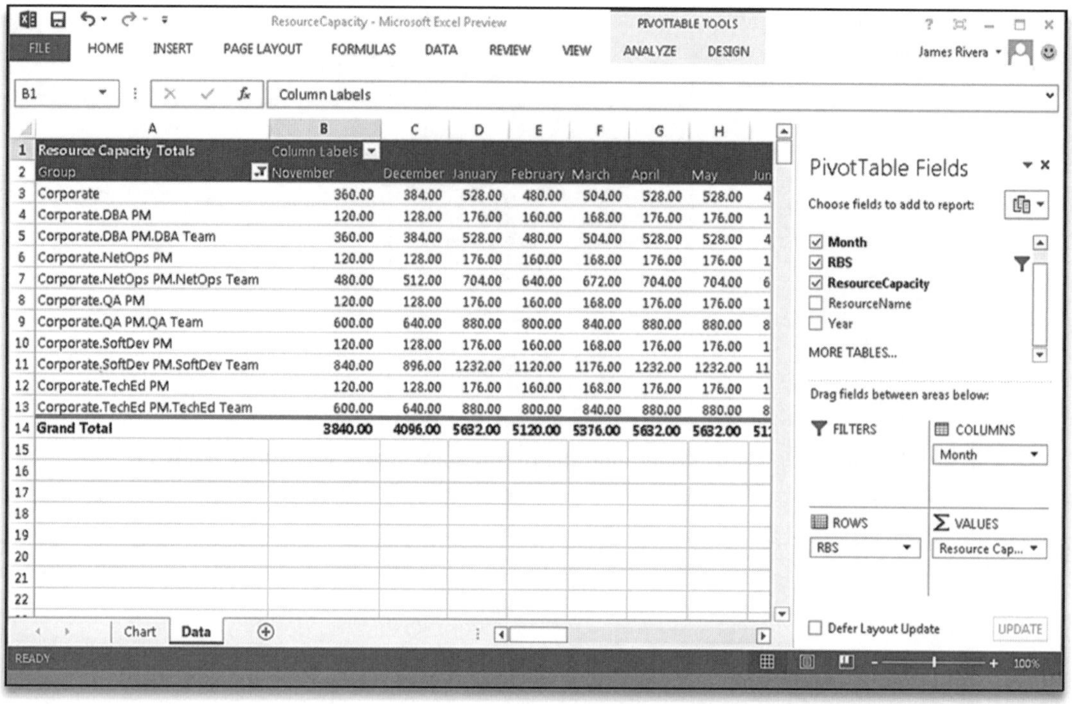

Figure 18 - 10: Excel 2013 PivotTable connected to a Project Server 2013 OLAP cube

The multi-dimensional cubes within the OLAP database contain analytical data used to create PivotTables, PivotCharts, and PivotDiagrams, allowing the breakdown of data across business dimensions. Data includes aggregate information, such as rollups of work and costs, for all projects, tasks, and resources in the system. The data also includes information stored in Project Sites relating to project deliverables, risks, issues, and documents. As an example of how you can use OLAP data to generate reports for detailed multi-dimensional analysis, consider the following reporting requirements for an organization:

- The organization must track the total amount of work for all projects in a portfolio of projects
- The organization must track the work by year for 2011, 2012, and 2013
- The organization must separate the work for its eastern and western regions
- The organization must capitalize certain types of work while expensing other types of work

The time dimension (2011, 2012, and 2013) is inherent to the system, but to help meet these reporting needs, the Project Server administrator must create two custom fields: an *Enterprise Project* field called *Region*, and an *Enterprise Task* field called *Expense Type*, each of which become dimensions in the multi-dimensional cube. The *Region* field includes a lookup table with the eastern and western regions listed. The *Expense Type* field contains a lookup table with the *Capital* and *Expense* items listed. The Project Server administrator must add these fields to the OLAP database configuration.

SQL Server Analysis Services rebuilds the OLAP database with the current data for all projects, enabling users to "slice and dice" the project work data according to their reporting needs. To illustrate this conceptually, Figure 18 - 11 shows the multi-dimensional cube of work data within the OLAP database, revealing 87,000 hours of total work across all projects in the Project Server database.

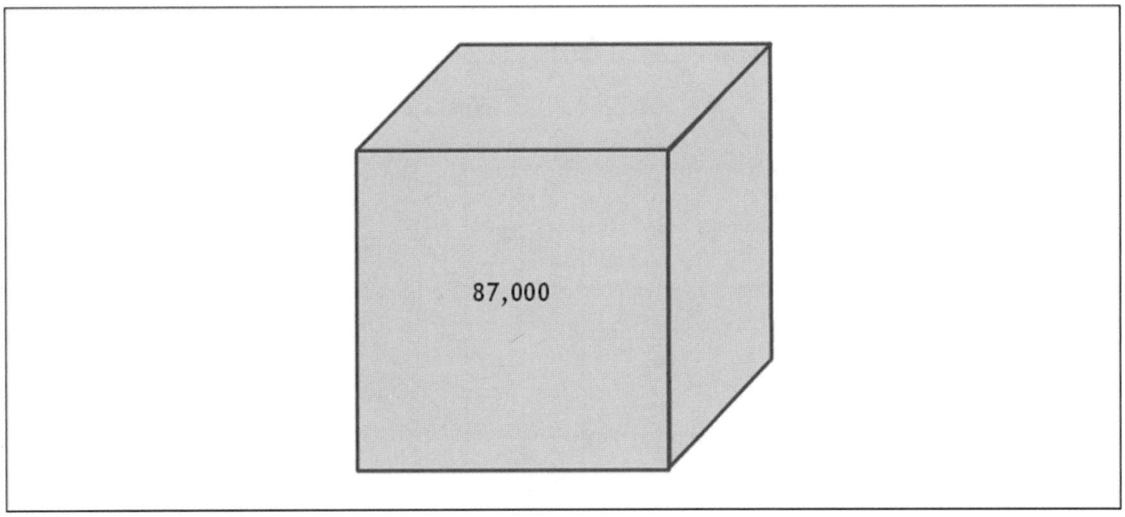

Figure 18 - 11: Multi-Dimensional Cube in OLAP database shows Total Work for all projects

Figure 18 - 12 shows the multi-dimensional cube within the OLAP database with the total project work broken down by year for 2010, 2011, and 2012.

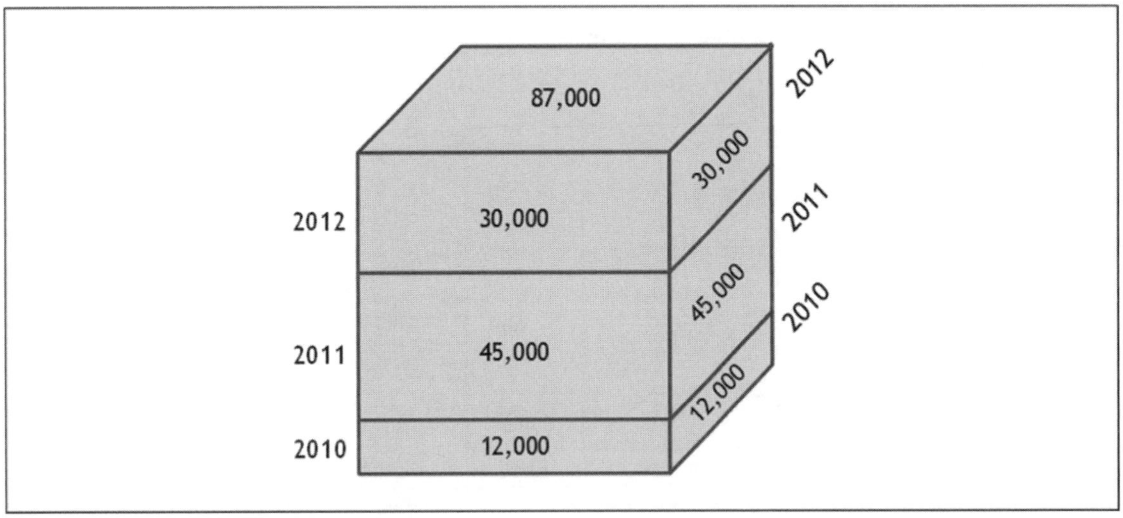

Figure 18 - 12: Multi-Dimensional Cube in OLAP database shows Total Work by Year

Figure 18 - 13 shows the multi-dimensional cube within the OLAP database with the total project work, broken down by both year and region.

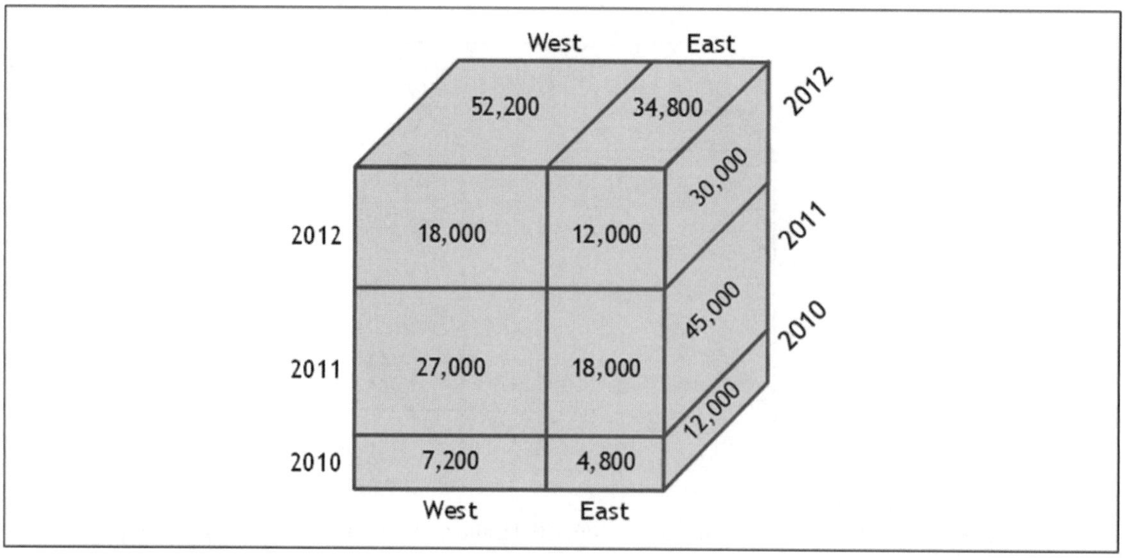

Figure 18 - 13: Multi-Dimensional Cube in OLAP database shows Total Work by Year and by Region

Figure 18 - 14 shows the multi-dimensional cube within the OLAP database with the total work broken down by year, by region, and amortization type.

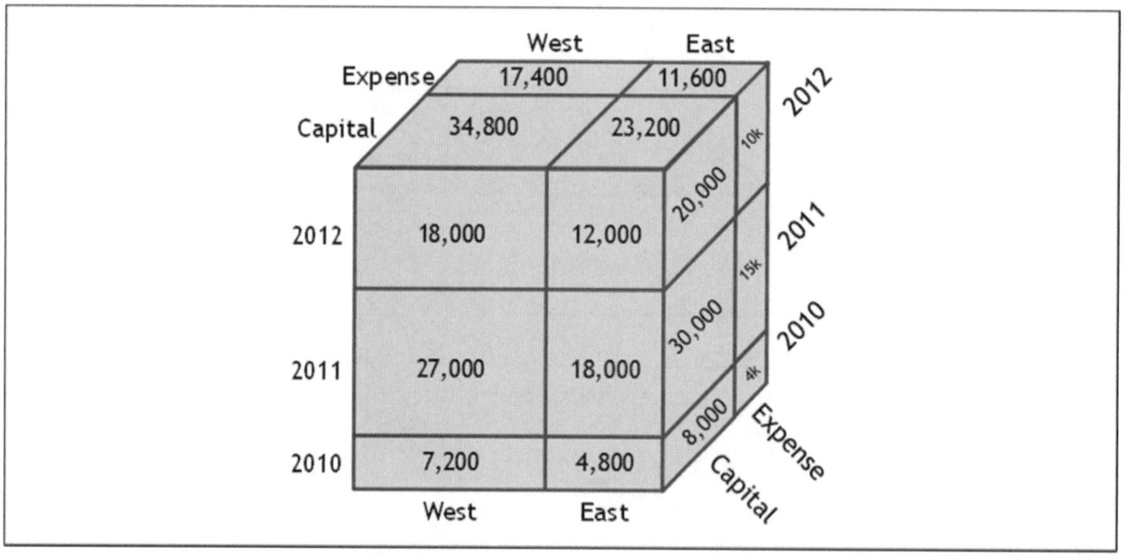

Figure 18 - 14: Multi-Dimensional Cube in OLAP database shows Total Work by Year, by Region, and by Amortization type

Multi-dimensional cubes contain data classifiable into two main categories:

- **Measures:** Measures are numeric data that you can aggregate into sums, averages and other mathematical aggregations, such as total work or total cost. You may see references to the *Totals* and *Measures* terms in OLAP or Analysis Services tools and documentation, and you may see references to the *Sum Values* term in Excel PivotTable or PivotChart tools and documentation. Be aware these terms describe actions you can only apply to measure data. In the previous example, the *Work* field is a measure.

- **Dimensions:** Dimensions enable you to group and summarize the measure data. Since you can combine dimensions, you can create different views of measure data for analysis. You may see location references to *Column Labels* or *Row Labels* terms in Excel PivotTable or PivotChart tools and documentation. These terms describe where you want the dimension data to appear in the visualization; but do not refer directly to the dimension. In the previous example, the *Year, Region,* and *Expense Type* fields are dimensions, where *Expense Type* and *Year* are *Row Labels* and *Region* is a *Column Label.*

Analytical (OLAP) Data

The OLAP data entities are similar to that present in the relational data where you see projects, tasks, resources, assignments, timesheet, and time itself. The system optimizes the organization of this data for analysis and exploration without the need for complex queries or knowledge of Structured Query Language (SQL).

Understanding how OLAP data is organized and the terms used helps you navigate your way to solving your information needs as well as making it easier for you to find additional information. A database contains each instance of OLAP data. Project Server 2013 supports multiple OLAP databases, so your particular OLAP instance may contain all Project Server data or just data related to your project and/or resource department.

There are fourteen OLAP cubes within each Project Server OLAP database. Each cube organizes the data to support a particular information need. An Excel report template for each cube within a particular OLAP database provides easy access to the data. In order to get the most from OLAP, you should understand four terms and what they mean. These terms relate to Excel functionality, which you learn about when you author reports. You structure OLAP data by:

- Measures
- Dimensions
- Attributes
- Attribute properties

Measures are the aggregated factual data upon which you base your analysis. In Project Server 2013, measures are *Cost, Duration,* or *Number* fields as the system can aggregate these values via summing, averaging, etc. Examples of measures are *Capacity* and *Work.*

Dimensions categorize and provide context to the underlying *Measure* data. For example, to break down *Capacity* and *Work* by project and resource, you use the project list and resource list dimensions to provide requisite data breakdown.

Attributes are values that make up dimensions and each attribute represents a unique value. You can also structure attributes as a hierarchy. The Resource Breakdown Structure (RBS) dimension illustrates how each RBS value (Corporate, Corporate.Sales, and Corporate.IT) represents an attribute as shown in Figure 18 - 15. Because RBS is a hierarchical dimension, the *Corporate at Level 1* RBS value results in a rollup of data from Corporate.Sales and Corporate.IT at Level 2.

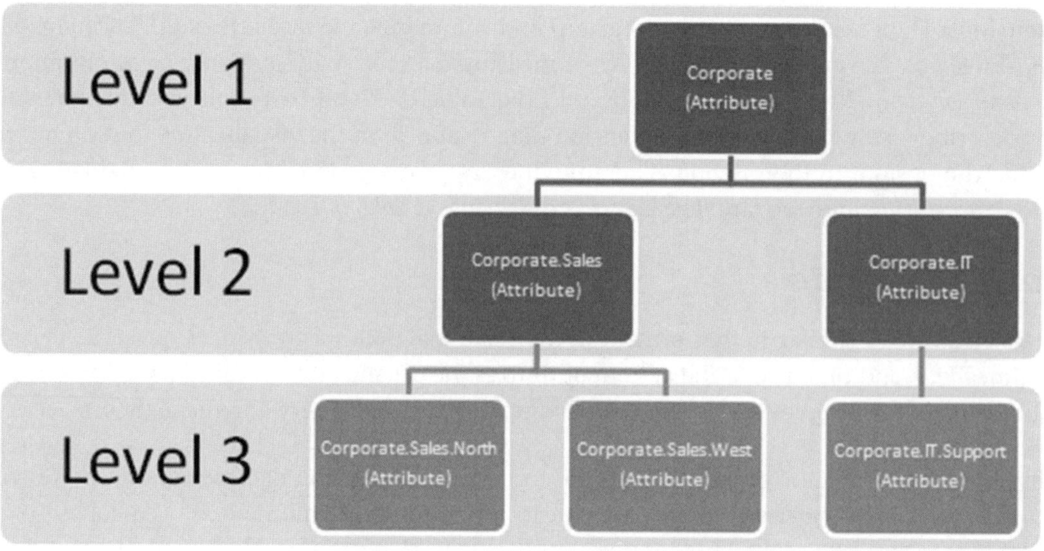

Figure 18 - 15: Example of the RBS Dimension with Hierarchy Levels and Attributes

Office Data Connections (ODC) Overview

Project Server 2013 pre-connects the sample Excel reports and report templates in the Business Intelligence Center to their respective data sources in the Project Server BI relational data store via an Office Data Connection (ODC) file. The Business Intelligence Center manages these data connections centrally in the *Data Connections* library so that you can share them between report authors.

The key benefit for external ODC files is that different reports can use one connection. Therefore, if you are writing a new report, you can use an existing ODC to get to your data. This eliminates the need for you to know things like database server names and SQL queries.

The ODC library contains six shared ODC files for connecting to the Project Server reporting database using the OData format. Another nine shared ODC files are available for connecting to the Project Server reporting database using SQL queries. Finally, there are fourteen shared ODC files for connecting reports to each OLAP database you create. I show the relationship between Excel reports, ODC's, and your data in Figure 18 - 16.

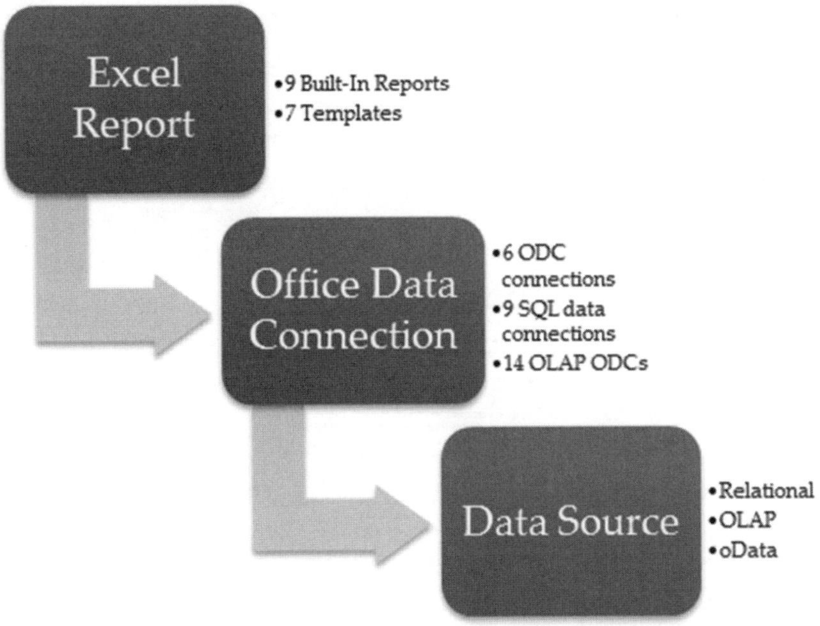

Figure 18 - 16: Excel - ODC - Data Source Relationship

To view these ODC files, navigate to the Business Intelligence Center and in the *Quick Launch* menu, click the *Data Connections* link. The system displays the *Data Connections* page shown in Figure 18 - 17.

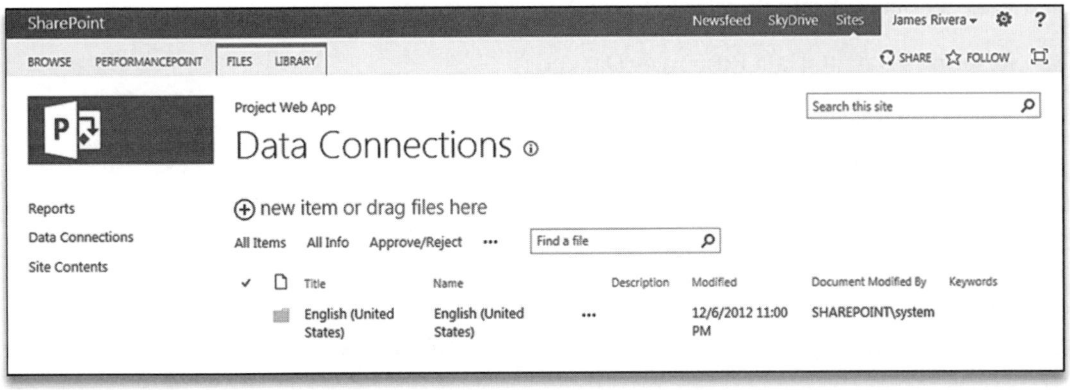

Figure 18 - 17: Data Connections page

To view the English language data connection files, in the *Data Connections* library, click the *English (United States)* folder. The system displays the *English (United States)* folder partially shown in Figure 18 - 18.

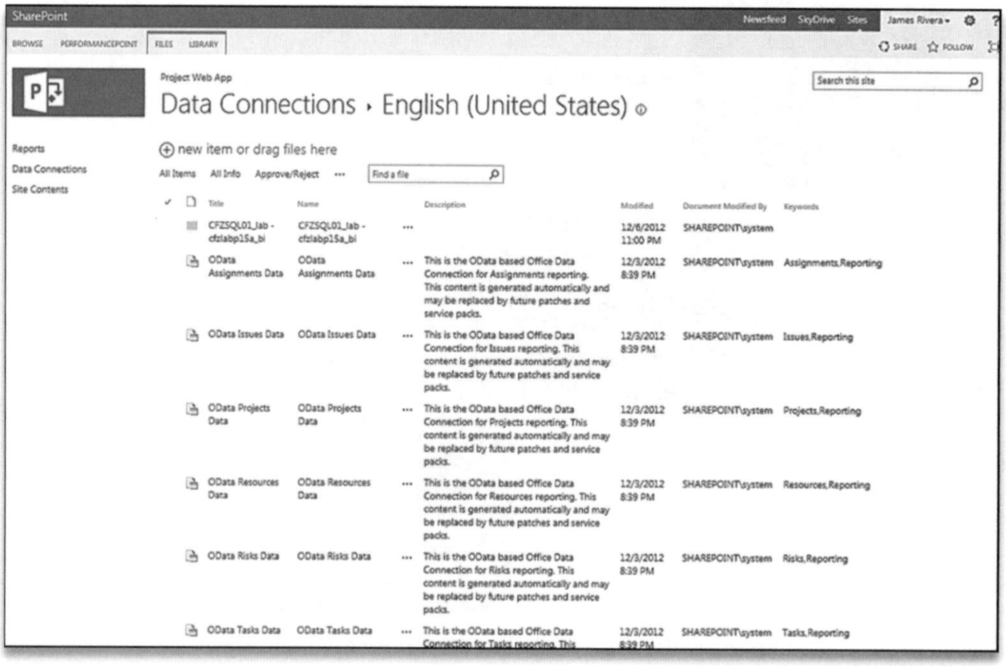

Figure 18 - 18: English language folder in the Data Connections library (partial)

The *English (United States)* folder contains fifteen ODC files for connecting reports to the Project Server BI relational data store:

- OData Assignments Data (OData Assignments Data.odc)
- OData Issues Data (OData Issues Data.odc)
- OData Projects Data (OData Projects Data.odc)
- OData Resources Data (OData Resources Data.odc)
- OData Risks Data (OData Risks Data.odc)
- OData Tasks Data (OData Tasks Data.odc)
- Project Server - Deliverables (Project Server - Deliverables.odc)
- Project Server - Issue Data (Project Server - Issue Data.odc)
- Project Server - Project And Task Data (Project Server - Project And Task Data.odc)
- Project Server - Project Assignment Data (Project Server - Project Assignment Data.odc)
- Project Server - Resource Capacity (Project Server - Resource Capacity.odc)
- Project Server - Resource Data (Project Server - Resource Data.odc)
- Project Server - Risk Data (Project Server - Risk Data.odc)
- Project Server - Simple Projects List (Project Server - Simple Projects List.odc)
- Project Server - Timesheet Data (Project Server - Timesheet Data.odc)

I summarize the ODC utilization in the built-in reports and report templates in Table 18 - 5.

ODC	Template Name	Description
Project Server - Deliverables.odc	Dependent Projects	Visualizes Project to Deliverable relationships
Project Server - Issue Data.odc	Issues	Visualizes Issues data with related Projects and Tasks data
Project Server - Project Assignment Data.odc	Projects and Assignments	Visualizes Project, Task, Assignment, and Resource relationship data
Project Server - Project And Task Data.odc	Projects and Tasks	Visualizes Project and Task relationship data
Project Server - Resource Data.odc	Resources	Visualizes Resource information
Project Server - Risk Data.odc	Risks	Visualizes Risks data with related Project and Tasks data
Project Server - Timesheet Data.odc	Timesheet	Visualizes Timesheet data with related Project and Resource data
Project Server - Deliverables.odc	Deliverables	Visualizes Deliverable data
Project Server - Issue Data.odc Project Server - Risk Data.odc	Issues and Risks	Visualizes Issues and Risks data
Project Server - Project And Task Data.odc	Milestones Due This Month	Visualizes all milestones across all projects due this month
OData Assignments Data OData Issues Data OData Projects Data OData Risks Data OData Tasks Data	Project Overview Dashboard	Visualizes project summary information in a Dashboard format
OData Assignments Data OData Issues Data OData Projects Data OData Risks Data OData Tasks Data	Project Overview	Visualizes project summary information in a table format

ODC	Template Name	Description
OData Assignments Data OData Resources Data OData Tasks Data	Resource Overview	Visualizes resource allocations for all project resources
Project Server - Resource Capacity.odc	Resource Capacity	Visualizes timephased resource capacity for all resources
Project Server - Simple Projects List.odc	Simple Projects List	Visualizes a simple list of projects
Project Server - Timesheet Data.odc	Timesheet Actuals	Visualizes all timesheet entries and their current process state by time reporting period

Table 18 - 5: ODC Reference Table

The *English (United States)* folder also contains a sub-folder for each OLAP database, each containing 14 data connection files for connecting reports to each of the 14 OLAP cubes in the OLAP database:

- OLAP Assignment Non Timephased (OlapAssignmentNonTimephased.odc)
- OLAP Assignment Timephased (OlapAssignmentTimephased.odc)
- OLAP Deliverables (OlapDeliverables.odc)
- OLAP EPM Timesheet (OlapEpmTimesheet.odc)
- OLAP Issues (OlapIssues.odc)
- OLAP Portfolio Analyzer (OlapPortfolioAnalyzer.odc)
- OLAP Project Non Timephased (OlapProjectNonTimephased.odc)
- OLAP Project SharePoint (OlapMSProjectSharePoint.odc)
- OLAP Project Timesheet (OlapProjectTimesheet.odc)
- OLAP Resource Non Timephased (OlapResourceNonTimephased.odc)
- OLAP Resource Timephased (OlapResourceTimephased.odc)
- OLAP Risks (OlapRisks.odc)
- OLAP Task Non Timephased (OlapTaskNonTimephased.odc)
- OLAP Timesheet (OlapTimesheet.odc)

OData Overview

OData is a new way to access reporting data in Project Server 2013. OData is a web-based open standard protocol that works over http or https to query and retrieve data without requiring direct access to the SQL Server. OData is the only reporting access method available for Microsoft's Project Online installations. The OData feature in Project Server 2013 provides data in Atom, JSON and XML formats. The default is Atom, which Excel can consume.

OData provides several advantages to the SQL method of access. Using OData for data access enables both report authors and report viewers to use the same data access method. OData reduces the overhead of maintaining custom fields as custom fields are automatically included in the feed. Lastly, OData provides language-specific support based on the language code at the end of the Uniform Resource Identifier (URI). If you specify no language code, the system uses the base server language.

The EntitySets (or Data Feeds in OData parlance) are collections of data for a given entity. A URI provides access to these EntitySets and looks much like a URL to we humans, as a URL is a type of URI. You use the URI to query the ProjectData service to return information from the Project Server reporting database. The URI for the ProjectData service is as follows:

```
http://ServerName/ProjectServerName/_api/
ProjectData/[LanguageCode](optional)/DataEntityName/$operation(optional)
```

To retrieve the OData schema for the ProjectData service, use the following URI, which displays the XML file where you can view all the available Entity Types and their associated properties as shown in Figure 18 - 19.

```
http://ServerName/ProjectServerName/_api/ProjectData/[EN-US]/$metadata
```

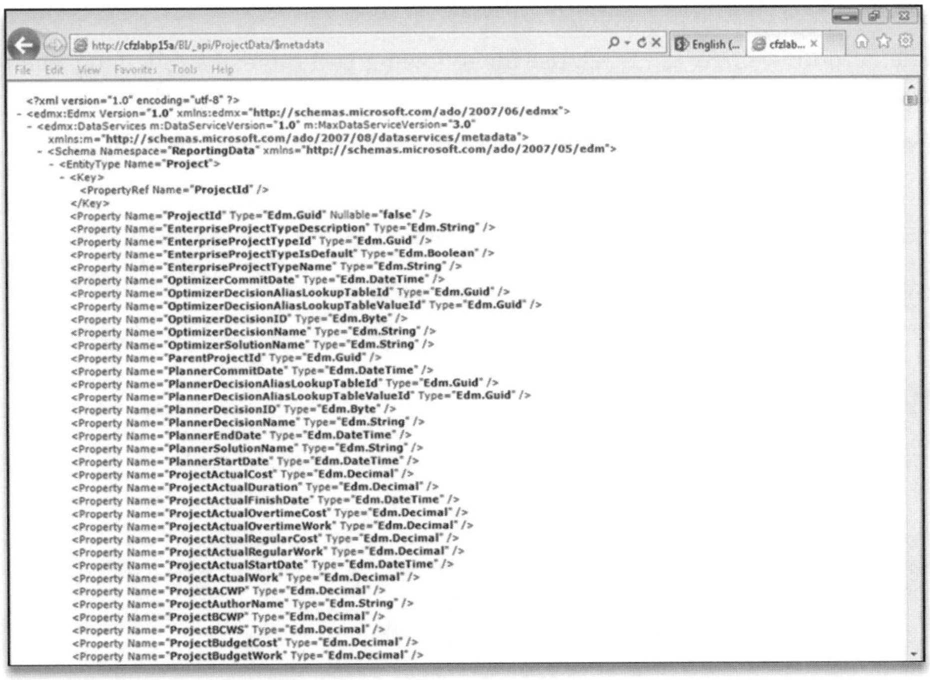

Figure 18 - 19: OData XML file - Project Entity Types

The list all the EntitySets (collections) of the ProjectData service, use the following URI:

```
http://ServerName/ProjectServerName/_api/ProjectData
```

Figure 18 - 20 shows the OData XML definition – EntityType Collections. This XML definition defines all the components of any project in the PPM system. For example, you can see by looking at the image that a project includes baselines, deliverables, issues, risks, and other elements.

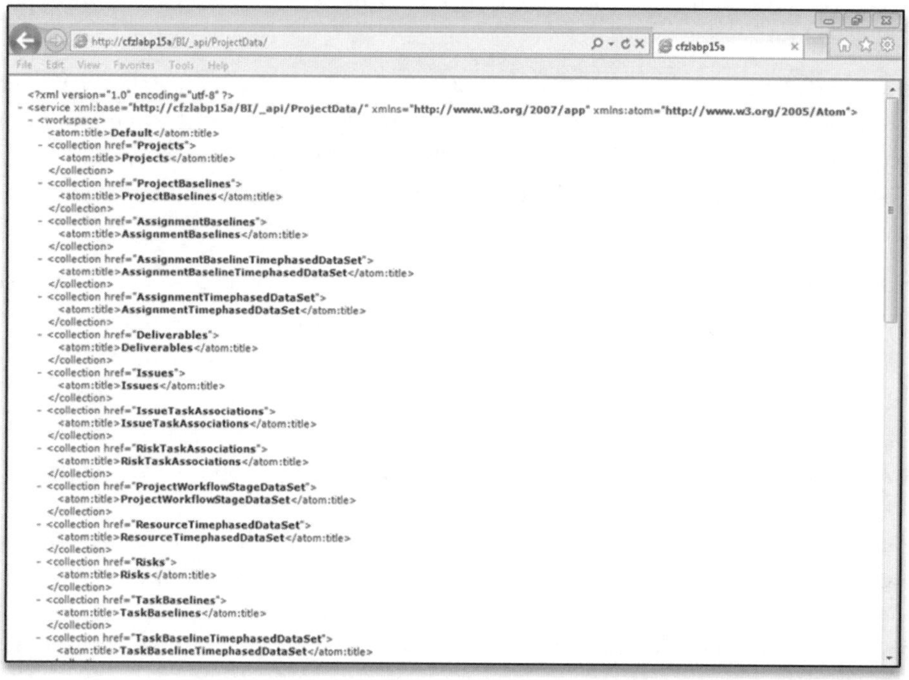

Figure 18 - 20: OData XML file - EntityType Collections

To retrieve the Data Feed for a single EntitySet, use the following URI (note: the following example retrieves the project's EntitySet).

```
http://ServerName/ProjectServerName/_api/ProjectData/[EN-US]/Projects
```

> **Information**: Entering this URI into a browser does not return any project information; it only displays the Data Feed. However, this can be very useful to test your syntax before you use the URI in Excel to retrieve external data. The data displays using this URI in an OData-aware tool such as Excel 2013.

OData EntitySets

OData enables access to the following Project Server 2013 EntitySet elements for the ProjectData service as shown in Table 18 - 6.

> **Information**: As of this writing, Microsoft has not completed the final reference. Refer to the following link for a complete list of EntitySets for the ProjectData service.
>
> http://msdn.microsoft.com/en-us/library/office/jj163048.aspx

OData EntitySet Name	Description
Assignments	Assignment details across all projects and resources
AssignmentBaselines	Assignment details for each baseline, across all projects and resources
AssignmentBaselineTimephasedData	Assignment baseline details by day for every existing baseline across all projects and resources
AssignmentTimephasedData	Assignment details by day across all projects and resources
BusinessDrivers	Business driver details and impact descriptions
BusinessDriverDepartments	Cross-reference of business drivers associated to specific departments
CostConstraintScenarios	Scenario summary information from the Optimizer for a given analysis
CostScenarioProjects	Project specific information for an Optimizer model, such as Project Force Status
Deliverables	Deliverable details across all projects
Issues	Issue details across all projects
PortfolioAnalyses	Describes the all of the core properties and characteristics of the Portfolio Analysis
PortfolioAnalysisProjects	Project specific information for a Portfolio Analysis such as priority and schedule constraints
Prioritizations	Prioritization session properties
PrioritizationDrivers	Business driver details and impact descriptions for a given prioritization
PrioritizationDriverRelations	Pairwise comparison data between business drivers
Projects	Project summary information
ProjectBaselines	Project baseline summary information
ProjectWorkflowStageDataSet	Workflow Phase and Stage status data across all projects
Resources	Resource summary
ResourceConstraintScenarios	Resource planner properties for a given scenario
ResourceScenarioProjects	Project specific information for a Resource Planner model
ResourceTimephasedDataSet	Resource capacity and work by day
Risks	Risk details across all projects
Tasks	Task details across all projects

OData EntitySet Name	Description
TaskBaselines	Task baseline details for every existing baseline across all projects and resources
TaskBaselineTimephasedDataSet	Task baseline details by day for every existing baseline across all projects and resources
TaskTimephasedDataSet	Task details by day across all projects
TimeSet	Time related information for fiscal period and calendar related questions
Timesheets	Timesheet summary information across all time reporting periods
TimesheetClasses	Cross-reference of timesheet classes by department
TimesheetLines	Timesheet line information across all timesheets for all time reporting periods
TimesheetLineActualDataSet	Timesheet line information by day across all timesheets for all time reporting periods
TimesheetPeriods	Time reporting period details

Table 18 - 6: OData EntitySets

Understanding the Toolset

Project Server 2013 has several Business Intelligence tools you can use to meet your needs. The primary tools covered in this topical section are the ones that project managers most commonly use.

Excel

The cornerstone of project reporting depends on Excel 2013 and its QueryTable/PivotTable/PivotChart functionality. You use Excel to author new reports, change existing reports, meet current needs, and view reports on your desktop. You use the Excel client exclusively to meet your personal Business Intelligence needs. Excel connects to the Project Server data stores via an ODC file that contains the connection string to the data source.

> **Information**: You cannot access OData using Excel 2010 without installing PowerPivot. You can download this add-on by visiting the Microsoft Download Center at *http://www.microsoft.com/downloads*. Power View is not available for Excel 2010.

Excel Services

Excel Services is a SharePoint functionality that enables you to publish and share Excel reports via a SharePoint site. When you create a report in the Excel client, it publishes the report through Excel Services. After you publish it, anyone with the appropriate security rights can use the interactive report. Once enabled on a SharePoint farm, a report author can host and render reports on any site within the farm. This flexibility provides project managers with the ability to customize reporting specific to the needs of each project that they manage.

The Business Intelligence Center

The Business Intelligence Center, a sub-site of your PWA site in the SharePoint hierarchy, organizes and provides immediate access to all of these report delivery tools in a single location. This site ties all of the BI tools together and provides a central point for a Project Server BI portal. The intent of the Business Intelligence Center is to provide a starting point for authors and to house BI content for *Enterprise* and *Collaborative* BI needs. The Business Intelligence Center also contains the central authorized library of all Office Data Connections used in the system.

Business Intelligence Center Security Overview

The Business Intelligence Center adheres to the SharePoint security model. It utilizes this model to grant people access to the site and all of its contents, and it utilizes the Secure Store Service to grant people access to the data in the Project Server BI relational data store.

Although a SharePoint sub-site typically inherits its security settings from its parent site (the PWA site, in this case), you can break the security inheritance and manage it separately using the SharePoint security model. If you must control access to specific items within the Business Intelligence Center site, such as specific report folders or individual reports within a folder, you can easily customize the SharePoint security permissions through the web interface. Having separate security also allows you to delegate Business Intelligence Center administrative duties to another person who is not a Project Server user.

Reporting Limitations

Microsoft recommends using Excel 2013 (preferred) or Excel 2010 as the primary tool to write reports for Project Server 2013. SharePoint 2013 can display Excel files so a user can view the report in a browser. Table 18 - 7 shows a list of the currently available data access methods and web-page refresh options when using Microsoft's Online (Office 365) services.

> **Warning**: In the RTM version of Project Server 2013, not all reports refresh without first opening them using Excel on the desktop client.

Online (Office 365)	
Report Types	**Can Refresh in the Browser?**
OData reports when displaying the Excel file in a browser	Yes
OData reports when displaying the Excel viewer web part	No
Reports accessing the database directly	No. You cannot access the database directly online.
Reports access the OLAP cube	No. There is no OLAP cube online.

Table 18 - 7: Data access and refresh capabilities and limitations when using Online (Office 365)

Table 18 - 8 shows a list of the currently available data access methods and web page refresh options when using an on-premises installation of Project Server 2013. To support most data refresh scenarios, you must use SQL Server 2012 Business Intelligence Center Edition or SQL Server 2012 Enterprise Edition.

On Premise (installed on your servers)	
Report Types	**Can Refresh in the Browser?**
OData Reports	No
Reports accessing the database directly	Yes
OLAP reports	Yes
Excel reports displayed using the Excel Web Part viewer in SharePoint	Partially. Direct SQL and OLAP work but OData does not. You should test using the web parts before committing them in your final design.

Table 18 - 8: Data access and refresh capabilities when using an on-premise installation

Preparing to View or Create Reports

Before you continue with this module, I highly recommend you prepare your workstation. Excel 2010 can read and create reports but you must install the *PowerPivot* add-on. While *Power View* is not necessarily required, I think it's important to have because this is the tool that allows you to join data. Therefore, I recommend you use Excel 2013 to create and view reports as the latest *Power View* and *PowerPivot* technologies are included in the base installation of the product. For this particular section, I use Excel 2013.

Best Practice: I recommend using Excel 2013 to create and manage reports for optimum use with SharePoint 2013 and Project Server 2013 reporting.

Enable Power View and PowerPivot for the first time

In order to connect to OData feeds, you run Excel 2013 and enable the *Power View* and *PowerPivot* add-ins. While these add-ins are an optional download for Excel 2010, they are now built in to Excel 2013. However, the system does not enable add-ins by default. Follow these steps to enable Power View and PowerPivot for the first time:

1. Log in to the workstation computer as an administrator. (Note anyone belonging to the *BIReportAuthors* group in SQL Server has rights to create reports.)
2. Press the **Windows** key on your computer keyboard and type *Excel 2013* to launch the *Excel 2013* program. The system displays the Excel *Backstage.*
3. Press the **Escape (Esc)** key on your computer keyboard. The system displays the Excel application.
4. Click the *File* ➢*Options* in the *Backstage.*

5. The system displays the *Excel Options* dialog shown in Figure 18 - 21. Click the *Add-Ins* tab located at the left of the dialog. The system displays the *View and manage Microsoft Office Add-ins* page. At the bottom of the page, click the *Manage* pick list, select the *COM Add-ins* item from the list and then click the *Go...* button.

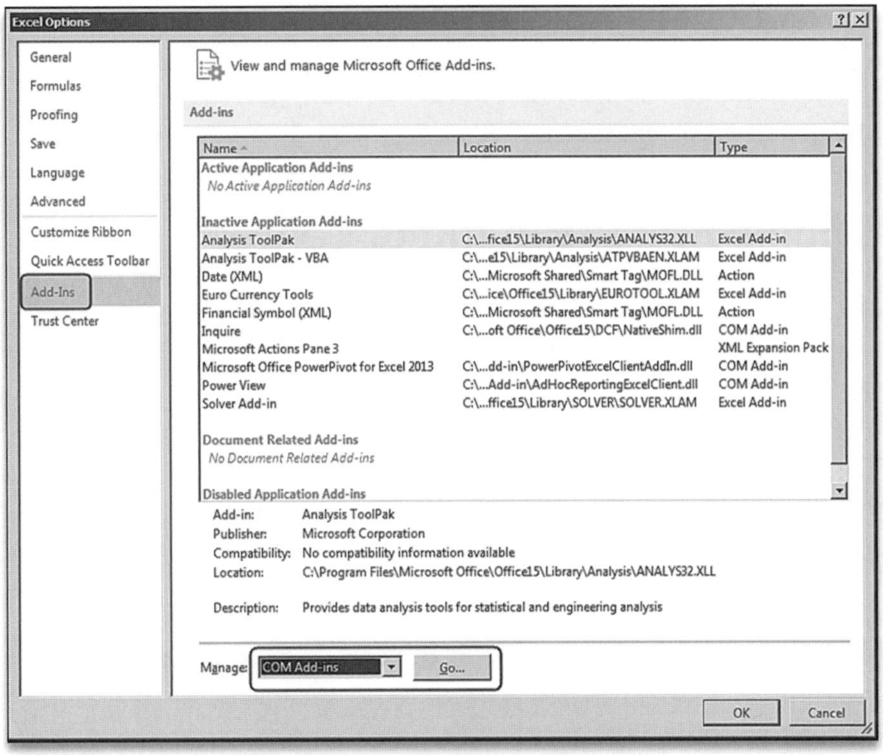

Figure 18 - 21: Excel Options dialog

6. The system displays the *COM Add-Ins* dialog shown in Figure 18 - 22. Select the *Microsoft Office PowerPivot for Excel 2013* and *Power View* options and then click the *OK* button.

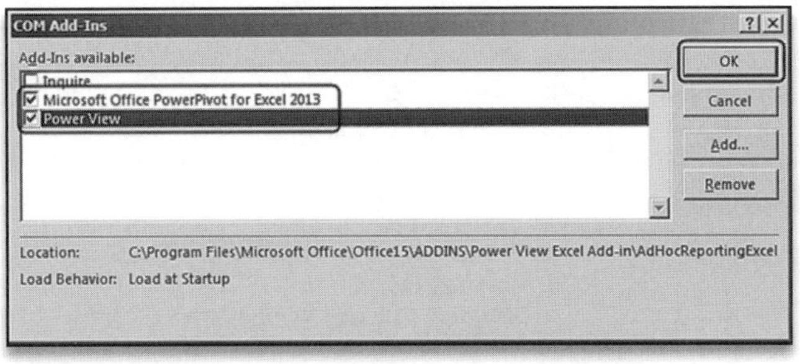

Figure 18 - 22: COM Add Ins dialog

7. In some circumstances where a computer may be limited in memory or other resources, the system may display the *Enable Power View Reports* dialog shown in Figure 18 - 23. If you receive this message, consider upgrading your computer with more memory and a more powerful processor. Click the *Continue* button.

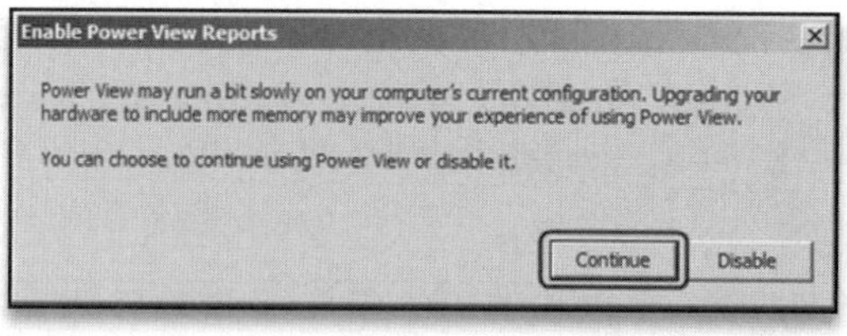

Figure 18 - 23: Enable Power View Reports dialog

8. Exit Excel 2013 so the system remembers your settings in the future.

Accessing Sample Reports in the BI Center

By default, all reports are stored in a *Reports* document library in PWA's BI Center (Business Intelligence Center). You can create your own document libraries or even create reports in other SharePoint sites but I recommend you consolidate your reports here. The BI Center supports multi-language reporting, and the sample *Reports* library contains a separate folder for each language pack that you configure for Project Server 2013. To access the BI Center, follow these steps:

1. Log in to PWA and click the *Reports* link on the *Quick Launch* menu.
2. The system displays the Business Intelligence Center home page shown in Figure 18 - 24. Click the *Reports* link on the *Quick Launch* menu one more time.

Figure 18 - 24: Business Intelligence Center - Navigate to sample Reports

3. The system displays the *Reports* page shown in Figure 18 - 25. To view the English language reports, click the *English (United States)* folder in the *Reports* library.

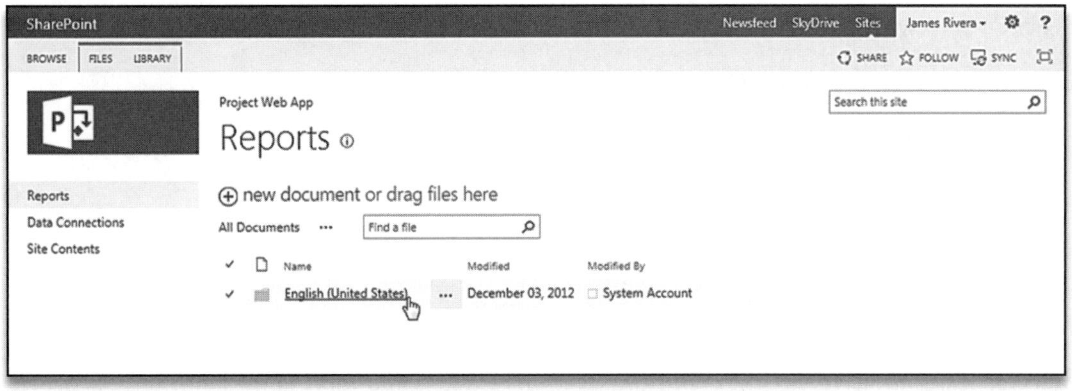

Figure 18 - 25: Select sample Reports folder by language

4. The system displays the sample *Reports* library shown in Figure 18 - 26.

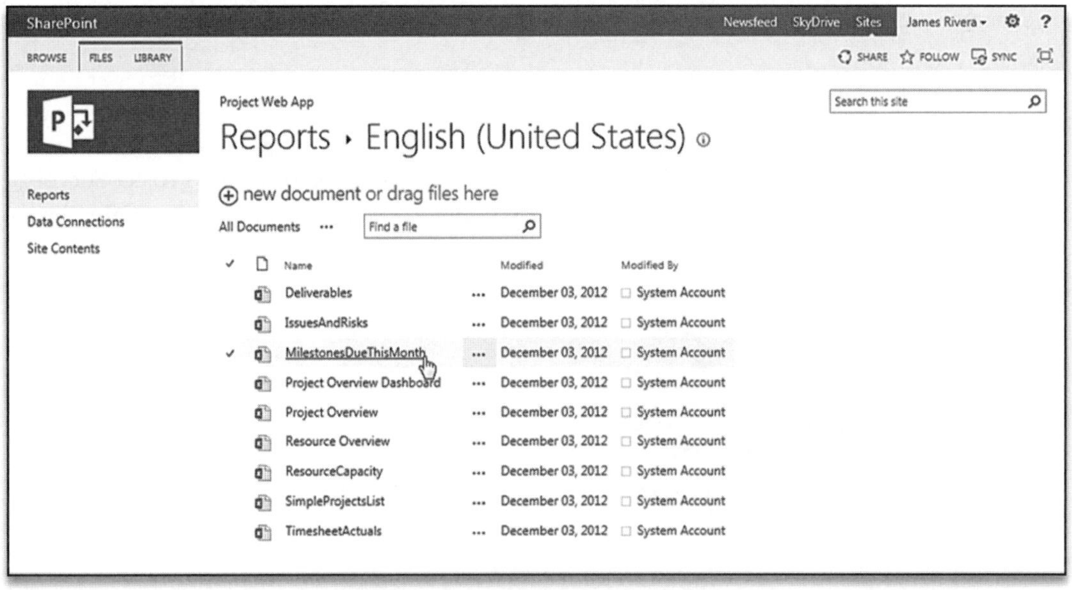

Figure 18 - 26: Select sample Report to view

Built-In Reports Overview

Project Server 2013 provides sample Excel reports that the system pre-connects to the Project Server reporting database through ODC and OData files saved in the Project Server BI relational data store. Microsoft intended that these reports provide the report author with a starting point for creating new reports. The system targets some of these reports to PMO usage scenarios and you can repurpose many of them for use on a specific project. The *Reports* library contains the following sample reports:

- Deliverables (Deliverables.xlsx)
- Issues and Risks (IssuesAndRisks.xlsx)
- Milestones Due This Month (MilestonesDueThisMonth.xlsx)
- Project Overview Dashboard (Project Overview Dashboard.xlsx)

- Project Overview (Project Overview.xlsx)
- Resource Overview (Resource Overview.xlsx)
- Resource Capacity (ResourceCapacity.xlsx)
- Simple Projects List (SimpleProjectsList.xlsx)
- Timesheet Actuals (TimesheetActuals.xlsx)

Accessing the Sample Reports

Before you access the sample reports, it is important to note that some reports may not refresh when you select them in the browser. I remain hopeful that Microsoft will enable these in future updates.

Information: You may receive error pages stating that the system cannot refresh reports, which is due to the limitations of OData refresh in SharePoint. If you receive this message, click the *Open in Excel* icon that appears on the page.

Deliverables Report

The *Deliverables* report extracts a listing of all Project Server 2013 deliverables from the Project Server BI relational data store and displays the data in an Excel PivotTable format in your web browser, as shown in Figure 18 - 27.

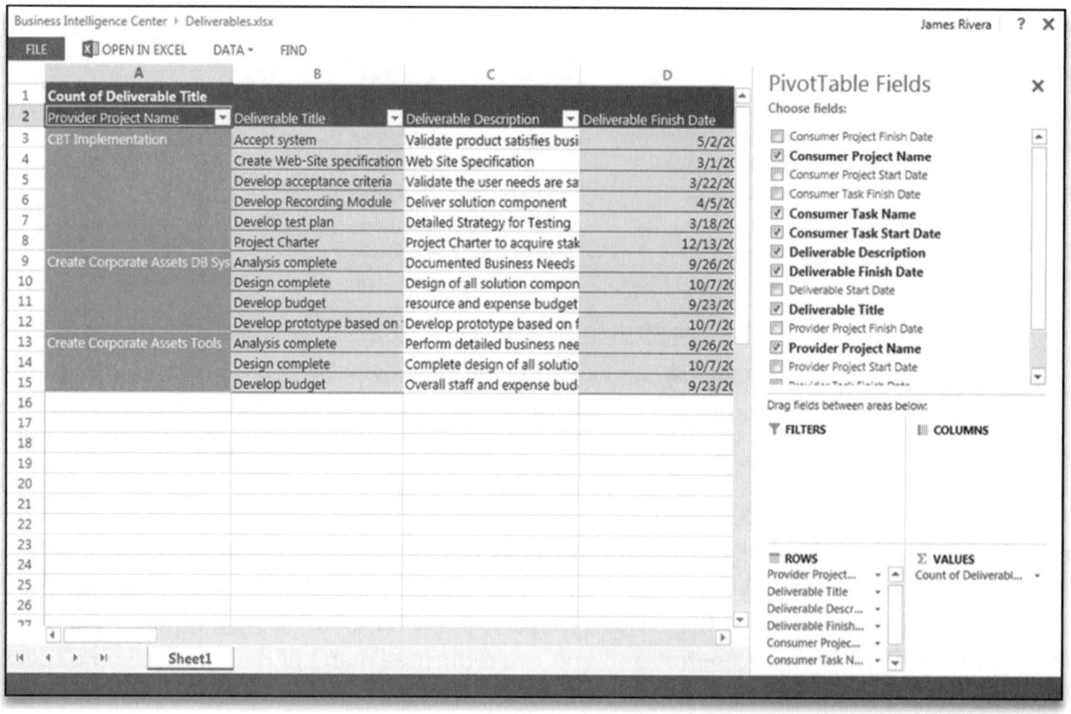

Figure 18 - 27: Deliverables report

Issues and Risks Report

The *Issues and Risks* report extracts a listing of all Project Server issues and risks from the Project Server BI relational data store and displays the data in Excel PivotTable format in your web browser, as shown in Figure 18 - 28 and Figure 18 - 29.

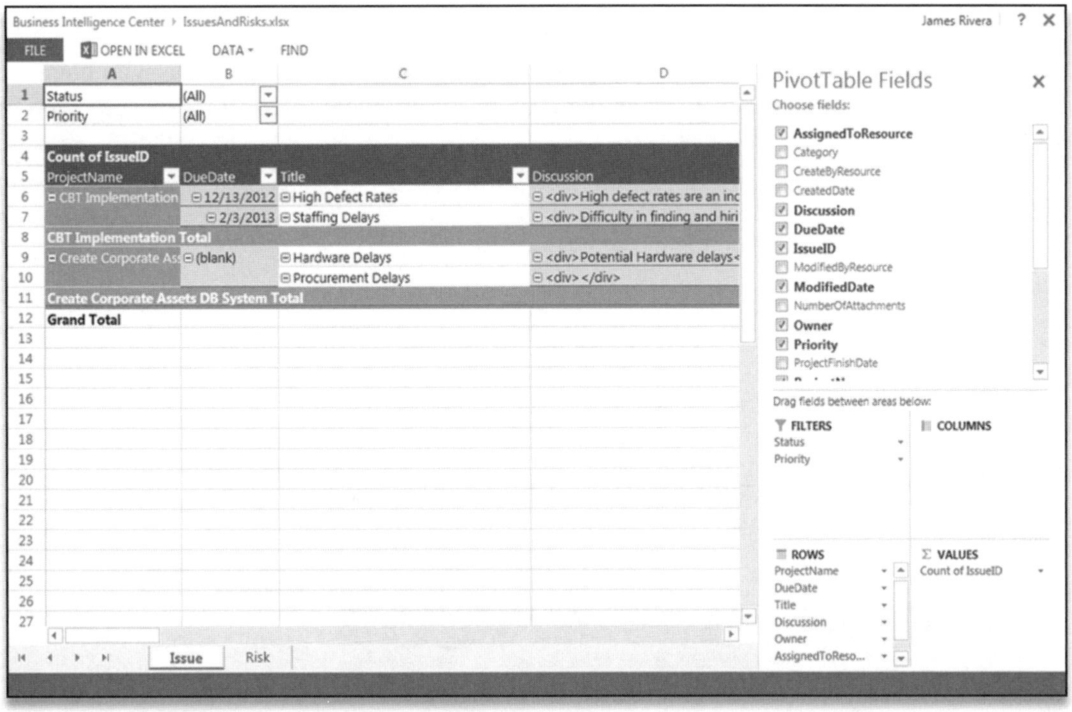

Figure 18 - 28: Issues and Risks report, Issue tab

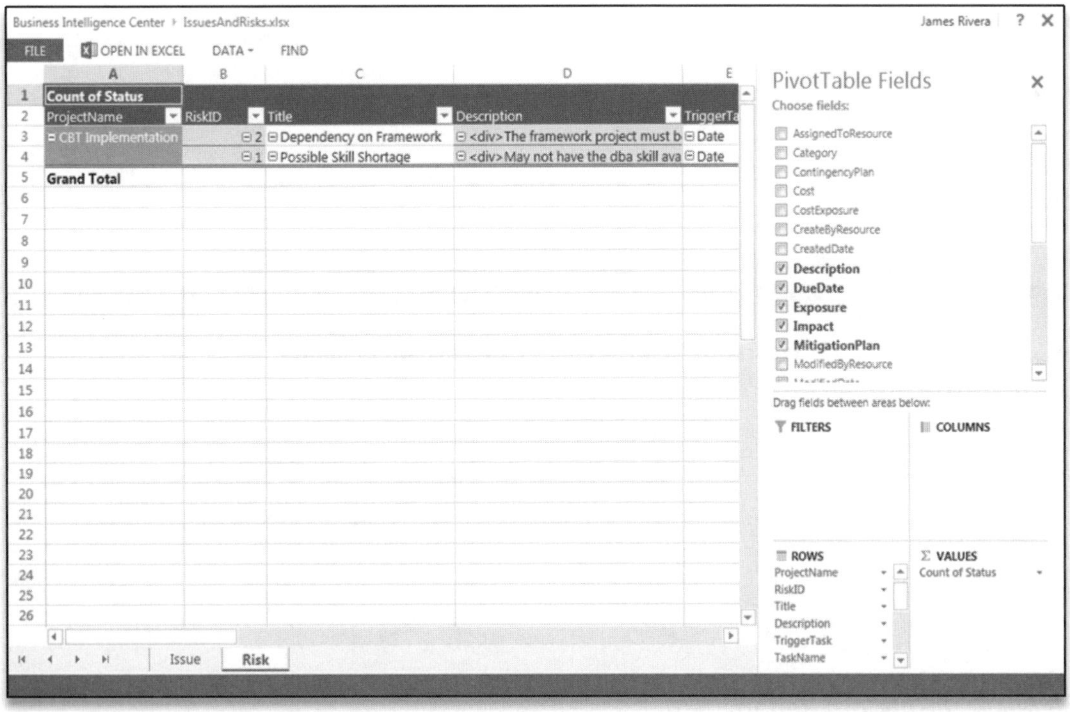

Figure 18 - 29: Issues and Risks report, Risk tab

Milestones Due This Month Report

The *Milestones Due This Month* report extracts a listing of all Project Server milestones that you have scheduled to complete during the current month and displays the data in Excel PivotTable format in your web browser, as shown in Figure 18 - 30.

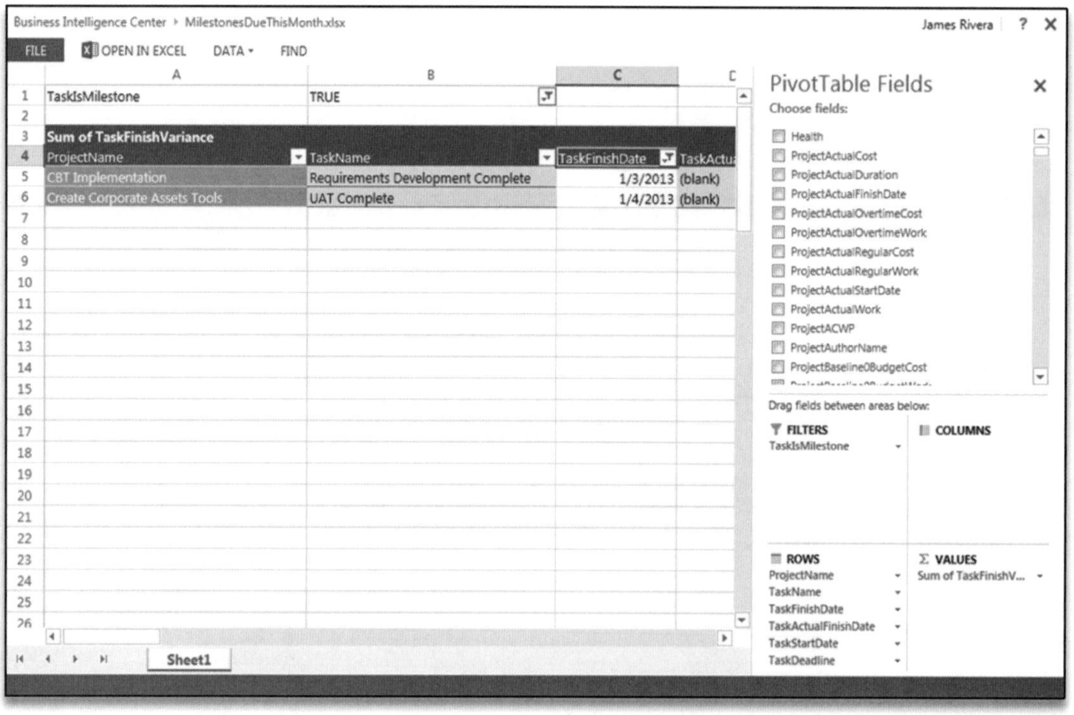

Figure 18 - 30: Milestones Due This Month report

Project Overview Dashboard Report

The *Project Overview Dashboard* report provides a summary view of the Project Server projects from the Project Server BI relational data store and displays the data in Excel 2013 Power View PivotChart, as shown in Figure 18 - 31.

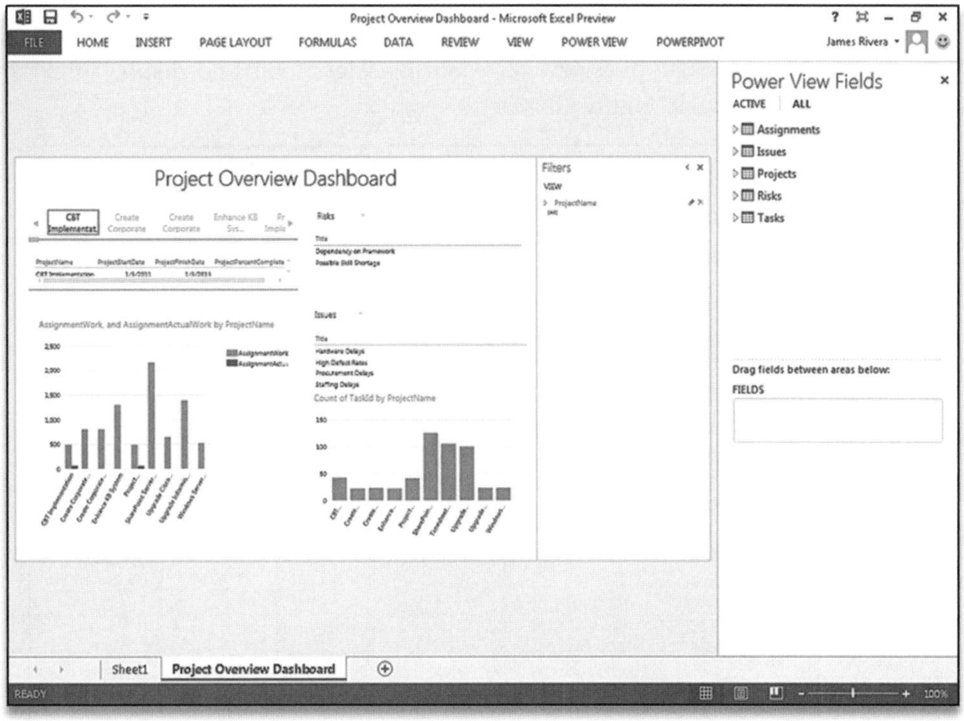

Figure 18 - 31: Project Overview Dashboard report

Project Overview Report

The *Project Overview* report provides an overview of project progress for all projects from the Project Server BI relational data store and displays the data in Excel PivotChart format in Excel 2013, as shown in Figure 18 - 32.

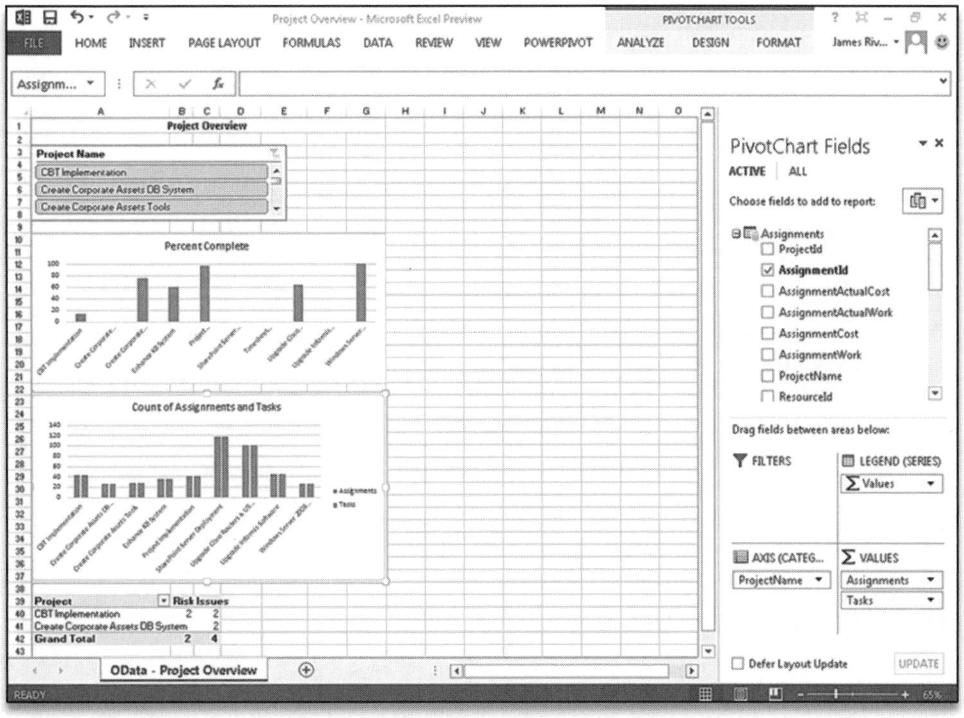

Figure 18 - 32: Project Overview report

Resource Overview Report

The *Resource Overview* report provides an overview of resource assignments and displays the data in Excel PivotChart format in Excel 2013, as shown in Figure 18 - 33.

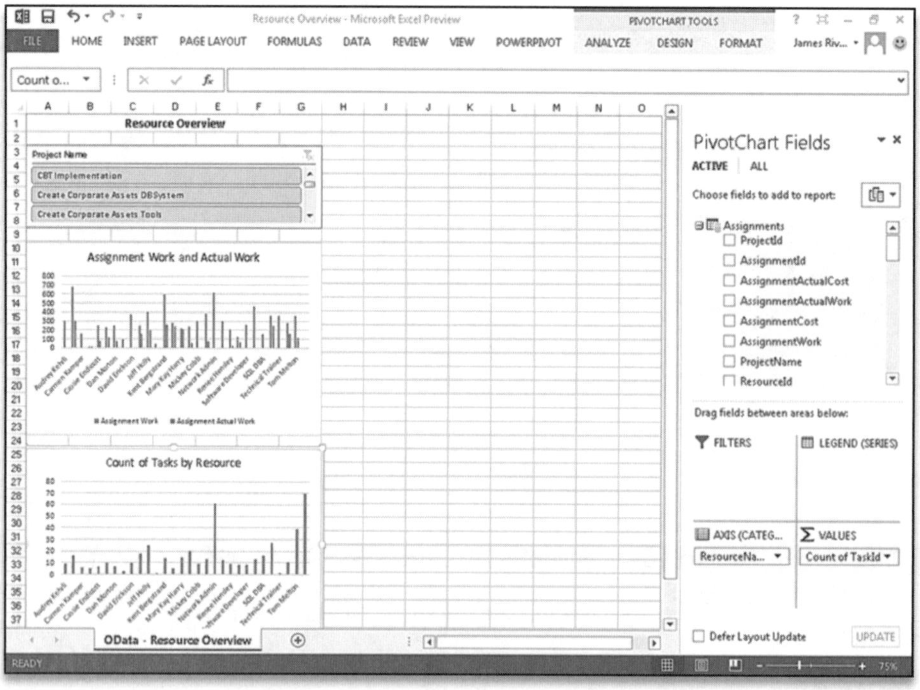

Figure 18 - 33: Resource Overview report

Resource Capacity Report

The *Resource Capacity* report extracts a listing of all Project Server resource capacities and displays the data in Excel PivotTable and PivotChart format in your web browser, as shown in Figure 18 - 34 and Figure 18 - 35.

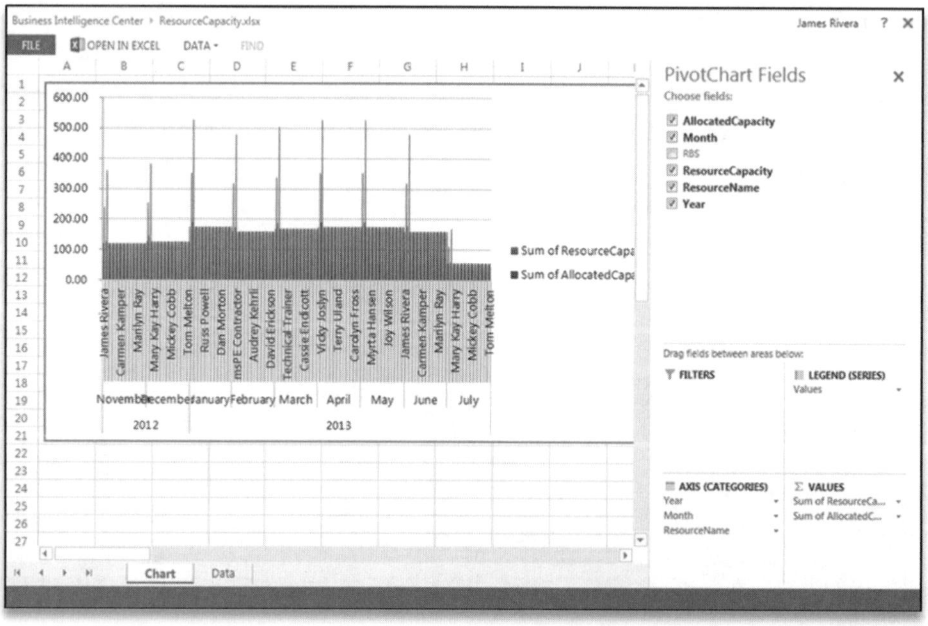

Figure 18 - 34: Resource Capacity report, chart tab

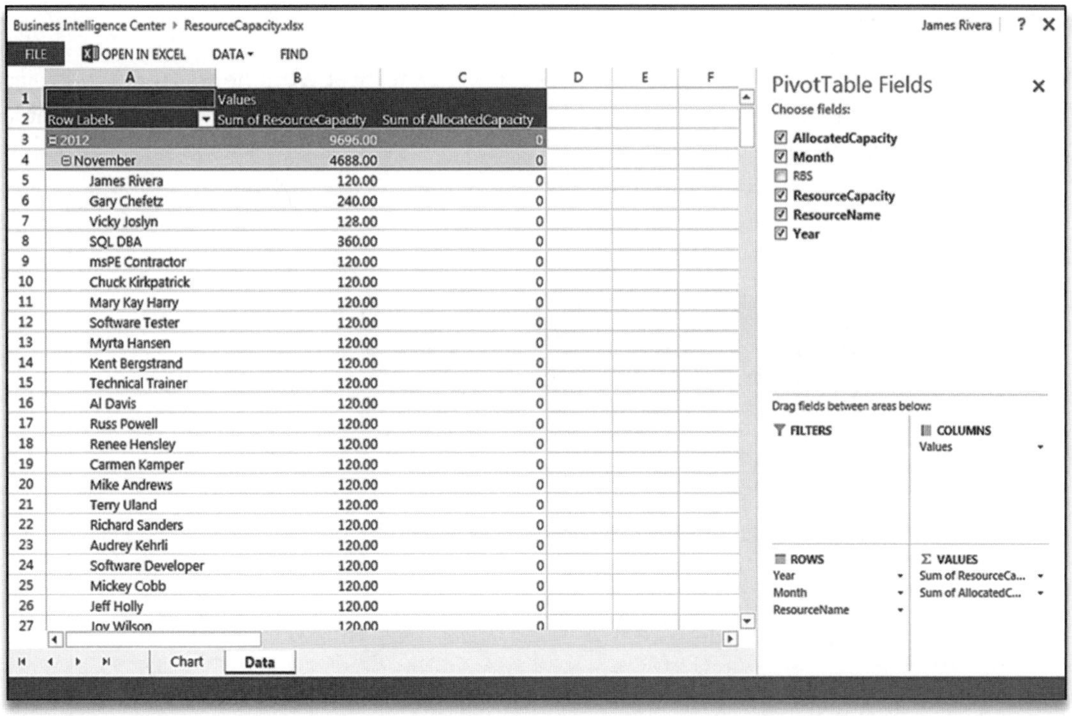

Figure 18 - 35: Resource Capacity report, data tab

Simple Projects List Report

The *Simple Projects List* report extracts a listing of all Project Server projects from the Project Server BI relational data store and displays the data in Excel PivotTable format in your web browser, as shown in Figure 18 - 36.

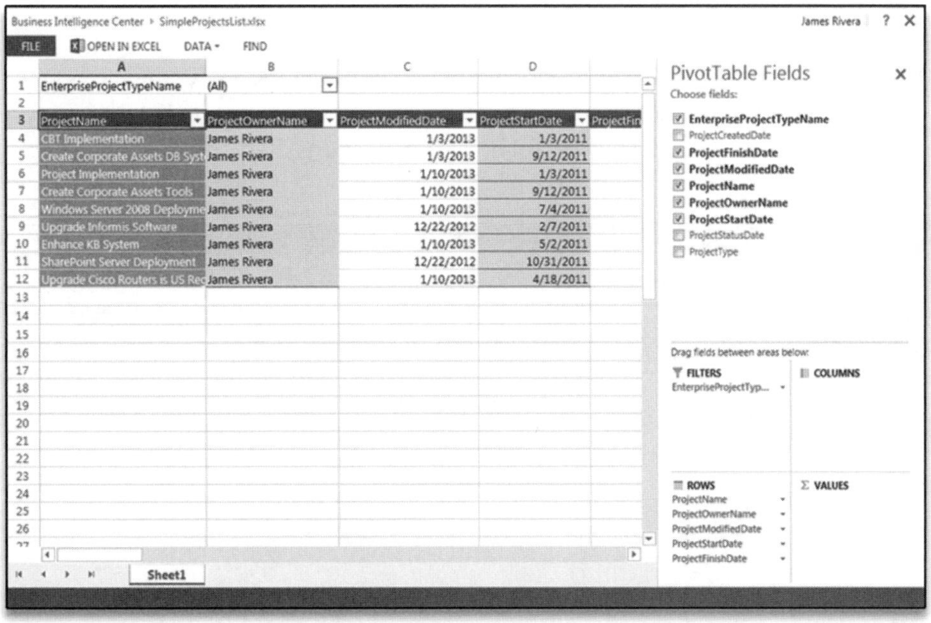

Figure 18 - 36: Simple Projects List report

Timesheet Actuals Report

The *Timesheet Actuals* report extracts a listing of all Project Server timesheet work hours from the Project Server BI relational data store and displays the data in an approval process step grouping, in Excel PivotTable format in your web browser, as shown in Figure 18 - 37.

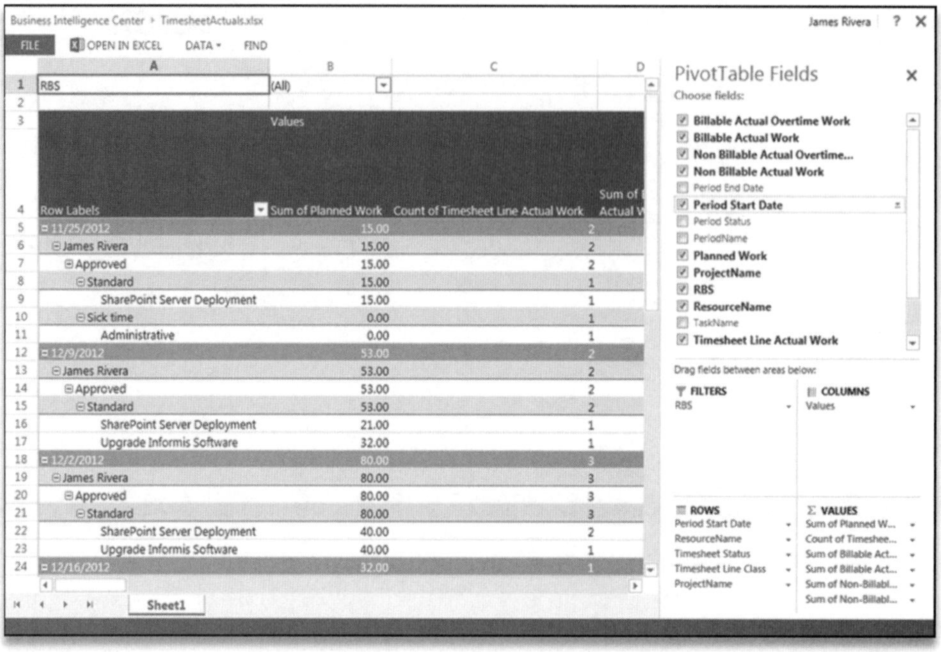

Figure 18 - 37: Timesheet Actuals report

About Report Templates

Project Server 2013 provides you with Excel report templates that use the ODC files to connect you quickly to your data. To view these report templates, from the Business Intelligence Center click the *Site Contents* link in the *Quick Launch* menu, then click the *Templates* folder. The system displays the *Templates* page shown in Figure 18 - 38.

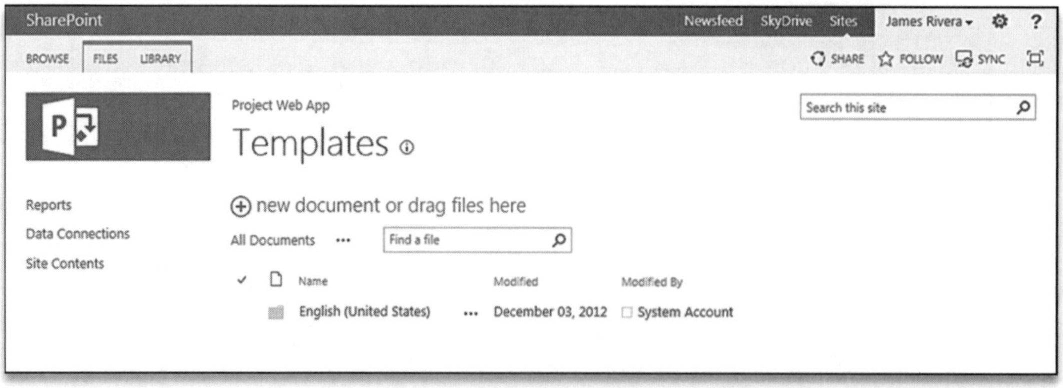

Figure 18 - 38: Templates page

The Business Intelligence Center supports multi-language reporting, and the *Templates* library contains a separate folder for each language pack that you provision for your Project Server database. To view the English language reports, click the *English (United States)* folder in the *Templates* library. The system displays the contents of the *English (United States)* folder as shown in Figure 18 - 39.

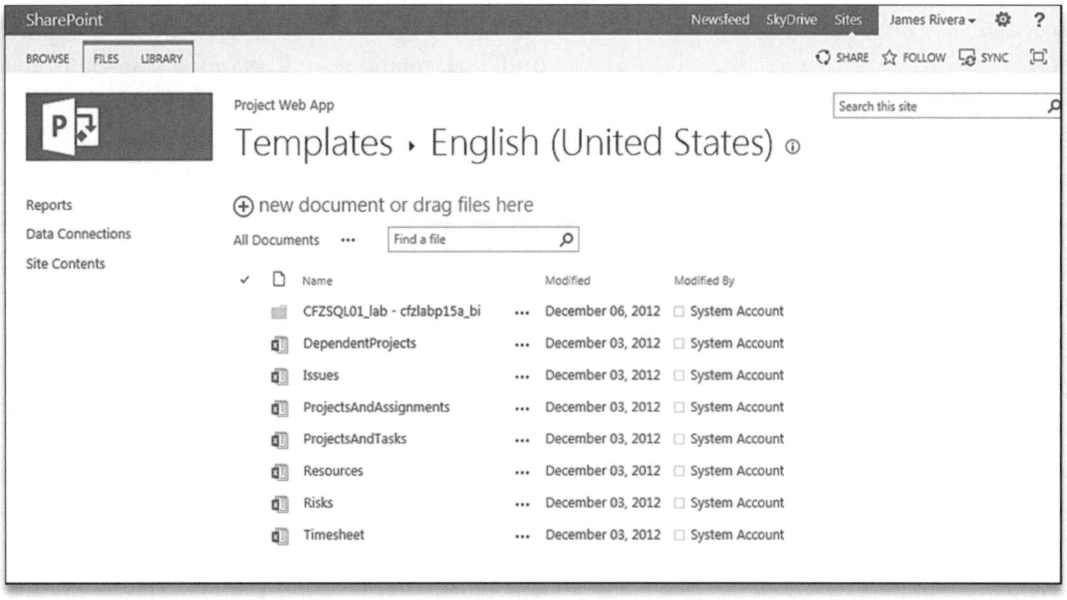

Figure 18 - 39: English language folder contents in the Templates library

The Excel report templates help you build new reports quickly. You can use these as starting points to develop your own custom reports. The system provides templates for each language available on the server.

The *English (United States)* folder contains seven report templates that arrive pre-connected to the Project Server BI relational data store as shown in Table 18 - 9.

Report Name	File	Description	Example Use
Dependent Projects	DependentProjects.xltx	Visualizes Project to Deliverable relationships	Report of projects, which have a dependency on your published deliverables
Issues	Issues.xltx	Visualizes Issues data with related Projects and Tasks data	Report of active issues by assigned resource across your projects
Projects and Assignments	ProjectsAndAssignments.xltx	Visualizes Project, Task, Assignment, and Resource relationship data	Report of projects and tasks by assigned resource in a given RBS node

Report Name	File	Description	Example Use
Projects and Tasks	ProjectsAndTasks.xltx	Visualizes Project and Task relationship data	Task analysis comparing planned start dates to actual start dates
Resources	Resources.xltx	Visualizes Resource information	Breakdown of Resource Standard Rates organized by Resource Breakdown Structure value
Risks	Risks.xltx	Visualizes Risks data with related Project and Tasks data	Average risk exposure by project
Timesheet	Timesheet.xltx	Visualizes Timesheet data with related Project and Resource data	Audit report comparing timesheet entered hours to planned hours

Table 18 - 9: Built-In Report Template Descriptions

Every time you create a new OLAP database, the system automatically creates another folder in the *Templates* library containing an additional 14 report templates for that new OLAP database. Each folder contains 14 templates pre-connected to each of the 14 OLAP cubes in each OLAP database as shown in Table 18 - 10.

Report Name	File	Description	Example Use
OLAP Assignment Non-Timephased	OlapAssignmentNonTimephased.xltx	Visualizes point in time Assignment data with related Project, Task and Resource data	Current Actual Cost total by project
OLAP Assignment Timephased	OlapAssignmentTimephased.xltx	Visualizes Assignment data over time with related Project, Task, and Resource data	Current Actual Cost total by project by month
OLAP Deliverables	OlapDeliverables.xltx	Visualizes Deliverable data	Count of projects consuming my project's deliverables

Report Name	File	Description	Example Use
OLAP EPM Timesheet	OlapEpmTimesheet.xltx	Visualizes Timesheet data with related Task, Project, and Resource data	Timesheet entries by project by month
OLAP Issues	OlapIssues.xltx	Visualizes Issue data	Active Issues for a particular vendor across projects
OLAP Portfolio Analyzer	OlapPortfolioAnalyzer.xltx	Visualizes Assignment and Resource data over time with related Project, Task, and Resource Plan data	Resources by project which have Resource Plan allocations
OLAP Project Non-Timephased	OlapProjectNonTimephased.xltx	Visualizes point in time Project data	Projects and Remaining Work grouped by Region custom field
OLAP Project SharePoint	OlapProjectSharePoint.xltx	Visualizes point in time Project data with related Risk, Issue, and Deliverable data	Project Summary with Issue, Risk, Deliverable counts, and Overall Risk Exposure
OLAP Project Timesheet	OlapProjectTimesheet.xltx	Visualizes Project data over time with related Resource, Timesheet, and Task measures	Analyze Capacity against Timesheet entries and Actual Work on Tasks against Capacity over time
OLAP Resource Non-Timephased	OlapResourceNonTimephased.xltx	Visualizes point in time Resource cost data	Standard rate and Overtime rate of all resources grouped by RBS
OLAP Resource Timephased	OlapResourceTimephased.xltx	Visualize Resource capacity data over time	Resource Capacity for Quarter 4 2011 by Skill resource custom field

Report Name	File	Description	Example Use
OLAP Risks	OlapRisks.xltx	Visualizes Risk data	List of risks across all projects, which have an exposure of 5 days or more
OLAP Task Non-Timephased	OlapTaskNonTimephased.xltx	Visualizes point in time Task data	Overallocated non-summary, active tasks across all projects
OLAP Timesheet	OlapTimesheet.xltx	Visualizes Timesheet data	Planned and actual administrative time by month

Table 18 - 10: Built-In OLAP Template Descriptions

Information: Note that the file extension for the Excel report templates is *.xltx, rather than *.xlsx, indicating that they are Excel template files.

Warning: When saving a report created from an Excel report template, verify that you have changed the file extension to *.xlsx. Otherwise, it will not render in Excel Services.

Interacting with Reports

In my organization Marian is a project manager who tracks project progress by milestones. Aware that there is a *Built-In* report that shows this information, she navigates to the sample *Reports* folder and selects the *MilestonesDuethisMonth* report. After a few seconds, Marian sees the report shown in Figure 18 - 40. If Marian receives an error that the system cannot refresh the data, she clicks the *Open in Excel* icon in the toolbar. From the report, Marian sees that there are several milestones across multiple projects that are due within the next few weeks.

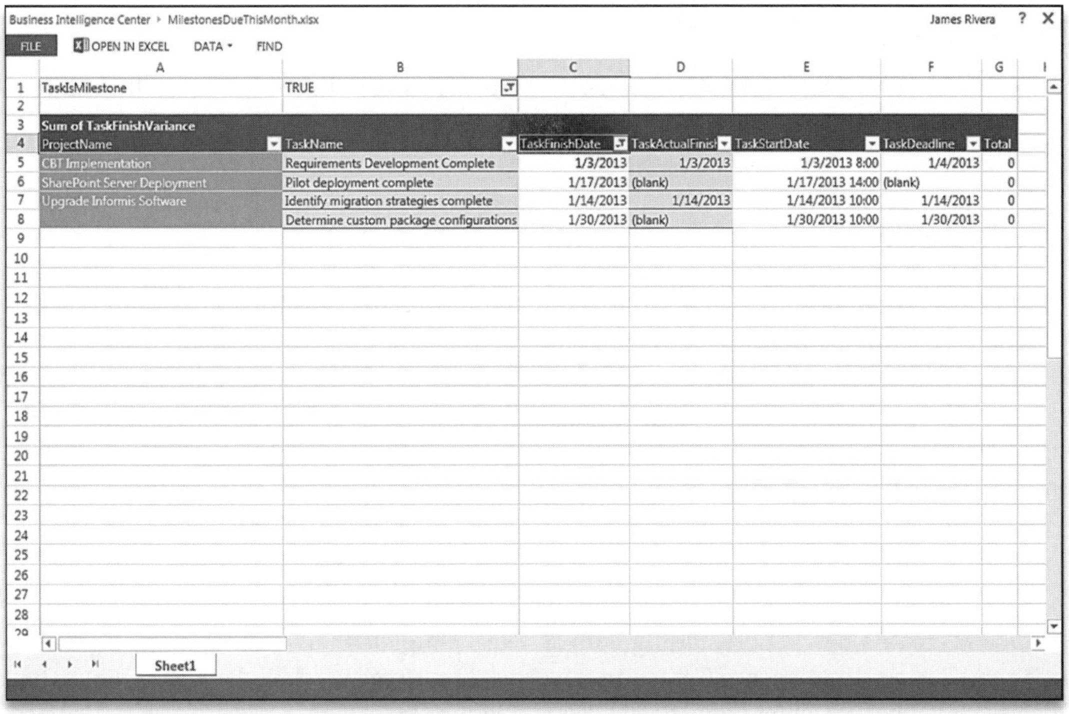

Figure 18 - 40: Web view of sample Report

Marian is also interested in viewing the milestones that are due next month, so she selects the *TaskFinishDate* filter pick list and selects the date filter for *Next Month* as shown in Figure 18 - 41.

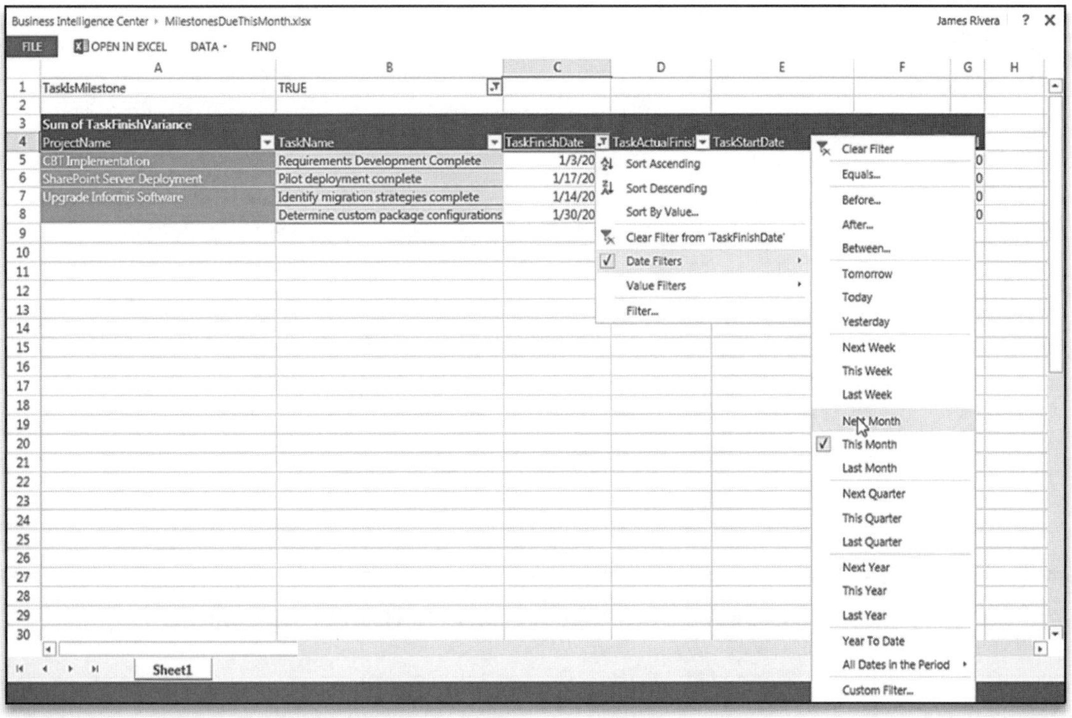

Figure 18 - 41: Example of Web Interactivity

Creating a Report from a Template

Creating a report from a template in Excel involves the three key steps shown in Figure 18 - 42. I cover each of these steps in detail in this topical section.

Open the Excel Template

Figure 18 - 42: High Level Edit Process

In the first step, you create a new report starting with an Excel template that you find in the Business Intelligence Center. To visit the Business Intelligence Center, in the *Quick Launch* menu, click the *Reports* link. The system displays the Business Intelligence Center home page shown in Figure 18 - 43.

Figure 18 - 43: Business Intelligence Center - Navigate to Site Contents

To visit the *Templates* library, click the *Site Contents* link to display the *Site Contents* page. Click the *Templates* tile as shown in Figure 18 - 44.

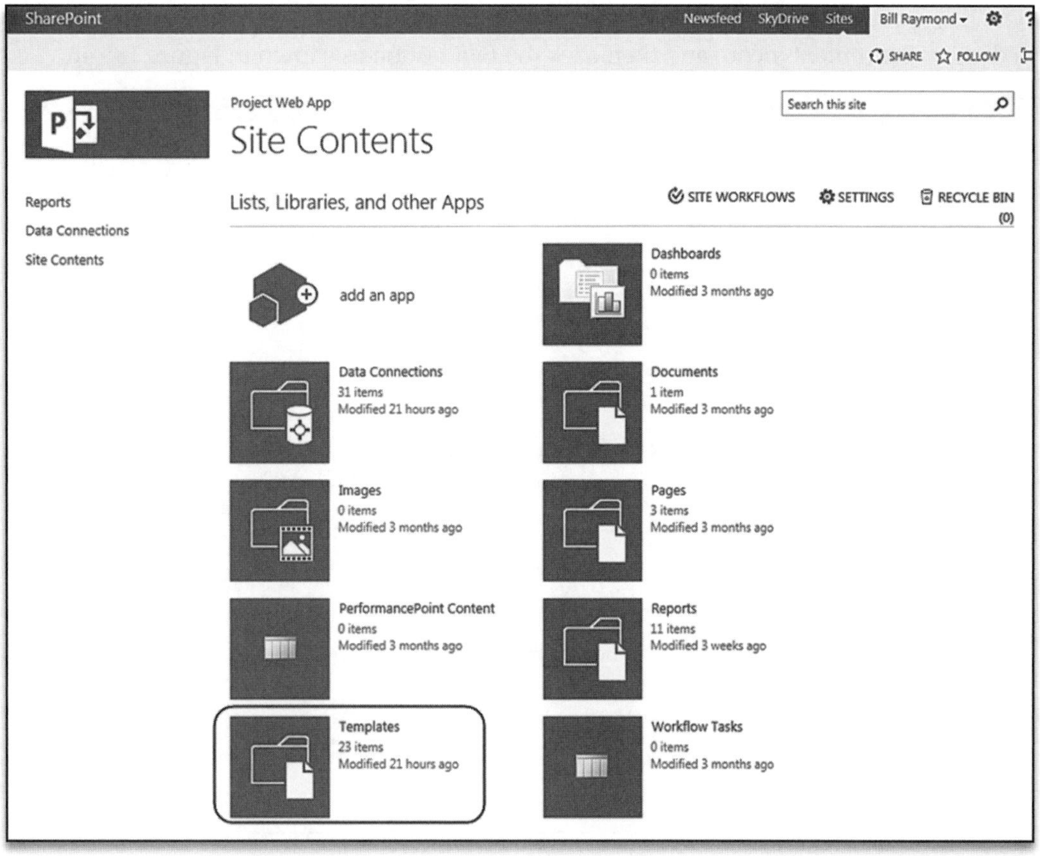

Figure 18 - 44: Site Contents page

The Business Intelligence Center supports multi-language reporting, and the *Templates* library contains a separate folder for each language pack that you configure for Project Server 2013. To view the English language reports, click the *English (United States)* folder in the *Templates* library as shown in Figure 18 - 45.

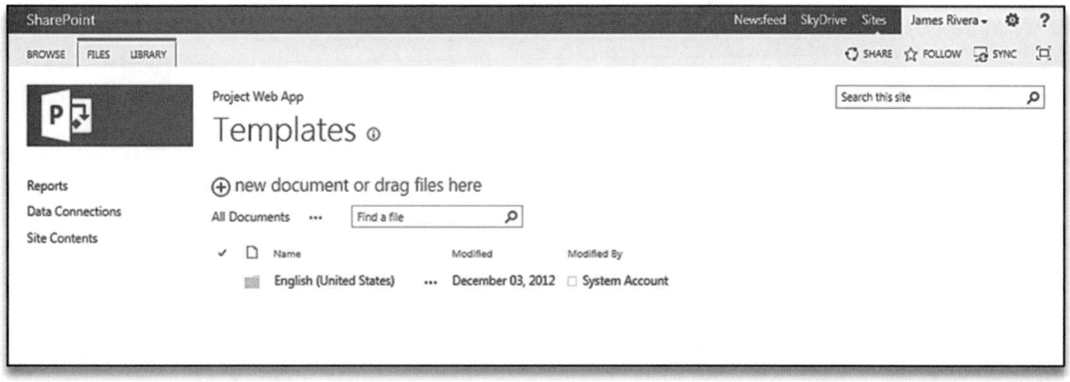

Figure 18 - 45: Templates Folder - Open Language Folder

Once you select the appropriate template for creating your report, click the ellipsis button (…) next to the template name to display the context menu, and then click the *Edit* button as shown in Figure 18 - 46.

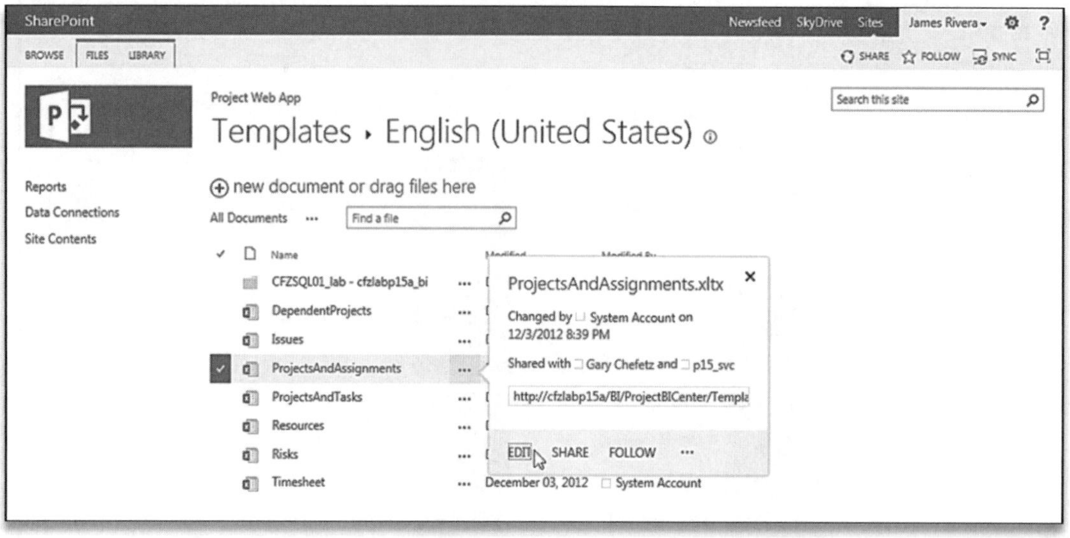

Figure 18 - 46: Edit Template in Microsoft Excel

The Business Intelligence Center prompts you with a security warning as shown in Figure 18 - 47. This prompt allows you to cancel the template "open" process in case you opened this file accidentally. Click the *Allow* button to continue the process and open the Excel client.

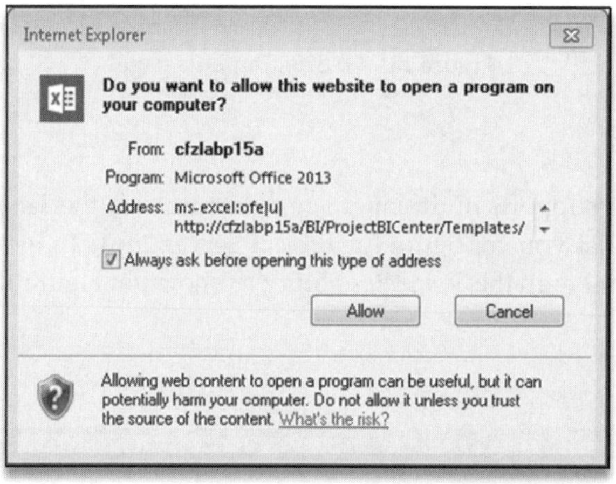

Figure 18 - 47: Open Document Confirmation

Depending on your system security configuration, Excel may disable data connections as a security precaution. This prevents you from accidentally opening a malicious file from the Internet. However, you must enable data connections for the template if you want to create a report.

The system prompts you with two warnings as shown in Figure 18 - 48 and Figure 18 - 49. Click the *Enable Content* button and Project Server 2013 presents you with the third security warning to make this a trusted document. As you are likely to use this template again, click the *Yes* button to make this template trusted and to begin writing your report.

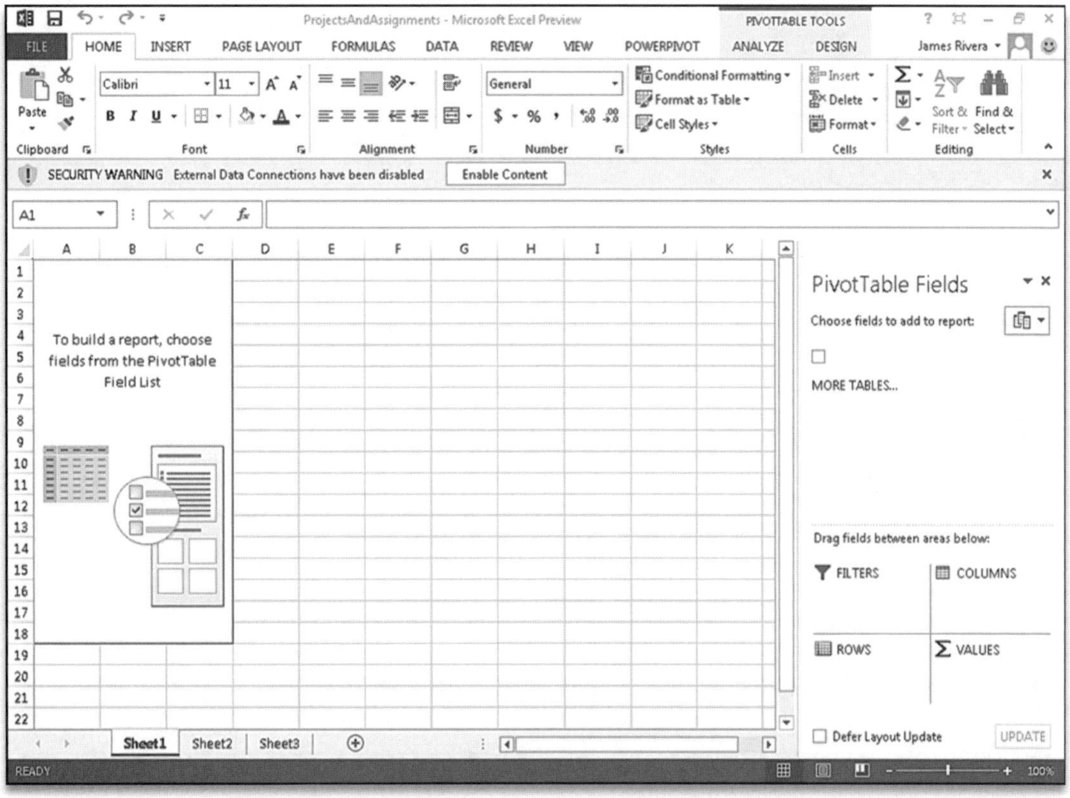

Figure 18 - 48: Data Connection Security Warning

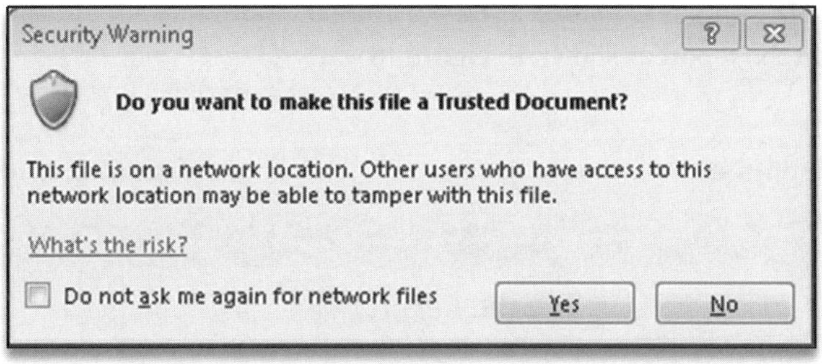

Figure 18 - 49: Make Template a Trusted Document

As the template continues to open, a series of messages appears in the Excel status bar, indicating that Excel is connecting to the data source. After a few seconds, you see the empty PivotTable shown in Figure 18 - 50, where you will begin creating your report.

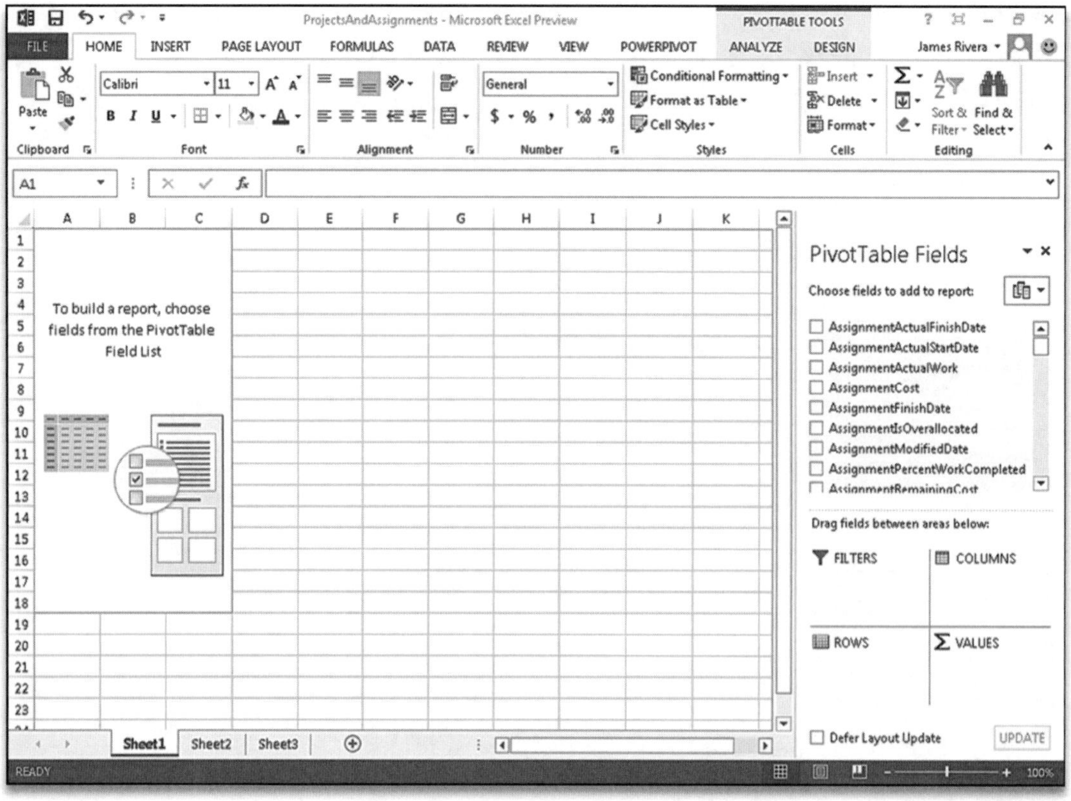

Figure 18 - 50: Template prior to making modifications

Edit the Report

In the second step, you edit the report as shown in Figure 18 - 51.

Figure 18 - 51: High Level Edit Process

The *PivotTable Fields* list is on the right side of the Excel template and is composed of six components, which you should understand in order to write a report. Figure 18 - 52 shows the list of available data fields for your report. The list is in alphabetical order to make it easier to find the data field you need. Product-generated data field names begin with the name of the data entity to which it belongs. For example, all project-related data fields have a name starting with Project. Therefore, Project Name is *ProjectName* in the list.

Figure 18 - 52: PivotTable Field List

Typically, you want to filter your data for relevancy to your report user. Report filters enable you to customize the data presented in the report. The *Filters* area, as shown in Figure 18 - 53, is where you designate fields as report filters. Any data field in this area appears above the PivotTable and acts as a filter for the report. While there are other ways to filter a report, this method is a good way to make common report filters very visible to the report user. To specify a data field as a report filter, drag the data fields from the *Field* list into this area as shown in Figure 18 - 53.

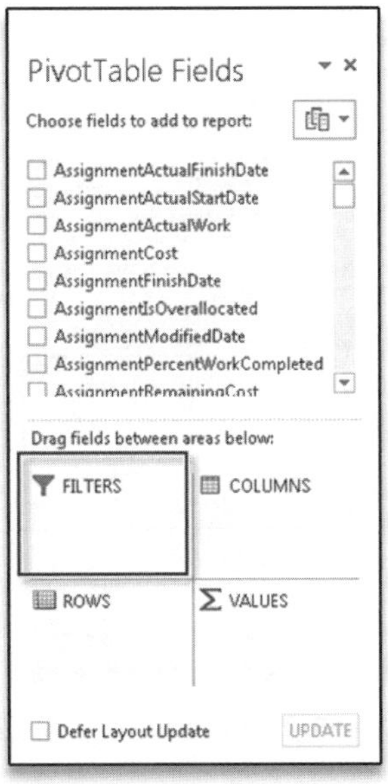

Figure 18 - 53: PivotTable Report Filters fields

To designate which data fields appear in the row, you must drag them into the *Rows* area as shown in Figure 18 - 54. The order of the data fields in this area determines where the field appears in the row. For example, if the topmost field is *ProjectOwnerName*, then *ProjectOwnerName* will be the left-most field in the report row. If you need to reorder the fields, you can drag them around in the *Rows* area.

Figure 18 - 54: PivotTable Report Rows

In some cases, you may need to create a *Cross-tabulation* or *Cross-tab* report. A *Cross-tab* report has both rows and columns where the intersection of the two values has meaning. A common column use is a time series where you need to show totals by month or by quarter. To designate a data field as a column, you drag it into the *Columns* area shown in Figure 18 - 55.

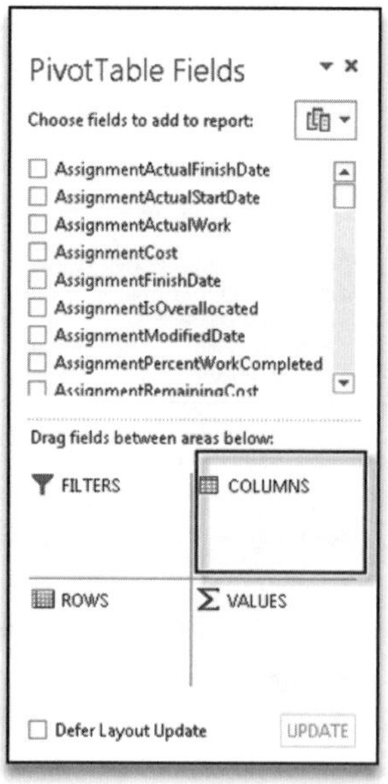

Figure 18 - 55: PivotTable Report Columns

If your report requires totals or averages of a particular data field, you should place that data field in the ∑ *Values* area as shown in Figure 18 - 56. Fields in this area should be numeric or date type fields since you can only aggregate those field types.

Figure 18 - 56: PivotTable Calculated Values

Each time you make a change in these four areas, the report re-queries the database. If your report queries a large dataset, this behavior may not be desirable. At the very bottom of the *PivotTable Fields* list is a checkbox and button, as shown in Figure 18 - 57. Selecting the *Defer Layout Update* option defers the data refresh process until you tell Excel to do so. This is very handy if you are making many changes or are creating a new report. To update the data once you make your changes, click the *Update* button. Deselecting the *Defer Layout Update* option returns the report to its normal behavior.

Figure 18 - 57: PivotTable Defer Layout Setting

Warning: In order to perform the steps outlined in this topical section, you must be a member of the Active Directory group that your organization uses for report authors.

Publish the Report

In the third step, you publish to SharePoint as shown in Figure 18 - 58.

Figure 18 - 58: High Level Edit Process

In order to make a report accessible to others, you publish the report to a SharePoint site by selecting the *Save As* option as shown in Figure 18 - 59. From the *Backstage,* you can publish to the SharePoint site where the report is currently saved by selecting the location displayed under the *Current Folder* section or you can publish to a recently accessed SharePoint site by selecting a location displayed under the *Recent Folders* section. The *Save* command saves the report to SharePoint but does not give you any additional options.

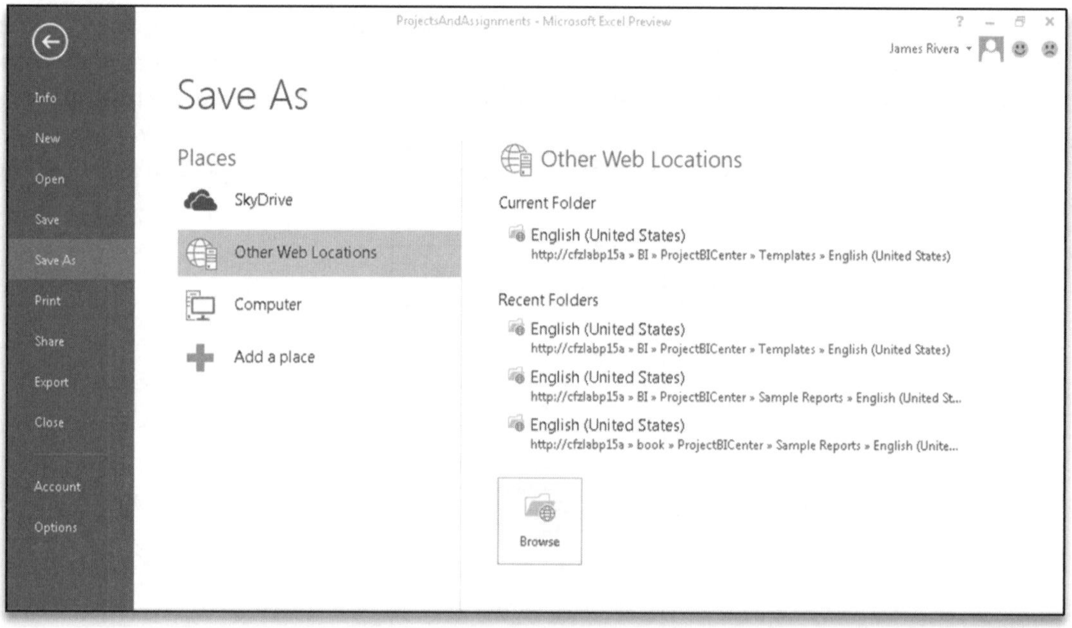

Figure 18 - 59: Publish to SharePoint with Save As

To publish a report, follow these steps:

1. Click the *File* ➤*Save As* in the *Backstage.*
2. Select the *Other Web Locations* item.
3. Click the *Browse* button and the *Save As* dialog appears as shown in Figure 18 - 60.

Because you opened a template from the *Templates* folder, Excel attempts to publish your report there by default. Do not save reports in the *Templates* folder.

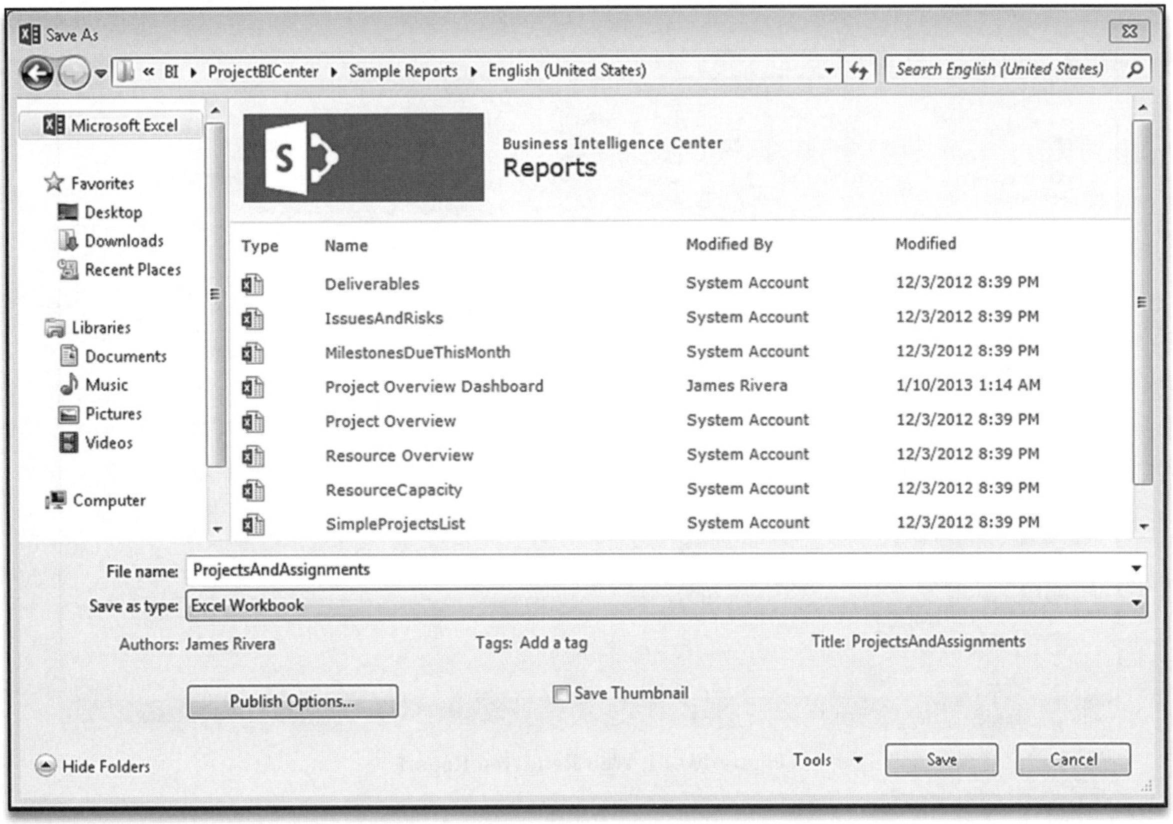

Figure 18 - 60: Browse to a Location dialog

4. Save your file to the following directory:

http://[*YourServerName*]/pwa/ProjectBICenter/Sample%20Reports/English%20(United%20States)/

5. Rename your report with a unique name.

6. In the *Save as type* field, select the *Excel Workbook* item.

7. Click the *Save* button.

To view the report, navigate to the SharePoint library where you saved the report and select the report to display in the browser. You will see a screen similar to Figure 18 - 61.

> **Warning**: You must change your *Save as type* field to Excel Workbook prior to saving! Otherwise, you will be saving a template to the BI Center, which will not render in the browser. Remember, to view a report in the browser, your file requires the .xlsx extension, not the .xltx extension.

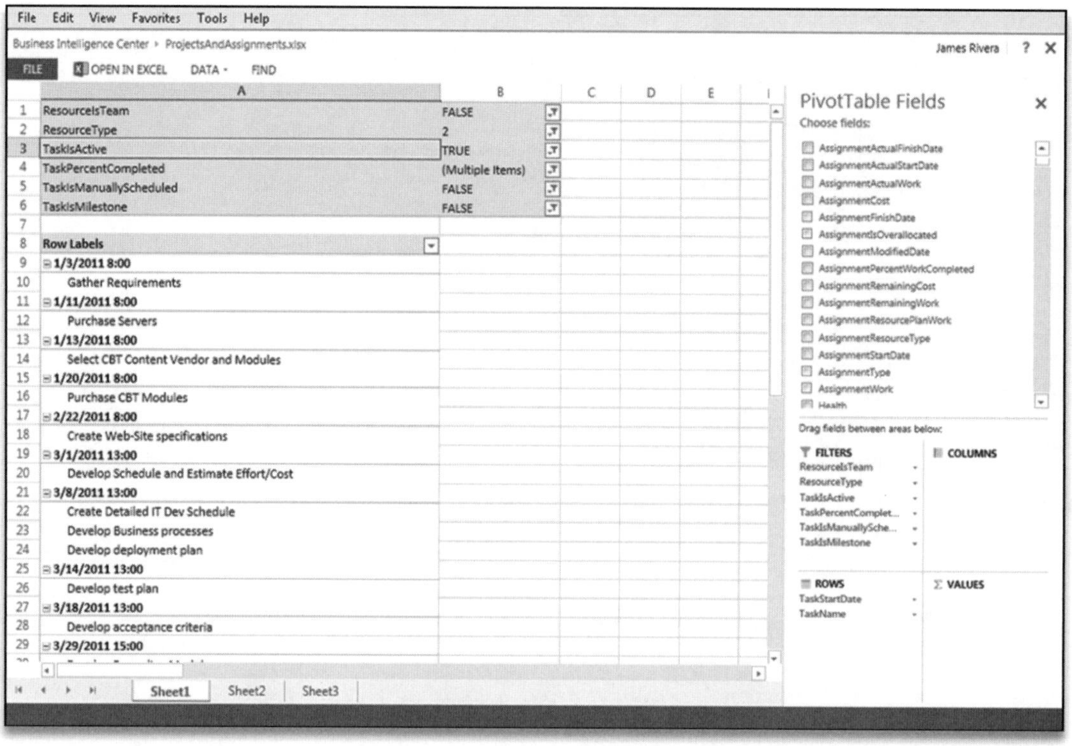

Figure 18 - 61: Web Rendered Report

Creating a New Report Using an OData ODC Connection

The Business Intelligence Center contains several Office Data Connection (ODC) files that Microsoft pre-installed and configured to use the OData service to retrieve data from an external data source such as the Project Server reporting database. When you connect the ODC file to an Excel workbook, you make the OData service available as a **Data Feed** within the Excel workbook. Connecting the ODC file to the Excel workbook involves the three key steps shown in Figure 18 - 62. I cover each of these steps in detail in this topical section.

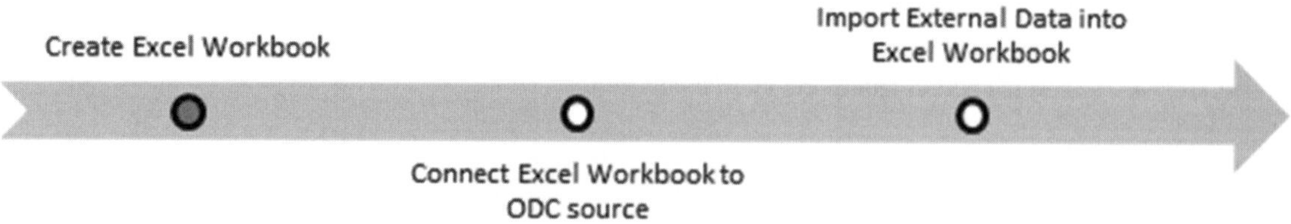

Figure 18 - 62: High Level Create Process

Create Excel Workbook

In the first step, you create a blank Excel workbook. Open Excel from your desktop by selecting the icon from the appropriate folder on the *Start* menu. Excel opens and displays the *Backstage* as shown in Figure 18 - 63.

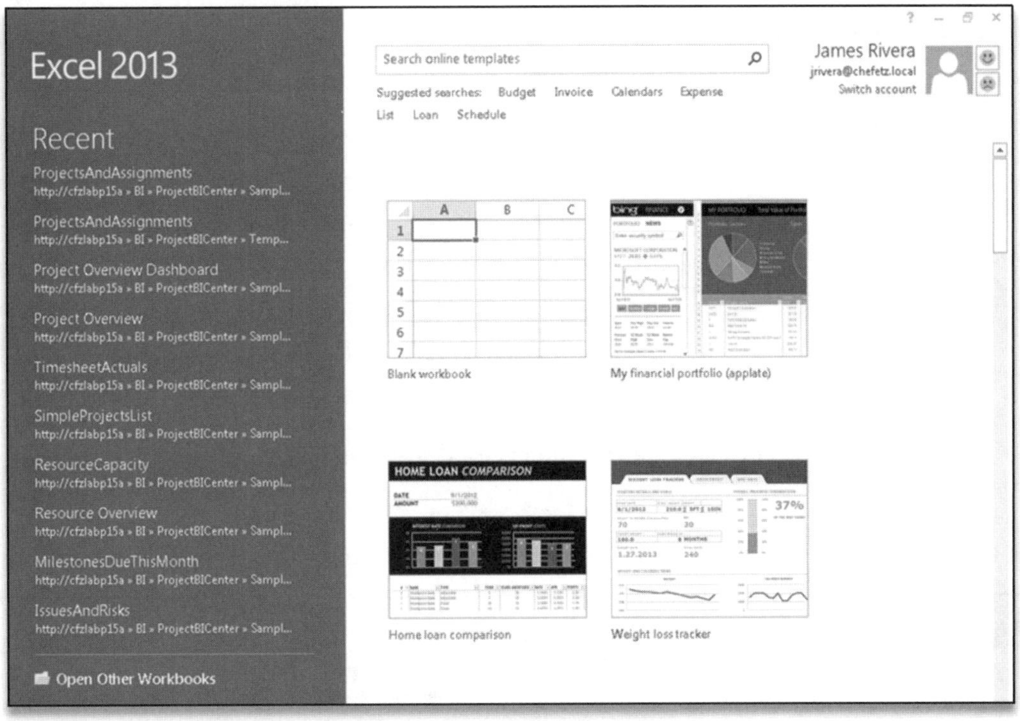

Figure 18 - 63: Excel Backstage

To create a blank workbook, click the *Blank workbook* link in the *Backstage*. Excel displays the blank workbook shown in Figure 18 - 64 and names it *Book 1 – Microsoft Excel Preview,* indicating that this is the first blank workbook created during the current Excel session.

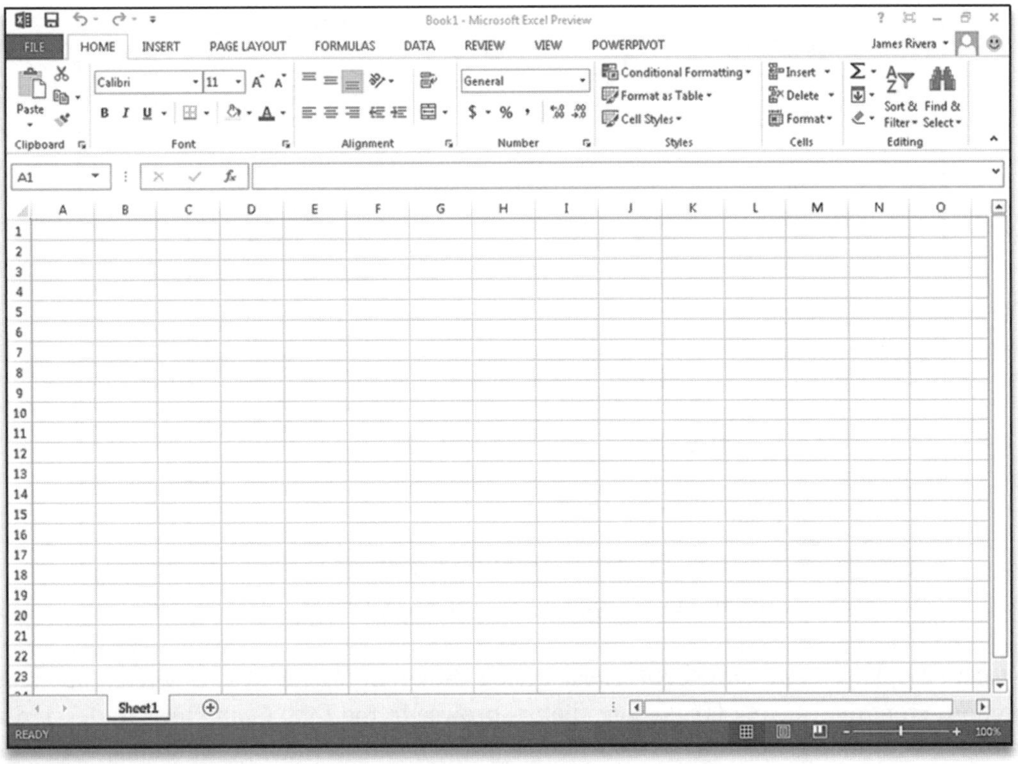

Figure 18 - 64: Blank Excel Workbook

Connect Excel Workbook to ODC Source

In the second step, as shown in Figure 18 - 65, you create a connection to an existing ODC source file in the *Data Connections* library in the Business Intelligence Center.

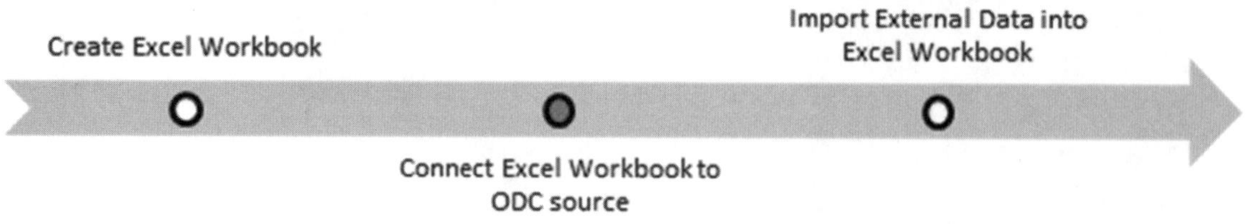

Figure 18 - 65: High Level Create Process

1. In the *Connections* section of the *DATA* ribbon, click the *Connections* button as shown in Figure 18 - 66.

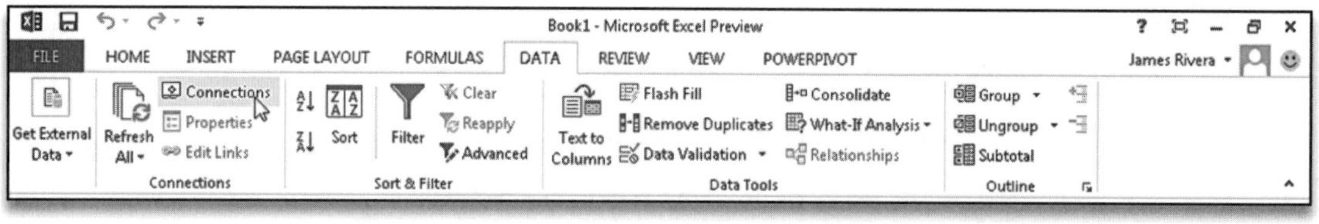

Figure 18 - 66: Connection button on Data ribbon

2. The system displays the *Workbook Connections* dialog shown in Figure 18 - 67. To add a new connection, in the dialog, click the *Add* pick list and select the *Add to the Data Model…* item.

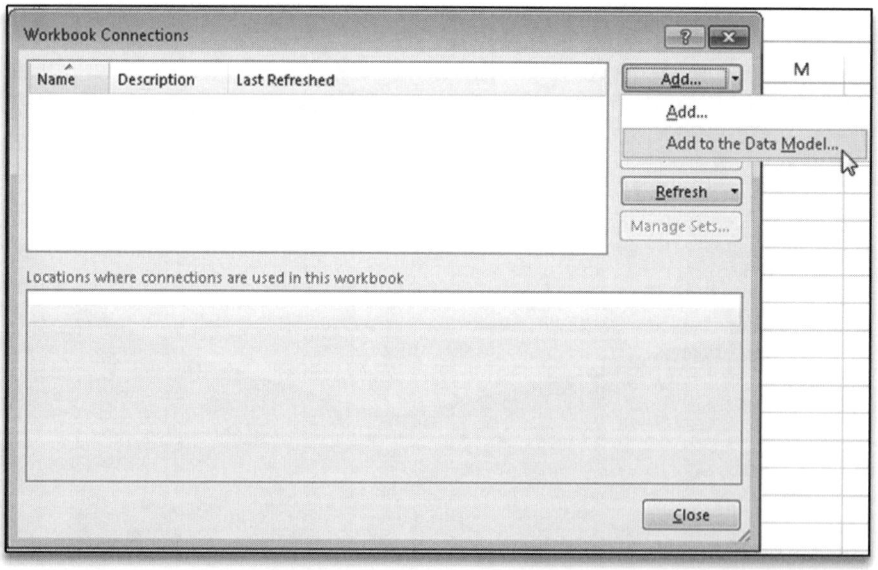

Figure 18 - 67: Workbook Connections dialog Add to the Data Model

3. The system displays the *Existing Connections* dialog shown in Figure 18 - 68 where you create your new connection. From the *Existing Connections* dialog, browse to the *Data Connections* folder and select an existing ODC file from the *Data Connections* library in the Business Intelligence Center. Click the *Browse for More…* button.

Information: When adding the connection using the *Add to Data Model...* option, the system creates an OData Data Feed in the PowerPivot window that you can use to create data models, PowerPivot tables, and PivotCharts.

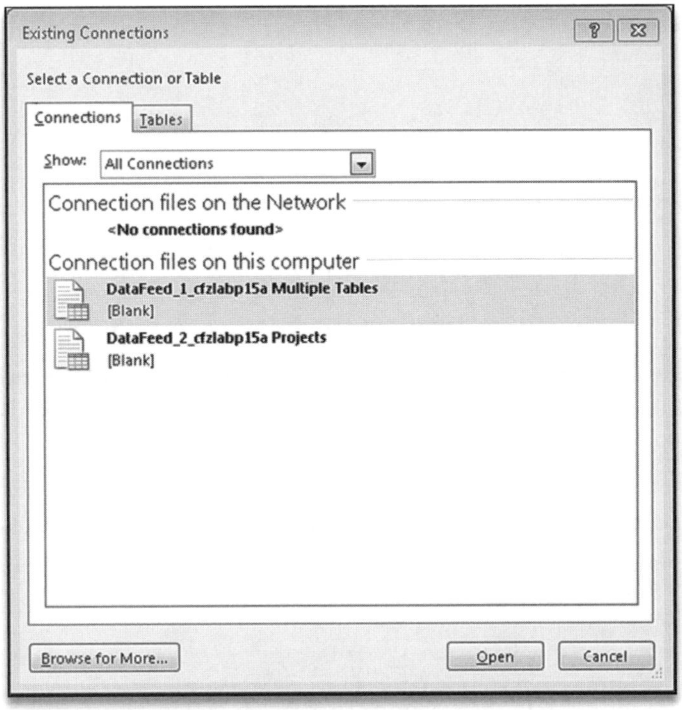

Figure 18 - 68: Existing Connections dialog

4. The system displays the *Select Data Source* dialog as shown in Figure 18 - 69. To navigate to the *Data Connections* library, type the URL in the *File name:* field and click the *Open* button. The URL format is as follows:

http://[*YourServerName*]/pwa/ProjectBICenter/ Data%20Connections/English%20(United%20States).

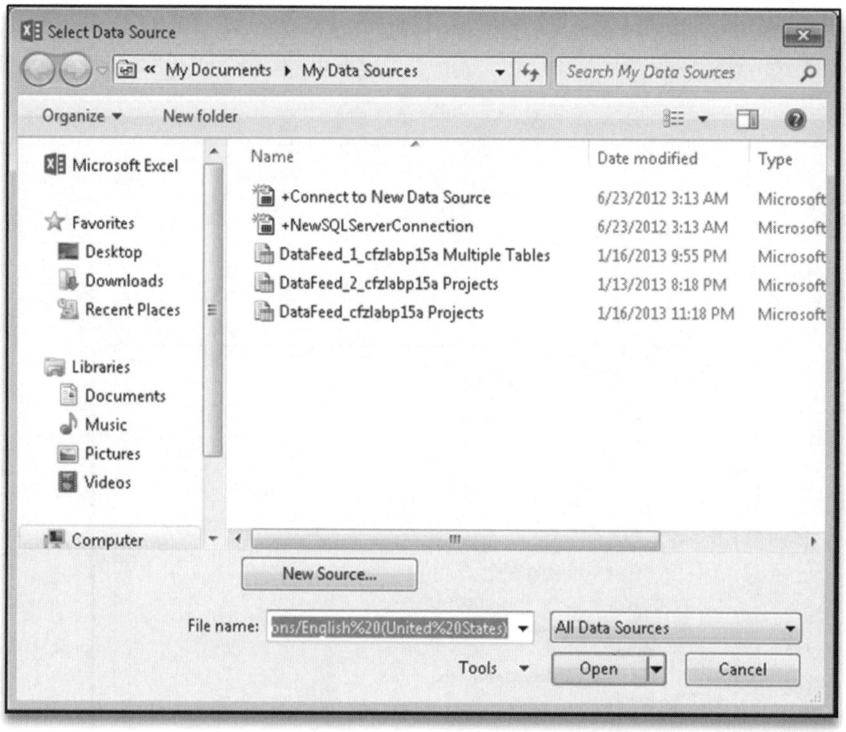

Figure 18 - 69: Select Data Source dialog

5. The system displays the contents of the *Data Connections* library as shown in Figure 18 - 70. Select the *OData Assignments Data* ODC file from the list of available ODC files, and click the *Open* button.

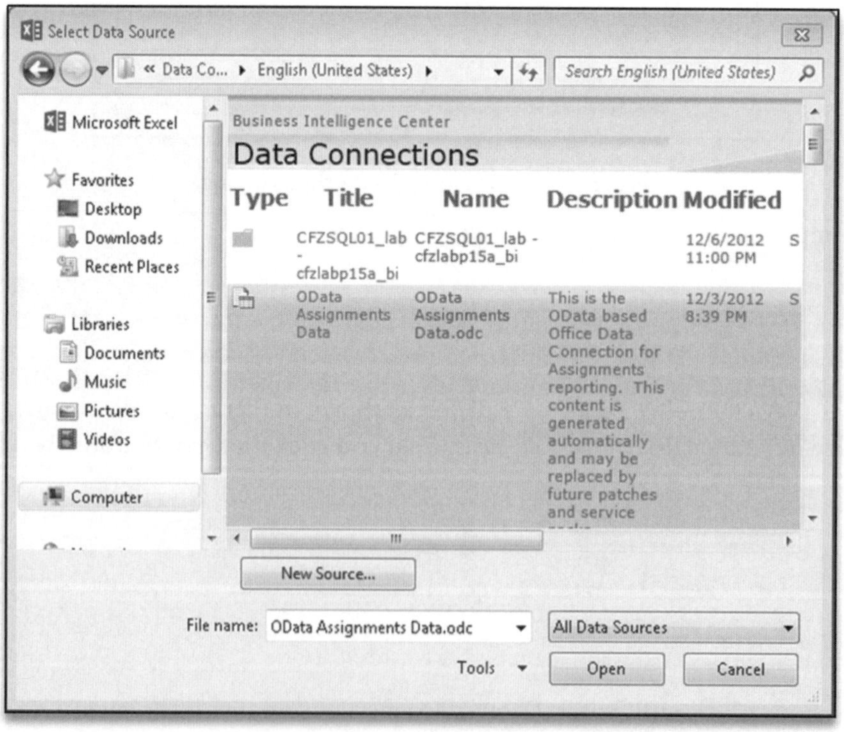

Figure 18 - 70: Select Data Source display Data Connections library

6. The system displays the *Workbook Connections* dialog containing the *OData Assignments Data* ODC file reference as shown in Figure 18 - 71.

> **Warning**: Be sure to click the *Title* of the OData ODC file and not the *Name* link. If you click the *Name* link of the ODC file, you will receive a java error.

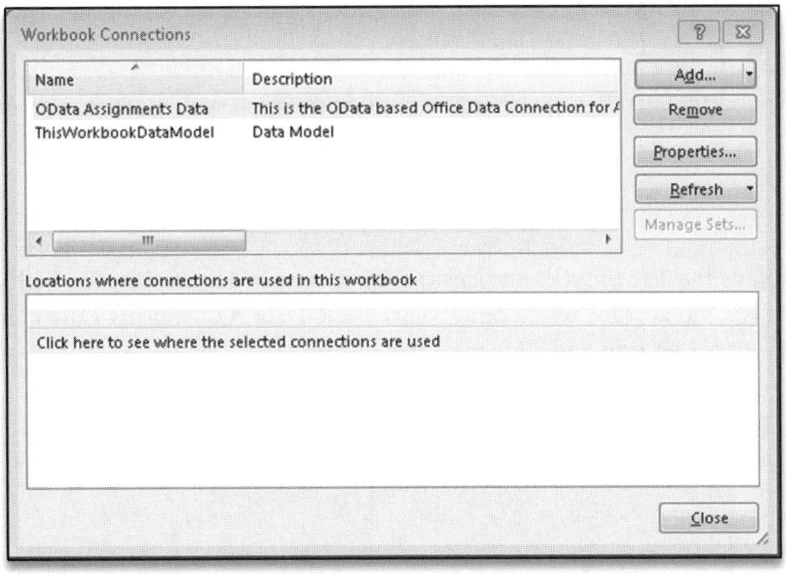

Figure 18 - 71: Workbook Connections OData Assignments Data

7. Click the *Close* button to close the *Workbook Connections* dialog.

Import External Data into Excel Workbook

In the third step, as shown in Figure 18 - 72, you create your report by importing external data into the Excel workbook using the connection you created in the previous step. The system configures this connection to use the OData Data Feed to import assignment data from the reporting database.

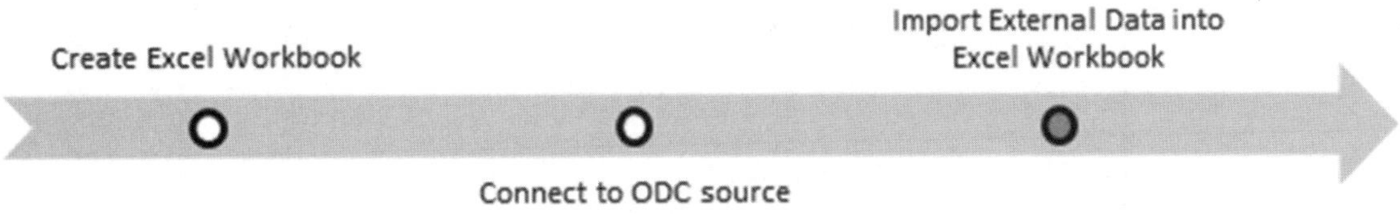

Figure 18 - 72: High Level Create Process

1. From the *DATA* ribbon, click the *Get External Data* pick list as shown in Figure 18 - 73.

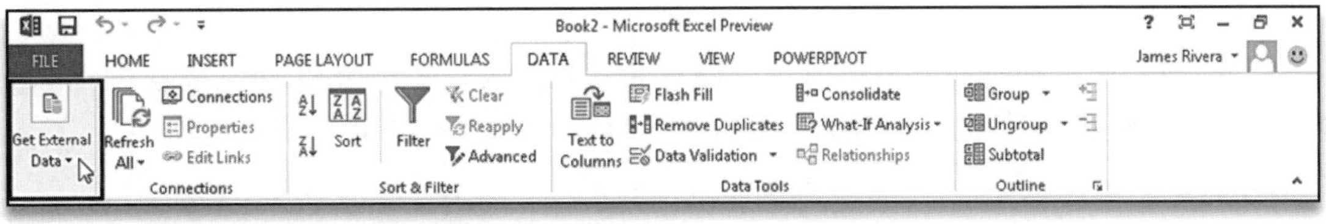

Figure 18 - 73: Get External Data item

2. Select the *Existing Connections* item from the *Get External Data* list as shown in Figure 18 - 74.

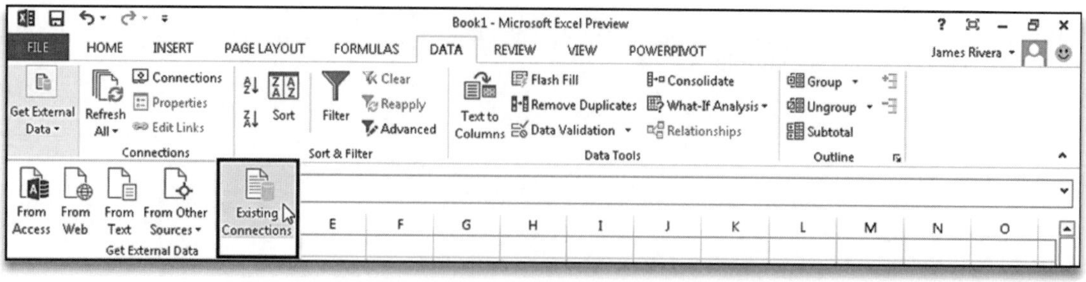

Figure 18 - 74: Existing Connections item

3. The system displays the *Existing Connections* dialog shown in Figure 18 - 75, with a listing of all connections configured for the current workbook. Select the *OData Assignments Data* connection from the *Connections in this Workbook* section and click the *Open* button.

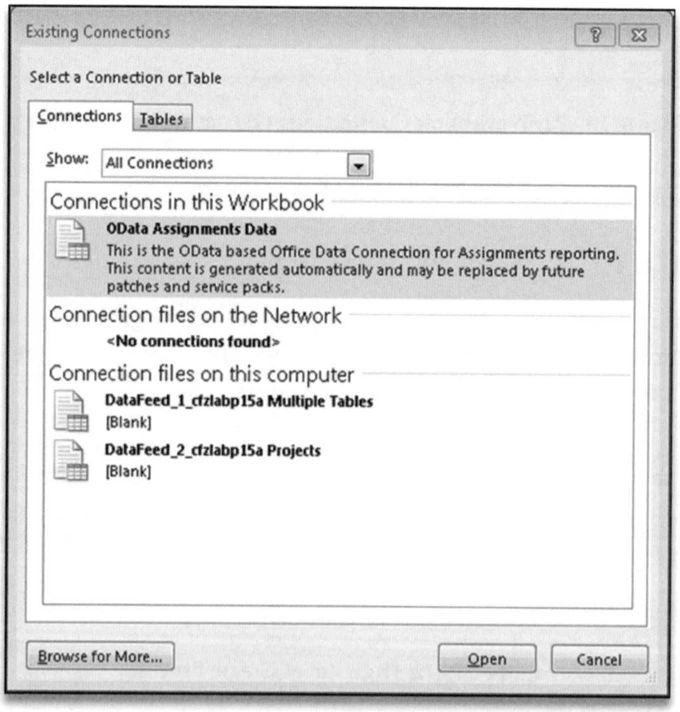

Figure 18 - 75: Existing Connections dialog OData Connection

4. The system displays the *Import Data* dialog shown in Figure 18 - 76. From the *Import Data* dialog, you have several options to display the data within the workbook, as outlined in Table 18 - 11.

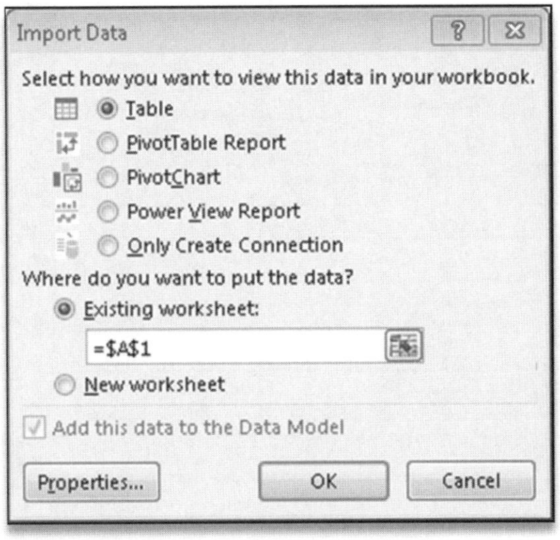

Figure 18 - 76: Import Data dialog

Import Data Option	Description
Table	The system displays the data in a tabular format beginning at the location referenced in the *Existing worksheet*: selection
PivotTable Report	The system displays the data in a PivotTable format beginning at the location referenced in the *Existing worksheet:* selection
PivotChart	The system displays the data in a PivotChart format beginning at the location referenced in the *Existing worksheet:* selection
Power View Report	The system displays the data in a new Power View worksheet

Table 18 - 11: Import Data Options

5. From the *Import Data* dialog, select the *PivotTable Report* option and click the *OK* button. The system displays the data in a PivotTable format in the Excel Worksheet as shown in Figure 18 - 77.

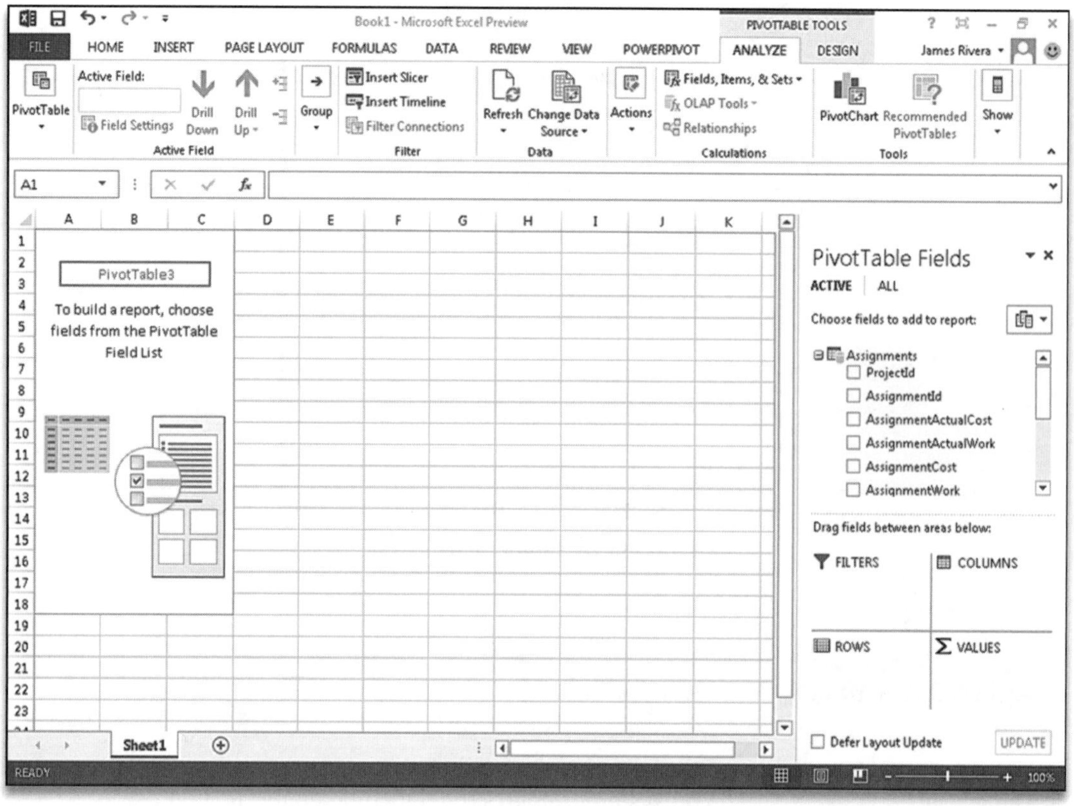

Figure 18 - 77: Excel OData PivotTable report

Creating a New Report from an OData Data Feed

Project Server 2013 provides an OData service that you can use to access the reporting database and import data into an Excel workbook. This method adds an OData Data Feed connection directly in the Excel worksheet, and does not require creating a connection to an external ODC file. When you connect the Data Feed to an Excel workbook, you make the OData service available within the Excel workbook.

Creating a Data Feed connection to an Excel workbook involves the three key steps shown in Figure 18 - 78. I cover each of these steps in detail in this topical section.

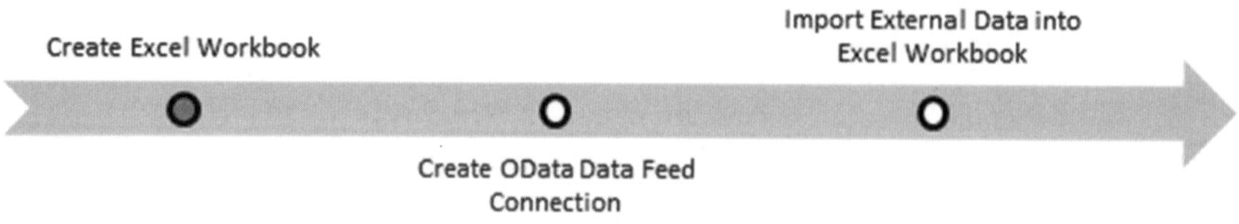

Figure 18 - 78: High Level Create Process

Create Excel Workbook

In the first step, you create a blank Excel workbook. Open Excel from your desktop by selecting the icon from the appropriate folder on the *Start* menu. Excel opens and displays the *Backstage* as shown in Figure 18 - 79.

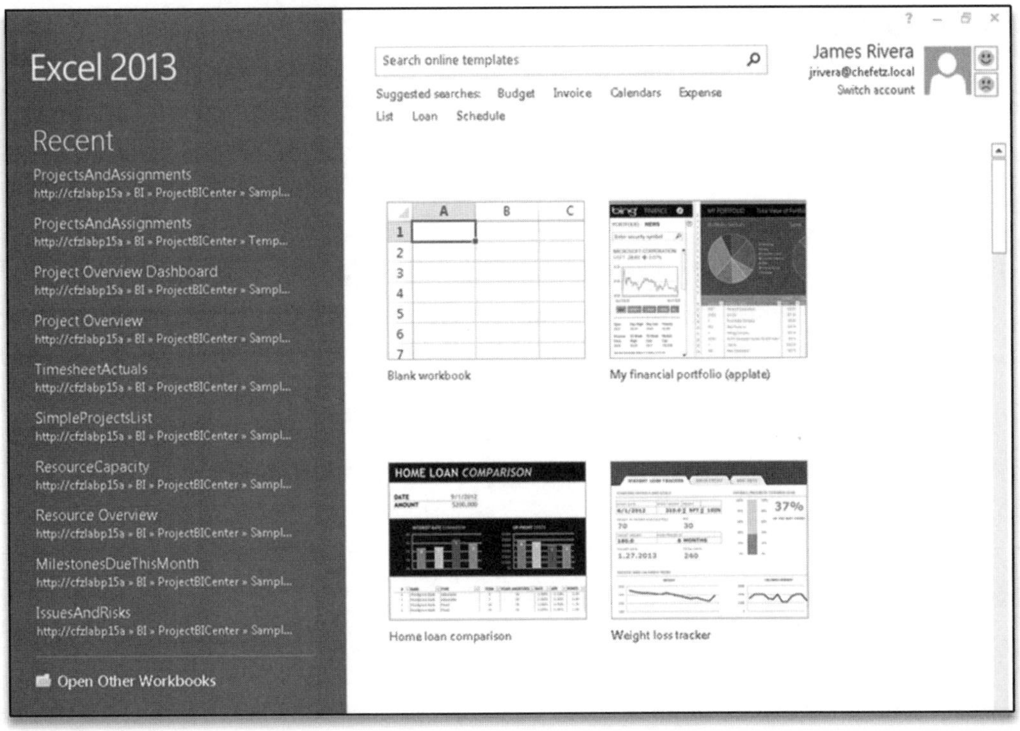

Figure 18 - 79: Excel Backstage

To create a blank workbook, click the *Blank workbook* link in the *Backstage*. The system displays the blank workbook shown in Figure 18 - 80. The system names the new workbook *Book 1 – Microsoft Excel Preview,* indicating that this is the first blank workbook created during the current Excel session.

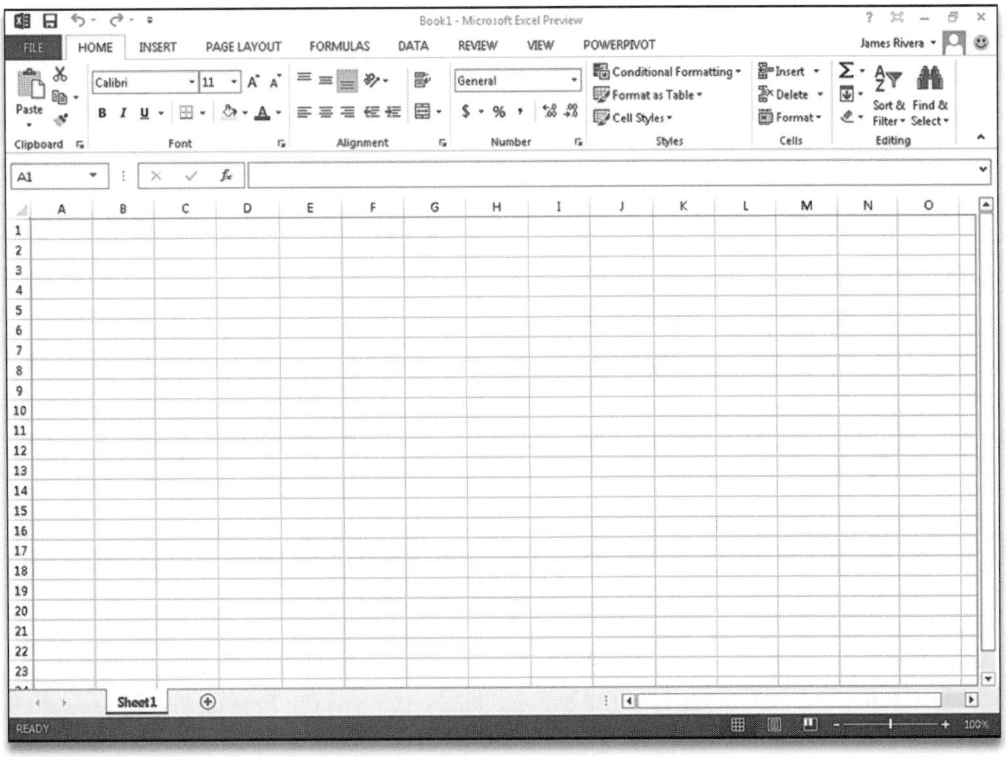

Figure 18 - 80: Blank Excel Workbook

Connect Excel Workbook to OData Data Feed

In the second step, as shown in Figure 18 - 81, you create a connection to an OData Data Feed by creating an *OData Data* connection.

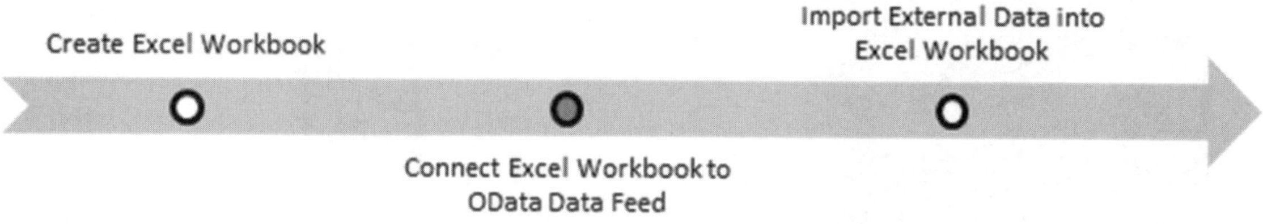

Figure 18 - 81: High Level Create Process

1. In the *Connections* section of the *DATA* ribbon, click the *Get External Data* pick list as shown in Figure 18 - 82.

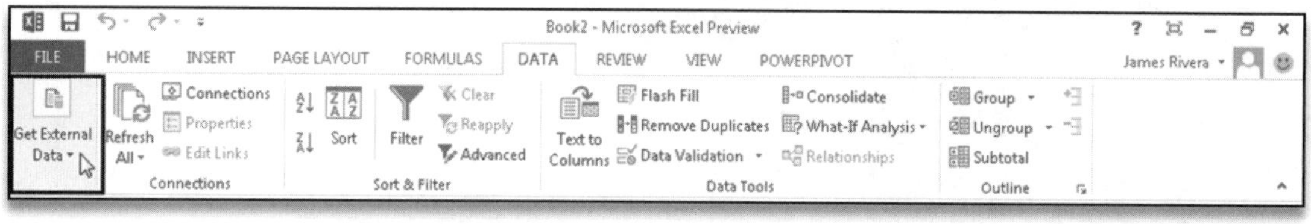

Figure 18 - 82: Get External Data pick list

2. Click the *From Other Sources* pick list and select the *From OData Data Feed* item as shown in Figure 18 - 83.

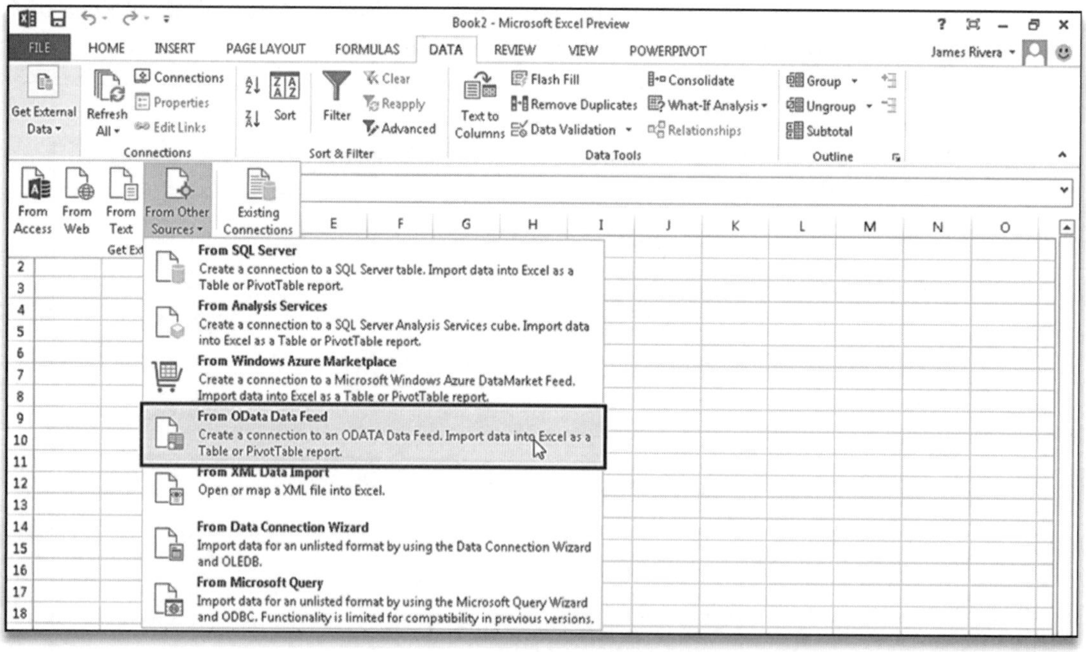

Figure 18 - 83: From OData Data Feed

3. The system displays the *Connect to a Data Feed* page in the *Data Connection Wizard,* as shown in Figure 18 - 84. Enter the OData URI for the ProjectData service in the *Link or File*: field and click the *Next >* button. The format for the OData URI for the ProjectData service is as follows:

```
http://ServerName/ProjectServerName/_api/ProjectData/
```

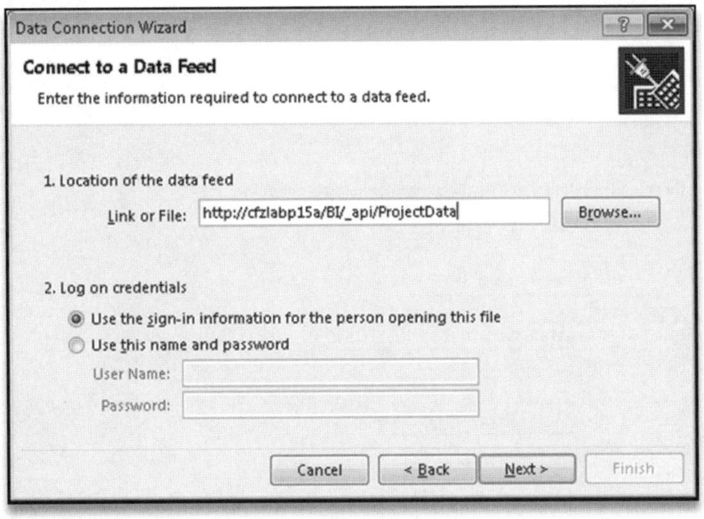

Figure 18 - 84: Data Connection Wizard – Connect to a Data Feed page

4. The system displays the *Select Tables* page in the *Data Connection Wizard* and lists all the available tables for the *ProjectData* service, as shown in Figure 18 - 85. Select only the *Projects* table from the list and click the *Next* > button.

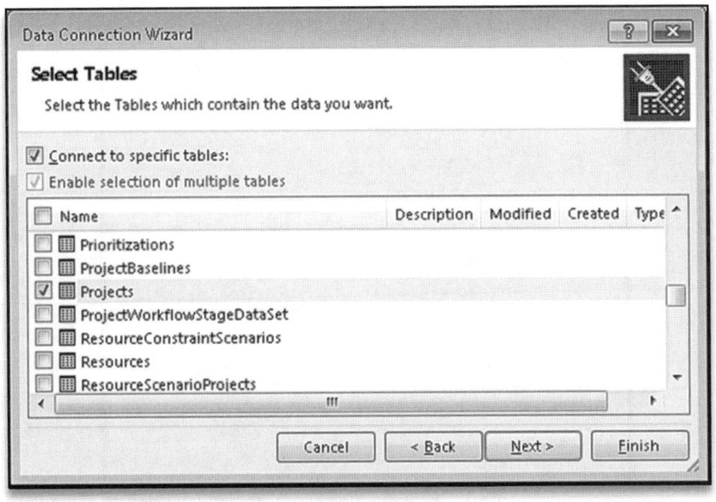

Figure 18 - 85: Data Connection Wizard - Select Tables page

5. The *Data Connection Wizard* displays the *Save Data Connection File and Finish* page, as shown in Figure 18 - 86. Enter a name for your data connection and click the *Finish* button.

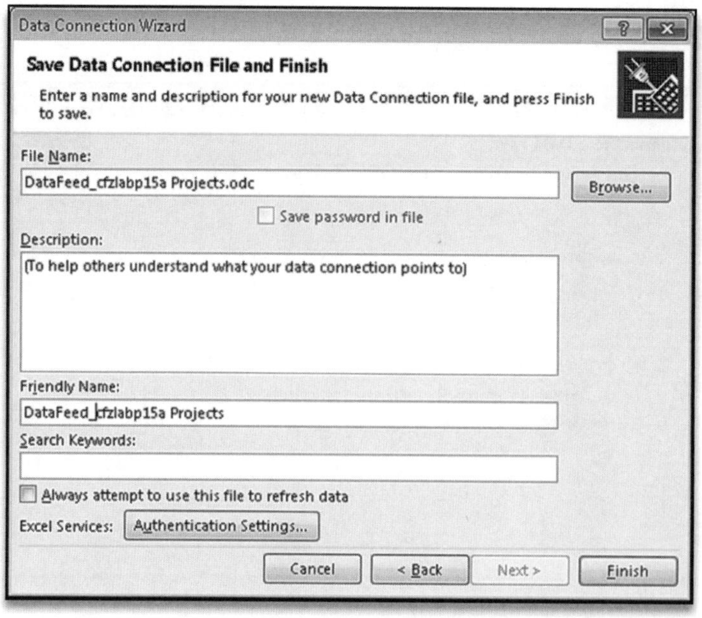

Figure 18 - 86: Data Connection Wizard - Save Data Connection File and Finish page

6. The system displays the *Import Data* dialog as shown in Figure 18 - 87. From the *Import Data* dialog, you have several options to display the data within the workbook, as shown previously in Table 18 - 11. From the *Import Data* dialog, select the *Power View Report* option and click the *OK* button.

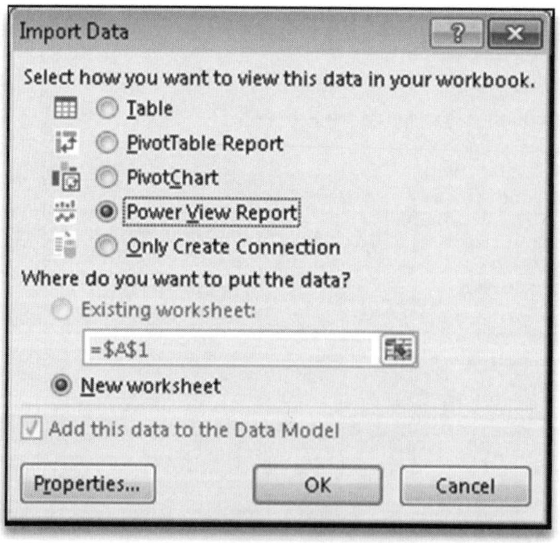

Figure 18 - 87: Import Data dialog – Power View

7. The system displays the data in a *Power View* format in a new Excel Worksheet as shown in Figure 18 - 88.

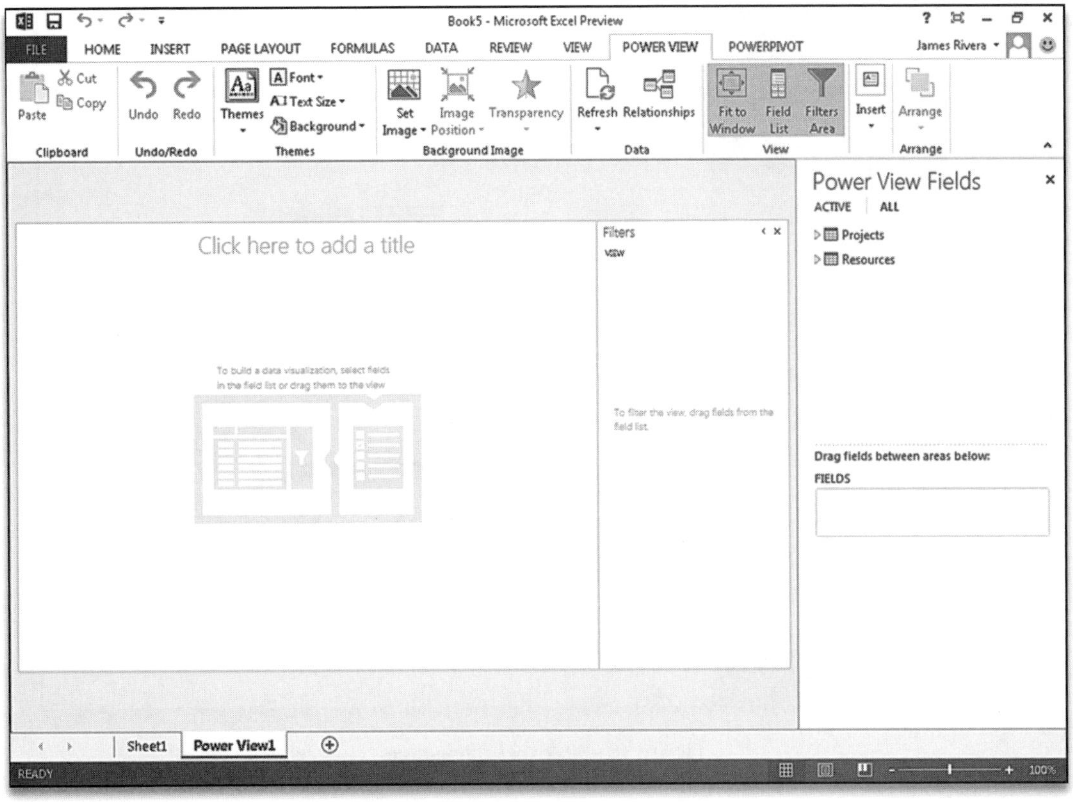

Figure 18 - 88: Excel OData Pivot View report

Creating a New PowerPivot Report

Creating a PowerPivot report in an Excel workbook involves the three key steps shown in Figure 18 - 89. I cover each of these steps in detail in this topical section.

Figure 18 - 89: High Level Create Process

Create Excel Workbook

In the first step, you create a blank Excel workbook. Open Excel from your desktop by selecting the icon from the appropriate folder on the *Start* menu. Excel opens and displays the *Backstage* as shown in Figure 18 - 90.

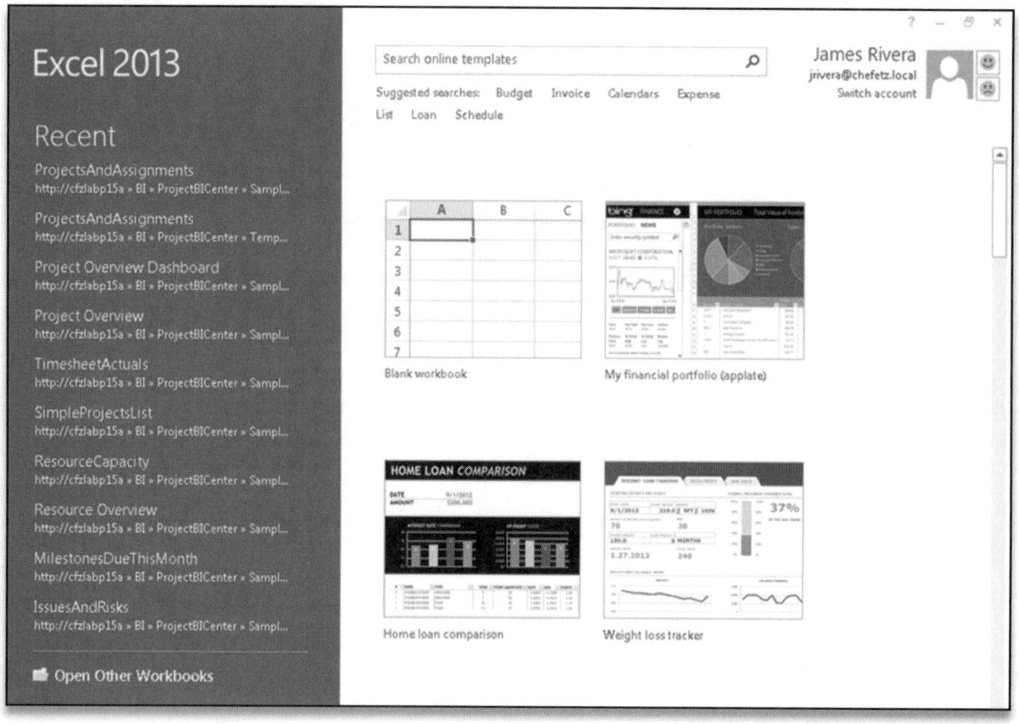

Figure 18 - 90: Excel Backstage

1. To create a blank workbook, click the *Blank workbook* link in the *Backstage*. The system displays a blank workbook as shown in Figure 18 - 91. Excel names the new workbook *Book 1 – Microsoft Excel Preview*, indicating that this is the first blank workbook created during the current Excel session.

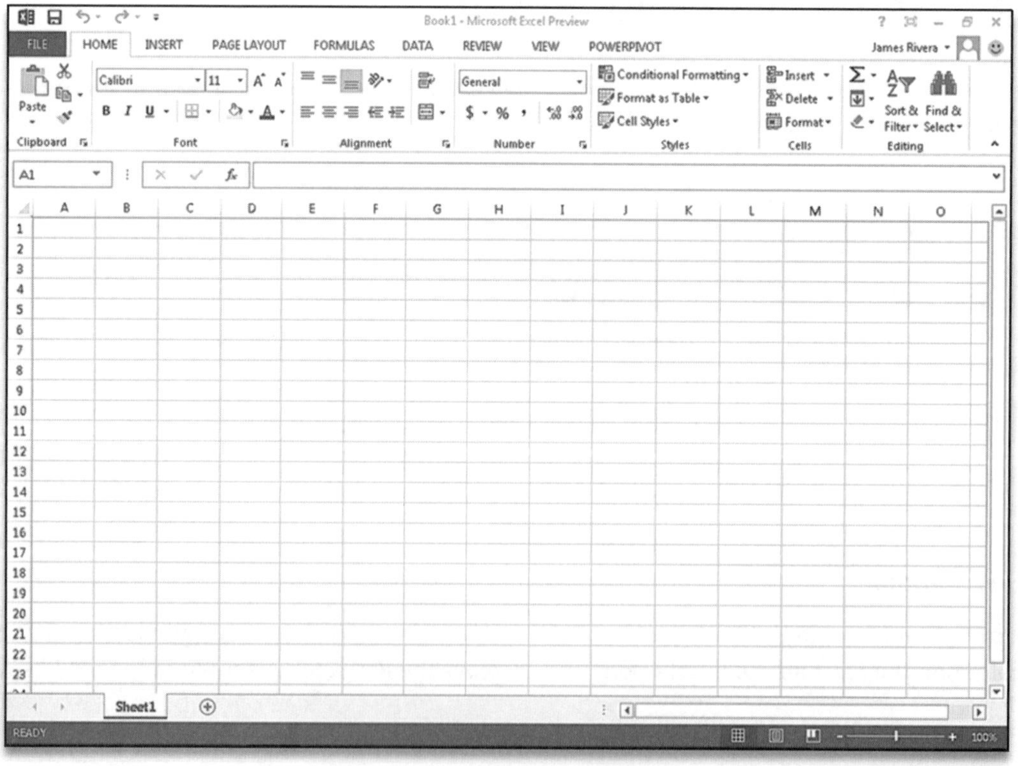

Figure 18 - 91: Blank Excel Workbook

2. In the *Data Model* section of the *POWERPIVOT* ribbon, click the *Manage* button as shown in Figure 18 - 92.

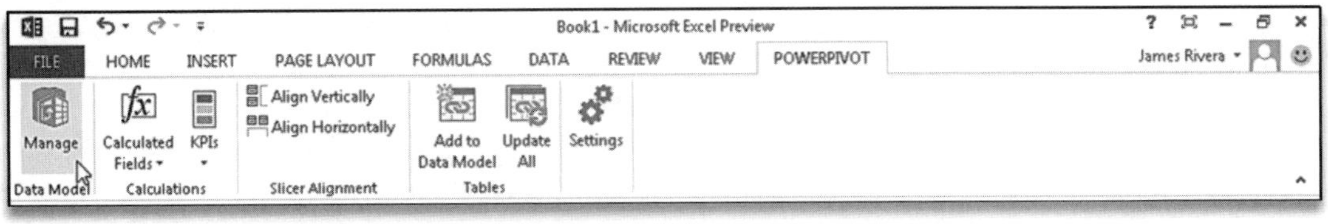

Figure 18 - 92: PowerPivot tab - Data Model

3. The system displays the PowerPivot window shown in Figure 18 - 93.

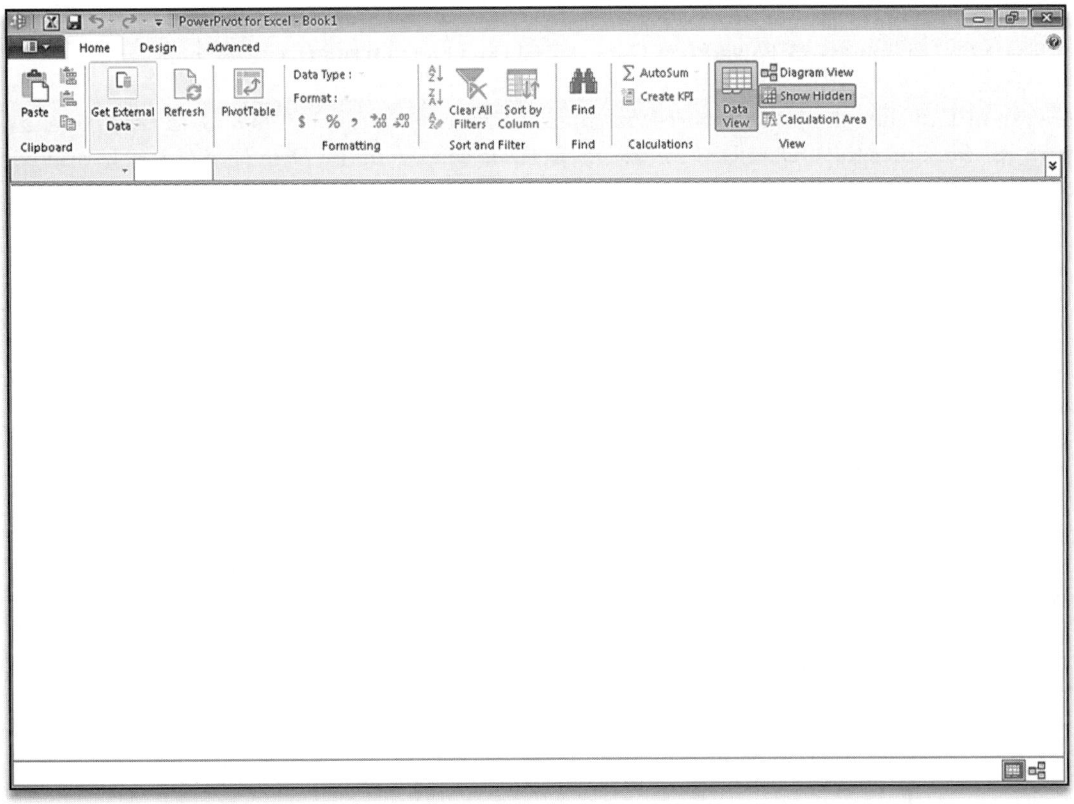

Figure 18 - 93: PowerPivot Window

4. In the *Connections* section of the *DATA* ribbon, click the *Get External Data* pick list as shown in Figure 18 - 94.

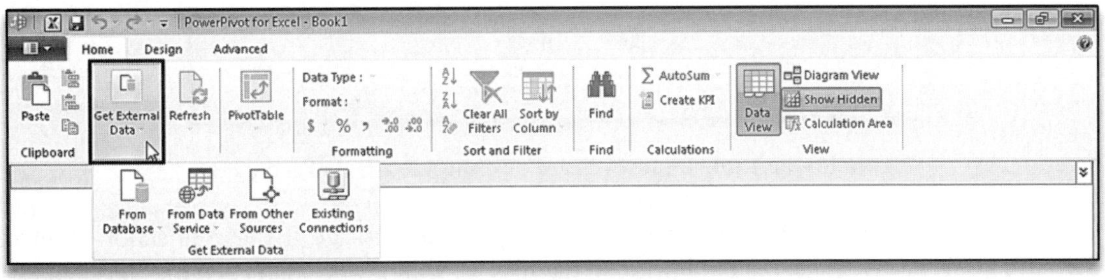

Figure 18 - 94: PowerPivot – Get External Data pick list

5. Click the *From Data Service* pick list and select the *From OData Data Feed* item as shown in Figure 18 - 95.

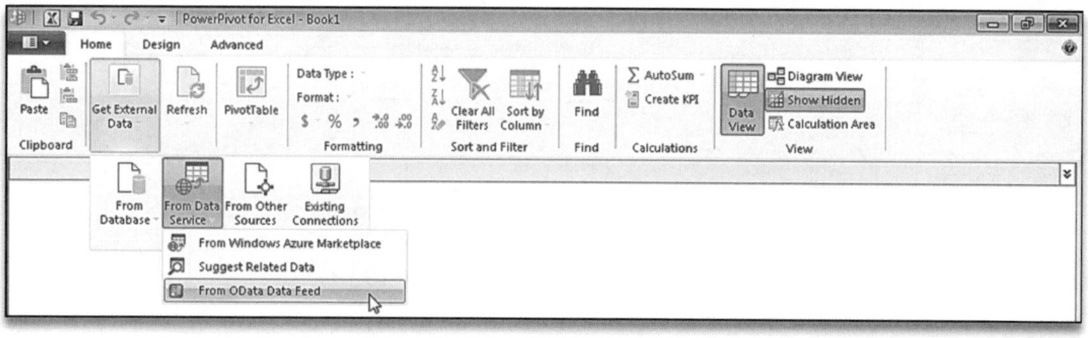

Figure 18 - 95: PowerPivot Get External Data From OData Data Feed item

6. The system launches the *Table Import Wizard* and displays the *Connect to a Data Feed* page, as shown in Figure 18 - 96. Enter the OData URI for the *ProjectData* service in the *Data Feed Url:* field and click the *Test Connection* button. The format for the OData URI for the *ProjectData* service is as follows:

```
http://ServerName/ProjectServerName/_api/ProjectData/
```

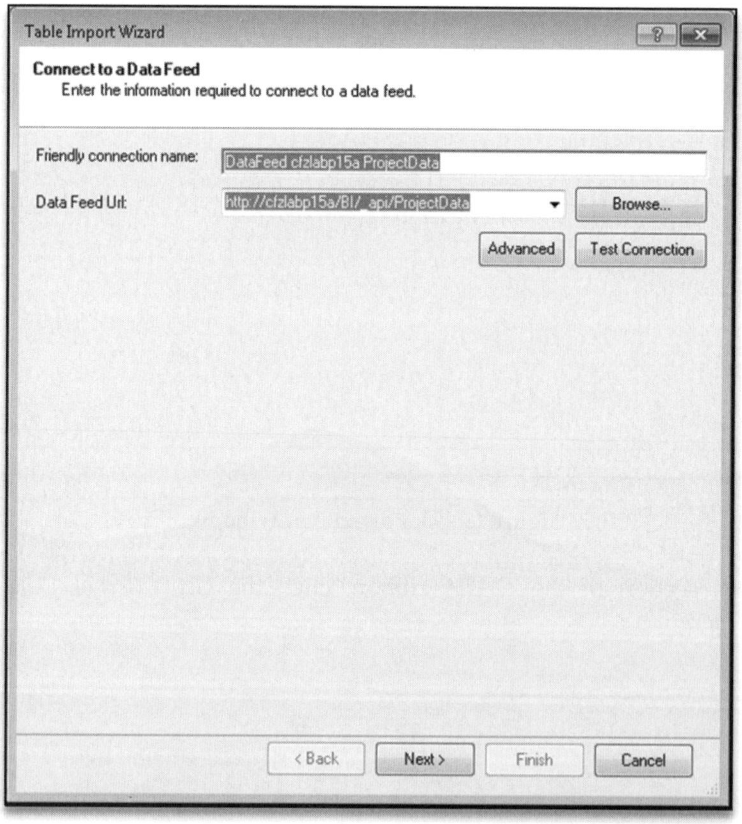

Figure 18 - 96: Table Import Wizard - Connect to a Data Feed page

7. The system validates the OData connection and displays a message if the connection is successful, as shown in Figure 18 - 97. Click the *OK* button to dismiss the dialog and then click the *Next >* button.

Figure 18 - 97: Test connection succeeded

8. The system displays the *Select Tables and Views* page of the *Table Import Wizard* and lists all the available tables for the *ProjectData* service, as shown in Figure 18 - 98. In the *Source Table* column, select the *Projects* item only and click the *Preview & Filter* button.

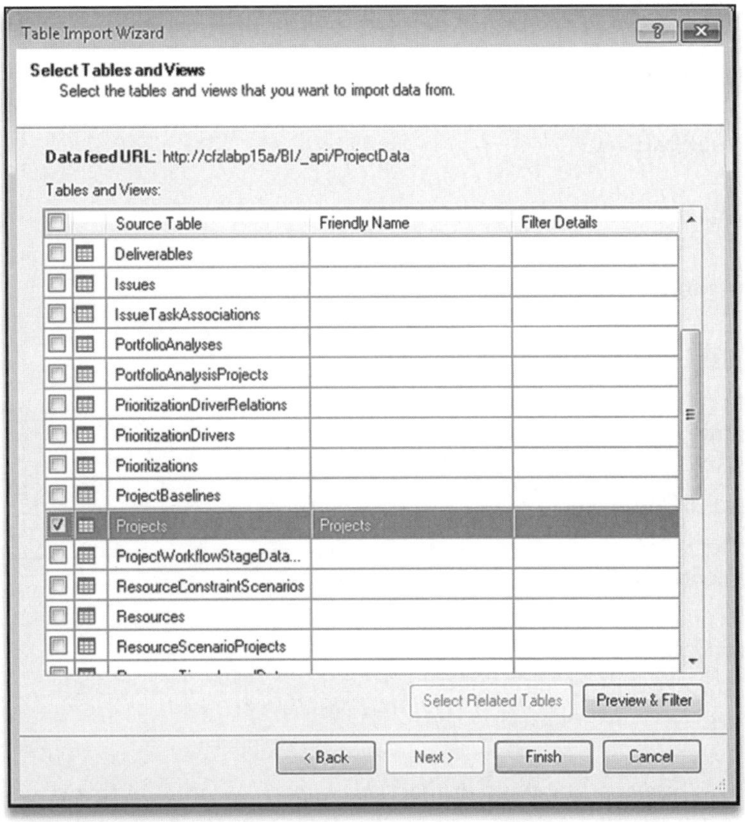

Figure 18 - 98: Table Import Wizard - Select Tables and Views page

9. The system displays the *Preview Selected Table* page in the *Table Import Wizard*, as shown in Figure 18 - 99.

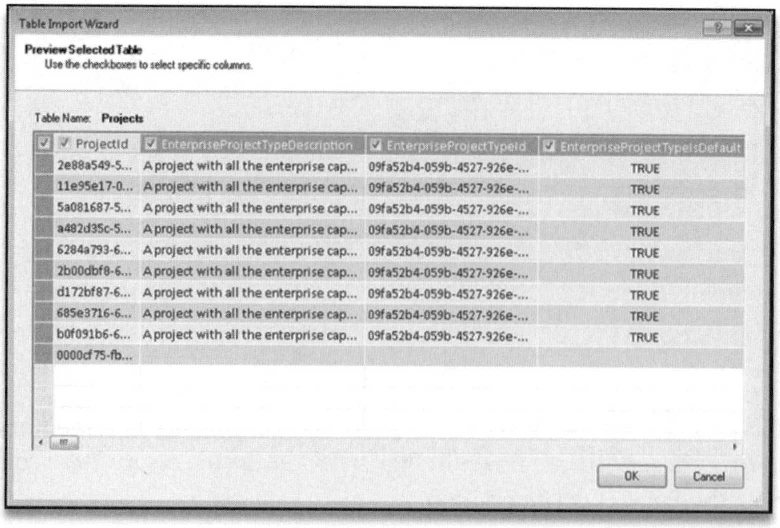

Figure 18 - 99: Table Import Wizard - Preview Selected Table page

10. Select the fields below, and click the *OK* button. Then click the *Finish* button.

- ProjectActualCost
- ProjectActualDuration
- ProjectActualStartDate
- ProjectActualWork
- ProjectDuration
- ProjectFinishDate
- ProjectName
- ProjectPercentCompleted
- ProjectPercentWorkCompleted
- ProjectStartDate
- ProjectWork

11. The system displays the *Importing* page of the *Table Import Wizard*. On this page, PowerPivot imports all the data and validates that the import was successful. Once the import has completed successfully, as shown in Figure 18 - 100, click the *Close* button to complete the import process.

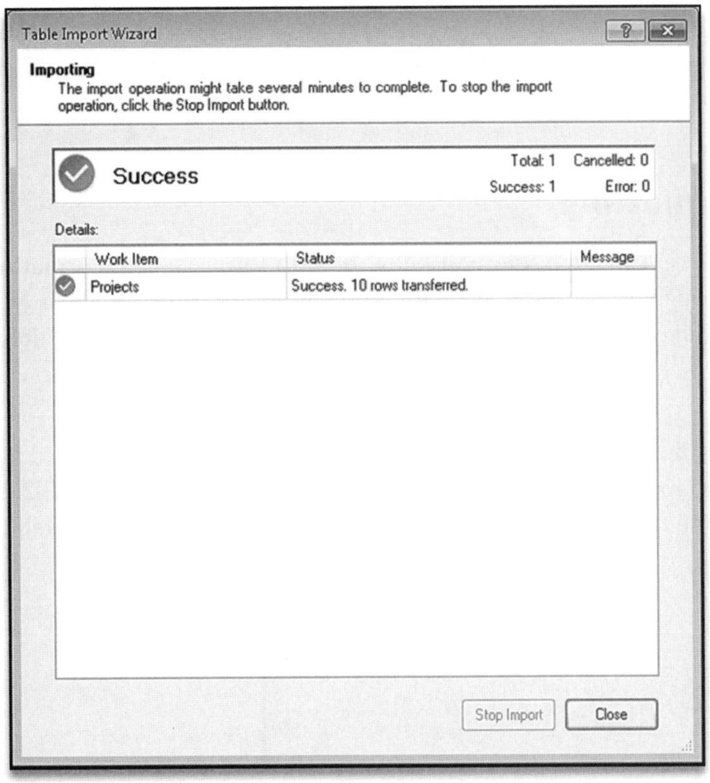

Figure 18 - 100: Table Import Wizard – Importing page

12. The system displays the OData results in a new PowerPivot worksheet, as shown in Figure 18 - 101.

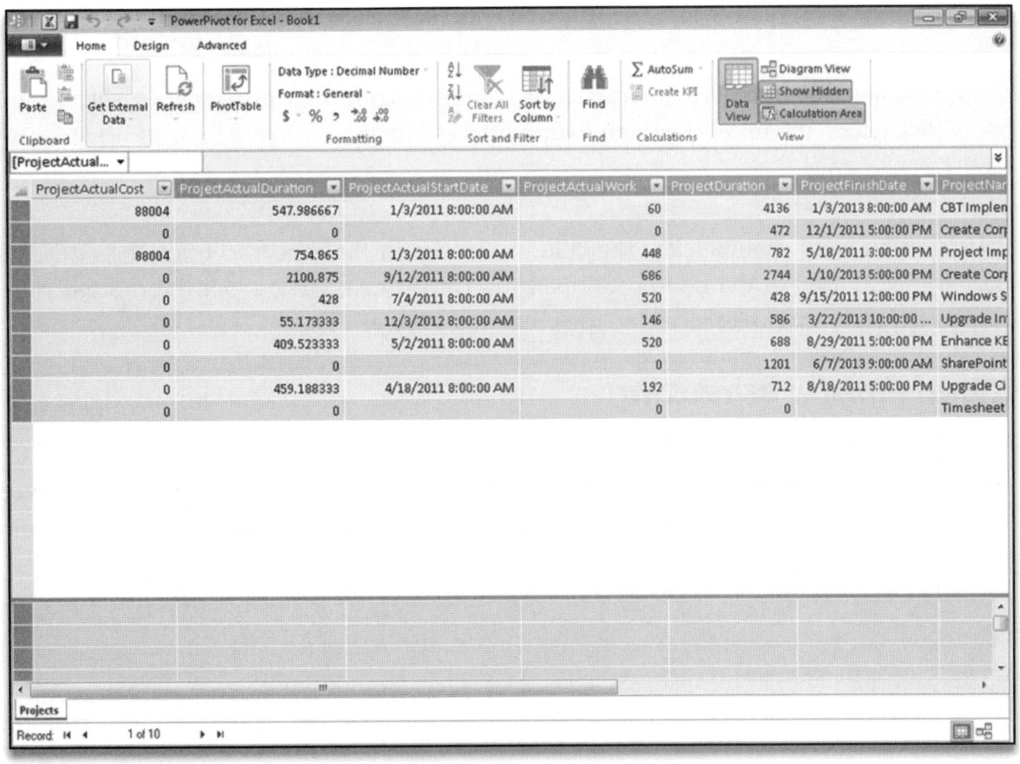

Figure 18 - 101: PowerPivot worksheet

Information: The worksheet in the PowerPivot window is actually a PowerPivot table. PowerPivot creates a separate worksheet (table) for each data source connection and allows you to create relationships between these tables creating a powerful data model that you can query to create Excel reports.

Applying Basic Formatting

If you have used Excel before, I assume that you know how to format a cell. Formatting a PivotTable is similar but has some oddities of which you should be aware. The method to format *Date* or *Number* values differs based on whether they are in the *Rows* area, *Columns* area or the ∑ *Values* area of the PivotTable.

Rows

To format a *Row Label* data field, float your mouse pointer over the top of the first data field instance to format. When the cursor changes to a downward pointing arrow, as shown in Figure 18 - 102, select the cell. The system highlights all instances of the data field. Use the *Format* pick list on the Excel *Home* tab to format the cells accordingly.

Figure 18 - 102: Selection cursor for Row Labels

Column Labels

In a *Cross-Tab* report, dates and numbers can appear as columns. To format these values, select the row selector and use the *Format* pick list on the Excel *Home* tab to format accordingly.

∑ Values

To format a ∑ *Values* data field, double-click the column header in the report to open the *Field Settings* dialog. Click the *Number Format* button at the bottom to open the *Format Cells* dialog. Set the desired numeric or date format and click the *OK* button twice to return to the [need word here].

Adding Fit and Finish Formatting

When you select a PivotTable, you see two new contextual tabs that appear in the Excel ribbon. Clicking these tabs displays the *Design* ribbon and *Options* ribbon shown in Figure 18 - 103 and Figure 18 - 104, respectively. The *Design* ribbon functionality focuses on the look of your report while the *Options* ribbon contains a number of functions that allow you to control the report experience.

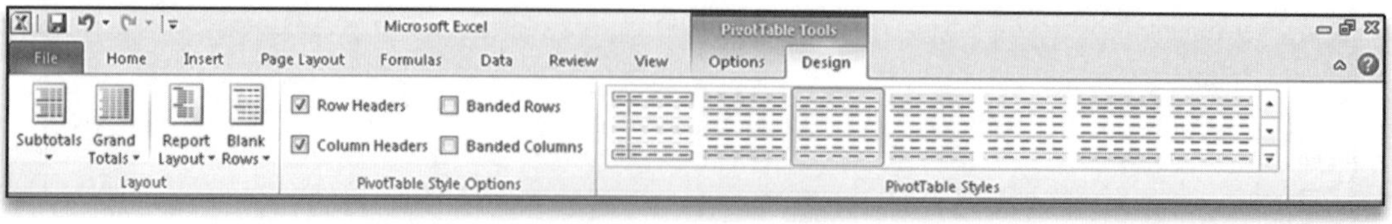

Figure 18 - 103: PivotTable Design ribbon

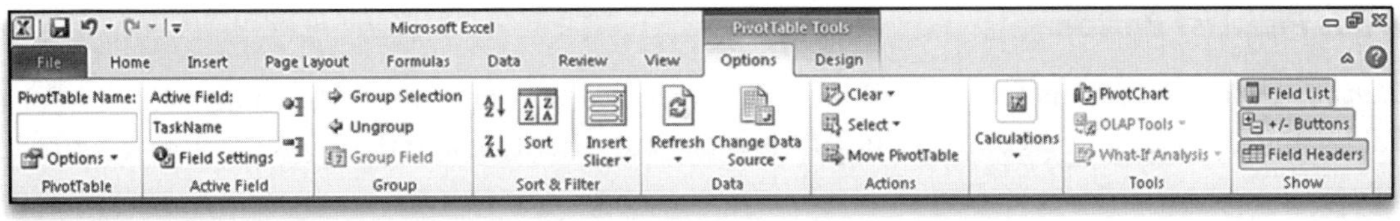

Figure 18 - 104: PivotTable Options ribbon

Using the Design Ribbon

The *Design* ribbon with *PivotTable Tools* applied contains functionality that controls the visual look of your report. I cover the most common options for report writing in this topical section.

Subtotals Pick List Button

The *Subtotals* pick list contains four options that control whether subtotals appear and where you would like them to appear in the report. This option is global for all fields in the report and requires a field in the ∑ *Values* area for you to see the impact. I list the options and their functionality in Table 18 - 12.

In a later section, you learn how to control this setting on a data field basis, providing you with more control over totaling. Unless you have a need for totals on every field, I suggest that you select the *Do Not Show Subtotals* option and control this on a data field basis.

Option	Functionality
Do Not Show Subtotals	Removes all subtotals for all fields in the PivotTable
Show all Subtotals at Bottom of Group	Inserts a totals row beneath each grouping data field in the report
Show all Subtotals at Top of Group	Displays a total in line with the grouping data field without inserting lines into the report
Include Filtered Items in Totals	This setting allows you to include items in the roll-up total, though you may have filtered them out of the report view

Table 18 - 12: Subtotals Menu Button options

Grand Totals Pick List Button

The *Grand Totals* pick list contains four options that control what and where grand totals appear in your report. The options, which are self-explanatory, are as follows:

- Off for Rows and Columns
- On for Rows and Columns
- On for Rows Only
- On for Columns Only

Report Layout Pick List Button

The *Report Layout* pick list contains five options, which control the presentation of the data fields in your report as shown in Table 18 - 13. This option controls one of the most important design decisions of your report.

You can also control this setting at the field level, which I cover in a later section of this module, providing finer control over presentation.

Option	Functionality	Example	Uses
Show in Compact Form	Shows all data fields in a compact tree structure	XXX XXX XXX	Works best when the number of data fields is greater than can be viewed horizontally and the report delivery is online Enables the report user to open and close groups
Show in Outline Form	Shows all data fields in a wide outline form, sometimes resembling a staircase	XXXXX XXXXX XXXXX	Works best with a small number of data fields and the report delivery is online. Enables the report user to open and close groups
Show in Tabular Form	Shows all data fields as a table but does not show repeating values by default	XXXX XXXX XXXXX XXXX XXXXX XXXXX	Works best for printed report delivery and a number of data fields that fit across the medium Can be used online with the open/close functionality

Option	Functionality	Example	Uses
Repeat All Item Labels	Note: This function has no impact on the Compact Form. Repeats all item labels for each group of repeating values	Outline Form looks like: XXXX XXXX XXXXX XXXX XXXXX XXXXX Tabular Form looks like: XXXX XXXX XXXXX XXXX XXXX XXXXX XXXX XXXX XXXXX	Can be very useful for printed reports for place keeping or where there are a lot of lines under a particular group and the group spans a page or screen Use cautiously in online reports as repeating data can make reports hard to read
Do Not Repeat All Item Labels	Default value that does not show all values for repeating values.	See defaults for Outline Form and Tabular Form above.	Useful for online report presentation where repeated same values can create visual clutter

Table 18 - 13: Report Layout options

Blank Rows Pick List Button

The *Blank Rows* pick list contains two options that control whether a blank line appears between data groups in your report. Blank lines provide additional visual breaks between data groups and are effective for printed reports. The options, which are self-explanatory, are as follows:

- Insert Blank Line after Each Item
- Remove Blank Line after Each Item

PivotTable Styles Gallery

The *PivotTable Styles* gallery is the quickest way to format the look and feel of your report as shown in Figure 18 - 105. Your report layout strongly influences how these gallery options appear to you. As you hover your mouse over each option, you can see the Active Preview of the selection's impact, if chosen. You should choose a style that makes the data presented as easy to view and understand as possible. Note also, that the system links colors for these gallery items to the *Page Layout* tab, *Colors* pick list. Any changes you make have an immediate impact on your report colors. Unless you truly desire a pink report, I advise caution.

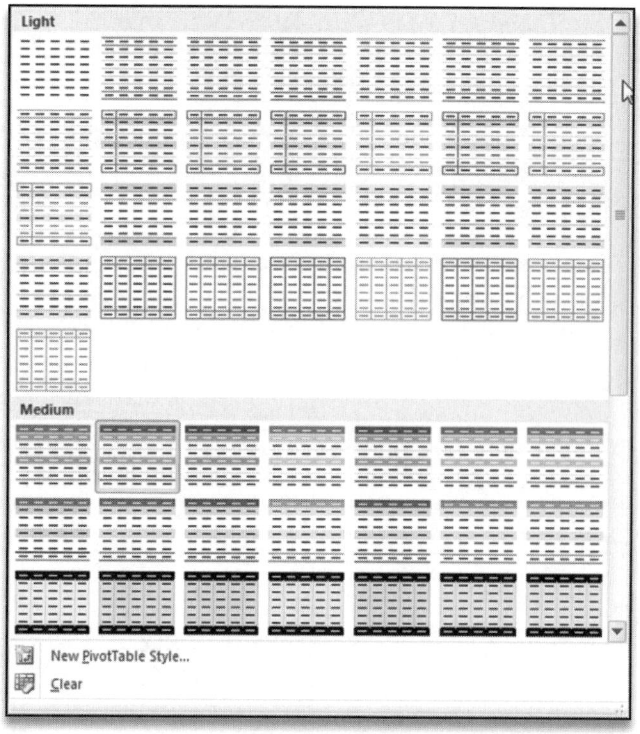

Figure 18 - 105: PivotTable Style gallery

Using the Options Ribbon

The *Options* ribbon with *PivotTable Tools* applied contains several functions that impact how the PivotTable behaves and what core elements appear. In this section, I cover the common options for report writing.

PivotTable Options

The PivotTable *Options* pick list, shown in Figure 18 - 106, is very important when creating a new report that you intend to use on a regular basis. You should review these settings during report creation as they control the basic visual properties and refresh data settings for the report. You typically set these only once during report creation.

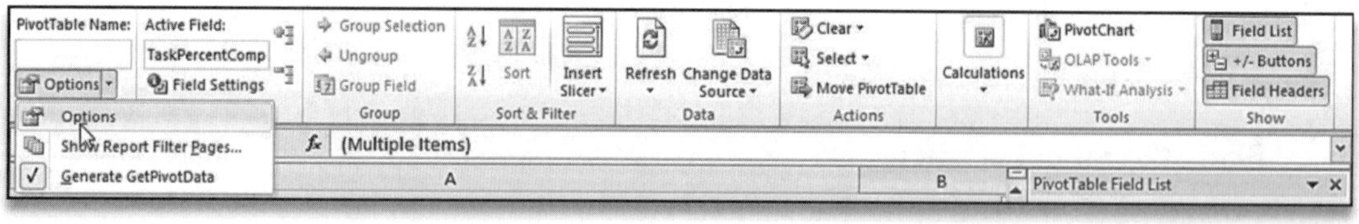

Figure 18 - 106: PivotTable Options - Options pick list

Click the *Options* pick list and select the *Options* item to display the *Pivot Table Options* dialog shown in Figure 18 - 107 and Figure 18 - 108. The first figure displays the *Layout & Format* page while the second figure shows the *Data* page.

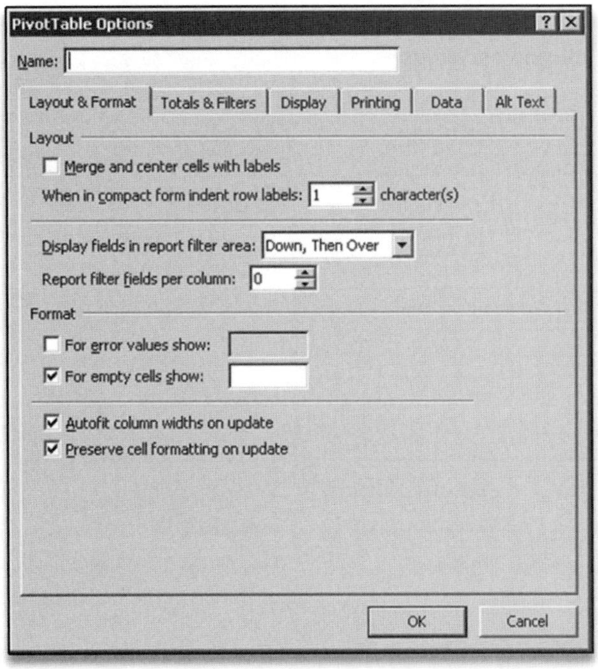

Figure 18 - 107: PivotTable Options dialog – Layout & Format page

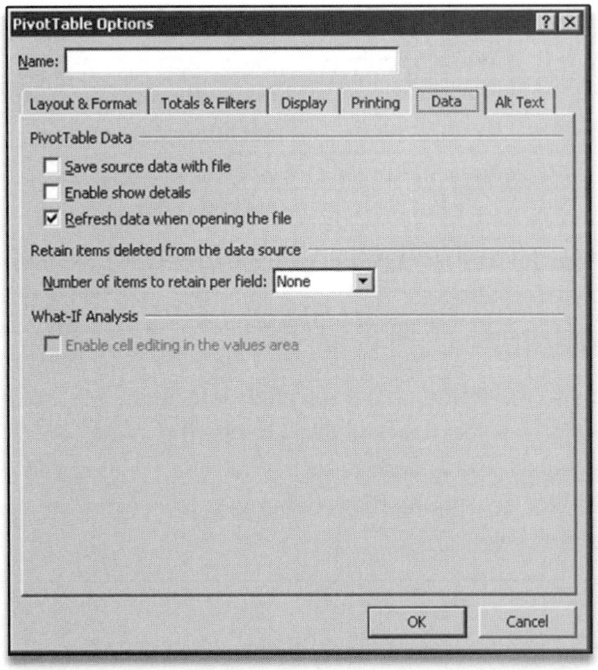

Figure 18 - 108: PivotTable Options dialog – Data page

I list the four most common settings found in the aforementioned pages in Table 18 - 14, along with explanations of their functionality and recommended settings.

Tab	Figure	Option	Function	Recommended Setting
Layout & Format	Figure 18 - 107	PivotTable Name	Enables you to designate a name for the PivotTable	**Recommend: Name your PivotTable** Give the PivotTable a name that you can easily identify. You will use this name later when I cover conditional publishing
Layout & Format	Figure 18 - 107	Autofit column widths on update	When selected, Excel autofits your columns automatically on data refresh	**Recommend: Deselect** This functionality makes it hard to control the format of the report, which can lead to the report being wider than your screen resolution
Layout & Format	Figure 18 - 107	Preserve cell formatting on update	When selected, prevents Excel from resetting the PivotTable formatting to the default settings on data refresh	**Recommend: Select** Otherwise, you lose any conditional formatting and other modifications on a data refresh
Data	Figure 18 - 108	Refresh data when opening the file	When selected, the Excel report automatically retrieves the latest data and gets rid of any cached data	**Recommend: Select** Otherwise, user confusion occurs when the system uses out-of-date data to make a decision

Table 18 - 14: List of Pertinent PivotTable Option Settings

Working with Field Settings

Use the *Active Field* field to change the name of the selected data field. For example, you decide that the *TaskWorkPercentComplete* name is too long; select the field and change the name to *% Work Comp*. When you press the **Enter** key on your computer keyboard, the system reflects your change in the PivotTable. Click the *Field Settings* button, shown in Figure 18 - 109, to see options that enable you to control the display of data at the individual data field level rather than the report level.

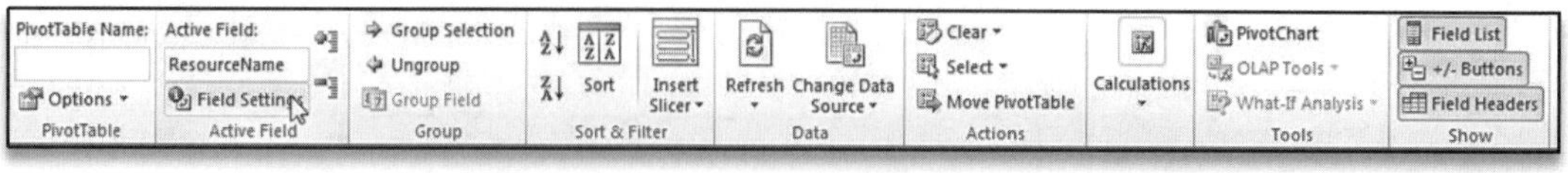

Figure 18 - 109: Field Settings button on the PivotTable Options tab

You can find the key settings on the *Layout & Print* page of the *Field Settings* dialog shown in Figure 18 - 110.

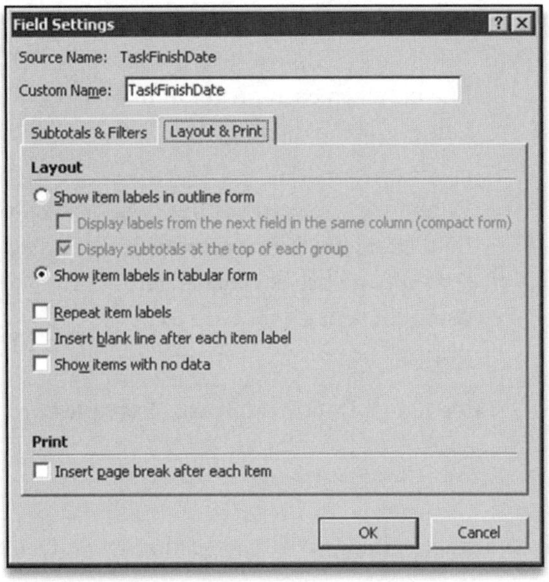

Figure 18 - 110: PivotTable Data Field Settings dialog, Layout & Print page

I list examples of how each setting affects the PivotTable in Table 18 - 15.

Setting	Effect	Example
Show item labels in outline form	When selected, the data field appears in a wide outline form, sometimes resembling a stair-case	XXXXX XXXXX XXXXX
Show item labels in tabular form	When selected, the data field appears as a table but does not show repeating values by default	XXXX XXXX XXXXX XXXX XXXXX XXXXX
Repeat item labels	When selected, the data field is repeated for each group of repeating values	Outline Form looks like: XXXX XXXX XXXXX XXXX XXXXX XXXXX Tabular Form looks like: XXXX XXXX XXXXX XXXX XXXX XXXXX XXXX XXXX XXXXX

Setting	Effect	Example
Insert blank line after each item label	When selected, inserts a blank line between each group of like values for the data field	XXXXX XXXXX XXXXX
Insert page break after each item	Whenever the value of the data field changes, the system inserts a page break. This is very useful in reports that are to be printed	XXXX XXXX -- YYYYY

Table 18 - 15: Data Field Setting Examples

Applying Grouping

On the *Options* ribbon with *PivotTable Tools* applied, the *Group* section contains three buttons:

- The *Group Selection* and *Ungroup* buttons enable you to dynamically group contiguous rows or columns into a collapsible group. If you are analyzing large amounts of data, you use these buttons to create dynamic groups that fit your analytical needs.

- The *Group Field* button enables you to meet a common project management reporting need of reporting data by week, month, and quarter. The *Group Field* button enables dynamic grouping of date data fields or number data fields into groups you specify.

You select the date or number field to group in the PivotTable by clicking the *Group Field* button. If you selected a date field, you see Figure 18 - 111. Note that the date groupings are *Days, Months, Quarters,* and *Years*. What happens if you want to group by week? Figure 18 - 111 illustrates the configuration for week grouping where you select *Days* and designate the number of days as *seven*. This approach enables other possibilities for date grouping such as bi-weekly reporting needs.

Best Practice: To group data by week, MSProjectExperts recommends you set the *By* field to *Days* and the *Number of days* field to *7*.

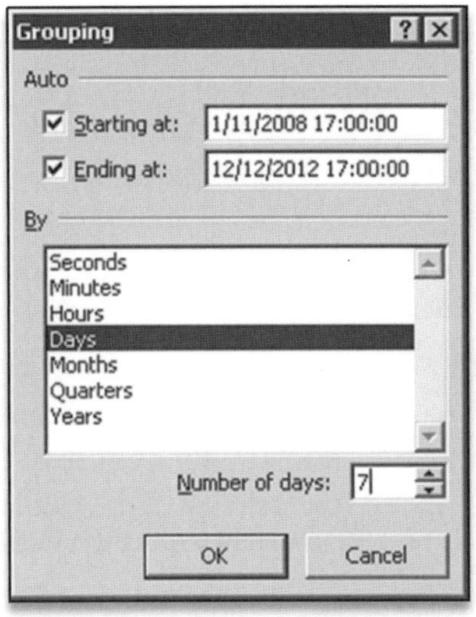

Figure 18 - 111: Grouping dialog Date by Week Grouping

If you selected a numeric field, you see Figure 18 - 112. You define the groups by starting and ending values and define how wide to make each group.

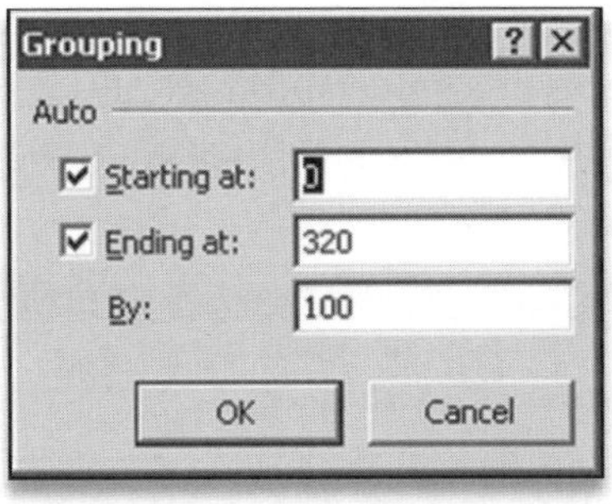

Figure 18 - 112: Grouping Dialog Example for Numeric Data

Summarizing Values

The *Summarize Values By* pick list button shown in Figure 18 - 113 enables the type of value aggregation performed on the selected field in the ∑ *Values* area of the PivotTable. You can also use this button to change the default calculation assigned by Excel to the numeric data field you placed in the ∑ *Values* area of the PivotTable in cases where it assigned an incorrect operation. Select the field in question in the PivotTable and use this button to correct the operation.

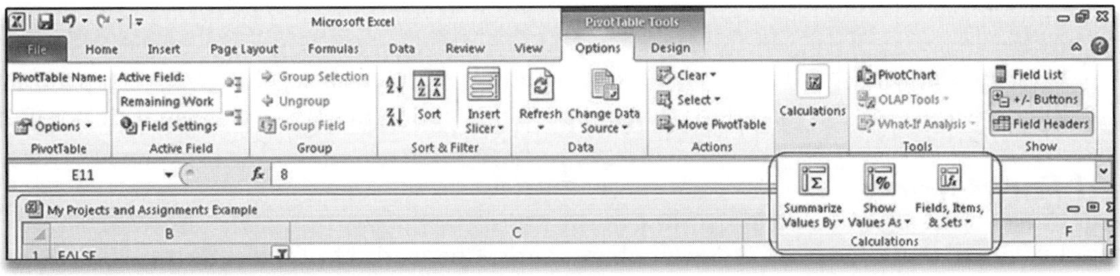

Figure 18 - 113: Calculations pick list of PivotTable Options tab

The most used choices in the *Summarize Values By* pick list are:

- Sum
- Count
- Average
- Min
- Max
- Product

There is also a *More options* selection to provide five more aggregation alternatives.

Fields, Items & Sets Pick List Button and Calculated Fields Menu Item

From the *Calculations* pick list, click the *Fields, Items & Sets* pick list button to create your own calculated fields in the ∑ *Values* area of the PivotTable. Figure 18 - 114 shows an example of a custom calculation where I compare *Baseline Work* to *Work*. The system calculates this value automatically when you refresh the PivotTable data. Most of the formula operators in Excel are available for use and Excel provides you with a list of data fields that you can use in a formula in the *Fields* list.

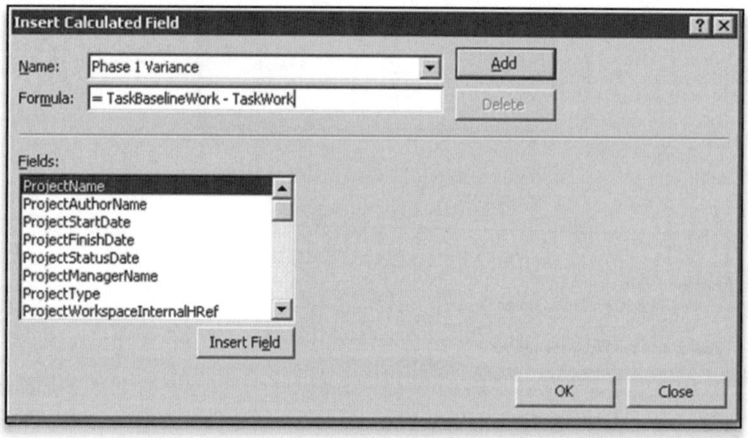

Figure 18 - 114: Insert Calculated Field dialog

+/- Buttons

On the right side of the *Options* tab, click the *+/- Buttons* button to hide or show the collapse/expand buttons next to each field in the PivotTable. If you intend to print a report, this option helps reduce visual clutter in the report.

Advanced Formatting

In this section, I cover advanced aspects of Excel where there is relevance to Project Server 2013 Business Intelligence.

Data Field Level Filtering for Date Fields

PivotTables offer support for special *Date* field filtering for *Date* data fields as shown in Figure 18 - 115. This feature enables you to restrict report data to the current month or quarter without user intervention. To specify a date filter:

1. In the PivotTable, select a *Date* data field.

2. In the data field heading, click the *Filter* pick list button.

3. Select the *Date Filters…* item.

4. Select the date filter to apply.

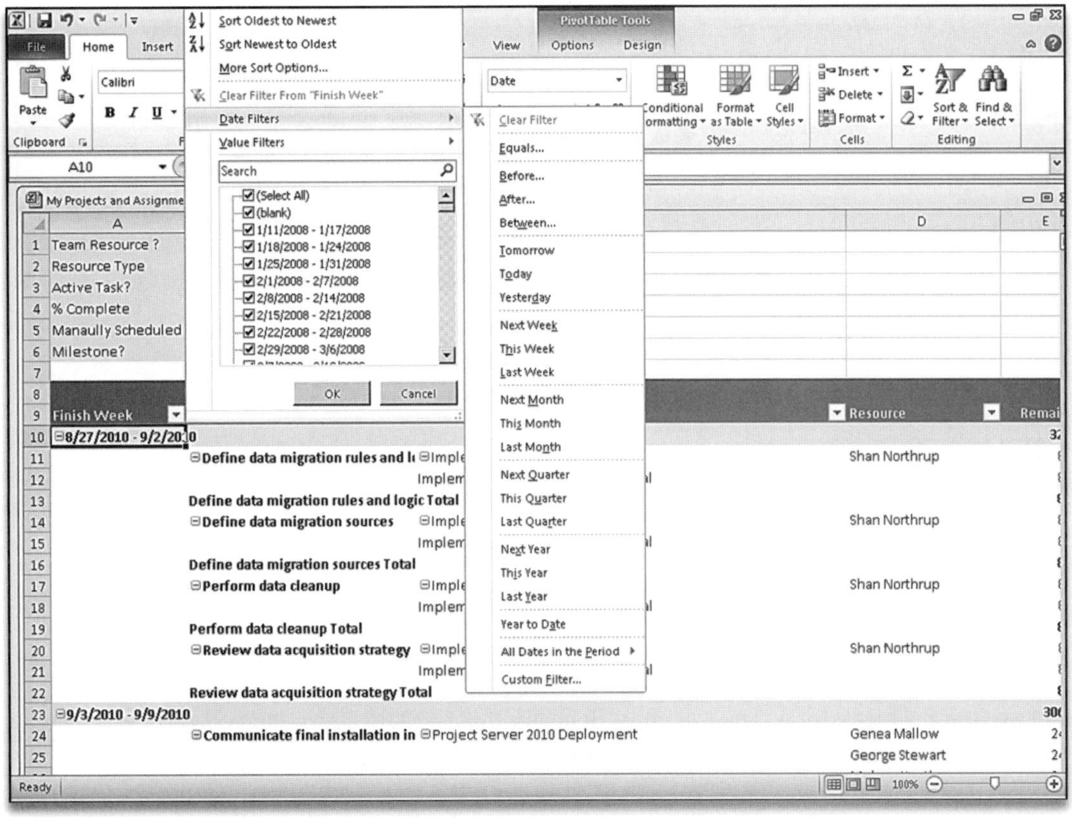

Figure 18 - 115: PivotTable Date filters for Date Data fields

Key Performance Indicators using Conditional Formatting

Your Business Intelligence most likely includes Key Performance Indicator (KPI) reporting. You can accomplish this type of reporting, in addition to other data visualizations, using an *Icon Set* conditional formatting as shown in Figure 18 - 116. KPI's, when used properly, provide visual indicators that draw the user's attention to significant data.

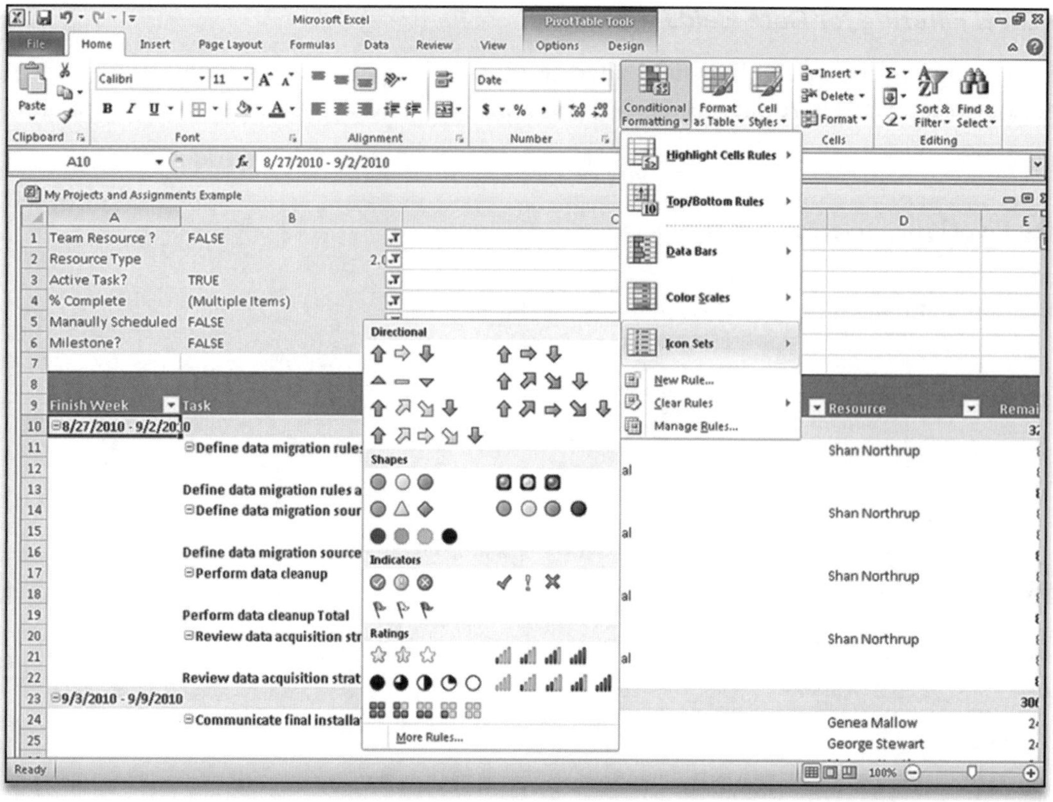

Figure 18 - 116: KPI Icon Sets for PivotTable Conditional Formatting

To apply *Icon Set* conditional formatting to a data field, do the following:

1. Select the top most cell of the data field to apply the formatting.

> **Warning**: Due to an Excel quirk, do not select the entire column, just the first value cell in the column.

2. On the *Home* tab, click the *Conditional Formatting* menu button.
3. Select the *Icon Sets…* item.
4. Select an *Icon Set* formatting. The system will apply this formatting to that cell. A new menu appears next to that cell as shown in Figure 18 - 117. Select the *All cells showing 'Remaining' values for 'Resource'* option.

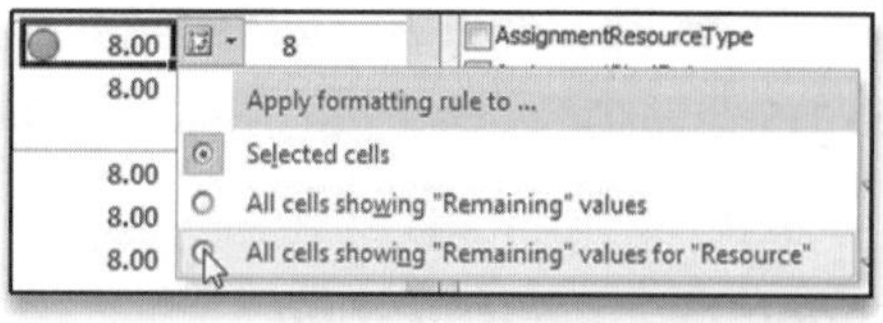

Figure 18 - 117: Icon Set Formatting menu

> **Information**: This procedure is to avoid the Excel quirk that applies conditional formatting to *Totals* rows. If you based your KPI on *% of Total*, including the *Column Total*, this calculation gives you incorrect results. If you follow this procedure, the system only applies conditional formatting to the detail rows.

5. The system applies conditional formatting to all detail rows.

The default *Conditional Formatting* rules applied are probably not using the criteria you desire. To change this, you need to edit the *Conditional Formatting* rule by doing the following:

6. On the *Home* tab, click the *Conditional Formatting* menu button.
7. Select the *Manage Rules...* item. The system displays the *Conditional Formatting Rules Manager* dialog shown in Figure 18 - 118.

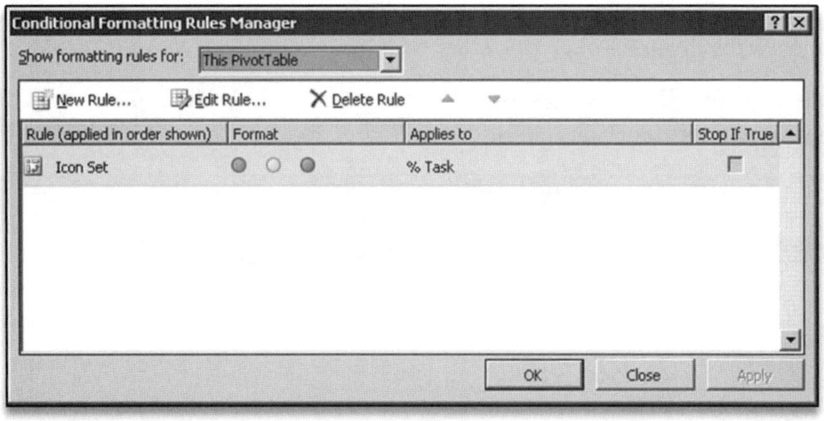

Figure 18 - 118: Conditional Formatting Rules Manger

8. Select the rule to edit and click the *Edit Rule* button to display the *Edit Formatting Rule* dialog shown in Figure 18 - 119. This dialog enables you to change the basis for displaying each icon, reversing the order of icons, and showing icons only.

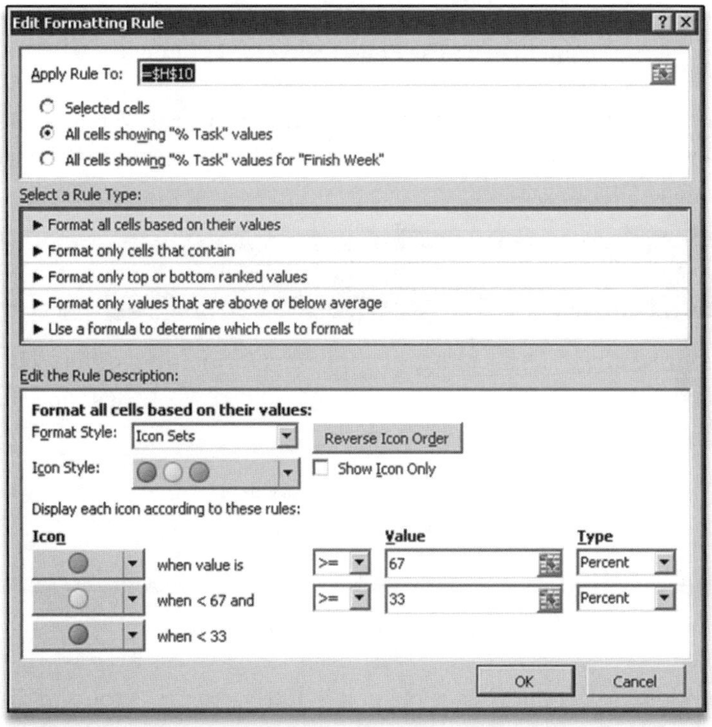

Figure 18 - 119: Edit Formatting Rule dialog

Adding Non-Project Server Users as Report Viewers

You can manage the security model in the Business Intelligence Center site separately from the Project Server 2013 security model, providing the ability to grant non-Project Server users such as executives, clients, or partners *Read-Only* access to the information stored in the site. It is an easy task to grant access to the BI Center site.

To grant the members of your *Report Viewers* group access to the BI Center site, follow these steps:

1. Log in to PWA as an administrator, such as the Farm Administrator service account, and in the *Quick Launch* menu, click the *Reports* link.
2. The system displays the *BI Center* as shown in Figure 18 - 120. At the top-right of the page, click the *Gear* icon and select the *Site Settings* menu item.

Figure 18 - 120: The Project Server 2013 BI Center

3. The system displays the *Site Settings* page shown in Figure 18 - 121. While the heading just above the text *Site Settings* displays the text *Project Web App*, you are actually managing the site settings for the BI Center. Click the *People and groups* link.

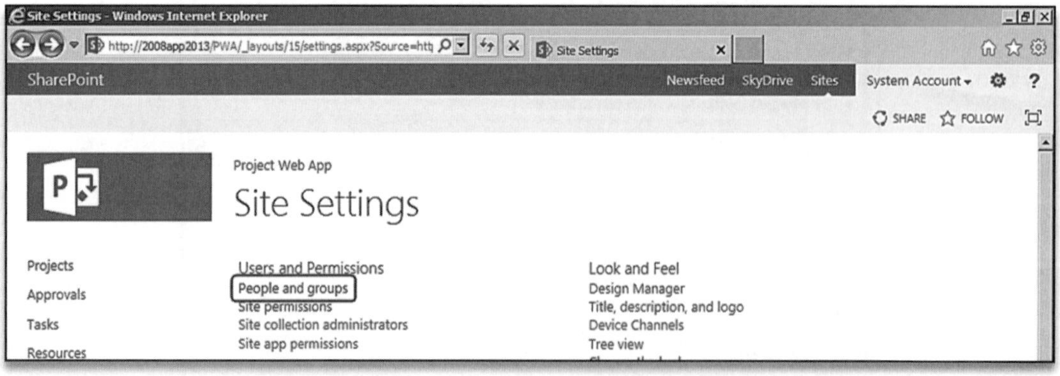

Figure 18 - 121: Site Settings page

4. The system displays the *People and Groups* page. It is likely the first group to display is the *Team Members for Project Web App*. Click the *Excel Services Viewers* link that appears at the left of the screen. The system displays the *People and Groups* page, allowing you to add *Excel Services Viewers* as shown in Figure 18 - 122.

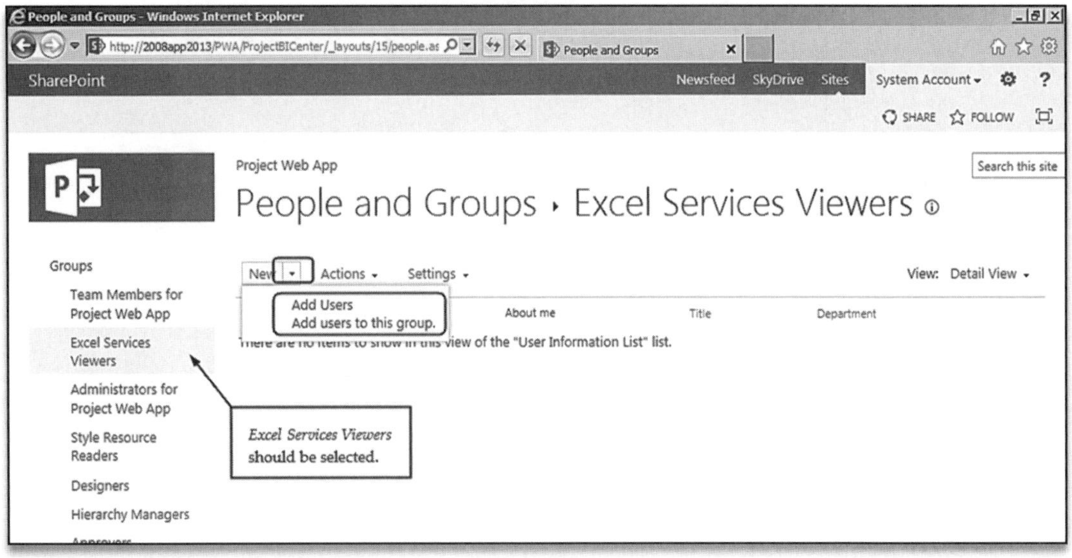

Figure 18 - 122: People and Groups management for Excel Services Viewers

5. The system displays the *Share 'Business Intelligence Center'* dialog shown in Figure 18 - 123. Using your keyboard, type the name of the individuals or groups you would like to have access to the *BI Center* reports. In my case, I add the *BI Report Viewers* active directory security group. Click the *Share* button.

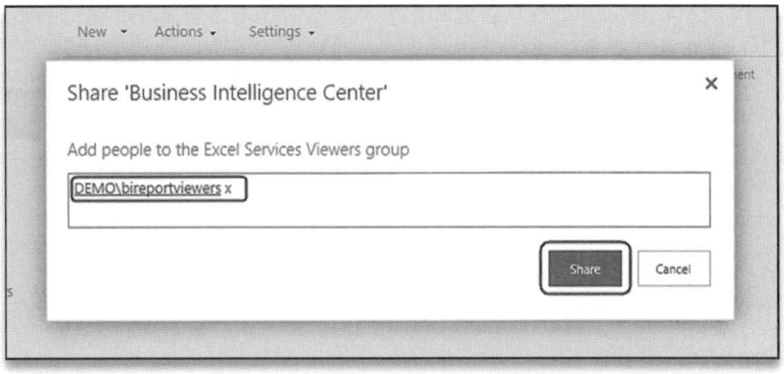

Figure 18 - 123: Share 'Business Intelligence Center' dialog

6. The system redisplays the *People and Groups* page with your new additions.

Index

Other Great books from msProjectExperts:

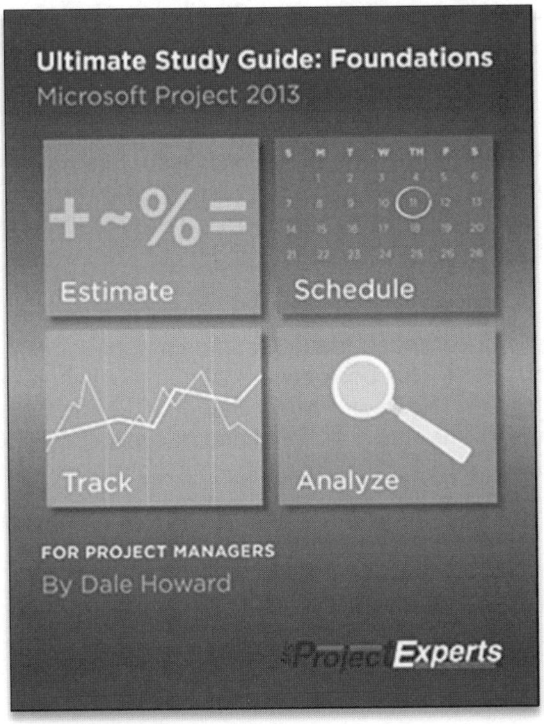

Ultimate Study Guide: Foundations Microsoft Project 2013

ISBN 978-1-934240-27-4

A comprehensive learning system for Microsoft Project 2013. The latest from the authoring team of Gary L. Chefetz and Dale A. Howard, is based on MSProjectExperts successful courseware series. Ultimate Study Guide combines a field-tested learning approach with in-depth reference to deliver the most comprehensive combined learning/reference manual ever published for Microsoft Project.

Prepare for Microsoft Exam 74-343

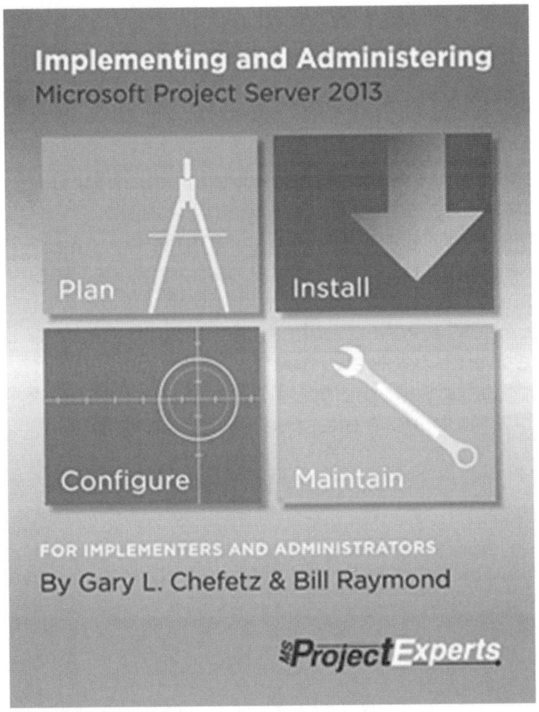

Implementing and Administering Microsoft Project Server 2013

ISBN 978-1-934240-25-0

The essential reference guide for installing, configuring, and deploying Project Server 2013 now covers Project Online. This book begins with the organizational strategies you need to succeed with a PPM deployment and follows through with an implementation plan and step-by-step instructions for installing, configuring and deploying the SharePoint 2013 and Project Server 2013 platform to your organization. Loaded with best practices, warnings and tips from Project Server gurus Gary Chefetz and Bill Raymond, *Implementing and Administering Microsoft Project Server 2013* sets the gold standard for PPM implementations using Project Server.

Prepare for Microsoft Exam 74-344

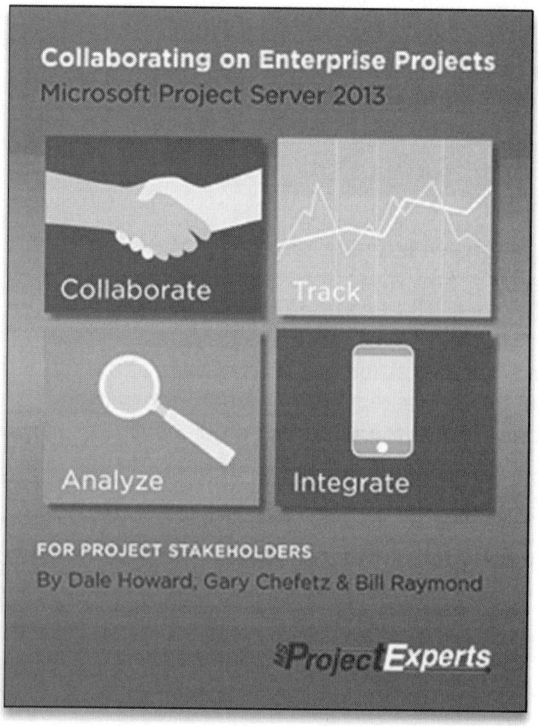

Collaborating on Enterprise Projects Microsoft Project Server 2013

ISBN 978-1-934240-29-8

This is the only book written specifically for managers and team members who use the Microsoft PPM platform, including SharePoint and Project Server 2013. Loaded with best practices, tips and tricks, and warnings, *Collaborating on Enterprise Projects Microsoft Project Server 2013* is a vital learning tool to help you educate your extended team, resource managers and senior staff. This book covers all of the collaborative features in Microsoft Project Server 2013, including SharePoint features for PPM and business intelligence tools.

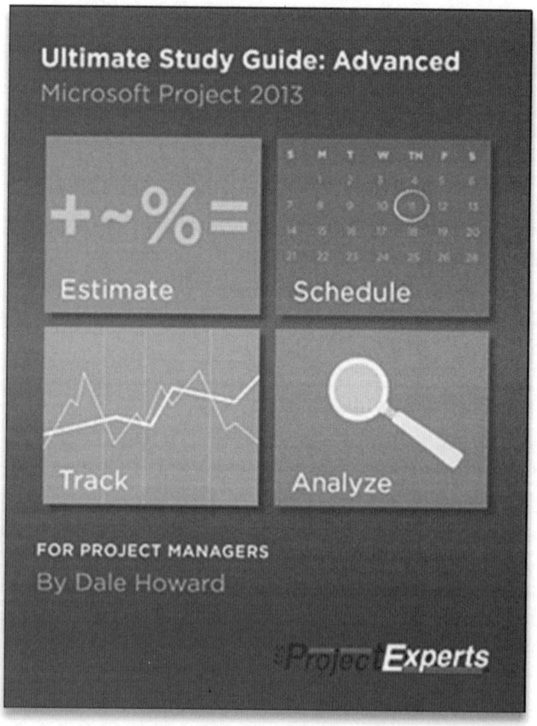

Ultimate Study Guide: Advanced Microsoft Project 2013

ISBN 978-1-934240-30-4

This book teaches you advanced techniques for using Microsoft Project 2013. You gain in-depth knowledge about standard and custom fields, calendars, scheduling, costing, critical path analysis, and exchanging project data with other applications. You learn advanced leveling techniques, how to create a shared resource pool, and how to record and write VBA macros for your project. After reading this book, you will be much more effective using Microsoft Project 2013.

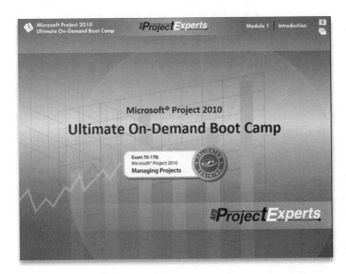